# Been in the Storm So Long

# Been in the Storm So Long

The Aftermath of Slavery

## LEON F. LITWACK

VINTAGE BOOKS
*A Division of Random House*
*New York*

First Vintage Books Edition, August 1980
Copyright © 1979 by Leon F. Litwack
All rights reserved under International and Pan-American
Copyright Conventions. Published in the United States by
Random House, Inc., New York, and in Canada
by Random House of Canada Limited, Toronto. Originally
published by Alfred A. Knopf, Inc., New York, in May 1979.

Library of Congress Cataloging in Publication Data
Litwack, Leon F.
Been in the storm so long.
Bibliography: p.
Includes index.
1. Afro-Americans—History—1863-1877.
2. Reconstruction.  3. Southern States—History—
1865-1877.  4. Southern States—Social conditions.
5. Afro-Americans—Southern States—History.
I. Title.
[E185.2.L57    1979b]    973′.0496073    80-11073
ISBN 0-394-74398-9

Manufactured in the United States of America

89

*For Rhoda with love*

# Been in the Storm So Long

---

I've been in the storm so long,
You know I've been in the storm so long,
Oh Lord, give me more time to pray,
I've been in the storm so long.

I am a motherless child,
Singin' I am a motherless child,
Singin' Oh Lord, give me more time to pray,
I've been in the storm so long.

This is a needy time,
This is a needy time,
Singin' Oh Lord, give me more time to pray,
I've been in the storm so long.

Lord, I need you now,
Lord, I need you now,
Singin' Oh Lord, give me more time to pray,
I've been in the storm so long.

My neighbors need you now,
My neighbors need you now,
Singin' Oh Lord, give me more time to pray,
I've been in the storm so long.

My children need you now,
My children need you now,
Singin' Oh Lord, give me more time to pray,
I've been in the storm so long.

Just look what a shape I'm in,
Just look what a shape I'm in,
Cryin' Oh Lord, give me more time to pray,
I've been in the storm so long.

—NINETEENTH-CENTURY BLACK SPIRITUAL

# Contents

# Preface

To DESCRIBE the end of slavery in the South is to re-create a profound human drama. The story begins with the outbreak of the Civil War, when the South's quest for independence immediately underscored its dependence on black labor and black loyalty and set in motion a social upheaval that proved impossible to contain. Throughout this devastating war, and in the immediate aftermath, the two races in the South interacted in ways that dramatized not only a mutual dependency but the frightening tensions and ambiguities that had always characterized the "peculiar institution." The extent to which blacks and whites shaped each other's lives and destinies and were forced to respond to each other's presence had never been more starkly apparent. The truth of W. J. Cash's observation—"Negro entered into white man as profoundly as white man entered into Negro, subtly influencing every gesture, every word, every emotion and idea, every attitude"—has never been more poignantly acted out. Under the stress of war, invading armies, and emerging black freedom, pretensions and disguises fell away and illusions were dissolved, revealing more about the character of slavery and racial relationships than many white men and women wished to know or to believe.

The various dimensions of slavery's collapse—the political machinations, the government edicts, the military occupation—should not be permitted to obscure the principal actors in this drama: the four million black men and women for whom enslavement composed their entire memory. For many of them, the only world they knew ended at the boundaries of the plantations and farms on which they toiled; most of them were several generations removed from the African immigrants who had been torn from their homeland and shipped in chains to the New World. The distant voices of Africa still echoed in their music, in their folk tales, in the ways they worshipped God, and in their kinship relationships. But in 1860 they were as American as the whites who lorded over them.

The bondage from which black men and women emerged during and after the Civil War had varied in conditions of living, in degrees of mental and physical violence, and in the character of ownership. But the education acquired by each slave was remarkably uniform, consisting largely of lessons in survival and accommodation—the uses of humility, the virtues of ignorance, the arts of evasion, the subtleties of verbal intonation, the techniques by which feelings and emotions were masked, and the occasions that demanded the flattering of white egos and the placating of white fears. They learned to live with the uncertainties of family life, the drab diet of "nigger" food, the whippings and humiliations, the excessive demands on their labor, the wiles and changing moods of masters and mistresses, the perverted Christianity of white preachers, and the inhumanities few blacks would ever forget—a spirited slave reduced to insensibility, a father helpless to protect his wife or children, a mother in the forced embrace of the master or his sons. Not only did most of the slaves learn to endure but they managed to create a reservoir of spiritual and moral power and kinship ties that enabled them under the most oppressive of conditions to maintain their essential humanity and dignity.

The slaves came to learn that the choices available to them were sharply constricted, that certain expectations would remain unrealized, that a lifetime could be spent in anticipation and disappointment, that to place any faith in the promises of white men and women or to misinterpret their occasional displays of patronizing affection might result in betrayals and frustrations that were psychologically debilitating. Each generation complied in its own ways with the demands and expectations of those who claimed to own them, sucked whatever joy they could out of their lives and families, and gave birth to still another generation of slaves. But for the black men and women who lived to experience the Civil War, there would be the moment when they learned a complex of new truths: they were no longer slaves, they were free to leave the families they had served, they could negotiate the terms of their future labor, and they could aspire to the same rights and privileges enjoyed by their former owners. It is that moment—and the days, months, and years that immediately followed—which this book seeks to capture: the countless ways in which freedom was perceived and experienced by the black men and women who had been born into slavery and how they acted on every level to help shape their condition and future as freedmen and freedwomen.

To describe the significance of freedom to four million black slaves of the South is to test severely our historical imagination. Perhaps only those who have endured enslavement and racial oppression are capable of fully appreciating the various emotions, tensions, and conflicts that such a dramatic change could provoke. The sources for assessing how black freedom traumatized the white South are abundant, for the war and postwar years produced a deluge of reactions in letters, journals, diaries, and the press; indeed, some whites could talk and write of little else in the aftermath of the war but the dimensions of their defeat and the loss of their chattel. For the slaves, the sources are no less plentiful but far more elusive. Newly freed slaves related their perceptions of freedom to Union soldiers, Freedmen's Bureau officers, northern visitors, newspaper reporters, clergymen, missionaries, teachers, and, with somewhat greater caution, to the masters and mistresses who had formerly owned them. More importantly, they acted on their perceptions in ways that could not escape the rapt attention and curiosity of contemporaries eager to ascertain how a once enslaved population would manifest their freedom and whether they could exercise responsibly the prerogatives of free men and women.

Some seventy years after the Civil War, the Federal Writers' Project (a New Deal agency) conducted interviews with more than two thousand surviving ex-slaves, most of them over eighty years of age. This book draws on those interviews (along with black testimony in the 1860s) in the belief that they are especially valuable for illuminating the experiences of freedmen and freedwomen. The reliability of such testimony has been questioned, reflecting concern about the memories of aged people, the biases and distortions of white interviewers, whether ex-slaves caught up in the Great Depression might not recall more favorably the relative security—food, clothing, and shelter—afforded them under bondage, and the likelihood that black men and women still seeking to survive in the racially oppressive South of the 1930s might choose to fall back on time-honored tactics of evasion and selectivity, thinking it expedient to tell whites what they thought the whites wanted to hear. Such objections suggest not that these records are invalid but only that historians need to use them with care and subject them to the same rigorous standards of historical criticism they would apply to other sources. Fortunately, and not surprisingly, neither old age nor the presence of a white interviewer seems to have dimmed the memories of such a critical event in their lives. Whether they chose to recall bondage with terror, nostalgia, or mixed feelings, their thoughts, concerns, and priorities at the moment they ceased to be slaves emerge with remarkable clarity and seldom conflict significantly with the contemporary historical evidence.

Whatever the surviving sources of black testimony, they have been compiled largely by white men and women. Not only could the reporter's race influence what he chose to record but his unfamiliarity with black speech patterns affected how he transmitted the material. No attempt has been made in this book to alter the transcription of Negro dialect, even in those instances where the white man's perception of black language seems obviously and intentionally distorted. But to transpose the dialect into standard English would only introduce other forms of distortion and project into black speech the biases and predilections of the modern observer. For that reason, the reader will simply be asked to keep in mind the conditions under which black people often related their experiences, including the circumspection some of them deemed necessary in the presence of whites.

Never before had black people in the South found any reason to view the future with more hope or expectation than in the 1860s. The war and freedom injected into their lives the excitement of anticipation, encouraged a new confidence in their own capabilities, and afforded them a rare insight into the vulnerability and dependency of their "white folks." For many, these were triumphs in themselves. If their optimism seems misplaced, the sights which greeted newly freed slaves suggested otherwise—black armies of occupation, families reunited, teachers offering to instruct them, Federal officials placing thousands of them on abandoned and confiscated lands, former masters prepared to bargain for their labor, and black missionaries organizing them in churches based upon a free and independent expression of their Christianity. To measure the significance of emancipation is not to compare the material rewards of freedom and slavery, as many contemporaries were apt to do, but to appreciate the many and varied ways in which the newly freed moved to reorder their lives and priorities and the new assumptions upon which they acted.

Even as many freed blacks found themselves exhilarated by the prospects for change, the old ways of living, working, and thinking did not die easily and those who had been compelled to free them immediately searched for alternative ways to exploit their labor and command their lives. Seldom in history have any people faced tasks so formidable and challenging as those which four million southern blacks confronted in the aftermath of the Civil War. This experience, like that of their enslavement, they could share with no other Americans. Nor was the dominant society about to rearrange its values and priorities to grant to black Americans a positive assistance commensurate with the inequalities they had suffered and the magnitude of the problems they faced. If the ex-slaves were to succeed, they would have to depend largely on their own resources. Under these constraints, a recently enslaved people sought ways to give meaning to their new status. The struggles they would be forced to wage to shape their lives and destinies as free men and women remain to this day an epic chapter in the history of the American people.

LEON F. LITWACK
*Berkeley, California*
*September 1978*

# Acknowledgments

---

A<small>T ITS INCEPTION</small>, this book was to have been a study of black life in the South from the Civil War to the turn of the century. But as the research progressed, the experience of the newly freed slaves took on a life of its own and became the primary focus. A John Simon Guggenheim Memorial Foundation Fellowship enabled me to devote a full year to research and writing. Funds provided by a grant from the National Institute of Mental Health and a Humanities Research Fellowship from the University of California at Berkeley afforded me additional time and support to reformulate the project, conduct further research, and complete the writing of the manuscript. The Institute of Social Sciences and the Committee on Research at the University of California also generously provided funds for research assistance, travel, and microfilming expenses.

My travels in search of materials ranged from manuscript libraries and state and federal archives to a remote United States Cemetery outside of Port Hudson, Louisiana, where the gravestones of black Union soldiers, many of them marked "unknown," stand as monuments to that dramatic moment in American history when armed black men, including recently freed slaves, marched through the southern countryside as an army of liberation and occupation. For the courtesies and generous assistance extended to me, I am grateful to the staffs of the Duke University Library; the Fisk University Library; the Henry E. Huntington Library; the Moorland Foundation Library at Howard University; the Louisiana State University Department of Archives and History; the Library of Congress; the National Archives; the Schomburg Center for Research in Black Culture, New York Public Library; the Southern Historical Collection at the University of North Carolina; the Historical Society of Pennsylvania; the South Caroliniana Library at the University of South Carolina; the South Carolina Department of Archives and History; and the Valentine Museum and State Library in Richmond, Virginia. I should also like to express my appreciation to the Board of Trustees of the Mother Bethel African Methodist Episcopal Church in Philadelphia for their kind permission to use and microfilm *The Christian Recorder,* a rare and major source of black testimony from the wartime and postwar South that proved indispensable to my work.

The opportunity to draw on the knowledge and insights of many friends and fellow teachers and scholars proved both rewarding and stimulating. Not all of them fully shared my views or approach but their suggestions and critical encouragement were deeply valued. For having first stimulated my interest in the history of slavery and the South, I remain indebted to my teacher and colleague, Kenneth M. Stampp. I am also grateful to Allan Nevins for having invited me to join the series he edited on the Impact of the Civil War—that proved to be the seed of the present volume. Among my associates at Berkeley, Paula S. Fass, Winthrop D. Jordan, Lawrence W. Levine, and Robert L. Middlekauff read and criticized the entire manuscript, bringing to it the insight, imagination, and sensitivity they have demonstrated so abundantly in their own published works. While completing his study of slavery, Eugene D. Genovese generously took time out to scrutinize early drafts of several chapters and to share with me his ideas on the "Moment of Truth"; he later read the completed manuscript and responded with his characteristically sharp and exacting criticism and warm encouragement. I am no less indebted to Eric Foner, Nathan I. Huggins, and Ronald G. Walters, each of whom expended considerable time and energy to read the manuscript and to suggest revisions which both improved the quality of the text and reduced its size. For their reactions to individual chapters, I would like to thank Herbert G. Gutman, James Kindregan, John G. Sproat, Peter H. Wood, and Arthur Zilversmit. During various stages of the book, I benefited from the assistance of Joseph Corn, Marina Wikramanayake Fernando, Susan Glenn, Alice Schulman, and Patricia Sheehan. For the thorough and perceptive reading of the book in page proofs, I am deeply grateful to Cornelia Levine. For sharing with me her skills in research and languages, Natalie Reid has my profoundest appreciation. I am also grateful to my editor at Knopf, Ashbel Green, for his careful reading of the manuscript and judicious comments.

But finally, this book belongs to my wife, Rhoda, who lived with it for more than a decade. Neither the dedication nor this brief acknowledgment adequately recognizes how much her love, personal insight, and support helped to ease the manuscript through its several passages.

# Been in the Storm So Long

# Chapter One

# "THE FAITHFUL SLAVE"

*Either they deny the Negro's humanity and feel no cause to measure his actions against civilized norms; or they protect themselves from their guilt in the Negro's condition and from their fear that their cooks might poison them, or that their nursemaids might strangle their infant charges, or that their field hands might do them violence, by attributing to them a superhuman capacity for love, kindliness and forgiveness. Nor does this in any way contradict their stereotyped conviction that all Negroes (meaning those with whom they have no contact) are given to the most animal behavior.*

RALPH ELLISON[1]

ROBERT MURRAY could already sense the change in his "white folks." As a young slave, dividing his time between running errands and tending the horses, he had been treated tolerably well. "Massa" had been generous in providing food and clothing, "missus" had ignored both law and custom to teach several of the slaves to read, and the slave children had usually found a warm welcome in the Big House. "Been treat us like we's one de fambly," Murray recalled. "Jus' so we treat de white folks 'spectable an' wu'k ha'hd." After the election of Abraham Lincoln, however, "it all diffrunt." The easy familiarity of the master and mistress gave way to suspicious glances, and the slaves were permitted less freedom of movement around the place. When the children ventured up to the Big House, as they had done so often in the past, the master or mistress now barred their way and offered excuses for not inviting them inside. "Don' go in de Big House no mo', chillun," Robert Murray's mother advised them. "I know whut de trouble. Dey s'pose we all wants ter be free."[2]

On the eve of the Civil War, the more than four million slaves and free blacks comprised nearly 40 percent of the population of the South. Although most slaveholders owned less than ten slaves, the majority of slaves worked as field hands on plantation-size units which held more than twenty slaves, and at least a quarter of the slave force lived in units of more than fifty slaves. Even without the added disruption of war, the awesome presence of so many blacks could seldom be ignored. While to the occasional visitor they might blend picturesquely into the landscape and seem almost inseparable from it, native whites were preoccupied with their reality. Oftentimes, in fact, they could talk of little else. Wavering between moods of condescension, suspicion, and hostility, slaveholding families acknowledged by their conversations and daily conduct a relationship with their blacks that was riddled with ambiguity. When the Civil War broke out, with the attendant problems of military invasion and plantations stripped of their white males, that ambiguity would assume worrisome dimensions for some, it would lure others into a false sense of security, and it would drive still more into fits of anguish.

Within easy earshot of the bombardment of Fort Sumter, Mary Boykin Chesnut, whose husband was an extensive planter and political leader in South Carolina, tried in vain to penetrate behind the inscrutable faces of her servants. Why did they not betray some emotion or interest? How could they go about their daily chores seemingly unconcerned that their own destiny might be in the balance but a few miles away? "Not by one word or look can we detect any change in the demeanor of these Negro servants. Lawrence sits at our door, as sleepy and as respectful and as profoundly indifferent. So are they all. They carry it too far. You could not tell that they even hear the awful noise that is going on in the bay, though it is dinning in their ears night and day. And people talk before them as if they were chairs and tables, and they make no sign." This almost studied indifference obviously troubled Mary Chesnut as much as it might have comforted and reassured her. "Are they stolidly stupid," she wondered, "or wiser than we are, silent and strong, biding their time?"[3]

The slaves were no less observant of their "white folks." Although blacks had always been aware of frailties in their owners, the system of slavery had been based on the acknowledged power of the white man. But the Civil War introduced tensions and tragedies into the lives of masters and mistresses that made them seem less than omnipotent, perhaps even suddenly human in ways blacks had thought impossible. Rarely had slaves perceived their owners so utterly at the mercy of circumstances over which they had no control. Never before had they seemed so vulnerable, so beleaguered, so helpless. Unprecedented in the disruptions, stresses, and trauma it generated among both whites and blacks, the Civil War threatened to undermine traditional relationships and dissolve long-held assumptions and illusions. Even if many slaves evinced a human compassion for masters and mistresses caught in the terrible plight of war, invasion, and death, how long before these same slaves came to recognize that in the very suffering of their "white folks" lay their own freedom and salvation?

## 2

DURING THE EARLY MONTHS, neither the whites nor the blacks appeared to grasp fully the nature of this war. The mobilization took on an almost festive air, exposing the slaves to unusual sights and sounds and affording them a welcome diversion from their day-to-day chores. They watched the military drills with fascination, learned the words of the patriotic songs, and stood with whites in the courthouse square to listen to the bombastic and confident speeches. "You'd thought the Confederates goin' win the War," John Wright speculated, after hearing Jefferson Davis address an enthusiastic crowd in Montgomery, Alabama. "But I notice Massa Wright look right solemn when we go back home. Don' believe he ever was sure the South goin' win." When the soldiers prepared to leave for the front, the festivities gave way to sobering farewells that made a deep impression on some of the blacks. "Mis' Polly an' de ladies got to cryin'," recalled Sarah Debro, who spent the war years as a young house slave in a North Carolina family. "I was so sad dat I got over in de corner an' cried too."[4]

The patriotic fervor and martial displays suggested a quick and glorious triumph. So confident was a North Carolina planter that he had his son candidly explain the issues to the slaves: "There is a war commenced between the North and the South. If the North whups, you will be as free a man as I is. If the South whups, you will be a slave all your days." Before leaving, the master jokingly told the slaves that he expected to "whup the North" and be back for dinner. "He went away," one of his slaves recalled, "and it wuz four long years before he cum back to dinner. De table wuz shore set a long time for him. A lot of de white folks said dey wouldn't be much war, dey could whup dem so easy. Many of dem never did come back to dinner."[5]

Neither white nor black Southerners were unaffected by the physical and emotional demands of the war. Scarcities of food and clothing, for example, imposed hardships on both races. But the slaves and their masters did not share these privations equally; black families could ill afford any reduction in their daily allowances, and they observed with growing bitterness that provisions needed to sustain them were often dispatched to the Army or hoarded for the comfort of their "white folks." Reduced diets opened the way for all kinds of ailments in weak and undernourished bodies, and yet there was no corresponding reduction in the hours of labor demanded of the slaves or in the diligence with which they were expected to carry out their assigned tasks. Later in the war, depredations committed by both Confederate and Union soldiers nearly exhausted the food supplies in some regions, and many a slave repeated the complaint made by Pauline Grice of Georgia: "De year 'fore surrender, us am short of rations and sometime us hungry. . . . Dey [the soldiers] done took all de rations and us couldn't eat de cotton." Even earlier, the shortage of food had driven slaves to the point of desperation; incidents of theft mounted steadily, some slaves went out on foraging missions (with the tacit consent of their owners), while still others preferred to risk flight to the Yankees rather than experience constant hunger. When asked if the Emancipation Proclamation had prompted his flight to the nearest Union camp, one slave responded, "No, missus, we never hear nothing like it. We's starvin', and we come to get somfin' to eat. Dat's what we come for."[6]

Despite the wartime shortages, slaves were reluctant to surrender the traditional privileges they had wrested from their owners. Any master, for example, who decided to dispense with the usual Saturday-night dances, the annual barbecue, the "big supper" expected after a slave wedding, or the Christmas holiday festivities might find himself unable to command the respect and labor of his slaves. Nor did servants who enjoyed dressing up in their master's or mistress's cast-off finery to attend church believe that the Confederacy's strictures on extravagance and ostentatious display applied to them. But no matter how disagreeable patriotic whites now found these displays, many slaveholders thought it best to tolerate them as a way of maintaining and rewarding loyalty in their blacks. When slaves dressed up in fine clothes, one white woman observed, they became "merry, noisy, loquacious creatures, wholly unconscious of care or anxiety." Such diversions presumably took their minds off the larger implications of the war and rendered them more content with their position—at least, many whites preferred to think so.[7]

The extent of the slaves' exposure to the war varied considerably, with those residing in the threatened and occupied regions obviously bearing the brunt of the disruptions along with the white families they served. In some sections of the South, however, life went on as usual, there were ample provisions, the white men remained at home, the slaves performed their daily routines, and the fighting remained distant. "The War didn't change nothin'," Felix Haywood of Texas recalled. "Sometimes you didn't knowed it was goin' on. It was the endin' of it that made the difference." By sharp contrast, a former Mississippi slave remembered feeling as though "the world was come to the end," and Emma Hurley, who had been a slave in Georgia, recalled the war years as "the hardest an' the saddest days" she had ever experienced. "Everybody went 'round like this [she took up her apron and buried her face in it]—they kivered their face with what-somever they had in their hands that would ketch the tears. Sorrow an' sadness wuz on every side."[8]

Even if the issues at stake were sometimes unclear, slaves could only marvel at a war that sent white men off to kill other white men, made a battleground of the southern countryside, and threatened to maim or destroy an entire generation of young free men. Recalling his most vivid impressions of the war, William Rose, who had been a slave in South Carolina, told of a troop train he had seen carrying Confederate soldiers to the front lines.

> And they start to sing as they cross de trestle. One pick a banjo, one play de fiddle. They sing and whoop, they laugh; they holler to de people on de ground, and sing out, "Good-bye." All going down to die. . . .
> De train still rumble by. One gang of soldier on de top been playing card. I see um hold up de card as plain as day, when de luck fall right. They going to face bullet, but yet they play card, and sing and laugh like they in their own house. . . . All going down to die.

The scenes witnessed by slaves in the aftermath of battles fought near their homes would never be forgotten. Martha Cunningham, who had been raised near Knoxville, Tennessee, recalled walking over hundreds of dead soldiers lying on the ground and listening to the groans of the dying. William Walters and his mother, both of them fugitives from a plantation in Tennessee, watched the wounded being carried to a clearing across the road from where they had sought refuge—"fighting men with arms shot off, legs gone, faces blood smeared—some of them just laying there cussing God and Man with their dying breath!"[9]

The tales of self-sacrifice and martial heroism that would inspire future generations hardly suggested the savagery, the destructiveness, the terrifying and dehumanizing dimensions of this war. The initial exultation and military pomp had barely ended before the streams of wounded and maimed returned to their homes. Few slaves were immune to the human tragedies that befell the families to whom they belonged. They had known them too well, too intimately not to be affected in some way. "Us wus boys togedder, me en Marse Hampton, en wus jist er bout de same size," Abram Harris recalled. "Hit sho did hurt me when Marse Hampton got kilt kase I lubed dat white man." The tragedies that befell the Lipscomb family in South Carolina provoked one of their slaves, Lorenza Ezell, beyond mere compassion to outright anger and a desire for revenge. As he would later remember that reaction:

> All four my young massas go to de war, all but Elias. He too old. Smith, he kilt at Manassas Junction. Nathan, he git he finger shot at de first round at Fort Sumter. But when Billy was wounded at Howard Gap in North Carolina and dey brung him home with he jaw split open, I so mad I could have kilt all de Yankees. I say I be happy iffen I could kill me jes' one Yankee. I hated dem 'cause dey hurt my white people. Billy was disfigure awful when he jaw split and he teeth all shine through he cheek.

The sight of a once powerful white man reduced to an emotional or physical cripple, returning home without a leg or an arm, looking "so ragged an' onery" as to be barely recognizable, generated some strong and no doubt some mixed emotions in the slaves, as did the spectacle of the whites grieving over a death. That was the first time, Nancy Smith recalled, "I had ever seed our Mist'ess cry. She jus' walked up and down in de yard a-wringin' her hands and cryin'. 'Poor Benny's been killed,' she would say over and over." After witnessing such scenes, another ex-slave recalled, "you would cry some wid out lettin your white folks see you."[10]

If the plight of their masters moved some slaves to tears, that was by no means a universal reaction. Grief and the forced separation from loved ones were hardly new experiences in the lives of many slaves. To witness the discomfiture of white men and women suffering the same personal tragedies and disruptions they had inflicted on others might produce ambiguous feelings, at best, or even be a source of immense gratification. Delia Garlic, for example, was working as a field hand on a Louisiana plantation when the war broke out. Born in Virginia, and sold three times, she had been separated from the rest of her family. "Dem days was hell," she would recall of her bondage.

> Babies was snatched from dere mother's breas' an' sold to speculators. Chilluns was separated from sisters an' brothers an' never saw each other ag'in. Course dey cry; you think dey not cry when dey was sold lak cattle? ... It's bad to belong to folks dat own you soul an' body; dat can tie you up to a tree, wid yo' face to de tree an' yo' arms fastened tight aroun' it; who take a long curlin' whip an' cut de blood ever' lick. Folks a mile away could hear dem awful whippings. Dey was a turrible part of livin'.

The most vivid impression she retained of the war was the day the master's two sons left for military service and the obvious grief that caused her owners. "When dey went off de Massa an' missis cried, but it made us glad to see dem cry. Dey made us cry so much." On the plantation in Alabama where Henry Baker spent his childhood, the news spread quickly through the slave quarters that Jeff Coleman, a local white man who once served on the detested slave patrols, had been killed in the war. "De 'niggers' jes shouted en shouted," Baker recalled, "dey wuz so glad he wuz dead cause he wuz so mean tuh dem."[11]

No matter how desperately white families might seek to hide or overcome their anguish and fear in the presence of the slaves, the pretense could not always be sustained. No one, after all, had more experience in reading their faces and discerning their emotions than the slaves with whom they had shared their lives. No one had a shrewder insight into their capacity for self-deception and dissembling. Even as the white South had mobilized for war, some slaves had sensed how a certain anxiety tempered the talk of Confederate invincibility. With each passing month, few slaves could have remained oblivious to the fact that the anticipated quick and easy victory had become instead a prolonged and costly slaughter. Nor could they fail to see with their own eyes how the realities of war had a way of mocking the rhetoric that celebrated its heroism, even robbing their once powerful "white folks" of the last remnants of human dignity. A former Tennessee slave remembered the death of Colonel McNairy, who had vowed to wade in blood before he would allow his family to perform the chores of servants. "He got blown to pieces in one of the first battles he fought in. They wasn't sure it was him but you know they had special kinds of clothes and they found pieces of his clothes and they thought he was blown to pieces from that." Bob Jones, who had been raised on a North Carolina plantation, would never forget the day some Confederate soldiers brought home the body of his master's son who had been killed in action. "I doan 'member whar he wus killed but he had been dead so long dat he had turned dark, an' Sambo, a little nigger, sez ter me, 'I thought, Bob, dat I'ud turn white when I went ter heaben but hit 'pears ter me lak de white folkses am gwine ter turn black.' "[12]

Although embellished considerably by postwar writers, those classic wartime scenes which depicted the faithful slaves consoling the "white folks" in their bereavement were by no means rare. With everyone weeping so profusely, white and black alike, and some whites on the verge of hysteria, Louis Cain, a former North Carolina slave, thought it "a wonder we ever did git massa buried." That blacks should have shared in the grief of the very whites who held them as slaves, in a war fought in large part over their freedom, underscored in so many ways the contradictions and ambivalence that characterized the "peculiar institution." Many of these same slaves, after all, would later "betray" their owners and welcome the Yankees as liberators. As a young slave on a Virginia plantation, Booker T. Washington listened to the fervent prayers for freedom and shared the excitement with which his people awaited the arrival of the Union Army. Yet the news that "Mars' Billy" had been killed in the war had profoundly affected these same slaves. "It was no sham sorrow," Washington would later write, "but real. Some of the slaves had nursed 'Mars' Billy'; others had played with him when he was a child. 'Mars' Billy' had begged for mercy in the case of others when the overseer or master was thrashing them. The sorrow in the slave quarter was only second to that in the 'big house.' " When two of the master's sons subsequently returned home with severe wounds, the slaves were anxious to assist them, some volunteering to sit up through the night to attend them. To Washington, there was nothing strange or contradictory about such behavior; the slaves had simply demonstrated their "kindly and generous nature" and refused to betray a trust. On the plantation in Alabama where she labored under a tyrannical master and mistress, a young black woman who had been separated by sale from three of her own four children grieved over the death of the master's son. "Marster Ben, deir son, were good, and it used to hurt him to see us 'bused. When de war came Marster Ben went—no, der ole man didn't go—an' he were killed dere. When he died, I cried. . . . He were a kind chile. But de oders, oh, dear."[13]

Whatever the degree of empathy slaves could muster for the bereavement of their "white folks," the uncertainty it introduced into their own lives could hardly be ignored. With the death of her master, Anna Johnson recalled, the mistress went to live with her parents and the plantation was sold "and us wid it." Pauline Grice remembered that her mistress eventually recovered from the death of her son "but she am de diff'rent woman." If only as a matter of self-interest, then, slaves were likely to view each new casualty list with considerable trepidation. Rather than unite blacks and whites in a common grief, news of the death of a master or a son might unsettle the remaining family members to the point of violent hysteria, with the slaves as the most accessible and logical targets upon whom they could turn their wrath. No sooner had the two sons of Annie Row's master enlisted than his behavior became even more volatile. "Marster Charley cuss everything and every body and us watch out and keep out of his way." The day he received news of the death of one of his sons proved to be particularly memorable:

Missy starts cryin' and de Marster jumps up and starts cussin' de War
and him picks up de hot poker and say, "Free de nigger, will dey? I free
dem." And he hit my mammy on de neck and she starts moanin' and
cryin' and draps to de floor. Dere 'twas, de Missy a-mournin', my mammy
a-moanin' and de Marster a-cussin' loud as him can. Him takes de gun
offen de rack and starts for de field whar de niggers am a-workin'. My
sister and I sees that and we'uns starts runnin' and screamin', 'cause
we'uns has brothers and sisters in de field.

Before the war, Mattie Curtis recalled, her mistress had been "purty good"
but the war turned her into "a debil iffen dar eber wus one," and after
hearing of the death of her son she whipped the slaves "till she shore nuff
wore out."[14]

The temperaments of white slaveholding families fluctuated even
more violently than usual, reflecting not only the casualty lists but news
of military setbacks, the wartime privations, the reports of slave disaffection, and the familiar problems associated with running a plantation. Every slave was subject to the day-to-day whims of those who owned him, and
even the kindest masters and mistresses had their bad days. "Dere was
good white folks, sah, as well as bad," an elderly freedman remarked, after
being asked his opinion of *Uncle Tom's Cabin*, "but when they was bad,
Lord-a-mercy, you never saw a book, sah, that come up to what slavery
was." If the Civil War could in some instances drive the plantation whites
and blacks closer together, revealing a mutual dependency and sympathy,
the shocks of war and invasion, coupled with the fears of emancipation,
were as likely to bring out the very worst in the human character. "You
see," a Virginia freedman explained, "the masters, soon as they found out
they couldn't keep their slaves, began to treat them about as bad as could
be. Then, because I made use of this remark, that I didn't think we colored
folks ought to be blamed for what wasn't our fault, for we didn't make the
war, and neither did we declare ourselves free,—just because I said that,
not in a saucy way, but as I say it to you now, one man put a pistol to my
head, and was going to shoot me. I got away from him, and left."[15]

The specter of emancipation, along with the increased demands of the
war, had a way of dissolving the posture of beneficence on the plantation.
Fearful of losing his slaves, a master might work them incessantly, determined to drain everything he could from his suddenly precarious investment. "Massa Jeems cussed and 'bused us niggers more'n ever," Wes Brady
recalled, "but he took sick and died and stepped off to Hell 'bout six months
'fore we got free." It had been bad enough before the war, Harry Jarvis said
of the plantation on which he worked, "but arter de war come, it war wus
nor eber. Fin'ly, he [the master] shot at me one day, 'n I reckoned I'd stood
it 'bout's long's I could, so I tuk to der woods. I lay out dere for three weeks."
Charlie Moses, who had been a slave in Mississippi, remembered only that
his master, after spending a year in the Army, returned home "even
meaner than before."[16]

If a master chose to serve in the war, his absence from the plantation for extended periods of time created a critical vacuum in authority. Although slaves might seek to exploit such a situation to their own advantage, the alteration of power relationships on the plantation did not always redound to their benefit. Unaccustomed to her new responsibilities, the plantation mistress was apt to be even more easily moved to ill temper than the master, possessing neither the patience nor the experience of her husband in dealing on a day-to-day basis with field slaves and work routines. "I tell [you] candidly," a South Carolina woman wrote her husband in the Confederate Congress, "this attention to farming is up hill work with me. I can give orders first-rate, but when I am not obeyed, I can't keep my temper. . . . I am ever ready to give you a helping hand, but I must say I am heartily tired of trying to manage *free* negroes." Equally dismayed at the "follies & sins" committed by black servants, a South Carolina widow thought the day might come when they would have to be eliminated "as rats & cockroaches are by all sorts of means whenever they become unbearable."[17]

If close contact had led some slaves to identify with the master or mistress, it had afforded others an education in the devious ways of their "white folks" and how even the best-intentioned and kindest of them could be transformed and degraded by the power they wielded. This was no less true of the mistress than the master. The gracious and maternal lady of southern legend, who reputedly tempered the harshness of slavery, was not entirely the figment of chivalrous white imaginations, but from the perspective of many black slaves, abnormal wartime conditions in some instances only exacerbated previously unstable personalities. It seemed to Lulu Wilson that her mistress "studied 'bout meanness" more than her master, and she blamed the blindness in her later life on the snuff her mistress had occasionally rubbed in her eyes as a punishment. With the master away during the war, the mistress's disposition only worsened. "Wash Hodges was gone away four years and Missus Hodges was meaner'n the devil all the time. Seems like she jus' hated us worser than ever. She said blabber-mouth niggers done cause a war."[18]

Confronted with a mistress who was "a demon, just like her husband," Esther Easter may not have been unique in the satisfaction she derived from playing one "demon" against the other. Taking advantage of the wartime disruptions and her access to the Big House, she finally found a way to even the score.

> While Master Jim is out fighting the Yanks, the Mistress is fiddling round with a neighbor man, Mister Headsmith. I is young then, but I knows enough that Master Jim's going be mighty mad when he hears about it.
> The Mistress didn't know I knows her secret, and I'm fixing to even up for some of them whippings she put off on me. That's why I tell Master Jim next time he come home.
> "See that crack in the wall?" Master Jim say yes, and I say, "It's just

like the open door when the eyes are close to the wall." He peek and see into the bedroom.

"That's how I find out about the Mistress and Mister Headsmith," I tells him, and I see he's getting mad.

"What you mean?" And Master Jim grabs me hard by the arm like I was trying to get away.

"I see them in the bed."

That's all I say. The Demon's got him and Master Jim tears out of the room looking for the Mistress. Then I hears loud talking and pretty soon the Mistress is screaming and calling for help . . .[19]

To maintain discipline and productivity among an enslaved work force under wartime conditions often required extraordinary efforts, for in the relative absence of white males with horses and firearms, slave restlessness, disaffection, and covert resistance might grow markedly. To a Virginia woman, it seemed like her slaves were trying "to see what amount of thieving they can commit"; to a North Carolina woman, the slaves had become, in her husband's absence, "awkward, inefficient, and even lazy"; to a Mississippi woman, pleading with the governor to release her overseer from militia duty, the slaves were not even performing half the usual amount of work. The women of the Pettigrew family of South Carolina, finding themselves suddenly in charge of the plantation, fought a losing battle to assert their authority among the slaves. As early as 1862, they confessed their doubts that "things will ever be or seem quite the same again." Later in the year, Caroline Pettigrew wrote her husband that she could feel no confidence in any of the slaves. "You will find that they have all changed in their manner, not offensive but slack."[20]

Not surprisingly, in the master's absence, the slaves were quick to test the mistress's authority, seeking to ascertain if she could be more easily outmaneuvered or manipulated than her husband. To those women forced to undergo such trials, the motivation of the slaves seemed perfectly obvious, with some of them relishing every moment of discomfiture evinced by their owners. After being left in charge of a plantation in Texas, Mrs. W. H. Neblett kept her husband informed of the steady deterioration of discipline and the heavy price she was paying in mental anguish. "[T]he black wretches [are] trying all they can, it seems to me, to agrivate me, taking no interest, having no care about the future, neglecting their duty." Neither her presence nor the harsh treatment meted out by the overseer had produced the desired results. The blacks refused to work, they abused and neglected the stock, they tore down fences and broke plows, and it did little good to give them any orders. "With the prospect of another 4 years war," she wrote her husband in the spring of 1864, "you may give your negroes away if you wont hire them, and I'll move into a white settlement and work with my hands. . . . The negroes care no more for me than if I was an old free darkey and I get so mad sometimes that I think I don't care sometimes if Myers beats the last one of them to death. I cant stay with them another year alone."[21]

Not all the women left in charge of plantations capitulated that easily. When unable to control their slaves, some mistresses called upon the assistance of local authorities or a neighboring planter to mete out punishment. After ordering local police to apprehend and jail a rebellious slave, a South Carolina woman derived considerable personal satisfaction from the way she had handled the matter. "What do you think," she wrote to her son, "I at last made up my mind to have Caesar punished, after daily provoking & impertinent conduct, . . . & it was all done so quietly, that the household did not know of it, though I let him stay 2 days in Confinement." Some women, on the other hand, needed little assistance or instruction in managing their enslaved labor but demonstrated a shrewdness and strength that compared favorably to that of their absent husbands. Refusing to panic or leave matters to the overseer, Ida Dulany, the mistress of a Virginia plantation, quelled a work stoppage by selling some of the slaves, hiring others out, removing a third group to a separate area, and whipping one of the leaders. To make certain that those who remained did their work properly, she visited the fields herself.[22]

Where overseers were employed, the absence of the master also disrupted the prevailing structure of authority. No longer able to play the overseer against the master, deriving what advantages they could from that division of power, slaves found themselves at the mercy of men who could finally rule them with an unrestrained hand. Andy Anderson, for example, recalled his experience on a cotton plantation in Texas, working for a master, Jack Haley, who was so "kind to his cullud folks" that neighbors referred to them as "de petted niggers." When the war broke out, Haley enlisted in the Army and hired a man named Delbridge to oversee the plantation.

> After dat, de hell start to pop, 'cause de first thing Delbridge do is cut de rations. . . . He half starve us niggers and he want mo' work and he start de whippin's. I guesses he starts to educate 'em. I guess dat Delbridge go to hell when he died, but I don't see how de debbil could stand him.

Unsuccessful in an escape attempt, Anderson was severely whipped and then sold, but when his old master returned from military service, he promptly admonished and fired the overseer.[23]

The enhanced authority of the overseer was as likely to disrupt as to secure a plantation. While the master remained away, slaves were even more sensitive to any action by an overseer that appeared to breach the normal limits of his authority. No longer able to appeal their differences with him to the master, the slaves on some plantations took matters into their own hands. After her master left for the war, Ida Henry recalled, the overseer tried to impress the slaves with his new importance and power. He worked them overtime and meted out harsh punishment to anyone who failed to meet his expectations, until "one day de slaves caught him and one held him whilst another knocked him in de head and killed him." On three large Louisiana plantations, near the mouth of the Red River, the slaves responded to the food shortage and a newly ordered reduction in rations by dividing up among themselves the hogs and poultry. When advised by the absent owner to punish these slaves, the overseers wisely refused on the grounds of personal safety.[24]

As an incentive to maintain order and maximize production, some masters chose to delegate authority in their absence to the slaves themselves. Andrew Goodman, who had worked on a Texas plantation, recalled not knowing "what the war was 'bout." But he readily appreciated its impact the day his master assembled the sixty-six slaves and told them of his plans to enlist in the Army, discharge the overseer, and leave the place in Goodman's hands. The master remained away for four years. Appreciating the confidence placed in them, the slaves left in charge of a plantation —often the same slaves who had been drivers or foremen—generally fulfilled the master's expectations, and in some instances even exceeded them. "I done the bes' I could," a former Alabama slave recalled, "but they was troublous times. We was afraid to talk of the war, 'cose they hung three men for talkin' of it, jest below here." With both the master and overseer absent, some slaves exulted in the greater degree of independence they enjoyed. The fact of a black "master," however, could prove to be a mixed blessing, with some drivers fulfilling their owner's expectations by maintaining a severe regime. When a former coachman took charge of a plantation in Alabama, one of the slaves recalled, "he made de niggers wuk harder dan Ole Marster did."[25]

Neither the expedient of a black driver nor an overseer necessarily resolved the dilemma posed by the absence of the master. To judge by the lamentations that abounded in the journals, diaries, and letters of women left in charge of plantations, many of them simply resigned themselves to an increasingly untenable situation over which they could exert a minimum of influence and authority. "We are doing as best we know," a Georgia woman sighed, "or as good as we can get the Servants to do; they learn to feel very independent as no white man comes to direct them." When slaves on a plantation in Texas openly resisted the overseer's authority, refusing to submit to any whippings, the mistress thought it best to avoid a showdown. Nothing would be gained by whipping the slaves, she wrote her husband, who was absent in the Army, "so I shall say nothing and if they stop work entirely I will try to feel thankful if they let me alone."[26]

Nor did the presence of the master necessarily help. The difficulties in maintaining control and discipline pointed up ambiguities that had always suffused plantation relationships. But the apprehensions now voiced by beleaguered owners had even larger implications. The spectacle of a master and his family tormented and rendered helpless in the face of wartime stresses and demands could not help but make a deep impression on the slaves. To what extent they would seek to exploit that vulnerability to their own advantage came increasingly to dominate the conversations of whites.

WITH TENS OF THOUSANDS of white men joining the Confederate Army, leaving their families behind them on isolated plantations and farms, the quality of black response to the Civil War assumed a critical and urgent importance. Few whites could be insensitive to the exposed position in which the presence of so many enslaved blacks placed them. "Last night," a Georgia woman wrote her son, "I felt the loneliness and isolation of my situation in an unusual degree. Not a white female of my acquaintance nearer than eight or ten miles, and not a white person nearer than the depot!" Amidst several hundred slaves, the mistress of a North Carolina plantation compared herself to "a kind of Anglo-Saxon Robinson Crusoe with Ethiopians only for companions—think of it!" Demonstrating a rare candor, a Confederate soldier from Mississippi, who had left his wife and children "to the care of the niggers," thought it *unlikely* that his twenty-five slaves would turn upon them. "They're ignorant poor creatures, to be sure, but as yet they're faithful. Any way, I put my trust in God, and I know he'll watch over the house while I'm away fighting for this good cause."[27]

This was hardly the time for self-doubt. Whatever previous experience might have suggested about the fragile nature of the master-slave relationship, an embattled Confederacy, struggling for the very survival of that relationship, preferred to think differently and employed a rhetorical overkill to attain the necessary peace of mind. "A genuine slave owner, born and bred, will not be afraid of Negroes," Mary Chesnut confided to her diary in November 1861. "Here we are mild as the moonbeams, and as serene; nothing but Negroes around us, white men all gone to the army." That was the proper spirit of confidence, voiced by a woman who had already confessed failure in her attempts to understand what the slaves thought of the war. Most whites, like Mary Chesnut, no matter what suspicions and forebodings they harbored, chose to put on the best possible face, to demonstrate their own serenity and composure. The alternatives were simply too horrible to contemplate. "We would be practically helpless should the Negroes rise," the daughter of a prominent Louisiana planter conceded, "since there are so few men left at home. It is only because the Negroes do not want to kill us that we are still alive."[28]

Whether to overcome their own anxieties or to silence the skeptics, many whites flaunted pretensions to security. "We have slept all winter with the doors of our house, outside and inside, all unlocked," a Virginia woman boasted in 1862. All too often, however, the incessant talk and repeated assurances betrayed something less than the confidence whites professed. Edmund Ruffin, for example, an ardent secessionist and defender of slavery, was obsessed with the question of security even as he sought to demonstrate his own unconcern. Almost daring the slaves to defy his expectations, he described in minute detail (albeit within the confines of his diary) the ease with which blacks could enter his room. Nor did he think himself unique in his unconcern. "[I]t may be truly said that every house & family is every night perfectly exposed to any attempt of our slaves to commit robbery or murder. Yet we all feel so secure, & are so free from all suspicion of such danger, that no care is taken for self-protection—& in many cases, as in mine, not even the outer door is locked."[29]

To have believed anything less would have been not only impolitic but subversive of the very institution on which the Confederacy claimed to rest. The "corner-stone" of the new government, affirmed Vice-President Alexander Stephens in March 1861, "rests upon the great truth, that the negro is not equal to the white man; that slavery—subordination to the superior race—is his natural and normal condition." Wherever he traveled in the South, an English visitor observed in 1861, he found absolute confidence that this subordination would be maintained. To resolve any doubts, a slaveholder might choose to parade some of his more obsequious specimens before the curious visitor, favor them with some humorous and familiar remarks, and then ply them with the obvious questions. In making his response, the slave usually had little difficulty in discerning what was expected of him. "Are you happy?" the slave is asked. "Yas, sar," he replies without hesitation. "Show how you're happy," the slaveholder demands. As if he had acted out this scenario many times before, the slave rubs his stomach and grins with delight, "Yummy! yummy! plenty belly full!" and the satisfied slaveholder turns to the visitor and remarks, "That's what I call a real happy feelosophical chap. I guess you've got a lot in your country can't pat *their* stomachs and say, 'yummy, yummy, plenty belly full!' "[30]

With few exceptions, the southern press expounded this kind of confidence, secure in the belief that "there was never a period in the history of the country when there was more perfect order and quiet among the servile classes." In the Confederate Congress, a Virginian boasted that the slaves' loyalty was "never more conspicuous, their obedience never more child-like." In the eyes of some slaveholders, of course, that observation might have prompted more alarm than relief. Rather than face up to such implications, however, the press and southern leaders made the most out of conspicuous examples of black support for the Confederacy, dutifully parading every such act as additional testimony to the beneficence of slavery and the attachment of slaves to their "white folks." When a slave became the first subscriber to the Confederate war loan in Port Gibson, Mississippi, for example, the local newspaper exulted: "The feeling at the South can be learned from this little incident. The negroes are ready to fight for *their* people, and they are ready to give money as well as their lives to the cause of their masters."[31]

If slaves deemed it politic to proffer their support and services, particularly in the early stages of the war, free blacks moved with an even greater sense of urgency to protest their loyalty and allay the suspicions of a white society which had always found them to be an anomaly and source of danger. In the decade preceding the outbreak of war, the more than 182,000 free blacks had faced growing harassment, increased surveillance, and demands for still further restrictions on their freedom. To identify with the white community in this time of crisis might hopefully serve to neutralize that opposition and improve their precarious position in southern society. In New Orleans and Charleston, where small colored elites had established churches, schools, and benevolent associations, the efforts to identify with whites were more conspicuous, their aloofness from the slaves was more pronounced, and their patriotic gestures tended to be more strident. In a memorial to the state governor, a group of free Negroes in Charleston, including a number of substantial property holders, could hardly have been more candid about their attachment to the common cause: "In our veins flows the blood of the white race, in some half, in others much more than half white blood, ... our attachments are with you, our hopes and safety and protection from you, ... our allegiance is due to South Carolina and in her defense, we will offer up our lives, and all that is dear to us."[32]

Clearly, the threat of invasion and the depredations of "alien" troops were capable of unifying diverse and conflicting groups in the South. Those free blacks who had managed to accumulate property were no doubt intent on protecting their investments, along with whatever privileges they enjoyed in a slave society. If some slaves and free Negroes later compared support of the Confederacy to the black driver forced to use the lash on his fellow slaves, still others made no apologies. When offering his support, Bowman Seals, a free black from Clayton, Alabama, claimed to understand fully "the quarrel" between the North and the South and how it affected his people. "I make no claim to be adversed to their best interests; but I know enough of Yankees and of their treatment of the starving blacks among them to understand that their war upon the South is prompted by no love of us, but only by envy and hatred, and by an intermeddling and domineering spirit." If the North should succeed, Seals warned, "disorder and ruin" and "extremist want and misery" would be visited upon all classes and both races.[33]

Had it not been for the exemplary conduct of "the faithful slave," some white Southerners doubted that the war could have lasted for more than ten months. Hence the paeans of praise that would be heaped upon those black men and women who had stood with their masters and mistresses, the oratorical tributes to their loyalty, the monuments erected to their memory, and the romantic images and legends that would be elaborated upon to comfort and entertain generations of whites. The proven fidelity of such individuals even permitted slaveholders to indulge themselves with the notion of slaves as part of the extended family. "We never thought of them as slaves," a Florida woman recalled, "they were 'ours,' 'our own dear black folks.'" Underscoring this same theme, a Richmond woman remembered her slaves as "the repositories of our family secrets. They were our confidants in all our trials. They joyed with us and they sorrowed with us; they wept when we wept, and they laughed when we laughed. Often our best friends, they were rarely our worst enemies." Even where the wartime evidence was at best inconclusive, many whites chose to dwell upon the supportive side of black behavior. When "massa" came home on leave, a Mississippi woman wrote, "no one showed himself [*sic*] more happy to see him than 'Mammy' as she fell upon the floor at his feet hugging and kissing him. 'My Massa come.' 'My Massa come.' I would be so glad if some of our northern friends could have seen her."[34]

If only masters and mistresses had been less insistent about their sense of security and equanimity, they might have been more believable. No matter how many times he heard slaveholders profess confidence in their blacks, William Russell, an English visitor, remained skeptical. After his extensive travels and conversations in the South during the early months of the war, he came away feeling that the very demeanor of the slaves suggested less than contentment with their lot. If these were the happiest creatures on earth, as he had been assured, how was he to explain the "deep dejection" he observed on so many of their faces. On a "model" Louisiana plantation he visited, where "there were abundant evidences that they were well treated," the slaves "all looked sad, and even the old woman who boasted that she had held her old owner in her arms when he was an infant, did not smile cheerfully." If these were such docile and passive people, moreover, as he had also been assured, how was he to explain the elaborate police precautions, the increased vigilance, the curfews, the night patrols. "There is something suspicious," Russell concluded, "in the constant never-ending statement that 'we are not afraid of our slaves.' "[35]

4

———————

EVEN AS MANY MASTERS and mistresses struck a pose of confidence and equanimity, few were unaware of the slaves' demonstrated capacity for evasiveness and dissimulation in the presence of whites. No matter how often slave owners kept reassuring themselves, the doubts and apprehensions were bound to surface. With each passing month, as the issues became clearer and the position of the Confederacy deteriorated, the ambiguities in the slave response would tend to dissolve and the whites who had proclaimed the loudest the faithfulness of their blacks were among those forced to reassess their perceptions in accordance with personal experiences. If the shock of recognition did not come easily for a people who had always claimed an intimate knowledge of the black personality, neither was it altogether unexpected; some whites, in fact, thought they knew their slaves too well to harbor any illusions about the future. "The tenants act pretty well towards *us*," a Virginia woman wrote early in 1862, "but that doesn't prevent our being pretty certain of their intention to stampede when they get a good chance—I, for one, won't care *one* straw—but for the expense of having to hire 'help.' They are nothing but an ungrateful, discontented lot & I don't care how soon I get rid of mine."[36]

To endure, perhaps even to survive, many slaves had learned from experience to anticipate the white man's moods and whims, to know his expectations, to placate his fears, to flatter his vanity, and to feed his feelings of superiority. As a slave, Henry Bibb recalled, he had come to realize the folly of openly resisting the white man. "The only weapon of self defence that I could use successfully, was that of deception." With considerable relish, a former Tennessee slave remembered the death of a particularly cruel mistress. The slaves on the plantation did what was expected of them when one of their "white folks" died; they solemnly filed into the Big House to pay their final respects, covering their faces with their hands as if to hide their tears and stifle their sobs. Once they were outside, however, the slaves made their feelings known to each other. "Old God damn son-of-a-bitch," one of them murmured, "she gone on down to hell."[37]

During the Civil War, when the master's temperament often experienced violent fluctuations, the slave had even more urgent reason to adhere to the time-tested imperatives: that he never appear to be too well informed, that he remain circumspect in his views, that he mask any feelings of hostility, that he feign stupidity at the right moment, that he "act the nigger" when the situation demanded it and punctuate his responses to whites with the proper comic mannerisms and facial expressions —the shuffling of the feet, the scratching of the head, the grin denoting incomprehension. The black man who invokes the "darky act," Ralph Ellison has suggested, is not so much "a 'smart-man-playing-dumb' as a weak man who knows the nature of his oppressors' weakness.... [H]is mask of meekness conceals the wisdom of one who has learned the secret of saying the 'yes' which accomplishes the expressive 'no.' " Although some slaves may well have internalized the ritual of deference, few whites could know for certain and that was a problem that would plague them throughout the war. "Oh, yes, massa!" a Virginia slave responded in 1863 when asked by a northern clergyman if she had heard of the Emancipation Proclamation, "we all knows about it; only we darsn't let on. We pretends not to know. I said to my ole massa, 'What's this Massa Lincoln is going to do to the poor nigger? I hear he is going to cut 'em up awful bad. How is it, massa?' I just pretended foolish, sort of." At the first opportunity, this slave fled to the Union lines.[38]

When questioned about the Civil War, as with any other subject the slave usually shaped his response to the tone of the question and the requirements of the occasion. He would tell his white listeners what he thought they wanted to hear. In the presence of southern whites, the slave was apt to proclaim his loyalty to the Confederacy (or to his "white folks" and the state in which he lived) in much the same way that he had denied on so many occasions (especially to northern visitors) the desire to be free. "The Yankees will be whipped," a South Carolina slave recalled assuring his master and mistress repeatedly, even as he prayed and believed otherwise. Whether in the presence of Southerners or Yankees, on the other hand, the slave might find it more politic to seek refuge in a pretense of ignorance or in evasiveness. "Why, you see, master," an elderly Louisiana slave told a Union reporter in 1863, " 'taint for an old nigger like me to know anything 'bout politics." When the reporter pressed him to indicate whether he favored the Confederacy or the Union, the slave maintained his "ineffable smile" for a moment, and then with a mock gravity replied, "I'm on de Lord's side, and He'll work out His salvation; bress de Lord." Framing his response with equal care, an elderly Georgia black told a Union officer who had questioned him about the war, "Well, Sir, what I think about it, is this—it's mighty distressin' this war, but it 'pears to me like the right thing couldn't be done without it."[39]

While military fortunes fluctuated with every skirmish and battle, so did the slaves' responses to the war, with many of them adopting a "wait and see" attitude and refusing to commit themselves irretrievably to either side. In 1862, for example, a correspondent traveling with the Union Army asked a Missouri slave if he favored the Union. "Oh! yes, massa," he replied, "when you's about we is." When asked what he would do if the Confederate troops returned, the slave quickly responded, "[W]e's good secesh then. Can't allow de white folks to git head niggers in dat way." The reporter went away impressed with how this slave perceived his role in the conflict. "These Missouri niggers know a great deal more than the white folks give them credit for, and whether Missouri goes for the confederacy or the Union, her slaves have learned a lesson too much to ever be useful as slaves. . . . The darkeys understand the whole question and the game played."[40]

The evasive stance assumed by slaves reflected not only their perception of reality but an initial confusion about the war and the issues over which it was being fought. How much of the war news a master thought advisable to share with his slaves varied considerably, and in some regions what one observer called "a stratum of ignorance" prevailed. The Georgia slave who in November 1864 had still not heard of the Emancipation Proclamation was by no means unique. "De white folks nebber talk 'fore black men," he explained; "dey mighty free from dat." Even if whites chose to be candid with their slaves, they were apt to find that anything they revealed about the war was greeted with suspicion. "I do not speak of the war to them," Mary Chesnut noted in November 1861; "on that subject, they do not believe a word you say." Perhaps more whites than blacks ultimately believed the rumors of Yankee atrocities; at least, the direful warnings voiced by slave owners would have little apparent effect on the steady stream of blacks to the Union lines. Nor did the master's confident talk about the progress of the war necessarily survive slave scrutiny. "I know pappy say dem Yankees gwine win, 'cause dey allus marchin' to de South, but none de South soldiers marches to de North," William Davis recalled. "He didn't say dat to de white folks, but he sho' say it to us."[41]

When the war began to turn against the Confederacy, even slaves with limited access to the news could sense it. In some regions, in fact, slaveholders had their hands full trying to reassure the blacks that the retreating

Confederate soldiers were not, as had been rumored, wantonly murdering slaves rather than see them freed. But the attempts to communicate with their slaves on such subjects often became an exercise in futility. "Would I kill you, or let anybody else kill you?" a South Carolina mistress asked her butler. He remained apprehensive. "We know you won't own up to anything against your side," he replied. "You never tell us anything that you can help." The white woman threw up her hands in exasperation, concluding that nothing more was to be expected of a slave who had been "a pampered menial" for twenty years. "His insolence has always been intolerable."[42]

That slaves should have doubted what their masters and mistresses told them reflected more than an intuitive skepticism. Despite their relative isolation and the prevailing degree of illiteracy, slaves over the years had devised various methods by which to keep themselves informed, not only of doings in the household but in the outside world. The servants enjoyed the most advantageous position, overhearing the conversations of the white folks while ostensibly preoccupied with their domestic duties, and then passing the information and gossip along to the slave quarters. "No, massa, we'se can't read, but we'se can listen," a South Carolina slave explained, after coming over to the Yankees.[43]

Within the master's house, numerous slaves formed their initial impressions of the war, why it was being fought, and how it might affect their own lives. Dora Franks, for example, who claimed to have been well treated in the Mississippi household in which she worked, overheard her master and mistress discuss the war: "He say he feared all de slaves 'ud be took away. She say if dat was true she feel lak jumpin' in de well. I hate to hear her say dat, but from dat minute I started prayin' for freedom." From the vantage of the house slave, news about the war sometimes consisted of overhearing angry outbursts and harangues by the whites, punctuated with wild talk about abolitionists seizing the South, Yankees coming to kill "us all," a war "to free the niggers," and how the Confederates intended to send "de damn yaller bellied Yankees" reeling back to the North. Despite such bombast, proximity to the conversations of whites usually helped to clarify the war issues and keep the slaves abreast of the military situation.[44]

When plantation whites became more guarded in their discussions, lest they be overheard, the slaves simply became more resourceful. "[T]he greater the precaution," a former South Carolina slave recalled, "the alerter became the slaves, the wider they opened their ears and the more eager they became for outside information." Many slaves would take considerable pride in how they had surreptitiously acquired the war news. "My father and the other boys," one recalled, "used to crawl under the house an' lie on the ground to hear massa read the newspaper to missis when they first began to talk about the war." On the occasion of festivities in the Big House like a dinner party, another slave recalled, he would climb into an oak tree, hide under the long moss, and wait until the master and his guests came out on the veranda for an after-dinner smoke. He would then invariably be treated to a full discussion of the latest war news and a frank appraisal of the military and political situation. An illiterate waiting maid experienced the frustration of hearing her master and mistress spell out certain words they did not want her to hear. This resourceful woman managed to memorize the letters, "an' as soon as I got away I ran to uncle an' spelled them over to him, an' he told me what they meant." No doubt some masters suspected the diligence with which slaves obtained news of the war but very few of them were able to adopt the tactic used by William Henry Trescot, a prominent South Carolinian. He had taken to sprinkling his conversation with French expressions. "We are using French against Africa," he explained to a perplexed friend. "We know the black waiters are all ears now, and we want to keep what we have to say dark. We can't afford to take them in our confidence, you know." Mary Chesnut, for one, found his explanation, also given in French, to be "exasperating."[45]

The local courthouse and post office, favorite meeting places for whites, were obvious and much-exploited sources of information and rumor. Like the body servants and conscripted laborers who brought home news from the front lines, slaves in town on errands for the master found it relatively easy to acquire information and form impressions about the progress of the war. The slaves who picked up the mail for their masters became in some instances couriers to the larger slave community. The post office, Booker T. Washington recalled, was located about three miles from the plantation, and the slave who was sent there lingered about long enough to catch the drift of the conversation of the many whites who gathered there and who invariably exchanged views about recent developments. On his way home, the mail carrier would share what he had heard with other slaves, and in this way, Washington claimed, blacks often heard the news before it reached the Big House. In Forsyth County, Georgia, young Edward Glenn fetched the newspaper for his mistress, and each day Walter Raleigh, the local black preacher, waited for him by the road and read the paper before the slave took it to the house. On the day Glenn would never forget, the preacher threw the newspaper on the ground after reading it, hollered "I'm free as a frog! " and ran away. The slave dutifully took the paper to his mistress, who read it and began to cry. "I didn't say no more," Glenn recalled.[46]

Although most slaves were illiterate, nearly every neighborhood contained at least one or more who had acquired reading and writing skills. Immediately after the war, when freed blacks no longer felt the need to conceal such matters, many a master would learn to his astonishment (often during contract negotiations) that a slave he had assumed to be illiterate had known for some time how to read. While in bondage, however, some slaves thought it impolitic to reveal such skills. Squires Jackson, a Florida slave who had kept his literacy from the whites, recalled how the master walked in upon him unexpectedly while he was reading the newspaper and demanded to know what he was doing. Equal to the moment, Jackson immediately turned the newspaper upside down and declared, "Confederates done won the war." The master laughed and left the room, and once again a slave had used the "darky act" to extricate himself from a precarious situation.[47]

Few plantation whites were fully aware of the inventiveness with which their slaves transmitted information to other blacks. Extensive black communication networks, feeding on a variety of sources, sped information from plantation to plantation, county to county, often with remarkable secrecy and accuracy. What slaves called the "grapevine telegraph" frequently employed code words that enabled them to carry on conversations about forbidden subjects in the very presence of their masters and mistresses. Although whites often failed to grasp the mechanics or vocabulary of slave communication, they did come to suspect that their slaves knew more than they revealed. With the outbreak of the war, slaveholders tried to curtail interplantation contacts between blacks, lest such fraternization—which had been generally tolerated—encourage a wide dissemination of news and permit concerted plans for flight to the Union lines. "When I first heard talk about the War," Mary Grayson recalled, "the slaves were allowed to go and see one another sometimes and often they were sent on errands several miles with a wagon or on a horse, but pretty soon we were all kept at home, and nobody was allowed to come around and talk to us." Despite these restrictions, she added, "we heard what was going on."[48]

Under wartime conditions, suspicions were more easily aroused and previously tolerated slave practices came under much closer scrutiny. Not long after the outbreak of war, for example, a black congregation in Savannah sang with particular fervor a traditional hymn,

> *Yes, we all shall be free,*
> *Yes, we all shall be free,*
> *Yes, we all shall be free,*
> *When the Lord shall appear.*

While the service was still in progress, local police entered the church, arrested those in attendance, and charged that the blacks were plotting freedom, singing "the Lord" instead of "the Yankees" in order to deceive any white observers in the audience. Even earlier, at the time of Lincoln's election, slaves in Georgetown, South Carolina, were whipped for singing the same song. The black youth who related this incident explained: "Dey tink *de Lord* mean for say *de Yankees.*" Whether the police overreacted is less important than the suspicions upon which their actions were based. Since long before the days of Nat Turner, blacks had been suspected of using their religious observances to communicate subversive sentiments. The most innocuous-sounding sermon, the most solemn, traditional hymns, might conceivably contain double meanings that were obvious only to the black parishioners. When they spoke and sang of delivery from bondage and oppression, with Old Testament allusions to Moses and the Hebrew children, the hope clearly lay in this world—"And the God dat lived in Moses' time is jus' de same today." The whites suspected as much, and wartime security demanded greater vigilance, including a more rigid enforcement of the statutes that required a white man's presence at a religious service conducted by a black.[49]

Whatever the potential risks, whites persisted in seeking comfort and reassurance in the religious enthusiasm of their slaves and in making it serve their own ends. During the war, participation of house slaves in the white family's devotion and in prayers for the safe return of the master or his sons helped to reinforce the notion of an extended family bound by affection, faithfulness, and loyalty. Similarly, white clergymen undertook the task of admonishing the slaves to be deferential and loyal to their owners in this time of crisis. Upon visiting the James Davis plantation in Texas, a white preacher explained the issues to the slaves with unmistakable clarity. "Do you wan' to keep you homes whar you git all to eat, and raise your chillen, or do you wan' to be free to roam roun' without a home, like de wil' animals? If you wan' to keep you homes you better pray for de South to win." At least, that was how William Adams, one of his slave parishioners, recalled the sermon. When the preacher then asked those slaves who were willing to pray for the South to raise their hands, everyone did so. "We was skeered not to," Adams recalled, "but we sho' didn' wan' de South to win."[50]

Nearly every white preacher faced a problem of credibility when he addressed the slaves. Not only did they perceive him as an instrument of the white master, capable of twisting the word of God to make it serve the white man's ends, but what he told them, particularly during the war, had little relevance for their own lives and hopes. With the prospect of emancipation looming larger, many slaves seized every opportunity to address God in their own ways. Charlotte Brooks, a Louisiana slave, bent down between the rows of sugarcane to pray for her liberation. "I knowed God had promised to hear his children when they cry, and he heard us way down here in Egypt." In Athens, Georgia, Minnie Davis and her mother dutifully attended the services in the First Presbyterian Church, where the slaves sat in the gallery and listened to the white preacher implore the Lord to drive the Yankees back to the North. "My mother said that all the time he was praying out loud like that, she was praying to herself: 'Oh, Lord, please send the Yankees on and let them set us free.' "[51]

Occupying a delicate position in the slave world, the black preacher and the black plantation exhorter might find themselves forced into compromises and duplicity in order to survive. If whites were present at the services, as the law so often commanded, the preacher or exhorter would have to be doubly cautious about what he told the blacks. The Civil War placed him in a particular dilemma, caught between increased white vigilance and the urge to articulate the uppermost thoughts of his parishioners. His attempts to resolve that conflict severely tested his powers of obfuscation. On the day of fasting and prayer ordered by President Jefferson Davis after a series of Confederate military reverses, whites and slaves gathered at the old Guinea Church in Cumberland County, Virginia. After the whites had said their prayers, seeking to turn the tide of battle, the time came for the blacks to make known their sentiments. The first black speaker, an old deacon, avoided the issue altogether with the simple prayer that "the Lord's will be done," which the parishioners could obviously interpret as they wished. But Armstead Berkeley, the pastor of the black Baptist church, when called upon to lead a prayer, pleaded with the Lord to "point the bullets of the old Confederate guns right straight at the hearts of the Yankees; make our men victorious on the battlefield and send them home in health and strength to join their people in peace and prosperity." That seemed clear enough; the black church deacons, in fact, were said to have reproached the pastor after the meeting for this apparent betrayal of the slaves' cause. "Don't worry, children," the pastor explained, "the Lord knew what I was talking about." The deacons were reportedly satisfied with the pastor's explanation. With a far clearer sense of purpose, an old plantation preacher in South Carolina complied with a request to pray for the Confederacy: "Bress, we do pray Thee, our enemies, de wicked Sesech. Gib dem time to 'pent, we do pray Thee, and den we will excuse Thee if Thou takes dem all to glory."[52]

Although forced at times to play a dual role, the black preacher usually commanded a leading place in the black community. Many former slaves recalled him as a man who had offered them hope for redemption and freedom in this world, even when the prospects seemed most dim. L. J. Coppin, who would later become a prominent cleric in the African Methodist Episcopal Church, remembered with particular admiration Christopher Jones, a Maryland black upon whom the slaves had come to rely not only for religious guidance and inspiration but for his knowledge of wartime developments. "He was not so much for resorting to the prophecies of Daniel for information," Coppin remarked, "as he was to the newspaper that secretly came weekly to him." Many of the whites with whom William Russell spoke, in his tour of the South in 1861, understood the power of the black preacher as well as his capacity for mischief. "They 'do the niggers no good,'" he was told, "'they talk about things that are going on elsewhere, and get their minds unsettled.'" Some whites in the Ogeechee District of Georgia were themselves so unsettled by a slave preacher who proclaimed the inevitability of a Yankee victory that they covered him with tar and set him afire.[53]

No matter how closely the master regulated the religious observances of his slaves, he could neither control every aspect of their lives nor filter the information and rumors that eventually reached the slave quarters. When asked if the masters knew anything of "the secret life of the colored people," Robert Smalls, a former South Carolina slave, would later testify: "No, sir; one life they show their masters and another life they don't show."

On the larger farms and plantations, where more than half the slaves lived, the social life of the quarters brought together house servants and field hands, artisans and carriage drivers, stableboys and cooks. The news gathered in the Big House that day or in the nearby town or from slaves on a neighboring plantation would be divulged and discussed, often with asides and stories at the expense of the master and mistress. Dilly Yellady's parents, who had been slaves in North Carolina, told her how "de niggers would git in de slave quarters at night an' pray fer freedom an' laf 'bout what de Yankees wus doin', 'bout Lincoln an' Grant foolin' deir marsters so."[54]

To attain a greater degree of privacy, the slaves might assemble "down in the hollow" or in the "hush-harbors," secluded meeting spots away from the Big House where the slaves would employ various devices to absorb the sounds. What transpired at such gatherings appears to have been a mixture of prayer, singing, and candid discussions (often whispered) about subjects that had to be repressed in the presence of the whites. On some plantations, it provided slaves with an opportunity to relieve themselves of the tensions and physical exhaustion that had accumulated over a long day and evening of hard labor. During the war, these gatherings took on even greater importance, serving not only to allow personal release and expression but also to convey and discuss the most recent news about the military situation, the proximity of Union troops, the prospect of emancipation, and the master's intentions. Traveling in the interior of Virginia, an "unobserved spectator" who happened upon such a gathering heard them pray for the success of the North, and one old woman wept for joy when told that the Yankees were soon coming to set them free. "Oh! good massa Jesus," she shouted, "let the time be short." After the white preacher on the Davis plantation in Texas led the slaves in prayers for the Confederacy, he left apparently confident of their faithfulness. That night, however, the slaves met secretly "down in de hollow" and Uncle Mack entertained them with a story.

> One time over in Virginny dere was two ole niggers, Uncle Bob and Uncle Tom. Dey was mad at one 'nuther and one day dey decided to have a dinner and bury de hatchet. So dey sat down, and when Uncle Bob wasn't lookin' Uncle Tom put some poison in Uncle Bob's food, but he saw it and when Uncle Tom wasn't lookin', Uncle Bob he turned de tray roun' on Uncle Tom, and he gits de poison food.

Looking out at the assembled group, Uncle Mack concluded: "Dat's what we slaves is gwine do, jus' turn de tray roun' and pray for de North to win."[55]

When the wartime experience began to reveal a diversity of slave response and behavior, whites were sometimes too incredulous to concede that they might have overextended themselves in the praise and confidence they had earlier lavished upon "the faithful slave." Victims of their own self-assurances, they seemed incapable of dealing with reality, refusing to believe that their slaves understood the implications of the war. "The truth is," Henry W. Ravenel of South Carolina insisted to the very end, "the negroes know but little of the cause & issues of the war." That assumption would enable Ravenel to blame the Yankee invaders for turning the heads of the blacks, leading them into acts of mischief and betrayal. But the impact of the war was simply too pervasive, and the sources of information too plentiful, to have kept the slaves in total ignorance of its meaning. As early as the election of 1860, in fact, several white observers had noted how slaves were "the most interested and eager listeners" at political gatherings, and numerous blacks recalled how their own masters had voiced fears that the election of Abraham Lincoln would doom slavery.[56]

Although slaves were reticent about openly revealing their feelings, they found it increasingly difficult to mask them. Even as their muscles remained faithful to the master, raising the crops that were both indispensable for the war effort and necessary for survival in the quarters, their faces and sometimes their words and actions threatened to betray their inner thoughts, particularly when the prospect of emancipation became clearer and the outcome of the war more predictable. The slaves appeared to sense when that turning point had been reached. "Damn the niggers," a Louisiana planter exclaimed, "they know more about politics than most of the white men. They know everything that happens." To a newspaper editor in Chattanooga, Tennessee, the progress of the war could be discerned by simply watching the faces of the local blacks: "The spirits of the colored citizens rise and fall with the ebb and flow of this tide of blue devils, and when they are glad as larks, the whites are depressed and go about the streets like mourners."[57]

Based upon the information they had pieced together from various sources, slaves not only kept themselves informed of the progress of the war but, more critically, they began to appreciate its implications for their own lives and future. By 1863, at least, the assumption prevailed among vast numbers of slaves (including even those who did not entirely welcome the prospect) that if the Union Army prevailed on the battlefields, the Confederacy and slavery would expire together. They appeared to understand, a Union officer reported, "that it was a war for their liberation; that the cause of the war was their being in slavery, and that the aim and result would be their freedom. Further than that they did not seem to have any idea of it."[58]

But that was more than enough to force the white South to consider the most expeditious means by which to maintain its internal security and calm the growing apprehension of its people.

## 5

NEVER HAD the slaveholding class permitted verbal expressions of faith in their blacks to blind them to the need for the utmost vigilance in controlling their movements and behavior. In the face of wartime disruptions, such vigilance became all the more imperative, if only to make certain that the loudly voiced self-assurances were neither misplaced nor betrayed. Although the Confederate Congress, like many states, initially exempted from military service one white man for every twenty slaves he supervised, the protest of less favored planters and farmers forced a sharp reduction in such exemptions, thereby shifting much of the burden of wartime surveillance to the citizens' patrols. Based on their previous experience with these patrols, few if any blacks had any reason to welcome this development.

Made up largely of nonslaveholding whites, many of them eager to vent their own grievances and frustrations on the blacks, the patrols had traditionally undertaken the responsibility for slave control outside the plantations. Aside from checking out rumors of insurrectionary plots, they seized runaways, broke up clandestine slave gatherings, and meted out punishment to blacks found off the plantations without a proper pass. Wherever the patrols operated, even if on an irregular basis, the slaves had come to fear them as legal terrorists who went out of their way to inflict brutalities and humiliation on any black people they encountered. With the outbreak of the war, state and local governments, recognizing the need to maximize police surveillance, moved to strengthen the patrols and to expand their operations. But these attempts came at precisely the moment army service depleted the number of eligible males, including many who had previously performed patrol duty. And as the prospect of controlling blacks sensing liberation diminished, the alarm of local white residents mounted. "I am afraid we will have troublesome times down here," a Louisiana woman wrote her husband. "[T]he men are patroleing [sic] all the time but the men are so few in the county that they can not do much good."[59]

Confronted with the actuality of a Yankee invasion and anxieties about the black response, white Southerners found themselves in an impossible situation. When the governor of Mississippi, for example, ordered the enlistment of still more men to resist the Yankees, he encountered a storm of protest from whites who gave every indication of fearing the slaves as much as the Union Army. An officer in the state militia privately warned the governor of the concern voiced by many of his soldiers: "the question is constantly asked 'what is to become of my wife & children when left in a land swarming with negroes without a single white man on many plantations to restrain their licentiousness by a little wholesome fear?'" The answer came soon enough, as letters poured in on the governor describing the virtual collapse of slave discipline and subordination in several counties. "If there is any more men taken out of this county," one resident warned, "we may as well give it to the negroes . . . now we have to patrole every night to keep them down." Such expressions of concern, coupled with demands that Confederate troops be placed in positions where they might most effectively combat epidemics of slave insubordination, multiplied as the Union Army (and the prospect of slave liberation) drew closer.[60]

Apprehension mounted, too, over the behavior and loyalty of slaves in the cities and towns. The objects of particular suspicion were those blacks permitted to hire out their time (with the owner receiving a specified rental payment), many of whom lived away from the premises of both the owner and the immediate supervisor and thereby acquired a degree of autonomy denied the rural slave. That autonomy, to believe the complaints of numerous white residents, had produced a dangerous class of people capable of undermining the entire system of racial control and discipline. After the outbreak of war, many planters heeded admonitions to withdraw their slaves from the contaminating influences of urban life; at the same time, newly strengthened state laws and local ordinances were designed to restrict the movement of black residents. Nevertheless, urban slaves capitalized on the shortage of policemen. Reports of theft, arson, and assault periodically revived fears of servile insurrection, and white residents were forced to alter old notions about the security of their homes. "There was a time," a Florida newspaper reminded its white readers, "when a man might go to sleep and leave his house open with impunity in this city, but we fear that time has passed away." Although still boasting that he never locked the apartment in which he slept, Edmund Ruffin confided to his diary that he had begun "to use means for defence which I never did before, in keeping loaded guns by my bedside."[61]

Despite the conspicuous efforts made by some free Negroes to allay white suspicions, the tensions created by the war eroded their legal position and subjected their daily lives to even closer scrutiny. To minimize the danger posed by this population, local and state authorities prepared to enforce the laws barring their entry into the state and prohibiting manumission by last will and testament; they also ordered free black residents to register and be properly licensed by county officials and threatened to remove any who exercised an "improper or mischievous influence upon slaves." The ultimate solution, adopted by several states, was to encourage free blacks to select a master and voluntarily enter into slavery. After all, a Savannah newspaper observed, "every day we hear our slaves pronounced the happiest people in the world. Why then this lamentation over putting the free negro in his only proper . . . condition?" Enforcement of the newly strengthened restrictions on free blacks varied considerably; nevertheless, the control machinery was readily available for those who wished to use it, whether for purposes of harassment or expulsion. And free blacks who might have entertained other notions had now been forcibly reminded that their position in southern society was analogous to that of the slave rather than the white man.[62]

Although legislation and patrol vigilance might check certain abuses, the swift punishment of troublesome blacks had always been thought to have a more immediate and enduring impact. The exigencies of war made it all the more urgent to maintain that "subjection through fear" long sanctioned by white public opinion and courts. If loyalty and subjugation could be exacted in no other way, plantation whites freely wielded the whip. Any violent altercation between a white person and a slave required no investigation of cause before meting out the appropriate punishment. "Jacob has had to fight with one of Mrs. Pickets Negroes," a Louisiana woman reported in May 1862, "and the Negro cut him seven times on the head and face. Jake gave him one hundred lashes for evry cut an fifty for the ballance of his misconduct." If only to preserve the prerogatives of the master class, some whites cautioned against summary justice meted out by a mob, but the overriding concern for internal security took its inevitable toll. Angry mobs did not hesitate to hang blacks accused of collaborating with the enemy, nor did they scruple about employing more brutal forms of punishment.[63]

Neither extraordinary legislative measures nor increased vigilance proved adequate to the impossible task of wartime slave control, and even the swift and summary punishment of recalcitrant workers hardly allayed growing apprehension over the behavior of the blacks. In some instances, the subjugation achieved by the use of the whip must have seemed less than satisfying to those inflicting the beating. In Nansemond County, Virginia, a slave known as Uncle Toliver had been indiscreet enough to pray aloud for the Yankees. The master's two sons ordered him to kneel in the barnyard and pray for the Confederacy. But this stubborn old man prayed even louder for a Yankee triumph. With growing exasperation, perhaps even bewilderment, the two sons took turns in whipping him until finally the slave, still murmuring something about the Yankees, collapsed and died. The "triumph" achieved by these two young white men sounded more like the death knell of the system they sought so desperately to maintain.[64]

Deprived of what they deemed essential protection, often frustrated in their attempts to anticipate black behavior, many anguished whites forgot all that talk about contented and loyal slaves and described a situation fraught with the most terrifying implications. Having heard that the home guard might soon be recalled to combat the Yankee invaders, the mistress of a plantation in the Abbeville district of South Carolina wondered how the remaining whites could possibly survive the internal enemy. "If the men are going, then awful things are coming, and I don't want to stay. My God, the women and children, it will be murder and ruin. There are many among the black people and they only want a chance."[65] If any additional evidence were needed, the obsession with internal security and, perhaps most ominous, the deployment in some regions of Confederate troops to resist *both* Yankee invaders and rebellious blacks suggested a white South desperately clinging to the fiction of the docile slave without in any way believing it.

6

REFUSING TO RESIGN THEMSELVES to the grim prospects of occupation and emancipation, numerous white families chose to remove their slaves to safer grounds. That was an abrupt change in his life that Allen V. Manning would never forget. Leaving the old plantation in Clarke County, Mississippi, Manning and his fellow slaves found themselves heading westward into a country they knew but little about. Several times the caravan halted in some place, while the master hired them out to planters trying to make a crop. Every time the Yankees came closer, he would move them out again until finally they crossed the Sabine River into Texas. That was where Manning's sister gave birth, and the master promptly named the new girl Texana. When they reached Coryell County, the master decided to settle and plant a crop, satisfied that the Yankees no longer posed an immediate threat to his slave property. And it was here, more than 600 miles from the plantation where he had spent most of his bondage, that Allen Manning would learn one day of his freedom. He never returned to Mississippi.[66]

The decision made by Allen Manning's master to run his slaves into Texas reflected the desperation with which numbers of planters sought to avoid the panic that often preceded the arrival of the Yankees and to find a place where they might keep their slave force intact and postpone for as long as possible the need to emancipate them. From the very outset of the war, some planter families anticipated the need for such a refuge and rented or purchased places to which they could move themselves and their slave property at the appropriate time. The first slaves to be relocated were often the most troublesome, those who were thought to have a demoralizing influence on the others and in whom the least amount of confidence could be placed. Louis Manigault, a Georgia rice planter, acting on the advice of his overseer, selected ten slaves he deemed "most likely would cause trouble" and dispatched them to an area "sufficiently remote from all excitement." A planter friend of Mary Chesnut searched for "a place of safety" to send 200 of his blacks who "had grown to be a nuisance," while still another South Carolinian, supervising the removal of his mother's slaves, chose "the primest hands & the most uncertain."[67]

Whether because of the threatened disruption of local and family ties or the proximity to freedom, few slaves relished the idea of being removed from the home farm or plantation. Sensing that reluctance, a Tennessee planter tried to ease the pain by sharing the remaining whiskey with his slaves before ordering their departure. Perhaps he had only intended to numb their senses; nevertheless, the act revealed a certain compassion, when compared to the owners who employed various deceptions to prepare their slaves for the arduous trek, telling them about the murderous Yankees and, as one slave recalled, "dat where dey is goin' de lakes full of syrup and covered with batter cakes, and dey won't have to work so hard." Rather than resort to such ruses, the proprietress of a plantation in central Georgia appealed to the faithfulness of her slaves and made removal a virtual test of their loyalty. "I reminded them of their master's absence; how he had committed his wife and children to their care; how desirous was I to be able to tell him on his return that they deserved his confidence to the last." All but two of the slaves left with her the next morning.[68]

Whatever their owners told them, the slaves seemed to know instinctively (if not from the "grapevine") why they were being sent away, and for some that proved to be sufficient reason to take immediate action to determine their own destinations. Stephen Jordon, who had been a slave in Louisiana, regarded his master as "a good man" but with a highly volatile temper. When slaves in the neighborhood ran off to Union-occupied New Orleans, however, he assured his master that he had no such intention. "I shall never leave you. Those Yankees are too bad, I hear." But when his master announced plans to remove all the slaves to Texas, Jordon had to reconcile his sense of obligation with his deep yearning for freedom.

> Of course I liked Mr. Valsin well enough, but I rather be free than be with him, or be the slave of any body else. So his word about going to Texas rather sunk deep into me, because I was praying for the Yankees to come up our way just as soon as possible. I dreaded going to Texas, because I feared that I would never get free. The same thought was in the mind of every one of the slaves on our place. So two nights before we were to leave for Texas all the slaves on our place had a secret meeting at midnight, when we decided to leave to meet the Yankees. Sure enough, about one o'clock that night every one of us took through the woods to make for the Union line.

In low-country South Carolina, a planter made the mistake of telling his slaves that he intended to move them into the interior after the crop had been completed; seventy-six of them left the night of his announcement and reached the Union lines. The steady movement of Louisiana planters into Texas and Arkansas was to have included the slaves belonging to John Williams of Assumption Parish; the morning of his intended departure, however, he awakened to discover that twenty-seven of them, including several of the family favorites, were nowhere to be found. "Will you ever have faith in one again?" his daughter thought to ask him. No matter how hard the planter tried to conceal his intentions, the information managed to reach the slave quarters. Only two days after making some discreet inquiries in town about a plantation to rent, John Berkley Grimball, a prominent South Carolina planter, learned that nearly every one of his slaves, including "the best of them," had disappeared during the previous night—"about 80 of them . . . men women and children." He quickly confined most of the remaining slaves to the workhouse in the nearby town until he found another place in the up-country. "This is a terrible blow and has probably ruined me," he sighed after adding up his losses.[69]

The wagon trains carrying the planter families and household goods, with the slaves, cattle, and horses trailing behind them, would become a familiar sight in parts of the wartime South. The fall of New Orleans and exposure to Federal raiding parties precipitated the largest exodus, with more than 150,000 slaves sent out of Louisiana and Mississippi, choking the roads and towns leading into Texas. "It look like everybody in the world was going to Texas," Allen Manning recalled. "When we would be going down the road we would have to walk along the side all the time to let the wagons go past, all loaded with folks going to Texas." The slaves who made these treks would long recall the crowded roads, the inhospitable towns, the mothers toting the children on their backs, the fathers tending the wagons and livestock, and the many difficult detours that were ordered to avoid Yankee raiding parties. "Dat was de awfullest trip any man ever make!" Charley Williams, a former Louisiana slave, recalled. "We had to hide from everybody until we find out if dey Yankees or Sesesh, and we go along little old back roads and up one mountain and down another, through de woods all de way." Virginia Newman remembered how "us all walk barefeets and our feets break and run they so sore, and blister for months. It cold and hot sometime and rain and us got no house or no tent." To compensate for the drudgery of the journey, the slaves invented some appropriate songs and sang them to the slow steps of the oxen pulling the wagons.

> *Walk, walk, you nigger, walk!*
> *De road am dusty, de road am tough,*
> *Dust in de eye, dust in de tuft;*
> *Dust in de mouth, yous can't talk—*
> *Walk, you niggers, don't you balk.*
>
> *Walk, walk, you nigger, walk!*
> *De road am dusty, de road am rough.*
> *Walk 'til we reach dere, walk or bust—*
> *De road am long, we be dere by and by.*

"We'uns don't sing it many times," Bill Homer remembered, " 'til de missy come and sit in de back of de wagon, facin' we'uns [who were walking], and she begin to beat de slow time and sing wid we'uns. Dat please Missy Mary to sing with us and she laugh and laugh."[70]

Although many of the elderly slaves had been left behind on the old plantations, relocation would take its toll in exhaustion, disrupted families, and lives. After two years on the road, the Miles family of Richmond, Virginia, finally reached Franklin, Texas, but not before the master had sold and traded both slaves and livestock along the way, retaining only his personal servants. Elvira Boles, who had been a slave in Mississippi, left her baby buried "somewhere on dat road" to Texas. Louis Love of Louisiana recalled the death of his brother before they reached the Trinity River. A North Carolina planter, who "didn' want to part with his niggers," failed to survive the trip to Arkansas, as did three of the slaves. "We buried the slaves there [on the road]," Millie Evans remembered, "but we camped while ol' master was carried back to North Carolina. When ol' mistress come back we started on to Arkansas an' reached here safe but when we got here we foun' freedom here too."[71]

Whether on the road or in the makeshift camps at night, the slaves had ample time to reflect over their situation—the places they had left behind, the breakup of families, the growing distance between themselves and the nearest Union troops, the uncertainty of what lay ahead. Their brooding boded only disastrous results for some slaveholders. Rarely a morning passed without the discovery that still more slaves had fled during the night, perhaps to the Union lines, perhaps even back to the old plantation. The difficulty in controlling their slaves on the road forced some owners to turn back; others simply tried to minimize their losses. With her husband in the Confederate Army, Mary Williams Pugh of Louisiana decided to attach her slaves to those of her parents, and the two families then set out for a month-long trip to Rusk, Texas. The morning they departed, her parents lost twenty-seven slaves. "The first night we camped Sylvester left —the next night at Bayou B. about 25 of Pa's best hands left & the next day at Berwick Bay nearly all of the women & children started—but this Pa found out in time to catch them all except one man & one woman. Altogether he had lost about sixty of his best men." Meanwhile, Mary Pugh's brother had encountered similar losses the first two days on the road and he decided to turn back, "as he was afraid of being left with only women & children." After these experiences, Mrs. Pugh could only be grateful for the "good behavior" of her own slaves. "[Y]ou have every reason to be proud of them," she wrote her husband, "as I have told them you would be. They are the talk of every neighborhood they pass through as they are such exceptions to other negroes."[72]

The decision to move the slaves, made in the interest of preserving the work force, could thus prove to be costly, and there appeared to be no way to predict accurately how the relocated blacks would respond. When two white men engaged in moving blacks from the South Carolina coast to the up-country made the mistake of laying down their weapons and going to sleep, the slaves seized the guns, shot and killed their escorts, and made off to the Yankees. Still further difficulties awaited masters at the end of these treks, when their slaves discovered something less than the land of milk and honey and the lakes filled with syrup they had been told to expect. Upon arriving in Texas, Van Moore recalled, a fellow slave tasted the water from a lake and spit it out in disgust. "I reckon he thinks dat funny syrup." If work routines differed from what they had known on the old place, they were not necessarily less arduous. Many owners, in order to sustain themselves, hired out their slaves by the day, week, and month to work in whatever jobs might be available. At the same time, some slaves who had been accustomed to specialized tasks now found themselves little more than common field hands. Bill Homer, for example, had been a coachman on the plantation in Shreveport, Louisiana, but in Caldwell, Texas, he became an ox driver and hoer.[73]

Rather than finding any relief from the customary problems of management and discipline, slaveholders were apt to discover that the new environment encouraged greater independence in the slaves. Even owners who removed their blacks only a short distance encountered unexpected problems. F. D. Richardson, a Louisiana planter, had moved the bulk of his work force from the Bayside plantation down a bayou and into the woods, in the hope that this more secluded spot would protect them from the Yankees; there he cleared some land, constructed a house and slave cabins, and hired an overseer. Four months later, his slaves pillaged the new place and fled; he subsequently located forty-five of them in nearby Opelousas, "together with six mule carts, two ox carts, one four horse wagon, twenty eight mules, eight yoke of oxen—mares & colts & saddle & buggy horses not to be found. This property I have lost and never expect to see it again."[74]

After assessing the various options open to him, John Berkeley Grimball found little reason to be optimistic. "To move or to stay seems to be equally ruinous to my prospects," he wrote in late February 1862. To compensate himself for the eighty slaves who had fled before he could move them, he sold nearly all his remaining slaves, retaining only the house servants and a few elderly blacks who would look after the old plantation. Like Grimball, a small minority of slave owners, rather than risk the perils of relocation or emancipation, turned to sale as a preferable if not altogether profitable alternative; perhaps as many, while retaining the bulk of their slave force, chose to rid themselves of the security risks, those who had already proven troublesome or whose past conduct raised questions about their dependability in a crisis. Louis Manigault of Georgia had no hesitation in selling a slave he considered "a most dangerous character & bad example to the others." Of the ten slaves belonging to a Missouri couple, only one had given them grounds for concern: "He used to wait in the house and was a likely boy and very smart. Well he must needs have his freedom—it was two years ago—so he bought a knuckleduster and was for killing my husband; but we found it out and sold him right off. We only got $700 for him, though." In the absence of any overt act, wartime tensions still had a way of magnifying suspicions. "*Sell Tom,*" a Florida woman advised her husband about his personal slave, "I am not happy with the thoughts of your being alone with him. . . . He will never abandon the hope of freedom, and if your life should stand in his way, you are not safe. . . . I would not have you between him and freedom for the wealth of the world. Tom must go out of our household."[75]

The wartime trade in slaves did not always suggest doubts about the future of the institution. In areas where the restricted acreage devoted to cotton, along with the concentration of relocated planters and their slaves, produced a surplus of slave laborers, purchasers were available to capitalize on good bargains. The market value of slaves remained relatively high, compared with prewar rates, but the prices paid for slaves reflected the rapid rate of inflation, the depreciated Confederate currency, and the military fortunes of the Confederacy; the slaves sold in Richmond in early 1865 for $10,000, for example, represented a real (gold) value of not more than $100. The capacity for self-deception proved limitless for those whites who chose to interpret the high prices as demonstrating confidence in the ultimate triumph of the Confederacy or as a firm rejection of the legality of Lincoln's Emancipation Proclamation. Most slaveholders, however, retained a sufficient business and political sense to know better. In December 1864, with the outcome of the war nearly decided, Edmund Ruffin, the staunchest Confederate patriot of them all, sold fifteen of his slaves, mostly women and children. His son made no attempt to conceal the reasons: "these were all consumers and likely to be for some time and were sold on account of the expense of keeping and the doubtful tenure of the property."[76]

When confidence in the survival of the Confederacy faltered, some slaveholders abandoned any patriotic or paternalistic pretenses and made a final, desperate effort to unload their slaves. "Us was sold on de block," Wash Wilson recalled, " 'cause Marse Tom say he gwine git all he done put in us out us, iffen he can 'fore de Yanks take dis country." Shortly before the shelling of Petersburg, Virginia, began, Fannie Berry remembered, "dey were selling niggers for little nothin' hardly," and as late as March 1, 1865, Mary Chesnut noted the "sale" of two slaves in besieged Richmond: a black woman traded for yarn, and a black man sold for a keg of nails. Although most slaveholders chose not to dispose of their property in this manner, they were hardly indifferent to the pecuniary consequences of emancipation. With an eye to the future, masters prepared for the Yankees by affixing a price to each of their slaves. If they could not retain them after the war, they would at least be in a position to claim compensation for their losses.[77]

7
————————

THE CONDITIONS CREATED by wartime dangers and necessities had few precedents in southern life or in the long history of slavery. If numerous blacks were removed to safe havens to keep them from the Yankees, still others were impressed into service as military laborers to help repel the Yankee invaders or kept in the fields to grow the crops necessary to feed the Army. Forced to muster every resource at its command, the white South would find itself in the position of debating the increased use of blacks in the military effort, even as fears mounted that blacks might, if given the opportunity, seek to undermine that effort. For the blacks, the situation and the choices were no less paradoxical, as they found themselves called upon to help sustain a war effort which, if successful, would perpetuate their bondage.

Appreciating the critical role of blacks in the economy, the white South, at the very outset of the war, pronounced slavery "a tower of strength" that would assure the ultimate triumph of independence. With enslaved workers providing the necessary labor at home, larger numbers of whites would be available for military service, thereby giving the slave South a decided advantage over the North. "The institution of slavery in the South," a Montgomery, Alabama, newspaper boasted, "alone enables her to place in the field a force so much larger in proportion to her white population than the North, or indeed than any country which is dependent entirely on free labor." Frederick Douglass, the leading black abolitionist, conceded as much when he called the black laborer "the key of the situation—the pivot upon which the whole rebellion turns." Without the immense human resources made available by slavery, he thought it unlikely that the Confederacy could sustain any prolonged military effort. "Arrest that hoe in the hands of the negro," Douglass advised early in the war, "and you smite rebellion in the very seat of its life."[78]

Not only did slaves constitute the mainstay of the agricultural economy—"the very stomach of this rebellion," said Douglass—but their services as military laborers more than justified the Union Army's belated decision to treat runaway slaves as "contraband of war." In the Confederate Army, slaves worked as cooks, teamsters, hospital attendants, musicians, and body servants; elsewhere, slaves were employed in a variety of skilled trades essential to the war effort. They labored in railroad construction and maintenance, in the extraction of raw materials, in the erection of fortifications, and in the manufacture of weapons of war. More than half the workers at the Tredegar Iron Works in Richmond were blacks, as were nearly three fourths of the employees in the naval ordnance plant at Selma, Alabama.[79]

Early in the war, when patriotism was at its peak, numerous slaveholders volunteered their blacks without wages (the government furnishing quarters and rations) or contracted (hired) them out to military authorities; at the same time, some free blacks sought to establish their loyalty by offering their services to strengthen defensive works around the cities and towns. When volunteers failed to meet increasing military needs, the Confederate government authorized the impressment of slaves and agreed to compensate the owners (thirty dollars a month and the full value of the slave in case of his death). The new law quickly fell victim to the growing conflict between state and Confederate authorities and failed to supply the necessary laborers. With somewhat greater success, local authorities and military commanders met emergency situations by arbitrarily mobilizing the available black laborers—free and slave alike—in a threatened region and forcing them into service. That was the fate of many blacks in Richmond, for example, as Union troops neared the city.

> The negroes were taken unaware on the street, at the market, from the shops, and at every point where they were found doing errands for themselves or their masters and mistresses. . . . In some cases the impressment agents acted with considerable indiscretion, snatching the negro from the marketing of his master, and leaving the marketing to take care of

itself; taking the negro from his perch on the cart and leaving the cart driverless behind.[80]

The growing reluctance of planters to part with their slaves, even to sustain a war for the preservation of that property, compounded the problem of meeting military labor requisitions. "Have you ever noticed the strange conduct of our people during this war?" a Confederate congressman from Georgia asked. "They give up their sons, husbands, brothers & friends, and often without murmuring, to the army; but let one of their negroes be taken, and what a howl you will hear." Still another legislator claimed to know a planter with five sons in the Army who resisted attempts to impress his slaves. "The patriotic planters," he observed, "would willingly put their own flesh and blood into the army, but when you asked them for a negro the matter approached the point of drawing an eye-tooth."[81] Neither waning patriotism nor constitutional scruples explain altogether the resistance of slaveholders to impressment. Although many did protest it as an interference with individual rights and property, the principal objections reflected a fear of pecuniary loss and the consequences of losing control over their slaves. Not only were slave laborers frequently impressed at a crucial time in plantation operations but the work patterns, rigors, and demands of military labor tended to injure their health, sometimes demoralized them, and all too often rendered them almost useless— if not downright dangerous—upon their return to the plantation.

Except for sale or removal, few wartime disruptions imposed greater hardships on the slaves than impressment. Made available to military authorities for a specified period of time, such slaves were invariably overworked, underfed, poorly clothed, brutally treated, exposed to enemy gunfire, and given inadequate medical attention. The deplorable condition and neglect of hospitalized slave military laborers in Richmond, for example, moved a local newspaper to denounce their treatment as "a disgrace to humanity." Letters poured in on the governor of Virginia from owners requesting that they be compensated for the slaves who had been laboring on fortifications and were lost because of disease, accident, exposure, and neglect. Ordered by local authorities to provide four blacks for the defense of Vicksburg, a Mississippi slaveholder noted their fate in his diary: "They were sent and put into the water up to the breast in the swamp below Vicksburg chop[p]ing trees the Consequence we have lost one by death the others are still ill one kept over there & got sick & we had to send a waggon & bed to bring him home."[82]

Even if slaves survived the physical ordeal of military labor, owners expressed concern about their state of mind and the unwholesome moral influences to which they might have been subjected. The information and ideas such slaves imbibed would be transmitted to the other slaves and threatened to undermine proper discipline and control. Nor could slave owners be certain that their impressed blacks would choose to return to the plantation. Proximity to Union lines afforded military laborers numerous opportunities for escape. The fact that some owners dispatched their troublemakers—the least intimidated slaves—made this all the more likely, but even the most carefully selected slaves found the prospect of freedom difficult to resist. [83]

Rather than flee to the Yankees, some impressed blacks who managed to escape headed for their homes. If they succeeded, they might then plead with their masters not to send them back to the fortifications, and some owners readily sympathized with such pleas. "[T]hey might kill him if they wanted to," a North Carolina slave told his master, "but . . . he would never go back to that work." Numerous slaves shared that aversion to military duty and did what they could to avoid it, often with the connivance of their masters. But for the many who served and survived, it proved to be an indelible experience.

> Dat was de worst times dat dis here nigger ever seen an' de way dem white men drive us niggers, it was something awful. De strap, it was goin' from 'fore day till 'way after night. De niggers, heaps of 'em just fall in dey tracks give out an' them white men layin' de strap on dey backs without ceasin'. Dat was zackly way it was wid dem niggers like me what was in de army work. I had to stand it, Boss, till de War was over.[84]

How a slave reacted to military labor depended to some degree on the kind of bondage he had known at home. Jacob Stroyer, for example, who had been raised on a plantation near Columbia, South Carolina, claimed to have "fared better" on the fortifications than on the plantation. He appreciated the spare time he had (in which he continued his quest for literacy), and he viewed the entire experience as a welcome diversion from the plantation routines. At the same time, he acknowledged the contradictions inherent in his role as a Confederate laborer:

> [A]lthough we knew that our work in the Confederate service was against our liberty, yet we were delighted to be in military service. We felt an exalted pride that, having spent a little time at these war points, we had gained some knowledge which would put us beyond our fellow negroes at home on the plantations, while they would increase our pride by crediting us with far more knowledge than it was possible for us to have gained.[85]

Of the slaves who served the Confederate war effort, none would rank higher in southern legend than the body servant. Accompanying his master (usually a more substantial planter or one of his sons) to military service, he performed the duties of a personal attendant and relieved the master of the more onerous camp chores; he might also be called upon to forage the countryside for food, entertain the soldiers, help care for the wounded, and dig trenches. Stephen Moore, servant to a South Carolina planter, informed his wife that he had been well treated in camp and enjoyed the leisure time available to him. "I have 3 meals of victuals to cook a day & the rest of the time is mine." Proud of his position, he asked his wife "to take this letter & read it to all my people. . . . Tell them all I have been on the Battle field."[86]

Since they would spend considerable time together and undergo the rigors of camp life and possibly enemy fire, a master took care in selecting the right slave for the position. Usually, the honor—for it was so considered by most—went to a slave who had already proven his fidelity, whose company the master enjoyed, and who could be expected to perform faithfully under the most trying circumstances; in many cases, he had previously served his master as a personal attendant, caring for his clothes, horses, and hounds. "Cyrus is a good boy indeed," a Georgia officer wrote of his servant, who had demonstrated both faithfulness and competence as a forager and cook.

> He has not had the first short word of dispute with a man since he left home. He gives me no trouble at all. Attends well to my horse and things general. I ask him sometimes if he does not want to go home—he replies not without I go. Him, I and Beauregard [the horse] form quite a trio. I will have to have our picture taken all together.

Overly pleased with the conduct and company of his body servant, a South Carolina master paid the highest compliment he could conceive: "Why weren't you white! Why weren't you white! Why weren't you white!"[87]

If the admonitions of some slave owners had been heeded, few of the body servants would have been provided with opportunities for wartime heroism. The usual procedure was to keep them behind the lines, not only to protect their lives but to safeguard the owners' investments as well. "I hear you are likely to have a big battle soon," a Virginia slaveholder advised his son, "and I write to tell you not to let Sam go into the fight with you. Keep him in the rear, for that nigger is worth a thousand dollars." Despite such considerations, the body servant often found himself sharing with his master the ordeal of battle and enemy fire. Like the white soldiers in his camp, he reacted with conduct that ranged from hysteria and flight to feats of incredible bravery. The stories of how he stood steadfast by his master and the instances in which he risked his life to recover the body of his slain master and carted him home for a proper burial would be accorded a prominent place in postwar recollections and tributes.[88]

The intimacy and affection that bound servant and master in the Army, like that which traditionally bound many house servants to the families residing in the Big House, could not escape the ambivalence that underlay the relationships formed in slavery. While most body servants remained loyal and faithful attendants, earning the laurels accorded them, significant numbers did not; in fact, some body servants calculatingly exploited the trust placed in them to desert to the Yankees at the first opportunity. Katie Darling, who had been a housegirl on a plantation in

Texas, recalled how her father ran away from "Massa Bill" while the two men were on their way to the battlefield. "Massa say when he come back from the war, That triflin' nigger run 'way and jines up with them damn Yankees." Lieutenant Theodorick W. Montfort, a Georgia farmer and lawyer, considered his body servant, Prince, to be "a most excellent" attendant. "You would be surprised to see how well he can cook & wash & how neatly he can iron & put up clothes. He can do it as well as any woman. I dont think you will want any better cook, washer & Ironer than he is by the time the war is over." But when the Yankees captured and then interned Lieutenant Montfort, his prize servant seized the opportunity to declare himself free. Not only did some body servants desert to the Yankees but they also provided them with information on the number and location of Confederate batteries; one such informer was subsequently recaptured, handed over to loyal servants for punishment, and reportedly "met a death at their hands more violent than any white person's anger could have suggested."[89]

When Confederate military fortunes declined and rations ran short, most of the body servants had to be sent home to help raise the necessary food supplies. In returning to the plantations, they imparted to their fellow slaves not only war experiences but the conversations they had overheard around the campfires and from captured Yankees about the prospects of a Union victory and emancipation. Although the white South would still accord the body servant a place in the pantheon of Confederate heroes, his conduct had often revealed an ambivalence that the coming of the Yankees would make even more explicit in the occupied South. That conflict between fidelity to the master and the yearning for freedom would manifest itself in numerous ways and deeply trouble both whites and blacks, leaving a bewildered white South to ponder, for example, over the behavior of a body servant who risked his life to carry his wounded master to safety and then remounted the master's horse and fled to the Yankee lines. Recalling his own experience, Martin Jackson, who had been a slave in Texas, spoke with considerable pride about the company in which he had served, but he made no effort to hide the conflict of loyalties he had felt. "Just what my feelings was about the War, I have never been able to figure out myself. I knew the Yanks were going to win, from the beginning. I wanted them to win and lick us Southerners, but I hoped they was going to do it without wiping out our company."[90]

Even as the white South persisted in touting the fidelity, contentment, and docility of its black population, there were limits to how much trust could be reposed in them and to what kinds of services they would be permitted to render. The employment of blacks as military laborers and body servants occasioned no particular alarm, as their duties were consistent with the servile position they occupied in southern society. But the proposal to enlist blacks as regular soldiers proved to be a different matter altogether. In opposing any such move, an Alabama legislator could think of no more effective argument than the example of his own body servant "who had grown up with him from boyhood, who had gone with him to the army and had shared with him, share and share alike, every article of food and clothing," and yet, inexplicably, "had seized the first opportunity which presented of deserting him, and joining the Yankees." Nevertheless, the Confederacy would have to confront the issue of slaves as soldiers, particularly after the Yankees began to reap such successes from the experiment.[91]

After the bombardment of Fort Sumter, free blacks in several towns organized themselves into military companies and offered their services to their respective states. The most notable example proved to be the free colored community of New Orleans, with its strong Creole element and the tradition of having fought under Andrew Jackson in 1815. After announcing early in the war their determination to "take arms at a moment's notice and fight shoulder to shoulder with other citizens" in defense of the city, two regiments of free colored men, known as the Native Guards, were soon parading the streets with white soldiers. Although formally incorporated into the Louisiana militia, the Native Guards were never called upon for combat duty. The same disinclination to employ black troops appeared elsewhere in the Confederacy. When sixty Richmond free blacks, bearing a Confederate flag, proffered their services as soldiers, the local authorities praised their loyalty and sent them home.[92]

Whether such volunteers were motivated by opportunism, a genuine patriotism, community coercion, or the prospect of better treatment is difficult to determine. By serving the Confederates, a New Orleans black leader later explained, they had hoped to improve their legal and social position; at the same time, almost in self-defense, they had felt the need to prove their fighting abilities and to learn the use of firearms, thereby raising their esteem among both the whites and their own people. "No matter where I fight," a New Orleans black later told the Yankees, "I only wish to spend what I have, and fight as long as I can, if only my boy may stand in the street equal to a white boy when the war is over." This may help to explain the ease with which the Native Guards quickly switched their loyalties after the fall of New Orleans; the colored troops—"the darkest of whom," said one Union general, "will be about the complexion of the late Mr. [Daniel] Webster"—were subsequently mustered into Federal service and sent into battle against the Confederates at Port Hudson, Louisiana.[93]

When Colonel James Chesnut's slaves volunteered in March 1862 "to fight for him if he would arm them," he professed to believe them. But one person could not make that decision, he told them. "The whole country must agree to it." Although there had been some proposals early in the war to enlist slaves, usually in the form of appeals from planters in threatened areas for permission to arm their slaves, the wisdom of such a drastic move was never seriously debated by the Confederacy until late in 1863. With the steady deterioration of the military effort, the question suddenly took on a new importance. In the ensuing and often far-reaching debate, the reasons advanced for slave enlistments ranged from the improved moral position of the South in the world community to how it might demoralize the black Yankees. But the most compelling argument, as it had been in the North, was that of military necessity. For some whites, at least, the urgent need to preserve the independence of the South took precedence over the institution upon which it was based, and the system they had initially viewed as the economic strength of the South now loomed as a critical source of military manpower as well. "The element which has been the foundation of wealth should now be made the instrument of our salvation," a Mississippi slaveholder told his fellow planters. "Arm our slaves." If the Confederacy failed to utilize this manpower, he warned, "the Yankees will, and the terminal scenes of this struggle . . . will be the subjugation of the Southern gentleman by his own slaves." It behooved every patriotic slaveholder, then, to "prepare the negro's mind for the position he is about to assume, and excite in him that love of country and of home which, I believe, exists strongly in the negro's breast." Having reprinted this slaveholder's appeal, the *New Orleans Tribune,* a black newspaper established in 1864, could not help but comment on its tragic irony: "The *chivalrous* Southerners, after bragging so long of their superiority above all other people, are now, in the pangs of agony, stretching their hands for help to those for whose enslavement they are trying to destroy their country. . . . They have, with their own lips and by their own acts, given the lie to their diabolical purpose."[94]

The gravity of the military situation notwithstanding, any proposal to enlist slaves as soldiers was bound to provoke strong opposition. When confronted with the prospect of armed slaves, in fact, many whites all too easily belied their previously expressed confidence in black loyalty and fidelity. "Would they not, with arms in their hands, either desert to the enemy or turn their weapons against us?" a prominent North Carolinian asked. By undertaking this experiment, opponents warned, the South will only have succeeded in introducing into the towns and countryside a veritable Trojan horse. "Are we prepared for this?" a Virginian asked. "To win their freedom with our own independence, to establish in our midst a half or quarter of a million of black freemen, familiar with the arts and discipline of war, and with large military experience!" At best, critics charged, black recruitment would exchange "a profitable laborer for a very unprofitable soldier," and, at worst, it leveled all distinctions and elevated blacks to equality with whites. If the Confederacy had to resort to such measures, thereby violating all previous practices and teachings, some whites thought it unworthy of survival. "The day you make soldiers of them is the beginning of the end of the revolution," General Howell Cobb warned. "If slaves will make good soldiers our whole theory of slavery is wrong."[95]

After the military reverses of late 1864, the Confederacy edged still closer to raising a black army. If nothing else, the heavy casualties they were sustaining impressed whites with the need to draw upon their immense reservoir of black manpower. Why condemn to destruction "the flower of our population, the hope of the country," a Virginia newspaper asked, "rather than mould to our use and make subsidiary to the great ends of independence, the inferior race that has so long acknowledged our guidance and control! Surely, they are good enough for Yankee bullets." What little was left of slavery, Mary F. Akin wrote her husband in the Confederate Congress, "should be rendered as serviceable as possible and for that reason the negro men ought to be put to fighting and where some of them will be killed. [I]f it is not done there will soon be more negroes than whites in the country and they will be the free race. I want to see them *got rid of soon.*" Walter Clark, a young Confederate officer, had initially opposed the enlistment of blacks but he now thought the policy deserved full support. "Let Negro fight negro," he advised. "This is an age of progressive ideas and mighty changes."[96]

The arguments grew increasingly bitter and vindictive as the war reached a desperate point. On March 13, 1865, the Confederate Congress, with the strong backing of Jefferson Davis and Robert E. Lee, finally authorized the enlistment of 300,000 additional troops "irrespective of color." To allay the fears of many whites, the act stipulated that no state was to enlist more than 25 percent of her able-bodied slave population between the ages of eighteen and forty-five. Within a few days, advertisements appeared in newspapers to urge the recruitment of blacks. In Richmond, a company of blacks in Confederate uniforms paraded in the streets to attract additional volunteers. Among those witnessing the spectacle was John S. Wise, a Confederate officer and the son of a former governor of Virginia. "Ah!" he thought, as he watched the "Confederate darkeys" drill in Capitol Square, "this is but the beginning of the end."[97]

Although the law authorizing black recruits avoided the question of emancipation, leaving that decision to the slave owners and the states, the clear implication was that slaves who served in the Confederate Army would be freed at the end of the war. But the promise of freedom as a reward for military service, whether by law or by implication, came too late to impress or deceive most slaves. "I'll work for Massa Randolph good 'nough," said a slave belonging to the former Confederate Secretary of War, "but no want to fight for Massa Davis." Bewildered by the remark, someone asked him how he could stand by idly while the Yankees robbed his master. "I knows nuthing 'bout politics," the slave replied. But when told that he might win his freedom by enlisting, this same slave suddenly revealed a sound grasp of politics: "We niggers dat fight will be free, course; but you see, massa, if some ob us don't fight, we all be free, Massa Lincum says." That same perception of reality had made Colonel James Chesnut's slaves far less enthusiastic about military service. When the question had first been broached, back in March 1862, they had talked enthusiastically about enlisting and securing their freedom and a bounty. More than two years later, however, with the military and political situation quite different, their tone had changed. "Now they say coolly that they don't want freedom if they have to fight for it. That means they are pretty sure of having it anyway."[98]

Even before the Confederate Congress authorized enlistments, some slaves found ways to communicate their aversion to fighting for their masters. In early 1865, a Richmond newspaper published a letter allegedly written by a black man to the president of the Confederate Senate:

> I hope you all will pass the law to arm the negro and the Day you do that We do intend to fight you all and We have made up our minds to do it when ever you all Will give us arms the Yankee is our friends, and you all is our enemy, and give us arms and we will rase war right here, and do you think we would fight again our friends for you all; no, never would I do so.[99]

When slaves were later questioned by Union soldiers about their willingness to bear arms for the Confederacy, they no doubt told them what they wanted to hear but there is little reason in this instance to suspect the blacks of duplicity. "My master offers me my freedom if I will take up arms," one slave told an escaped Union prisoner, "but I have a wife and five children, and he does not offer them their freedom, and we have come to the conclusion that there is no use fighting for our masters and our freedom when any children we may have are to be made slaves, and we have thought when we get arms and are allowed to be together in regiments, we can demand freedom for our wives and children, and take it." The day the Confederacy arms its slaves, a Georgia black assured General Sherman, "*dat day de war ends!*" Equally explicit, another slave vowed that his people would never have fought the Yankees. "I habe heard de colored folks talk of it. They knowd all about it; dey'll turn the guns on the Rebs."[100]

The Confederacy had anticipated little difficulty in mobilizing slaves for military duty. Nor did the proponents of black enlistments doubt the efficiency with which such soldiers would serve. After all, an Alabama newspaper suggested, "masters and overseers can marshal them for battle by the same authority and habit of obedience with which they are marshalled to labor." The end of the war, however, rendered such questions academic. Few slaves were ever enlisted, and none of them apparently had the opportunity to fight. Had the Confederacy managed to raise a black army, it would seem unlikely, particularly after 1863, that it could have fought with the same sense of commitment and self-pride that propelled the black troops in the Union Army. When he first heard of the act to recruit blacks for the Confederate Army, a Virginia freedman recalled, he had suddenly found himself unable to restrain his emotions. "They asked me if I would fight for my country. I said, 'I have no country.' "[101]

8

WHILE BLACKS WERE RELUCTANT to take up arms to perpetuate the bondage of their people, many were to regret that they had not struck harder for their liberation. If only there had been a massive upheaval, undermining the Confederacy and expediting a Union victory, what wonders that might have achieved for black self-pride. Felix Haywood, a former Texas slave, tried to sort out his thoughts about that failure.

> If every mother's son of a black had thrown 'way his hoe and took up a gun to fight for his own freedom along with the Yankees, the war'd been over before it began. But we didn't do it. We couldn't help stick to our masters. We couldn't no more shoot 'em than we could fly. My father and me used to talk 'bout it. We decided we was too soft and freedom wasn't goin' to be much to our good even if we had a education.

Only in retrospect, too, did Robert Falls, who had endured a harsh bondage in North Carolina, regret the essentially submissive role he had played during his more than twenty years as a slave. "If I had my life to live over," he reflected, "I would die fighting rather than be a slave again. . . . But in them days, us niggers didnt know no better. All we knowed was work, and hard work. We was learned to say, 'Yes Sir!' and scrape down and bow, and to do just exactly what we was told to do, make no difference if we wanted to or not." His father, in whom he had considerable pride, had symbolized for Falls the virtues and perhaps the futility of the slave rebel's usually lonely struggle. "Now my father, he was a fighter. He was mean as a bear. He was so bad to fight and so troublesome he was sold four times to my knowing and maybe a heap more times."[102]

The extent of black insurrectionary activity during the Civil War remains a subtle question. What is nearly impossible to determine in each instance is whether the reported revolt or plot was actually consummated, whether it existed only in the fevered imaginations of war-weary whites, or, far more commonly, whether "insurrection" simply became a way to define "suspicious activity," "insubordination," and organized flight to the Yankees. None of the wartime slave plots and uprisings achieved any spectacular results. But the psychic impact was formidable, each report and rumor reminding the white South of the potential that resided in its black population. The specter of servile insurrection hovered over the debate on enlisting blacks into the Confederate Army and intruded itself on the confidence with which whites periodically congratulated themselves over the docility of their slaves. The many reports that quantities of arms, gunpowder, knives, and hatchets had been found secreted under the floors of slave cabins revived traditional fears, and some planters ordered that hoes, axes, and other implements that might serve as weapons be locked up at night. The sound of fire bells excited still more panic, with the increase in arson attempts ascribed to blacks, particularly after it became known that slave rebels in Mississippi had planned to inaugurate an insurrection by burning the city of Natchez.[103]

The initial fears stemmed from reports that slaves in certain regions were preparing to wage insurrectionary warfare the moment the white volunteers left for military service or as soon as Yankee troops came into the vicinity. Within months after the bombardment of Fort Sumter, rumors of a black uprising placed Charleston residents on alert, and insurrectionary plots were uncovered in Georgia, Virginia, Arkansas, Kentucky, South Carolina, Louisiana, and Mississippi.[104] In May 1861, a citizens' committee in Kingston, Georgia, ordered the hanging of a slave after hearing evidence that pointed to "one of the most diabolical schemes ever devised by any fiend to murder the citizens of this county, and take possession of their property." That same month, Edmund Ruffin reported the discovery of a conspiracy in Virginia which had been organized at "night meetings for pretended religious worship." But he claimed to be unshaken by the news.

> A conspiracy discovered & repressed is better assurance of safety than if no conspiracy had been heard of or suspected. While I deem there is not the least ground for alarm & that this conspiracy, if undiscovered, would have had no dangerous results—still we ought to be always vigilant, & be ready to meet attacks, whether from northern invaders or negro insurgents.

With less equanimity, a white family in Bossier Parish, Louisiana, described the slaves in their neighborhood as "verry bold" and "trying to make up a company to rise." When overtaken, one of the conspirators "abused his Master to the last and told him that the North was fighting for the Negroes now [and] that he was as free as his Master." The accused rebel was then bound and left behind while the whites pursued the remaining conspirators. Upon their return, they found that "he had got loos and taken the cords that he was tied with and hung him self." Not far from this scene, and at nearly the same time, a Louisiana planter, having crawled under a slave cabin, overheard his slaves plotting a revolt.[105]

Although whites tried to downplay the impact of the Emancipation Proclamation, President Lincoln's preliminary announcement in September 1862 promptly set off a new wave of rumors and reports of insurrection. "It was very weak and ill-arranged," Emma Holmes of Camden, South Carolina, said of a plot discovered in her district, and several blacks were scheduled to hang. In December, one month before the Proclamation took effect, a Confederate militia unit from Mississippi requested that it be permitted to disband and return home for the Christmas holiday, not for purposes of merriment but to forestall an anticipated slave uprising. "[W]e deem it highly necessary that we should be there for the defense of our families," a spokesman for the group advised the governor, "as the negroes are making their brags that by the first of January they will be free as we are and a general outbreak is expected about that time." No doubt this was not the only militia unit which preferred to take its chances with slave rebels rather than Yankee soldiers.[106]

With emancipation an avowed Union objective, persistent reports circulated that blacks intended to stage a general revolt that would affect every part of the South and begin with the destruction of railroad tracks, telegraph lines, and bridges. Julia LeGrand, a young white woman, heard that the revolt would fall on New Year's Day 1863, and no place would be safe, not even the Union-occupied New Orleans in which she resided.

> I feel no fear, but many are in great alarm. . . . Fires are frequent—it is feared that incendiaries are at work. Last night was both cold and windy. The bells rang out and the streets resounded with cries. I awoke from sleep and said, "Perhaps the moment has come." . . . Mrs. Norton has a hatchet, a tomahawk, and a vial of some kind of spirits with which she intends to blind all invaders. We have made no preparations, but if the worst happen we will die bravely no doubt.[107]

Reinforcing the rumors of an impending general insurrection, reports mounted during the last two years of the war of the existence of "underground" organizations among the slaves. An escaped Union prisoner related how he had been assisted by a secret society which included "men whom their masters trusted in important transactions." In Livingston Parish, Louisiana, a woman informed her husband of "a terrible stir" involving more than a hundred slaves belonging to two planters; the conspirators organized a company, elected officers, stole guns and horses, and were "all ready just as quick as the word was given to go to work." Local whites put down the uprising, numerous slaves were whipped "very bad," and five were scheduled to hang.[108]

If whites tended to blur the distinction between an "insurrection" and an organized escape to the enemy, they often had good reason. In Amite County, Mississippi, some thirty or more armed slaves seized their masters' horses and "openly with boldness, cheers and shouting" made their way toward Union-occupied Natchez; within fifteen miles of their destination, however, the slaves were overtaken and most of them killed. With far greater success, Elijah Marrs mobilized twenty-seven slaves in Simpsonville, Kentucky, for an escape to the Union lines nearby; they used the local church for a headquarters, elected Marrs their captain, and accumulated an arsenal of "twenty-six war clubs and one old rusty pistol." Reaching Louisville before their owners, the slaves marched to the recruiting office and enlisted in the Union Army.[109]

The awesome number of mass punishments meted out to suspected black rebels often reflected nothing more than sheer hysteria. Although some whites thought their worst fears were about to be realized, the fact remains that the slaves failed to execute a major wartime rebellion. That failure was something the postwar white South chose to recall, as did certain black leaders eager to calm post-emancipation fears of a wave of black terror. "We never inaugurated a servile insurrection," Georgia freedmen would memorialize the legislature in 1866, exaggerating their race's submission.

We stayed peaceably at our homes, and labored with our usual industry. While you were absent fighting in the field, though we knew our power at the same time, and would frequently speak of it. We knew then it was in our power to rise, fire your houses, burn your barns, railroads, and discommode you in a thousand ways, so much so, that we could have swept the country, like a fearful tornado. But we preferred then as we do now, to wait on God, and trust to the instincts of your humanity.[110]

With different degrees of emphasis, some observers ascribed the absence of any large-scale servile insurrection to "the habit of patience" that bondage had instilled in black people. Thomas Wentworth Higginson, for example, an abolitionist Union officer commanding a black regiment in the South, often asked himself why "this capacity of daring and endurance" he observed in his soldiers had not kept the South "in a perpetual flame of insurrection." One answer, he reflected, must lie somewhere "in the peculiar temperament of the races, in their religious faith, and in the habit of patience that centuries had fortified."[111]

But the discussions which Colonel Higginson had with his own men revealed that "the habit of patience" explained rather little. Around the campfires, at least, when any of the black soldiers broached the subject of insurrection, they spoke of a lack of information, money, arms, drill, organization, and mutual confidence—"the tradition" that nearly every revolt had been betrayed at the outset. "The shrewder men all said substantially the same thing," Higginson observed. "What was the use of insurrection, where everything was against them?" To many blacks, in fact, talk of rebellion was simply "fool talk," a suicidal form of resistance. By mid-1862, the *Christian Recorder*, a black newspaper in Philadelphia, had lost its patience with those northern whites who envisioned a slave uprising as the death gasp of the Confederacy. When the war first broke out, the editor noted, and the North had expected a quick triumph, the mere hint of a slave rebellion would have aroused nationwide indignation.

Now, that same people want the slaves to rise up and fight for their liberty. Rise against what?—powder, cannon, ball and grape-shot? Not a bit of it. They have got too much good sense. Since you have waited till every man, boy, woman and child in the so-called Southern Confederacy has been armed to the teeth, 'tis folly and mockery for you *now* to say to the poor, bleeding and downtrodden sons of Africa, "Arise and fight for your liberty!"

The point was well made. From the outset of the war, it had been apparent to many observers, white and black, that the Yankees were as likely to betray a rebellion as some slave informer. The President, anxious to hold the border states in line, had made it clear on numerous occasions that this war was not being waged to provoke servile insurrection. Had there been a slave rebellion, Colonel Higginson conceded, it would surely have divided northern sentiment, "and a large part of our army would have joined with the Southern army to hunt them down." It was not, then, a black journalist explained, that the slaves were too ill informed to revolt. "They are too well informed and too *wise* to court destruction at the hands of the combined Northern and Southern armies."[112]

The absence of any major slave revolts during the Civil War should in no way obscure the nature and extent of the resistance that accompanied, often in the same person, the more celebrated slave virtues of obedience, fidelity, and patience. Not all slaves waited for freedom to be thrust upon them, nor did pro-Union blacks necessarily confine their activities to secretive prayers and midnight meetings. Where it was possible to expedite the Union cause, there were almost always some slaves and free blacks willing to take the risks. While a few operated as Union spies, still larger numbers provided the Union Army with valuable information about Confederate campsites, troop movements, and morale and guided Union forces when they came into the vicinity. "A negro brought the Yankees from Pineville," a white South Carolinian noted with dismay, "and piloted them to where our men were camped, taking them completely by surprise, capturing Bright and killing two of his men." Alarmed at the effective use made of slave informants by the Union Army, Confederate officials urged severe punishment of any blacks found engaged in such activity, and soldiers resorted to various ruses to ferret them out. In Berkeley County, South Carolina, where a black driver had come under suspicion as an informant, Confederate scouts disguised as Yankees went to his cabin, offered to pay him if he could lead them to a reported Confederate camp in the swamps, and then "hung the traitor" when he did so. By early 1864, however, a Confederate officer thought slave activity on behalf of the Union Army had reached the point of "an omnipresent spy system, pointing out our valuable men to the enemy, revealing our positions, purposes, and resources, and yet acting so safely and secretly that there is no means to guard against it."[113]

The literature of the Civil War is replete, too, with stories of how slaves and free blacks rendered invaluable assistance to Union soldiers who had escaped from Confederate prisons. Several such prisoners testified that their escape would have been impossible had it not been for the blacks who fed them and guided them to the Union lines. "George has brought us food during the day, and will try to get us a guide to-night," an escaped Union soldier noted in the diary he kept during his flight. "Sometimes," another escapee reported, "forty negroes, male and female, would come to us from one plantation, each one bringing something to give, and lay it at our feet, in the aggregate corn bread and potatoes enough to feed a regiment." Fearing the consequences if they were detected, some slaves proved less helpful, while still others treated the Yankees as enemies and reported escapees to local authorities. One Union soldier who managed to escape from Andersonville recalled an uncooperative black woman who proclaimed her hatred for all white men, Yankees and Confederates alike, and refused to assist him in any way. "She was the only one of the race I ever applied to in vain for assistance."[114]

Judged by the reaction it generated, the most spectacular and celebrated exploit of a black man during the Civil War concerned the delivery of a Confederate steamer to the Union Navy. The protagonist in this drama was Robert Smalls, a Charleston slave who had been hired out on the waterfront for several years and had acquired a boatman's skills. In 1862, impressed into service, Smalls worked as an assistant pilot on the *Planter,* a cotton steamer converted by the Confederate government into an armed transport. On the night of May 12, 1862, the ship was docked in Charleston with some artillery newly loaded aboard. The officers and white crewmen had gone ashore, leaving Smalls to prepare the vessel for departure the next day. But the black crew, including the families of Robert Smalls and his brother, chose to leave prematurely aboard the *Planter*, thereby culminating Smalls's plan to deliver the steamer intact to the Union ships blockading Charleston harbor. "I thought the *Planter* might be of some use to Uncle Abe," he remarked afterwards. The North hailed him as a hero, and the government commissioned him an officer in the United States Colored Troops. Smalls returned at the helm of the *Planter* to witness the United States flag raised over Fort Sumter, and by this time he was well on his way toward becoming a legendary figure among South Carolina blacks. "Smalls ain't God!" a skeptical black told one of Smalls's admirers. "That's true, that's true," he replied, "but Smalls' young yet." To the white South, the entire episode seemed impossible to grasp. Emma Holmes of Camden, South Carolina, confided her "horrified" reaction to the diary she kept, pronouncing Smalls's act "most disgraceful" and "one of the boldest and most daring things of the war."[115]

Few slaves were in a position to emulate the heroism of Robert Smalls. If they manifested their desire for freedom, it would have to take less spectacular forms. No less dramatic, however, and equally far-reaching, was the decision made by tens of thousands of slaves not to wait for the Yankees but to expedite liberation by fleeing to the Union lines. "We had heard it since last Fall," an escaped slave told the Yankees in May 1861, "that if Lincoln was elected, you would come down and set us free. And the white-folks used to say so, but they don't talk so now; the colored people have talked it all over; we heard that if we could get in here [the Union camp] we should be free, or at any rate, we should be among friends." With the advance of the Union Army, the legendary North Star that had once illuminated the road out of bondage lost its strategic importance; freedom was as close as the nearest Union camp, perhaps only down the road or across a nearby swamp or river. "See how much better off we are now dan we was four years ago," a successful runaway exulted. "It used to be five hundred miles to git to Canada from Lexington, but now it's only eighteen miles! *Camp Nelson* is now *our* Canada."[116]

UNTIL AT LEAST MIDWAY through the war, Federal policy toward slave runaways remained unclear and inconsistent. Although the Lincoln administration endorsed the decision of General Benjamin F. Butler to treat them as "contraband of war," Union commanders in the field persisted in making their own judgments, with some officers returning fugitives and upholding the legal right of loyal slaveholders to their property. The Fugitive Slave Act remained operative until mid-1864, though only *loyal* masters (as defined usually by local commanders) could seek to reclaim runaways under its provisions. Federal legislation in 1862, however, barred military personnel from participating in the return of fugitive slaves and decreed that the escaped slaves of disloyal masters would be forever free.[117]

Whether defined as "contraband of war," "fugitives," or "freedmen," they ceased to be slaves when they reached the Union lines. That was the news the "grapevine telegraph" quickly circulated, thereby swelling the number of slaves seeking out the Yankees. The "exodus" affected some plantations and regions far more severely than others, with those more remote from the war and the advancing Union Army recording the fewest successful escapes. In King William County, northeastern Virginia, nearly half the able-bodied male slaves between the ages of eighteen and forty-five fled in the first two years of the war, and a white resident of northern Virginia thought scarcely any slaves remained in that section of the country—"they have all gone to Canaan, by way of the York River, Chesapeake Bay, and the Potomac." In North Carolina, a Confederate officer estimated in August 1862 that one million dollars' worth of slaves were fleeing every week. By 1863, Union-occupied Vicksburg and Natchez had become centers for slave runaways in Mississippi, and that same year thousands of Louisiana slaves entered the Union lines at Baton Rouge and New Orleans. After its capture in early 1862, Fernandina, Florida, served as a haven for fugitives from Georgia and Florida, much as Beaufort did for South Carolina slaves.[118]

Although some runaways traveled in well-organized and armed contingents, this was largely a spontaneous movement, made up of single persons and groups of families. Slaves would leave the plantations at night, conceal themselves in the woods or swamps during the day, and seek out the nearest Yankee camp or Union-held town. The more fortunate fled in horse carts and ox carts, or even in the master's buggy, while still others made use of boats, rafts, and canoes and their knowledge of the local waterways. Determined to enter the Union lines at Hilton Head, South Carolina, Jack Flowers hid in the rice swamps during the day and crept along at night until he reached the woods and a nearby river; he then made a basket boat, woven out of reeds cut in the swamp, caulked with cotton picked from the fields, and smeared with pitch from the pine trees, and successfully paddled his way to freedom. With few resources at their command, many refugees had to walk long distances on swollen and bleeding feet, carrying bundles of clothing or children on their shoulders. Two Louisiana families waded six miles across a swamp, spending two days and nights in mud and water to their waists, their children clinging to their backs. Some managed to carry away their few belongings, usually old rags, bedding, and furniture, which were piled onto carts and wagons. Several of the women attired themselves in their mistress's clothes, and the men occasionally raided the master's wardrobe before departing. Many, however, left with nothing but the clothes they were wearing: "Well, massa, we'd thought freedom better than clothes, so we left them."[119]

To succeed required not only the physical strength to endure the trek but the ingenuity that might be necessary to elude pursuers. They devised various ruses and concoctions by which to throw off the bloodhounds, or simply clung to the swamps and rivers to cover up their tracks. They were known to dress themselves in Confederate uniforms and flee on their masters' horses. They took advantage of the confusion and panic caused by the movement of troops and the sound of gunfire. Mary Lynn, a forty-five-year-old Virginia field hand, used the Christmas holiday festivities, when her absence for several days would not be noticed, to effect her escape. On some plantations, the slaves derived what initial advantages they could by tying up their master and overseer before fleeing. In Colonel Higginson's black regiment, a freed slave named Cato related, to the obvious pleasure of his audience, the tale of his escape and how he had used some time-honored strategy to deceive and extract information from a white planter he encountered along the way. Overhearing the story, while standing in the background of the gathering, Higginson noted not only the freedman's words but how they were received.

"Den I go up to de white man, berry humble, and say, would he please gib ole man a mouthful for eat?

"He say he must hab de valeration ob half a dollar.

"Den I look berry sorry, and turn for go away.

"Den he say I might gib him dat hatchet I had.

"Den I say" (this in a tragic vein) "dat I must hab dat hatchet for defend myself *from de dogs!*"

(Immense applause, and one appreciating auditor says, chuckling, "Dat was your *arms*, ole man," which brings down the house again.)

"Den he say de Yankee pickets was near by, and I must be very keerful.

"Den I say, 'Good Lord, Mas'r, am dey?' "

Commenting on the soldier's conclusion of the story, Higginson conceded that words alone could hardly capture "the complete dissimulation with which these accents of terror were uttered,—this being precisely the piece of information he wished to obtain."[120]

If slavery was really so disagreeable, Mary Chesnut suggested rather smugly in July 1861, "why don't they all march over the border where they

would be received with open arms. It amazes me." For all of her insights
into the "inscrutable" slave, she was in no position to perceive the daring
and courage required for a successful escape, the magnitude of the risks,
and the certainty of severe punishment for those who failed. "Ah, you
know, my bredren," an elderly runaway told a group of freedmen, "how dey
try to keep us from gittin' to Camp Nelson. Some o' you hev only jist got
from behind; where Massa ask you, 'Would you like to be free, David?' O'
course I should; but den, if I say so, dey jist cross my hands, tie 'em up, strip
me; den whip me wid the cowhide, till I tell a lie, and say 'No.' " That only
a small percentage of slaves chose flight suggests the kinds of obstacles they
faced. There were mounted citizens' patrols, river patrols, and Confederate
sentinels that had to be eluded, as well as pursuing bloodhounds ("the
detective officers of Slavery's police," one freedman called them); some of
the boats used by runaways broke apart or overturned, drowning the occupants; and nervous Union guards sometimes mistook escapees for enemy
soldiers and shot and killed them. While attempting to escape across a river
to the Union lines, a young slave and his mother were fired upon by the
master's son; the mother managed to reach the other bank safely but her
son died soon afterwards from bullet wounds. Some years before, her husband and two other sons had been sold, and she was now left to lament her
most recent and ironic fate:

> My poor baby is shot dead by that young massa I nussed with my own
> boy. They was both babies together. Missus made me nuss her baby, an'
> set her little girl to watch me, for fear I'd give my baby too much, no
> matter how hard he cried. Many times I wasn't allowed to take him up,
> an' now that same boy has killed mine.

Even if certain and severe punishment awaited apprehended runaways,
they might have counted themselves fortunate to be returned to their
masters; in numerous instances, mounted slave patrols ran them down
with their horses, shot them on the road, or tied them to the horses and
dragged them to the nearest jail.[121]

Although hardly unique to the Civil War, the slave runaway most
vividly demonstrated to an already apprehensive white South the breakdown and possible collapse of discipline and control. To many whites, in
fact, there was little to distinguish the runaway from the rebel; both threatened to bring down the system, and reports of new desertions invariably
fueled talk of subversion, insurrection, and the very death of slavery.
"They are traitors who may pilot an enemy into your *bedchamber!*" the
Reverend C. C. Jones of Georgia warned. "They know every road and
swamp and creek and plantation in the county, and are the worst of spies.
If the absconding is not stopped, the Negro property of the county will be
of little value." This usually reserved churchman, who prided himself on
his religious work with the slaves, became so deeply disturbed over the
mounting reports of runaways in the neighborhood that he suggested the

need to define them as insurrectionists and mete out summary justice. After all, he wrote his son in the Confederate Army, "they declare themselves enemies and at war with owners by going over to the enemy who is seeking both our lives and property." Responding to his father's concerns, Charles C. Jones, Jr., who had served as mayor of Savannah before enlisting in the Army, disdained anything that would "savor of mob law" but agreed that defectors who evinced sufficient intelligence and leadership qualities to devise "a matured plan of escape" and to influence others to flee should be treated as armed insurrectionists and executed. "If insensible to every other consideration," Colonel Jones suggested, "terror must be made to operate upon their minds, and fear prevent what curiosity and desire for utopian pleasures induce them to attempt."[122]

Nearly everyone loyal to the Confederacy conceded that the effectiveness of any system designed to thwart slave desertions rested ultimately on local and individual vigilance. While some whites might choose to debate legal niceties, most of them were concerned only with achieving immediate and conclusive results. Henry A. Middleton, a South Carolina planter, obviously appreciated the dispatch with which Georgetown County had dealt with apprehended runaways.

> [O]f the people who went away three men, returned to the plantation of Dr. McGill and carried away their wives—the six were taken together making their way to the enemy. The men were tried yesterday by the provost martials court—they were sentenced to be hung—to day one oclock was fixed for the execution that no executive clemency might intervene ... there was a crowd—the blacks were encouraged to be present—the effect will not soon be forgotten.[123]

On the nearby Allston rice plantation, Stephen (the valet) had defected with his wife and children, and the effect on the other slaves, according to the overseer, had been noticeable: "I Can see since Stephn left a goodeal of obstanetry in Some of the Peopl. Mostly mongst the Woman a goodeal of Quarling and disputeing & teling lies." That was all the more reason for Adele Petigru Allston, who had become the mistress of the plantation upon the death of her husband, to act firmly in this matter. Unable to apprehend Stephen, she resolved to make an example of his wife's mother, not so much out of spite as the conviction that parents and relations should be held responsible for the actions of their families. "You know all the circumstances of Stephen's desertion," she wrote the local magistrate.

> You know that his wife is Mary's daughter and she is the third of her children who have gone off. . . . It is too many instances in her family for me to suppose she is ignorant of their plans and designs. She has been always a highly favoured servant, and all her family have been placed in positions of confidence and trust. I think this last case should be visited in some degree on her.

At the same time, Adele Allston informed Jesse Belflowers, the overseer, of her decision to remove Mary and James (Stephen's father) to "some place of confinement" in the interior of the state and hold them there "as hostages for the conduct of their children." If by making an example of these individuals, she had thought to instill proper subordination in the remaining slaves, subsequent events on the Allston plantations, particularly with the coming of the Yankees, would prove less than reassuring.[124]

What compounded the problem of control was the difficulty of anticipating defections; every slave owner would have to make his own determination and act accordingly. Anxious about retaining his house servant and cook, a Georgia planter put heavy iron shackles on her feet while she worked and locked her in the cornhouse at night. In the Mississippi River region, a Union officer who returned from a raid with two hundred slaves reported having found twenty-five of them chained in a cane brake. On the plantation in Virginia where Susie Burns labored, any slave contemplating an escape during the war years needed to elude the vigilant eye and drunken wrath of the master. "Used to set in his big chair on de porch wid a jug of whiskey by his side drinkin' an' watchin' de quarters to see that didn't none of his slaves start slippin' away." More commonly, a slave owner made an example of runaways who were apprehended and returned to the plantation. If not immediately sold, they were liable to be whipped, chained at night, put to work on Confederate fortifications, or removed for safekeeping to non-threatened areas. After thwarting an attempted escape, the son of a South Carolina planter sold two of the leaders in Charleston and punished the others "by whips and hand-cuffing," making certain that they were chained and watched at night. But some planters, acting as though their tenure as slave owners might be short-lived, were so unnerved by defections that they vented all of their frustrations on those they could apprehend. "W'en de Union soldiers wur near us," a freedwoman named Affy recalled, "some o' de young han's run off to git to de Union folks, an' massa ketch dem an' hang dem to a tree, an' shoot dem; he t'ink no more'n to shoot de culled people right down. . . . But t'ank God, I got away, an' him won't git me agin."[125]

Even in the face of danger and repeated failures, the slaves persisted in their attempts to reach the Union lines. Having been thwarted in their initial attempt to escape from a plantation near Savannah, a seventy-year-old black woman and her husband immediately made plans to try again. While the plantation whites were meting out punishment to her husband, she collected their twenty-two children and grandchildren in a nearby marsh. After drifting some forty miles down the river in a dilapidated flatboat, the family was rescued by a Union gunboat. "My God!" she exclaimed as they came aboard, "are we free?" Her husband subsequently made good on his second escape attempt. No less persistent was a Maryland servant who tried to join others in a mass escape despite the fact that his hands and feet had been amputated some years before because of severe frostbite. "Well, I got him back and had him tied up," the owner told a visiting Englishman, "for I thought he must be mad. But it was no use, he got away again, and walked to Washington." How, asked the curious visitor, could he have managed such a remarkable deed? The answer no doubt must have seemed equally incredible.

> Oh, he just stumped along. He was always a right smart nigger, and he could do many things after he lost his limbs. He could attend to the cooking and sew with his teeth very well, and could get on a horse and ride as easy as look. He was always a remarkably strong nigger. Why, even after he lost his hands, he could kill a man, almost, with a blow of one of his knobs.

The persistence of some black runaways came at the expense of their white pursuers. After overtaking his slave in a swamp, a South Carolina master found himself engaged in a fierce struggle. He managed to shoot the slave in the arm, shattering it badly. Knowing what awaited him if captured, the fugitive grimly fought on, unhorsed his master, and then beat him "until he was senseless."[126]

Rather than flee to the Yankees, numerous slaves responded to particular provocations, as they had before the war, by decamping for the nearby woods or swamps, where they might hide out for extensive periods of time. After all, even the much-hunted Nat Turner had managed to elude his pursuers for nearly eight weeks. Near the end of the war, Anna Miller recalled, "my sis and nigger Horace runs off. Dey don' go far, and stays in de dugout. Ev'ry night dey'd sneak in and git 'lasses and milk and what food dey could. My sis had a baby and she nuss it ev'ry night when she comes. Dey runs off to keep from gettin' a whuppin'." Far more dangerous were the colonies of runaways that formed in some areas, from which slaves would forage the countryside for provisions. While searching for runaways, a group of whites in South Carolina found such a settlement in a nearby swamp, "well provided with meal, cooking utensils, blankets, etc.," as well as twelve guns and an ax. In Surry County, Virginia, a scouting party investigated a similar runaway camp but never lived to report their findings; the fugitives killed them.[127]

Assumptions about slave contentment, docility, or indifference prepared few whites for the extent of the runaway problem. "Unlettered reason or the mere inarticulate decision of instinct brought them to us," thought one Union officer, while a white resident of Natchez deemed it little wonder "that they long to throw aside their chains and 'live like white people' as they say." The slaves themselves had little difficulty in explaining why they had fled. Reflecting upon their escapes, exchanging stories across the campfires in the contraband villages, answering the queries of Union officers and reporters, they usually talked about the oppressiveness of enslavement, the difficulties of carrying out plantation duties while freedom was so close at hand, and the determination to liberate themselves rather than wait for the Yankees.

Massa wanted we niggers to go 'way with him, but we want come to
Yankees 'cause he treat us too bad. We hear you come down 'long time
ago. Massa said de Yankees would take de niggers and sell us in Cuba,
and want us to fight, but we talk it over, and agreed to come to de
Yankees. When Massa ran away he shot one man' lip off, who refused to
follow him. I want to be free. I know freemen have to work—can't live
without work. Dere's great difference between free and slave. When you
free you work and de money b'long to yourself.[128]

Fearing imminent removal or sale, some slaves chose to escape. The
moment her master ordered all the house servants into wagons, a Virginia
slave went into hiding. Thomas Pritchard, a carpenter, disappeared while
the master and a slave broker were discussing the terms of his sale. Some
slaves had heard rumors that they were about to be conscripted for military
service or put to work on Confederate fortifications. "They's jest takin' me,
sir," Tom Jackson of Virginia explained, "an' I run off." Some were eager
to locate their families or join the slaves from their plantation who had
already escaped. "All of our friends were ober here," a runaway explained.
Isaac Tatnall, who had been hired out, fled when his master refused to pay
him his share of the wages. "Last month," Tatnall remarked, "master took
him all, but he lost by dat, cause dis month I runned away, and he's lost
$1,880."[129]

The uncontrolled rage of their masters, often for no easily ascertain-
able reason other than the imminent loss of the war, hastened the departure of many slaves. "They does it to spite us," a runaway woman testified, " 'cause you come here. Dey spites us now 'cause de Yankees come."
This woman had just escaped with two of her children, leaving behind her
eldest son whom the master had just "licked" almost to death because he
suspected him of wanting to join the Yankees. Stories of recent beatings
ran through the testimony of numerous newly arrived refugees. "Master
whipped me two or three weeks ago," a freedwoman declared, "because I
let the cows from the bog road into the yard. Struck me and knocked me
down with his fist. Left Monday night, and walked all the way. I am free;
come here to be protected; was not safe to stay." On the morning of his
escape, a Georgia slave noted, he had been promised a whipping, but "when
de time came dis chile was about five miles from dar, and he nebber stopped
until las night." Among the slaves who fled after harsh treatment were
those who felt compelled to contain their anger rather than risk the consequences of direct retaliation. "They didn't do something and run," a former
slave suggested. "They run before they did it, 'cause they knew that if they
struck a white man there wasn't going to be a nigger."[130]

Although specific provocations helped to sustain the steady movement
toward the Union lines, the overriding consideration remained the prospect of freedom and the pride that a slave took in expediting his or her own
liberation. "I wants to be free," a South Carolina runaway kept repeating.
"I came in from the plantation and don't want to go back; I don't want to

go back; I don't want to be a slave again." The intensity of this feeling even induced elderly slaves to make the perilous trek, refusing to postpone any longer that dream that had eluded them for a lifetime. "Ise eighty-eight year old," one refugee told the Yankees. "Too ole for come? Mas'r joking. Neber too ole for leave de land o' bondage." Near Vicksburg, where slaves had been deserting in substantial numbers, a planter went out to the quarters and asked the "patriarch" among his slaves, "Uncle Si, I don't suppose you are going off to those hateful Yankees, too, are you?" "O no, marster," he replied, "I'se gwine to stay right here with you." When the planter visited the quarters the next morning, he found that every one of his slaves had left that night, including Uncle Si and his wife. Searching the nearby woods for them, he came across Uncle Si, bending over the prostrate body of his wife, weeping. The planter wondered why he had subjected her to such a difficult and now fatal journey. "I couldn't help it, marster," the old man replied; "but then, you see, she died free."[131]

Whether or not a slave chose to desert his master did not necessarily reflect a personal history of brutal treatment. Alex Huggins, who ran away in 1863 at the age of twelve, recalled no complaints about the way his master and mistress had treated him: "Twa'nt anythin' wrong about home that made me run away. I'd heard so much talk 'bout freedom I reckon I jus' wanted to try it, an' I thought I had to get away from home to have it." The verbal exchange that took place in late 1861 between a Union soldier and a runaway revealed as vividly what many whites would find so difficult to understand and forgive in their slaves.

> "How were you treated, Robert?"
> "Pretty well, sar."
> "Did your master give you enough to eat and clothe you comfortably?"
> "Pretty well, till dis year. Massa hab no money to spend dis year. Don't get many clothes dis year."
> "If you had a good master, I suppose you were contented?"
> "No, sar."
> "Why not, if you had enough to eat and clothes to wear?"
> "Cause I want to be *free*."[132]

## 10

NEITHER THE NUMBER of reported "insurrections" nor an accurate count of the runaways could adequately measure slave resistance and disaffection during the final years of the "peculiar institution." Equally significant for slaveholders were the kinds of rumors that circulated, the fears that were generated, the outbreaks of "insolence" and "insubordination" which could drive individual families and entire communities to the brink of hysteria,

and the various ways in which enslaved blacks—consciously or otherwise
—brought anguish and frustration to those who claimed to own them.

Even before the Emancipation Proclamation, slaves perceived on the
faces of their "white folks" a growing uneasiness and resignation. The
certainty of Confederate victory seemed far less pronounced, the patriotic
oratory less believable, and there crept into the conversations of white men
and women the apprehension that life as they had known it might never
survive this war. No matter how desperately slaveholding families wanted
to believe in the faithfulness of their blacks, and despite the patriotic and
loyal models they could display and would forever venerate, there persisted
an undercurrent of suspicion and fear that could never be successfully
repressed and that surfaced with every rumor of an uprising, every case of
insubordination, and every report of an escape. "The runaways are numerous and bold," Kate Stone confided to her diary. "We live on a mine that
the Negroes are suspected of an intention to spring on the fourth of next
month. The information may be true or false, but they are being well
watched in every section where there are any suspects. Our faith is in
God."[133]

Nor were the fears of white men and women entirely illusory; they
could on occasion assume a terrible reality. The war was not even a year
old when Mary Chesnut heard that her cousin—Betsey Witherspoon of
Society Hill—had been found dead in her bed, although she had been "quite
well" the previous night. Two days later, the frightening news reached
Mary Chesnut that her cousin had met a violent death. "I broke down;
horror and amazement was too much for me. Poor cousin Betsey Witherspoon was murdered! She did not die peacefully in her bed, as we supposed,
but was murdered by her own people, her Negroes." With the arrest of two
house servants, the details began to emerge. On the day of the murder, Mrs.
Witherspoon's son (who resided nearby) had charged several of his mother's slaves with misusing and breaking some of the household china while
giving a party in their mistress's absence, and he promised to return the
next day to give them a severe thrashing. Although Mrs. Witherspoon had
interceded on their behalf, thinking it "too late to begin discipline now,"
that news had not reached the slaves, one of whom allegedly told the
others: "Mars' John more than apt to do what he say he will do, but you
all follow what I say and he'll have something else to think of beside
stealing and breaking glass and china. If ole Marster was alive now, what
would he say to talk of whipping us!" That night, the slaves methodically
carried out the murder, smothering Betsey Witherspoon so as to make it
appear like a natural death.

News of the murder forced Mary Chesnut to reexamine many of her
previous assumptions about the "placid, docile, kind and obedient" slaves
she had known. "Hitherto I have never thought of being afraid of Negroes.
I had never injured any of them; why should they want to hurt me? Two
thirds of my religion consists in trying to be good to Negroes, because they
are so in our power, and it would be so easy to be the other thing." But as

of this day, she confessed, "I feel that the ground is cut away from under my feet. Why should they treat me any better than they have done Cousin Betsey Witherspoon?" While Mary Chesnut and her sister, Kate Williams, sat up late that night and discussed the murder, Kate's maid ("a strong-built, mulatto woman . . . so clever she can do anything") dragged a mattress into the room and insisted that she spend the night with her mistress. "You ought not to stay in a room by yourself these times," she told her. "Missis, as I have a soul to be saved, I will keep you safe. I will guard you." When the maid left for more bedding, Kate turned to her sister and exclaimed, "For the life of me, I cannot make up my mind. Does she mean to take care of me, or to murder me?" Unable to sleep, whether because of the murder or the maid's presence, or both, Kate went into her sister's bedroom, and the two women tried to comfort each other, both of them haunted by "the thought of those black hands strangling and smothering Mrs. Witherspoon's grey head under the counterpane." One month later, the details of the murder remained as vivid in Mary Chesnut's mind as if it had occurred the day before. "That innocent old lady and her grey hair moved them not a jot. Fancy how we feel. I am sure I will never sleep again without this nightmare of horror haunting me. . . . If they want to kill us, they can do it when they please, they are noiseless as panthers." And yet, she confided to her diary, although "we ought to be grateful that anyone of us is alive, . . . nobody is afraid of their own Negroes. I find everyone, like myself, ready to trust their own yard. I would go down on the plantation tomorrow and stay there even if there were no white person in twenty miles. My Molly and all the rest I believe would keep me as safe as I should be in the Tower of London."

But as she had feared, the specter of Mrs. Witherspoon's death remained with them, manifesting itself in different ways at different times. There was the day, for example, when Mary Chesnut's mother-in-law had "bored" her with incessant talk about "the transcendant virtues of her colored household"; that night, the woman suddenly warned everyone at the dinner table not to touch their soup: "It is bitter. There is something wrong about it!" The family tried to calm her and continued with their meal, while the black waiters "looked on without change of face." Kate whispered to her sister, "It is cousin Betsey's fate. She is watching every trifle, and is terrified." Afterwards, Kate told Mary of a Dr. Keith, "one of the kindest of men and masters," who had discovered one day that his slaves were slowly trying to poison him and had thrown a cup of tainted tea in the face of a suspected servant; the next morning, the doctor was found with his throat cut. "Mrs. Witherspoon's death," Mary Chesnut noted, "has clearly driven us all wild." On Christmas Day 1861, she duly recorded that the slaves charged with the murder of her cousin had been hanged. That same day, the servants rushed in with cries of "Merry Christmas" and "Christmas Gift." "I covered my face and wept."

Despite the confidence she still reposed in her own servants, Mary Chesnut began to entertain doubts about what she might expect of them in the future. Nearly a year after Mrs. Witherspoon's death, with all the terror that had generated, she found herself reading a book about the Sepoy Mutiny in India, in which the Bengal Army had turned upon its British officers.

> Who knows what similar horrors may lie in wait for us? When I saw the siege of Lucknow in that little theatre at Washington, what a thrill of terror ran through me as those yellow and black brutes came jumping over the parapets! Their faces were like so many of the same sort at home. To be sure, John Brown had failed to fire their hearts here, and they saw no cause to rise and burn and murder us all, like the women and children were treated in the Indian Mutiny. But how long would they resist the seductive and irresistible call: "Rise, kill, and be free!"[134]

It was precisely an incident like the Witherspoon murder, no matter how isolated, no matter how exceptional within the full record of slave behavior, that prompted white men and women, while publicly praising the exemplary behavior of their blacks, to reflect upon the combustible and unpredictable nature of a society in which the most devoted, the most pampered, the most humble slaves could strike terror and fear into a family whose confidence they commanded. Despite the accumulating evidence of betrayal, most slaveholders might have readily agreed that the faithful slave still constituted the vast majority of the black population; they could, as one Virginian did, dismiss any other thought from their minds.

> Were not the negroes perfectly content and happy? Had I not often talked to them on the subject? Had not every one of them told me repeatedly that they loved "old Marster" better than anybody in the world, and would not have freedom if he offered it to them? Of course they had,—many and many a time. And that settled it.

But how could anyone be certain that the exception was not on his own plantation or in his own household? That was the essential problem, and it had plagued the white South for generations. Far more terrifying than Nat Turner and his "deluded and drunken handful of followers," a Virginia legislator declared in 1832, was "the suspicion eternally attached to the slave himself, the suspicion that a Nat Turner might be in every family, that the same bloody deed could be acted over at any time and in any place, that the materials for it were spread through the land and always ready for a like explosion." That was no less true in 1861 than it had been thirty years before.[135]

And there appeared to be no way to resolve this dilemma. Many a master was driven to sleepless nights in his attempt to penetrate behind the masks of his blacks, attaching significance to nearly every movement or word, and perhaps even more significance to their silence or apparent indifference. The meekest, the most passive, the most submissive slaves could unsettle a household. The very appearance of fidelity was sometimes suspect. "They carry it too far," Mary Chesnut had written of her servants on the first day of the war. Not until nearly two years later did she begin to discern changes in them, and even then only in her father's butler. Although he remained "inscrutably silent" about the war, she sensed a difference. "I taught him to read as soon as I could read myself, perched on his knife board; but he won't look at me now. He looks over my head, he scents freedom in the air.... He is the first Negro that I have felt a change in."[136]

The approach of the Union Army would raise new concerns for white families but the traditional fears remained paramount. "I am afraid of the lawless Yankee soldiers," a Virginia woman confessed, "but that is nothing to my fear of the negroes if they should rise against us."[137]

Slaves were no less apprehensive, and their concern was by no means limited to what they might expect from an invading army made up largely of whites. The Civil War would not last forever, a Texas slave advised his son, but "our forever was going to be spent living among the Southerners, after they got licked."[138]

# Chapter Two

---

# BLACK LIBERATORS

*Now we sogers are men—men de first time in our lives. Now we can look our old masters in de face. They used to sell and whip us, and we did not dare say one word. Now we ain't afraid, if they meet us, to run the bayonet through them.*

—SERGEANT PRINCE RIVERS,
1ST SOUTH CAROLINA VOLUNTEERS,
UNITED STATES COLORED TROOPS[1]

*Lieutenant, de old flag neber did wave quite right. There was something wrong about it,—there wasn't any star in it for the black man. Perhaps there was in those you made in de North; but, when they got down here, the sun was so hot, we couldn't see it. But, since the war, it's all right. The black man has his star: it is the big one in the middle.*

—TOM TAYLOR,
UNITED STATES COLORED TROOPS[2]

*How extraordinary, and what a tribute to ignorance and religious hypocrisy, is the fact that in the minds of most people, even those of liberals, only murder makes men. The slave pleaded; he was humble; he protected the women of the South, and the world ignored him. The slave killed white men; and behold, he was a man.*

—W. E. B. DU BOIS[3]

ON APRIL 12, 1864, George W. Hatton found cause for celebration and reflection. Three years had passed since Confederate batteries opened fire on Fort Sumter, and he could only marvel at the changes which had taken place in his own life and in the lives of his people. "Though the Government openly declared that it did not want the negroes in this conflict," he noted, "I look around me and see hundreds of colored men armed and ready to defend the Government at any moment; and such are my feelings, that I can only say, the fetters have fallen—our bondage is over." Hatton was a sergeant in Company C of the 1st Regiment, United States Colored Troops. The regimental chaplain—among the first black men ever so designated—was Henry McNeal Turner, a native of South Carolina but most recently pastor of the Israel Bethel Church in Washington, D.C.

Encamped near New Bern, North Carolina, the regiment awaited the orders that would take them into Virginia for what promised to be the final assault on the Confederacy. To many of the soldiers in this regiment, it all seemed incredible. "Who would not celebrate this day?" Sergeant Hatton asked. "What has the colored man done for himself in the past three years? Why, sir, he has proved ... that he is a man."

Less than a month later, Hatton's regiment reached Wilson's Landing, only a few miles from Jamestown, where (as the sergeant duly noted) some 264 years earlier "the first sons of Africa" had been landed on American soil. The region took on a special meaning, too, for several of the soldiers in the regiment who had labored as slaves there. The memories they retained of those years were no doubt revived when several black women entered the camp, still bearing the marks of a severe whipping recently administered to them. While out on a foraging mission the next day, the soldiers captured the man who had meted out that punishment—"a Mr. Clayton, a noted reb in this part of the country, and from his appearance, one of the F.F.V.'s [First Families of Virginia]." Before an obviously appreciative audience, which included the black women he had whipped, the slaveholder was tied to a tree and stripped of his clothes; William Harris, one of his former slaves before fleeing to enlist in the Union Army, took up a whip and lashed him some twenty times, "bringing the blood from his loins at every stroke, and not forgetting to remind the gentleman of days gone by." The whip was then handed over to the black women, who "one after another," as Sergeant Hatton afterward wrote, "came up and gave him a like number, to remind him that they were no longer his, but safely housed in Abraham's bosom, and under the protection of the Star Spangled Banner, and guarded by their own patriotic, though once down-trodden race."

That night, Sergeant George Hatton tried to sum up his impressions of this almost unreal experience. He confessed that he was at a loss for the proper words. "Oh, that I had the tongue to express my feelings while standing upon the banks of the James river, on the soil of Virginia, the mother state of slavery, as a witness of such a sudden reverse! The day is clear, the fields of grain are beautiful, and the birds are singing sweet melodious songs, while poor Mr. C. is crying to his servants for mercy."[4]

The war to save the Union had become, for scores of black people at least, nothing less than a war of liberation. This far-reaching change in the nature of the Civil War, like emancipation itself, had been achieved neither quickly nor easily.

2

WHEN THE CIVIL WAR BROKE OUT, Frederick Douglass, a black abolitionist leader and former slave, immediately called for the enlistment of slaves and free blacks into a "liberating army" that would carry the banner of emancipation through the South. Within thirty days, Douglass believed, 10,000 black soldiers could be assembled. "One black regiment alone would be, in such a war, the full equal of two white ones. The very fact of color in this case would be more terrible than powder and balls. The slaves would learn more as to the nature of the conflict from the presence of one such regiment, than from a thousand preachers." But the North was not yet prepared to endorse such a revolutionary move, any more than it could conceive of the necessity or wisdom of embracing a policy of emancipation.[5]

Along with most northern whites, even ardent Union patriots tended to view the enlistment of blacks into the armed forces as an incendiary act contrary to accepted modes of warfare and "shocking to our sense of humanity." The specters of Nat Turner and Santo Domingo were regarded as sufficient warnings of what might happen if armed black men were unleashed upon white slaveholding families. The history of slave insurrections, a Republican senator from Ohio reminded his colleagues, demonstrated that "Negro warfare" inevitably produced "all the scenes of desolation attendant upon savage warfare." Besides, a border state congressman told his constituents, "to confess our inability to put down this rebellion without calling to our aid these semi-barbaric hordes" would prove "derogatory to the manhood of 20 millions of freemen."[6]

Early conceptions of the Civil War as "a white man's war" with limited objectives were not the only deterrent to raising a black army. Even if black enlistments should be deemed desirable, few whites believed that black men possessed the necessary technical skills, intelligence, and courage to become effective soldiers. "If we were to arm them," President Lincoln conceded in September 1862, "I fear that in a few weeks the arms would be in the hands of the rebels." No less threatening to many whites was the possibility that they were wrong and that the black man might actually prove himself in combat. "If you make him the instrument by which your battles are fought, the means by which your victories are won," an Ohio congressman warned, "you must treat him as a victor is entitled to be treated, with all decent and becoming respect." The use of black troops also threatened to undermine the morale of white Union soldiers, many of whom recoiled at the thought of serving alongside black comrades. "[I]t Will raise a rebelion in the army that all the abolisionist this Side of hell Could not Stop," one Union soldier predicted. "[T]he Southern Peopel are rebels to the government but they are White and God never intended a nigger to put white people Down."[7]

The exclusion of blacks from the armed forces, like President Lincoln's reluctance to make emancipation a war objective, worked only so long as the government and northern whites remained confident of their ability to win the war. In the aftermath of Fort Sumter, with patriotic whites rallying to the flag, there seemed little reason to doubt that the rebellion would be easily and speedily crushed. Eighteen months later, the expected quick victory had not materialized, the war still raged with no end in sight, and a weary, frustrated North was forced to think about a different kind of war. Mounting casualties, the return home of the maimed and wounded, the alarming increase in desertions (more than 100,000 away without leave at the end of 1862), and the growing difficulty in obtaining enlistments encouraged a reassessment of the military value of emancipation and black recruitment. "If a bob-tail dog can stick a bayonet on his tail, and back up against a rebel and kill him, I will take the dog and sleep with him," a Union officer declared, "and if a nigger will do the same, I'll do the same by him. I'll sleep with any thing that will kill a rebel." Although this may have been a curious kind of recognition, the argument gained increasing acceptance with every casualty list. To enlist blacks was to preserve the more valuable lives of white men. The best men of the North were dying in the swamps of the South, an officer observed, and this was a loss the nation could ill afford. "[Y]ou can't replace these men, but if a nigger dies, all you have to do is send out and get another one."[8]

The same Administration that had summarily rejected black volunteers at the outset of the war began in mid-1862 to consider the employment of blacks in the armed forces. The initial proposals contemplated using such troops primarily for menial labor and for garrison duty in areas deemed unfit for white men, such as the malarial regions along the Gulf of Mexico and the Mississippi River. The advantages of deploying blacks in these ways were obvious. "The blacks," said the *New York Times,* "thoroughly acclimated, will be saved from the risks of the climate, while in the well-defined limit of fortifications they will be restrained from the commission of those revengeful excesses which are the bug-aboos of the Southern people." In a series of articles on "Colored Troops," a columnist for the *Christian Recorder,* the voice of the African Methodist Episcopal Church, seemed to share the prevailing belief that blacks were "especially adapted to service in the South" because they were less susceptible to diseases which easily felled white men. When Vicksburg surrendered, the black columnist noted, the hospitals were filled with southern white soldiers suffering from malarial diseases and fevers "from which colored men are almost exempt." Citing the many advantages of black troops, he welcomed the proposal to use them to guard prisoners of war and to protect garrisons in the occupied areas. Such duty, he thought, would be especially "pleasant" to the emancipated slaves, enabling them "to stand guard over those who have so long abused the power they held over them."[9]

To resolve the doubts which persisted about the military capabilities of black men, some suggested that they first be tested in battle against the Indians. If the experiment proved successful, black troops could then be deployed for combat duty in the South. Nothing came of this proposal, and it won little favor among blacks themselves. "I am very doubtful whether the negro could display his bravery as well against his co-sufferer, as he could against his enemy," wrote Henry M. Turner, the black clergyman. "Like us," the Indian has been "scattered and peeled." How could blacks, of all people, share in a deliberate policy of racial extermination? The Indians, Turner observed, "cherished no special hatred against my race," and the "scalping knife and tomahawk were not shaped nor moulded to injure us." Rather than wage war on the Indians, Turner suggested that black people might well learn to emulate their bravery. "If we had one half of the Indian spunk, to-day slavery would have been among the things of the past." Whatever the merits of Turner's argument, blacks had been used to fight Indians in the past, and they would do so again in the postwar Indian wars, but to have employed them for this purpose in 1863 must have struck some blacks as a perversion of priorities.[10]

While the President refused to alter his position on emancipation and black enlistments, the Union Navy was using "contraband" slaves as apprentice seamen and the Army began to employ them extensively as laborers and officers' servants. Limited and unauthorized attempts, moreover, had been undertaken in Kansas, Louisiana, and South Carolina to arm, drill, and use black soldiers. After General Benjamin Butler overcame his initial reluctance to enlist blacks, three regiments made up of free colored militiamen (previously organized by Confederate authorities) and even larger numbers of freed slaves were organized in Louisiana. With unconcealed enthusiasm, General David Hunter sought to mobilize blacks in the Sea Islands of South Carolina, explaining to the War Department that he had recruited no "fugitive slaves" but "a fine regiment of loyal persons whose late masters are fugitive rebels." The Hunter project proved short-lived, largely because the government refused to recognize or assist it in any way, and aggressive recruitment tactics had antagonized both the freedmen and many of the northern white missionaries and teachers stationed there.[11]

Responding to new military reverses and stalemates, the War Department in August 1862 authorized the recruitment of a slave regiment in the Union Army—the 1st South Carolina Volunteers. In compliance with the proviso that white men serve as officers, Thomas Wentworth Higginson was appointed to command the regiment. Appropriately, this New England intellectual was also a fervid abolitionist and an old friend of John Brown. He eagerly accepted the commission, considering it a challenge that might well influence the entire course of the war and the destiny of black people in the United States. "I had been an abolitionist too long, and had known and loved John Brown too well," he later wrote, "not to feel a thrill of joy at last on finding myself in the position where he only wished to be."[12]

The 1st South Carolina Volunteers drew its recruits largely from the Sea Islands freedmen. Higginson insisted that his white officers treat the soldiers with respect, refer to them by their full names and never as "nigger," and eschew any "degrading punishments." After assuming command in November 1862, his first impressions were favorable, though heavily overladen with a condescending paternalism that characterized his New England contemporaries' views of black people. He marveled at the religious devotions, songs, and "strange antics" that emanated from "this mysterious race of grown-up children." He admired their inexhaustible "love of the spelling book." He was impressed by their aptitude for drill and discipline and their capacity for imitativeness. To Higginson, they were always "a simple and lovable people, whose graces seem to come by nature, and whose vices by training." He came to love them both as a military commander and as a father figure. "I think it is partly from my own notorious love of children that I like these people so well." The immediate task at hand, as he interpreted his mission, was to educate these "perpetual children, docile, gay, and lovable," to manhood and to mobilize them into an effective fighting force. He was fully confident of success.[13]

Against a background of military setbacks, mounting casualty lists, and unfilled recruitment quotas, President Lincoln issued in September 1862 a Preliminary Proclamation of Emancipation which stipulated that on January 1, 1863, in those states or portions of states still engaged in rebellion, the slaves would be "forever free." Not only were Tennessee and the loyal border slave states thereby excluded but also the slaves in designated portions of Louisiana, Virginia, and West Virginia. Limited though it was and justified only as "a fit and necessary war measure," the Proclamation marked a strategic shift in the President's thinking about the military uses of black men. Henceforth, he decreed, they would be accepted into the armed forces for garrison duty and to man naval vessels. This fell far short of a commitment to a black army, but the wording was sufficiently vague to invite a variety of interpretations and proposals. "The best thing in the proclamation," wrote a northern lawyer, "is the annunciation that the southern garrisons are to be *Negros*. We ought to have our standing army (after the rebellion) composed *exclusively* of Negros—a regular Janissary Corps, who propagate & recruit themselves." The news was greeted with far less enthusiasm in the Union Army camps in the South, where white troops needed to weigh the advantages of combat replacements and labor relief against deeply entrenched racial attitudes. "The truth is," one army private wrote, "none of our soldiers seem to like the idea of arming the Negros. Our boys say this [is] a white mans war and the Negro has no business in it."[14]

After the Administration committed itself to the military employment of blacks as soldiers, the changes came so rapidly that Frederick Douglass could only describe them as "vast and startling." Less than three weeks after the Emancipation Proclamation went into effect, the 1st South Carolina Volunteers marched through the streets of Beaufort, with a white regimental band leading the way. "And when dat band wheel in before us, and march on," a black sergeant remarked afterwards, "my God! I quit dis world altogeder." The astonishment of the native whites at this awesome spectacle was matched only by the obvious pride manifested in the eyes of the black soldiers, their faces set rigidly to the front. "We didn't look to de right nor to de leff," one of them recalled. "I didn't see notin' in Beaufort. Eb'ry step was worth a half a dollar." Several weeks later, they made their initial contact with the enemy, and Colonel Higginson was deeply impressed. "Nobody knows anything about these men who has not seen them in battle. I find that I myself knew nothing. *There is a fierce energy about them beyond anything of which I have ever read,* unless it be the French

Zouaves. It requires the strictest discipline to hold them in hand." There could no longer be any doubt in Higginson's mind that "the key to the successful prosecution of this war" lay in the unlimited use of black troops.

> Their superiority lies simply in the fact that they know the country, which White troops do not; and, moreover, that they have peculiarities of temperament, position, and motive, which belong to them alone. Instead of leaving their homes and families to fight, they are fighting for their homes and families; and they show the resolution and sagacity which a personal purpose gives. It would have been madness to attempt with the bravest White troops what I have successfully accomplished with Black ones.[15]

The "vast and startling" changes manifested themselves throughout the occupied South. While black troops marched in Beaufort, a regiment recruited largely from fugitive slaves out of Arkansas and Missouri went into combat as the Kansas 1st Colored Volunteers Infantry. "I believe the Negro may just as well become food for powder as my son," the commander of this regiment had previously declared. In the lower Mississippi Valley, meanwhile, the thousands of slaves crowding the Union camps were being mobilized into military units, and in Louisiana the previously organized free colored and slave regiments were augmented despite bitter objections from native whites. "When we enlisted," one black soldier wrote, "we were hooted at in the streets of New Orleans as a rabble of armed plebeians & cowards." On May 27, 1863, two of the Louisiana black regiments joined in the assault on Port Hudson, a major Confederate stronghold on the lower Mississippi River. That morning, Henry T. Johns, a white private, wrote: "I am glad to know that on our right and on our left are massed *negro* regiments, who, this day, are to show if the inspiration of Freedom will lift the serf to the level of the man. Whoever else may flinch, I trust *they* will stand firm and baptize their hopes in the mingled blood of master and slave. Then we will give them a share in *our* nationality, if God has no separate nationality in store for them." Although the attack was repulsed with heavy losses, the blacks had proven themselves in battle, and a Union officer confessed that his "prejudices" in regard to black troops had been dispelled in a single day. Private Johns thought, too, that the question of black troops had been firmly settled, "and many a proud master found in death that freedom had made his slave his superior." To many observers, in fact, Port Hudson was the turning point in white recognition of the Negro as a combat soldier. And when two regiments made up of freedmen successfully resisted a Confederate assault on Milliken's Bend the following month, even the Confederate officer commanding the attack was duly impressed. "This charge was resisted by the negro portion of the enemy's force with considerable obstinacy, while the white or true Yankee portion ran like whipped curs almost as soon as the charge was ordered."[16]

Six months after the Emancipation Proclamation, more than thirty black regiments had been organized, camps had been established to receive and train them, recruiting was taking place almost everywhere, and several units had already participated in combat action. That was only the beginning. By December 1863 over 50,000 blacks had been enrolled in the Union Army, and the President was assured that this number would rapidly increase as Federal troops moved deeper into the Confederacy. Before the end of the war, more than 186,000 would be enlisted, including 24,000 in Louisiana, 17,800 in Mississippi, and 20,000 in Tennessee. The President even overcame his initial reluctance to organizing black regiments in the loyal border states of Kentucky, Missouri, and Maryland. Although he tried to restrict enlistments in those states to the slaves of disloyal masters, army recruiters made little or no effort to enforce such discrimination, and the promise of freedom to enlistees and their families went far, in fact, to undermine the entire institution of slavery in those regions excluded from the Emancipation Proclamation. "I claim not to have controlled events, but confess plainly that events have controlled me," President Lincoln wrote to a Kentucky newspaper. "Now, at the end of three years struggle the nation's condition is not what either party or any man devised, or expected." Christopher A. Fleetwood, a Baltimore free black who had enlisted in the Union Army, voiced almost the same sentiments when he noted in his diary at the end of 1863: "This year has brought about many changes that at the beginning were or would have been thought impossible. The close of the year finds me a soldier for the cause of my race."[17]

The transformation of public sentiment on the enlistment of blacks pointed up the extent to which military necessity managed to surmount prevailing racial attitudes. The passage of the Draft Act in March 1863, reflecting as it did the desperate need for more troops, broke down still further the remaining objections to blacks as soldiers. For many war-weary Northerners, especially those who were now subject to military conscription, the arming of the black man suddenly took on a new meaning. The immediate and widespread popularity of a song ascribed to Irish Americans testified not so much to its melodic quality as to its persuasive logic:

> *Some tell us 'tis a burnin shame*
> *To make the naygers fight;*
> *An' that the thrade of bein' kilt*
> *Belongs but to the white;*
> *But as for me, upon my soul!*
> *So liberal are we here,*
> *I'll let Sambo be murthered instead of myself*
> *On every day in the year.*[18]

Capitalizing on the apparent changes in public sentiment, black spokesmen and newspapers in the North insisted that the very nature of the Civil War had been fundamentally altered. "The strife now waging is not between North and South," a black meeting declared in mid-1863, but between "barbarism and freedom—civilization and slavery." For the North to lose this war would "rivet our chains still firmer" and seal "our perpetual disfranchisement." The most effective remedy for what ailed blacks, the meeting resolved, was "warm lead and cold steel, duly administered by two hundred thousand black doctors." Now that the Civil War promised to liberate the slaves, the necessity for defeating the Confederacy was coupled with the urgency of black people helping to strike the decisive blow and setting themselves free. "Liberty won by white men," Douglass maintained, "would lose half its luster." But by breaking the chains themselves, he told prospective black volunteers, "you will stand more erect, walk more assured, feel more at ease, and be less liable to insult than you ever were before." Few welcomed this opportunity more readily than did many of those who had only recently been slaves. "A year ago, where was we?" asked a soldier with the 7th Regiment Corps d'Afrique. "We was down in de dark land of Slavery. And now where are we? We are free men, and soldiers of de United States. And what have we to do? We have to fight de rebels so dat we never more be slaves."[19]

Although emancipation did not directly affect northern blacks, they were urged to act upon the sympathy they had long expressed for their enslaved southern brethren. Participation in the war, moreover, could not help but improve their own precarious place in American society and break down the barriers white Northerners had erected against them. "There never was, nor there never will be, a better opportunity for colored men to get what they want, than now," the Washington, D.C., correspondent of the *Christian Recorder* wrote in June 1863. "Suppose," he asked, "500,000 colored men were under arms, would not the nation really be under our arms, too? Would the nation refuse us our rights in such a condition? Would it refuse us our vote? Would it deny us any thing when its salvation was hanging upon us? No! never!" Whether in the North or in the South, then, the prospects for black Americans seemed inseparable from their military exploits—the way to the ballot box, into the classroom, and onto the streetcar was through the battlegrounds of the Confederacy. The rifle and the bayonet, Douglass insisted, would speak more forcefully for civil rights than any "parchment guarantees."

> Once let the black man get upon his person the brass letters, U.S.; let him get an eagle on his button, and a musket on his shoulder and bullets in his pocket, and there is no power on earth which can deny that he has earned the right to citizenship in the United States.

To learn the use of arms, moreover, was "to become familiar with the means of securing, protecting and defending your own liberty. . . . When it is once found that black men can give blows as well as take them, men will find more congenial employment than pounding them."[20]

Once an advocate of nonresistance and only recently a major critic of President Lincoln for refusing to endorse emancipation, Frederick Douglass agreed in early 1863 to become a recruiting agent for the United States Army. "There is something ennobling in the possession of arms," he told a meeting in Philadelphia, "and we of all other people in the world stand in need of their ennobling influence." Having undertaken the mission of enlisting blacks in the newly formed 54th Massachusetts Regiment, Douglass toured western New York seeking volunteers. "In Rochester," he wrote in April 1863, "I have thirteen names, my son heading the list."[21]

## 3

THE CIVIL WAR provided Americans with various opportunities to exploit the nation's military needs for personal profit and advantage. That white men should have used the recruitment of black regiments for such purposes is not altogether surprising. With the end of racial restrictions on enlistments, state and local bounties and military conscription instantly made black men valuable and marketable commodities. Capitalizing on the law which permitted a draftee to send a person in his place, the "substitute broker" viewed the black man as a likely candidate; his lowly economic position often made him easier and cheaper to purchase, some were intimidated into enlisting, and the broker's commission for finding a "substitute" justified whatever method he needed to employ. The practice became so widespread, in fact, that the War Department finally interceded and ruled that Negroes could substitute only for other Negroes. That decision not only forced brokers to look elsewhere but depressed the price which some blacks had been asking (and obtaining) for a substitute enlistment.[22]

Mixing patriotism and personal profit in varying degrees, more than a thousand "state agents" combed the cities and countryside, particularly in the occupied South, for prospective black soldiers. The incentive was a new congressional law, enacted on July 4, 1864, which provided that blacks recruited in the Confederate states could be credited to the draft quotas of the loyal states. Acting sometimes as emissaries of northern governors and authorized to offer handsome bounties, the "state agents" used every conceivable method to obtain recruits and often defrauded them of the promised bonus. The number of military officers who accepted bribes to turn over slave refugees "to *particular* agents" will never be known. But one court-martial trial revealed how a Massachusetts white man had formed a thriving business by purchasing blacks in New Bern, North Carolina, from a Union officer, inducting them into the Army, and then crediting them to the quotas of various Massachusetts towns in proportion to the amount of money the townspeople had contributed for bounty payments. The agent in this case testified that his share of the profits had amounted to $10,000. Stories such as these prompted one Massachusetts officer to express his revulsion at "this traffic of New England towns in the bodies of wretched negroes, bidding against each other for these miserable beings who are deluded, and if some of the affidavits I have in my office are true, tortured into military service."[23]

Employing both persuasion and strong-arm methods, the Army sought most of its black recruits in the occupied South. With "soul-stirring music and floating banners," a correspondent reported from Maryland, recruiting parties would march through a neighborhood and "sweep it clean of its black warriors." Wherever the Union Army was in control, recruitment offices were opened and specially designated agents (or raiding parties made up of a dozen men and a noncommissioned officer) were dispatched to the countryside to round up potential recruits. The usual procedure was for the agent to enter a town, address a hastily convened meeting of local blacks, tell them what the President had done for the colored people, display the attractive recruitment poster, and promise anyone who joined both financial and moral compensation. Appointed to recruit black troops in northern Alabama, James T. Ayers found himself frequently forced to adopt direct personal pleading. "I want your man," he told a black woman who had urged her husband not to enlist. "You ought to be a slave as long as you live and him too if he is so mean as not to help get his Liberty." Far more effective, in some instances, was the use of black soldiers to obtain additional recruits. Not only were black troops frequently dispatched with instructions to enlist any able-bodied slaves they could locate but they might be necessary to protect the recruits from white retaliation. The black soldier also often appeared as the featured speaker at meetings of his people, and invariably he would appeal to the race pride and manhood of his audience. "Don't you remember how afraid they used to be that we would rise?" Jerry Sullivan asked a Nashville gathering in 1863.

> And you know we would, too, if we could. (Cries of "that's so.") I ran away two years ago. . . . Come, boys, let's get some guns from Uncle Sam, and go coon hunting; shooting those gray back coons that go poking about the country now a days. (Laughter.) . . . Don't ask your wife, for if she is a wife worth having she will call you a coward for asking her. (Applause, and waving of handkerchiefs by the ladies.)[24]

The job of a recruiting agent in the South was beset with difficulties, frustrations, and personal danger. The whites regarded him as an incendiary (he proposed, after all, to arm black men), and slaveholders were naturally incensed by anyone who threatened to make soldiers of their laborers. Unless accompanied by a detachment of troops, both the agent and his prospective recruits might find it difficult to return to the nearest Union camp. In Kentucky, the provost marshal enumerated cases in which slaves had been whipped, mutilated, and murdered for trying to enlist and recruiting agents had been "caught, stripped, tied to a tree and cowhided" before being driven out of town. What made the work of the agent all the more exasperating was his frequent lack of success in obtaining many enlistments. The reports of white violence no doubt discouraged prospective volunteers but this may not adequately explain the disturbing report of a Federal official that in nearly four months of recruitment work, more than a thousand men had been employed to enlist a total of 2,831 blacks. More likely, many blacks simply shared with their white countrymen an aversion to the hardships and risks of military service. "The negroes re-indicate their claim to humanity," an officer wrote from South Carolina, "by shirking the draft in every possible way; acting exactly like *white men* under similar circumstances." He conceded, however, that the black con-script was less likely to desert than his white counterpart. Some recruiting agents came away disgusted with the refusal of blacks to yield to their appeals. Initially enthusiastic about his recruiting mission in northern Alabama, James T. Ayers, who had been an antislavery Methodist preacher in Illinois, urged blacks to accept the responsibility for liberating their brethren from bondage. But his best efforts did not produce the results he had expected, and less than a year after his appointment Ayers was a thoroughly disillusioned man. "I feel now much inclined to go to Nashville and throw up my papers and Resign, as I am hartily sick of Coaxing niggers to be Soaldiers Any more. They are so trifleing and mean they dont Deserve to be free."[25]

After making their way to the Union camps, many slave refugees eagerly volunteered for military service, believing that this act would con-firm their freedom. The more reluctant blacks might be inducted anyway. "It seems that pretty nearly all the refugees join the army," a Federal official wrote from South Carolina. "You wish to know whether the ref-ugees are kept in the guard house until they are willing to volunteer. I do not know whether they are kept confined till they do volunteer but I know that they always let them out when they do volunteer." Increasingly, the Army resorted to forcible impressment, though in some regions they would try to balance the demand for recruits with the need to maintain planta-tion labor. The effectiveness of the recruitment campaign in the lower Mississippi Valley rested partly on the insistence that slaves who had left their masters should be forced to serve either as soldiers or as military laborers; the methods employed by officers in this region were often ques-tionable but they achieved spectacular results. "The plan for 'persuading' recruits," one officer wrote from Memphis, "while it could hardly be called the shot-gun policy was equally as convincing, and never failed to get the 'recruit.' " The commissioner entrusted with raising black troops in Mary-land simply conceded that "no recruits can be had unless I send detach-ments to particular localities and compel them to volunteer."[26]

Despite assurances to South Carolina blacks of voluntary enlistment, freedmen in the Sea Islands region stood in perpetual fear of raiding par-ties—often composed of black soldiers—which descended upon communi-ties and plantations in the dead of night to carry them away to nearby military camps. "Not a man sleeps at night in the houses," a missionary teacher wrote, "except those too old to be taken. They have made a camp somewhere and mean never to be caught." Prospective recruits here and elsewhere often hid out in the woods or swamps.for considerable periods of time rather than be inducted into the Army. Having already experienced forced separations from their loved ones, black women did not necessarily look with favor upon similar disruptions undertaken by their professed liberators; in South Carolina, women field workers attacked a black impressment party with their hoes, shouting that white men were too frightened to fight and only wanted blacks to do their dirty work for them. "The womens all hold back der husbands," a black sergeant complained, "didn't want them to go sogering, 'cause they get killed. Women worse than the men, and some hide the men in the woods.... I feel 'shamed for our women."[27]

Impressment of Sea Islands freedmen not only alarmed the intended victims and forced many of them into hiding but provoked some furious protests from the white teachers and missionaries who had come there from the North to ease their transition to freedom. The coercive recruitment practices reminded them, they said, of what they had only recently criticized in their indictments of slavery. What was impressment, after all, if not the forcible enslavement of blacks, albeit under different auspices? After Union troops had carried away still another black man during the night, one missionary observed that only recently Confederate soldiers had shot and killed black men for refusing to go along with them. How were the freedmen, she asked, to know the difference? "It strikes me as very important," a high-ranking Federal official wrote to a Union officer, "to avoid all things likely to impair the self respect of the emancipees. Fresh from slavery, if they *enlist freely* they must feel themselves very different persons from what they would regard themselves if *forced into the ranks*."[28]

Despite a flurry of protests, army commanders defended their conduct not only on the grounds of military necessity but as in the best interests of the blacks. That recruitment had been progressing more slowly than expected was only one reason why General Hunter wanted to impress all blacks not regularly employed as officers' servants or military laborers. Military discipline, Hunter insisted, was the best way to lift these people to "our higher civilization." The slaves, moreover, could never adequately appreciate freedom until they realized "the sacrifices which are its price." And finally, he noted, the recruitment of black men made a servile insurrection less likely. In defending the conduct of impressment parties in Washington, D.C., a black resident singled out the contemptuous way in which some of his people responded to recruitment appeals. When asked to enlist, they would "make light" of the proposal and demand to know "what am I going to fight for? this is a white man's war," and accompany their response with verbal abuse. "Well, now," the observer added, "the colored soldiers think this is too much; they suffer enough at the hands of the white race, without being buffeted by their own race, whose sympathies should be in their behalf."[29]

Less coercive methods were employed in the North, where state governors and patriotic citizens' committees were initially responsible for mounting recruitment campaigns. To mobilize support among northern blacks, mass meetings were called, broadsides were circulated (the most popular of which was written by Frederick Douglass), and the few black newspapers sought to inculcate their readers with the obligations of black men in a war of liberation. Although the *Christian Recorder* had initially disapproved of the war and the resort to violence, it now urged black men to take up arms for their country and race. "Shame on him who would hang back at the call of his country," the newspaper declared, in supporting the efforts to raise a black regiment in Philadelphia. "Go with the view that you will return freemen. And if you should never return, you will die with the satisfaction of knowing that you have struck a blow for freedom, and assisted in giving liberty to our race in the land of our birth."[30]

Critical to the raising of a black army in the North were, in fact, the black recruitment agents. When Governor John A. Andrew of Massachusetts was authorized in January 1863 to organize a Negro regiment, he immediately recognized the far-reaching implications of his new responsibility. Since this would be the first black regiment raised in the North, he thought the success or failure of the effort would "go far to elevate or to depress the estimation in which the character of the Colored Americans will be held throughout the World." Although two companies were quickly formed in Boston and New Bedford (including black men whom the governor had been forced to reject at the outset of the war), there were insufficient numbers of blacks in Massachusetts to make up an entire regiment. The governor thereupon secured the support of a wealthy abolitionist who agreed to help finance the enlistment of blacks throughout the North, largely by employing as recruitment agents such leading black spokesmen as Martin R. Delany, John Mercer Langston, John S. Rock, William Wells Brown, Charles Lenox Remond, Henry Highland Garnet, and Frederick Douglass. These were all familiar names in black abolitionism, most of them had worked actively to eradicate racial discrimination in the North, and several of them had only recently endorsed emigration to Haiti or Central America before being dissuaded by the reality of an antislavery war. "Action! Action! not criticism, is the plain duty of this hour," Douglass declared, in a broadside intended to attract blacks to the Massachusetts regiment. "The iron gate of our prison stands half open. One gallant rush from the North will fling it wide open, while four millions of our brothers and sisters shall march out into liberty."[31]

The recruitment drive was highly successful. By May 1863, the 54th Massachusetts Regiment, the most celebrated of the northern black regiments, was ready to leave Boston for Hilton Head, South Carolina, where it had been ordered to report to General David Hunter. With some 20,000 cheering Bostonians lining the streets, and the regimental band playing the John Brown anthem, the troops made their way to the Battery Wharf. "Glory enough for one day; aye, indeed for a lifetime," remarked William C. Nell, a veteran black abolitionist. Frederick Douglass was there, not only to view the results of his recruitment activities but to see off his two sons, Lewis and Charles, who had been the first New York blacks to enlist in the regiment. Martin R. Delany's eighteen-year-old son, Toussaint L'Ouverture Delany, had left his school in Canada to join the regiment. And on the balcony of Wendell Phillips' house, overlooking the parade, stood none other than William Lloyd Garrison, who was observed resting his hand on a bust of John Brown.[32]

Two months later, the 54th Massachusetts Regiment made its famous assault on Fort Wagner, a Confederate stronghold situated at the entrance to Charleston harbor. The attack was repulsed, with considerable loss of life (Robert Shaw, the white regimental commander, was among those killed), but black troops had fought valiantly. And that was what mattered. "It made Fort Wagner such a name to the colored race," proclaimed a New York newspaper, "as Bunker Hill has been for ninety years to the white Yankees." Even the enormous expenditure of black lives could be viewed as a necessary sacrificial offering. "Do you not rejoice & exult in all that praise that is lavished upon our brave colored troops even by Pro-slavery papers?" abolitionist Angelina Grimké Weld asked Gerrit Smith. "I have no tears to shed over their graves, because I see that their heroism is working a great change in public opinion, forcing all men to see the sin & shame of enslaving such men." Two days after the battle, Lewis Douglass informed Amelia Loguen, his future wife, that he had not been wounded. "Men fell all around me. A shell would explode and clear a space of twenty feet, our men would close up again, but it was no use we had to retreat, which was a very hazardous undertaking. How I got out of that fight alive I cannot tell, but I am here. . . . Remember if I die I die in a good cause. I wish we had a hundred thousand colored troops we would put an end to this war."[33]

With the successful organization of two Massachusetts regiments (the surplus of volunteers for the 54th became the 55th Massachusetts Regiment), several northern states undertook to form similar contingents and employed black leaders to find the necessary men. The enthusiasm which brought about the Massachusetts regiments, however, proved to be less contagious than had been expected. Although several thousand northern blacks did respond to the call for military service, the anticipated stampede to the recruitment offices failed to materialize. "Before an opportunity was presented for them to do so," a disillusioned black soldier told a gathering of his people in Washington, D.C., "many of the black people were spoiling for a fight—they were ready and anxious to die for their race—but now whar are dey? What do you want Mr. Linkun to do—feed you on ice-cream? Suppose these white men here were about to be drove into Slavery, wouldn't they fight? Certainly they would; but you—you would stand tamely and let your hands be crossed behind your back, and told to go on dar, nigger, without resisting it."[34]

If this disgruntled soldier had looked around him, he might have perceived why some blacks had declined to enlist. The Civil War had expanded economic opportunities, and black people shared to some extent in the wartime prosperity. While a black resident of Washington, D.C., described a substantial increase in black employment, a white Bostonian was complaining that "the blacks here are too comfortable to do anything more than talk about freedom." Nor did northern blacks feel as intensely that inducement of freedom which moved their southern brethren to enlist in far greater numbers; some insisted that they could serve their race more effectively if they remained at home, where important campaigns also needed to be waged. "I am pleased to learn that you were fortunate enough to escape the draft," William H. Parham, a black school principal in Cincinnati, wrote to a prominent Philadelphia black leader, "as I believe you will be able to do more for the race where you are than you could by going to the battlefield. When this war is over, the next struggle will be against prejudice, which is to be conquered by intellect and we shall need all the talent that we have among us or can possibly command. Then will be your time to be found in the thickest of the fight; where the battle rages fiercest and the danger is most imminent." When Parham himself was enrolled under the Conscription Act and thereby made subject to the draft, he searched desperately for some way to avoid military service. "Many have escaped the enrollment," he wrote, "but I am not one of the fortunate ones. . . . If I am drafted, I do not think I shall go." Aside from his obvious reluctance to serve in the Army, Parham had heard "discouraging" reports that black soldiers were not being accorded the same pay, bounties, and treatment as white recruits.[35]

# 4

WITH THE ENLISTMENT of black men, the question of how they would be treated in the United States Army quickly surfaced. It was understood from the outset that blacks would serve in separate regiments and be commanded largely by white officers. But still other questions required clarification, and some blacks demanded answers before committing their services. "What are to be the immunities of the colored soldiers?" one black newspaper asked. "Will they receive bounties, as well as the white? If they are maimed for life, will they receive pensions from the Government? If they are captured by the enemy, will they be treated as prisoners of war? —or will they be hung up by the rebels, shot or quartered, as the case may be, without redress?"[36] These were not easy questions to answer, and many of the problems they raised were never satisfactorily resolved.

Although the War Department stipulated on several occasions that black soldiers were entitled to the same pay and benefits accorded whites, there was no legal basis for such promises. But most of the recruits had no way of knowing this, and they generally assumed they would be treated like other troops. After all, one black soldier wrote, "we were mustered in as Massachusetts volunteers, not as the United States colored forces or as military laborers"; moreover, Governor Andrew had promised them "the same treatment, in every respect, as the white volunteers receive." In the appeals for enlistments, recruiters repeatedly assured blacks of the same wages, rations, equipment, protection, bounties, and treatment as enjoyed by white troops. "I have assured myself on these points," Frederick Douglass told prospective black recruits, "and can speak with authority. More than twenty years unswerving devotion to our common cause, may give me some humble claim to be trusted at this momentous crisis."[37]

The promises seemed sufficiently clear, and Douglass and other recruiters no doubt believed in them, but the equal treatment they insisted upon never came to pass. And since such promises had comprised a considerable element of the recruitment appeals, initial disappointments had a way of turning into a sense of betrayal. Substantial numbers of black soldiers, mostly those recruited in the North, charged that they had been deceived. "We were promised three hundred dollars bounty and thirteen dollars a month, or whatever the white soldiers got," a Pennsylvania soldier declared; "but, God help their poor lying souls! Now that they have us where they want us, they have forgotten all their promises." His complaint was well grounded. Whatever the assurances upon enlisting, the experience of the black soldier revealed a double standard in enlistment bounties, benefits for dependents, promotions, pay, and time spent in fatigue duty. And since blacks were called upon to perform the same duties as white soldiers, these distinctions made no sense at all. "Do we not fill the same ranks?" asked one soldier. "Do we not cover the same space of ground? Do we not take up the same length of ground in the grave-yard that others do? The ball does not miss the black man and strike the white, nor the white and strike the black. . . . [A]t that time there is no distinction made."[38]

Who had betrayed them? Although the Federal government obviously reneged on its promises, dissatisfied soldiers tended to place much of the responsibility on the recruitment agents who had beguiled them with visions of patriotic service, handsome bounties, and equal rights. "They made us a great many sweet and charming promises just to get us into the service," one soldier charged, "which they were very anxious to do, as it saved them from going themselves." The active role played by black leaders in their recruitment only compounded the bitterness. Before the 14th Rhode Island Regiment had even left for the South, Martin R. Delany, the principal recruitment officer, stood accused of having betrayed young men "taught to hold his name sacred." Of those who had participated in organizing the regiment, one soldier observed, Delany was "the most heartily despised." The complaints of the soldiers were legitimate, but the charges leveled at the black recruitment agents were, most likely, closer to half-truths. "Some unprincipled agents" acting "under me" or "even in *my name,*" Delany conceded, may have been guilty of deceiving black recruits, but he vigorously defended his own record as "the constant and consistent defender of colored soldiers' rights and claims." Rather than accept a

reduction in the bounties paid to black enlistees, Delany refused to do any
more recruiting for the Rhode Island regiment. Frederick Douglass, after
protesting the failure of Federal authorities to ensure equal protection and
treatment to black troops, also vowed to discontinue his recruitment activities. "I owe it to my long abused people, and especially those of them
already in the army," he explained, "to expose their wrongs and plead their
cause. I cannot do that in connection with recruiting. . . . The impression
settles upon me that colored men have much overrated the enlightenment,
justice and generosity of our rulers at Washington. In my humble way I
have contributed somewhat to that false estimate." Hoping to regain his
faith in the government's assurances, Douglass requested a meeting with
President Lincoln.[39]

Readily conceding that inequalities existed between white and black
soldiers, Federal officials argued that expediency justified and perhaps
even demanded the maintenance of racial distinctions, for the self-respect
of the common Yankee soldier was being sorely tested. The fact that he was
now asked to live and fight alongside blacks not only challenged his deeply
held racial prejudices but also raised the humiliating implication that he
had not been able to win the war without black support. To place the two
races on the same level, some argued, was to degrade and demoralize the
white soldier. The inequalities, President Lincoln told Frederick Douglass,
were a regrettable but necessary concession to popular prejudices; nevertheless, he suggested, blacks had more compelling motives to enlist and
should be willing to serve under almost any conditions. Ultimately, he
promised Douglass, black soldiers would be accorded equal treatment. That
vague assurance was good enough for Douglass, who resumed his recruitment activities.[40]

But many of the black troops in the field, especially those from the
North, found themselves unable to share Douglass' renewed confidence. "I
have always been ready for any duty that I have been called upon to
perform," a soldier wrote from Jacksonville, Florida, "but things work so
different with us from what they do with white soldiers, that I have got
discouraged; and not only myself, but all of our company." Comparing their
condition and treatment with that of whites, black soldiers could not understand why they should receive less pay ("We do the same work they do, and
do what they cannot"), spend more time in fatigue duty ("I fancy, at times,
that we have exchanged places with the slave"), eat inferior food ("All the
rations that are condemned by the white troops are sent to our regiment"),
and be subjected to inferior officers ("They try to perpetuate our inferiority,
and keep us where we are").[41]

Of the many grievances, the most deeply felt and resented was the
inequality in pay—the fact that white privates were paid $13 a month plus
a $3.50 clothing allowance, while blacks received $10 a month, out of which
$3.00 might be deducted for clothing. This was not only "an unequivocal
breach of contract," blacks charged, but a hardship on their families at
home. "I could not afford to get a substitute, or I would not be here now,"

a draftee wrote from Yorktown, Virginia. Although "it made me feel some-what proud to think that I had a right to fight for Uncle Sam, . . . my wife's letters have brought my patriotism down to the freezing point," and he indicated that most of his regiment shared this feeling of despair. If they were at home, a number of soldiers insisted, they would at least make enough to provide adequately for their families. "I am not willing to fight for anything less than the white man fights for," a Massachusetts soldier declared. "If the white man cannot support his family on seven dollars per month, I cannot support mine on the same amount."[42]

The inequality in pay assumed a significance for many soldiers that went beyond the question of dollars and cents and family support. The distinction branded them as second-class soldiers and citizens, and this seemed particularly galling at a time when the nation called upon them for patriotic service, perhaps even the sacrifice of their lives. "When the 54th left Boston for the South," a soldier wrote, "they left many white men at home. Therefore, if we are good enough to fill up white men's places and fight, we should be treated then, in all respects, the same as the white man." Nor did blacks find altogether persuasive the oft-repeated argument (which the President himself had made to Douglass) that they had greater motives for fighting this war and should thus be willing to serve under any conditions. Why should they necessarily feel a greater obligation than the white man to preserve the Union or even to liberate the slaves? "I want to know if it was not the white man that put them in bondage?" a Massa-chusetts soldier asked. "How can they hold us responsible for their evils? and how can they expect that we should do more to blot it out than they are willing to do themselves?" Besides, he argued, "if every slave in the United States were emancipated at once they would not be free yet. If the white man is not willing to respect my rights, I am not willing to respect his wrongs."[43]

How to combat the government's discriminatory policy while fighting an antislavery war posed a real dilemma for the black soldier. Not only would a refusal to fight subject him to a court-martial and probable execu-tion, but any serious interruption of the war effort would delay the libera-tion of his enslaved brethren. "Shall it be said that when adversity overshadowed our land, when four million bondmen prayed for deliver-ance, that the free colored man looked on calmly and with folded arms on account of a paltry dollar or two?" This question, raised by a black newspa-per, could not be easily dismissed. Yet to submit to these racial distinctions was to confirm their inferiority. The experience of black people in Ameri-can society afforded certain lessons which a Pennsylvania soldier, sta-tioned in South Carolina, hoped his men would heed: "Our regiment is to be pitied, for we are always ready to take hold of any thing we are ordered to do, and never have we refused to obey orders. This is why we are imposed on; for the horse that draws the most willingly, generally gets the lash the most freely, and the least recompense for it." Shortly after their arrival in the South, this soldier noted, his unit was notified that they would receive less pay than the white troops. Immediately, "despair passed over the whole regiment," and on payday only a few men signed the payroll, "and those who did a great many of us tried to influence to the contrary."[44]

Even as the black regiments went into combat, the reaction to unequal pay assumed the form of organized protest. Until Congress recognized the legitimacy of their position, several regiments refused to accept any pay at all. "The enemy is not far off, and we expect an attack every day," a soldier with the Rhode Island regiment reported, after which he noted that the paymaster had offered them their seven dollars a month "and the boys would not take it." What was at stake, black troops insisted, was nothing less than their self-respect. Although the protest was largely confined to the northern regiments, Colonel Higginson reported that at least one third of the 1st South Carolina Volunteers, "including the best men in the regiment," had quietly refused to accept the government's pay. "We's gib our sogerin' to de Guv'ment, Cunnel," one of the men told him, "but we won't 'spise ourselves so much for take de seben dollar." With such convictions, many of the regiments held out, some for as long as eighteen months. "Here we are," a sergeant with the 54th Massachusetts Regiment reported, "toiling and sweating beneath the burning rays of the sun, for nothing . . . but our hard tack and salt pork, and a constant attendance of the blues."[45]

While Congress failed to act on their grievances, resentment among the black troops mounted. "Fifty-two of the non-commissioned officers are going to hold a meeting upon the subject," a soldier with the 1st District of Columbia Regiment reported; "we don't feel like serving the United States under such an imposition." Henry M. Turner, who was serving as a chaplain to that regiment, confirmed growing apprehension that the hitherto peaceful protests might assume other forms. Unless the troops received their full pay soon, Turner wrote, "*I tremble with fear for the issue of things.*" Discontent in the 54th Massachusetts Regiment reached mutinous proportions, with reports that one soldier had been court-martialed and executed and two had been shot and wounded for refusing to obey orders. "The fact is," a corporal reported, "this regiment is bordering on demoralization." The commanding officer confessed his sympathy with the men, "and yet," he added, "military necessity has compelled me to shoot two of them." Conditions in the 55th Massachusetts Regiment were also close to open rebellion, with more than half the men indicating they were ready to stack arms and perform no more duties unless fully paid. Sergeant William Walker of the 3rd South Carolina Volunteers did more than threaten action; he marched his company to the captain's tent and ordered them to stack arms and resign from the Army. Since the government had broken its contract with his men, he explained, it had no right to demand their allegiance. Sergeant Walker was court-martialed and shot for mutiny.[46]

Confronted with growing resentment of discrimination and the still pressing need to attract more recruits to a war of liberation, black spokesmen on the home front pressed for equal rights in the Army while at the same time urging more enlistments. After assuring black recruits that the "magnanimity" of this nation would speedily grant them equal pay, Frederick Douglass suggested that some blacks might be overreacting to the issue. "Do you get as good wages now as white men get by staying out of the service? Don't you work for less every day than white men get? You know you do." Similarly, the influential *Christian Recorder,* which had wavered between protest and patriotic accommodation, lamented the inequality in pay but fully supported black enlistments and expressed the hope "that our men will not stand now on dollars and cents." What greater inducement was necessary to fight, John S. Rock asked a black regiment, than "two centuries of outrage and oppression and the hope of a glorious future?" What greater inducement was necessary, a black newspaper in New York asked, than "a chance to drive a bayonet or bullet into the slaveholders' hearts?" It was even possible to argue, as did a broadside calling for black volunteers, that the inequality in pay and bounties should, "rightly considered," act as "a fresh incentive" to enlist. Here was the opportunity to demonstrate "that you are actuated not by love of gain but by promptings of patriotism."[47]

That the refusal to accept unequal pay was essentially a northern protest is undeniable. This raised the inevitable charge that, not being slaves, northern blacks had less of a stake in the war and were more apt to be moved by such mundane matters as pay, bounties, and benefits. Disagreement prevailed among the various black regiments as to how they should respond to unequal treatment, whether this was the proper time or place for protests, and whether the grievances warranted any kind of protest. "Those few colored regiments from Massachusetts make more fuss, and complain more than all the rest of the colored troops in the nation," observed Garland H. White, a former Virginia slave who had escaped to Ohio before the war. He regarded their protests as a disservice to the great mass of black people, whom he urged to rebuke the "spirit of dissatisfaction and insolence" and compel the "rebellious" troops "to be quiet and behave themselves like men and soldiers."[48]

With an even greater sense of urgency, the regiments made up largely of former slaves questioned the protests of their northern brethren. After noting "some pretty hard grumbling" among the northern regiments in South Carolina, two soldiers with the 78th United States Colored Troops (recruited from slaves and free Negroes in Louisiana) conceded "that we are pretty much in the same boat with them" but thought they had "put it on a little too thick." Although their own regiment had enlisted under the same expectations of full pay, the two soldiers suggested that southern blacks had entered military service with more compelling motives than those which moved the northern blacks.

> They seem to be fighting for one thing, and we for another. They, for the money they are to get, and we, to secure our liberation. Tell them to hold up a little on grumbling. They say a great deal about the distress of their

families at home. They don't know any thing about distress, till they
come to look at ours. There is not a man of them but knows where his
family is; but hundreds of us don't know where our families are. When
they came away from home, they left their families in the care of their
friends; but we left ours among their enemies, looking only to God to
preserve them.[49]

When Congress finally acted in June 1864 to resolve the controversy
over unequal pay, the resulting legislation only partially satisfied black
demands. Although racial distinctions in pay were abolished, the new law
made a curious distinction in retroactive payments between free Negroes
(those free before April 19, 1861), who would be paid from the date of their
enlistment, and freedmen, whose retroactive payments would begin on
January 1, 1864. This posed a considerable problem in the regiments which
included both free Negroes and ex-slaves. It "divides the colored soldiers
into two grades," one abolitionist charged, and "does honor to injustice
with a vengeance." In the 54th Massachusetts Regiment, Colonel E. N.
Hallowell worked out a rather ingenious solution. Since the commanders
of black regiments were to determine which of their men were free
Negroes, he simply had them all take an oath that on or before April 19,
1861, they "owed no man unrequited labor." This was satisfactory for the
54th, which included very few former slaves, but such a solution was
deemed unacceptable in the regiments made up almost exclusively of freedmen. "If a year's discussion . . . has at length secured the arrears of pay for
the Northern colored regiment," an irate Colonel Higginson remarked,
"possibly two years may secure it for the Southern." Still, the action of
Congress placated the northern regiments, and the first payday (October
1864) under the new law took on a festive air. "Two days have changed the
face of things," an officer with the 54th Massachusetts Regiment observed.
"The fiddle and other music long neglected enlivens the tents day and
night. Songs burst out everywhere; dancing is incessant; boisterous shouts
are heard, mimicry, burlesque, and carnival; pompous salutations are
heard on all sides."[50]

Perhaps, though, the real struggle had only begun. Despite the equali-
zation of pay, black soldiers had not yet been accorded the same rights and
recognition as whites. The question of equal protection for black prisoners
of war persisted, as did the absence of black representation in court-martial
proceedings, the exclusion of blacks from the military academies, and the
small number of black commissioned officers. Both race pride and the
brutal conduct of some white officers prompted increasing demands for
the appointment of blacks to command black troops. But even some of
the firmest advocates of black recruitment found the idea of black officers
difficult to accept, violating as it did the white man's sensibilities and racial
stereotypes in ways that enlisting blacks as common soldiers had not. Since
childhood, blacks had been trained "to obey implicitly the dictates of the
white man" and to believe that they belonged to an inferior race. This

might still make them good soldiers but hardly leaders of men. "Now, when organized into troops," a Union officer observed, "they carry this habit of obedience with them, and their officers being entirely white men, the negro promptly obeys his orders." The impression that blacks would naturally serve white officers more loyally was difficult to dispel, and some observers seriously questioned if black troops would be willing to serve under black officers. In the 1st South Carolina Volunteers, "the universal feeling among the soldiers," a regimental officer told an antislavery meeting, was that they did not want "a colored man to play the white man over them." But many blacks denied these inferences, charged that the relative absence of black officers helped to perpetuate the idea of racial inferiority, and insisted that blacks be judged for promotions and commissions on the same basis as whites. "We want black commissioned officers," one soldier argued, "because we want men we can understand, and who can understand us. . . . We want to demonstrate our ability to rule, as we have demonstrated our willingness to obey."[51]

Shortly after the Civil War broke out, Martin R. Delany, still reflecting the racial pride that had made him an emigrationist and black nationalist in the 1850s, contemplated "a corps d'Afrique" modeled after the black Zouaves who had served the French in the Algerine War. Characteristically, he stressed that the origin, dress, and tactics of the Zouaves d'Afrique were uniquely African. Along similar lines, Henry M. Turner, whose racial pride matched that of Delany but whose advocacy of emigration still lay in the future, expressed the hope that there would be no racial intermingling in the newly organized black regiments. "If we do go in the field, let us have our own soldiers, captains, colonels, and generals, and then an entire separation from soldiers of every other color, and then bid us strike for our liberty, and if we deserve any merit it will stand out beyond contradiction." But Turner's proposal, like Delany's, was premature. Having made the decision to use blacks as soldiers, the government was not prepared to flaunt numbers of black officers before an already apprehensive white public.[52]

No sooner had Congress equalized the pay of white and black soldiers than various schemes for a black army were revived, the most ambitious plan remaining Martin Delany's "corps d'Afrique." This time he took his idea directly to President Lincoln. What he proposed was a black army commanded by black officers that would operate essentially as a guerrilla-type force in the interior, emancipating and arming the slaves wherever they went. "They would require but little," Delany assured the President, "as they could subsist on the country as they went along." President Lincoln, as Delany described his reaction, could barely contain his enthusiasm. "This is the very thing I have been looking and hoping for," he told Delany, "but nobody offered it." Having agreed to command and raise such an army, Delany was commissioned a major and ordered to South Carolina. The war ended before he could put his plan into operation, but Delany remained in South Carolina and subsequently embraced and acted upon still another vision—political power in a state where blacks comprised a majority of the population.[53]

## 5

WHEN 1,100 UNION PRISONERS OF WAR were marched through Petersburg, Virginia, in August 1864, the spectators who lined the streets viewed with particular curiosity and mixed emotions the 200 black soldiers. To the whites in the crowd, few sights could have been more distasteful. At the very least, a Richmond newspaper observed, the black prisoners should have been separated from the white Yankees and driven "into a pen" until their status was determined and their owners located. "Two hundred genuine Eboshins sprinkled among the crowd of prisoners, and placed on the same footing, was a sight, the moral effect of which upon the slaves of Petersburg could not be wholesome." Equally concerned, Emma Holmes of South Carolina wondered how Confederate authorities would deal with the black prisoners recently brought in—"barefoot, hatless and coatless and tied in a gang like common runaways." To have them treated like other prisoners, she confessed, was not only "revolting to our feelings" but "injurious in its effects upon our negroes."[54]

The Confederacy faced a real dilemma. When the North chose to enlist blacks as soldiers, the white South immediately conjured up visions of thousands of armed black men descending upon defenseless families. To contemplate one rebellious Nat Turner was sufficient cause for alarm, but to think that the same government which had been empowered by the Constitution to help suppress insurrections was now arming slaves and using them to fight white men provoked cries of disbelief. "Great God, what a state of helpless degradation," a Virginia slaveholder exclaimed, "our own negros—bought by our own ancestors from the Yankees, the purchase money & interest now in their pockets, who first rob us of the negros themselves, & then arm them to rob us of every thing else—even our lives." Although the white South kept insisting that the Negro would fail as a soldier, fears were expressed that he might succeed. There was an obvious urgency, then, about the question of how to dispose of captured black soldiers. What was said to be at stake was not only the security of white men, women, and children but also the well-being of the slave population.[55]

No matter how the black soldier might perform in combat, the initial reaction of the Confederacy was to call for "sure and effective" retaliation. Since the North had determined to arm blacks and wage a war of extermination, there was little left for the white South to do but wage "a similar war in return." Nor was there any reason to be overly scrupulous about this problem. Once the black man became a soldier, he was as much an outlaw as the men who trained and commanded him. And once black men, whether northern freedmen or southern slaves, were corrupted by military

service, an Atlanta newspaper declared, they could "scarcely become useful and desirable servants among us." The message was clear enough.[56]

But the Confederacy was never able to resolve this question in any
consistent manner. When the North began to recruit black regiments in
the Mississippi Valley, the Confederate Secretary of War informed the
commanding officer at Vicksburg that captured black soldiers were not to
be regarded as prisoners of war. The official position of the Confederate
government, as stated on numerous occasions, was in no way ambiguous:
captured black soldiers (usually designated as "slaves in arms") and their
commissioned officers had forfeited the rights and immunities enjoyed by
other prisoners of war. Any officer who helped to drill, organize, or instruct
slaves, with the intention of using them as soldiers, or who commanded
Negro units, was defined as an "outlaw" and deemed guilty of inciting
servile insurrection. Upon capture, he was to be executed "or otherwise
punished at the discretion of the court." But black captives were to be
turned over to state authorities and treated in accordance with the laws
of the state in which they had been taken prisoner. These laws invariably
demanded their execution as incendiaries or insurrectionists.[57]

Although this official position was never repealed, authorities chose to
modify its enforcement. Whatever the guidelines or legislation, most of the
actual decisions were made in the field by unit commanders and lesser
officers. How many blacks were held as captives was never easy to determine, largely because Confederate officials refused to report such captives
as prisoners of war. Some black soldiers and military laborers were executed or sold into slavery, but most of them were held in close confinement,
handed over to civilian authorities, or put to work on military fortifications. "After arriving at Mobile," one black captive testified, "we were
placed at work on the fortifications there, and impressed colored men who
were at work when we arrived were released, we taking their places. We
were kept at hard labor and inhumanly treated; if we lagged or faltered,
or misunderstood an order, we were whipped and abused; some of our men
being detailed to whip others." In the aftermath of the assault on Fort
Wagner, eighteen black soldiers were placed on trial under the insurrectionary laws of South Carolina but the state failed to win a conviction and
the men were interned as prisoners of war. For many whites, including
some of the highest-ranking Confederate officials, it was preferable to think
that blacks, especially former slaves, who served in the Union Army had
been duped. And since they were little more than "deluded victims of the
hypocrisy and malignity of the enemy," the Confederate Secretary of War
advised, they should be treated with mercy and returned to their previous
owners, "with whom, after their brief experience of Yankee humanity and
the perils of the military service, they will be more content than ever . . ."[58]

The Confederate government refused to agree to any general exchange
of black prisoners of war for prisoners held by the Union Army. This
attitude reflected to some degree a distinction made by Confederate officials between free Negroes and slaves. That the North might employ its

own black residents for military service seems to have been conceded; that is, the North had as much right to use black men against them as it did to use elephants, wild cattle, or dogs. But the North had no right to arm a slave against his master. Nor did the South have any obligation to return such slaves. In a war, property recaptured from the enemy reverted to its owner, or could be disposed of in any way the captor deemed proper—and slaves were property. In March 1864, a Confederate lieutenant inquired of his commanding officer if he could sell the four black soldiers he had captured and divide the profits among those who had participated in the mission; the commanding officer advised him "not to report any more such captures." What complicated the question of prisoner exchange were certain principles said to be immutable that outweighed any legal considerations. To argue an equality between white and black prisoners, as one Richmond newspaper observed, was nothing less than an act of northern insolence. "Confederates have borne and forborne much to mitigate the atrocities of war; but this is a thing which the temper of the country cannot endure."[59]

The most efficient way to deal with the vexing issue of black prisoners was to take no prisoners. This was not even necessarily a racial matter but a time-honored military principle. Few wars have failed to arouse charges and countercharges regarding the disposition of soldiers after they have surrendered. In the Civil War, the presence of armed black men, most of them former slaves, thereby aggravated an already sensitive issue. For the common Confederate soldier, the need to confront blacks in armed combat was still difficult to accept, and the military setbacks he suffered exacerbated his frustrations and hatreds. "I hope I may never see a Negro soldier," a Mississippian wrote to his mother, "or I cannot be . . . a Christian Soldier." After the Battle of Milliken's Bend, in which black troops distinguished themselves, the Confederate commander reported that substantial numbers of blacks had been killed and wounded; "unfortunately," he added, "some fifty, with two of their white officers were captured." The nature of warfare dictated that such matters could not be easily controlled by official edicts, whether these emanated from Richmond or from the immediate commanding officer. Every black prisoner "would have been killed," a Confederate soldier wrote after the Battle of the Crater, "had it not been for gen Mahone who beg our men to Spare them." Still, as he noted, one of his fellow soldiers, who had already killed several blacks, could not restrain himself. Even when General Mahone told him "for God's sake" to stop, the soldier asked to kill one more, as "he deliberately took out his pocket knife and cut one's Throat." Late in the war, as white southern frustrations mounted, a clash with black troops at Mark's Mill, Arkansas, resulted in a battlefield "sickening to behold." "No orders, threats, or commands," a Confederate soldier reported, "could restrain the men from vengeance on the negroes, and they were piled in great heaps about the wagons, in the tangled brushwood, and upon the muddy and trampled road."[60]

Whether or not these were the normal atrocities of warfare, the reports out of the South aroused blacks already deeply disturbed over other manifestations of unequal treatment for black soldiers. The failure of the government to guarantee protection for black troops, in the event of their capture, had already reportedly caused a slackening in the recruitment campaigns. To ensure "full rights and immunities" for all prisoners, regardless of color, black spokesmen urged the Lincoln administration to adopt a policy of retaliation: "For every black prisoner slain in cold blood, Mr. Jefferson Davis should be made to understand that one rebel officer shall suffer death, and for every colored soldier sold into slavery, a rebel shall be held as hostage." When Frederick Douglass resigned his post as a recruiting agent, he was most emphatic about this particular issue. Even "the most malignant Copperhead," Douglass charged, could hardly criticize President Lincoln for "any undue solicitude" for the rights and lives of black soldiers. The Confederates murdered blacks in cold blood, shot down black military laborers, threatened to sell black prisoners into slavery, and yet, Douglass noted, "not one word" from the President. "How many 54ths must be cut to pieces, its mutilated prisoners killed and its living sold into Slavery, to be tortured to death by inches before Mr. Lincoln shall say: 'Hold, enough!' " Until that time, Douglass declared, "the civilized world" would hold the President and Jefferson Davis equally responsible for these atrocities.[61]

Calling the attempts to enslave prisoners "a relapse into barbarism and a crime against the civilization of the age," Lincoln decreed in July 1863 that for every Union soldier killed "in violation of the laws of war," a Confederate soldier would be executed; and for every Union soldier enslaved or sold into slavery, a Confederate soldier would be placed at hard labor on the public works. Although this pronouncement appeared to satisfy black demands, the President, as well as some black leaders, fully recognized that the real problem lay with implementation. "The difficulty is not in stating the principle," Lincoln remarked, "but in practically applying it." And once applied, he advised Douglass, there was no way to know where it might end. Among the questions raised by the President's order was whether the northern white public was actually prepared to accept this kind of retaliation. At least one black newspaper remained skeptical. If any attempts were made to retaliate for the murder of black soldiers, the editor suggested, Confederate authorities were counting on the probability "that Northern sentiment, already weak on the subject, will revolt against taking the life of white men for 'Niggers.' "[62]

The battle fought on April 12, 1864, at Fort Pillow, Tennessee, where blacks comprised nearly half the garrison, provoked the most bitter black protest of the Civil War. "We had hoped," a black newspaper declared, "that the first report might have been exaggerated; but, in this, we have been doomed to disappointment." Nearly 300 Union soldiers (the precise number varied with every report) were slain after they had thrown down their arms and surrendered. The conflicting accounts of what happened were never satisfactorily resolved. Subsequent testimony, however, leaves little doubt as to the indiscriminate slaughter undertaken by Confederate troops. Only the extent of the annihilation remains uncertain. To black people, and to much of the white northern public, it became known as the "Fort Pillow Massacre." But to General Nathan Bedford Forrest, who commanded the Confederate forces, it was simply that place on the Mississippi River, "dyed with the blood of the slaughtered," where his troops had conclusively demonstrated "to the Northern people that negro soldiers cannot cope with Southerners." The total number of Union dead, Forrest observed, "will never be known from the fact that large numbers ran into the river and were shot and drowned." The casualness with which the general treated the massacre suggested no need to defend his conduct or the murders committed under his command.[63]

Although shocked by the Fort Pillow Massacre, angry blacks expressed little surprise. Since the United States government refused to recognize black soldiers as equal to whites, why should the Confederacy? The tragedy, blacks charged, only underscored the tardiness with which the Lincoln administration and Congress had acted upon their demands for equal protection, equal treatment, and equal rights. "I do not wonder at the conduct and disaster that transpired at Fort Pillow," a Massachusetts soldier wrote from South Carolina. "I wonder that we have not had more New York riots and Fort Pillow massacres." Perhaps, though, these deaths had not been in vain, suggested Richard H. Cain, a black clergyman. At the very least, he hoped, what transpired at Fort Pillow might serve to educate the northern public. "None but the blacks of this land, have heretofore realized the hateful nature of the beast: but now, white men are beginning to feel, and to realize what its beauties are." From these deaths, the Reverend Cain vowed, a new spirit would pervade black troops, and he offered them some words of advice. In future clashes with the enemy, "give no quarter; take no prisoners; make it dangerous to take the life of a black soldier by these barbarians." When that happens, he promised, "they will respect your manhood, and you will be treated as you deserve at the hands of those who have made you outlaws."[64]

Several months after the Fort Pillow affair, the anger had not yet subsided. In the wake of new reports of black soldiers "mown down like grass at Petersburg," the Reverend H. H. White told a mass meeting called by Boston Negro leaders that a sense of despair prevailed among the people. But he refused to be discouraged. Whatever the losses sustained by black people, the thought that should remain uppermost in their minds is that God had brought about the sacrifice of millions of men in other countries "for the cause of liberty and humanity." The speakers who followed, however, found it impossible to share the Reverend White's optimism or explanation. The most forceful disclaimer came from William Wells Brown, a veteran black abolitionist and former advocate of emigration who had recently helped to recruit the 54th Massachusetts Regiment. "Mr. White's God is bloodthirsty!" Brown charged. "I worship a different kind of God. My God is a God of peace and good will to men." Although he had once urged black men to fight, in order to convince "this God-forsaken nation" that they could be as courageous as other men, he now confessed his doubts and disillusionment. "Our people have been so cheated, robbed, deceived, and outraged everywhere, that I cannot urge them to go. . . . We have an imbecile administration, and the most imbecile management that it is possible to conceive of. If Mr. White's God is managing the affairs of this nation, he is making a miserable failure."[65]

Since editorial outrage, mass meetings, and executive decrees were obviously insufficient to deal with the problem, black troops were left to consider actions that might produce the effect initially intended by the President's order. An officer with the 22nd United States Colored Troops made explicit a growing feeling among many of the black soldiers: "Sir, we can *bayonet* the enemy to terms on this matter of treating colored soldiers as prisoners of war far sooner than the authorities at Washington can bring him to it by negotiation. This I am *morally persuaded of.*" Six days after the fall of Fort Pillow, Confederate troops in Arkansas routed Union forces in the Battle of Poison Spring, including soldiers belonging to the 1st Kansas Colored Regiment. Not only were some black prisoners summarily executed but captured Union wagons were also driven back and forth over the bodies of wounded blacks. That was more than sufficient inducement for the men of the 2nd Kansas Colored Regiment to vow to take no more prisoners, and in a subsequent clash at Jenkins Ferry, Arkansas, the black regiment charged the Confederate lines, shouting "Remember Poison Spring," and inflicted heavy losses on the enemy. But they fell slightly short of their avowed goal; one Confederate prisoner was taken—apparently by mistake—and he was returned to his regiment to impart the lessons of this battle. When black troops at Memphis reportedly took an oath "on their knees" to avenge Fort Pillow and show no mercy to the enemy, General Nathan Bedford Forrest, of all people, lodged a Confederate protest, charging that the oath had been taken in the presence of Union officers. "From what I can learn," a Union general replied, "this act of theirs was not influenced by any white officer, but was the result of their own sense of what was due to themselves and their fellows who had been mercilessly slaughtered."[66]

The Fort Pillow Massacre obviously had a different impact than General Forrest intended. If blacks were not to be treated as prisoners of war, they would fight that much harder to avoid capture. "As long as we are not recognized by the Federal Government," a black corporal wrote, "we do not expect the enemy to treat us as prisoners of war; and, as there is no alternative left for us, we will kill every rebel we capture." Writing from his camp near Petersburg, Virginia, a black sergeant noted that his regiment had gone into battle shouting "Remember Fort Pillow!" and that "more rebels gave themselves up that day than were actually taken prisoners." No matter how inflated may have been some reports of black vengeance, sufficient instances were recorded to suggest that black troops fought with even greater ferocity and determination, some of them apparently convinced that to be captured was to be murdered in cold blood. The fact that Confederate officers tried to disclaim any such intentions partly reflected a growing concern over the morale of their own troops. "The Johnnies are not as much afraid of us as they are of the Mokes [black troops]," a white Union soldier wrote from Petersburg. "When they charge they will not take any prisoners, if they can help it. Their cry is, 'Remember Fort Pillow!' Sometimes, in their excitement, they forget what to say, when they catch a man they say: 'Remember what you done to us, way back, down dar!' "[67]

# 6

WHEN UNION GUNBOATS came up the Combahee River in South Carolina, the slave laborers on the rice plantations dropped their hoes and ran. Few of them knew what to expect of the Yankees, and some no doubt believed the atrocity stories related by their masters and mistresses. Imagine the surprise of these slaves when they finally caught their first glimpse of the invaders. None of their "white folks" had thought to tell them that the Yankee devils might also be black men. In this instance, the soldiers belonged to the newly formed 2nd South Carolina Volunteers, which had been recruited largely from former slaves. Colonel James Montgomery, the white commanding officer, had fought with John Brown in the Kansas guerrilla wars. And the "scout" who accompanied him on this raid was none other than Harriet Tubman, known to many of the slaves as "Moses" for the forays she had made into the South before the war to escort fugitives to freedom. This time she had the backing of Federal guns as she supervised the removal of slaves from the Combahee River plantations.

The slaves looked on in amazement as armed black men came ashore and burned down the homes of white men. "De brack sojer so presumptious," one slave kept muttering, his head shaking with admiration and disbelief at what he was witnessing. "Dey come right ashore, hold up dere head. Fus' ting I know, dere was a barn, then tousand bushel rough rice, all in a blaze, den mas'r's great house, all cracklin' up de roof." It had to be an impressive spectacle, and this slave seemed to relish every minute, making no move to put out the flames. "Didn't I keer for see 'em blaze?" he exclaimed. "Lor, mas'r, didn't care notin' at all. *I was gwine to de boat.*" For the soldiers, as for the slaves who were now rushing to the gunboats, a holiday atmosphere prevailed. "I nebber see such a sight," an exultant Harriet Tubman declared—"pigs squealin', chickens screamin', young ones squallin'." Elderly couples vied with the young to reach the boats, determined to leave "de land o' bondage"; numerous women came aboard, one of them balancing a pail on her head ("rice a smokin' in it jus' as she'd taken it from de fire"), most of them loaded down with baskets and bags containing their worldly possessions. "One woman brought two pigs, a white one an' a black one," Harriet Tubman recalled; "we took 'em all on board; named de white pig Beauregard, and de black pig Jeff Davis." With more than 700 slaves aboard, the gunboats finally set out for Beaufort.[68]

Nowhere in the Confederate South was the impact of the Civil War more graphically demonstrated than in the sight of armed and uniformed black men, most of them only recently slaves, operating as a liberation and occupation army. The grievances of the black soldier often took on a diminished importance when he contemplated his role in this war. "Men and women, old and young, were running through the streets, shouting and praising God," one soldier wrote after his regiment had entered Wilmington, North Carolina. "We could then truly see what we had been fighting for, and could almost realize the fruits of our labors." With his regiment nearing Richmond, another soldier exulted, "We have been instrumental in liberating some five hundred of our sisters and brethren from the accursed yoke of human bondage." The scenes which greeted black soldiers in their march through the South—abandoned plantation houses, joyous celebrations of freedom, reunions of families separated by slavery, the shocked and angry faces of white men and women—were bound to make a deep and lasting impression. For many of the northern blacks, this was their first look at the South and the Southerner. "I have noticed a strange peculiarity among the people here," a soldier with the 54th Massachusetts Regiment noted. "They are all the most outrageous stutterers. If you meet one and say, 'How are you?' as you pass, you could walk a whole block before he could sputter out the Southern, 'Right smart, I thank-ee.' " The soldiers were moved not only by the effusive welcomes they usually received from the slaves but also by observing at first hand the effects of a lifetime of bondage. "I often sit down and hear the old mothers down here tell how they have been treated," a Pennsylvania soldier wrote. "It would make your heart ache. . . . They have frequently shown me the deep marks of the cruel whip upon their backs." Many of the black soldiers located family members and revived old friendships, while some began courtships that would result in new relationships.[69]

Perhaps most memorable were the occasions on which the soldiers who had once been slaves were afforded the opportunity to manifest their contempt for the relics and symbols of their enslavement. "We is a gwine to pay our respectable compliments to our old masters," one soldier declared, summing up the sentiments of his regiment. While marching through a region, the black troops would sometimes pause at a plantation, ascertain from the slaves the name of the "meanest" overseer in the neighborhood, and then, if he had not fled, "tie him backward on a horse and force him to accompany them." Although a few masters and overseers were whipped or strung up by a rope in the presence of their slaves, this appears to have been a rare occurrence. More commonly, black soldiers preferred to apportion the contents of the plantation and the Big House among those whose labor had made them possible, singling out the more "notorious" slaveholders and systematically ransacking and demolishing their dwellings. "They gutted his mansion of some of the finest furniture in the world," wrote Chaplain Henry M. Turner, in describing a regimental action in North Carolina. Having been informed of the brutal record of this slaveholder, the soldiers had resolved to pay him a visit. While the owner was forced to look on, they went to work on his "splendid mansion" and "utterly destroyed every thing on the place." Wielding their axes indiscriminately, they shattered his piano and most of the furniture and ripped his expensive carpets to pieces. What they did not destroy they distributed among his slaves. And when the owner addressed one of the soldiers "rather saucily," he was struck across the mouth and sent reeling to the floor. Chaplain Turner, who witnessed the action, obviously thought no explanation was necessary for the punishment meted out to this planter. "It was on Sabbath," he noted, and "as Providence would have it," the men had halted their march to eat and rest near the home of this "infamous" slaveholder.

> Oh, that I could have been a Hercules, that I might have carried off some of the fine mansions, with all their gaudy furniture. How rich I would be now? But I was not. When the rich owners would use insulting language, we let fire do its work of destruction. A few hours only are necessary to turn what costs years of toil into smoke and ashes.

Besides, after observing the work of General Sherman's armies, Chaplain Turner concluded that "we were all good fellows."[70]

Had such scenes been imagined at the outset of the Civil War, the sensibilities of white Americans would no doubt have been shocked. Yet, but two years later, black soldiers of the United States Army, most of them freed slaves, engaged their former masters in combat, marched through the southern countryside, paraded and drilled in southern towns and villages, and brought the news of freedom to tens of thousands of slaves. "The change seems almost miraculous," a black sergeant conceded. "The very people who, three years ago, crouched at their master's feet, on the accursed soil of Virginia, now march in a victorious column of freedmen, over the same land." When violating southern codes and customs, black soldiers appeared to be fully aware of the significance of their actions. "We march through these fine thoroughfares," a soldier wrote from Wilmington, North Carolina, "where once the slave was forbid being out after nine P.M., or to puff a 'regalia,' or to walk with a cane, or to ride in a carriage! Negro soldiers!—with banners floating." And with unconcealed delight, James F. Jones wrote from New Orleans how he had "walked fearlessly and boldly through the streets of a southern city ... without being required to take off his cap at every step, or to give all the sidewalks to those lordly princes of the sunny south, the planters' sons!"[71]

Nor would any black soldier soon forget that exhilarating moment when he and his men marched into a southern city amidst crowds of cheering slaves who rushed out into the streets to embrace them and to clasp their hands. It seemed to one soldier that the slaves "look for more certain help, and a more speedy termination of the war, at the hands of the colored soldiers than from any other source; hence their delight at seeing us." Although some slaves greeted them initially with suspicion and disbelief ("Are you the Yankees?") or even with hostility ("wild Africans"), the restraints broke down quickly in most places and what ensued were celebrations that lasted far into the night. "I was indeed speechless," a black sergeant wrote from Wilmington after the tumultuous reception given his regiment. "I could do nothing but cry to look at the poor creatures so overjoyed." To the disgust of a white resident of Camden, South Carolina, the black troops staged a regular camp meeting to which local blacks were invited—"tremendous excitement prevailed, as they prayed their cause might prosper and their just freedom be obtained."[72]

When black troops entered Charleston singing the John Brown song, they found themselves immediately surrounded by the black residents. Upon seeing the soldiers, one elderly slave woman threw down her crutch and shouted that the year of the Jubilee had finally arrived. Some of the soldiers and their officers, after what they had witnessed, confessed that "the glory and the triumph of this hour" simply defied description. "It was one of those occasions which happen but once in a lifetime." Several weeks later, newly commissioned Major Martin R. Delany arrived in Charleston, still hoping to consummate his vision of a "corps d'Afrique." He could barely restrain himself at the thought of entering the city "which, from earliest childhood and through life, I had learned to contemplate with feelings of the utmost abhorrence." After pausing momentarily to view "the shattered walls of the once stately but now deserted edifices of the proud and supercilious occupants," he found himself "dashing on in unmeasured strides through the city, as if under a forced march to attack the already crushed and fallen enemy."[73]

After a Virginia planter heard from his father alarming reports of black occupation troops, he vowed to keep the letter for his children in order to aid him "in cultivating in their hearts an *eternal hatred* to Yankeedom." The expression "What I most fear is not the Yankees, but the negroes" summed up the apprehensions that gripped southern whites as Union troops neared their homes. Having expected little else, black soldiers grew accustomed to the cold stares and defiant looks on the faces of the defeated whites. "You cannot imagine, with what surprise the inhabitants of the South, gaze upon us," a black sergeant remarked. "They are afraid to say anything to us; so they take it out in looking." The sight of black troops patrolling the city streets and passing through the plantations, and the fact that many of their own slaves were among these regiments, constituted for many whites the ultimate humiliation of the Civil War. "There's my Tom," one planter muttered, his face reddening, as he viewed some passing soldiers. "How I'd like to cut the throat of the dirty, impudent good-for-nothing!" Some of the whites he observed, Henry M. Turner noted, appeared to be uncertain "as to whether they are actually in another world, or whether this one is turned wrong side out."[74] No matter how hard whites tried to keep their thoughts to themselves, the indignation they felt could not always be contained. They shook their fists at the passing troops, spit at them from behind the windows where they were standing, ordered them to stay out of their yards, and expressed rage and disbelief whenever any black regiment was kept in the town or neighborhood as an occupation force. "Those dreadful negro wretches, whose very looks betokened their brutal natures," one white woman observed, "caused an indefinable thrill of horror and loathing."[75]

Although the black soldier made few attempts to provoke the whites, he, too, had difficulty in containing his feelings. The position he now held, moreover, gave him a novel opportunity to demand obedience from whites and impress upon them how the old relationships had been rendered obsolete. When several "white ladies and slave oligarchs" came to Henry M. Turner at regimental headquarters to request government rations, they entered his office, he said, "in the same humiliating custom which they formerly would have expected from me." And it gave him immense satisfaction, he confessed afterwards, to see them "crouching before me, and I a negro." Several weeks later, Chaplain Turner accompanied his regiment as they crossed a river near Smithfield, North Carolina. Before wading through the stream, the men stripped off their clothes. "I was much amused," Turner wrote, "to see the secesh women watching with the utmost intensity, thousands of our soldiers, in a state of nudity."

> I suppose they desired to see whether these audacious Yankees were really men, made like other men, or if they were a set of varmints. So they thronged the windows, porticos and yards, in the finest attire imaginable. Our brave boys would disrobe themselves, hang their garments upon their bayonets and through the water they would come, walk up the street, and seem to say to the feminine gazers, "Yes, though naked, we are your masters."[76]

With obvious pride and satisfaction, some black soldiers chose to visit their old masters and mistresses. After the Battle of Nashville, a nineteen-year-old black youth from Tennessee used his furlough for this purpose. His former mistress seemed happy to see him. "You remember when you were sick and I had to bring you to the house and nurse you?" she asked him. He replied affirmatively. But now, she exclaimed, "you are fighting me!" "No'm, I ain't fighting you," he replied, "I'm fighting to get free."[77]

## 7

---

BY THE END of the Civil War, more than 186,000 black men, most of them (134,111) recruited or conscripted in the slave states, had served in the Union Army, comprising nearly 10 percent of the total enrollment. Almost as many blacks, men and women, mostly freedmen, were employed as teamsters, carpenters, cooks, nurses, laundresses, stevedores, blacksmiths, coopers, bridge builders, laborers, servants, spies, scouts, and guides. "This army would be like a one-handed man, without niggers," a Union soldier conceded. "We have two rgts. of fighting nigs. and as many more of diggers. . . . The nigs. work all night, every night, planting guns and building breast-works." Seldom paid (if at all), herded together and marched from their tents to work, sometimes under the watchful eyes of overseers, black military laborers often perceived little change in their lives, except for the acknowledgment of their "freedom."[78]

Among both the soldiers and the laborers, the Civil War exacted a heavy price in human lives. Some one third of the black soldiers—an estimated 68,178 men—were listed as dead and missing, 2,751 of them killed in combat. For both white and black soldiers, the overwhelming majority of deaths resulted from disease rather than military action. Among the more unglamorous statistics of the Civil War is the fact that deaths from diarrhea and dysentery alone exceeded those killed in battle. And most diseases did not discriminate according to race any more than enemy fire in their devastation of the ranks. Despite the claim that blacks were less susceptible to diseases which felled whites, the death rate from disease was nearly three times as great for black soldiers as for whites.[79]

When blacks were first recruited, considerable doubt prevailed as to how they would perform as soldiers, particularly under enemy fire. "Many hope they will prove cowards and sneaks," a New York newspaper perceived, while "others greatly fear it." Two years of experience with black troops made believers of most of the doubters. The evaluations made by Union officers, while agreeing rather remarkably on the military capabilities of blacks, also revealed that the very qualities often stressed in racial stereotypes as marking blacks different from (hence "inferior" to) whites made them commendable soldiers. Since they were "more docile and obedient," blacks were thought to be easier to control and command. "Their docility, their habits of unquestioning obedience," one soldier observed, "pre-eminently fit them for soldiers. To a negro an order means obedience in spirit as well as letter." Accustomed as they were to heavy menial labor, black soldiers were found to work "more constantly" and "obediently" than whites and to offer fewer "complaints and excuses." Although blacks were considered to be excessive in their religious worship ("Their singing, praying, and shouting in camp had to be arrested, sometimes, at the point of the bayonet"), this characteristic, too, could be viewed as a military virtue. The fact that blacks were "a religious people" suggested to one Union officer "another high quality for making good soldiers," while it prompted Major General David Hunter, who had organized the first slave regiment in South Carolina, to observe that "religious sentiment—call it fanaticism, such as you like . . . made the soldiers of Cromwell invincible." The white man had also conceded to blacks a natural gift for music and rhythm, and this helped to explain their aptness for military drill and marching. "In mere drill they must beat the whites," one soldier conceded; "for 'time,' which is so important an item in drilling, is a universal gift to them." But even if blacks clearly had the potential for becoming good soldiers, the assumption prevailed that only white men could properly lead them, largely because blacks were accustomed to obeying whites and had too little regard for their own race. "They certainly need *white* officers for a while, and the best of officers, too," a sympathetic white soldier argued, "for they will, like children, lean much on their superiors."[80]

Although former slaves made up the largest portion of black troops, disagreement prevailed over whether they were better soldiers than the northern blacks who had never experienced bondage. Ignoring the question of motivation (which black commentators usually cited), a Union officer from New York thought the northern blacks had more self-reliance and came closer "to the qualities of the white man in respect to dash and energy"; several other officers in his unit concurred with this judgment and they unanimously agreed that slaves were less desirable as soldiers. The most vigorous defense of the slave as soldier was made by Colonel Higginson, whose South Carolina regiment consisted almost exclusively of recently held bondsmen. He preferred them as soldiers, he explained, because of "their greater docility and affectionateness" and "the powerful stimulus" which prompted men to fight for their own homes and families. The demeanor of his men, moreover, he considered superior to "that sort of upstart conceit which is sometimes offensive among free negroes at the North, the dandy-barber strut." But Higginson refused to argue, as did some Union officers, that slavery with its emphasis on submission and obedience had prepared slaves for military service. "Experience proved the contrary," he insisted. "The more strongly we marked the difference between the slave and the soldier, the better for the regiment. One half of military duty lies in obedience, the other half in self-respect. A soldier without self-respect is worthless."[81]

The prevailing assessment of the black soldier in combat was that he conducted himself as well as the white man. That in itself was a substantial concession. "They seem to have behaved just as well and as badly as the rest and to have suffered more severely," concluded a white officer who but two years earlier had warned that the use of blacks as soldiers would be a serious blunder (like "Hamlet's ape, who broke his neck to try conclusions"). Some black soldiers deserted under fire, though proportionately fewer than in the white regiments. Much like the white soldiers, blacks complained of camp conditions, oppressive officers, and punishments out of proportion to the offenses committed—and some blacks argued that racial discrimination aggravated each of these grievances. Like the white soldiers, blacks suffered the moments of disillusionment, frustration, and weariness that are characteristic of any war, particularly a struggle as agonizing and brutal as the Civil War. "More than one half of our whole command was . . . sacrificed without gaining any particular object," a black soldier remarked after a battle in which 231 of the 420 men in his outfit had been killed or wounded. The same observation might have been made by the common soldier of any war in history.[82]

Both white and black soldiers shared a capacity for incredible valor (seventeen black soldiers and four black sailors were awarded Congressional Medals of Honor), battle fatigue, and outright fear. "I prayed on the battle field some of the best prayers I ever prayed in my life," one black soldier readily confessed, and "made God some of the finest promises that ever were made." And for some blacks, as for some whites, the level of violence and inhumanity reached in this war was too much to bear. "I sho' wishes lots of times I never run off from de plantation. I begs de General not to send me on any more battles, and he says I's de coward and sympathizes with de South. But I tells him I jes' couldn't stand to see all dem men layin' dere dyin' and hollerin' and beggin' for help and a drink of water, and blood everywhere you looks." But when it came down to the real test, most of the black soldiers fought, and many of them died, and that was all the evidence most observers required. Nor did the black soldier who had been a slave evince any hesitation about facing his former master in the field of combat. "Our masters may talk now all dey choose," a black soldier replied when told that slaves loved their old masters too much to fight them; "but one ting's sartin,—*dey don't dare to try us.* Jess put de guns into our hans, and you'll soon see dat we not only knows *how* to shoot, but *who* to shoot. My master wouldn't be wuff much ef I was a soldier."[83]

The white Yankee soldier gradually grew accustomed to the sight of uniformed blacks. In some regions, the initial hostility subsided when black regiments relieved the whites of fatigue and garrison duties and did a disproportionate share of the heavy labor. "Never fear that soldiers will be found objecting to negro enlistments," a Massachusetts private noted. "One hour's digging in Louisiana clay under a Louisiana sun, and we are forever pledged to do all we can to fill up our ranks with the despised and long-neglected race." With additional experience, moreover, impressions of the military capabilities of blacks also became more favorable. When he first undertook to train black troops in South Carolina, Lieutenant Colonel John S. Bogert thought it would take some time "to make soldiers of my darkies" but he was determined to succeed. "I will either make soldiers of them or make them wish they were slaves again." Two weeks later, he was confident of making a disciplined regiment out of them. "You would be surprised to see how they improve by being kindly treated, they begin to act like men & they soon feel that they are of some account & have very curious ways of showing their dignity."[84]

But even as black soldiers were said to be creating "a revolution in thinking" in the Union Army, the initial sources of hostility were not so easily displaced, and deeply entrenched racial antipathies still had a way of surfacing. For some whites, the black soldiers were never more than comic relief. "There are about three regiments of darkies raised here for Wilde's brigade," a Massachusetts soldier wrote home, "regular Congoes with noses as broad as a plantation and lips like raw beefsteaks, Yah!"

Although some white officers warned that they would withhold their troops from any engagement in which blacks were placed in command as commissioned officers, this never became a problem. Far more serious were the racial antagonisms that erupted into bloody encounters between white and black soldiers. After cne such clash at Ship Island, Mississippi, white gunners disregarded orders to cover the advance of three black companies; instead, they turned the field pieces on their black comrades.[85] But such occurrences proved to be rare. The conduct of the black soldier was such as to convince even white Yankees who refused to give up their racial hatreds that military necessity dictated a policy of recognition and cooperation. "I never believed in niggers before," a Wisconsin cavalry officer confessed, "but by Jasus, they are hell in fighting."[86]

Not only did the black soldier impress many of his white comrades but he proved himself to his own people, did wonders for their racial pride, and gave them some genuine heroes and prospective leaders. "Dey fought and fought and shot down de 'Secesh,' and n'er a white man among 'em but two captains," a newly freed slave boasted to one of the white missionary teachers. When Robert Smalls, hero of the *Planter* affair, visited New York City in 1862, he was acclaimed and feted by the black populace for having performed a military feat "equaled by only a few events in any other war." The black people of his native South Carolina would honor him in the next several decades by electing him to the state legislature and to the United States Congress. But even if few blacks reached such heights, the uniform and the rifle, as Douglass had predicted, were capable of effecting significant changes in the demeanor of many black men. "Put a United States uniform on his back and the *chattel* is a *man*," one white soldier observed. "You can see it in his look. Between the toiling slave and the soldier is a gulf that nothing but a god could lift him over. He feels it, his looks show it."[87]

The fact that black men had played a significant role in liberating their enslaved brethren and preserving the Union would remain a source of considerable pride, even as it led them to expect much of the future. Once the war ended, the black soldier expected that a grateful nation would accord him and his people the rights of American citizens. He had demonstrated his loyalty. He had fought for his country's survival. On the battlefields of the South—at Port Hudson, Battery Wagner, Milliken's Bend, Olustee, and Petersburg—he had disproved those widely held notions about his inability to handle firearms or meet the test of fire. What more could white Americans expect of him? Like any victor, was he not entitled to share in the triumph? If he expected much of the United States, it was because he had served its citizens well. Reflecting upon the role of blacks in the war, Thomas Long, a former slave and a private in the 1st South Carolina Volunteers, suggested to the men of his regiment that they had faced and surmounted obstacles almost unprecedented in the history of warfare—the test of enemy fire and the suspicions and hostility of their own comrades.

We can remember, when we fust enlisted, it was hardly safe for we to pass by de camps to Beaufort and back, lest we went in a mob and carried side arms. But we whipped down all dat—not by going into de white camps for whip um; we didn't tote our bayonets for whip um; but we lived it down by our naturally manhood; and now de white sojers take us by de hand and say Broder Sojer. Dats what dis regiment did for de Epiopian race.

If we hadn't become sojers, all might have gone back as it was before; our freedom might have slipped through de two houses of Congress and President Linkum's four years might have passed by and notin' been done for us. But now tings can neber go back, because we have showed our energy and our courage and our naturally manhood.

Whatever happened to them after the war, Private Long declared, the memory of their participation in that conflict would be handed down to future generations of black people. "Suppose," he speculated, "you had kept your freedom witout enlisting in dis army; your chilen might have grown up free and been well cultivated so as to be equal to any business, but it would have been always flung in dere faces—'Your fader never fought for he own freedom'—and what could dey answer? Neber can say that to dis African Race any more."[88]

That black men managed to win the respect of white America only by fighting and killing white men was an ironic commentary on the ways in which American culture (like many others) measured success, manliness, and fitness for citizenship. "Nobly done, First Regiment of Louisiana Native Guard!" a New York newspaper proclaimed after the assault on Port Hudson. "That heap of six hundred corpses, lying there dark and grim and silent before and within the works, is a better proclamation of freedom than President Lincoln's." Some seventy years after the Civil War, W. E. B. Du Bois suggested that it may have required "a finer type of courage" for the slave to have worked faithfully while the nation battled over his destiny than for him to have plunged a bayonet into the bowels of a complete stranger. But the black man, Du Bois noted, could prove his manhood only as a soldier. When he had argued his case with petitions, speeches, and conventions, scarcely a white man had listened to him. When he had toiled to increase the nation's wealth, the white man had compensated him with barely enough for his subsistence. When he had offered to protect the women and children of his master, many white men had considered him a fool. But when the black man "rose and fought and killed," Du Bois observed, "the whole nation with one voice proclaimed him a man and brother." Nothing else, Du Bois was convinced, had made emancipation or black citizenship conceivable but the record of the black soldier.[89]

Recognizing his former master among the prisoners he was guarding, a black soldier greeted him effusively, "Hello, massa; bottom rail top dis time!" Observing black soldiers with rifles and bayonets demanding to verify the passes of white men and women, a Confederate soldier returning home after a prisoner exchange could hardly believe his eyes. "And our own niggers, too," he exclaimed. "If I could have my way, I'd have a rope around every nigger's neck, and hang 'em, or dam up this Mississippi River with them. Only eight or ten miles from this river slaves are working for their masters as happily as ever." Both scenes, each of them incredible in its own way, pointed up much of the confusion into which a rigidly hierarchical society had been thrown. Nor would that confusion of roles end with the war itself. "I goes back to my mastah and he treated me like his brother," recalled Albert Jones, who had spent more than three years in the Union Army. "Guess he wuz scared of me 'cause I had so much ammunition on me."[90]

Whether by guarding prisoners, marching through the South as an army of occupation, or engaging Confederate troops in combat, the black soldier represented a sudden, dramatic, and far-reaching reversal of traditional roles—as spectacular as any in the history of the country. What made this reversal even more manifest, however, was the conduct of the slaves on the plantations and farms that lay in the path of the advancing Union Army. Once the Yankees made their presence felt, or earlier, at the first sound of distant guns, the ties that bound a slave to his master and mistress, including loyalties and mutual affections that had endured for decades, would face their most critical test.

# Chapter Three

# KINGDOM COMIN'

*We'll soon be free,*
*We'll soon be free,*
*We'll soon be free,*
*When de Lord will call us home.*

*My brudder, how long,*
*My brudder, how long,*
*My brudder, how long,*
*'Fore we done sufferin' here?*

*It won't be long,*
*It won't be long,*
*It won't be long,*
*'Fore de Lord will call us home.* [1]

AFTER SEARCHING the slave quarters, the overseer solved the mystery of the missing ammunition. Ishmael had been accumulating shot and powder with the intention, as he confessed, to desert to the enemy. That had been the first indication of trouble on the Manigault rice plantations, located in coastal Georgia along the Savannah River. The war was in its seventh month, the slaves had been "working well and cheerfully," and no desertions had been reported. But the Yankees were moving into the Sea Islands, black field hands had reportedly sacked the town of Beaufort, and a panicky Savannah feared imminent attack. Equally ominous were the reports of "murmuring" and disaffection among the slaves working the Savannah River plantations. "We had no trouble with our own Negroes," Louis Manigault noted, "but from clear indications it was manifest that some of them were preparing to run away, using as a pretext their fear of the Yankees." In the months that followed, Manigault, like so many plantation managers, came to discover that the always arduous task of controlling enslaved workers took on new dimensions under wartime conditions. His own slaves would teach him that much and more.

Seeking to minimize potential slave defections, Manigault conferred with his overseer, William Capers, a "remarkable" man and "perfect Gentleman" in whom he had complete confidence. The previous overseer had foolishly placed himself "on a par with the Negroes," participating in their

prayer meetings and "breaking down long established discipline." Capers
was not so easily misled. He claimed to know the Negro character, arguing
that "if a Man put his confidence in a Negro He was simply a Damned
Fool." Only by understanding and acting upon that proven proposition, he
believed, had he achieved success in managing slaves. In late 1861, convinced that "all was not quite correct" among the Manigault slaves, he
advised that those most likely to cause trouble be removed to a safer area.
Manigault agreed, and the two men soon learned how accurately they had
appraised the character of some of those selected. That night, three of them
attempted to escape; they were quickly apprehended and forcibly removed
in handcuffs. The remaining seven "came very willingly."

Despite these precautions, trouble persisted on the Manigault plantations. On February 21, 1862, Jack Savage, the head carpenter, ran away.
That came as no surprise to Manigault, who said he epitomized the "bad
Negro." "We always considered him a most dangerous character & bad
example to the others. . . . I think Jack Savage was the worst Negro I have
ever known. I have for two years past looked upon him as one capable of
committing murder or burning down this dwelling, or doing any act." At
the same time, he was "quite smart" and "our best plantation Carpenter,"
and that presumably was why he had been retained. Savage did not flee to
the Yankees; instead, he secluded himself in the nearby swamplands,
where other neighborhood runaways soon joined him, including Charles
Lucas, a Manigault slave ("one of our Prime Hands") who had been entrusted with the plantation stock and who had recently been punished
after the mysterious disappearance of some choice hogs. "His next step,"
Manigault guessed, "was to follow the animals which he had most probably
killed himself, and sent to the retreat where he expected soon to follow."
Shortly after this incident, Manigault sold a large portion of the livestock.
"This was," he explained, "through fear of their being all stolen some night
by our Negroes." On August 16, 1863, nearly eighteen months after his
escape, Jack Savage returned to the plantation, "looking half starved
and wretched in the extreme," but acting with such impertinence that
Capers suspected he would soon flee again. With Manigault's approval,
Capers quickly sold him in Savannah for $1,800, despite Savage's attempt
to depress that price: "It would have provoked you," the overseer wrote, "to
have heard Jack's lies of his inability &c." That same month, Charlie Lucas
was apprehended.

While trying to anticipate runaways among the field hands, Manigault
also had to deal with defections among his household servants. The disappearance of "his Woman 'Dolly' " must have particularly perplexed him,
as the description which he posted in the Augusta and Charleston police
stations indicates:

> She is thirty years of age, *of small size, light complexion,* hesitates some-
> what when spoken to, and is not a very healthy woman, but rather good
> looking, with a fine set of teeth. Never changed her Owner, has been
> always a house Servant, and no fault ever having been found with her.

At a loss for a plausible explanation, Manigault finally concluded that she had been "enticed off by some White Man." Although such defections annoyed Manigault, he found even more incredible the strange behavior of Hector, who for nearly thirty years had been his "favorite Boat Hand" and "a Negro We all of us esteemed highly." He had been a good worker, a trusted slave, "always spoiled both by my Father and Myself, greatly indulged," and "my constant companion when previous to my marriage I would be quite alone upon the plantation." And yet, he was "the very first to murmur" and "give trouble" after the outbreak of the war. Only after considerable personal anguish did Manigault agree to remove him to Charleston; there was no question in his mind but that Hector "would have hastened to the embrace of his Northern Brethren, could he have foreseen the least prospect of a successful escape."

The wartime experience with his slaves unsettled Manigault. The unexpected behavior of Hector proved to be "only One of the numerous instances of ingratitude evinced in the African character." In the end, he would no longer harbor any illusions about the depth of slave fidelity. "This war has taught us the perfect impossibility of placing the least confidence in any Negro. In too numerous instances those we esteemed the most have been the first to desert us."

When Manigault paid his last wartime visit to his Georgia properties, the sound of cannon fire could be heard in the distance. He thought the slaves still seemed pleased to see him. More than two years would elapse before he would see any of them again; meanwhile, on Christmas Eve 1864, Yankee troops left a trail of destruction as they moved through the largely abandoned Savannah River plantations.[2]

2

---

"DE WAR COMES ter de great house an' ter de slave cabins jist alike," recalled Lucy Ann Dunn, a former slave on a North Carolina plantation. When the Yankees were reported to be approaching, even the less perceptive whites might have sensed the anxiousness, the apprehension, the excitement that gripped the slave quarters. "Negroes doing no good," a Tennessee planter reported. "They seem to be restless not knowing what to do. At times I pity them at others I blame them much." The tension was by no means confined to the fields but entered the Big House and affected the demeanor of the servants, including some who had hitherto betrayed few if any emotions about the war. "I tole you de Nordern soldiers would come back; I tole you dose forts was no 'count," Aunt Polly, a Virginia house slave, exclaimed to the master's son. "Yes," he replied, obviously taken aback by her bluntness, "but you told me the Southern soldiers would come back, too, when father went away with them." "Dat because you cried," she explained, "and I wanted to keep up your spirits." With those words, Aunt Polly, a long-time family favorite for whose services her master said he could set no price, prepared to leave her "accustomed post" in the kitchen.[3]

Although few slaves demonstrated such "impertinence" in the presence of the master's family, they did appear to be less circumspect in expressing their emotions. The pretenses were now lowered, if not dropped altogether. "The negroes seem very unwilling for the work," a young white woman confided to her journal; "some of their aside speeches very incendiary. Edward, the old coachman, is particularly sullen." On some plantations, the once clandestine prayer meetings were noticeably louder and more effusive, and there appeared to be fewer reasons to muffle the sounds before they reached the Big House. The singing in the slave quarters, Booker T. Washington remembered, "was bolder, had more ring, and lasted later into the night." They had sung these verses before but there was no longer any need to conceal what they meant by them; the words had not changed, only their immediacy, only the emphasis with which certain phrases were intoned. "Now they gradually threw off the mask," Washington recalled, "and were not afraid to let it be known that the 'freedom' in their songs meant freedom of the body in this world."[4]

The mood of the slaves often defied the analysis of the master. On certain plantations, the slaves continued to act with an apparent indifference toward the war and the approaching Union troops, leaving their owners to speculate about what lay behind those bland countenances. In early 1865, as General Sherman's troops moved into South Carolina, a prominent rice planter observed little excitement among his slaves; in fact, they seemed "as silent as they had been in April, 1861, when they heard from a distance the opening guns of the war." Each evening the slave foreman dutifully obtained his instructions for the next day, and the work proceeded smoothly and silently. "Did those Negroes know that their freedom was so near? I cannot say, but, if they did, they said nothing, only patiently waited to see what would come." A neighboring planter found his slaves performing little work but they "appear to be calm and are quite lively. They are orderly and respectful more so than one could expect under the circumstances." With Yankee raiding parties reported a few miles away, the daughter of a Louisiana planter observed the slaves busily engaged in preparations for a Christmas party. That night, after hearing that a nearby town had been virtually destroyed, the white family witnessed the slave festivities with mixed feelings.

We have been watching the negroes dancing for the last two hours. Mother had the partition taken down in our old house so that they have quite a long ball room. We can sit on the piazza and look into it. I hear now the sounds of fiddle, tambourine and "bones" mingled with the shuffling and pounding of feet. Mr. Axley is fiddling for them. They are having a merry time, thoughtless creatures, they think not of the morrow.

On New Year's Day 1864, Catherine Broun gave her servants their custom-ary party—"everything I would prepare for a supper for my own company" —even as she wondered how many of them would be with her by the end of the year; the "general opinion" in her neighborhood was that few of the slaves would remain. "I sometimes think I would not care if they all did go, they are so much trouble to me we have such a host of them."[5]

Before the arrival of the Union Army, the roadsides were apt to be filled with the retreating columns of Confederate troops, their condition imparting most vividly and convincingly the visage of defeat. For many slaves, that sight alone confirmed what the "grapevine" and the demeanor of their "white folks" had earlier suggested, and the contrast with the initial predictions of ultimate victory could hardly have been more strik-ing.

> I seen our 'Federates go off laughin' an' gay; full of life an' health. Dey was big an' strong, asingin' Dixie an' dey jus knowed dey was agoin' to win. I seen 'em come back skin an' bone, dere eyes all sad an' hollow, an' dere clothes all ragged. Dey was all lookin' sick. De sperrit dey lef' wid jus' been done whupped outten dem.[6]

But even the anticipation of freedom did not necessarily prompt slaves to revel in the apparent military collapse of the Confederacy. Whether from loyalty to their "white folks," the need to act circumspectly, or fear of the Yankees, many slaves looked with dismay at the ragged columns of Confed-erate soldiers passing through the towns and plantations. For some, faith-fulness may have been less important than simply pride in their homeland, now being ravaged by strangers who evinced little regard for the property and lives of Southerners, black or white.[7]

The ambivalence that characterized the reaction of some slaves to the demise of the Confederacy reflected an understandable tension between attachment to their localities and the prospect of freedom. Three years after the war, an English visitor asked a Virginia freedman his opinion of Robert E. Lee. "He was a grand man, General Lee, sah," the ex-slave replied without hesitation. "You were sorry when he was defeated, I sup-pose?" the visitor then asked. "O no, sah," the freedman quickly retorted; "we were glad; we clapped our hands that day." If few slaves yearned for a Confederate victory, they did nevertheless view themselves as Southern-ers, they did sense that their lives and destinies were intricately bound with the white people of the South, and some even shared with whites the humiliation of defeat. "Dere was jes' too many of dem blue coats for us to lick," a former Alabama slave tried to explain. "Our 'Federates was de bes' fightin' men dat ever were. Dere warn't nobody lak our 'Federates."[8]

When the unfamiliar roar of gunfire echoed in the distance, the emo-tions of individual slaves ranged from bewilderment and fear to uncon-cealed elation. In eastern Virginia, within earshot of the battle raging at Manassas, an elderly slave "mammy" preparing the Sunday dinner greeted each blast of the cannon with a subdued "Ride on, Massa Jesus." When the guns were heard near Charleston, a sixty-nine-year-old woman exclaimed, "Come, dear Jesus," and she later recalled having felt "nearer to Heaben den I eber feel before." The younger slaves were apt to be less certain about what was happening around them. The strange noise, the hasty preparations, the talk in the slave quarters were at the same time exciting and terrifying. Two young slaves who lived in different sections, Sam Mitchell of South Carolina and Annie Osborne of Louisiana, each heard what sounded like thunder when the Yankees approached, and both of them sought an explanation. "Son," Sam's mother assured him, "dat ain't no t'under, dat Yankee come to gib you Freedom." When the cannons ceased booming, Annie's brother told her, "We's gwine be all freed from old Massa Tom's beatin's." No amount of time could dim those recollections, any more than Sarah Debro, who had been a slave in North Carolina, could forget the moment she asked her mistress to explain the thunder that had frightened her "near 'bout to death." Those were Yankee cannons killing "our men," the woman replied, before breaking down in tears. Alarmed by this unusual sight, Sarah ran to the kitchen, where Aunt Charity was cooking, and told her what had just happened. "She ain't cryin' kaze de Yankees killin' de mens," the black woman declared, "she's doin' all dat cryin' kaze she skeered we's goin' to be sot free."[9]

To perform the usual plantation routines under these conditions proved to be increasingly difficult. Although planters and overseers tried to maintain business as usual, and some succeeded, the reported approach of the Union Army tended to undermine slave discipline and in some places it brought work to a complete standstill. From the moment Yankee soldiers were sighted in the vicinity, John H. Bills, a Tennessee planter, found he could exert little authority over his slaves. "My people seem Contented & happy, but not inclined to work. They say 'it is no use' the *Yankeys* will *take it all.*" Moble Hopson, who had been a slave in Virginia, recalled how they had paid little attention to the war until the day they reported to the field and found no one there to supervise them. "An' dey stand 'round an' laugh an' dey get down an' wait, but dey don' leave dat field all de mawning. An' den de word cum dat de Yankees was a comin', an' all dem blacks start tuh hoopin' an' holl'rin', an' den dey go on down to deer shacks an' dey don' do no work at all dat day."[10]

The approach of the Union Army forced planters and slaves alike into a flurry of last-minute activity. " 'Fore they come," a former Georgia slave recalled, "the white folks had all the niggers busy hidin' everything they could." On the assumption, which proved to be incorrect, that the Yankees would not disturb the slaves' possessions, many white families secreted their valuables in or under the slave cabins or on the very persons of the slaves. "Miss Gusta calls me and wrops my hair in front and puts her jewelry in under the plaits and pulls them back and pins them down so you couldn't see nothin'." With Union troops sighted nearby, a South Carolina planter moved some of his house furniture into the cabin belonging to

Abram Brown, the driver and headman on the plantation, and told him to claim ownership if the Yankees asked any questions. To the Union soldiers, it must have looked like the best-furnished slave cabin in the South, and they refused to believe Brown's story. Knowing the risks, some slaves simply refused to accept such responsibilities, using time-honored devices. "Mamma Maria was too nervous," her mistress wrote, "and cried too much to have any responsibility put on her."[11]

During those tense, anxious days of waiting, there were slaves who provided whatever encouragement and support they could muster for their masters and mistresses. With the Yankees expected any moment, Emma LeConte, the daughter of a prominent South Carolinian, found great comfort in the declaration of her servant, Henry, that he would stand by the family, whatever the consequences. "I believe he means it, but do not know how he will hold on." On the day the Union Army entered Columbia, the LeConte servants (including Henry) returned from the center of town laden with looted provisions which they then shared with the white family. "How times change!" a grateful Emma LeConte wrote in her diary that night. "Those whom we have so long fed and cared for now help us." Where the mistress and her daughters were the only remaining whites on the plantation, the slave women sometimes reversed paternalistic roles and insisted upon moving into the Big House, even into the same room, to afford them a greater degree of security. And with so many strangers prowling through the neighborhood, including Confederate Army stragglers and deserters, the slaves often treated with apprehension anyone who approached the plantation. On one Georgia plantation, a "suspicious-looking character" asked for food, only to be told by the servants that the master was not at home. But the mistress, who remained upstairs at the insistence of the servants, sent word to them to feed the stranger. "They made him sit in the piazza," she wrote her son afterwards, "and when he attempted to come into the house (as he said, 'to see how it looked') Flora and Tom barred the front door. I could see him from the balcony, and when his dinner was ready they . . . would not even trust him with a knife or fork, but gave him only an iron spoon."[12]

Not only did some slaves vow to protect their "white folks," as though the imminent arrival of the Yankees required a reaffirmation of loyalty, but they did what they could to ensure their safety. Preparing for the Union soldiers, a maid in Mary Chesnut's household urged her mistress to burn the diary she had been keeping lest it fall into the hands of the enemy. During the siege of Vicksburg, Mary Ann Loughborough, along with her daughter and servants, took refuge in a cave and remained there during the Yankee bombardment; one of the servants stood guard, gun in hand, assuring his mistress that anyone who entered "would have to go over his body first." No one had more experience in anticipating the changing moods of a master than did his slaves, and this valuable asset enabled some of them to save the lives of their masters. When the Yankees were sighted, Charley Bryant, a Texas slaveholder, ran into the house and grabbed his gun. But George Price, the head slave on the plantation, fearing for the safety of his volatile master, disarmed him and locked him in the smoke-house. "He ain't do dat to be mean," a former slave recalled, "but he want to keep old massa outten trouble. Old massa know dat, but he beat on de door and yell, but it ain't git open till dem Yankees done gone."[13]

Anticipating the path of the Union Army, many planters had already removed the bulk of their slaves to safer areas. If that proved impractical, some attempted to hide them, along with the family jewels, money, and livestock, until the Yankees had passed through the neighborhood. Revers-ing traditional roles, the planter himself might seek refuge in the nearby woods or swamp, depending upon the slaves to supply him with food and not to betray his hiding place. Rather than take such chances, Amanda Stone and her family, like so many others, chose to abandon their planta-tion in Louisiana. In helping them to prepare for the hasty evacuation, the slaves proved helpful—almost too helpful. The family claimed not to be deceived. "You could see it was only because they knew we would soon be gone. We were only on sufferance. Two days longer and we think they would all have gone to the Yankees, most probably robbing and insulting us before they left." Only two of the remaining slaves agreed to accompany them. "So passes the glory of the family," Kate Stone sighed. Appearances could, indeed, be deceptive. John S. Wise, the son of a prominent Virginian, recalled the abandonment of the family plantation near Norfolk and how Jim, the butler, had diligently assisted them. "Jim my father regarded as his man Friday. Nobody doubted that one so faithful and so long trusted would prove true in this emergency." But after helping to load the carriage with silverware and valuables, and just before they were to depart, Jim disappeared. "In vain we called and searched for him. We never saw him again. The prospect of freedom overcame a lifetime of love and loyalty."[14]

The flight of the white families evoked a variety of responses in their slaves. Some claimed to understand the decision, though it seemed like a strange turnabout to remain on the plantation while the white folks ran. "Funny how they run away like that," a former North Carolina slave reminisced. "They had to save their selves. I 'member they [the Yankees] took one old boss man and hung him up in a tree across a drain of water. . . . Those white folks had to run away." Still other slaves came away with contempt for their masters for having fled and abandoned them, while some thought it highly amusing, even ludicrous, and most certainly an admission of defeat. The scene lent itself, in fact, to one of the most popular wartime songs, "Kingdom Comin'," in which it was even suggested that some of the fleeing masters tried to pass themselves off as "contrabands."

> *Say, darkies, hab you seen de massa,*
> *Wid de muffstash on his face,*
> *Go along de road some time dis mornin',*
> *Like he gwine to leab de place?*
> *He seen a smoke way up de ribber,*
> *Whar de Linkum gunboats lay.*

*He took his hat, an' lef' berry sudden,*
*An' I spec' he run away!*

CHORUS

*De massa run! ha, ha!*
*De darkey stay! ho, ho!*
*It mus' be now de kingdom comin'*
*An' de year ob Jubilo!*

*He six foot one way, two foot tudder,*
*An' he weigh t'ree hundred pound.*
*His coat so big, he couldn't pay de tailor,*
*An' it won't go half way round.*
*He drill so much, dey call him Cap'n,*
*An' he get so drefful tanned,*
*I spec' he try an' fool dem Yankees,*
*For to tink he's contraband.*

*De darkeys feel so berry lonsome,*
*Libing in de log house on de lawn.*
*Dey move dar tings to massa's parlor,*
*For to keep it while he's gone.*
*Dar's wine an' cider in de kitchen,*
*An' de darkeys dey'll hab some;*
*I spose dey'll all be confiscated,*
*When de Linkum sojers come.*

*De oberseer he make us trouble,*
*An' he dribe us round a spell;*
*We lock him up in de smoke-house cellar,*
*Wid de key trown in de well.*
*De whip is lost, de han'cuff broken,*
*But de massa'll hab his pay.*
*He's old enuff, big enuff, ought to know better*
*Dan to went an' run away.*[15]

Nor did the irony of their masters suddenly becoming fugitives seem to escape the slaves. In the newspaper edited by Frederick Douglass, who had himself once been a fugitive, there appeared an advertisement purportedly written by a slave in Beaufort, South Carolina, offering a reward for the return of his "runaway master." Whatever the authenticity of the item, the point could not have been made more graphically.

$500 REWARD.—Rund away from me on the 7th of dis month, my massa Julian Rhett. Massa Rhett am five feet 'leven inches high, big shoulders, brack hair, curly, shaggy whiskers, low forehead an' dark face. He make big fuss when he go 'mong de gemmen, he talk very big, an' use de name ob de Lord all de time. Calls heself "Suddern gemmen," but I 'spose will try now to pass heself off as a black man or mulatter. Massa Rhett has a deep scar on his shoulder, from a fight, scratch 'cross de left eye, made by Dinah when he tried to whip her. He neber look people in de face. I more dan spec he will make track for Bergen kounty, in the furrin land of Jersey, whar I 'magin he hab a few friends.

I will [give] $100 for him if alive, an' $500 if anybody show [him] dead. If he come back to his kind niggers without much trouble, dis chile will receive him lubbingly.

SAMBO RHETT
Beaufort, S.C., Nov. 9, 1861[16]

Before a master fled, he might entrust the plantation or town house to some responsible slave, usually the driver or house servants, in the hope that his property could be kept intact until his return. Such confidence in most instances was not betrayed, with the slaves demonstrating what few masters had willingly conceded them—the ability to look after themselves and the plantation without any whites to advise or direct them. If the able-bodied hands had been removed earlier, however, the only remaining slaves were apt to be "the old and sickly," the very young, and a few house servants. This could result in a precarious existence, particularly in those regions where the dreaded "paterollers" and Confederate guerrillas were active. In the Mississippi River parishes, the frequency with which the slaves left on abandoned plantations were kidnapped, taken to Texas, and sold finally forced the governor to send troops to curtail such activity and, if possible, to recover the slaves.[17]

When white families abandoning the plantations tried to take slaves with them, they often encountered the same resistance that had greeted earlier attempts to remove slaves to safer areas. The classic example occurred early in the war, when the sudden appearance of Union warships at the Sea Islands off the coast of South Carolina precipitated a mass exodus of planters and their families. Despite pleading, threats, and violence, however, the slaves stubbornly refused to accompany their owners to the mainland, many of them hiding in the swamps and fields rather than be taken. With freedom perhaps only a few hours or days away, this reluctance was not surprising. After being ordered to row his master to the mainland, Moses Mitchell, a carpenter and hoer, heeded his wife's suggestion to "go out dat back door and keep a-going." Equally determined, a slave named Susannah, valued as the family seamstress, refused to leave with her master and mistress despite their dire warnings about what would happen if she remained. Several days later, when her master's son returned and ordered the slaves to destroy the cotton lest it fall into the hands of the Union Army, they refused to cooperate. "Why for we burn de cotton?" they asked. "Where we get money then for buy clo' and shoes and salt?" Rather than burn the cotton, the slaves took turns guarding it, "the women keeping watch and the men ready to defend it when the watchers gave the alarm." In some instances, however, slaves who resisted removal were shot down, even burned to death in the cotton houses. On Edisto

Island, where a Confederate raiding party had tried to remove some blacks, "the women fought so violently when they were taking off the men," a white Charlestonian wrote, "that they were obliged to shoot some of them."[18]

Not only did the areas of comparative safety within the Confederacy shrink with the advance of the Union Army but there were more compelling reasons why most slaveholding families chose not to flee. To stay was to try to save their homes and plantations from destruction and to preserve their slaves from the fearful epidemic whites diagnosed as "demoralization." By remaining at home, a Mississippi planter decided, he would be in a position to prevent his slaves "from denuding my place." Henry W. Ravenel of South Carolina entertained more lofty thoughts. Still imbued with the old paternalism, he thought it wrong—morally as well as practically—to desert his slaves at this time. "We know that if left to themselves, they cannot maintain their happy condition. We must reward their fidelity to us by the same care & consideration we exercised when they were more useful." Apart from economic considerations, slavery had long been defended as a necessary instrument of social control that benefited both races. And now, with the Yankees not far away, some slaveholders deemed it their duty to protect their blacks from vices that would inevitably accompany liberation and freedom.[19]

Whether the master and mistress chose to stay or flee, they might lecture the slaves on how to behave when the Yankees arrived. Although they were to avoid impertinence, that did not require them to welcome the invaders as they did most guests. Traditional plantation hospitality was to be extended most discriminately. "Dey ain't our company," a former North Carolina slave remembered being told. A Virginia master, after reciting the "barbarities" of the Yankees, threatened to punish anyone who suggested to the enemy that they had not been content as slaves. "Dey tol' us to tell 'em how good dey been to us," a former Alabama slave recalled, "an' dat we liked to live wid 'em." Rivana Boynton, who had been a house slave on a plantation near Savannah, remembered the day her mistress, Mollie Hoover, assembled the slaves and instructed them on what to tell the approaching Yankees. "If they ask you whether I've been good to you, you tell 'em 'yes.' If they ask you if we give you meat, you say 'yes.'" Most of the slaves did not get any meat, the former servant recalled, "but I did, 'cause I worked in the house. So I didn't tell a lie, for I did git meat." Most importantly, the white family warned the slaves not to divulge where the valuables had been hidden, no matter what the Yankees told them. "We knowed enough to keep our mouths shut," a former Georgia slave remarked. But a Tennessee slave, named Jule, who claimed not to fear the Union soldiers, had some different ideas. As the Yankees neared the plantation, the mistress commanded the slaves to remain loyal. "If they find that trunk o' money or silver plate," she asked Jule, "you'll say it's your'n, won't you?" The slave stood there, obviously unmoved by her mistress's plea. "Mistress," she replied, "I can't lie over that; you bo't that silver plate when you sole my three children."[20]

When the Union Army was nearby, slaves were quick to discern any changes in the disposition of their owners. In some places, the frequency and the severity of punishments abated, and the masters—perhaps fearing slave retaliation—assumed a more benign attitude, prepared for the eventuality of free labor, and even offered to pay wages. After the Yankees had been sighted less than two miles away, a Tennessee planter who had beaten one of his slaves that morning apologized to him and begged him not to desert. But as slaves had learned so well, usually from bitter personal experience, the moods of their "white folks" were capable of violent fluctuations. If the wartime disruptions, privations, and casualties had earlier provoked fits of anger, the impending disaster they now faced and the knowledge that they were about to lose both the war and their slaves rendered even some usually self-possessed whites unable to contain their emotions. That was how Katie Darling, a nurse and housegirl on a Texas plantation, recalled her mistress. When the Yankees drew near, "missy go off in a rage. One time when a cannon fire, she say to me, 'You li'l black wench, you niggers ain't gwine be free. You's made to work for white folks.' " A former Georgia slave recalled a "good master" who broke under the strain and tension that preceded the Union soldiers. "Marse William ain't eber hit one of us a single lick till de day when we heard dat de Yankees was a'comin'." When one of the slaves jumped up and shouted "Lawd bless de Yankees" on that day, the master lost his composure. Shouting "God damn de Yankees," he slapped the slave repeatedly. "Ever'-body got outen dar in a hurry an' nobody else dasen't say Yankees ter de marster."[21]

Not knowing what to expect of the invading army but fearing the worst, white families, in those final days and hours, often verged on panic and hysteria. At least that was how some of their slaves perceived them. In exasperation, masters were known to have lashed out at men and women who were too quick to celebrate their imminent release from bondage, while others refused to acknowledge either defeat or emancipation. After hearing of a new Confederate setback in the vicinity, Katie Rowe's master mounted his horse and rode out onto the plantation where the slaves were hoeing the corn. He instructed the overseer to assemble the hands around the lead row man—"dat my own uncle Sandy"—and what he told them on that occasion Katie Rowe could recall vividly many years later:

> You niggers been seeing de 'Federate soldiers coming by here looking purty raggedy and hurt and wore out, but dat no sign dey licked! Dem Yankees ain't gwine git dis fur, but iffen dey do you all ain't gwine git free by 'em, 'cause I gwine free you befo' dat. When dey git here dey going find you already free, 'cause I gwine line you up on de bank of Bois d'Arc Creek and free you wid my shotgun! Anybody miss jest one lick wid de hoe, or one step in de line, or one clap of dat bell, or one toot of de horn, and he gwine be free and talking to de debil long befo' he ever see a pair of blue britches!

Not long after that warning, the master was "blowed all to pieces" in a boiler explosion, "and dey jest find little bitsy chunks of his clothes and parts of him to bury." And when the Yankees finally arrived, the overseer who had previously terrorized them "git sweet as honey in de comb! Nobody git a whipping all de time de Yankees dar!"[22]

Looking on with a growing sense of incredulity, slaves observed the desperation, the anguish, the helplessness that marked the faces and actions of their "white folks." A Tennessee slave recalled how her mistress, at the sight of Union gunboats, suddenly "got wild-like" and "was cryin' an' wringin' her han's," while at the same time she kept repeating to her slaves, "Now, 'member I brought you up!" Although the slaves shared much of the uncertainty that pervaded the Big House, the quality of their fears and the anticipation they felt were quite different. When Margaret Hughes, who had been a young slave in South Carolina, heard that the Union soldiers were coming, she ran to her aunt for comfort. Much to Margaret's surprise, she found her in the best of spirits and not at all dismayed by the news. "Child," she reassured her, "we going to have such a good time a settin' at de white folks' table, a eating off de white folks' table, and a rocking in de big rocking chair."[23]

With Union soldiers already in the vicinity, Emma Holmes, a twenty-six-year-old white woman of "aristocratic" tastes and breeding, calmly attended the Methodist services in Camden, South Carolina. On that day, the Reverend Pritchard delivered a "thoroughly practical sermon" to the slaves in the audience, drawing his illustrations from "daily life," warning them about lying, stealing, cursing, and quarreling, and telling them that the Yankees had been "sent by the devil." But, like Job, they were all to bear their losses. Overhearing her servants discuss the sermon afterwards, Emma Holmes was both "amused" and "interested," and concluded "that good seed had been sowed and was bearing fruit." The attire worn by many of the black women at the service, however, deeply distressed her. Rather than wear "the respectable and becoming handkerchief turban," they had appeared "in the most ludicrous and disgustingly tawdry mixture of old finery, aping their betters most nauseatingly—round hats, gloves and even lace veils." They would do best to adopt "a plain, neat dress for the working classes, as in other countries, and indeed among our country negroes formerly." Even as the death of slavery appeared imminent, the thoughts uppermost in this woman's mind after attending church that day hardly conceded as much. "If I ever own negroes, I shall carry out my father's plan and never allow them to indulge in dress—it is ruin body and soul to them."[24]

The appearance of the first Yankee soldier symbolized far more than the humiliation of military defeat. No matter how certain they were of their own slaves, nearly every master and mistress sensed that the old loyalties and mutual dependencies were about to become irrelevant. "Negro slavery is about played out," John H. Bills, the Tennessee planter, observed, "we being deprived of that Control needful to make them happy and prosperous." And Sarah Morgan, the daughter of a slaveholding family, could find solace only in recalling the past. "No more cotton, sugarcane, or rice!" she lamented. "No more old black aunties or uncles! No more rides in mule teams, no more songs in the cane-field, no more steaming kettles, no more black faces and shining teeth around the furnace fires!" The previous night, she had sat around the fire with a crowd of family slaves, singing with them, enjoying their company. "Poor oppressed devils!" she thought. "Why did you not chunk us with the burning logs instead of looking happy, and laughing like fools?"[25]

Preparing to abandon the family plantation, as the Yankees approached, Eliza Andrews took time to note in her journal: "There is no telling what may happen before we come back; the Yankees may have put an end to our glorious old plantation life forever." That night, she paid a final visit to the slave quarters to bid her blacks farewell. "Poor things, I may never see any of them again, and even if I do, everything will be different. We all went to bed crying ... " Four months later, returning to her home, she confided to her journal: "It is necessary to have some nickname to use when we talk before the servants, and to speak very carefully, even then, for every black man is a possible spy. Father says we must not even trust mammy too far."[26]

## 3

---

*Don't you see the lightning flashing in the cane brakes,*
*Looks like we gonna have a storm*
*Although you're mistaken it's the Yankee soldiers*
*Going to fight for Uncle Sam.*
*Old master was a colonel in the Rebel army*
*Just before he had to run away—*
*Look out the battle is a-falling*
*The darkies gonna occupy the land.*[27]

THE LONG, often excruciating wait was nearly over. On plantations and farms in the path of the Union Army, the tension and uneasiness, albeit in different degrees, pervaded both the Big House and the slave quarters. Mary Brodie, a thirteen-year-old slave in Wake County, North Carolina, could easily sense the change that had come over the plantation on which she resided. "Missus and marster began to walk around and act queer. The grown slaves were whisperin' to each other. Sometimes they gathered in little gangs in the grove." In the next several days, the noise of distant gunfire grew louder, everybody "seemed to be disturbed," the slaves walked about aimlessly, nobody was working, "and marster and missus were crying." Finally, the word went out for every slave to assemble in front of "the great house." Sam and Evaline Brodie came out on the porch and stood side by side facing their more than 150 slaves. "You could hear a pin drop," Mary recalled, "everything was so quiet." After greeting them, the master explained why he had called them together. "Men, women and children, you are free. You are no longer my slaves. The Yankees will soon be here." There was no more to be said. The master and mistress went back into the house, picked up two large armchairs, placed them on the porch facing the road, and sat down to wait. "In about an hour," Mary recalled, "there was one of the blackest clouds coming up the avenue from the main road. It was the Yankee soldiers."[28]

When Union gunboats were sighted coming up the Combahee River in South Carolina, the overseer frantically assembled the slaves. "The Yankees are coming!" he told them. "You must all keep out of sight. Don't let them see you. If they land near here, cut and run and hide where nobody can find you. I tell you them Yanks are the very devil! If they catch you they will sell you to New Orleans or Cuba!" The slaves assured the overseer that they would run so fast "de Debil hisself" would be unable to catch them. "Don't you worry, Massa Jim," the old slave cook added. "We all hear 'bout dem Yankees. Folks tell we they has horns an' a tail. I is mighty skeery myself, an' I has all my t'ings pick up, an' w'en I see dem coming I shall run like all possess." Reassured, the overseer announced that he was going to the mainland and would leave everything in their care. The slaves gathered to watch him ride off. "Good-by, ole man, good-by," they shouted as he disappeared down the road. "That's right. Skedaddle as fas' as you kin. When you cotch we ag'in, I 'specs you'll know it. We's gwine to run sure enough; but we knows the Yankees, an' we runs that way." And so they did, directly toward the Union gunboats.[29]

When former slaves recalled the war years, what remained most vivid in their memories—"just as good as it had been dis day right here"—was that moment when freedom from bondage suddenly became a distinct possibility in their own lifetimes. The first slaves who experienced that sensation were usually those whose homes lay in the path of the Union Army. "We hear'd 'bout de Yankees fightin' to free us," remembered Berry Smith of Mississippi, "but we didn' b'lieve it 'til we hear'd 'bout de fightin' at Vicksburg." When the "freedom gun" was fired, and Sherman's troops came through the plantation, Susan Hamilton was scrubbing the floors. "Dey tell me I wus free but I didn't b'lieve it." While driving the cows to pasture, Rilla Pool, a North Carolina slave, glanced down the railroad tracks and "everything was blue"; she ran home to tell the others, and heard her grandmother exclaim, "Well I has been prayin' long enough for 'em [and] now dey is here." Hester Hunter, a South Carolina slave, recalled the day her grandmother ran into the house with news that the Yankees were on their way, after which the mistress screamed, fetched her valuables, and told the slave to sew them up in the feather bed. Still another South Carolina slave was about to be whipped by his master for misconduct when they heard the shout that Union gunboats were coming up the river; both fled, but in opposite directions.[30]

Uncertainty, skepticism, and fear marked the initial reaction of many slaves to the Yankee invaders. The first impulse was often to hide. "I done what all of de rest o' de slaves done," recalled a former slave who had fled to the nearby woods. Young Margaret Lavine remembered how her mother grabbed her in her arms; indeed, some slave women ordered their children to bed, told them to feign illness, and warned the Union soldiers not to enter the cabin because "dere's de fever in heah!" Neither ignorance nor devotion to their "white folks" necessarily explains the caution with which many slaves greeted their liberators. The activities of the much-feared "paterollers," who roamed the countryside to keep the blacks in check, had already made the slaves exceedingly wary of approaching strangers, even those claiming to be Yankees; the citizens' patrols, as well as Confederate guerrillas (sometimes wearing Yankee uniforms), were known to have beaten and murdered slaves who mistook them for Union soldiers and prematurely rejoiced over their liberation, and some slaves had been tricked into giving information to alleged Yankees, only to find themselves strung up as spies and informers. Many a slave suffered, too, at the hands of white stragglers and deserters, and General Joe Wheeler's Confederate cavalry had become notorious for the ways in which it pillaged and terror-ized the countryside, leaving in some areas of South Carolina and North Carolina little for the Yankees to plunder. "Dey was 'Federates but dey was mean as de Yankees," Sarah Debro recalled. "Dey ax de niggahs if dey wanted to be free. If dey say yes, den dey shot dem down, but if dey say no, dey let dem alone. Dey took three of my uncles out in de woods an' shot dey faces off."[31]

If the approaching soldiers were, in fact, Yankees, there remained compelling reasons why the slaves might act cautiously. Although freedom appeared to be at hand, uncertainty about what forms that freedom would take, how their "liberators" would treat them, and what would happen to them once the soldiers departed suggested the need to adopt that noncom-mittal stance that had served them so well in relations with the "white folks." Realizing that their master would most likely regain control after the soldiers moved on, slaves had good reason to fear that a terrible revenge might be visited upon those who behaved contrary to expectations. Despite reassurances by General Sherman himself that the Yankees came as friends, an elderly Georgia slave remained skeptical. "I spose dat you'se true," he told the General; "but, massa, you'se 'll go way to-morrow, and anudder white man 'll come." Experience with both Yankees and Confeder-ates led one former slave to conclude, "Dem 'Blue-coats' wuz devils, but de 'gray-coats' wuz wusser," and it prompted many slaves to maintain a safe distance between themselves and either army.

> One night there'd be a gang of Secesh, and the next one, there'd come
> along a gang of Yankees. Pa was 'fraid of both of 'em. Secesh said they'd
> kill 'im if he left his white folks. Yankees said they'd kill 'im if he didn't
> leave 'em. He would hide out in the cotton patch and keep we children
> out there with him.[32]

If a slave chose to believe only half of what he had been told about the approaching Union soldiers, there was every reason to be apprehensive. On the day the Yankees were expected, Betty Roach, a housegirl and nurse for the children on a small plantation in Tennessee, asked how she might be able to tell them apart from other whites. That would be easy, her mistress explained. "They got long horns on their heads, and tushes in their mouths, and eyes sticking out like a cow! They're mean old things. And Betty—if they come to the house, don't dare tell them the babies' names—you hear? [The children had been named after two prominent Confederate generals.] If you do, they will kill the babies—and you too!" This same woman had previously assured Betty that if she worked hard and behaved herself, she would eventually turn white. Not at all uncommon, then, was the experience of a Union officer near Opelousas, Louisiana, when he wandered off the road to a shed in search of a cup of water. Seeing him, the slave women and children fled, leaving behind a small child who was trying desperately to join the others. The officer patted the child on the head and tried to assure him that he was perfectly safe. Emerging from their hiding places, the slaves who had run away explained that their master and mistress had told them that Union soldiers killed black children, sometimes even roasted and ate them.[33]

Since the outbreak of the war, white families had tried to frighten their slaves about the consequences of Yankee occupation, warning them to expect atrocities, forced labor, and military conscription. Since some slaves had come to expect anything of white men and women, the terrifying images of Yankee white devils might have seemed entirely plausible. But the slave's perception of his master and mistress, based on years of close observation, and the information he gathered from a variety of alternative sources provided ample grounds for skepticism if not outright disbelief. Even with a limited access to the news, many slaves dismissed the atrocity stories because they simply made no sense. "Massa can't come dat over we," a Georgia slave told a Union officer; "we know'd a heap better. What for de Yankees want to hurt black men? Massa hates de Yankees, and he's no fren' ter we; so we am de Yankee bi's fren's." After hearing those direful predictions of a Yankee hell, Aunt Sally, a Virginia slave, assumed a "darky" countenance and assured her mistress that there was nothing to fear from the enemy soldiers. "I done tell her what'd dey go to do to an ol' good-for-nuffin nigger like me. Dey wouldn't hab no use for me, I'se thinkin'. I'll stay by de stuff." The same master who warned his slaves about the Yankees, moreover, might have also boasted of the invincibility of Confederate arms, assuring them that the war would be brief and victorious. Why should they place any more confidence in their master's word now than they had before? "They told her a heap more'n she believed," a Louisiana freedwoman remarked after the war.[34] And if the Yankees brought with them a promise of freedom, as everyone seemed to concede, why should the slaves fear them?

The first glimpse usually convinced even the more skeptical slaves, if not their masters, that the Yankees, in physical appearance at least, were less than the monsters they had been warned to expect. "Why dey's folks," one slave shouted with delight, as she ran down the road to greet them. Not knowing what he might see, Abram Harris, a former South Carolina slave, remembered his surprise at discovering that the Yankees were "jes lak my white folks." Still not entirely convinced, Mittie Freeman, who had been a slave in Mississippi, recalled how she refused to come down from a tree until the Union soldier had removed his hat to show her he had no horns. Lingering suspicions of white men, whether Yankees or Confederates, were not always so easily set aside. Although anxious to celebrate their freedom, Gus Askew and his friends preferred not to do so in the presence of the Yankees. "We went on away from the so'jers and had a good time 'mongst ourselves, like we always done when there wasn't any cotton pickin'." The slaves were sometimes more restrained in their welcomes if their master or mistress happened to be present, and that may also account for the indifference with which some disappointed Yankees thought they had been received. "On our way up from Carrollton," a Massachusetts soldier wrote, "one [slave] got the woodpile between him and the whites, and then vigorously waved his hat in welcome. It was our only welcome."[35]

If the Yankees' physical appearance seemed reassuring, the promise of freedom they had come to symbolize overcame for scores of slaves any doubts or suspicions. Without the slightest hesitation, many of them flocked to the roadsides, waved their hats and bonnets, greeted the soldiers with shouts of "God bress you; I is glad to see you," threw their arms about in jubilation, stretched out their hands to touch them, even tried to hug them. "Massa say dis bery mornin', 'De damn Yankees nebber get up to here!' " a slave in the Teche country of Louisiana shouted at the passing troops, "but I knowed better; we all knowed better dan dat. We's been prayin' too long to de Lord to have him forgit us; and now you'se come, and we all free." At the sight of Sherman's army, one slave recalled, the whites fled to the woods and most of the slaves ran to their cabins, "but I'se on top o' a pine stub, ten feet high, an' I'se jes' shoutin' 'Glory to God! take me wid ye! Glory to God! Glory Glory!' " Eliza Sparks, who had been a slave in Mathews County, Virginia, recalled most vividly the Union officer who wanted to know the name of the baby she was nursing. "Charlie, like his father," she told him. "Charlie what?" the officer asked. "I tole him Charlie Sparks." After presenting the baby with a copper coin, the officer rode off, but not before bidding the slave a farewell she would long remember. "Goodbye, Mrs. Sparks," he yelled. That was what impressed her. "Now what you think of dat? Dey all call me 'Mrs. Sparks'!"[36]

When the Yankees entered Charleston, a sixty-nine-year-old slave woman greeted them with a simple, repetitive chant:

> *Ye's long been a-comin',*
> *Ye's long been a-comin',*
> *Ye's long been a-comin',*
> *For to take de land.*

*And now ye's a-comin',*
*And now ye's a comin',*
*And now ye's a-comin',*
*For to rule de land.*

That the coming of the Yankees should have been suffused with religious significance for many slaves is hardly surprising. "Us looked for the Yankees on dat place," a former South Carolina slave recalled, "like us look now for de Savior and de host of angels at de second comin'." To the elderly, those who had endured nearly a lifetime of bondage, what they were now witnessing appeared to be nothing less than acts of divine intervention, with the Yankees cast as "Jesus's Aids," General Sherman as Moses, and Lincoln as "de Messiah." That was the only way some slaves could explain what was happening to them, the only way they could render comprehensible these remarkable and dramatic events. Seldom had their prayers been answered so concretely. "I'd always thought about this, and wanted this day to come, and prayed for it and knew God meant it should be here sometime," a Savannah slave declared as she shook her head in disbelief, "but I didn't believe I should ever see it, and it is so great and good a thing, I cannot believe it has come now; and I don't believe I ever shall realize it, but I know it has though, and I bless the Lord for it."[37]

But the arrival of the Yankees on many plantations and farms came to be viewed, by slaves and their owners alike, as the visitation of God's wrath. The soldiers would assemble the white family and the slaves, demand to know where the valuables were hidden, threaten them if they refused to divulge the information, and then commence to ransack the entire plantation, venting their anger on whatever or whoever got in the way. "De worst time we ever had," recalled Fannie Griffin, who had been a slave in South Carolina. "De Yankees 'stroyed 'most everything we had." On the plantation in Alabama where Walter Calloway worked as a plow hand, Confederate soldiers had already taken off the best livestock, making it "purty hard on bofe whites an' blacks," but the Yankees proved to be even more thorough, "smashin' things comin' an' gwine."[38]

What the Yankees did not take they might distribute among the slaves, even urging them to join in the pillaging. With their restricted diet having been further reduced by wartime scarcities, some slaves found it impossible to resist the invitation to partake of the food supply created by their own labor or the Big House furnishings accumulated through generations of their unpaid labor. When the soldiers broke open the storeroom on the Pooshee plantation in South Carolina, the slaves seized nearly everything in sight, much to the shock of the owner, who had to witness the scene. Afterwards, his granddaughter informed a friend of what had happened: "It must have been too mortifying to poor Grand Pa for his negroes to behave as they did, taking the bread out of our mouths. I thought better of them than that." After the Yankees passed through her rice plantations, Adele Allston learned that the blacks had divided among themselves the furniture and livestock. But even when slaves were afforded these rare opportunities, their behavior defied predictability; many of them refused to have anything to do with such "looting" and were reluctant to accept any of the master's property. In some instances, the slaves took what the soldiers gave them, so as not to anger them, but subsequently returned the goods to their owners, whether out of loyalty or because they feared the repercussions once the Union Army moved on.[39]

When Yankee troops looted the Morgan home in Baton Rouge, a faithful servant stood all he could before he exclaimed, "Ain't you 'shamed to destroy all dis here, that belongs to a poor widow lady who's got two daughters to support?" No matter how each slave felt inwardly, the sight of Yankees pillaging the plantation and perhaps humiliating the white residents had to be a unique experience. The way the soldiers "jes' natcherly tore up ol' Marster's place," as though they had a "special vengeance" for their "white folks," left many slaves quite incredulous. So did the treatment of the women.

> Upstairs dey didn't even have de manners to knock at Mist'ess' door. Dey just walked right on in whar my sister, Lucy, wuz combin' Mist'ess' long pretty hair. They told Lucy she wuz free now and not to do no more work for Mist'ess. Den all of 'em grabbed dey big old rough hands into Mist'ess' hair, and dey made her walk down stairs and out in de yard, and all de time dey wuz a-pullin' and jerkin' at her long hair . . .

With equal "impertinence," the soldiers might force the white women to prepare meals and serve both them and the slaves. That was a sight Mary Ella Grandberry, a former Alabama slave, would never forget. "De Yankees made 'em do for us lak we done for dem. Dey showed de white folks what it was to work for somebody else."[40]

Upon observing "the gloomy ebony scowl" on the faces of the slaves, a Union officer thought it arose from "jealousy at the liberties, taken by us, with what they consider their own plantations and possessions." He was no doubt correct in his assumption. The slaves might have marveled at the audacity of the Yankees, and some perhaps derived pleasure from the discomfiture of their owners, but the indiscriminate and wasteful destruction of the food supply and what many regarded as their home struck them as excessive and unnecessary. The Yankees called it "a holy war," a former South Carolina slave observed, "but they and Wheeler's men was a holy terror to dis part of de world, as naked and hungry as they left it." It was the pillaging, a former Mississippi slave recalled, that turned him against the Yankees, and he shared, too, the resentment of numerous blacks that the soldiers destroyed what they had worked so hard to produce. "We helped raise that meat they stole. They left us to starve and fed their fat selves on what was our living." No less disturbing had been those planters and Confederate soldiers who had ordered the destruction of crops rather than leave them to the Yankees. "It made my innards hurt," Charlie

Davenport recalled, "to see fire 'tached to somethin' dat had cost us Niggers so much labor an' hones' sweat."[41]

What compounded the bitterness was that the Yankees pillaged both whites and blacks, the Big House and the slave cabins alike. "The negroes all share the same fate as ourselves," Emma Holmes noted after the Yankees had passed through Camden, South Carolina, "everything ransacked and whatever was wanted stolen, though the Yankees told them they had come to free them and called them 'sis,' talking most familiarly." That they should be robbed and defrauded by those who claimed to be their liberators, that their cabins should be searched and ransacked, their wives and daughters insulted and abused, came as a shocking revelation to many slaves, leaving them both angry and confused. "I always bin hear dat de Yankees was gwine help de nigger!" one of the Allston servants exclaimed to her mistress after the Yankees had seized her few possessions. "W'a' kynd a help yu call dis! Tek ebery ting I got in de wurld." The depth of black disillusionment with the Yankees is suggested by the number of slaves who compared them to the much-despised and degraded poor whites. "By instinct," Andy Brice of South Carolina observed, "a nigger can make up his mind pretty quick 'bout de creed of white folks, whether they am buckra or whether they am not. Every Yankee I see had de stamp of poor white trash on them." Perhaps that was what a Mississippi slave had in mind after a Union soldier had addressed her as "Auntie." "Don't you call me 'Auntie,' " she retorted, "I ain't none o' yo' kin."[42]

With considerable ingenuity, based on years of experience with their own "white folks," some slaves managed to preserve their few possessions from the clutches of the Yankees. In Camden, South Carolina, for example, the soldiers seized the blankets belonging to an elderly black shoemaker. But he proved more than equal to the crisis. Feigning "a tone of terror," he warned them not to mix his blankets with theirs, "as all the house girls had some catching disease." On hearing this, the alarmed Yankees not only returned the blankets but presented the black with the mule on which they had placed the loot. Equally artful were the servants in the Mary S. Mallard household in Montevideo, Georgia, who sought both to avoid conscription into the Union Army and to save their belongings.

> From being a young girl she [the cook] had assumed the attitude and appearance of a sick old woman, with a blanket thrown over her head and shoulders, and scarcely able to move. Their devices are various and amusing. Gilbert keeps a sling under his coat and slips his arm into it as soon as they appear; Charles walks with a stick and limps dreadfully; Niger a few days since kept them from stealing everything they wanted in his house by covering up in bed and saying he had *"yellow fever"*; Mary Ann kept them from taking the wardrobe of her deceased daughter by calling out: "Them dead people clothes!"[43]

Although the vast majority of slaves welcomed the Union soldiers, albeit with varying degrees of enthusiasm, experience would reveal that their "liberators," like their previous owners, might display moments of kindness, tenderness, generosity, and paternal benevolence but their racial beliefs and temperaments made them at the same time unpredictable and capable of a wide range of conduct. When an Arkansas slave confronted a Yankee who had stolen her quilts, she voiced the frustration of many of her brethren who had experienced a similar betrayal of expectations: "Why, you nasty, stinkin' rascal. You say you come down here to fight for the niggers, and now you're stealin' from 'em." But the soldier had the final word, aptly summing up his conception of the war and that of thousands of his comrades: "You're a God Damn liar, I'm fightin' for $14 a month and the Union."[44]

# 4

---

BEFORE ENTERING THE SOUTH, few Yankee soldiers had ever seen so many blacks, such concentrations of them, appearing almost everywhere they marched. The tens of thousands who greeted them along the roadsides, the "contrabands" who flocked to their camps, the refugees who followed their columns, the sullen-looking figures who gazed at them from a distance provided most Union soldiers with their initial view of the "peculiar institution." It was as if Harriet Beecher Stowe's characters had suddenly materialized before their very eyes. "I never saw a bunch of them together," a Wisconsin youth wrote, "but I could pick out an Uncle Tom, a Quimbo, a Sambo, a Chloe, an Eliza or any other character in Uncle Tom's Cabin."[45]

Although curious about what he would find in the South, the average Union soldier brought with him certain notions about black people, based largely on the racial beliefs and exaggerated caricatures with which he had been inculcated since childhood. His first impressions of the slaves he encountered invariably confirmed and reinforced those caricatures, and the descriptions he provided the folks at home dwelled upon them. If anything, their physical "peculiarities" struck him as even more pronounced than he had imagined; they were "so black that 'charcoal would make a white mark on them,' " their mouths were excessively large, their lips excessively thick, and their noses excessively broad and flat. "They are the genuine Negro here," a Pennsylvania soldier wrote from South Carolina, "as black as tar and their heels stick out a feet behind." A New England soldier in Louisiana wrote his brother with a mixture of revulsion and attraction: "If I marry any one at all I believe I'll marry one of these nigger wenches down here. One that grease runs right off of, one that shines and one that stinks so you can smell her a mile, and then you can have time to get out of the way." Such disparagements were neither uncommon nor limited to Negrophobes. Even those Yankee soldiers who claimed to be antislavery expressed their amusement at the physical appearance and

demeanor of the enslaved blacks, revealing more about their own back-
grounds and biases than about the objects of their sympathy. "There is
something irresistibly comical in their appearance," wrote one such soldier, "they are so black, and their teeth are of such dazzling whiteness,
their eyes so laughing and rolling, their clothes so fantastic, and their
whole appearance so peculiar."[46]

The Yankees expected to find a degraded, inferior, primitive people,
who were at the same time picturesque, comical, indolent, and carefree,
always wearing "a happy and contented expression," displaying their
broad grins, touching their hats to the white folks, answering questions
politely and humbly. That was the kind of Negro they had seen cavorting
across the minstrel stages of the North and pictured in the popular literature, and now they were simply viewing Sambo and Dinah in their natural
habitat. "Until I saw and conversed with the greater number of these
persons," a northern reporter wrote from South Carolina, "I believed that
the appearance and intelligence of Southern field hands were greatly li-
beled by the delineators of negro character at the concert saloons. Now I
cannot but acknowledge that instead of gross exaggerations the 'minstrels'
give representations which are faithful to nature. There were the same
grotesque dresses, awkward figures, and immense brogans which are to be
seen every night at Bryant's or Christy's." Nor did the Yankees obviously
expect to find any particular intelligence exhibited by these minstrel-like
characters, quite apart from the laws that barred them from learning to
read or write. Thus did a Union soldier, who was himself barely literate,
inform his parents that the "niggers" he had encountered "dont no as
much as a dumb bruit."[47]

Unlike many southern whites, the Yankees had little awareness of the
complexity of the slave's demeanor and personality. They still had some
hard lessons to learn in the kind of dissembling and deception that enslaved blacks often practiced on whites. That would come with time and
experience. "One of these blacks, fresh from slavery, will most adroitly tell
you precisely what you want to hear," a northern journalist discovered in
South Carolina. "To cross-examine such a creature is a task of the most
delicate nature; if you chance to put a leading question he will answer to
its spirit as closely as the compass needle answers to the magnetic pole."
Still other revelations would emerge with additional exposure to the variety of black folk. Although Union soldiers were quick to note the blackness
of the slaves, the gradations in color did not escape them, and the abundant
evidence of miscegenation would evoke considerable comment and curiosity. "Many of the mongrels are very beautiful," a Massachusetts soldier
conceded, "with their fine hair, straight or wavy, and their blue or dark
eyes, always soft and lustrous and half concealed by the long lashes. They
look more like voluptuous Italians than negroes." He had been told by one
"Southern gentleman" that the mulattoes were "more docile and affectionate" than "the unmixed negro," although "less hardy" and "generally
unchaste." Whatever "handsome" qualities the mulattoes and quadroons

possessed, the Yankees naturally attributed them to their white ancestry. How else could they explain the startling incongruity in the appearance of a mulatto child with his mother? "Judging by the extreme hideousness of some of these mothers," a soldier wrote, "I was led to conclude that Southern passion was superior to Southern taste."[48]

Although the prevailing image pictured blacks as a happy-go-lucky and carefree race, at best a source of amusement, some Yankee soldiers came away with altogether different impressions. The slaves they saw did not resemble "the rollicking, joyous, devil-may-care African" they had anticipated, nor did they hear any of the laughter and jubilant songs that were said to radiate from the slave cabins. When he had come to the South, Private Henry T. Johns of Massachusetts, like most of his comrades, had believed that the blacks, "if not a happy race, were at least careless and light-hearted." But the longer he remained in the South, the more skeptical he became of that stereotype. "I have been with them a great deal," he wrote from Louisiana, "and never before saw so much of gloom, despondency, and listlessness. I saw no banjo, heard none but solemn songs. In church or on the street they impress me with a great sadness. They are a sombre, *not* a happy, race." Several weeks later, when his regiment was encamped near Baton Rouge, he attended a black religious service and described the "mingled excitement and devotion," the shouting, the clapping of hands, the jumping, the often wild and excited singing. It all impressed him, however, as "a *mournful* joy," and the hymns seemed "more a loud wail than a burst of joyous melody."

> When praying about their enslaved condition, or for the dying, or for the salvation of poor sinners, they unitedly break out into the most plaintive chorus imaginable. I can't describe it, but to my dying hour I shall remember it. It seemed like the *incarnation of sadness.* I could think of nothing but a mother in heaven wailing for her *lost* son. . . . Almost like a nightmare it clings to me, ever presenting depths of sadness and resignation beyond my conception.[49]

The degree of enthusiasm with which slaves greeted their "liberators" created something of a paradox. If they acted indifferently or hostilely, as some did, the Yankees concluded they were too ignorant to appreciate or recognize freedom. But if they were effusive in their response, the Union soldiers often mocked their behavior. The typical Yankee was at best a reluctant liberator, and the attitudes and behavior he evinced did not always encourage the slaves to think of themselves as free men and women. Although Union propagandists and abolitionists might exult in how a war for the Union had been transformed into a crusade for freedom, many northern soldiers donned the crusader's armor with strong misgivings or outright disgust. "I dont think enough of the Niggar to go and fight for them," an Ohio private wrote. "I would rather fight them." Few Northerners, after all, had chosen to wage this kind of war. "Our government has broken faith with us," a Union deserter told his captors. "We enlisted to fight for the Union, and not to liberate the G–d d—d niggers." Rather than view emancipation as a way to end the war, some Yankee soldiers thought it would only prolong the conflict. Now that the very survival of the southern labor system was at stake, not to mention the proper subordination of black people, the prospect of a negotiated peace seemed even more remote, and southern whites could be expected to fight with even greater intensity and conviction.[50]

That most Union soldiers should have failed to share the abolitionist commitment is hardly surprising. What mattered was how they manifested their feelings when they came into direct contact with the slaves. The evidence suggests one of the more tragic chapters in the history of this generally brutalizing and demoralizing war. The normal frustrations of military life and the usually sordid record of invading armies, when combined with long-held and deeply felt attitudes toward black people, were more than sufficient to turn some Union soldiers into the very "debils" the slaves had been warned by their masters to expect. Not only did the invaders tend to view the Negro as a primary cause of the war but even more importantly as an inferior being with few if any legitimate human emotions—at least none that had to be considered with any degree of sensitivity. Here, then, was a logical and convenient object on which disgruntled and war-weary Yankees could vent their frustrations and hatreds. "As I was going along this afternoon," a young Massachusetts officer wrote from New Orleans, "a little black baby that could just walk got under my feet and it look so much like a big worm that I wanted to step on it and crush it, the nasty, greasy little vermin was the best that could be said of it." And if anything, additional exposure to blacks appeared to strengthen rather than allay racial antipathies. "My repugnance to them increases with the acquaintance," a New England officer remarked. "Republican as I am, keep me clear of the darkey in any relation." Praying for an early end to the war, a Union soldier stationed in Missouri declared that he had had his fill of colored people. "I never want to see one of the animals after I leave here."[51]

The thousands of slaves who flocked to the Union lines were apt to encounter the same prejudices, the same exploitation, the same disparagement, the same capacity for sadistic cruelty which they thought they had left behind them on the plantations and farms. To belittle the slave's character, dress, language, name, and demeanor, to make him the butt of their humor, to ridicule his aspirations, to mock his religious worship, to exploit his illiteracy were ways of passing the duller moments of camp life and military occupation. Besides, the manipulation of blacks for the amusement of white audiences had a long and accepted tradition behind it. "There were five negroes in our mess room last night," a New England soldier wrote from Virginia, "we got them to sing and dance! Great times. Negro concerts free of expense here." Sarah Debro, who had been a slave in North Carolina, recalled the Yankee soldiers who threatened to shoot her toes off unless she danced for them, and other former slaves remembered, too, how the Yankees forced them to sing and dance and called them "funny names." The soldiers who shared in these diversions did so regardless of their feelings about slavery and emancipation. Henry M. Cross constantly deplored racist sentiment in his regiment; what he had seen of the slaves, he wrote, made him despise even more intensely the bondage "which has brought them to their miserable condition." But even as he made that comment, Private Cross wrote of a sixteen-year-old black youth attached to the adjutant in his camp:

> He is filthy and lazy and seems to know as much as a child of four years, and yet once in a while shows gleams of intelligence beyond his years and condition. He never looks at you when talking, but shifts uneasily from one leg to the other and turns his head from side to side, rolling his eyes and grunting queer laughs. We make all kinds of sport of him.[52]

To strip the slave of his dignity and self-respect was not enough. Some Yankees exploited his ignorance and trust to defraud him of what little money or worldly goods he possessed. They might, for example, persuade him to exchange his money for certificates that turned out to be soap wrappers, or sell him equally worthless passes that permitted him to travel freely, or offer for a price to reunite him with his family. Some slaves were less gullible than the Yankees thought but were in no position to challenge their authority, while a few slaves managed to turn the tables on their liberators, like the elderly black man who claimed to be the original Uncle Tom and sold a souvenir-hunting Yankee the whip with which he had allegedly been beaten.[53]

To debauch black women, some Yankees apparently concluded, was to partake of a widely practiced and well-accepted southern pastime. The evidence was to be seen everywhere. Besides, Yankees tended to share the popular racist notion of black women as naturally promiscuous and dissolute. "Singular, but true," a Massachusetts soldier and amateur phrenologist observed, "the heads of the women indicate great animal passions." Although some Union officers made no secret of their slave concubines, sharing their quarters with them, a black soldier noted that they usually mingled with "deluded freedwomen" only under the cover of darkness, while they openly consorted with white women during the day. The frequency with which common soldiers mixed with black women prompted some regimental commanders to order the ejection of such women from the camp because their presence had become "demoralizing." "I won't be unfaithful to you with a Negro wench," a Pennsylvania soldier assured his wife, "though it is the case with many soldiers. Yes, men who have wives at home get entangled with these black things." Marriages between Yankees and blacks were rare, but when they did occur southern whites made the most of them.

Two of the Brownfields former negroes have married Yankees—one, a light colored mustee, had property left her by some white man whose mistress she had been—she says she passed herself off for a Spaniard and Mercier Green violated the sanctity of Grace Church by performing the ceremony—the other, a man, went north and married a Jewess—the idea is too revolting.

Not surprisingly, Union soldiers often shared the outrage of local whites at such liaisons. In November 1865, a black newspaper in Charleston reported that an Illinois soldier had been tarred and feathered by his own comrades for having married a black woman. "He was probably a Southern man by birth and education," the newspaper said of the victim, "and Hoosiers and Suckers don't take readily to Southern habits."[54]

Whatever the reputation of black women for promiscuity, sexual submission frequently had to be obtained by force. "While on picket guard I witnessed misdeeds that made me ashamed of America," a soldier wrote from South Carolina; he had recently observed a group of his comrades rape a nine-year-old black girl. Not only did some Union soldiers sexually assault any woman they found in a slave cabin but they had no compunctions about committing the act in the presence of her family. "The father and grandfather dared offer no resistance," two witnesses reported from Virginia. In some such instances, the husband or children of the intended victim had to be forcibly restrained from coming to her assistance. Beyond the exploitation of sexual assault, black women could be subjected to further brutality and sadism, as was most graphically illustrated in an incident involving some Connecticut soldiers stationed in Virginia. After seizing two "niger wenches," they "turned them upon their heads, & put tobacco, chips, stocks, lighted cigars & sand into their behinds." Without explanation, some Union soldiers in Hanover County, Virginia, stopped five young black women and cut their arms, legs, and backs with razors. "Dis was new to us," one of the victims recalled, "cause Mr. Tinsley [her master] didn' ever beat or hurt us." Most Union soldiers would have found these practices reprehensible. But they occurred with sufficient frequency to induce a northern journalist in South Carolina to write that Union troops had engaged in "some of the vilest and meanest exhibitions of human depravity" he had ever witnessed. If such incidents were rare, moreover, the racial ideology that encouraged them had widespread acceptance, even among those who deplored the excesses.[55]

The actions of white men could not surprise some blacks. Many of those who hailed the Yankees as their champions and liberators nevertheless were to experience a rude awakening. In Norfolk, Virginia, the slaves had rejoiced at the coming of the Yankees. "There was nothing we would not do for them," one black resident remarked; "and they knew it, too. We were humble, grateful and respectful." But the soldiers destroyed their property, shot at them, and abused them "in every possible way," and it now appeared to him "as if we had no one to protect us, and there's nothing left us but to protect ourselves." Such experiences were more than unsettling; they raised real questions about the quality of the newly acquired freedom. What were the blacks to think when "those individuals whom we all regarded as our friends, and hailed as our deliverers," broke up their celebrations, heaped physical and mental abuse on them, shoved them off sidewalks, cursed them as "niggers" and "mokes," robbed them of their few belongings, and ravished their women? It was as if one set of masters had been replaced by another, and that was precisely how a Norfolk black woman viewed the change in her status: "I reckon I'm Massa Lincoln's slave now."[56]

Reflecting the wide range and diversity of northern opinion, the Union Army also contained in its ranks men who were imbued with abolitionist ideals, who were anxious to wage an antislavery war, and who would have resented any implication that they harbored racist attitudes. "I tell the boys right to their face I am in the war for the freedom of the slave," a Wisconsin soldier boasted. Initially indifferent or hostile to emancipation, some Union soldiers were won over by military considerations, while others resolved their doubts when they came face to face with the victims of the "peculiar institution." After hearing from slave runaways the stories of their escape and the bondage they had left behind them, a Union soldier in North Carolina wrote his parents that "every man in our army is *now* an abolitionist." Even more convincing than the familiar tales of whippings and the separation of families was the direct physical evidence of how slaves had been treated. Upon visiting several plantations near New Orleans, where he released slave prisoners from heavy chains and weights, one Union soldier said he had seen "enough of the horrors of slavery to make one an Abolitionist forever." When several new black recruits stripped for a physical examination in Louisiana, prior to their induction, a Union soldier afterwards described in detail the marks which bondage had left on the bodies of these men. It was a depressing sight.

> Some of them were scarred from head to foot where they had been whipped. One man's back was nearly all one scar, as if the skin had been chopped up and left to heal in ridges. Another had scars on the back of his neck, and from that all the way to his heels every little ways; but that was not such a sight as the one with the great solid mass of ridges from his shoulders to his hips. That beat all the antislavery sermons ever yet preached.[57]

The more sympathetic Union soldiers tried to alleviate the condition of the slave refugees who flocked in ever greater numbers to their camps. Anticipating the movement of teachers and missionaries into the South, they volunteered their time to establish informal classes for the slaves in reading and writing, and some insisted on giving them religious instruction. The life of an abolitionist in the Union Army, however, much like that of his counterpart in the North, was never very comfortable, particularly if he sought to proselytize his fellow soldiers, and he almost always sensed that he was in a small minority. "Most of the boys have their laugh at me for helping the 'Niggers,'" a Wisconsin soldier confessed. The hostility toward abolitionism and blacks that so many Northerners carried with them into the war was sometimes vented on those who tried to agitate the subject in the Army. "If some of the niger lovers want to know what the most of the Solgers think of them," an Ohioan informed his father, "they think about as much as they do a reble. They think they are Shit asses."[58]

The abolitionist Yankee found himself troubled by more than the hostility of his fellow soldiers. Mirroring the ambivalence of the antislavery movement itself, he often found it easier to preach abolitionism than to accept the black man as an equal or to mix with him socially. Henry T. Johns, the well-meaning and sympathetic Massachusetts soldier, frankly confessed near the end of the war, "I know I always revolt at shaking hands with a darkey or sitting by him, but it is a prejudice that should shame me." To free the slaves, he recognized approvingly, was to grant them equality. "There is no help for it, and the sooner we get rid of our foolish prejudices the better for us. In me those prejudices are very strong. I can fight for this race more easily than I can eat with them." As they moved through the South and ultimately became an army of occupation, Union soldiers, like the North itself, failed to agree on the proper place of black people—both freed slaves and free blacks—in American society. If there was anything approaching a typical attitude, a Union Army physician stationed in Virginia may have come close to capturing it. He did not regard himself as proslavery. He wanted to see the institution of slavery abolished. But he found it difficult to view blacks as people possessing emotions, sensitivities, and aspirations like everyone else: "He thinks they are nobody and ought never to be anybody."[59]

The attitudes and behavior of the Union soldiers varied considerably, ranging from condescension to outright brutality. That made the Yankees no different in the eyes of many slaves than their own masters and mistresses. Despite the uncertainties that awaited them, the movement of slaves toward the Union lines that had begun in the early months of the war continued unabated, with growing numbers now running away with Yankee raiding parties, or following Union troops when they passed through the vicinity, or seeking out the Union gunboats plying the southern rivers. The exodus reached such proportions in some regions that it took on all the drama and tragedy of the most classic wartime refugee scenes. When Sherman's army moved through Georgia and the Carolinas, tens of thousands of slaves tried desperately to keep up with the marching columns, many of them carrying their household goods and children, fighting off hunger, exhaustion, exposure, harassment, and the efforts of Union officers to drive them off. "[W]e only wanted the able-bodied men (and to tell you the truth the youngest and best looking women)," one officer wrote. "Sometimes we took off whole families and plantations of niggers, by way of repaying some influential secessionist. But the useless part of these we soon manage to lose—sometimes in crossing rivers—sometimes in other ways." This letter, allegedly found in the streets of Camden after the Yankees departed, may have been fabricated by Confederate propagandists but other evidence suggests little distortion of what took place on Sherman's march. Numbers of slaves were left behind on the roads and at the river crossings, where they subsequently fell prey to General Wheeler's Confederate raiders, and some drowned while attempting to cross the rivers. "The waters of the Ogeechee and Ebenezer Creek," one of Sherman's officers wrote, "can account for hundreds who were blocking up our columns, and there abandoned. . . . Many of them died in the bayous and lagoons of Georgia." The terrible plight of the Georgia refugees moved a young Boston teacher to observe that "freedom means death to many."[60]

Exulting over the mass desertion of slaves to the Union Army, a black newspaper in New Orleans proclaimed, "History furnishes no such intensity of determination, on the part of any race, as that exhibited by these people to be free." But historical comparisons immediately came to mind, and abolitionist-minded northern whites and black leaders made the most of them. This "vast hegira" of slaves, they agreed, resembled the movement of the Israelites out of Egypt and to the Promised Land. The differences, however, seemed almost as striking. "There was no plan in this exodus, no Moses to lead it," observed a Union officer who had been entrusted with the supervision of over 20,000 black refugees in the Mississippi Valley. Nor did it appear to have a Promised Land. By the time they reached the Union camps, the refugees were exhausted, half starved, frightened, and sick. It was not uncommon for malnutrition and pulmonary disease to claim the lives of three or four blacks every day in the hastily constructed and congested contraband villages. "The poor Negroes die as fast as ever," a missionary teacher reported. "The children are all emaciated to the last degree and have such violent coughs and dysenteries that few survive."[61]

The number of slaves entering the Union lines provoked considerable dismay among commanding officers who found their camps overrun and the movement of their troops impeded. "What shall I do with my niggers?" asked one beleaguered commander, while another complained that he had more blacks in his camp than whites and no rations to feed them. What to do with these slaves proved to be a formidable problem that would never be satisfactorily resolved. The most immediate solution took the form of the contraband camps in which slaves were put to work as government laborers, paid wages, fed on army rations, and clothed by philanthropic agencies. The camps soon became overcrowded, disease took a heavy toll, the promised wages were often not paid, and many slaves came to feel they had been defrauded.

> Dey said that we, de able-body men, was to get $8 a month, an' de women, $4 and de ration; only we was to allow $1 de month to help de poor an' de old—which we don't 'gret—an' one dollar for de sick ones, an' den

anudder dollar for *Gen'l Purposes.* We don't zactly know who dat Gen'l
is, but 'pears like dar was a heap o' dem Gen'ls, an' it takes all dar is to
pay 'em, 'cause we don't get nuffins.

That was only a precursor of the problems that would beset Federal policy
toward the "contrabands." By the end of the war, with more than a million
ex-slaves under some form of Federal custody, the initial confusion regarding their status, disposition, and future remained unresolved, thereby frustrating anything approaching a genuine social reconstruction.[62]

What might have induced so many slaves to leave the relative security
of the farm and plantation for the uncertainty of the Union Army and the
contraband camps deeply troubled some slaveholding families. The most
convenient explanation was that the Yankees forcibly removed them, and
there were sufficient examples to warrant such a charge; some slaves, on
the other hand, were thrown off the plantations by their owners, particularly the women and children of men who had run off or had enlisted in
the Union Army. After the way the Yankees had stripped the plantations
bare, some masters also pleaded poverty, claiming they simply could not
feed or support the blacks. Recognizing this, numerous slaves had already
left, deciding they might fare better on army rations. But most whites
suspected that the prospect of immediate freedom, and the fear of losing
it if they remained, induced many of their slaves to follow the Yankees.
"Generally when told to run away from the soldiers, they go right to them,"
Kate Stone observed in Louisiana, "and I cannot say I blame them." More
ominously, a Louisiana planter, after watching the slaves in his neighborhood for a week, thought many of them decided to leave with the Yankees
because they feared retaliation for the outrages they had committed and
they had heard that "the 'rebel' soldiers were coming on down and killing
negroes as they came." That may also help to explain why some slaves
balked at Yankee questions about the names of their owners.[63]

The decision to desert their "home," locale, and "white folks," however, did not always come easily. Every slave would have to determine his
own priorities. Near Milledgeville, Georgia, in the path of Sherman's
march, a staff officer came upon a scene that could have been enacted
almost anywhere the Union soldiers appeared. In a hut he found a slave
couple, both of them more than sixty years old. Nothing they said to him
suggested that they were displeased with their situation; if anything, like
many of the elderly slaves he had encountered, they were content to spend
their remaining years in the service and care of those who had exploited
them for a lifetime of labor. But as the troops prepared to move on, the
woman suddenly stood up, and a "fierce, almost devilish" look came across
a face that only minutes before had been almost devoid of expression.
"What for you sit dar?" she asked, pointing her finger at the old man
crouched in the corner of the fireplace. "You s'pose I wait sixty years for
nutten? Don't yer see de door open? I'se follow my child; I not stay. Yes,
anudder day I goes 'long wid dese people; yes, sar, I walks till I drop in my

tracks." Only a Rembrandt, the officer later wrote, could have done justice to this scene. "A more terrible sight I never beheld."[64]

If the Civil War initially drew some masters and slaves closer together, with both now sharing privations and suffering, the approach of the Union Army underscored the ambiguous nature of that relationship and forced the master to reevaluate not only individual slaves in whom he had placed his confidence but the entire system of racial subordination. Both sides in the war had an obvious stake in how the slaves responded to the Yankees. The faithful black reinforced the conviction that the great mass of slaves (there had always been some "bad niggers") were perfectly content and had no real wish to alter their status; the fidelity and steadiness demonstrated by the slaves, a North Carolinian argued, "speaks not only well for themselves but well for their training and the system under which they lived." Union propagandists and abolitionists, on the other hand, viewed the exodus of slaves to and with the Union Army as an oppressed and brutalized population welcoming its release from bondage. In that spirit, a Union reporter wrote of a recent victory:

> The moment our forces defeated the enemy at Labadieville, hundreds of negroes, besotted by the most severe system of Slavery, were in a moment left to themselves, and in a delirium of excitement, they first threw themselves in an ecstacy of joy, on their knees, and "bressed God that Massa Linkum had come," and then, as semi-civilized people would naturally do, they commenced indulging in all sorts of excesses, the first fruits of their unrestricted liberty.[65]

That captured the public mood in the North perfectly, indicting the enemy (slaveholders) while at the same time explaining black excesses in ways that reinforced prevailing racial beliefs and suggested the need for some form of continued racial control.

Caught between these polar positions were the slaves themselves, many of whom were sufficiently familiar with the expectations of white people to frame an appropriate response.

## 5

THE EXPERIENCE of Wilmer Shields, who managed several plantations in Louisiana in the absence of the owner, suggests only the magnitude of the problem that thousands of masters and overseers had to confront when Union soldiers passed through the vicinity. "You can form no idea of my situation and the anxiety of my mind," he informed his employer on December 11, 1863. "All is anarchy and confusion here—everything going to destruction—and the negroes on the plantation insubordinate—My life has been several times in danger." Several weeks later, Shields confessed that he felt powerless to deal with "the outrageous conduct of the Negroes who will not work for love or money—but who steal every thing they can lay their hands on." Although he offered to pay them for their labor, those who continued to work did so at their own pace; they reported to the fields in the late morning, picked a little cotton, and then returned to the quarters to cook the hogs and beef they had killed that day. "You have no idea of the mental agony I endure under this state of affairs," Shields repeated, in still another dismal report to the absentee owner. "Neither life, liberty, or property is valued a pin here—bands of thieves stroll about the country plundering in every direction—and I have not been allowed a single weapon for self defense—I know not at what moment my time may come."

When the local Union commander backed Shields's authority "to make the people work," conditions improved perceptibly, but the officer's departure prompted a return to the earlier manifestations of disaffection. "Let me again repeat," Shields advised the owner, "that but very very few are faithful—Some of those who remain are worse than those who have gone—And I think that all *who are able* will leave as soon as the warm weather sets in—in no other way can I account for their present course of conduct for they will not even gather food for themselves." Like the field hands, most of the house servants left when they pleased and did little when they remained. "I do not miss her," Shields said of a departed servant, "for she had long since ceased to attend to her duties here. . . . When all leave me, if they do, I will be compelled to hire one or two, and they if possible shall be White servants."

After the war, a disillusioned Shields compiled for his employer a list of the ex-slaves who remained on the plantations, and he affixed next to each name a mark denoting his evaluation of their wartime conduct and dependability. Of the 146 adult slaves on four plantations, 16 had been "perfectly faithful," 30 had "done well *comparatively,*" and the other 100 had "behaved *badly;* many of them Outrageously." Nearly every slave on this list, Shields noted, had absented himself from the plantation at some time and then returned, "some of them half a dozen times." So grateful was he to those few who had remained "perfectly faithful" that he now urged his employer to present medals to four of them, with some "appropriate" inscription testifying to their loyalty. "The Medals coming from me," he explained, "would be but little valued, from you greatly." More than eighteen months after the war, Shields remained obsessed with how the slaves had behaved during that crisis, and he was perfectly willing to use it as a standard by which to judge the blacks under his supervision. When his employer instructed him to give five dollars to one of the freedmen, Shields retorted: "Robin was always one of my favorites, and I have ever thought him honest, but it is a question whether he was faithful to you or me—True he did not betray or *rob* us, as a great many others did, but *he* deserted us in two or three weeks after the Federal occupation of Natchez—for gain —instead of remaining here, as Ellen and Frank, and two or three others did, assisting me in protecting and saving the place and property. . . . This was fidelity."[66]

What transpired on the plantations managed by Wilmer Shields would be repeated on countless places lying in the path of the Union Army. Far more than any Federal proclamation, the slaves themselves undermined the authority of the planter class. In Mississippi and Louisiana, for example, the many reports of slave "demoralization" and "defection" came close to suggesting a coordinated withdrawal of labor and efficiency. When a large Union force passed through the Bayou Lafourche region in late 1862, A. Franklin Pugh, the part owner and manager of four sugar plantations, first noted "great excitement" among the slaves; the next day, he found them "in a very bad way"; two days later, they were "completely demoralized," some of them leaving and more preparing to depart. "I fear we shall lose them all. They go off in carts." Before the week had ended, one of his plantations had been virtually "cleaned out," with many of the slaves fleeing at night, and conditions steadily deteriorated at the other places. In what Pugh perceived as "a rebellion," the slaves on a neighboring plantation overpowered their master and overseer, tied them up, and tried to remove them to a nearby town. Elsewhere in the rich plantation parishes, slaves refused to work without pay (or for worthless Confederate currency) and were generally found to be "demoralized," "refractory," and "in a state of mutiny"—that is, if they remained at all. "The negroes have all left their owners in this parish," a planter's son reported from Bayou Plaquemine. "Some planters have not even one servant left. Our wives and daughters have to take the pot and tubs; the men, where there are any, take to the fields with the plough and hoe."[67]

When Union forces in 1863 undertook an expedition into central and northern Louisiana, the news of their approach reportedly "turned the negroes crazy." Not only did the slaves refuse to work, John H. Ransdell informed an absentee owner, but "they became utterly demoralized at once and everything like subordination and restraint was at an end." The slaves who did not flee with the Yankees, he observed, "remained at home to do *much worse.*" For nearly a week, Ransdell, like other planter families in Rapides Parish, had to stand by helplessly (usually secluded in their homes) while the blacks engaged in "a perfect jubilee." Some planters lost "nearly every movable thing," as the slaves destroyed property, killed much of the livestock, and emptied the storerooms. "Confound them," Ransdell wrote the governor of Louisiana, who owned the neighboring plantation, "they deserve to be half starved and to be worked nearly to death for the way they have acted. . . . The recent trying scenes through which we have passed have convinced me that *no dependence is to be placed on the negro*—and that they are the greatest hypocrites and liars that God ever made." After enumerating his "considerable" losses, however, he thought them "*nothing in comparison to those of the planters below us*—and we really have great cause of thankfulness that we came off so well."[68]

The heavy concentrations of slaves in parts of Louisiana and Mississippi help to account for the extent of the "demoralization"—that popular term used by whites to describe the disaffection of enslaved black workers. Even some ardent defenders of the "peculiar institution" might have agreed that slavery worked its greatest excesses in these regions and made the most impossible demands on black laborers. Not surprisingly, then, the brutalizing nature of the labor system in the Deep South supposedly made for a more volatile situation than elsewhere, and slaveholders were now reaping the consequences of years of abuse. Perhaps, too, the recalcitrant slaves who had been sold here from the more "benign" slaveholding states provided leadership or in some way influenced those who had known no other kind of bondage.

The problem with such explanations is that the excesses of bondage in the Deep South might have conceivably yielded some different results. As a number of fugitive slaves argued, the labor system in the Louisiana sugar parishes was calculated to produce the most docile, abject, obsequious, and degraded bondsmen, totally lacking in hope. If any system might have been expected to produce a crop of model Sambos, it should have been this one. But the reaction of these slaves at the approach of the Union Army, and the testimony of Louisiana and Mississippi planters, suggest that a people apparently broken in body and spirit had even more reason to contemplate the benefits of freedom and to hasten their liberation.

Every plantation, every farm, every town no doubt had its own version of how the slaves behaved. Until the Union Army made its presence felt, plantation life tended to remain relatively stable, crops were made, and most slaves went about their daily tasks. The Emancipation Proclamation by itself did little to alter this situation, with most slaves preferring to wait for a more propitious moment. But news that Yankee soldiers were somewhere within reach precipitated the rapid depopulation of the slave quarters, often without the slightest warning. "They have shown no signs of insubordination," one observer noted. "Down to the last moment they cut their maize and eat their corn-cake with their old docility—then they suddenly disappear." The experience of John H. Bills, the Tennessee planter, resembled that of his Mississippi neighbors and illustrated a pattern of slave response that crippled the labor system in substantial portions of the occupied South. With the appearance of the Yankees, the restlessness and reluctance to work he had observed during the past several months suddenly flared into "wild confusion" and "a general stampede." In less than six weeks, more than twenty slaves left him (he estimated his loss at nearly $22,000), and those who remained might as well have gone, "they being totally demoralized & ungovernable." Like the field hands, the servants worked erratically if at all: "the females have quit entirely or nearly so, four of the men come & go when & where they please. . . . I talk to them Earnestly but fear it will do no good." Some six months later, "a wretched state of idleness" prevailed, and Bills found himself unable to exert any control. After still another six months, he conceded that slavery on his plantations was "about played out."[69]

The epidemic of "demoralization" and "desertion" varied little from state to state (except for those regions untouched by the Union Army), nor did it make any perceptible distinctions between reputedly "cruel" and "benign" masters. When the Yankees approached her Georgia residence, Mary Jones might have wondered whether the many years of solicitude and concern with which the family had treated the slaves would now be sufficient to meet the test. Before his death in 1863, her husband—the Reverend C. C. Jones—had devoted much of his life to the spiritual uplift of the slaves. Upon the arrival of the troops, however, the slaves belonging to Mary Jones, and those in the immediate vicinity, exhibited a range of behavior that left her bewildered, hurt, and angry. "The people are all idle on the plantations, most of them seeking their own pleasure." Although relatively few of her slaves had yet defected, Mary Jones was sufficiently dismayed by the behavior of some of those who remained to wonder if she would not be better off if they left. "Their condition is one of perfect anarchy and rebellion. They have placed themselves in perfect antagonism to their owners and to all government and control. We dare not predict the end of all this, if the Lord in mercy does not restrain the hearts and wills of this deluded people. They are certainly prepared for any measures."[70]

# 6

AFTER ONLY A BRIEF FLIRTATION with "freedom," some slaves drifted back to the plantations and farms from which they had fled. On a number of places, nearly every slave left at some point during the war, not necessarily together, but most of them returned within several weeks or months. "Father had eighty five negroes gone for a while," the son of a Louisiana planter reported, "but about twenty have returned since." Nor was it uncommon for slaves to return only to leave again. Homesickness, the families they had left behind, and disillusionment with the empty content of their freedom, compounded still further by near starvation and exhaustion, drove many back to the relative security of the plantation. The Yankees "didn't show no respec' for his feelin's," a Georgia slave explained, and he voiced the discouragement of many who had sought refuge in the Federal camps only to be subjected to hard work and personal abuse.[71]

Once having left the plantation and tasted even a semblance of freedom, the blacks who returned often behaved in a way that caused their owners considerable anxiety. On a Louisiana plantation, Mary C. R. Hardison complained that the servants heaped abusive language on her and did everything but strike her; the "leader" was thought to be a young black who had recently returned to the plantation declaring he had had enough of the Yankees. John H. Bills, the Tennessee planter, came to regret his decision to re-admit "My Woman Emmeline" after her brief stay in a Federal camp where her husband had died. Upon her return, the woman acted "verry Contrary," refused to obey his commands, and threatened to "jump off the Waggon" if he tried to return her to the Yankees. "I feel that my desire to oblige has gotten me into trouble," Bills concluded from this experience. Perceiving the changed demeanor of the returnees, or unwilling to forgive them for having once deserted, some masters simply refused to permit them back on the plantation or else kept them under constant scrutiny. "Jane returned to Arcadia," a Georgia woman noted, "but as she has been to Savannah and returned before, I fear she may have come to steal." Even more galling for masters were slaves like James Woodson, who returned to Fluvanna County, Virginia, with a detachment of Union troops, led them to the place where the valuables had been hidden, and then stood by while the Yankees whipped his ex-owner. That display of "insolence" was exceeded only by the former slaves who returned to the old plantation not *with* but *as* Union soldiers.[72]

After what many planters had experienced, the number of slave defections seemed less important than the behavior of those who remained. More often than most whites wished to believe or to concede publicly, the "demoralization" (as they preferred to call it) of the slave population took a violent and destructive bent. The victims of such depredations took little comfort in the ready explanation that these were exceptional cases. Nor was their anguish necessarily mitigated by the popular view that only the Yankees could have instigated the blacks to behave so outrageously. If only the slaves had been left alone, Henry W. Ravenel kept telling himself, they would have obeyed their natural instincts and remained "a quiet, contented, & happy people." But Ravenel, a native of South Carolina, should have known better. The sacking of nearby Beaufort, early in the war, illustrated the capacity of the slaves for destructive activity in the days *preceding* the arrival of Union troops. (Local planters had already set an example by trying to burn down the cotton barns before their hasty departure.) If slaves in the Sea Islands region usually refrained from destroying the plantations on which they lived, the many who poured into Beaufort had little compunction about occupying and ransacking the stately town houses of well-to-do planters. When one planter momentarily returned to his home, he found a slave seated at the piano "playing away like the very Devil" and two young black women upstairs "dancing away famously"; he also discovered that many neighboring houses had been "completely turned upside down and inside out" and the local churches had been vandalized. When a Union landing party finally came ashore, they were startled by the extent of the devastation.

> We went through spacious houses where only a week ago families were living in luxury, and saw their costly furniture despoiled; books and papers smashed; pianos on the sidewalk, feather beds ripped open, and even the filth of the Negroes left lying in parlors and bedchambers.

Much of the destruction, one reporter suggested, could not be defined as "plunder" but only as a "malicious love of mischief gratified." When news of the sacking reached the North, Henry M. Turner, an outspoken black clergyman, was equally startled; in fact, he refused to believe the "ridiculous, outrageous, and cannibalistic reports" of slave excesses. Having been a resident of South Carolina for more than twenty years of his life, he could attest to the fact that "there are no class of colored people south of Mason and Dixon's line, where more sound sense, morality, religion, and refined taste, prevails, than in Beaufort." The slaves themselves said little about the fury they had unleashed on some of the more imposing symbols of the slaveholding aristocracy. Nor did they apparently deem an explanation necessary.[73]

Although the extent of slave "pillaging" in the South was sometimes exaggerated, or confused with Yankee depredations, that any should have occurred aroused consternation. "The Moorfield negroes are crazy quite," a South Carolinian wrote; "they have been to Pinopolis, helping in the sacking of the houses." In some areas, the slaves singled out the popular summer retreats for wealthy planters, where the quality of the furnishings provided sufficient temptation. Where white families had abandoned their homes, the slaves in many instances preferred occupation to pillage, moving from their own cramped quarters into the more commodious and comfortable lodgings which they had previously envied from a distance; the slaves who flocked into the towns from the outlying plantations, seeking the protection of Federal authority and a more congenial atmosphere in which to spend their first days of freedom, found an instant answer to their housing problem by occupying the elegant town houses of absent owners. To sleep in the master's bed and eat at the dining-room table with the family silver and china was a novel and exhilarating experience. "Mamma's house is occupied by *freedmen,* cooking in every room," reported a South Carolina woman who had only recently heard from a friend in a nearby town that "all the houses around them are occupied by negroes." Already in shock over the apparent collapse of the social order, native whites now listened to reports that slaves were using the baronial town houses to give "Negro balls" and dinner parties. "The whites [presumably Yankees] and blacks danced together," a friend wrote Adele Allston of a recent "ball" in Georgetown, South Carolina.[74]

Where would it all end? The events of the past several weeks, Henry W. Ravenel confided to his diary, reminded him of the horrors of the French Revolution. "White man is nigger—and nigger is white man" was the way another South Carolinian chose to describe "the state of things." Whether in the towns or in the countryside, the welcome accorded the Union troops by many slaves had not been confined to prayers and singing but had included as well the expropriation of nearly everything belonging to their masters and mistresses that could be moved. With a feeling of utter helplessness, Amanda Stone's family, after abandoning the family home in Louisiana, heard how the slaves had quarreled over the division of clothes and how the house had been stripped of furniture, carpets, books, the piano, "and everything else." Nor did the presence of the white family necessarily restrain the slaves. "The Negroes as soon as they heard the guns," a rice planter in South Carolina reported, "rushed to my house and pillaged it of many things and principally wearing apparel"; he felt certain that the entire affair had been "pre-arranged."[75]

For the masters, what proved most difficult to accept was the gratification some slaves derived from these attacks on property. "Many of them," John H. Bills thought, "do all they can to have us destroyed & delight in seeing the work of destruction." Upon returning to their plantation home, the Allston family suddenly understood the overseer's report that their slaves had "behaved Verry badly."

> We looked at the house; it was a wreck,—the front steps gone, not a door nor shutter left, and not a sash. They had torn out all the mahogany framework around the doors and windows—there were mahogany panels below the windows and above the doors there were panels painted—the mahogany banisters to the staircase going upstairs; everything that could be torn away was gone.... It was a scene of destruction, and papa's study, where he kept all his accounts and papers, as he had done from the time he began planting as a young man, was almost waistdeep in torn letters and papers.[76]

The systematic nature of much of the black pillaging suggests that it was frequently neither indiscriminate nor simply a matter of gratified revenge but rather an opportunity to supplement their meager diets and wardrobes and improve their standard of living. Why they killed the livestock, emptied the meat houses and storerooms, and expropriated the liquors and wines would seem sufficiently obvious. The furniture and materials removed from the Big House were often used to make their own cabins more habitable. One South Carolina slave explained that after the master departed, they stripped boards from his house in order to floor their own cabins and put in lofts. Similarly, when the slaves broke into closets, bureaus, trunks, and desks, ripped open the bedding, or scattered the master's private papers, they were frequently seeking money, jewelry, or silverware that might be traded for needed commodities. When the slaves seized the mules, horses, and wagons, it was often with the idea of making their escape from the plantation, taking with them whatever the carts could carry. On A. F. Pugh's plantation, an enterprising former slave accumulated a cartload of articles from several neighboring plantations and bartered them with other blacks in the vicinity; the overseer was powerless to stop this apparently flourishing business based on loot.[77]

What the whites defined as theft might be viewed by the slaves as long-overdue payments for past services. Adele Allston conceded almost as much when she wrote her son about the destruction visited upon their Chicora Wood plantation. "The conduct of the negroes in robbing our house, store room meat house etc and refusing to restore anything shows you they think it right to steal from us, to spoil us, as the Israelites did the Egyptians." The slaves simply suggested that the question of theft be placed in its proper perspective, like the old Gullah preacher who asked his congregation, "Ef buckra neber tief, how come nigger yer?" That the constraints of slave life had made "thieves" of them some slaves readily conceded, though always stressing the conditions that had made this necessary. "We work so hard and get nothing for our labor but jes our 'lowance, we 'bleege to steal," a South Carolina slave explained in 1863, "and den we must keep from dem ebery ting or dey suffer us too much. But dey take all our labor, and steal our chil'ren, and we only take dare chicken." To attempt to reason with a slave on this sensitive matter could be an exasperating, if sometimes illuminating experience for a white. In Tennessee, a slave rode into a Union camp on a horse he had taken from his owner. Upon being questioned, presumably by a Union soldier or reporter, the slave insisted only that the usual notions of morality had little relevance to his action.

> "Don't you think you did very wrong, Dick, to take your mistress' horse?"
> "Well, I do' know, sah; I didn't take the bes' one. She had three; two of 'em fuss-rate hosses, but the one I took is ole, an' not berry fast, an' I offe'd to sell him fo' eight dolla's, sah."
> "But, Dick, you took at least a thousand dollars from your mistress, besides the horse."
> "How, sah?"
> "Why, *you* were worth a thousand dollars, and you should have been satisfied with that much, without taking the poor woman's horse," said I, gravely.
> The contraband scratched his woolly head, rolled up his eyes at me, and replied with emphasis.
> *"I don't look at it jis dat way, massa.* I wo'ked ha'd fo' missus mor'n thirty yea's, an' I reckon in dat time I 'bout pay fo' meself. An' dis yea' missus guv me leave to raise a patch o' 'baccy fo' my own. Well, I wo'ked nights, an' Sabbaths, an' spar' times, an' raised a big patch (way prices is, wuff two hun'red dolla's, I reckon) o' 'baccy; an' when I got it tooken car' of dis fall, ole missus took it 'way from me; give some to de neighbors; keep some fo' he' own use; an' sell some, an' keep de money, an' I reckon dat pay fo' de ole hoss!"
> Failing to find any conscience in the darkey, I gave up the argument.[78]

Even where slaves refrained from expropriating and destroying property, they often behaved in ways that troubled and infuriated their masters and mistresses. The decision of a slave to remain on the plantation was no guarantee of his fidelity or steady labor. The Reverend Samuel A. Agnew, a Mississippi slaveholder, understood that all too well. "Some of our negroes will not go to the Yankees," he thought, "but they may all prove faithless." For many slave owners, as for Agnew, the ability to retain the bulk of their blacks proved to be no cause for self-congratulation. Despite the concern voiced over the "stampede" of the slaves, some white families might have found reasons to be grateful, if only because they avoided the anguish experienced by so many of their neighbors.

> Oh! deliver me from the "citizens of African descent." I am disgusted forever with the whole race. I have not faith in one single dark individual. They are all alike ungrateful and treacherous—every servant is a spy upon us, & everything we do or say is reported to the Yankees. They know everything.[79]

# 7

THE TERMS with which slave-owning families described the conduct of their blacks—"insolence," "impertinence," "impudence," and "ingratitude"—had been used often and indiscriminately to denote slave transgressions or departures from expected behavior. Once the Yankees arrived, masters and mistresses detected examples of such behavior almost everywhere—in the defection of the favorites, in the demeanor and language of the slaves who remained, in their refusal to submit to punishment, in their failure to obey orders promptly (or at all), and, most frequently, in their unwillingness to work "as usual." To a Louisiana planter, traveling from Ascension Parish to New Orleans in mid-1863, the slaves he observed along the way were nearly all "insolent & idle," which he defined as "working not more than half a day, yet demanding full rations of every thing." To the wife of a prominent Alabama planter, the slaves behaved in "an insolent manner" by taking off whenever there was work to be done. "The negroes are worse than free," she informed her son. "They say they *are* free. We cannot exert any authority. I beg ours to do what little is to be done." To a Virginia white woman, the blacks were acting "very independent and impudent," and like most whites she equated the two traits. To slave owners everywhere, the defections were difficult enough to understand but the ways in which some slaves chose to depart invariably provoked the most grievous charge of all—"ingratitude." Few stated it more succinctly than Emily C. Douglas, a resident of Natchez who had earlier extolled the loyalty of her slaves: "They left without even a good-bye."[80]

The "delirium of excitement" set off by the arrival of the Yankees gave scores of slaves a much-welcomed respite from their usual labors and momentarily paralyzed agricultural operations. That was the day, a former Florida slave remembered, when they dropped their plows and hoes, rushed to their cabins, put on their best clothes, and went into town to join with other slaves in a "joyous and un-forgettable occasion." If the slaves did not stop work altogether, they often slowed down the pace and made only sporadic appearances in the fields, "going, coming, and working when they please and as they please," sometimes spending the day in their cabins, sometimes venturing into town for a week at a time. The attempts to make a crop under these conditions were futile. On the Magnolia plantation in Louisiana, the overseer first complained that the slaves were "very slow getting out"; three weeks later, "the ring of the Bell no longer a delightful sound," and the slaves were "moving very slowly"; more than a month later, in utter exasperation, he could only *"wish every negro would leave the place* as they will do only what pleases them, go out in the morning when it suits them, come in when they please, etc." The erratic performance of the slaves even dismayed some northern observers, who wondered if this augured trouble for a free labor system. The Negroes' idea of freedom, an alarmed Union reporter observed, "is that of unrestrained license to do as they please, and go where they choose." The slaves might well have agreed, after having watched their masters and other whites for so many years interpret freedom in precisely that manner.[81]

To mark their release from bondage, blacks not only withheld their labor but in some instances vented their frustrations and bitterness on the most glaring and accessible symbols of their past labor—the Big House, which they might pillage; the cotton gin, which they might deliberately destroy; the slave pens and cotton houses, which in some cases were converted into freedmen schools and churches; and the overseer, who often represented the sole authority left on a plantation and who had come to personify the excesses of bondage. Many overseers clearly deserved their reputation for cruelty; nevertheless, the discipline they enforced, the punishments they meted out, and the labor they exacted from the slaves almost always reflected their need to meet the expectations of their employers. Rather than share the responsibility for any excesses that might result from his often inordinate demands, the planter all too readily permitted his overseer to assume the blame; indeed, the owner might even intercede at times to soften the overseer's punishments, thereby enhancing his own sense of paternalism and "humanity" while reinforcing the image of the overseer as an uncaring brute.[82]

Neither the slaves nor the overseers were necessarily oblivious to this kind of deception, but the flight of the masters often left the overseer by himself to absorb the slaves' wrath. Regardless of what whites remained on the plantation, the coming of the Yankees encouraged slaves to act as though there were alternatives in their lives: if they chose not to desert, they might simply refuse to submit to the usual discipline and punishments. On the C. C. Clay plantation in Alabama, the slaves had become "so bold," the mistress informed her son, that they threatened to kill the overseer if he tried to punish them for disobedience. That these were not empty threats is borne out by what took place on the Millaudon plantation in Louisiana, where "bad feelings" between the overseer and the slaves had prompted the absentee owner to pay a visit to his place. When Millaudon tried to reprimand the "ringleader," the slave responded "with insolence." Unaccustomed to such conduct, the planter then struck him with a whip. This time the slave responded by furiously charging Millaudon, who finally felled him with a stick. "This seemed to bring the negro to his senses, and

he took refuge in his cabin; but he presently came out with a hatchet . . ."
One of the other slaves interceded at this point and grabbed the hatchet,
the rebellious slave fled into the cane field, and Millaudon departed from
the plantation, thinking he had suppressed "the affair." He had not gone
far, however, before the report reached him that his slaves were now "in
full revolt" and had killed the overseer. Returning once again to the plantation, this time with Union soldiers, Millaudon beheld an extraordinary
scene: a large number of his blacks, with their possessions and quantities
of plantation goods, were walking alongside a cart on which lay the body
of the murdered overseer, wrapped in a flag. "It appears that he had been
attacked by five of them while he was at dinner, his head being split open
by blows with a hatchet, and penetrated by shots at his face." The "assas-
sins" reportedly "rejoiced" over their success, and "the whole gang" of
some 150 slaves had left the plantation.[83]

Anticipating acts of vengeance, some overseers fled shortly before the
Yankees reached their plantations. Those who remained were apt to find
themselves in an uncertain and often perilous situation. If the slaves did
not drive the overseer forcibly off the plantation, they conducted themselves in ways that undermined his authority and left him powerless. On
the Nightingale Hall plantation, one of several rice plantations in South
Carolina owned by Adele Allston, the slaves imprisoned the overseer in his
own house. "Mr. Sweat, was a very good, quiet man, and had been liked by
all the negroes," Adele Allston's daughter wrote of him, "but in the intoxi-
cation of freedom their first exercise of it was to tell Mr. Sweat if he left
the house they would kill him, and they put a negro armed with a shotgun
to guard the house and see that he did not leave alive." Watching from his
window, the conscientious overseer kept a journal of the activities of the
blacks, hoping someday to hold them to account.[84]

Conditions were no different on the Allstons' Chicora Wood plantation,
where Jesse Belflowers, reputedly one of the most efficient overseers in the
South Carolina low country, had been in charge since 1842. Having been
compelled to surrender the barn keys to the slaves, he confessed to his
employer that the workers had become unmanageable. "I am not allowed
to say any [thing] a bout Work and have not been to the Barn for the last
five days. Jacob is the worst man on the Place, then comes in Scipio Jackey
Sawney & Paul." And in a "P.S." he added: "Most all of them have arms."
Although Adele Allston continued to support him, she wondered in the
aftermath of the war if Belflowers had not outlived his usefulness to the
plantation now that the blacks considered themselves to be free. "Belflowers is cowed by the violence of the negroes against him," she wrote to her
son, "and is *afraid* to speak openly. He is trying to curry favour. His own
morals are impaired by the revolution, and he always required *backing* as
your father expressed it. *You* must tell him what to *do* and *support* him
in carrying it out." This proved to be an accurate assessment. Belflowers
never really recovered from his wartime experience and he found it impossible to adapt himself to the post-emancipation changes. "[I]t Looks Verry

hard to Pull ones hat to a Negro," he conceded in April 1865. Within a year, he was dead—by natural causes. "He is one of our *true* friends," Adele Allston wrote when she learned he was seriously ill, "and a link connecting us with the past."[85]

Not surprisingly, the war and emancipation played upon and exacerbated white fears and fantasies that were as old as slavery itself. Despite the apprehensions they voiced, far fewer masters and mistresses were murdered and assaulted than expected to be. While hiding from the Yankees, Joseph LeConte encountered a fellow South Carolinian who lived from day to day in a state of terror, convinced that a neighbor's slave he had once flogged would now murder him. "We tried to reason with him and show him the absurdity of his fears," LeConte recalled, "but all in vain. He looked upon himself as a 'doomed man.' " Although the planter escaped the anticipated vengeance, the fears he had felt were neither unique nor groundless. Always eager for news from her beloved Charleston, Emma Holmes recoiled at the reported murder of "my old friend" William Allen, "who was chopped to pieces in his barn." Still other reports and rumors of murder and assault dominated the conversations of whites, including the ominous story of a planter who "narrowly escaped being murdered by two of his most trusty negroes." In a South Carolina community, the Union commander reported that whites were imploring him for protection from the blacks, "who were arming themselves and threatening the lives of their masters," and one slaveholder had requested protective custody "to save his life." In nearly all instances of slave violence against their owners, whites tended to blame the Yankees, as did Emma Holmes, for having aroused "the foulest demoniac passions of the negro, hitherto so peaceful and happy." At least, such explanations preserved whites from what would have otherwise been a most excruciating self-examination.[86]

Rather than murder their masters, some slaves preferred to expose them to the humiliations they had once meted out so freely. In Choctaw County, Mississippi, slaves administered several hundred lashes to Nat Best, a local planter; in nearby Madison County, two slaves, one of them disguised as a Union soldier, were reported to have "mercillesly whipped" an elderly white woman; and in Virginia, near Jamestown, the former slaves of a reputedly cruel master whipped him some twenty times to remind him of past punishments. When the Yankees arrived, a former Virginia slave recalled, the mistress on a neighboring plantation was whipping a housegirl. "The soldiers made the house girl strip the mistress, whip her, then dress in her clothes. She left with the soldiers." Young Sarah Morgan reacted with horror rather than skepticism to the reports from Baton Rouge, her home town, that blacks were stopping ladies on the street, cutting the necklaces from their necks, stripping the rings from their fingers, and subsequently bragging of these feats.[87]

That these proved to be exceptional and isolated examples made them no less sensational and ominous. Although most slave owners did not meet personal violence at the hands of their slaves, the persistent reports and rumors of murder, insubordination, insolence, and plunder sustained the threat and the genuine fear that black freedom might degenerate into insurrectionary violence. "We are afraid now to walk outside of the gate," a South Carolina woman confessed, after hearing that field hands in the immediate vicinity were "in a dreadful state." To listen to jubilant slaves welcome the Yankees by singing (to the tune of a Methodist hymn) "We'll hang Jeff Davis on the sour apple tree" may have been more of an irritation than an overt threat, but on the Magnolia plantation in Louisiana the slaves erected a gallows intended for their master. To achieve their freedom, the slaves on this plantation had come to believe, according to their master, that they must first hang him and expel the overseer. "[N]o one now can tell what a Day may bring Forth," the threatened master wrote, "we are all in a State of Great uneasiness." The gallows was never used, but that became less important than the vivid impression the sight made on the local populace, both whites and blacks.[88]

The activities of armed groups of slaves operating out of outlaw settlements helped to sustain the fears of insurrection. In some areas they concealed themselves in the swamps, cane brakes, and woods, periodically raiding nearby plantations and farms for provisions. Where planters had abandoned their homes, the slaves belonging to these and adjoining plantations would sometimes congregate to test their newly won freedom and to organize themselves into bands of marauders that roamed the countryside, seizing plantations and parceling out the land and terrorizing the white populace. Even after Union occupation, the threat posed by these outlaw gangs and communities persisted. Early in September 1865, a low-country planter in South Carolina informed the absentee owner of a neighboring plantation that it was "being rapidly filled up by vagabond negroes from all parts of the country who go there when they please and are fast destroying what you left of a settlement. They are thus become a perfect nuisance to the neighborhood and harbor for all the thieves and scamps who wont work."[89]

The point at which "insubordination" or "insolence" became "insurrection" was always somewhat obscure. Perhaps no real distinction existed in the white man's mind, except for the number of blacks involved. When the slaves on the David Pugh plantation in Louisiana took their master and overseer prisoners, that was called "a rebellion." When slaves on the nearby Woodland sugar estate refused to work without pay, that was termed "a state of munity [sic]." When a large group of slaves in low-country South Carolina indulged themselves in the wines and liquors obtained from the homes of former masters, they were perceived as laying the groundwork for "open insurrection at any time." And when a group of Louisiana slaves, "armed with clubs and cane knives," poured into New Orleans, a frightened white citizen wrote in his diary of "servile war" in parts of the city.[90]

If anything was calculated to revive the specter of black rebellion, it had to be the knowledge that substantial numbers of slaves now had access to weapons or were already in possession of them. "Molly tells me all of the men on our plantation have Enfield rifles," Mary Chesnut noted bitterly, and perhaps now the enemy will get that "long hoped for rising against former masters." To the shock of Henry W. Ravenel, blacks in a nearby town not only were armed but openly displayed their weapons and drilled, apparently modeling themselves after the black troops they had only recently observed. It became clear to Ravenel, as it eventually did to Union commanders, that some way would have to be found to deal with such an ominous situation. The "summary executions" of some of the leaders, Ravenel thought, had already had "a beneficial effect" and he suggested more of the same.[91]

Like the gallows the slaves in Louisiana had erected for their master, the terror and suspicions aroused by the fears of slave violence became more important than the actual number of incidents. The anticipated uprisings never materialized in New Orleans, Charleston, Wilmington, Lynchburg, and other localities where rumors to that effect had kept white residents in a constant state of anxiety and readiness. Nonetheless, the fears never seemed to subside, even after the much-dreaded day had passed without incident. "We are slumbering on a volcano," the newspaper in Wilmington editorialized. "[T]he general eruption is likely to occur at any time." The mere sight of unfamiliar blacks in the vicinity was enough to unsettle the local whites. "As we passed through our quarters," Kate Stone wrote, "there were numbers of strange Negro men standing around. They had gathered from the neighboring places. They did not say anything, but they looked at us and grinned and that terrified us more and more. It held such a promise of evil."[92]

Recognizing the unpredictability of black behavior, there was every reason for slaveholding families to be apprehensive. After the experiences some of them had endured, and the incredible scenes they had witnessed, they also came to be that much more appreciative of those slaves whose attachment to the family never seemed to waver. The "faithful few" stood out. That in itself had to be a frightening comment on the system the slave owners had so methodically erected.

8

---

ALTHOUGH WHITE SOUTHERNERS would weave heroic images and tales into the legend of the faithful slave, both exaggerating and simplifying his wartime behavior, they did not simply create him out of a vivid imagination or a troubled conscience. Such slaves existed in sufficient numbers to warrant the oratorical tributes and legislative resolutions of gratitude. Whether their loyalty rested on genuine attachment, habit, fear, or sheer opportunism usually defied detection. What mattered to whites was that they fulfilled the highest expectations of their masters and mistresses. The runaways, the pillagers, the insubordinate could be charged to subversive Yankee influences. How much more comforting and reassuring it was to recall those slaves who remained "faithful through everything," proving themselves "superior to temptations which might have shaken white people" and "shirking no debt of love and gratitude" to those who owned them. Risking even the hostility of their own people, the "faithful few," including those legendary white-haired "uncles" and devoted "mammies," tried to protect their "white folks," stood in the doorway of the Big House to block the entrance of the soldiers, refused to divulge where the valuables were hidden, and scolded the Yankees for their "insolence."[93] With one leg bandaged, and feigning lameness (to avoid conscription), the servant of Mary Kirkland advised his mistress to stand up, keep her children in her arms, and remain calm while the Yankees pillaged the house. He then imparted to her a valuable lesson he had learned as her slave: "Don't answer 'em back, Miss Mary. Let them say what they want to. Don't give 'em any chance to say you are impudent to 'em."[94]

To dissemble or "play dumb" had been effective ploys during slavery to mislead the master and obtain special advantages. The same kind of deception was now used by some slaves, particularly the house servants, to mislead the Yankees and protect the master and mistress. To save the family's silverware which he had secreted, an elderly slave on a South Carolina plantation tried to impress the Yankee soldiers with how much he hated his "white folks," even slapping the master's children to demonstrate his loyalty to the Union cause. (He was said to have "cried like a child afterwards because he 'had to hit Mas' Horace's children.' ") In Richmond, to preserve his mistress's house, a servant deceived the Yankees into thinking she was "a good Union woman." (Actually, the family was passionately pro-Confederate and had to be restrained from hanging the flag outside their window.) When asked about the location of the silver (which she had helped to hide), Hannah, a Mississippi house servant, told the Yankees it had all been sent "to Georgia or somewhyar a long time ago." ("The silver and plate had been in Hannah's charge for years," her mistress explained, "and she did not wish to see it go out of the family.") To thwart Yankee pillagers, Ida Adkins abandoned deception for direct action—she turned over the beehives: "Dey lit on dem blue coats an' every time dey lit dey stuck in a pizen sting. De Yankees forgot all about de meat an' things dey done stole; they took off down de road on a run." The grateful mistress rewarded her with a gold ring.[95]

When confronted with Yankee threats and insolence, the "faithful few" often stood their ground and defended the lives and property of their owners. Booker T. Washington would later try to explain such loyalty: "The slaves would give the Yankee soldiers food, drink, clothing—anything but that which had been specifically intrusted to their care and honour." Hoisted up by his two thumbs, a South Carolina slave still refused to divulge where he had hidden his master's money and gold watch. After her master had been taken prisoner, a loyal housegirl clung to the trunk filled with valuables, thereby earning for herself the highest possible praise a slave owner could bestow: "She's black outside, but she's white inside, shore!" Individual feats of heroism would become legendary, along with the tales of how the slaves pleaded with the Yankees not to burn the master's house and the ways in which they came to the defense of the white women. Even the most grateful white families might have found it difficult to fathom the quality of loyalty that could induce a young slave on a South Carolina plantation to save her mistress from rape by taking her place! That same kind of loyalty may have saved the life of John Williams, a Louisiana planter, whom the Yankees had ordered either to dance for them or to make his slaves dance.

> Dar he stood inside a big ring of dem mens in blue clothes, wid dey brass buttons shining in de light from de fire dey had in front of de tents, and he jest stood and said nothing, and it look lak he wasn't wanting to tell us to dance.
>
> So some of us young bucks jest step up and say we was good dancers, and we start shuffling while de rest of de niggers pat.
>
> Some nigger women go back to de quarters and git de gourd fiddles and de clapping bones made out'n beef ribs, and bring dem back so we could have some music. We git all warmed up and dance lak we never did dance befo'! I speck we invent some new steps dat night!

The slave performers appear to have satisfied the soldiers; more importantly, they felt they had saved their master from unnecessary humiliation and physical violence. "We act lak we dancing for de Yankees," one of the slaves later recalled, "but we trying to please Master and old Mistress more than anything, and purty soon he begin to smile a little and we all feel a lot better."[96]

The tales of slave heroism and sacrifice made the rounds of southern white society and no doubt cheered many a listener who had yet to face his moment of crisis. But the reassurances were at best ephemeral, and the doubtful remained doubtful. Unlike the popular toy Negro that danced minstrel-style when wound up, black men and women refused to conform to any predictable pattern of behavior. If they had, the white South might have felt less compelled to celebrate the feats of loyalty as though they were extraordinary and exceptional rather than what anyone should have expected of his slaves. "Such faithfulness among so faithful few deserves to be recorded," Emma Holmes wrote of a slave who had saved the valuables of the family to whom he belonged. What made the behavior of the "faithful few" so praiseworthy was the mounting evidence of desertion, disaffection, and "betrayal." "Five thousand negroes followed their Yankee brothers from the town and neighborhood," Sarah Morgan noted; "but ours remained." Mary Chesnut contrasted the exemplary conduct of her blacks with stories of recent outrages, and concluded that she had been among the fortunate.

They [her friends] talked of Negroes who flocked to the Yankees and showed them where the silver and valuables were hid by the white people; lady's maids dressing themselves in their mistress's gowns before their very faces and walking off. Before this, everyone has told me how kind and faithful and considerate the Negroes had been. I am sure, after hearing these tales, the fidelity of my own servants shines out brilliantly. I had taken it too much as a matter of course.[97]

From the outset of the war, the character of the slaves' affections for their "white folks" had been a common topic of conversation and speculation. With the steady advance of the Union Army, particularly after 1863, the conversations turned increasingly gloomy as the behavior of the slaves became increasingly inexplicable. Previous assumptions needed to be reexamined, and new answers were required for the old questions. What lay behind the professions of fidelity? What lurked beneath the slaves' apparent indifference? How genuine was their attachment to the master and his family? How far could they be trusted? The answers did not come easily. After observing the conduct of the slaves in his region, Henry W. Ravenel found two "exhibitions of character" he had never anticipated. On many plantations "where there was really kind treatment & mutual attachment," the coming of the Yankees suddenly snapped the old ties. At the same time, numerous slaves resisted the temptations placed before them and remained, in his view, docile and submissive. With the blacks exhibiting such contradictory tendencies, Ravenel seemed to suggest the utter impossibility of calculating their loyalty.[98]

The "defections" were bad enough. But the "betrayals" within the plantation and Big House proved even more troubling, in part because they were more brazen, might be committed in the presence of the white family, and often involved the most trusted blacks. Even on the places where most slaves remained loyal, the fact that only one did not might spell the difference between a family keeping or losing its most valuable possessions. "All of our servants remained faithful except the cook," a North Carolina woman wrote, but it was the cook who told the Union soldiers where the meat was hidden. On the plantation of Joseph Howell, the Yankees held "a court of inquiry," questioned each slave individually about the location of the master's valuables, and then went directly to the spot where they had been hidden. "Must have been a Judas 'mongst us," recalled Henry D. Jenkins, who had been a slave there.[99]

For the white families, as they came to understand more fully the explosive potential of each of their slaves, such experiences were both bewildering and humiliating. How were the stalwart defenders of the "peculiar institution" to evaluate the behavior of those "petted and trusted" slaves in Virginia who burned the overseer's house and deserted their aged, bedridden mistress after stripping the woman of her clothing? No less perplexed had to be the Confederate officer in South Carolina, the owner of several plantations, who found himself a prisoner of his own slaves, the very same slaves whose virtues and fidelity he had only recently praised. Manifesting their delight over this turnabout, they even improvised some verses while taking him to the nearest Union camp.

> *O Massa a rebel, we row him to prison.*
> *Hallelujah.*
> *Massa no whip us any more.*
> *Hallelujah.*
> *We have no massa, now; we free.*
> *Hallelujah.*
> *We have the Yankees, who no run away.*
> *Hallelujah.*
> *O! all our old massas run away.*
> *Hallelujah.*
> *O! massa going to prison now.*
> *Hallelujah.*

Stories such as these confirmed the increasingly gloomy talk about the fragile nature of the black man's affections for his "white folks." Were these truly the same individuals they had known so intimately as slaves, who had assured them of their loyalty, who had repeatedly denied any desire to be free? Little wonder that some whites simply threw up their hands in utter disgust over such examples of ingratitude and treachery. "Those their masters had put most confidence in," a Virginia woman wrote, had revealed everything to the Yankees; the soldiers located pistols, guns, and uniforms in a secret place "that no one but the servants knew anything about. I am beginning to lose confidence *in the whole race.*"[100]

Few thought to ask the slaves to explain their apparent "betrayal" of the white families they had once served so faithfully. It remained easier to blame the Yankees and to cling to the notion that most slaves retained an affection for their "white folks" but feared to show it in the presence of the soldiers. Near Opelousas, Louisiana, a black youth rushed out of his cabin to tell a passing Union officer where his master had hidden two splendid horses. Although grateful for the information, the officer thought to ask the youth why he had betrayed his master's prize possession: "You ought to have more love for him than to do such a thing." Without the slightest hesitation, the slave replied, "When my master begins to lub me, den it'll be time enough for me to lub him. What I wants is to get away. I want you to take me off from dis plantation, where I can be free." Few whites were privy to the private conversations of their slaves; in the master's presence, of course, a slave chose his words carefully and rarely betrayed his real feelings if they seemed inappropriate at the time. When Kate Stone's brother ventured back to the family home in Louisiana, which they had abandoned, he had the rare opportunity to overhear a conversation between two of the remaining servants, one of whom was Aunt Lucy, the principal housekeeper. The two slaves sat before a fire drinking coffee and discussing the merits of their mistress, Amanda Stone. Remaining well hidden, James Stone heard enough to make a full report when he returned to the exiled family. Not only had Lucy and Maria abused his mother verbally but they referred to her always as "that Woman," talked exultantly of strutting about in her clothes and replacing her as the mistress, and heaped scorn upon the entire family.[101]

The number of slaves who "betrayed" their masters, ran away, became insubordinate, or remained faithful defies any precise statistical breakdowns. Conceivably, if slave behavior could be quantified, the results might suggest that a majority of slaves (particularly in the areas untouched by the Union Army) remained with their masters, at least for the duration of the war. But this would prove to be a highly misleading criterion for determining loyalty or fidelity. The master cared less about percentages of faithfulness in the neighborhood than how he could be reasonably certain of the conduct of his own slaves. More than anything else, the uncertainty depressed him. Manifestations of disaffection could sometimes be dismissed with the observation that the slave in question "had always been a bad Negro," or "we always considered him a most dangerous character," or he "has been a runaway from childhood." The mounting anguish of the master, however, often coincided with the realization that the previous demeanor of his slaves, the efficiency and loyalty with which they had served him, the antebellum record of mischief and devotion simply offered no reliable clues as to how they would behave when the Union Army came into the neighborhood or when they were informed of their freedom.[102]

Within the same household and plantation, the pattern of "betrayal" and "loyalty" created bewilderment, dismay, and surprise. The old distinctions a master had been able to draw between the "good slaves" and the "bad niggers" were no longer dependable. "Jonathan, whom we trusted, betrayed us," Mary Chesnut wrote. "The plantation house and mills, and Mulberry House were saved by Claiborne, that black rascal who was suspected by all the world." Few of Adele Allston's slaves behaved more faithfully than did Little Andrew, "whom we never had felt sure of" and had thought would desert to the Yankees. In Camden, South Carolina, Emma Holmes wrote of a family in which "the old, favored family servant" betrayed them while a young slave "formerly so careless and saucy, proved true as steel."[103]

If slaveholding families came to be alarmed by the extent of the disaffection, the implications for their self-image as benign and benevolent patriarchs could be even more disturbing, sometimes downright traumatizing. No more plaintive cry resounded through slaveholding society than that the slaves in whom they had placed the greatest trust and confidence were the very first to "betray" them. If this complaint recurred most frequently, perhaps that was because it seemed least comprehensible. "Those we loved best, and who loved us best—as we thought—were the first to leave us," a Virginian lamented, voicing an experience that would leave so many families incredulous. To Robert P. Howell, a North Carolina planter who had lost a number of slaves, the behavior of Lovet "disappointed" him the most. "He was about my age and I had always treated him more as a companion than a slave. When I left I put everything in his charge, told him that he was free, but to remain on the place and take care of things. He promised me faithfully that he would, but he was the first one to leave ... and I did not see him for several years." To the wife of a prominent Louisiana slaveholder, the most troubling defection was that of "a colored woman born in the same house with me, always treated as well as me, always till my marriage slept in the same bed with me, and now, she is the first to leave." John H. Bills, the Tennessee planter, least expected to hear of Tom's departure—"he is the first to leave me & had thought would have been the last one to go"—while Louis Manigault, the rice planter, found himself at a loss to explain why the slave he esteemed most highly should have been "the very first to murmur" and "give trouble."[104]

To whom could masters and mistresses turn for comfort and reassurance if not to the old family favorites, the legendary "aunties" and "uncles," with whom they had lived so intimately, who had reared them as children, who had regaled them so often with their stories and songs, and who had shared with them the family tragedies and celebrations. But these slaves, too, refused to comply with the expectations of those who claimed to own them. "Even old Cirus went," a perplexed Mississippian observed. "I reckon he is over a hundred years old." Equally bewildered, Alexander and Cornelia Pope of Washington, Georgia, learned of "the rascality" of Uncle Lewis. This "old gray-haired darkey," wrote Eliza Andrews, a neighbor and niece of the Popes, "has done nothing for years but live at his ease, petted and coddled and believed in by the whole family. The children called him, not 'Uncle Lewis,' but simply 'Uncle,' as if he had really been kin to them." During the family prayers, he sat in a special place and was frequently called upon to lead the worship. "I have often listened to his prayers when staying at Aunty's, and was brought up with as firm a belief in him as in the Bible itself." Here, then, was the very prototype of the faithful servant, venerated by his owners and the townspeople as "an honored institution." With the coming of the Yankees, Uncle Lewis not only deserted but told "a pack of lies" about his mistress and claimed a portion of the family lands. Although the Popes no longer tolerated his presence, the memories of their "fallen saint" and his startling betrayal lingered on.[105]

The behavior of an Uncle Lewis clearly overshadowed in significance if not in actual numbers those celebrated examples of wartime fidelity. The planter found it easier to resign himself to the defection of the field hands, for he may have had little direct contact with them, particularly if he employed an overseer or driver, and they could not be expected to have as strong an attachment to their "white folks." But the conduct of the house servants, whom he thought he knew so well and no doubt felt he had pampered, most of whom had given him years of loyal service, raised questions which few slaveholding families wanted to confront. After awakening one morning to discover that every one of his servants had decamped, a Georgia planter found himself revising assumptions he had never thought to question. "We had thought there was a strong bond of affection on their side as well as ours! We have ministered to them in sickness, infancy, and age." Not all masters failed to appreciate the attraction of freedom, and a few treated the slaves' aspirations with the respect they deserved. After losing a trusted slave, James Alcorn, a Mississippi planter, experienced the usual humiliation over being deceived but he stopped short of condemnation and had little difficulty in ascertaining the cause. "I feel that had I been in his place I should have gone, so good by Hadley, you have heretofore been faithful, that you should espouse your liberty but shows your sense. I wish you no harm." Unlike Alcorn, most planters reacted with outrage and bewilderment, suffering a severe shock to their egos as well as their pocketbooks, and demanded to know why their trusted servants fled a situation in which they appeared to be perfectly content.[106]

The house servants achieved a reputation as the "white niggers" and "Uncle Toms" of slavery, who identified with and tried to emulate their masters, and whose disdain for the field hands was exceeded only by the pride they felt in their quality "white folks." "We house slaves thought we was better'n the others what worked in the field," a former Tennessee bondsman recalled. "We really was raised a little different, you know ..." From the vantage point of the fields, a former South Carolina slave confirmed a common impression: "De house servants put on more airs than de white folks." Contrary to this image of a slave hierarchy, house servants and field hands actually spent a great deal of time together, not only in the slave quarters which they often shared (sometimes as husband and wife, with one working in the house and the other in the field) but in the daily agricultural operations, with the servants often called upon to help at harvest time. In the few urban centers (like Charleston, New Orleans, and Richmond) and on the relatively small number of large "aristocratic" plantations (like those of low-country South Carolina and the Mississippi River), house servants approximated an elite class that lived up to the legend. Elsewhere, the lines were not so clearly drawn between field and house slaves. Typically, the slave quarters rather than the Big House constituted the real social world for most slaves; consequently, few house servants were unconcerned about how their fellow slaves judged them and many of them acted as an intermediary between the Big House and the quarters. Although some field hands spoke scornfully of the superior airs of house slaves, many relished the tales of life inside the Big House and took a vicarious delight in watching house slaves deceive their masters and mistresses.[107]

The distinctions between house and field slaves seem more pronounced in the literature than in the day-to-day operations of slavery. Sufficient examples of the elite house servant lording it over his or her fellow slaves were always on hand, however, to sustain and reinforce the prevailing image. The accounts of both fugitive slaves and planter families lent further "inside" credence to that view. While the number of defections increased each day, Susan Smedes wrote, George Page, her father's servant, "tried to make up in himself for what he looked on as the lack of loyalty on the part of the other servants. They were field Negroes; he belonged to the house." Similarly, in the Allston household, Mammy Milly "held herself and her family as vastly superior to the ordinary run of negroes, the aristocracy of the race." Nevertheless, surprisingly large numbers of house servants fled at the first opportunity, sometimes entire households, and if they remained, many of them refused to wait upon their masters and mistresses, coveted possession of the Big House and its contents (even Mammy Milly fell under suspicion), and "behaved outrageously." After being told by Union soldiers that he was free, the coachman of a Virginia family headed directly for his master's chamber, attired himself in the master's finest clothes, and took his watch and chain and walking stick. Returning to the parlor, where his master sat, the slave "insolently" informed him that henceforth he could drive his own coach.[108]

The range of conduct exemplified by George Page and the Virginia coachman prompted whites to seek some plausible explanation that might be translated into appropriate action. But the initial assumptions they made about slave behavior rendered any real analysis impossible. What they found so difficult to believe was that their slaves might have developed their own standards of accepted behavior and evolved their own concepts of freedom. It was so much easier to think that the troublesome slaves, the defectors, and the rebels were simply not themselves, that they had been misled, that their minds had been contaminated by outside influences. After a Richmond slave denounced Jefferson Davis and refused to serve any white man, a local editor demanded that he "be whipped every day until he confesses what white man put these notions in his head." There had to be an explanation which slaveholding families could accept without in any way compromising their self-esteem or the fundamental conviction that slavery was the best possible condition for black people. To pretend that the Yankees instigated slave aggression and enticed and forced slaves to desert their masters proved to be a highly popular explanation, since it contained a semblance of truth and conveniently evaded the hard questions. "The poor negroes don't do us any harm except when they are put up to it," Eliza Andrews thought. "Even when they murdered that white man and quartered him, I believe pernicious teachings were responsible."[109]

Although many whites gave public voice to this charge, few thought it adequately explained the rate of desertion and betrayal. The more they reflected over their own experiences, as well as their neighbors', slaveholders came increasingly to question the lax discipline and familiarity which, they now argued, had produced pampered, spoiled, and overly indulged servants. "It has now been proven," Louis Manigault maintained, "that those Planters who were the most indulgent to their Negroes when we were at peace, have since the commencement of the war encountered the greatest trouble in the management of this species of property." Nor was that observation peculiar to Manigault's rice plantations, for Julia LeGrand made precisely the same point based on her experience in New Orleans. "So many people have been betrayed by *pet* servants. Strange that some of the most severe mistresses and masters have kept their servants through all this trying year." After noting how the most indulged slaves had turned out to be "the meanest" and least trustworthy, a Georgia planter indicated that his wartime experience left him with only one conclusion: "A nigger has got to know you're his master, and then when he understands that he's content. . . . Flail a nigger and he knows you." That was, of course, time-honored advice. By nature, it had long been held, blacks required rigid discipline and the full exercise of the master's authority; without those restraints, they would revert back to the barbarism from which they had emerged. The closer blacks approached a state of freedom, the more un-manageable and dangerous they became.[110]

To understand why their most trusted slaves turned against them, most masters need not have looked beyond their own households. The answer usually lay somewhere in that complex and often ambivalent relationship between a slave and his "white folks," in the intimacy and dependency which infused those relations and created both mutual affection and unbearable tension in the narrow quarters of the Big House. Unlike the field slave, who enjoyed a certain degree of anonymity and a prescribed leisure time, the house servant stood always at the beck and call of each member of the master's family, worked under their watchful eyes, and had to bear the brunt of their capricious moods. The very same family that petted and coddled him might at any time make him the butt of their jokes, the object of their frustrations, the victim of their pettiness. He had to learn how to be the "good nigger," to submit to indignities without protest, to submerge his feelings, to repress his emotions, to play "dumb" when the occasion demanded it, to respond with the proper gestures and words to every command, to learn the uses of flattery and humility, to never appear overly intelligent. He was expected to acquire and to exhibit at all times what a Georgia slaveholder defined as "a *house look.*" The quality of bond-age to which he submitted could be measured neither by the number of beatings he sustained nor by the privileges and indulgences he enjoyed. What took the heaviest toll, as W. E. B. Du Bois observed, had to be "the enforced personal feeling of inferiority, the calling of another Master; the standing with hat in hand. It was the helplessness. It was the defenseless-ness of family life. It was the submergence below the arbitrary will of any sort of individual."[111]

That a certain intimacy characterized the slave-master relationship in the Big House reveals little about the conflicting feelings it generated and the precarious base on which it often rested. To live in close day-to-day contact with his master, to know his capacity for deceit and cunning, to know him as few of the field hands could, enabled some slaves to hate him that much more, with an intensity and fervor that only intimate knowledge could have produced. Recalling her many years as the cook in a North Carolina family, Aunt Delia suggested ways in which a house slave might choose to manifest that feeling: "How many times I spit in the biscuits and peed in the coffee just to get back at them mean white folks." The easy familiarity that pervaded service in the Big House made not only for ambiguity but for a potentially volatile situation.[112]

Even if the master had been a model of virtue and propriety, there was no assurance that the blacks he had most indulged would remain faithful to him. Recalling their own experiences, William Wells Brown and Frederick Douglass, both of whom ultimately escaped to the North, testified that beneficent treatment, much more than abuse, had intensified their dissatisfaction with bondage. The better treated he was, Brown explained, the more miserable he became, the more he appreciated liberty, the more he detested the bondage that confined and restrained him. "If a slave has a bad master," Douglass observed, "his ambition is to get a better; when he gets a better, he aspires to have the best; and when he gets the best, he aspires to be his own master." To make a contented slave, he added, was to make a thoughtless slave. Rather than being grateful for his ability to read and write, he recalled those times when he envied the "stupidity" of his fellow slaves. "It was this everlasting thinking of my condition that tormented me." On this point, then, Brown, Douglass, and the slaveholding class found themselves in unusual agreement, and the wartime experience demonstrated in scores of instances the validity of their observation: the best-treated, the most indulged, the most intelligent slaves might be expected to be the first ones to "betray" their masters.[113]

No plantation slave exercised greater authority than did the driver or foreman. The position he occupied as the director of labor and as an intermediary between the Big House and the quarters made him a crucial figure in the wartime crisis and in the subsequent transition to free labor. The driver dispatched the slaves to the fields, set the work pace and supervised performance of the daily tasks, maintained order in the quarters, settled disputes among slaves, and shared supervisory duties with the overseer or, quite commonly, combined the functions of driver and overseer. In a conflict between the overseer and the driver, the driver's judgment might in many instances prevail; the very maintenance of discipline often demanded that his authority be sustained. "I constantly endeavored to do nothing which would cause them [the slaves] to lose their respect for him [the driver]," the manager of a plantation in South Carolina noted. With that same objective in mind, many planters provided the driver with better clothing, granted certain privileges to his wife, and always made a point of reprimanding him in private rather than in the presence of other slaves.[114]

In the literature and folklore of slavery, the driver enjoyed at best a mixed reputation, usually reflecting the ways in which he exerted his power to exact labor and mete out punishments. If the "Uncle Toms" came to dominate the legend of the house slave, the black "Simon Legrees" seemed to prevail in the characterization of the driver. Henry Cheatam, a former Mississippi slave, recalled the driver as "de meanest debil dat eber libbed on de Lawd's green earth. I promise myself when I growed up dat I was agoin' to kill dat nigger iffen it was de las' thing I eber done." To make matters worse, that driver along with the mistress ran the plantation after the death of the master in the war. In a song overheard by Colonel Thomas Higginson, some of his black troops improvised verses that reflected the prevailing image of the driver. And as with the house slave, sufficient examples abounded to make it quite plausible.

> O, de ole nigger-driver!
>   O, gwine away!
> Fust ting my mammy tell me,
>   O, gwine away!
> Tell me 'bout de nigger-driver,
>   O, gwine away!
> Nigger-driver second devil,
>   O, gwine away!
> Best ting for do he driver,
>   O, gwine away!
> Knock he down and spoil he labor,
>   O, gwine away!

After the war, on those plantations where the driver had a reputation for cruelty, the freedmen demanded his removal before they would consent to work.[115]

If a master maintained confidence in any of his slaves, outside of a few of the venerable "uncles" and "aunties," he most likely trusted the driver. He had personally chosen this man for his loyalty, competence, and dependability, believing him capable of managing the plantation in his absence. But the master also selected a driver who commanded the respect and obedience of the slaves, and this leadership role was apt to create conflicting loyalties. When the Yankees arrived, numerous drivers exercised leadership and influence in ways few masters had dared to contemplate. On one of the Allston plantations, Jesse Belflowers, the much-harassed overseer, traced the prevailing disorder and the misconduct of the slaves to the driver. He "is not behaveing write," Belflowers reported, "he doant talk write before the People." Not far from this scene, Confederate scouts captured and hanged a driver for his "treachery." When a number of slaves fled a Georgia plantation to join General Sherman's army, "the leading spirit" as well as the youngest of the group was the driver, described by one Union officer as a "very quick and manly fellow, a model, physically." Not only did some drivers desert to the Yankees, but they were likely as well to take other slaves with them, and in several instances the driver directed the seizure of deserted plantations and helped to wreak vengeance on masters and overseers. A South Carolina planter and his son were shot and seriously wounded while riding in their carriage near the plantation; the band of blacks who ambushed them had been "led on by his Driver." After blacks had seized one of his plantations, Charles Manigault accused the driver of aspiring to be *"lord & master of everything there."*

> *Frederick* (the Driver) was ringleader, & at the head of all the iniquity committed *there*. He encouraged all the Negroes *to believe* that the Farm, and everything on it, *now since Emancipation*, belonged *solely to him*, & *that their former owners* had now no rights, or control there whatever.

No less dismayed, Edmund Ruffin described the exodus of blacks from his son's plantation, Marlbourne, along with the decision of those who remained to refuse to work. "My former black overseer, Jem Sykes," he added, "who for the last seven years of my proprietorship, kept my keys, & was trusted with everything, even when I & every other white was absent from 4 to 6 weeks at a time, acted precisely with all his fellows." If the driver remained on the plantation, as he usually did, he might also assume the responsibility for informing the slaves of their freedom and initiating negotiations with the master for a labor contract.[116]

When some planters came to assess the wartime disaster that deprived them of an enslaved work force, they did not hesitate to project much of their anger and frustration on the trusted drivers. "The *drivers* everywhere have proved the worst negroes," a Louisiana planter concluded. Actually, the record varied considerably, and as many planters voiced satisfaction and admiration for the ways in which their drivers managed to sustain agricultural operations and control the labor force during the war and in some instances run the entire plantation in their absence. With a number of slaves manifesting their discontent, Louis Manigault was much relieved to learn that Driver John "is still the same"; and since he deemed John "a Man of great importance" to the plantation, Manigault advised his father to furnish him with all the items the driver had requested—boots, a coat, a hat, a watch, and ample clothing. On the South Carolina Sea Islands, particularly on the smaller plantations, the drivers remained after the masters fled and succeeded in supervising and planting food crops and in maintaining a semblance of order and discipline. Impressed with the leadership and knowledge of plantation operations exhibited by these drivers, Union officers viewed them as a crucial stabilizing factor in the transition to free labor and tried to bolster their authority, particularly on the larger plantations where it had been seriously undermined by the absence of whites.[117]

Recognizing the influence many of the drivers retained over the freed slaves, planters went to considerable lengths after the war to maintain their services. Once again, the driver found himself caught between conflicting loyalties. Through the driver, the planter hoped to retain the bulk of his labor force on the most favorable terms, though in a few instances he would have to dismiss an unpopular driver to keep any of his former slaves. Through the driver, on the other hand, many former slaves hoped to present a united front to the employer and exact concessions from him that would make their labor sufficiently remunerative and less arduous. In many of these postwar arrangements, the planter and the driver, both leaders in their own ways, seemed to have reached a tacit understanding about the division of power. On a plantation near Lexington, Tennessee, the driver—Jordan Pyles—had fled with the Yankees and had served in the Union Army. When he returned to the plantation after the war, he "was a changed nigger and all de whites and a lot of de niggers hated him," his stepson recalled. "All 'cepting old Master, and he never said a word out of de way to him. Jest tol him to come on and work on de place as long as he wanted to." Whatever the hostility that initially greeted him, Jordan Pyles must have retained much of the leadership quality and influence he had previously exercised, for in 1867 he would be elected a delegate to the Radical state convention.[118]

Among the field hands, the house servants, the skilled black artisans, and the slave drivers, the Civil War provoked a wide range of behavior. Contrary to the legends of "docility" and "militancy," the slaves did not sort themselves out into Uncle Toms and Nat Turners any more than masters divided neatly into the "mean" and the "good." Rebelliousness, resistance, and accommodation might manifest themselves at different times in the same slave, depending on his own perception of reality. Rare was that slave, no matter how degraded, no matter how effusively he professed his fidelity, who did not contain within him a capacity for outrage. Whether or not that outrage ever surfaced, how much longer it would remain muted was the terrible reality every white man and woman had to live with and could never really escape. The tensions this uncertainty generated could at times prove to be unbearable. "The loom room had caught from some hot ashes," Kate Stone confided to her diary, "but we at once thought Jane [the slave cook] was wreaking vengeance on us all by trying to burn us out. We would not have been surprised to have her slip up and stick any of us in the back." If the vast majority of slaves refrained from aggressive acts and remained on the plantations, most of them were neither "rebellious" nor "faithful" in the fullest sense of those terms, but rather ambivalent and observant, some of them frankly opportunistic, many of them anxious to preserve their anonymity, biding their time, searching for opportunities to break the dependency that bound them to their white families. "There is quite a difference of manner among the negroes," a South Carolina white woman noted in March 1865, "but I think it proceeds from an uncertainty as to what their condition will be, they do not know if they are free or not, and their manner is a sort of feeler by which they will find out how far they can go."[119]

The war revealed, often in ways that defied description, the sheer complexity of the master-slave relationship, and the conflicts, contradictions, and ambivalence that relationship generated in each individual. The slave's emotions and behavior invariably rested on a precarious balance between the habit of obedience and the intense desire for freedom. The same humble, self-effacing slave who touched his hat to his "white folks" was capable of touching off the fire that gutted his master's house. The loyal body servant who risked his life to carry his wounded master to safety remounted his master's horse and fled to the Yankees. The black boatman lionized by the Richmond press for his denunciation of the Yankees and enlistment as a Confederate recruit deserted to the Union lines with valuable information and "twenty new rebel uniforms." The house slave who nursed her mistress through a terrible illness, always evincing love and affection, even weeping over her condition, deserted her when the moment seemed right—"when I was scarce able to walk without assistance—she left me without provocation or reason—left me in the night, and that too without the slightest noise." On the Jones plantation, near Herndon, Georgia, the house servant had given no warm welcome to the Union soldiers. She dutifully looked after the white children entrusted to her care. "I suckled *that* child, Hattie," she boasted, "all these children suckled by colored women." And yet, when the Yankees threatened to burn down her master's house, Louisa made no protest. "It ought to be burned," she told a Union officer. "Why?" the astonished officer asked her, for he had been rather moved by her fidelity to the family and her apparent devotion to the children. "Cause there has been so much devilment here," she replied, "whipping niggers most to death to make 'em work to pay for it."[120]

To place the blame for slave disaffection on lax discipline or outside influences, as so many slaveholders chose to do, was to make the same false assumptions about blacks. If the war taught slaveholders anything, it should have revealed how little they actually knew their blacks, how they had mistaken the slave's outward demeanor for his inner feelings, his docility for contentment and acquiescence, and how in numerous instances they had been deliberately deceived so that they might later be the more easily betrayed. The conduct of slaves during the recent crisis, a South Carolina planter conceded, should have impressed upon every slaveholding family that "we were all laboring under a delusion."

> Good masters and bad masters all alike, shared the same fate—the sea of the Revolution confounded good and evil; and, in the chaotic turbulence, all suffer in degree. Born and raised amid the institution, like a great many others, I believed it was necessary, to our welfare, if not to our very existence. I believed that these people were content, happy, and attached to their masters. But events and reflection have caused me to change these opinions. . . . If they were content, happy and attached to their masters, why did they desert him in the moment of his need and flock to an enemy, whom they did not know; and thus left their, perhaps really good masters whom they did know from infancy?[121]

Whatever happened in the future, no matter what kind of South emerged from the ruins, it seemed certain that the relations which masters and slaves alike had enjoyed or tolerated in the past would never be quite the same again.

WHEN THE UNION ARMY neared his Savannah River plantations, Louis Manigault fled. That was December 1864. More than two years later, having leased the plantations to a former Confederate officer, Manigault decided to visit the place for the first time since his hasty departure and assess the impact of the war. Traveling along the familiar roads between Savannah and his plantations, he noted traces of previous army encampments, the twisted ruins of the Charleston and Savannah Railroad, and the remains of what had once been a magnificent neighboring mansion. Upon entering the plantations, he was greeted enthusiastically by his former slave cooper, George, who still called him "Maussa." Standing next to the ruins of his country house, Manigault recalled how he had spent here "the most happy period" of his childhood. All that remained of the house was a tall chimney and some scattered bricks which the slaves had not stolen and sold in Savannah. Except for the "Negro Houses," which he had constructed just before the war, the entire settlement had "a most abandoned and forlorn appearance."

As he approached the old slave quarters, some of the blacks came out of their cabins, hesitant in their greetings, "not knowing whether under the new regime it would be proper to meet me politely or not." Manigault shook hands with them, called each by his name ("which seemed to please them highly"), and joked with them about his present plight. "Lord! a Massy!" he mocked when asked why he had not returned earlier. "You tink I can lib in de Chimney." Near the center of the plantation, twelve of his former slaves greeted him. "They all seemed pleased to see me, calling me 'Maussa' & the Men still showing respect by taking off their caps." He spotted "Captain" Hector, "as cunning as Negroes can be," his "constant companion" until the war transformed him into "a great Rascal" and troublemaker. Hector was now a foreman.

Much to Manigault's surprise, Jack Savage, the slave he had sold in Savannah, had returned. "Tall, black, lousy, in rags, & uncombed, kinky, knotty-hair," this man had been "the most notoriously bad character & worst Negro of the place," the one slave he had thought capable of murder and arson, and yet acknowledged to be intelligent and an able carpenter. The two men now shook hands and exchanged "a few friendly remarks." To Manigault, it seemed highly ironic that Jack Savage, "the last one I should have dreamt of," greeted him, "whilst sitting idly upon the Negro-House steps dirty & sluggish, I behold young Women to whom I had most frequently presented Earrings, Shoes, Calicos, Kerchiefs &c, &c,—formerly pleased to meet me, but now not even lifting the head as I passed."

Unlike many slaveholders, Louis Manigault had never pretended to understand his blacks. Before the war, he reflected, fear had largely shaped the behavior of the slaves, and "we Planters could never get at the truth."

Those who claimed to know the Negro were simply deceiving themselves. "Our 'Northern Brethren' inform us that we Southerners knew nothing of the Negro Character. This I have always considered *perfectly true*, but they further state that They (the Yankees) have always known the true Character of the Negro which I consider *entirely false* in the extreme. So deceitful is the Negro that as far as my own experience extends I could never in a single instance decipher his character." Conversing now with his former slaves, Manigault was suddenly overcome by a strange feeling. "I almost imagined myself with Chinese, Malays or even the Indians in the interior of the Philippine Islands." It was as though he were on alien turf and had never really known these people who had once been his slaves.[122]

Before setting out to make a new life for himself, William Colbert, a former Alabama slave, looked back for a last time at the old plantation on which he had spent more than twenty years. He had no reason to regret his decision to leave. The bondage he had endured had been harsh, reflecting the temperament of a master who had never hesitated to whip his slaves severely. "All de niggers 'roun' hated to be bought by him kaze he wuz so mean," Colbert recalled. "When he wuz too tired to whup us he had de overseer do it; and de overseer wuz meaner dan de massa." The arrival of the Yankees had not materially affected their lives. After a few days of looting, the soldiers had suddenly left "an' we neber seed 'em since." After the war, the blacks only gradually left and the plantation slowly deteriorated. Many years later, reflecting on his experience, Colbert captured with particular vividness the ambivalence that had necessarily characterized a slave's attachment to his master. His recollections were tinged neither with romantic nostalgia nor with abject hatred. Whatever bitterness he still felt may have been dissipated both by the passage of time and by the knowledge that Jim Hodison, his former master, had come to learn in his own way the dimensions of human tragedy. And that was an experience William Colbert could easily share with him.

> De massa had three boys to go to war, but dere wuzn't one to come home. All the chillun he had wuz killed. Massa, he los' all his money and de house soon begin droppin' away to nothin'. Us niggers one by one lef' de ole place and de las' time I seed de home plantation I wuz a standin' on a hill. I looked back on it for de las' time through a patch of scrub pines and it look' so lonely. Dere warn't but one person in sight, de massa. He was a-settin' in a wicker chair in de yard lookin' out ober a small field of cotton and cawn. Dere wuz fo' crosses in de graveyard in de side lawn where he wuz a-settin'. De fo'th one wuz his wife. I lost my ole woman too 37 years ago, and all dis time, I's been a carrin' on like de massa— all alone.[123]

After the war, Savilla Burrell left the plantation near Jackson's Creek, South Carolina, on which she had been raised as a slave. Not until many years later did she return to visit her old master, Tom Still, in his final days. Sitting there by his side, trying to keep the flies off him, she could clearly see the lines of sorrow "plowed on dat old face" and she recalled that time when he had looked so impressive as a captain in the Confederate cavalry. "It come into my 'membrance de song of Moses: 'de Lord had triumphed glorily and de hoss and his rider have been throwed into de sea.' "[124]

# Chapter Four

# SLAVES NO MORE

*Slavery chain done broke at last!*
*Broke at last! Broke at last!*
*Slavery chain done broke at last!*
*Gonna praise God till I die!*

*Way up in that valley,*
*Pray-in' on my knees,*
*Tell-in' God a-bout my troubles,*
*And to help me if He please.*

*I did tell him how I suffer,*
*In the dungeon and the chain;*
*And the days I went with head bowed down,*
*An' my broken flesh and pain.*

*I did know my Jesus heard me,*
*'Cause the spirit spoke to me,*
*An' said, "Rise, my chile, your children*
*An' you too shall be free."*

*I done 'p'int one mighty captain*
*For to marshal all my hosts;*
*An' to bring my bleeding ones to me,*
*An' not one shall be lost.*

*Now no more weary trav'lin',*
*'Cause my Jesus set me free,*
*An' there's no more auction block for me*
*Since He give me liberty.* [1]

ON THE NIGHT of April 2, 1865, Confederate troops abandoned Richmond. The sudden decision caught Robert Lumpkin, the well-known dealer in slaves, with a recently acquired shipment which he had not yet managed to sell. Desperately, he tried to remove them by the same train that would carry Jefferson Davis out of the Confederate capital. When Lumpkin reached the railway station, however, he found a panic-stricken crowd held back by a line of Confederate soldiers with drawn bayonets.

Upon learning that he could not remove his blacks, the dealer marched them back to Lumpkin's Jail, a two-story brick house with barred windows, located in the heart of Richmond's famous slave market—an area known to local blacks as "the Devil's Half Acre." After their return, the slaves settled down in their cells for still another night, apparently unaware that this would be their last night of bondage. For Lumpkin, the night would mark the loss of a considerable investment and the end of a profession. Not long after the collapse of the Confederacy, however, he took as his legal wife the black woman he had purchased a decade before and who had already borne him two children.[2]

With Union soldiers nearing the city, a Confederate official thought the black residents looked as stunned and confused as the whites. "The negroes stand about mostly silent," he wrote, "as if wondering what will be their fate. They make no demonstrations of joy." Obviously he had not seen them earlier that day emerging from a church meeting with particular exuberance, "shaking hands and exchanging congratulations upon all sides." Nor had he heard, probably, that familiar refrain with which local blacks occasionally regaled themselves: "Richmond town is burning down, High diddle diddle inctum inctum ah." Whatever the origins of the song, the night of the evacuation must have seemed like a prophetic fulfillment. Explosions set off by the retreating Confederates left portions of the city in flames and precipitated a night of unrestrained looting and rioting, in which army deserters and the impoverished residents of Richmond's white slum shared the work of expropriation and destruction with local slaves and free blacks. Black and white women together raided the Confederate Commissary, while the men rolled wheelbarrows filled with bags of flour, meal, coffee, and sugar toward their respective shanties. Along the row of retail stores, a large black man wearing a bright red sash around his waist directed the looting. After breaking down the doors with the crowbar he carried on his shoulder, he stood aside while his followers rushed into the shops and emptied them of their contents. He took nothing for himself, apparently satisfied to watch the others partake of commodities long denied them. If only for this night, racial distinctions and customs suddenly became irrelevant.[3]

Determined to reap the honors of this long-awaited triumph, white and black Yankees vied with each other to make the initial entry into the Confederate capital. The decision to halt the black advance until the white troops marched into the city would elicit some bitter comments in the northern black press. "History will show," one editor proclaimed, "that they [the black troops] were in the suburbs of Richmond long before the white soldiers, and but for the untimely and unfair order to halt, would have triumphantly planted their banner first upon the battlements of the capital of 'ye greate confederacie.' " Many years later, a former Virginia slave still brooded over this issue. "Gawdammit, 'twas de nigguhs tuk Richmond," he kept insisting. "Ah ain't nevuh knowed nigguhs—even all uh dem nigguhs—could mek such uh ruckus. One huge sea uh black faces filt de streets fum wall tuh wall, an' dey wan't nothin' but nigguhs in sight."

Regardless of who entered Richmond first, black newspapers and clergy-men perceived the hand of God in this ironic triumph. The moment the government reversed its policy on black recruitment it had doomed the Confederacy. And now, "as a finishing touch, as though He would speak audible words of approval to the nation," God had delivered Richmond— "that stronghold of treason and wickedness"—into the hands of black sol-diers. "This is an admonition to which men, who make war on God would do well to take heed."[4]

To the black soldiers, many of them recently slaves, this was the dramatic, the almost unbelievable climax to four years of war that had promised at the outset to be nothing more than a skirmish to preserve the Union. Now they were marching into Richmond as free men, amidst throngs of cheering blacks lining the streets. Within hours, a large crowd of black soldiers and residents assembled on Broad Street, near "Lumpkin Alley," where the slave jails, the auction rooms, and the offices of the slave traders were concentrated. Among the soldiers gathered here was Garland H. White, a former Virginia slave who had escaped to Ohio before the war and now returned as chaplain of the 28th United States Colored Troops.

> I marched at the head of the column, and soon I found myself called upon by the officers and men of my regiment to make a speech, with which, of course, I readily complied. A vast multitude assembled on Broad street, and I was aroused amid the shouts of ten thousand voices, and proclaimed for the first time in that city freedom to all mankind.

From behind the barred windows of Lumpkin's Jail, the imprisoned slaves began to chant:

> *Slavery chain done broke at last!*
> *Broke at last! Broke at last!*
> *Slavery chain done broke at last!*
> *Gonna praise God till I die!*

The crowd outside took up the chant, the soldiers opened the slave cells, and the prisoners came pouring out, most of them shouting, some praising God and "master Abe" for their deliverance. Chaplain White found himself unable to continue with his speech. "I became so overcome with tears, that I could not stand up under the pressure of such fulness of joy in my own heart. I retired to gain strength." Several hours later, he located his mother, whom he had not seen for some twenty years.[5]

The white residents bolted their doors, remained inside, and gained their first impressions of Yankee occupation from behind the safety of their shutters. "For us it was a requiem for buried hopes," Sallie P. Putnam conceded. The sudden and ignominious Confederate evacuation had been equaled only by the humiliating sight of black soldiers patrolling the city streets. For native whites, it was as though the victorious North had conspired to make the occupation as distasteful as possible. Few of them could ever forget the long lines of black cavalry sweeping by the Exchange Hotel, brandishing their swords and exchanging "savage cheers" with black residents who were "exulting" over this dramatic moment in their lives. After viewing such spectacles from her window, a young white woman wondered, "Was it to this end we had fought and starved and gone naked and cold? To this end that the wives and children of many dear and gallant friends were husbandless and fatherless? To this end that our homes were in ruins, our state devastated?" Understandably, then, local whites boycotted the military band concerts on the Capitol grounds, even after Federal authorities, in a conciliatory gesture, had barred blacks from attendance.[6]

Four days after the entry of Union troops, Richmond blacks assembled at the First African Church on Broad Street for a Jubilee Meeting. The church, built in the form of a cross and scantily furnished, impressed a northern visitor as "about the last place one would think of selecting for getting up any particular enthusiasm on any other subject than religion." On this day, some 1,500 blacks, including a large number of soldiers, packed the frail structure. With the singing of a hymn, beginning "Jesus my all to heaven is gone," the congregation gave expression to their newly won freedom. After each line, they repeated with added emphasis, "I'm going to join in this army; I'm going to join in this army of my Lord." But when they came to the verse commencing, "This is the way I long have sought," the voices reached even higher peaks and few of the blacks could suppress the smiles that came across their faces. Meanwhile, in the Hall of Delegates, where the Confederate Congress had only recently deliberated and where black soldiers now took turns swiveling in the Speaker's chair, T. Morris Chester, a black war correspondent, tried to assess the impact of these first days of liberation: the rejoicing of the slaves and free blacks, the tumultuous reception accorded President Lincoln when he visited the city, the opening of the slave pens, and the mood of the black population. "They declare that they cannot realize the change; though they have long prayed for it, yet it seems impossible that it has come."[7]

It took little time for the "grapevine" to spread the news that Babylon (as some blacks called it) had fallen. When black children attending a freedmen's school in Norfolk heard the news, they responded with a resounding chorus of "Glory Hallelujah." Reaching the line "We'll hang Jeff Davis to a sour apple tree," one of the pupils inquired if Davis had, indeed, met that fate. The teacher told her that Davis was still very much alive. At this news, the pupil expressed her dismay "by a decided pout of her lips, such a pout as these children only are able to give." Still, the news about Richmond excited them. Most of the children revealed that they had relatives there whom they now hoped to see, several looked forward to reunions with fathers and mothers "dat dem dere Secesh carried off," and those who had neither friends nor relatives in the city were "mighty glad" anyway because they understood the news to mean that "cullud people free now."[8]

When the news reached a plantation near Yorktown, the white family broke into tears, not only over the fall of Richmond but over the rumor that the Yankees had captured Jefferson Davis. Overhearing the conversation, a black servant rushed through the preparation of the supper, asked another servant to wait on the table for her, and explained to the family that she had to fetch water from the "bush-spring." She walked slowly until no one could see her and then ran the rest of the way. Upon reaching the spring, she made certain she was alone and then gave full vent to her feelings.

> I jump up an' scream, "Glory, glory, hallelujah to Jesus! I's free! I's free! Glory to God, you come down an' free us; no big man could do it." An' I got sort o' scared, afeared somebody hear me, an' I takes another good look, an' fall on de groun', an' roll over, an' kiss de groun' fo' de Lord's sake, I's so full o' praise to Masser Jesus. He do all dis great work. De soul buyers can neber take my two chillen lef' me; no, neber can take 'em from me no mo'.

Several years before, her husband and four children had been sold to a slave dealer. Her thoughts now turned to the possibility of a reunion.[9]

Only a few miles from the Appomattox Courthouse, Fannie Berry, a house servant, stood in the yard with her mistress, Sarah Ann, and watched the white flag being hoisted in the Pamplin village square. "Oh, Lordy," her mistress exclaimed, "Lee done surrendered!" Richmond had fallen the previous week, but for Fannie Berry this was the day she would remember the rest of her life.

> Never was no time like 'em befo' or since. Niggers shoutin' an' clappin' hands an' singin'! Chillun runnin' all over de place beatin' tins an' yellin'. Ev'ybody happy. Sho' did some celebratin'. Run to de kitchen an' shout in de winder:
>
> > *Mammy, don't you cook no mo'*
> > *You's free! You's free!*
>
> Run to de henhouse an' shout:
>
> > *Rooster, don't you crow no mo'*
> > *You's free! You's free!*
> > *Ol' hen, don't you lay no mo' eggs,*
> > *You's free! You's free!*
>
> Go to de pigpen an' tell de pig:
>
> > *Ol' pig, don't you grunt no mo'*
> > *You's free! You's free!*

Tell de cows:

> *Ol' cow, don't you give no mo' milk,*
> *You's free! You's free!*

Meanwhile, she recalled, some "smart alec boys" sneaked up under her mistress's window and shouted, "Ain't got to slave no mo'. We's free! We's free!" The day after the celebration, however, Fannie Berry went about her usual duties, as if she hadn't understood the full implications of what had transpired. And as before, she permitted her mistress to hire her out. Finally, the woman for whom she was working told her she was now free, there was no need to return to her mistress, and she could stay and work for room and board. "I didn't say nothin' when she wuz tellin' me, but done 'cided to leave her an' go back to the white folks dat furst own me."[10]

Unlike many of their rural brethren, who evinced a certain confusion about the implications of freedom and when to claim it, the blacks in Richmond had little difficulty in appreciating the significance of this event. And they could test it almost instantly. They promenaded on the hitherto forbidden grounds of Capitol Square. They assembled in groups of five or more without the presence or authorization of a white man. They sought out new employers at better terms. They moved about as they pleased without having to show a pass upon the demand of any white person. "We-uns kin go jist anywhar," one local black exulted, "don't keer for no pass—go when yer want'er. Golly! de kingdom hab kim dis time for sure —dat ar what am promised in de generations to dem dat goes up tru great tribulations." And they immediately seized upon the opportunity to educate themselves and their children, to separate their church from white domination, and to form their own community institutions.[11]

Less than two years after the fall of Richmond, a Massachusetts clergyman arrived in the city with the intention of establishing a school to train black ministers. But when he sought a building for his school, he encountered considerable resistance, until he met Mary Ann Lumpkin, the black wife of the former slave dealer. She offered to lease him Lumpkin's Jail. With unconcealed enthusiasm, black workers knocked out the cells, removed the iron bars from the windows, and refashioned the old jail as a school for ministers and freedmen alike. Before long, children and adults entered the doors of the new school, some of them recalling that this was not their first visit to the familiar brick building.[12]

2

---

DESPITE THE IMMEDIATE GRATIFICATION experienced by the black residents of Richmond, the death of slavery proved to be agonizingly slow. That precise moment when a slave could think of himself or herself as a free person was not always clear. From the very outset of the war, many slaves assumed they were free the day the Yankees came into their vicinity. But with the military situation subject to constant change, any freedom that ultimately depended on the presence of Union troops was apt to be quite precarious, and in some regions the slaves found themselves uncertain as to whose authority prevailed. The Emancipation Proclamation, moreover, excluded numbers of slaves from its provisions, some masters claimed to be unaware of the emancipation order, and still others refused to acknowledge it while the war raged and doubted its constitutionality after the end of hostilities. "I guess we musta celebrated 'Mancipation about twelve times in Harnett County," recalled Ambrose Douglass, a former North Carolina slave. "Every time a bunch of No'thern sojers would come through they would tell us we was free and we'd begin celebratin'. Before we would get through somebody else would tell us to go back to work, and we would go. Some of us wanted to jine up with the army, but didn't know who was goin' to win and didn't take no chances."[13]

Outside of a few urban centers, Union soldiers rarely remained long enough in any one place to enforce the slave's new status. Of the slaves in her region "who supposed they were free," a South Carolina white woman noted how they were "gradually discovering a Yankee army passing through the country and telling them they are free is not sufficient to make it a fact." Nor was the protection of the freedman's status the first priority of an army engaged in a life-and-death struggle. When the troops needed to move on, many of the blacks were understandably dismayed, confused, and frightened. "Christ A'mighty!" one slave exclaimed in late 1861 when told the troops were about to depart. "If Massa Elliott Garrard catch me, might as well be dead—he kill me, certain." Even if Union officers assured him of his safety, the slave had little reason to place any confidence in the word of someone who would not be around on that inevitable day of reckoning. While encamped in the North Carolina countryside, the black regiment to which Henry M. Turner was attached had attracted nearly 700 slaves from the immediate vicinity. "To describe the scene produced by our departure," he wrote, "would be too solemn, if time and space permitted. Suffice it to say, many were the tears shed, many sorrowful hearts bled. . . . God alone knows, I was compelled to evade their sight as much as possible, to be relieved of such words as these, 'Chaplain, what shall I do? where can we go? will you come back?' "[14]

Widespread dismay at the impending departure of the Yankees reflected not only the prevailing uncertainty about freedom but the very real fear that their masters or the entire white community might wreak vengeance on them for any irregular behavior during the brief period of occupation. In a Mississippi town near Vicksburg, a number of slaves had joined with the Yankees to plunder stores and homes, apparently assuming that the soldiers would be around to protect them. But now the troops were moving on, leaving the looters with their newly acquired possessions and all the slaves, regardless of what role they had played in the pillaging, at the mercy of whites who felt betrayed and robbed. With "undisguised amazement," the blacks watched the soldiers leave, and within hours one of them caught up with the Yankee columns and reported that a number of his people had already been killed. On a plantation near Columbia, South Carolina, the master and mistress waited until the Yankees departed and then vented their anger on a young slave girl who had helped the soldiers to locate the hidden silverware, money, and jewelry. "She'd done wrong I know," a former slave recalled, "but I hated to see her suffer so awful for it. After de Yankees had gone, de missus and massa had de poor gal hung 'till she die. It was something awful to see." With similar swiftness, a slaveholder who was reputedly "very good to his Negroes" became so enraged over the behavior of a black that the moment the Yankees left the area he strung him up to the beams of a shed.[15]

Where slave misbehavior had been particularly "outrageous," as in northern Louisiana and the adjoining Mississippi counties, the Yankee raiding parties had no sooner returned to their bases than local whites demanded swift and severe retaliation. Not content to leave such matters entirely in the hands of the planters, a newspaper in Alexandria urged that public examples be made of "the ungrateful and vindictive scoundrels" who seized their masters' property, volunteered information to or acted as guides for the enemy, and "were seen armed or participated in any active demonstration."

> The uppermost thought in every one's mind before the Yankee invasion of our Parish was, what will be the conduct of the slaves. The most important consideration for all of us now that the invasion has swept by, is what conduct are we to pursue to them? . . . Some offences have been committed that cannot be atoned for but by death. Others may be safely expiated by the lash or other corporeal punishment. Others may safely be left to the milder discipline of the plantation. The punishment for each proper to its kind, should be inexorably and unflinchingly afflicted.

The newspaper advised whites to scrutinize recent slave conduct and then select a particularly "diabolical" offender for immediate and public punishment. "This will inspire wholesome terror. Its example will be long remembered." Acknowledging the losses already suffered by some masters and the fear of losing still more, the editor asked the planter class to place the security of the entire white population above any pecuniary considerations: "Here and there the life of a slave forfeited by his crime will entail a loss, but a great and good result will be attained, and those who are instrumental in engraving a wholesome lesson on the minds of this impressionable population will have cause to be thankful hereafter for this suggestion."[16]

Requiring little prompting, some slaveholders had already acted in this spirit. In Rapides Parish, which included the town of Alexandria, John H. Ransdell moved very quickly to reassert his authority after the Yankees departed. "Things are just now beginning to work right," he informed his absentee neighbor, Governor Thomas O. Moore. "The negroes hated awfully to go to work again. Several have been shot and probably more will have to be." Less than a month later, he concurred with the governor that the recent Yankee raids had left him thoroughly disillusioned with the blacks. Even when two of the governor's runaways returned, expressing pleasure at having escaped from the Yankees, Ransdell doubted their story and suspected "deep laid villany at the bottom of it." In neighboring Mississippi, James Alcorn, a planter in Coahoma County, thought the recent Union raids had "thoroughly demoralized" the slaves, rendering them "no longer of any practical value to this vicinity." Less than a month later, he informed his wife: "Hadley, Anthony & Bill are very faithful, about ten days since I whipped several in the field house including your filthy, lazy Margaret; it helped them greatly."[17]

Nearly a year elapsed before the Union Army returned to these regions, and this time some of the slaves insisted that they be permitted to accompany the soldiers rather than be left behind. Near Alexandria, an elderly slave told a Union correspondent, "Oh, master! since you was here last, we have had dreadful times." Several other slaves who had gathered around him corroborated his narration of a reign of terror.

> We seen stars in the day time. They treated us dreadful bad. They beat us, and they hung us, and starved us. . . . Why, the day after you left, they jist had us all out in a row and told us they was going to shoot us, and they did hang two of us; and Mr. Pierce, the overseer, knocked one with a fence rail, and he died next day. Oh, Master! we seen stars in de day time. And now we going with you, we go back no mo'![18]

Even if such stories were exaggerated for northern consumption, the fact remains that many slaves realistically perceived the degree to which their "freedom" rested on a Yankee presence. Once the troops moved on, despite the assurances of Union officers and regardless of how exemplary black behavior might have been, the status and conditions of labor of the slaves tended in many regions to revert back to what they had been, sometimes with painful consequences for those who insisted upon asserting their freedom or who were thought to have been "spoiled" by the Yankees. "The negroes' freedom was brought to a close to-day," a South Carolina white woman reported with relief, noting that as soon as the Yankees moved on, Confederate "scouts" assembled the slaves, told them the Union soldiers had no right to free them, and advised them to return to their usual tasks. Many former slaves recalled precisely that experience. "They tol' us we were free," an ex-North Carolina slave testified about the Yankees, but the master "would get cruel to the slaves if they acted like they were free." Although recognizing that he was free, a former Alabama slave knew better than to claim that freedom in the presence of his master. "Didn't do to say you was free. When de war was over if a nigger say he was free, dey

shot him down. I didn't say anythin', but one day I run away." After
Confederate troops briefly reoccupied several parishes in southern Louisiana, James Walkinshaw, an overseer, quickly made it clear to the blacks
he supervised that the Yankee invasion had changed nothing. "Don't contradict me," he shouted at a slave who protested his order to work harder.
"I don't allow anybody white or black to do that; if you contradict me again,
I'll cut your heart out; the Yankees have spoiled you Niggers but I'll be
even with you." Apparently the verbal reprimand was not sufficient, for
the overseer terminated the incident by stabbing the "spoiled" slave in the
breast.[19]

The racial tensions exacerbated by black behavior during the Yankee
invasion persisted long after the troops had moved elsewhere. With even
greater vigilance, slaveholders and local whites scrutinized the remaining
blacks, looking for any actions, words, or changes in their demeanor that
suggested Yankee influences. Eliza Evans, a former Alabama slave, could
recall quite vividly the day she first used the surname which a Yankee
soldier had persuaded her to assume. "Jest Liza," she had told the soldier
when he asked for her name. "I ain't got no other names." After ascertaining that she worked for a John Mixon, the Yankee had told her, "You are
Liza Mixon. Next time anybody call you nigger you tell 'em dat you is a
Negro and your name is Miss Liza Mixon." The idea appealed to the young
slave. "The more I thought of that the more I liked it and I made up my
mind to do jest what he told me to." Several days later, after the Yankees
had withdrawn from the area, Eliza was tending the livestock when her
master approached. "What you doin', nigger?" he demanded to know. "I
ain't no nigger," she replied. "I'se a Negro and I'm Miss Liza Mixon."
Startled by her response and sensitive to any signs of post-Yankee insolence, the master picked up a switch and ran after her. "Law', but I was
skeered!" she recalled. "I hadn't never had no whipping so I ran fast as I
can to Grandma Gracie." She reached her grandmother about the same
time her master did. "Gracie," he charged, "dat little nigger sassed me."
When Eliza explained what had happened, revealing the conversation with
the soldier, her grandmother decided to mete out the punishment herself.
"Grandma Gracie took my dress and lift it over my head and pins my hands
inside, and Lawsie, how she whipped me and I dassent holler loud either."
Still, as she recalled the incident many years later, Eliza Evans suggested
that she had derived considerable self-pride from this initial assertion of
freedom. "I jest said dat to de wrong person," she concluded.[20]

What, then, was "freedom" and who was "free"? The fluctuating
moods of individual masters, unexpected changes in the military situation,
the constant movement of troops, and widespread doubts about the validity
and enforcement of the Emancipation Proclamation were bound to have a
sobering effect on the slaves' perceptions of their status and rights, leaving
many of them quite confused if not thoroughly disillusioned. The sheer
uncertainty of it all prompted blacks to weigh carefully their actions and
utterances, as they had earlier in the war, even in some instances to

disclaim any desire to be free or to deny what the Yankees told them. "Sho' it ain't no truf in what dem Yankees wuz a-sayin'," Martha Colquitt recalled her mother telling her, "and us went right on living just like us always done 'til Marse Billie called us together and told us de war wuz over and us wuz free to go whar us wanted to go, and us could charge wages for our work."[21]

Only with "the surrender," as they came to call it, did many slaves begin to acknowledge the reality of emancipation. The fall of Richmond and the collapse of the Confederacy broke the final links in the chain. With freedom no longer hanging on every military skirmish, slaves who had shrewdly or fearfully refrained from any outward display of emotion suddenly felt free to release their feelings and to act on them. Ambrose Douglass, who claimed to have celebrated emancipation every time the Yankees came into Harnett County, North Carolina, sensed that this time it was different, and he proposed to make certain. "I was 21 when freedom finally came, and that time I didn't take no chances on 'em taking it back again. I lit out for Florida." The day the war ended, Prince Johnson recalled, "wagon loads o' people rode all th'ough de place a-tellin' us 'bout bein' free." When the news reached Oconee, Georgia, Ed McCree found himself so overcome that he refused to wait for his master to confirm the report of Lee's surrender: "I runned 'round dat place a-shoutin' to de top of my voice."[22]

In the major cities and towns, far more than in the countryside, the post-Appomattox demonstrations resembled the Jubilees that would become so firmly fixed in black and southern lore. If only for a few days or hours, many of the rural slaves flocked to the nearest town, anxious to join their urban brethren in the festivities and to celebrate their emancipation away from the scrutiny of their masters and mistresses. When news of "the surrender" reached Athens, Georgia, blacks sang and danced around a hastily constructed liberty pole in the center of town. (White residents cut it down during the night.) Although urban blacks had enjoyed a certain degree of autonomy in the past, military occupation afforded them the first real opportunity to express themselves openly and freely as a community, unhampered by curfews, passes, and restrictions on assemblages. Even before Appomattox, many of them made full use of such opportunities.[23]

The largest and most spectacular demonstration took place in Charleston, less than a month after Union occupation. More than 4,000 black men and women wound their way through the city streets, cheered on by some 10,000 spectators, most of them also black. With obvious emotions, they responded to a mule-drawn cart in which two black women sat, while next to them stood a mock slave auctioneer shouting, "How much am I offered?" Behind the cart marched sixty men tied together as a slave gang, followed in turn by a cart containing a black-draped coffin inscribed with the words "Slavery is Dead." Union soldiers, schoolchildren, firemen, and members of various religious societies participated in the march along with an impressive number of black laborers whose occupations pointed up the important role they played in the local economy—carpenters, butchers, tailors, teamsters, masons, wheelwrights, barbers, coopers, bakers, blacksmiths, wood sawyers, and painters. For the black community of Charleston, the parade proved to be an impressive display of organization and self-pride. The white residents thought less of it. "The innovation was by no means pleasant," a reporter wrote of the few white onlookers, "but they had sense enough to keep their thoughts to themselves."[24]

Less than a week after the end of the war, still another celebration in Charleston featured the ceremonial raising of the United States flag over the ruins of Fort Sumter. Far more dramatic than any of the speeches on this occasion was the presence of such individuals as William Lloyd Garrison, the veteran northern abolitionist, for whom this must have been a particularly satisfying day. Robert Smalls, the black war hero who had delivered a Confederate steamer to the Union Navy, now used that same ship to convey some 3,000 blacks to Fort Sumter. On the quarterdeck stood Major Martin R. Delany, who had once counseled emigration as the only alternative to continued racial oppression and enslavement and who would soon take his post as a Freedmen's Bureau agent in South Carolina. Next to Delany stood another black man, the son of Denmark Vesey, who some thirty-three years before had been executed for plotting a slave insurrection in Charleston.[25]

Nearly a week after the fall of Richmond, the Confederate dream lay shattered. When the news reached Mary Darby, daughter of a prominent South Carolina family, she staggered to a table, sat down, and wept aloud. "Now," she shrieked, "we belong to Negroes and Yankees." If the freed slaves had reason to be confused about the future, their former masters and mistresses were in many instances absolutely distraught, incapable of perceiving a future without slaves. "Nobody that hasn't experienced it knows anything about our suffering," a young South Carolina planter declared. "We are discouraged: we have nothing left to begin new with. I never did a day's work in my life, and don't know how to begin." Often with little sense of intended irony, whites viewed the downfall of the Confederacy and slavery as fastening upon them the ignominy of bondage. Either they must submit to the insolence of their servants or appeal to their northern "masters" for protection, one white woman wrote, "as if we were slaves ourselves—and that is just what they are trying to make of us. Oh, it is abominable!"[26]

Seeking "*temporary* relief" from the recent disasters, including the loss of "many of our servants," Eva B. Jones of Augusta, Georgia, immersed herself in fourteen volumes of history. But she found little comfort in a study of the past, only additional evidence of human depravity.

> How vice and wickedness, injustice and every human passion runs riot, flourishes, oftentimes going unpunished to the tomb! And how the little feeble sickly attempts of virtue struggle, and after a brief while fade away, unappreciated and unextolled! The depravity of the human heart

is truly wonderful, and the moiety of virtue contained on the historic page truly deplorable.

If she found any consolation in her readings, it was only to know how often "these same sorrows and unmerited punishments that we are now undergoing [have] been visited upon the brave, the deserving, the heroic, and the patient of all ages and in all climes!" Returning to the history that was being acted out in her own household, she bemoaned the abolition of slavery as "a most unprecedented robbery," intended only for the "greater humiliation" of the southern people. "However, it *is* done," she sighed; "and we, the *chained witnesses,* can only look on."[27]

With such thoughts preying upon them, slave-owning families prepared to surrender their human property but not the ideology that had made such possessions possible and necessary.

3

———————

WHATEVER DOUBTS persisted in the minds of slave owners about the status of their blacks were largely resolved in the aftermath of the Confederate collapse. On the day he heard of General Lee's surrender, Thomas Dabney, a prominent Mississippi planter, rode out into his fields and informed the slaves that they were free; at the same time, his daughter recalled, he advised them "to work the crop as they had been doing" and he promised to compensate them "as he thought just." Not all masters acted with such decisiveness, even after Appomattox. Only gradually, often belatedly, did many of them concede freedom to their slaves, but not without considerable self-torment, bitterness, and anxiety about the future. After Union troops occupied Augusta, Georgia, some three weeks after Lee's surrender, Jefferson Thomas read the edict from the commanding officer and only then did he feel compelled to call his slaves together to talk to them about the *probability* of freedom. When David G. Harris, a South Carolina planter, first heard about the emancipation edict in early June 1865, he said nothing to his slaves; not until mid-August, four months after the end of the war, and only after Union troops stationed nearby ordered the planters to inform their slaves, did most of them in his vicinity do so.[28]

Although they had anticipated it for some time, many slaveholding families still expressed incredulity when emancipation became a reality. "If they don't belong to me, whose are they?" one woman asked, clinging to the certainty that black people had to belong to someone. To be deprived of property some of them had worked hard to accumulate struck them with particular dismay. "I tell you it is mighty hard," a dispossessed slave owner averred, "for my pa paid his own money for our niggers; and that's not all they've robbed us of. They have taken our horses and cattle and sheep *and every thing.*" Even when they faced up to the inevitable, some had no way of knowing how to go about freeing their slaves. "This is more than I anticipated," the widowed mistress of a Georgia plantation wrote on May 17, 1865, "yet I trust it will be a gradual thing & not done all at once." Twelve days later, she remained undecided on how to proceed. "What I shall do with mine is a question that troubles day & night. It is my last thought at night & the first in the morning." After finally telling them they were free and promising to look after them, she wondered how she could possibly survive without them.[29]

The way to retain their slaves, some families determined, was to make freedom a vague and frightening prospect. Not until nearly two months after Union occupation and the end of the war did the Elmore family of Columbia, South Carolina, "talk very freely" to their servants about "the probability of freedom," and then only to make clear to them that they would find freedom "much harder than slavery." Even as some of their blacks were taking the initiative to claim their freedom, the Elmores waited until the end of May to inform the remaining servants that they were no longer slaves. In nearby Camden, Emma Holmes heard that an emancipation edict had been issued in Columbia, "but we have not yet seen it, nor have any Yankees been here"; in the meantime, Emma and her mother warned the servants that in the event of freedom they would have to pay their own expenses. The uncertainty about emancipation did not deter them from dismissing two servants for insubordination, nor did it inhibit several of their slaves from leaving in mid-June without saying a word to anyone. To retain Chloe, a valued servant and cook, they told her that freedom for the blacks remained uncertain until Congress acted and most likely "negroes [would] still [be] obliged to remain with their masters." They also pleaded with Chloe "not to sneak away at night as the others had done, disgracing themselves by running away." When the Yankees finally arrived, the commanding officer, as Emma Holmes understood him, declared that the slaves were not yet free but "shall work and behave properly, though on a different footing with their former masters." Nevertheless, Chloe left in late August, after giving two days' notice, and Ann, the laundress and a "poor deluded fool," departed without even finishing her ironing.[30]

Henry W. Ravenel, the prominent South Carolinian who thought of himself as a benevolent master, was typical of those who refused to rush headlong into an acknowledgment of emancipation. "Many negroes in Aiken," he wrote in early May 1865, "hearing they were free in Augusta have gone over to hear from the Yankees the truth. Some are returning disappointed. . . . Most that we hear is mere rumor." The Union officers stationed nearby claimed to have received no instructions regarding emancipation. Thinking the issue still in doubt, Ravenel opted for delay. "My negroes have made no change in their behaviour, & are going on as they have always hitherto done. Until I know that they are legally free, I shall let them continue." After the local Union Army commander ordered that the slaves be set free, Ravenel took the required oath of allegiance to the

United States Constitution in late May and only then did he resolve his doubts about emancipation. "It is the settled policy of the country," he concluded. "I have today formally announced to my negroes the fact, & made such arrangements with each as the new relation rendered necessary."[31]

While slave-owning families determined how and whether to break the news, the blacks themselves were not necessarily passive spectators. Most often, they first heard about their freedom when the Yankee soldiers passed through the vicinity. "We's diggin' potatoes," a former Louisiana and Texas slave recalled, "when de Yankees come up with two big wagons and make us come out of de fields and free us. Dere wasn't no cel'bration 'bout it. Massa say us can stay couple days till us 'cide what to do." In the cities and towns, the presence of Union troops both confirmed and helped to enforce black freedom; many rural slaves, in fact, learned of their freedom by accompanying their master to town on some errand. "No Negro is improved by a visit to Columbia, & a visit to Charleston is his certain destruction," an up-country South Carolinian concluded, after he had observed the demoralizing effects of such a visit on a neighbor's slave who now talked wildly about making a "bargain" before working any more.[32]

The same network of communications developed by slaves to keep themselves informed of the war also helped to spread the news about freedom to plantations and farms bypassed by the Yankees. The conversations of the "white folks" remained a prime source of information, and many body servants returning with their masters from the war front were feted by their fellow slaves not only for their heroism but for the valuable information they brought. "All de slaves crowded 'roun me an' wanted to know if dey wus gonna be freed or not an' when I tol' 'em dat de war wus over an' dat dey wus free dey wus all very glad." Charlotte Brooks had been sold at the age of seventeen to a hard-driving Texas planter. Working in the house as a cook, she overheard a conversation about freedom, immediately ran into the field to inform the other slaves, and they all quit work together. Still another source of information was employers seeking to hire black laborers. Taking advantage of the momentary absence of a master, who had refused to tell his slaves they were free, two white men representing a nearby mill informed Lizzie Hughes's mother she was a free woman, handed her "a piece of paper" to prove it, and offered to pay her twelve dollars a month if she would cook for the mill hands.[33]

Whatever the source, the news reached some slaves at a most opportune time. During an altercation with her mistress, Annie Gregg, a Tennessee slave, watched as she picked up a handful of switches with the intention of meting out the usual punishment for insolence. "I picked up the pan of boiling water to scald the chickens in. She got scared of me, told me to put the pan down. I didn't do it." Quickly called to the scene, the master scolded his wife rather than the slave, reminding her that the slaves were now "as free as you are or I am." To Annie Gregg, the intervention of her master, whom she had always considered "cruel," was only slightly less startling than the news itself. "That is the first I ever heard about freedom," she recalled. The news of freedom had immediate significance, too, for the Louisiana slaves hiding out in the cane brakes along the Mississippi River, for the Texas mother who dreaded having to send her small child out into the fields to work, for the North Carolina slave still wearing a ball and chain after trying to run away (a Yankee officer had to take him to town to cut it off), and for the many slaves who suddenly found themselves released from slave pens and jails—among them, "Uncle Tom," an Arkansas slave, "the best reader, white or black, for miles," who had made the mistake of reading a newspaper with the latest war news to a gathering of blacks. And for a Tennessee slave who had been purchasing her freedom, the news relieved her of the need to pay any more. "De rest ain't paid yet," she said with a smile. "No, sah! leave dat to de judgment-day."[34]

While their "white folks" refused to confirm their freedom, numbers of slaves continued to strike out on their own. The many blacks who flocked to the Union camps or left with the Yankee soldiers had acted to determine their own status, as did the slaves in Kentucky and Missouri and other states and regions unaffected by the Emancipation Proclamation. Yet despite examples of slave initiative, the habits and dependency learned as slaves, as well as the need to survive, prompted many blacks to refrain from any premature or hasty assertion of their freedom. If doubts persisted, both reason and fear sustained those doubts. Even when the Yankees informed them of freedom, they often accompanied the announcement with admonitions that left some blacks understandably confused. In explaining their new status to them, a Union officer in Liberty County, Georgia, reportedly warned the blacks "to stay at home and work harder than they had ever done in their lives." The soldiers, he added, were there to make certain "that they behaved themselves." A white resident who overheard the talk observed, "They (the Nigs) were quite disgusted."[35]

The example of blacks who were beaten for claiming their freedom prematurely tended to make the others cautious about how they acted and what they said. Again, the temperaments of individual masters and mistresses varied considerably, particularly when they had to face still further losses from a war that had already cost them dearly. While some tried to deny or distort the news of freedom, others backed their denials with a show of force. The master on a Tennessee plantation interpreted a slave's assertion of freedom as a display of insolence and slapped the woman across the face—the first time he had ever laid hands on her. Only after a visit to the nearby town did he reluctantly accept the fact of emancipation. "Seemed like he couldn't understand how freedom was to be," one of his former slaves recalled. No matter what they heard, however, some slave-owning families resisted the advent of freedom and used every wile and device to postpone or deny it. "Ed," a Georgia mistress inquired of a young slave, "you suppose them Yankees would spill their blood to come down here to free you niggers?" That question he could not answer, but "I'se free anyhow," he insisted. At that, the mistress dropped any further attempt to reason with him. "Shut up," she ordered, or "I'll mash your mouth." Not until midsummer 1865, and only after the arrival of Union troops, did she acknowledge his freedom.[36]

With the end of the war, Federal officials attempted in various ways to impress upon slaves and masters that emancipation was now the law of the land. That ran contrary, however, to the persistent belief in some regions that slavery remained a legal institution until the new state legislatures and perhaps eventually the Supreme Court of the United States resolved the question. By offering inducements to their blacks to remain with them, some planters evidently hoped not only to complete the current crops but to reap the benefits of court decisions which might invalidate the Emancipation Proclamation. The only real question to be decided, according to the leading newspapers of Jackson, Mississippi, was whether or not the state should adopt a system of gradual and compensated emancipation. After visiting three counties in that state, a Union officer thought such opinions "to be the views of the people generally" and that the prospects for an early recognition of emancipation were quite dim. "Nowhere that I have been do the people generally realize the fact that the negro is Free."[37]

Disturbed by the apparent resiliency of the "peculiar institution," the Freedmen's Bureau, a new Federal agency designed to ease the slave's transition to freedom, undertook the task of publicizing and enforcing the abolition of slavery. In late May 1865, Bureau officers warned that any person employing freedmen who failed to compensate them for their labor would be adjudged disloyal to the United States government and risked having his or her property seized and divided among the freedmen. In Louisiana, Bureau agents were asked to read the Emancipation Proclamation on every plantation within their jurisdiction and to leave copies (in French and English) with the freedmen as well as the planters. At the same time, Bureau officers in Mississippi distributed circulars to black preachers and urged that meetings of freedmen be convened at which the Proclamation would be read and explained.[38]

For numerous slaves, in fact, freedom came only when "de Guvment man" made his rounds of the plantations and forced the planters to acknowledge emancipation. The mere threat of such visits and the rumors that Union soldiers were patrolling the countryside in search of offenders prompted a number of holdouts to free their slaves. The day she knew she was a free woman, Sarah Ford recalled, a Union officer came onto the plantation and read the Emancipation Proclamation to the assembled slaves. "Dat one time Massa Charley can't open he mouth, 'cause de captain tell him to shut up, dat he'd do de talkin'." On a Louisiana plantation, "way after freedom," the same scene was acted out, except that the planter's wife emerged from the house after the officer left and told her newly freed blacks: "Ten years from today I'll have you all back 'gain." Although most masters no doubt resented the interference of Federal officers and would have preferred to tell the slaves in their own time and way, Henry W. Ravenel requested the presence of a Union officer in order to make clear to his blacks that they were entitled to none of his land, they were expected to remain at work, and they were free to serve him without fear of reprisals. (The rumor had circulated, allegedly the work of black troops, that slaves found working for their previous owners would be shot.) The officer happily obliged Ravenel, warning the newly freed slaves of "the trouble & sufferings they would encounter if they left their homes."[39]

The old order died slowly, often with considerable resistance. In the remote and relatively isolated interior counties and parishes where Yankee troops had rarely if ever been seen, the war had barely interrupted the old routines and the patrollers made certain that the blacks remained on the plantations. The news of emancipation, like much of the war news, had been delayed and sometimes deliberately suppressed or distorted. "De Yankees never come into de 'dark corner,'" a black resident of Chester County, South Carolina, recalled, and not until two years after the war did they learn of their freedom—"then we all left." In the up-country of North Carolina, a freedman remarked several years after the war, "the whip is a-goin' and the horn a-blowin' just as it used to be." On some plantations, the owners barred all visitors, locked their slaves in the yards at night, and intimidated them with stories of how the Yankees intended to sell them to defray the cost of the war. Traveling through the upper and interior sections of Georgia in August 1865, James Lynch, a missionary for the African Methodist Episcopal Church, found that "in some places the people do not know really that they are free, and if they do, their surroundings are such that they would fear to speak of it."[40]

Nowhere was the problem more persistent than in Texas, which had been relatively untouched by the war. The slave population, however, had swelled after many planters in neighboring states moved their chattel there in the hope of avoiding both the Yankees and emancipation. Not until June 19, 1865, more than two months after Appomattox, would black freedom be acknowledged in Texas. "Dat a long year to wait, de las' year de war," recalled Henry Lewis, who had been a slave in Jefferson County. But even then, some planters clung to the notion that "niggers would never be free in Texas" and acted in that belief. Wash Ingram, who had faithfully toted water for Confederate soldiers during the war, claimed that his master did not free the more than three hundred slaves on the plantation until at least a year after Lee's surrender. Sometime around September, Susan Merritt recalled, "a gov'ment man" came to the plantation in Rusk County and demanded to know why the slaves had not yet been informed of their freedom. The master replied that he had first wanted to complete the crop. That day, the slaves were called out of the fields and told the news—"but massa make us work sev'ral months after that. He say we git 20 acres land and a mule but we didn't git it." What compounded the problem for the slaves in Rusk County, Susan Merritt remembered, was that freedom had been acknowledged several months earlier in neighboring counties. "Lots of niggers was kilt after freedom, 'cause the slaves in Harrison County turn loose right at freedom and them in Rusk County wasn't. But they hears 'bout it and runs away to freedom in Harrison County and they owners have 'em bushwhacked, that shot down. You could see lots of niggers hangin' to trees in Sabine bottom right after freedom, 'cause they cotch 'em swimmin' 'cross Sabine River and shoot 'em."[41]

Even where the slaves realized they were free, some preferred to wait until their masters had confirmed their new status. Hearing about freedom from others, whether they be Yankees or even neighboring slaves, seemed somehow less satisfying, perhaps less believable. Morris Sheppard, a former Oklahoma slave, claimed to have learned about Lincoln the Emancipator only from what his children were later taught in school. "I always think of my old Master as de one dat freed me, and anyways Abraham Lincoln and none of his North people didn't look after me and buy my crop right after I was free like old Master did. Dat was de time dat was de hardest and everything was dark and confusion." The number of blacks who responded to questions about their freedom by declaring, "Mas' Henry ain't told me so yit," often infuriated postwar visitors to the South, as it did black clergymen like James Lynch and Henry M. Turner who reproached their people for the way they still cringed before their old masters and mistresses. Near Lexington, North Carolina, a northern correspondent encountered a seventy-year-old black ferryman who had outlived seven masters and who for forty-three years had conveyed passengers across the Yadkin River. Although freedom had been declared in this region, he had not yet severed his ties with the woman who owned him.

"Well, old man, you're free now."
"I dunno, master. They say all the colored people's free; they do say it certain; but I'm a-goin on same as I allus has been."
"Why, you get wages now, don't you?"
"No, sir; my mistress never said anything to me that I was to have wages, nor yet that I was free; nor I never said anything to her. Ye see I left it to her honor to talk to me about it, because I was afraid she'd say I was insultin' to her and presumin', so I wouldn't speak first. She ha'n't spoke yet."

Bewildered by these responses, the reporter finally asked him if he intended to work on "just the same" until he died. At this point the loyal slave made it clear that although good manners and a sense of mutual obligations had kept him from asserting his freedom, he was quite prepared to impose deadlines on his patience.

"Ye see, master, I am ashamed to say anything to her. But I don't 'low to work any longer than to Christmas [1865], and then I'll ask for wages. But I want to leave the ferry. I'm a mighty good farmer, and I'll get a piece of ground and a chunk of a hoss, if I can, and work for myself."[42]

The number of slaves who waited for the master to confirm their freedom, rather than assert it independently, is not altogether surprising. Whether the enslaved worker had labored on a plantation or a farm, he had been brought up to view his master as the primary source of authority—the provider and the protector, the lawmaker and the enforcer, the judge and the jury, and most masters had deliberately cultivated feelings of dependency and helplessness in their slaves. No edict of emancipation could immediately obliterate the habits of obedience and deference with which many slaves had been inculcated since childhood. Nor could it in some instances destroy a familiar relationship worked out over a period of time, involving mutual obligations of service, sustenance, and protection. The defeat of the Confederacy and the abolition of slavery no doubt weakened the master's stature in the eyes of many slaves. But it did not necessarily lessen the respect, fear, and obedience he commanded by virtue of his authority and economic power. "A lot o' de niggers knowed nothin' 'cept what missus and marster tole us," a former Georgia slave observed. "What dey said wus just de same as de Lawd had spoken to us." And in this instance, he told them that Lincoln was dead, they were still slaves, and he would distribute black cloth so they could mourn both Lincoln and their freedom.[43]

But there were sharply contrasting stories, too, which revealed the compelling need some slaves felt to confront their masters and mistresses with the truth about freedom, if for no other reason than to remove the last doubts and to observe their reactions. Hired out to another family during the war, a Virginia slave had been working in the fields when a friend informed her that she was now free. "Is dat so?" she exclaimed. Dropping her hoe, she ran the seven miles to her old place, found her mistress, "looked at her real hard," and then shouted, "I'se free! Yes, I'se free! Ain't got to work fo' you no mo'. You can't put me in yo' pocket now!" Her mistress broke into tears and ran into the house. That was all the slave needed to see. The momentary doubt at hearing the news had been resolved, and for the first time she could begin to think of herself as a free woman.[44]

The legends that grew out of emancipation would assume a special place in the folk history of Afro-Americans. Like their white owners, they retained strong, often emotionally charged memories of this critical moment in their lives. In the interviews with former slaves conducted more than seventy years later, no event would stand out with greater clarity in their minds than the day they heard of their freedom. Even as many of the slave descendants moved into the urban North in the next century, the stories of emancipation would follow them. That was how Kathryn L. Morgan came to learn of her great-grandmother Caddy, a strong-willed and defiant slave who had been sold many times in her life but never ceased to torment her owners. Of the many tales about this remarkable woman, the one that became the favorite among her children, grandchildren, and great-grandchildren was about the day she learned of her freedom.

Caddy had been sold to a man in Goodman, Mississippi. It was terrible to be sold in Mississippi. In fact, it was terrible to be sold anywhere. She had been put to work in the fields for running away again. She was hoeing a crop when she heard that General Lee had surrendered. Do you know who General Lee was? He was the man who was working for the South in the Civil War. When General Lee surrendered that meant that all the colored people were free! Caddy threw down that hoe, she marched herself up to the big house, then, she looked around and found the mistress. She went over to the mistress, she flipped up her dress and told the white woman to do something. She said it mean and ugly. This is what she said: *Kiss my ass!*[45]

## 4

ALTHOUGH THE TIME and manner varied from place to place, the majority of masters eventually got around to informing their slaves that emancipation had become the law of the land. Occasionally, they did so under the compulsion of a Federal order, upon the visitation of a Freedmen's Bureau officer, or at the demand of their own slaves. Usually, the master himself decided how and when to make the announcement. When he sent out the word for his slaves to assemble the next day, nearly everyone knew what to expect. "There was little, if any, sleep that night," Booker T. Washington recalled. "All was excitement and expectancy." Except perhaps for the coming of the Yankees, it was like no other day in their lives. Outside the Big House, the master waited for them on the front porch, often with his entire family standing beside him. To the very end, he would invariably act the role of the patrician, even as he presided over the dispersion of his flock and the sundering of traditional and even intimate ties. Observing how their master "couldn't help but cry" or "couldn't hardly talk," some former slaves confessed to having felt a certain compassion for him at this moment, putting the best possible face on his previous treatment of them. "We couldn't help thinking about what a good marster he always had been," a former Georgia slave recalled, "and how old, and feeble, and gray headed he looked as he kept on a-talkin' that day." Such sentiments were not shared by all slaves, not even on the same plantation, and each black had a different way of recollecting a master's or mistress's tears at the moment of emancipation. "Missy, she cries and cries, and tells us we is free," a former Louisiana slave recalled, "and she hopes we starve to death and she'd be glad, 'cause it ruin her to lose us."[46]

Once the slaves had been assembled for the master's announcement, most of them stood quietly and anxiously, waiting to hear how he would choose to tell them of their freedom. Some of them remained apprehensive, recalling that the only previous occasion for such a gathering had been to tell them they had been sold. Before his master could say a word, Robert Falls remembered questioning him in a mocking manner, "Old Marster, what you got to tell us?" His mother quickly warned him that he would be whipped but the slave owner decided instead to use the outburst to make his point. As Falls recalled his words:

> No I wont whip you. Never no more. Sit down thar all of you and listen to what I got to tell you. I hates to do it but I must. You all aint my niggers no more. You is free. Just as free as I am. Here I have raised you all to work for me, and now you are going to leave me. I am an old man, and I cant get along without you. I dont know what I am going to do.

In less than ten months, he was dead. "Well, sir," Falls explained, "it killed him."[47]

What the slaves recalled most vividly, "jes like it yestiddy," was the manner in which the master recognized their freedom, both his words and temperament at that moment. The way he imparted the information revealed much about his state of mind, the kind of relationship he thought he enjoyed with his slaves, and how he viewed the future. He first read to them some official-looking paper setting forth the details of emancipation. It might have been the Emancipation Proclamation itself or a recent Federal circular; in any event, the language was cold, detached, bureaucratic, and often incomprehensible. After the formal reading, Silas Smith of South Carolina remembered, "us still sets, kaise no writing never aggrevated us niggers way back dar." Since such a moment called for absolute clarity, most masters obliged with their own explanation, and those were the words the slaves had waited to hear. "We didn't quite understand what it was all about," a former Missouri field hand recalled, "until he informed us that it meant we were slaves no longer, that we were free to go as we liked, to work for anyone who would hire us and be responsible to no one but ourselves." As if to underscore the significance of his remarks, and perhaps in some instances to commemorate the slave's graduation to a different status, some masters ceremonially presented to each of them "de age statement," which included his or her name, place of birth, and approximate age or date of birth. "I's 16 year when surrender come," Sam Jones Washington told an interviewer many years later. "I knows dat, 'cause of massa's statement. All us niggers gits de statement when surrender come."[48]

To free his blacks was not to surrender the convictions with which he had held them as slaves. In explaining to them the circumstances that now made freedom necessary, most masters made it abundantly clear that their actions did not flow from some long-repressed humanitarian urge. "We went to the war and fought," a Texas planter declared, "but the Yankees done whup us, and they say the niggers is free." That was the typical explanation, as most ex-slaves recalled it: they were now free " 'cause de gov'ment say you is free" or " 'cause the damned Yankees done 'creed you are." If some slaves had felt that only "massa" could free them, many masters insisted that the Yankees had set them free. That they chose to view emancipation in these terms was perfectly consistent with their own self-image. "I have seen slavery in every Southern State," a prominent

Virginian concluded in June 1865, "and I am convinced that for the slave it is the best condition in every way that has been devised." The "tens of thousands" of old men, women, and children he expected would now starve for lack of support only made him that much more certain. "A Farmer now has to pay his hands and he will keep none but such as will work well, women with families and old men are not worth their food and they are being turned adrift by the thousands." As many masters viewed this moment, then, if they had acted from humanitarian considerations, they would have retained slavery, because of the protection and sustenance it afforded a people incapable of caring for themselves.[49]

If slaveholders felt morally reprehensible or guilt-ridden, they evinced no indication of it at the moment they declared their blacks to be free. Nothing in the postwar behavior and attitudes of these people suggested that the ownership of slaves had necessarily compromised their values or tortured their consciences. Nor was there any reason to suspect hypocrisy or self-deception in the "strong conviction" of Henry W. Ravenel, for example, "that the old relation of master & slave, had received the divine sanction & was the best condition in which the two races could live together for mutual benefit." Any detectable twinges of conscience in the slaveholding class largely stemmed from the realization that some had abused the institution. But like any northern employer, the master maintained that the excesses of the few should not be permitted to question or undermine the system itself. Nor were most of them intent on foisting the responsibility for bondage on the New Englanders who had initially supplied them. After all, a New Orleans newspaper observed several years after the war, the transplantation from Africa to North America had "humanized" the Negro, regenerating him in body, mind, and morals. Rather than confess any misgivings about their slaveholding past, most masters at this moment viewed themselves as decent men, good Christians who had performed a useful, necessary, and benevolent task, fulfilling an obligation to an inferior people which more than compensated for the labor they had received in return. There was nothing for which they needed to apologize. As George A. Trenholm proudly told the Chamber of Commerce of Augusta, Georgia, in early 1866, "Sir, we have educated them. We took them barbarians, we returned them Christianized and civilized to those from whom we received them; we paid for them, we return them without compensation. Our consciences are clear, our hands are clean."[50]

If any slave owner felt the need to reassure himself, he might use the occasion of emancipation to remind the assembled blacks how well they had fared under his tutelage. After making precisely that point, a Texas planter who had moved his slaves there from Virginia during the war asked them if he had ever treated anyone meanly. Every one of the slaves, Liza Smith recalled, shouted, "No, sir!" and that brought a smile to their master's face. Equally confident of his image, Isaiah Day, known to his slaves as "Papa Day" because he never liked the title of master, read the official proclamation and then told them, as one of his slaves recalled: "De gov'ment don't need to tell you you is free, 'cause you been free all you days. If you wants to stay you can and if you wants to go, you can. But if you go, lots of white folks ain't gwine treat you like I does." With slightly less confidence, a Georgia planter, proud of the behavior of his slaves during the Yankee occupation, confessed to them, as he freed them, that he had never realized the extent of their love for him. "He told us he had done tried to be good to us and had done de best he could for us," one of his former slaves recalled. John Bonner, an Alabama planter, after reminding his slaves how well he had provided for them, simply warned any who now chose to leave that they would "jes' have to root, pig, or die."[51]

To impress his freed slaves with the bounties and security they had enjoyed was less designed to assuage any feelings of guilt than to entice them to remain with him. That prime consideration elicited many a personal note in the master's announcement of freedom. With tears in his eyes, his head bowed, and his hands clasped behind his back, the Reverend Robert Turner, a preacher, farmer, and storekeeper, told his newly freed slaves how much he admired each of them, appreciated their faithfulness, and hated to lose them. The appeal had no apparent effect, as nearly every one of his blacks left him. To remind their slaves of the "good life" they had provided them, some masters chose to celebrate emancipation with a bountiful feast or party. On a plantation in Harnett County, North Carolina, Taylor Hugh McLean called his slaves out of the fields, met them at the gate, told them they were free, and invited them to eat dinner. It proved to be a feast few of them could forget.

> He had five women cooking. He told them all he did not want them to leave, but if they were going they must eat before they left. He said he wanted everybody to eat all he wanted, and I remember the ham, eggs, chicken, and other good things we had at that dinner. Then after the dinner he spoke to all of us and said, "You have nowhere to go, nothin' to live on, but go out on my other plantation and build you some shacks."

With similar generosity, John Thomas Boykin, a substantial Georgia planter, turned emancipation into "a big day," killed several hogs for the occasion, rolled out barrels of whiskey, and invited his freed slaves to enjoy themselves and consider his proposal to stay with him and work for pay.[52] Whether or not a master consciously used such festivities to seduce his newly freed work force, none of those ex-slaves who recalled them claimed it influenced their decision to stay on or leave.

Few slave owners, in any case, thought it necessary or desirable to accompany the announcement of freedom with a lavish entertainment. Maintaining the posture of the protective father, addressing his "children" who might soon experience the cruel and inhospitable world outside the plantation, many masters preferred to use this solemn occasion to offer advice and moral instruction. This was "no time for happiness," a Mississippi planter told his former slaves, for they had no experience with freedom. Albert Hill, who had been a slave in Georgia, recalled how his master tried to explain to them on this day the difference between freedom ("hustlin' for ourselves") and slavery ("dependin' on someone else"). Even as the master stressed the problems his slaves were liable to confront as freedmen and freedwomen, he seldom suggested, at least not in their presence, that he may have been negligent in preparing them to assume the responsibilities of freedom. Rather, he reminded his blacks how he had raised them to be honest, to work diligently, and to lead moral and Christian lives. But at the same time, and without perceiving any contradiction, he usually urged them to remain on the plantation until, as one former slave recalled, "dey git de foothold and larn how to do"—that is, until they learned how to take care of themselves.[53]

The least any gentleman planter could do at this time was to invite his "people" to stay with him and continue to share in the comforts, sustenance, and protection the old "home" supposedly afforded them. He acted, in other words, to preserve his source of labor in the guise of protecting his former slaves from the inevitable hardships and snares of freedom. Claiming a responsibility toward them as dependents, which emancipation should in no way compromise, some masters tried to ease the "burden" of freedom on the older slaves and the children. "Old Amelia & her two grandchildren," Henry W. Ravenel wrote, "I will spare the mockery of offering freedom to. I must support them as long as I have any thing to give." Whether from a sense of paternal obligation or to exploit their labor, some masters insisted that the children remain with them until they reached the age of twenty-one, and the apprenticeship laws usually permitted them to do so if the parents were missing or unable to support the children. Silas Dothrum, a former Arkansas slave who could not recall ever seeing his parents, was about ten years old when freedom came: "They kept me in bondage and a girl that used to be with them. We were bound to them that we would have to stay with them. They kept me just the same as under bondage. I wasn't allowed no kind of say-so." In some instances, the attempt to retain the children amounted to little less than kidnapping, with the masters resisting the efforts of parents to claim them. Millie Randall, a former Louisiana slave, recalled how her master "takes me and my brother, Benny, in de wagon and druv us round and round so dey couldn't find us." Finally, their mother induced the justice of the peace to intervene on her behalf.[54]

Although a confusion of values often marked their efforts, many slaveholders perceived the need to accommodate their old views and moral justifications to the reality of freed blacks. Few planters embodied the paternal ideal more faithfully in this moment of transition than Myrta Lockett Avary's father, a Virginia slaveholder. His daughter's recollection of the day freedom came to the plantation testified quite vividly to what the South wanted so desperately to believe—the enduring strength and viability of the traditional ties that had bound the white family and their blacks. Although the Yankees had already told the slaves they were free, they waited to hear the master make it so. On the night of the announcement, Myrta Avary recalled, the slaves assembled in the back yard, many of them holding pine torches. On the porch of the Big House stood her father, next to a table on which a candle had been placed. Looking out at a "sea of uplifted black faces," all of them now fastened on him, the planter first read from a formal document, presumably the Emancipation Proclamation, after which he spoke to them in a trembling voice.

> You do not belong to me any more. You are free. You have been like my own children. I have never felt that you were slaves. I have felt that you were charges put into my hands by God and that I had to render account to Him of how I raised you, how I treated you. I want you all to do well. You will have to work, if not for me, for somebody else. Heretofore, you have worked for me and I have supported you, fed you, clothed you, given you comfortable homes, paid your doctors' bills, bought your medicines, taken care of your babies before they could take care of themselves; when you were sick, your mistress and I have nursed you; we have laid your dead away. I don't think anybody else can have the same feeling for you that she and I have. I have been trying to think out a plan for paying wages or a part of the crop that would suit us all; but I haven't finished thinking it out. I want to know what you think. Now, you can stay just as you have been staying and work just as you have been working, and we will plan together what is best. Or, you can go. My crops must be worked, and I want to know what arrangements to make. Ben! Dick! Moses! Abram! line up, everybody out there. As you pass this porch, tell me if you mean to stay; you needn't promise for longer than this year, you know. If you want to go somewhere else, say so—and no hard thoughts!

After their master completed his talk, the blacks, who had "listened silently," passed before him, each one of them indicating that he intended to remain. Uncle Andrew, the black patriarch on this plantation, no doubt spoke the sentiments of most of them when he explained his decision: "Law, Marster! I ain' got nowhar tuh go ef I was gwine!" The next morning, the freedmen went about their regular duties, except for Uncle Eph, who was nowhere to be found. Several days later, he returned, a disillusioned man and "the butt of the quarters for many a day." On this Virginia plantation, the transition from slavery to freedom had been completed.

It was the perfect picture, embodying the notions of white nobility, black humility, mutual obligations, faithful service, and the extended family unit—black and white. The slaves had reacted precisely as any "grateful" and properly trained people would have been expected to react. And Uncle Eph had discovered for all of them the advantages of the old home compared to the uncertainty and insecurity that lay outside. "I jes wanter see whut it feel lak tuh be free," he explained after his brief sojourn, "an' I wanter to go back to Ole Marster's plantation whar I was born. It don' look de same dar, an' I done see nuff uh freedom."[55]

If every planter could have been reasonably confident of this kind of scenario, the anxieties and fears which gripped so many of them in the aftermath of emancipation might have been avoided. But that was not to be. Neither the dispossessed slaveholders nor their newly freed slaves were always willing or able to play the roles expected of them.

5

─────────

NO MATTER HOW EASILY the old paternalism might adapt itself to new realities, the death of slavery remained difficult to accept. The slave-owning class had always included in its ranks men and women of varying degrees of temperament and mental stability, with the vast majority falling somewhere between the legendary gentlemen and sadists. Understandably, wartime tensions, privations, and personal tragedies had taken their toll and left many white families shattered, bitter, angry, and betrayed. Now, in addition to the other calamities which had been visited upon them, they faced the loss of their slave property and perhaps their labor force. That proved to be more grief than some masters and mistresses were capable of handling. After acknowledging their freedom, "Big Jim" McClain, a Virginia planter, asked his more than one hundred slaves to continue to work for him. None of them expressed a willingness to remain, not even to harvest the current crops. At this affront, the pent-up bitterness in McClain suddenly exploded. Seizing his pistol, he fired wildly into a crowd of terrorized blacks, killing some outright and wounding others. When finally restrained, McClain tried to take his own life. At this point, several blacks promised to stay for another year and that seemed to placate him. But Union troops would have to intervene before he would permit any of his former slaves to leave the plantation.[56]

Although few of their masters reacted as violently, newly freed slaves had little way of knowing what to expect. The violent outburst of a McClain, based on his record as a slaveholder, probably surprised none of his blacks. But Matt Gaud, on the other hand, had treated his three slave families like they were members of his own family. At least, that was how Anderson Edwards remembered him. "The other niggers called us Major Gaud's free niggers." Gaud had no sooner heard of emancipation, however, than he began to curse his blacks vigorously, proclaiming that the Almighty had never intended such a thing as "free niggers." And, as Edwards recalled, his master "cussed till he died." Having endured a hard bondage, which included being sold six times, Jane Simpson expected no help from her last owners—a temperamental mistress and alcoholic master. Anticipating no change in their attitudes, she learned soon after emancipation how accurately she had assessed their character. Like most of the slaveholding families in the neighborhood, she recalled, "dey was so mad 'cause dey had to set 'em free, dey just stayed mean as dey would 'low 'em to be anyhow, and is yet most of 'em." Not surprisingly, the plantation mistresses, many of whom suddenly faced the unpleasant prospect of doing the cooking and housework themselves, often reacted with even greater resentment than their husbands, belying what may have been left of their reputation as the benevolent half of the household. Although the master "took it well," a former South Carolina slave recalled, the mistress (who had lost two sons in the war) "just cussed us and said, 'Damn you, you are free now.'" At the same time, the mistress of a Georgia plantation, where some two hundred slaves had resided, gave every indication of losing her mind after her husband acknowledged the emancipation decree. "I 'members how she couldn't stay in the house," Emma Hurley remarked, "she jest walked up an' down out in the yard a-carrin'-on, talkin' an' a-ravin'."[57]

To believe the testimony of former slaves, some of their masters and mistresses never did recover from emancipation but died shortly afterwards from "heartbreak" and grief. "Miss Polly died right after the surrender," a former Virginia slave recalled. "She was so hurt that all the negroes was going to be free. She died hollering 'Yankee!' She was so mad that she just died." Similarly, Isaac Martin, who had been a slave in Texas, remembered that his master "didn' live long atter dey tek his slaves 'way from him. Well, it jis' kill him, dat's all." In these instances, as in many others, it remains unclear whether the "heartbreak" was induced by the loss of slaves with whom the white owners thought they had intimate ties, the loss of property and suddenly dim economic prospects, or the fears engendered by the thought of four million free blacks. More than likely, the grief stemmed largely from a sense that the world as they had known it was collapsing all around them. Nevertheless, whatever the actual cause of death, the former slaves had their own ideas. Within ten or fifteen days after his freed slaves began to leave him, "Massa" Harry Hogan was dead, and one black he had owned attributed it to "all de trouble comin' on him at once." Within three weeks after the slaves on an Arkansas plantation heard they were free, they buried their mistress. "The news killed her dead," one of them recalled. And when "Marster" Billy Finnely returned from the war (his brother had been killed in action), only to find the slaves freed and most of them leaving the plantation, he seemed unable to cope with reality; his mother found him one day in a shed, his throat slashed, and beside him the razor and a note which revealed that he did not care to live " 'cause de nigger free."[58]

To attribute the deaths of masters or mistresses to grief over the loss of their slaves poses obvious difficulties, despite the exactitude with which some blacks were able to pinpoint the occurrence. Still, the reported instances of this kind in the recollections of former bondsmen occur too frequently to dismiss them altogether as flights of fantasy or faulty memory. What remains crucial is that so many ex-slaves chose to recall the death of a master or mistress in this way, as if to suggest that their "white folks" had been so dependent on them that they were unable to conceive of a future without them. "Old Mistress never git well after she lose all her niggers," Katie Rowe recalled, "and one day de white boss [the overseer] tell us she jest drap over dead setting in her chair, and we know her heart jest broke." Such testimony differed in no significant respect from how Duncan Clinch Heyward remembered the death of his grandfather, who had been one of the largest rice planters in South Carolina.

> As my grandfather sat on the piazza of his house at the Wateree, his former slaves stopped on their way to the station to bid him goodbye. All they said was that they were going home, and would look for him soon. He never returned to Combahee and did not see them again. Broken in health and staggered by his losses, Charles Heyward could not recover under the final blow. The emancipated slave could look forward to a better day for himself and his descendants, but the old slaveholder's day was done. He soon went to his grave and his traditions and his troubles were buried with him.[59]

Although dismay and anxiety over emancipation were hardly uncommon, not all slaveholders shared these fashionable ailments in the same degree and only a very few permitted the shock to drive them to suicide or a premature death. Several months after Appomattox, Josiah Gorgas, the former Confederate chief of ordnance, discussed recent events with a wealthy Alabama planter and found him very much troubled, both about himself and about the future of the white race in the South. Now that his slaves had been freed, he seemed to think that his entire life had been "wasted." "This state of mind is natural, and leads to despondency in his case," Gorgas confided to his journal after the conversation, "but not so in the case of most planters." In his recent travels, Gorgas had been generally pleased by the conduct of the planter class, particularly their equanimity in the face of disaster. Here were Yankee officers coming onto their plantations, meeting and talking with the slaves, telling them they were free and promising to protect their new rights, while the former masters made no protest but avidly questioned the officers about their new relations with the blacks. It all seemed like "a gigantic dream." Four months ago, Gorgas reflected, "that Yankee Captain attempting to make such an address to their slaves, would have been hung on the nearest tree, and left there."[60]

But the readiness with which Gorgas perceived the planters adapting themselves to the new conditions could manifest itself in many different ways, not all of them consistent with the image this class had long tried to cultivate. As slaveholders, many of them had preferred to view the "peculiar institution" as an obligation and a burden, binding them to feed, clothe, and protect the blacks in return for their labor and obedience. The plantation mistress who in a moment of exasperation screamed, "It is the slaves who own me," gave perfect expression to that sense of burden. The slaveholding class had always taken considerable pride in its treatment of elderly slaves, contrasting such benevolence with the crassness of northern employers who cared neither for the aged nor the sick but turned workers onto the streets when they ceased to be productive. Actually, few slaves lived long enough to constitute a burden on their owners, and even the aged slaves often performed tasks that defrayed the cost of their upkeep. When his grandmother was no longer able to work, Frederick Douglass recalled, her owners manifested their gratitude for her many years of service by removing her to the woods, where they "built her a little hut, put up a little mud-chimney, and then made her welcome to the privilege of supporting herself there in perfect loneliness." Whatever the quality of care owners had bestowed on their elderly slaves, emancipation, as some viewed it, absolved them of any further responsibility. If the blacks were no longer his slaves, the master might feel neither the compassion, the gentlemanly compulsions, nor the economic need to provide them with the same degree of protection, sympathy, and support. None expressed it more graphically than the Georgia planter who burned the slave cabins to the ground and expelled the occupants from the plantation. Nor did Will Davison, a Texas planter, refrain from making himself clear on the day he freed his slaves. "Well, you black sons-of-bitches, you are just as free as I am," he declared, and he promised to horsewhip any of them he found on the place the next morning.[61]

Upon freeing their slaves, the expressions of relief voiced by some white families drowned out or blended indistinctly with the painful cries of betrayal and ingratitude. But this reaction reflected not so much a sense of guilt as a welcome respite from the vexations of managing troublesome blacks, as if they—the slave owners—had been emancipated. "I was glad and thankful—on my own account—when slavery ended and I ceased to belong, body and soul, to my negroes," a Virginia woman declared. With a fine ironic twist, many a master and mistress thus managed to turn the trauma and financial loss of black freedom into deliverance from the chains that had bound them to their black folk. Cornelia Spencer, a prominent resident of Chapel Hill and a future educator, hailed emancipation for the benefits it would bestow upon all whites; slavery, she insisted, had been "an awful drag" on the proper development of the South. "And because I love the white man better than I do the black, I am glad they are free." Nor could she help but add, "And now I wish they were all in—shall I say Massachusetts?—or Connecticut? Poor things! We are doing what we can for them." The equally high-minded Henry A. Wise, whose popularity in Virginia remained undiminished, told a meeting in Alexandria more than a year after the war that he praised God daily for having delivered him from the "negrodom and niggerdom" of slavery. But he claimed to feel some compassion for the real victim. "He is now a freedman but without a friend. But he is a freedman. I am now free of responsibility for his care and comfort, and, I repeat I am content." The expressions of relief tended to grow more vociferous as they became purely self-serving, designed only to cover a family's losses and to compensate shattered egos for the black betrayals. "I lost sixteen niggers," a Charleston resident remarked; "but I don't mind it, for they were always a nuisance, and you'll find them so in less than a year.... I wouldn't give ten cents apiece for them." Similarly, Emma Holmes expressed pleasure over the departure of several house slaves, "for we do not want unwilling, careless, neglectful servants about us," and a Georgia woman described the loss of a maid as "Good riddance: all parties quite *relieved.*"[62]

But relief from the anxieties of supervising blacks could last only so long as white families managed to perform the house and field labor themselves or find suitable white replacements. That proved to be a painfully brief period of time. Even as planters recognized the need to maintain a work force, however, they were now in a position to make some important decisions, not only about the disposition of the old and the very young but how many and which of the able-bodied ex-slaves they wished to retain. Noting how her neighbor had been "awfully sanguine" over losing his slaves, Mary Chesnut thought she knew why. "His main idea is joy that he has no Negroes to support, and can hire only those that he really wants." Although she had always had reservations about slavery, Mary Chesnut found no difficulty in sharing her neighbor's realistic appraisal of emancipation. "The Negroes are a good riddance," she confided to her diary. "A hired man is far cheaper than a man whose father and mother, his wife and his twelve children have to be fed, clothed, housed, nursed, taxes paid and doctors' bills." [63]

Whatever the former slaveholders thought of emancipation, it afforded them a convenient way out of supporting nonproductive laborers. Hence, a wealthy Richmond resident, who had owned large numbers of slaves, could suggest that the Emancipation Proclamation provided more immediate relief for the masters than for the intended benefactors of freedom. "It will prove a good thing for the slave-owners," he explained; "for it will be quite as cheap to hire our labor as to own it, and we shall now be rid of supporting the old and decrepit servants, such as were formerly left to die on our hands." Not all masters rushed to evict their older slaves, and some would have found it repugnant to their moral sensibilities, but many had no qualms about driving them off their plantations or thinking in such terms, even as they regretted the circumstances that made it necessary and claimed to sympathize with the victims. But why as employers should they assume any greater responsibilities than their far wealthier counterparts in the North? "We are to hire them just as free labor is hired in the North," Elias Horry Deas reasoned, as he tried to resume rice cultivation in South Carolina. "I hope this may be so for if it is, I think we will be better off, & be able to plant more successfully than we have ever yet done, as we will not have a crew of old idle lazy negros with their children to feed & clothe."[64]

Now that the blacks were no longer a financial investment, they suddenly became expendable—but only some of them. While freedmen made decisions about whether to remain on the same plantation, their former masters determined whom they wished to keep with them, based largely on previous records of behavior. "Now that they are all free," Charles C.

Jones, Jr., wrote his mother, "there are several of them not worth the hiring." She agreed, and named one in particular: "Cato has been to me a most insolent, indolent, and dishonest man; I have not a shadow of confidence in him, and will not wish to retain him on the place." If any planter felt uneasy about evicting the elderly, he might still eagerly avail himself of the opportunity to purge the work force of the proven troublemakers, the least efficient, and the bad influences, as well as those who were too quick to drop the old deference after emancipation. The sudden discovery that one of his former slaves had deceived him was sufficient provocation to discharge him. On an Alabama plantation, the newly freed workers affixed their marks to a labor contract, except for Arch, who signed his full name. That was too much for his former master, who ordered him off the place. "You done stayed in war wid me four years," he told him, "and I ain't known that was in you. Now I ain't got no confidence in you." The tribulations that awaited the employers of free black labor would provide still other excuses for discharging their former slaves. Thus did an elderly Virginia freedman find himself on the road to Richmond without a home. His master had become enraged after the able-bodied hands left him rather than work without wages, and he had countered this affront by driving everyone off the plantation, including the sick and the aged, declaring that he had no use "fo' old wore-out niggers."

> I knowed I was old and wore-out, but I growed so in his service. I served him and his father befo'e nigh on to sixty year; and he never give me a dollar. He's had my life, and now I'm old and wore-out I must leave. It's right hard, mahster!

Although not knowing what to expect now, he made it clear that he had no desire to return to the old bondage. "I'd sooner be as I is to-day." And with those words, he placed his bundle on his back and made his way along the road to Richmond.[65]

When it came to making practical decisions about the ideal labor force, planters divided sharply over whether to retain their former slaves or seek an entirely new group of blacks. Having known them so intimately as slaves, and accustomed to their deference, some families were disturbed at the idea of living with these same people as free laborers with the same rights as themselves. Perhaps, they reasoned, the former slaves knew *them* too intimately as well. Without citing any specific reason, Elias Horry Deas, the South Carolina rice planter, informed his daughter that "the general feeling on the river" was to discharge all the hands at the end of the season. "There are a very few of mine that I think I will hire again, & there is many *an old one* that will have to quit." At the same time, Edward Lynch, also a rice planter, returned from a meeting in Savannah where the assembled planters concluded that "the worst possible labor for a man to employ was the labor formerly belonging to him."[66]

But the clear preference in most instances was to retain the slaves they had known and supervised in the past. On the same day the master informed them of their freedom, he usually asked them to remain and work for some kind of compensation, with perhaps an added inducement to complete the current crops. How the freed slaves would respond, however, remained questionable. Although the "old ties" binding blacks and their "white folks" persisted long after the war, each freedman and each former owner clearly felt them in different degrees, and many felt nothing at all. It was possible for a freed slave to retain a certain affection for the old master without feeling any obligation to continue to serve him. To place any confidence in him—or perhaps in any white man or woman—was something altogether different. "You jes' let 'em 'lone, ma'am," a freedwoman observed of white people. "Yur never know which way a cat is going to jump."[67]

6

—————

NOT LONG AFTER THE WAR, the wife of a former slave trader watched in horror as a freedman in Petersburg, Virginia, skinned a live catfish. Clearly upset, she asked him how he could be so cruel. "Why, dis is de way dey used to do me," he replied, "and I's gwine to get even wid somebody." Judging by the way many whites talked in the aftermath of emancipation, that was the fate that awaited them at the hands of blacks, who would now wreak a terrible revenge on those who had kept them in bondage. The South Carolina planter who glimpsed in the "looks and language" of the freed slaves "great bitterness toward the whites" gave voice to familiar fears that mounted with every report of a disorder, every act of "insolence," and every jubilant black chorus promising to hang Jefferson Davis—and presumably the leading "rebels" along with him. Once again, there was no way the blacks could win the debate over whether they intended to avenge bondage by turning emancipation into a racial bloodbath. If they retaliated for the wrongs visited upon them and sought to punish their former masters, they revealed their ingratitude and savage natures. If they refrained from violence and showed compassion for their former owners, they revealed their natural docility, slavish mentality, and inferiority as men.[68]

In observing the black regiment he commanded, almost all of them former slaves, Colonel Higginson expressed surprise over the absence of any feelings of affection or revenge toward their former masters and mistresses. On one occasion, during a raid in Florida, a black sergeant had pointed out to him the spot where whites had hanged his brother for leading a band of runaway slaves. What impressed Higginson was the sergeant's remarkable composure and self-control as he related the story. "He spoke of it as a historic matter," Higginson recalled, "without any bearing on the present issue." None of his men, he noticed, ever spoke nostalgically about slavery times but neither did they evince in his presence any desire to seek a violent revenge on their former owners. Rather, they tended in their conversations to discriminate between various types of slaveholders, with some of them claiming to have had "kind" owners who had bestowed occasional favors upon them. But that in no way lessened their hatred of the institution of slavery. "It was not the individuals," wrote Higginson, "but the ownership, of which they complained. That they saw to be a wrong which no special kindnesses could right."[69]

But if Higginson detected no mood of vengeance, other whites were less certain. While the North engaged in a furious debate over what to do with the South and the Confederate leaders, more than one curious northern visitor thought to ask the freedmen they encountered what kind of punishment should be meted out to their former masters. The question itself made many blacks visibly uncomfortable, as though torn between what they really felt and what they thought the white reporters wanted to hear. Not being certain, many chose obfuscation. Although a few openly declared that hanging would be "too good" for their masters, the general response was that the Yankees should settle this question. If any slaveholders were to be punished, few if any of their former slaves wished to be around for the event, either to carry it out or to witness it. The same ex-slave who thought hanging was "too good" for his master rejected the invitation (no doubt made in jest) of a Union officer to inflict the punishment himself. "Oh, no, can't do it," he replied, "can't do it—can't see massa suffer. Don't want to see him suffer." With similar expressions of horror, a group of South Carolina blacks responded to a Yankee soldier who had promised to return their master to them for any action they deemed appropriate.

> "Oh! don't massa, don't bring him here; we no want to see him nebber more," shouted a chorus of women.
> "But what shall we do with him?"
> "Do what you please," said the chorus.
> "Shall we hang him?"
> "If you want, massa"—somewhat thoughtfully.
> "But shall we bring him *here* and hang him?"
> Chorus—much excited and shriller than ever—"no, no, don't fetch him here, we no want to see him nebber more again."

Since these freedmen were also occupying and working the land of their absent master, their reaction made considerable sense.[70]

As for punishing Confederate leaders, blacks may have sung about hanging Jeff Davis to a crab-apple tree but a black preacher came closer to capturing popular feelings: "O Lord, shake Jeff Davis ober de mouf ob Hell, but O Lord, doan' drap him in!" Except for the confiscation of land, most freedmen saw little to gain by the punishment of ex-Confederate leaders; on the contrary, some feared that an aroused white populace would surely visit its rage on the most vulnerable targets—the newly freed slaves. Gertrude Thomas, a white resident of Augusta, Georgia, had only to watch the cheering blacks running down the street, all of them eager for a glimpse of Jefferson Davis as a prisoner, to wish at that moment she could have destroyed the whole motley group with a volley of gunfire. Recognizing how intensely whites felt about this issue, blacks who thought about it at all tended to view such matters in personal and pragmatic terms, calculating the effect it might have on their own lives and destinies. Few expressed that more pointedly than the freedmen of Claiborne County, Mississippi, when they petitioned the governor in 1865 to relieve them of oppressive laws and dishonest employers. "All we ask is justice and to be treated like human beings," they pleaded, while making it clear they extended those principles to all people and bore no animosity toward their former masters.

> We have good white friends and we depend on them by the help of god to see us righted and we not want our rights by Murdering. We owe to[o] much to many of our white friends that has shown us Mercy in bygon dayes To harm thaim.... Some of us wish Mr. Jeff Davis to be Set at liberty for we [k]no[w] worse Masters than he was. Altho he tried hard to keep us all slaves we forgive him.

Elizabeth Keckley, who had worked as a maid for Davis, thought singling him out for punishment was simply irrelevant to the noble cause that had prompted her to leave his service. "The years have brought many changes," she reflected; "and in view of these terrible changes even I, who was once a slave, who have been punished with the cruel lash, who have experienced the heart and soul tortures of a slave's life, can say to Mr. Jefferson Davis, 'Peace! you have suffered! Go in peace.'" Regardless of how blacks had viewed the war, most of them could concur with the idea of amnesty for Jefferson Davis, if only because they intended to remain in a society made up largely of people of his color and outlook.[71]

The ambivalence that had always characterized the relations between slaves and their white families, along with the pragmatic need to placate an angry and bitter white South, was bound to affect how freedmen perceived their beaten and discouraged former masters and mistresses. The way in which Samuel Boulware, a former South Carolina slave, recalled the day the Yankees pillaged his master's plantation typified a widely felt reaction. "Us slaves was sorry dat day for marster and mistress. They was gittin' old, and now they had lost all they had, and more than dat, they knowed their slaves was set free." Even so, many white families were left to question the depth of such feelings, particularly after what some of them had endured at the hands of their blacks, and came away with altogether different impressions. While a South Carolina planter saw hatred of whites in the faces of the freedmen, a North Carolinian expressed the certainty that they "felt for their masters and secretly sympathized with their ruin," and she appreciatively noted what local blacks had written on a huge banner they unfurled at a recent celebration: "Respect for Former Owners."[72]

That "respect" might assume more tangible forms than commiserations and banners. Much as the wartime distress had sometimes brought masters and slaves closer together, the hard times that followed the war taxed the charitable instincts of both races. Although some freedmen returned to the old place seeking help to tide them over a difficult period, the need for assistance worked both ways. Numerous white families, reduced to economic privation by the war and the loss of their property, felt no compunctions (at least, none they admitted) about calling on their former bondsmen for help. Whether out of affection, pity, or that old sense of mutual obligations, ex-slaves invariably responded with generosity to the plight of their old masters and mistresses, at least to the extent they could afford to be generous. Had it not been for a former slave who shared his earnings with her, a North Carolina woman confessed, the family could hardly have survived the loss of their property. Two years after the war, her black benefactor died. "But even at the last," the grateful woman recalled, "he had not forgotten us. He left $600 to me, and $400 to one of my family."[73]

No doubt many freedmen derived a certain satisfaction from extending a helping hand to those who had once held them in bondage. On the Sea Islands, for example, the success of blacks in working the abandoned plantations made them "objects of attention" to the dispossessed planters, who paid occasional visits to the old places, often to seek material assistance while they waited to reclaim their lands. Some women even went from cabin to cabin among their former slaves, pleading the family's poverty and eagerly collecting food, silverware, dishes, and a little money. Such donations, a Federal official observed, were made partly out of pity but also to impress upon the owners how well they were managing themselves as free people—"an intense satisfaction if a little boastful." On one plantation, Jim Cashman welcomed his former master back, offering him the same courtesies and warm hospitality any southern gentleman might extend to a visitor and proudly reciting his achievements.

> "The Lord has blessed us since you have been gone. It used to be Mr. Fuller No. 1, now it is Jim Cashman No. 1. Would you like to take a drive through the island Sir? I have a horse and buggy of my own now Sir, and I would like to take you to see my own little lot of land and my new house on it, and I have as fine a crop of cotton Sir, as ever you did see, if you please—and Jim can let you have ten dollars if you want them, Sir."

The former owner graciously accepted both his hospitality and his assistance. In still another instance, a Georgia freedman amassed some savings from working in a sawmill while at the same time planting cotton in a small lot he had purchased. Upon the death of his former master, he came to the aid of the mistress, who had been left without any land and apparently penniless. He supported her until the woman's death some two years later. Only when it came to paying the cost of her funeral did local residents balk, saying, "He done his share already," but her own kind would bury her.[74]

While serving the Freedmen's Bureau in South Carolina, John William De Forest, a white agent, recalled a former slave who appeared at his office, not to pick up rations for himself, but to make a personal appeal on behalf of the Jacksons, a local white family in dire need of help. Except for the sudden plunge in the fortunes of this family, their plight and incapacity for steady labor, as described by this freedman, resembled the pessimistic white accounts of postwar blacks.

> "They's mighty bad off. He's in bed, sick—ha'n't been able to git about this six weeks—and his chil'n's begging food of my chil'n. They used to own three or four thous'n acres; they was great folks befo' the war. It's no use tellin' them kind to work; they don't know how to work, and can't work; somebody's got to help 'em, Sir. I used to belong to one branch of that family, and so I takes an interest in 'em. I can't bear to see such folks come down so. It hurts my feelings, Sir."[75]

Even compassion had its limits. If some freed slaves manifested sympathy for their broken and impoverished or dead masters and mistresses, there remained those who saw no reason to feel remorse of any kind. "I never had no whitefolks that was good to me," Annie Hawkins recalled of her bondage in Georgia and Texas. "Old Mistress died soon after the War and we didn't care either. She didn't never do nothing to make us love her. We was jest as glad as when old Master died." On the Sea Islands, the generosity displayed by freedmen and freedwomen went only so far, and they made clear the distinction between serving their former masters and helping them. When a former resident sent word that "she thought some of her Ma's niggers might come to wait upon her," none volunteered; instead, some of them went to see her and offered some food, money, and clothes, and the woman in return swallowed her pride and position and agreed to become a dressmaker for the blacks. After the initial gestures of goodwill, moreover, freedmen became concerned lest their generosity be misunderstood and abused. "They say that two come for every one they send away relieved," a Freedmen's Bureau agent reported from the Sea Islands, "and that it is a new way 'maussa' has of making them work for him."

> Although the "masters" weep with joy at the sight of their humble friends, and though one of them said he "should go away and cut his throat if they looked coldly upon him," yet the people are only transiently touched by this manifestation of affection. They look very jealously and uneasily upon all who return, often ask why Government lets them come back to trouble the freedman.

Near Beaufort, a former owner visited the old place, shook the hands of his former slaves, pleaded his poverty, and asked for sympathy and spare change. After all, he told them, they should realize that he and his wife knew nothing of work and had never done any. The ex-slaves needed no reminder, nor did they respond favorably to his plight when it became clear that he coveted the return of his lands upon which they were now working.[76]

Whatever the mixed emotions with which freedmen viewed their former owners after emancipation, nothing could obliterate the slave experience from their minds, and it would continue to shape the attitudes and behavior of many of them long after their old masters and mistresses had passed from the scene. Some preferred to put the past behind them, if only to contain their emotions and memories. Nearly a decade after the war, an older student at Hampton Institute, a black college, told a teacher that he preferred not to talk about slavery times. "I feel as if folks mightn't believe me, and then, if I think too much about them myself, I can't *keep feeling right,* as I want to, toward my old masters. I'd do any thing for them I could, and I want to forget what they have done to me." When in the twentieth century ex-slaves reminisced about the old days, they were apt to be less harsh in their judgments, though Martin Jackson, who recalled "good treatment," suspected many of them deliberately refrained from telling everything they knew.

> Lots of old slaves closes the door before they tell the truth about their days of slavery. When the door is open, they tell how kind their masters was and how rosy it all was. You can't blame them for this, because they had plenty of early discipline, making them cautious about saying anything uncomplimentary about their masters. I, myself, was in a little different position than most slaves and, as a consequence, have no grudges or resentment. However, I can tell you the life of the average slave was not rosy. They were dealt out plenty of cruel suffering. Even with my good treatment, I spent most of my time planning and thinking of running away.

But in the immediate aftermath of the war, memories were quite short, in some instances as short as the tempers of ex-slaves. All that might be required to set them off was the casual pronouncement by some northern visitor or reporter that many masters had been kind to their slaves. "Kind!" one freedman cried, not believing the naiveté and ignorance of the person who made the observation of his former master. "Kind! I was dat man's slave; and he sold my wife, and he sold my two chill'en . . . Kind! yes, he gib me corn enough, and he gib me pork enough, and he neber gib me one lick wid de whip, but whar's my wife?—whar's my chill'en? Take away de pork, I say; take away de corn, I can work and raise dese for myself, but gib me back de wife of my bosom, and gib me back my poor chill'en as was sold away!"[77]

To forgive their former masters and mistresses for past wrongs was to forget neither the wrongs nor the men and women who had inflicted them.

Forgiveness, like compassion, could be extended only so far. For many former slaves, the teachings of Christianity and their recollections of bondage would never be easily reconciled. Harry Jarvis remembered working for "de meanest man on all de Easte'n sho', and dat's a heap to say." Early in the war, he fled the plantation, eventually joined the Union Army, and lost a leg in the Battle of Folly Island. Some years later, two white schoolteachers questioned him about slavery days, his escape and army service, and his intense religious conversion immediately after the war. "As you have experienced religion," one of the teachers asked him, "I suppose you have forgiven your old master, haven't you?" The question came unexpectedly, the glow immediately left the man's face, and he dropped his head. Upon recovering his composure, he straightened himself and gave his reply. "Yes, sah! I'se forgub him; de Lord *knows* I'se forgub him; but"—and now his eyes suddenly blazed—"but I'd gib my oder leg to meet him in battle!" The schoolteachers thought it best at this moment to terminate the conversation.[78]

## 7

HOW THEIR FORMER SLAVES would perceive them had to be uppermost in the minds of the absentee planter families returning to their homes after the war. Where owners had abandoned their plantations, the slaves had often remained and continued to work the land, and in some regions they had been encouraged to believe that the land and the crops would remain in their hands. Now that the war had ended, however, the planters returned to reclaim their property—all but the slaves, whose freedom they were forced to acknowledge. Before long, many of the white families expected that life on the plantations would be very much as they had known it before the war. But success, as they clearly understood, still rested on the availability of labor—free black labor. As they approached the familiar surroundings, they had little way of knowing how many of their former slaves had remained, how they would be greeted, the extent to which the "old ties" had survived the crisis, and the kind of relationship they would be able to establish with those they had once called their "people." The range of reactions they encountered suggested the diversity of black response and expectations elsewhere in the South.

Except for the physical devastation, some families found that little had changed since their hasty departure. Some of their slaves had left, never to be seen again, but substantial numbers had remained and still others would shortly return. The homecoming proved in some instances to be a most pleasant occasion, exceeding the expectations of the white family and allaying whatever fears they might have entertained. When he came onto his plantations near Natchez, a former Confederate general encountered "a perfect jubilee" celebrating his return. "They picked me up and carried me into the house on their shoulders, and God-blessed me, and tanked de Lo'd for me, till I thought they were never going to get through." Returning to his "large and elegant" town house in Charleston, a former South Carolina slave owner found it occupied by his servants, "who were as humble, respectful and attentive as of old"; in his absence, they had kept the place "in the neatest and cleanest style." No doubt his gratitude over-flowed when he compared his situation with that of his far less fortunate neighbors, who found their places occupied by strange blacks cooking their meals in the drawing rooms.[79]

Despite the effusive homecomings, some planters quickly perceived that appearances could be quite deceiving. When Stephen Elliott returned to his father's plantation at Beaufort, South Carolina, he found the former slaves comfortably settled and in good spirits. "They were delighted to see me, and treated me with overflowing affection." The scene seemed to sug-gest that nothing had happened in his absence. But he soon learned other-wise, and in a most abrupt and unexpected manner. Although they greeted him warmly, the newly freed blacks combined their hospitality with an explicit statement of how matters now stood between them and their for-mer owner. "They waited on me as before, gave me beautiful breakfasts and splendid dinners; but they firmly and respectfully informed me: 'We own this land now. Put it out of your head that it will ever be yours again.' "[80]

The initial difficulty for some planters lay less in reclaiming their land than in dealing with changes in the demeanor of their former slaves. That "total change of manner" surprised and hurt Edward Barnwell Heyward "most of all" when he arrived to take over the Combahee rice plantations in South Carolina he had only recently inherited from his father. Only a year before, he had seen these people at the plantation to which they had been removed during the war, and they had seemed faithful and content. But now, as he wrote his wife, "Oh! what a change. It would kill my Father and worries me more than I expected or rather the condition of the Negroes on that place is *worse* than I expected. It is very evident they are disap-pointed at my coming there. They were in hopes of . . . having the place to themselves." Not only did they refuse at first to come out of their cabins but when they did deign to speak with him, the old deference had given way to a provoking familiarity. "If I could meet with impudence, accompanied with intelligence," Heyward told his wife, "it would not be so bad but to find the brutish rice field hands familiar, is perfectly disgusting. I have seen nothing like it before . . ."[81]

Rather than manifest any feelings of remorse or hatred for their for-mer masters, many of the newly freed slaves would have been perfectly content never to see them again. Nowhere was this feeling more pervasive, of course, than on those lands they had been working and claiming as their own. The night before Captain Thomas Pinckney returned to El Dorado, his plantation fronting the Santee River in South Carolina, he stayed at the home of a neighbor who had overseen the property in his absence. His report was less than reassuring. "Your negroes sacked your house, stripped it of furniture, bric-a-brac, heirlooms, and divided these among themselves. They got it into their heads that the property of whites belongs to them; and went about taking possession with utmost determination and insolence. Nearly all houses here have been served the same way." Proceeding to his plantation the next day, Pinckney could immediately sense how much the times had changed. Where he had once been welcomed by crowds of slaves shouting, "Howdy do, Marster! Howdy do, Boss!" only silence now greeted him. None of his former slaves was in sight. In the house, he found a solitary servant, and she seemed pleased to see him. But she claimed to know nothing about where the others had hidden themselves. The dinner hour passed but still none of the blacks ventured forward. Finally, the exasperated planter told his servant that he would come back in the morning and expected to see every one of his former slaves.

When Pinckney returned, he was armed. Since he had often carried a gun as a huntsman, he thought he could do so now "without betraying distrust" or causing any undue alarm among his men. But even as he armed himself, he tried to deny the necessity for doing so.

> Indeed, I felt no fear or distrust; these were my own servants, between whom and myself the kindest feelings had always existed. They had been carefully and conscientiously trained by my parents; I had grown up with some of them. They had been glad to see me from the time that, as a little boy, I accompanied my mother when she made Saturday afternoon rounds of the quarters, carrying a bowl of sugar, and followed by her little handmaidens bearing other things coloured people liked. At every cabin that she found swept and cleaned, she left a present as an encouragement to tidiness. I could not realise a need of going protected among my own people, whom I could only remember as respectful, happy and affectionate.

After telling the servant to summon the men, he waited for them under the trees. Slowly, they began to appear, and Pinckney could see only sullen and defiant faces, none of them showing the slightest trace of that "old-time cordiality." No longer, as he quickly noted, did they address him as "Marster" but instead made a point of referring to him as "you" or "Cap'n." That was not all he noticed. His former slaves, too, had brought their guns. "Men, I know you are free," he told them. "I do not wish to interfere with your freedom. But I want my old hands to work my lands for me. I will pay you wages." The blacks remained silent. "I want you to put my place in order," he continued, "and make it as fruitful as it used to be, when it supported us all in peace and plenty. I recognise your right to go elsewhere and work for some one else, but I want you to work for me and I will on my part do all I can for you."

This time they responded; their remarks were brief, punctuated with defiance, and accompanied by none of the old "darky" antics. "O yes, we

gwi wuk! we gwi wuk all right," one of them assured him, but in a tone that
suggested trouble rather than compliance. "We gwi wuk. We gwi wuk fuh
ourse'ves. We ain' gwi wuk fuh no white man." If they refused to work for
any white man, Pinckney asked them, where did they intend to go and how
would they support themselves? He had only to look at their faces to
anticipate their reply. "We ain' gwine nowhar," they declared. "We gwi
wuk right here on de lan' whar we wuz bo'n an' whar belongs tuh us." Some
of them had not been born on this land, Pinckney recalled to himself, but
had been purchased by him during the war—"in the kindness of his heart"
—to avoid the division of a family in the settlement of an estate. If such
thoughts crossed the minds of any of the blacks, there was nothing to
indicate it. One of them, dressed in a Union Army uniform and carrying
a rifle, made it clear that he would work or not as he pleased, come and
go as he pleased, and he claimed a portion of the land as his own. And then,
as if to underscore these words, he went to his cabin, stood in the doorway,
looked his former master in the eye, brought his gun down with a crash,
and declared, "Yes, I gwi wuk right here. I'd like tuh see any man put me
outer dis house!"

After giving the blacks some time to reconsider their position, Pinckney assembled them once again. If anything, their attitude had grown
"more insolent and aggressive." Failing to reach any understanding with
them, he now gave his former slaves ten days, after which those who
remained unwilling to work for him would be forced off the plantation.
Meanwhile, Pinckney heard of neighbors having similar experiences, some
of them "severer trials" than his own. Where only a few years before
"perfect confidence" had characterized slave-master relations, or so he
thought, almost every white man now went armed, with his weapon exposed to view, and so presumably did most of the blacks. After consulting
among themselves, the planters finally appealed directly to the Union
Army commander at Charleston, and he agreed to send a company of
troops and to address the blacks himself.

Despite the "Federal visitation," which Pinckney thought had a
"wholesome effect," the blacks still refused to work. He decided now to wait
them out until "starvation" brought about their capitulation. He did not
have to wait long. One day, his former head plower came to see him,
claiming that he could no longer feed his wife and children. When Pinckney reminded him that he had brought this grief on himself and could
return to work at any time, the former slave replied, "Cap'n, I'se willin'.
I been willin' fuh right smart while. I ain' nuvver seed dis way we been
doin' wuz zackly right. I been 'fused in my min'. But de other niggers dee
won' let me wuk. Dee don' want me tuh work fuh you, suh. I'se feared."
Although Pinckney considered distributing some food rations "without
conditions," he decided that this might be interpreted as a sign of weakness. Several days later, as he no doubt expected, his head plower reap-
peared. "Cap'n, I come tuh ax you tuh lemme wuk fuh you, suh." The
planter assented, told him the plow and mule were ready, and he could now.

draw his rations. Having broken the back of the resistance, Pinckney now had the final satisfaction of watching his former slaves slowly drift back to their cabins and out into the fields. "They had suffered," he recalled, "and their ex-master had suffered with them."[82]

The ordeal of Adele Allston, like that of Thomas Pinckney, suggested comparable situations, particularly in low-country South Carolina, where the reluctance of freed slaves to yield their brief occupation of the plantations often reached the dimensions of outright rebellion. The death of Robert F. W. Allston had left his wife with the responsibility of managing the several plantations belonging to the family, located in a section of South Carolina where blacks outnumbered whites by six to one. When the Yankees came into this region, many of the planter families had fled. On the Allston plantations, the slaves plundered the houses, seized the barn keys, locked up the overseer at Nightingale Hall, and completely intimidated the overseer at Chicora Wood. With the end of the war, Adele Allston moved almost immediately to reclaim her property and reestablish her authority. The initial skirmishes were fought over the keys to the barns, which contained the crops that the blacks had already made. Union soldiers had turned the keys over to the slaves, encouraging them in some instances to distribute the contents among themselves. Both the freed slaves and the planters recognized that whoever controlled those keys exercised more than symbolic authority over the plantations themselves. "This would be a test case, as it were," wrote Elizabeth Allston, who would accompany her mother on the trip. "If the keys were given up, it would mean that the former owners still had some rights."

After taking the oath of allegiance to the United States and securing a written order which commanded the blacks to surrender the keys, Adele Allston and her daughter set out for the plantations. They were under no illusions as to what they might expect to find there. "If you come here," a close friend had warned, "all your servants who have not families so large as to burthen them and compel a veneering of fidelity, will immediately leave you. The others will be more or less impertinent as the humor takes them and in short will do as they choose." If she still insisted on returning, her friend offered some advice: "I warn you ... not to stir up the evil passions of the blacks against you and your family if you wish to return here. The blacks are masters of the situation, this is a conquered country and for the moment law and order are in abeyance." And one sure way "to stir up the evil passions," she believed, was to attempt to dispossess the blacks of the property they had seized. "The negroes would force you to leave the place, perhaps do worse. I have not been in my negro street nor spoken to a field hand since 1st March. The only way is to give them rope enough, if too short it might hang us. No outrage has been committed against the whites except in the matter of property." If her friend's warnings were not sufficiently alarming, Adele Allston had only to read a recent letter from the overseer at Chicora Wood, in which he related how the blacks permitted him to say nothing to them about work. Despite these ominous reports, Adele Allston remained adamant in her determination to return and face her former slaves. It was bound to be a memorable experience.

Arriving first at the Nightingale Hall plantation (where the blacks had been "specially turbulent"), Adele and Elizabeth Allston encountered less trouble than they had anticipated. Stepping out of the carriage (but insisting that her daughter remain inside), Mrs. Allston stood in the midst of her former slaves, spoke to each of them by name, and inquired after their children. Gradually, the initial tension eased, the black foreman surrendered the keys, and the Allstons quickly moved on. "She did not think it wise to go to the barn to look at the crops," Elizabeth wrote of her mother. "Having gained her point, she thought it best to leave." At the Chicora Wood plantation, the keys were handed over with even less difficulty. The Allstons concluded that was because Daddy Primus, the head carpenter, who held the keys, "was a very superior, good old man." Although the blacks here "seemed glad" to see them, the house which they had helped to plunder stood there for everyone to view, and many of the furnishings now adorned their cabins.

That left the most formidable challenge, the Guendalos plantation, which belonged to Adele Allston's son, Benjamin, whose service in the Confederate Army had kept him away from home during most of the war. With no whites present, the slaves had been reportedly "turbulent and excited." As they neared the plantation, the two Allston women had only to look around them to confirm their worst fears. The former slaves lined the road on both sides, a mood of defiance clearly reflected in their "angry, sullen black faces." What a contrast, Elizabeth thought, between their present demeanor and "the pleasant smile and courtesy or bow to which we were accustomed." Instead of the usual warm welcome, only an "ominous silence" prevailed. As the carriage passed the blacks, they formed a line behind it and followed it into the plantation.

Stopping in front of the barn, the two women found themselves suddenly surrounded by several hundred blacks. The mistress stepped down from the carriage and asked to see Uncle Jacob, the former black driver who had been left in charge of Guendalos during the war. After he showed her the rice and corn barns, she complimented him on the condition of the stored crops. But when Adele Allston then demanded the keys, the driver refused to give them up unless ordered to do so by a Federal officer. After reading the written order which Mrs. Allston had procured, however, he finally relented and slowly drew the keys from his pocket. Before he could hand them over, a young black man who had been standing nearby shook his fist at the driver and warned him, "Ef yu gie up de key, blood'll flow." The crowd immediately shouted its agreement until it became "a deafening clamor." The driver thought it best to pocket the keys, while the blacks, now "yelling, talking, gesticulating," pressed closer around the two women, leaving them virtually no standing room. Finally, the mistress ordered her carriage driver to bring her son, Charles, to the place. At the same time, the blacks decided to send for the nearest Union officer. Before leaving, however, the black envoys admonished the crowd, "Don't let no white man een dat gate," and the remaining blacks responded, "No, no, we won't let no white pusson een, we'll chop um down wid hoe—we'll chop um to pieces sho'." Adding emphasis to their threat, some of them held up their sharp and gleaming rice-field hoes, while others brandished pitchforks, hickory sticks, and guns.

With no white person within five miles, the Allstons waited. While strolling about the plantation, they found themselves again surrounded by a shouting "mob of men, women, and children," some of them dancing, some singing. To the two white women, the scene took on an eerie and unreal dimension.

> They sang sometimes in unison, sometimes in parts, strange words which we did not understand, followed by a much-repeated chorus:
>
> > *"I free, I free!*
> > *I free as a frog!*
> > *I free till I fool!*
> > *Glory Alleluia!"*
>
> They revolved around us, holding out their skirts and dancing—now with slow, swinging movements, now with rapid jig-motions, but always with weird chant and wild gestures.

The Allston carriage driver returned alone, unable to locate the mistress's son. "It was a great relief to me," Elizabeth recalled, "for though I have been often laughed at for the opinion, I hold that there is a certain kind of chivalry in the negroes—they wanted blood, they wanted to kill some one, but they couldn't make up their minds to kill two defenseless ladies; but if Charley had been found and brought, I firmly believe it would have kindled the flame." Now determined to wait for the Union Army officers, the two women tried to ignore the "blasphemous mutterings and threats" they heard around them as they paced the plantation grounds. Finally, word reached the plantation that the officers could not be located but that the driver and one other black (perhaps to look after him) had gone to Georgetown to seek assistance.

Exhausted by the long ordeal, the two Allston women slept that night in their nearby Plantersville home, "which had no lock of any kind on the door." Early the next morning, a knock at the door awakened them. Before they could reach the hallway, the door opened and a black hand held out the keys to Guendalos. "No word was spoken—it was Jacob," Elizabeth Allston recalled; "he gave them in silence, and mamma received them with the same solemnity. The bloodless battle had been won."[83]

To the Allstons, as to Thomas Pinckney and others, the battles they waged and won to reclaim their lands could easily be viewed as a struggle of wills in which the character and superiority of white men and women inevitably prevailed. But to the blacks, the defeats they sustained resulted not from a failure of will but from the readiness of Federal authorities to back up the legal claims of whites to their land. Nevertheless, even if planters remained certain of their land titles, they came to fear the turbulence which so often marked the efforts to reestablish a semblance of authority over their former slaves. The range of receptions accorded white families returning to their homes after the war suggests only one dimension in the unraveling of the complex relationships that had made up the "peculiar institution." On most plantations and farms, the whites had remained, along with their slaves, and the issue at the moment of freedom was not so much who owned the land and the crops but on whose land the newly freed slaves would continue to plant and harvest the crops.

## 8

WHERE THE MASTER assembled the blacks to tell them they were no longer his slaves, the reactions he provoked gave rise to the legendary stories of a "Day of Jubilo," in which crowds of ecstatically happy blacks shouted, sang, and danced their way into freedom. Large numbers of former slaves recalled no such celebration. Although not entirely myth, the notion of a Jubilee, with its suggestion of unrestrained, unthinking black hilarity, tends to neglect if not demean the wide range and depth of black responses to emancipation, including the trauma and fears the master's announcement produced on some plantations. The very nature of the bondage they had endured, the myriad of experiences to which they had been exposed, the quality of the ties that had bound them to their "white folks," and the ambivalence which had suffused those relationships were all bound to make for a diverse and complex reaction on the day the slaves were told they no longer had any masters or mistresses.

Capturing nearly the full range of responses, a former South Carolina slave recalled that on his plantation "some were sorry, some hurt, but a few were silent and glad." From the perspective of the mistress of a Florida household, "some of the men cried, some spoke regretfully, [and] only two looked surly and had nothing to say." Although celebrations seldom followed the master's announcement, numerous blacks recalled taking the rest of the day off, if only to think through the implications of what they had been told. Still others, like Harriett Robinson, remembered that before the master could even finish his remarks, "over half them niggers was gone." But the slaves on an Alabama plantation stood quietly, stunned by the news. "We didn' hardly know what he means," Jenny Proctor recalled. "We jes' sort of huddle 'round together like scared rabbits, but after we knowed what he mean, didn' many of us go, 'cause we didn' know where to of went." None of them knew what to expect from freedom and they interpreted it in many different ways, explained James Lucas, a former slave of Jefferson Davis, who achieved his freedom at the age of thirty-one.

> Dey all had diffe'nt ways o' thinkin' 'bout it. Mos'ly though dey was jus' lak me, dey didn' know jus' zackly what it meant. It was jus' somp'n dat de white folks an' slaves all de time talk 'bout. Dat's all. Folks dat ain' never been free don' rightly know de *feel* of bein' free. Dey don' know de meanin' of it. Slaves like us, what was owned by quality-folks, was sati'fied an' didn' sing none of dem freedom songs.

How long that sensation of shock or incredulity lasted would vary from slave to slave. "The day we was set free," remembered Silas Shotfore, "us did not know what to do. Our Missus said we could stay on the place." But his father made one decision almost instantly: no matter what they decided to do, they would do it somewhere else.[84]

Suspicious as they might be of the white man's pronouncements, some blacks were initially skeptical, thinking it might all be a ruse, still another piece of deception calculated to test their fidelity. With that in mind, some thought it best to feign remorse at the announcement, while others needed to determine the master's veracity and sought confirmation elsewhere, often in the nearest town, at the local office of the Freedmen's Bureau, or on another plantation. When his master explained to him that he was now a free man, Tom Robinson refused to believe him (" 'You're jokin' me,' I says") until he spoke with some slave neighbors. "I wanted to find out if they was free too. I just couldn't take it all in. I couldn't believe we was all free alike."[85]

Although most slaves welcomed freedom with varying degrees of enthusiasm, the sense of confusion and uncertainty that prevailed in many quarters was not easily dispelled. The first thought of sixteen-year-old Sallie Crane of Arkansas was that she had been sold, and her mistress's reassurance that she would soon be reunited with her mother did little to comfort her. "I cried because I thought they was carrying me to see my mother before they would send me to be sold in Louisiana." The impression deliberately cultivated by some masters that the Yankees intended to sell freed slaves to Cuba to help defray war costs may have had some impact. No matter what they were told, a former North Carolina slave recalled of the master's announcement, he and his mother were simply too frightened to leave the premises. "Jes like tarpins or turtles after 'mancipation. Jes stick our heads out to see how the land lay."[86]

Nor did some slaves necessarily welcome the news when they fully understood its implications for their own lives. The sorrow which some displayed was not always pretense. To those who were reasonably satisfied with their positions and the relations they enjoyed with the white family, freedom offered no immediate cause for rejoicing. "I was a-farin' pretty well in de kitchen," Aleck Trimble remarked. "I didn' t'ink I eber see better times dan what dem was, and I ain't." That was how Mollie Tillman also recalled the advent of freedom, since, as she boasted, "I warn't no common eve'yday slave," and her mistress refused to let her work in the fields. "I wuz happy den, but since 'mancipation I has jes' had to scuffle an' work an' do de bes' I kin." To Moses Lyles, a former South Carolina slave, emancipation undermined the mutual dependency upon which slavery had rested and neither class benefited from the severance of those ties. "De nigger was de right arm of de buckra class. De buckra was de horn of plenty for de nigger. Both suffer in consequence of freedom."[87]

Standing on the porch of the Big House and watching her fellow slaves celebrate their emancipation, Sara Brown wondered why they thought the event worthy of such festivities. "I been free all de time," she thought. This insistence that they were already as free as they wanted to be repeated an old article of faith which some slaves had recited almost habitually in antebellum days when northern visitors pressed them on the subject of slavery. Disillusionment and "hard times" in the post-emancipation period helped to keep this perception of slavery alive. But for certain ex-slaves, the attachments went much deeper, and neither "good times" nor a bountiful freedom would most likely have altered the relationships and position they had come to cherish. To some of the strong-willed "mammies," whose dominance in the white household was seldom questioned and whose pride and self-respect remained undiminished, emancipation threatened to disrupt the only world and the only ties that really mattered to them and they clung all the more stubbornly to the past. Even death would not undo such relationships, as some of them anticipated a reunion in an all-white heaven.

> Who says I'se free? I warn't neber no slabe. I libed wid qual'ty an' was one ob de fambly. Take dis bandanna off? No, 'deedy! dats the las' semblance I'se got ob de good ole times. S'pose I *is* brack, I cyan't he'p it. If mah mammy and pappy chose for me ter be brack, I ain't gwine ter be lak some white folks I knows an' blame de Lord for all de 'flictions dat comes 'pon 'em. I'se put up wid dis brackness now, 'cordin' to ol' Mis's Bible, for nigh on ter ninety years, an' t'ank de good Lord, dat eberlastin' day is mos' come when I'll be white as Mis' Chloe for *eber mo*'! [Her mistress had died some years before.] What's dat, honey? How I knows I'se gwine ter be white? Why, honey, I'se s'prised! Do you s'pose 'cause Mammy's face is brack, her soul is brack too? Whar's yo' larnin' gone to?

Many of the freed slaves who viewed emancipation apprehensively readily confessed that they had escaped the worst aspects of bondage. "I ain't never had no mother 'ceptin' only Mis' Patsey," a Florida freedwoman remarked, "an' I ain't never felt lak' a bond slave what's been pressed—dat's what dem soldiers say we all is."[88]

The mixed emotions with which slaves greeted their freedom also reflected a natural fear of the unknown, along with the knowledge that "they's allus 'pend on Old Marse to look after them." For many blacks, this was the only life they had known and the world ended at the boundaries of the plantation. To think that they no longer had a master or mistress, while it brought exuberance and relief to many, struck others with dismay. "Whar we gwine eat an' sleep?" they demanded to know. And realizing they could not depend on the law or on other whites for protection, who would now stand between them and the dreaded patrollers and "po' buckra"? After hearing of their freedom, Silas Smith recalled, "de awfulest feeling" pervaded the slave quarters that night as they contemplated a future without masters or mistresses. "You felt jes' like you had done strayed off a-fishing and got lost." Fifteen years after emancipation, Parke Johnston, a former Virginia slave, vividly recalled "how wild and upset and *dreadful* everything was in them times."

> It came so sudden on 'em they wasn't prepared for it. Just think of whole droves of people, that had always been kept so close, and hardly ever left the plantation before, turned loose all at once, with nothing in the world, but what they had on their backs, and often little enough of that; men, women and children that had left their homes when they found out they were free, walking along the road with no where to go.[89]

Since emancipation threatened to undermine the mutual obligations implicit in the master-slave relationship, some freed blacks responded with cries of ingratitude and betrayal that matched in fury the similar reactions of white families to the wartime behavior of certain slaves. When Yankee soldiers told an elderly South Carolina slave that she no longer had a master or mistress, the woman responded as though she had been insulted: "I ain' no free nigger! I *is* got a marster an' mistiss! Dee right dar in de great house. Ef you don' b'lieve me, you go dar an' see." Like so many of the older slaves, this woman felt that her services and devotion to the "white folks" over many years had more than fulfilled her part of the relationship. For the family to abandon her now and deprive her of the security, care, and protection she clearly thought she had earned would be, in her view, the rankest form of ingratitude. On a plantation in South Carolina, the oldest black on the place reacted with downright indignation when his former master read the terms of a proposed labor contract; indeed, few blacks expressed the idea of mutual obligations more clearly:

> Missis belonged to him, & he belonged to Missis, & he was not going to leave her. . . . Massa had brought him up here to take care of him, & he had known when Missis' grandmother was born & she was 'bliged to take care of him; he was going to die on this place, & he was not going to do any work either, except make a collar a week.[90]

The uncertainties, the regrets, the anxieties which characterized many of the reactions to emancipation underscored that pervasive sense of dependency—the feeling, as more than one ex-slave recalled, that "we

couldn't do a thing without the white folks." Slavery had taught black
people to be slaves—"good" slaves and obedient workers. "All de slaves
knowed how to do hard work," observed Thomas Cole, who had run away
to enlist in the Union Army, "but dey didn't know nothin' 'bout how to
'pend on demselves for de livin'." Of course, the very logic and survival of
the "peculiar institution" had demanded that nothing be done to prepare
slaves for the possibility of freedom; on the contrary, they had been taught
to feel their incapacity for dealing with its immense responsibilities. Many
years before the war, a South Carolina jurist set forth the paternalistic
ideal when he advised that each slave should be taught to view his master
as "a perfect security from injury. When this is the case, the relation of
master and servant becomes little short of that of parent and child." The
testimony of former slaves suggests how effectively some masters had been
able to inculcate that ideal and how the legacy of paternalism could para-
lyze its victims.[91]

Nor did Federal policies or programs in the immediate aftermath of
emancipation address themselves to this problem. Whatever the freedman's desire or capacity for "living independently," he would in scores of
instances be forced to remain dependent on his former masters. It was
precisely through such dependency, a North Carolina planter vowed, that
his class of people would be able to reestablish on the plantations what they
had ostensibly lost in emancipation, "until in a few years I think every
thing will be about as it was."[92]

Upon hearing of their freedom, some slaves instinctively deferred to
the traditional source of authority, advice, sustenance, and protection—the
master himself. Now that they were no longer his slaves, what did he want
them to do? Few freed blacks, however, no matter how confused and apprehensive they may have been, were altogether oblivious to the excitement
and the anticipation that this event had generated. At the moment of
freedom, masses of slaves did not suddenly erupt in a mammoth Jubilee but
neither did they all choose to be passive, cowed, or indifferent in the face
of their master's announcement. Outside of the prayer meetings and the
annual holiday frolics, plantation life had afforded them few occasions for
free expression, at least in the presence of their "white folks." If only for
a few hours or days, then, many newly emancipated slaves dropped their
usual defenses, cast off their masks, and gave themselves the rare luxury
of acting out feelings they were ordinarily expected to repress.

Once they understood the full import of the master's words, and even
then perhaps only after several minutes of stunned or polite silence, many
blacks found they could no longer contain their emotions. More importantly, they felt no need to do so. "That the day I shouted," was how
Richard Carruthers of Texas recalled his emancipation. Booker T. Washington stood next to his mother during the announcement; many years
later, he could still vividly recall how she hugged and kissed him, the tears
streaming down her face, and her explanation that she had prayed many
years for this day but never believed she would live to see it. Freedom took

longer to reach Bexar County, Texas, where the war had hardly touched the lives and routines of the slave. But Felix Haywood, who worked as a sheepherder and cowpuncher, recalled how "everybody went wild" when they learned of freedom. "We all felt like horses and nobody had made us that way but ourselves. We was free. Just like that, we was free."[93]

If neither words nor prayers conveyed the appropriate emotions, the newly freed slaves might draw on the traditional spirituals, whose imagery easily befitted an occasion like emancipation. The triumph had come in this world, not in the next. The exuberance and importance of such a moment also inspired updated versions of the spirituals and songs especially composed for the occasion. Out in Bexar County, Felix Haywood heard them sing:

> *Abe Lincoln freed the nigger*
> *With the gun and the trigger;*
> *And I ain't goin' to get whipped any more.*
> *I got my ticket,*
> *Leavin' the thicket,*
> *And I'm a-headin' for the Golden Shore!*

Harriett Gresham, who had belonged to a wealthy planter in South Carolina, remembered hearing the guns at Fort Sumter that inaugurated the war, as well as the song that sounded the death of slavery:

> *No slav'ry chains to tie me down,*
> *And no mo' driver's ho'n to blow fer me.*
> *No mo' stocks to fasten me down,*
> *Jesus break slav'ry chain, Lord.*
> *Break slav'ry chain, Lord,*
> *Break slav'ry chain, Lord,*
> *Da Heben gwinter be my home.*

"Guess dey made 'em up," Annie Harris said of many of the songs she heard in those days, " 'cause purty soon ev'ybody fo' miles around was singin' freedom songs."[94]

Although the classic version of the Jubilee featured large masses of people, some newly freed slaves only wanted to be alone at this moment. Neither fear of the master nor deference to his feelings entirely explains this preference. Overwhelmed by what they had just heard, some needed a momentary solitude to reflect on its implications and to convince themselves that it had really happened, while others simply preferred to express themselves with the least amount of inhibition. Lou Smith recalled running off and hiding in the plum orchard, where he kept repeating to himself, "I'se free, I'se free; I ain't never going back to Miss Jo." After hearing of his freedom, an elderly Virginia black proceeded to the barn, leaped from one stack of straw to the other, and "screamed and screamed!" Although confined to bed, Aunt Sissy, a crippled Virginia slave, heard the celebration outside, limped out the door, and then simply stood there praying. "Wouldn't let nobody tetch her, wouldn't set down. Stood dere swayin' fum side to side an' singin' over an' over her favorite hymn."

> *Oh, Father of Mercy*
> *We give thanks to Thee*
> *We give thanks to Thee*
> *For thy great glory.* [95]

Like Aunt Sissy, many slaves viewed their deliverance as a sign of divine intervention. God's will had been heeded, if belatedly, and in this act lay final proof of His omnipresence. Few expressed it more eloquently than the Virginia black woman who looked upon emancipation as something approaching a miracle. "Isn't I a free woman now! De Lord can make Heaven out of Hell any time, I do believe." In addressing his Nashville congregation, a black preacher interpreted emancipation as a result of his people having kept the faith, even when it appeared as though there was no hope and that the Lord had forsaken them.

> We was all like de chil'en of Israel in Egypt, a cryin' and cryin' and a gronin' and gronin', and no Moses came wid de Lord's word to order de door broke down, dat we might walk t'rough and be free. Now de big ugly door is broke down, bress de Lord, and we know de groans of de captive is heard. Didn't I tell you to pray and not to faint away, dat is not to doubt, and dat He who opened de sea would deliber us sure, and no tanks to de tasker massas, who would nebber let us go if dey could only hab held on to us? But dey couldn't—no dey couldn't do dat, 'cause de Lord he was wid us, and wouldn't let us be 'pressed no more ... [96]

Even as many slaves reveled in their newly proclaimed freedom, few of them made any attempt to humiliate or unduly antagonize their newly dispossessed owners. Appreciating this fact, some masters and mistresses felt both grateful and immensely relieved. "Whilst glad of having freedom," Grace Elmore said of her servants, "they have never been more attentive or more respectful than now, and seem to wish to do all in their power to leave a pleasant impression." That the newly emancipated slaves had largely confined their release of emotion to a few relatively harmless celebrations encouraged some planters to think they could ease through the transition from bondage to freedom with a minimum of concession and change. Once the initial excitement subsided, they fully expected that economic necessity if not the "old ties" and attachment to the "home" would leave their blacks little choice but to carry on much as they had before the war. "We may still hope for a future I think," a prominent Alabaman confided to his journal. Since on many plantations and farms the day after freedom very much resembled the days that had preceded the master's announcement, such confidence appeared to be well founded. Even where a Jubilee atmosphere had prevailed, the blacks were no less appreciative of the immense problems they faced in acting on their new status. Like the other slaves on her Texas plantation, Annie Hawkins had shouted for joy; nevertheless, she recalled, none of them made any move to leave "for fear old Mistress would bring us back or the pateroller would git us."[97]

What masters and mistresses perceived as blacks fulfilling obligations learned under the tutelage of slavery might have been viewed differently by the former slaves themselves. In agreeing to stay until the planted crops had been harvested or until their assigned tasks in the household had been completed, many field hands and servants not only confirmed the freedom of choice now available to them but also exhibited a dignity and self-respect commensurate with their new status. Several of Grace Elmore's servants promised to give sufficient notice before leaving so as to enable their mistress to make other arrangements. The DeSaussure family of Charleston lost every servant but the nurse, and she agreed to stay only "as a favor until they could hire white servants." Few freed slaves, however, thought it necessary to emulate the attentiveness of a South Carolina woman who prepared to leave the family she had served for thirty-six years; before departing to join her husband and son, she made certain that all the clothes had been washed, she distributed gifts to the white children, and she left two of her children behind to wait on the family.[98]

Despite the debilitating effects of dependency and the confusion which persisted over the precise nature of their new status, the freedmen were neither helpless, easily manipulated, nor frightened into passivity. Although some still deferred to the advice of the old master, many did not. During slavery, they had often survived only by drawing on their own inner resources, their accumulated experience, and the wisdom of those in their own ranks to whom they looked for leadership and counsel. Upon being told of their freedom, the blacks on many plantations retired to their quarters to discuss the announcement, what if any alternatives were now open to them, and the first steps they should take to test their freedom. On a plantation in Georgia, for example, where the owner had asked his former slaves to remain until they finished the current crop, they discussed his proposal for the next several days before reaching a common decision. "They wasn't no celebration 'round the place," William Hutson recalled, "but they wasn't no work after the Master tells us we is free. Nobody leave the place though. Not 'til in the fall when the work is through."[99]

The possibilities that suddenly presented themselves, the kinds of questions that freedom posed, the sheer magnitude of this event in their lives could not always be readily absorbed. Recounting his own escape to freedom, more than two decades before the war, William Wells Brown never forgot the strange sensations he experienced: "The fact that I was a freeman—could walk, talk, eat and sleep as a man, and no one to stand over me with the blood-clotted cowhide—all this made me feel that I was not myself." For the newly emancipated blacks, however, most of whom chose to remain in the same regions in which they had been slaves, the problems they faced were far different and more formidable than those which had confronted the fugitives upon reaching the North. Experiencing her first days of freedom, a Mississippi woman voiced that prevailing uncertainty as to how to give meaning to her new status: "I used to think if I could be free I should be the happiest of anybody in the world. But when my master come to me, and says—Lizzie, you is free! it seems like I was in a kind of daze. And when I would wake up in the morning I would think to myself, Is I free? Hasn't I got to get up before daylight and go into the field to work?"[100]

The uncertainties plagued both blacks and whites. Under slavery, the boundaries had been clearly established and both parties understood them. But what were the proper boundaries of black freedom? What new forms would the relationship between a former slave and his former master now assume? How would the freed blacks be expected to interact with free whites? Neither the blacks nor the whites were altogether certain, though they might have pronounced views on such matters. Now that black freedom had been generally acknowledged, it needed to be defined. The state legislatures, the courts, and the Federal government offered some direction. But freedom could ultimately be defined only in the day-to-day lives and experiences of the people themselves. "De day of freedom," a former Tennessee slave recalled, the overseer came out into the fields and told them that they were free. "Free how?" they asked him, and he replied, "Free to work and live for demselves."[101] In the aftermath of emancipation, the newly freed slaves would seek to test that response and answer the question for themselves.

## Chapter Five

# HOW FREE IS FREE?

*No more peck o'corn for me,*
*No more, no more,—*
*No more peck o'corn for me,*
*Many thousand go.*

*No more driver's lash for me,*
*No more, no more,—*
*No more driver's lash for me,*
*Many thousand go.*

*No more pint o'salt for me,*
*No more, no more,—*
*No more pint o'salt for me,*
*Many thousand go.*

*No more hundred lash for me,*
*No more, no more,—*
*No more hundred lash for me,*
*Many thousand go.*

*No more mistress' call for me,*
*No more, no more,—*
*No more mistress' call for me,*
*Many thousand go.*

—FREEDMEN SONG, CIRCA 1865[1]

*What my people wants first, what dey fust wants is de right to be free.*

—FREEDMAN IN SALISBURY, NORTH CAROLINA, FALL 1865[2]

Not long after hearing of their freedom, two young house servants on a plantation in Florida, unaware that they were being overheard, sat on the back porch one evening and exchanged thoughts about the kind of future they envisioned for themselves. One of them, Frances, had been a childhood gift to her equally young mistress, Martha, who had taught her to read and write. Like so many newly emancipated slaves, Frances had her full share of fantasies about a new life under freedom. To talk about them, as she did with another servant, had a way of making them seem almost real.

Frances:    "Bethiah, isn't that a pretty piece Miss Martha is playing on the piano?"

Bethiah:    "I dunno. I wasn't a-lisenin'."

Frances:    "Well, you listen, Beth. It's such a pretty piece, and it's a new piece, too. But I can sing every note of it. Lieutenant Zachendorf says this time next year all the white folks will be at work in the fields, and the plantations and the houses, and everything in them will be turned over to us to do with as we please. When that time comes I'm going straight in the parlor and play that very piece on the piano."

Bethiah (scoffing):  "You cain't do it—you dunno how!"

Frances:    "Yes, I do, too. You'll see—but what are you going to do?"

Bethiah:    "I'se a-gwine upstairs an' dress up in de prittiest cloes dey-all is got, an' den I'se a-gwine ter ax my beau ter walk rite in de parler an' set down on de white folks sofy, an' I gwine ter pull up one o' dem fine cheers what we-all ain't 'lowed ter set in, rite long-side o' dem an' us 'ill lissen ter you play de pi-an-ner!"

Frances (thoughtfully):  "I don't believe I would like to see my young lady working in the field—don't mind about the rest of them —but I think I'll keep her in the house for my maid."

Bethiah:    "No, let 'em all work—it'll do 'em good! I 'spect dey will soon be ez black ez me when de sun teches 'em hot an' steddy."

Frances:    "Le's take a walk out to Camp."

The two young women then vanished into the darkness. Several months after their conversation, without saying anything to the former owner, every freed slave on the plantation had left for new jobs and places. The day on which they made their mass exodus seemed somehow appropriate: New Year's Day 1866, the third anniversary of the Emancipation Proclamation. Several of them would soon return, however, their bodies lean with hunger and ravished by disease, their expectations shattered and their hopes deferred. Frances and Bethiah were apparently not among them, but they, too, like so many others, were bound to discover that "revolutions may go backward."[3]

## 2

EVEN AS SLAVES, black people had often tried to conceptualize for themselves a life outside of bondage and beyond the plantations and farms which constituted the only world they knew. After learning of their freedom, however, the conversations in the quarters, in the fields, and in the kitchens turned to alternatives that were suddenly real, to new ways of living and working, and to aspirations they might hope to satisfy in their own lifetimes. To talk about the possibilities could be downright exhilarating, even infectious. But when it came to acting out these feelings, the old fears and insecurities and the still pervasive dependency on their former owners would first have to be surmounted. That came easily for some but not for most. "They were like a bird let out of a cage," a Virginia freedman explained. "You know how a bird that has been long in a cage will act when the door is opened; he makes a curious fluttering for a little while. It was just so with the colored people. They didn't know at first what to do with themselves. But they got sobered pretty soon." That same imagery of birds freed from a cage occurred to a white Georgian, but she could think only of birds who were "helpless" and others, like the hawk, whose release would most likely inflict "mischief" on everyone.[4]

The Confederacy lay in ruins. The white South, however, demonstrated remarkable intransigence and evinced few signs of repentance or enlightenment. Rather than rethink their values and assumptions, most whites preferred to romanticize about the martyred Lost Cause. Although resigned to legal emancipation for nearly four million black men and women, most whites clung even more tenaciously to traditional notions of racial solidarity and black inferiority. Whatever "mischief" emancipation unleashed, what it could not do, as a Georgia editor suggested, was far more crucial: it could not transform the Negro into a white man.

> The different races of man, like different coins at a mint, were stamped at their true value by the Almighty in the beginning. No contact with each other—no amount of legislation or education—can convert the negro into a white man. Until that can be done—until you can take the kinks out of his wool and make his skull thinner—until all these things and abundantly more have been done, the negro cannot claim equality with the white race.

Even the white conquerors of the South might not have thought to question the universal wisdom of that comforting observation. The *Cincinnati Enquirer*, in fact, offered its own variant of a popular theme: "Slavery is dead, the negro is not, there is the misfortune. For the sake of all parties, would that he were."[5]

To what, then, could freed blacks aspire in a society dominated by white men and women intent on using any means to perpetuate that domination? For any freedman or freedwoman to linger too long over that question might be both demoralizing and self-deprecating. If emancipation by itself could touch their lives and destinies in any significant way, some blacks expressed the hope that it would turn them white. In one Virginia household, a young servant expressed her disappointment over the failure of emancipation to do precisely that. Nor did the reassuring words of her mistress—"You must not be ashamed of the skin God gave you. Your skin is all right"—make any impression on the young woman. "I druther be white," she persisted. Reflecting later upon this incident, the mistress's daughter concluded that there had been "something pathetic in the aspiration."[6]

But what this discouraged black youth had suggested, in her own unique way, were simply the dimensions of the problem her people now faced. Despite emancipation, she realized that to be free was not to be like everyone else. With equal clarity, she perceived that to be white in American society was to be something, perhaps everything. That was a doctrine more fundamental and far-reaching in its implications than scores of emancipation proclamations, constitutional amendments, legislative enactments, and court decisions. George G. King, a former South Carolina slave, knew that only too well from his own experience. Born on a plantation appropriately called "two-hundred acres of Hell," he had been subjected to a "devil overseer," a "she-devil Mistress," and a master who "talked hard words." He would never forget the sight of his mistress walking away laughing while his mother screamed and groaned after a brutal whipping. Having witnessed and endured all of this, how much could he have expected of emancipation? His master had tried to allay any initial misconceptions. "The Master he says we are all free," King recalled of that day, "but it don't mean we is white. And it don't mean we is equal. Just equal for to work and earn our own living and not depend on him for no more meats and clothes."[7]

Although emancipation left skin hues unaltered, freedmen might still wish to fashion their aspirations and way of life after those who had always enjoyed freedom and whose comforts, diversions, and manners they had observed for so many years. To be free invited flights into fantasy, grandiose visions of a new life, not a life in which oppression and exploitation are vanquished but in which the roles are reversed and the blacks find themselves in the seats of power and the whites are relegated to the kitchens and fields.

> Hurrah, hurrah fer freedom!
>   It makes de head spin 'roun'
> De nigga' in de saddle
>   An' de white man on de groun'.

After all, only a few years before, who would have thought it conceivable that slaves would be armed and would march through the countryside to do battle with their "masters"? Nothing seemed impossible any longer, not even the division of the master's lands among his former slaves. "It's de white man's turn ter labor now," an ex-slave preacher told a torch rally near the Lester plantation in Florida, and that was as it should be.

> When de white man set on de piazzy an' de Nigger sweated in de sun— when de white man rode it through de sand—when de Nigger made de cotton, an' de white man spen' de money—now, Glory, halleluyer, dere ain't no marster an' dere ain't no slave! Glory, halleluyer! From now on, my brudders an' my sisters, old things have passed away an' all things is bekum new.

The elderly slave woman in South Carolina who had welcomed the Yankees with visions of "settin' at de white folks' table, a eating off de white folks' table, and a rocking in de big rocking chair" might have witnessed such scenes by visiting the plantations and town houses abandoned by the owners and occupied by former slaves. Whatever had induced such visions was less important than the way in which freed blacks chose to manifest them. The housemaid who had experienced a lifetime of reprimands, the field hands who knew no other routines, the urban laborers whose earnings had been pocketed by their owners might now aspire to something different. After still another scolding for her alleged incompetence, a servant finally turned on her mistress and retorted, "I expect the white folks to be waiting on me before long!"[8]

To indulge in such fantasies might be momentarily satisfying but it did nothing to resolve the slave's immediate predicament after emancipation. At some point, he would have to appraise his position realistically and define for himself the content of his freedom. After three days of "shoutin' an' carryin' on," the blacks at Wood's Crossing, Virginia, began their first Sunday as free men and women in a reflective mood. "We was all sittin' roun' restin'," Charlotte Brown recalled, "an' tryin' to think what freedom meant an' ev'ybody was quiet an' peaceful." Suddenly, Sister Carrie, an elderly black woman, began to chant:

> *Tain't no mo' sellin' today,*
> *Tain't no mo' hirin' today,*
> *Tain't no pullin' off shirts today,*
> *It's stomp down freedom today.*
> *Stomp it down!*

When she came to the words "Stomp it down!" the others began to shout along with her until they finally made up music to accompany their words. Like Sister Carrie's chant, the initial attempts to define freedom drew largely on the most familiar images of slavery. If the future still seemed clouded with uncertainty, what blacks had experienced as slaves remained abundantly clear and vivid, so that freedom in its most immediate and meaningful sense could best be understood in terms of the limitations placed on white behavior. On the Sea Islands, slaves had interpreted the flight of their masters as meaning "no more driver, no more cotton, no more lickin'," and with freedom they were "done wid massa's hollerin'" and "done wid missus' scoldin'." The popular wartime spiritual "Many Thousand Go" similarly dwelled on freedom as a release from the most oppressive aspects of bondage: the inadequate rations, the whippings, the work routines, and the harassment—"No more peck o'corn for me," "No more driver's lash for me," "No more pint o'salt for me," "No more hundred lash for me," and "No more mistress' call for me." Even the "hard times" and arduous labor that would characterize the postwar years in no way diminished the value ex-slaves placed on their freedom. "I's mighty well pleased tu git my eatin' by de 'sweat o' my face,' " a newly freed slave wrote his brother, "an' all I ax o' ole masser's tu jes' keep he hands off o' de Lawd Almighty's property, fur *dat's me.*"⁹

Although former slaves chose to manifest their freedom in many different ways, with each individual acting on his or her own set of priorities, nearly all of them could subscribe to the underlying principle that emancipation had enabled them to become their own masters. And those were precisely the terms they most often employed to define their freedom. When the earliest contrabands reached Fortress Monroe, they testified that the most compelling idea in their minds had been "to belong to ourselves." To the familiar question so often put to them as slaves, "Who do you b'long to, boy?" a Georgia freedman responded in 1865, "Ise don't b'longs to nobody, Missus. Ise owns self, en b'longs to Macon." For many of the emancipated slaves, freedom of action—the chance "to do something on their own account"—went to the very heart of their new condition. Not surprisingly, few other manifestations of black freedom would prove more irritating to their previous owners, many of whom failed to appreciate the importance of this concept in the lives of people whose actions they had tried so rigidly to control. " 'Twould be amusing if it were not too pitiful to hear their idea of freedom," sighed Grace Elmore, a South Carolina woman, after she discussed the question with one of her servants. "I asked Phillis if she likes the thought of being free. She said yes, tho she had always been treated with perfect kindness and could complain of nothing in her lot, but she had heard a woman who had bought her freedom from kind indulgent owners, say it was a very sweet thing to be able to do as she chose, to sit and do nothing, to work if she desired, or to go out as she liked, and ask nobody's permission. And that was just her feeling. 'She wished the power to do as she chose.' "¹⁰

When asked what price tag he now bore, an Alabama freedman replied, "I's free. Ain't wuf nuffin." The northern visitor who asked the question did so after hearing that plantation hands in the Black Belt districts had no real understanding of freedom. Whatever remained vague about their new status, every freedman realized that he was no longer an article of merchandise, subject to sale at the whim, bankruptcy, or death of his owner. He understood, too, that freedom secured his family from involuntary disruption. If the freedman could not immediately support his wife and children, he at least had the satisfaction of knowing that any income or property he henceforth accumulated from his labor would be his to retain. That realization was in itself immensely gratifying. After earning his first dollar, working on the railroad after the war, a former Arkansas slave recalled that he "felt like the richest man in the world!" Even ex-slaves who had been treated well readily appreciated this crucial difference between bondage and freedom. "I was brought up with the white folks, just like one of them," declared a slave refugee who had fled to the Union lines; "these hands never had any hard work to do. I had a kind master; but I didn't know but any time I might be sold away off, and when I found

I could get my freedom, I was very glad; and I wouldn't go back again, because now I am for myself." That same point was made by a South Carolina freedman when a reporter asked him why he did not want to return to a mistress who, by his own admission, had treated him well. "Why, sar," he explained, "all I made before was Miss Pinckney's, but all I make now is my own."[11]

Other than instructing them to "labor faithfully for reasonable wages" and "to abstain from all violence, unless in necessary self-defence," the Emancipation Proclamation provided newly freed slaves with no real guidelines. Nor did subsequent Federal policies provide any underpinning for their new status. Clearly, black people were now free. But how free? Few knew for certain, though many whites had ideas about both the quality and the durability of black freedom. "These niggers will all be slaves again in twelve months," a Mississippi planter told a Union officer. "You have nothing but Lincoln's proclamation to make them free." He had, in fact, made a telling point. No official document by itself could turn a slave into a free man, nor could the Yankees, the white missionary teachers, or the most sympathetic southern whites perform that feat. To know "de feel of bein' free" demanded that the ex-slave begin to act like a free man, that he test his freedom, that he make some kind of exploratory move, that he prove to himself (as well as to others) by some concrete act that he was truly free. The nature or the boldness of that act was far less important than the feeling he derived from it. The action undertaken by Exter Durham of North Carolina, for example, could hardly be described as a startling break with the past. Upon being informed of his new status, he gathered his few belongings together and left the Snipes Durham plantation in Orange County for the George Herndon plantation in adjoining Chatham County. But to Exter Durham and his wife, Tempie Herndon, who had belonged to different masters, this move meant everything—"kaze den me an' Exter could be together all de time 'stead of Saturday an' Sunday."[12]

By enlarging the freedman's sense of what was attainable, desirable, and tolerable, emancipation encouraged a degree of independence and assertiveness which bondage had sharply contained. To leave the plantation without a pass, to slow the pace of work, to haggle over wages and conditions, to refuse punishment, or to violate racial etiquette were all ways of testing the limits of freedom. No doubt a Mississippi freedman derived considerable satisfaction from refusing to remove his hat when ordered to do so in the presence of a white man, as did a Richmond black who turned down the request of a white man to help him lift a barrel, telling him at the same time, "No, you white people think you can order black people around as you please." To those long accustomed to absolute control, even the smallest exercise of personal freedom by a former slave, no matter how innocently intended, could have an unsettling effect.[13]

Acting as individuals and families, usually without the semblance of organized effort, freed slaves began the arduous process of ascertaining the boundaries of freedom. If few of them indulged in land seizures, arson, or physical attacks on whites, this suggests that most blacks perceived the need to exercise their freedom with some degree of appreciation for where the power still rested in their communities. But whatever action a freedman deemed appropriate, no matter how restrained or insignificant it may have appeared to others, the objective remained essentially the same—to achieve some recognition, even if only grudgingly given, of that new sense of dignity and self-respect which emancipation encouraged in them. Few expressed it more graphically than an elderly freedman in South Carolina when he explained to a black schoolteacher why he rejoiced over his new status: "Don't hab me feelins hurt now. Used to hab me feelins hurt all de time. But don't hab em hurt now, no more." Whenever he reflected back on slavery, Stephen McCray testified many years later, he thought invariably of the story of the coon and the dog. "The coon said to the dog: 'Why is it you're so fat and I am so poor, and we is both animals?' The dog said: 'I lay round Master's house and let him kick me and he gives me a piece of bread right on.' Said the coon to the dog: 'Better then that I stay poor.' Them's my sentiment. I'm lak the coon. I don't believe in 'buse."[14]

To dwell only on the most dramatic manifestations of freedom would distort the experience entirely. If a former slave should decide, for example, to change his employer, that might simply entail a move from his old plantation to the next one down the road. This was not about to alter in any significant degree his day-to-day life but to many a freedman, as to Ambus Gray of Alabama, that had been the "one difference" between freedom and bondage: "You could change places and work for different men." Even if a slave chose to stay with his master after emancipation, even if his demeanor remained unchanged, even if his fidelity to the "white folks" stood unshaken, this did not necessarily mean that nothing had happened to him or that he failed to grasp the meaning of his freedom. "When you'all had de power you was good to me," an elderly black man told his former master in May 1865, "and I'll protect you now. No niggers nor Yankees shall touch you. If you want anything, call for Sambo. I mean, call for Mr. Samuel—that's my name now."[15]

To determine the "one difference" between freedom and bondage, the ex-slaves found themselves driven in many directions at the same time. But the distance they placed between themselves and their old status could not be measured by how far they traveled or even if they left the old plantation. That "difference" could most often be perceived in the choices now available to them, in the securing of families and the location of loved ones who had been sold away, in the sanctification of marital ties, in the taking of a new surname or the revelation of an old one, in the opportunity to achieve literacy, in the chance to move their religious services from "down in the hollow" to their own churches, in sitting where they pleased in public places, in working where the rewards were commensurate with their labor. What emancipation introduced into the lives of many black people was not only the element of choice but a leap of confidence in the ability to effect changes in their own lives without deferring to whites. "What I likes bes, to be slave or free?" Margrett Nillin, a former Texas slave, pondered over that question many decades after her emancipation. "Well, it's dis way," she answered. "In slavery I owns nothin' and never owns nothin'. In freedom I's own de home and raise de family. All dat cause me worryment and in slavery I has no worryment, but I takes de freedom."[16]

3

───────────

NOTHING EXHILARATED Charlie Barbour more in the aftermath of emancipation than to know "dat I won't wake up some mornin' ter fin' dat my mammy or some ob de rest of my family am done sold." With even more vivid memories, Jacob Thomas, who had seen his parents separated by sale, had no difficulty many decades later in relating what for him had been the overriding significance of freedom: "I has got thirteen great-gran' chilluns an' I knows whar dey ever'one am. In slavery times dey'd have been on de block long time ago." For the tens of thousands of slaves who had been involuntarily separated from their loved ones, freedom raised equally exciting prospects. Rather than have to wait for the heavenly reunions they had sung about, they might anticipate seeing each other again in this world. To William Curtis, a former Georgia slave whose father had been sold to a Virginia planter, "dat was de best thing about de war setting us free, he could come back to us."[17]

Few scenes acted out in the post-emancipation South exceeded the drama, the emotion, the poignancy that marked the reunions of families which had been torn asunder by slavery. The last time Ben and Betty Dodson had seen each other, they had begged their master to sell them together; twenty years passed before the couple met again—in a refugee camp. "Glory! glory! hallelujah," Ben Dodson shouted as he alternated between embracing his wife and stepping back to reassure himself that it was really she. "Dis is my Betty, shuah. I foun' you at las'. I's hunted an' hunted till I track you up here. I's boun' to hunt till I fin' you if you's alive." In many such reunions, the passage of time and the effects of bondage made recognition nearly impossible. Not until the woman at the door removed her hat and the bundle she carried on her head did a young Tennessee freedwoman discern the scar on her face, and only then did she know for certain that she was gazing upon her mother, whom she had not seen since childhood. In a Virginia refugee camp, a mother found her daughter, now eighteen years old, who had been sold away from her when only an infant. "See how they've done her bad," the mother declared to anyone who would listen. "See how they've cut her up. From her head to her feet she is scarred just as you see her face."[18]

Each reunion had its own incredible story, revealing the extraordinary resourcefulness with which husbands and wives, parents and children, brothers and sisters sought each other out in the immediate aftermath of

Union occupation and emancipation. Family members embarked on these searches, a much-impressed Freedmen's Bureau officer reported, "with an ardor and faithfulness sufficient to vindicate the fidelity and affection of any race—the excited joys of the regathering being equalled only by the previous sorrows and pains of separation." The attempts freedmen made to relocate loved ones forcefully belied the commonly held theories about a race of moral cripples who placed little value on marital and familial ties. Even some of the most dedicated abolitionists subscribed to these theories, attributing the blacks' moral insensibility, "licentiousness," and "false ideas touching chastity" to the evil influences of bondage. Like most whites, they tended to underestimate the depth of familial love and emotional attachment that induced so many former slaves to make the location of relatives their first priority after emancipation. "They had a passion, not so much for wandering, as for getting together," a Freedmen's Bureau agent in South Carolina wrote of the postwar migrations of blacks; "and every mother's son among them seemed to be in search of his mother; every mother in search of her children. In their eyes the work of emancipation was incomplete until the families which had been dispersed by slavery were reunited." In North Carolina, a northern journalist encountered a middle-aged freedman—"plodding along, staff in hand, and apparently very footsore and tired"—who had already walked nearly six hundred miles in his determination to reach the wife and children he had been sold away from four years before.[19]

Although viewed as a post-emancipation phenomenon, the attempt to reunite with loved ones actually represented an ongoing impulse that had frequently manifested itself in the antebellum period. Except for punishment, no other factor had accounted for as many runaway slaves; indeed, a significant number of such escapes came immediately after a master had sold a spouse, a parent, or a child.[20] Equally important, the strong commitment to family ties had kept thousands of slaves from resorting to flight. Emancipation made the search for lost relatives less perilous, though not necessarily more successful. Where contact had been maintained during the period of separation, either through letters or the "grapevine," reunions were effected with little difficulty. The wartime contraband camps, by bringing together thousands of uprooted and "runaway" slaves, provided valuable information about separated families and reunited many of them.

For countless numbers of freed slaves, however, the attempt to find lost relatives became an arduous, time-consuming, and frustrating task, requiring long and often fruitless treks into unfamiliar country, the patience to track down every clue and follow up every rumor, and the determination to stay on a trail even when it suddenly appeared to vanish. "Dey was heaps of nigger families dat I know what was sep'rated in de time of bondage dat tried to find dey folkses what was gone," Tines Kendricks recalled. "But de mostest of 'em never git togedder ag'in even after dey sot free 'cause dey don't know where one or de other is." Of the "dozens of children" Jennie

Hill knew who searched for parents "sold 'down the river,' " as well as parents who looked frantically for their children, she could remember only one case in which the family was reunited. "Some perhaps were killed in the battles but in the majority of the cases the children of slaves lost their identity when they were taken from the place of their birth into a new county." Martha Showvely, who was twenty-eight years old at the time of emancipation, had not seen her mother since they were separated by sale in 1846. After the war, she reached the county where her mother reportedly resided, only to learn that death had claimed her life three years earlier. The efforts to reunite with loved ones sometimes involved risks other than disappointment over failure. Hoping to find any members of his family, James Curry ventured back to the county in North Carolina from which he had escaped more than twenty years before the war; whether provoked by his earlier escape or by his association with northern abolitionists, enraged local whites assaulted him.[21]

Despite herculean efforts, the prospects for a successful reunion remained slim. Many years had passed since relatives had last seen each other and inevitable changes had altered physical appearances. The searcher usually carried with him only a visual image of what a spouse, a child, or a parent had looked like numerous years, even decades, earlier. No sooner had a missionary teacher in South Carolina returned from a trip to Virginia than an elderly black woman tearfully pleaded for any information she might have gathered about the whereabouts of her daughter.

> As soon as she heard I had travelled through Virginia, she came to me to know if I had ever seen her "little gal." . . . And she begged me to look out for her when I went back. She was sure I should know her, she "was such a pretty little gal." It was useless to tell her the girl was now a woman, and doubtless had children of her own. She always had been and always would be her "baby."[22]

The Freedmen's Bureau did what it could to help, acting as a clearinghouse of information and providing free transportation in some cases; at the same time, northern teachers and missionaries, many of them stationed in the contraband camps, frequently spent entire days writing letters for ex-slaves who were trying to make contact with a relative, invariably on the basis of the scantiest information. "Ellen Cummins; least dat *was* her name, w'en dey dun toted her off to Florida," an elderly black woman replied when asked for the address of her daughter, who had been sold away from her twenty years before at the age of four. Upon learning that his brother, whom he had not seen for twenty years, was in Virginia, a Mississippi freedman immediately dictated a letter in the hope of effecting an early reunion.

> I's gwine tu buy a lot, an' build me a hut on it; an' den, Jack, you is wanted down yere, tu see you' ole brudder. Fur de last time he seed you, he wuz

standin' on de auction block, an' Mass'r Bill was a turnin' he round, like
a 'possum on de spit, so's de driber'd see me fa'r an' squar'. Neber min',
Jack. I's tryin' tu let by-gones go, an' jes' look out fur number one; an' I's
powerful glad I's a free man now, for shore. Come a Christmas, ef ye kin,
Jack.[23]

If the initial efforts proved unsuccessful, the search for family members might span several decades. Until well into the 1870s and 1880s, the
newly established black newspapers, both in the South and in the North,
abounded with advertisements in which relatives requested any information that might assist them. If physical descriptions were given at all, they
tended to be sparse and badly outdated; more often, family members had
to content themselves with listing whatever leads they had accumulated
over the years about the location of loved ones.

Information Wanted, of Caroline Dodson, who was sold from Nashville,
Nov. 1st, 1862, by James Lumsden to Warwick, (a trader then in human
beings), who carried her to Atlanta, Georgia, and she was last heard of
in the sale pen of Robert Clarke, (human trader in that place), from which
she was sold. Any information of her whereabouts will be thankfully
received and rewarded by her mother. Lucinda Lowery, Nashville.

$200 Reward. During the year 1849, Thomas Sample carried away from
this city, as his slaves, our daughter, Polly, and son, Geo. Washington, to
the State of Mississippi, and subsequently, to Texas, and when last heard
from they were in Lagrange, Texas. We will give $100 each for them to
any person who will assist them, or either of them, to get to Nashville,
or get word to us of their whereabouts, if they are alive. Ben. & Flora
East.

Saml. Dove wishes to know of the whereabouts of his mother, Areno, his
sisters Maria, Neziah, and Peggy, and his brother Edmond, who were
owned by Geo. Dove, of Rockingham county, Shenandoah Valley, Va.
Sold in Richmond, after which Saml. and Edmond were taken to Nashville, Tenn., by Joe Mick; Areno was left at the Eagle Tavern, Richmond.
Respectfully yours, Saml. Dove, Utica, New York.[24]

Not only had physical features changed in the intervening years but
new loyalties and emotional commitments had often replaced the old. Husbands and wives who had given up any hope of seeing each other again
were apt to have remarried, and children sold away from their parents had
been raised by other black women or by the white mistresses, creating
innumerable post-emancipation complications. Even if the search for family members succeeded, then, the reunions might be less than joyous occasions, and some couples who had remarried thought it best to avoid seeing
each other again. Few revealed the emotional torment raised by such
problems more graphically than the husband of Laura Spicer. Several
years after their forced separation, he had remarried in the belief that his

wife had died. When he learned after the war that she was still alive, the news stung him, prompting both joy and remorse. "I read your letters over and over again," he wrote her. "I keep them always in my pocket. If you are married I don't ever want to see you again." But in other letters, he revised that hasty warning and urged her to remarry. "I would much rather you would get married to some good man, for every time I gits a letter from you it tears me all to pieces. The reason why I have not written you before, in a long time, is because your letters disturbed me so very much." Even as he urged her to find another man, however, he professed his undying love for her.

> I would come and see you but I know you could not bear it. I want to see you and I don't want to see you. I love you just as well as I did the last day I saw you, and it will not do for you and I to meet. I am married, and my wife have two children, and if you and I meets it would make a very dissatisfied family.

Although they did not see each other, the correspondence continued. He requested her to send him locks of the children's hair with their names attached. He again urged her to remarry, if only for the sake of the children. But whatever she did, he insisted, their love for each other would remain undiminished.

> You know it never was our wishes to be separated from each other, and it never was our fault. Oh, I can see you so plain, at any-time, I had rather anything to had happened to me most than ever have been parted from you and the children. As I am, I do not know which I love best, you or Anna. If I was to die, today or tomorrow, I do not think I would die satisfied till you tell me you will try and marry some good, smart man that will take good care of you and the children; and do it because you love me; and not because I think more of the wife I have got than I do of you. The woman is not born that feels as near to me as you do. Tell them [the children] they must remember they have a good father and one that cares for them and one that thinks about them every day.

> My very heart did ache when reading your very kind and interesting letter. Laura I do not think that I have change any at all since I saw you last—I thinks of you and my children every day of my life. Laura I do love you the same. My love to you *never* have failed. Laura, truly, I have got another wife, and I am very sorry, that I am. You feels and seems to me as much like my dear loving wife, as you ever did Laura.[25]

Perhaps as tragic were the "reunions" in which marital partners accused each other of betrayal, infidelity, and desertion since their forced separation. After four years of absence, a freedman in North Carolina located his wife, only to find that she had borne two children by her master. Refusing to support the children, the husband took the case to the Freedmen's Bureau in Raleigh, which decided that the woman in such cases could name the father and force him to assume paternal responsibility and support. "This decision is not yet generally known," a reporter noted, "but when it is I fancy that it will create quite a flutter." Near Woodville, Mississippi, Fanny Smart learned that her husband, Adam, whom she had presumed to be dead, was still alive. Although not displeased by this news, she had been hurt by his failure to contact her earlier and by his apparent indifference to the children he had fathered.

> I received your letter yesterday. I was glad to hear from you. I heard that you was dead. I now think very strange, that you never wrote to me before. You could not think much of your children, as for *me*, I dont expect you to think much of as I have been confined, just got up, have a fine *daughter*. . . . I expect to stay here this *year*. I have made a contract to that effect. I am doing very well. My children I have all with *me*, they are all well, and well taken care of, the same as ever, if one get sick, they are well nursed. I now have eight children, all dependent on me for a support, only one, large enough to work for herselfe, the rest I could not hire for their victuals and clothes. I think you might have sent the children something, or some money. Joe can walk and talk. Ned is a great big boy, *bad as ever*. My baby I call her Cassinda. The children all send howda to you they all want to see you.

The circumstances surrounding their separation may have accounted for Adam Smart's failure to contact his wife earlier, perhaps even for the rumor that he had died. At least, the man who had been his master suggested as much in the postscript he added to Fanny Smart's letter.

> Adam you have acted the damn rascal with me in ever way   you trid to make the Yanks distroy ever thing I had   I know worn you to neve put you foot on my place   i think you a nary raskal   after this yer you can send an git you your famley if they want to go with you.[26]

Far more serious complications were introduced into postwar reunions by masters who had insisted that their slaves have marital partners, regardless of compatibility or depth of affection, and who had forbidden interplantation relationships. On some plantations, "marriages" were forced upon men and women who had spouses in other places from whom they had been separated by sale. Stephen Jordon, a former Louisiana slave who had been sold away from both his mother and his wife, found himself in such a predicament.

> I myself had my wife on another plantation. The woman my master gave me had a husband on another plantation. Every thing was mixed up. My other wife had two children for me, but the woman master gave me had no children. We were put in the same cabin, but both of us cried, me for my old wife and she for her old husband. As I could read and write I used to write out passes for myself, so I could go and see my old wife; and I

wrote passes for the other men on the place, so they could go and see their
wives that lived off the place.

Even as Jordon and his second wife shared the same cabin, he wrote out
passes that enabled her to slip out and visit her husband on a nearby
plantation. When conditions "got to be so tight" that he could no longer see
his wife as often as he wished, Jordon resolved to escape. Upon being
apprehended, however, he was sold even further away from his wife until
finally both of them remarried "during the long years of our enforced and
hopeless separation."[27]

Where husbands and wives had lived on separate but nearby plantations, their marital relationship rested on the willingness of two masters
to permit weekend visitations. Understandably, as a former South Carolina
slave explained, "a man dat had a wife off de place, see little peace or
happiness. He could see de wife once a week, on a pass, and jealousy kep'
him 'stracted de balance of de week, if he love her very much." Such
relationships, recalled Millie Barber, whose parents had lived five miles
apart, often produced "confusion, mix-up, and heartaches."

> My pa have to git a pass to come to see my mammy. He come sometimes
> widout de pass. Patrollers catch him way up de chimney hidin' one night;
> they stripped him right befo' mammy and give him thirty-nine lashes,
> wid her cryin' and a hollerin' louder than he did.

After emancipation, husbands and wives who had lived in this manner
quickly seized the opportunity to spend more than weekends together and
settled down, usually, on one or the other place.[28]

Upon learning of their freedom, a former slave recalled, the older
blacks "knowed what it meant, but us young ones didn't." Many of them
would learn soon enough, often in ways that proved to be quite memorable
and traumatic. Husbands and wives not only located each other in the
aftermath of emancipation but made what one Federal officer described as
"superhuman efforts" to find the children who had been sold away from
them; indeed, numerous ex-slaves would recall that their first realization
of freedom came when a parent, a sibling, or an aunt or uncle suddenly
appeared to take them away.[29] Depending on the circumstances of their
separation, such reunions could result in outbursts of unbounded joy or
produce very mixed emotions, particularly in young blacks who had little
or no recollection of their parents. Having been raised by someone else, to
whom firm emotional commitments may have been made, the sudden appearance of a strange man or woman who claimed to be a father or mother
was a terribly confusing and agonizing moment, even more so if faced with
the prospect of separation from those they had grown to love.

Since infancy, when her mother had been sold away, Frankie Goole
had been reared by her white mistress, slept in the same room with her,
and she came to regard her with considerable affection. At the age of

twelve, with the war over, Frankie found herself in a courtroom standing next to a woman who claimed to be her mother and facing a judge who asked her to verify it. "I dunno, she sezs she ez," Frankie remembered having told him. Reflecting back on that moment many years later, she summed up the confusion she had felt: "W'at did I know ob a mammy dat wuz tuk fum me at six weeks ole." When Harriet Clemens fled a plantation in Mississippi before the war ("It was on 'count o' de Nigger overseers. Dey kep' a-tryin' to mess 'roun' wid her an' she wouldn' have nothin' to do wid 'em"), she left her small child in the care of an elderly woman addressed as Aunt Emmaline, who "kep' all de orphunt chillun an' dem who's mammas had been sent off to de breedin' quarters." As soon as the war ended, she returned to claim her daughter. "At firs' I was scared o' her, 'cause I didn' know who she was," the daughter recalled. "She put me in her lap an' she mos' nigh cried when she seen de back o' my head. Dey was awful sores where de lice had been an' I had scratched 'em. She sho' jumped Aunt Emmaline 'bout dat. Us lef' dat day ..."[30]

On some plantations, the mistress had made a practice of selecting certain young slaves and moving them into the Big House to train them to be maids. Sarah Debro, a former North Carolina slave, recalled being separated from her mother for that purpose. "De day she took me my mammy cried kaze she knew I would never be 'lowed to live at de cabin wid her no more." While life in the Big House had both advantages and disadvantages, depending on the moods of the "white folks," the impressions it made on a young slave could be incalculable.

> My dresses an' aprons was starched stiff. I had a clean apron every day. We had white sheets on de beds an' we niggers had plenty to eat too, even ham. When Mis' Polly went to ride she took me in de carriage wid her. De driver set way up high an' me an' Mis' Polly set way down low. . . . I loved Mis' Polly an' loved stayin' at de big house.

After the war, her mother immediately came to claim her. But Sarah refused to leave, crying and holding on to the dress of her mistress, who pleaded for the right to retain her. Despite the tears and pleas, Sarah's mother remained firm and reminded the mistress that only her callousness had made this scene possible. "You took her away from me an' didn' pay no mind to my cryin', so now I'se takin' her back home. We's free now, Mis' Polly, we ain't gwine be slaves no more to nobody." With those words, she dragged her daughter out of the house. "I can see how Mis' Polly looked now," Sarah Debro recollected. "She didn' say nothin' but she looked hard at Mammy an' her face was white." That night, in the windowless "mud house" to which they moved, Sarah lay on her straw mattress and looked up through the cracks in the roof. "I could see de stars, an' de sky shinin' through de cracks looked like long blue splinters stretched 'cross de rafters. I lay dare an' cried kaze I wanted to go back to Mis' Polly."[31]

The close relationships that sometimes developed between slave children and the white mistress could be even more psychologically damaging than separation by sale. Where a master or mistress made "pets" out of certain favorites, indulging them in ways their parents could not, a conflict of loyalties became highly possible. Jane Sutton, a former Mississippi slave, contrasted her master, who provided the blacks with "plenty t'eat an' wear" and gave the children candy and presents when he returned from town, with her father, who belonged to a neighboring planter and visited on weekends. "He jus' come on Satu'd'y night an' us don' see much of 'im. Us call him 'dat man.' Mammy tol' us to be more 'spectful to 'im 'cause he was us daddy, but us aint care nothin' 'bout 'im. He aint never brung us no candy or nothin'." Rather than live with her father after emancipation, Jane ran away and returned to the old plantation. With equally conflicting emotions, Lizzie Hill, who had been a slave in Alabama, ran away from her mother three times after the war in order to return to the plantation where she had been accorded the same food and clothes as the white children with whom she had played and slept. Nor could Lou Turner easily give up the life she had led as a young slave on a Texas plantation, where the mistress had fed her well, dressed her in nice clothes, and insisted on her sleeping in the same room. "Old missy have seven li'l nigger chillen what belong to her slaves, but dey mammies and daddys come git 'em. I didn't own my own mammy. I own my old missy and call her 'mama.' Us cry and cry when us have to go with us mammy."[32]

But for most young blacks and children, slavery had been something less than a playground. The examples of brutal treatment, abuse, and neglect were no mere figments of the abolitionist imagination. If some absorbed the cultural ethos of the white family from constant contact with it, the vast majority of black children formed their view of the world in the quarters and usually within their own family groupings. More often than not, the child's teacher, school, and family were all the same, and the values and warnings with which he or she was inculcated reflected the experience of parents and grandparents who had themselves learned these lessons in the same way. In the absence of parents, the child was still more likely to obtain the love and learning he needed from other blacks than from his "white folks."[33] Not only did many black youths embrace the chance to sever the ties with their master and mistress but those who had been separated from loved ones often took the initiative to find them. After learning of her freedom in 1863, for example, Mary Armstrong, a seven-teen-year-old Missouri youth, went in search of her mother, who had been sold and taken to Texas. Several years later, she tracked her down in Wharton County. "Law me, talk 'bout cryin' and singin' and cryin' some more, we sure done it," she recalled of their reunion. Whatever the wishes of parents or children, some dispossessed masters insisted on keeping the young blacks until the age of twenty-one. The various state apprenticeship laws came close to legalized kidnapping in many instances, depriving parents of children if a white judge deemed it "better for the habits and comfort" of a child to be bound out to a white guardian. Protests over

arbitrary apprenticeship mounted in the postwar years, with parents frequently appealing to the local provost marshal or the Freedmen's Bureau
for custodial rights to their children.[34]

Few memories of bondage elicited greater pain in black parents than
the humiliation they had suffered in watching their children whipped or
abused by a member of the white family. After emancipation, if they decided to remain with the same master or if they hired out elsewhere,
freedmen families often made their labor contingent on the abolition of
such practices and a recognition of their exclusive right to manage and
discipline their own children. Employers who violated that understanding
were apt to find themselves with fewer laborers the next morning or when
the time came to renew a contract. With equal fervor, parents committed
themselves in the immediate aftermath of emancipation to provide an
education for their children, not only in the numerous schools established
by northern whites but in schools which employers were forced to establish
on their plantations in order to retain and attract a labor force.

Deprived of any legal standing, stripped of any means to protect itself,
faced always with the specter of forced breakup, the black family under
slavery needed to demonstrate remarkable resiliency to withstand the
often debilitating and debasing experience of white ownership. While some
slaveholders recognized and encouraged strong family ties for the stabilizing influence they exerted, many others were either indifferent, thought
their blacks to be emotionally incapable of sustaining the necessary affection, or resented any attempts by them to ape the social norms of their
superiors. "I was once whipped," a black servant in New Orleans remarked, "because I said to missis, 'My mother sent me.' We were not
allowed to call our mammies 'mother.' It made it come too near the way
of the white folks." Whatever the prevailing attitudes of individual masters
or mistresses, every black family had to find ways to counter the sense of
powerlessness imparted by white ownership. Not only did they lack control
over separation by sale but the people who owned them were free to inflict
indignities, both physical and verbal, as their moods dictated, and they
were apt to do so in the presence of the entire family. To calculate the
brutalities of the "peculiar institution" by counting the number of whippings meted out by a master or overseer would be to miss the point altogether, as nearly every slave who wrote about his or her experience
would testify.[35]

Although some slave families were disrupted, by irreparable psychic
damage if not by sale, what seems so remarkable is that most of them
endured the experience of bondage. On most plantations and farms, the
lives of the slaves—field hands, house servants, and artisans alike—revolved around family units, the two-parent household predominated, and
the black husband and father exerted in his own way the dominant influence in that household. If he could not always provide for his family as he
wished, he tried to supplement their diets by hunting, fishing, and theft.
If he could not always protect his family as he wished, he often managed

to lay down a line of tolerated behavior beyond which masters and overseers proceeded at their own risk. Sam Watkins, a Tennessee planter, was
among those who flagrantly crossed that line once too often.

> He would ship their husbands (slaves) out of bed and get in with their
> wives. One man said he stood it as long as he could and one morning he
> just stood outside, and when he got with his wife he just choked him to
> death. He said he knew it was death, but it was death anyhow; so he just
> killed him. They hanged him.[36]

Few wives expected their husbands to sacrifice their lives in this way. Fully
aware of the master's power, most couples made the necessary accommodation. That reflected not indifference to family ties but the simple resolve
to keep the family together and alive. The same consideration would im-
pede escape until the proximity of the Union Army enabled entire families
to leave the plantations.

During the Civil War, the black family had to withstand attacks from
various sources. Numbers of slaves who accompanied their masters to the
front lines never returned, nor did many of those impressed into Confederate labor battalions. "Father wus sent to Manassas Gap at the beginning
of de war," a former Virginia slave recalled, "and I do not 'member ever
seein' him." When freedmen attempted to trace lost family members after
emancipation, the trail often started and ended with the information that
he was last seen in "a gang [that] was taken away de firs year of de war."
The wartime decisions to remove slaves to Texas or to some "safe" place
in the interior resulted in still further disruptions, with the women, children, and elderly blacks often left on the old place. Nor did the coming of
the Union Army necessarily secure black families; instead, some of the
men enlisted or were forcibly impressed into service as military laborers
and soldiers. Whatever the commitment of slaves to the Union cause, many
of them feared that service in the Union Army would place their wives and
children in immediate jeopardy from hostile whites and deprive them of
necessary support. Such fears were not illusory. Enraged over losing any
of their slaves, particularly to the Union Army, masters were known to
avenge themselves on the soldiers' wives and children, either by abusing
them, refusing to support them, or expelling them from the premises. Only
after strong pressure from black soldiers who threatened mutiny and desertion did the Federal government belatedly guarantee freedom to the
families of black volunteers, make them eligible for rations, and try to
ensure their safety. By this time, however, numerous families had already
been disrupted.[37]

When weighed against the enormous tensions to which slave marital
ties were subjected, the prospects for success under any circumstances
might have seemed dim. The very words by which marriages were solemnized indicated their vulnerability. "Don't mean nothin' less you say,
'What God done jined, cain't no man pull asunder,' " a former Virginia

slave observed. "But dey never would say dat. Jus' say, 'Now you married.' " The classic account of the slave preacher in Kentucky who united couples "until death or *distance* do you part" had its equivalent in the Virginia master who, as one of his former slaves recalled, devised his own marriage vows by which he united slave couples:

> *Dat yo' wife*
> *Dat yo' husban'*
> *Ise yo' Marser*
> *She yo' Missus*
> *You're married.*

If they achieved nothing else, the mock wedding rites, highlighted by "jumping the broomstick," sanctioned such marriages in the eyes of the man and woman and their fellow slaves. But the white owner determined the longevity of their relationship, and the forcible breakup of slave marriages occurred with sufficient regularity to warrant the casualness of the ceremony, the fears of the couple, and some bitter recollections:

> One night a couple married an' de next mornin' de boss sell de wife. De gal ma got in de street an' cursed de white woman fur all she could find. She said: "dat damn white, pale-face bastard sell my daughter who jus' married las' night," an other t'ings.

The police had to be summoned to restrain the grief-stricken mother and remove her to the local workhouse.[38]

No sooner had emancipation been acknowledged than thousands of "married" couples, with the encouragement of black preachers and northern white missionaries, hastened to secure their marital vows, both legally and spiritually. "My husband and I have lived together fifteen years," the mother of a large family remarked, "and we wants to be married over again now." Mildred Graves, a former Virginia house servant, remembered her courtship, the broomstick ceremony, and the cast-off dress her mistress gave her as a wedding present; nevertheless, after the war, she also recalled, "we had a real sho' nuff weddin' wid a preacher. Dat cost a dollar."[39] The insistence of teachers, missionaries, and Freedmen's Bureau officers that blacks formalize their marriages stemmed from the notion that legal sanction was necessary for sexual and moral restraint and that ex-slaves had to be inculcated with "the obligations of the married state in civilized life." But many of the couples themselves, who needed no instruction in such matters, agreed to participate in formalizations of their unions for more practical reasons—to legitimize their children, to qualify for soldiers' pensions, to share in the rumored forthcoming division of the lands, and to exercise their newly won civil rights. Whatever the most compelling reason, mass wedding ceremonies involving as many as seventy couples at a time became a common sight in the postwar South.

> One evening four couples came to the schoolhouse to meet "the parson" who was to perform the marriage ceremony for them. They came straight from the field, in their working-clothes; the women, as was their custom, walking behind the men.... When they left the schoolhouse the women all took their places by the side of the men, showing that they felt they were equal in the eyes of the law.[40]

Native whites looked upon these spectacles with a mixture of amusement, disdain, and indifference. Having forbidden legal marriages, condoned the breakup of families, and demeaned family relationships, some former masters and mistresses now mocked the efforts of ex-slaves to dignify with proper ceremony and affidavit marital ties of long standing. "They take the white man's notions as they copy his manners, not for what they are but for the impression that's made by them on the world," a South Carolina white woman observed of the interest taken by blacks in solemnizing their marriage relationship.

> Now what [is] more common than to hear "I must go with my wife," not because they have investigated the matter and seen the right of the thing, but such is the view of the white and the view suits present circumstances, and is therefore adopted by the negro. One wife is as good as another to them ...

Like most whites, she seemed incapable of explaining the actions of the freedmen except as a desire to imitate their superiors—and moral exemplars. Even the northern missionaries, who liked to think of themselves as rescuing the ex-slaves from the sins of concubinage, shared many of the prevailing assumptions about the moral depravity of blacks. Nevertheless, white Southerners and northern observers alike would hardly have disagreed with the potential benefits that flowed from stable black families. "Marital relations are invaluable as a means of promoting industry," a northern correspondent wrote from Louisiana. "Morality encourages industry and prosperity. Immorality in the sexual relations produces idleness, intemperance, and apathy."[41]

Not all slave couples hastened to legalize their marriages, at least not until they resolved the many complications stemming from multiple liaisons in a lifetime of bondage. The question facing numerous freedmen and freedwomen was not whether to formalize their slave marriage but which one should take precedence. With numerous spouses having remarried since their forced separation, that would frequently be a difficult and agonizing decision to make. Nor could they resolve the dilemma, as a South Carolina woman attempted to do, by alternating between two spouses on separate plantations. Newly enacted state laws usually validated unions between persons of color who were living together at the time of emancipation and required ex-slaves with multiple spouses to make an immediate decision about which "marriage" they wished to legitimate; Federal authorities, who tended to take these matters more seriously, recognized the right of a husband or wife to leave a childless marriage to return to a previous partner by whom they had had children. "Whenever a negro appears before me with two or three wives who have equal claim upon him," a Freedmen's Bureau officer in North Carolina reported, "I marry him to the woman who has the greatest number of helpless children who otherwise would become a charge on the Bureau."[42]

Although black preachers, white missionaries, and Bureau officials helped some couples to resolve these difficulties, the final decision was generally made by the partners themselves, who would have to reconcile conflicting emotions compounded by the manner in which they had initially been separated and the presence of children. In the District of Columbia, for example, a man who had been separated from his first wife for twenty-two years resolved to annul his present marriage "and live with the first by whom he has several grown children." On the Sea Islands, Jane Ferguson, after hearing that her first husband had returned, had no hesitation in making a decision. "Martin Barnwell is my husband, ma'am," she told a missionary teacher. "I am got no husband but he. W'en de secesh sell him off we nebber 'spect to see each odder more. He said, 'Jane take good care of our boy, an' w'en we git to hebben us will lib togedder to nebber part no more.'" When she subsequently married Ferguson, they had agreed that Martin's return would annul their ties. "I told him I never 'spects Martin *could* come back, but if he did he would be my husband above all others." But what if Ferguson refused to give her up? the teacher asked her. "Martin is my husband, ma'am, an' the father of my child," the woman replied; "and *Ferguson is a man*." But the matter was not so easily resolved, as Ferguson, a Union soldier, pleaded with his wife not to abandon him: "Martin has not seen you for a long time. He *cannot* think of you as I do. O Jane! do not go to Charleston. Come to Jacksonville. I will get a house and we will live here. Never mind what the people say. Come to me, Jane." But Jane dictated a response that terminated both the correspondence and their marriage: "Tell him, I say I'm sorry he finds it so hard to do his duty. But as he does, I shall do mine, an' I shall always pray de Lord to bless him. . . . I shall never write to him no more. But tell him I wish him well."[43]

Emancipation functioned in some cases as an instant and convenient divorce, enabling a couple to dissolve their marriage by mutually agreeing not to formalize it. Some freedmen and freedwomen seized the chance to annul an incompatible and loveless marriage, which in several instances had been forced upon them by their owner. In a "divorce" case argued before a Union officer in Louisiana, the husband claimed he had done everything in his power for the comfort of his wife and wished to retain her, but the woman declared she could now take care of herself and refused to stay with a man whom she did not love.[44] Among families that had survived bondage intact, the difficult post-emancipation decision about whether to stay with their last master also produced conflicts which were sometimes resolved by divorce. More often than not, however, those who lived together at the end of the war did not avail themselves of the opportunity to dissolve those ties, suggesting the extent to which their marriages had been based on considerations other than the convenience of the master.

During slavery, interracial sexual liaisons—usually between slave women and white men, sometimes between slave men and white women —had occasionally developed into affectionate and lasting relationships. Obviously, such ties could neither be solemnized nor legalized, and few even cared to admit that they were based on genuine feelings of love, particularly those involving white women. Emancipation permitted interracial couples to formalize those relationships, at least to the extent state laws and public opinion would tolerate them. When the daughter of a former slave owner in Mississippi announced her intention to marry one of their former slaves, with whom she had already established a relationship, a local judge refused to believe her avowal of love for the man and ordered the arraignment and trial of the couple. With different results, a quadroon mistress of a planter in Mississippi refused to continue a relationship with her master after the war unless he agreed to marriage; they finally prevailed upon a reluctant army chaplain to perform the necessary rites after the master claimed he had "married her in the sight of God five years ago." The difficulties that confronted a white woman and a black man made any permanent relationship almost impossible in the postwar South. Although the courts always dealt harshly with attacks on whites, whatever the evidence, a court in Fredericksburg, Virginia, acquitted a black woman accused of assaulting a white woman who had "stolen the affections" of her black husband, prompting him to leave her for the white woman. That came about as close to justifiable assault in the eyes of the white community as any black person could commit.[45]

Neither the legalization nor the sanctification of black marriages necessarily moved the ex-slaves to adopt in full the sexual code of upper-class whites. "The negroes had their own ideas of morality, and held to them very strictly," the proprietress of a Georgia plantation observed; "they did not consider it wrong for a girl to have a child before she married, but afterwards were extremely severe upon anything like infidelity on her part. Indeed, the good old law of female submission to the husband's will on all points held good." While both races frowned upon certain sexual practices (such as adultery), the differences which persisted in defining moral behavior (such as the condoning of prenuptial sex among blacks) and the post-emancipation complications surrounding polygamy help to explain the intensity with which white missionaries and black preachers dwelled on black "moral vices" and admonished the ex-slaves to conform in every respect to the Victorian moral code. When Clinton B. Fisk, a sympathetic Freedmen's Bureau officer, counseled freedmen and freedwomen that God would no longer close his eyes to "adultery and fornication" among them, he was saying little that black preachers had not already said on numerous occasions. "Look at de white folks," one such

preacher told his congregation. "D'ye eber see a *white* man want to marry
a woman when he had a lawful wife a libing? Neber! I neber heared ob sech
a thing in all my life. A white man is 'structed; he knows dat's agin de law
and de gospil."[46]

Although reports of rampant "polygamy, adultery, and indiscriminate
sexual intercourse" among the ex-slaves would reinforce white notions of
black moral laxity, some Freedmen's Bureau officers readily conceded that
a disproportionate number of such cases came to their attention. "If I
exaggerate in this matter," a Bureau officer in South Carolina wrote, "it
is because, like most officers of justice, I saw chiefly the evil side of my
public—all the deserted ones coming to me for the redress of their grievances or for help in their poverty." Actually, the seriousness with which
most blacks assumed and sustained their marital vows, like the intense
interest they had shown in locating family members, surprised and elated
many Bureau officers and northern missionaries, who had come to the
South prepared for the worst. If Horace Greeley, the New York editor,
thought "enslaved, degraded, hopeless races or classes are always lewd,"
that was far from the conclusion reached by a white teacher in postwar
Virginia. "The colored people easily assume the responsibilities, proprie-
ties, and graces of civilized life. As a class, their tastes are comely, though
they are acquainted with filth. I fancy they see the moral significance of
things quite as readily as white people." And if white masters and mistresses claimed credit for the "civilizing influences" they had exerted on
their slaves, the freedmen and freedwomen took some pride in the moral
values they had managed to sustain in the quarters, often in the face of the
grossest forms of white savagery.[47]

The eagerness of blacks to assume the "graces of civilized life" manifested itself in ways that native whites found most disturbing. "The black
women do not like to work," an Alabama planter reported, "it is not lady-
like." The phenomenon he described was real enough, though whites
tended to exaggerate its prevalence. With the acknowledgment of emancipation, many black women did withdraw their labor from the fields and the
white man's kitchen in order to spend more time tending to their own
husbands and children. If the women themselves did not initiate such
moves, the men often insisted upon it, and husbands and wives together
effected arrangements that would be more compatible with freedom. Mary
Jones, the Georgia proprietress, tersely summed up the changes affecting
her own household: "Gilbert will stay on his old terms, but withdraws
Fanny and puts Harry and Little Abram in her place and puts his son
Gilbert out to a trade. Cook Kate wants to be relieved of the heavy burden
of cooking for two and wait on her husband." No less distraught, an Alabama planter claimed he had lost one fourth of his labor because the men
regarded it as "a matter of pride" to exact from their employers a new
division of labor that would exempt their women from field work. Where
women continued to work, the men often insisted during contract negotiations that wives and mothers be given time off during the regular workweek to tend to their housekeeping chores.[48]

That the withdrawal of women from the labor force was frequently made at the insistence of the men reflected a determination by many husbands and fathers to reinforce their position as the head of the family in accordance with the accepted norms of the dominant society. The place for the woman was in the home, attending to the business of the home. "When I married my wife," a Tennessee freedman told his employer, in rejecting his request for her services, "I married her to wait on me and she has got all she can do right here for me and the children." Like many outside observers, Laura Towne, a northern white teacher in the Sea Islands, explained such developments as a natural reaction to the dominant place she had assumed black women had occupied in the slave household. In wishing to "rule their wives," the men could thus hardly be blamed for exercising "an inestimable privilege" of freedom. "In slavery the woman was far more important, and was in every way held higher than the man. It was the woman's house, the children were entirely hers, etc., etc." Since emancipation, however, Laura Towne had observed the frequency with which black leaders urged black men "to get the women into their proper place—never to tell them anything of their concerns, etc., etc.; and the notion of being bigger than women generally, is just now inflating the conceit of the males to an amazing degree."[49]

If the spectacle of black marriages amused former masters and mistresses, the inclination of black women "to play the lady" did not, particularly when it made it more difficult for white women to do so. On a Mississippi plantation, where the black women suddenly refused to work, the employer (who had been their former master) ordered them to resume their positions in the field or leave the premises. They left. What whites contemptuously called "playing the lady" occasionally took the form of black women cavorting about town in the cast-off finery of their last mistress. Despite these much-publicized examples, however, most black women charged with "playing the lady" had simply opted to spend more time in their own households and made labor arrangements that would permit them to do so. A Georgia planter, for example, managed to hire four "good hands," only to discover that their wives had no intention of cooking for him, at least not until they had discussed the matter with him. Aware of his inability to hire a cook, the women took advantage of their bargaining position and exacted promises to pay them "their own price" and, equally important, to permit them to divide the housework and cooking among themselves. Presumably, this arrangement would have given each of them ample time to meet her own domestic responsibilities. Such experiences, not at all uncommon, revealed that many black women, rather than withdraw from work altogether, used the threat quite successfully to obtain better terms from an employer.[50]

Few black leaders, clergymen, or editors would have disputed the "plain counsels" offered by a Freedmen's Bureau officer to the emancipated black woman about her proper role in the home. Before marriage, she should learn to knit, sew, mend clothes, bake bread, keep a clean house, cultivate a garden, and read and write, while at the same time remaining "a true woman"—that is, protecting her chastity. After marriage, she would be expected to take proper care of her person, to appear always clean, neat, and tidy, and to look "as pretty as possible." That was simply another way of saying that black women should aspire to be like their white counterparts and abide by the conventional wisdom and experience of mid-nineteenth-century American society. Not all black women, however, willingly assented to such a narrow definition of their roles, few of them had the means to become "ladies" of leisure, and some did not look upon white women as the most desirable models to imitate; indeed, their previous experiences with white "ladies" had not necessarily filled them with awe, admiration, or even respect. Whatever black men might have preferred, most black women could not afford to withdraw from outside labor after emancipation; many continued to work in the fields alongside their men, while others moved into the towns in the hope of obtaining more remunerative employment.[51]

Out of economic necessity and the experience of slavery, black women fashioned a place for themselves in the post-emancipation family and community. Invariably, it would be a more important position than that occupied by their white counterparts. If fewer black women labored in the fields, they often cared for the family garden plot, worked as washerwomen or wet nurses, and performed other jobs that were necessary to supplement the family income. If they deferred to the men and absented themselves from the political discussions, they might still guard the rifles stacked outside the meeting places. And in the waning years of Reconstruction, when whites threatened to regain power, black women in Charleston were sighted "carrying axes or hatchets in their hands hanging down at their sides, their aprons or dresses half-concealing the weapons." Exhorting a large audience to defend the work of Reconstruction, a black clergyman would warn of "80,000 black men in the State who can use Winchesters and 200,000 black women who can light a torch and use a knife."[52]

No matter how they manifested their freedom, black men and women found themselves in a better position to defend their marital fidelity, to maintain their family ties, and to control their own children. That in itself ensured an enhanced dignity and pride as a family that slavery had so often compromised. But nothing could erase the still vivid memories of the fear and experience of forced separation from loved ones and the innumerable tragedies and complications which such separations, as well as the day-to-day indignities of slave life, had inflicted upon their families. More than the memories of those years remained to haunt them. Near Norfolk, Virginia, a long-separated couple found each other near the end of the war. "Twas like a stroke of death to me," the woman said afterwards. "We threw ourselves into each others arms and cried. His wife looked on and was jealous, but she needn't have been. My husband is so kind, I shouldn't leave him if he hadn't had another wife, and of course I shouldn't now. Yes, my husband's very kind, but I ain't happy." The momentary reunion had been painful for both of them. Reflecting back upon her first marriage, the days they had spent together, and the forced separation, she could only say, "White folk's got a heap to answer for the way they've done to colored folks! So much they wont never *pray* it away!"[53]

4

COMPARED TO THE MANY acute problems facing the freedman, the question of his name might have seemed the least consequential. But the newly freed slaves thought otherwise, sharing a concern with names and naming voiced nearly a century later by Ralph Ellison.

> For it is through our names that we first place ourselves in the world. Our names, being the gift of others, must be made our own. . . . They must become our masks and our shields and the containers of all those values and traditions which we learn and/or imagine as being the meaning of our familial past.
>
> And when we are reminded so constantly that we bear, as Negroes, names originally possessed by those who owned our enslaved grandparents, we are apt . . . to be more than ordinarily concerned with the veiled and mysterious events, the fusions of blood, the furtive couplings, the business transactions, the violations of faith and loyalty, the assaults; yes, and the unrecognized and unrecognizable loves through which our names were handed down unto us.[54]

Rather than reveal a sordid past, the names assumed or revealed after emancipation reflected a new beginning—an essential step toward achieving the self-respect, the personal dignity, and the independence which slavery had compromised. "We hardly knowed our names," recalled Sallie Crane, a former Arkansas slave. "We was cussed for so many bitches and sons of bitches and bloody bitches, and blood of bitches. We never heard our names scarcely at all." Describing "the most cruel acts" inflicted upon him as a slave, William Wells Brown singled out the order that he drop the name his mother had given him. (The master had wished to placate his nephew, also named William, who had recently taken up residence on the plantation.) "I received several very severe whippings for telling people that my name was William, after orders were given to change it. Though young, I was old enough to place a high appreciation upon my name." Until his escape, he went by the name of Sandford, but the moment he reached a safe haven he adopted his old name "and let Sandford go by the board, for I always hated it. Not because there was anything peculiar in the name; but because it had been forced upon me."[55]

During slavery, many blacks only had a given name. Although most slaves appear to have named their own children, the master might arbitrarily assign a name, borrowing heavily from classical, biblical, and simplified Anglo-Saxon appellations; the naming process also afforded him a chance to indulge in some humorous whims, and some did so at the expense of the slave's dignity. Masters might permit certain favorites and slaves who exercised authority over other slaves to adopt their own surnames; the less privileged were apt to have the same surname as the master—a convenient way to identify the plantation to which they belonged. To allow the slave to use his own surname, Jacob Stroyer recalled, "would be sharing an honor which was due only to his master, and that would be too much for a negro, said they, who was nothing more than a servant. So it was held as a crime for a slave to be caught using his own name, a crime which would expose him to severe punishment." Numerous ex-slaves, then, like Wash Ingram of Texas, recalled only that "we always went by the name of whoever we belonged to." In South Carolina, a teacher in a freedmen's school tried without success to induce one of the pupils to state her surname. "Only Phyllis, ma'am," she would reply. Finally, an older student interceded, exclaiming, "Pshaw, gal! What's you'm title?" The pupil then understood what was demanded, and she gave the name of her former master.[56]

More often than many masters realized, slaves adopted their own surnames. "When the white folks speak of them they say 'John, that belongs to Mr. So and So,'" Robert Smalls testified during the war. "But among themselves they use their titles. . . . Before their masters they do not speak of their titles at all." Plantation records rarely listed slaves by surnames, and the vast rice plantations owned by the Heyward family in South Carolina were no exception. Some of the more prominent blacks, however, like "old blacksmith Caesar," were known by both their given names and their surnames. And "among themselves," Duncan Clinch Heyward conceded, "the slaves all had surnames, and immediately after they were freed these names came to light. The surnames were selected by the Negroes themselves. Scarcely ever did a Negro choose the name of his or her owner, but often took that of some other slaveholding family, of which he knew." Occasionally, surnames other than that of the master would surface beyond the confines of the slave quarters, much to the surprise of the white family. "Mammy, what makes you call Henry Mr. Ferguson," Susan Dabney Smedes remembered asking her "usually indulgent" mammy, who had taken her to a slave wedding. "Do you think 'cause we are black that we cyarn't have no names?" she replied indignantly. Usually, however, such names were not publicly revealed until after emancipation.[57]

Although family pride was reason enough, certain practical considerations also encouraged the selection of names after emancipation. Whether to enlist in the Union Army, live in the contraband camps, apply for relief at the Freedmen's Bureau office, or, some years later, vote in an election, blacks needed to register both a given name and a surname with Federal authorities. Henry Banner took his surname under the erroneous impression that it would qualify him for a government bounty of forty acres and a mule. "He told me never to go by any name except Banner. That was all the mule they ever give me." Midway through the war, Federal officials expressed some consternation over the number of contrabands who gave them false names. "Perhaps, after all, no false motive influences them," a white missionary teacher tried to explain, "as they may bear many names in a lifetime." Still, she found herself repeatedly frustrated in trying to ascertain the full names of the freedmen and freedwomen she encountered. "They are Judith or John, and nothing more." Not at all hesitant about adopting or revealing surnames were scores of ex-slaves who considered this step necessary to demonstrate and ensure their newly won freedom. "No man thought he was perfectly free," the overseer on a Louisiana plantation observed, "unless he had changed his name and taken a family name. Precious few of 'em ever took that of their old masters." If any doubts remained about the validity of emancipation, some freed slaves came up with the ingenious idea that a new name might be a useful device to retain their freedom and avoid re-enslavement. "When us black folks got set free," Alice Wilkins recalled, "us'n change our names, so effen the white folks get together and change their minds and don't let us be free any more, then they have a hard time finding us."[58]

The notion that blacks marked their emancipation by repudiating their slave names distorts the significance those names had assumed for large numbers of slaves, particularly the ways in which they often reflected a deeply felt familial consciousness. Although some freedmen quickly dropped the whimsical names their masters had bestowed on them, nearly everyone else retained his or her previous given name. This had been their sole identity during bondage, often the only remaining link to parents from whom they had been separated and who had initially named them. No matter how harsh a bondage they had endured, few freed slaves revealed any desire to obliterate their entire past or family heritage, and those whose given names or surnames reflected kinship ties tended to guard them zealously. Many freedmen, on the other hand, adopted surnames for the first time, often choosing a name that would set them off as a discrete family, some began to use openly the surnames they had assumed as slaves, and still others slightly altered their names to symbolize their right to do so. Once they knew of their freedom, Lee Guidon recollected, "a heap of people say they was going to name their selves over. They named their selves big names. . . . Some of the names was Abraham an' some called their selves Lincum. Any big name 'ceptin' their master's name. It was the fashion." If that was "the fashion," Lee Guidon's father decided to be the exception—he kept the name of his master, because "fine folks raise us an' we goiner hold to our own names."[59]

If freedmen retained or adopted their master's surname, this did not necessarily reflect any deep affection for him or the conditions of bondage on that plantation. In many instances, the name of the ex-slave's parents or grandparents was the same as that of the master, and that alone was sufficient reason to hold on to it. Martin Jackson, who had been a slave on the Fitzpatrick plantation in Texas, thought many years later that taking the master's name after emancipation had reflected expediency more than anything else. "This was done more because it was the logical thing to do and the easiest way to be identified than it was through affection for the master. Also, the government seemed to be in a almighty hurry to have us get names. We had to register as someone, so we could be citizens." When forced to choose his own surname, however, Jackson thought about all the slaves who would assume the name Fitzpatrick. "I made up my mind I'd find me a different one. One of my grandfathers in Africa was called Jeaceo, and so I decided to be Jackson."[60]

The freedman who took the name of an earlier owner, perhaps the first owner he could recall, often made that choice out of a sense of historical identity, continuity, and family pride—the reputation of the particular master notwithstanding. The idea was not to honor a previous master but to sustain some identification with the freedman's family of origin.

> I don't know whether my father used his master's name or his father's name. His father's name was Jerry Greene, and his master's name was Henry Bibb. I don't know which name he went by, but I call myself Greene because his father's name was Jerry Greene.

After emancipation, Aleck Gillison adopted the surname of a previous master who had sold him; so did Jim Henry's father, who had once belonged to the Patrick Henry family of Virginia; Isaac Thomas, the slave of I. D. Thomas, a Texas planter, returned to his old home in Florida, where he "find out he people and git he real name, and dat am Beckett." Similarly, Anson Harp had belonged to Tom Harp, a Mississippi planter, before being separated from his parents and sold to James Henry Hammond, a prominent South Carolina planter. After the war, he refused to take the name of Hammond, " 'cause too many of his slaves do," and decided to keep the name of his old master. That was "the one my daddy and mammy had," he explained, though he never saw them again after their forced separation.[61]

In adopting surnames, as in other manifestations of their new freedom, the ex-slaves defied any easy categorization. If, for a variety of reasons, some took the names of old or recent masters, many openly repudiated such names. "That's my ole rebel master's title," a young South Carolina black protested after he used the name of Middleton in a freedmen's school. "Him's nothing to me now. I don't belong to he no longer, an' I don't see no use in being called for him." While enrolling a freedman in the Union Army, a recruiting officer in Tennessee demanded that he take a surname and suggested that of his previous master. The proposal struck the young black man with obvious dismay. "No, suh," he replied emphatically. "*I'se had nuff o' ole massa.*" In some instances, Federal officials expedited the naming process by furnishing the names themselves, and invariably the name would be the same as that of the freedman's most recent master. But these appear to have been exceptional cases; the ex-slaves themselves usually took the initiative—like the Virginia mother who changed the name of her son from Jeff Davis, which was how the master had known him, to Thomas Grant, which seemed to suggest the freedom she was now exercising. Whatever names the freed slaves adopted, whether that of a previous master, a national leader, an occupational skill, a place of residence, or a color, they were most often making that decision themselves. That was what mattered.[62]

That freedmen should have assumed the surnames of prominent white families might have flattered the patriarchal ego and self-image of the planter class, but it also left some whites in utter dismay and few of them had any notion of the considerations that entered into such decisions. "I used to be proud of my name," Caroline Ravenel wrote a close friend. "I have ceased to be so. I fear it will no longer [be] spotless, as the two meanest negroes on the place have appropriated it." Eliza Frances Andrews, the daughter of a prominent Georgian, expressed some amusement over the names taken by the family's former slaves but she also proved to be far more perceptive than most whites. In the Andrews household, the family servant, Charity, announced on her wedding day that she had two names, like her "white folks"; she would henceforth be addressed as Mrs. Tatom, while her husband, Hamp, a field hand, would now be known as Mr. Sam Ampey Tatom. Trying to keep a straight face, Eliza Andrews asked her how they had come by the name of Tatom. "His grandfather used to belong to a Mr. Tatom," she replied, "so he took his name for his *entitles*." The blacks "seldom or never" adopted the names of their most recent owners, Miss Andrews observed; almost always, they would take the name of some former master, "and they go as far back as possible." After all, she surmised, "it was the name of the actual owner that distinguished them in slavery, and I suppose they wish to throw off that badge of servitude. Then, too, they have their notions of family pride." But even as these changes both amused and impressed her, Eliza Andrews had to confess to herself that they were not altogether pleasing.

> All these changes are very sad to me, in spite of their comic side. There will soon be no more old mammies and daddies, no more old uncles and aunties. Instead of "maum Judy" and "uncle Jacob," we shall have our "Mrs. Ampey Tatoms," and our "Mr. Lewis Williamses." The sweet ties that bound our old family servants to us will be broken and replaced with envy and ill-will.[63]

## 5

BEING FREE was often a day-to-day struggle, if only to understand the new possibilities and dangers. The achievement of an individual dignity and self-respect commensurate with their legal status demanded of black peo-

ple much more than the adoption or revelation of family names. Now that
they were free, some thought the old pretenses and demeanor could be
dropped. The need to cringe in the presence of whites or to respond obsequi-
ously to their whims and petty humiliations seemed less compelling. Freedom, as a former Georgia slave defined it, meant taking "no more
foolishment off of white folks." Early in 1865, two white men were walking
along a street in Helena, Arkansas, when they encountered a freedman.
"How do ye do, Mr. Powell," the black man greeted one of them. "Howdy,
uncle," Powell replied. Several months earlier, that familiar exchange of
greetings would have terminated the conversation, but not in this first year
of emancipation. Much to Powell's astonishment, the black man cursed
him, denied that he was his uncle, and made it clear that he did not permit
such people to claim kinship with him. When Powell protested that he was
only trying to be "civil," the freedman angrily retorted, "Call me Mister."
And with that parting salvo, the men went their respective ways. The
much-perturbed Powell turned to his companion and exclaimed, "Oh my
God; how long before my ass will be kicked by every negro that meets
me?"[64]

Comparable incidents and confrontations were bound to arise while
former slaves explored the content of their freedom. This was the appropriate time, some of them thought, to give substance to their new status, even
to challenge and revamp the traditional and seemingly inviolate code of
racial etiquette. Of what use was a family name if white people seldom used
it in addressing blacks, if they persisted in referring to adult black men and
women as "boy," "girl," or "nigger," while reserving the honorific titles of
"auntie" and "uncle" for the venerable few. After emancipation, Emma
Watson recalled, she perceived few changes in her status, except that the
mistress both acknowledged and demeaned her freedom at the same time,
as in the command: "Come here, you li'l old free nigger." Even without the
benefit of organized or coordinated action, freedmen and freedwomen made
known their objections to these linguistic relics of bondage, some of them
insisting that they be addressed by their surnames (preceded by the appropriate mister, missus, or miss), that they no longer be identified by the
plantation or the master for whom they worked (as in Colonel Pinckney's
Ned), that they be treated, in other words, as mature men and women
rather than as children or pets. For whites to address adult black men as
"boys," a black clergyman declared, was to evince a "spirit of malice" he
deemed incompatible with the rights of free "colored men." The use of such
terms, he charged, assumed that a black man was little more than "a
six-year-old stripling or a two-year colt," and it reminded him of the Irishman who testified that "in the 'ould counthry,' when they whistled for him
to come to dinner, he never knew whether it was himself or the hogs they
wanted." With unjustified optimism, the clergyman warned that "white or
colored Christians" would no longer tolerate such terms of address.[65]

The problem defied any early resolution. Not only did whites persist
in using the familiar terms of address but the blacks themselves found it

difficult to discard the titles by which they had customarily known their former owners. As slaves, they had addressed them as "master" and "mistress," or even more familiarly as "marster" or "mars" and as "mistis," "miss," or "missy," usually followed only by the Christian name, as in "Miss Ann" or "Mars Bill." Customarily, they had used titles like "boss," "cap'n," "major," and "colonel" in addressing white men of high rank with whom they were less acquainted. (The term "boss" might be reserved for whites who were neither slaveholders nor "poor buckra.") After learning of his freedom, a Georgia black wanted to know, "You got to say master?" to which a fellow freedman responded in the negative. "But they said it all the same," Sarah Jane Paterson recalled. "They said it for a long time." In Virginia, a Union officer in charge of freedmen affairs reproached some ex-slaves for referring to him as "massa," explaining that they were no longer slaves. "No, massa," one of them replied, "but I'm so used to it." Searching for alternatives to the traditional "marsa" and "missus," but not wishing to incur the charge of insolence, some freedmen, especially the younger ones, resolved the dilemma by addressing their former masters as "boss" or "cap'n" and their former mistresses as "ma'am." Since those titles had often been used in the past when speaking with strangers, they suggested less intimacy and seemed more appropriate to the new relationships.[66]

With some exceptions, the men and women who had once owned slaves evinced no urgent desire to alter the traditional forms of deference and recognition. If nothing else, whites clung to social usages which reminded them of happier and more orderly times. The language and demeanor of the blacks had always defined their place in society and their relationship with whites, and in the chaotic postwar years, many whites preferred to think that a semblance of sanity and good manners might have survived emancipation. Louis Manigault, the Georgia planter, thus confessed his pleasure at being called "Maussa" and at seeing his former slaves "still showing respect by taking off their caps." Some planters even went so far as to stipulate in the labor contracts they drew up with the freedmen that they be addressed as "master." Seeking to accommodate himself to emancipation, Thomas Dabney, the prosperous Mississippi planter, advised his ex-slaves they no longer had to call him "master," but he seemed reassured by the chorus of "Yes, marster" that greeted his admonition. "They seem to bring in 'master' and say it oftener than they ever did," he observed, and Dabney preferred to accept it in good faith as a sign of affection; indeed, as his daughter noted, the term "seemed to grow into a term of endearment," and former slaves Dabney had never known became tenants on the plantation and also called him "master." With equal pride, a Mississippi white woman displayed her "little Confederate nigger," as she called her, to a northern visitor. "She is the only one I have been able to keep, and I only have her because her parents haven't yet been able to coax her away." The young black girl still called her "Missey," and the mistress proclaimed this fact with unconcealed delight, as if it were a singular achievement in the post-emancipation South. Perhaps it was. "All the niggers have been trying to break her of that, but they can't. They tell her to call me Miss Lizzie, but she says 'she may be your Miss Lizzie, but she's my Missey.' " One day in church, her servant left the other blacks, declaring loudly for everyone to hear that she preferred to sit with her "Missey." That created quite a stir, the mistress conceded. "You should have seen everybody's head turning to see who it was, in these sorrowful times, that was still fortunate enough to be called Missey!"[67]

Dismayed by the post-emancipation behavior of her fellow servants, particularly their truckling manner and continued use of terms like "master" and "mistress," a Mississippi black woman admonished them in the very presence of the white family to change their ways. They had "no master or mistress on earth," she informed them, and "they were fools" to act as though they did. But the old habits proved difficult to break, even as the old fears of the power wielded by their former masters proved difficult to surmount. "My master would kill any-body who called *any-body* but a white person Missis," a Virginia freedwoman declared. How blacks addressed each other often prompted equal dismay among black clergymen and northern white emissaries. Seeking to check the frequent use of the term "nigger," Colonel Higginson, the well-intentioned commander of a black regiment, instructed his white officers to address the black soldiers by their full names. But he found that the blacks themselves used derogatory terms like "nigger" with little hesitation, and he was at a loss to know how to combat such behavior. "They have meekly accepted it," he sighed. To a postwar English visitor, the derogatory terms used by blacks reflected the value they placed on color. "White was the tint of nobility; black the symbol of degradation. If one coloured man wanted to insult another, he called him a nigger. To call him 'a charcoal nigger' was the blackest insult of all, making him the furthest remove from the nobility of whiteness." Based upon his experiences in postwar South Carolina, Sidney Andrews, a northern correspondent, offered a more positive view of black terminology. He discovered that the terms "cousin" and "brother" were commonly used and "seem to be expressive of equality." Although "the older and more trusted blacks" on the plantation seldom referred to a field hand as "cousin," the field hands themselves frequently addressed each other as "Bro' Bob, Bro' John, Co'n Sally, Co' Pete, &c." What Andrews described, however, was less a phenomenon of emancipation than the continuation of traditional practices.[68]

The term "nigger," as used by blacks, had varying inflections, implications, and definitions, ranging from a description of slavish personalities to an expression of endearment. To a South Carolina freedman, the term had class connotations and suggested dependency on the white man. "Dey be niggers still, and dey will be for great many year, and dey no lib togeder widout de white man to look arter 'em. You take ten colored folks an tree of 'em may stop being nigger, but de rest allers be nigger and dere chil'n be nigger." Whatever blacks meant by the term, they almost all detested its use by whites, but the very fact of emancipation appears to have increased its popularity in white circles. Early in 1865, Mary Chesnut claimed to have heard the word used for the first time "by people *comme il faut*. Now it is in everybody's mouth, but I have never become accustomed to it." No doubt the term became more popular as whites searched for ways to address those who had been slaves. Ethelred Philips, a Florida physician and farmer, stubbornly refused to call them "freedmen" or even "colored people," a term which they preferred to "negroes." "I never will call them 'colored people,'" Philips vowed. "It sounds too much like a Yankee, besides, they are but negroes and never can be anything else."[69]

Responding to a sympathetic Quaker missionary from Massachusetts who had rebuked her for referring to the freedmen as "niggers," an elderly black woman in Savannah defended her use of the term as appropriate to the condition of her people. No matter what they might be called, she suggested, and regardless of what emancipation might bring, deeply entrenched views would not be easily given up. "We *are* niggers," she insisted. "We always was niggers, and we always shall be; nigger here, and nigger there, nigger do this, and nigger do that. We've got no souls, we are animals. We are black and so is the evil one." The missionary interrupted her at this point to explain that nothing in the Bible indicated that the devil might be black. "Well, white folks say so," the freedwoman replied, "and we'se bound to believe 'em, cause we'se nothing but animals and niggers. Yes, we'se niggers! niggers! niggers!" Whether this Quaker missionary understood what the black woman was trying to tell her is not clear. Fortunately for the well-meaning emissary from New England, she could turn to some of the more attractive features of Savannah, like the "excellent music in a fine colored church," to take her mind off this unpleasant encounter with "an old cotton-picking 'auntie.'"[70]

# 6

WHILE PROBING the limits of their freedom, black people quickly discovered that the line between impudence and the traditional subservience expected of them was perilously narrow, that matters of racial etiquette could seldom be compromised, and that whites were more sensitive than usual to any behavior which suggested social equality or manifested an unbecoming assertiveness, familiarity, or lack of respect. To have lost the war and suffered the humiliation of Yankee occupation had been penance enough. "It is hard to have to lay our loved ones in the grave, to have them fall by thousands on the battle-field, to be stripped of everything," a Savannah white woman declared, "but the hardest of all is nigger equality, and I won't submit to it."[71]

That did not mean, as a farmer in North Carolina assured two northern visitors, whites in the South wished to return the blacks to slavery, only that they had no desire to mix with them socially. He expected any white man in the country could readily appreciate that principle without ascribing evil intent or inhumanity to those who merely wished to implement it in day-to-day life.

> I haven't any prejudices against 'em because they're free, but you see I can't consider that they're on an equality with a white man. I may like him, but I can't let him come to my table and sit down like either of you gentlemen. I feel better than he is. The niggers has a kind of a scent about him that's enough for me. You Northern men needn't think that we hate 'em; I rather like 'em myself, and I believe we treat 'em better than you would.

As if to underscore his decent instincts, the farmer reminded his guests that during slavery blacks had usually been tried by a jury of slaveholders. "That don't look much as if we were inclined to be too hard on 'em, does it?" If blacks or Yankees tried to force equal rights upon the South, the Speaker of the Virginia House of Delegates warned, they would only poison the good feelings that now prevailed between the races. "There is no unkind feeling towards the negro in a position where he is not asserting an equality; but the best friend a negro ever had in the world, the kindest friend he ever had, a young boy or girl raised by a negro mammy, and devotedly attached to her, would become ferociously indignant if the old mammy were to claim equality for a moment."[72]

To free the slaves did not make them equal. That was a maxim to which all classes of whites could subscribe, and any actions by freed blacks to the contrary broke the limits of toleration and invited not only condemnation but vigilant action. Recognizing the universality of that sentiment, many freedmen who were eager to test their freedom hesitated to provoke post-emancipation white sensitivities. Since the slightest deviation from "normal" behavior might be deemed impudent or presumptuous, they often found themselves forced to act with even greater caution than usual. But black tolerance, too, had its limits. Without necessarily flaunting their freedom, blacks demanded, at the very least, a respect that would be commensurate with their new status. In a hotel dining room in Knoxville, Tennessee, for example, a white guest requested service by calling out to the black waiter (who was about thirty years old), "Here, boy!" That familiar greeting had no doubt been uttered thousands of times in this setting, but the "boy's" response had few if any precedents. "My name is Dick," he announced. Whether irritated at being corrected or at the tone of the black man's voice, the hotel guest quickly turned into an irate defender of his race. "You'll answer to the name I call you," he roared, "or I'll blow a hole through you!" When the waiter ignored him and went about his business, the much-disgusted white man addressed the other dining-room patrons on the proper treatment of impudent freedmen:

"Last week, in Chattanooga, I said to a nigger I found at the railroad, 'Here, Buck! show me the baggage-room.' He said, 'My name a'n't Buck.' I just put my six-shooter to his head, and by ——! he didn't stop to think what his name was, but showed me what I wanted."

Upon hearing his story, the other hotel guests "warmly applauded" his sentiments, except for one unenlightened white man who failed to perceive the impudence in the freedman's response.[73]

Even if the ex-slave made no overt move to exercise his freedom, even if his demeanor remained virtually unchanged, that in itself might be greeted with suspicion, as though he were masking his real feelings behind the old "darky" façade. All too often, in fact, the freedman did not have to say anything in order to displease or raise suspicions in the whites; he only had to look a certain way or fail to exhibit the expected lowered head and shuffling feet. "They perceive insolence in a tone, a glance, a gesture, or failure to yield enough by two or three inches in meeting on the sidewalk," a visitor to Wilmington, North Carolina, observed. Some of his fellow whites, a Virginian remarked, "can't see a nigger go along the street now-a-days that they don't damn him for putting on airs." To defy the expectations of whites had always been a highly dangerous undertaking, even when no "offense" had been intended, but to do so in the wake of the recent military disaster and emancipation was to invite an even more volatile response.[74]

The behavior of white men and women underscored the tacit assumption most of them embraced with a kind of religious zeal—that neither the Civil War nor emancipation had in any way altered the time-honored etiquette of racial relations. "With us, the death of slavery is recognized," affirmed a South Carolina Unionist and former slaveholder, "but we don't believe that because the nigger is free he ought to be saucy; and we don't mean to have any such nonsense as letting him vote. He's helpless and ignorant, and dependent, and the old masters will still control him." If anything, in fact—and innumerable whites testified to this effect —the need to maintain the traditional code regulating the relations between the races was now more urgent than ever before, perhaps even a matter of self-preservation. After all, a North Carolina farmer warned, seemingly unaware of the implications of what he was saying, "If we let a nigger git equal with us, the next thing we know he'll be ahead of us. He's so impudent and presumin'."[75]

During slavery, custom and habit had largely defined the behavior expected of blacks, and the rules had been sufficiently understood to make special laws unnecessary. The slave addressed his owners in respectful terms; he never sat down or kept his hat on in the presence of whites; he never initiated a conversation with them unless first addressed; if he accompanied his master or mistress to town or to church, he walked several steps behind them; if he encountered any whites on the sidewalk, he made ample room for them to pass, stepping down into the street if necessary;

and he never suggested by any words, looks, or mannerisms anything less than the respect, humility, and cheerful obedience expected of him at all times. From his own experience, Frederick Douglass had described the circumscribed world of the slave:

> A mere look, word, or motion,—a mistake, accident, or want of power,— are all matters for which a slave may be whipped at any time. Does a slave look dissatisfied? It is said, he has the devil in him, and it must be whipped out. Does he speak loudly when spoken to by his master? Then he is getting high-minded, and should be taken down a button-hole lower. Does he forget to pull off his hat at the approach of a white person? Then he is wanting in reverence, and should be whipped for it. Does he ever venture to vindicate his conduct, when censured for it? Then he is guilty of impudence,—one of the greatest crimes of which a slave can be guilty. Does he ever venture to suggest a different mode of doing things from that pointed out by his master? He is indeed presumptuous, and getting above himself . . .[76]

And it was out of this world that the slave stepped into freedom and tried to define its dimensions.

Whether emancipation warranted deviations from the traditional code of racial etiquette prompted sharp differences among whites and blacks and invited immediate misunderstandings and confrontations. The way most whites chose to view these matters, any breaches of expected behavior or decorum in their former slaves, no matter how trivial they seemed, threatened to disrupt the entire fabric of a society based on racial subordination. What was permissible behavior for a white person, in other words, was not necessarily permissible behavior for a black man or woman. When freedmen declined to remove or touch their hats upon meeting a white person, or if they failed to stand while they spoke with whites, they were "growing too saucy for human endurance." When freedmen took to promenading about the streets or public places, refusing to give up the sidewalks to every white who approached, that was "impudence" of the rankest sort. ("It is the first time in my life that I have ever had to give up the sidewalk to a man, much less to negroes!" Eliza Andrews wrote. "I was so indignant that I did not carry a devotional spirit to church.") When black women attired themselves in fancy garments, carried parasols, and insisted upon being addressed as "ladies" (or "my lady" rather than "my ole woman"), that was "putting on airs"; and when black men dressed themselves conspicuously, that was sufficient provocation to cut the clothes from their backs. When white "gentlemen" engaged in hunting encountered freedmen "enjoying themselves in the same way" (with shotguns and a pack of dogs), that was called still another instance of "insubordination and insolence." When freedmen staged parades, dances, and barbecues, like those scheduled to commemorate the Emancipation Proclamation, whites invariably characterized them as "orgies" or "outrageous spectacles." When freedmen roamed about at night, disregarding the old curfew and refusing orders to return to their quarters, that was "a terrible state of insubordination" bordering on insurrection. And when freedmen attended meetings in which they openly talked about "perfect equality with the whites," acquiring land, and even voting, that was an incitement to race war. "Such incendiary and revolutionary language," a white Louisianan wrote of one such meeting in New Orleans, "was enough to freeze the blood. I fear they will have trouble there soon."[77]

What the white South characterized as "insolence," "sauciness," and "putting on airs" were more often than not simply the ways many ex-slaves chose to demonstrate their freedom. To refuse to touch their hats to whites, to ignore their former masters or mistresses in the streets, to remain seated while speaking with whites, or to neglect to yield the sidewalks to them were not so much discourtesies or intended provocations as positive assertions of their new status as free men and women. But each of these actions violated the white man's double standard. That is, although few whites would have thought of extending any of these social courtesies to black men or women, they insisted that the freedmen comply, as before, with the traditional and one-sided code of etiquette. The failure of blacks to do so, or still worse their open refusal, constituted further evidence of how emancipation had "ruined" them and filled their heads with mistaken notions about their place in society. "Their freedom's made 'em so sassy there's no livin' with 'em," an exasperated North Carolinian declared. Even the usually mild-mannered, gentlemanly Henry W. Ravenel, who had often expressed his pleasure at the "good" conduct of the ex-slaves, could scarcely believe what he saw during a visit to Charleston several months after the end of the war.

> It is impossible to describe the condition of the city—It is so unlike anything we could imagine—Negroes shoving white persons off the walk —Negro women drest in the most outré style, all with veils and parasols for which they have an especial fancy—riding on horseback with negro soldiers and in carriages. The negro regiments have just been paid off which gives them money to indulge their elegant tastes ...

As if this were not bad enough, his own personal servant became "excessively insolent" after being exposed to city life. "So much for the fidelity of indulged servants," Ravenel sighed. "I bought him at his own request and he had always fared as I had. I am utterly disgusted with the race, and trust that I may some day be in a land that is purged of them."[78]

Rather than confess their sense of betrayal, many whites preferred another explanation, one that had served them well during the war. The "insolent" freedmen were exhibiting the natural effects of contamination from Yankee soldiers (white and black) and northern missionaries and teachers. After being shoved off the sidewalk by blacks, Eliza Andrews recalled "a time when such conduct would have been rewarded with a thrashing—or rather, when such conduct was unheard of, for the negroes generally had good manners till the Yankees corrupted them." Although southern whites had frequently blamed "outside influences" for their troubles, the evidence now seemed more compelling than ever before, particularly with all the wild talk about granting privileges and rights to the newly freed slaves. As a New Orleans newspaper quickly noted, only "wicked demagogues" could induce otherwise innocent and well-behaved blacks to entertain ideas about "rights."

> Negroes care nothing for "rights." They know intuitively that their place is in the field; their proper instruments of self-preservation, the shovel and the hoe; their *Ultima Thule* of happiness, plenty to eat, a fiddle, and a breakdown.
> 
> Sambo feels in his heart that he has no right to sit at white man's table; no right to testify against his betters. Unseduced by wicked demagogues, he would never dream of these impossible things.
> 
> Let us trust that *our* Legislature will make short work of Ethiopia. Every real white man is sick of the negro, and the "rights" of the negro. Teach the negro that if he goes to work, keeps his place, and behaves himself, he will be protected by *our* white laws; if not, this Southern road will be "a hard one to travel," for the whites must and shall rule to the end of time, even if the fate of Ethiopia be annihilation.[79]

With some justification, white Southerners accused the North of hypocrisy in seeking to impose upon them a racial equality which most Northerners would have abhorred. Everyone knew, a South Carolina magistrate averred, that in northern schools, street railways, steamers, and hotels, racial distinctions were maintained "which we have been accustomed to observe at the South. . . . This is all we ask—no more, no less, than our northern brethren claim for themselves." Whatever use whites made of this charge, some came to question its veracity, particularly after watching certain Yankee officers, missionaries, and teachers overindulge the freedmen, mix with them socially, and encourage their "impudence." The Reverend Samuel A. Agnew of Mississippi found incredible the reports that Federal authorities had fined a "gentleman" for merely "slapping a negroe off the pavement" and that Yankees had "cruelly beaten" a white clergyman "because his wife whipped a little negroe." Apparently, Agnew concluded, "the negroe is a sacred animal. The Yankees are about negroes like the Egyptians were about cats. Negrophilism is the passion with them. When they come to their senses they will find that the negroe must be governed in the same way." But the chances of Yankees coming to their senses seemed rather dim to Ethelred Philips, the Florida farmer and physician, after observing in his wife's "Lady's book" that "the most fashionable head dress" in the North had become "the *African*," because the "very *short curls*" were meant to imitate the "beauty of the negro's kinks of wool!" The next "rage," he assumed, would be "to marry no other color."[80]

If the North seriously intended to recast the South in its own image, that could conjure up all kinds of "mongrel" images in the minds of whites already made uneasy by the actions of the freedmen. Even as some southern newspapers and orators chided the North for oppressing its own blacks, white visitors to that region wrote home alarming reports of the veritable Negro haven they had uncovered in Yankeedom.

> Here you can see the negroe all [on an] equal footing with white man. White man walking the streets with negro wenches. White man and negroe riding together. White man and negroe sit in the same seat in church or in a word the negroe enjoys the same privileges as the white man. They address each other as Mr and Miss. . . . I long for the day to come when I will leave this abominable place.[81]

With nearly 4,000,000 newly freed blacks in the South, as contrasted with less than 400,000 blacks in the North, this surely was for southern whites a most frightening vision of the future.

7

---

THE SPECTER of Africanization lurked behind every assertive move made by blacks in the aftermath of emancipation. When they chose to test their freedom by entering public places from which they had previously been barred or by sitting indiscriminately in public conveyances where their presence had previously been restricted, the worst fears of the white South were realized and the utmost vigilance demanded. Under slavery, the body servants or maids who accompanied their masters or mistresses into these places or conveyances had seldom aroused any comment or controversy. But once blacks ceased to be slaves, traveling in the company of their owners, their presence suddenly became an intrusion and a source of contamination, symbolizing an equality most whites found threatening. With emancipation, then, exclusion and segregation became even more firmly embedded in the lives of black people, barring some of them from privileges they might have exercised as slaves. That is, the context in which blacks traveled and used public facilities became all-important, with the intermixing of races permitted only in those situations where the superiority of whites was clearly understood. The Mississippi law of 1865 that barred blacks from railroad cars "set apart, or used by, and for white persons" thus exempted "Negroes or mulattoes, travelling with their mistresses, in the capacity of nurses," and a Savannah ordinance prohibiting blacks from entering the public park exempted those who accompanied a white child.[82]

With large numbers of freedmen on the move after emancipation, the controversy over their use of public conveyances and their behavior on the principal urban promenades came almost immediately to a head.

I have seen in a Southern street-car all blacks sitting and all whites standing; have seen a big black woman enter a car and flounce herself down almost into the lap of a white man; have seen white ladies pushed off sidewalks by black men. The new manners of the blacks were painful, revolting, absurd. The freedman's misbehaviour was to be condoned only by pity that accepted his inferiority as excuse. Southerners had taken great pains and pride in teaching their negroes good manners. . . . It was with keen regret that their old preceptors saw them throw all their fine schooling in etiquette to the winds.[83]

The indignity of it all was more than most whites could bear and they quickly moved to lay down a color line that would maintain the old racial distinctions and impress upon the newly freed slaves their place as a separate and inferior people. In most instances, the "color line" simply perpetuated distinctions that had been made during slavery. On the city streetcars, blacks were forced to ride on the open platforms or in separate and specially marked cars. (In New Orleans, for example, blacks rode only on cars marked with a black star.) On the railroads, blacks were excluded from first-class accommodations (the "ladies' car") and relegated to the smoking compartments or to freight boxcars in which seats or benches had been placed. On the steamboats plying the waterways and coasts, blacks were expected to sleep on the open deck and to eat with the servants, although they paid the same fares as white passengers.[84] Seldom written into law (only Florida, Mississippi, and Texas thought it necessary to enact "Jim Crow" laws in 1865 and 1866), the practices and customs governing racial contact in public places and accommodations acquired the force of statutes, backed as they were by a nearly unanimous white public opinion and local police power. If any black passengers protested these inferior accommodations, they faced the likelihood of expulsion, violence, or verbal harassment. "You're free, aint you?" a railroad conductor mocked one such passenger. "Good as white folks, aint ye! Then pay the same fare, and keep your mouth shut." With equal clarity, a Richmond newspaper advised black passengers not to trouble themselves "about first class seats until they are fully recognized as a first class people."[85]

The restrictions imposed on the freedmen never approximated the thoroughness with which southern legislatures and communities segregated the races in the late nineteenth and early twentieth centuries. The racial distinctions that characterized the immediate post-emancipation years were almost always understood rather than stated. But to the blacks themselves, the differences might have seemed minimal and the risks incurred in flaunting deeply rooted social customs were no less pronounced than those which would later inhibit a successful challenge to Jim Crow laws. What whites aspired to in both instances was a separation of the races, and the post-emancipation restrictions were by no means limited to public transportation. If admitted at all to public places, such as theaters and churches, blacks sat in separate and inferior sections, usually the rear seats or the balcony. Few if any public inns or restaurants accommodated them, except for those which catered exclusively to blacks. (The Union Hotel in Augusta, Georgia, for example, advertised itself as a first-class hotel "for the special accommodation of the Citizen and Travelling Public of Color.")[86] Not knowing what to expect, some hotels and public inns had considered reclassifying themselves as private houses in order to exclude black patrons. Knowing what to expect, most blacks avoided such places rather than be insulted and ejected. The ludicrous extent to which legislatures segregated the races later in the century was clearly anticipated in the instructions given black people in Natchez in 1866 that henceforth the promenades along the river and the bluff to the right of Main Street would be reserved "for the use of the whites, for ladies and children and nurses —the central Bluff between Main Street and State for bachelors and the colored population, and the lower promenade for the whites." Not far behind, Georgia decreed that black and white patients in the "Lunatic Asylum" be kept separate—a decision justified as "in the wisest sanitary policy"—and in Richmond, Virginia, blacks and whites applied for "destitute rations" at separate places.[87]

The determination of whites to maintain a color line in public places and conveyances conflicted with the desire of many ex-slaves to utilize facilities from which they had been barred and to achieve a public equality that seemed justified by their new status. To press their demands for equal access, blacks questioned the logic that underlay segregationist and exclusionist practices. Why, for example, did black men and women traveling by themselves in public conveyances pose a danger, whereas black maids, nurses, and servants accompanying a white mistress or white children did not? "If the idea is so dreadful," a black newspaper in Georgia asked, "why should poor little children be forced to draw sustenance from black breasts, be kissed by black lips, and hugged by black arms?" Apparently, another black editor suggested, colored people in the act of nursing white children were noncontagious. Some decades would elapse before the wet nurse herself became suspect. "We gave our infants to the black wenches to suckle," an elderly South Carolinian reflected in 1885, "and thus poisoned the blood of our children, and made them *cowards* . . . it will take 500 years, if not longer, by the infusion of new blood to eradicate the hereditary vices imbibed with the blood (milk is blood) of black wet nurses."[88]

By choosing to make an issue of racial separation in public places, black men and women in the aftermath of Union occupation provoked a prolonged and often heated controversy that sometimes spilled out into the streets of southern communities. By 1867, on the eve of Radical Reconstruction, blacks in such cities as Mobile, New Orleans, Savannah, Richmond, Charleston, Nashville, and Baltimore had already challenged the ordinances, company rules, and customs barring them from or segregating them in the horse-drawn streetcars. "For as long as distinctions will be kept on in public manners," the black newspaper in New Orleans announced, "these discriminations will react on the decisions of juries and courts, and make impartial justice a lie."[89]

If unable to obtain court injunctions against the operation of exclusive city railway lines, blacks boarded the streetcars, ignored the conductor's order to leave, waited to be forcibly removed, and then sued the company for assault and battery. Hoping to avoid such confrontations, the newly launched City Railway Company in Charleston initially proposed to establish separate and equal cars or to partition the same cars between blacks and whites. But blacks rejected these proposals as demeaning and in violation of their newly acquired civil rights and demanded nothing less than fully integrated facilities. In April 1867, the attempt of police to eject two blacks who had refused to leave a streetcar precipitated a riot in which crowds of blacks tried to force their way into the police station to release their brethren who had been arrested. The police finally restored order, the blacks decided to press their case in the courts, and the City Railway Company announced a month after the "riot" that it had decided to eliminate all racial distinctions on its cars.[90]

Despite the force of custom and white opinion, blacks managed to win a sufficient number of court decisions and favorable rulings from local Union Army commanders to compel the transportation companies to reconsider their racial policies. Seeking to retain a semblance of distinction between blacks and whites, the streetcar company in Richmond provided two classes of cars, one of which would be confined to white women and white men accompanying them while the other would be open to all persons. In a variation of that system, Richmond also established alternate cars for white and black passengers, with the cars for the latter distinguishable by a black ball perched on the roof.[91] That resembled the "black star" cars in New Orleans, which had come under steady attack from blacks since the early days of Union occupation. The *New Orleans Tribune*, the voice of the influential colored community, not only denounced the "black star" cars in its editorials but permitted its columns to be used to advocate direct action: "Let every colored citizen of New Orleans, on and after the fifteenth of August [1865], enter into any car of the C.R.R.C., and if ordered out—take a seat, and if afterwards ejected, sue the company." Nearly two years later, after considerable litigation and numerous confrontations, the superintendent of a local railway company informed the mayor that blacks had threatened to force their way onto the cars reserved for whites "and that should the driver resist or refuse their passage, they would compel him to leave the car and take forcible possession themselves." Fearing a riot, he requested the mayor to take all measures necessary to preserve the peace. Several days later, the chief of police issued an order forbidding any interference with blacks riding on the streetcars. After hailing this triumph of equal justice, the black newspaper turned its editorial fire on racial distinctions in the public schools.[92]

To the blacks, freedmen and freeborn alike, the challenges to segregated seating in public conveyances were inseparable from the issues over which they claimed the war had been fought. But to many whites, this flagrant disregard for racial etiquette gave rise to even more fearful apprehensions about the results of emancipation and the extent to which they would be able to exert power over the former slaves. Few whites needed to be reminded of what was ultimately at stake. Behind every discussion and skirmish involving racial separation lurked the specter of unrestrained black lust and sexuality, with that most feared of consequences—racial amalgamation or, as it was now popularly called, miscegenation. Now that enslavement no longer marked a distinction between blacks and whites, the implications of physical contact were sufficiently obvious to whites. Equal access to public vehicles, theaters, restaurants, hotels, schools, parks, and churches would eventually open the door to the home, the parlor, and the bedroom. The absence of distinctions in public life thus prepared the way for no distinctions at all. "If we have social equality," one native white warned, "we shall have intermarriage, and if we have intermarriage we shall degenerate; we shall become a race of mulattoes; we shall be another Mexico; we shall be ruled out from the family of white nations. Sir, it is a matter of life and death with the Southern people to keep their blood pure."[93]

Much of the furor over racial separation in public vehicles grew out of fears that white women and black men might otherwise find themselves seated next to each other. In the absence of restrictions, blacks would gain access to the "ladies' car" (hitherto reserved for nonsmoking men and for women) on the railroads and to the sleeping compartments on the steamboats. The issue in both cases was eminently clear. On a Mississippi River steam packet running between Memphis and Vicksburg, the white passengers applauded the action of the captain in refusing to grant a stateroom to a black couple. Expressing his relief at the decision, one of the passengers posed the central question to a skeptical northern visitor, "How would you feel to know that *your wife was sleeping in the next room to a nigger and his wife?*" After reflecting over that question, the visitor realized soon enough that his fellow passengers expected no response. "The argument was unanswerable: it was an awful thought!" As for the unwelcome couple, they were cast ashore to wait for still another boat but their chances seemed dim. "They won't find a boat that'll take 'em," the captain declared. "Anyhow, they can't force their damned nigger equality on to me!"[94]

In playing upon postwar fears of miscegenation, whites seemed almost oblivious to the hypocrisy of their sudden concern for the survival of the Anglo-Saxon race. Among others, Mary Chesnut knew better than to press this argument too far. "Like the patriarchs of old," she had confided to her diary in March 1861, "our men live all in one house with their wives and their concubines; and the mulattoes one sees in every family partly resemble the white children. Any lady is ready to tell you who is the father of all the mulatto children in everybody's household but her own. Those, she seems to think, drop from the clouds."[95] Actually, whites made no attempt to deny the presence of a substantial mulatto population; those transgressions, however, had violated black women, not the prevailing racial code, and they had taken place in a rigidly controlled setting, with white men exercising a power which the prevailing relationships in their society permitted them. But in this same context, with men setting the sexual code and regulating their own behavior, black male sexuality assumed even more menacing proportions, precisely because it was deemed to be uncontrollable.

With so much evidence to the contrary around them, blacks found it hard to take seriously the white man's sudden preoccupation with racial purity. But if whites were serious in their protestations, they were advised to direct that concern to the principal source of the problem—themselves. "The white man says he don't want to be placed on equality with the negro," Abraham H. Galloway, a mulatto, told a convention of freedmen in North Carolina in 1865. "Why, Sir, if you could only see him slipping around at night, trying to get into negro women's houses, you would be astonished." The other delegates indicated their agreement, one of them shouting out, "That's the truth, Galloway." The *New Orleans Tribune* thought it highly ironic that some of the most "devoted apostles of miscegenation" now proclaimed themselves as the principal defenders of the white race.

> When you speak of separation, it is your illegitimate children and their unfortunate mothers that you propose to banish from among you. The talk is idle and senseless. The attraction between both races has proved too strong for their ever being severed. . . . You are ashamed of it! Why? Because the great mass of the blacks—or more exactly of the browns— had no liberty, no education and no social status. But now they will enjoy, as any white man or woman, these advantages, and become your equals. Let us tell you the truth, gentlemen: you will never let them go.

Looking to the future, a Virginia freedman testified that he apprehended no greater danger of racial amalgamation now than during slavery. "It was nothing but the stringent laws of the south that kept many a white man from marrying a black woman." He thought the strongest inclination to interracial sexual relations still rested with whites, though he would not deny the possibility that some blacks might wish to indulge themselves in what whites had already made fashionable. "I will state to you as a white lady stated to a gentleman down in Hampton, that if she felt disposed to fall in love with or marry a black man, it was nobody's business but hers; and so I suppose that if the colored race get all their rights, and particularly their equal rights before the law, it would not hurt the nation or trouble the nation."[96]

Despite white apprehensions, few blacks rushed into sexual liaisons or marital relationships with white partners. If anything, the abolition of slavery tended to diminish such contacts by freeing black women from the whims and lusts of their masters; moreover, as a Freedmen's Bureau agent

in South Carolina reported, "young gentlemen did not want mulatto children sworn to them at a cost of three hundred dollars apiece." When it
came to domestic relationships at least, blacks welcoméd the implementation of racial separation. To the charge that they coveted the daughters and
sisters of white men, Henry M. Turner replied that black men wished only
to live with and love their own women without having to fear white intervention. "What do we want with their daughters and sisters? We have as
much beauty as they. Look at our ladies, do you want more beauty than
they? The difficulty heretofore has been, our ladies were not always at our
own disposal. All we ask of the white men is to let our ladies alone, and they
need not fear us."[97]

No matter how carefully or eloquently blacks tried to clarify the differences between "social equality" and "public equality," insisting that they
had already suffered "social equality with a vengeance," whites would
continue to raise the bugaboo of miscegenation and to press for legislation
to outlaw it. It was as though they could not trust themselves to heed their
own warnings. "By his loud out-cry against the *dreadful* thing," the black
newspaper in Augusta, Georgia, said of the white man, "he seems to be
afraid that some of his daughters may do what a good many of his sons and
himself has done time and again, and therefore he wants laws made to
prevent *them* doing so."[98] Actually, the white man's rhetorical concern for
racial purity served him well by helping to mask his own complicity in its
compromise. At the same time, the obsession with miscegenation and racial supremacy proved to be effective banners around which whites could
be mobilized to resist any encroachments on the traditional practices and
social usages governing race relations. During the next decade, whites
would be repeatedly rallied to those banners to combat the more threatening manifestations of black freedom, but in the immediate aftermath of the
war they singled out for special attention the black soldier, whose continued presence most graphically symbolized their defeat and humiliation and
whose behavior set the most dangerous example for their former slaves.

8

WHEN ASKED TO EXPLAIN the origins of the rapist, Myrta Lockett Avary
immediately thought of the black soldier. "The rapist is a product of the
reconstruction period. His chrysalis was a uniform; as a soldier he could
force his way into private homes, bullying and insulting white women; he
was often commissioned to tasks involving these things. He came into life
in the abnormal atmosphere of a time rife with discussions of social equality theories, contentions for coeducation and intermarriage." Asked to
comment on the rampant violence that prevailed in the postwar South,
Governor Benjamin Humphreys of Mississippi thought the presence of
black troops sufficient explanation. "Everyone is afraid of the negro sol-

diers—they crowd everybody off the sidewalks, and shoot and kill us, and protect the freedmen in their indolence and acts of crime." Despairing over the breakdown of the plantation labor system, Edmund Rhett of South Carolina placed the blame directly on the influence of the black troops. "If your desire is to restore quiet, and orderly labor to the land," he advised the Freedmen's Bureau commissioner in Charleston, "nothing in my judgment is more pernicious in its effect than the example, and presence of colored troops, amongst a class of colored agricultural laborers."[99]

If Avary, Humphreys, and Rhett were oblivious to the tradition of the white rapist and vigilante in the South and the deeper roots of violence, sexual exploitation, and labor troubles, they nevertheless voiced the prevailing outrage and despair over the continued presence of more than 80,000 black occupation troops. Nothing seemed more contrived to humiliate white manhood, insult white womanhood, and demoralize the ex-slave than the "vindictive and revengeful" act of Federal authorities in stationing black troops in their midst. Nothing could evoke more terror in a southern community than the rumor that black troops might be sent there. "Think of a lot of negroes being brought here to play master over us!" young Eliza Andrews exclaimed, and few whites needed to be reminded of the terrible implications of what she had said. Nor were they oblivious to the fact that many of the soldiers were northern blacks who had been raised outside the plantation tradition and discipline. "Few of them perhaps have had opportunities of spiritual instruction," Henry Ravenel observed, "or of forming attachments to their masters, or of being benefitted by that domestic relation which the presence of the master on the plantation always creates."[100]

Regardless of how they conducted themselves, black soldiers by their very presence violated tradition and provoked a vehement response in a people who had always viewed armed blacks as insurrectionists. After all, a New Orleans newspaper explained, white men and women in the South had customarily encountered blacks "only as respectful servants," and now they were understandably "mortified, pained, and shocked" to find some of those same blacks in the towns and villages and on the public roads "wearing Federal uniforms, and bearing bright muskets and gleaming bayonets. They often recognized among them those who had once been their own servants." Few Confederate Army veterans were able to maintain their composure when they returned to their homes to find armed, uniformed black men patrolling the streets, jostling their women from the sidewalks, and claiming authority over their families. "Boy, le' me see your gun," a recently paroled Confederate soldier declared with disdain as he moved to examine the rifle of a black soldier. Not knowing what the white man's intentions might be, the soldier stepped back and readied his gun for possible use. Hastily departing, the ex-Confederate murmured, "How the war *has* demoralized the cussed brutes!"[101]

The catalogue of "atrocities" and "daily outrages" for which black soldiers were held responsible seemed limitless, with nearly every white man and woman prepared to relate some still more horrible tale. While sometimes exaggerated or invented, the stories usually contained an element of truth; their authenticity, however, was less important than how whites chose to define an "outrage." The black soldier mixed indiscriminately with whites, occasionally at "miscegenation" dinners and dances; he did not always wait to be addressed before he deigned to speak to whites; he might reprimand and harass whites in the city streets, perhaps even arrest them for a trivial offense; and in several communities, he conspired to release black prisoners from the jails, charging that they could not obtain impartial justice, and he clashed openly with the authority of local police.[102] No white man who witnessed the incident was likely to forget that day in Wilmington, North Carolina, when a black sergeant arrested the chief of police for carrying a weapon illegally and then escorted him as a prisoner through a throng of cheering freedmen. Nor were black soldiers immune to meting out extralegal justice if they thought local courts and officials would fail to punish whites for offenses against black persons. In Victoria, Texas, they entered the jail, dragged out a white man accused of murdering a freedman, and lynched him. With equal dispatch, black soldiers in South Carolina disposed of an ex-Confederate soldier who had fatally stabbed a black sergeant after he had refused to leave a railway car in which several white women sat; the soldiers tried him by "drumhead courtmartial" and then shot and buried him.[103]

That black soldiers exercised a subversive influence on the recently freed slaves seemed obvious to most whites. During the war, slave owners had often blamed the massive desertions from the plantations on outside influences, preferring to think that black soldiers "intimidated" faithful slaves who had otherwise wished to remain in their service. And now, in this critical period of transition, the conduct of the black troops allegedly encouraged impressionable freedmen to defy white authority. By insulting whites in the presence of the ex-slaves, the soldiers created erroneous illusions of power and even superiority. By making black laborers dissatisfied with their working conditions and telling them they would soon obtain the lands of their masters, the soldiers encouraged false expectations and the withdrawal of steady labor. By boarding the trains and streetcars and sitting indiscriminately in public places, they encouraged the violation of time-honored southern customs. By their behavior, Henry Ravenel believed, these "diabolical savages" had turned "a quiet, contented, & happy people" into "dissatisfied, unruly, madmen intoxicated with the fumes of licentiousness, & ready for any acts of outrage." Eliza Andrews readily agreed, after observing events in the Georgia community where her family resided. What appalled her was not simply that black soldiers cursed and threatened whites on the public streets but that they did so "while hundreds of idle negroes stood around, laughing and applauding it." Nor did the Reverend John H. Cornish of Mississippi think it altogether coincidental that the day after black troops created a disturbance by violating seating arrangements in the local Baptist church, one of his own servants suddenly turned on him.[104]

Not all whites shared an excessive concern for the demoralizing impact of black troops. On the contrary, some even hoped that such troops, if properly disciplined, might restrain the ex-slaves by their example and instruct them in the ways of responsible behavior. Even without black troops, a South Carolina planter thought, the freedmen were bound to test their newly won rights, and his fellow whites deceived themselves to think otherwise.

> There is considerable difference of opinion here as to the good or evil influences of black troops upon the negroes. I see only this, that the presence of the troops brings out openly what I believe was hidden in them before. The spirit of liberty was in them and if not brought out in this way probably would have burst out in a general insurrection . . .

That was putting the best possible face on black occupation, but most whites, if judged by their often hysterical letters and appeals to be relieved of black troops, were unable to share the South Carolinian's insight and equanimity. The problem, as many whites viewed it, lay precisely in the ability of the black troops to command the loyalty of the freedmen for whatever purposes they deemed appropriate. In urging the removal of those troops, the planters on Edisto and Wadmalaw islands, off the coast of South Carolina, complained of how their presence and influence undermined "the little control we had over the labor." Endorsing their petition, a Freedmen's Bureau officer agreed that white troops would more effectually secure "good order" and prove less troublesome to the planter class.[105]

That some black soldiers, particularly the ex-slaves, derived considerable satisfaction from the power they exerted over the white population was doubtless true. Conscious of the explosive potential in such a situation, and not averse to placating native whites, Union Army commanders placed restrictions on the black troops, forbade them in some areas from fraternizing with the local blacks, and severely punished any offenses they committed against the white populace. The tensions between black and white soldiers frequently erupted into violent clashes, and native whites readily exploited those antagonisms to their own advantage. "Never have I witnessed such lack of confidence as is beginning to dawn here with us," a black soldier wrote from Louisiana in August 1865, "and if there ever was a time that we felt like exterminating our old oppressors from the face of the earth, it is at this present time. The overthrow of the rebellion is consigning us to perpetual misery and distraction." Despite their proven service to the Union, another soldier protested, they were "still compelled to feel that they are black, and the smooth oily tongue of the white planter is enough to condemn any number of them . . ."[106]

Not only did black soldiers complain about the insults to which white citizens daily subjected them but their own officers rendered them virtually defenseless in responding to such provocations. It simply made no sense. Traitors to the country, whom they had been asked to exterminate only a few months before, suddenly became their principal accusers and, even more disturbingly, commanded greater respect and credibility in the eyes of the white Yankees than the black men who had fought to save the Union. "A report from any white citizen against one of our men, whether it be credible or not, is sufficient to punish the accused," a black soldier charged, and the punishments inflicted upon them were as severe as anything they had experienced or witnessed during slavery. "Men have been bucked and gagged in their company streets, exposed to the scorching rays of the sun and the derision of the majority of the officers, who seem to take delight in witnessing their misery." By the eve of Radical Reconstruction, a white newspaper in Wilmington, North Carolina, was able to exult, "The true soldiers, whether they wore the gray or the blue, are now united in their opposition . . . to negro government and negro equality. Blood is thicker than water."[107]

The pride black soldiers once derived from military service quickly dissipated. Since the end of the war, William P. Green wrote, "our task has become more laborious, our treatment more severe," and he saw little reason to expect any improvement. Neither did Christian A. Fleetwood, a sergeant major and one of the recipients of the Congressional Medal of Honor for valiant conduct in battle. "No matter how well and faithfully they may perform their duties," he wrote of his fellow soldiers, "they will shortly be considered as 'lazy nigger sojers'—as drones in the great hive." Rather than "remain in a state of marked and acknowledged subserviency," he decided that he might better serve his race outside the Army. Like Fleetwood, many blacks asked to be discharged rather than serve as second-class soldiers under the command of white men who no longer made any attempt to mask their racial antipathies.[108]

If disillusionment drove many blacks out of the Army, the mounting aggression and hostility of white citizens made life intolerable for those who remained. Even before the war had ended, the white South placed no higher premium on any demand than the removal of the black troops from their midst. "Why are these savages still kept here to outrage & insult our people?" Henry Ravenel asked. The matter assumed greater urgency with every new report of an "outrage" and every new rumor of an impending black insurrection. "They were taught during the war that it was their duty to kill the whites & they cant learn now that the war is over," Ravenel confided to his journal. "Their shooting propensities still continue strong, showing a tendency toward reversion to the savage state." Finding that reports of "outrages" secured results, whites besieged Federal authorities with their protests and petitions, often with the backing of local Union Army commanders and Freedmen's Bureau agents. And with President Johnson adopting an avowedly conciliatory policy, the demobilization of black troops proceeded rapidly. By 1866, most of them had been mustered out of service or transferred to posts outside the South. The nightmare had ended, Governor Humphreys of Mississippi seemed to suggest in his report to the legislature; the removal of black troops had freed the white race from "insults, irritations and spoliation," while the ex-slaves were now free to pursue "habits of honest industry" and to enjoy the "friendship and confidence" of their former masters.[109]

Now that they were being discharged, the black soldiers lined up to receive the appropriate papers and their final pay. Around many of the camps, guards had been posted with orders to exclude peddlers, who were said to be lying in wait. "Beware of these unprincipled knaves!" a black newspaper warned of the "modern Shylocks" who sought to swindle the soldiers out of their discharge pay. But the black veteran had far more to fear than peddlers as he left his camp and entered civilian life. If he remained in the South, he entered a society in which the dominant population only grudgingly recognized his freedom, refused to admit him as an equal, and remembered all too vividly his service in the Union Army. To many whites, at least, he was a traitor and more than likely a potential troublemaker. As a soldier, he had been feared; as a civilian, he seemed no less dangerous. A prominent South Carolinian had predicted a race war if the troops were not removed; now that they had been mustered out, another South Carolinian feared the discharged black soldier would contribute his services to the agitation for land.[110]

Although the black soldier had fought to preserve the Union, he found himself with less voice in the government, in the courts of law, and in the work place than those he had only recently vanquished. "The great question with us is: Shall traitors to our country hold the balance of power again?" a black minister in North Carolina asked. "I give you the unequivocating answer, No! They shall die so dead, so dead, so dead." Not nearly as confident, a black veteran in Beaufort, South Carolina, addressed an appeal to President Johnson, reiterating his devotion to the Union and requesting some clarification of black freedom. "We Want to Know Some thing A Bought our Rites." But as the President's policy for the South unfolded, J. H. Payne, a black sergeant stationed in North Carolina, found himself placing what faith he had left in God rather than in Andrew Johnson.

> I remember reading an old history one time, where there was a certain king who had signed an unalterable decree for the destruction of a certain race of people; and yet, through the instrumentality and prayers of a certain woman, the great curse was removed. So let there be days of fasting and prayer proclaimed . . . among the colored race, and let them call upon the name of Elijah's God, until the fulness of their rights is maintained. . . . O! that God would awaken in us a spirit of independence to ask of the white man no favors but ask all from God . . .

Whether blacks appealed to Johnson or to God, the results were less than reassuring. Not only did the veteran find himself restricted in his access to public facilities, the ballot, and the jury box but his military service made him an obvious target for the frustrations of whites. "When they commenced mustering out the colored troops," one veteran recalled, "they told us to go back as close to the old masters as we could get. I didn't like that much. Then the next hard times that come up was the mobbing and lynching of Negroes."[111]

To former slaves who had served in the Union Army, the question of what they should do with themselves after leaving military service defied any easy resolution. "I didn't want to be under the white folks again," a former Tennessee slave and soldier remembered as his most vivid thought at that time. Three soldiers on active duty in South Carolina typified the dilemma of others as they prepared in 1866 to return to civilian life. None of them relished the idea of returning to the old plantations where they had worked as slaves, particularly if any of them had fled to join the Army. Having seen too many hired men "turned off without being paid," Melton R. Lenton wanted to avoid contract labor. "They try to pull us down faster than we can climb up." He thought his military service entitled him to a plot of land, as did his previous labor for white men. "They have no reason to say that we will not work, for we raised them, and sent them to school, and bought their land, and now it is as little as they can do to give us some of their land—be it little or much." H. D. Dudley, who had risen to the rank of sergeant, recalled that, in the battles he had fought, racial distinctions had no place. "That was so in battle, but it is not so now. If any man believes that there is no distinction in regard to color now, let him approach the cars, or enter a hotel or a steamboat, and he will be set right upon that matter." Like Sergeant Dudley, W. W. Sanders wondered if he had reaped any rewards for his years of service. He doubted it. "It seems that all our fighting has done us but little good. Our politicians and leading men seem to be doing but little for us. Our trust is in God and our own good conduct. Let us convince the world that we are worthy to enjoy the rights we ask for." Whether he would be in any position to prove anything remained a troublesome question.[112]

If many whites thought the former soldier a potentially dangerous citizen, they were in less agreement about his desirability as a laborer. Despite the proscriptions visited upon allegedly exploitative peddlers at the army camps, no such restrictions were placed on planters and speculators, many of whom inundated the military installations around discharge time with contracts in hand, eager for the services of the blacks. "The negro was king," a northern traveler wrote after witnessing the ways in which Mississippi and Louisiana planters had descended upon a black regiment being mustered out near Natchez.

> Men fawned upon him; took him to the sutler's shop and treated him; carried pockets full of tobacco to bestow upon him; carefully explained to him the varied delights of their respective plantations. Women came too—with coach and coachmen—drove into the camp, went out among the negroes, and with sweet smiles and honeyed words sought to per-

suade them that such and such plantations would be the very home they
were looking for.

Ironically, some planters thought them more desirable laborers because
they had been soldiers and might be able to exert restraint and discipline
on the other workers. For that reason, the higher the rank, the better offer
a black veteran might expect. "I told a nigger officer that I'd give him thirty
dollars a month just to stay on my plantation and wear his uniform,"
remarked a substantial planter from Jackson, Mississippi. "The fellow did
it, and I'm havin' no trouble with my niggers. They're afraid of the shoul-
der-straps."[113]

If black soldiers had known what awaited them in civilian life, they
might have kept more than their uniforms upon being mustered out of the
Army. The rewards of plantation labor would prove disappointing; whites
retained economic power and returned political and police power to those
who had wielded it before the war; and as black dissatisfaction mounted,
so did the white man's recourse to physical violence, legal repression, and
vigilante justice. For many freedmen, self-preservation took precedence
over self-employment. "As one of the disfranchised race," a Louisiana black
advised, "I would say to every colored soldier, 'Bring your gun home.' "[114]

## 9

---

SEVERAL MONTHS after the end of the war, two white men overtook an
elderly black woman who had insisted on leaving her former master's
plantation near Washington, Georgia. While one of the men shot her, the
other broke her ribs and beat her on the head with a stone until she died;
they left her body unburied in a secluded spot. Ten days later, the body was
discovered and military authorities arrested the two assailants. Whether
the brutal murder or the subsequent arrests excited more public indignation and concern is not entirely clear. "She certainly was an old fool," Eliza
Andrews said of the victim, "but I have never yet heard that folly was a
capital offense." Judge Garnett Andrews, Eliza's father and a former state
legislator who had opposed secession, agreed to defend the two men
charged with the crime, not because he approved of their deed but because
he felt they deserved a fair trial. He said very little about the case, his
daughter observed, "because conversation on such subjects nearly always
brings on a political row in the family."

Although Eliza Andrews thought the murder had been "a very ugly
affair," her sympathies almost instinctively went out to the accused. After
all, "there is only negro evidence for all these horrors, and nobody can tell
how much of it is false." As for the two defendants, one of them was a family
man whose "poor wife is ... almost starving herself to death from grief"
and whose children were reportedly frightened into convulsions when the

soldiers arrested their father, while the other was a twenty-year-old youth whose "poor old father hangs around the courtroom, putting his head in every time the door is opened, trying to catch something of what is going on." Judge Andrews thought it unfortunate that the trial should take place at this time, for the Yankees would no doubt "believe everything the negroes say and put the very worst construction on it." His daughter agreed. "Brutal crimes happen in all countries now and then," she confided to her journal, "especially in times of disorder and upheaval such as the South is undergoing, but the North, fed on Mrs. Stowe's lurid pictures, likes to believe that such things are habitual among us, and this horrible occurrence will confirm them in their opinion."

Eliza Andrews made no mention of the verdict handed down in the murder case, except to note that her father believed one of the defendants would surely hang and entertained little hope of saving the other. But she did record still another "unfortunate affair" that occurred at the same time in adjoining Lincoln County. Having learned that freedmen were holding a secret meeting, "which was suspected of boding no good to the whites," a group of local youths resolved to break up the gathering; one of them, in his attempt to frighten the blacks, "accidentally" shot and killed a woman. "He didn't mean to hurt anybody," Miss Andrews had heard, "but the Yankees vow they will hang the whole batch if they can find them. Fortunately he has made his escape, and they don't know the names of the others."

> Corrie Calhoun says that where she lives, about thirty miles from here, over in Carolina, the men have a recipe for putting troublesome negroes out of the way that the Yankees can't get the key to. No two go out together, no one lets another know what he is going to do, and so, when mischievous negroes are found dead in the woods, nobody knows who killed them.[115]

Many freedmen quickly discovered in the aftermath of emancipation how much more vulnerable and expendable their lives had suddenly become. "Nigger life's cheap now," a white Tennessean observed. "Nobody likes 'em enough to have any affair of the sort [murder] investigated; and when a white man feels aggrieved at anything a nigger's done, he just shoots him and puts an end to it."[116] Whether previously expressed in martial displays, bellicose oratory, battlefield valor, family feuds, personal vengeance, or in the whipping of slaves, violence lay close to the surface of southern life and culture. Neither whites nor blacks had been exempt from its influence, whether as perpetrators or victims, and the prevalence of frontier conditions, the remoteness of many regions from local government and military occupation, the memories of the Lost Cause, and the felt need to control and discipline freed blacks militated against any decline of violence in the postwar years.

The question of how a highly volatile white population might respond to emancipation had been an immediate concern of nearly every freedman and freedwoman. During slavery, they had been exposed to violence on the plantations and farms where they worked and from the dreaded patrollers if they ventured off those plantations. But the financial investment each of them represented had operated to some degree as a protective shield. Before the war, a Tennessee farmer explained, the slave "was so much property. It was as if you should kill or maim my horse. But now the nigger has no protection." With black men and women no longer commanding a market price, the value placed on black life declined precipitately, and the slaves freed by the war found themselves living among a people who had suffered the worst possible ignominy—military defeat and "alien" occupation. Many whites, moreover, thought the abolition of slavery had doomed the African race in the South to extinction, and all too many of them seemed eager to expedite that prophecy. "If I could get up tomorrow morning and hear that every nigger in the country was dead, I'd just jump up and down," the wife of a South Carolina planter exclaimed after hearing that Yankee soldiers had recently shot several blacks who were "getting very impudent."[117]

The apparent indifference with which some whites regarded the fate of the ex-slave dismayed many visitors to the postwar South. "He is actually to many of them nothing but a troublesome animal," Sidney Andrews wrote from South Carolina; "not a human being, with hopes and longings and feelings . . . 'I would shoot one just as soon as I would a dog,' said a man to me yesterday on the cars. And I saw one shot at in Columbia as if he had been only a dog,—shot at from the door of a store, and at midday!" Nor did visitors find this behavior confined, as they had expected, to the lower classes of whites; in many instances, it reached into the highest circles of southern society. In Alabama, for example, a planter found himself embroiled in a controversy with one of his former slaves over ownership of a horse left behind by the Yankees; the evidence clearly favored the freedman's claim, the local Freedmen's Bureau agent agreed and awarded him the horse, but the former master thought otherwise and for him the issue obviously went beyond rightful ownership of the animal. "A nigger has no use for a horse like that," he explained. "I just put my Spencer to Sip's head, and told him if he pestered me any more about that horse, I'd kill him. He knew I was a man of my word, and he never pestered me any more." The planter enjoyed a reputation in the community as a just, upright, and honorable man, and that fact disturbed the visitor more than anything else. "No doubt if I had had dealings with him I should have found him so. He meant to give the freedmen their rights, but he was only beginning dimly to perceive that they had any rights; and when it came to treating a black man with absolute justice, he did not know the meaning of the word." If a "just and upright" man could have so little regard for the rights of the freedmen, their fate in the hands of less paternalistic whites suggested a difficult and violent period ahead.[118]

How many black men and women were beaten, flogged, mutilated, and murdered in the first years of emancipation will never be known. Nor could any accurate body count or statistical breakdown reveal the barbaric savagery and depravity that so frequently characterized the assaults made on freedmen in the name of restraining their savagery and depravity—the severed ears and entrails, the mutilated sex organs, the burnings at the stake, the forced drownings, the open display of skulls and severed limbs as trophies. "The negro was murdered, beheaded, skinned, and his skin nailed to the barn," a Freedmen's Bureau officer wrote of a case in Mississippi, as he supplied the names of the murderers and asked for an investigation. Reporting on "outrages" committed in Kentucky, a Bureau officer confined himself to several counties and only to those cases in which he had sworn testimony, the names of the injured, the names of the alleged offenders, and the dates and localities.

> I have classified these outrages as follows: Twenty-three cases of severe and inhuman beating and whipping of men; four of beating and shooting; two of robbing and shooting; three of robbing; five men shot and killed; two shot and wounded; four beaten to death; one beaten and roasted; three women assaulted and ravished; four women beaten; two women tied up and whipped until insensible; two men and their families beaten and driven from their homes, and their property destroyed; two instances of burning of dwellings, and one of the inmates shot.

Because of the difficulty in obtaining evidence and testimony, the officer stressed that his report included only a portion of the crimes against freedmen. "White men, however friendly to the freedmen, dislike to make depositions in these cases, for fear of personal violence. The same reason influences the black—he is fearful, timid, and trembling. He knows that since he has been a freedman he has not, up to this time, had the protection of either the federal or State authorities; that there is no way to enforce his rights or redress his wrongs."[119]

Neither a freedman's industriousness nor his deference necessarily protected him from whites if they suspected he harbored dangerous tendencies or if they looked upon him as a "smart-assed nigger" who needed chastisement. "The fact is," a Freedmen's Bureau officer in North Carolina reported, "it's the first notion with a great many of these people, if a Negro says anything or does anything that they don't like, to take a gun and put a bullet into him, or a charge of shot." In those instances where the reasons for an assault on blacks could be determined, the provocations ranged from disagreements over wages, working conditions, and the quality of work performed to the presence of black troops, black political and religious meetings, resistance to punishment, and suspicion of theft, murder, and rape. What proved even more alarming were the numerous instances of violence in which no reason could be easily ascertained, except perhaps the frustration of military defeat and emotional and recreational deprivation. The ferocity of the attacks on freedmen and the ecstasy with which the mobs meted out their punishment reached a point where it dismayed as many native whites as northern visitors and Freedmen's Bureau officers. "The American Indian," wrote a white public official in Georgia, "is not more delighted at the writhings and shrieks of his victim at the stake, than many Georgians are at the agonizing cries of the African negro at the whipping post."[120]

The violence inflicted upon freedmen seldom bore any relationship to the gravity of the alleged provocation. Of the countless cases of postwar violence, in fact, the largest proportion related in some way to that broad and vaguely defined charge of conduct unbecoming black people—that is, "putting on airs," "sassiness," "impudence," "insolence," "disrespect," "insubordination," contradicting whites, and violating racial customs. Behavior which many blacks and outside observers deemed relatively inoffensive might be regarded by certain native whites as deserving of a violent censure. "The truth is," a Tennessee farmer explained, "a white man can't take impudence from 'em. It may be a long ways removed from what you or I would think impudence, but these passionate men call it that, and pitch in." Near Corinth, Tennessee, for example, "an old nigger" working in a sawmill "got his head split open with an axe" for having "sassed" a white man. Near Fredericksburg, Virginia, a white man shot and wounded a former black soldier after overhearing him "boast" of his service in the Union Army. In South Carolina, a former slave was shot for requesting that a Federal officer examine the contract he had negotiated with his employer, and still other blacks were beaten for no greater offense than refusing to sign a contract. "You must expect such things to happen when the niggers are impudent," a South Carolinian said of reports of violence in his state, but a white farmer who overheard the remark thought otherwise. "The niggers a'n't to blame," he explained. "They're never impudent, unless they're trifled with or imposed on. Only two days ago a nigger was walking along this road, as peaceably as any man you ever saw. He met a white man right here, who asked him who he belonged to. 'I don't belong to anybody now,' he says; 'I'm a free man.' 'Sass me? you black devil!' says the white fellow; and he pitched into him, and cut him in four or five places with his knife. I heard and saw the whole of it, and I say the nigger was respectful, and that the white fellow was the only one to blame."[121]

Much of the violence inflicted on the freedmen had been well organized, with bands of white men meting out extralegal "justice" and anticipating the Klan-type groups that would operate so effectively during Radical Reconstruction. The names by which these paramilitary self-styled vigilantes were known varied from place to place—"reformers," "regulators," "moderators," "rangers"—but the tactics of random terrorism and assassination they employed barely differed and they tended to attract men of all social classes. The "justice" they enforced resembled that of the hastily formed mobs who lynched blacks suspected of more serious offenses like rape, murder, and arson. With increasing regularity, however, white terrorists focused their violence on blacks in leadership positions who sym-

bolized to them the excesses of the present and the dangers of the future
—teachers, clergymen, soldiers, and political activists. In Opelika, Alabama, four local whites repeatedly beat and stabbed Robert Alexander, a
twenty-six-year-old black minister, leaving him close to death. No black
schools would be allowed in the community, they warned him, nor would
they tolerate the presence of a black preacher who stirred up the people.
When Henry M. Turner, an organizer for the African Methodist Episcopal
Church in Georgia, met him several days later, the Reverend Alexander
resembled "a *lump of curdled blood*," and the local Freedmen's Bureau
agent had refused to intervene in the case. "The picture is too sad for me
to draw," Turner wrote. "O God! where is our civilization? Is this Christen-
dom, or is it hell? Pray for us." If black teachers and clergymen were not
themselves mobbed or threatened, their schoolhouses and churches were
often burned to the ground, and black pupils were apt to be assaulted or
intimidated even when attending separate schools. Some years after the
New Orleans race riot of 1866, Douglass Wilson, a former black soldier,
could still vividly recall the anxiety with which parents had sent their
children to school, not knowing what they might encounter.

> We had no idea that we should see them return home alive in the eve-
> ning. Big white boys and half-grown men used to pelt them with stones
> and run them down with open knives, both to and from school. Some-
> times they came home bruised, stabbed, beaten half to death, and some-
> times quite dead. My own son himself was often thus beaten. He has on
> his forehead to-day a scar over his right eye which sadly tells the story
> of his trying experience in those days in his efforts to get an education.
> I was wounded in the war, trying to get my freedom, and he over the eye,
> trying to get an education. [122]

Charging that northern propagandists distorted or even fabricated
stories of "outrages" in the South, some whites chose not to believe any of
them, while others ascribed them to lower-class whites or defended them
as a proper response to black impudence and lawlessness. "Don't you believe your 'eye-witnesses and ear-witnesses' of our cruelty," a prominent
North Carolina woman advised her friend in Connecticut. "Exceptional
cases there are no doubt, as in everything, but *believe me*, nine hundred
and ninety in every thousand of our people are kindly disposed to them, and
if they behave themselves will befriend them." It was grossly unfair to the
South, an irate planter observed, for newspaper reporters to view "solitary
instances" of brutality as typical of "the condition of the niggers and the
disposition of the whites." After all, he added, if "some impudent darkey,
who deserves it, gets a knock on the head," that did not mean "that every
nigger in the South is in danger of being killed." With absolute confidence,
a magistrate in South Carolina insisted that blacks faced no danger to their
lives unless they themselves provoked it. [123]

Even allowing for some exaggeration in the news accounts of white "atrocities," the number of assaults and murders never reported, whether because of fear of retaliation or the disappearance of the victims, approximated or exceeded those later found to be unfounded or distorted. Without intending to do so, a Georgia farmer suggested the difficulty in accurately measuring the full extent of white violence.

> A heap of 'em [freedmen] out in my country get into the swamps and get lost. I don't know as it's true, but I've heard that there's men out there that haven't got anything else to do, and if you mention any nigger to 'em, and give 'em twelve dollars, the nigger's sure to be lost in a very few days.
>     I know four right here in Barnwell that have been drowned some way within the last two months. Niggers never were so careless before. They go into the swamps and nobody can find out anything about 'em till by-and-bye they're seen floating down the river. Going to the coast, I reckon; that's where they're fond of going.

After reporting the brutal rape of a black woman, in which the attackers had vowed vengeance on the families of men who had served in the "God damned Yankee army," the black newspaper in Savannah declared that all too often such reports were suppressed, lest they incriminate the entire white population and "make capital" for the Radicals. "This is a miserable plea," the editor wrote, "for shielding criminals and thwarting the demands of justice." Nor could whites explain away the violence by placing the onus on the so-called dregs of the white population. To do so would have slighted some of the best families and demeaned their contribution to the maintenance of racial solidarity. Although "gentlemen" and "ladies" tended to deplore the excesses, many of them assumed an indifference that came close to approval or sympathy. No matter how hard some whites claimed to have tried, it remained difficult for them to view the murder of a black person as comparable to the murder of a white. The wave of postwar violence in Wilkes County, Georgia, for example, prompted considerable outrage among "the more respectable class" of whites and resulted in a protest meeting. "This class is ashamed of such outrages," a Freedmen's Bureau officer observed, "but it does not prevent them, and it does not take them to heart; and I could name a dozen cases of murder committed on the colored people by young men of these first families."[124]

When violence reached the dimensions of race war, few could remain indifferent. Emancipation introduced into the South a phenomenon already well known to Northerners—the race riot. Appropriately, the first such outbreaks—in Charleston and Norfolk in 1865—pitted white Union soldiers against black soldiers and freedmen. By 1867, however, native whites had fought freedmen in the streets of several southern cities and towns, among them Charleston, Norfolk, Richmond, Atlanta, Memphis, and New Orleans. Whatever the precipitating incident, nearly every riot reflected that growing conflict between how ex-slaves and whites chose to define emancipation and the determination of whites to retain the essentials of the old discipline and etiquette.[125]

The most far-reaching disturbances broke out in Memphis in early May 1866 and in New Orleans several months later. In Memphis, trouble began when freedmen and recently discharged black soldiers clashed with local police over the arrest of a black man; the forcible release of the prisoner triggered pent-up emotions and frustrations, aggravated by large numbers of black refugees, economic distress, and the enforcement of vagrancy laws. The riot took the lives of forty-six blacks (including two children and three women) and two white men (a policeman and a fireman), with many of the casualties incurred when white mobs invaded the black section of the city and burned homes, churches, and schoolhouses while terrorizing the residents. The Union Army commander, who had demobilized many of the black soldiers stationed near Memphis, initially refused to intervene to halt the violence, explaining to the local Freedmen's Bureau agent that "he had a large amount of public property to guard; that a considerable part of the troops he had were not reliable; that they hated Negroes too." While applauding his actions ("He knows the wants of the country, and sees the negro can do the country more good in the cotton fields than in the camp"), the local newspaper also expressed satisfaction with the overwhelming lesson taught by the riot. "The late riots in our city have satisfied all of one thing: that the southern men will not be ruled by the negro. . . . The negroes now know, to their sorrow, that it is best not to arouse the fury of the white man."[126]

The pattern of race rioting seldom varied in these years. When relations between the freedmen and the whites reached a breaking point, the slightest incident might be seized as a pretext for an organized assault upon the entire black community. In New Orleans, tension had mounted over warring political factions, the convening of a constitutional convention in 1866, and the aggressive demands of the colored community. When black laborers paraded to press their demands for equal suffrage on the convention, that was sufficient provocation. Confronted by a mob of hostile whites, the paraders dispersed, street fighting broke out, and numerous delegates and black spectators trying to flee the convention hall were shot and killed. By the end of the affray, 48 men had been killed and 166 wounded, and Federal authorities had distinguished themselves largely by their indecision and belated intervention. What began as a "riot," a congressional inquiry later concluded, ended as a "massacre."[127]

If the postwar riots and violence were intended to teach the freedman "not to arouse the fury of the white man," they taught him that and considerably more. Law enforcement agencies and officers, if not co-conspirators in violating the civil rights of ex-slaves, might be expected to protect or ignore the violators. Neither the Union Army nor the Freedmen's Bureau could be trusted to afford them adequate protection; instead, Union troops in some localities alternated with native whites as the principal aggressors. To seek a redress of grievances in the courts of law, as many freedmen also quickly discovered, resulted invariably in futility if not personal danger.

10

––––––––

NOTHING SEEMED BETTER DESIGNED to drive blacks into total exasperation and ultimately into lawlessness than the law itself. In the experience of many freedmen at least, the differences between the law and lawlessness often became so blurred as to be indistinct. Not surprisingly, the legal system and its enforcement agents reflected, as they always had, the domination and the will of the white man. Few voiced that conviction more eloquently than an illiterate rural delegate to a freedmen's convention in Raleigh, North Carolina. Although confessing his "ignorance" and lack of skill in oratory, he insisted upon sharing his observations with the other delegates.

> Yes, yes, we are ignorant. We know it. I am ignorant for one, and they say all niggers is. They say we don't know what the word constitution means. But if we don't know enough to know what the Constitution is, we know enough to know what justice is. I can see for myself down at my own court-house. If they makes a white man pay five dollars for doing something today, and makes a nigger pay ten dollars for doing that thing tomorrow, don't I know that ain't justice? They've got a figure of a woman with a sword hung up thar, sir; Mr. President, I don't know what you call it—["Justice," "Justice," several delegates shouted]—well, she's got a handkercher over her eyes, and the sword is in one hand and a pair o' scales in the other. When a white man and a nigger gets into the scales, don't I know the nigger is always mighty light? Don't we all see it? Ain't it so at your court-house, Mr. President?[128]

Upon examining the quality of postwar justice, some blacks compared it unfavorably to what they had known as slaves. The comparison revealed far more about the bleakness of the present than the brightness of the past. Although the slave codes had imposed penalties on slave owners who failed to treat their slaves humanely or who killed them maliciously, the protection such provisions afforded black men and women had been minimal, largely because they could neither file a formal complaint nor testify against a white person; moreover, the need to maintain racial unity and control made white witnesses reluctant to testify and white juries even more reluctant to convict.[129]

While blacks had been slaves, the self-interest, if not the paternal instincts, of the master had often prompted his intervention to protect his property. "Our former masters," a group of Richmond blacks declared after the war, "did once protect us from the tyrant that now rules in the Mayor's Court, and those who sit in the Hustings Court and those in the jury box.

because we were their property." This same point was made repeatedly by former slaveholders, as if to warn their now emancipated slaves of the fragile nature of their freedom and to impress upon them their state of dependency. Before emancipation, an Alabama judge observed in 1865, "the wrong done by a third party to a negro, was a wrong done to the owner or master, and the negro was merged in the Master, the black man in the white man—and the controversy was really between the two, although a third person was involved. The white man, recognized as master, felt a pride in the very dependence of the slave—the slave must appear thro' the master in court, in all contracts. He could not speak, act, or be spoken to or acted with, except by the consent, express or implied, of the owner." A Georgia newspaper editor made the point even more precisely: "when detected in his frequent delinquencies, Sambo will now have no 'maussa' to step in between him and danger."[130]

But in some crucial respects emancipation made little difference. Whether dealing with slaves or freedmen, southern courts and jurists seldom wavered from the urgent need to solidify white supremacy, ensure proper discipline in blacks, and punish severely those who violated the racial code. In his charge to a postwar jury, a South Carolina judge managed to combine these imperatives with the old paternalism.

> We belong to the master race of mankind—that race which, ruling all the waters of the world, its seas and oceans, without dispute, dominates equally upon the land, and plants its yoke at will upon the neck of all the other tribes and kindreds and races of men. We make, we administer the law. We judge; we have all the responsibility of superior power—of power. How appealingly, then, does every sentiment of magnanimity persuade us to exercise that power justly, forbearingly, mercifully, kindly and charitably, whether on the Bench or in the Jury box, or in the common affairs of life.

Whatever the magnanimous spirit in which the judge made his charge, the judicial system rarely reflected it. Even the most conscientious jurists, who were able to reconcile their belief in white supremacy with a commitment to equal justice and protection for blacks, often had to confess their helplessness. Julius J. Fleming, for example, a magistrate and lawyer in Sumter, South Carolina, conceded that despite his best efforts, wrongs were inflicted upon freedmen "with absolute impunity," few of them had the funds to meet litigation costs, and many of them were swindled out of legal claims to wages because they could not post the necessary bond as plaintiffs. "It is a stupendous wrong to emancipate & then desert them," Fleming concluded. "The master's interest was once their protection—but that is now gone. My interest in their behalf has not added to my business or popularity—but I care not."[131]

Until the civil courts were thought to be ready to protect the legal rights of the freedmen, the provost courts (operating under military authority) and the Freedmen's Bureau dispensed justice in the postwar South. While in many ways fairer toward the freedmen, the quality of that justice varied according to the competence and commitment of the particular officers and depended on their success in securing the cooperation of the Union Army to enforce their decisions. Like many such officials, John De Forest, a Freedmen's Bureau agent in South Carolina, thought his primary obligation was to teach the whites to accord equal protection under the law to the freed slaves. "I so interpreted my orders as to believe that my first and great duty lay in raising the blacks and restoring the whites of my district to a confidence in civil law." When Cato Allums, a freedman, shot and killed a white man in self-defense, De Forest permitted civil authorities to handle the case. But he followed their actions carefully, warned them that they were on trial as much as the freedman, and attempted in every way to protect Allums' rights when he was indicted for murder. The refusal of several white witnesses to testify ultimately resulted in the dismissal of the indictment. De Forest hailed the outcome as "a triumph of justice, public conscience, and public sense" and a vindication of his decision to allow local whites to resume judicial power. Although grateful for his release, Allums resented his lengthy confinement and the expenses he incurred in his defense. Unlike De Forest, he deemed the outcome less than a triumph of white justice. "I never was treated like most niggers was," he told De Forest. "Mighty few white men has tried to ride over Cato." By 1866, in most sections of the South, civil courts had resumed their jurisdiction, although the Freedmen's Bureau reserved the right to intervene if it thought blacks had been denied impartial justice. That it seldom did so revealed more about the predilections of Bureau officers than the impartiality of civil justice.[132]

After their initial experiences with the judicial system, many freedmen found little reason to place any confidence in it. The laws discriminated against them, the courts upheld a double standard of justice, and the police acted as the enforcers. Arrested often for the most trivial offenses (for which whites would rarely be apprehended), blacks found themselves in jail for months without a trial, denied the right to competent counsel (lawyers feared losing their white clients), charged exorbitant legal fees, and sentenced as much for their race as for the nature of their crime.[133] Upon entering the town of Selma, Alabama, a northern journalist came across a gang of black prisoners at work in the street, each of them linked to the other by a long chain. Anxious to learn what they had done to deserve such "ignominious" punishment, he obtained a list of their crimes, the most serious of which was "using abusive language towards a white man"; the other offenses included disorderly conduct, vagrancy, petty theft, and selling farm produce within the town limits (the offender had been unable to pay his fine of twenty dollars). "But it was a singular fact," the visitor learned, "that no white men were ever sentenced to the chain-gang,—being, I suppose, all virtuous." The all-black chain gang, like the two Bibles required in some courtrooms, one for white witnesses and the other for black witnesses, symbolized all too graphically the kind of justice many freedmen had come to expect.[134]

If only because they feared Federal intervention, some courts made scrupulous attempts to guard the rights of accused blacks. But the infrequency with which whites were apprehended, tried, and convicted of crimes against freedmen made a mockery of equal justice and encouraged still more white violence. At nearly every step in the judicial process, the victims of such violence found themselves frustrated, even in swearing out a complaint against a white man.

> It is difficult to get an officer to arrest a white man when he has assaulted and beaten a colored man; the magistrates will not give warrants for the arrest of white men without long interrogation. We are bound to know a stranger's name—if not, no warrant, when he is white; but if he be colored, they will quickly give warrants that the colored man may be put in jail. Oh, how quickly the officers will catch him!

To lodge a complaint against a white person was also to invite harassment and sometimes violence. "The idea of a *nigger* having the power of bringing a *white man* before a tribunal!" a Georgian exclaimed. "The Southern people a'n't going to stand that." Moreover, as a Freedmen's Bureau officer in Alabama observed, anyone making a complaint had to provide bail to appear as a witness or be kept in jail until the trial. "As no white man will give bail for a negro to appear as a witness against a white man, and as they don't fancy lying perhaps weeks in jail in order to be heard, they prefer to suffer wrong rather than seek redress."[135]

Even when the names of the offenders were known, whites could be expected to abide by a "gentlemen's agreement" not to cooperate with the authorities in apprehending them, and the police were often less than eager to pursue the matter and in some instances conspired to effect the escape of a white prisoner accused of a serious crime. When murders were committed, neighbors and friends would invariably hide the offenders, and few men possessed the necessary courage to expose the guilty parties lest they share the same fate. Without military protection for himself and the witnesses, no freedman could be expected to help prosecute a white man for assault, murder, or any other crime. That was the conclusion reached by a Freedmen's Bureau officer in Grenada, Mississippi. "As against freedmen the majority of whites are a unit and even honorable men, otherwise, will vouch for persons of, to say the least, doubtful character as 'high social Gentlemen.' "[136]

If a white man should be apprehended and tried for offenses committed against freedmen, the chances of convicting him were slight so long as whites dominated the juries. And if convicted, the penalties assessed against him were likely to be far less than the gravity of the crime warranted or that would have been imposed upon a black person. The double standard of white justice was nowhere clearer, in fact, than in the disparate punishments meted out to whites and blacks convicted of similar crimes. In Marion County, Florida, for example, James J. Denton, after being convicted of the slaying of a black man, had to pay a fine of $250 and serve one minute in prison; most blacks found guilty of petty theft could expect a more severe sentence. (In nearby Lake City, two blacks convicted of stealing several boxes of goods from a railroad company were fined $500; unable to pay the fine, their services were sold to the highest bidder.) No doubt many whites still needed to learn that killing a black person amounted to murder. But a Freedmen's Bureau officer in Georgia despaired of any early or mass conversion to that principle. "The best men in the State admit that no jury would convict a white man for killing a freedman, or fail to hang a negro who had killed a white man in self-defence." The need to demonstrate to the satisfaction of a white jury that the defendant had been "animated by the intention to kill" complicated the conviction and punishment of any white person for murder, as did the underlying principle of slave law that a master's severe chastisement of his blacks did not justify resistance. As the Georgia Supreme Court had once ruled, even if the owner should "exceed the bounds of reason . . . in his chastisement, the slave must submit . . . unless the attack . . . be calculated to produce death."[137]

Rather than press for a diminution or increase in the penalties assessed by the courts, blacks simply insisted that the punishment fit the crime and be applied equally to both races. In New Orleans, the local criminal court sentenced a white person convicted of theft (a pair of shoes valued at $13) to one day in prison; the same court on the same day committed a black person found guilty of theft (shirts and petticoats valued at $18) to three months in prison—or, as the local black newspaper noted, "three days for the stealing, and eighty-seven days for being colored." The disparity in punishments, however, was not confined to the regular courts; in many regions, the provost marshals adopted the same double standard. In Salisbury, North Carolina, a white woman killed a black mother who had tried to rescue her child from a severe beating; a military court found her guilty of manslaughter and fined her $1,000, and within several days the white community had collected and paid the fine. In Natchez, a white man who brutally assaulted an elderly black woman was fined $15 ($5 for the provost marshal who sentenced him and $10 for the injured woman); the victim contributed her award to the Lincoln Monument Fund, exclaiming, "I don't want money, but justice."[138]

When blacks drew up their postwar demands, equal justice almost invariably superseded all others. Even those who argued the primacy of the suffrage or economic grievances conceded that without equal protection under the law, neither the property they accumulated, the wages they were promised, nor the vote they might someday cast would be safe. "To be sure, sah, we wants to vote," a black barber observed, "but, sah, de great matter is to git into de witness-box." The price exacted of the white South in exchange for the reinstatement of civil courts was the admissibility of black testimony. Like emancipation and later the suffrage, whites viewed it as a consequence of military defeat and occupation. But that hardly made it a popular concept. "Nothing would make me cut a nigger's throat from ear to ear so quick," said a white shoemaker in Liberty, Virginia, "as having him set up his impudent face to tell that a thing wasn't so when I said it was so."[139]

With the right of testimony, blacks had hoped to secure the equal protection which the Constitution ensured all citizens. The credibility accorded such testimony by white judges and juries, however, made this substantially less than the triumph freedmen had imagined. "Why, no nigger can be believed whether he is under oath or not," a Virginian observed. "No one that knows a nigger will ever think of believing him if it's for his interest to lie." Making essentially the same point, a resident of Charlotte, North Carolina, perhaps said more than he intended when he argued that white people were simply not ready to admit black testimony against other whites. "What would be the good of putting niggers in the witness-box?" he asked. "You must have niggers in the jury-box, too, or nigger evidence will not be believed. I don't think you could find twelve men in the whole State who would attach any weight to the testimony of ninety-nine niggers in a hundred."[140]

Few blacks might have disagreed with that assessment of the minimal impact of their testimony. Unless they were admitted to the juries, too, they realized, equal justice would remain a mockery. "It is the right of every man accused of any offence, to be tried by a jury of his peers," the Reverend J. W. Hood told a black convention in North Carolina. "I claim that the black man is my peer, and so I am not tried by my peers unless there be one or more black men in the jury box." By the eve of Radical Reconstruction, blacks were already sitting on some juries, though not without vehement white objections, and still more would be added after the Radical governments took power. In some states, as in South Carolina, Federal authorities stipulated that every person registered as a taxpayer or voter also qualified as a juror. Like the admission of black testimony, the appearance of blacks in the jury box signaled still another encroachment on the white man's domain. To a Louisiana planter and judge, it all seemed like a steady descent into total anarchy and depravity, and he could trace every step along the way. "The fortune of war has materially changed my circumstances. My niggers used to do as I told them, but that time is passed. Your Northern people have made soldiers of our servants, and will, I presume, make voters of them. In five years, if I continue the practice of law, I suppose I shall be addressing a dozen negroes as gentlemen of the jury."[141]

If black jurors and testimony could soften the abuses of the courts, many blacks also contended that only biracial police forces could ensure a semblance of equality in law enforcement. Until that objective had been realized, at least, freedmen would remain vulnerable to harassment, violence, and discriminatory arrests by police officers who acted as the instruments of white control and repression. "The police of this place make the law to suit themselves," a black teacher in Wetumpka, Alabama, protested, citing arrests of freedmen for minor offenses which were ignored when committed by whites. "From what I can see and hear among the Col[ore]d people of this place," he added, "something serious will grow out of this if we do not get the proper protection." In some communities, blacks complained that policemen regularly invaded their homes, ostensibly in search of weapons and to quiet the insurrectionary fears of white citizens. The black newspaper in New Orleans charged the police with "a provoking series of petty persecutions" as well as participation in the riot of 1866 and expressed particular outrage over the disarming of blacks while whites openly displayed their weapons without fear of arrest. The black protests, from wherever they emanated, agreed that law and order could not be established in their communities without some restraints being placed on the police. A resident of Charleston commended the military commander there for having found one constructive solution to the problem of police violence—he ordered the arrest of any policeman found in possession of a revolver or club.[142]

Despite black testimony and some black jurors, the quality of justice on the eve of Radical Reconstruction largely reflected white power and the determination to preserve it. If anyone thought the freedmen were enjoying equal protection under the law, a black resident of Macon, Georgia, invited him to visit the local courtroom and observe the proceedings. "A white man may assault a colored gentleman at high noon, pelt him with stones, or maul him with a club, without any provocation at all; and if it has to be decided by rebel justice, the colored man is fined or imprisoned, and the white man is justified in what he and his friends call a 'narrow escape.' " To many blacks, that remained the crux of their problem—the black plaintiff appeared to have less of a chance for legal redress than the defendant. If he hesitated to file a complaint against a white person or to involve himself in any way with the legal process, that was because he feared ending up in jail rather than the offender. When the victims of white violence demanded that action be taken against white assailants, some of them were dismissed with the advice to avoid contact with individuals who were apt to harm them.[143] That was surely one way to avoid trouble, though difficult to achieve without becoming a recluse; some blacks suggested another alternative, far more in keeping with the values and tradition of white America—they could shoot the assailant in self-defense.

11

AFTER STILL ANOTHER violent clash in Norfolk, in which Yankee troops had vowed to "clear out all the niggers," a black resident of that city voiced his despair at such betrayal and at the same time warned all whites—

Yankees and natives alike—not to push the freedmen too far. "We are a nation that loves the white people," he declared, "and we would never attack them, but if we are driven to exasperation we know our duty." Although emancipation and the gradual reduction of Union troops made blacks more vulnerable to attack, most of them had enjoyed freedom, however briefly, and refused to surrender their newly acquired rights without a struggle. It seemed like an appropriate time, then, to invoke such time-honored concepts and virtues as self-defense.

> A kind of general serfdom and humiliation of the colored race is about to take the place of slavery—if we do not check the tendency toward that course. . . . If there is no protection for us at the hands of the municipal police or the military guard, if there is no redress for our people before the Criminal Courts in cases of murder and rape, then let us form at once societies for self-protection and have recourse to personal defense.

That sentiment, voiced by the black newspaper in New Orleans, accorded with advice to discharged black soldiers to retain their guns and its call for Home Guard units which would mobilize whenever circumstances demanded their presence. After all, why should not those who had defended their nation on the battlefields likewise defend their families and friends at home. "In times of peace prepare for war," a black resident of New Orleans suggested. "They have burned our churches, murdered our friends in their own yards, in the presence of their own family, and yet our civil government is still running, and the murderers are still allowed to roam our streets undisturbed."[144]

Not surprisingly, blacks vented much of their anger and "lawlessness" on the law itself. Since they could not expect impartial justice in the courtroom, groups of blacks in some communities invaded the jails and courtrooms to release their accused brethren. At the same time, they evinced a determination to mete out extralegal justice if the white police and courts failed to do their duty. In Selma, Alabama, blacks threatened to burn down the town unless a known white murderer was turned over to them or brought to justice; Federal troops intervened and the suspected murderer escaped. After a white mob in Jeffersonton, Georgia, removed a black youth from the jail and hanged him, allegedly for having killed a farm animal, more than a hundred blacks, all of them armed with guns and pistols, appeared to demand the prosecution of those responsible for the lynching. Although Federal authorities persuaded the blacks to disperse, a still larger crowd gathered the next day, and this time the local Freedmen's Bureau agent requested Federal troops. Only the presence of such troops prevented a riot in Wilmington, North Carolina, after blacks tried to halt the public whipping of five men found guilty in a trial where black testimony had been excluded; in three Virginia counties, the Freedmen's Bureau quickly resumed judicial power because the blacks had threatened to retaliate for the injustices committed by the civil courts; and in several communities, blacks armed themselves to resist attacks on their schools and churches.[145]

The threats of black retaliatory violence obviously concerned native whites and military authorities and gave rise in the postwar years to new rumors and reports of insurrectionary activity. But little was done to attack the sources of black discontent. In Columbia, South Carolina, blacks reacted with outrage when in May 1866 the chief of police shot and killed a young freedman while arresting him for a misdemeanor. Both the coroner's jury and local military authorities acquitted the police chief, setting off a new wave of anger in the black community. On the morning of May 30, a Union officer was "startled" to find that a notice had been posted during the night in the local post office.

> We the Coloured Men of Columbia, were Advised to whate [wait] and see what would be said or done a bout that act of Murder committed *by Green*. We have Seen and heard! *We* know it to be a mock trial and we will trie him next. He has committed Cold and Willful Murder and if not removed, we can and will have revenge. . . . By one thousand true and reddy We will have his Blood, Green the Murderer.

Two companies of Federal troops were brought into the city, the police chief secluded himself, and the black threats of violence failed to materialize. But "the worst feature in the case," a black woman wrote the Freedmen's Bureau, was that nothing had been done to satisfy the grievances of the black residents, thereby encouraging the whites to think themselves immune to prosecution or control.

> We have very dark days here; the colored people are almost in despair. . . . The rebels here boast that the negroes shall not have as much liberty now, as they enjoyed during slavery. We can not have a party or gathering of any kind, unless we ask leave of the Mayor, & the men that the United States send here to keep things straight, wink at, & allow these things to go on thus.
>
> God knows how we will do. We are not allowed to have arms; if a white man strikes us, & we attempt to defend ourselves, we are carried to Provost Court, & fined ten or twenty dollars. It is hard I tell you. Our friends in Congress are wasting time & breath, & all the bills they may pass, will do us no good, unless men are sent here, that will see those laws enforced.
>
> Col. Greene [the Union commander] cares not a fig for a colored person. It is very seldom you can get a word with him. He spends all his time in the Billiard Saloon. . . .
>
> I will tell you, if things go on thus, our doom is sealed. God knows it is worse than slavery. The negro code is in full force here with both Yankees and rebels.[146]

This graphic description of conditions in the capital of South Carolina in mid-1866 might have been duplicated in countless communities and regions. Neither her assessment nor her despair were unique. Although the talk of armed retaliation might evoke images of black "minutemen" and "regulators," the freedmen possessed neither the weapons nor the power to offset the better organized whites. Nor could they successfully contend with the threat of Federal intervention to suppress them if they took the law into their own hands. Despite the rhetoric of violence, the great mass of blacks recognized where the power still resided.

If confronted with an intolerable situation on the plantation or in the neighborhood, alternatives other than armed resistance were presumably available to black people. Freedom permitted them to take their labor elsewhere. For many freed slaves, in fact, this right constituted the very essence of their new status, and they proposed to use such a weapon to carve out a greater degree of independence for themselves and their families. Not all freedmen exercised this prerogative in the same way, or at the same time, and some did not exercise it at all. Neither the former slave nor his former master, however, could easily predict the precise moment when confrontation and separation would become unavoidable.

## Chapter Six

---

# THE FEEL OF FREEDOM: MOVING ABOUT

*So long ez de shadder ob de gret house falls acrost you, you ain't gwine
ter feel lak no free man, an' you ain't gwine ter feel lak no free 'oman.
You mus' all move—you mus' move clar away from de ole places what
you knows, ter de new places what you don't know, whey you kin raise
up yore head douten no fear o' Marse Dis ur Marse Tudder.*

—RICHARD EDWARDS,
BLACK PREACHER, FLORIDA, 1865[1]

*Sun, you be here an' I'll be gone,*
*Sun, you be here an' I'll be gone,*
*Sun, you be here an' I'll be gone.*
*Bye, bye, don't grieve arter me,*
*Won't give you my place, not fo' your'n,*
*Bye, bye, don't grieve arter me,*
*'Cause you be here an' I'll be gone.*

—FREEDMEN SONG,
VIRGINIA, CIRCA 1865[2]

To THROW OFF A LIFETIME of restraint and dependency and to feel like free men or free women, newly liberated slaves adopted different priorities and chose various ways in which to express themselves, ranging from dramatic breaks with the past to subtle and barely perceptible changes in demeanor and behavior. But even as they secured family ties, sanctified marriage relations, proclaimed surnames, and encroached on the white man's racial etiquette, black men and women grappled with the most critical questions affecting their lives and status. To make certain of their freedom, would they first need to separate themselves physically from those who had only recently owned them? If so, where would they go, how would they protect themselves from hostile whites, for whom and under what conditions would they work? If they remained on the old place, what relations would they now enjoy with their former owners and how could they safely manifest their freedom?

Having lived in close, sometimes intimate contact with their "white folks," dependent on them for daily sustenance, conditioned by their demands and expectations, freedmen could not always quickly or easily resolve such questions. For many of them, however, that tension between the urge toward personal autonomy and the compulsions of the old dependency grew increasingly intolerable, and nearly every slaveholding family could affix a date to the moment when their former slaves resolved the tension. "On the 5th of August [1865] one of our young men left for Albany," the Reverend John Jones reported, "and on the 8th inst. (or night before) nine more took up the line of march, carrying our house boy Allen and a girl sixteen years old (Amelia, the spinner). This girl had been corrected for being out the most of Saturday night previously." Once that "dark, dissolving, disquieting wave of emancipation" (as he called it) broke over a particular region or plantation, many a planter family watched helplessly as the only world they had known collapsed around them. "I have been marking its approach for months," the Georgia clergyman wrote, "and watching its influence on our own people. It has been like the iceberg, withering and deadening the best sensibilities of master and servant, and fast sundering the domestic ties of years."[3]

To experience the phenomenon was traumatic enough, but to seek to understand it could be a totally frustrating and impossible task. Ella Gertrude Thomas, the wife of a Georgia planter, tried her best, while viewing from day to day, and then confiding to her diary, the rupture of those affective ties which had provided her with such fond memories of a past now apparently beyond recovery. The experience of Jefferson and Gertrude Thomas reveals only the disruption of one household. But their ordeal, as they came to realize, was not unique. Like so many former slaveholders, the Thomases suffered the ingratitude of favorites, the impertinence of strangers, the exasperation of new "help," and the fears of race war. And like many others, Gertrude Thomas reached that point when nothing surprised her any longer and she could only utter the familiar cry of postemancipation despair—"And has it come to this?" Most importantly, the legacy of distrust, bitterness, and recrimination emerging out of experiences like these helped to shape race relations in the South for the next several decades.

Except for those who had already experienced the anguish of wartime "betrayal," few knew what to expect from their black servants and laborers in the first months of emancipation. "Excitement rules the hour," Gertrude Thomas observed in May 1865. "No one appears to have a settled plan of action, the Negroes crowd the streets and loaf around the pumps and corners of the street. . . . I see no evidence of disrespect on the part of the Negroes who are here from the adjoining plantations." During the war, nearly all the Thomas slaves, both at the Augusta house and plantation (some six miles outside of town) and on the plantation in Burke County, had "proved most faithful." Only when Union troops entered Augusta, more than three weeks after the end of the war, did Gertrude Thomas resign herself to the inevitability of emancipation. While Yankee soldiers and blacks filled the streets, Jefferson Thomas performed the familiar rites of emancipation, advising the house staff that he would just "as soon pay them wages as any one else." The servants received the news with little show of emotion, though they evinced "a more cheerful spirit than ever" and Sarah "was really lively while she was sewing on Franks pants." Still, their apparent "faithfulness" pleased the Thomases, even as the future seemed dim. "Our Negroes will be put on lands confiscated and imagination cannot tell what is in store for us."

The news of freedom precipitated no spontaneous celebration or Jubilee among the Thomas blacks. None of them suddenly rushed out to test their new status. When they severed their ties with the Thomases, they did so quietly with a conspicuous absence of fanfare. There was no insubordination, there were no bursts of insolence, and the Thomas property remained undisturbed. Nor were there any tearful farewells. Like many freed slaves elsewhere, the Thomas servants did not betray their emotions, at least not in the presence of their former owners. Within less than a month after the Union occupation, nearly all of them left in much the same manner as they had received the news that they were free.

Among the most faithful and best liked of the slaves had been Daniel, the first servant Jefferson Thomas had ever owned. "When we were married," Gertrude Thomas recalled, "his Father gave him to us to go in the Buggy." Daniel was the first servant to depart, and he did so at night "without saying anything to anyone." He remained in town but the Thomases had no wish to see him again. "If he returns to the yard he shall not enter it." The day after Daniel's unexpected departure, Betsy went out to pick up the newspaper, "as she was in the habit of doing every day." This time, she never returned. "I suppose that she had been met by her Father in the street and taken away but then I learned that she had taken her clothes out of the Ironing room under the pretense of washing them." Shortly afterwards, Mrs. Thomas learned that the "disappearance" had been "a concerted plan" between Betsy and her mother, who had once been a servant in the house ("an excellent washer and ironer") but was found to be "dishonest" and had been transferred to the plantation in Burke County. "She left the Plantation, came up and took Betsy home with her." While disclaiming "any emotion of interest" in Betsy's departure, this loss obviously troubled Mrs. Thomas. Nor did the thought that familial ties had superseded those of mistress and slave console her in any way. "I felt interest in Betsy, she was a bright quick child and raised in our family would have become a good servant. As it is she will be under her Mothers influence and run wild in the street."

If the Thomases wondered who might leave them next, they did not have long to wait. But this time, at least, they had a premonition. Several days after Betsy's disappearance, Aunt Sarah seemed more diligent and cheerful than usual. "Sarah has something on her mind," Gertrude Thomas remarked to her husband. "She has either decided to go or the prospect of being paid if she remains has put her in a very good humor." That night, she left. By now, the Thomases were making a conscious effort to conceal their disappointment from the remaining servants, apparently in the belief that the others derived some pleasure from their discomfort. Meanwhile, Nancy had become a problem. After the departure of Sarah, she had been instructed to take over the cooking as well as perform her usual duties. Perhaps dismayed by her doubled work load, Nancy claimed that she was not well enough to work. When the "illness" persisted and the unwashed clothes accumulated in the ironing room, the much-annoyed mistress decided to take action. "Nancy," she asked, "do you expect I can afford to pay you wages in your situation, support your two children and then have you sick as much as you are?" Nancy stood there and made no reply. The next day, she left with her two children, claiming that she would return shortly. That was the last Mrs. Thomas saw of her, and upon entering Nancy's room she discovered not unexpectedly that "all her things had been removed." Less than a week later, Willy departed, thereby spurning the Thomases' offer of clothing and a silver quarter every Saturday night. The next day, Manly left with his two children, apparently without any explanation.

"Out of all our old house servants," Gertrude Thomas noted near the end of May 1865, "not one remains except Patsy and a little boy Frank." Gradually and unspectacularly, nearly all of the servants had grasped their freedom by completely severing the old ties. The Thomases could only console themselves with the knowledge that many other white families were experiencing similar losses. For Gertrude Thomas, in fact, the departure of Susan from her mother's household truly marked the end of an era. "I am under too many obligations to Susan to have hard feelings towards her. During six confinements Susan has been with me, the best of servants, rendering the most efficient help. To Ma she has always been invaluable and in cases of sickness there was no one like Susan. Her husband Anthony was one of the first to leave the Cuming Plantation and incited others to do the same. I expect he influenced Susan." Now that Susan had left, Gertrude Thomas recalled the number of times her father had warned the family about this slave. "I have often heard Pa say that in case of a revolt among Negroes he thought that Susan would serve as ringleader. She was the first servant to leave Ma's yard and left without one word."

By late July 1865, Gertrude Thomas hoped that "the worst of this transition state of the Negroes" had been reached. "If not," she sighed, "God have mercy upon us." But her conversations with friends and relatives, as well as the news from the plantation in Burke County, were anything but reassuring; indeed, one close friend speculated that "things would go on so until Christmas" and then she expected real trouble, underscoring her warning with a gesture across the throat. As if to confirm such fears, a delegation of field hands from the plantation came to the Augusta house, entered the yard, and handed Jefferson Thomas a summons from the local Union Army commander, ordering him to appear and answer the demand of these blacks for wages. Incensed by the impertinence of the delegation, Thomas ordered them out of his yard. Before leaving, however,

one of them shouted out an insult, hoping—or so the Thomases thought—
to provoke him into a confrontation. "And this too we had to endure," Mrs.
Thomas wrote of the incident. "As it could not be resented it was treated
with the silence of contempt. And has it come to this?" After reflecting over
her experience of the past several months, Gertrude Thomas, who had once
confessed her ambivalence about slavery, decided that she would just as
soon never have to look at a black man or woman again. "Every thing is
entirely reversed, I feel no interest in them whatever and hope I never
will."[4]

While every experience had its own unique qualities, the odyssey of
Jefferson and Gertrude Thomas through the first months of emancipation
revealed a pattern of behavior—white and black—that would be repeated
on farms and plantations and in town houses throughout the South. Once
emancipation had been acknowledged, what mattered was how many freed
slaves would find separation indispensable to their new status. With the
wartime experience still vivid in many minds, few whites now thought they
knew their former slaves well enough to speculate with much confidence
on this troublesome question. "Some folks think free labour will be cheap
& that the freedmen will gladly hire out for food and clothing," a South
Carolinian wrote. "But I think not, they seem so eager to throw off the yoke
of bondage they will suffer somewhat, before they will return to the plantations. . . . It seems like a dream, dear Aunt, we are living in such times."[5]

## 2

THE FLAMES from a pitch-pine bonfire illuminated the woods near the
Lester plantation in northern Florida. Hundreds of men, women, and children came from every direction to attend this late-night meeting, gathering
around a makeshift speaker's platform—the trunk of a fallen pine tree.
Mounting that rostrum, Richard Edwards, a black preacher, looked out at
the faces of these people only recently freed from bondage. With their cries
of "Dat's so" and loud "Amens" punctuating his remarks, he told them of
the glories of their triumph. He welcomed the new era in which black men
and women no longer cringed in the presence of the white man. He urged
them to embrace their liberty. He insisted that only they—not the Yankees, not Lincoln, not the northern teachers—could make themselves free.

You ain't, none o' you, gwinter feel rale free till you shakes de dus' ob
de Ole Plantashun offen yore feet an' goes ter a new place whey you kin
live out o' sight o' de gret house. So long ez de shadder ob de gret house
falls acrost you, you ain't gwine ter feel lak no free man, an' you ain't
gwine ter feel lak no free 'oman. You mus' all move—you mus' move clar
away from de ole places what you knows, ter de new places what you
don't know, whey you kin raise up yore head douten no fear o' Marse Dis

ur Marse Tudder. Take yore freedom, my brudders an' my sisters. You-all is jis' ez good ez ennybody, an' you-all is jis' ez free! Go whey you please —do what you please—furgit erbout de white folks—an' now stan' up on yore feet—lif' up yore eyes—an' shout wid me Glory, halleluyer! AMEN![6]

Within the first year of freedom, thousands of blacks exercised that option in precisely that spirit. If they were truly free, they could walk off the plantation on which they had labored as slaves and never return. Whatever else they did, that remained the surest, the quickest way to demonstrate to themselves that their old masters and mistresses no longer owned or controlled them, that they were now free to make their own decisions. Although the black preacher in Florida had talked about "new places what you don't know," most of those who left preferred the localities they knew, where they could still retain their familial ties and friendships; they might simply move to the next plantation or to the nearest town. In separating themselves from their previous owners, not from the region itself, they had begun to feel like free men and women.

Explaining the movement of blacks in his region, a Florida planter and physician made the essential point. "The negroes don't seem to feel free unless they leave their old homes," he informed his cousin in North Carolina, "just to make it sure they can go when and where they choose." Elsewhere in the South, white families and Federal officials observed the same phenomenon: many freedmen were acting on the assumption that to stay with their former masters was to remain slaves. Once a black man or woman made the critical decision to leave, not even the most handsome of offers from the former master was likely to keep them on the old place. In South Carolina, a white family proposed to pay their valuable cook nearly twice the amount she had been offered in the nearby village. But this woman, who had served the family faithfully for many years, could not be persuaded to stay. "No, Miss, I must go," she insisted. When pressed to give some reason for spurning such a generous offer, the woman had little difficulty in making her motives absolutely clear: "If I stay here I'll never know I am free." Without even pretending to understand the deeply felt yearnings that prompted such behavior, some whites chose to dismiss the departures as foolish or even amusing, much as they previously had belittled the humanity of their slaves. "In almost every yard servants are leaving," Emma Holmes observed in Camden, South Carolina, "but going to wait on other people for food merely, sometimes with the promise of clothing, passing themselves off as free, much to our amusement."[7]

To leave the plantation or farm, his worldly possessions stuffed into a small bundle slung over his shoulder, came easily to some, not so easily to most. On numerous places, the entire black population decamped at the same time, as if prearranged, leaving the owners to wallow in self-pity and to utter those familiar cries of betrayal. "Every Negro has left us," the wife of a South Carolina planter exclaimed in July 1865. "I have never in my life met with such ingratitude, every Negro deserted."[8] But the postwar "exodus" usually reflected individual and family decisions and often sharply divided the ex-slaves on the same plantation. Typically, as a former Mississippi slave recalled, "they didn't go off right at first. They was several years getting broke up. Some went, some stayed, some actually moved back. Like bees trying to find a setting place."[9] For white families to make sense out of those who left and those who stayed proved no less frustrating after emancipation than during the Yankee invasion. Again, previous records of behavior were misleading, verbal expressions of loyalty counted for little, and familial ties could induce various responses. No archetypal "deserter" emerged: the faithful and the troublesome left, the most and the least trusted, those who had endured a harsh bondage and those who counted themselves among the relatively well treated.

The "exodus" affected every kind of master. Those who had acquired notorious reputations, however, usually sustained the earliest and the largest losses. Austin Grant, who had worked as a field hand in Mississippi and Texas, recalled that his master had been "a pretty good boss" because he had fed them well. But he had also made frequent use of the "black snake" (a bullwhip) to maintain discipline and production, and he worked them hard.

> We got up early, you betcha. You would be out there by time you could see and you quit when it was dark. They tasked us. They would give us 200 or 300 pounds of cotton to bring in and you would git it, and if you didn' git it, you better, or you would git it tomorrow, or your back would git it. Or you'd git it from someone else, maybe steal it from their sacks.

When the master informed them of their freedom, he made himself quite clear: "Now, you can jes' work on if you want to, and I'll treat you jes' like I always did." That was all they needed to hear. "I guess when he said that they knew what he meant. The' wasn't but one family left with 'im. They stayed about two years. But the rest was just like birds, they jes' flew." On an Alabama plantation, Aunt Nellie, a "nurse girl" who had alternated between tending a temperamental mistress and her equally obnoxious children, left as soon as she learned of her freedom but not before giving the children a long-overdue thrashing.[10]

Whatever the pathos and nostalgia conveyed by the popular minstrel ballad "I Lost My Massa When Dey Set Me Free," newly freed slaves, as the ballad itself suggested, might have felt and acknowledged a certain affection for their "white folks" but still left them. "It ain't that I didn't love my Marster," Melvin Smith recalled, "but I jest likes to be free," and when told that he "didn't b'long to nobody no more" he immediately left his home plantation in South Carolina and headed for Tallahassee, Florida. Reputedly humane and generous masters who had expected to retain their former slaves were thus in numerous instances doomed to a bitter disappointment. "As a general rule," a white woman in Virginia wrote of the "defections" in her region, "they are all anxious to leave home and many that seemed perfectly contented in slavery are now dissatisfied, and many humane kind masters, who owned large numbers of servants, have been left without a single one." Having always thought of himself as a good master, a planter in Amelia County, Virginia, tried to understand why he had lost all but six of his 115 slaves. "My people were always well treated, and never were worked hard. A number of them had been with my father, and there were a good many that I had grown up with from boyhood. I loved some of them." Although many of his slaves seemed to share this affection, they were no less adamant in their decision to leave, even as they came to him with tears in their eyes to shake his hand and bid him farewell.[11]

The good reputation of a former slaveholder was not necessarily irrelevant when blacks formulated their post-emancipation plans. It simply was not always enough. The decisions made by black people were not always in reaction to the abuse, kindness, or indifference of white men; their behavior in the aftermath of freedom reflected a diversity of considerations, not the least of which were familial ties, attachment to particular locales, and the perfectly natural urge to explore the forbidden and the unknown and to grasp new and hopefully more remunerative opportunities. Again, Mary Chesnut seemed more perceptive than most whites when she observed in June 1865, "In their furious, emotional way they swore devotion to us to their dying day. All the same, the moment they see an opening to better themselves, they will move on." Moreover, as the freed blacks perceived the situation, the previous good works and present good intentions of a former master counted for less than their confidence in his ability and willingness to compensate them properly for any future labor. If freed slaves suspected that their old master might be on the verge of bankruptcy (and the blacks usually surmised correctly), they saw little reason to stay with him. Sarah Ann Smith, for example, acknowledged that her master had been a decent man but he was simply "too busted ter hire us ter stay on, so we moved over ter Mr. Womble's place." Despite the "good white folkses" Anna Parkes had served, she realized that most of the master's money "wuz gone," he could obviously not afford to pay most of his laborers, and she and her mother therefore moved to the nearby gun factory and began to take in washing.[12]

Even if their former masters were able and willing to pay them, they might choose not to stay if they had any reason, based on their previous experience, to doubt his word. Significant numbers of ex-slaveholders failed to pass that test. After all, a freedman from Petersburg, Virginia, explained, so many masters had broken so many promises in the past that they had forfeited the confidence of their blacks, and those who had been victimized in this way "won't stay with their old masters on any terms." On a plantation in Crawford County, Georgia, the freedmen were promised a plot of land and a mule by their former owner. But they knew from experience that the mistress was "de real boss" and they suspected she would not agree to such a generous offer. And when those suspicions were confirmed, Tines Kendricks recalled, "every nigger on dat place left. Dey sure done dat; an' old mars an' old mis', dey never had a hand left there on that great big place, an' all that ground layin' out."[13]

With emancipation, many blacks redefined the mutual obligations which had been implicit in the slave-master relationship. They were now apt to demand not only the protection and care to which they had been accustomed but a compensation, respect, and autonomy that would be commensurate with their new status. If they thought their former master incapable of such concessions, or if he violated their expectations (as on the first payday), that was sufficient reason to sever the old ties. Even if the master proved agreeable, some blacks found it impossible to give full expression to their freedom in the presence of people who had only recently demanded their absolute obedience and subserviency. All too often, as the freedmen quickly discovered, their previous owners, no matter how well-intentioned, were willing to do everything for them except accord them the same dignity and respect they demanded for themselves. Trying to make some sense out of his recent losses, a South Carolina planter explained to a northern visitor how he had made such a good home for his slaves and how he had cared for them in health and sickness. With a note of pride in his voice, he declared that he had been so solicitous of his slaves that they had never been obliged to think for themselves. And yet, "these niggers all left me," and they did so at the first opportunity.[14]

Rather than accept their losses as an inevitable consequence of emancipation, many planter families viewed them as betrayal of a mutual trust. Provoked by such charges, the black newspaper in New Orleans asked the white South what it might have expected from a people who had spent a lifetime in bondage. If the freed slaves had remained passive, that would only have confirmed their inferiority as a race, incapable of appreciating the value of freedom. But in choosing to exercise that freedom and the rights belonging to free Americans, they stood convicted of moral treason and ingratitude.

> Four or five years ago, there was nothing but praise coming forth from the lips of the Southern people when alluding to the colored population. The negro was a good-natured being; he was a faithful and devoted servant; he would sacrifice his life, if necessary, to save his masters, . . . and on many a battle-field, it was recorded that some negro boy had gallantly fought in the ranks of the Confederates, by the side of his owner; and so forth.
>
> The Northern soldier came down to the cotton and sugar plantations, and made the black man free. And, lo! for the great crime of accepting the boon of freedom, the negro can expect nothing but hatred, insults and contumeliousness at the hands of his former well-wishers. Would the Southerner esteem the black man more, if the latter had esteemed his freedom less? if he was less of a man? if he cared not for his human dignity? if he had less self-respect? if he was ready to sacrifice his rights?[15]

Even if the former slaveholders would have regarded these as valid questions, which is doubtful, they were in no emotional state to venture any answers.

3

SINCE THE END OF THE WAR, nothing had seemed quite the same to the old slaveholding families. Even if they pretended to understand the fragile nature of the old ties, that could not make the losses any more bearable. "Something dreadful has happened dear Diary," confided a Florida woman in May 1865.

> I hardly know how to tell it, my dear black mammy has left us. . . . I feel lost, I feel as if someone is dead in the house. Whatever will I do without my Mammy? When she was going she stopped on the doorstep and, shaking her fist at Mother [with whom she had had an altercation], she said: "I'll miss you—the Lord knows I'll miss you—but you'll miss me, too —you see if you don't."

With equal consternation, a young Virginia woman returned home from school to find "everything strange" in the household; the cook, who had "reigned" in the kitchen for some thirty years, had gone to Richmond, as had most of the servants. "I cannot tell you how it oppressed me to miss the familiar black faces I have loved all my life, and to feel that our negroes cared so little for us, and left at the first invitation."[16]

Although many families had anticipated losses, they may have underestimated how they would feel when the blacks actually confirmed their fears. Despite the wartime lessons, which should have forced some humility upon the slaveholding class, they still had enormous self-pride invested in the postwar behavior of the freed slaves, along with an image of themselves that they expected their blacks to authenticate. But the first waves of postwar departures failed to sustain that image in numerous instances, and the cries of ingratitude and betrayal were repeated with even greater vigor and frequency than during the war, compounded this time by a growing feeling of helplessness. "Just imagine," a Virginia woman wrote of herself and her husband, "two forlorn beings as we are, neither of us able to help ourselves, left without a soul to do anything for us." The same themes of despair and disbelief thus persisted. That those for whom they had done the most should have demonstrated the greatest degree of ingratitude still perplexed them. Even more inexplicable, many of the servants who had stood by their white families in the worst period of the war, who had given them comfort and support when it was badly needed, were now abandoning them. No sooner had the war ended than the servant of Emma LeConte who had foraged for food to nourish the child entrusted to her care became "a great nuisance" and then departed "unexpectedly."[17]

It was all like a horrible dream, Grace Elmore lamented, "this breaking up of old ties, the giving up of those with whom your life has been spent, and making a new and wholly unknown start." Even if the bulk of the work force remained with them, the departure of certain individuals gave former masters and mistresses little reason to place much confidence in the others. In the Elmore household in South Carolina, the fidelity of most of the servants seemed almost forgotten amidst the distress over the departure of "Old Mary," the reliable nurse "of whom we expected most because of her age and the baby."

> Saturday evening she was told of her freedom & expressed quiet satisfaction, but said none could be happy without prayer (the hypocrite) and Monday by daylight she took herself off, leaving the poor baby without a nurse. I feel so provoked, of course one cannot expect total sacrifice of self, but certainly there should be some consideration of others. Old Mary is off my books for any kindness or consideration I may be able to show her in after years. I would not turn on my heel to help her, a more pampered indulged old woman one could find no where.... I think a marked difference should be shown between those who act in a thoughtful and affectionate manner, and those who show no thought or care for you.

With her servants gradually leaving, Mary Jones reached essentially the same conclusion in her Georgia home; in fact, she thought it a triumph of sorts that she had managed to overcome any "anxieties" she might have once felt for this race of people. "My life long (I mean since I had a home) I have been laboring and caring for them, and since the war have labored with all my might to supply their wants, and expended everything I had upon their support, directly or indirectly; and this is their return."[18]

Whether provoked by the departures or by the behavior of the blacks who remained, white families looked on with emotions that varied from outrage to resignation to sorrow, and many ran the entire gamut of emotions. The tearful postwar separations between some of the freed slaves and their "white folks" did so much to reinforce the self-image of the slaveholding class that such scenes became a common theme in late-nineteenth-century southern romanticism. While the stories were often embellished and exaggerated, they were not without some basis in fact. But with the passage of time, the chroniclers who regaled new generations with those scenes tended to forget their exceptional quality. That is, the affections held by masters and mistresses for their former slaves were almost always reserved for certain favorites, usually a few of the "uncles" and "aunties" who had a long record of service to the family. But that said very little about the ways in which these same masters and mistresses regarded the bulk of their blacks. On a plantation in Florida, Susan Bradford, a young white woman, described the "pitiful" scene in which one of the family servants left them. The tears flowed freely, there were embraces, and everyone in the family shared in the prevailing sorrow over losing Nellie. But this same Susan Bradford, who had been deeply touched by this emotional parting, thought little about swinging a whip into a group of black children who had offended her by singing "We'll hang Jeff Davis to a sour apple tree." If anything, she seemed to relish the opportunity to vent her anger in this way. "Laying the whip about me with all the strength I could muster I soon had the whole crowd flying toward the Quarter, screaming as they went." The family that bestowed such affection on the parting Nellie watched the proceedings and thought it amusing that nineteen-year-old Susan should be striking a black for the first time.[19]

If some ex-slaves still commanded the affection and appreciation of their masters and mistresses because of the quality of their previous service to the family, many others forfeited such consideration by their post-emancipation behavior. During slavery, white families had demanded obedience and passive submission from their blacks. After emancipation, it proved difficult if not impossible for these same families to accept the idea that a presidential proclamation, a military order, or even a constitutional amendment could free the blacks from obligations that they presumed immutable. What outraged them was not simply that many blacks left but that they did so despite the urgent pleas to remain and in a manner often not in keeping with the deference and humility whites expected of their black folk. The line between leaving the plantation and insolence was never altogether clear, as more than one black victim would discover.[20]

Disgruntled planters, or agents acting on their behalf, were not averse to using forcible means to keep the blacks on the plantations and to punish those who left. Six former slaves in the Clarendon district of South Carolina expressed their dissatisfaction with the overseer by leaving the plantation in a body; the overseer and several neighbors pursued them with dogs, captured the entire group, shot one who tried to escape and hanged the others by the roadside. That show of force was sufficient to keep the remaining hands on the plantation, at least for another month. In Gates County, North Carolina, a planter explained to his freed slaves that "he was better used to them than to others" and he urged them to remain for board, two suits of clothing, and a bonus of "one Sunday suit" upon completion of the crop. When one of the hands exercised his prerogative as a free man to decline the offer, the master's son "flew at him and cuffed and kicked him"; the others heeded the lesson and indicated they were "perfectly willing to stay," but the master still thought it advisable to have them closely watched. Few masters pursued such matters as relentlessly as the planter who located in a nearby city the black woman who had left him and then shot her when she refused to return with him. In reporting this incident for a northern audience, the *New York Times* correspondent tried very hard to maintain his detachment—and he succeeded. "Whipping, paddling, and other customs, peculiar to the palmy days of the institution, are practiced, and the negro finds, to his heart's sorrow, that his sore-headed master is loath to give him up. There is fault on both sides and equal exaggerations in the representations of difficulties, by both master and servant."[21]

If the planter could not induce his freed slaves to remain, either by persuasion or forcible means, he might then call upon local or Federal officials for assistance, and all too often they readily complied with such requests. Local police and Home Guard units (often made up of ex-Confederate soldiers) proved particularly effective in "persuading" many freedmen to return to the plantations on which they had previously worked; the more recalcitrant ones were likely to be flogged or shot. In Northampton County, Virginia, the Home Guards shot three freedmen when they refused to return to their old master after having accepted employment elsewhere. And in Edgefield, South Carolina, a guerrilla band headed by Dick Colburn made it "their business" to compel the freed slaves to remain with their former masters. Much to the bewilderment and consternation of the freedmen, Federal authorities—both Union Army and Freedmen's Bureau officers—actively conspired with planters in numerous instances to accomplish the same objective, though they were apt to defend their actions as in the best interests of the freedmen and the experiment in free labor.[22]

Despite these efforts, many freedmen persisted in separating themselves from their places of bondage. The white South viewed them as taking to the road without purpose or destination, except to leave those who had previously cared for them in favor of settling in the nearest town. For the whites, this aspect of the migration created the most consternation. To see their former slaves abandon them for no better assurances or offers anywhere else did little for the master's view of himself and simply heightened the bitterness and reinforced the sense of personal "betrayal." After seeing a number of blacks leave his plantation, a proprietor in Georgia rode up to them and demanded to know where they were going. "I don't know where I will get to before I stop," one of the freedmen replied, apparently in a tone of voice that suggested anything but deference to a superior. Recounting the incident, Gertrude Thomas explained that only a white Southerner could have possibly appreciated "the feelings" such a reply provoked in the offended white man. "Buddy fired his pistol twice," she reported, "and created much alarm among them."[23]

That so many ex-slaves left their "white folks" for a difficult and unknown alternative attests to their remarkable courage and determination and to the brittle quality of the "old ties." Unaccustomed to such displays of black independence, the old slaveholding class moved quickly to save itself—to check the movements of the freedmen and to restore stability to the shattered labor system.

To LOOK AT the congested railroad depots, the makeshift camps along the tracks, the hastily constructed freedmen villages, and the stragglers crowding the country roads, bundles under their arms or slung over their shoulders, many of them hungry, sick, and barely clad, the impression conveyed was that of an entire people on the move. Such scenes took on, in fact, all the dimensions of the more classic postwar movements of refugees. Traveling between Jackson and Vicksburg, a Union Army officer found the roads filled with "hungry, naked, foot-sore" freedmen and their families, "aliens in their native land, homeless, and friendless," some of them becoming "vagabonds and thieves from both necessity and inclination." Less sympathetic was the Freedmen's Bureau officer who thought most of the ex-slaves left their homes under the impression "that Freedom relieved them from Labor."[24]

If native whites and Federal officials perceived thousands of freedmen on the road with no purpose but to experience the sensation of freedom, they tended to exaggerate the numbers of such migrants and failed to appreciate many of the more substantial reasons for moving. For many black men and women, the post-emancipation migration represented something more than mere caprice or wanderlust. To move was to improve their economic position, to locate family members, to return to the homes from which they had been removed during the war, and to relocate themselves in places where they could more readily secure their newly won rights. "I met men plodding along Virginia and North Carolina roads," a northern reporter wrote, "who had come from distant parts of those States, or from distant States, seeking work or looking for relatives. One man I remember who had walked from Georgia in the hope of finding at Salisbury a wife from whom he had been separated years before by sale. In Louisiana, I met men and women who since the war had made long journeys in order to see their parents or children. . . . These were sights that seemed to fill every white Southerner with anger."[25]

During the war, thousands of slaves had been removed from the threatened regions, like the South Carolina low country, to the more remote sections of the state, where they would be out of the path of the Union Army, insulated from dangerous influences, and still available for some kind of labor. With the confirmation of their freedom, many of these "refugeed" blacks wanted to return to their old homes and friends and to the type of labor with which they were familiar. Not only did they seek employment "in labor which they understood better," one observer noted, but "it might easily be that no place could well be worse than the region in which they found themselves when the war closed." Near Kingsville, South Carolina, a black refugee camp was made up almost exclusively of men and women who had worked for a rice planter on the Combahee River before

being removed to the Richland district, where they were put to work raising other crops. For several days, they had been waiting beside the railroad
tracks for transportation to their old residences. "All we gang o' nigger is
rice nigger," they declared, as if that were sufficient explanation. If he
could not obtain a piece of land for himself upon his return, one of the
freedmen declared, he preferred to go back to the old rice plantation and
labor there with his fellow workers for money or shares.[26]

With some 125,000 slaves having been removed to Texas during the
war, many of these now joined the steady stream of migrants traveling
along the old San Antonio road, eager to get back to their old homes in
Louisiana, Mississippi, and elsewhere—"or, at all events, to get out of
Texas." To undertake the trek required considerable fortitude, many freedmen preferred to take their chances in Texas, and the decision in some
instances split families asunder, with some returning to the old places and
others remaining in their new homes. "Pappy, him goes back to Louisiana
to massa's place," Fred Brown recalled. "Dat am de las' we hears from him.
Mammy and I goes to Henderson [Texas] and I works at dis and dat and
cares for my mammy ten years, till she dies. Den I gits jobs as cook in Dallas
and Houston and lots of other places." After being abandoned by their
master in the regions to which he had removed them, some freedmen were
more than justified in invoking the cry of "ingratitude" and did so. Near
Macon, Georgia, a northern traveler encountered a group of twenty-six
former slaves who had come from Mississippi and were determined to
reach their old homes in South Carolina. "My young master moved to
Mississippi and took us with him," an elderly freedman explained. "He had
a great many slaves. When de Lord brought freedom to us, why my young
master turned us out, said we was no good, we couldn't work any, and said
go away." Such instances may have been exceptional. If the planter did not
feel responsible for his former slaves, he might be sufficiently anxious for
their continued labor to arrange for their transportation to the regions
from which he had removed them.[27]

Rather than return to the plantations from which they had recently
been moved, some freedmen chose, as did Cheney Cross's father, to "put out
for de place where he fust belong"—that is, to the old plantations on which
they had once labored before being sold away. Such destinations were not
nearly as inexplicable as some observers thought. When Jane Sutton, a
Mississippi slave who had been given to her master's married daughter,
walked "all de way back" to the old place, she had a clear purpose in mind.
"I wanted to see Old Mis' an' my Mammy an' my brothers an' sisters." For
a different reason, Andy J. Anderson resolved to return to the plantation
in Williamson County, Texas, from which he had been sold several years
before. After his first master, Jack Haley, had left for military service, the
overseer made life intolerable for the slaves; Anderson was sold to a man
"what hell am too good for" and then sold again to a "good" master. Once
the war ended, he traveled at night and hid by day to avoid the patrollers
and headed back to the old place, where he remained in hiding until Haley

returned and fired the overseer. Emerging from his father's cabin, Andy Anderson then greeted his old master—a day he would recall many decades later as "de happies' time in my life."[28]

When Louisa Adams, a North Carolina freedwoman, returned with her parents to the same region in which they had been slaves, they did not go back to the old plantation, which had nothing but bad memories for them, but went to work for a neighboring planter. This typified the attachment which numerous ex-slaves felt not so much to the old master or mistress but to the region they knew most intimately, the familiar surroundings in which they had been raised. Attachments to "the old range," as they called it, often took priority over attractive offers made by planters elsewhere who were reputed to be good employers. Joseph Maxwell, a Georgia planter, urged the slaves he had removed to Early County during the war to stay with him and "be well cared for." But most of them insisted on leaving, not because they respected him any less ("We lub de massa an' work ha'd fo' him"), but because they wanted to return to "de place whar we libed befo'—Liberty County." To the astonishment of a Freedmen's Bureau officer in South Carolina, the blacks who had been removed to the up-country "were crazy to get back to their native flats of ague and country fever," while the "Highland darkeys who had drifted down to the seashore were sending urgent requests to be 'fotched home again.' "[29]

Even if only partially understood, the pervasive quality of local attachments provided some convenient answers to some troublesome questions about post-emancipation behavior. After examining the prevailing discontent among the blacks in a freedmen's camp near Goodrich's Landing, Louisiana, a northern reporter ascribed it all to "homesickness," for few of them had been raised in this region. "Perhaps the most marked trait in the negro character," he suggested, "is his love of home and of the localities to which he is accustomed. They all pine for their homes. They long for the old quarters they have lived in; for the old woods they have roamed in, and the old fields they have tilled." Several of the physicians in charge of these camps came up with still another malady peculiar to the Negro psyche— "homesickness" and "nostalgia." "They get thinking of their old homes and if they have left their families, or any part of them behind, they long to see them, and so they become depressed in spirits and yield readily to the first attack of disease, or succumb to the depression alone." Only this strong local attachment could presumably explain why Lucy Sanders' mother returned to her first master, though he had sold his slaves "to obtain the cash value" in the expectation that they might be emancipated. Whatever the most compelling reasons for these moves, the results proved quite acceptable to the planters who stood to gain by their labor. "This love for home," a Freedmen's Bureau official in Meridian, Mississippi, predicted, "will be of great service to us in reorganizing this Country under the new order of things." In the lexicon of the Bureau, that meant getting the ex-slaves back to work.[30]

When the war ended, Simon Crum, a black corporal in Higginson's regiment, vowed to leave the South altogether. "I'se made up my mind," he declared, "dat dese yere Secesh will neber be cibilized in my time." Although the explanation seemed plausible enough to many ex-slaves, particularly after the first year of "freedom," few of them acted out his conclusion. Both during and after the war, several groups of freed slaves, largely women and children, were shipped to northern cities, where they were placed under the supervision of various benevolent societies. But this never became a significant movement. The few who did come North in this fashion were usually employed in domestic jobs. Before the expected arrival of a hundred Virginia blacks, a New York newspaper announced that applications were being accepted in the basement of Brooklyn's Methodist Episcopal Church for "first-rate domestics." Most freedmen and freedwomen, however, if they even considered the possibility, rejected migration to the North as neither feasible nor desirable. Whatever the mammoth problems of transition they now faced, the ex-slaves seemed to suggest by their actions that following the North Star no longer constituted the only way to achieve their freedom.[31]

If the North seemed unattractive or impractical, Africa was even more so. Although several prominent northern blacks had maintained their commitment to African emigration through the first years of the war, few of them remained active in the movement after the Emancipation Proclamation. Between 1866 and 1871, however, several thousand blacks, many of them from South Carolina, did accept the offer of the American Colonization Society for free transportation to Liberia. The explanation offered by a black colonizationist repeated the familiar argument. "We do not believe it possible, from the past history and from the present aspect of affairs, for our people to live in this country peaceably, and educate and elevate their children to that degree which they desire." But most of the black leaders in the North who had enunciated the same position only a few years back no longer thought it applicable, at least not until disillusionment with the overthrow of Reconstruction forced a few of them—like Henry McNeal Turner—to reassess the situation. With black interest in African emigration sharply reduced, and in part because of that fact, President Lincoln's scheme for removing the bulk of the freed slaves to Africa or Central America came to very little in the postwar years. "They say that they have lived here all their days, and there were stringent laws made to keep them here," a Virginia freedman explained to a congressional committee, "and that if they could live here contented as slaves, they can live here when free. . . . If we can get lands here and can work and support ourselves, I do not see why we should go to any place that we do not want to go to." Nearly every postwar black convention repeated that same sentiment.[32]

For the postwar migrants, Mecca lay neither in the North nor across the seas but southward, where Florida, Louisiana, Mississippi, Arkansas, and Texas vied for needed laborers by promising "enormous" wages and evoked images of opportunity and even lushness. And as with so many subsequent black migrations, the participants would find upon reaching their destinations that the attractions had been exaggerated and the short-comings minimized. "I got to Texas and try to work for white folks and try to farm," a former Virginia slave recalled. "I couldn't make anything at any work. I made $5.00 a month for I don't know how many year after the war." The image of Texas as a "land of milk and honey" that had sustained so many involuntary wartime migrants gave way after the war to Florida as the "land of plenty," where homesteads were plentiful, wages high, and laborers scarce. But the rewards proved to be far less than the promise, the homesteads less than plentiful and difficult to clear and sustain, and many of the disappointed freedmen had to settle for labor on the plantations. At the very least, the migrants who reached states like Florida, Arkansas, and Mississippi secured terms of labor that compared favorably to what they would have received had they remained in the older states. The Georgia planters, a northern traveler reported, "haggled at paying their freedmen six or seven dollars a month, while Arkansas and Mississippi men stood ready to give twelve and fifteen dollars, and the expenses of the journey."[33]

Throughout those older states, labor agents eagerly sought recruits and advertised the advantages of their respective regions. All he had to do to obtain laborers, a Mississippi planter boasted from Eufaula, Alabama, was to send his "nigger" to talk with the local freedmen. "They had nothin' to do," he said of the Alabama blacks, and he could easily outbid his Georgian competitors who offered only board and clothing. The planter left Eufaula the next day with sixty-five black recruits. Not all the labor re-cruiters were quite this successful; they were apt to encounter not only the hostility of local whites but the suspicions of blacks who had heard tales of enticing offers that eventually resulted in sale to Cuba. Nevertheless, many freedmen listened eagerly to the promises of agents of their own race, accepted their assurances, and learned something about the biracial na-ture of deceit and betrayal.

> De white folks would pay niggers to lie to the rest of us niggers to git der farming done for nothing. He'd tell us come on and go with me, a man wants a gang of niggers to do some work and he pay you like money growing on trees. Well we ain't had no money and ain't use to none, so we glad to hear dat good news. We just up and bundle up and go with this lying nigger. Dey carried us by de droves to different parts of Alabama, Arkansas and Missouri. After we got to dese places, dey put us all to work allright on dem great big farms. We all light in and work like old horses, thinking now we making money and going to git some of it, but we never did git a cent. We never did git out of debt. . . . All over was like dat. Dem lying niggers caused all dat. Yes dey did.

Reflecting on the exaggerated claims of labor agents, white and black, John F. Van Hook, who learned about their operations from his parents in North Carolina, tended to be more philosophical about the consequences. "Some of those labor agents were powerful smart about stretching the truth," he recalled, "but those folks that believed them and left home found out that it's pretty much the same the world over, as far as folks and human nature is concerned."[34]

Despite the alarm they generated among whites, the numbers of ex-slaves who moved from state to state never reached the proportions suggested by contemporary accounts. The reports that blacks were leaving Georgia "by thousands," that at least that many South Carolina freedmen were heading southward, and that Virginia had suffered massive losses, while essentially accurate in themselves, obscured the fact that most freed slaves, if they migrated at all, confined those movements within their respective states and counties. Most significantly, perhaps, they tended to seek out the counties where their people were already heavily concentrated and to abandon the areas of white preponderance. That they settled where the demand for black labor was greatest only partially explains their preference; equally important in some regions, racial violence and white hostility prompted ex-slaves to seek security in numbers, and that in turn drove them into the Black Belt counties, as in Alabama, and increasingly into the cities and towns—where, as many blacks thought, "freedom was free-er."[35]

5

---

IT MIGHT HAVE BEEN any southern town in 1865. Walking through the outskirts of Macon, Georgia, where the half-built Confederate arsenal aptly memorialized the recent past, a northern reporter came upon a small hut in which eleven freedmen resided—an elderly man, a middle-aged man, three women, and six children. Bundles of old rags provided the only bedding; several stools, one chair, and half a dozen cooking utensils comprised the furnishings, and a bag of meal and a few pounds of bacon were on hand to sustain them. That was the extent of their worldly possessions. The reporter seemed astonished that anyone would have given up the security of the old plantation for this kind of precarious existence. And being a reporter, he searched for a plausible explanation.

> "Well, Uncle, what did you come up to the city for? Why didn't you stay on the old place? Didn't you have a kind master?"
>
> "I's had a berry good master, mass'r, but ye see I's wanted to be free man."
>
> "But you were just as free there as you are here."
>
> "P'r'aps I is, but I's make a livin' up yer, I dun reckon; an' I likes ter be free man whar I's can go an' cum, an' nobody says not'ing."
>
> "But you would have been more comfortable on the old place: you would have had plenty to eat and plenty of clothes to wear."
>
> "Ye see, mass'r, de good Lo'd he know what's de best t'ing fur de brack, well as fur de w'ite; an' He say ter we dat we should cum up yer, an' I don't reckon He let we starve."

Not satisfied with the old man's explanation, the reporter discussed with other members of the family the comparative comfort and security afforded by the old plantation and the town. No matter how he phrased the question, their responses never varied: they had come to Macon to experience freedom. Near Milledgeville, the reporter encountered still more rural blacks, living in overcrowded cabins, trying to make a new life for themselves, and he asked the same question of them. Although conceding that they lived in "hard times," none of them regretted having left the countryside for the city. "Wa'l now ye see, sah," a father of seven children tried to explain, "das a Scriptur' what says if de man hab a little to eat, an' he eat with a 'tented mind, he be better off dan de man what hab de fat ox an' isn't 'tented."[36]

The size of the city or town to which many blacks flocked after emancipation mattered less than the freedom, the opportunities, the protection, and the camaraderie they expected to find there. "Nobody took our homes away, but right off colored folks started on the move," Felix Haywood recalled. "They seemed to want to get closer to freedom, so they'd know what it was—like it was a place or a city."[37] Even the smallest village had a certain attractive quality about it, particularly for the ex-slaves whose previous world had been restricted to the boundaries of the plantation. But most of the migrants to the towns appear to have come from the nearby plantations; some of them had been hired out before the war as slaves to city employers, they were largely familiar with the offerings of the city, and they knew from their own observations that some free blacks had fared comparatively well there.

Regardless of where they came from, or their degree of familiarity with urban life, the compulsions that had driven them to the nearest town or village varied but slightly. When Henry Bobbitt, who had spent his bondage in Warren County, North Carolina, walked all the way to Raleigh, he recalled the need "ter find out if I wuz really free." Jordon Smith, who had been sent from Georgia to Texas during the war, headed straight for Shreveport, Louisiana, because he knew Yankee soldiers were stationed there. Several freedmen who left Dinwiddie County, Virginia, were determined to reach Richmond, if only because it had to be better than what they had left behind them. "I thought I couldn't be no wus off than whar I was," one of them explained; "and I hadn't no place to go. You see, mahster, thar a'n't no chance fo' people o' my color in the country I come from." An Alabama planter, distraught over his losses, looked on helplessly as the blacks in his region headed for Selma "to be free" and "to embrace the *nigger lovers.*" Equally concerned, a former Confederate officer found the roads to Vicksburg clogged with blacks anxious "to get their freedom," and a Freedmen's Bureau officer in Coahoma County, Mississippi, encountered four field hands on the road who had little idea of what they would do when they reached the city but assumed that "once in Memphis and they are all right." He ordered them all to return to the plantation.[38]

The popular idea that "freedom was free-er" in the towns and that they could live "much easier" there helped to sustain the migrants, even as native whites, Federal officials, and northern reporters dismissed their assumptions as "absurd." The blacks clearly had reason to think otherwise. After describing the brutal treatment accorded freed slaves in Warren County, Georgia, the black newspaper in Augusta found it hardly surprising that so many freedmen would prefer to take their chances in the city rather than on the more remote and exposed plantations and farms. With violence and confusion rampant in some regions, the mere presence of a small detachment of Federal troops in the nearest town might turn it into a freedmen's refuge; they "seek the safe shelter of the cities," a traveler wrote from Charleston, "solely from the blind instinct that where there is force there must be protection." The nearest town also often housed the local Freedmen's Bureau office, to which blacks could bring their problems, settle conflicts over wages, and obtain some measure of relief in the form of government food rations. "Beaufort was their Mecca," an observer wrote of black refugees in the Sea Islands region, "and their shrine the office of the General Superintendent of Freedmen, who at this period worked eight days a week, besides Sundays."[39]

No doubt many blacks simply wanted the comfort of numbers, the chance to live with large groups of their own race away from the constant scrutiny of the master or overseer. Outside of the largest plantations, the city afforded freedmen expanded opportunities to think and act as part of a black community; moreover, they felt free to exercise their newly won liberties in ways that would invite trouble in the countryside. To be in the city gave them readier access to the black churches and the black benevolent societies; they could partake more freely of the growing interest in political questions, and, most important of all, they were able to send their children to the newly established freedmen's schools. In describing black life in postwar Macon, a northern reporter may have inadvertently hit upon precisely the combination of attractions that lured so many plantation freedmen to the city: four "prosperous" churches (one Methodist, one Presbyterian, and two Baptist); several benevolent societies (which contributed monthly support to the "parentless and indigent"); and five schools, four of which were taught by blacks. In addition, a Freedmen's Bureau officer willingly listened to their grievances.[40]

Whether they had worked for "kind" or "mean" masters, significant numbers of freed slaves resolved to abandon plantation labor altogether. Heading for the urban centers, they hoped to secure positions that afforded more pay, personal independence, and a welcome relief from the plantation routines. Those who had labored on the plantations as blacksmiths, millers, mechanics, carpenters, and wheelwrights hoped to capitalize on the same skills in the cities, where they would join black artisans who had long dominated several of the skilled urban occupations. Former house servants, on the other hand, tended to seek similar positions in the cities or worked as waiters, hackmen, and seamstresses, while field hands might become stevedores, porters, laundresses, or menial laborers.[41] In Richmond, blacks still comprised nearly half the work force of the Tredegar Iron Works, and the manager showed no inclination to reduce that proportion, despite the reluctance of newly imported white workers from Philadelphia to labor alongside blacks. "We dont want any men to come here who object to working with a colored man," the manager insisted. "We Southern men regard Negroes as an inferior race, but we make no distinction of color in employing men and pay all the same wages as all have to live."[42]

Although coming to the city hardly made any of the freedmen rich, and despite the many betrayed expectations, some nevertheless managed to achieve for themselves and their families a more meaningful and satisfying way of life than they would have enjoyed on the plantations. When Charles Crawley accompanied his family to Petersburg, two weeks after Lee's surrender, he left behind a master and mistress who "wus good to me as well as all us slaves," but the Crawleys were determined "to make a home fo' ourselves." After working "here an' dar, wid dis here man an' dat man," they purchased a home and remained there for the rest of their lives. As slaves, Mary Jane Wilson's parents were owned by different masters and hence lived separately; after the war, her father reunited the family in Portsmouth, Virginia, went to work in the Norfolk navy yard as a teamster, purchased a lot and built his own house. "He was one of the first Negro land owners in Portsmouth after emancipation," she proudly recalled. After attending the local school, Mary Jane Wilson graduated from Hampton Institute and then returned to Portsmouth as one of the first black teachers in that town. "I opened a school in my home, and I had lots of students. After two years my class grew so fast and large that my father built a school for me in our back yard.... Those were my happiest days."[43]

Frequently, success in the city consisted more of personal satisfaction than significant material gain. But the examples of blacks who achieved both goals encouraged still others to take their chances. Between 1860 and 1870, census statistics confirmed what the white South had already strongly suspected—a striking increase in the black urban population. In Mississippi, for example, the black population of Vicksburg, to which so many slaves had fled during the war, tripled while that of Natchez more than doubled; the four largest cities in Alabama—Mobile, Montgomery, Selma, and Huntsville—showed an increase of more than 57 percent in black residents; three of Virginia's principal cities—Richmond, Norfolk, and Lynchburg—now had nearly as many blacks as whites, and Petersburg found itself with a black majority; in Charleston, too, blacks moved into a majority position, while the black population of Memphis increased with a rapidity that made it a likely candidate for a race riot.[44] In the smaller towns and villages, comparable and more keenly felt increases in black residents took place. Even if the actual number of blacks moving into a town remained relatively small, it might be sufficient to change the character of the community. The Black Belt town of Demopolis, Alabama, where the slaves were observed in a "state of excitement and jubilee" after being told of their freedom, had but one black resident officially listed in 1860; within the next decade, however, nearly a thousand blacks settled in

Demopolis, perhaps in part because of the decision of the Freedmen's Bureau to locate a regional office there.[45]

If whites had exercised some perspective in viewing these increases, they might have been less alarmist in their reactions. Despite the number of new black urbanites, the overwhelming majority of black people remained in the rural areas. To have heard the whites talk, however, any observer might have thought that the fields were being literally emptied of laborers. "They all want to go to the cities, either Charleston or Augusta," Henry Ravenel complained. "The fields have no attractions." The very language employed by Freedmen's Bureau officials and native whites to describe the black migration to the cities suggested something akin to an invasion. The freed slaves were reported to be "crowding every road" in Alabama leading to the principal towns, and Montgomery had become "crowded, crammed, packed with multitudes of lazy, worthless negroes"; they were also sighted "flocking" to Savannah, Atlanta, and Houston; "an exodus" threatened to flood Albany, Georgia; Charleston had been "overrun" by blacks of "all sorts and conditions," while Mobile reeled under waves of immigrants. "Mobile is thronged to a fearful excess," a Freedmen's Bureau official reported, "their manner of living there is destructive to their morals and life. These noisome tenements are overcrowded with these miserable people."[46]

Even an insignificant number of black migrants aroused cries of inundation, partly out of the expectation that many more would follow. What they were viewing seemed clear enough to the white South: a once productive labor force, released from proper supervision, filled the cities and towns as vagrants, thieves, and indigents, threatening to place an intolerable burden on taxpayers and charitable services. "Before the war," a newspaper in Baton Rouge observed, "there were but six hundred Negroes in this place. Now there are as many thousand. . . . We have to support them, nurse them, and bury them." With increasing reports of petty crimes committed by the newcomers, the outrage mounted, and the ways in which blacks allegedly comported themselves in the cities fired the indignation in places like Memphis until it reached explosive dimensions.

> The streets [of Memphis] are filled with them, and at every corner are seen knots of them playing, idling, and sleeping in the sun. The shops are overflowing with them, squandering on themselves and each other what little money they have acquired in anything that strikes their fancy. On the outskirts of the city are small towns made up of rude and wretched hovels that have been collected during the war, built by the negroes themselves, in which a very considerable population live, and where disease and vice in their most loathsome and revolting characters abound.

That observation, in a leading Memphis newspaper, appeared less than two months before the violent riot that would claim forty-eight lives.[47]

Not only were these country invaders said to be rude and impertinent, but their penchant for ostentatious display affronted a people long accustomed to monopolizing such behavior.

> You will see faces black as ebony arrayed in silks & satins, of all the colors of the rainbow, with little white chip hats streaming with ribbons of all colors perched on their heads, & their faces covered with blue & brown veils, (to prevent their black faces, I suppose, from being bleached)—in fact Ring St. is crowded with them all day, it is their great promenade.

Still worse, blacks allegedly adopted a "manner of living" in the cities that would inevitably lead to the moral degeneration of both races. "For a plantation girl to go to Beaufort and stay six months," a northern lessee wrote in September 1865, "is almost sure ruin," and the whites, he added, were not without blame. "If you hear a man cursing the race as a lying, thieving, licentious race, you may be almost sure that he is paying money to a black woman." It seemed to him, in fact, that at least half of Beaufort, Yankee officers and native whites alike, were "corrupt with this infernal lust for black women." With the infusion of country blacks, city dwellers also complained of noisy nights and entire neighborhoods kept awake by drunken frolics and "orgies." "Truly freedom down in the low country has passed from the Southerner to the negro," a South Carolina woman confided to her diary, "and our beloved city has become Pandemonium."[48]

Whether in Chicago and New York in the next century or in southern cities in the post-Civil War years, black residents of long standing tended to give the new arrivals a mixed reception, even sharing at times with the whites a disdain for the rustic manners, crude life styles, and shabby attire of the newcomers. To a white observer in Charleston, for example, it seemed as if the older black residents found the newly freed slaves a source of embarrassment.

> The really respectable class of free negroes, whom we used to employ as tailors, boot makers, mantua makers, etc. wont associate at all with the "parvenue free" ... They are exceedingly respectful to the Charleston gentlemen they meet—taking their hats off and expressing their pleasure at seeing them again, but regret that it is under such circumstances, enquiring about others, etc.

Nor did the older black residents necessarily welcome the prospect of competing with the migrants for the available jobs, and some would recall with bitterness how the new arrivals had subsisted on the government's bounty during and immediately after the war.

> The slaves that was freed, and the country Negroes that had been run off, or had run away from the plantations, was staying in Augusta in Guv'ment houses, great big ole barns. They would all get free provisions

from the Freedmen's Bureau, but people like us, Augusta citizens, didn't get free provisions, we had to work. It spoiled some of them.[49]

To many apprehensive whites, the city had always undermined the manners and discipline of rural black folk. The way in which a South Carolina planter described the "defection" of one of his servants after the war typified this attitude: "Bob is somewhere about the City [Charleston], going to ruin." Since at least the 1850s, if not earlier, city officials had tried to restrict the movement and activities of urban blacks, encouraging and in some instances virtually forcing slave owners to move their city slaves back to the plantations, where they could be more easily controlled. The city, these whites had insisted, bred only discontent and independence, and that was the stuff of which insurrections were made. With equal alarm, whites responded to the postwar movement of freed slaves into the urban centers and resolved to check it. "At one time," Elias Horry Deas of Charleston informed his daughter, "I was opposed to the expelling of *all* Negroes from the City but now that I know them, I am fully for doing so except those that may be personally attending on you. A negro . . . has not as much gratitude about him as many of the inferior animals." With that observation, he not only caught the urgency of the problem but the spirit in which native whites and Federal officers sought to overcome it.[50]

6

_____

ALTHOUGH SOMETIMES MOTIVATED by different considerations, Federal authorities and native whites often worked in close harmony to curb black movement into the cities and to force the freed slaves back onto the plantations. Few northern whites espoused the cause of the ex-slave more forcefully than Clinton B. Fisk, a Freedmen's Bureau officer who commanded the respect of most blacks. And when he admonished them to remain on the plantations, few doubted that he thought this the best way for them eventually to realize their aspirations. In the congested cities, Fisk warned, "you will wear your lives away in a constant struggle to pay high rent for miserable dwellings and scanty allowances of food. Many of your children, I greatly fear, will be found wandering through the streets as vagrants— plunging into the worst of vices, and filling the workhouses and jails."[51]

Invoking almost the same images, black leaders, newspapers, and conventions repeated the same advice and affirmed the agrarian mystique to which most Americans—white and black—still adhered. "He that tilleth the land shall have plenty of bread," declared the black newspaper in Augusta, Georgia, and others played on that same theme. The freed slaves who came to the cities exposed themselves to "high rents," "exorbitant prices," and unemployment, whereas in the country they "can always make a living," perhaps even save enough to purchase at some future date

their own farms. "You have no trade adapted to city life," one black editor
advised the freedmen. That being the case, he warned, they would be
compelled to find alternatives to legitimate occupations if they persisted in
settling in urban centers.

> Many who flock to these large cities are very apt to partake of all the vices
> prevalent, such as rum drinking, playing cards, picking pockets, and
> knocking men down with bludgeons for the sake of a little recreation. . . .
> What little money you may have will soon be squandered in loathsome
> rumshops, generally kept by those who are negro-haters, although they
> profess to be "frinds" while your money lasts. . . . If you carry on in this
> way, you will soon become strolling vagabonds, and honest men will shun
> you.

Few agrarian leaders set forth as cogently the evils that lurked in the city.
In addressing the recently freed blacks of Maryland, Frederick Douglass,
who had himself drifted toward the city as a fugitive slave, tried to disabuse
their minds of the notion that urban living and freedom were somehow
inseparable. "I believe $150 in the country is better than $400 in the city,"
he insisted. Since fewer temptations existed in the country to lead them
astray, they would live more economically, accumulate their savings, and
become landowners. "If the colored people of Maryland flock to Baltimore,
crowding the alleys and by-streets, woe betide them! Sad, indeed, will be
their fate! They must stick to the country, and work." Whoever they listened to, whites or blacks, the freedmen might have heard those words
repeated in various forms.[52]

To make certain that the ex-slaves heeded this advice, city authorities
moved to restrict, harass, and expel them, not always bothering to distinguish between the older black residents and the newcomers or even between the gainfully employed and the "vagrants." In Richmond, the
post-emancipation "jubilee" had hardly ended before black residents complained of treatment "worse than ever we suffered before," including daily
mounted patrols reminiscent of the much-dreaded patrollers and the revival of the old pass system.

> We are required to get some white person to give us passes to attend to
> our daily occupations, without which we are marched off to the Old Rebel
> Hospital, now called the negro bull pen. . . . We saw women looking for
> their husbands, children for parents, but to no purpose—for they were in
> the bull pen. . . . All that is needed to restore Slavery in full is the auction-
> block as it used to be.

The white residents of Richmond, another black protested, still clung to
and acted by the old motto: "Hickory stick growing in the ground, if you
aint got one cent keep the nigger down." Despite personal appeals to President Johnson, including a delegation of Richmond blacks, little was done
to resolve their grievances; by August 1865, local blacks met again, this

time to protest a series of outrages, involving not only the white citizenry and police but Union soldiers—"those individuals whom we all regarded as our friends, and hailed as our deliverers."[53]

If freedmen came to the cities because of the reassuring presence of Union troops and a Freedmen's Bureau office, and some apparently did, they might be bitterly disappointed over the quality of their reception and treatment. Not only did Federal authorities afford them minimal protection or none at all but Union commanders were most likely to greet the new arrivals by advising them to return to work for their former masters, who knew them best and would thus be more sympathetic to their problems. The slaves who had fled during the war to places like New Orleans and Natchez had already seen such advice translated into orders and vigorously enforced. Consistent with wartime policies, Federal officials were as eager as the planters themselves to return the freed slaves to plantation labor and they willingly supplied the necessary force to implement such decisions. Scarcely a day passed without complaints by urban blacks of mistreatment, arbitrary arrests, the suspension of food rations, robbery, and outright brutality at the hands of occupation troops. "It appears that all the jail birds of New York, and the inmates of Moyamensing had been left in this State to guard the freedmen's interest," a black correspondent wrote from South Carolina in July 1866. "No Southern white man in Charleston, has heaped as much insult upon colored females passing the streets, as those foul-throated scamps who guard this city."[54]

The vigor with which Union officers acted to restrain urban blacks won some grudging admiration from local whites. When the Union commander in Galveston ordered freedmen with neither a "home" nor a "master" to be put to work on the streets, a Houston newspaper was both relieved and grateful that the blacks had been brought "to common sense in a summary manner." Nor were Galveston's mayor and city council displeased when the Union commander suggested that they adopt an ordinance punishing "all hired servants" who left their employers before the expiration of their contracts. But for the recently freed slaves, the actions of the Union Army deepened their disillusionment and frustrations. "It is not the Southerners we dread but the Federal soldiers," a group of blacks in Mobile, Alabama, declared as they petitioned the Freedmen's Bureau for help. Not long after the war had ended, Henry McNeal Turner, while still a chaplain in a black regiment, insisted that white troops were unfit to garrison the South. Not one in twenty, he thought, would treat the freedmen with any justice or respect; many soldiers, in fact, cursed, threatened, and whipped blacks "to gratify some 'secesh belle,' or to keep the good will of some Southerner who can keep a sumptuous table. I have been told, over and over, by colored persons, that they were never treated more cruelly, than they were by some of the white Yankees."[55]

Whether undertaken by Federal authorities or by native whites, the efforts to control urban blacks and to forestall the urbanization of blacks began to assume a familiar pattern throughout the South. In Mobile, the mayor instructed the police to arrest "vagrants" and warned freedmen either to find employment, leave the city, or be forced to work on the streets. "If the white class was treated in the like manner," a black resident observed, "I would not complain." If black "vagrants" were not fined and sent to the workhouse (as in Nashville and New Orleans), they were put to work on the streets to pay for their room and board at the jail (as in San Antonio and Montgomery) or simply compelled to return to their previous owners (as in Lexington, Kentucky).[56] Rather than enforce the vagrancy laws against freedmen, numerous communities (such as New Orleans and Savannah), often with the full support of military authorities, preferred to revive the old curfew and pass regulations, resorting at times to mass arrests of blacks found on the city streets after a certain hour without the permission of their employers. Faced with the possibility of overcrowded jails, city authorities happily complied with the offers of local residents and planters to pay the fines of the blacks in exchange for their employment as virtual indentured servants.[57]

If enforcement of vagrancy and curfew laws proved insufficient to deal with the problem, or if Federal officials were unwilling to approve such laws, urban whites relied on more ingenious and imaginative solutions to check the number of black residents in their midst. Imposing heavy license fees and taxes on the occupations which freedmen were most likely to enter might produce the desired results and also suggested that whites were less concerned about "vagrancy" than about ex-slaves working in non-agricultural pursuits. Without the need for any special laws, community pressure was often sufficient to deny jobs and housing to incoming blacks; any whites who defied those pressures were apt to find themselves homeless—the victims of organized arsonists. In New Orleans, insurance companies considered withdrawing coverage from all dwellings in which blacks resided, on the pretext that colored people were "inflammable matter." In reporting this threat, the local black newspaper urged black citizens to form their own insurance companies.[58]

To break up the urban black settlements, like the shanty villages appearing on the edges of numerous towns, local authorities might simply order their demolition. To justify such arbitrary actions, they would cite the outbreak of disease among malnourished and ill-clad freedmen and the need to protect the health of the community. That was the only excuse officials in Meridian, Mississippi, needed before they broke up the freedmen's camps, burned down the makeshift dwellings, and drove the inhabitants from the town. To protect the townspeople of Selma, Alabama, allegedly from a smallpox epidemic, city officials barred any freedmen who did not have the written approval of an employer. Why an employer's consent would have made the community less susceptible to disease was not explained.[59]

No doubt some communities simply took their cue from the Union Army's wartime experiment in preventive medicine in Natchez. To protect both the Union troops and the city's residents, A. W. Kelly, an army surgeon and the chief health officer, thought it essential to remove any possible sources of "pestilential diseases," and there was no question in his mind about where to look—in precisely the same places nearby planters were looking for needed laborers.

> Large numbers of *idle* negroes ... now throng the streets, lanes and alleys, and over-crowd every hovel. *Lazy* and *profligate,* unused to caring for themselves; thriftless for the present, and recklessly improvident of the future, the most of them loaf idly about the streets and alleys, prowling in secret places, and lounge lazily in crowded hovels, which soon become dens of noisome filth, the hot beds, fit to engender and rapidly disseminate the most *loathsome* and *malignant* diseases.

No "contraband" would be permitted to remain in Natchez unless employed by a "*responsible white person* in some legitimate business" and unless he or she lived with the employer. Clearly, then, household servants and virtually no one else would be exempt, even if that meant arbitrarily separating families. The first roundup, in fact, took place appropriately enough at the freedmen's school, with the children herded off to a nearby contraband camp. Although they were subsequently returned, the potential of the order had been clearly revealed. Not only did the action alarm the black residents of Natchez but it infuriated the black soldiers stationed nearby, many of whom had wives and children in the city. "I heard colored soldiers yesterday in their madness swear desperately that they would have revenge," a white missionary reported. "*And they will.* I tremble as do so many of the officers in the colored regiments, when I witness such expressions & conduct of the soldiers." Perhaps only the threatened mutiny of these black troops prompted a modification of the order and the dismissal of both the health officer and the Union commander who had supported him. More than a year later, however, in June 1865, a black correspondent in Natchez described a deplorable state of affairs which suggested how much local authorities had learned from their Yankee conquerors.

> A rebel doctor is appointed on the Health Board. The consequence is, on the pretext of generating the yellow disease among them, (which is not an epidemic with colored people,) the colored people are forcibly carried out of the town. Many are taken from their employment, and their humble, though comfortable houses, built by their own industry, are torn down before their tearful eyes, and they are huddled into a swamp or plain, some distance from town, without employment, to starve, or return to their rebel master.

And this time, no black soldiers were in the vicinity to check such activities.[60]

Although some of the older black residents liked to think of themselves as different from the new arrivals from the countryside, they quickly discovered that the restrictions, harassment, and violence were directed against the entire black community. Enforcement of the vagrancy laws revealed an all too familiar double standard. If a white man was out of work, as many were in 1865, that was simply unemployment, but if a black man had no job, that was vagrancy. If a planter refused to till the fields himself, that was understandable, but if a former slave declined to work for him, that was idleness if not insolence. Having perceived the rationale that guided the actions of white authorities, a black editor angrily denounced the arrest of black "vagrants" in Mobile. The laziest class in society, he charged, had to be the planters themselves. "They are lazy enough not to work themselves; but they want to live as parasites on the proceeds of other people's labor. This time is past; *inde irae.* Laziness, gentlemen, is on your side. We want to work, but not for you; we want to work freely and voluntarily—for ourselves." Nevertheless, the arrest of "vagrants" persisted, cheered on by groups of unemployed whites loitering nearby.[61]

Under circumstances that were difficult and often perilous, urban blacks tried to develop some community strength and response. In Tuscaloosa, Alabama, black residents met to protest illegal house searches and legislation that would deny them the right to rent either land or houses within the town limits. In petitioning the Freedmen's Bureau for help, they simply noted that "this is not the pursuit of happiness, therefore We hope you will help us out." After enduring a series of "abuses," including the arrest of blacks coming into town to make some purchases, Vicksburg freedmen held a public meeting in which they protested police harassment and "disgraceful proceedings" in the civil courts. In the smaller towns, often removed from any Federal "protection," the complaints sounded far more desperate. From Tuscumbia, Alabama, Jim Leigh and forty-seven other black residents voiced their disappointment over the limited amount of freedom they were permitted to enjoy. Local stores would sell them nothing ("We get a White man to get it for us"), and although some of them paid taxes like the white residents, they were still unable to get a school for their children. Nor could they purchase liquor without an order from a white man, or establish an independent business, such as a grocery. They could not even act in their own self-defense. "If a White Man Strik you With a Rock you are not Lowed to Look mad at him." What was left but for them to appeal to the Freedmen's Bureau, the agency which had been established, they had heard, to look after their interests. "Send us Sum help. We want Justice. We Want Justice. Gennel you can Send us one Company if you please. We are treted here like dogs."[62]

Whatever their expectations in coming to the cities, many of the migrants discovered that their new freedom counted for far less than they had imagined. Former field hands were forced to eke out an existence in the most menial jobs, at least those they could wrest from the former residents who had been practicing them. To a black woman in Atlanta, for example, a mother of six children, whose husband had died "fighting for de Yankees," survival depended essentially on how much wash she could take in each day. "Sometimes I gits along tolerable," she sighed; "sometimes right slim; but dat's de way wid everybody;—times is powerful hard right now." Even the plantation artisans and mechanics who had come to the cities with higher expectations found, along with the older residents, declining opportunities to practice those skills. With emancipation, whites began to challenge the virtual monopoly which blacks had enjoyed in various urban occupations, not only in the skilled trades but in the menial jobs once considered beneath the dignity of whites. Of course, if those jobs could be reserved for whites, that would lend them sufficient dignity. In Petersburg, Virginia, the local newspaper perceived significant changes in urban labor as early as August 1865:

> Formerly a white drayman or cartman or hack-driver was a sight unknown to our streets, now they share these employments with the blacks, and eventually will monopolize them. . . . Formerly, most, if not all, of our bars were tended by colored men, though owned by whites; now, the cobblers and juleps are mixed, as well as the rent paid, and the stock kept up by white men in many instances. Formerly, the restaurants of Petersburgh were almost exclusively in the hands of the colored people; now, we believe, there is but one establishment of the sort in the city. Formerly, we had only colored barbers; now, the native whites seek, generally, barbers of their own color, and eventually, they will do so exclusively.[63]

The black families which migrated to the cities and decided to remain were apt to discover that the struggle for survival deprived them of some of the advantages that had initially attracted them there. After the war, Jennylin Dunn recalled, her parents moved into the nearest city—Raleigh, North Carolina. Although they managed fairly well in their new environment, Jennylin Dunn never realized her ambition to attend any of the schools the Yankees had established for the freed slaves. The reason she cited told the story of countless others. "Most o' us wuz so busy scramblin' roun' makin' a livin' dat we ain't got no time fer no schools."[64]

7

---

DESPITE THE ALARM over inundation of the towns and cities, the ex-slaves who moved immediately after emancipation generally confined themselves to the countryside and traveled only a short distance.[65] No matter how close they stayed to the old place, however, the farmers and planters who had lost them as laborers were as distressed as if they had moved to the nearest town. To check such interplantation movement, some former slave-holders, as in Lowndes County, Alabama, agreed among themselves not to hire any freedman within ten miles of his former home. But to implement that decision, the labor supply would have to be plentiful and the planters would have to remain unified, and such situations were uncommon, especially in the immediate aftermath of the war.[66]

Within several months after the end of the war, the first wave of post-emancipation migration subsided, most of the migrants having resettled in areas with which they were familiar. H. R. Brinkerhoff, a Union officer stationed near Clinton, Mississippi, initially accepted the prevailing view that freed slaves from all parts of the countryside were converging on the towns and cities. After further observation, however, he realized that he had exaggerated both the numbers of blacks involved and the extent of their movements. The migrants who came to the cities, he concluded in July 1865, comprised "a very small part of the whole," and almost all of these had previously worked on plantations nearby. By the end of 1865, the chief of the Freedmen's Bureau in Alabama claimed to have "no further fear of the wandering propensities of the negro"; the end of slavery, he reported, had been "naturally followed by a jubilee; but that is over now." Actually, his optimism proved to be unjustified. Once the 1865 crops were completed and new contracts had to be negotiated, many freedmen who had stayed on the plantations after emancipation chose this moment to move elsewhere, not so much to seek their fortunes in the cities as to improve their prospects on another place. But movement in itself, as many of them discovered, only assured them of different faces directing their labor rather than significant changes in the labor itself or in the rewards they reaped from it. "It wus like dis," a former North Carolina slave explained, "a crowd of tenants would get dissatisfied on a certain plantation, dey would move, an' another gang of niggers move in. Dat wus all any of us could do. We wus free but we had nothin' 'cept what de marsters give us."[67]

If any "new" migrants headed for the cities in late 1865, they most likely encountered many of their people on the roads going in the other direction—back to the old places. Mounting pressure from Federal authorities to contract with an employer or be arrested as vagrants, the hostile reception they had received in the urban centers, and the declining hope for any kind of land distribution had forced many ex-slaves to reassess their lives, recognize the limitations of their freedom, and face up to the urgent need to survive. Near Mobile, Alabama, 900 freedmen held a mass meeting to voice their disappointment over the government's failure to provide for them and voted 700 to 200 to return to their former masters. The stories of disillusioned migrants soon assumed a familiar pattern. After spending one year in a nearby town, Jacob and Lucy Utley decided they had had enough. Cramped conditions in a rat-infested dwelling and a steady diet of hardtack and pickled meat finally persuaded them to return to the old plantation. With equal dismay, John Petty, a former slave in Spartanburg County, South Carolina, was forced to reexamine the decision he had made. The one slave who chose to leave the plantation immediately after the war had returned with a glowing picture of opportunities for young blacks in the cities. "Up in Winston," he had reported, "all the niggers make five dollars a day; how come you don't go up there and git rich like I is." The other blacks had laughed at his story, refusing to believe any portion of it. But young Petty—eighteen years old at the time of emancipation—waited for the crop to be completed and then informed his old master that he intended to leave for the "north" to make his fortune. He promised the others that he would return and bring them "something." But Winston proved to be less of a Promised Land than he had expected.

> It was that hard, a-cleaning and a-washing all the time. 'Cause I never knowed nothing 'bout no 'baccy and there wasn't nothing that I could turn off real quick that would bring me no big money. It got cold and I never had no big oak logs to burn in my fireplace and I set and shivered till I lay down. Then it wasn't no kivver like I had at Marse Jim's. Up there they never had 'nough wood to keep no fire all night. Next thing I knowed I was down with the grippe and it took all the money dat I had and then I borrowed some to pay the doctor.

He returned to the plantation, empty-handed, thinking himself "a fool" for ever having left. "I ax where that nigger what 'ticed me off to the north and they all 'low that he done took the consumption and died soon after I done gone from home. I never had no consumption, but it took me long time to git over the grippe. I goes to old Marse and hires myself out and I never left him no more till the Lawd took him away."[68]

Like John Petty, many of the migrants drifted back to the old places, their dreams and expectations of a different way of life having yielded them only frustration and a sense of betrayal. To return to the familiar surroundings often became a matter of survival rather than homesickness or attachment to "old Marse." "The Freedmen's Bureau helped us some," Squire Dowd recalled, "but we finally had to go back to the plantation in order to live." Along the wharves in Charleston, a northern visitor encountered some 1,500 freedmen waiting for transportation back to their old homes, some of them also resigned to resuming the old way of life, others hopeful they might attain something better. "We wants to git away to work on our own hook," one of them explained. "It's not a good time at all here. We does nothing but suffer from smoke and ketch cold. We wants to begin de planting business." An elderly black woman, who had been waiting here for more than two weeks, poured out her feelings of frustration and concluded with a dim view of her future prospects. "De jew and de air hackles we more 'n anyting. De rain beats on we, and de sun shines we out. My chil'n so hungry dey can't hole up. De Gov'ment, he han't gib we nottin'. . . . Some libs and some dies. If dey libs dey libs, and if dey dies dey dies."[69]

The sight of former slaves returning, many of them thoroughly disillusioned with "freedom" and Yankee promises, no doubt pleased and reassured planter families. That some of their former slaves should have traveled a great distance to be back on the old place impressed the daughter of a Georgia planter as "a fact that speaks louder than words as to their feeling for their old master and former treatment." The talk in the Chesnut family was of the plight of "poor Old Myrtilia," who had left with the Yankees and now wrote "the most pathetic letters" asking to be returned. When no one in the Chesnut family offered to help her, she managed to get back on her own. That impressed Mary Chesnut, who concluded that Myrtilia, like so many ex-slaves after the "first natural frenzy of freedom," had simply discovered "on which side her bread was buttered" and "where her real friends were." With similar confidence, former slaveholders looked upon the return of blacks as a step closer to a resumption of the old relationships that had characterized bondage. "My own negro boy, whom I have owned since infancy," a Virginia physician testified, "has returned to me. . . . He has returned to his old status. The feeling between the negroes and their former masters seems to be perfectly kind; I see the negroes working as usual."[70]

That confidence rested in some instances on the satisfaction evinced by their former slaves in returning to the old places and positions. If some still harbored feelings of bitterness and disappointment over their fate, they seemed to appreciate the greater measure of security they now enjoyed and the chance to renew old friendships among those with whom they had shared bondage. Not long after the war, Mary Anderson recalled, her former master and mistress went out in a carriage to relocate their former slaves. With apparent ease, they persuaded many of them to return, and it seemed as if little had changed, with the blacks still addressing the whites as "master" and "missus" and resuming their usual tasks and demeanor. "My father and mother, two uncles and their families moved back," Mary Anderson remembered. "Also Lorenza Brodie, and John Brodie and their families moved back. Several of the young men and women who once belonged to him came back. Some were so glad to get back they cried, 'cause fare had been mighty bad part of the time they were rambling around and they were hungry."[71]

Not every planter welcomed back the freedmen who had left him. If their departure had been interpreted as betrayal or ingratitude, the former owners might not wish to see them again; some eagerly anticipated their ex-slaves begging to return and prepared to turn them off, while still others expressed a willingness to hire them but would not entrust them with positions of responsibility. "They'll all be idle before winter," predicted a South Carolina "gentleman," who had apparently lost the bulk of his slave force. "I don't look for nothing else when cold weather comes but to have them all asking me to take them back; but I sha'n't do it. I wouldn't give ten cents apiece for them." Even if dispossessed planters shared similar feelings about hiring back their former slaves, most of them could ill afford such thoughts in regions where labor was scarce. Not only did planters seek out the blacks who had left them after emancipation but a few went so far as to try to lure back some able slave who had fled before or during the war.

If former slaveholders found this a disagreeable and even demeaning task, many of the freedmen they sought were no less chagrined by the thought of working on the old places again. No matter how enticing the offer or how desperate their own situation had become, they might choose to cling stubbornly to whatever degree of separation from the old way of life they had managed to attain. With emancipation, Archie Millner's father, who had been a slave in Virginia, took his family, crossed the county line, and fixed up a shanty for them on the edge of the woods. His former master, who became "hard fixed fo' someone to work fo' him," located the Millner family and pleaded with them to return to the plantation, even offering them the overseer's house. "Pa listened to him through but shook his head. 'Reckon I better stay here,' said pa. Ole man Brown say, 'All right, John, I see how you feel 'bout it. But it's all right; I kin make out somehow, an' if you ever need anything come on over to de place an' git it.' But pa never would go back."[72]

Where the ties between the "white folks" and the slaves had been fairly close, some of the freedmen returned to the old places but with no intention of staying. That is, they might choose to pay a social visit, perhaps to let their former master and mistress know how they were faring in freedom or to see their old friends who had remained after emancipation. Several years after leaving her mistress, Mandy Hadnot, a former Texas slave, still thought of her often "all 'lone in de big house" and finally resolved to see her again. "I go to see her and took a peach pie, 'cause I lub her and I know dat's what she like better'n anything." The two women said the Lord's Prayer together, as they had often done before, and parted knowing they would never see each other again. At times, the situation would be reversed, with former masters and mistresses calling on their former slaves. Many years after emancipation, Jim Leathers, a North Carolina planter, decided to visit his old hands, most of whom were concentrated in Dix Hill, near Raleigh. "We had a big supper in his honor," John Coggin recalled. Few of them could have imagined how this memorable reunion would end. "Dat night he died, an' 'fore he died his min' sorta wanders an' he thinks dat hit am back in de slave days an' dat atter a long journey he am comin' back home. Hit shore wuz pitiful an' we shore did hate it."[73]

If the return of former slaves, whether to stay or to pay a friendly visit, suggested the durability of the "old ties," planter families found even more compelling evidence in the number of blacks who had not moved at all but continued with their usual tasks in the usual way, seemingly oblivious to their freedom and the world outside the plantation. Not all the freed slaves who chose to remain, however, would have shared that view of their decision. Whatever the degree of their commitment to the old ties, many of them perceived all too accurately what lay beyond the boundaries of the plantation and opted for the relative security of the old place, at least until they ascertained how compatible this might be with the exercise of their newly won freedom.

AFTER THE SHOUTING and singing had ended, a former Mississippi field hand recalled of emancipation, "we got to wonderin' 'bout what good it did us. It didn' feel no diffrunt; we all loved our marster an' missus an' stayed on wid 'em jes' lak nothin' had happened." The same story was related on numerous farms and plantations in the post-emancipation South. Not only did many freed slaves remain on the same place but they said "marse" and "missus" to the same white folks, worked under the same overseer and driver, lived in the same quarters, performed the same tasks, and suffered the same punishments for the same offenses. After agreeing to remain with his former master for forty cents a day, James Green, a twenty-five-year-old Texas field hand who had been sold from his Virginia home some thirteen years before, perceived "no big change" on the plantation. "De same houses and some got whipped but nobody got nailed to a tree by de ears, like dey used to." But to Levi Pollard, a former Virginia slave, who also remained on the same place, the few changes he did discern made a significant difference. "Us live in de same fine house en do the same kinda work, but us git real money fer hit, a hundred dollars a year. Den, us wuz us own boss, en could [come] en go like us any white, jus' so's us put in time dat us wuz paid fa. En on top er dat, us could have crops, en a garden 'round de house."[74]

Whether to justify the confidence placed in them or from considerations of age, infirmity, or self-interest, some freedmen never seem to have entertained the thought of leaving the farms and plantations on which they had labored as slaves. In their minds, as in their day-to-day lives, the terms "our white folks" and "our home" had become synonymous, and they saw no reason to alter a relationship and situation they deemed favorable to their own best interests. "We was just one fam'ly an' had all we needed," explained John Evans, a former North Carolina slave. "We never paid no 'tention to freedom or not freedom." The recollections of former slaves who remained on the same places after emancipation repeated the same themes. This was their home, "these were our folks," this was the only kind of life they had known, their relatives and friends were here, and to abandon the known and the familiar for uncertainty and danger seemed both foolish and irresponsible. The day of emancipation, Ed McCree remembered, was "a happy day" on the plantation, but he remained there with his parents for more than a year and thought he understood the reason. "If us had left, it would have been jus' lak swappin' places from de fryin' pan to de fire, 'cause Niggers didn't have no money to buy no land wid for a long time atter de war."[75]

For some freed slaves, however, to remain on the same plantations was neither an easy nor a popular decision. Not only might they find themselves isolated from their fellow blacks who had left but they could be subjected to criticism and harassment if the departure of the others had been designed to protest the cruelty of the master or to press him into more favorable contractual terms. Her decision to remain with the same master, Adeline Blakely recalled, placed her in "a wrong attitude" with local blacks, most of whom had not shared her "happy" days in the Big House. "I was pointed out as different. Sometimes I was threatened for not leaving." But she endured the name-calling and harassment to stay with the white folks she thought of as "my people." If remaining with a former owner subjected some ex-slaves to the hostility of their fellow blacks, the decision to leave, as many freedmen discovered, exposed them to the violence of hostile whites. In choosing to stay on the same place, black families expected from their former master the same protection from gangs of roving whites that he had provided them from the patrollers. Her old master had little money after emancipation, Virginia Bell recalled, and "things was mighty hard for a while," but those who stayed with him "wasn' as bad off as some, 'cause white folks knew we was Massa Lewis' folks and didn' bother us none."[76]

Not all the freedmen who remained with their previous owners felt the same degree of attachment or sense of obligation. But no matter how they viewed the old ties, they were all likely to agree on the absence of realistic alternatives. After assessing their chances elsewhere, even some of the more independent-minded freed slaves might opt for certainties and survival. To dwell too long on other possibilities seemed like an exercise in futility. "Us had no education, no land, no mule, no cow, not a pig, nor a chicken, to set up house keeping," Violet Guntharpe recalled. "De birds had nests in de air, de foxes had holes in de ground, and de fishes had beds under de great falls, but us colored folks was left widout any place to lay our heads."[77] The decision to stay on the same plantation was never an accurate measure of fidelity nor did it necessarily stem from ignorance or an innate docility. But it could serve as a reliable measurement of disillusionment with "freedom."

> De slaves, where I lived, knowed after de war dat they had abundance of dat somethin' called freedom, what they could not eat, wear, and sleep in. Yes, sir, they soon found out dat freedom ain't nothin', 'less you is got somethin' to live on and a place to call home. Dis livin' on liberty is lak young folks livin' on love after they gits married. It just don't work. No, sir, it las' so long and not a bit longer. Don't tell me! It sho' don't hold good when you has to work, or when you gits hongry.

Some years after the death of his master, this former slave finally achieved his ambition of farming on his own—and that made all the difference. "If a poor man wants to enjoy a little freedom, let him go on de farm and work for hisself. It is sho' worth somethin' to be boss, and on de farm you can be boss all you want to."[78]

Although postwar hardships in the South affected both races, blacks were sufficiently realistic to recognize that the brunt of the suffering would be borne by those without any land or means of support. Jane Johnson, a former South Carolina slave, voiced the sentiments of thousands of freedmen and freedwomen when she recalled the "hard times" after the war as "de worse kind of slavery."[79] If nothing else, then, the old plantation still symbolized for some ex-slaves a minimal but fairly reliable source of daily sustenance, and that kind of security could easily outweigh other considerations. Regardless of the harshness or benevolence of the former master, if he appeared to be reasonably solvent and provided his blacks with their immediate needs, that might be reason enough to stay with him, at least for a time. Cecelia Chappel, a former Tennessee slave, had little reason to feel any affection for her master and mistress (they had whipped her often and she still had the scars to prove it), but she remained with them for a number of years after emancipation. Despite their uneven temperament, she would recall, "I allus had good clothes en good food en I didn' know how I'd git dem atter I lef'." Nor did Daniel Lucas, who had worked for a reputedly harsh master and overseer, choose to join the other slaves on the plantation who quickly scattered after emancipation. "He pays me ten dollars every month, gives me board and my sleeping place just like always, and when I gets sick there he is with the herb medicine for my ailment and I is well again." Like many former slaves who stayed, he finally left the plantation only when he married.[80]

What the freedmen saw and heard of those who left immediately after emancipation tended to reinforce the decision many had made to stay where they were. The stragglers who came begging for food, the sight of wagons loaded with the coffins of cholera and smallpox victims, the reports of new murders and drownings, and the stories of migrants subsisting on cornmeal mush, salt water, and pickled horsemeat, using the marrow from discarded bones to season their greens, served as daily reminders of the perils and uncertainty that lay down the road. "What I care 'bout freedom?" asked Charlie Davenport, as he reminisced about the Mississippi plantation where he remained after the war, even though his father had run off with the Yankees. "Folks what was free was in misery firs' one way an' den de other." Like many slaves on the plantation, he had responded with enthusiasm at the first news of freedom.

> I was right smart bit by de freedom bug for awhile. It sounded pow'ful nice to be tol': "You don't have to chop cotton no more. You can th'ow dat hoe down an' go fishin' whensoever de notion strikes you. An' you can roam 'roun' at night an' court gals jus' as you please. Aint no marster gwine a-say to you, 'Charlie, you's got to be back when de clock strikes nine.' " I was fool 'nough to b'lieve all dat kin' o' stuff.

But he quickly revised his expectations about freedom, and the example of those who had gone elsewhere influenced his thinking. "Dem what lef' de old plantation seemed so all fired glad to git back dat I made up my min' to stay put. I stayed right wid my white folks as long as I could." Besides, he recalled with pride, his master would have been helpless without him.[81]

The ironic twists of these years exceeded the most vivid of imaginations. The same class that took such pride in how it looked after old and decrepit slaves would now behold the spectacle of former slaves caring for and refusing to abandon old and decrepit whites who had only recently been their masters and mistresses. Even as white families wrestled with the problem of what to do about their aged blacks after emancipation, many freed slaves were torn between their desire to make a new start and the obligations they still felt toward masters and mistresses unable to look after themselves. "Marster was too old to wuk when dey sot us free," Nicey Kinney recalled, "so for a long time us jus' stayed dar and run his place for him." Similarly, Charlie Davenport, upon learning of his freedom, appreciated the dependency of the "white folks" on his labor. "When I looked at my marster an' knowed he needed me, I pleased to stay." Where the master had been killed in the war, leaving his wife in charge of the plantation, many freed slaves thought it would be heartless and a betrayal of mutual trust to abandon her at this critical time. "Mist'ess, she jus' cried and cried," Elisha Doc Garey recalled of the death of his master. "She didn't want us to leave her, so us stayed on wid her a long time."[82] Even if the necessary compassion for a widowed proprietress might be lacking, some freedmen sensed that they were in an advantageous bargaining position and decided to stay, at least until they saw how the new arrangement worked out.

Not only did many freed slaves remain to help their "white folks" through the first difficult postwar years but some apparently felt that only the death of their old master and mistress could truly break the relationship. Typical in this respect was Simon Walker, one of the more than one hundred slaves belonging to Hugh Walker, an Alabama planter. The war brought hard times to the plantation; the Yankees pillaged the place thoroughly and the master's son returned from military service with only one leg. On the day Walker freed his slaves, he asked those willing to remain to raise their hands, and nearly all of them did so. "Mos' all de hans stayed on de plantation 'tell de Cun'l died, and de fambly sorter broke up. Dat wuz fo' yeahs atter de Surrender." Ellen Betts and her mother, Charity, also remained with "old Marse" until his death. And when the end came, he insisted upon seeing Ellen's mother. "He won't die till ma gits there. Dey fotch ma from de cane patch and she hold Marse's hand till he die." Even after the death of the master and mistress, some former slaves continued to serve the family. When "young Master" took over the farm, William Curtis, a former Georgia slave recalled, that was all the more reason why he had to stay. "He couldn't a'done nothing without us niggers. He didn't know how to work."[83]

No matter how eloquently former slaveholders praised the fidelity of those who remained, thinking the old ties had survived still another disruptive challenge, the most faithful often turned out to be the elderly, the infirm, and the very young, those who felt least compelled to uproot themselves. Although many of the older slaves embraced emancipation, for their children and grandchildren if not for themselves, some thought it too late to aspire to anything beyond the security afforded by the master and mistress. While the former master might feel obliged to retain and look after these people, he also recognized how little labor was left in them. "My crowd of darkies is rapidly decreasing," a South Carolina lawyer and politician informed his brother. "Almost two weeks ago, my cook departed with her child. Last week, our house girl left, and this morning, another girl, lately employed in the culinary department, vacated. We still have six big and little—one old, three children, one man sick, so that you may perceive there are mouths and backs enough, but the labor is very deficient." Anticipating future losses, Emma Holmes thought in May 1865 that every servant would leave except for Ann, "who is lame, solitary, very dull, slow, timid and friendless." In some instances, the few remaining slaves shared the dismay of their "white folks" over the departures, but for altogether different reasons. "I was de only nigger left on de place," recalled Esther Green, who was ten years old at the time. "I jus' cried and cried, mostly because I was jus' lonesome for some of my own kind to laugh and talk wid."[84]

To remain might be less of a commitment to the old place and the old ties than a necessary holding action, until the confusion surrounding emancipation had been clarified. After being informed of his freedom, Robert Glenn, a young Kentucky black, agreed to remain on the same plantation. But he spent much of his time, as he recalled, considering a different kind of life for himself. "I took my freedom by degrees and remained obedient and respectful, but still wondering and thinking of what the future held for me. After I retired at night I made plan after plan and built aircastles as to what I would do." Nearly a year later, having failed to heed the first work call, he found himself awakened one morning by the foreman's slap across the head. Glenn went about his usual tasks that day, feeding the stock and cutting firewood. His employer then ordered him to hitch a team of horses to a wagon and proceed to a neighboring farm where he was to pick up a load of hogs. Perhaps Glenn himself could not have anticipated his response. He refused to carry out the command. "They called me into the house and asked me what I was going to do about it. I said I do not know. As I said that I stepped out of the door and left." He never returned.[85]

With sufficient time, freedmen like Robert Glenn gained additional confidence in themselves, learned more about the opportunities made possible by their freedom, and determined to take their chances elsewhere. After spending the first year on the plantation or farm of their bondage, scores of blacks in every section of the South chose to leave. Even larger numbers, however, began to stake out a greater degree of autonomy for themselves without moving at all. The more perceptive white families could discern the changes in those who had remained, often quite gradual and subtle but no less threatening and disconcerting. "Henney is still with me," a South Carolina woman informed her niece, "but not the same person that she was."[86]

## Postscript: Four Letters

WHETHER OR NOT the freed slave and the former owner ever met again after emancipation, each of them retained his or her own memories of the old times and places and the quality of the "old ties" that had bound them together. For generations, members of slaveholding families and their descendants would regale the reading public with period pieces and reminiscences in which their "black folk" figured conspicuously, most often appearing as the authors had always wished to perceive them. Unfortunately, few former slaves kept any written records of their thoughts during the critical juncture of their lives when they became free men and women. But the "old ties" occasionally yielded a letter written by a former slave to those who had once owned their bodies (though never wholly their minds); in some instances, the communications were barely legible or had been dictated to a friend, a teacher, or a clergyman. But if the black correspondents were at times illiterate, they seldom suffered from inarticulateness. Reflecting the experiences of the nearly four million black people who had endured bondage, the authors of these four letters revealed a wide range of emotions and perceptions about slavery, freedom, and the quality and endurance of the old relationships, and these in turn were profoundly influenced in each case by the fate of their post-emancipation expectations and aspirations.

Liberty, Va. July 10th/1865

Master Man,

I have the honor to appeal to you one more for assistance, Master. I am cramped hear nearly to death and no one ceares for me heare, and I want you if you pleas Sir, to Send for me. I dont care if I am free. I had rather live with you. I was as free while with you, as I wanted to be. Mas. Man you know I was as well Satisfied with you as I wanted to be. Now Affectionate Master pleas, oh, pleas come or Sind for me. John is still hired out at the Same and doing Well and well Satisfied only greaving about home, he want to go home as bad as I do, if you ever Send for me I will Send for him immediately, and take him home to his kind Master. Mas, Man. pleas to give my love to all of my friends, and especialy to my young mistress dont forget to reserve a double portion for yourself. I Will close at present, hoping to bee at your Service Soon yes before yonders Sun Shal rise and Set any more.

May I Subscribe myself your Most affectionate humble friend and Servt.

Isabella A. Soustan[87]

Montgomery, February 10, 1867

My Dear Old Master,—I am anxious to see you and my young masters and mistresses. I often think of you, and remember with pleasure how kind you all ever were to me. Though freedom has been given to the colored race, I often sigh for the good old days of slave-times, when we were all so happy and contented. . . . I am tolerably pleasantly situated. I am hired to a Mr. Sanderson, who treats me very well. I am very well, and hope I may have an opportunity of coming to see you all next Christmas. I am still single and don't think much about beaux. I don't think the men in these days of freedom are of much account. If I could find one whom I think a real good man, and who would take good care of me, I would get married. Please, dear old master, ask some of my young mistresses to write to me.

My kind and respectful remembrances to all.

Your former servant and friend,
Alice Dabney[88]

February 5, 1867

Mas William

I guess you will be somewhat surprised to receive a letter from me. I am well & doing just as well as I could expect under the circumstances, one blessing is I have plenty to eat & have plenty of work to do, & get tolerable fair prices for my work. I have but two children, they are good size boys, able to plough & help me out a great deal. I still work at my trade. I once thought I wanted to come back to that old country, but I believe I have given up that notion. Give my best respects to old Mas Henry & his family Miss Jane & all the family.

Tell Austin howdy for me & tell him I want him to write to me & give me all the news of that old country who has married who has died give me all the news I am anxious to hear from them all tell Austin to give them all my love to all I havent time to mention all ther names, but I wish to hear from all remember me to Coleman especialy. As I am in a great hurry I will close please send me word, direct your letter to Camden in the Case or in the name of S. B. Griffin, Camden, Washita County, Arksas.

I remains as ever Respt

Your humble Servant

Jake[89]

Dayton, Ohio, August 7, 1865

To My Old Master, Colonel P. H. Anderson,
Big Spring, Tennessee

Sir: I got your letter and was glad to find you had not forgotten Jourdon, and that you wanted me to come back and live with you again, promising to do better for me than anybody else can. I have often felt uneasy about you. I thought the Yankees would have hung you long before this for harboring Rebs they found at your house. I suppose they never heard about your going to Col. Martin's to kill the Union soldier that was left by his company in their stable. Although you shot at me twice before I left you, I did not want to hear of your being hurt, and am glad you are still living. It would do me good to go back to the dear old home again and see Miss Mary and Miss Martha and Allen, Esther, Green, and Lee. Give my love to them all, and tell them I hope we will meet in the better world, if not in this. I would have gone back to see you all when I was working in the Nashville hospital, but one of the neighbors told me Henry intended to shoot me if he ever got a chance.

I want to know particularly what the good chance is you propose to give me. I am doing tolerably well here; I get $25 a month, with victuals and clothing; have a comfortable home for Mandy (the folks here call her Mrs. Anderson), and the children, Milly, Jane and Grundy, go to school and are learning well; the teacher says Grundy has a head for a preacher. They go to Sunday-School, and Mandy and me attend church regularly. We are kindly treated; sometimes we overhear others saying, "Them colored people were slaves" down in Tennessee. The children feel hurt when they hear such remarks, but I tell them it was no disgrace in Tennessee to belong to Col. Anderson. Many darkies would have been proud, as I used to was, to call you master. Now, if you will write and say what wages you will give me, I will be better able to decide whether it would be to my advantage to move back again.

As to my freedom, which you say I can have, there is nothing to be gained on that score, as I got my free-papers in 1864 from the Provost-Marshal-General of the Department at Nashville. Mandy says she would be afraid to go back without some proof that you are sincerely disposed to treat us justly and kindly—and we have concluded to test your sincerity by asking you to send us our wages for the time we served you. This will make us forget and forgive old scores, and rely on your justice and friendship in the future. I served you faithfully for thirty-two years and Mandy twenty years. At $25 a month for me, and $2 a week for Mandy, our earnings would amount to $11,680. Add to this the interest for the time our wages has been kept back and deduct what you paid for our clothing and three doctor's visits to me, and pulling a tooth for Mandy, and the balance will show what we are in justice entitled to. Please send the money by Adams Express, in care of V. Winters, esq, Dayton, Ohio. If you fail to pay us for faithful labors in the past we can have little faith in your promises in the future. We trust the good Maker has opened your eyes to the wrongs which you and your fathers have done to me and my fathers, in making us toil for you for generations without recompense. Here I draw my wages every Saturday night, but in Tennessee there was never any pay day for the negroes any more than for the horses and cows. Surely there will be a day of reckoning for those who defraud the laborer of his hire.

In answering this letter please state if there would be any safety for my Milly and Jane, who are now grown up and both good-looking girls. You know how it was with poor Matilda and Catherine. I would rather stay here and starve and die if it comes to that than have my girls brought to shame by the violence and wickedness of their young masters. You will also please state if there has been any schools opened for the colored children in your neighborhood, the great desire of my life now is to give my children an education, and have them form virtuous habits.

P.S.—Say howdy to George Carter, and thank him for taking the pistol from you when you were shooting at me.

From your old servant,

Jourdon Anderson[90]

Few individuals—white or black—have ever articulated the meaning of freedom more clearly or more precisely than Jourdon Anderson. How many such people came out of slavery remains difficult to determine. But as former slaveholders assumed the role of employers and prepared to deal with the freed slaves as workers, they sometimes found their plantations and farms overrun with men and women who evinced the same spirit and the same determination to work under conditions that would in no way compromise their newly won freedom. What happened to that spirit and to that determination would profoundly affect race relations and the nation for more than a century.

# Chapter Seven

# BACK TO WORK: THE OLD COMPULSIONS

*We have been faithful in the field up to the present time, and think that we ought to be considered as men, and allowed a fair chance in the race of life. It has been said that a black man can not make his own living, but give us opportunities and we will show the whites that we will not come to them for any thing, if they do not come to us. We think the colored people have been the making of them, and can make something of ourselves in time. The colored people know how to work, and the whites have been dependent upon them. They can work again, and will work. A white man may talk very well, but put him to work, and what will he say? He will say that hard work is not easy. He will say that it is hard for a man who has owned so many able-bodied negroes to have the Yankees come and take them all away.*

—CORPORAL JACKSON CHERRY, COMPANY I, 35TH REGIMENT, UNITED
STATES COLORED TROOPS, DECEMBER 16, 1865[1]

"OLD LETITIA is with me still on the old terms and declines to make any change in consequence of her freedom," William L. DeRosset, a former North Carolina slaveholder, informed his brother. "I can see no difference in her at all, and I notified her when I first saw the order freeing them, that she was at liberty to go, but that if she staid with me it must be as she had before & if she misbehaved I would not hesitate to flog her. She acquiesced fully & I have had no trouble." With several of the other servants, however, he had been less successful. "Susie became impudent & I drove her off," while Louisa "wanted to make a change" and left. To replace them, he managed to hire "two of the best servants I ever saw, both young mulatto women, & real niggers." Having already surrendered the use of his right leg, the still unrepentant DeRosset remained willing to sacrifice his right arm if it would help to ensure the ultimate triumph of the Lost Cause. With blacks in his region abandoning the rice fields for more desirable labor, he recognized that unwelcome changes lay ahead. But DeRosset remained confident of the outcome and he would manage his laborers in that spirit. "The Negroes over the entire South are beginning to awaken to a sense of their still dependant position towards the whites and consequently are much more respectful and steadily improving in this respect. So that in a few years I think every thing will be about as it was except that we can not control their entire time."[2]

To listen to the former slaveholder, emancipation had changed only the method of compensation, not the basic arrangement, not the mutual understanding that had underlain the old system. If he continued to meet his obligations to his freed blacks and provide for their daily needs, if he agreed to pay them in some way for their labor (whether by wages or shares), he expected them to maintain the old demeanor and to comply with his expectations, regulations, and demands. "My own servants on the lot have not said a word about wages nor changed at all in their deportment or duty," a Florida farmer and physician advised his cousin in North Carolina. The one problem he had encountered was a former slave who "was very idle & a little impertinent to my wife," but he resolved the matter quickly and in a familiar fashion. "I gave her a moderate thrashing a few days ago and we have had no more trouble yet." That same remedy, when coupled with the traditional reliance on mutual obligations, provided a Mississippi planter with all the security he needed to continue his agricultural operations. "We go right on like we always did," he explained, "and I pole 'em if they don't do right. This year I says to em, 'Boys, I'm going to make a bargain with you. I'll roll out the ploughs and the mules and the feed, and you shall do the work; we'll make a crop of cotton, and you shall have half. I'll provide for ye, give ye quarters, treat ye well, and when ye won't work, pole ye like I always have.' They agreed to it, and I put it into the contract that I was to whoop 'em when I pleased."[3]

Even as Henry W. Ravenel argued that both whites and blacks now needed to unlearn the old relationship, he had nothing drastic in mind. He insisted that the freed blacks were to show "deference, respect & attachment," while their former masters, in return, would exercise "kindliness, care, & attention." But there was little question as to where the ultimate authority lay. Like most planters, William Henry Stiles of Georgia prepared to manage his working force much as he had in the past. If the blacks were no longer legally bound to him, as he finally and only grudgingly conceded, neither did he feel obligated to employ them if they proved troublesome. After reprimanding his newly freed slaves for their independent work habits, such as taking more time off for meals than he permitted, Stiles advised them that they were perfectly free to leave. But if they chose to stay, he made clear, "they should work as they had obligated themselves to do—that is to work in the same manner as they always had done." This kind of advice became commonplace, and the phrase "to work in the same manner as they always had done" was often written into newly devised labor contracts. To many planters, in fact, the principle was sufficiently important to risk their entire labor force. "Our freedmen will leave us," J. B. Moore, an Alabama planter, confided to his diary. "They will not agree to work and be controlled by me, hence, I told them I would not hire them."[4]

Whatever the legal status of the freedmen, then, the planter class made every effort to retain the essential features of the old work discipline. To tolerate the slightest deviation, no matter how trivial, was to unhinge the entire network of controls and restraints and thereby undermine the very basis of the social order as well as the labor system. What most whites found difficult to accept was not so much the freedom of the slaves as the determination of the ex-slaves to act as though they were free. "Our Negroes remain in status quo," Donald MacRae, a North Carolina commission merchant, observed in September 1865, "except that I imagine they feel a little disposition to show their freedom." He determined to impress upon every one of his former slaves that there were restraints on that freedom. "Yesterday," he related to his wife, "Zielu—without asking—told me she was going to church at Cool Spring. She did what work she had to do ahead, left at daylight, and did not return till after supper. I told her this morning that though I acknowledge her freedom, I do not acknowledge her right to do as she wishes without my consent, and that if she tried it again she should not come back." He could hardly have been clearer, and few whites accustomed to the ownership of slaves would have dissented from his position. Even the most "humane" among them, "conscious of none but the friendliest and best intentions" toward their blacks, a traveler in Virginia observed in 1865, insisted on "nothing less than complete deference" and resisted "anything resembling independence and self-reliance in them. . . . In short, he wishes still to be master, is willing to be a kind master, but will not be a just employer."[5]

If the former master preferred to view the new relationship within the old work discipline, the newly freed slaves were apt to have some different notions about how matters now stood. Although as slaves they had been subject to the arbitrary powers and caprice of their owners, even then many of them had managed to establish a line of toleration beyond which few masters or overseers might wish to move; and as freedmen, they sought to achieve a sense of personal autonomy while widening the area of maneuverability. No matter how many of them still worked for the same "white folks" and still depended on white men for support and protection, few were unaffected by the change in their legal status. Even if the aspiration of ex-slaves to eradicate the old dependency was but barely realized, the vast majority of them, according to the testimony of two black leaders in July 1865, "knew pretty well in what respects their present differed from their former situation. They all knew they were their own men."[6]

The crucial difference could not be measured by the amount of compensation they now received but involved a different perception of themselves and their relationship to whites. The freedmen on the Sneed plantation, near Austin, Texas, expressed no desire to leave the place on which they had labored as slaves but they had every intention of moving out of their slave quarters. On the plantation of Joseph Glover in South Carolina, a slave named Abraham had served with considerable distinction during the war, managing the place in his master's absence and even berating "the bad behaviour of some of the people." With the advent of freedom, Abraham informed his former master that he neither wished nor intended to leave but would await his return "to hear what proposal you may make." No less ready to assert her new status was a black woman named Rose, who worked as a servant on a plantation in Louisiana and also performed the duties of midwife, attending both the slaves and several "white ladies" in the neighborhood. For assisting the white women, she had been paid ten dollars each time, half of which her mistress had retained. With freedom, her new employer promised her the entire ten dollars. "Didn't you say the black people are free?" she asked him. When he agreed, she inquired, "White people are free, too, ain't they?" When he again replied in the affirmative, Rose both asked and demanded, "Then why shouldn't you pay me ten dollars every time I 'tend upon *the black folks* on the plantation?" None of these instances constituted startling or even dramatic manifestations of independence, any more than the action of some Alabama slaves who chose to stay with "massa" but demanded and secured the right to celebrate each year the anniversary of their freedom. ("Every 19th of June he would let us clean off a place and fix a platform and have dancing and eating out there in the field.") But in each case, if only symbolically, the freedmen had made their point; they had acted on their freedom, they had asserted their individual worth, and they had no doubt derived considerable personal satisfaction and pride from doing so.[7]

To remain on the same farm or plantation, to work for the old master or for any white man, was not necessarily to forfeit, postpone, or compromise their freedom. No matter how each ex-slave chose to express this fact, many of them insisted that it be understood and acknowledged, even at the cost of severing the relationship altogether. "Whose servant are you?" the Reverend John Hamilton Cornish, an Episcopalian minister in Aiken, South Carolina, demanded to know of his former slave after reprimanding her for using profane language in his presence. "My own servant," she replied. Seeking clarification, he asked her if she intended to remain with him. "I am willing to live with you as I have always done, & know you will pay me proper wages," she replied. Not satisfied with that answer, the minister insisted, "If you remain with me, you will be my servant, & conduct yourself accordingly, & will receive just what you have been accustomed to receive. Nothing more." If this had been calculated to impress her with his undiminished authority, the result must have been discouraging. "I'll leave then," she promptly announced. Having stood enough of her "impertinence," the clergyman told her to "seek a better place" and to have her belongings removed by the end of the week. And still to his surprise, she did precisely that.[8]

Whether in the fields or in the house, the most disturbing manifestations of black freedom were the breakdown of the old discipline, the refusal to obey orders promptly if at all, and the disinclination to regard "massa" and "missus" with the same degree of fear, awe, and respect previously expected of black subordinates. "My niggers used to do as I told them, but that time is passed," a Louisiana planter lamented. The number of black laborers dismissed for "bad work & insolent language" may have been limited only by the difficulty in replacing them. Neither the formerly free Negroes nor the freed slaves, a northern observer wrote, "seem to recognize any obligations they may be under to employers." Not only had they "appropriated" chickens, eggs, milk, and vegetables "to an amount fully equal to their wages" but any attempt to discipline them proved futile as long as some neighboring planter was anxious to hire them. Where slaves had behaved "outrageously" during the war, as on the Louisiana plantation of Governor Thomas O. Moore, the efforts of local whites to restore the old discipline met with only partial success. The conduct of black workers on the Moore place had become so "*disobedient*, defiant, [and] disrespectful" that the manager preferred to deal with them through an agent. "I go but seldom where they are at work," he confessed.[9]

Comparisons of productivity under slave and free labor, a favorite pastime of postwar commentators of all persuasions, clearly favored the old system. With near unanimity, the planters themselves testified in the aftermath of the war that their former slaves did "half their former work"; the estimates ran both higher and lower but that average tended to prevail.[10] A Mississippi planter told of a slave who had once picked thirty bales of cotton in one season but freedom reduced that figure to three bales; on the other hand, he praised three black families (also his former slaves) "who from nothing, are worth from $1,000 to $1,500 in money, stock, etc., to-day. They yielded to my advice. This number, out of 225 (which I was relieved of without any effort on my part); the balance are all trash, paupers, consumers, worse than army worms, and strange to say, they are quite as intelligent as the prosperous ones; but generally good slaves made poor freedmen."[11]

To place any considerable weight on these initial assessments of the productivity of freedmen would be to minimize the ways in which a destructive war might have disrupted any kind of labor system. The statistics of output, moreover, could tell different stories, depending on who collected them and for what purpose. Abolitionists and Union officials eager to prove the advantages of free labor were not necessarily more accurate in their computations than those who looked back with nostalgia to the old days and the Lost Cause. No doubt productivity declined under freedom, but to many of the ex-slaves comparative labor efficiency seemed less important in 1865 than the conditions under which they would work as free men and women and the rewards they would reap from their labor.

With the scarcity of laborers in many sections of the postwar South, the former slaves appeared to be in an excellent bargaining position. "The cry on all sides, is for laborers," a much-perplexed Mississippi planter observed, and yet the freedman, "finding himself master of the situation," preferred to use his new power to reduce his labor rather than increase his compensation. The problem, most observers agreed, lay not so much in the number of working hours (the ten-hour day, six-day week still prevailed) as in the inclination of the freedmen to labor less arduously. Even as patient and systematic a planter as Edward B. Heyward, who prided himself on his unique understanding of the rice-field blacks, almost despaired of extracting more labor from them.

> The work progresses very slowly and they seem perfectly indifferent. Oh! no one away from "the scene of operations" can have any conception of the difficulties we have to encounter. . . . I allude especially to our Rice field negro, a real gang worker, a perfect machine or part of a machine rather. He never thinks, never did, perhaps never will. The women appear most lazy, merely because they are allowed the opportunity. They wish to stay in the house or in the garden all the time. . . . The men are scarcely much better. They go out, because they are obliged to. They feel bound as a slave and work under constraint, are impudent, careless and altogether very provoking.

What most planters suspected and many freedmen readily conceded was a general and deliberate slowdown—the development of a work pace consistent with and reflective of their new status as free men and women. "Their idea of freedom," a Federal official reported from Bolivar County, Mississippi, in July 1865, "is that they are under no control; can work when they please, and go where they wish."[12]

With careful training, and with force if necessary, the planter class thought it could instill a discipline and attitude in their slaves that would overcome the blacks' traditional notions about work and time. But to listen to the former masters in the aftermath of the war, that discipline came unhinged the moment their blacks began to act on their freedom. "Negroes know nothing of the value of time," a Texas planter proclaimed, and on countless farms and plantations that seemed to translate into less work and lost days, with laborers reporting to the fields late, remaining out longer at mealtime, and refusing to labor on Saturday afternoons.[13] Pierce Butler, the large Georgia rice planter, wondered how he could possibly make a crop when most of his hands left the fields in the early afternoon, even at the busiest time of the season. When his daughter returned to the plantation after the war to assist him, she shared his exasperation, particularly in view of the loyalty the blacks had shown him as slaves.

> The negroes talked a great deal about their desire and intention to work for us, but their idea of work, unaided by the stern law of necessity, is very vague, some of them working only half a day and some even less. I don't think one does a really honest full day's work, and so of course not half the necessary amount is done and I am afraid never will be again. . . . I generally found that if I wanted a thing done I first had to tell the negroes to do it, then show them how, and finally do it myself.

Their way of managing not to do it was very ingenious, for they always were perfectly good-tempered, and received my orders with, "Dat's so, missus; just as missus says," and then always somehow or other left the thing undone.[14]

Few planters appeared to comprehend fully why this was happening, only that their experiences confirmed what they had long suspected—that black slaves were productive laborers while free blacks were not. After thirty-seven years devoted to raising sugarcane and cotton, a Louisiana planter found himself unable to induce his seventy-five blacks, almost all of them his former slaves, to produce even a fraction of the prewar crops. Not only did they work slowly but they took no interest in maintaining the plantation fences ("all rotting down") or buildings ("decaying and going to ruin"). It was as though they no longer cared. "Wherever you look the eye rests on nothing but the relics of former things fast passing to destruction." Neither "moral suasion" nor wage incentives had induced them to work harder. "The nature of the negro cannot be changed by the offer of more or less money," he concluded, repeating the familiar excuse of employers everywhere, "all he [the Negro] desires is to eat, drink and sleep, and perform the least possible amount of labor." But even if the ultimate responsibility lay with racial characteristics, that made the experience no less wrenching, the humiliations endured no less trying. "I have the heart-break over things," one disillusioned planter wrote. "I see this big planta-tion, once so beautifully kept up, going to rack and ruin. I see the negroes I trained so carefully deteriorating every day. We suffer from theft, are humiliated by impertinence; and cannot help ourselves. . . . This is the first rule in their lesson of freedom—to get all they can out of white folks and give as little as possible in return."[15]

Where planters, overseers, and managers failed to induce the blacks to maintain the old pace of labor, the black drivers fared little better, provided they were tolerated at all. On a Louisiana sugar plantation, Jim had long held the position of driver, and he was proud of the way he had exercised his duties—no prouder than his master, who thought him the most intelligent and skillful slave he had ever known. After the war, however, Jim found his people unresponsive to his demands, and he could only shake his head in disbelief:

I sposed, now we's all free, dey'd jump into de work keen, to make all de money dey could. But it was juss no work at all. I got so 'scouraged sometimes I's ready to gib it all up, and tell 'em to starve if dey wanted to. Why, sah, after I'd ring de bell in de mornin' 'twould be hour, or hour 'n half 'fore a man 'd get into de fiel'. Den dey'd work along maybe an hour, maybe half hour more; and den dey'd say, "Jim, aint it time to quit?" I say, "No, you lazy dog, taint ten o'clock." Den dey'd say, "Jim, I's mighty tired," and next thing I'd know, dey'd be pokin' off to de quarters. When I scold and swear at 'em, dey say, "We's free now, and

we's not work unless we pleases." Sah, I got so sick of deir wuflessness
dat I sometimes almost wished it was old slavery times again.

That was the driver's view of how matters stood; the remaining field hands,
however, thought him a hard taskmaster—"harder on them than white
folks." Few of them, moreover, expected to contract for a new year unless
they were accorded certain privileges, like their own tracts of land to
cultivate for their own benefit. Nevertheless, the driver expected that in
time these freedmen would come to their senses, particularly with a white
overseer now on the premises. "Dey wants a white man to gib orders," he
explained. "Dey wouldn't min' me las' yeah, 'cause I's nigger like demselves. I tink dey do better dis yeah."[16]

Although the rate of "desertion" appears to have been lower in the
fields than in the households, few planters could assume in mid-1865 that
any of their hands would be on the same plantation at the end of the year.
Within a period of five months, the Beaver Bend plantation, a once flourishing enterprise, was brought to a point of virtual ruin. Before the war, Hugh
Davis had reaped substantial profits out of his 5,000 acres of rich Black Belt
land; in 1862, he died of an apoplectic stroke, and an administrator and
overseer managed the plantation while Hugh Davis, Jr., eighteen years old
when the war broke out, served in the Confederate Army. After the war,
Davis found that the slaves in this region had "all become monomaniacs
on the subject of freedom," thousands of them flocking to Selma "to be free"
and "to embrace the *nigger lovers,*" only to discover Yankee freedom to be
a "delusion" and to hasten back to the old plantation. Of the seventy-eight
Davis slaves, some thirteen men and thirteen women were persuaded to
remain and contract to work "as they have heretofore done" for provisions
and a share (one fifth) of the crop. Within several weeks after Davis' return
to the plantation, continual movement and malingering among the former
slaves seriously interfered with the completion of the crop. "Negroes will
not work for pay, the *lash* is all I fear that will make them," he wrote on
May 30, 1865. Five weeks later, the same problems plagued him, with
seventeen of his "best hands" having left for Selma. The Davis plantation,
like so many others, experienced a turbulent period in which freedmen—
both the old hands and the newly hired workers—came and departed with
an exasperating regularity. After sustaining still further losses, the young
planter finally threw up his hands in disgust and left the plantation to take
up residence in nearby Marion, where he remained the rest of his life. On
October 3, 1865, some five months after his return from military service,
Davis made his final journal entry as a prospective postwar planter: "Farewell Old Farm Book! to record the future work of free negroes beside your
content would disgrace the past. The work and profits of the best labor
system ever established have been written on these pages—the past was
brilliant but the future is dismal, gloomy."[17]

With undisguised smugness (as if they had anticipated precisely this
outcome), punctuated with proper expressions of alarm, outrage, and exas-

peration, occasionally tempered with a degree of commiseration, the dispossessed slaveholding class observed the fatal effects of emancipation on
the Negro character and the plantation economy. Everywhere he went in
the South, a northern journalist reported, people talked about little else.
"Let conversation begin where it will, it ends with Sambo." Expecting the
worst, the white South prepared to believe almost anything, and with few
exceptions it heard only an accumulation of irritations, grievances, and
horror tales. The incidents and themes kept repeating themselves, resting
as they did on long-held assumptions about the character and limited
capacity of the African race. Released from the care and discipline of the
master, "no longer stimulated by the 'Must!'," the freedman by his behavior revealed how necessary that bondage had been. He refused to work,
preferring a life of idleness, dissipation, and vagrancy; and even when he
worked, "what is done is badly done." He entertained extravagant notions
about his freedom—"idleness, plenty of good food and fine clothes," not to
mention that imminent forty acres and a mule. His natural inclination to
theft manifested itself even more blatantly in freedom. "I'm sure they were
all thieves in Africa. Wherever you read about them they're always the
same." Freed from all restraint, he had become "fearfully licentious,"
"saucy and rude," "insubordinate and insolent," "lazy, thieving, lying,
ignorant, brutish," "shiftless, improvident, idle," "skulking, shuffling, and
worthless," and "an unmitigated nuisance." After all that had been done
for him, he evinced "not as much gratitude . . . as many of the inferior
animals." Although his legal status had been altered, his basic character
remained the same, and that only invited future troubles. "Thar ain't no
good side to 'em," an old South Carolina planter explained. "You can't find
a white streak in 'em, if you turn 'em wrong side outwards and back
again. . . . All the men are thieves, and all the women are prostitutes. It's
their natur' to be that way, and they never'll be no other way. They ain't
worth the land they cover."[18]

If planters suspected their blacks of deliberately slowing the pace of
labor, few of them cared to deal with the more obvious implications of such
a move. Rather, they preferred to assign responsibility not only to peculiar
racial characteristics but to lax discipline, Federal interference, and, perhaps most critically, a rising generation of blacks who had not been inculcated with a proper regard for time, industry, and the Protestant work
ethic. "The old hands are passing away," a Texas planter lamented. "The
young ones do not learn to work. No authority is exercised by parents to
teach them to work or understand the value of time, industry and economy." Under present conditions, an Arkansas planter concurred, the number of blacks "trained from childhood to hard labor" was rapidly
diminishing and the new generation was therefore bound to be "worthless." The same considerations prompted an Alabama planter to rely on his
"old, trained hands" to make a crop. "Such as were once considered second-
rate," he observed, "are now the best." Actually, these were simply variations on what had become a popular postwar theme among whites—that

unless blacks were properly controlled and trained, the African race under conditions of freedom would revert back to barbarism.[19]

But if whites quickly interpreted the work habits of their former slaves as conclusive proof of racial degeneration, the newly freed black workers chose to view their introduction to free labor quite differently. What many planters defined as a slowdown was often the freedmen's refusal to work up to their previous exploitative level. And what many planters viewed as an unwillingness to work and rebellious behavior proved in some instances to be nothing more than a well-earned, albeit brief respite from the rigorous plantation routines that had characterized the freedmen's previous lives. "No rest, massa, all work, all de time; plenty to eat, but no rest, no repose," was the way an elderly South Carolina freedman described his life as a slave; he was much happier now, he added, if only for the "chance for [a] little comfort." How could the planter class, moreover, deny to their former slaves a privilege they had flaunted so often in their presence? If there were "lazy" and "improvident" freedmen, a black clergyman declared, they were simply modeling themselves after the masters and mistresses they had observed for so many years. "They never worked for their own living," he said of the planters, "and hence their slaves imitate their former owners. Who is to blame?" Slavery itself, another observer noted, had taught that a gentleman was a person who lived without working. "Is it wonderful," he then asked, "that some of the negroes, who want now to be gentlemen, should have thought of trying this as the easiest way?"[20]

Even if few ex-slaves had the wherewithal to aspire to be "gentlemen," they did have certain strong convictions about the perquisites of their new status. What was freedom all about if not the chance to work less than they had as slaves and to have more leisure time for themselves, their families, and their garden plots? As one freedwoman in South Carolina remarked, she had not yet experienced any freedom, for she was working just as hard as ever. When pressed to work harder, a Georgia freedman "indignantly" inquired of his new employer, who happened to be a Northerner, "what the use of being free was, if he had to work harder than when he was a slave." More often than not, the slowdown was a way for newly freed black men and women to dramatize to themselves the distinction between their former and present positions—to know "de feel of bein' free." The inclination to work at their own pace also reflected for many ex-slaves the limited possibilities for achievement as landless agricultural laborers—if freedom could not mean "getting ahead," it could at the very least mean not working hard.[21]

While planters preferred to compare how many bales of cotton were produced under slavery and under freedom, their former slaves searched for ways to break away from a dependency and a day-to-day routine that seemed all too familiar. "Missus done keep me in slave times totin' milk, an' pickin' cotton, an' now de black 'uns is free, . . . 'pears like we hev tu tote all de milk, an' pick de cotton, an' work jes' de same."[22] Within the closer confinement and supervision of the households, where it proved difficult for blacks to reconcile their new freedom with the demands of domestic service, the quest for personal autonomy and individual worth often took on an even greater urgency than in the fields.

2
———————

AFTER THE WAR, Charles and Etta Stearns, both of them "uncompromising" abolitionists, came to the South, where they acquired ownership of a plantation in Columbia County, Georgia. The name they gave to their place, "Hope On Hope Ever Plantation," signified their optimism about the transition to free black labor. Within days after their arrival, Etta began to reorder the household. That was when the trouble began. Margaret, the cook, was a woman of considerable independence and sensitivity, outspoken on behalf of her rights and prerogatives, and determined that no person should infringe upon them without her consent. It required only a minor incident—an order to wash the dishes in a different way—to bring to the surface her feelings about the new arrangements and her new mistress. Planting herself in the middle of the room, facing Etta Stearns, Margaret made it clear that she was "gwine to be cook ob dis ere house, and Ise want no white woman to trouble me. You white folks spose, cause you white, and we all black, that us dunno noffin, and you knows eberyting." Removing her yellow turban from her head, and waving it in her hands, she declared in a voice loud enough to reach the more than attentive black laborers outside:

> Now missus, youse one bery good white woman, come down from de great Nc•th, to teach poor we to read, and sich as that; but we done claned dishes all our days, long before ye Yankees heard tell of us, and now does ye suppose I gwine to give up all my rights to ye, just cause youse a Yankee white woman? Does ye know missus that we's free now? Yas, free we is, and us ant gwine to get down to *ye,* any more than to them ar rebs.

Upon hearing "this harangue," the overseer rushed in, seized Margaret by the neck of her dress, and dragged her out unceremoniously, while exclaiming, "Shut up, you damn black wench, or I'll beat your brains out." Turning to his employers, he remarked, "Never mind her, Mrs. Stearns; these niggers have no more sense or manners than a mule; but I'll teach her not to insult white people." When Margaret subsequently returned to the house, she was "mild as a lamb" and washed the dishes as ordered but when told the next day to clean the cupboards, rebellion flared again. "Black folks don't work on Sunday," she announced. Etta Stearns cleaned the cupboards.[23]

The refusal to take any more "foolishment off of white folks" (native whites and Yankees alike) reflected the determination of many freedmen and freedwomen to stake out a larger degree of personal autonomy for themselves. Families accustomed to servants and absolute obedience often had to look no further than to their own households to observe the strange, ominous, sometimes shocking manifestations of black freedom. How was any family to know when a long-time black faithful had reached the breaking point, and as a free person no longer felt obliged to contain the rage and resentment within her? "You betta do it yourself," a Charleston servant suddenly told her mistress after being ordered to scour some pots and kettles. "Ain't you smarter an me? You think you is—Wy you no scour fo you-self." On the Pine Hill plantation in Leon County, Florida, Emeline had served as the cook for many years; the white family thought of her as "a great pet," a favorite of the children, and a faithful worker. On May 20, 1865, around dinnertime, the mistress's daughter searched for Emeline ("who has always professed to love me dearly") in her accustomed place in the kitchen but failed to find her. Hastening to Emeline's house, she found her dressed in her best Sunday clothes, preparing to attend an emancipation picnic sponsored by three regiments of black soldiers stationed nearby. When reminded of her kitchen obligations and the expected guests for dinner, the long-time servant retorted, "Take dem [storeroom and pantry] keys back ter yer Mother an' tell her I don't never 'spects ter cook no more, not while I lives—tell her I'se free, bless de Lord! Tell her if she want any dinner she kin cook it herself." Admittedly "hurt and dazed" by this encounter, the white woman left silently. "They are free, I thought; free to do as they please. Never before had I had a word of impudence from any of our black folks but they are not ours any longer.... I have learned a lesson today: we must not expect too much of 'free negroes.' "[24]

Although such outbursts from servants were rare, many white families might have preferred them to the more subtle transformation by which their once faithful domestics became unrecognizable men and women. After five months with his freed slaves, a Georgia planter found them "obviously changing in character every day." Even Frances Butler Leigh, who had been so impressed with the devotion of her father's slaves, wondered if she had been premature in her judgment. Visiting the plantation on St. Simon's Island, she found her household staff reduced both in numbers and in the quality of their service: Alex "invariably is taken ill just as he ought to get dinner," while Pierce "since his winter at the North is too fine to do anything but wait at table. So I cook, and my maid does the housework ..." Emma Holmes, on the other hand, described in admiring detail the faithful service rendered by "the few who remain with us," including a servant who still asked permission to leave the premises and apologized profusely when he once returned late. But she added: "These things are so unusual, that I have noticed them particularly."[25]

The rate of "desertion" among the house servants during and after the war should have given sufficient warning that this traditionally loyal class of blacks could behave in independent and unpredictable ways. That was no less true of those who chose to remain with the families they had served as slaves. Like Adele Allston of South Carolina, many a plantation mistress came away with mixed emotions about the postwar conduct of their household staffs.

> I can never feel kindly towards Nelly again.... Phebe gets into an ill humor occasionally and *jaws* me, but on the whole she is very good. I have agreed to give her $50 a year and Aleck the same, but Aleck has been gone for a week and I think he will possibly not return.... I fear Milly is tired being good and faithful. She appears discontented.

Within the intimacy and closeness of the Big House, the slightest incident, misunderstanding, or exchange of words could precipitate a confrontation, and in the aftermath of emancipation the sensibilities of both whites and blacks could be easily provoked. Even while ostensibly carrying on their normal duties, domestics had a way of irritating their mistresses or arousing their suspicions. "The servants torment me," a South Carolina woman wrote her sister, "but I suppose they do the same to everybody." The household in Augusta, Georgia, over which Eva B. Jones presided underwent a crisis when some money she had carefully saved and secreted suddenly disappeared. The only question was which of the servants might be the thief, and the evidence pointed to a freedwoman who was about to become a bride "and has therefore indulged in some extravagancies and petty fineries." Upon hearing of this incident, Mary Jones, Eva's mother-in-law, responded with that familiar sigh, "We cannot but feel such ingratitude." If she offered little more comfort, that may have reflected preoccupation with her own persistent domestic irritations: Flora was "most unhappy," working very little, and apparently ready to leave; Jack had moved into a Savannah boardinghouse, "where I presume he will practice attitudes and act the Congo gentleman to perfection"; and Kate and Flora, in "an amusing conversation" she overheard, talked about how "they are looking forward to gold watches and chains, bracelets, and *blue veils* and silk dresses!" To Mary Jones, it all seemed rather hopeless, and she had given up trying to anticipate the behavior of her domestics. "It is impossible to get at any of their intentions, and it is useless to ask them. I see only a dark future for the whole race."[26]

As long as their servants retained the precious right of mobility, neither the master nor the mistress could determine or control the outcome of domestic conflicts. If servants felt insulted or compromised, or if the employer resorted to the whip, they often chose to leave. Until additional help could be hired, the mistress might try various expedients to fill the gap. Eva Jones distributed the household duties among the remaining servants and even assumed a few of the tasks herself. "Our menage has been frightfully reduced," she informed her mother-in-law, "and of our numerous throng there remains a seamstress (who has had to lay aside her old calling to become cook, washer, and chambermaid) and one who attends to everything else about this unfortunate establishment." Nor was it uncommon to transfer field hands to the house and make domestics of them. To replace the "faithful" Patty, the Grimball family of South Carolina hired a field hand and his family. With less success, Frances Butler Leigh employed several "raw field hands, to whom everything was new and strange, and who were really savages." Sara Pryor, ill in bed and unable to care for her children, replaced her maid (who left on Christmas morning) with a field hand named Anarchy, but she soon determined that the new servant's hands, "knotted by work in the fields, were too rough to touch my babe."[27]

Unprepared for the frustrations that close contact with whites could provoke, some initiates into domestic service had brief tenures. On a Mississippi plantation, the wife of a field hand was transferred to the house; within a short time, troubles developed, words were exchanged, she claimed she had been insulted, and she left her household duties undone and remained in the quarters "doing nothing." Some domestics, on the other hand, found even more traumatic a sudden transfer from the house to the fields to replace defecting laborers. Lizzie Hill, who had been a slave in Alabama, remembered vividly the change in her duties after she returned to the plantation to be back with "Old Mistis" again; the position she had previously occupied in the house had been filled, and "I's had a hard time workin' in de field." The more typical experience was that of Dora Franks, a former Mississippi slave, who left her household duties to accompany her brother after the war. Upon resettling on a new plantation, she found herself in the fields and she would never forget her initiation into that kind of labor: "I'd faint away mos' ever' day 'bout eleven o'clock. It was de heat. Some of 'em would have to tote me to de house. I'd soon come to. Den I had to go back to de fiel'." Such considerations may well have been in the minds of some domestic servants when they chose to remain in their same positions after emancipation.[28]

Now that the last vestiges of old-time fidelity and devotion—however tenuous these proved to be—were being stripped from the master-servant relationship, white families needed to develop new sources of labor. When Gertrude Thomas resorted to hiring, she found herself dismayed by the experiment, and yet she revealed more about her own exploitative standards than the incapacity of the employee.

> Monday I had a woman to wash for me. Hired her for thirty cts a day. I think it probable that she was one of the recently made free negroes. I had no idea what was considered a task in washing so I gave her all the small things belonging to the children ... She was through by dinner time [and] appeared to work steady. I gave her dinner and afterwards told her that I had a few more clothes I wished washed out. Her reply was that "she was tired." I did not for a minute argue with her. Said I "If you suppose I engaged a woman to wash for me by the day and she stops by dinner time, If you suppose I intend paying for the days work you are very mistaken." Turning from her I walked into the house. She afterwards

sent in for more clothes and washed out a few other things. So much for hiring by the day.

But to her delight, she managed to hire a cook—an elderly mulatto woman who claimed that her previous employer had sent her off to procure a new position. Unfortunately, when Mrs. Thomas informed her husband of the new acquisition, he insisted that the woman obtain a note from her old employer before he would consent to hire her. This was not an uncommon practice among white families after emancipation, partly a matter of personal security but also intended to check the propensity of newly freed blacks to change or improve their positions. To no one's surprise, the cook never returned.[29]

In view of the experiences of some women, Gertrude Thomas might have considered herself fortunate. After hiring new servants, several Florida women found it necessary to count their spoons and forks every night before locking them up in their bedrooms; Julia LeGrand of New Orleans wondered if there was any alternative to "locking up and watching," and a South Carolina woman complained that her servants "don't work very hard, but I do." Emma Holmes would have little to do with her newly hired washer after the woman complained of arduous labor; "we have a constant ebb and flow of servants," she noted, "some staying only a few days, others a few hours—some thoroughly incompetent, others though satisfactory to us, preferring plantation life." Not surprisingly, the new servants simply reinforced for many white families the prevailing belief about the incapacity of free blacks for any kind of labor and even provoked some of the old wartime laments. "Three have run away during the last few months that we had clothed up to be decent," the wife of a North Carolina planter wrote her mother. "They came to us all but naked. They are an ungrateful race. They drive me to be tight and stingy with them." This woman, until recently a resident of New York, needed little time to learn that the frustrations of the employer class easily cross sectional lines.[30]

None of this came as any surprise to Grace Elmore. "The negro as a hireling will never answer," she confided to her diary in May 1865. "They have not principle enough, nor character enough to stand temptation. So long as master and servant were one you could find honesty among the race and even so it was a rarity." But the times had clearly changed, the old ties had been irrevocably severed, the blacks entertained strange, crude, and false notions about work and freedom, and she doubted if they could really survive the curse of emancipation. "[N]ow that he has power to change his place, and to escape punishment when detected, now that his and the master's interest are separate and there is no bond but dollars and cents between them, I think the house servants will be chosen from the whites, and that immediately." Although she had not yet yielded to such logic, she thought it only a matter of time before blacks were forced out of domestic service altogether. After all, she asked, "Who would employ the negro, unless his slave, in any work that could be done by a white? . . . Who would choose the black in any capacity except to be held as slave and so bound to her obedient and faithful?"[31]

3

———

THE TROUBLESOME QUALITY of black labor, both in the houses and in the fields, encouraged experiments in the employment of whites for positions traditionally held by blacks. After hiring two white girls, both of whom had been seeking employment at a nearby factory, Donald MacRae, a North Carolina merchant and planter, exulted in that novel feeling of independence from his former slaves. His new servants were not at all disdainful about performing the daily chores, they willingly did the kind of work reserved for blacks, and they claimed competence in spinning, weaving, cooking, washing, housework, tending children, and even plowing. While they remained with him, MacRae felt no need to make any concessions to retain his increasingly restless black help.[32]

If nothing else, the absence of blacks in a household might soothe otherwise shattered nerves and be a much-welcomed relief from daily irritations. To Ethelred Philips, the Florida farmer and physician, emancipation had resulted in "worthless servants," and he feared their continued presence in his household. Now that he had hired a white girl, however, "we find it so quiet and so comfortable to be rid of the negro." He rested much easier about the safety of his family, and he gloated over his pioneering success: "The white women are taking the place of the negroes in our village," he informed his cousin, "and I take some credit for being the first to make the experiment in the face of every body—not a man but declared it would never do, yet I took a girl about 18 as ignorant and poor as any cornfield negro, but respectable and willing to do any work to support herself and mother and 6 children." To transform a piney-woods girl into an efficient domestic servant had been no inconsiderable task, but MacRae boasted that his wife, "one of the most industrious and skillful housewives I ever saw, has made her serve her purpose much better than a negro and no darky dares enter my lot for fear of my dog."[33]

Within the first year of emancipation, and periodically thereafter, the introduction of whites, especially immigrants, into the fields and households of former slaveholders came to be viewed as a panacea that would surely strengthen the labor system, force the ex-slave to make a realistic accommodation to freedom, and provide white planters with an alternative to the increasingly humiliating and degrading dependency on black labor. That is, the employment of whites, or perhaps only the threat to do so, was a way to control the labor of the freedmen. "If white labor is generally introduced into the upper District," a South Carolina rice planter vowed, "it will drive the Negro down, and then the competition for labor will oblige them to work for very little." White labor, moreover, would provide the permanent and stable working force the South so desperately required for the successful cultivation of its crops. Compared to the freedmen, who "love change, and a month's work at a place," white people "love home, take interest in making it pleasant, comfortable—as the spot from which issue all their money and comforts."[34]

For those who accepted these assumptions, the proposition made good sense, both racially and economically, and white Southerners certainly enjoyed talking about it. In northern Florida, planters eager for white laborers prepared to apply to New York City for help; a group of Tennessee planters welcomed immigrants from the "industrious Germanic race" to replace "the now indolent negro"; and the Virginia legislature resolved in March 1866 that "the recent radical change in the labor system of the South has rendered the introduction of a new class of laborers necessary." Principal attention focused for a time on the bold efforts of Mississippi and Alabama planters to import Chinese laborers to work their fields. If racial peculiarities had made black slaves ideal workers, similar characteristics would enable the Chinese to answer the southern need for a docile, tractable, adaptable labor force, with superior enduring powers and less propensity than blacks to fraternize with or intermarry with whites. "We've got to change our whole system of labor," an Alabama planter declared. "Why, I was talking, down to Selma, the other day, with Jim Branson, up from Haynesville. We figured up, I don't know how many millions of coolies there are in China, that you can bring over for a song. It will take three of 'em to do the work of two niggers; but they'll live on next to nothing and clothe themselves, and you've only got to pay 'em four dollars a month. That's our game now. And if it comes to voting, I reckon we can manage that pretty well!"[35]

This was bold talk, indeed, and it proved to be mostly talk. How to rid themselves of the presence of the Negro was always a favorite topic of conversation, permitting planters to share their frustrations, anger, and fantasies with others, but few took it seriously. To talk about it perhaps served a therapeutic need, if nothing else. "To get the privilege of governing him [the Negro] as they pleased," a Freedmen's Bureau official in Mississippi observed of the local planters, "they will express their anxiety to get rid of him and many other foolish things; but come to the point— they want and must have the negro to work the plantation." Actually, some Chinese laborers were imported, and small numbers of Swedes, Germans, Dutchmen, and Irishmen were also induced to come to the South. But the results of these experiments were less than gratifying and more often than not failed to meet the expectations or needs of the planters. The new immigrants were no more tractable than many of the freedmen, and replacing troublesome blacks with troublesome immigrants not only made little sense but the cost was apt to be higher. "They cost me $35 each to bring them to Charleston from New York," a South Carolina planter said of the Dutchmen he had hired. "I fed them far better than ever I thought of feeding my hands, even gave them coffee and sourkrout, when, what should they do but demand butter for their bread and milk for their coffee, and the next thing the whole crowd left me." The Freedmen's Bureau in Virginia concluded that recent efforts to recruit foreign immigrants to replace blacks had been unsuccessful, and an English traveler in that state thought he knew why: "Swedes, Germans, and Irishmen had been imported; but the Swedes refused to eat cornbread, the Germans sloped away north-west-ward, in the hope of obtaining homesteads, and the Irishmen preferred a city career. It seems that the South will have need of Sambo yet awhile . . ." Nor did the attempts to recruit native whites for domestic service successfully overcome the stigma that still attached itself to that kind of labor. "I tried to hire some white women to live with & assist my family with their work," a South Carolina planter testified. "They do not like the idea of becoming 'Help.' "[36]

The more the white South experimented with white labor, the more the employer class came to appreciate the relative advantages of black labor, free or slave. Such admissions did not always come easily, and whites hastened to add that in "the professions, in the counting house, in the workshops of the artisan, in the factory, and on the wave," the white man had no superior. But in the fields, as the cultivator of the great southern staples, the Negro remained "unequalled," both for his skills and his enduring powers. The experience of a Louisiana sugar planter prompted him to estimate that "one able-bodied American negro of ordinary intelligence is worth at least two white emigrants. He understands the business, and he has the advantage of being acclimated." Appreciative of this fact, he was willing to pay even higher wages for blacks than for whites. "You may think this extravagant; but during the unsettled state of affairs for the last two years, I have had to try both, and I base my opinion not on my prejudices, but on my experience." With equal candor, the president of the Virginia Agricultural Society reminded the delegates to a State Farmers' Convention in 1866 that "we have in the labor of the freedmen a decided advantage over other portions of the world." After employing both foreign and native white workers, he concluded that "the world cannot produce a more skillful and efficient farm laborer than a well-trained Virginia negro who is willing and able to work." And for all the difficulties he had encountered with his freedmen, Edward Barnwell Heyward, the South Carolina rice planter, remained convinced that he could turn them into a productive labor force. "The negroes themselves begin to see our superiority and recognise in us their true *Master*. We are the only people who can ever get them to do any thing, and I confess I do not look with much pleasure to the time when their places will be supplied by these still more savage Germans as white labourers."[37]

Despite the experiments with white workers, despite all the talk about replacing blacks, despite the calumnies heaped on the freedmen, the conclusion reached by most practical-minded ex-slaveholders was that the Negro remained ideally suited for their purposes. He had already proven himself "peculiarly adapted by nature" to the cultivation of cotton, rice, and sugar, working under temperatures and conditions that would wilt any white man. "The African don't mind it," an Alabama planter noted, "the white man won't stand it." And so it came down to familiar discussions of racial traits. When a Virginia planter and manufacturer affirmed that the African race made ideal agricultural laborers, he enumerated their principal virtues as "docility, tractability and affectionate disposition"—that is, "just the material desirable and necessary." Nor were blacks any less valuable, some insisted, as domestics: the black nurse was "more affectionate, more attached, and more devoted than the white," while the black servant was "more faithful and has less thought of self in his devotion to his master and employer."[38]

If a Grace Elmore still insisted that the "separate" interests of blacks and whites doomed the Negro as the principal laborer of the post-emancipation South, the argument made little sense to planters who chose to view the entire matter in businesslike terms. "There is now nothing between me and the nigger but the dollar—the almighty dollar," a Florida planter declared, "and I shall make out of him the most I can at the least expense." That was a principle to which any nineteenth-century American employer could have readily subscribed.[39]

4
───────

TO DISCOVER ONE DAY, as did so many white women, that "I have not one human being in the wide world to whom I can say 'do this for me' " had to be a most disheartening realization. "We have truly said good bye to being ladies of leisure," Grace Elmore lamented, as she sought to adjust to her new daily routine. "My time seems fully occupied and often I do not have time to sleep even. My hour for rising is 5 o'clock." Embittered by the continuing defection of their servants, exasperated by the behavior of those who remained, and unable to find satisfactory replacements, many families found themselves forced into the unfamiliar role of doing the housework themselves. No matter how they rationalized this change in their lives, and whatever the orgy of self-congratulation that often accompanied the assumption of household responsibilities, the unprecedented nature of their predicament provoked considerable dismay and disbelief.[40]

To assume responsibility for the daily chores—to cook a meal, to dust and sweep, to wash the clothes, to feed the horses and milk the cows—was to undertake tasks they had previously watched their black folk perform. "I always had thirty or forty niggers," the wife of a Louisiana planter declared. "I never even so much as washed out a pocket handkerchief with my own hands, and now I have to do all my work." With considerable anguish, a Virginia woman admitted to her cousins in the North that it would require "some time for us to get fixed to do our own house work or to do with a few servants"; if nothing else, she noted, the distances separating the kitchen, the spring, and the dining room seemed all too formidable. Like so many "ladies" she knew, Gertrude Thomas found herself sharing the household chores with the few remaining servants. The sheer novelty of the experience struck her with wonderment. Not only did she assist in washing the breakfast dishes—"a thing I never remember to have done except once or twice in my life"—but she startled one of the servants by announcing that she intended to do the ironing. "It was amusing to see his look of astonishment but indeed the necessity for it appeared qu[i]te im[m]inent." That night, she described the experience in her journal, concluding, "I am tired and sleepy."[41]

To hear white families relate their experiences, the initiation into domestic labor had its moments of self-satisfaction and even triumph. The spectacle of "fragile women," left without any servants, "cooking and washing without a murmur," moved Emma Holmes to extol the "heroism and spirit" of southern womanhood. With less flourish, a Virginia woman described how she missed "the familiar black faces" she had grown to love. "Domestic cares are making me gray! But I get some fun trying to do things I never did before." Eva Jones had to tell her mother-in-law how she expected "to become a very efficient chambermaid and seamstress," though she confessed that the sewing came "very hard to my poor unused fingers."[42]

The first days of performing domestic chores could even be an exhilarating experience. Charlotte S. J. Ravenel took pride in "how nicely" she had prepared a meal, while another South Carolina woman, after scrubbing the wash "until my poor hands are skinned," took some consolation in how "white and clean" the clothes looked. None of these women, however, matched in exuberance the triumph felt by William Heyward, the elderly rice planter who had taken up residence in Charleston. Disgusted with the familiarity, deficiencies, and insolence of the black waiters, he gave up boarding at a local hotel and resolved to cook his own meals. Although he kept an old Irish chambermaid to tidy his room, Heyward learned to do his own shopping, washing, and cooking. After a month, he claimed "perfect success" and hailed his achievement as a personal victory. "A part of the satisfaction," he confessed, "is, that I am perfectly independent of having Negroes about me; if I cannot have them as they used to be, I have no desire to see them except in the field."[43]

Few took up the challenge more diligently than the Andrews family in Washington, Georgia. Of the twenty-five servants who had formerly been their slaves, only five remained, and two of these were too ill to work. Young Eliza Andrews found herself cleaning the downstairs with her sister, while her mother washed the dishes. At first, it all seemed quite strange. "It is very different from having a servant always at hand to attend to your smallest need," Miss Andrews confided to her journal, "but I can't say that I altogether regret the change; in fact, I had a very merry time over my work." To this proud young Georgia woman, the menial tasks she now performed were nothing less than a challenge to her race and sex.

I don't think I shall mind working at all when I get used to it. Everybody else is doing housework, and it is so funny to compare our experiences. Father says this is what has made the Anglo-Saxon race great; they are not afraid of work, and when put to the test, never shirk anything that they know has got to be done, no matter how disagreeable.[44]

Whatever the enthusiasm that marked these work experiences, few white men or women who had once owned slaves could overcome the feeling that they were demeaning themselves in performing the tasks thought to be fit only for black hands. Having reassured herself that southern white womanhood had more than met the test, Eliza Andrews wondered why young ladies like herself should be placed in the predicament of performing labor that was clearly unworthy of them.

[I]t does seem to me a waste of time for people who are capable of doing something better to spend their time sweeping and dusting while scores of lazy negroes that are fit for nothing else are lying around idle. Dr. Calhoun suggested that it would be a good idea to import some of those man-apes from Africa and teach them to take the place of the negroes, but Henry said that just as soon as we had got them tamed, and taught them to be of some use, those crazy fanatics at the North would insist on coming down here to emancipate them.[45]

If some white women initially derived satisfaction from domestic labor, steady exposure to that kind of work took its inevitable toll, not only in physical and mental exhaustion but in frayed temperaments. After failing to iron some items properly, Julia LeGrand confessed to feeling "anything but spiritual-minded. I got angry with my irons which would smut my muslins, and then got angry with myself for having been angry —finally divided the blame, giving a part to Julie Ann for running away and leaving me to do her work . . ." The more the women worked, the more they came to resent these new demands on their time and the less able they were to enjoy the usual pastimes of "ladies." When Eliza Andrews attended the "charming" party to which she had been invited, she found herself "too tired" to enjoy or partake of the dancing. And when she retired that night, she was too exhausted to sleep, her legs "ached as if they had been in the stocks," and she wondered how long she could maintain this grueling pace. "[W]hen I become more accustomed to hard work, I hope it won't be so bad. I think it is an advantage to clean up the house ourselves, sometimes, for we do it so much better than the negroes." The next few days, however, hardly reassured her. The morning after the party, Eliza arose long before her accustomed hour and helped to clean the house. When guests dropped in that day as she prepared to take a nap, there was still more work to do. "I never was so tired in my life; every bone in my body felt as if it were ready to drop out, and my eyes were so heavy that I could hardly keep them open." Finally, she confessed to herself, "I don't find doing housework quite so much of a joke as I imagined it was going to be, especially when we have company to entertain at the same time, and want to make them enjoy themselves." After dinner, Eliza reluctantly went off to a dance she had promised to attend. "I was so tired that I made Jim Bryan tell the boys not to ask me to dance." The next morning, the same seemingly endless routine repeated itself. "I had to be up early and clean up my room, though half-dead with fatigue." That evening, she went to bed as soon as she had eaten her supper.[46]

Like Eliza Andrews, the outspoken Emma Holmes of Camden, South Carolina, had performed her first household tasks with considerable zeal and a sense of personal commitment. "Of course it occupies a good deal of time," she observed in May 1865, "but the servants find we are by no means entirely dependent on them." That feeling in itself gave her immense satisfaction. Less than a month later, some of that enthusiasm had waned: "I was very tired yesterday, after my various pieces of manual labor, but hope they will drive off headache as medicine wont. I was up at five to-day ···." Still, she persisted, trying to put the best face on her labors as still another servant left the household. "[W]e girls went to ironing, and though of course it was fatiguing, standing so long, it was not near as difficult nor as hard work as I fancied." But by mid-August, after another day of household chores, she sounded a rather different note. "I dont like cooking or washing, even the doing up of muslins is great annoyance to me and I do miss the having all ready prepared to my hand. I generally rise at five or before, though sometimes not till six, when very tired, but often rouse servants and household by going to sweep the drawing room." Later that month, the initial excitement had all but vanished. "I am very weary, standing up washing all the breakfast and dinner china, bowls, kettles, pans, silver, etc. and minding Sims, churning, washing stockings, etc.—a most miscellaneous list of duties, leaving no time for reading or exercise ···."[47]

Never once did Emma Holmes or any of the other women who described their admittedly difficult experiences with housework think to question how their black help had for so many years performed these same duties, day after day, while also caring for a husband and children. Perhaps the question never even entered their minds. This was, as they had discovered, labor suited only for black hands—or, as Eliza Andrews suggested, for "negroes that are fit for nothing else." Mary Chesnut, who never suffered these ordeals, seemed to understand better than most what housework entailed. "Ellen is a poor maid, but if I do a little work, it is quite enough to show me how dreadful it would be if I should have to do it all." Only many years later, when she reflected over the black folks who had served her, did Kate Stone begin to realize the monstrous demands she had made on them.

> Even under the best owners, it was a hard, hard life: to toil six days out of seven, week after week, month after month, year after year, as long as life lasted; to be absolutely under the control of someone until the last breath was drawn; to win but the bare necessaries of life, no hope of more,

no matter how hard the work, how long the toil; and to know that nothing could change your lot. Obedience, revolt, submission, prayers—all were in vain. Waking sometimes in the night as I grew older and thinking it all over, I would grow sick with the misery of it all.

Nor, as she now realized, had the domestics escaped arduous labor. The seamstress always had "piles of work ahead," while the washerwoman labored all week to keep the family in clean clothes. And the cook needed to prepare three abundant meals a day for the thirteen to twenty whites who were almost always present, not to mention the more lavish dinners and entertainments. "Thinking it over by the light of later experience, I know our cook was a hardworked creature. Then, we never thought about it."[48]

To the women who had been accustomed to domestic help, self-reliance never came easily, if at all. The early exuberance and self-congratulation turned into deep resentment and cries of despair, reflecting both physical exhaustion and psychic humiliation. "I am tired—tired tonight, will all the days of the year be like this one?" the young mistress on a Florida plantation asked. "What are we going to do without the negroes?" Many years later, she could still recall "the wearisome hours, when only pride kept us up! . . . oh, the trials of those days to the housekeepers who had always been accustomed to first-class service!" The women who had derived such satisfaction from "trying to do things I never did before" turned before long to more somber reflections and more realistic appraisals. That brave talk about Anglo-Saxon adaptability and how it had been "a great relief to get rid of the horrid negroes" turned increasingly to nostalgic recollections of how much easier and simpler life had been before the disruption of the labor system and the loss of their servants.[49]

"Slavery was bad economy, I know," a Tennessee woman conceded. "But oh," she added, "it was glorious! I'd give a mint of money right now for servants like I once had,—to have one all my own! Ladies at the North, if they lose their servants, can do their own work; but we can't, we can't!" The housegirl who had once served her so faithfully had now taken up dressmaking in St. Louis. "She could read and write as well as I could. There was no kind of work that girl couldn't do. And so faithful!—I trusted everything to her, and was never deceived." Although revealing how dependent she had been on black labor, this woman thought emancipation had been a cruel blow to the slaves who had served their white folks so well. "Emancipation is a worse thing for our servants than for us. They can't take care of themselves."[50]

5

-------

RATHER THAN RENDERING THEM INDEPENDENT of their former slaves, the attempts of white families to hire white replacements or to work themselves only underscored their dependency. The incessant talk about ridding themselves of the ex-slaves may have impressed certain northern reporters but it never fooled the blacks. "Dey was glad to have a heap of colored people bout dem, cause white folks couldn' work den no more den dey can work dese days like de colored people can," recalled Josephine Bacchus, a former South Carolina slave. With equal cogency, a plantation mistress, in expressing gratitude for the blacks who had remained with her, acknowledged that "*they* can't spare *me,* and *I* can't spare *them.*"[51]

The sense of responsibility, obligation, and duty, invoked so often by the slaveholding class to justify keeping an "inferior, helpless and childlike" race in bondage, could obviously work both ways. The dependency of white families helps to explain the outrage and cries of ingratitude that greeted defecting and troublesome blacks, as it does the immense comfort those same families derived from some of their former slaves who chose to remain. Concerned for the welfare of her mother, Eliza Huger Smith of South Carolina went to considerable lengths to persuade a valuable servant to stay in the household after emancipation. "Hennie's decision to remain with me," she said afterwards, "is a great relief on Mamma's account as she is as dependent on her as a baby—more so." In a Georgia household, where all the servants had left, Hope L. Jones thought it a sad blow to her Aunt Bella, "since she is old and needs them more than ever."[52]

Even as whites acknowledged, at least to themselves, the urgent need to retain their black laborers and servants, they recognized the continued importance of controlling that labor. With emancipation, the pecuniary loss had been difficult enough to absorb. But to lose control over their former slaves, to be deprived of the necessary disciplinary powers, to be subject to their "insolence," to be forced to endure their work slowdowns and other manifestations of independence, to be compelled to deal with them as equals was to demand too much, even as the price of military defeat. "We can't feel towards them as you do," a young South Carolina planter tried to explain to a northern visitor. "I suppose we ought to, but 't is n't possible for us. They've always been our owned servants, and we've been used to having them mind us without a word of objection, and we can't bear anything else from them now. If that's wrong, we're to be pitied sooner than blamed, for it's something we can't help." Although discouraged by the postwar conduct of his former slaves, he could not conceive of doing without them. "I never did a day's work in my life, and don't know how to begin."[53]

Realizing how dependent they remained on black labor, those who had once held slaves concluded that the freed blacks needed them more urgently now than ever before. To make this absolutely clear, the planter class devised a rationale as familiar and elaborate as the argument they had used to justify slavery. What they wished to demonstrate, however, seemed so obvious to them as to require little proof—that the Negro as a free person could neither survive nor be a serviceable worker unless he remained under their care and protection. "The Negro stands as much in need of a master to guide him as a child does," a Virginia planter explained. "When I look at my servants, I feel weighing upon me all the responsibili-

ties of a parent. . . . The Negro will always need the care of someone superior to him, and unless in one form or another it is extended to him, the
race will first become pauper and then disappear." Along similar lines, the
provisional governor of South Carolina, no doubt with his conquerors in
mind, asked the obvious question: "If all the children in New York City
were turned loose to provide for themselves, how many would live, prosper,
and do well? The negroes are as improvident as children, and require the
guardian protection of some one almost as much as they do."[54]

To retain the laborers he needed so badly, "old massa" once again cast
himself in the familiar role of the beneficent protector, exercising a paren-
tal and providential vigilance over a helpless, childlike, and easily misled
race. He could do no less for those who had been accustomed to look to him
for direction and sustenance. "They are the descendants in a great degree
of the woman who nursed me," a Maryland congressman declared. "They
. . . look upon me as their protector. I am in truth their only friend. Am I
to turn them off as outcasts on the world? I have been my whole life
engaged in their protection. I have an affection for them, and have a duty
to perform for them. . . . They have labored for me, it is true, but they have
in turn received from me quite as much as they have given me." Consistent
with their view that slavery had been the best possible condition for a
people unable to look after themselves, the former masters viewed emancipation as an unfortunate if not tragic consequence of the war. But the
Negro, they emphasized, should not be held responsible. "It is not their
fault they are free," the new governor of Florida asserted; "they had nothing to do with it; that was brought about by 'the results and operations of
the war.' "[55]

Although revealing an abysmal ignorance of black attitudes and actions, the argument that Negroes had nothing to do with their freedom
would be repeated in many different forms, the principle itself would be
written into several of the new state constitutions, and it reflected an
abiding faith in the black laborer if only left in the hands of those who knew
him best. "The negro isn't to blame for his freedom," a Georgia planter told
a northern reporter. "He served us faithfully all through the war, and I
sincerely believe very few planters have any desire to see him injured. We
know his ways; and if you give us time, I think we shall be able to get him
back into his place again,—not as a slave, but as a good producer." Freedom
had been forced upon the slave, an Alabama judge told a grand jury in Pike
County, and it behooved the South to show compassion for the "faithful old
negro" who was now an involuntary freedman without the experience, the
self-reliance, or the ability to understand and appreciate his new status.
"He may have been the companion of your boyhood," he reminded them;
"he may be older than you, and perhaps carried you in his arms when an
infant. You may be bound to him by a thousand ties which only a southern
man knows, and which he alone can feel in all their force." Nor could the
freedman be blamed for the "excesses" that had characterized the transition in his status. "He has always been a child in intellect," Charles C.

Jones, Jr., explained to his mother, while sympathizing with "severe trials" she had experienced, "improvident, incapable of appreciating the obligations of a contract, ignorant of the operation of any law other than the will of his master, careless of the future, and without the most distant conception of the duties of life and labor now devolved upon him."[56]

Even if whites chose to view the old ties with varying degrees of sympathy, they could readily appreciate the forcefulness and timeliness of the argument. Now that the slaves had been freed, through no fault of their own, the burden of emancipation demanded of the old slaveholding class the same exercise of paternal solicitude and authority; indeed, the need had never been greater. If anything, the very suddenness of freedom, thrust upon an unprepared people, had increased the master's obligations and duty to a race possessing neither the physical nor the mental resources to care for themselves. "They are like grown up children turned adrift in the world," Eliza Andrews observed. "The negro is something like the Irishman in his blundering good nature, his impulsiveness and improvidence, and he is like a child in having always had someone to think and act for him." What had characterized slavery, many whites continued to argue, had been a kind of benevolent patriarchy. Even if slavery had been sometimes oppressive, even if it had not been free of excesses and defects, even if it had brutalized some bondsmen, this much-maligned institution, according to its practitioners, had given the bulk of the race a necessary protection which freedom now threatened to remove. "How much better off they were when slaves!" a Mississippi planter affirmed. "A man would see to his own niggers, like he would to his own stock. But the niggers now don't belong to anybody, and it's no man's business whether they live or die."[57]

If dependency on the master had protected and sustained the Negro as a slave, what would happen to him as a freedman? How would he manage to survive in a hostile and competitive environment, exposed now to unfriendly whites, his own innate vices, and a free-market economy? Such questions grew out of a tradition of proslavery argument, and the answer seemed no less obvious after emancipation. Without the patriarchal guidance and support of the former master, the African race would surely exterminate itself. "The child is already born who will behold the last negro in the State of Mississippi," a Natchez newspaper affirmed in early 1866. Whatever agreement existed among whites about the future of the Negro as a free man invariably revolved around the conviction that he would sink lower and lower in the social scale, that he would dissipate the civilizing influences he had acquired from contact with his master, and that he could never survive the competitive struggle for life with a superior race. The antislavery movement, in other words, would soon discover that in abolishing slavery it had abolished the race itself.[58]

Historical analogies came quickly to mind. The freed slaves now faced a doom not unlike that of the other inferior and degraded species in their midst—the Indian. If anything, the African race might diminish at an even more rapid rate. "They're a-goin' faster'n the Injins," a Georgia planter insisted. "The negro is the most inferior of the human races," Grace Elmore argued from her home in South Carolina several months before the first of her servants defected, "far beneath the Indian or Hindu, and how can it be expected that they will be the white mans equal. It will be with them as with the Indian." But like most, she held out a modicum of hope: "The negro will disappear except where he is kept in subjection, and consequently where it will be [in] the interest of the master to promote the welfare of body and soul."[59]

The logic of the argument seemed irresistible. If a master did not look out for the welfare of the ex-slave, no one else would, including the ex-slave himself. Nor could the unfortunate Negro be blamed for the innate vices and defects he shared with most tropical peoples—what a Mississippi planter called the "indisposition to provide for the future by sustained industry and persevering efforts." The typical Negro, as the whites viewed him, worked only to satisfy immediate wants; he was careless or thoughtless of anything beyond the present. Unlike most whites, he was not motivated by a desire for gain; hence, he was apt to do nothing after earning a little money until starvation forced him back to work.[60] If the arguments about improvidence and the absence of initiative had a familiar ring about them, they had traditionally characterized upper-class and employer attitudes toward laboring peoples, white and black. A Georgia planter reflected this view when he advised some fellow planters that the problems they now faced were class rather than racial in nature. "I'll tell you how 't is: a free nigger's jest like any low-down white fellow,—pull off your coat and work with him, and he does well enough; put it on and go off to town, and he shirks."[61]

In forecasting the doom of the Afro-American race, many whites hastened to add their regrets that this should be the outcome of emancipation. The paternal spirit manifested itself in expressions of sympathy and remorse and in outbursts of nostalgia. "If you had seen them in slave days," one planter told an English visitor, "what a merry, rollicking, laughing set they were! Now they are care-worn and sad. You hardly hear them laugh now as they used to do." When the first postwar governor of Mississippi declared that the Negro was "destined to extinction, beyond all doubt," he thought it "alarming" and "appalling" and hoped he might be mistaken; a South Carolina magistrate "pitied" the freedmen for their inability to understand the freedom thrust upon them; and the Virginia planter who expected the race to "first become pauper and then disappear" still wished the freedmen well and "sincerely" hoped they would disappoint his expectations. But there was good reason to suspect that professions of this kind were not altogether sincere. That is, the former ruling class had a peculiar stake in black failure.[62]

While traveling by rail through the countryside of western Tennessee, J. T. Trowbridge, the northern journalist and author, caught occasional glimpses of homeless ex-slaves huddled around the campfires in their makeshift settlements, warming their hands and watching with curiosity as the train rolled by them. The conversation he overheard of his fellow passengers might have been repeated almost anywhere in the South when native whites came across such scenes:

> "That's freedom! that's what the Yankees have done for 'em!"
> "They'll all be dead before spring."
> "The Southern people were always their best friends. How I pity them! don't you?"
> "Oh, yes, of course I pity them! How much better off they were when they were slaves!"

What dismayed Trowbridge were not the remarks themselves (he had heard them so often) but the expressions of "grim exultation" and the " 'I-told-you-so!' air of triumph" that accompanied them, as though their prophecies were their desires. "The slave-owners, having foretold that freedom would prove fatal to the bondman, experienced a satisfaction in seeing their predictions come true. The usual words of sympathy his condition suggested had all the hardness and hollowness of cant."[63]

To think that the freedmen could possibly succeed defied logic and nature and contradicted the very reasons they had been held as slaves. How much more reassuring to argue that emancipation—unless properly controlled—sealed the race's doom and that the abolitionists had succeeded only in expediting racial suicide. This belief rested, of course, on the popular assumption that the character and capacity of the Negro remained immutable; emancipation only filled his head with dreams and aspirations which could never be fulfilled. But that in itself raised a potentially dangerous situation requiring the utmost vigilance and understanding. If blacks should aspire to rise above their appointed station in life, the results were predictable. "Of course, they'll fail," an Alabama planter assured a northern visitor; "we have no uneasiness on that score; but we are the friends of these people, and we are sorry to see them expose themselves to so much misery in making attempts that we know from the outset must be abortive. Isn't it better to have the laws in some way take the matter out of their hands and make them work?"[64]

If the African race was to survive, then, the old slaveholding class deemed it essential that they determine the conditions of survival—preferably a forced dependency allowing the freedman little or no opportunity to prove his own individual worth. Before emancipation, the planters had argued that they kept the Negro in bondage for his own benefit. Now they could contend that the freedman's welfare demanded a condition of tutelage and a system of constructive compulsion. After all, to expect that self-interest alone would motivate ex-slaves, as it did whites, to be productive laborers was to betray ignorance of the race itself. "You don't know the niggers," a young Virginian told a northern reporter. "No nigger, free or slave, in these Southern States, nor in any part of the known world, ever would work or ever will work unless he's made to."[65]

ALTHOUGH THE FORMER SLAVEHOLDERS constituted a small minority of the white population of the South, nearly everyone still looked to them for leadership and supported the urgent need to impose controls on the newly freed blacks. To play on white fears of the Negro, moreover, as most planters recognized, served an important function in maintaining their own supremacy and in muting class antagonisms. Despite the abolition of slavery, the attitudes, fears, and assumptions which had helped to shape and reinforce that institution for over two centuries remained virtually unaffected. When the Freedmen's Bureau commissioner in Mississippi and Louisiana commented on the state of white opinion in the post-emancipation South, he invited attack as a northern partisan but the evidence was altogether too compelling to discount his conclusions:

> Wherever I go—the street, the shop, the house, the hotel, or the steamboat—I hear the people talk in such a way as to indicate that they are yet unable to conceive of the negro as possessing any rights at all. Men who are honorable in their dealings with their white neighbors will cheat a negro without feeling a single twinge of their honor. To kill a negro they do not deem murder; to debauch a negro woman they do not think fornication; to take the property away from a negro they do not consider robbery. The people boast that when they get freedmen affairs in their own hands, to use their own classic expression, "the niggers will catch hell."
>
> The reason of all this is simple and manifest. The whites esteem the blacks their property by natural right, and however much they may admit that the individual relations of masters and slaves have been destroyed by the war and by the President's emancipation proclamation, they still have an ingrained feeling that the blacks at large belong to the whites at large, and whenever opportunity serves they treat the colored people just as their profit, caprice or passion may dictate.[66]

No doubt some southern whites might have thought this a crude characterization of their thinking, but nearly every white man and woman readily agreed to the wisdom of restraining and controlling black men and women in ways that were not thought to be necessary for themselves. "The whites seem wholly unable to comprehend that freedom for the negro means the same thing as freedom for them," a northern reporter concluded after his travels in the postwar South. "I did not anywhere find a man who could see that laws should be applicable to all persons alike; and hence even the best men hold that each State must have a negro code."[67]

Despite a white rhetoric that doomed the freedmen to self-extinction, most planters needed and demanded their labor. And despite all the talk about a childlike race, most whites expected blacks to work and behave like mature adults. Although the war and emancipation had, in the view of whites, filled the heads of their former slaves with unrealistic expectations and rendered their labor erratic, they refused to give up on them altogether, at least not until time-honored remedies proved ineffectual. Whether he had ever owned slaves or not, almost every white man remained convinced that only rigid controls and compulsion would curtail the natural propensity of blacks toward idleness and vagrancy, induce them to labor for others, and correct their mistaken notions about freedom and working for themselves. Claiming an intimate and exclusive knowledge of the Negro's character ("We are the only ones that understand the nigger"), the former slaveholder demanded the necessary force to back up the traditional rights of authority over "his people," including the punishment of deviant behavior. Without compulsion of some kind, the experiment in free labor could not succeed. It was as simple as that.[68]

The self-evident truth which the planter class now imparted to the freed slaves was that they must either work for white folks or starve. That advice differed in no significant way from what Federal officials had been telling blacks since the moment of liberation. "When that lesson has been thoroughly learned and inwardly digested," a Macon newspaper declared, "the negro may perhaps be of some value." Whatever sympathies Northerners pretended for the Negro, southern whites assumed they could not object to a principle so universally accepted. "All we want," a South Carolina planter told a northern visitor, "is that our Yankee rulers should give us the same privileges with regard to the control of labor which they themselves have." When pressed for his understanding of northern labor controls, he indicated that laborers were bound by law to make an annual contract and could be punished for any violations. Told that no such laws existed in the North, the planter seemed incredulous. "How do you manage without such laws? How can you get work out of a man unless you compel him in some way?" The visitor replied that "Natural laws" sufficed, with the best laborers commanding the best wages. "You can't do that way with niggers," the planter immediately retorted. When comparing the two labor systems, some southern whites insisted, in fact, that this distinction be understood—the presence of the African race made the southern situation unique and demanded a unique response. "Northern laborers are like other men," one planter explained, but "southern laborers are nothing but niggers, and you can't make anything else out of them. They're not controlled by the same motives as white men, and unless you have power to compel them, they'll only work when they can't beg or steal enough to keep from starving."[69]

The urgency of the situation seemed obvious enough. To plant a crop without knowing how many laborers might be around to harvest it made postwar agricultural operations a highly risky venture. Henry W. Ravenel, for example, thought no planter would want to engage in such operations "without some guarantee that his labour is to be controlled & continued under penalties & forfeitures." To make the free labor system work, some

planters suggested that the ex-slaves be apprenticed to their former masters or to an employer of their choice. The apprenticeship laws enacted by
a number of states imposed such controls on blacks under eighteen years
of age who were orphans or whose parents could not or refused to support
them. Such laws provided some planters with a cheap supply of involuntary labor (if he were deemed a "suitable" person, the former owner of
the minor was given preference); at the same time, the arbitrary power
these laws usually gave to the courts to bind out such children without the consent of their parents revived the specter of families forcibly separated.[70]

The idea of apprenticing nearly four million ex-slaves to their former
masters never received serious consideration. Nor did the proposals to
distribute the freed blacks equally around the country or to colonize them
elsewhere make any sense to planters who desperately needed laborers.[71]
Anxious to regain control over their blacks, but not entirely indifferent to
northern reactions, the planter class preferred to establish a docile black
labor force in the guise of fulfilling their Christian duties and obligations
to those who had once served them so well. Claiming sympathy for their
former slaves, they demanded the controls necessary to make them once
again "happy and prosperous." To control and regulate the freedmen was
to advance and protect the best interests of this unfortunate race, to help
them restrain their "worst passions," to redeem them from certain relapse
into semi-barbarism, to save them from "inevitable failure," to disabuse
their minds of false illusions, and to assist them in finding their proper
place in postwar southern society. "If they cannot (as they never can)
occupy the places of legislators, judges, teachers, &c.," a North Carolina
planter explained, "they may be useful as tillers of the soil, as handicrafts-
men, as servants in various situations, and be happy in their domestic and
family relations. . . . It is our Christian duty to encourage them to these
ends."[72] That was putting the best possible face on the legislation adopted
by most of the ex-Confederate states to regulate the freedmen—laws that
came to be known collectively as the Black Codes.

To the white South, the principle seemed altogether clear and fair-
minded: "Teach the negro that if he goes to work, keeps his place, and
behaves himself, he will be protected by *our* white laws." Although borrowing heavily from antebellum restrictions on free Negroes, as well as from
northern apprenticeship laws and Freedmen's Bureau and War Department regulations, the Black Codes were still very much a product of postwar southern thinking, both a legal expression of the lingering paternalism
(to protect the ex-slave from himself) and a legislative response to immediate and pressing economic problems. While the Codes defined the freedman's civil and legal rights, permitting him to marry, hold and sell
property, and sue and be sued, the key provisions were those which defined
him as an agricultural laborer, barred or circumscribed any alternative
occupations, and compelled him to work. "Upon this point turns the entire
question," a South Carolina newspaper said of the principle of compulsion,

"and as that is decided, so is the safety or ruin of this country." If the Codes did not reestablish slavery, as some northern critics charged, neither did they recognize the former slaves as free men and women, entitled to equal protection under the law. As if to underscore how little had changed, a South Carolina law defined the two parties to a labor contract as "servants" and "masters."[73]

Although the laws differed from state to state, the underlying principles and the major provisions remained the same. If found without "lawful employment," a freedman could be arrested as a common vagrant, jailed and fined; if unable to pay the fine, he would be hired out to an employer who in turn assumed the financial liability and deducted it from the laborer's wages. The Mississippi law also defined as vagrants any blacks unable or unwilling to pay a new tax to support Negro indigents, while the Alabama code included as vagrants "any runaway, stubborn servant or child" and any laborer "who loiters away his time" or fails to comply with the terms of his employment. Several of the codes also set down the hours of labor (from sunrise to sunset), the duties, and the behavior expected of black agricultural workers. With a sliding scale of fines for violations, the Louisiana code employed the kind of language a master might have once used in his instructions to the overseer:

> Bad work shall not be allowed. Failing to obey reasonable orders, neglect of duty, and leaving home without permission will be deemed disobedience; impudence, swearing, or indecent language to, or in the presence of the employer, his family, or agent, or quarreling and fighting with one another shall be deemed disobedience.[74]

Rather than expedite the slave's transition to freedom or help him to realize his aspirations, the Black Codes embodied in law the widely held assumption that he existed largely for the purpose of raising crops for a white employer. Although the ex-slave ceased to be the property of a master, he could not aspire to become his own master. No law stated the proposition quite that bluntly but the provisions breathed that spirit in ways that could hardly be misunderstood. If a freedman decided that agricultural labor was not his special calling, the law often left him with no practical alternative. To discourage those who aspired to be artisans, mechanics, or shopkeepers, or who already held such positions, the South Carolina code, for example, prohibited a black person from entering any employment except agricultural labor or domestic service unless he obtained a special license and a certification from a local judge of his "skill and fitness" and "good moral character." This provision, of course, threatened to undermine the position of the old free Negro class which had once nearly dominated the skilled trades in places like Charleston. With unconcealed intent, the Mississippi law simply required special licenses of any black wishing to engage in "irregular or job work." To discourage freedmen who aspired to raise their own crops, Mississippi barred them from renting or leasing any land outside towns or cities, leaving to local authorities any restrictions they might wish to place on black ownership of real estate.

By adopting harsh vagrancy laws and restricting non-agricultural employment, the white South clearly intended to stem the much-feared drift of freedmen toward the cities and to underscore their status as landless agricultural laborers. Even as Mississippi forbade them to lease lands outside towns or cities, local ordinances there and in neighboring Louisiana made black residency within the towns or cities virtually intolerable if not impossible. The ordinance adopted in Opelousas, Louisiana, deservedly served as a model and inspiration for other communities. To enter the town, a black person needed his employer's permission, stipulating the object of the visit and the time necessary to accomplish it; any freedman found on the streets after ten o'clock at night without a written pass or permit from his employer would be subject to arrest and imprisonment. No freedman could rent or keep a house within the town limits "under any circumstances," or reside within the town unless employed by a white person who assumed responsibility for his conduct. To hold any public meetings or to assemble in large numbers for any reason, blacks needed the mayor's permission, as they also did to "preach, exhort or otherwise declaim" to black congregations. Nor could they possess weapons or sell, barter, or exchange any kind of merchandise without special permits. A freedman found violating these ordinances could be punished by imprisonment, fines, and forced labor on the city streets. Virtually identical ordinances were adopted in several Louisiana towns and parishes, with St. Landry Parish adding its own brand of punishment: "confining the body of the offender within a barrel placed over his or her shoulders, in the manner practiced in the army," for a period not to exceed twelve hours. While finding the ordinances "incompatible with freedom," the black newspaper in New Orleans noted that freedmen could walk the streets up to ten o'clock at night—one hour later than under slavery. "This additional hour is the fruit of our victories in the field," the editor declared; "four years of a bloody war have been fought to gain that one hour. The world certainly moves in that quarter."[75]

With the adoption of the Black Codes, the place of the ex-slave in postwar southern society had been fixed in law, his mobility checked, his bargaining power sharply reduced, and his rights of appeal hedged with difficulties. Any freedman who refused to work at the prevailing wage in a particular area could be defined as a vagrant, and there was little to protect him from combinations of employers setting wages and conditions. To many in the North, the Codes smacked of the old bondage, and even some southern whites thought them ill-advised, impractical, or at least badly timed. *"We showed our hand too soon,"* a Mississippi planter conceded. "We ought to have waited till the troops were withdrawn, and our representatives admitted to Congress; then we could have had everything our own way." Unmoved by the criticism they anticipated, the authors of the Florida code thought it "needless to attempt to satisfy the exactions of the fanatical theorists—we have a duty to perform—the protection of our wives and children from threatened danger, and the prevention of scenes which may cost the extinction of an entire race." The special committee preparing the Mississippi code conceded that some of the proposed legislation "may seem rigid and stringent" but only "to the sickly modern humanitarians."[76]

To the former slaves, whose opinions carried little weight, the Codes clouded the entire issue of freedom and left them highly dubious of what rights if any they could exercise without fear of arrest or legal harassment. In petitioning the governor, the freedmen of Claiborne County, Mississippi, thought it necessary to ask for a clarification: "Mississippi has abolished slavery. Does she mean it or is it a policy for the present?" By barring them from leasing or renting land, the petitioners charged that the legislature had left them with no choice but to purchase land, knowing full well that "not one of us out of a thousand" could afford the price of even a quarter of an acre. If any of them deserted an employer because of cruel treatment, they could be arrested and forcibly returned to him. How could this be reconciled with their newly won freedom? "Now we are free," they insisted, "we do not want to be hunted by negro runners and their hounds unless we are guilty of a criminal crime." To read the daily newspapers, the petitioners asserted, was to learn only of "our faults" rather than of the many blacks who worked to enrich the very people seeking to circumscribe their liberties. Who made possible the comforts of the planter class if not hard-working black men and women?

> If every one of us colored people were removed from the state of Mississippi our superiors would soon find out who were their supporters. We the laborers have enriched them and it is as much impossible for them to live with out us as it is for we to be removed from them.

The petitioners assured the governor of their willingness to work for anyone who treated them well and paid them adequately; they reminded him, too, of how the slaves had stood by their white families in troublesome times. Although they recognized the presence of some "good and honest" employers among the whites, such men were "not the majority" and the "good" employer could be easily intimidated and "put down as a negro spoiler." Finally, the petitioners thought Jefferson Davis, a fellow Mississippian, should be set free, if only because "we [know] worse Masters than he was. Altho he tried hard to keep us all slaves we forgive him."[77]

But even as black petitioners and conventions condemned the Black Codes, or appealed for an amelioration of the laws, few expected a receptive audience among the planters and white farmers who controlled the legislative and executive branches of the new southern governments. After all, a black editor in Charleston observed of the "Colored Code" in his state, "it expresses an average of the justice and humanity which the late slaveholders possess." But if "the right will prevail and truth triumph in the end," as this editor firmly believed, most blacks came to look to the halls of Congress rather than to the state capitol for relief. If southern whites could easily dismiss the pleas of black meetings and politically powerless black leaders, they could not afford to ignore the way in which the black newspaper in Georgia chose to frame its editorial attack on the Black Codes: "Such legislation can but tend to keep the State out of the Union, retain troops in our houses and public buildings, and increase taxation to maintain a large standing army."[78]

The Black Codes proved to be short-lived, largely because the South had moved precipitately, impetuously, and carelessly. Although Federal officials, both in the Freedmen's Bureau and the Union Army, had implemented labor policies which were strikingly similar, the Codes were deemed too blatantly discriminatory and overly repressive. Not long after the Codes were adopted, Federal officials ordered many of them suspended, nearly always on the grounds that freedmen should be subject to the same regulations, penalties, punishments, and courts as whites. Several of the state legislatures, too, had second thoughts about their actions, particularly after the initial insurrection panic subsided and the labor situation improved; the legislators themselves repealed or revised some of the more obnoxious clauses, and the Codes passed by a number of states in 1866 proved less harsh.[79]

Despite Federal and court orders suspending their operation, the Codes were nonetheless enforced in regions where Freedmen's Bureau officials refused to intervene and where blacks found it difficult to appeal local decisions. Since some of the new laws, moreover, theoretically applied to both races, they were permitted to stand, with local authorities deciding how and when to enforce them. The most obvious example was the vagrancy law; although largely enforced against blacks, authorities could if they chose enforce it against whites. The mayor of Aberdeen, Mississippi, rounded up hundreds of freedmen in early 1866, gave them a few hours to contract with an employer for the year, and put the others to work sweeping the city streets. The local ordinances in Louisiana "still hold good in many parishes," the *New Orleans Tribune* charged, despite a War Department order countermanding them; however, the ordinances were no longer published in the local newspapers and thus had to be "carried on in the dark." When dealing with blacks under contract who left their employers, both local and Federal officials could be expected to act within the spirit and provisions of the Codes. The appearance in a Mississippi newspaper of an advertisement asking for the apprehension of a runaway laborer, complete with a description and sketch of the culprit, stirred old memories. "It is positively refreshing to look at it," one editor remarked. No less familiar, a black man in Natchez served a jail sentence for harboring and feeding an apprentice who had run away from "a most estimable lady."[80]

If the Codes were dead, the sentiment which had created them was still very much alive. Whether enforced, set aside, or amended, the Black Codes had revealed how the ruling class expected to perpetuate that rule. The setback, then, could be viewed as but temporary, a concession to expediency. If statutes proved unavailing in returning the ex-slaves to the fields and kitchens where they belonged, economic necessity and the enforcement of contracts could achieve the same goals within an ideological framework familiar and acceptable to the North. Neither during slavery days nor in the immediate postwar years, moreover, did the planter rely entirely on legislative enactments to maintain the order and discipline he deemed essential. When it came to managing blacks, experience taught him that the place to establish his authority was in the field and the kitchen, not simply in the courthouse.

7
_____

FACED WITH troublesome laborers after the war, a Louisiana sugar planter mused over the changed situation and how he would have dealt with such problems in better days. "Eaton [an overseer] must find it very hard to lay aside the old strap—As for myself, I would give a good deal to amuse myself with it, a little while. I have come to the conclusion that the great secret of our success was the great motive power contained in that little instrument." Few of the former slaveholders would have disputed that observation. To maintain a disciplined and docile labor force, they had long acknowledged their reliance on "the power of fear." Nor had the emancipation of the slaves lessened the need to exercise their traditional prerogatives. "They can't be governed except with the whip," one planter explained. "Now on my plantation there wasn't much whipping, say once a fortnight; but the negroes knew they would be whipped if they didn't behave themselves, and the fear of the lash kept them in good order."[81]

When Federal officials suspended the newly enacted Black Codes, southern whites greeted the decision with predictable expressions of dismay but few were altogether surprised and some felt the states had acted foolishly. But when Federals in some regions reprimanded employers for using the whip on black laborers or forbade any kind of corporal punishment, that was truly hard to accept—even to comprehend. "I know the nigger," a Mississippi planter pleaded with a Freedmen's Bureau official. "The employer must have some sort of punishment. I don't care what it is. If you'll let me tie him up by the thumbs, or keep him on bread and water, that will do.... All I want is just to have it so that when I get the niggers on to my place, and the work is begun, they can't sit down and look me square in the face and do nothing."[82]

To manage black laborers, numerous planters agreed, was not unlike handling mules; both could be stubborn, even insolent, and experience suggested that they were most serviceable and contented when they had "plenty of feed, plenty of work, and a little licking." What these planters now demanded was simply the necessary authority to exact the fear and the deference always considered essential to racial control. Like the Black Codes, corporal punishment would benefit the blacks by restraining their worst passions and forcing them to acknowledge authority. "A nigger has got to know you're his master," a Georgia planter still insisted, "and then when he understands that he's content." Still another former slaveholder attributed his postwar success in managing thirty-five freedmen to their *fear* of punishment: "You see I never let myself down to 'em."[83]

If the old discipline in any way contradicted the new freedom, few of the former slaveholders cared to admit it. To them, emancipation had only made more urgent the need to exercise traditional authority. Although employers made less use of the whip than before the war, they managed to find equally effective and less controversial alternatives. After serving a fifteen-day jail sentence for lashing a former slave ("was there ever such a damned outrage!"), a South Carolina planter claimed to have "larnt a trick" that exacted the proper respect of his blacks. "I jest strings 'em up by the thumbs for 'bout half an hour, an' then they are damned glad to go to work." Since the Union Army used that method to discipline its own men as well as recalcitrant blacks, the South Carolinian obviously expected no interference. Fearful of whipping their freed slaves, lest they lodge a complaint with Federal officials, some planters took out their frustrations in verbal abuse. "Can't lick free niggers, but I don't know if there's any law ag'in cussin' 'em, and I believe it does 'em a heap o' good," a Georgian suggested to a group of fellow planters. "It's next best to lickin'. Jest cuss one o' 'em right smart for 'bout five minutes, and he'll play off peart." Unfortunately for this planter, emancipation had left him without a black to curse and he could only fantasize about how to bring the freedmen under control. "I should like to lick a hundred free negroes jest once all 'round. If I didn't bring 'em to know their places, I'd pay ten dollars apiece for all I failed on."[84]

The degree to which emancipation altered the day-to-day behavior and temperament of the former slaveholder became a matter of immediate concern to black men and women. On numerous farms and plantations, they soon discovered that the potential of the white family for volatile behavior had in no way been abated and it seemed like the old times again. Katie Darling, a former Texas slave, remembered staying with her "white folks" for six years after the war "and missy whip me jist like she did 'fore." If Anna Miller perceived any change in her master after emancipation, it was only his rapid mental deterioration. "De marster gets worser in de disposition and goes 'roun' sort of talkin' to hisse'f and den he gits to cussin' ev'rybody." Within a year after vowing that he would not live in a country "whar de niggers am free," her master killed himself.[85]

The previous behavior of their masters, as many ex-slaves suddenly discovered, often proved an unreliable guide to how they would now conduct themselves and manage their freed blacks. Frank Fikes, for example, claimed to have suffered few hardships or beatings as a slave. "Old miss and mars was not mean to us at all until after surrender and we were freed.

We did not have a hard time until after we were freed. They got mad at us because we was free . . ." Nor were some of the former masters oblivious to how emancipation could work curious changes in their attitudes and temperament. When he had held slaves, a South Carolina planter recalled, he had always thought of himself as a model master and only once had he resorted to whipping one of his blacks. But now, in his relations with these same people as freedmen and freedwomen, he found himself increasingly moody and temperamental. On one occasion, he misinterpreted what a former slave told him and had to be restrained by several friends who were present from shooting the man on the spot; instead, he calmed himself by administering 130 lashes to him, "hard as I could lay on." But if the whipping relieved this planter of his anger, it also left him displeased with his loss of self-control. "I was wrong, I know, but I was in a passion. That's the way we treat our servants, and shall treat them, until we can get used to the new order of things,—if we ever can."[86]

Although Federal officials were inclined to overlook how an employer chose to discipline his laborers, the blacks themselves refused to be passive spectators. If a planter relied on the old discipline, confident that fear and punishment could still maintain a captive labor force, he might discover that his intended victims, often his former slaves, no longer felt compelled to submit. After what they had endured as slaves, they saw no reason to tolerate such treatment as freedmen. "Damn him," a South Carolina black remarked after an altercation with his old master, "he never done nufin all his damned life but beat me and kick me and knock me down; an' I hopes I git eben with him some day." In Mississippi, an overseer who responded to a disobedient field hand by threatening him with an ax suddenly found himself facing the laborer's daughter and several other blacks, all of them holding axes. "I had to run for my life," the overseer testified. On the Brokenburn plantation in Louisiana, John B. Stone, the highly temperamental son of the mistress, shot a black youth after an argument in the fields. That so infuriated the other hands that they turned upon Stone and might have killed him had not some others intervened. Still, Kate Stone would never forget the sight of her brother being escorted to the house by "a howling, cursing mob with the women shrieking, 'Kill him!' and all brandishing pistols and guns." The family thought it best to send John away to school, at least until a semblance of calm had been restored. Upon his return, he seemed a much-changed and subdued young man. "He never speaks now of killing people as he formerly had a habit of doing," his sister wrote of him.[87]

If open resistance invited severe reprisals, the freedmen could exercise the power to withhold their labor or leave the premises and never return. The ties that kept former slaves on the plantation were often so tenuous that an employer's threat or attempt to inflict punishment might end the relationship altogether. Faced with the imminent loss of their laborers, many a former master and mistress suddenly became "very con'scending" after the war, learned to address their blacks in terms of respect, and banished both the whip and the overseer. "I told my overseer the old style wouldn't do,—the niggers wouldn't stand it,—and he promised better fashions," an Alabama planter remarked; "but it wasn't two days before he fell from grace, and went to whipping again. That just raised the Old Scratch with them; and I don't blame 'em." In explaining the changed attitudes of their old masters, some former slaves suggested that fear itself could have been a motivating factor. "He never was mean to us after freedom," a former Tennessee slave recalled, along with the many beatings she had once endured. "He was 'fraid the niggers might kill him." Rather than trust their former master to exercise proper judgment, many blacks extracted from him, as a condition of employment, assurances that he would refrain from corporal punishment and discharge the overseer.[88]

By these and other demands, the freedmen suggested the need not only to abolish the relics of bondage but to give substance to their position as free workers, with the same rights and prerogatives they had observed white laborers exercising. Nowhere would they manifest this determination more vividly than in the new economic arrangements they worked out with their employers. Unfortunately, the former slaveholding class seemed in many respects less equipped to make the transition to freedom than their former slaves. No matter how hard some tried, few of them were capable of learning new ways and shaking off the old attitudes. Even if they could, they found themselves increasingly trapped into an untenable position. Desperately needing to exact enough labor from their former slaves to meet a brutally depressed market, employers now encountered free workers who looked first to their own subsistence and refused to work up to an exploitative level they deemed incompatible with their new status. When these conflicting needs created an impasse, as they often did, the employer class was forced to look elsewhere for the kind of compulsion and guidance that might once again produce a stable and tractable labor force. How ironic that none other than the much-hated Yankee conquerors should have ultimately shown them the way.

## 8

NOT LONG AFTER Federal authorities set aside the Black Code of South Carolina, Armisted Burt, who had helped to frame the new laws, noted with obvious satisfaction that the Union commander had ordered freedmen to contract with an employer or be sentenced to hard labor on public projects. "I have no doubt the Yankees will manage them," he concluded. The confidence he expressed was not misplaced. No matter how much whites chafed under military rule and occupation, the planter class—native whites and northern lessees alike—often acknowledged its indebtedness to the Union Army for controlling the otherwise restless and rebellious dispositions of the freed slaves. After conversing with the local

commander on steps that had been taken to suppress a feared black uprising, the manager of a plantation in low-country South Carolina breathed
much easier: "Our people object to the troops being sent here. I thank God
they are here." No sooner were cases of "insubordination" reported to
Federal authorities, a Georgia clergyman and planter informed his sister,
than forceful steps were taken to suppress the troublemakers. "The effect
has been a remarkable quietude and order in all this region. The Negroes
are astounded at the idea of being whipped by Yankees. (But keep all this
a secret, lest we should be deprived of their services. I have not called on
them yet, but may have to do so.)"[89]

If the Black Codes had not been the edicts of legislatures dominated
by ex-Confederate leaders, they might not have suffered the fate of nullifi-
cation. The problem lay not so much in specific provisions as in what the
total product came to symbolize to the victorious North—white southern
intransigence and unrepentance in the face of military defeat. But the
suspension of the Codes in no way diminished the need to reactivate and
control black labor. Almost every Federal official recognized that necessity,
and Union commanders moved quickly to expel former plantation hands
from the towns and cities, to comply with the requests of planters to force
their blacks to work, and to punish freedmen for disobedience, theft, vagrancy, and erratic labor.[90] "Their idea of freedom," the provost marshal
of Bolivar County, Mississippi, said of the recently freed slaves, "is that
they are under no control; can work when they please, and go where they
wish. . . . It is my desire to apply the Punishments used in the Army of the
United States, for offences of the Negroes, and to make them do their duty."
Empowered to settle disputes between employers and laborers, the provost
marshals invariably sustained the authority of the planters. In Louisiana,
for example, plantation laborers testified to the hopelessness of appealing
any grievances they might have to the nearest Federal official:

> Q. Have you any white friend, in your parish, who will support your
> claims or take your defense?
> A. We have no white friends there.
> Q. Have you any colored friend who could do so?
> A. No colored man has any thing to say; none has any influence.
> Q. Is not the Provost Marshal a protector for your people?
> A. Whenever a new Provost Marshal comes he gives us justice for
> a fortnight or so; then he becomes acquainted with planters, takes din-
> ners with them, receives presents; and then we no longer have any rights,
> or very little.[91]

If Union officers eschewed the whip as an instrument of slavery, they
did not hesitate to employ familiar military punishments to deal with
"disorderly" blacks. "What's good enough for soldiers is good enough for
Niggers," a sergeant told a Florida woman who had expressed shock over
seeing her "negligent" servant hung up by the thumbs. Upon witnessing

a similar punishment meted out to two laborers he had reported for loitering on the job, a South Carolina planter heard them plead to be flogged instead. But if Yankee "justice" dismayed or surprised some native whites, a Mississippi hotelkeeper marveled at the way the local provost marshal had dealt with a "sassy" black who refused to work. "We've got a Provo' in our town," he boasted, "that settles their hash mighty quick. He's a downright high-toned man, that Provo', if he is a Yankee. . . . He tucked him [the black] up, guv him twenty lashes, and rubbed him down right smart with salt, for having no visible means of support." That evening, the black victim returned quite willingly to his job.[92]

Since the early days of occupation, Federal authorities had shared with planters a concern over how to keep the ex-slaves in the fields and impress upon them the necessity of labor. "The Yankees preach nothing but cotton, cotton," a Sea Islands slave exclaimed, voicing the dismay of many blacks over how quickly their liberators returned them to the familiar routines. Soon after the troops occupied a region, Union officers confronted the problem of what to do with the "contrabands" pouring into their camps. Although many of them were conscripted for military service and labor, the vast majority found themselves working on abandoned and confiscated plantations. The Federal government supervised some of these plantations, while leasing most of them to private individuals, including a number of northern whites intent on maximizing profits as quickly as possible. Thomas W. Knox, a white Northerner who tried his hand at plantation management, characterized most of his colleagues in the business as "unprincipled men" who had little regard for the former slave. "The difference between working for nothing as a slave, and working for the same wages under the Yankees," he observed, "was not always perceptible to the unsophisticated negro."[93] Small numbers of black farmers also managed to obtain leases, all of them eager to demonstrate the feasibility of free and independent labor. The most successful of such experiments took place at Davis Bend, Mississippi, where blacks secured leases on six extensive plantations, including two belonging to Joe and Jefferson Davis; the blacks repaid the government for the initial costs, managed their own affairs, raised and sold their own crops, and realized impressive profits.[94]

Whatever the promise of Davis Bend, neither the Union Army nor the Freedmen's Bureau thought to question the basic assumption underlying the discredited Black Codes—that the ex-slaves were fit only to till the land of others as agricultural laborers and that only compulsion would exact the necessary work and discipline. The proven success of black lessees at Davis Bend and elsewhere, no matter how widely applauded, failed to stem the steady drift toward restoration. Even before the termination of the war, loyal planters and those who took the oath of allegiance to the United States government were permitted to retain their plantations and to work the blacks on a wages or shares basis; Federal officials intervened only to provide planters with the necessary laborers, to suppress any disorders, and to provide guidelines for the management of the ex-slaves. In the view of some Union officers, only if the former master and his former slaves agreed to a separation should the blacks be permitted to leave the plantations on which they had worked. That was how Emma Holmes interpreted Federal policy in her region, and her mother accordingly reported to the local Union officer a black man who had taken a job elsewhere: "By yesterday morning he had found out the Yankees were his masters, and he walked back here to his work."[95]

Based on early experiences with the freedmen, the labor system established during the war by successive Union commanders in Louisiana proved far more typical of the Federal approach than the short-lived Davis Bend experiment. To meet the problem of growing numbers of black refugees and of plantations disrupted by black defections and erratic labor, General Nathaniel P. Banks promised to return the ex-slaves to the fields and to enforce "conditions of continuous and faithful service, respectful deportment, correct discipline, and perfect subordination on the part of the negroes." The regulations he issued manifested precisely that spirit: a contract system binding the ex-slaves to the land, compensating their labor with wages or shares, and assuring them of just treatment, adequate rations and clothing, medical attention, and education for their children. Although the freedman could select an employer, he was bound to him for the remainder of the year, during which time he was expected to perform "respectful, honest, faithful labor." To encourage compliance, one half of his wages would be withheld until the end of the season; any black refusing to enter into a contract, violating its terms, or found guilty of "indolence, insolence, and disobedience" would forfeit his pay and be subject to military arrest and employment without wages on public works. Conceding little else to emancipation, the new rules forbade employers from flogging their laborers or separating families; in numerous instances, however, freedmen were returned to their old masters with little concern for their subsequent treatment.[96]

Even if conceived in "a benevolent spirit," the labor system envisioned by these regulations struck some black critics as "freedom by toleration" and a "mitigated bondage" analogous to Russian serfdom. That was how the *New Orleans Tribune,* the articulate organ of the free colored community, chose to characterize the new rules. "Strange freedom indeed! Our freedmen, on the plantations, at the present time, could more properly be called, mock freedmen." If a laborer were truly free, the editor observed, he should be able to choose his place of residence and his trade or occupation, negotiate his own terms with an employer (including wages, conditions, and term of service), and bring court action against anyone who tried to defraud him; moreover, he should be paid the full value of his labor, not a wage stipulated by planters' meetings or Federal rules. Under the current regulations, the editor contended, blacks would have to work for wages which barely sustained them. But that deplorable fact seemed even less important than the ways in which the new system perpetuated and enforced the dependency of the freedmen on their former masters:

He does not wear his own clothes; but, as the slave, he wears his master's clothes. He does not eat his own bread, the bread he won by the sweat of his brow; he eats his master's bread. He is provided for like the mules and cattle on the plantations. And it is said that this is the way some people intend to follow to make men!

Finally, black critics thought it highly ironic but not altogether surprising that such a labor system should have been instituted and defended by white men who never ceased to display their abolitionist credentials as evidence of their good faith. "I despise a man who pretends to be an abolitionist, and who is only a deepskin abolitionist," a black clergyman told a meeting in New Orleans called to protest the labor regulations. "We have good friends, who will work with us till this country be a free country; but we have unfaithful friends also. A wolf came, one day, among sheep, in sheep's clothing; but he had a strange foot, and the sheep wondered at that. We, too, are ready to watch this foot."[97]

In defending the labor system of Louisiana, a Union officer not only alluded to his "life-time Anti-Slavery" but curtly dismissed the black critics in New Orleans as "a class of colored people who, with all their admirable qualities, have not yet forgotten that they were, themselves, slaveholders." But if the urban black elitists could be dismissed, Federal authorities would still have to contend with the black laborers themselves, most of whom had never read a newspaper and needed no one to remind them of the oppressive nature of the system under which they were now told to work. The kind of resistance they undertook varied from mass defections to open revolt; most of them, however, took out their grievances in the erratic work habits about which their employers continued to complain. Rather than submit to the new regulations, the blacks on a plantation south of New Orleans threw down their tools, vowed they would never work under such terms, and "left in a body." In Plaquemines Parish, field hands lodged the familiar complaint that they had not yet received their share of the previous season's crops; when they then refused to work, a civilian police officer attempted to arrest the ringleaders, only to find himself "beset upon by at least twenty—with hoes, shovels and hatchets" and forced to leave. Whether directed at specific labor regulations or reflecting general conditions, such outbreaks in Louisiana and elsewhere in the South would require the continued intervention of Federal authorities.[98]

Neither the charges of black critics nor the resistance of black laborers effected any significant changes in a labor system calculated to subordinate black labor to white planters and lessees. The advocates of that system persisted in the assumption that only coercion and rigid controls could assure the triumph and vindication of free labor in the South. When in mid-1863, at General Banks's request, two abolitionists evaluated the labor system of Louisiana, they reported with praise that on those plantations where the regulations had been faithfully implemented, the black laborers appeared to be "docile, industrious, & quiet." By 1865, the initial experiment in labor relations undertaken in Louisiana had evolved into a system of contracts between laborers and employers not unlike that being instituted elsewhere in the occupied South under the 'auspices of Federal authorities. Although the format and the specific terms might differ, the nature of the relationship remained essentially the same, as did the role of the Federal government and the sources of black discontent.[99]

Even as Federal authorities sought to keep the freed slaves on the plantations under a contract labor system, they were not able to guarantee to planters the quality of the labor performed. And to the planter class, caught up in depressed prices and the demands of a free market, that consideration remained critical. "Every abolitionist of New England believes that by thus merely changing slave labor to hireling labor ... everything will work well," Edmund Ruffin of Virginia said of the newly instituted labor system in Louisiana. The assumption would be proven false, he maintained, if only because black workers would "presume on their new rights of freedom" and fail to pass through a necessary "intermediate condition—which would be that of hunger & general privation & suffering, next to starving." After all, he noted, "few white laborers, of the lowest classes, will labor continuously unless under the compulsion of hunger & suffering of themselves & their familys. Still fewer free negroes will labor without this compulsion." Rather than view the disaster he predicted for plantation labor, Ruffin chose to put a bullet through his head several months after Appomattox. But few of his fellow planters chose that way out of their dilemma, preferring instead to employ every means at their disposal to regain control over both the movements and the labor of their former slaves.[100]

9

With the end of the war, the Bureau of Refugees, Freedmen and Abandoned Lands (commonly known as the Freedmen's Bureau) undertook to complete the transition to "free labor" initially begun under the direction of the Union Army. "The freedmen in a few instances are doing well," Thomas Smith reported in November 1865, not long after he had assumed his post as a Bureau subcommissioner in charge of northern Mississippi. He found many of the freedmen to be "indolent," some of them "disrespectful and totally unreliable," and almost all of them "greatly in need of instruction." But like most Bureau agents, he thought his primary concern was not to make literates of the freed slaves but to teach them to be reliable agricultural laborers. "They have very mistaken notions in regard to freedom. ... They ask, 'What is the value of freedom if one has nothing to go on?' That is to say if property in some shape or other is not to be given us, we might as well be slaves." He needed to disabuse their minds of such notions while at the same time restoring their faith in the former masters.

"The colored people lack confidence in the white man's *integrity;* they fear that, were they to hire to him, and work for him, that he would not pay them for their labor. . . . The more quickly, and the more perfectly, *that* confidence is restored, the better will it be for all classes." He could conceive of no more important task he faced in his new position.[101]

If "instruction" could cure the propensity of the ex-slaves toward "indolence" and "unreliable" labor, the agents of the Freedmen's Bureau eagerly assumed the role of teachers and disciplinarians. The lessons they imparted seldom varied and rarely departed from what Union officers and planters had been telling the slaves since the first days of liberation. "He would promise them nothing, but their freedom, and freedom means work," General Oliver O. Howard, the Bureau commissioner, explained to the freedmen of Austin, Texas, and he offered them, too, the classic maxim of nineteenth-century employers: "The man who sits about the streets and smokes, will make nothing." That very morning, Howard said, he had attended church services in different parts of the city and had heard a black clergyman and a white clergyman preach the gospel of love. "Oh, if you will only practice what you preach," the commissioner told the freedmen, "it will all be well." But if they refused to work, a Bureau officer warned the blacks of Mississippi, they should expect neither sympathy, love, nor subsistence. "Your houses and lands belong to the white people, and you cannot expect that they will allow you to live on them in idleness." Nor should the ex-slave expect the state or Federal government "to let any man lie about idle, without property, doing mischief. A vagrant law is right in principle. I cannot ask the civil officers to leave you idle, to beg or steal. If they find any of you without business and means of living, they will do right if they treat you as bad persons and take away your misused liberty."[102]

Upon assuming office, the local Freedmen's Bureau agent seized every opportunity to preach the gospel of work to the blacks in his district, often visiting the plantations themselves at the invitation of the grateful proprietors. In addressing the assembled laborers, he would familiarize them with their "duties and obligations," seek to correct their "exaggerated ideas" of freedom, impress upon them the need to be "orderly, respectful, and industrious," and assure them of protection and compensation "commensurate with their industry and demeanor." At the same time, Bureau commissioners implored the freedmen, in words that would become all too familiar, to exhibit those traditional virtues of patience and forbearance, no matter what the provocation.

> Your freedom will expose you to some new troubles. Bad men will take advantage of your ignorance and impose upon you. Some will try to defraud you of your wages, and a few may be wicked and cowardly enough to revenge their losses upon you by violence. But let none of these things provoke you to evil deeds. It is better to suffer wrong than to do wrong.

No doubt many Bureau agents took comfort in the impact of their message. "The Negro is often suspicious of his former master and will not believe him," the subcommissioner in Jackson, Mississippi, observed, "but when assured by the Federal authorities that he must go to work and behave himself, he does so contentedly." That made it all the more imperative, he thought, "for the good of the Negro and the peace of the Country," to have Bureau representatives visit every part of their districts.[103] The manager of a plantation in Bolivar County, Mississippi, heartily agreed. "If you would send an agent here to look into matters, and give some advice, I would be pleased to have him make his quarters with me for a week or two." With unconcealed enthusiasm, a planter near Columbia, South Carolina, welcomed the advice a Bureau official gave to his laborers. "You're their best friend, they all know," he told him, "and I'm very glad you've come down this way." The planter had good reason to be grateful. Until the official's visit, the freedmen had thought they owned the plantation.[104]

Acting in what they deemed to be the best interests of the ex-slaves, the strongest and proven advocates of the freedmen's cause admonished them to prove their fitness for freedom by laboring as faithfully as they had as slaves—and even more productively. "Plough and plant, dig and hoe, cut and gather in the harvest," General Rufus Saxton urged them. "Let it be seen that where in slavery there was raised a blade of corn or a pound of cotton, in freedom there will be two." Along with Saxton, few whites were more committed to the freedmen than Clinton B. Fisk, a Bureau official who subsequently helped to found one of the first black colleges. And he doubtless thought himself to be speaking in their best interests when he advised the freedmen to remain in their old places and work for their former masters.

> You have been associated with them for many years; you are bound to the old home by many ties, and most of you I trust will be able to get on as well with your late masters as with anyone else. . . . He is not able to do without you, and you will, in most cases, find him as kind, honest, and liberal as other men. Indeed he has for you a kind of family affection. . . . Do not think that, in order to be free, you must fall out with your old master, gather up your bundles and trudge off to a strange city. This is a great mistake. As a general rule, you can be as free and as happy in your old home, for the present, as any where else in the world.[105]

Consistent with such advice, Freedmen's Bureau officials made every effort to rid the urban centers of black refugees and to force them back onto the plantations. (Ironically, the very presence of the Bureau in the towns and villages had induced many ex-slaves to settle there, thinking they might be more secure with Federal protection nearby.) A successful Bureau officer in Culpeper, Virginia, was able to report that "this village was overrun with freedmen when I took charge here, but I have succeeded in getting the most of them out into the country on farms. The freedmen are, almost without an exception, going to work, most of them by the year."[106]

Having been established to facilitate the transition from slavery to freedom, the Bureau faced an admittedly immense task. With limited personnel and funds, it was forced to operate on a number of levels, providing the newly freed slaves with food rations and medical care, assisting them in their education, helping to reunite families, relocating thousands of ex-slaves on abandoned lands, and transporting still more to areas where the scarcity of labor commanded higher wages. In its most critical role as a labor mediator, the Bureau set out to correct abuses in contracts, establish "fair" wage rates, force employers to pay what they had promised, and break up planter conspiracies to depress wages. "What we wish to do is plain enough," a Bureau officer in North Carolina announced. "We desire to instruct the colored people of the South, to lift them up from subserviency and helplessness into a dignified independence and citizenship."[107]

The attempts to implement these policies and lofty objectives revealed varying ranges of competence and dedication within the Bureau's personnel. In theory, a northern reporter wrote, the Bureau unquestionably "stands as the next friend of the blacks," but "practically, and in the custom of the country," he concluded after several months of observation, "it appears to stand too often as their next enemy." The agent he met in a South Carolina community typified for him the Bureau mentality. Empowered to examine labor contracts and determine the validity of planter and freedmen grievances, he demonstrated little or no sympathy for the very people he had been dispatched to protect. "He doesn't really intend to outrage the rights of the negroes, but he has very little idea that they have any rights except such as the planters choose to give them." Henry M. Turner, the prominent black clergyman, shared this dim view of the Bureau in operation. Based upon his travels in Georgia and his conversations with numerous freedmen, Turner concluded that although Bureau agents professed "to do much good," many of them appeared to be "great tyrants" who were utterly incapable of understanding the problems of his people.[108]

Whatever directives flowed out of the national office, the crucial power of the Freedmen's Bureau rested with the state and local officials, many of whom were former soldiers and officers who looked upon their positions as sinecures rather than opportunities to protect the ex-slaves in their newly acquired rights. The competence of individual agents varied enormously, as did the quality of the commitment they brought to their jobs. Under difficult, even hazardous circumstances, some Bureau agents braved the opposition of native whites as well as Federal authorities to protect the freedmen from fraud, harassment, and violence; among these agents were whites imbued with the old abolitionist commitment and a small group of blacks, including Martin R. Delany, B. F. Randolph, and J. J. Wright, all of them holding posts in South Carolina.[109] But many of the field agents of the Freedmen's Bureau coveted acceptance by the communities in which they served and became malleable instruments in the hands of the planter class, eager to service their labor needs and sharing similar views about the racial character and capacity of black people and the urgent need to control them. The *New Orleans Tribune* tried to be as sympathetic toward the Freedmen's Bureau as its observations would permit: in the midst of a hostile population, the agents had little choice but to act cautiously; their acquaintances were almost always whites and each day they were subjected to "false impressions and misrepresentations." Under such conditions, the editor charged, the legitimate grievances of black laborers were understandably "treated with contempt"—that is, if they were considered at all. In a recent visit to Amite City, in St. Helena Parish, he found that most of the blacks were unaware of the presence of the Bureau. "The representatives of the federal power are lost in the crowd," the editor observed; "and feeling themselves powerless, they are wasting time the best they can, and do not hurt the feelings of any body." To "make Abolition a truth," he suggested that black troops be stationed there. "Up to this time, Emancipation has only been a lie—in most of our parishes."[110]

No matter how a Bureau agent interpreted his mission, the tasks he faced were formidable. At the very outset, the extent of territory for which he was responsible reduced his effectiveness. "My satrapy," a South Carolina agent recalled, "contained two state districts or counties, and eventually three, with a population of about eighty thousand souls and an area at least two thirds as large as the state of Connecticut. Consider the absurdity of expecting one man to patrol three thousand miles and make personal visitations to thirty thousand Negroes." The questions an agent needed to answer and act upon were equally demanding. If a slaveholder had removed his blacks during the war to a "safe" area, who bore the responsibility for returning them to their original homes? If blacks had planted crops in the master's absence, who should reap the profits? Could a former master confiscate the personal possessions a black had accumulated as his slave? If a black woman had borne the children of a master, who assumed responsibility for them in freedom? Could the ex-slaveholders expel from their plantations the sick and elderly blacks no longer able to support themselves? Compared to the numerous disputes involving the interpretation of contracts, the division of crops, and acts of violence, these were almost trivial questions, but even the best-intentioned agents had few guidelines to help them reach a decision. The Bureau officer, a South Carolina agent recalled, needed to be "a man of quick common sense, with a special faculty for deciding what not to do. His duties and powers were to a great extent vague, and in general he might be said to do best when he did least."[111]

No sooner had he taken office than the typical Bureau agent found himself besieged by planters wanting to know what terms and punishments they could impose on their blacks. That would constitute the bulk of his work, along with the many complaints of freedmen who had suffered fraud, abuse, and violence at the hands of their employers. Unfortunately, few Bureau agents possessed the ability, the patience, or the sympathy to deal with the grievances of the freedmen, even to recognize their legitimacy, and the ex-slave had no way of knowing what to expect if he should file a complaint. To do so, he might have to travel anywhere from ten to fifty miles to the nearest Bureau office, where he was apt to find an agent "who rides, dines, and drinks champagne with his employer" and viewed any complainant as some kind of troublemaker. Even the more sympathetic agents were not always able to consider the freedman's grievances with the seriousness they deserved.

> The majority of the complaints brought before me came from Negroes. As would naturally happen to an ignorant race, they were liable to many impositions, and they saw their grievances with big eyes.... With pomp of manner and of words, with a rotundity of voice and superfluity of detail which would have delighted Cicero, a Negro would so glorify his little trouble as to give one the impression that humanity had never before suffered the like.[112]

The ways in which a local Bureau agent or provost marshal considered the grievance of a freedman often differed markedly from the deference paid to a prominent planter. In Liberty, Virginia, for example, the local superintendent of freedmen's affairs—a sergeant in the Union Army—listened to a black laborer's account of a severe beating he had suffered at the hands of his employer.

> "What did you do to him? You've been sassy?"
> "No, boss; never was sassy; never *was* sassy nigger sence I'se born."
> "Well, I suppose you were lazy."
> "Boss, I been working all de time; ask any nigger on de plantashn ef I'se ever lazy nigger. Me! me and dem oder boys do all de work on de plantashn same as 'foretime."
> "Well, then, what did he strike you for?"
> "Dat jest it, sah. Wot'd he strike me for? Dar ar jest it. I done nothin'."
> "How many of you are there on the plantation?"
> "Right smart family on de plantashn, sah. Dunno how many."
> "Did he strike any other boy but you?"
> "No, sah, me one."
> "You must have been doing something?"
> "No, boss; boss, I tell you; I'se in at de quarters, me and two o'dem boys, and he came in de do', jump on me wid a stick, say 'he teach me.'"
> "What did you do then?"
> "Run, come yer."
> "Well, now you go back home and go to your work again; don't be sassy, don't be lazy when you've got work to do; and I guess he won't trouble you."[113]

This freedman fared better than the many blacks who testified that local agents refused even to listen to their complaints but ordered them back to work and threatened them with deportation. Confronted with an employer unwilling to pay him his share of the crop and with threats to burn down his house (because he conducted classes there), a North Carolina freedman carried his appeal to General Oliver O. Howard, the Bureau's head commissioner, after the local agent had refused to intercede.[114]

Even where a Bureau official tried to act on behalf of a freedman, he might find himself frustrated by military authorities, whose support he needed to enforce his decisions but whose sympathies often lay with the native whites. In some regions, military officers not connected with the Bureau collected fees for approving labor contracts and paid little attention to the provisions. Captain Randolph T. Stoops, the provost marshal in Columbia, Virginia, readily conceded his lack of concern in such matters but thought it perfectly justified. "As to the price of labour I have nothing to do with it. The citizens held a meeting some time since and made a price to suit themselves. . . . When Farmers bring the negro before me to have written agreements between them whatever price is agreed upon between them I enter on the article and consider them bound to fulfill the agreement whatever it may be." Often over the protests of sympathetic Bureau agents, military authorities permitted employers to mete out punishments to recalcitrant blacks or imposed their own form of discipline. That was how Captain Stoops dealt with the problem of blacks "swarming the streets" of the town in which he was stationed. "There being no jail or place of confinement I resorted to the wooden horse and making them work on the streets. Such punishment I found beneficial for in a short time I found almost every negro for some distance, had gone to work and was doing well. . . . Fright has more to do with it than anything else."[115]

To keep the freed slaves on the old plantations and to force them into contracts with an employer doubtless helped a local Bureau official to win a degree of toleration in an otherwise hostile community. But at the same time, he easily persuaded himself that he was acting in the best interests of the freedmen. After all, the Bureau officer in Vicksburg observed, wherever the freedmen were "submissive and perform the labor they contract to do in good faith," the native whites treated them "with kindness." If the blacks themselves remained unconvinced of the Bureau's good intentions, an official could reason that they had only recently been released from bondage and were in no position to know what was best for them. The more the freedmen resisted their advice, the more Bureau officials insisted on it, justifying their positions by the number of ex-slaves they had induced to return to work. Upon assuming his post in Jackson, Mississippi, Captain J. H. Weber found the city "full to overflowing with stragglers from the plantations." He immediately ordered the troops under his command to round up the "stragglers" and put them to work on the city streets.

> The result was surprising; it stopped in short order the influx of stragglers, and saved the soldiers the labor of cleaning up the City. The stragglers began to learn, and those coming in learned from them that they

could not remain here in idleness—they went back to their homes contented to go to work again. I have gathered up in this way, more than three hundred, and as planters and others have called for laborers, I have turned those thus gathered up over to them ...

With equal satisfaction, a Bureau officer in southern Mississippi boasted that his "presence and authority," backed by troops when needed, had "kept the negroes at work, and in a good state of discipline." If it had not been for the Bureau, he added, "I feel confident there would have been an uprising upon the part of the negroes."[116]

Established to ease the ex-slaves' transition to freedom, the Freedmen's Bureau ultimately facilitated the restoration of black labor to the control of those who had previously owned them. "They are, in fact, the planter's guards, and nothing else," the *New Orleans Tribune* concluded, almost two years after expressing its initial doubts about the Bureau. "Every person acquainted with the regime of our country parishes knows what has become of the Bureau's agencies and the Agents." The potential for a different course of action had been present from the outset. Although the President's liberal pardon policy necessarily frustrated any radical redistribution of land, the Freedmen's Bureau had been in a position to effect significant changes in labor relations, particularly during the chaotic aftermath of emancipation. "In my opinion," a Bureau official wrote from Meridian, Mississippi, in June 1866, "you could inflict no more severe punishment on a planter than to take from him the negroes that work the place. They will do anything, rather than this, that is possible or reasonable. They feel their utter helplessness without them to do the work." But even the best-intentioned of the commissioners and local agents manifested their sympathy for the freedmen in curious and contradictory ways, embracing a paternalism and a contract labor system that could only perpetuate the economic dependency of the great mass of former slaves.[117]

"Philanthropists," a black newspaper observed in 1865, "are sometimes a strange class of people; they love their fellow man, but these to be worthy of their assistance, must be of an inferior kind. We were and still are oppressed; we are not demoralized criminals." Nor did black people need to be reminded to avoid idleness and vagrancy; the repeated warnings, preached by native whites and Federal authorities alike, were all too reminiscent of the white preacher's sermons during slavery. After all, the newspaper concluded, "the necessity of working is perfectly understood by men who have worked all their lives."[118]

# Chapter Eight

---

# BACK TO WORK:
# THE NEW DEPENDENCY

*"Now children, you don't think white people are any better than you because they have straight hair and white faces?"*

*"No, sir."*

*"No, they are no better, but they are different, they possess great power, they formed this great government, they control this vast country.... Now what makes them different from you?"*

*"MONEY." (Unanimous shout)*

*"Yes, but what enabled them to obtain it? How did they get money?"*

*"Got it off us, stole it off we all!"*

—FREEDMEN SCHOOL, LOUISVILLE, KENTUCKY, 1866[1]

*You know it is better to work for Mr. Cash than Mr. Lash. A black man looks better now to the white than he used to do. He looks taller, brighter, and more like a man. The more money you make, the lighter your skin will be. The more land and houses you get, the straighter your hair will be.*

—REV. HENRY HIGHLAND GARNET,<br>AT THE CENTER STREET METHODIST EPISCOPAL CHURCH,<br>LOUISVILLE, KENTUCKY, SEPTEMBER 20, 1865 [2]

ON A PLANTATION in South Carolina, an elderly black woman known as Aunt Phillis told how her master had built his new house only a year before the outbreak of the Civil War. Like those slaves who habitually boasted of the wealth of their "white folks," she dwelled on the fact that her master had paid a great deal of money for this house, as much as $20,000. "Where did your master get so much money?" a northern journalist asked the old woman. The question obviously agitated her. Although confined to bed because of an illness, she managed to raise herself up and with considerable excitement in her voice she kept repeating the question: "Whar he git he money? Whar he git he money? Is dat what you ask—whar he git he money? *I* show you, massa." Pushing up her sleeve, she revealed a gaunt, skinny arm. Tapping it vigorously with her forefinger, she exclaimed, "You see dat, massa? Dat's whar he got he money—out o' dat black skin he got he money."[3]

Few ex-slaveholders ever paused to scrutinize their own lives and dependency, and still fewer would have perceived any reason to do so. But their former slaves had been quite observant, and no one knew their "white folks" better than they did. "Oh, massa ain't old as me," an elderly black woman explained. "Us been playfellows togedder. But massa ain't stan' lika me, ma'am. Hard work an' beatin' about make us grow ole too fast. Us been ole w'en him young. Massa lib soft w'en us lib hard." Wherever the freedmen turned, it seemed, white men who claimed to be their best friends and emancipators were on hand to advise them to work diligently and thereby prove themselves fit for freedom. The former slaves usually listened politely and nodded their heads in acquiescence. But occasionally their anger surfaced, and few charges infuriated them more than that of idleness, particularly when their former masters leveled the accusation. "They take all our labor for their own use and get rich on it and then say we are lazy and can't take care of ourselves," was the way a South Carolina freedman expressed his rage. Why should the ex-slave have to prove himself, others asked, when the evidence of his labor was everywhere to be seen? Indeed, if the freedman needed only to work to prove himself fit to enjoy the blessings of liberty, he should have been free for more than two centuries. After observing how "the flippant class that talks so loud of the idleness of the negro" finds itself unable to do anything without him, the *New Orleans Tribune* reminded the planters: "The time has come when *the cash,* and not *the lash* commands labor. The blacks are no longer required to rise at four and work, work, work all day, till it is too dark to see; and then get up frequently during the night to wait upon the caprices of an indolent master or mistress to whom surfeiting forbids sleep."[4]

Having been exposed to regular dosages of advice from white men, more than five hundred freedmen on St. Helena Island, South Carolina, listened with particular attentiveness when Major Martin R. Delany, the outspoken black nationalist and abolitionist who returned to his native South as a Freedmen's Bureau officer, addressed them in the summer of 1865. "I want to tell you one thing," he began. "Do you know that if it was not for the black man this war never would have been brought to a close with success to the Union, and the liberty of your race? I want you to understand that. Do you know it? Do you know it? Do you know it?" Cries of "yes," "yes," "yes," greeted his question. With the crowd obviously in his grasp, shouting out their encouragement and approval, Delany assailed the southern planters and northern speculators who exploited their labor, and he urged them to be skeptical even of those who claimed to be their best friends—the schoolteachers and ministers, "because they never tell you the truth," and the cotton agents, "who come honey mouthed unto you, their only intent being to make profit by your inexperience." With even greater forcefulness, however, Delany reminded his audience of the heritage of bondage, the white man's indebtedness to their labor, and the power they held in their hands.

People say that you are too lazy to work, that you have not the intelligence to get on for yourselves. They have often told you, Sam, you lazy nigger, you don't earn your salt. . . . *He* never earned a single dollar in his life. You men and women, every one of you around me, made thousands and thousands of dollars. Only *you* were the means for your master to lead the idle and inglorious life, and to give his children the education which he denied to you for fear you may awake to conscience. If I look around me, I tell you, all the houses on this Island and in Beaufort, they are all familiar to my eye, they are the same structures which I have met with in Africa. They have all been made by the Negroes, you can see it by their rude exterior. I tell you they (White men) cannot teach you anything, and they could not make them because they have not the brain to do it. . . .

Now I look around me and I notice a man, bare footed covered with rags and dirt. Now I ask, what is that man doing, for whom is he working. I hear that he works for 30 cents a day. I tell you that must not be. That would be cursed slavery over again. . . . I tell you slavery is over, and shall never return again. We have now 200,000 of our men well drilled in arms and used to warfare, and I tell you it is with you and them that slavery shall not come back again, and if you are determined it will not return again.

The few local whites who were present, according to one witness, listened to Delany "with horror depicted in their faces." No less alarmed were two Freedmen's Bureau officers who had been dispatched to the scene to impart their impressions of this most recent addition to their ranks. If Delany's words disturbed them, the crowd's reaction seemed even more portentous. "The excitement with the congregation was immense," one officer noted, "groups were formed talking over what they have heard, and ever and anon cheers were given to some particular sentences of the speech"; he overheard one freedman remark that Delany was "the only man who ever told them the truth," while others vowed "they would get rid of the Yankee employer." Little wonder that the officers dutifully reported the contents of Delany's speech to their superior with a warning that such "discourse" produced "*discontent* among the Freedmen," generated "feelings of indignation toward the white people," and could only incite the ex-slaves to insurrection. "My opinion of the whole affair," one of them concluded, "is, that Major Delany is a thorough hater of the White race, and tries the colored people unnecessarily."[5]

To judge the freedmen by their actions, on St. Helena Island and elsewhere in the South, Martin Delany had articulated feelings that were only beginning to surface in the negotiations over the terms of free labor. Neither Delany nor the host of Bureau officers and missionaries who had descended upon the South were in any real position to do for the freedman what he would have to do for himself—that is, work out some kind of arrangement with the former masters that would be commensurate with his new legal status and his aspirations. Even with the presence of Federal

authorities, whose attitudes varied enormously, the ultimate settlement—
barring any redistribution of land—would have to be made between those
who worked and those who owned the land and the tools. And, as a black
newspaper in Georgia observed, "*no* man loves work naturally. Interest or
necessity induces him to labor. If the laborer has no inducement to be
faithful, he should not be censured for neglect. . . . Why does the *white man*
labor? That he may acquire property and the means of purchasing the
comforts and luxuries of life. The *colored man* will labor for the same
reason."[6]

Actually, despite the gloomy talk and predictions, there was never
really any question about whether the freedmen would work. Unlike many
of their former masters, they had never known anything but work, and
most of them did not view this as a question at all. From the moment of
their emancipation, the bulk of the ex-slave population had little choice but
to labor for old and new employers under a variety of arrangements. Some
of the very planters who forecast the Negro's doom were successfully using
free black labor; indeed, a Virginia planter seemed stunned and almost
indignant that his blacks were working with a diligence they had denied
him when they were his slaves. The son of a former slaveholder on the Sea
Islands made the same observation when he returned in 1863 and began
to cultivate the plantation with the newly freed blacks. The acknowledgment of their freedom and the promise of compensation appeared to be
sufficient inducement.

> I never knew, during forty years of plantation life, so little sickness.
> Formerly, every man had a fever of some kind; and now the veriest old
> cripple, who did nothing under secesh rule, will row a boat three nights
> in succession to Edisto, or will pick up the corn about the corn-house.
> There are twenty people whom I know who were considered worn out and
> too old to work under the slave system, who are now working cotton, as
> well as their two acres of provisions; and their crops look very well. I have
> an old woman who has taken six tasks (that is, an acre and a half) of
> cotton, and last year she would do nothing.[7]

Although obviously searching for evidence of black industry, sympathetic northern observers did not have to fabricate their reports. The evidence was all around them, not only in the fields but in the towns and cities,
where blacks were most prominently employed in the reconstruction of a
war-ravaged South. Watching the rebuilding of the burned-out district of
Richmond, a traveler came away impressed with the fact that black men
comprised a majority of the workers. "They drove the teams, made the
mortar, carried the hods, excavated the old cellars or dug new ones, and,
sitting down amid the ruins, broke the mortar from the old bricks and put
them up in neat piles ready for use. There were also colored masons and
carpenters employed on the new buildings." And yet, he reflected, despite
such scenes, "I was once more informed by a cynical citizen that the negro,
now that he was free, would rob, steal, or starve, before he would work."[8]

If the Negro existed only to make cotton, sugar, and rice, as so many whites professed to believe, that would have sentenced to immediate oblivion thousands of skilled black workers and artisans, as well as the far larger number of menial laborers who performed the arduous tasks shunned by white people. In the skilled trades, the principal questions revolved not around the black man's willingness to work or his ability but how much longer he would be permitted to compete with white artisans and mechanics and the degree to which his compensation permitted him to support himself. "By de time I pays ten dollars a month rent fo' my house, an' fifteen cents a poun' for beef or fresh po'k, or thirty cents fo' bacon, an' den buys my clo'es, I doesn't hab much leff," a hod carrier in Selma, Alabama, declared. "I's done tried it, an' I knows brack man cant stan' dat." Nor did black workers in a Richmond tobacco factory, engaged in labor that white men rejected as too difficult, fare much better.

> We the Tobacco mechanicks of this city and Manchester is worked to great disadvantage. . . . They say we will starve through laziness that is not so. But it is true we will starve at our present wages. They say we will steal we can say for ourselves we had rather work for our living. give us a Chance. We are Compeled to work for them at low wages and pay high Rents and make $5 per week and sometimes les. And paying $18 or 20 per month Rent. It is impossible to feed ourselves and family—starvation is Cirten unles a change is brought about.

That constant advice to work or starve, which their white "friends" so freely imparted, never seemed to anticipate the plight of people who did little more than work and yet stood on the brink of starvation. "I keeps on washin for em," remarked a laundress in Richmond, who spent most of her day stooped over a washtub, "for if I leave em they'll never pay me what they owe me."[9]

On the plantations and farms, where the bulk of black laborers still resided, the issue was not whether the freedmen would work but rather for whom, at what rates, and under what conditions, and those were different questions altogether, requiring answers from a class of Southerners who had little experience in dealing with such matters. "Can a planter be expected to treat the laborers under his control in any other way to-day than he has treated them for the last twenty years?" the *New Orleans Tribune* asked. "He and they are the same men, in the same place, bearing to each other, in all respects, the same apparent relations. No visible change has passed off between them. The Proclamation of Emancipation did not invest the slave with a physical sign of freedom. It was a metaphysical endowment."[10] But if the relationship between "master" and laborer remained essentially unaltered by emancipation, so did the mutual dependency upon which it had always rested, and that raised the most crucial question of all. Could the former slave transform the white man's dependence on him into a formidable weapon with which to expand his personal autonomy, improve his day-to-day life and his prospects for the future, and thereby redefine if not sever altogether the old relationship? Whatever the degree of success attained toward these ends, the effort itself marked a significant break with the past.

## 2

WHEN WILLIAM ELLIOTT tried to persuade Jacob to work for him, he ran into unexpected difficulties. As his slave, Jacob had served him faithfully over many years, and Elliott, a South Carolina planter, wished not only to retain a valuable laborer but to have him use his influence to convince the other blacks to return to work. Before he would agree to terms, however, Jacob demanded certain concessions—like the right to keep the provisions he made for himself—that would have lessened his dependency on the old master. He asked for them, moreover, in consideration of his previous record of service to the family. To Elliott, that might have suggested a demand for retroactive compensation, and he viewed the question quite differently than his former slave. "I told him I thought the obligation lay the other way. He is eaten up with self-esteem & selfishness."[11]

If the incident be judged by the content of the postwar debate, William Elliott clearly had the advantage. Although dispossessed slaveholders thought themselves entitled to compensation for their losses (President Lincoln had once proposed it as a way to encourage voluntary emancipation), the question of remunerating the slaves for past labor never reached the level of serious consideration. But if the freedmen were not to be paid for their work as slaves, and few of them ever pressed the matter, they could be quite adamant about being paid for any future labor. As slaves, each of them had borne a price tag; as free men and women, they now felt entitled to wages or crop shares commensurate with the labor they performed. To settle for anything less was to compromise their freedom.

During the Civil War, often at the first sighting of Yankee troops, slaves refused to work without some form of compensation. What a Louisiana overseer described in 1863 as "a state of mutiny" on a neighboring plantation proved to be the failure of the blacks to report to the fields one morning; instead, they appeared before the overseer and insisted they would no longer work without pay. At the same time, the workers on a South Carolina plantation turned down the wage offer of their master. "I mean to own my own manhood," one of them explained, "and I'm goin' on to my own land, just as soon as when I git dis crop in, an' I don't desire for to make any change until den." Besides, he added, "I'm not goin' to work for any man for any such price [25 cents a day]." That was how the others felt, too, as a fellow laborer quickly indicated: "I won't work for no Man for 25 cents a day—not dis chile—unless he gib me my rations too!"[12]

Even while their legal status remained clouded, newly freed slaves articulated their dissatisfaction with the past by conditioning any future labor on the fulfillment of certain immediate demands, such as payment in good wages (not in worthless Confederate bills), adequate food and clothing, additional time off for meals and holidays, and the abolition of gang labor and the position of overseer. If the employer expected his free laborers to demonstrate that habitual deference and compliance, he might find himself deeply disappointed if not at times outraged. Early in 1864, for example, a planter in Louisiana addressed a group of prospective field hands in the hope of hiring them. "All listened attentively," noted a reporter present at the scene, "and there was no stupidity apparent in their faces. They seemed to hear every adjective." After listening to the explanation of terms, the laborers countered with questions which revealed their most immediate concerns: "When will our wages be paid?" "What clothing are we to have?" "What land are we allowed?" "Can we keep our pigs?" The women insisted they would no longer work on Saturdays; the men indicated their unwillingness to perform any plantation chores on Sunday. Finally, the planter asked them to raise their hands if they agreed to the terms. At first, a number of them, including most of the women, refused to do so, holding out for a five-day week, but they finally assented on condition they could work less than the full time.[13]

The initial give-and-take between planters and laborers in wartime Louisiana impressed a northern observer for the ways in which the blacks were rapidly learning their own power and worth. "They have a mine of strategy," he reported, "to which the planter sooner or later yields." He cited the example of a planter who had hired a new overseer; the choice proved to be obnoxious to the blacks because of his reputation for wielding the whip and using abusive language in addressing black women. When a delegation of field hands demanded the overseer's dismissal, the planter refused in the strongest possible language. After vowing that he would hire anyone he chose to be overseer, he ordered the hands back to work. Rather than return to the fields, however, the blacks went to their cabins, packed up their belongings, and started down the road; they had not gone far before the owner called them back and promised them a voice in the selection of a new overseer.[14]

If the South wanted some indication of what it might expect from the new labor relations, there was also that unique experiment on the Sea Islands off the coast of South Carolina, where the freed slaves and a select group of largely northern employers tried to make a success out of cotton cultivation by free black labor. Not long after the Federal occupation, and still quite early in the war, a Sea Islands black made clear the prevailing sentiment about returning to work: "I craves work, ma'am, if I gets a little pay, but if we don't gets pay, we don't care—don't care to work." But even when compensated for their labor, some of the blacks thought the pay to be inadequate, particularly in comparison to the profits reaped by their new employers. And when they resolved to make their feelings known, the laborers did so with sufficient force and unanimity to alarm those highminded missionaries who thought themselves the best friends and emancipators of this oppressed race. Early in 1864, Harriet Ware recorded the "injudicious" way in which a group of these "poor, ignorant creatures" confronted Edward Philbrick, a Boston entrepreneur and a firm believer in free labor who had obtained extensive acreage on St. Helena Island.

> The women came up in a body to complain to Mr. Philbrick about their pay,—a thing which has never happened before and shows the influence of very injudicious outside talk, which has poisoned their minds against their truest friends. The best people were among them, and even old Grace chief spokeswoman.

Before Philbrick left the islands, he leased out his plantation and tried to induce the blacks to contract with the new superintendent; instead, the two men found themselves surrounded by disaffected field hands who were shouting, "A dollar a task! A dollar a task!"—substantially more than they had been earning. When Philbrick explained to them how the proceeds of last year's crop had been spent in carrying on the current work, they refused to believe him; one of the blacks, in fact, insisted that "they [the employers] had been jamming the bills into that big iron cage [Philbrick's safe] for six months, and there must be enough in it now to bust it!" Still refusing to budge, Philbrick opened his door several days later only to confront a delegation of twenty women. Once again, "old Grace" spoke for the group:

> I'se come to you, sir. [pause] I'se been working fer owner three years, and made with my chillun two bales cotton last year, two more this year. I'se a flat-footed pusson and don't know much, but I knows those two bales cotton fetch 'nough money, and I don't see what I'se got for 'em. When I take my leetle bit money and go to store, buy cloth, find it so dear, dear Jesus!—the money all gone and leave chillun naked. Some people go out yonder and plant cotton for theyself. Now they get big pile of money for they cotton, and leave we people 'way back. That's what I'se lookin' on, Marsa. Then when I come here for buy 'lasses, when Massa Charlie sell he sell good 'lasses, then when Mister W. sell he stick *water* in 'em, *water enough*. Molasses turn thin, but he charge big price for 'em. Now I'se done working for such 'greement. I'se done, sir.

But Philbrick remained unmoved, rejected the demands for higher pay, restated his terms, and told those who found them unacceptable that they were free to go elsewhere. "I told them, too, that if some of those people who made so much noise didn't look out, they would get turned off the place, just as Venus and her gang got turned off last year." Before long some of the women returned to inform him of their decision to remain and accede to his terms. "The fact is," Philbrick confided to a friend, "they are trying to play brag, as such people often will; but they will all go to work in a few days, I feel sure."[15]

Whether expressed collectively or individually, the threat by former slaves to make their continued labor contingent on a white employer complying with their demands was in itself almost unprecedented. The implications of such bargaining were certainly not lost on the native whites, some of whom chose to expel blacks who refused to work "as usual" or who deigned to approach them about an agreement. No sooner had Richmond fallen than the slaves in one household selected a committee of three to inform their owner that they expected wages for any future services. Infuriated at this display of insolence, he ordered them from the room. "Well I told the whole crew to go to hell, and they left," he later explained; "its my opinion they'll all get there soon enough." Still recouping from the shock of emancipation, some employers were in no mood to offer their newly freed slaves anything more than the usual quarters, provisions, and clothing, and scores of freedmen did agree to such terms during and immediately after the war, at least until the current crop had been completed. But that arrangement failed to satisfy Ann Ulrich, who told her master "dat since freedom we git a little change"; he responded with a torrent of "all de low names he could think of" and ordered her off the plantation. Nor was Mary Love satisfied with the new dress her mistress had given her, along with the promise to feed and house her. "After while I asked her ain't she got some money for me, and she say no, ain't she giving me a good home? Den I starts to feeling like I ain't treated right." Some days later, without saying "nothing to nobody," she placed the new dress in a bundle and headed for the nearest town. "Its ten miles into Bonham, and I gits in town about daylight. I keeps on being afraid, 'cause I can't git it out'n my mind I still belong to Mistress."[16]

Community pressures—both white and black—often inhibited any early agreement on paid labor. While the status of slavery and the possibility of compensation remained unclear, many planters held back, preferring to dismiss recalcitrant slaves rather than bargain with them. When blacks in Fredericksburg, Virginia, defected in large numbers and demanded wages, white residents responded by agreeing among themselves not to hire their own or other people's slaves. After one resident broke that pact and agreed to hire his servants, "the gentlemen of the town" warned him that he was establishing a dangerous precedent and violating the laws of Virginia, and that his action would mark him as a traitor to the state. "So the old man refused to hire them," a neighbor wrote, "and they all left him." Such understandings among whites were a forerunner of postwar agreements not to tamper with each other's former slaves and to set maximum wage and share rates. But the pressures could work both ways. That is, blacks who continued to work when others refused to do so were apt to encounter the hostility of their own people. Thus did a South Carolina proprietress observe "the faithful few" among her slaves to be "uneasy," fearing repercussions from those who had left. "Rius gave his wife (Ellen) a fearful beating because she came to wait on Aunt Nenna. Those who are faithful suffer so much from the rebellious ones, and we can do nothing to protect them."[17]

Confronted with the departure of their laborers, growing numbers of planters would have to face up ultimately to the necessity of reaching some kind of agreement with them. Late in the war, Henry W. Ravenel, the introspective South Carolina slaveholder, acknowledged the need to effect "a radical change" in the labor system. The reason for his decision was clear enough: "Since Thursday the negroes have not been at work. . . . The negroes are on a 'strike' for terms & until an agreement can be made, matters will be no better." His blacks objected to "gang work," they wanted no overseer or driver, and they demanded a plot of land "to work for their own use." Although anxious to retain their labor, Ravenel, for all his brave talk about "a radical change," feared any concessions which would be "incompatible with discipline & good management." While the impasse continued, he detected a "sullenness" in his laborers "which I dislike to see," and he heard that many blacks in the neighborhood, including presumably some of his own, were now armed. The house servants belonging to a Georgia woman determined to test their freedom by suing her for wages. "A most unwarrantable procedure," her son-in-law wrote afterwards, but he agreed that henceforth "we must pay for services rendered."[18]

With the acknowledgment of emancipation, most planters gradually resigned themselves to some form of compensated labor. When the master assembled his newly freed slaves to inform them of his offer, he might also use the occasion to remind them of their new responsibilities and to introduce them to some of the harsher realities of free labor. Thus did a planter in Lowndes County, Alabama, explain to his blacks the new situation in which they now found themselves:

> Formerly, you were my slaves; you worked for me, and I provided for you. You had no thought of the morrow, for I thought of that for you. If you were sick, I had the doctor come to you. When you needed clothes, clothes were forthcoming; and you never went hungry for lack of meal and pork. You had little more responsibility than my mules.
>
> But now all that is changed. Being free men, you assume the responsibilities of free men. You sell me your labor, I pay you money, and with that money you provide for yourselves. You must look out for your own clothes and food, and the wants of your children. If I advance these things for you, I shall charge them to you, for I cannot give them like I once did, now I pay you wages. Once if you were ugly or lazy, I had you whipped, and that was the end of it. Now if you are ugly and lazy, your wages will be paid to others, and you will be turned off, to go about the country with bundles on your backs, like the miserable low-down niggers you see that nobody will hire. But if you are well-behaved and industrious, you will be prosperous and respected and happy.

If only every planter adopted this approach, he assured a northern visitor, there would be a harmonious transition to free labor. "They all understood this talk," he added, "and liked it, and went to work like men on the strength of it. . . . There's everything in knowing how to manage them."[19]

The transition to free labor would seldom be as smooth as this Alabama planter envisioned. Not only was the situation without any clear precedent but the sharp divisions of race and class, exacerbated by the heritage of slavery and wartime memories, were bound to complicate the new relationship of white employer and black laborer. "I do not like the negro as well free as I did as a slave," a Virginian conceded, "for the reason that there is now between us an antagonism of interest to some extent, while, before, his interest and mine were identical. Then, I was always thinking of how I could fix him comfortably. Now, I find myself driving a hard bargain with him for wages; and I find that sort of feeling suggested directly by motives of interest coming in between the employer and the employed." When the former master came around to compensated labor, he would have to calculate precisely how much his ex-slaves were worth to him as free workers. That created some obvious conflicts, with employers and laborers entertaining different notions of value and both determined to stand by their estimates. "They have what seem to me to be extravagant ideas as to what they ought to receive," a North Carolinian observed, and scores of planters would register the same complaint. But surely, some freedmen suggested, they should not be worth any less now than the price for which their masters had occasionally hired them out as slaves. If the planter pleaded financial difficulties, as so many did, the freedmen had only to look out into the fields and calculate the value of the expected crops. "Massa fust said he find all de family food and house for our work," a Virginia black remarked; "den I think that, as him grow 4,000 bushels corn, near 10,000 lbs. clover, and odder tings 'sides, he can 'ford to pay me better dan dat, so I no go with him. Me tell him me worth more, and p'raps he give me some of crop."[20]

Accustomed to holding the upper hand in all dealings with blacks, the former slaveholder preferred to make his own decision about compensation rather than suffer the audaciousness of freedmen who confronted him with demands or ultimatums. In his region, a Florida farmer and physician revealed, the planters usually refused to pay "any who demand it" but several had promised to supply their freedmen with provisions at the end of the year if they worked faithfully. Even relationships of long standing, which had survived the war and the first years of emancipation, could fall apart when the ex-slave raised the question of additional pay. Within that tightly knit Jones clan of Georgia, for example, Kate had remained "faithful" to Mary Jones's daughter while many others defected. Not until late in 1867 did she assert herself on the wage question: "I wish to tell you if you will give me twelve dollars per month [an increase of three dollars] I will stay with you; but if not, I have had good offers and I will find another place." Despite the years of loyal, unpaid labor this servant had rendered, the mistress of the household turned down her request for a raise. When Kate then left her, the mistress noted that she did so "with a very impertinent air."[21]

The sheer novelty of free black labor introduced complexities and nuances into the issues that traditionally separated employers and workers. The proposed compensation mattered less to some freedmen than what form it would take (crop shares or cash), when it would be paid (monthly or after completion of the crop), and the often arbitrary nature of the employer's deductions (for the provisions he supplied and the fines he levied for negligent work). Of equally vital concern to the freedman might be the kinds of crops he could now grow (the old staples or food), the quality of the provisions he received, the availability of schools for his children, the right to unrestricted travel, and freedom from verbal and physical abuse. Inseparable from all these considerations, and for many the most crucial, was the degree of personal autonomy he could now enjoy.[22] The only way to keep the ex-slaves on the plantations without compromising their freedom, the *New Orleans Tribune* boldly suggested, was not simply to compensate them but to make them full partners in the management and in the crop yields; freedom implied the abolition of both "slaves" and "masters," the "democratization" of the plantations, and the opportunity for blacks to control their own crops, lands, and lives. Unless "the necessary step" was taken to free the workingman, the newspaper concluded, emancipation would remain "a mockery and a sham." By "the necessary step," the editor envisioned the free colored community of New Orleans investing their money in land and managing that land in partnership with the former slaves, who would perform the labor.[23]

Early in the postwar period, at least, that ultimate question of who controlled the crops and the lands remained unresolved in the minds of many freedmen. After noting that planters now intended to pay their ex-slaves with crop shares, Henry M. Turner, the outspoken black clergyman, refused to applaud their action; instead, he dismissed the proposal as an "ingenious trickery . . . designed to keep the old master fat doing nothing, making the Yankees believe 'dis old nigga no wants to leave massa,' and for the purpose of fizzling them out of all their claims upon the real estate." Rather than settle for compensation in wages or shares, the freedmen in some areas were already insisting that the crops they had planted in 1865, if not the land itself, rightfully belonged to them. "Some of them," wrote the police chief in Duplin County, North Carolina, "are declaring they intend to have lands, even if they shed blood to obtain them. Some of them are demanding all of the crop they have raised on the former master's lands, and in some cases, so obstinate are they in these demands, that I have had to arrest them before they would come to terms."[24]

With emancipation, many former slaves obviously sensed a new power and evinced a determination to test it. The mere offer of compensation would not assure the employers of a stable and contented labor force. To pay them for their labor, after all, did not resolve all fundamental questions about authority, autonomy, and control of the land. Whether provoked by a wage dispute or some other grievance, freedmen continued to leave the old places, sometimes en masse. Still more remained and worked indifferently, reserving any enthusiasm they might have for their own individual garden plots. Looking at those small gardens, which they had tended and cherished as slaves, many freedmen had heard enough to imagine them expanded into forty-acre farms. That remained the most exciting prospect of all, exceeding in importance and in emotional investment any question of wages.

Shortly after the fall of Richmond, the scene acted out on the nearby Rosewood plantation posed the problem a number of landowners would have to face soon enough. After having promised to remain and work, a freedman named Cyrus absented himself from the fields. When Emma Mordecai, the plantation mistress, questioned him about his conduct, he replied by advancing his own perception of how matters stood between them.

> Seems lak we'uns do all the wuck and gits a part. Der ain't goin' ter be no more Master and Mistress, Miss Emma. All is equal. I done hear it from de cotehouse steps. . . . All de land belongs to de Yankees now, and dey gwine to divide it out 'mong de colored people. Besides, de kitchen ob de big house is my share. I help built hit.[25]

## 3

EVEN AS THEY TOILED in the same fields, performed the familiar tasks, and returned at dusk to the same cabins, scores of freedmen refused to resign themselves to the permanent status of a landless agricultural working-class. Like most Americans, they aspired to something better and yearned for economic independence and self-employment. Without that independence, their freedom seemed incomplete, even precarious. "Every colored man will be a slave, & feel himself a slave," a black soldier insisted, "until he can raise him own bale of cotton & put him own mark upon it & say dis is mine!" Although often expressed vaguely, as if to talk about it openly might be unwise, the expectation many ex-slaves shared in the aftermath of the war was that "something extraordinary" would soon intervene to reshape the course of their lives. In the Jubilee they envisioned, the government provided them with forty-acre lots and thereby emancipated them from dependency on their former masters. "This was no slight error, no trifling idea," a Freedmen's Bureau officer reported from Mississippi in 1865, "but a fixed and earnest conviction as strong as any belief a man can ever have."[26] The feeling was sufficiently pervasive, in fact, to prompt thousands of freedmen in late 1865 to hold back on any commitment of their labor until the question of land had been firmly resolved.

The only real question among some blacks was not whether the lands belonging to the former slaveholders would be divided and distributed, but when and how. Freedmen in South Carolina heard that the large plantations along the coast were to be distributed. Equally persistent reports suggested that the lands on which the ex-slaves were working would be divided among them. Few blacks in Mississippi, a Bureau officer reported in November 1865, expressed any interest in hiring themselves out for the next year. "Nearly all of them have heard, that at Christmas, Government is going to take the planters' lands and other property from *them,* and give it to the colored people, and that, in this way they are going to begin to farm on their own account." In a Virginia community, the freedmen had reportedly deposited their savings with "responsible" persons so as to be in the most advantageous position to purchase lots of "de confiscated land, as soon as de Gov'ment ready to sell it." And in Georgia a black laborer was so certain that he "coolly" offered to sell to his former master the share of the plantation he expected to receive "after the division."[27]

Although confident of retaining their lands, planters expressed growing concern over the extent to which the freedmen's aspirations interfered with the normalization of agricultural operations. It proved difficult to raise crops when laborers went about "stuffed with the idea of proprietorship" and the anticipation of soon becoming their own employers. "You cannot beat into their thick skulls that the land & every thing else does not belong to them," a South Carolina planter wrote his daughter. Since many whites refused to believe their blacks capable of formulating perceptions of freedom, they blamed the land mania on "fanatical abolitionists," incendiary preachers, and the Yankee invaders. But those who had overheard the "curious" wartime discussions in which the blacks apportioned the lands among themselves knew better, as did the victims of black expropriation. Where planters had fled, abandoning their properties, the freed slaves had in numerous instances seized control and they gave little indication after the war of yielding their authority to the returning owners. Along the Savannah River, blacks under the leadership of Abalod Shigg seized two major plantations on the assumption that they were entitled to "forty acres and a mule." Federal troops had to be called in to dislodge them. Elsewhere, similar seizures revealed the intensity of black feelings about the land and created a volatile situation that many native whites and Federal officials feared might erupt into armed confrontations.[28]

As if to confirm black land aspirations, the Federal government adopted an ambitious settlement program in direct response to the thousands of unwanted and burdensome freed slaves who had attached themselves to the Union Army in the wake of General Sherman's march to the sea. On January 12, 1865, Sherman and Secretary of War Stanton conferred with twenty black ministers and church officers in Savannah to ascertain what could be done about these people. The delegation suggested that land was the key to black freedom. "We want to be placed on land until we are able to buy it, and make it our own," the spokesmen for the group declared. Several days later, Sherman issued Special Field Order No. 15, a far-reaching document that set aside for the exclusive use of the freedmen a strip of coastal land abandoned by Confederate owners between Charleston, South Carolina, and Jacksonville, Florida, granting black settlers "possessory titles" to forty-acre lots. Although intended only to deal with a specific military and refugee problem, the order encouraged the growing impression among the freedmen that their Yankee liberators intended to provide them with an essential undergirding for their emancipation. That impression gained still further credence when Congress made the newly established Freedmen's Bureau the custodian of all abandoned and confiscated land (largely the lands seized for nonpayment of the direct Federal tax or belonging to disloyal planters who had fled); ex-slaves and loyal Unionists could pre-empt forty-acre lots, rent them at nominal rates for three years, and purchase them within that period at a fair price (about sixteen times the annual rent). If the Bureau had implemented this provision, and if blacks had been able to accumulate the necessary funds, some 20,000 black families would have been provided with the means for becoming self-sustaining farmers.[29]

To apportion the large landed estates among those who worked them and who had already expended years of uncompensated toil made such eminent sense to the ex-slave that he could not easily dismiss this aspiration as but another "exaggerated" or "absurd" view of freedom. "My master has had me ever since I was seven years old, and never give me nothing," observed a twenty-one-year-old laborer in Richmond. "I worked for him twelve years, and I think something is due me." Expecting nothing from his old master, he now trusted the government to do "something for us." The day a South Carolina rice planter anticipated trouble was when one of his field hands told him that "the land ought to belong to the man who (alone) *could work it,*" not to those who "sit in the house" and profit by the labor of others. Such sentiments easily translated into the most American of aspirations. "All I wants is to git to own fo' or five acres ob land, dat I can build me a little house on and call my home," a Mississippi black explained. With the acquisition of land, the ex-slave viewed himself entering the mainstream of American life, cultivating his own farm and raising the crops with which to sustain himself and his family. That was the way to respectability in an agricultural society, and the freedman insisted that a plot of land was all he required to lift himself up: "Gib us our own land and we take care ourselves; but widout land, de ole massas can hire us or starve us, as dey please." And what better way to confirm their emancipation than to own the very land on which they had been working and which they had made productive and valuable by their own labor.[30]

The expectation of "forty acres and a mule" may have been sheer delusion, but the freedmen had sufficient reason to think otherwise. Since the outbreak of the war, many of them had overheard their masters talk in fearful tones about how the Yankees, if successful, would divide up the land among the blacks. The Freedmen's Bureau, in fact, blamed the false expectations of land on Confederate slaveholders who had exploited the fear of confiscation during the war to arouse propertied whites to greater exertions and sacrifices. The deception was deliberately cultivated in some instances by planters who were determined to keep their ex-slaves until the

postwar crops had been harvested; at least, numerous disappointed freedmen recalled how they had been assured the Federal government would
grant them plots of land after the completion of the agricultural season.
When the Yankees finally arrived, they reinforced the land fever by assuring the freed slaves of their right to forty acres and a mule. When a Union
soldier asked him if he had ever been whipped, West Turner of Virginia
recalled, he had replied, "Yessir, boss, gimme thirty and nine any ole time."
Upon hearing this, the soldier advised him to take one acre of land for each
time he had been whipped and an extra acre as a bonus. "So I measure off
best I could forty acres of dat corn field an' staked it out. De Yanks give
all Fayette Jackson's land away to de Negroes an plenty mo' other Secesh
land. But when Marse Jackson come back, we had to give it all up."[31]

Although they might have had good reason to doubt the word of their
masters and even the white Yankee troops, some freedmen claimed to have
heard the same promises repeated by their own leaders. The fleeing slaves
who boarded the Union gunboats on the Combahee River heard the reassuring refrain with which the much-idolized Harriet Tubman welcomed
them:

> Of all the whole creation in the East or in the West,
> The glorious Yankee nation is the greatest and the best.
> Come along! Come along! don't be alarmed,
> Uncle Sam is rich enough to give you all a farm.

Still further encouragement came from black soldiers and black missionaries, who sought to prepare their people for the responsibilities they would
soon assume and placed particular emphasis on the imminent division of
the lands. "It's de white man's turn ter labor now," a black preacher in
Florida told an assemblage of field hands. "He ain't got nuthin' lef' but his
lan', an' de lan' won't be his'n long, fur de Guverment is gwine ter gie ter
ev'ry Nigger forty acres of lan' an' a mule."[32]

Within the first two years after the war, freedmen who embraced and
acted upon the expectation of "forty acres and a mule" learned soon
enough to face up to the possibility of disappointment. When some former
Alabama slaves staked off the land they had been working and claimed it
as their own, the owner quickly set matters straight: "Listen, niggers,
what's mine is mine, and what's yours is yours. You are just as free as I
and the missus, but don't go foolin' around my land." Of course, planters
derived considerable comfort from the knowledge that Federal officials
were prepared to confirm their property rights. Until the blacks acknowledged the futility of land expectations, the Freedmen's Bureau recognized
how difficult it would be to stabilize agricultural operations. With that
sense of priorities, the Bureau instructed its agents to do everything in
their power to disabuse the ex-slaves of any lingering illusions about taking
over their masters' lands. "This was the first difficulty that the Officers of
the Bureau had to contend with," a Mississippi officer wrote, "and nothing

but their efforts and explanations, kept off the storm. Even now, it is but a temporary settlement." If the blacks refused to believe their old masters, Bureau agents were quite prepared to visit the plantations in person and impart the necessary confirmation: "The government owns no lands in this State. It therefore can give away none. Freedmen can obtain farms with the money which they have earned by their labor. Every one, therefore, shall work diligently, and carefully save his wages, till he may be able to buy land and possess his own home." The blacks he encountered held so tenaciously to their illusions, a Bureau officer in Alabama observed, that "unless they see me and hear me refute the story, they persist in the belief." Still other officers reported that the freedmen refused to believe them, too, or thought the question of land might be negotiable. After being told of the government's policy, a Virginia freedman offered to lower his expectations to a single acre of land—"ef you make it de acre dat Marsa's house sets on."[33]

As an alternative to confiscation, Freedmen's Bureau officers and northern white missionaries and teachers advanced the classic mid-nineteenth-century self-help ideology and implored the newly freed slaves to heed its lessons. Rather than entertain notions of government bounties, they should cultivate habits of frugality, temperance, honesty, and hard work; if they did so, they might not only accumulate the savings to purchase land but would derive greater personal satisfaction from having earned it in this manner. Almost identical advice permeated the editorials of black newspapers, the speeches of black leaders, and the resolutions adopted by black meetings. "Let us go to work faithfully for whoever pays fairly, until we ourselves shall become employers and planters," the *Black Republican,* a New Orleans newspaper, editorialized in its first issue. With an even finer grasp of American values, a black Charlestonian thought economic success capable of overriding the remaining vestiges of racial slavery. "This is the panacea which will heal all the maladies of a Negrophobia type. Let colored men simply do as anybody else in business does, be self-reliant, industrious, producers of the staples for market and merchandise, and he will have no more trouble on account of his complexion, than the white men have about the color of their hair or beards."[34]

To provide proper models for their people, black newspapers featured examples of self-made freedmen who had managed to accumulate land and were forming the nucleus of a propertied and entrepreneurial class in the South. Actually, a number of blacks had done precisely that, some of them fortunate enough to have purchased tax lands and still others who had taken advantage of the Homestead Act or who had made enough money to purchase a plot in their old neighborhoods.[35] But the number of propertied blacks remained small, and some of these found they had been defrauded by whites who had an equal appreciation of the self-help philosophy and made the most of it.[36] Even the blacks who obtained legitimate title to lands soon discovered the elusive quality of economic success. The land often turned out to be of an inferior quality, the freedman usually lacked the capital and credit to develop it properly, and he might consequently find himself enmeshed in the very web of indebtedness and dependency he had sought to escape. By the acquisition of land, he hardly avoided the same problems plaguing so many white farmers.[37]

No matter what the freedmen were told or what precepts they were admonished to follow, the belief in some form of land redistribution demonstrated a remarkable vitality. The wartime precedents and promises were apt to speak louder in some regions than the insistent postwar denials. Thousands of ex-slaves had been placed on forty-acre tracts under Sherman's program, the earlier experiments at Davis Bend and on the Sea Islands persisted into 1865, and the stories of individual and collective success by the black settlers who worked these lands would seem to have assured the continuation and expansion of such projects. But even if few blacks elsewhere in the South knew of them, even if still fewer were aware of the congressional debate on Thaddeus Stevens' ambitious land confiscation program or of the immense generosity of the Federal government in awarding millions of acres to railroad corporations, the idea of "forty acres and a mule" simply made too much sense and had become too firmly entrenched in the minds of too many freedmen for it to be given up at the first words of a Bureau underling. Nor could the thousands of ex-slaves on abandoned and confiscated lands in 1865 understand that the Federal policies which made their settlement possible had not been long-term commitments but rather temporary military expedients, designed to keep them working on the plantations and away from the cities and the Union Army camps.

Resilient though they were, the hopes of the freedmen could withstand only so many shocks. When the governor of Florida told them, "The President will not give you one foot of land, nor a mule, nor a hog, nor a cow, nor even a knife or fork or spoon," he could be dismissed as a mouthpiece of planters who stood to lose the most from a confiscation scheme. When a Bureau officer told some Georgia blacks essentially the same thing, one disbelieving freedman remarked, "Dat's no Yank; dat just some reb dey dressed in blue clothes and brought him here to lie to us." But the denials began to assume a substance that could no longer be ignored. On May 29, 1865, President Andrew Johnson announced his Proclamation of Amnesty, whereby most former Confederates were to be pardoned and recover any of their lands which might have been confiscated or occupied. That had to be taken seriously—as seriously as the Federal officers who now prepared to implement the order. In some communities, the news coincided with a rumor, said to have been circulated by planters, that the President had revoked the Emancipation Proclamation. To many freedmen, contemplating what would happen to the lands they had worked and expected to own, that was no rumor at all. "Amnesty for the persons, no amnesty for the property," the *New Orleans Tribune* cried. "It is enough for the republic to spare the life of the rebels—without restoring to them their plantations and palaces." Under Johnson's magnanimous pardoning policy, any faint hope of a land division collapsed, along with the promising wartime precedents. Rather than confirm the settlers in possession of the land they had cultivated and on which they had erected their homes, the government now proposed to return the plantations to those for whom they had previously labored as slaves. Not satisfied with having their lands returned, some of the owners displayed their own brands of "insolence" and "ingratitude" by claiming damages for any alterations made by the black settlers and by suing them for "back rents" for the use of the land.[38]

The freedmen found themselves incredulous at this apparent betrayal of expectations and trust. At first, some of them could not believe or fully grasp the implications of the restoration. When a Bureau officer addressed the freedmen in one South Carolina community, the blacks came in their best clothes and in high spirits, obviously expecting a very different kind of announcement. "If the general don't tell them cuffees they're to have their share o' our land and hosses and everything else," a local planter warned, "you'll see a hell of a row today." No "row" took place but the faces of the assembled freedmen, after being told there would be no land division, said it all. The more Federal officers tried to explain and defend the decision, the less sense it made to the black audiences and the less able they were to contain their rage. "Damn such freedom as that," a Georgia black declared after a Bureau agent had addressed them.[39]

Where substantial numbers of freedmen had settled on abandoned lands, as in the Sea Islands, the disappointment was bound to be felt most keenly. Appreciating that fact, General O. O. Howard, who headed the Freedmen's Bureau and may have been second only to Lincoln in the esteem of the ex-slaves, decided to pay a personal visit to Edisto Island to inform the settlers that they must give up the lands they had been cultivating as their own. Perhaps only Howard could possibly make them believe it. As if to prepare the assemblage for the ordeal ahead, he thought it might be appropriate for them to begin the meeting with a song. Suddenly an old woman on the edge of the crowd began to sing, "Nobody knows the trouble I've seen," and the entire throng of more than two thousand soon joined in a resounding chorus. Whether it was the song, the look of dismay on their faces, or the shouts of "No! No!" that greeted his announcement, Howard found himself so flustered that he could barely finish his speech. But he had nevertheless articulated the government's position. They should lay aside any bitter feelings they harbored for their former masters and contract to work for them. By working for wages or shares, he assured them, they would be achieving the same ends as possession of the soil would have given them. If the freedmen found Howard's advice incomprehensible, that was only because they understood him all too clearly.[40]

The hope Bureau officials held out for the freedmen was largely a cruel delusion. The same men who had been disabusing the minds of the ex-slaves of their land expectations now urged them to bind themselves to the white man's land. That was another way of saying they should give up the struggle altogether. Not all of them were willing to do so, at least not at the outset. What the freedmen on Edisto Island found most offensive in Howard's speech, apart from having to give up their claims to the land, was the suggestion that they should now work for their former masters. In the petition they addressed to the President, the Edisto blacks argued that no man who had only recently faced his master on the field of battle should now be expected to submit to him for the necessities of life. He was more than willing to forgive his old master, another freedman remarked, but to have to submit to his rule again demanded too much. "He had lived all his life with a basket over his head, and now that it had been taken off and air and sunlight had come to him, he could not consent to have the basket over him again." Rather than face that eventuality, the blacks on several islands near Edisto rowed themselves to Savannah, leaving behind their household goods and the crops they had made.[41] But some of the freedmen had worked too long and too hard on these lands to give them up so easily, and they resolved to remain and fight.

To inform the blacks that their land aspirations were all a delusion was difficult enough. But to remove them from the lands they had come to regard as their own often required more than verbal skills. In Norfolk County, Virginia, the freedmen who had settled on Taylor's farm refused to leave, ignoring the court orders and ousting the sheriffs and Federal officers who tried to enforce them. After assembling together, the blacks refused offers of compromise, questioned the President's right to pardon the original owner, and resolved to defend their property. At this meeting, Richard Parker ("better known as 'Uncle Dick,' " said the Norfolk newspaper) explained to his fellow freedmen that the white man had secured this land only by forcibly expelling the Indians and he suggested that they now exercise the same prerogative.

> We don't care for the President nor the Freedmen's Bureau. We have suffered long enough; let the white man suffer now. The time was when the white man could say, "Come here, John, and black my boots," and the poor black man had to go; but, my friends, the times have changed, and I hope I will live to see the day when I can say to the white man, "Come here, John, and black my boots," and he must come. I will never be satisfied until the white man is forced to serve the black man, as the black was formerly compelled to serve the white. Now, my friends, we must drive them away.

After a pitched battle with county agents, the black settlers were finally driven off the land.[42]

Along the South Carolina coast, blacks barricaded themselves on the plantations, destroyed the bridges leading to them, and shot at owners seeking to repossess them. On several of the Sea Islands, they organized along military lines to hold their lands and treated any claimants as trespassers. "They use threatening language, when the former residents of the Islands are spoken of in any manner," a Bureau officer reported, "and say openly, that none of them, will be permitted to live upon the Islands. They are not willing to be reasoned with on this subject." On Johns Island, the blacks in early 1866 persisted in refusing to contract, insisted they would work only for themselves, and refused to surrender ownership of the land —in theory or in fact. When "a party of Northern Gentlemen" proposed to look over real estate prospects on the island, they were made "prisoners" the moment they landed, disarmed, and advised never to return. With similar vigilance, the blacks on James Island repelled the first landing party of planters who had come to recover their lands. The battle over restoration of the lands soon resembled a series of mopping-up operations, with the Freedmen's Bureau and Federal troops always ready to guarantee the safety and property of the returning owners, and the blacks able to hold out only for so long against the dictates of the law and the force of an army.[43]

If blacks could not acquire land by government action, neither would they find it easy to obtain it by any other means, even if they adopted the self-help precepts and accumulated the necessary funds. Appreciating the threat black proprietorship posed to a dependent, stable, and contented work force, and the feelings of "impudence and independence" it might generate, many planters refused to sell or to rent any land to blacks. Such a policy was in accordance with "the general good," a South Carolina rice planter insisted, for once lands were leased to freedmen, "it will be hard ever to recover the privileges that have been yielded." When whites tried to restrict landownership in the Black Codes or in combinations among themselves, the Federal government revoked their actions. But community pressures often achieved the same results. "I understand Dr. Harris and Mr. Varnedoe will rent their lands to the Negroes!" a much-scandalized Mary Jones wrote her daughter. "The conduct of some of the citizens has been very injurious to the best interest of the community." If whites persisted in such behavior, they faced social ostracism or violence to their property. Any white man found selling land in his parish, a Louisiana plantation manager observed, would "soon be dangling from some trees." Of course, restrictions on the sale and rental of land to blacks could not always be applied with the rigidity some whites desired, particularly when landowners found that leasing might be the only way to keep their land in productive use.[44]

Within a year of the war's end, the planter class had virtually completed the recovery of its property. But repossession would be of limited value without a productive and regulated black laboring force to work the lands. Few stated the problem more candidly than Allen S. Izard, a Georgia planter. Now that the "game of confiscation" had been settled, his fellow planters needed most urgently to consolidate their triumph.

> Our place is to work; take hold & persevere; get labour of some kind; get possession of the places; stick to it; oust the negroes; and their ideas of proprietorship; secure armed protection close at hand on our exposed

River, present a united and determined front; and make as much rice as
we can. . . . Our plantations will have to be assimilated to the industrial
establishment of other parts of the world, where the owner is protected
by labour tallies, time tables, checks of all kinds, & constant watchful-
ness. Every operator will steal time and anything else.[45]

The terms he chose to describe the challenge facing planters in the postwar
South suggested the need to adopt modern industrial techniques to ensure
their continued mastery over a class of workers who had only recently
broken the chains of bondage. That the ideal binding force should have
been introduced by Northerners would seem, therefore, to have been less
ironic than logical. Like the planters, Federal authorities appreciated full
well the need to guarantee and compel black labor. When the officers of the
Freedmen's Bureau enlightened the ex-slaves in the fall of 1865 on the
futility of their land expectations, they supplied at the same time the forms
that the new dependency would assume.

## 4

WHEN THE POSTWAR southern legislatures adopted measures to compel
blacks to contract with an employer or face arrest as vagrants, they had
merely written into law what the Union Army and the Freedmen's Bureau
had already demanded of the freed slaves. Despite the virtual abrogation
of the Black Codes, the contract system remained very much intact. In
South Carolina, for example, the Union commander voided the Codes but
simultaneously ordered freedmen to contract in the next ten days or leave
the plantations on which they lived. The Codes had contained clauses
which offended northern standards of justice and fairness. The contract, on
the other hand, was a much-venerated instrument of law which enjoyed
high standing both in the North and in the South. Embodying as it did a
voluntary agreement between two parties, in which the terms and conditions were spelled out, the contract suggested what the Codes had not—
impartiality, equality before the law, and the traditional American virtues
of give-and-take and compromise.

Federal authorities introduced the contract into wartime labor relations in the South as a way of protecting the newly freed slaves, easing the
transition from slave to free labor, and compelling former owners to recognize emancipation and compensate their workers. Drawn up initially by
Union Army officers and Freedmen's Bureau agents, the contract also
came to be accepted as the most expedient way to get the blacks back to
the fields, to regulate the quality of their labor, and to ensure a stable
working force for the highly seasonal agriculture of the South. With often
the noblest of intentions, then, the Freedmen's Bureau, from the moment
of its inception, urged the ex-slaves to sign contracts, assured them they

would be treated fairly, and warned them of the consequences of noncompliance. "Your contracts were explained to you, and their sacredness impressed upon you, again and again," the Bureau commissioner for Mississippi told the freedmen. "If you do not have some occupation you will be treated as vagrants, and made to labor on public works."[46]

The planters were in such perfect agreement about what they expected of their freed black laborers that they often used the same language in the contracts. By affixing his signature to the agreement, the freedman invariably promised to render "perfect obedience," to be "prompt and faithful" in the performance of his duties, and to maintain a proper demeanor. On the Heyward plantations in South Carolina, the laborers not only recognized the "lawful authority" of the employer and his agents but agreed to conduct themselves "in such manner as to gain the good will of those to whom we must always look for protection."[47] Few employers went so far as the South Carolina planter who bound his blacks to be "strictly as my slaves" in obeying his instructions. Nor did many think it necessary to adopt the proviso which another planter insisted upon—that the freedmen always address him as "master." But few would have dissented from the spirit that had inspired such stipulations. It made little difference to H. A. Moore, a South Carolina planter, if his freedmen addressed him and his wife as "Mr. & Mrs. Moore" or simply as "Massa Maurice & Miss Bettie," but they were always to "speak politely to us."[48]

Lest the freedman be in any way tempted to compromise his "perfect obedience," most contracts barred him from possessing "deadly weapons" or "ardent spirits," and the employer reserved the right to enter the freedman's cabin at any time. During working hours, moreover, the laborer agreed to have no visitors and to obtain his employer's permission before leaving the plantation for any reason (numerous contracts required such permission at all times). In some regions, the freedmen agreed to submit to punishment for contract violations—"our employer being the judge whether we are to be punished or turned off." But most contracts could not provide corporal punishment for violations, if only because a Bureau official might disallow the entire agreement; however, employers did specify fines for any absenteeism, negligence in work, or breakdowns in expected demeanor. For the more serious offenses, like insubordination or desertion, the laborer could be dismissed, thereby forfeiting all or a portion of his wages and crop shares for the year.[49] In some rare instances, as on one South Carolina plantation, the employer agreed to submit cases of misconduct and conflicts between himself and the freedmen to a jury of his own laborers, whose judgments would be binding on both parties. The "model" contract drawn up by Martin Delany in South Carolina stipulated that the panel adjudging such disputes include the employer, a freedman, and a third party acceptable to both of them. But if the offense warranted dismissal or a forfeiture of pay, an officer of the Freedmen's Bureau would preside and make the final decision.[50]

Under the old task system, which some contracts maintained, a laborer had been expected to complete a prescribed amount of work each day, with the rest of the time his own. To determine how much work a free laborer, as distinct from a slave, should perform each day raised some obvious difficulties, but some enterprising planters and overseers resolved the dilemma by borrowing from past experience. "There's a heap in hum-buggin' a nigger," a Mississippi overseer advised. "I worked a gang this summer, and got as much work out of 'em as I ever did. I just had my leading nigger, and I says to him, I says, 'Sam, I want this yer crop out by such a time; now you go a-head, talk to the niggers, and lead 'em off right smart, and I'll give you twenty-five dollars.' Then I got up a race, and give a few dollars to the men that picked the most cotton, till I found out the extent of what each man could pick; then I required that of him every day, or I docked his wages." Precisely because the task and gang systems remained vivid reminders of slavery, both came into growing disrepute after the war; most contracts stipulated a six-day workweek and a ten- to twelve-hour workday—usually from sunrise to sunset, with an hour or more for dinner. The question of time off on Saturday would take on increasing importance in the annual negotiations over a new contract.[51]

Reacting against the close personal supervision that had characterized slavery, the freedmen had already expressed strong reservations about the presence of an overseer on the plantation. During the war, newly freed slaves had vented much of their anger on their overseer, and in some instances they had either driven him off or refused to work until he had been removed. After the war, antipathy to the overseer in no way diminished, despite the efforts of some planters to make the position more palatable and more consistent with emancipation by redesignating the overseer as a superintendent. "With the negroes a name is imposing," one observer wrote. "Many would engage cheerfully to work under a 'superintendent,' who would not have entered the field under an 'overseer.' " But the distinction escaped many ex-slaves, and this same observer conceded that "it is easier to change an odious name than an odious character." As a Mississippi planter confided to him, "I should get along very well with my niggers, if I could only get my superintendent to treat them decently. Instead of cheering and encouraging them, he bullies and scolds them, and sometimes so forgets himself as to kick and beat them. Now they are free they won't stand it. They stood it when they were slaves, because they had to." On a plantation in Coahoma County, Mississippi, a Freedmen's Bureau agent endeavored to ascertain why the laborers objected to the employment of a former overseer to supervise the work. "I made inquiries regarding the treatment of the hands, by Mr. Hogan, and found no complaint whatever; the only objection was that he was an old overseer. The Freedmen have an idea that overseers are no longer allowed." He lectured the freedmen on their obligation to obey "whoever their employer chose to employ as their superintendent."[52]

Where an overseer no longer supervised the field hands, black dissatisfaction would now most likely fall directly on the employer himself or on the black driver. Like the overseer and the task and gang systems, the driver symbolized for many blacks the excesses and close supervision of slavery; nevertheless, he enjoyed considerably more 'staying power than the overseer, and the freedmen tended to view his presence with fewer misgivings. The typical contract obligated laborers to obey a driver selected from their ranks, but "out of compliment to the changed times" he would now be known as a foreman or captain. That satisfied some freedmen, but only if a change in personnel accompanied the new appellation. In the Sea Islands, a group of laborers told a Union officer that "the drivers ought now to work as field hands, and some field hands be drivers in their place." Already convinced that the old ways of managing blacks would no longer suffice, Edward B. Heyward, the South Carolina rice planter, acknowledged the importance of naming as his foreman an individual who had never before held that position. "Had he turned loose old 'Wasp' [the former driver] on the plantation," Heyward's son recalled, "I am quite sure he would have had few Negroes in his fields. But how Wasp would have enjoyed it!" On many plantations, however, the old driver still commanded the respect and loyalty of the blacks, and employers relied heavily on his leadership to continue agricultural operations with the least amount of disruption; in some places, as on the Manigault rice plantations, the land-owner made a contract with a black foreman or manager, in which he entrusted the entire agricultural operation to him, including the hiring and disciplining of the hands. At the end of the year, the owner retained one half of the net profits, while the blacks divided the rest among themselves. "Little or no intercourse is thus held between Gen'l Harrison [the employer] and the Mass of the Negroes," Manigault wrote of that unique arrangement on his old place, "and provided the Work is performed it is immaterial what Hands are employed."[53]

If the constraints imposed by contracts upon the movements and behavior of black laborers assumed a near uniformity, the amount and the method of compensation tended to vary considerably, even within the same region. "I furnish everything but clothes, and give my freedmen one third of the crop they make," an Arkansas planter declared, but "on twenty plantations around me, there are ten different styles of contracts." The compensation offered a freedman reflected the scarcity of labor in the district, the planter's ability to pay, agricultural prospects, how successfully the laborers pressed their demands, and how effectively planters were able to decide among themselves on maximum rates. Despite variations within regions, the wage rates and crop shares tended to be higher in the lower than in the upper South: a first-class male field hand could generally expect to make no more than $5–$10 a month in Virginia, North Carolina, and Tennessee; $8–$12 in South Carolina and Georgia; $10–$18 in Mississippi, Alabama, Florida, and Louisiana; and $15–$25 in Arkansas and Texas. On the same plantation, however, wage scales fluctuated according to how the employer classified his laborers; on a Mississippi plantation, for example, the employer paid first-class male laborers $15 a month, first-class women $10, and drivers $40, while the average hand netted about $10.[54]

The value of these wages obviously depended upon the degree to which the employer maintained his laborers—that is, whether he furnished the lodgings, food, clothing, and medical care or deducted those items from wages. On a plantation in Louisiana, for example, field hands earned $25 a month but they had to purchase their food, clothing, and other provisions, and each hand paid a tax to ensure regular visits by a doctor; most of the wage, they testified, went for food, they could ill afford a contemplated tax for schools, and it was "pretty tight living." The method and time of payment reflected an employer's dim view of black character. The alleged propensity of blacks to spend their wages quickly and foolishly induced employers to insert clauses in contracts whereby they would provide certain necessities "at the current prices" and deduct the expense from the freedmen's pay. And to ensure compliance with the contract, they preferred to pay the laborer half of his earnings on a quarterly or monthly basis, withholding the rest until the end of the year; in many cases, they withheld all payments until the crop had been completed, although advancing money or provisions against the final settlement. If a laborer worked for a portion of the crop rather than wages, his share usually ranged from one fifth (with board) to one half (less the deductions made for provisions). Since the agreed-upon share would be divided among all the laborers on the plantation, individuals received amounts commensurate with the work they performed and their position and sex.[55]

With the advent of paid labor, planters and freedmen failed to agree even among themselves on the respective merits of compensation in cash wages or in shares of the crop. To the planters, many of them desperately short of cash after the war, payment in shares reflected at first nothing more than economic necessity. But some came to prefer this method of payment, thinking it might ensure a more stable work force and stimulate the freedmen by giving them "an interest and pride in the crop." The planters who remained skeptical feared that payment in shares would encourage the hands to think they had an interest in the land as well as the crop, make them even more presumptuous and independent, and increase the difficulty of discharging inefficient workers. Both methods of payment remained popular, with some planters trying both at various times and assessing the results. That neither system exacted the desired amount of labor they attributed largely to the freedman's slovenly work habits and racial traits rather than to his inevitable disappointment on payday. Based upon the freedman's experience with wages or shares, the issue took on growing importance in the negotiations that preceded a new contract.[56]

Although running the risk of having a Federal official disallow the contract, some planters tried to capitalize on the freedman's illiteracy and the Freedmen's Bureau's indifference. On one plantation, the contract awarded to the laborers one third of seven twelfths of the crop; in another instance, four freedmen contracted to work for one fifth of one third of the crop and failed to realize their error until the final settlement. "Contracts which were brought to me for approval contained all sorts of ludicrous provisions," a Freedmen's Bureau agent in South Carolina recalled. "The idea seemed to be that if the laborer were not bound body and soul he would be of no use." The rumors that circulated among freedmen that a contract would bind them for life or a seven-year apprenticeship were based in part on the efforts of certain employers to do precisely that. "Master," an Alabama freedman declared as he packed his belongings to leave the plantation, "they say if we make contracts now, we'll be branded, and made slaves again." Some Bureau officials spent nearly as much time reassuring freedmen on this point as they did explaining the terms of contracts.

> Some of you have the absurd notion that if you put your hands to a contract you will somehow be made slaves. This is all nonsense, made up by some foolish or wicked person. There is no danger of this kind to fear; nor will you be branded when you get on a plantation. Any white man treating you so would be punished.[57]

In numerous instances, however, freedmen affixed their names to contracts which only perpetuated the terms by which they had served as slaves. "Heap of 'em, round here, just works for their victuals and clothes, like they always did," a South Carolina planter observed. "I reckon they'll all be back whar they was, in a few years."[58]

Although designed to protect the interests of planters and freedmen alike, the contract in practice gave employers what they had wanted all along—the crucial element of control by which they could bind the ex-slaves for at least a year and compel them to work and maintain proper behavior. Nor did the presence of a Freedmen's Bureau officer necessarily make the contracts any less oppressive; after all, one agent conceded, the objective of the contract was to prevent black laborers from deserting their employers "at a critical time" in the making of the crop. Whatever the initial intent, the contract system embodied that universally accepted dictum that only compulsion and discipline could induce free blacks to work. Unlike the northern worker who entered into a verbal contract with an employer, the black laborer in the postwar South was bound by a legal instrument which not only stipulated objective terms of service (compensation, hours, and duties) but imposed conditions of demeanor and attitude on the laborer and not on the employer. That feature in itself made the question of compliance or noncompliance necessarily arbitrary and revealed the contract as something less than a bilateral agreement between equals. In so many ways, in fact, the new arrangements simply institutionalized the old discipline under the guise of easing the ex-slave's transition to freedom. After comparing the regulations under slavery with those which now controlled free labor, the *New Orleans Tribune* found but few differences: "All the important prohibitions imposed upon the slave, are also enforced against the freedman. . . . It is true that the law calls him a freeman; but any white man, subjected to such restrictive and humiliating prohibitions, will certainly call himself a slave."[59]

By hedging the freedman's newly acquired rights, by narrowing his room for maneuverability, by robbing him of his principal bargaining strengths, by seeking to control both his social behavior and his labor, the contract between a former master and his former slaves reminded one observer of a "patent rat-trap." No one, he noted, could have devised a surer instrument to compel black labor. "Rats couldn't possibly get out of it. The only difficulty was that they declined to go in."[60]

## 5

ONCE THE CONTRACT had been prepared, the employer assembled the laborers on his place (most of them his former slaves), explained the terms, and urged them to sign. The response was likely to be mixed, with some freedmen walking back to their quarters only to pack their belongings and take to the road, unwilling to commit their labor and lives to an agreement they could not even read. The very formality, obscure legalisms, and binding nature of the contract provoked skepticism and dismay, even in ex-slaves who fully intended to remain with their former master. In Burke County, Georgia, Willis Bennefield would have nothing to do with a contract. "What you want me to sign for? I is free," he told the man who had owned him as a slave. Nor did the master's explanation that the contract held both of them to their word satisfy him. "If I is already free, I don't need to sign no paper," he insisted. "If I was workin' for you and doin' for you befo' I got free, I kin do it still, if you wants me to stay wid you." If he refused to sign a contract, his mother warned him, he might forfeit his pay. "Den I kin go somewheh else," the ex-slave replied.[61]

Rather than objecting to a specific clause, large numbers of freedmen feared that the contract, as a binding legal agreement, compromised their newly won liberties, and perhaps even forfeited their rights to the expected distribution of land among them. In his section of Virginia, a Union officer reported, the blacks refrained from contracting for any length of time "in the expectation of some indefinable but great benefits to be bestowed on them by the Government." Nor would they place any great faith in the employer's assurance that the contract protected their best interests. The freedmen lacked confidence "in the white man's *integrity,*" a Bureau commissioner in Mississippi concluded, and the suspicion, other agents reported, often extended to "papers of any description, in which their former masters are in any way concerned." On Edisto Island, South Carolina, several freedmen declared at a meeting with Federal officials that they bore no personal enmity toward their old masters but they had no desire to contract with men who had once owned and abused them, or even with those who might have treated them reasonably well but in whom they had no confidence.[62]

With numbers of ex-slaves refusing to sign contracts, many of them hoping to obtain better terms, the planter class counted heavily on the ultimate weapons of necessity and compulsion. To hasten that moment of decision, Federal authorities complied all too readily with the demands of planters that they apprehend black vagrants and cease issuing food rations to freedmen, thereby forcing them to depend once again upon their old masters for daily subsistence. Ironically, that policy accorded with the growing conviction of the Freedmen's Bureau and northern freedmen's aid societies that to distribute food and clothing among the ex-slaves made them less independent, reduced their incentives to work, and demoralized them. "The most dangerous process through which the negro goes when he becomes a freedman is that of receiving the gratuities of benevolence in the shape of food and clothing," a missionary wrote late in 1865. "If you wish to make them impudent, fault-finding and lazy, give them clothing and food freely." Once the freedmen had to depend upon his bounty, the planter reasoned, he had only to withhold such support to induce his laborers to agree to terms. That proved to be a sound conclusion, though the results were not always gratifying. When Stephen Doan, a South Carolina proprietor, decided to withhold food rations to force his men to abide by a contract, they killed him.[63]

To counter the freedman's principal bargaining strength—the threat to take his labor to the highest bidder—planters often effected combinations or understandings among themselves not to contract with any former slave who failed to produce a "consent paper" or a proper discharge from his previous owner. The white citizens of Nelson County, Virginia, acting "to prevent improper interference with each other's arrangements," resolved that "in *no case*" would they hire a laborer who failed to supply "a certificate of character, and of permission to rehire himself." More often, as in the Clarendon district of South Carolina, local planters simply reached a verbal understanding "not to hire their neighbour's negroes."[64] Such an agreement, in one bold stroke, would effectively reduce the freedman's chances of either improving or changing his position, while it obviously enhanced a planter's ability to exact for himself the most favorable terms. "The nigger is going to be made a serf, sure as you live," vowed the owner of a cotton factory and two plantations in Alabama.

> It won't need any law for that. Planters will have an understanding among themselves: "You won't hire my niggers, and I won't hire yours"; then what's left for them? They're attached to the soil, and we're as much their masters as ever. I'll stake my life, this is the way it will work.[65]

Appreciating the need to coordinate their efforts, planters in numerous regions also met to fix maximum wages, to draw up model contracts, to agree on penalties for violations of contracts, and to pledge themselves not to lease or rent any land to a freedman. Although the Freedmen's Bureau frowned upon such combinations and in some instances banned them, local agents might choose to look the other way; after all, the ends they wished to achieve were almost identical. In Clarke County, Alabama, a Labor Regulating Association formed by local planters appeared to be on good terms with the Bureau agent and hoped to obtain his approval for apprenticing the orphan children of ex-slaves. But even where the Bureau broke up such combinations, planters kept themselves informed of what their neighbors were paying and paid no more. Still other pressures were brought to bear on recalcitrant blacks. In a South Carolina community, physicians agreed not to treat freedmen unless the planters authorized their visits. "They adopt this course," a local resident explained, "to bring to the notice of the negroes, their dependent condition & to check the feeling of irresponsibility now prevalent." And if other measures proved unavailing, some employers, particularly in areas remote from a Freedmen's Bureau office, had no hesitation in employing violent methods to force their laborers to agree to terms. In Surrey County, Virginia, a black farmer testified, "they are taking the colored people and tying them up by the thumbs if they do not agree to work for six dollars a month; they tie them up until they agree to work for that price, and then they make them put their mark to a contract.... A man cannot endure it long." In some regions, patrols of white men meted out summary justice to blacks who were not under contract to an employer or who were found to be in violation of a contract.[66]

Although the vast majority of freedmen eventually agreed to terms, that hardly ended the difficulties. During the first postwar agricultural season, with both sides testing the effects of emancipation, the reports mounted of freedmen unable to appreciate the binding character of a contract and leaving the plantations "on the most trifling pretext" before their terms of service had expired. (One planter still referred to such workers as "runaways.") "They are constantly striking for higher wages," a Georgian observed of the black laborers in his state.

> The great difficulty is that they will not stick to a contract; they are fickle; they are constantly expecting to do better; they will make a contract with me to-day for twelve or fifteen dollars a month, and in a few days somebody will come along and offer a dollar or two more, and they will quit me—never saying anything to me, but leave in the night and be gone.

The most persistent complaints revolved around those laborers who remained on the plantations, worked "only when they please, and as little as they please," feigned sickness to avoid labor, and had a habit of carrying pistols with them to the fields (allegedly to shoot stray rabbits or squirrels). Unaccustomed to black labor, a northern lessee and former abolitionist who operated a plantation in Georgia found himself annoyed by the sight of laborers dropping their shovels and hoes in the fields to sing "a religious song." Still other employers fretted over the propensity of their workers to do as little as possible in the expectation of "a better time coming"—the anticipated division of the land among the freedmen.[67] "Every contract made in 1865 has been broken by the freedmen," a Freedmen's Bureau agent reported from the Georgetown district of South Carolina, and one local proprietor, Jane Pringle, derived little satisfaction from the willingness of Federal authorities to arrest and jail black violators: "Of what earthly benefit is it to us that men who should be laboring are thrown into prison, they can't till the land there and I assure you that a prison life is rather a pleasure to a negro than a punishment, since they are fed without working." As an alternative to the "tedious law process," she proposed the establishment of military posts "at small distances for instant relief" and "double labor on the land" as proper punishment.[68]

No matter how explicitly a contract defined the freedmen's rights, duties, and compensation, many laborers persisted in following their own notions about how and when they wished to work. Although most freedmen contracted to work a six-day week, many of them refused to labor for the employer on Saturdays, preferring to confine their efforts to their own garden plots and to household chores. More commonly, disputes arose over whether freedmen were obliged to perform tasks not actually stipulated in the contract. On a Georgia farm, for example, the refusal of a freedman to work on Sunday precipitated a confrontation with his employer that required the intervention of the Freedmen's Bureau. By the terms of the contract, he had agreed to perform "any and every duty that may, at any time, be required," including "the customary labors on the Sabbath" such as caring for the livestock. Claiming that he had "his own business" to look after, the freedman rejected Sunday work; when the farmer then insisted on reading the contract to him, the laborer refused to listen, left the place, and took his case to the local Bureau agent, who immediately advised him to return to work. But when his employer insisted that he now acknowledge the error and the commitment to work on Sunday, the freedman said he "would promise nothing and agree to nothing." To have to listen to such "insolence" from a former slave proved to be more than many planters could tolerate. When a freedman in low-country South Carolina insisted that the contract did not oblige him to perform certain kinds of work, his employer beat him over the head and shoulders with a club; on another plantation, an employer shot a freedman who insisted upon consulting the local Bureau agent about the interpretation of a certain clause in the contract. The tenuous peace that existed in the aftermath of emancipation could be easily broken over such matters, but with alarming regularity the violence would not remain one-sided.[69]

Whatever the constraints of a contract, the eagerness and determination of black people to reunite their families and to regularize family relations took precedence. For the planters, on the other hand, the need to retain their labor force intact could not be compromised. On a plantation in upper Georgia, William Henry Stiles thus rejected the plea of a former slave (who had fled during the war) that he be permitted to take his wife with him to Savannah; the planter countered that he needed her labor and he intended to hold her to the contract that bound her to his place until the end of the year. Nor would a Louisiana planter assent to the request of an elderly black woman who wished to be paid so she could move to another place and be closer to her husband. "Don't you know that you contracted with me for a year?" he asked her. "Don't know nuffin about it. I wants to go 'way," she replied. But the planter remained unyielding, and the law clearly backed him. "Well, I'm keeping my part of the contract, and you've got to keep yours," he warned the woman. "If you don't, I'll send you to jail, that's all."[70]

Although claiming that the ignorant and backward Negro could not be made to respect the sanctity of a written agreement, employers were not necessarily the innocent victims of black deceit. If the contract stipulated food rations, for example, it guaranteed neither the quality nor the quantity of the food. That was "de fust dif'culty," a South Carolina freedman contended when asked about contract violations, "we gits no meat." Investigating a disturbance on a plantation in the Beaufort district, the Freedmen's Bureau agent reported that the laborers thought their employer to be dishonest, and they complained of overwork and being fed "musty" corn and "rotten" bacon. Although the Freedmen's Bureau threatened to disallow contracts which empowered employers to use corporal punishment, that did not protect the freedmen from other forms of abuse. After being berated for negligence, a Mississippi freedman replied that he was a free man, he refused to be insulted as though he were still a slave, and he left. His decision could not have been made lightly. Not only did he face arrest and prosecution for violating the contract but he lost his remaining pay.[71]

The thought occurred to more than one planter that a way to avoid paying his laborers was to provoke them to break the contract near the end of the season. Asked to explain "the real cause" of labor turbulence in his area, a black worker who lived near Florence, South Carolina, singled out that particular grievance.

> Well, sah, there's a many masters as wants to git de colored peoples away, ye see; an' dey's got de contrac's, an' dey can't do it, ye see, lawful; so dey 'buses dem, an' jerks 'em up by de two fums, an' don't give 'em de bacon, an' calls on 'em to do work in de night time an' Sun'ay, till de colored people dey gits oneasy an' goes off.

On a Mississippi plantation, the manager expelled some blacks who had expressed dissatisfaction over working conditions, refusing to pay them for the three months they had already labored. (The Bureau agent ordered their reinstatement.) And in South Carolina, Martin Delany heard numerous complaints that near the completion of the crop, the employer brought "some frivolous" charge against freedmen and discharged them, thereby making them forfeit their share of the forthcoming division of the crop. The practice reached such proportions, in fact, that the Freedmen's Bureau found it necessary to require that employers show "sufficient cause" before discharging contracted laborers and pay them what they had earned. When one Bureau agent tried to explain this policy to local planters, he reported that they found it "quite incomprehensible from the old-fashioned, patriarchal point of view."[72]

Although the Freedmen's Bureau insisted that both planters and laborers comply with contract terms, local agents thought their primary mission was to keep the blacks at work and punish them for violations. "Doing justice," an observer sympathetic to the blacks reported, "seems to mean . . . seeing that the blacks don't break contract and compelling them to submit cheerfully if the whites do." Nothing seemed to disturb Bureau agents more about the postwar black "migration" than the tendency of freedmen to leave employers with whom they had agreed to complete the current crop. Consistent with their vigorous suppression of black vagrancy and their regular pronouncements on the necessity of labor, Bureau officials impressed upon blacks the sanctity of contracts and moved quickly to apprehend non-signers and violators as vagrants. While employers might be reprimanded or even fined for violating a contract, the freedman usually found himself in far deeper trouble, perhaps incarcerated for a period of time or forced to work on the public roads without pay. After a "contrary" freedman in a Florida community spent a week in jail on a diet of bread and water, he was said by the local Bureau agent to have been "very willing" to return to the fields. If evidence reached the nearest office of the Freedmen's Bureau that laborers had left a plantation, refused to contract or work, or were creating a disturbance, that was all the agent needed to know to justify his intervention, with troops if he deemed them necessary. Upon hearing that some freedmen near Meridian, Mississippi, had left their jobs for "frivolous and insufficient causes," the Bureau agent requested the names of the "guilty" parties and ordered their arrest. In many instances, Bureau officials acted in good conscience to exact a fair settlement of the grievances which had required their intervention but seldom would they tolerate any violation of a contract, no matter how relatively trivial the nature of the offense or how unreasonable the contract.[73]

The Freedmen's Bureau defended its policies in the name of stabilizing labor relations. But the overly zealous commitment of its agents to the inviolability of contracts and the double standard they often applied in enforcement and in the punishment of offenders proved of immeasurable benefit to the employers. After reviewing the work of the Bureau, a conservative Memphis newspaper could not help but applaud its accomplishments: "The chaotic condition of the labor system is being reduced to order. It gives the employer the means of compelling the fulfillment of engagements on the part of the employee." Such intervention was particularly welcomed in the initial experiments with contract labor, when violations and plantation disturbances loomed as a critical test of the entire labor

system. The need to make examples of "turbulent negroes," lest they influence others to "go astray," seemed all the more urgent. When two of his
contracted freedmen fled "without any provocation," Lorenzo James, an
Alabama planter, wished to have them arrested, punished severely, and
sent back "as an example to those remaining." He knew precisely in what
terms to frame his appeal to the Freedmen's Bureau for assistance:

> There is every reason to believe that these two negroes were induced to
> leave by the other negroes, to test this question and see if any punish-
> ment could be inflicted upon them for a violation of their contract. If they
> go unpunished, it will have a very bad effect upon, not only my planta-
> tion, but upon the surrounding country; and if they are allowed to violate
> a contract made in good faith whenever they see fit to do so, the agricul-
> tural interest throughout the country must necessarily suffer to a very
> great extent.

His friendship with the Bureau's regional commissioner no doubt helped
to ensure prompt compliance with his request.[74]

The sanctity of contracts proved of little avail to the freedmen on the
day they settled their accounts with the employer. With the approach of
Christmas each year and the division of the crop and the final wage payment, the dire predictions of "a heap o' trouble" proved all too prophetic.
"They'll be awfully defrauded," a Virginia poor white thought, perhaps
reflecting his own experiences with the planter class. "I know houses yer
whar they keep a nigger till his month's most out, and then they make a
muss with him, and kick him out without any wages. Poor men like me has
got to pay for it. Of course, if they don't pay, the niggers can't keep themselves, and it'll come on us. They'll be cheated all kinds o' ways. Don't I
know it?"[75]

6

---

IF HIS NEWLY FREED SLAVES remained with him until the end of the season,
a Tennessee planter promised, they would be awarded a share of the crop.
"Most of them left," Lorenzo Ivy recalled; "they said they knew him too
well." But this sixteen-year-old black youth and his father stayed on and
worked "just as if Lee hadn't surrendered." By Christmas 1865, they had
raised a large crop of corn, wheat, and tobacco, they had shucked the corn
and stored it in the barn, and they had stripped all the tobacco. "I never
worked harder in my life, for I thought the more we made, the more we
would get." But when the two freedmen stood before their former master
to obtain the promised shares, he refused to pay them anything, declared
he could no longer support them, and ordered them off his land. Thinking
few grievances could be more legitimate or clear-cut, they appealed to the

local officer of the Freedmen's Bureau. He refused to help them. "The officer," Lorenzo Ivy recalled, "was like Isaac said to Esau: 'The voice is like Jacob's voice, but the hands are the hands of Esau.' So that was the way with the officer—he had on Uncle Sam's clothes, but he had Uncle Jeff's heart."[76]

Large numbers of freedmen shared the experience of Lorenzo Ivy and his father. With the completion of the crops, some planters defaulted on promised payments or pleaded inability to pay, and still more reduced the payments drastically through arbitrary and inflated deductions. The initial victims were ex-slaves like the Ivys who had agreed to stay on after emancipation in return for a share of the crop. But now they were left with nothing, and even driven from the plantation. When the Freedmen's Bureau launched its operations, local agents found their offices besieged by blacks testifying to the extent and persistence of this grievance. "The old story has been repeated thousands of times," one officer reported, "no definite bargain made—no wages promised; but 'massa said, stay till the crop is made and he would do what was right.'" That proved to be the downfall of many a freedman. Popular in verbal understandings though seldom written into contracts, the employer's promise to pay his laborers "what was right" left him free to pay them nothing or very little; indeed, he might even persuade himself that to pay his workers any more could only demoralize them and encourage indulgences not befitting inferiors. The Mississippi planter who deprived his ex-slaves of the crop shares he had promised still thought of himself as an honest man; he simply presumed, a neighbor said of him, that northern capitalists always treated free laborers in this way.[77]

If the planter pleaded financial poverty and indebtedness, he might place the blame on falling cotton prices, a bad crop, or the slovenly work habits of his laborers. Not uncommonly, an employer would charge that the work of his blacks had not even paid for the food he gave them. The problem with confessing an inability to pay, even when justified, was that few of his laborers chose to believe him. And if they did believe him, why should they work for him another year on the vague assurance that conditions would improve? That made no sense at all. The "impoverished" planter might discover soon enough that he had become an undesirable risk among all the freedmen in the vicinity, even more so if they suspected him of deceit or fraud. The much-heralded contract, moreover, seemed less than sacrosanct when it denied them the very fruits of their labor. Such initial experiences, a black man wrote from Helena, Arkansas, in early 1866, would not be soon forgotten. "They may cheat the poor negro out of a year's work, but in spite of them he has gained a year's experience, and had the advantage of being thoroughly acquainted with that system of morals, that teaches the negro to observe and fulfill the moral obligations of a contract, but has no meaning or significance when applied to the white man."[78]

Although most employers agreed to compensate their laborers on the basis of the contract, the annual settlement of accounts, in itself an unprecedented event, produced new disappointments, angry confrontations, and near rebellion on some places. Even as the freedmen eagerly looked forward to this day, the employer found it unnerving if not downright humiliating. "Staid on New Hope Plantation all day preparing to settle with the Negroes," a Louisiana planter confided to his diary. "I had almost as lief be shot as to do it, but it must be done." Equally depressed, Wilmer Shields, who had managed several plantations through a turbulent war-time experience, anticipated nothing but trouble as the dreaded payday approached. "I do not expect to satisfy any of them," he informed the owner, "for each one seems to think his share will be a fortune." Whatever the planter's financial position, he came to look upon this day as an un-avoidable ordeal. Unaccustomed to dealing with blacks over such matters, his demeanor was all too likely to crack under the torrent of complaints and challenges—what a South Carolina planter described as "the most gross abuse."[79]

But to the ex-slave, "countin' day" set off his new status from the old, and his expectations were high—almost always too high. Outside the main house the freedmen would assemble and face the table where the planter or his agent sat, holding in his hands the payroll and store book. As each laborer heard his name called, he would step forward to be informed of the number of days he had worked, the debts he had accumulated, the fines assessed against him, and the precise amount he had earned after deduc-tions. That was when the trouble began. If he barely comprehended the often complicated balancing of debts and earnings, he understood the final sum soon enough, his face suddenly assuming an expression of utter dis-may and incredulity. "Ain't got nary a hundud dollars! Ain't got nary a hundud dollars! Done wucked all de year an' ain't got nary a hundud dollars!" a Florida freedwoman kept shouting, waving the dollar bills wildly above her head. On a Louisiana plantation, one of the laborers thought there had to be a mistake: "I done wuck mighty hard fo' you, chop briars and roll logs, and you haint paid me nuffin at all." On a Georgia plantation, the laborers failed to discern any relationship between what they had been paid and the labor they had performed.

> Ole mass'r had 'greed to give we one tird de craps, an' we dun got 'em all up,—got de corn shucked, an' de tatees digged, and de rice trashed; an' ole mass'r he dun gone sold all de craps, an' he bringed we all up yere yes'erday, an' gif we seven dollar fur de man an' he wife to buy de cloth wid to make we clofes, an' he say may be he gif we some shoes; an' he dun gif we'n none o' de craps, none o' de rice, none o' de corn, none o' de tatees.

The same incomprehension gripped the laborers on the Butler plantation in Georgia, each one convinced he had been cheated, invariably greeting his payment with some variation of the remark: "Well, well, work for massa two whole years, and only get dis much."[80]

Puzzled, bitter, angry over the settlement, the freedmen might insist that their employer had erred in his calculations. If he deigned to respond to such charges, he would hold up the ledger and explain to his laborers how the advances of food, clothing, seed, tools, and fuel, in addition to other deductions, had consumed the greater part of their wages or shares. He would remind them of the items they had purchased and the number of days they had lost because of illness. He might even scold them for their thriftlessness and indulgences. "Now, auntie, you have a right to spend your earnings any way you please; you're free. It's none of my business what you do with your money. But if you would let me give you a little advice, I'd tell you all not to waste your money on fish, and candy, and rings, and breastpins, and fine hats. If you will have them, we'll sell them to you, but you had better not buy so freely." Denying any intent to deceive his laborers, the employer would contend in this instance and others that he had simply enforced the contract, which stipulated the amount of compensation and enumerated the deductions.[81]

Unfortunately, the contract said nothing about the cost of the provisions the employer agreed to furnish his laborers. Although the culprit may have been the supply merchant rather than the planter, the fact remained that provisions were sold at highly inflated prices and the laborer had no recourse but to trade where he could obtain credit. "I have neighbors," a Mississippi planter conceded, "who keep stores of plain goods and fancy articles for their people; and, let a nigger work ever so hard, and earn ever so high wages, he is sure to come out in debt at the end of the year." Even if the laborer could understand the deductions for actual purchases, he found far less comprehensible if not fraudulent the fines for negligence, the number of days or hours allegedly absent from work, and even in some cases charges for items like bagging and ropes; in Mississippi, planters reportedly gave "presents" to certain laborers during the season to accelerate the pace of work and then charged the cost of these gifts to their accounts. After the various deductions and charges had been assessed, the most brutal truth that greeted the laborer on the long-awaited "countin' day" was that he stood in debt to the planter! That revelation created such a reaction on a Virginia plantation that the employer, fearing trouble, agreed to pay a token amount ($2 to $5) to each worker.[82]

No matter how carefully his employer explained the situation, the laborer still found it difficult to understand why his months of hard work should have left him with so little or actually in debt. After what seemed like endless disputations over each settlement, Frances Butler thought it useless to argue any further; henceforth, she would pay her father's laborers and refuse to discuss the matter. Besides, she had concluded that the freedmen indulged in these discussions not because they thought they had been cheated but only "with an idea of asserting their independence and dignity." If an aggrieved laborer appealed his case to the Freedmen's Bureau, and many did, he might obtain a measure of relief—but only after proving he had been defrauded. That obstacle proved insurmountable, with the plantation ledger winning out easily over the freedman's recollections, as it would have in any court of law. Even the most sympathetic Bureau officials confessed their helplessness in such cases. Thomas H. Norton, who supervised freedmen's affairs in Meridian, Mississippi, suspected that many blacks had been "meanly defrauded" of their earnings and he could readily understand their discouragement. But he could offer them little but his sympathy.

> Whenever cases of this kind are presented to the Sub Commissioner for investigation he will find himself involved in such a "Milky Way" of figures, admissions and denials, criminations and recriminations, that it will be almost impossible, considering the length of time that has elapsed, and the inability of the freedmen to bring the necessary witnesses to testify to their statements, to arrive at any just conclusion or settlement of the case.[83]

A Bureau officer in South Carolina, John William De Forest, recalled how exasperated he became after arbitrating "a hundred or two" such cases, spending in some instances "an entire forenoon" trying to convince a laborer that his employer had not cheated him. "I read to him, out of the planter's admirably kept books, every item of debit and credit: so much meal, bacon, and tobacco furnished, with the dates of each delivery of the same; so many bushels of corn and peas and bunches of 'fodder' harvested. He admitted every item, admitted the prices affixed; and then, puzzled, incredulous, stubborn, denied the totals." Meanwhile, the laborer's wife stood next to him, "trembling with indignant suspicion," until she could contain herself no longer. "Don' you give down to it, Peter," she exhorted her husband. "It ain't no how ris'ible that we should 'a' worked all the year and git nothin' to go upon." But it was no use. The Bureau agent finally advised the couple to throw themselves upon "the generosity" of their employer.[84]

If the experience of payday exhausted planters and exasperated Bureau officials, it left the freedmen disillusioned, frustrated, and outraged —and in many cases penniless if not in debt. But no matter how hard they tried or to whom they appealed, there was simply no way to make the figures come out differently. "The darkey don't understand it," a Mississippi planter remarked, "he has kept no accounts; but he knows he has worked hard and got nothing. He won't hire to that man again." The thousands of freedmen who left at the expiration of the contract often cited as the principal reason their dissatisfaction over the final settlement. "I'm willin' to wu'k, sah, and I want to wu'k, 'cos I'm mighty ill off," a Virginia freedman declared, but after his employer had reneged on a promised half of the crop he resolved not to work another year "till I knows I'm gwine to get paid at the end of it." Wherever they chose to contract for the next year, including the places on which they had worked, freedmen evinced a determination to do so only after some hard bargaining. "We all gits fooled on dat first go-out!" Katie Rowe recalled, but the following year "we all got something left over." Nor would the freedmen necessarily confine themselves in future confrontations to a refinement of their verbal skills. On Edisto Island, for example, the blacks who worked the Rabbit Point plantation found a different way to make certain that the division of the crops reflected the labor they had expended.

> The moment the Cotton house was opened the people rushed in and a number of them took forcible possession of their cotton and carried it off without division and all refused to allow any division to take place, threatened to knock my brains out and forcibly resisted me. Not having any force at my command I was obliged to close the house and await the arrival of a guard.[85]

With the end of each agricultural season, the tenuous peace that had existed on the plantations suddenly seemed more precarious. The wage settlement, the division of the crops, the need to negotiate new contracts, and the persistent expectations of a land division pitted laborers against employers in ways that violated accepted customs and threatened to undermine the prevailing racial code. Both whites and blacks would have to contend with the fear that traditional antagonisms of race, now aggravated by a new kind of class conflict, might at any time assume more violent forms. Each Christmas season somehow occasioned a new alarm.

7

———

ALTHOUGH DISCERNING FEW CHANGES in his laborers, Donald MacRae, a North Carolina merchant, conceded in September 1865 a widespread sense of uneasiness in the white population. He suspected that the source of the anxiety lay in the expectation of blacks that they would ultimately share in if not possess entirely the lands and goods of their former masters. That expectation had become so pervasive, MacRae believed, that the disappointment, when it came, could only produce the most dreaded of consequences—a black uprising. Fortunately, the local military commander had warned the freedmen not to entertain or act upon such foolish notions. "This may quiet it down," MacRae thought. But if it did not, he anticipated an insurrection that would exceed the worst horrors of the Civil War, "for total annihilation would be the war cry on both sides." Preparing for such an eventuality, Ethelred Philips, the Florida farmer and physician, decided to teach his wife, "timid as she has always been," to use a revolver. "She took the first lesson a few days ago with a rifle and was delighted to find shooting so easy, and when she saw the ball had struck in a few inches of the mark she was quite encouraged, tho she had spoiled her sleeve by the powder. . . . She shall become a sure shot—how many hours of fright may be avoided when a woman feels she holds her safety in her own hand."[86]

The approach of the Christmas holiday in 1865, coinciding as it did with payday, new contract talks, and new land expectations, produced the first major postwar insurrection panic. Now that the blacks were no longer bound by the old restraints, many whites feared they would vent their frustrations and disillusionment over the betrayal of expectations by plunging the South into a racial holocaust. "If they dont massacre the white Race, it is not because the desire dont exist," a South Carolina Unionist observed as he appealed to President Johnson to provide whites with the means to protect themselves from the fury of a race that had become "worse than Devels." Newspapers fed the prevailing anxiety by claiming exclusive knowledge of sinister plots. "We speak advisedly," one of them warned, "we have authentic information of the speeches and conversations of the blacks, sufficient to convince us of their purpose. *They make no secret of their movement.* Tell us not that we are alarmists." For many whites, however, the idea of black insurrection had become such a self-fulfilling prophecy that they needed no fire-eating editors to tell them what they had long suspected would flow naturally out of emancipation. "It will begin the work of extermination," sighed a South Carolina planter, without indicating which race he expected to survive.[87]

With imaginations running rampant, whites found no difficulty in conjuring up horrors and demons befitting the expected bloodbath. The slightest change in a freedman's demeanor, the most trivial incident, the most innocent display of independence could trigger new rumors and fears. The mistress of a plantation near Columbia, South Carolina, had only to listen to the freedmen singing in their quarters—"as only they could sing in these times"—to imagine "a horde pouring into our houses to cut our throats and dance like fiends over our remains." The sight of his former slaves "talking together, sometimes in whispers and sometimes loudly," ignoring his orders to retire to their cabins by the curfew hour, prompted a Georgian to suspect "conspiracies" and to fear "an outbreak every moment." Near Fort Motte, South Carolina, a young planter who had served in the war heard that his blacks planned to attack the barns later in the month; in the meantime, he encountered only their "sour looks" and "uncivil words." One day, he watched as they carried out his order to slaughter some hogs. He found the scene disturbing, impossible to forget. The next day, he still "shuddered" as he recalled "the fiendish eagerness" the blacks had evinced "to stab & kill, the delight in the suffering of others."[88]

In their fevered minds that fall and winter, whites fanned the flames of the conflagration they had largely created themselves. The black man moving through the woods hunting squirrels suddenly became thousands of armed blacks hunting their old masters. The Mississippi planter missing for several days was presumably a victim of murderous blacks, several of whom were arrested and threatened with a lynching until the "martyr" returned home after an extended stay "with some prostitutes." The Yankee soldier who answered the summons of a planter distraught over suspicious black movements was himself mistaken for one of the rebels and shot and killed. The gatherings of blacks to plan for the forthcoming Emancipation Day celebration on January 1 found their way into the conversations and newspapers of whites as meetings to complete the plans for an uprising. The rusty army musket discovered in a freedman's cabin became overnight a vast arsenal to supply the arms for the revolt. Even blacks at work in the fields could be projected into guerrilla armies wielding their spades, pitchforks, and scythes to kill their masters and seize the lands they had been denied. The most persistent rumors stemmed from reports of armed blacks drilling for the coming showdown, but Federal investigators found in one instance a group of young freedmen playing soldier with sticks and unserviceable army rifles, while in another the blacks had, indeed, armed themselves—in fear of a white insurrection.[89]

Much as they had at the outbreak of the war, native whites tried to project a feeling of confidence. Even as Eliza Andrews prepared for a race war, with the tales of the Sepoys, Lucknow, and Cawnpore still quite vivid in her mind, she claimed in June 1865 to have conquered much of the anxiety she had once felt. "Now, when I know that I am standing on a volcano that may burst forth any day, I somehow, do not feel frightened. It seems as if nothing worse could happen than the South has already been through, and I am ready for anything, no matter what comes." Despite the fears of imminent insurrection, Pierce Butler left his daughter and her maid alone on St. Simon's Island with no white person within eight miles, as if to demonstrate the confidence he still reposed in his former slaves. At least, that was how his daughter, Frances, interpreted his action, and she shared his equanimity. "Neither then nor afterwards," she wrote, "when I was alone on the plantation with the negroes for weeks at a time, had I the slightest feeling of fear, except one night, when I had a fright which made me quite ill for two days." The momentary panic had been triggered by a noise emanating from a raft loaded down with mules. Even after discovering the source of the clamor, she recalled, "I had been too terrified to laugh." But if Frances Leigh still enjoyed a feeling of relative security, the many letters and conversations that passed between whites in this period revealed considerable anguish and a growing fear that "no plantation will be a safe residence this Winter."[90]

Fear of insurrection had a long tradition in the South. The new hysteria fed largely on emancipation, black disenchantment with the meager economic rewards of freedom, and the knowledge that tens of thousands of ex-slaves had come into possession of firearms. "Our negroes certainly have guns and are frequently shooting about," the Reverend Samuel A. Agnew of Mississippi observed in November 1865. "Brice had some women go to Corinth recently and they have returned bringing, it is said, ammunition. A good many look for trouble about Christmas." When local whites

disarmed the blacks later that month, Agnew noted that some of the freedmen were "in high dudgeon" over this action, claiming they now had
"equal rights with a white man to bear arms." The reports of armed blacks
were not necessarily exaggerated. With emancipation, large numbers of
freedmen had acquired the weapons denied to them as slaves. "These guns
they prize as their most valued possessions next to their land," a Bureau
agent reported from the Sea Islands, "and to take them away would leave
a lasting and bitter resentment, and sense of injustice."[91] But that was
precisely what the whites intended to do, refusing to believe that when
laborers carried weapons into the fields with them they wished only to
shoot at stray rabbits and squirrels. Heeding the popular outcry, state
governors ordered the militias to patrol the countryside and disarm blacks,
legislatures rewrote and strengthened patrol laws, towns authorized the
employment of additional police, and planters urged the white citizenry to
fill the ranks of the militia. Although some Union Army officers and Bureau agents tried to calm the populace, perhaps as many shared the prevailing fears and cooperated with civil authorities and volunteer patrols to
search the homes of blacks for guns. The occasional discovery of a cache
of arms confirmed the worst fears and intensified the campaign to disarm
the black population. In the Wilmington district of North Carolina, the
Union commander went so far as to urge white citizens to form voluntary
military companies as a precaution against the feared black uprising, and
he promised them arms and ammunition as well as "the entire power at
his command."[92]

Although whites verged on panic, some moving their families to safer
areas, many others volunteering for local patrols, none looked upon the
rumors of impending insurrection with greater apprehension than the
freedmen themselves. Previous experience had revealed all too vividly that
whites had a way of exorcising imagined black demons by exterminating
those within reach who most closely resembled them. And the purgation
—with the inevitable floggings, beatings, and assassinations—would most
likely exceed in brutality the terrors which whites had concocted in anticipation of a black uprising. Unaware of conspiracies in their midst, realizing
the false basis of white fears, drawing upon their own intimate knowledge
of the white man, some blacks concluded—logically enough—that the fear
of insurrection served only the purposes of their former masters, providing
them with the opportunity to invade their homes, to seize their weapons,
to make examples of their leaders, and to otherwise terrorize and harass
them until they revised their notions about the perquisites of freedom.[93]
When the white citizens of two Louisiana parishes appealed to the governor
for arms, ammunition, and the authority to organize for "self preservation," they cited the urgent need "to overawe the colored population, and
thereby avoid the effusion of blood and all the horrors of a cruel insurrection." To force blacks to stand in awe of the white man had of course been
a vital ingredient of racial control under slavery. With that memory of

bondage still vivid in their minds, blacks in some areas began to drill and accumulate arms in preparation for any eventuality. "We'ns smart nuff t' hold 'r own," a South Carolina freedman remarked, and the reporter who heard him thought the optimism justified. "Moreover," the reporter observed, "the whites of all these low-country districts know that fact, too."[94]

On the night of December 27, 1865, the widowed mistress of a plantation in the interior of Georgia sat up until after midnight, "fearing that something sad must occur with so many freedmen about me." But the night passed "and with it all my fears." Throughout the South, Christmas passed without the slightest hint of a contemplated black uprising. Only a few sporadic incidents, almost all of them provoked by overzealous whites, disturbed an otherwise quiet and orderly holiday season. Federal authorities who took the time to investigate the many rumors of black military preparations found no justification for white fears, only a few organizations that blacks had formed for self-defense and with which they hoped to advance their prospects in the forthcoming negotiation of contracts. Perhaps the vigilance of the white community, the vigorous patrolling of the countryside, and the presence of reinforced police, militias, and volunteer patrols had saved the white South from a certain conflagration. Some whites began to suspect that was not the case, that the victory had been something of a sham. "It appears that there has been a great alarm without any cause," the Reverend Samuel A. Agnew of Mississippi confided to his diary; the many reports of imminent insurrection, he now concluded, "were only the creations of the imaginations of timid people." The white hysteria and the extraordinary measures it had provoked, he thought, might in their own way have constituted a tactical victory for the blacks. "As affairs have turned out the negroes must think that the white people are afraid of them."[95]

Although the fears of insurrection proved to be unfounded, whites could never quite surmount them. The circumstances which had fed the rumors would persist. During the next several years, any new epidemic of restlessness, any new manifestation of discontent, any new report of black organization would precipitate still another crisis. If anything, the fears would take on even more lurid dimensions, no doubt reflecting growing apprehension over black political power. As the Christmas season of 1866 approached, James R. Sparkman, a plantation proprietor in South Carolina, shared his apprehensions with a long-time friend. While in town recently, he had attended "a *secret conference*" at which three "respectable citizens" described "an insurrectionary movement, wide spread, and terrible in its plot." Within the next two months, the blacks planned to rise on a certain night and massacre the male adults and children, while retaining many of the females "for servile and licentious purposes." By 1868, even Frances Leigh's confidence and equanimity had ebbed considerably. If in 1865 she had felt "not the slightest" fear of the blacks on the Butler plantations, three years later she refused to sleep without a loaded pistol by her bed.

> Their whole manner was changed; they took to calling their former owners by their last name without any title before it, constantly spoke of my agent as old R——, dropped the pleasant term of "Mistress," took to calling me "Miss Fanny," walked about with guns upon their shoulders, worked just as much and when they pleased, and tried speaking to me with their hats on, or not touching them to me when they passed me on the banks. This last rudeness I never permitted for a moment.

Frances Leigh thought that if she relaxed her vigilance for even a moment, she would lose control over the blacks altogether. For the next two years, she recalled, "I felt the whole time that it was touch-and-go whether I or the negroes got the upper hand."[96]

It was not as though the blacks had no reason to revolt. Even as they persisted in testing their freedom, they had not succeeded in breaking the bonds that tied them to the farms and plantations as agricultural laborers. That had to be the uppermost thought in their minds after each settlement, about the same time whites were fashioning new notions of conspiracy and rebellion. On New Year's Day 1866, black people commemorated emancipation, not by overturning their masters in a violent upheaval, but by attending appropriate ceremonies and listening to appropriate speeches. In Charleston, more than ten thousand assembled at the racecourse to hear their "best friends" advise them on future prospects. General Rufus Saxton implored them to be honest, industrious, and sober; if they wanted land, they would have to work for it, filling their pockets with greenbacks until they had enough to purchase a lot. Colonel Ketchum counseled them to emulate their brethren on Edisto Island who had met the loss of their lands with "remarkable dignity." But easily the most stirring moments that day belonged to Colonel Trowbridge, the commander of a black regiment, who took the stand to bid an emotional farewell to his soldiers, most of whom were about to be discharged. When he finished, the large crowd sat "hushed and silent" for several minutes until a voice rang out:

> Blow ye the trumpet, blow!
> The gladly solemn sound.

The entire throng then joined in the singing, reaching a loud crescendo as they came to the refrain:

> The year of jubilee has come,
> Return, ye ransomed sinners, home.[97]

With the speeches and songs of Emancipation Day still ringing in their ears, the blacks returned to their respective places and prepared to work the fields of the white man for still another year.

LESS THAN TWO WEEKS after dismissing the talk of insurrection as the product of white hysteria, the Reverend Samuel A. Agnew found the laborers on his father's plantation in Mississippi to be "disobedient, idle and puffed up with an idea of their own excellence." After receiving their shares from the sale of the crops, the blacks were "disinclined" to commit their entire time for still another year. "They have exalted ideas," Agnew wrote in disgust. On the several plantations in Louisiana managed by Wilmer Shields, the laborers held back on signing a new contract and refused to reveal their intentions. When they assembled one Sunday "to express themselves" on the matter, Shields thought their propositions "too absurd and inadmissible to be repeated." Although Adele Allston had managed to repossess her plantations earlier that year, the approach of December found her pessimistic about future prospects. No matter what she said or did, it all seemed in vain. None of the blacks wished to contract for another year, and even Milly, a servant who had been with her for many years, "is tired being good and faithful. She appears discontented. It seems to me she wants the whole of the stock, the profits of it at least." Upon investigating conditions in the South Carolina low country, a Freedmen's Bureau agent found the planters "uniformly ready and anxious" to contract but the freedmen almost all refused, except "upon such terms as the Bureau cannot justly require" of the employers.[98]

With the completion of the crops, the labor system seemed destined each year to undergo a new series of convulsions, many of them precipitated by those persistent visions of land distribution, independent farming, and higher wages. Although the ultimately compelling need to test the boundaries of freedom surfaced at different times for different blacks, it continually frustrated any regularization of labor relations. Thousands of freedmen, including many who had stayed on with their old masters after emancipation, would now seek places elsewhere, leaving "in squads of five or ten at a time" and sometimes in sufficient numbers to render entire plantations and farms devoid of laborers. Such movements, for example, virtually sealed the fate of the rice industry in South Carolina.[99] The familiar refrain "Every Negro has left us" once again punctuated the letters, private journals, and conversations of the former slaveholding class. The element of surprise seemed less pronounced now in view of the shared experiences of so many white families, though many who had survived the wartime and post-emancipation departures were to awaken one morning to find none of their laborers and servants present. On the Pine Hill plantation in Florida, Christmas had been a traditionally festive occasion, involving considerable interchange between the white and black families. But in 1865 the white family sensed a difference. When the blacks came to the Big House to pick up their gifts, they did so with little of the old enthusiasm, and, uncharacteristically, they quickly returned to their quarters. On the surface, at least, the plantation appeared to be peaceful, free of the fears of insurrection that had unsettled other regions, and the servants had performed their duties faithfully. "Adeline cooked us an elegant Christmas dinner and Bill served it to perfection. Each man and maid were in place, attending to their various duties, but the atmosphere of merriment and good-will was lacking." Within the month, Adeline and Bill, along with the other blacks, departed, leaving the white folks "all alone on the hill."[100]

The need to break away from the places where they had served as slaves still had a way of overcoming specific economic considerations. Nevertheless, disillusionment over the paltry rewards of the first years of free labor added considerable impetus to the desire for some kind of change. "We worked hard for two years and didn't make nothing by contracts," a black family in Georgia declared; "we are now gwine to try it ourselves." And like a growing number of ex-slaves, they had resolved to improve their situation by moving into town. "Even the cornfield negro has a great dislike to go into the field," a white physician in Atlanta, Georgia, observed in early 1866; "he wants to get into the towns and do little errands and jobs. They have, as a class, a great thirst for the towns and cities; they like company; they are very social creatures—like to job about during the day, and be where they can go to a party at night." The principal attractions of the city remained the greater feeling of security it afforded and the chances for more remunerative employment and a more active social life. Even if the freedman did not move into an urban center, he often preferred to contract on a plantation nearby, so as to be in a position to enjoy the advantages of a town while still performing the kind of labor he knew best. After an unsuccessful attempt to hire laborers in Vicksburg, a Mississippi planter conceded his problems might have been minimal if he could have picked up his plantation and moved it closer to the city. Still another disappointed employer came away convinced "the black rascals wouldn't trust themselves the width of my plantation away from town for fear I would eat 'em up."[101]

Whether the freedman moved or not, the end of each agricultural season set off a new round of contract talks, invariably preceded by an employer's complaint that his hands "positively" refused to agree to terms. During the negotiations, employers would learn soon enough how successfully they had placated their working force over the past year; indeed, that was precisely why these annual talks took on such importance for the freedmen, not only as a way to better their terms but for the rare opportunity it afforded them to express their grievances and suggest how conditions might be improved. In settling the accounts with the laborers on the Butler plantations, Frances Leigh had learned not to respond to their exclamations of doubt and disapproval. But when it came to negotiating a new contract with them, she discovered that they would not be put off so easily. This time they insisted upon being heard, and Frances Leigh had little choice but to listen.

> For six mortal hours I sat in the office without once leaving my chair, while the people poured in and poured out, each one with long explanations, objections, and demonstrations. I saw that even those who came fully intending to sign would have their say, so after interrupting one man and having him say gravely, " 'Top, missus, don't cut my discourse," I sat in a state of dogged patience and let everyone have his talk out, reading the contract over and over again as each one asked for it, answering their many questions and meeting their many objections as best I could. One wanted this altered in the contract, and another that. One was willing to work in the mill but not in the field. Several would not agree to sign unless I promised to give them the whole of Saturday for a holiday. Others . . . would "work for me till they died," but would put their hand to no paper. And so it went on all day, each one "making me sensible," as he called it.

Through it all, she remained "immovable," insisting that they agree to the contract as it stood. On the first day, she managed to sign sixty-two of the field hands—"good work," she thought, "though I had a violent attack of hysterics afterwards, from fatigue and excitement." Only once did she lose her composure and that was when a freedman, "after showing decided signs of insolence," finally declared, "Well, you sign my paper first, and then I'll sign yours." She ordered him off the plantation, only to have him return minutes later "with a broad grin on his face" and prepared to sign the contract. After several days of negotiation, she claimed to have broken "the backbone of the opposition," and all but two of the laborers went back to work under the new contract; one left from "imagined ill-health" and the other she dismissed for "insubordination."[102]

The economic necessity which forced planters to bargain with their former slaves did not make the experience any less demeaning or exasperating. A Louisiana planter confided to his diary how he had "purposely" stayed away from the sugar house "to avoid talking to the negroes about a contract before I was ready to make one." When he finally did so, he found the final terms to be "distasteful" but unavoidable. "Every body else in the neighborhood has agreed to pay the same and mine would listen to nothing else." The task of having to deal with their former slaves at the bargaining table could be further aggravated by the obvious delight the laborers derived from the proceedings and the breakdown in the traditional forms of deference. When Daniel Heyward, the South Carolina planter, met with his blacks, the word soon got around that they had been "kind enough but spoke to him sitting, and with their hats on." Not only did they seem "confounded and incredulous as to *his* ownership of the land" but they shook their heads when he suggested they work in much the same way as they had before emancipation. "Oh no, neva work as they did," they replied, "and no overseer and no drivers." Upon hearing this story, an acquaintance of the Heyward family expressed no surprise: "Now all this strikes me as being exactly what was to be expected. That feeling of security and independence has to be eradicated; and if it should survive after January [1866], I think with proper management it will be effectually extirpated before we wish to put seed in the ground in March or April."[103]

Employers evinced the most resistance to precisely those demands—less supervision, more free time, and the opportunity to lease lands—that might ultimately lead to a greater measure of independence and self-reliance for their black workers. To the freedmen, these issues naturally took on added significance with each new contract year, reflecting their discouragement over the most recent settlement, the failure of their land aspirations, and their precarious economic position. If planters grew to fear that crop shares, as a substitute for cash wages, compromised the proper relationship between themselves and the laborers, growing numbers of freedmen turned to that form of compensation as affording them an enhanced feeling of independence. After charging that indebtedness now characterized the monthly wage system, the black newspaper in South Carolina advised agricultural laborers to work the land on shares or leases and thereby "retrieve the mistakes of the past season." About the same time, late in 1865, on a cotton plantation near Beaufort, the freedmen countered the planter's wage offer by demanding half the crop instead. Upon being turned down, they appealed to the local Union commander, who advised them to agree to the employer's fair offer. Still refusing to concede anything, the laborers crowded around the planter when he visited their quarters, shouting their demand for "half the crop." With the planting season about to begin and the freedmen refusing to sign the contract, Federal troops were dispatched to remove the rebellious blacks from the plantation and make room for more compliant workers. The show of force and the threat to displace them from their jobs broke the resistance effectively, and the laborers reluctantly gave up their fight for a share of the crop.[104]

The questions of greater independence, more free time, and less supervision proved to be inseparable. After the first agricultural season, planters and Freedmen's Bureau agents noted the persistence with which blacks refused to labor on Saturday for anyone but themselves, preferring to tend their own garden plots or to sell in town some of the produce they had raised. "Five days I'll work," a Mississippi field hand insisted, in refusing to sign a new contract, "but I works for no man on Saturday." If he worked on Saturday, another freedman told his employer, he expected additional compensation. On Johns Island, the issue even assumed religious proportions in May 1866 when an elderly black woman claimed a revelation from heaven forbidding work on Fridays and Saturdays; many of the freedmen hailed the revelation as "God's truth" and ceased to work on those days until Federal authorities threatened to intervene and drive the blacks off the island. The way in which some planters and freedmen finally resolved this demand was to compromise in favor of half a day's work on Saturday or to excuse one member of a family, usually the wife or oldest daughter, on Saturday afternoon so that she could attend to domestic duties. The idea of a five-day workweek, like the share system, imparted to many freedmen a greater feeling of independence even as their economic situation remained the same, and for some it reflected a growing assumption that they were perfectly capable of managing agricultural operations without white interference. On plantations where overseers had been retained, for example, the objections were directed not so much to the quality of the individual hired to fill that position, which had once been the principal issue, but to supervision by any white man. "Some of the best hands told me," a Bureau officer reported from Mississippi in 1866, " 'they would not have a superintendent to direct them as they knew how to do the work as well as any white man.' " More than a year later, after investigating labor troubles on several Louisiana plantations, a Bureau officer thought the freedmen were "greatly to blame, as they would not, as a general rule, be dictated to either by their employers or their agents; in fact, they will not have a white man dictate to them."[105]

The refusal to sign a contract was the freedman's principal bargaining weapon and he could wield it but once a year. The longer he held out, the later the planting season began, and many laborers obviously hoped to use such leverage to exact the desired concessions. If the planter remained unyielding, he would have to face the arduous and urgent task of hiring new laborers, and in some instances the replacements would come onto plantations littered with the charred remains of what had once been the farm buildings. If the evicted blacks could no longer use the facilities, nobody else would. Shortly after a planter in South Carolina ousted the laborers for their refusal to work, the house in which he and his sons were living suddenly erupted into flames; several nights later, he bent down to pick something up "just in time to escape a whistling bullet." On still other plantations, after being ordered to leave for refusal to sign contracts, black laborers burned down the employer's house and entrenched themselves in their quarters. Little wonder that a planter should have advised his colleagues to use "forbearance and management" in dealing with their laborers, for "a recourse to other means may cause the buildings to be laid in ashes, as was the case in my late brother's place near Mobile, Alabama."[106]

On the plantations in Louisiana he managed for the absentee owner, Wilmer Shields experienced that now characteristic period of indecision and maneuvering before obtaining any success with the laborers. The almost always exhausting process of negotiating a contract would begin in the early fall and continue into the next year. In mid-September 1866, for example, Shields already despaired of retaining most of the laborers beyond the present crops. Not only did he find the blacks "very fond of change" but "*all* of our neighbors want them, and some are offering every inducement they can to get them away—promising teams and horses to take them to town every Saturday." By November, only a few laborers had indicated they intended to remain, "most of *these* worth but little—being either old or sickly." The others had begun to make clear the new conditions they would insist upon—a five-day workweek, the use of horses and teams for occasional trips to Natchez, more pay, a school, "and many other things." If Shields refused to budge on these demands, the freedmen threatened to take their labor elsewhere, and he knew only too well how willing his neighbors were to oblige.

> Metcalfe I hear is making efforts to get a very large force, offering inducement, with plenty of whiskey and every latitude & liberty to do as they please if they work for him. And Hutchins tampers with our Negroes and those who left us . . . , offering to furnish mules, utensils and all plantation gear & tools for half the cotton made. I mention only two.

In mid-December, a laborer told Shields he thought "the *whole of Saturday* and a school would keep nearly all." The manager had no objection to a school but he strongly advised his employer against any concessions to a five-day workweek; meanwhile, he prepared to stop issuing any food rations to laborers who refused to sign after the old contract expired. On January 1, the moment of decision neared. "The cry with our people now is, that we are too strict and do not pay enough." Several of the neighboring planters, in the meantime, had made offers that proved to be irresistible. "He has nothing whatever to do with his place," Shields said of one nearby planter. "Not a word to say—The Negroes manage all and are to give him one half." When the expected "stampede" came to his plantations, Shields was thus not altogether surprised. But a sufficient number remained, largely because they wished "to be at home" and they doubted the honesty of the neighboring planters. The final settlement closely resembled the original proposal, with the hands choosing between cash wages (double the previous year's rates) and an interest in the crop; the employer did concede the establishment of a school, though the freedmen were to pay for the teacher and his tenure would rest on his "good behaviour." To replace the losses, Shields tried to hire other laborers but with little success. "They demand exorbitant wages—And the more the white owner of the soil yields, the more they require."[107]

Where a considerable demand for black labor prevailed, planters found it difficult to sustain a united front against potentially ruinous competition. Vying with each other for scarce field hands, very much as Shields's neighbors had, employers sometimes assumed the most solicitous airs to induce blacks to contract with them. No doubt to incur favor with his freedmen, John H. Bills, the Tennessee planter, found himself driving a wagonload of them to a nearby community, where they could attend a "Negro barbecue" and dance through the night. Adele Allston tried to satisfy her laborers by stocking the plantation with "some extras, such as beef etc.," while another South Carolina planter modified his original terms by giving a freedman "more time to work for himself." The Reverend Samuel Agnew thought his father "had no alternative" but to accede to the extravagant demands of a valued laborer, although he thought he had reached an agreement with the man for a lesser sum the previous week. "But he [the laborer] could get more and he took advantage of circumstances." Hard-pressed for laborers, a Mississippi planter ventured to New Orleans and offered a black labor agent five dollars a head for all the men he could obtain; the agent prepared to accommodate the planter but upon learning where the freedmen were to be sent he refused any further assistance, saying he would not send a black man to Mississippi for a hundred dollars a head. "And why?" the outraged planter bellowed afterwards. "All because the sassy scoundrel said he didn't like our Mississippi laws."[108]

Where employers had gained a reputation for abusing their laborers, whether with the whip or the pen, they might lose all of them at the end of the season and find it exceedingly difficult to attract any replacements. "The Negroes have a kind of telegraph by which they know all about the treatment of the Negroes on the plantations for a great distance around," a Florida planter observed. And they obviously availed themselves of such knowledge before they contracted with anyone, the local Bureau agent added, after finding some planters unable to secure a single laborer. If the freedmen decided to remain with such an employer or hire out to him, they were apt to do so only after driving a hard bargain. In the Ogeechee district of Georgia, a planter with a notorious reputation among the local blacks had to offer one half the crop rather than the customary one third; at the same time, he agreed to divide his land into plots and permit the blacks to work them as they chose without any white supervisors. That seemed eminently fair to one local freedman; after all, he remarked, "when a man has been burned in the fire once you cannot make him run in again."[109]

9

———————

ALTHOUGH SLAVERY had never precluded a certain amount of bargaining, culminating at times in verbal understandings about work routines and the limits of authority, the first years of emancipation created new possibilities and a host of novel experiences in labor relations. When former slaves and former slaveholders confronted each other as employees and employers, conflicts were bound to arise and in numerous instances the deadlocks which resulted clearly resembled strikes and lockouts. After investigating disturbances on plantations in Coahoma County, Mississippi, a Freedmen's Bureau officer came away deeply impressed with the sense of unity manifested by the black laborers. "I find that when one or more Freedman becomes dissatisfied others are very liable to sympathize with him, and in case one leaves, others will follow." That same inclination to vent their grievances and press their demands collectively rather than as individuals pervaded low-country South Carolina, where the freedmen finally gave up the expectation of land only to demand control of the crops. "It is really wonderful how unanimous they are," a sympathetic Bureau agent reported; "communicating like magic, and now holding out, knowing the importance of every day in regard to the welfare of the next crop;—thinking that the planters will be obliged to come to their terms."[110]

Apart from the obvious advantages of collective action at contract time, the same unity would be maintained during the year to protect laborers from physical abuse and to support them in any reinterpretation of the contract they deemed essential to their welfare. On a Mississippi plantation, the employer managed somehow to write into the contract a stipulation that if the freedmen failed to work satisfactorily, she reserved the right to hire additional laborers at their expense. But when she invoked the clause, the freedmen threatened to drive the new men off the plantation and eventually won a favorable decision from the local Bureau agent. Nor could a planter, as in the old days, single out a freedman for punishment and gather the other hands around to witness the proceedings as a lesson to all of them. When a Mississippi proprietor (a former Union officer) attempted to tie a freedman up by the thumbs for his impudence and refusal to work, nearly every laborer quit work and several of them went to an adjoining plantation to mobilize assistance; the planter soon faced a formidable group armed with rifles "and other war-like weapons" and immediately called upon the Bureau to rush him some support.[111] With similar displays of unity and various degrees of success, freedmen protested delays in paying them for their work, forcibly resisted attempts by Union soldiers to search their cabins for furniture allegedly belonging to their employer, and refused to work on the public roads (charging that most whites were exempted from such labor).[112]

When "a very large assemblage" of blacks convened in a South Carolina community in late 1866, the speakers dwelled on the inadequacy of one third of the crop as compensation for the labor they had performed the previous year. The only conditions under which they should now contract, they agreed, would be for an equal division of the crops among those who labored and those who owned the land. To a local white who observed the proceedings, the meeting assumed "the character of a strike for higher wages" but he found no cause for alarm and applauded the speakers for their advice to act calmly, prudently, and in conformity with the law. Whether or not such meetings were specifically intended to counter similar "combinations" among white employers, black laborers in various parts of the South thought they could strengthen their bargaining position by agreeing on a common set of demands, including the minimum amount of compensation for which they were willing to work. Significantly, they understood the need to involve all the plantations in the region and even to agree on penalties that would be meted out to those blacks who broke their solid front. In Cherokee County, Alabama, the blacks pledged themselves not to work for less than $2.00 a day during the harvest and assessed a penalty of fifty lashes for any among them who agreed to work for less. (White laborers subsequently gathered the harvest at $1.50 a day.) In Rowan County, North Carolina, the freedmen simply resolved that anyone

who worked for less than a certain sum would "have to abide the consequences."[113] Although such examples (unique even for white workers)
might well have been exceptional, they suggested a potential that could
have had a profound impact on labor and race relations. At least, the
prospects were sufficiently alarming to prompt many whites to concoct new
notions of conspiracy and revolution.

Aside from the freedmen's work habits, nothing concerned planters
and Federal authorities more in 1866 and 1867 than the widely reported
proliferation of organizations among plantation laborers. Since most of
them were not easily identifiable, they seemed all the more menacing.
Near the end of 1866, alarming reports reached the Charleston office of the
Freedmen's Bureau that freedmen in the Kingstree region were organized
into six armed military companies which drilled and marched "under Red
flags," threatened white families, and intimidated blacks who refused to
join them. Upon investigating these sensational rumors, the Bureau officer
found that the freedmen in this region did, indeed, meet regularly to agree
on minimal demands for the next year of labor; the sole threat they had
issued was to migrate to Florida if they could not obtain "reasonable and
just" terms. If any of them possessed arms, the agent reported, they did so
with no violent intent but from "the foolish habit into which they have
fallen of carrying guns wherever they travel." Still, the Bureau agent
thought it advisable to station a detachment of Union troops in the area
for "the moral effect" it might have on both white and black residents.[114]

Any kind of organization among plantation hands, whether intended
for protective, benevolent, or economic purposes, was bound to create consternation in the white populace and revive old specters. The conclusion of
Bureau officers that most of the organizations rumored to be military in
nature were actually designed to exact economic concessions hardly allayed white fears. The ostensible purpose of meetings of black laborers may
be "a strike for higher wages," a white resident of Halifax County, North
Carolina, warned the governor, "but I believe the real design is to organize
for a General massacre of the White population. Nearly every negro is
armed not only with a Gun, but a revolver. . . . I am not one to get up an
alarm for a trifle, or to raise a noise because some one else does, but the
meeting of a thousand or two of negroes every other Sunday, with Officers
and Drilling, I think a serious matter. . . . *I hope you will not use my name*
in connection with this matter, as it may cost me my life."[115]

The fears provoked by organized action among black laborers proved
to be more than illusory. Since the early days of emancipation, whites and
Federal authorities alike had considerable difficulty distinguishing between black work stoppages and insurrections. The confusion was at times
perfectly understandable. When a South Carolina planter heard that
blacks on a nearby plantation were "organized after military fashion" and
had posted guards on the roads leading to the place, he could hardly be
blamed for thinking in terms of an insurrection rather than a strike. The
events that transpired on a plantation near Georgetown could also easily

evoke the old fears. On March 31, 1866, a freedman named Abram left the field on which he had been working and called the other laborers out with him; after arming themselves with axes, hatchets, hoes, and poles, they drove the black agent of the proprietor off the premises. Finally, two Union soldiers were called in to help quell the uprising, and the planter and his agent prepared to restore order. "As soon as we entered the street the people collected with axes, hoes, sticks and bricks and pelted us with bricks and stones and poles, and took the gun away from one of the soldiers." The reports of blacks taking possession of plantations were not uncommon in the postwar years, but the purpose of their action was not always clear. In a number of instances, at least, the blacks did not actually lay claim to the land but challenged the proprietor's right to dictate to them and to dispose of the crops they had raised.[116]

The plantation "strike," not always easy to define, could be a complex affair, testing the ability of the workers to maintain a solid front against the planter's threat to evict them and the probability of Federal intervention. On a Louisiana plantation, when the hands struck for the immediate payment of their wages and the right of each of them to have an acre of land for his exclusive cultivation, the proprietor retaliated by refusing to meet with them, calling in the Freedmen's Bureau, and locking up the mules—that is, turning a "strike" into a "lockout" and preventing the workers from returning to their tasks without his permission. The Bureau agent resolved the crisis, largely by rebuking the strike leader for his insolent language and threatening to arrest him for breach of contract; at the same time, he sought to exploit differences among the blacks about the advisability of their action. "Dey didn't want to quit," several of them indicated, "but dere was no use in deir wuckin' by demselves, cause de rest 'd say dey was a turnin' gin deir own color an' a sidin' wid de wite folks." To a northern visitor, who had witnessed the strike, the Freedmen's Bureau had once again proven its worth. "I knew that but for this very agent not less than a dozen heavy planters would have been compelled to suspend operations. All availed themselves of his services."[117]

Along with evidence of collective action, the plantations would also yield leaders capable of mobilizing black laborers. Although some drivers and preachers retained the influence they had exercised before the war, the continuity in leadership is difficult to determine. On the Sea Islands, a Bureau officer investigating labor troubles placed the blame on "oracles" among the freedmen, "and as *they* go, so go the whole without stopping to consider." Not uncommonly, a Bureau officer would determine that a particular individual on the plantation had provoked the others to action and he would dismiss him from the place. On the "old Combahee" plantation, near Beaufort, South Carolina, a planter complained of "insolent" laborers who appeared to follow in the steps of Bob Jenkins, a black "firebrand" he had previously ordered off his place. Two Bureau agents investigated the dispute, one of them J. J. Wright, a black man who would subsequently play an important role in the Radical state government. In his report,

Wright cited the testimony of the foreman, who claimed that the planter had tried to speed up the work and Jenkins "knew a great deal and that was the reason he was called a firebrand." Several weeks later, a white Bureau agent visited the same place, ordered the people to return to work, and quickly disposed of Jenkins. "This man's influence was so evidently bad that I ordered him to leave the place."[118]

Of growing concern, too, were black agitators who belonged to no plantation but who allegedly aroused the freedmen. Aaron Bradley, who had migrated from Massachusetts to Georgia, remained a controversial figure throughout Reconstruction; as early as 1865, he elicited strong reactions from Bureau officers:

> A man named Bradley has been making speeches at S[avannah] to the colored people criticising President's policy, advising Negroes not to make contracts except at point of bayonet, and to disobey your orders; have arrested him, he does not deny charges, proof conclusive. Genl Steedmen has ordered him to be tried by Military Commission.

Two years later, after Bradley encouraged blacks to take possessory title of certain lands, Bureau officers again cited his "pernicious influence over the more ignorant of the freed people" and asked for authority to banish him from the region.[119]

The organized efforts of black laborers to improve working conditions were not limited to the plantations. Again, the number of successes achieved may have been less important than the possibilities revealed by such efforts. The "new phenomenon" of black stevedores in Charleston refusing to work for less than two dollars a day was sufficiently spectacular to be noted in the leading northern working-class newspaper, as was the decision of the Freedmen's Bureau in Memphis to break a strike of levee workers before it erupted into a full-scale riot. In 1866 and 1867, strikes also broke out among city laborers in Nashville, tobacco workers in Richmond, lumberyard workers in Washington, D.C., and stevedores in New Orleans, Richmond, and Savannah. The Savannah strike elicited particular attention, if only because white and black stevedores combined to resist a new tax imposed on their occupation; the police intervened but confined its arrests and beatings to the black workers.[120] In New Orleans, black stevedores had to be restrained from lynching a contractor who had allegedly defrauded them of their wages; the police rescued the contractor, while a detachment of troops dispersed the more than five hundred stevedores who had assembled to express their grievances. In late 1865, even as many whites feared an imminent black uprising, New Orleans looked upon the rare sight of black and white stevedores joining forces to strike for higher wages. The mayor himself conceded the impressive quality of such an event, particularly the demonstration of racial unity among the workers. "They marched up the levee in a long procession, white and black together. I gave orders that they should not be interfered with as long as they interfered with nobody else; but when they undertook by force to prevent other laborers from working, the police promptly put a stop to their proceedings."[121]

Whatever the promise of such combined efforts, neither white trade unions nor the black press would permit them to herald a new era in urban labor relations. When it came down to admitting blacks into the few existing trade unions, the racial barriers were impregnable. "At present, we have nothing to do with the negro," a white carpenter in Richmond declared at a meeting of his union, "but the time is coming, and we must prepare ourselves to say to this dark sea of misery, 'thus far shalt thou come, but no farther.' " Noting that sentiment, a Richmond black predicted "an irrepressible conflict between the white and the black mechanics of the South," now that the whites had been contaminated by the same "devilish prejudice" that ostracized black mechanics in the North. In New Orleans, meanwhile, the *Tribune,* voice of the free colored community, adopted a stance during the stevedores' strike that anticipated the generally hostile attitude of black middle-class leadership toward trade unions and strikes. "Poor negroes," it said of blacks beaten for continuing to work, "abused when suspected of being unwilling to work, and mauled when ready to labor!" When stevedores took to the streets to mobilize support for their strike, the newspaper lamented the number of blacks among them, noting how "their white fellow-workers despise them under ordinary circumstances." After the laborers returned to their jobs at the old wages, the newspaper could only conclude, "Such is generally the folly of strikes."[122]

Whether on the plantations or in the cities, black workers confronted obstacles not unfamiliar to white laborers in the North. Since any work stoppage during the agricultural season necessarily required a breach of contract, field hands found themselves in an even more precarious position. The decision to cease work could not be made easily, involving as it did the possibility of eviction with a loss of accrued wages and the probability of Federal intervention. Not long after a Union commander announced his intention to remove all laborers who failed to conclude agreements with their employers, a group of freedmen near Savannah refused to renew a contract they thought to be unfair. But neither were they willing to move, even when a Bureau agent and five soldiers ordered them to do so. The agent returned with fifty soldiers, the blacks "crowded together in solid phalanx and swore more furiously than before that they would die where they stood," each side leveled guns at the other, and the soldiers withdrew. But the point had been made, and blacks knew full well they could not stand for long against an entire army.[123]

If judged by certain isolated examples, the possibilities might have seemed truly promising, perhaps even momentous. The planters owned the land, while the freedmen commanded the labor, and each side reserved the right to use that power to exact concessions from the other, with the differences finally resolved through negotiations. That state of affairs encouraged the black newspaper in South Carolina to think that a new day had dawned. "It takes two to make a bargain now-a-days," the editor exulted after noting that the former slaves no longer had to contract with their former owner simply because he desired it. But the new era envisioned by this newspaper died in infancy. Appreciating where the power still resided, the employer could hold out against the "extravagant" demands of his laborers, thinking that by January they would be forced to work at whatever terms he dictated. More often than not, that turned out to be a correct assumption. "They thought, by standing out, they could force me to terms about their mules and cotton," the agent of a Louisiana planter remarked. "But I soon undeceived them. I rigged up the carts, packed their traps into them, and sent them bag and baggage off the place. . . . Now they're sneaking back every day and asking leave to enter into contract."[124]

Despite the triumphs scored by the field hand on some plantations, particularly in regions where a scarcity of labor prevailed, the bargaining power he wielded with his right to reject a contract proved far less formidable in practice than in theory. "What kin we do, sah?" an underpaid laborer in Virginia asked; "dey kin give us jes what dey choose. Man couldn't starve, nohow; got no place to go; we 'bleege to take what dey give us." In the North, white workers came to learn comparable lessons about that much-cherished right to bargain with an employer—that is, they could work at whatever wages and under whatever conditions their hungriest competitors were willing to accept or not work at all. In the postwar South, the options seemed even more limited. If the laborer chose to hold out for better terms, he could be evicted, with the planter free to call on Federal authorities for assistance. If the laborer voluntarily left the plantation, dissatisfied with the previous year's meager earnings and disinclined to contract for still another year of the same, how would he support himself? To whom could he turn? Although the Freedmen's Bureau recognized his right to contract elsewhere, it insisted that he contract with some employer; if not, he could be arrested for vagrancy, incarcerated for a brief time, forced to work on the public streets, and finally hired out to an employer under a contract arbitrarily prepared by the Bureau officer. If he chose to work elsewhere, he also faced in some regions the possibility of being blacklisted by other planters, particularly if he had a previous record as a malcontent or rebel. Dissatisfied with conditions, a laborer in Guilford County, North Carolina, left his place of employment and settled a few miles down the road. "I gathered up some o' our boys," his former employer declared, "and we went down to this place whar I thought he was at, and told him he'd make tracks before night, and if he was found in this neighborhood arter next day we'd shoot him wherever we found him. . . . We a'n't agoin' to let niggers walk over us." Finally, if laborers combined among themselves to resist a contract they considered unacceptable, they faced the likelihood of intervention by local militia units or Federal troops.[125]

Having found no alternative that could sustain them, the vast majority of blacks returned each year to their familiar labors under a contractual arrangement. But it often proved to be a precarious truce rather than a planters' jubilee. Although blacks found their bargaining power sharply circumscribed, that did not guarantee the quality of their subsequent labor or an orderly plantation. The opprobrium heaped upon black labor in 1865 would be repeated with even greater regularity and the usual expressions of dismay in subsequent years—disregard for contracts, erratic work, arrogant behavior, insolent language, and a contempt for any kind of authority. Few planters considered themselves more exemplary in their behavior and attitudes than Everard Green Baker of Panola, Mississippi. As a slaveholder, he claimed to have made every effort to keep his blacks "joyous and happy," and the wartime experience no doubt solidified his self-image. While the slaves of neighboring planters fled, his blacks showed "their good sense & stood true to mine & their interests." After emancipation, they remained with him, and in January 1866 he noted how "cheerfully" they went to work—"perhaps better than any others in the neighborhood." Six months later, however, for reasons Baker found inexplicable, his freedmen worked only "tolerably," failing to report early in the morning and remaining in their cabins for two or three hours at noon. "I do not think I will be bothered any more with freedmen," the discouraged planter confided to his diary. One year later, he added a footnote to that entry: "I had better have adhered to the above resolution. I did not & much regret it."[126]

Even if they successfully contracted with their work force, some planters found little relief in the day-to-day ordeal of supervising free black laborers, many of whom refused to surrender their newly acquired prerogatives or accommodate themselves to a contract they had been compelled to sign. On the plantations in South Carolina she had managed since the death of her husband in 1864, Adele Allston had endured work stoppages and near rebellions. With each new crisis her confidence ebbed still further until finally her patience ran out. "Negroes will soon be placed upon an exact equality with ourselves," she wrote in late 1866, "and it is in vain for us to strive against it." In 1869, after most of her properties had been sold at auction, she retired to Chicora Wood, her sole possession, and planted a few acres of rice. With similar resignation, Ethelred Philips, the Florida physician and farmer, replaced his "worthless" black servants with "a poor ignorant white girl" and contemplated removing himself and his family to California, where they might be free of "the *everlasting negro*" rather than have to wait out his inevitable extinction. "They have the China man in place of the African and do what they please with *him* and no one cares about it—he does not happen to be fashionable color."[127]

Few gave up the struggle with greater reluctance and internal torment than Mary Jones, the deeply religious owner of three plantations in Liberty County, Georgia. After the death of her husband in 1863, she had resolved to carry on the family tradition of paternal affection and beneficent regard for the black children of God. If only they had not also been her laborers, acting all too often as adult men and women, the rewards might have been greater. The plantations languished, the freedmen manifested their discontent with the conditions of labor, and an incident early in 1866 proved to be a turning point. Shortly after two blacks—July and Jesse—asked to see a copy of the contract, the black foreman reported to his employer that the laborers "one and all" refused to work; they were dissatisfied with the contract and thought she intended to deceive them. Along with July and Jesse (whom she suspected as the "ringleaders"), Mary Jones proceeded to the nearest office of the Freedmen's Bureau, where the local agent advised them that the contract was perfectly legal, even if other planters in the area had offered a greater share of the crop to their laborers. That ended the affair and the freedmen returned to work, but for Mary Jones it had obviously been a demeaning experience.

> I have told the people that in doubting my word they offered me the greatest insult I ever received in my life; that I had considered them friends and treated them as such, giving them gallons of clabber every day and syrup once a week, with rice and extra dinners; but that now they were only laborers under contract, and only the law would rule between us, and I would require every one of them to come up to the mark in their duty on the plantation. The effect has been decided, and I am not sorry for the position we hold mutually. They have relieved me of the constant desire and effort to do something to promote their comfort.

The relief this may have afforded Mary Jones failed to instill in her workers any greater appreciation for the conditions under which they labored. Several months after the incident, Charles C. Jones, Jr., advised his mother to avoid still another skirmish with the "ingrates" and sell the plantations. Problems would persist everywhere in the South, he warned, as long as whites allowed themselves to be "led by the Negroes" rather than direct and control their labor.

But Mary Jones held on, sustained by her faith in "His infinite wisdom and special guidance," even as she lost all faith in the ability of her former slaves to become intelligent and reliable free workers.

> The whole constitution of the race is adverse to responsibility, to truth, to industry. He can neglect duty and violate contracts without the least compunction of conscience or loss of honor; and he can sink to the lowest depths of want and misery without any sense of shame or feeling of privation which would afflict a sensitive Caucasian.

After still more outbreaks of disaffection ("they dispute even the carrying out and spreading the manure"), new fears ("they all bear arms of some sort"), new losses ("Gilbert is very faithful, and so is Charles. They are the exceptions"), she acceded to her son's warning that they would all face troublesome times "before the white race regains its suspended supremacy." Early in 1868, Mary Jones gave up the plantations, which had now become for her "the grave of my buried hopes and affections."[128]

ONLY A FEW YEARS after the war, the sight of an old master gathering around him his former slaves, all of whom still maintained that same deference in his presence, filled a white observer in South Carolina with nostalgic memories. He had seen more than enough, he conceded, to know that such exhibitions of the old affections stood out "like an oasis in the desert." On the eve of Radical Reconstruction, most planters and freedmen appeared to be dissatisfied in various degrees with the workings of the new labor system. While planters fretted over erratic work habits, freedmen complained of little inducement to work. Where it had only recently been popular to contemplate the rapid demise of the African race under freedom, the talk now turned increasingly to the demise of the plantation system, if only because the blacks refused to work as slaves, rebelled against white authority, and rejected any organization of labor that resembled the old times. "If a man got to go crost de riber, and he can't git a boat, he take a log," a freedman on James Island, South Carolina, declared after the planters had repossessed their lands. "If I can't own de land, I'll hire or lease land, but I won't contract."[129]

Even as the freedman returned to work for wages or shares, disillusionment with the meager rewards of his labor kept alive that persistent "mania for owning a small piece of land" and farming for himself. That is, he retained an aspiration he had seen many whites and even a few blacks realize. With the end of each agricultural season, the aspiration seemed to take on a new life. While trying to explain the unwillingness of blacks to contract in early 1866, a Freedmen's Bureau officer in South Carolina made a revealing observation, perhaps without fully appreciating its implications: "They appear to be willing to work, but are decisive in their expressions, to work for no one but themselves." Only a week earlier, another Bureau officer noted the unanimity with which the laborers refused to contract unless they could control the crops they made. After considering the options open to them, the freedmen on Edisto Island, who were about to lose the lands they had been cultivating, declared that nothing could induce them to work again for their former masters under the old system. But if they could rent the lands they now worked, they were willing to remain. It was the only way to retain at least a semblance of the independence they were now being asked to surrender.[130]

The experiences of planters in various sections of the South testified to the determination of the freedman to "set up for himself." After paying wages for three years and treating his hands "with the utmost kindness," a planter in Maury County, Tennessee, seemed perplexed by their "growing dislike to being controlled by or working for white men. They prefer to get a little patch where they can do as they choose." Before his laborers would agree to contract, a Louisiana planter reported, they insisted on having tracts of land set off for their exclusive use. No sooner had she paid off her hands, Frances Leigh noted, than a number of them took their money and purchased small, inadequate lots out in the pine woods, "where the land was so poor they could not raise a peck of corn to the acre." Although she thought they had been defrauded, she was still impressed by the obvious enthusiasm with which her former laborers cleared the lots, built their log cabins on it, and prepared to live "like gentlemen." With similar amazement, she had previously witnessed the remarkable transformation that came over former slaves she thought "far too old and infirm to work for me" when they came into possession of any land. "Once let them get a bit of ground of their own given to them, and they became quite young and strong again."[131]

The drift of these experiences, reflecting both old aspirations and recent disappointments, was unmistakable. Unable to acquire ownership of land, whether because he lacked the funds or local custom barred him, the black laborer increasingly resolved on an alternative that would provide him with the feeling if not the actual status of a family farmer. He became a sharecropper. In the usual arrangement, the planter divided his land into small units or "farms" and rented them to individual black families; he also furnished the necessary implements, work animals, and seed. In return, the tenant or "farmer" paid the planter one half of the crops he raised; if he supplied his own tools and animals, he generally paid one fourth to one third of his crops. In either case, he might have to pledge another portion of the prospective crops to the supply merchant (or the landowner serving in that capacity) for the food and clothing he purchased.[132]

After several years of highly precarious planting, the landowner was nót necessarily averse to the rental system, preferring to reorganize the plantation rather than continue an increasingly unprofitable arrangement. At best, he hoped to achieve a modicum of economic success without compromising his ownership of the land and without having to suffer the ordeal of supervising black labor. Such a decision, nevertheless, was not always reached easily. Only when he despaired altogether of operating the place successfully along the old lines did the planter usually agree to divide and rent. That was the only way he could procure labor "under any terms," an Alabama planter conceded, and still realize "a *bare support*" from his land. Despite the anguish that often accompanied such decisions, however, the plantation system itself remained very much intact. Only apportionment of land and responsibility on the plantation had been altered.[133]

But to many freedmen, the new arrangement—tenant farming— seemed promising at first glance because of the feelings of independence it imparted, making them in effect mock farmers and freeing them from the cultivation of staple crops and from working in field gangs under supervision. As if to underscore such feelings, the new tenant might move his cabin from the old slave village out onto the plot of land he had rented or else build a new cabin to symbolize his new autonomy. In opting for this arrangement, moreover, he fully expected to make this plot of land his own through hard work and frugality—precisely as his leaders and many of his white friends from the North had advised him. But in most instances, such aspirations remained unfulfilled and the tenant found himself little better off than he had been under the previous arrangement. "We made crops on shares for three years after freedom, and then we commenced to rent," Richard Crump recalled. "They didn't pay everything they promised. They taken a lot of it away from us. They said figures didn't lie. You know how that was. You dassent dispute a man's word then."[134]

No matter how often the black press celebrated the few examples of economic success and landownership, the great mass of laboring freedmen, whether they rented lands or worked for wages or shares, remained laborers—landless agricultural workers. Even the illusion of independence imparted by tenant farming could not obscure for very long the fact that the black "farmer" enjoyed neither ownership of the soil nor the full rewards of his labor. He worked the white man's land, planted with the white man's seeds, plowed with the white man's plow and mules, and harvested a crop he owed largely to the white man for the land, the seeds, the plow, and the mules, as well as the clothes he wore and the food he consumed. And if his own leaders could offer him little more than the mid-nineteenth-century shibboleths of hard work, perseverance, frugality, and honesty, to whom could he turn? How could he be frugal if he had no money to save? Why should he be honest only to have the white man defraud him? Why should he work hard and persevere if the results of that labor left him even further removed from acquiring the land on which he toiled? "The negro's first want is, not the ballot, but a chance to live,—yes, sir, *a chance to live*," a prominent white Georgian declared in late 1865. "Why, he can't even live without the consent of the white man! He has no land; he can make no crops except the white man gives him a chance. He hasn't any timber; he can't get a stick of wood without leave from a white man. We crowd him into the fewest possible employments, and then he can scarcely get work anywhere but in the rice-fields and cotton plantations of a white man who has owned him and given up slavery only at the point of the bayonet. . . . What sort of freedom is that?"[135]

If the freedman's "mania" for renting or owning land came to symbolize his yearning for economic independence and personal freedom, the betrayal of those expectations confirmed the persistence of the old dependency. The former slave found that all too little had changed. By resorting to a sharecropping arrangement, he had hoped to achieve a significant degree of autonomy; instead, he found himself plunged ever deeper into dependency and debt, pledging his future crops to sustain himself during the current crop. In that brief flurry of excitement and anticipation at the moment of freedom, there had been all kinds of talk about land and "living independently" and being able to do what the white folks did. But the talk was now of survival, their principal hopes remained unfulfilled, and some freedmen were certain they had been hopelessly betrayed. "We thought we was goin' to get rich like the white folks," recalled Felix Haywood, who had been a slave in Texas. "We thought we was goin' to be richer than the white folks, 'cause we was stronger and knowed how to work, and the whites didn't and they didn't have us to work for them anymore. But it didn't turn out that way. We soon found out that freedom could make folks proud but it didn't make 'em rich."[136]

More than seventy years after emancipation, Thomas Hall, who had been born a slave in Orange County, North Carolina, could still shake with anger when he thought about the way his people had been freed. "Lincoln got the praise for freeing us, but did he do it? He give us freedom without giving us any chance to live to ourselves and we still had to depend on the southern white man for work, food and clothing, and he held us through our necessity and want in a state of servitude but little better than slavery. Lincoln done but little for the negro race and from living standpoint nothing." While relating a history of white betrayal, North and South, the bitterness overflowed and he finally turned it upon the white interviewer.

> You are going around to get a story of slavery conditions and the persecutions of negroes before the civil war and the economic conditions concerning them since that war. You should have known before this late day all about that. Are you going to help us? No! you are only helping yourself. You say that my story may be put into a book, that you are from the Federal Writers' Project. Well, the negro will not get anything out of it, no matter where you are from. Harriet Beecher Stowe wrote Uncle Tom's Cabin. I didn't like her book and I hate her. No matter where you are from I don't want you to write my story cause the white folks have been and are now and always will be against the negro.[137]

# Chapter Nine

# THE GOSPEL
# AND THE PRIMER

*Wealth, intelligence and godliness combined, make their possessors in-
dispensable members of a community.*

> —ADDRESS OF THE BISHOPS OF THE AFRICAN
> METHODIST EPISCOPAL CHURCH, MAY 2, 1866[1]

*Wat's de use ob niggers pretendin' to lurnin? Dey's men on dis yeah
plantation, old's I am, studyin' ober spellin'-book, an' makin' b'lieve 's
if dey could larn. Wat's de use? Wat'll dey be but niggers wen dey gits
through? Niggers good for nothin' but to wuck in de fiel' an' make cotton.
Can't make white folks ob you'selves, if you is free.*

> —BLACK DRIVER, FISH POND PLANTATION,
> LOUISIANA, APRIL 1866[2]

WHEN THE CIVIL WAR ENDED, Henry McNeal Turner sensed that his
work had only begun. He thought he knew how and where he could
best serve his people. Two years earlier, he had preached his farewell
sermon as pastor of Israel Bethel Church in Washington, D.C., and within
weeks he had returned to his native South as a chaplain assigned to the
1st Regiment, United States Colored Troops. While serving in that post, he
manifested a racial pride that would distinguish his thoughts and actions
for the remainder of his life. Never would he relent in the conviction that
the African race possessed the capacity for intellectual and material greatness. "I claim for them," he wrote in August 1865, "superior ability." None
of the renowned orators, ministers, and statesmen he had heard in the
North, not even a Henry Ward Beecher or a Charles Sumner, compared in
his estimation with the simple eloquence he had once heard from the lips
of a black slave in South Carolina. Nor did he consider the celebrated work
of architects and mechanics in the North superior to the skills demonstrated by many slave artisans. While conceding that these were "exceptional" blacks who had "mastered circumstances," Turner liked to think
of them nevertheless as "extraordinary projections" who suggested the still
largely unrealized potential of his people.

Even with emancipation, he realized, this vast potential would be difficult to tap. No matter how often he celebrated the achievements of individual blacks, he remained deeply troubled in 1865 by the condition of the great mass of recently freed slaves, especially those outside of the urban centers who had spent a lifetime laboring in the fields, sustained only by the will to survive. Almost everywhere he traveled in the postwar South, Turner found freedmen still embracing and cherishing the old slave habits, exhibiting little of the racial pride he felt so intensely; some of them were too "timid," "doubtful," and "fearful" to exercise their freedom, preferring instead to defer to their old masters or to transfer their feelings of dependency to their new Yankee masters.

> That old servile fear still twirls itself around the heart strings, and fills with terror the entire soul at a white man's frown. Just let him say stop, and every fibre is palsied, and this will be the case till they all die. True, some possessing a higher degree of bravery may be killed or most horribly mutilated for their intrepidity, but should this be the case, the white man's foot-kissing party will be to blame for it. *As long as negroes will be negroes* (as we are called) *we may be negroes.*

That so many of his brethren should behave in this way came as no surprise to him. "Oh, how the foul curse of slavery has blighted the natural greatness of my race!" he wrote in early 1865, while his regiment was camped in North Carolina. "It has not only depressed and horror-streaked the should-be glowing countenance of thousands, but it has almost transformed many into inhuman appearance."

By the close of the war, the rapidly proliferating northern benevolent societies were actively engaged in tending to the religious, educational, and relief needs of the freedmen. Turner knew of their activities, and he welcomed the diligence, commitment, and resources they brought to the freedman's cause. But he perceived, too, that hundreds of thousands of newly freed slaves remained beyond the reach of these societies. Enjoying only a superficial freedom, they survived as best they could without money, land, or homes; they had never seen the inside of a schoolhouse, they either embraced primitive notions of Christian worship or attended a white man's church (where they heard their bondage sanctified), and they had little or no appreciation of the responsibilities and liabilities they had incurred with emancipation. "They want to know what to do with freedom," Turner observed. "It is not natural that a people who have been held as chattels for two hundred years, should thoroughly comprehend the limits of freedom's empire: the scope is too large for minds so untutored to enter upon at once." If Turner understood better than most the magnitude of the problem, that necessarily tempered his optimism and prepared him for a long and demanding ordeal. "I do not expect a high state of things, in this day at most; it will be impossible for the present generation to become wonders of the world. Nothing more than a partial state of civilization and moral attainment can be hoped for by the most sanguine."

That was more than sufficient inducement, however, for Turner to enlist his efforts in the critical work of redeeming the nearly four million slaves from the moral and spiritual degradation which their condition had forced upon them. Upon resigning his chaplaincy in 1865, he chose to remain in the South to organize freedmen into the African Methodist Episcopal Church and subsequently into the Republican Party.[3]

The prospects for a reformation in the post-emancipation South seemed auspicious, even exhilarating. While the Union soldier completed the liberation of the slaves from physical bondage, the teacher would free them from mental indolence and the missionary would lead them out of the "Synagogues of Satan." Both the teacher and the missionary would assume the responsibility for instilling in their minds the personal habits, moral values, and religious character deemed necessary to dignify and implement their new legal status. Although a formidable undertaking, the recruits were available and eager to begin their work—several thousand men and women of both races, some of them attached to the Freedmen's Bureau, some the designated agents of a church or a freedmen's aid society, and some initially unaffiliated but ready to serve in any capacity. "I dont ask position or money," a chaplain in a black regiment wrote a Freedmen's Bureau officer. "But I ask a place where I can be most useful to my race. My learning, my long experience as a teacher North, and my faithful service as Chaplain, demand that I seek such a place among my race."[4] For many of the recruits, their previous involvement in the abolitionist movement made this southern pilgrimage a particularly satisfying and fulfilling experience. No less gratified were those in the black contingent who were now returning to the places from which they had escaped as slaves or from which they had exiled themselves as free blacks.

The vision that bound them together was that of a redeemed South. Like the Puritans of seventeenth-century New England, with their vision of a "city on a hill," this modern Gideon's Band proposed to establish beachheads of Christian piety and Yankee know-how in the moral wilderness of the defeated Confederacy, dispelling the darkness which two centuries of human slavery had cast over the region. Teachers and missionaries alike, whatever their race or affiliation, could agree on the critical need to provide the recently freed slaves with prerequisites of civilization and citizenship, and these would be nothing less than the virtues esteemed by mid-nineteenth-century Americans and taught in nearly every school and from every pulpit—industry, frugality, honesty, sobriety, marital fidelity, self-reliance, self-control, godliness, and love of country. "Hitherto their masters have acted and done for them," a black religious journal observed, "but now that they are free they must be taught how to be free." A white missionary educator in South Carolina said as much when he defined what had to be done for the freedmen—"to *unlearn* them and learn them *from,* the vices, habits and associations of their former lives." And if the white evangels could talk in terms of supplying enough teachers "to make a

New England of the whole South," a black bishop of the African Methodist Episcopal Church could anticipate that glorious day when "New England ideas, sentiments, and principles will ultimately rule the entire South."[5]

Whatever the optimism and confidence with which the missionaries and teachers began their work, sectarian rivalries, racial tensions, personality clashes, and differences over tactics and roles would take their toll within the ranks of this strong-willed group of individuals. Even the most dedicated and best-intentioned of them experienced their moments of discouragement, not only in seeking to minimize native white opposition and internal dissension but in bridging the cultural gulf which separated them from the former slaves. To communicate with the freedmen could be in itself a tiring and exasperating ordeal. "We are not as yet like *skilled* in *negro-talk,*" one missionary teacher wrote home soon after arriving in Virginia. The wonder perhaps is not that so many problems surfaced or that some evangels fell from grace but rather that so many of them held on and persevered under the most formidable challenges, sustained by the depth of their commitment alone. "Ours is truly a missionary work," C. M. Shackford reported from Mississippi, "in our isolation from society, in teaching the ignorant, in deprivation of many comforts, and in being the scorn and derision of the community. There is a glory, excellence, and satisfaction in the work."[6]

The same sense of high purpose that found this white missionary laboring among the freedmen in Okolona, Mississippi, also nourished Richard H. Cain, a black minister who had transplanted his pastorship from Brooklyn, New York, to South Carolina. "I have often thought of my kindred at home—of the happy associations left behind. While I have toiled through the hot sun and over the dense sands of the South, hungry and weary, I have met hundreds of my brethren far away from their homes, awaiting my arrival, that they might hear the truths of the Gospel. I have forgotten my own trials in the flush of joy which thrilled my heart as I gazed on the vast sea of upturned eyes and radiant, expectant faces. I have exclaimed, 'Truly, the harvest is ripe, but the laborers are few.' "[7]

The newly freed slaves viewed with varying degrees of marvel, gratitude, and suspicion this strange army of men and women who came into their midst carrying Bibles and spelling books instead of rifles. They were clearly not like the white folks they had known; some of them, in fact, seemed almost incongruous in a southern setting, antiseptic in appearance, and stiff and formal in their manners and conversation. The language they spoke, and the way in which they formed their words, confirmed their alien appearance and made it difficult at times to make any sense out of what they were saying. "Dey didn't talk like folks here and didn't understan' our talk," recalled Wayman Williams, who had been a slave in Mississippi and Texas, and he suggested that both sides would need to develop some patience and a degree of compassion before the barriers of communication would break down.

> Dey didn't know what us mean when us say "titty" for sister, and "bud-der" for brother, and "nanny" for mammy. Jes' for fun us call ourselves big names to de teacher, some be named General Lee and some Stonewall Jackson. We be one name one day and 'nother name next day. Until she git to know us she couldn't tell de diff'rence, 'cause us all look alike to her.

The learning process, as Williams also remembered, proved quite often to be reciprocal. While the teacher tried to instill proper English and pronun-ciation into them, the pupils introduced her to southern ways and to the mysteries of black magic and conjuration. "De teacher from de North don't know what to think of all dat. But our old missy, who live here all de time, know all 'bout it. She lets us believe our magic and conjure, 'cause she partly believe it, too."[8]

Nor were the black emissaries from the North necessarily any less alien to the freedmen, though they might have recognized the type at least from some of the free Negroes they had known. Previous experience with black drivers, black overseers, and even free Negroes had a way of temper-ing the initial enthusiasm with which the freedmen welcomed the black teachers and missionaries; at the same time, the old slave preachers and exhorters would resist any attempt to supplant them in position and influ-ence with their people. The northern black might also share with his white co-workers a similar difficulty in bridging the cultural gulf between himself and his southern brethren. "I cannot worship intelligently with the colored people," Thomas W. Cardozo confessed, "and, consequently, am at a loss every sabbath what to do." The educated black minister from the North who soon found himself castigating the crude, unruly, and heathen worship of his fellow blacks was no different than the black teacher from the North who found himself suddenly and unexpectedly wielding the whip to enforce discipline in the classroom.

> I know not why, but I felt as it were, driven to it the first day. I cannot attempt to philosophize on the matter. I shall have a long talk with you when I return. Suffice it to say, in part, it is accountable to my inexperi-ence of the vices to which these children have been reared and hence of their general characteristics. I suppose in governing children as well as adults much of our success depends on our ability to read human nature.

During the past six years in the North, he went on to explain, he had been engaged largely in "theoretical pursuits"; although this had made him confident of his intellectual abilities, he thought the transition to "practi-cal life" had simply been too abrupt. But he remained determined to suc-ceed, if only because he recognized the unique opportunity he had been afforded. "Here I am at last in a Slave State. How strange are the workings of Providence! Who would have thought three years ago that such mighty and important changes would so soon take place?"[9]

No matter how they defined success, and this tended to vary, the missionaries and teachers who descended upon the post-emancipation South would express considerable gratification over the progress of their efforts, even as the records they left behind also revealed moments of frustration, doubt, and discouragement. For the freedmen, of course, the opportunity to worship in their own churches and to be taught in their own schoolhouses had to be one of the supreme manifestations of their new status. Not surprisingly, though, any attempt to impose "civilizing" influences on a "backward" people is bound to produce its share of misunderstandings and tensions between the evangels and their wards, in part because that was invariably how the evangels viewed the relationship. Whether to appease the hostility of native whites or to placate the cultural biases and psychic needs of their northern friends, the freedmen would be forced to pay some price in violated sensitivities and prolonged dependencies. Regardless of whether they were treated with disdain, a benign tolerance, or exaggerated praise and condescension, there would be the many occasions on which a freedman or freedwoman might have easily identified with the protagonist in Ralph Ellison's *Invisible Man,* who observed, "When they approach me, they see only my surroundings, themselves, or figments of their imagination—indeed, everything and anything except me."[10]

2

SINCE EARLY IN THE WAR, the black South had loomed as a fertile field for missionary labor. None recognized this potential more readily than did the black churchmen of the North. *"The Rubicon is passable,"* exulted the Reverend James Lynch in September 1861, after noting how his African Methodist Episcopal Church had been compelled for years to operate on the northern side of the Potomac River. "With God for our guide, and his promises for our specie currency, *we will cross,* and carry there the legacy of the sainted Allen, our church government, and the word of God." Although the black church acted initially with caution, pending a clarification of the war's objectives, the Emancipation Proclamation and the enlistment of blacks in the Union Army removed any lingering doubts. Within several months of these developments, James Lynch was on his way to South Carolina. "My own heart has been fired by our brethren here," he soon reported. "Ignorant though they be, on account of long years of oppression, they exhibit a desire to hear and to learn, that I never imagined. Every word you say while preaching, they drink down and respond to, with an earnestness that sets your heart all on fire, and you feel that it is indeed God's work to minister to them."[11]

Although other denominations were no less zealous in bringing the freed slaves into their respective folds, the Methodists and the Baptists enjoyed a clear advantage from the outset. If the Baptists offered greater organizational flexibility and more easily accommodated native black preachers, the Methodists provided, as the founder of the AME Church once explained, "the plain simple gospel" which "the unlearned can understand, and the learned are sure to understand." Both of these pietistic sects also found it necessary to spend less time in conversion than in simply providing the organizational structure that would accommodate the tens of thousands of slaves already committed to their faiths. When the Reverend Lynch, for example, sought to organize the 800 black residents of Helenaville, into the AME Church, he would report that "they all readily assented, with the exception of a few Baptists." At the same time, he continued, "I licensed two local preachers, and two exhorters who had been previously verbally licensed; I never saw men appreciate anything so much in my life."[12]

No matter what denominations they represented, the black missionaries found upon entering the South a ready confirmation of the marvelous workings of the Divine Spirit. To look around them, to witness at first hand this "most terrible retribution" which God had inflicted on the white South for the "cruel barbarities" of slavery, more than fulfilled the warnings they had hurled against Babylon from their pulpits in the North. What more dramatic proof of His presence and the triumph of His justice than to see for themselves Pharaoh's hosts engulfed and vanquished. After the Reverend Richard H. Cain walked through the streets of Charleston and gazed at the ruins that were once "the dwellings of the proud and defiant manstealers," he could only conclude that this city had become "a monument of God's indignation and an evidence of His righteous judgments." For the slave, he added, a new era had dawned, the day of redemption was at hand, and the prophet's proclamation had come to be realized: "Arise, shine: for thy light is come, and the glory of the Lord has risen upon thee." And those who wished to oversee the fulfillment of this prophecy had only to "go among this redeemed people; enter their humble homesteads; sit down with them and listen to their stories of wrong and their songs of rejoicing; [and] gain their confidence." For the Reverend Cain, Charleston was the place to establish his church for the freedmen.[13]

Although some of the black missionaries had once resided in the South as slaves or free Negroes, many of them were native Northerners who had formed their impressions of slavery in the abolitionist movement. Upon entering the South, then, they expected to find a people degraded and scarred—physically and psychically—by a lifetime of bondage and in desperate need of "regeneration and civilization." No proclamation or legislative act, they assumed, could get at the evils that had accumulated and festered over many decades. "As a malignant cancer leaves its roots after being apparently cured," the Reverend James W. C. Pennington observed from Jacksonville, Florida, "so Slavery has left its barbarisms which are in danger of being mixt up with all that is now being done for the advancement of christian civilization among the people." The breakup of slavery, he believed, had uncovered "a fearful moral chaos" in the South, and only education and "the *Remedial power of the Gospel*" could accomplish for the African race in the United States what they had already achieved for the Anglo-Saxon race. Repeatedly, clerics and teachers alike would define the task before them as undoing the moral depravity, self-debasement, and dependency which slavery had fostered in its victims, and the Reverend Cain, for one, thought no vestiges of bondage more resistant to reform than these. *"The people are emancipated but not free!"* he wrote from Charleston. *"They are still slaves to their old ideas,* as well as to their masters. The great masses have, by the old systems, been taught that they were inferior to the whites in everything, and they believe it still."[14]

If instruction in the spelling book could be left to the teacher, the work of moral reformation belonged properly to the clergyman, but in the post-emancipation South such distinctions in roles were seldom deemed necessary or even desirable and the teacher and the minister in some instances were the same person. In any event, both the school and the church declared open war on the "rum-suckers, bar-room loafers, whiskey-dealers, and card players among the men, and those women who dressed finely on *ill-gotten* gain." The best weapon by which to combat these evils was instruction at every level in the virtues of temperance, marital fidelity, chastity, and domestic economy. The larger and the more urgently this task loomed, the more frequently went out the appeals for assistance—for more individuals like themselves who would dedicate their lives to the work of redemption. "The only thing I regret is, that there are not more Baptist and Methodist ministers down here," the Reverend Arthur Waddell wrote from Beaufort, South Carolina. "When I say this, I mean *colored ministers,* and I do not mean the *silk-gloved* kind, and those who come down here to buy farms, and to cheat these poor people out of their rights. But I mean those who come down here to preach Christ in the way that St. Paul commanded Timothy."[15]

But the work of moral reformation was considered too vast and too critical to leave to "colored ministers" alone. The white benevolent societies placed the highest priority on this kind of missionary labor. That was why Marcia Colton, upon arriving in Virginia, found herself assigned not to a classroom or to a church but to Craney Island, in Norfolk harbor, where she assumed responsibility for reforming a group of black prostitutes. In a prison-like encampment, she would attempt to direct these fallen women into "the paths of virtue" and toward "Christ the Fountain that cleaneth from all Sin."

> The Military & *Moral* authorities think it is a Military necessity to have a Magdalen Camp on Craney Island, a sort of out-door Prison Life where they can send these Women who having just emerged from Slavery, are beset by bad Men (& many of *these* are connected with the Federal Army,) led astray from the paths of virtue. And the influence of those who have thus fallen being contagious with others, it is decided to arrest & send them [without a trial] to the Island.

Although not relishing the assignment, Miss Colton accepted it "in the name and for the sake of Christ." Her task was made no easier by the conduct of the soldiers guarding the encampment, some of whom effected sexual liaisons with the black women. "Alas—alas!" reported Miss Colton, "that Sin,—the Sin of Sodom is so common in our Army. It's a Sore trial to Me that I do not have any Christian on the Island amongst the Guard and no one even comes near Me to offer Me any support." Moreover, she complained, the officers in charge of the camp viewed the problem "with Man's judgment," while "I from a Christian & moral standpoint, with Woman's Pity for the degraded and fallen of our own sex." Whatever methods she adopted to enlighten the women in the ways of virtuous living, the results were less than gratifying. Upon serving out their "sentences," the women often returned to their "old haunts" in Norfolk, where they would soon be arrested again and returned to the island. "There are so many temptations in Norfolk, and they have so little moral power that it's hardly possible for them to resist. . . . I am not able to spend much time in instructing them. They are not disposed to listen much to instruction." Despairing over her ineffectuality, Miss Colton suggested that the source of the problem might lie in the African heathenism to which these "poor degraded freedwomen" clung. "I am aware when I say this that you will repel the Idea from your Mind as quickly as possible," she wrote to her supervisor. "Yet nevertheless I think it *True.* How else can I get any excuse for this predominance of Animal habits which show themselves all the while with most of them?"[16]

Not the least of the "barbarisms" associated with slavery that dismayed both white and black missionaries was, in fact, the excessive emotionalism, frenzy, and "heathenism" they claimed to find in the religious practices of the freedmen. Upon visiting a service on Roanoke Island, Henry M. Turner thought the black parishioners worshipped "under a lower class of ideas" and entertained crude conceptions of God. "Hell fire, brimstone, damnation, black smoke, hot lead, &c., appeared to be presented by the speaker as man's highest incentive to serve God, while the milder and yet more powerful message of Jesus was thoughtlessly passed by." No revival was considered complete, Turner observed on another occasion, without some blacks indulging in the most ludicrous capers. "Let a person get a little animated, fall down and roll over awhile, kick a few shins, crawl under a dozen benches, spring upon his feet, . . . then squeal and kiss (or buss) around for awhile, and the work is all done." If they had acted with less zeal, Turner surmised, the legitimacy of their conversion might have been questioned. It was this kind of "ignorant" and frenzied worship that led Thomas W. Cardozo to avoid the freedmen's church in Charleston and that prompted an educated black woman to remark, "I won't go to the colored churches, for I'm only disgusted with bad grammar and worse pronunciation, and their horrible absurdities."[17]

Neither the Methodists nor the Baptists were strangers to emotional fervor in worship; indeed, that had been a source of their appeal to the slaves. What many of the missionaries now appeared to suggest, however, was that emancipation demanded a new dignity and decorum in religious worship, and that these objectives could best be attained through instruction by an educated clergy. The *Christian Recorder,* as the official spokesman for the AME Church, deemed this point particularly critical as it described the activities of the church's missionaries in the South.

> There was a time when white ministers thought any kind of preaching would do for colored people, and they would deal in small talk. There was a time when colored ministers could glory in their own ignorance before a congregation, and succeed in making the people believe they were Divinely inspired, and secure their respect and homage. There was a time when clownishness and incorrect speech were admired, and a swollen pomposity and conceit were mistaken for ability.

Such primitive conceptions of worship, the newspaper suggested, would now have to be discarded, along with the other relics of bondage. By exposing the freedmen to higher standards of worship, a white cleric hopefully declared, they would learn the meaning of order and restraint—prerequisites of freedom whose importance went beyond the realm of religion. "Order in one kind of gathering will tend to the same in other things. They are ignorant & unaccustomed to plan & manage for themselves and I cannot help feeling strongly that their greatest need is *orderly Churches,* under the care of educated men. For the effects of such religious order is not easily overestimated, as it regards both spiritual things and temporal."[18]

Until such order prevailed in the freedmen's worship, both black and white northern missionaries would share some common concerns. Upon visiting their first black prayer meeting in the South, white ministers conceded a certain admiration for the "simple and childlike" faith of the freedmen, their evident "sincerity and earnestness," their "implicit belief in Providence," their demonstrated love of prayer, and the powerful emotional impact of their music and hymns. "It took me nearer to heaven than I had been for years," one missionary said of the singing he had heard. Still another spectator at a black religious service came away impressed not only by the "purity and simplicity" of the slaves' faith but also by its practicality. "They believe simply in the love of Christ, and they speak of Him and talk to Him with a familiarity that is absolutely startling. They pray as though they thought Christ himself was standing in the very room." Even though he considered the preachers "very rude and uncultivated," exhibiting little understanding of the Bible, he would conclude from his observations that the freedmen were "the only people I ever met whose religion reacted on their daily life."[19]

What appalled the white missionaries and visitors about black religious worship made by far the deeper impression—the emotional wildness and extravagance, the unlettered preaching, the "incoherent speeches and prayers," the "narrowness" of the religious knowledge, and the evidently strong survivals of supersitition and paganism. "My spirit," said one missionary, "sinks within me in sorrow to think of their noisy extravagance around the altar of my blessed Lord, who is the God of *order* not confusion." While some observers claimed to be deeply moved by the *"soul thrilling"* hymns and the "melodious responses" to the sermons, others found them "ludicrous." While some thought the shuffling, clapping, cries, shouts, and groans blended into "a kind of natural opera of feeling," others considered them a vulgar display of paganism without any redeeming religious virtue. Rather than try to understand the role of tone, gesture, and response in the blacks' worship, it would be far easier to ridicule it or to dismiss it altogether. "I never saw anything so savage," the usually tolerant Laura Towne wrote of the first "shout" she witnessed after coming to the Sea Islands. No less dismayed, Lucy Chase came away from her first prayer meeting convinced that the religious feeling of the freedmen was "purely emotional, void of principle, and of no practical utility"; at the same time, her supervisor seized every opportunity to impress upon black worshippers "that boisterous Amens, wild, dancing-dervish flourishes ... and pandemoniamics generally, do not constitute religion."[20]

What the well-intentioned northern emissaries failed to appreciate was precisely the degree to which the freedmen considered the emotional fervor inseparable from worship because it brought them that much closer to God. It was almost as though white people wished to maintain a distance.

> White folks tells stories 'bout 'ligion. Dey tells stories 'bout it kaise dey's 'fraid of it. I stays independent of what white folks tells me when I shouts. De Spirit moves me every day, dat's how I stays in. White folks don't feel sech as I does; so dey stays out. . . . Never does it make no difference how I's tossed about. Jesus, He comes and saves me everytime. I's had a hard time, but I's blessed now—no mo' mountains.

The testimony of this former South Carolina slave suggests what so many of the missionaries appeared to have missed—that the slaves over more than a century had fashioned a Christianity adapted to their circumstances. Thomas Wentworth Higginson, a missionary of a very different sort as commander of a black regiment, may have been unique in this respect. Unlike Lucy Chase, he had no difficulty in finding a "practical utility" in black religious worship; in fact, he would be forced to conclude, in retrospect, that "we abolitionists had underrated the suffering produced by slavery among the negroes, but had overrated the demoralization. Or rather, we did not know how the religious temperament of the negroes had checked the demoralization."[21]

But such insight was all too rare. When a teacher in Beaufort, South Carolina, suggested that "our work is just as much missionary work as if we were in India or China," she actually underestimated the task many missionaries thought they faced in the post-emancipation South. If it were only a matter of introducing Christianity to heathens, that was a work with which they were familiar and, as one missionary conceded, "we should know how to proceed." How to bring order, decorum, and intelligence into Christian worship, how to show the freedmen the difference between "sense and sound," and how to eradicate the "mass of religious *rubbish*" which had collected over two centuries of slavery posed some very different problems from those encountered in missionary endeavors overseas. After all, these people had already been won over to Christ, they had for many years attended some kind of church or service, and they had experienced either a white minister or a slave preacher—and often both. Even if usually "unlettered," the slave preacher or plantation exhorter had shared with them some trying times, he may have introduced them to the Gospel, and, most importantly, he knew how to communicate with them—and with God. With that in mind, a missionary in Norfolk, Virginia, warned that a strange minister who presumed to question how the former slaves chose to manifest their belief in God might not be welcomed into their community.

> They feel that religion is something they possess—they do not feel their need of religious instruction from the pulpit—for they have always had it here—they have been obliged to listen to white ministers provided, or placed over them by their masters, while they have had men among themselves whom they believe were called of God to preach, who were kept silent, by the institution from which they are now freed—& to have white preachers still placed over them, is too much like old times to meet with their approval. Their long silent preachers *want* to preach & the people prefer them.

While agreeing that educated ministers were preferable, she advised her supervisors in the North that the freedmen would have to be educated themselves before they could appreciate that virtue in their ministers. That being the case, she requested that no more clergymen be dispatched to her region, "unless they are specially asked for—by the church over which they are to preside as pastors."[22]

Whatever church they chose to affiliate with, and whether a northern minister or a native preacher presided, the freedmen would not give up easily the religious practices and fervor that had sustained them through so many trials. It was not that they were unwilling to learn new ways but only that they often found these new ways too far removed from God's presence. Not long after the close of the Civil War, a black woman rose during a religious meeting and felt called upon, perhaps because of the presence of some northern white visitors, to defend the worship to which she still felt committed.

> I goes ter some churches, an' I sees all de folks settin' quiet an' still, like dey dunno know what de Holy Sperit am. But I fin's in my Bible, that when a man or a 'ooman gets full ob de Holy Sperit, ef dey should hol'

dar peace, de stones would cry out; an' ef de power ob God can make de
stones cry out, how can it help makin' us poor creeturs cry out, who feels
ter praise Him fer His mercy. Not make a noise! Why we makes a noise
'bout ebery ting else; but dey tells us we mustn't make no noise ter praise
de Lord. I don't want no sich 'ligion as dat ar. I wants ter go ter Heaben
in de good ole way. An' my bruddren an' sisters, I wants yer all ter pray
fer me, dat when I gits ter Heaben I wont nebber come back 'gain.

No sooner had she taken her seat than the congregation added their confirmation in song.

> *Oh! de way ter Heaben is a good ole way;*
> *Oh! de way ter Heaben is a right ole way;*
> *Oh! de good ole way is de right ole way;*
> *Oh! I wants ter go ter Heaben in de good ole way.*

After the service, which ended in a wild emotional outburst, complete with
shrieks, shouts, and the stamping of feet, the white visitors stood outside
the church shocked and shaken by what they had seen and heard. "A few
moments more, and I think we should have shrieked in unison with the
crowd. . . . More than one of the party leaned against the wall, and burst
into hysterical tears; even strong men were shaken, and stood trembling
and exhausted." Several years later, however, this spectator lamented that
the missionaries and benevolent societies had not done enough to correct
such perversions of Christianity. "By our presence and silence," she wrote
in 1870, "we sanctioned their extravagances; and they stand now self-
confident, proof against remonstrance and instruction."[23]

## 3

EVEN BEFORE they embarked for the South, most of the missionaries and
teachers—whites and blacks alike—assumed that nothing short of a massive moral and religious transformation could liberate southern blacks
from the remaining vestiges of slavery. But the question of how to structure
that transformation and whether whites or blacks should assume primary
responsibility and leadership precipitated tensions within this biracial
movement that would persist into the Reconstruction Era, with implications for the political as well as the moral reformation of the postwar
South. Since early in the war, the appeal had gone out in the northern
black communities for qualified men and women to form their own Gideon's Band. "I argue the peculiar fitness of the colored man for that position," the Reverend Henry M. Turner wrote, "because about him the most
incredulous would have no doubt. Neither could he be bribed by the deceptive flippancy of the oily-tongued slaveocrats, who too often becloud the
understanding of the whites."[24]

Although nearly every postwar black convention and newspaper praised the white benevolent societies for their efforts, these same spokesmen insisted that "the great work of elevating our race" properly belonged to black people. If the freedmen were to be taught self-respect, if they were to be inculcated with pride in their race and begin to view themselves as the equals of whites, what better examples for them to follow than those who had already demonstrated in their own lives the capacity for improvement and leadership. If the freedmen were to be introduced to new forms of church government and worship, would not black ministers be the ideal guides, since they would at once remove "the greatest stigma" that could be attached to such reforms—"that of being a 'white man's religion.' " And if the freedmen were to be encouraged to drop "the old broken brogue language" of slavery, they should listen to "enlightened" and educated ministers of their own color who spoke "in plain English."[25]

With blacks undertaking responsibility for their own people, the potential for a conflict of interest would also be minimized. Although the emissaries of both races in the South stressed the importance of former slaves returning to work and proving their capacity for free labor, the suspicion grew that some white missionaries stood to profit materially from such counsel. Economic and moral objectives were not always easy to separate, as in the Sea Islands, for example, and if the same people who supervised black laborers in the field sometimes taught in the classroom or preached in the church, the distinctions blurred even more. "The danger now seems to be—not that we shall be called enthusiasts, abolitionists, philanthropists," Laura Towne noted with concern, "but cotton agents, negro-drivers, oppressors." Not far from where Miss Towne taught school in the Sea Islands, the Reverend A. Waddell preached in the First African Baptist Church, and he obviously thought her concern more than justified.

> Some of our white ministerial friends do more in the way of procuring farms, and keeping our poor race in ignorance, than any thing else. They are more concerned about the *cotton bag* than they are about *souls*. They pretend, when they are North, that they would come down here and do any thing for our race in the way of enlightening them; but, instead of this, when they see the cotton bag, they forget all about Christ and Him crucified, and the saving of souls.

Equally concerned with "pretended benefactors of the colored race" who "make lucre the chief idol of their devoted shrine," Henry M. Turner voiced the not uncommon fear that white missionaries and teachers, by virtue of their color and eagerness to be accepted in the communities in which they worked, might naturally gravitate toward the native whites and be the more easily beguiled by them. For the black missionary, however, as Turner quickly noted, "no sumptuous tables, fine chambers, attractive misses, springy buggies, or swinging carriages" would distract him from his labors, since "he would find his level only among the colored race." Not only would he gain easier access to the homes and social gatherings of the freedmen but "his influence and personal identification with them would go farther than the white man's" and he would be more apt to expose and resist schemes which exploited the labor of the freed slaves in the guise of philanthropic enterprise.[26]

The black missionary moved quickly to exploit a critical advantage he had over his white denominational rivals. He could offer the freedmen an immediate alternative to the white man's church and to the white minister. "The Ebony preacher who promises perfect independence from White control and direction carries the col[ore]d heart at once," an officer in the American Missionary Association observed. Near Columbia, Kentucky, a newly freed slave who had some years before been ordained as a deacon and elder in the white Methodist Episcopal Church needed little persuasion to transfer his loyalties to the African Methodist Episcopal Church. "I was offered liberal inducements to continue in the M.E. Church and preach to my people," he explained, "but I preferred to come out from under the yoke. I had been there long enough." That was reason enough for tens of thousands of freedmen and freedwomen to abandon the white-dominated churches for their own facilities, organizations, and preachers; indeed, such a move became for some as important and symbolic an assertion of freedom as the decision to separate from the scene of their bondage. For years they had listened to the white preachers admonish them to embrace their situation and obey their worldly masters in order to gain admission to "the kitchen of heaven."

> When the white preacher come he preach and pick up his Bible and claim he gittin the text right out from the good Book and he preach: "The Lord say, don't you niggers steal chickens from your missus. Don't you steal your marster's hawgs." That would be all he preach.

For years, too, they had put up with the deception and hypocrisy of these professed men of God, some of whom were themselves slaveholders. "The man that baptized me," Susan Boggs observed, "had a colored woman tied up in his yard to whip when he got home, that very Sunday and her mother belonged to that same church. . . . That was our preacher!" Nor did the stale and empty sermons of the white minister and his manner of worship succeed in moving them spiritually or emotionally. "Dat ole white preachin' wasn't nothin'," Nancy Williams recalled. "Ole white preachers used to talk wid dey tongues widdout sayin' nothin', but Jesus told us slaves to talk wid our hearts." Inevitably, then, as a former Texas slave suggested, "the whites preached to the niggers and the niggers preached to themselves."[27]

With many slaves preferring one of their own to preach God's word, the arrangement worked out in some churches before the Civil War permitted the black worshippers to convene separately with their own preacher or exhorter, though a white man would presumably be present to oversee the proceedings. Typically, a former Alabama slave recalled, "white fo'ks have deir service in de mornin' an' 'Niggers' have deirs in de evenin', a'ter dey clean up, wash de dishes, an' look a'ter ever'thing. . . . Ya'see 'Niggers' lack'ta shout a whole lot an' wid de white fo'ks al'round'em, dey couldn't shout jes' lack dey want to." Where such liberties were not permitted the slaves, the master might hire a white preacher to visit the plantation, or the slaves would simply accompany the master's family to the white church and sit in the gallery overlooking the white worshippers. Later in the day or that night, without the master's knowledge, the slaves would gather in their quarters or in the nearby woods to hold the "real meetin'." Emancipation, however, enabled blacks to dispense with the secrecy and the pretense. The black preacher and exhorter no longer needed to accommodate sermons to the needs and presence of the master, nor did black worshippers need to fear an imminent intrusion by white men into their services. "Praise God for this day of liberty to worship God!" was how one freedman described his new status, while another placed his hand on the shoulder of the black preacher and remarked, "Bless God, my son, we don't have to keep watch at that door to tell us the patrollers are coming to take us to jail and fine us twenty-five dollars for prayin' and talkin' of the love of Jesus. O no, we's FREE!"[28]

Where blacks had once been obliged to worship under a white preacher, they were now in a position to depose him, hire their own preacher, and choose their own organizational affiliation. For both the white minister and the black congregation, the transition of a church from slavery to freedom could be as traumatic as the simultaneous upheavals affecting the masters of the plantations and their field hands and servants. Several days after the fall of Wilmington, North Carolina, nearly 1,600 blacks filled the Front Street Methodist Church, where the Reverend L. S. Burkhead, a white minister, regularly presided over the predominantly black congregation. Traditionally, every Sunday morning the class leaders, all of whom were black, would conduct the sunrise prayer meeting. But the mood of the assemblage on this first Sunday after Union occupation suggested at once to the Reverend Burkhead, as he took his seat near the altar, that this would be a unique service. "The whole congregation was wild with excitement," he recalled, "and extravagant beyond all precedent with shouts, groans, amens, and unseemingly demonstrations." After the already excited throng joined in the singing of a hymn appropriate for the occasion, "Sing unto the Lord a New Song," the Reverend William H. Hunter, a chaplain in one of the black regiments which had helped to liberate the city, strode to the pulpit upon the invitation of the class leaders. No military triumph could have afforded him any greater personal satisfaction than the return to a region in which he had once been a slave, and he made this immediately clear in his address, with the crowd enthusiastically chanting their responses.

A few short years ago I left North Carolina a slave. (Hallelujah, oh, yes.) I now return a man. (Amen) I have the honor to be a regular minister of the Gospel in the Methodist Episcopal Church of the United States (glory to God, Amen) and also a regularly commissioned chaplain in the American Army. (Amen) I am proud to inform you that just three weeks ago today, as black a man as you ever saw, preached in the city of Washington to the Congress of the United States; and that a short time ago another colored man was admitted to the bar of the Supreme Court of the United States as a lawyer. (Long, loud and continued applause, beating on benches, etc.) One week ago you were all slaves; now you are all free. (Uproarious screamings) Thank God the armies of the Lord and of Gideon has triumphed and the Rebels have been driven back in confusion and scattered like chaff before the wind. (Amen! Hallelujah!) I listened to your prayers, but I did not hear a single prayer offered for the President of the United States or for the success of the American Army. (Amen! O, yes, I prayed all last night, etc.) But I knew what you meant. You were not quite sure that you were free, therefore a little afraid to say boldly what you felt. I know how it is. I remember how we used to have to employ our dark symbols and obscure figures to cover up our real meaning. The profoundest philosopher could not understand us. (Amen! Hallelujah! That's so.)

After "the tumultuous uproar" subsided, the Reverend Burkhead, visibly shaken by the proceedings, retired to his parsonage to consider the implications. He thought he had known his parishioners, and he had accepted in good faith their pledge a few weeks earlier to stand behind him. But that was before the Union Army appeared and before the black chaplain had been permitted "to unsettle all their former principles and ideas of subordination." Now, he surmised from what he had heard, the newly freed slaves seemed to anticipate a new era in which the whites who had owned them surrendered their churches, dwellings, and lands and bowed down to them "to receive the manacles of slavery." Had the Reverend Burkhead known the outcome of his speculations and fears, he might have praised God and rested comfortably. But for the moment, at least, like so many of the white clergymen who had presided over black congregations, he would have more urgent matters to consider, such as a formal demand by his congregation that he be deposed and that the church be permitted to affiliate with the African Methodist Episcopal Church.[29]

4

WITH SOME FOUR MILLION souls at stake, the struggle for supremacy among the several Protestant denominations often took on the spirit and the language associated with the prosecution of a war. Into the breach left by departing and deposed "rebel" ministers poured native black preachers and both white and black northern missionaries, and each congregation captured would be hailed as though an enemy had been routed. "Our cause has been gaining daily," the Reverend Cain reported from South Carolina.

"In Columbia, the capital of the State, we have captured all the Methodists, and are laying the foundation for an immense congregation." Less than forty-eight hours after General Sherman entered Savannah, the Reverend James Lynch was in the city to claim Andrew's Chapel, previously affiliated with the Methodist Episcopal Church; the white minister had fled, and under the Reverend Lynch's exhortations the black congregation voted overwhelmingly to align itself with the African Methodist Episcopal Church. Consolidating the gains made by previous missionaries, the Reverend Henry M. Turner reported in early 1866 that Georgia had been secured for the AME Church. "I have visited every place it was safe to go, and sent preachers where it was thought I had better not venture. Last night was the first quiet night I have had for five weeks in succession."[30]

Few triumphs, however, were more gratifying to the African Methodist Episcopal Church than the day in September 1865 when the cornerstone was laid for a new church building in Charleston. Not only did this mark the return of the AME Church to a city from which it had been banished some forty years earlier for complicity in the Denmark Vesey insurrection plot but the new building would be erected exclusively by black labor and the architect was none other than Robert Vesey, the son of the executed insurrectionist. Some three thousand black Charlestonians listened that day to speeches from a group of black clergymen who would for the next decade play a dominant role in both the religious and the political history of the state. By September 1866, a black Charlestonian could proudly describe eleven colored churches in his city—five Methodist (two of them affiliated with the AME Church), two Presbyterian, two Episcopalian, one Congregational, and one Baptist. "The flower of the city," he also noted, worshipped at the Episcopalian Church (St. Mark's), some of "the wealthiest colored families" attended the Methodist Episcopal Church (which had been reorganized by northern white missionaries), and the Reverend Cain's AME Church was made up largely of newly freed slaves. In Charleston, as in other urban centers where a free Negro community had thrived before the war, church affiliation often reflected divisions of class, status, and color within the black community. And if the experience of Ed Barber some years after the war was in any way typical, those who crossed those lines in choosing a church might come away disappointed.

> When I was trampin' 'round Charleston, dere was a church dere called St. Mark, dat all de society folks of my color went to. No black nigger welcome dere, they told me. Thinkin' as how I was bright 'nough to git in, I up and goes dere one Sunday. Ah, how they did carry on, bow and scrape and ape de white folks. . . . I was uncomfortable all de time though, 'cause they was too "hifalootin" in de ways, in de singin', and all sorts of carryin' ons.[31]

Almost conceding defeat at the outset, the Methodist Episcopal Church (South) did little to check the mass withdrawal of blacks from its ranks.

Within a year after the end of the war, in fact, it had already lost more than half of its black membership; those who remained would soon be reorganized into a separate Colored Methodist Episcopal Church.[32] To win over the departing black Methodists, an often furious battle ensued between the Methodist Episcopal Church (North) and the African Methodist Episcopal Church. Despite the impressive number and quality of the missionaries dispatched South by the northern Methodists and their clear superiority in financial resources, the black Methodist organizations also did quite well, demonstrating to their satisfaction that "blood is always more potent than money." In some communities, the rivals worked out a "compromise" by which preachers of both denominations used the same building and took turns at the pulpit. But at least one black minister who experimented with that arrangement found it unworkable. "The Apostle said, 'Be not unequally yoked together with unbelievers.' But in an accommodating sense, I say be not unequally yoked together with a white man." Even less charitable, the Reverend Richard H. Cain viewed his Methodist rival in Charleston as "this Judas, who comes here to rule over our people with his Yankee rod of iron," acting "more like Barnwell Rhett with his slaves, than a minister of Christ."[33]

What exacerbated the denominational rivalries was the unresolved question of who had the legal and moral right to the property of those churches which had formerly serviced the slaves. Although blacks had often built them, title to the land and the building had invariably been held in trusteeship for the black congregations by the whites. This issue assumed particular importance now that black congregations were searching for places in which to meet. Wherever possible, they would seek to establish new church structures to make absolutely clear their break with the past and their new independence in religious affairs. But even where the will and the labor existed to build their own churches, the resources were not always available. Until land could be acquired by purchase or rental and a building erected, blacks would be forced to hold their services in improvised "brush arbors," abandoned warehouses, and in their own cabins. On a plantation in Louisiana, a double cabin which had previously housed two slave families was subdivided so that black worshippers could meet in one of the rooms. "As you entered," a visitor noted, "you had your choice—you could visit the family or go to church." In many communities, moreover, the black preacher might be kept in quarters and food by his parishioners but he would have to appeal elsewhere for anything approaching a salary. "We are not doing so Well here," one such preacher wrote to the nearest Freedmen's Bureau officer, "the People of Smithville are very Poor so much so that they cannot suport me as their Preacher. For the last three month I have not had but $8.78. cents from my congregation. I do not know how I shall get along at this rate."[34]

The spectacle of overwhelming numbers of blacks withdrawing from the established churches in order to worship by themselves provoked a mixed response in the white South. Faced with the choice of permitting the black congregations to depart or granting them equal privileges and seating within the old churches, most whites preferred separation. But the social convenience this afforded them would have to be weighed against the risks incurred, and these covered an assortment of fears. If black laborers without white supervision reverted to indolence and vagrancy, as many whites expected, black worshippers freed from white surveillance might presumably fall into the vices of heathenism. Recalling the exodus of blacks from the white churches, Myrta Lockett Avary thought that was precisely what happened.

> With freedom, the negro, *en masse,* relapsed promptly into the voodooism of Africa. Emotional extravaganzas, which for the sake of his health and sanity, if for nothing else, had been held in check by his owners, were indulged without restraint. It was as if a force long repressed burst forth. "Moans," "shouts" and "trance meetings" could be heard for miles. It was weird.

Voicing an even more common concern, she noted how the blacks who had participated in these orgies would return to their homes late at night or at dawn, "exhausted, and unfit for duty."[35]

The political implications of separation revived even graver concerns among some native whites. Before the war, recognition of the dangers posed by independent black religious expression and organization had resulted in placing them under rigid surveillance and regulation. With emancipation, however, those restraints could no longer be enforced, and black-controlled churches and preachers not responsible to the master would become principal influences in the lives of the freedmen. Much as the whites had feared, rumors and reports of what transpired in the black churches suggested not only emotional extravagance but political subversion. In Mobile, Alabama, for example, several black preachers were accused of inculcating the freedmen with doctrines of murder, arson, violence, and hatred of white people. Not only were whites described in their sermons as "white devils," "demons," or "pro-slavery devils" but the preachers talked of an impending race war in which the whites would be exterminated. "He [the black preacher] frequently cried out 'In this hour of blood who will stand by me?' and his question ever met with most enthusiastic replies of 'I will, bless God!' from the assembled auditory."[36]

Whatever the proven capacity of black preachers for insurrectionary activity, whites had always been aware of that potential but had also learned over the years to encourage the religious enthusiasm of their slaves as a way of curbing any revolutionary impulses. Even with separation, the ability of the church to impose restraint and to divert people from their own grievances and oppression might still prove to be serviceable to whites. After describing the organization of several new black churches in Columbia, South Carolina, a northern correspondent reported how the whites had encouraged these efforts in the hope that "they will keep the attention of restless spirits from speculative politics, which promise so much harm to the poor negro." When the Reverend Henry M. Turner organized Georgia blacks into the AME Church and sought to train local preachers to preside over the new congregations, he found his efforts applauded by the southern white churches. "They were pleased to see that we were endeavoring to elevate the colored preachers of the South, instead of flooding the country with Northern ministers, many of whom might be 'too radical' for the times."[37]

Not only did the Union Army and the Freedmen's Bureau recognize the authority exercised by the black preacher but they sought to exploit his influence to restrain recalcitrant blacks and to disabuse the minds of the freedmen of any extravagant notions about freedom. The black preacher might be asked, for example, to explain the new labor contracts to the field hands and to urge their compliance, while at the same time he would correct any mistaken expectations they still held about the disposition of the lands of their former masters. In the presence of a Union officer, who no doubt nodded his head in approval, a black minister in Louisiana told a large gathering of freedmen not to delude themselves into thinking they no longer had a master—they had only changed their master. "Everything must have a head," he explained. "The plantation, the house, the steamboat, the army, and to obey that head was to obey the law; to disobey lawful commands was to disobey the law." In praising God for their freedom, the minister concluded, "they must not forget to honor Him by doing their duty."[38]

But the number of preachers beaten and the many churches burned to the ground by irate whites testified to the fact that the black minister did not always play the role expected and demanded of him. If he viewed himself as the moral and religious caretaker of his people, he would be drawn inexorably into the political arena. For black churchmen to have drawn a line between political and religious concerns in the years immediately following emancipation would have been ideologically and tactically impossible. After all, one black journal asked, how could the church stand apart from politics when the issues in question were civil rights, the suffrage, education, and equal protection under the law?[39] Not surprisingly, then, in state after state, the political and religious leaders were the same men. For many of them, preaching the gospel in the aftermath of emancipation proved to be only a prelude to preaching civil rights in the constitutional conventions, in the state legislatures, and in the United States Congress.

With justification, the AME Church boasted in 1870 that it had sent the first missionaries, black chaplains, and the highest black commissioned officers to the South. More recently, to cap this "glorious record," it had provided the first black postmaster in the South, the first black delegate to a constitutional convention, numerous state legislators, and a United

States senator—Hiram R. Revels of Mississippi, who only a few years earlier had been organizing AME churches in Vicksburg and Jackson. "A remarkable feature of all these promotions," the journal of the AME Church added, "is, that all the men remembered the 'rock whence they were hewn'—they remain strong African Methodists, and are using their increased influence to spread its borders." After assuming his duties as an organizer for the AME Church in Georgia, the Reverend Henry M. Turner would become an active figure in the Republican Party and subsequently serve in the state constitutional convention and in the legislature. The Reverend Richard H. Cain established a political base in Charleston, where his Emmanuel Church soon became "one of the strongest political organizations in the State"; he would serve in the state constitutional convention and in the state senate. The Reverend Jonathan C. Gibbs, who came to the South as a Presbyterian missionary, would rise to political power in Florida as secretary of state and superintendent of public instruction. After years of missionary work in the South, the Reverend James Lynch returned to Philadelphia to edit the *Christian Recorder,* but in June 1867 he announced that "convictions of duty to my race" impelled him to relinquish his editorial post "to go to a Southern State, and unite my destiny with that of my people, to live with them, suffer, sorrow, rejoice, and die with them." That would take him to Jackson, Mississippi, where he quickly became a leading Republican politico whose popularity elevated him to the state senate and to the position of secretary of state of Mississippi.[40]

With the withdrawal of thousands of blacks from the white-dominated churches, the black church became the central and unifying institution in the postwar black community. Far more than any newspaper, convention, or political organization, the minister communicated directly and regularly with his constituents and helped to shape their lives in freedom. Not only did he preach the gospel to the masses in these years but he helped to politicize and educate them. Many of the black missionaries and clergymen also assumed the position of teachers, and very often the classrooms themselves were housed in the only available quarters in town—the church. While northern black missionaries envisaged in an educated ministry and congregation an end to the excesses that marked the religious worship of southern blacks, even the old slave preachers, many of whom were illiterate, understood the value of knowledge and implored their people to make certain that the new generation learned the word of God in ways that had been denied the parents. "Breddern and sisters!" one such preacher declared. "I can't read more'n a werse or two of dis bressed Book, but de gospel it is here—de glad tidings it is here—oh teach your chill'en to read dis yar bressed Book. It's de good news for we poor coloured folk."[41] If some elderly blacks flocked to the newly opened freedmen's schools in the hope of reading the Bible before they died, the young thirsted for a knowledge not only of the Scriptures but of those subjects that would help them to improve their lot in this world.

"CHARLES, you is a free man they say, but Ah tells you now, you is still a slave and if you lives to be a hundred, you'll STILL be a slave, cause you got no education, and education is what makes a man free!" Nothing that any missionary educator or Freedmen's Bureau officer might have told Charles Whiteside about the value of schooling could have made as deep an impression as these words with which his master informed him of his freedom. Few freedmen, in fact, would have failed to appreciate the thrust of the slaveholder's remarks. If they looked to any panacea (outside of land) to free them from mental and physical dependency, they fastened their hopes on the schoolhouse. The Reverend Richard H. Cain pronounced education as second only in importance to godliness, but many newly freed slaves might have found it difficult to rank such priorities. "If I nebber does do nothing more while I live," a Mississippi freedman vowed, "I shall give my children a chance to go to school, for I considers education next best ting to liberty."[42]

Although most masters had managed to overcome their fears of religious worship among the slaves, only a very few had dared to extend such toleration to teaching blacks to read and write. "Everything must be interdicted which is calculated to render the slave discontented," was the explanation once offered by a Supreme Court judge in Georgia for the legislative restrictions placed on black literacy. Notwithstanding the elaborate precautions and legislation, some slaves and larger numbers of freeborn blacks managed to acquire a smattering of education, whether in clandestine schools, in the several schools for the freeborn tolerated in certain communities, or because of the indulgence of a member of the master's family. By virtue of their duties and access to the Big House, the plantation slaves most likely to have acquired a competence in reading and writing were the drivers, house servants, and artisans. Whenever the opportunity was there, some blacks had made the most of it. "These whites don't read and write because they don't want to," a black preacher observed in 1865; "our people don't, because the law and public feeling were against it. The ignorant whites had every chance to learn, but didn't; we had every chance to remain ignorant, and many of us learned in spite of them."[43] At the time of emancipation, however, the vast majority of southern blacks were illiterate—a triumph of sorts for the masters, legislatures, and courts who had deemed such a condition essential to the internal security of their society.

Like most young slaves, Booker T. Washington had viewed the mysteries of reading and writing from a distance. But the very fact that he was forbidden these practices of white people excited his curiosity. And when his mother explained that whites considered reading too dangerous for black people, that made him even more anxious to acquire this skill. "From that moment," he would recall, "I resolved that I should never be satisfied until I learned what this dangerous practice was like." On several occasions, he accompanied his master's daughter to the schoolhouse door, and the sight of the young white children inside made an impression upon him that he would never forget. "I had the feeling that to get into a schoolhouse and study in this way would be about the same as getting into paradise." That opportunity came for many young blacks in the aftermath of emancipation, though not all of them were in the best position to enjoy its benefits. After his family moved away from the farm on which they had been slaves, young Washington went to work in the salt furnaces and tried on his own to make some sense out of the spelling book his mother had acquired for him. When finally permitted to enroll in the newly opened freedmen's school, he still had to work in the furnaces for five hours in the early morning and for two more hours after classes. Because work demands made it impossible for him to continue his studies in the day school, he enrolled in the night school, and it was there, he later recalled, that he acquired "the greater part" of his elementary education.[44]

Nothing could have been more calculated to impress upon slaves the value of education than the extraordinary measures adopted by their "white folks" to keep them from it. Even if blacks simply drew on their own experiences and observations, they had come to recognize that power, influence, and wealth in southern society were invariably associated with literacy and monopolized by the better-educated class of whites. "My Lord, ma'am, what a great thing larning is!" a freed slave exclaimed to a white teacher in South Carolina. "White folks can do what they likes, for they know so much more'na we." No less impressed were some "contraband" children at Fortress Monroe early in the war. When placed in schools, one freed slave suggested, these children "thought it was so much like the way master's children used to be treated, that they believed they were getting white."[45]

The practical value of education never seemed clearer than in the aftermath of emancipation, when illiterate black laborers learned from bitter experience, especially on payday and at contract time, how white people used "book-larnin' " to take advantage of them. To an elderly Louisiana freedman, that was reason enough to send the children to school, even if their absence from the fields deprived the parents of their earnings. "Leaving learning to your children was better than leaving them a fortune; because if you left them even five hundred dollars, some man having more education than they had would come along and cheat them out of it all." Nearly every convention of freedmen in the postwar years dwelled incessantly on this point, seeking to drive home to every black family that "knowledge is power." Of course, nearly every black family that had survived slavery could readily understand that maxim. "They had seen the magic of a scrap of writing sent from a master to an overseer," a missionary in the Sea Islands noted, "and they were eager to share such power if there were any chance."[46]

To remain in ignorance was to remain in bondage. That conviction

alone drew hundreds of thousands, adults and children alike, to the freedmen's schools from the moment they opened, some of the prospective students making a pilgrimage of several miles, and many of them forced to
combine their schooling with rigorous work schedules. The very intensity
of their commitment caught both teachers and native whites by surprise.
"They will endure almost any penance rather than be deprived of this
privilege," a missionary educator in North Carolina observed. To a school
official in Virginia, trying to convey his thoughts about the freedmen's
enthusiasm for education, the phrase "*anxious* to learn" was insufficient;
"they are *crazy* to learn," he reported, as if their very salvation depended
on it. No doubt many ex-slaves were certain that it did. When asked why
he wished to enroll in a school, an elderly black man quickly replied,
"Because I want to read de Word of de Lord." That would permit him,
moreover, as an old Mississippi black man noted, to read all of the Bible,
not simply the portions the master and mistress had always selected for
their slaves.

> Ole missus used tu read de good book tu us, black 'uns, on Sunday eve-
> nin's, but she mostly read dem places whar it says, "Sarvints obey your
> masters," an' didn't stop tu splane it like de teachers; an' now we is free,
> dar's heaps o' tings in dat ole book, we is jes' sufferin' tu larn.[47]

If some southern blacks viewed with suspicion the ministers from the
North who presumed to "civilize" their religious worship, they usually
extended an effusive welcome to both white and black teachers. Unable in
many regions to pay the salaries of the teachers, black parents did what
they could to sustain them with gifts of eggs, vegetables, and fruit—anything that might persuade them to remain. "The people sent for tuition 5
eggs and a chicken," a black teacher in Virginia noted. Delighted that a
school had been opened in her neighborhood, a freedwoman vowed to
"work her fingers off" if necessary to send her children there. This was the
first time in her life, she told the teacher, that any white person had shown
any interest in her or in her children; until now, she had been driven,
kicked about, and made to work for others for nothing. When teachers
encountered resistance from native whites, freedmen in some places stood
guard outside their lodgings and the schoolhouse, alternating day and
night shifts with their own work schedules. In Augusta, Georgia, Asa B.
Whitfield, who had learned to write in a freedmen's school, expressed his
gratitude to the teacher in the terms he knew best. "We know that Christ
is our best friend because he suffered the most painful treatment for us.
Now I will say that the teachers are suffering on the account of us. And
they are our most perticular friends."[48]

But no matter how fully committed they might be to the principle of
schooling, not all black parents could afford the luxury of losing the labor
of their children. As teachers and school officials would quickly discover,
the turnover in students and erratic attendance usually reflected work

demands and planting seasons, and in some places teachers tried to adjust
their instruction to accommodate the laborers. "We work all day," a group
of freedmen in Macon, Georgia, explained to the teacher, "but we'll come
to you in the evening for learning, and we want you to make us learn; we're
dull, but we want you to beat it into us!" Many of her students, a teacher
reported from New Bern, North Carolina, were unable to leave work before
eight o'clock in the evening but they still insisted on spending at least an
hour afterwards "in earnest application to study." Even when at work,
however, some freedmen took their primers with them, much to the neglect
of their duties. "I dont wonder E. learns so fast and reads so well," one pupil
told his teacher, "for while she sits in the field watching the crows, she
minds her book so hard they come and eat up her corn."[49]

The demand for schools increased so rapidly that the initial problem
lay not in finding willing students but in hiring teachers and locating
quarters to house the classes. Until new structures could be built with
money raised by the freedmen or donated by the northern benevolent
societies, almost any place would have to suffice—a mule stable (Helena,
Arkansas), a billiard room (Seabrook plantation, Sea Islands), a courthouse
(Lawrence, Kansas), an abandoned white school (Charleston), the plantation cotton house (St. Simon's Island), warehouses and storerooms (New
Orleans), and, most commonly, the black church. Where buildings could
not be found, whether because of the expense or white opposition, classes
might alternate from day to day in the cabins of the freedmen. Some of the
more unusual temporary school quarters evoked memories that would be
lost on neither teachers, students, nor visitors. In Savannah, the Bryant
Slave Mart was converted into a school; the windows in the three-story
brick structure still had their iron grates, the handcuffs and whips found
inside became instant museum pieces, and the children were taught in
what had been the auction room. In New Orleans, a slave pen became the
Frederick Douglass School, with the auction block now serving as a globe
stand. And when the old cotton house on Tom Butler King's plantation in
Georgia was turned into a Sabbath school, a missionary teacher was moved
to write: "Strange transition from the rattle of the cotton gin, to the sweet
songs of Zion, but this is a day of great changes, when God is overturning
old systems, old practices, to give place to new, and I trust better." Not far
from this scene, a visitor in Augusta, Georgia, observed classes in a small
room above a store—the same place where the teacher had imparted lessons clandestinely during the war. "I was shown the doors and passages by
which they used to escape and disperse, at the approach of white persons."[50]

When field hands on a plantation near Selma, Alabama, erected a
schoolhouse near where they worked, they were fulfilling an agreement
made with their employer: he would furnish the materials and they would
perform the labor and pay for the teacher out of their earnings. Such
arrangements were by no means rare in the postwar South. Whether to
entice his former slaves to remain with him or to attract laborers, the

planter might offer them facilities for the education of their children. More often, the blacks themselves demanded a plantation school as a condition of employment and insisted that such a clause be written into the contract. Not all planters were necessarily averse to such an arrangement, for they believed it would help to keep laborers content, discourage premature departures from the plantation, and enable them to retain "the better class" of former slaves to perform the work. Even where such agreements were reached, however, implementation tended to vary from place to place, depending on the attitude of the planter and the persistence of his laborers. Once a contract had been signed, a Freedmen's Bureau superintendent of education reported from Arkansas, "the school is, in some cases, purposely left to run down under an incompetent or intemperate teacher." Nor were the results always satisfactory when the planter himself undertook to teach the school. "Massa teach school for us at night," a former Texas slave recalled. "Us learn A B C and how spell cat and dog and nigger. Den one day he git cross and scold us and us didn't go back to school no more."[51]

Although a few states began to take some faltering steps toward establishing schools for whites and blacks, the development of a system of tax-supported public education would be largely an achievement of Radical Reconstruction. During the interim years, the work of educating the newly freed slaves would have to be undertaken by the freedmen themselves, and by that host of white and black teachers who came to the South in the wake of Union occupation. As the northern emissaries boarded the ships and trains that brought them to their various destinations, and as they began their work, they came increasingly to believe that the very wisdom of emancipation itself was at stake—whether or not black people possessed the capacity for mental improvement and would be able to function as citizens and free workers in a competitive, white-dominated civilization.

6

―――――――

"THE BEST WAY to take Negroes to your heart," Mary Chesnut once observed, "is to get as far away from them as possible." When this plantation mistress confided these remarks to her diary in 1862, she had in mind not herself but those northern do-gooders like Harriet Beecher Stowe who wrote so authoritatively about people of whom they were personally ignorant and from whom they would no doubt recoil at meeting face to face.

> Topsys I have known, but none that were beaten or ill-used. Evas are mostly in the heaven of Mrs. Stowe's imagination. People can't love things dirty, ugly, and repulsive, simply because they ought to do so, but they can be good to them at a distance; that's easy. You see, I cannot rise very high; I can only judge by what I see.

But even Mary Chesnut, for all of her insights into the character of whites and blacks, could not have anticipated the sight of scores of Yankee "schoolmarms" descending upon her native South to work on a day-to-day basis with the same people who had previously been the objects of distant solicitude and verbal indulgence. "I have written and politized about them," a teacher wrote from Norfolk in 1864, "but now I see the reality and that has the highest coloring of all! ... O Mr. Whipple! what shall I say? my heart is full. My sensitive spirit was lacerated through and through by the sights and sounds I heard and witnessed last Sunday. No Eva shed more tears in one day than fell streaming down my cheeks last Sabbath."[52]

To redeem the oppressed, the ignorant, and the fallen was the finest kind of missionary work, and since the early days of Union occupation various evangelical and nonsectarian societies in the North had begun to dispatch teachers to the South to instruct the newly freed slaves in the ways of "civilization" and freedom. The American Missionary Association, the most prominent of these societies, set the proper tone for the entire missionary effort when it called upon its people in 1863 to take the freedmen "by the hand, to guide, counsel and instruct them in their new life, protect them from the abuses of the wicked, and direct their energies so as to make them useful to themselves, their families and their country." Recognizing the stabilizing influence of education, as well as the demonstrated eagerness for it, the Freedmen's Bureau made its best effort in this field of activity, providing materials, facilities, rations, transportation for teachers, and considerable encouragement and supervision, while the northern freedmen's aid societies supplied and paid the teachers.[53]

Like the Union soldiers who preceded them, the missionary teachers and educators came to the South with a number of assumptions and expectations about the people they sought to elevate to a higher level of intellect and morality. The effects of a lifetime of bondage, they suspected, had dulled the minds of its victims, debased their morals, demeaned their character, destroyed their self-respect, and rendered them incapable of taking care of themselves. Marcia Colton, a missionary worker in Virginia, claimed that her conversations with returned missionaries from Africa and her previous familiarity with Negroes as slaves permitted her to minister to the freedmen "with more Charity, & less expectation" than most of her co-workers. "I did not expect to find with them generally, any nice distinction of propriety or Chastity." Nor did Lydia Maria Child, a veteran abolitionist, think any of her friends who chose to teach in the South should harbor any false illusions about what they would find there. "I doubt whether we *can* treat our colored brethren *exactly* as we would if they were white, though it is desirable to do so. But we have kept their minds in a state of infancy, and children *must* be treated with more patience and forbearance than grown people." Much like their antislavery antecedents, the freedmen's aid societies, as "the wisest and best friends" of the Negro, refused to claim that the African race was the equal of the Anglo-Saxon. But neither would they concede that blacks were necessarily inferior.

"They simply assert that the negro must be accorded an opportunity for development before his capacity for development can be known.".This was, of course, sound abolitionist gospel, steeped in the conviction of antebellum reform that untrammeled individual development alone should determine place in society.[54]

For many of the missionary teachers, this was their first visit to the South, and the initial impressions they formed of the blacks they encountered would tap a wide range of emotions. At the outset, the sheer numbers, blackness, and demeanor of these people would have to be absorbed. Elizabeth Botume, for one, tried hard.

> Negroes, negroes, negroes. They hovered around like bees in a swarm. Sitting, standing, or lying at full-length, with their faces turned to the sky. Every doorstep, box, or barrel was covered with them. . . . Words fail to describe their grotesque appearance. Fortunately they were oblivious to all this incongruity. They had not yet attained distinct personality; they were only parts of a whole; once "massa's niggers," now refugees and contrabands.

Although experience would force the teachers to revise some of the assumptions they brought with them to the South, what they espied in the condition and moral deportment of the freed slaves tended to confirm the previous image of "helpless grown up children" with well-developed habits of indolence, dependency, and licentiousness and skilled in the arts of deception and thievery. But like any good abolitionist, the missionary teacher regarded these vices as the natural consequences of a lifetime of slavery, not innate racial characteristics. If these people were childlike, that was because they had been denied the necessary tools for development. If they were sometimes thieves, they had acquired the habit to supplement their meager rations. If they were easily led into unchastity, they had only modeled their behavior after their masters'. If they dissembled and shielded each other, they had developed those arts in order to survive. If they were ragged and dirty in appearance, they had "lived so long in a filthy condition they don't know what it is to be clean." Besides, much of what the teachers saw seemed almost surprisingly familiar, and they were quick to compare the freedmen with the Irish who inhabited the northern cities. After noting that the southern blacks looked "wretched and stupid," a Boston teacher in South Carolina added that "to those who are accustomed to many Irish faces, these except by their *uniformity* c[oul]d suggest few new ideas of low humanity."[55]

Even if the first impressions tended to confirm expectations, that did not always diminish the shock or revulsion a number of the teachers experienced in their daily encounters with the freedmen. "It is *one* thing to sit in ones office or drawing room and weave fine spun theories in regard to the Negro character," a teacher wrote from Beaufort, North Carolina, "but it is quite another to come into actual contact with him. I fail to see those beauties and excellencies, and the 'Uncle Toms,' that some do. Is it reasonable, in short, to suppose that people brought up, or rather who have come up under such influences, would be altogether lovely." That was the kind of observation a Mary Chesnut might have pounced upon to prove her point that northern reformers dealt best with their wards at a distance. What she may not have been prepared for, however, was how these missionary teachers would act upon their feelings of shock and dismay. The more they saw and experienced, in fact, the more many of them came to believe that there could be no greater missionary field anywhere in the world; the shock and dismay many of them confessed to only seemed to heighten their sense of purpose, even driving them into outbursts of sheer exultation over their work. "The prattle of infancy has always been pleasant to me," one teacher wrote, "yet to live in daily communion with two or three hundred of this infant race, to watch the latent fires of intelligence in their first development, is happiness." No less inspired, a teacher in Louisiana found himself "happy when surrounded with their dusky faces and glistening eyes"; a teacher in South Carolina found her work to be "a joy and glory for which there are not words"; a teacher in North Carolina claimed to have overcome in two months the doubts and "personal antipathies" with which she began her mission; and a teacher in Virginia reported, "I think I shall stay here as long as I live, and teach this people. I have no love or taste for any other work, and am happy only here with them."[56]

Neither the magnitude nor the complexity of the task they faced seemed nearly as awesome to the missionary teachers and educators as the opportunity to stamp their image on nearly four million newly freed slaves. "We can make them all that we desire them to be," exulted a teacher in New Bern, North Carolina. That thought alone helped to sustain the northern emissaries in their daily labors and to overcome the disappointments and frustrations they would experience. To make the freedmen "all that we desire them to be" was to instruct them not only in the spelling book and the gospel but in every phase of intellectual and personal development —in the virtues of industry, self-reliance, frugality, and sobriety, in family relations and moral responsibility, and, most importantly, in how to conduct themselves as free men and women interacting with those who had only recently held them as slaves. In seeking to enlist the support of a prominent planter in his district, a freedmen's educator in North Carolina phrased educational objectives in such a way as to disarm any potential critics.

> We start with the principle that to rescue the Freedmen from vice and crime, they must be intelligent and virtuous. To become intelligent and virtuous they must be taught. . . . Their [the teachers'] business is not only to teach a knowledge of letters, but to instruct them in the duties which now devolve upon them in their new relations—to make clear to their understanding the principles by which they must be guided in all their intercourse with their fellowmen—to inculcate obedience to law

and respect for the rights and property of others, and reverence for those
in authority; enforcing honesty, industry and economy, guarding them
against fostering animosities and prejudices, and against all unjust and
indecorous assumptions, above all, indoctrinating them in the Gospel of
our Lord and Saviour Jesus Christ.[57]

Both the northern societies and the Freedmen's Bureau recognized the
value of education in preparing the blacks for practical life, and neither
would have understood the need to draw any distinctions between teaching
freedmen to read and write and making productive free laborers of them.
The education of the freedmen, as many a school official argued, should in
fact be designed to ensure their diligence and faithfulness in the workplace.
Any teacher, then, might be called upon to lecture the blacks on the need
to comply with the terms of labor contracts. When field hands in the Sea
Islands grew restive over a recent wage settlement, Laura Towne, along
with several other teachers, found herself "borrowed and driven to the
different plantations to talk to and appease the eager anxiety." For the few
teachers who felt ill-used when asked to perform such duties, the resentment might manifest itself in spending more time teaching the freedmen
how to protect themselves from unscrupulous employers who manipulated
figures and the language of contracts to keep their workers in perpetual
debt. Had only more teachers addressed themselves to such concerns, a
black North Carolinian argued some years later, the difficulties encountered by freedmen in the making and enforcing of contracts might have
been minimized. "What we want among freedmen," he added, "is an education that will not only look after their immortality, but also their cor-
poreity. The denomination that will bless the freedmen most is the one that
looks most after soul and body."[58]
      Although priorities differed among individual teachers, many of them
did feel compelled not only to impart universal middle-class values but to
attack the special deficiencies they perceived in a people who had been
denied the barest rudiments of learning. Based on their assessment of the
needs of their students, that would entail instruction in the days of the
week, the months, weights, measures, and monetary values, how to calculate their ages, the shape of the world, proper forms of address, and the
history of mankind. "Suffice it to say," the Reverend Henry M. Turner
counseled prospective teachers and missionaries, "they need instruction in
every thing, and especially the little things of life, such points of attention
as thousands would never stoop to surmise." Moreover, a people "who had
never had a country to love" needed to be taught sentiments of patriotism
and an appreciation of how they came to be freed. Rather than separate
such lessons from the basic skills of reading and writing, teachers would
invariably combine them, much as the primers they used did. Through
appropriate readings, songs, and exercises, positive moral and patriotic
images would be implanted in the minds of the pupils. In teaching the
alphabet, each letter might introduce a couplet conveying some moral or

value, and in at least one instance an elderly black student composed his own twenty-six verses, with the letters "G," "K," and "Q," for example, communicating thoughts few of his classmates could have failed to comprehend.

> *God* fix all right
> Twix' black and white.
>
> *King* Cotton's ded
> And Sambo's fled.
>
> *Quashee* was sold
> When blind and old.

Similarly, teachers devised dialogues which their pupils would memorize and then often recite to visitors, and many of these consisted of historical lessons with an undisguised New England bias.

> Q. Where were slaves brought to this country?
> A. Virginia.
> Q. When?
> A. 1620.
> Q. Who brought them?
> A. Dutchmen.
> Q. Who came the same year to Plymouth, Massachusetts?
> A. Pilgrims.
> Q. Did they bring slaves?
> A. No.[59]

To succeed in the classroom, many teachers felt they needed only to capitalize on the eagerness with which their pupils had grasped the opportunity to come to them. If additional incentives were deemed necessary, instructors and school officials were apt to differ whether or not these should be largely psychological, material, or corporal. To impress upon his students the need to learn their lessons well, a teacher in North Carolina warned them that they were being watched closely by enemies who wished to see the entire experiment in black education fail. Edwin S. Williams, teaching in St. Helena Village, South Carolina, claimed success in using more substantial rewards to emphasize certain lessons, as in accompanying "a piece of beef with an injunction to make it relish by industry," or by providing the pupils with extra molasses while giving them "a vigorous stirring up about their smoky rooms & dirty clothes." Nevertheless, some teachers frankly confessed their inability to maintain classroom discipline, and others felt their effectiveness impaired by the need to teach large numbers of pupils of various ages and grade levels in the same room. "I acknowledge that it was *not* a very pleasant one," a black teacher wrote of her first day in the classroom. "Part of my scholars are very tiny,— babies, I call them—and it is hard to keep them quiet and interested while I am hearing the larger ones."[60]

Traditionally, teachers seldom hesitated to mete out a sound thrashing to enforce their authority and maximize their instruction. But corporal punishment might have a very different meaning for a former slave than for a white youth, and that consideration alone prompted some freedmen's school officials to forbid it. The reports of teachers, however, suggest that this prohibition was neither universally obeyed nor respected. In Charleston, a teacher insisted that whipping a freedman in the classroom could not be compared with whipping a slave in the field, especially if "a kind and serious talk" with the recalcitrant pupil followed the thrashing. That, she observed, "seems to astonish them into good behavior, for they appear to have been accustomed to threats rather than kindness, and have been driven to feel that anger rather than love governed those who whipped them." Whether deservedly or not, black teachers were reputed to be the harshest disciplinarians, and some of them refused to be defensive about it. After all, a black teacher in New Orleans noted, many of his pupils had been plantation slaves and consequently knew no motive for obedience other than fear of punishment. "Coax 'em and they'll laugh at you; you've got to knock 'em about, or they won't think you've got any power over 'em." Nor were black parents necessarily averse to seeing their children punished, if necessary to instill proper learning habits, but they made it clear that they would tolerate a whipping only if meted out by "a Yankee teacher" and not by a native white.[61]

Fully aware of the pervasive theories in American society which assumed the mental inferiority of the African race, the teachers and supervisors in the freedmen's schools needed periodically to assess the results of their efforts and to report them to a curious and skeptical public. But measuring success and progress was not always easy, and each teacher had different priorities. For many, the acquisition of basic learning skills—reading and writing—was sufficient proof of success; still others looked to the performance of black pupils in advanced subjects or chose to stress perceptible improvements in physical appearance, demeanor, and personal habits. "We now see civilization stamped on these schools," a superintendent reported from Fernandina, Florida. "Instead of rags and filth, there is decent clothes and cleanliness; instead of the vacant half-frightened stare and low slavish tone, there is an intelligent eye and more erect bearing, and full tone." Antoinette Turner, a teacher in New Bern, North Carolina, derived particular satisfaction from the efforts her pupils made to discard "the 'dis' and 'dat,' so peculiar to them," while an equally gratified instructor in Maryland noted his success in persuading the adults in his class to discard common nicknames like "Uncle Jack" and "Aunt Sallie" in favor of "the respectable names of Mr. and Mrs. Brown."[62]

But the critical question, as every educator understood, came down to a comparison of their pupils with white students in the North, both in the rapidity with which they acquired basic skills and their demonstrated aptitude in more advanced subjects. Few needed to be reminded that the manner in which they decided this issue went to the very heart of their efforts, indeed to the legitimacy of the "experiment" itself. Nearly every teacher and supervisor made the inevitable comparison, some with greater detail than others. The clear consensus was that black pupils learned as rapidly as the average white child in a northern school. When they proceeded to particularize that observation, however, many of them seemed to suggest an inequality of intellectual talents and perhaps even of capacity. Not unlike the stereotype already formed of black pupils in northern schools, the freedmen were generally thought to excel in subjects entailing rote memory and imitation and to be less proficient than whites in fields of study requiring the application of logic and induction, "powerful reasoning," and "inventive" and reflective powers. Having made these distinctions, some teachers added that such powers were not beyond the reach of blacks once they were permitted to develop their full potential. In the meantime, black pupils might have taken some consolation in the observations of their teachers that they were more emotional and affectionate than whites, more "graphic and figurative in language," and clearly superior in wit, cunning, and musical expression. "How musical they are!" more than one teacher would remark, and Mary E. Burdick apparently exploited that faculty every chance she had. "I doubt if the same number of whites could produce half the melody they can in simply singing the multiplication table. I thought it exceeded every thing!"[63]

To display the talents of their students, both white and black teachers in the freedmen's schools scheduled periodic programs and recitations, many of them specifically designed to impress the host of northern visitors, officials, and correspondents who descended upon these schools. No day passed without some visitation, Elizabeth Botume observed, and she confessed a low regard for the ways in which the guests often conducted themselves in the presence of her pupils.

> I wish to ask why so many well-intentioned people treat those who are poor and destitute and helpless as if they were bereft of all their five senses. This has been my experience. Visitors would talk before the contrabands as if they could neither see nor hear nor feel. If they could have seen those children at recess, when their visit was over, repeating their words, mimicking their tones and gestures, they would have been undeceived.

In the typical school program, the students recited various exercises, engaged in carefully rehearsed dialogues with their teacher, and culminated the proceedings with a rousing chorus of "John Brown's Body" or perhaps an old spiritual. And the northern guests would invariably leave the school very much impressed with this "startling" exhibition of black talent.[64]

But these displays raised a troublesome question. Did the "surprise" and "astonishment" registered by teachers, superintendents, and visitors alike over the intellectual attainments of black pupils reflect a different standard of expectation and measurement than they would have applied to white pupils? Long before the Civil War, a black newspaper in the North had raised this question in noting the praise lavished on black students by school visitors and wondered if the same performance from white pupils would have excited the slightest attention. If anything, the temptation to magnify black achievements in the classroom would have been far greater in the postwar South, and some teachers frankly thought the emphasis on producing measurable results as quickly as possible was not only educationally unsound but demeaning to black people.

> I find it a great fault, in nearly all the schools for Freedmen, that the children are advanced too rapidly. Before they can read one book with any degree of care and fluency, they are pushed into another still more difficult. Teachers do not seem to care about *quality* but have a great desire to send home reports of scholars beginning with the alphabet and their being able to read in the 3rd 4th or 5th readers—in as many months.

After visiting several freedmen's schools in North Carolina, Jonathan C. Gibbs, a black minister, thought the pupils were "doing well as could be expected, and some much better than I had anticipated," but he felt the teachers were doing far too much, "seemingly, for the sake of present impression, rather than for the solid interests of the children. When I remember that in a few years these black children will control largely the future destiny of this southern country and will make it either a hell upon earth or a paradise, I tremble for the responsible trust which has been placed in the hands of these improper persons."[65]

That the quality of instruction varied with each teacher was hardly unique to the education of freedmen. For some teachers, the challenge of educating recently freed slaves demanded an understanding and patience they simply did not possess, resulting in a total breakdown in communication and an early return to the North. Nor did the often inadequate living quarters, the shortages of books and materials, and the open displays of white hostility make the life of a freedmen's teacher any easier. For most of them, however, the level of commitment remained high enough to withstand the inconveniences, the threats, and, in a few instances, the initial suspicions of the pupils and their parents. The white teacher in Beaufort, South Carolina, suspended for using derogatory language in referring to blacks and for habitually using opium was quite exceptional, though such cases no doubt confirmed the black critics who thought some of the teachers academically sound but morally weak. Nor would it be easy to assess the charge of a black preacher in Wilmington, North Carolina, that "some of the teachers were setting the devil into his people."[66] In gauging black reaction to this massive educational effort, far more typical would be the consternation that swept over a black community when a teacher announced his or her departure. Although he loved his "southern friends," a black student in Augusta, Georgia, wrote his former teacher, he knew

that none of them could have faced up to the ordeal experienced by many
of the Yankee teachers.

> Now the white people south says that the yankee are no friend to the
> southern people. That's a mistaken idea. The northerners do not advise
> us to be at enmety against any race. They teach us to be friends.... If
> you say the yankee is no friend how is it that the ladies from the north
> have left there homes and came down here? Why are they laboring day
> and night to elevate the collord people? Why are they shut out of society
> in the South? The question is plain. Answer it.... I'm going to school now
> to try to learn some thing which I hope will enable me to be of some use
> to my race. These few lines will show that I am a new beginner. I will try,
> and do better.... Thank God I have a book now. The Lord has sent us
> books and teachers. We must not hesitate a moment, but go on and learn
> all we can.[67]

## 7

LEAST IMPRESSED by the public displays of black intellectual capabilities
were the native whites, many of whom reacted to the educational experiment in their midst with varying degrees of amusement, skepticism, suspicion, and outright hostility. For some whites, the only uncertainty was
whether to fear or to ridicule the strange spectacle of black youths and
adults, only recently their slaves, marching off to places where they would
imbibe lessons from Yankee schoolmarms. "I have seen many an absurdity
in my lifetime," remarked a Louisiana legislator upon viewing his first
black pupils, "but this is the climax of absurdities!" Once white Southerners grew accustomed to such sights, if they ever could, they would differ
about the benefits and dangers black education posed. Voicing a position
that would gain a respectable hearing in some circles, a magistrate in
Sumter, South Carolina, argued that the same concern for public safety
which had once required Negroes as slaves to be kept ignorant now required that Negroes as freedmen be enlightened in the responsibilities of
citizenship.[68]

Consistent with this theme of accommodation, the "better class" of
whites suggested that with "the right kind of teachers," the newly freed
slaves could be taught a proper deference for their superiors, fidelity to
contracts, respect for property, the rewards of industriousness, and other
virtues calculated to ensure an orderly transition to free labor. That prospect could induce a Florida planter to believe "the best way to manage the
Negroes now is to educate them and increase as far as practicable their
wants and dependence upon the white man." With an equal appreciation
for proper priorities, a planter in North Carolina informed a freedmen's
educator that "a due observance of law and order, an improvement in

morals, and decent respect for the rights and opinions of others—properly inculcated & impressed on the minds of the Freedmen," would no doubt be tolerated in his community, though he cautioned the official not to expect "any demonstrations of *delight.*" Rather than openly oppose the education of the freedmen, then, some whites insisted on withholding their judgments until they could begin to ascertain the results. While "decidedly in favor" of black parents educating their children, a newspaper in Waco, Texas, made it clear that "we do not approve their sending their children to school from a mere hifalutin idea of making them smart and like white folks."[69]

Even if the education of the freedmen was a laudable objective, calculated to impress upon them their new duties and responsibilities, many native whites remained skeptical of the experiment and confidently predicted its failure. "I do assure you," a white woman advised one teacher, "you might as well try to teach your horse or mule to read, as to teach these niggers. They *can't* learn." The laws prohibiting the instruction of slaves, she explained, had been aimed at the house servants and urban blacks. "Some of these were smart enough for anything. But the country niggers are like monkeys. You can't *learn* them to come in when it rains." Of course, the inferior mental capacity of Negroes had long been a staple of the proslavery argument, confirming as it did their inability to look after themselves and their need to defer to the superior judgment and wisdom of their owners. To think now that the minds of black people might be susceptible to classroom instruction not only contradicted theories which had the highest academic standing but posed more immediate and more troublesome questions. If this experiment should prove successful, how would it affect the proper subordination of blacks in southern society? If their ambitions were heightened, how could they remain satisfied with their low economic, social, and political position? Inflated with ideas of their own importance and capability, would they not certainly become even more discontented and impudent? "The cook, that must read the daily newspaper, will spoil your beef and your bread," a southern educator noted; "the sable pickaninny, that has to do his grammar and arithmetic, will leave your boots unblacked and your horse uncurried."[70]

Whatever accommodations whites might make to black education, such apprehensions never really subsided. The warning sounded by a white educator late in the century only echoed concerns that were frequently expressed in the post-emancipation years. "Suppose our educational schemes succeeded," he asked; "suppose we elevate him as a race until he has the instincts and drives of a white man? . . . Being trained for office he will demand office. Being taught as a Negro child the same things and in the same way as the white child, when he becomes a Negro man he will want the same things and demand them in the same way as a white man." That was reason enough to be doubly cautious about the teachers and curriculum in the education of blacks. And if the path from the schoolhouse led to the courthouse and the white man's parlor and bedroom, then perhaps this enterprise should be resisted before it gained any foothold in southern society.[71]

Although whites continued to disagree about the wisdom of educating black children, the opposition mounted in some areas made it virtually a moot question. "There are no colored schools down in Surry county," a Virginia black testified; "they would kill any one who would go down there and establish colored schools. . . . Down in my neighborhood they [the blacks] are afraid to be caught with a book." Those whites who opposed his efforts, a freedmen's school official observed, were usually more "tacit and concealed" in their methods than violent, manifesting their resistance in agreements among themselves not to rent homes or buildings that might be used for schools and to declare as "nuisances" any schoolhouses erected by the black residents. Even some of the black churches which had initially permitted classes to meet in their basements were forced to reconsider the offer in the wake of threats to deny them insurance because they had suddenly become fire risks. To read the daily press or the reports of freedmen's school officials was to appreciate, in fact, why any building housing classes for black pupils became by definition a poor actuarial risk.[72]

In nearly every part of the South, but especially in the rural districts, the destruction of schoolhouses, usually by fire, only begins to suggest the wave of terror and harassment directed at the efforts to educate blacks. "We are advised by friends not to be out evenings," a white teacher wrote from Little Rock, Arkansas. Amos McCollough, an aspiring black teacher in Magnolia, North Carolina, pleaded for Federal troops to protect him in his efforts to establish a school: "I [intended] to open school here in Magnolia which I did but only proceeded one day. Why? Because the house which I taught in was threatened of being burnt down." If not humiliated, beaten, or forced into exile, many teachers found it nearly impossible to obtain credit in local stores or to find living quarters, thus forcing them to board with black families and subjecting them in some states and counties to arrest as vagrants for cohabiting with black women. The mayor of Enterprise, Mississippi, defended the arrest of a freedmen's teacher by noting that he had been "living on terms of equality with negroes, living in their houses, boarding with them, and at one time gave a party at which there were no persons present (except himself) but negroes, all which are offences against the laws of the state and declared acts of vagrancy." At the same time, the mayor affirmed his belief that no one had any objection— "None whatever"—to a Negro school in the town.[73]

The case of the Mississippi teacher illustrates only the more absurd manifestations of native white resistance to schools for the freedmen. More often than not, the violence and harassment required no explanation. When blacks in Canton, Mississippi, raised money among themselves to build a schoolhouse, they were told that the structure would be burned to the ground, and a citizens' committee headed by a local attorney warned the prospective teacher to leave on the first train or face a public hanging. When a young female teacher in a freedmen's school in Donaldsonville, Louisiana, was killed by a militia patrol, authorities called it an "accidental" shooting, thereby moving the *New Orleans Tribune* to observe: "This is a series of 'accidents' as seldom accidentally occur in this world." After describing a number of recent beatings, stabbings, and whippings, most of them in the outlying parishes, the same newspaper concluded: "The record of the teachers of the first colored schools in Louisiana will be one of honor and blood." Although many native whites discountenanced attacks on schools, a missionary educator in Grenada, Mississippi, voiced a common belief among teachers that such protests were almost always to no avail. "Tho they [the perpetrators] may be a small minority, the majority dare not move their tongues against them; but must tacitly consent to what they do. The colored people are in perpetual fear of them, & well they may be; for they kill them with almost perfect impunity." Even where freedmen schools were tolerated, moreover, teachers found themselves treated by these same "respectable" whites with "a studious avoidance," and many a teacher and superintendent considered the maintenance of their schools dependent on the nearby Federal garrison.[74]

Despite the fears of educators, the withdrawal of Union Army garrisons did not result in a massive dismantlement of the freedmen's schools. With each passing year, in fact, additional numbers of native whites came around to the view that the education of blacks—at least on a rudimentary level—had become an unavoidable consequence of emancipation and that the white South had best accommodate itself to this reality. That accommodation would be expedited and the dangers minimized, they suggested to their people, if steps were taken to control the educational apparatus and staff the schools with their own kind. This was not necessarily inconsistent with the belief of some Freedmen's Bureau educational officers that more native whites should be employed as teachers, since "they understand the negro" and would be in a good position to combat the strong feelings against his education. But others were quick to point out that such teachers would also be in an ideal position to vent their own frustrations on those who had previously been their slaves, and there were sufficient examples to underscore that concern. In one school taught by two native whites, the children were not only whipped frequently but forced to address their teachers as "massa" and "missus."[75]

Although some time would elapse before large numbers of native whites could be induced to teach in black schools, the number steadily grew in the immediate postwar years, in part because of the feverish search by some impoverished whites for any kind of remunerative employment. "While I am on the nigger question," Sallie Coit wrote a friend, "I must tell you that my school for them [Negroes] still flourishes.... I hope I can do them some good. I have the satisfaction of knowing that I put good books into their hands, while if they went to Yankees they would doubtless have books tainted with Abolitionism." Outright control of the school systems, along the lines suggested by Sallie Coit, would have to await the overthrow of Radical Reconstruction; in the meantime, native whites tried to accommodate themselves to the idea of paying taxes for the support of public schools for both races. "Every little negro in the county is now going to school and the public pays for it," wrote one disgruntled planter. "This is a hell of [a] fix but we cant help it, and the best policy is to conform as far as possible to circumstances." Considering other possible reactions, this represented a triumph of sorts for the cause of black education in the South.[76]

Whatever toleration and public support native whites chose to accord the freedmen's schools depended in large measure not only on the conduct of the teachers but on maintaining a strict segregation between white and black pupils. "Sir, we accept the death of slavery," a prominent Savannah citizen explained, as he remonstrated against the proposed admission of blacks to the public schools; "but, sir, surely there are some things that are not tolerable. Our people have not been brought up to associate with negroes. They don't think it decent; and the negroes will be none the better for being thrust thus into the places of white men's sons." Pending the establishment of public school systems, some white parents unable to afford private instruction for their children chose to send them to the only available alternative—the freedmen's schools, where they were sometimes taught in the same classrooms as the black pupils. Almost as often, however, the white parents were forced to withdraw their children because of overwhelming community pressure. The townspeople "made so much fuss," one mother told a teacher, that she had no choice. "I would not care myself, but the young men laugh at my husband. They tell him he must be pretty far gone and low down when he sends his children to a 'nigger school.' That makes him mad, and he is vexed with me."[77]

Seeking to allay native white fears, and well aware of the strong feelings on the question of race mixing, the freedmen's aid societies would have preferred to avoid the issue. Although official policy called for integrated schools, implementation varied with local circumstances and also depended on the willingness of missionary teachers to undertake the instruction of poor whites as well as blacks. The controversy that erupted in Beaufort, North Carolina, was unique only because H. S. Beals, an educational officer of the American Missionary Association, maintained a separate school for poor whites and because a co-worker chose to make an issue of it. Defending the schools, Beals considered them an accommodation to white sensitivities and to the urgent need to educate any child, white or black, who chose to come to them. To integrate the white school, he warned, would "scatter that school in a day." (That was precisely what had happened in nearby Raleigh.) He did not question the *ideal* of integrated education but thought it less important than reaching as many children as possible.

*We* are right, but the prevailing sentiment of the white people *here,* is *wrong.* Shall we wait to convert them to our ideas, before we give them what alone will secure that conversion. . . . The whole race of poor white children are crying out for this life giving influence. Is it our policy, or our principle, to hold this multitude, clamoring for intellectual light, outside the benign influence of schools, till we force them to adopt our ideas?

Whatever the merits of that question, the Reverend S. J. Whiton, also an AMA representative in Beaufort, felt a critical principle had been sacrificed, and he charged that the two schools provoked "much excitement and hard feeling" among the blacks. "The colored people here are watching curiously to see the result. In their minds the AMA is convicted of saying one thing and through its agents doing another." But Whiton's protest to AMA officers resulted only in a reprimand for "meddling" and for making "a very unfortunate and unwise" issue out of a delicate matter, and he thereupon submitted his resignation from the AMA rather than be identified with the perpetuation of racial distinctions. Several black students also indicated their displeasure with "the White School," among them Hyman Thompson, who urged the AMA to return to its original principles. More of his brethren would have joined the protest, he added, but they feared "Mr. Beals will not give them clothes or hire them to work if they do."[78]

To black parents, the opportunity to educate their children seemed to take precedence over whether they would share the same classrooms with whites. Even while pressing for full and equal access to public facilities and transportation, without regard to color, many blacks willingly conceded and some even preferred separate schools, but only if those schools were equal in quality, comfort, and the allocation of funds to the schools reserved for whites. In opting for separation, some parents simply wanted to avoid subjecting their children to the taunts, derision, and harassment of white pupils. "No, Sir," a black woman in New Orleans responded when asked if she would like to see the school system integrated. "I don't want my children to be pounded by dem white boys. I don't send them to school to fight, I send them to learn."[79]

During the early years of Radical Reconstruction, black delegates to the constitutional conventions and black legislators in several states would argue vigorously to outlaw racial distinctions in the schools, and in New Orleans, the only city where such a system was maintained for a time, the black newspaper had been an early advocate of integration. In urging the mayor in 1867 to reject a city ordinance establishing separate schools, the *Tribune* maintained that equality before the law would never be fully realized until an equality of rights pervaded the entire community—"in customs, manners, and all things of everyday life." Two years later, in commemorating the twenty-fifth anniversary of the successful integration of public schools in Boston, the same newspaper wondered how much longer the white people of the South would be willing to pay for two sets of teachers and two sets of schools.[80] Three more generations, in fact, would attend separate schools before that dual system began to collapse under a decision of the United States Supreme Court which echoed the editorial sentiments of the *New Orleans Tribune*.

8

No LESS DISTURBING to whites than race mixing in the classroom was the spectacle of Yankee schoolmarms fraternizing with local blacks and flaunting their notions of social equality. "They went in among the negroes, ate and slept with them, paraded the streets arm-in-arm with them," one white southern woman recalled. If some white teachers indulged in such behavior, native whites relished every opportunity to report it, and the missionary teachers themselves were not above being "gossipy" about such matters. "To-day I am informed by letter of an engagement between a Colored physician and a Yankee teacher," wrote a concerned instructor from Columbus, Georgia, to her supervisor. "What do you think of such alliances? . . . The rebs have reported a number of such matches. Now they can have their sensation and a real cause."[81]

The problem did not lie in liaisons between Yankee schoolmarms and black men, for these were rare. But the question of social intercourse between teachers and freedmen outside the classroom and how far professed principles needed to be compromised to appease native whites surfaced frequently enough to become divisive issues within the ranks of the freedmen's aid movement. Nor were those who challenged the wisdom of such fraternization necessarily any less zealous in their efforts to educate the freedman or less dedicated to the ideal of equal rights. This was a matter of tactics, they insisted, not principle. Few stated the view more clearly than G. L. Eberhart, superintendent of the freedmen's schools in Georgia and also a Freedmen's Bureau officer. To disarm the white critics, he maintained, "[w]e must be governed in this work by great prudence, and, so far as we possibly can without any compr[om]ise of principle, or conflict with truth, be controlled by policy and expediency." It was not a matter of rights but of whether the exercise of those rights helped or hindered the cause to which they had dedicated themselves in the South.

> I have, for instance, a perfect right, if my taste run in that way, to publicly kiss a negro child on the street, or to board and live, on terms of perfect social equality, with colored people; yet here, I think, every consideration of prudence and expediency, *for the sake of the freed people alone,* forbids the *exercise* of any such right—forbids it, too, in the most peremptory manner.

For Eberhart, this was no abstract issue; he voiced his views in a letter requesting the transfer of several teachers under his jurisdiction who, in his estimation, had exceeded "the limits of prudence and propriety." Among them was a teacher who had "totally disqualified" herself, not only by her arrogant manner in and out of the classroom but by the easy familiarity she had assumed with the blacks, totally disregarding local feelings and customs. "For a white Northern lady here to kiss a colored child is very *imprudent* to say the least of it, and, in reply to an insulting remark made by a white person, to say that the negroes are as good as that white person, is *entirely unnecessary.*"[82]

Although some of Eberhart's associates in the educational movement might have chosen to be more circumspect in voicing their views on this delicate matter, few of them would have denied the logic or the necessity of his position. To listen to some of the missionary educators, the initial call of their societies to take the black man "by the hand" was to be exercised with considerable restraint. Any ostentatious display of affection for the freedmen or violation of local racial codes suggested, in their view, self-indulgence rather than genuine commitment to the cause and helped neither the blacks nor the image of the teacher. But to advise teachers, as did one educational officer, to "conform to local customs and practices wherever such conformity will not compromise principle" was to invite disagreement and controversy over the precise point at which principle had been compromised. Rather than submit to an order that she refrain from social intercourse with blacks outside the school (such as receiving them in the parlor or eating or walking with them), Martha L. Kellogg, a teacher in Wilmington, North Carolina, requested a new assignment, even if it be "an isolated position." And if she could be boarded with a black family in her new post, that would be all the better. "I desire not [to] be identified with any policy that ignores or repudiates social equality, and I desire to be, where I can act freely in the matter, according to conscience and the gospel idea—to treat the colored people as I should whites in the same circumstances.... It seems to me that unless one engaged in mission work does feel this freedom, true effort is in a measure paralysed."[83]

Any veteran of the antislavery movement, remembering those abolitionists who made a point of parading their fraternization with blacks before a hostile northern public, would have recognized the problem instantly. He would have recalled how that question had plagued them throughout their history, producing divisiveness and even sundering numerous friendships. He might have named the prominent abolitionists who despite their zealous commitment to the cause, or because of it, scorned social relations with Negroes as impolitic and detrimental to the objectives for which both white and black activists fought. But for those who chose to question such tactics, whether in the abolitionist movement or in the freedmen's aid movement, the implications remained absolutely clear. Would not the measures deemed necessary to make the movement palatable to a hostile public reinforce the very conditions and attitudes the movement had initially set out to undermine? That question defied any easy resolution in the 1860s, much as it had in antislavery circles before the war.[84]

Having struggled through such problems in the old antislavery days, and eager to bury the sources of divisiveness, Lewis Tappan, who had made the transition from abolitionism to the freedmen's aid movement, drew upon his experience to advise prospective missionary teachers in the South.

> People of color have an intuitive apprehension of the feelings of those who profess to labor for their instruction and moral elevation. They are quick to distinguish between affected and real zeal on their behalf, between condescension and true regard, between outward conduct and the emotions of the heart, and, while confiding, they are also very jealous lest the inward should not correspond to the outward in our treatment of them. Little things often betray the actual state of the mind. Unsympathetic, cold and selfish persons can not, with all their pretense, deceive the instincts of those unsophisticated children of nature.

No matter how well-intended the advice, this veteran abolitionist failed to appreciate the still larger problem that would surface again in the postwar years and, even more forcefully, during Radical Reconstruction. For all of its good works and sacrifices, the freedmen's aid movement, like its antislavery predecessor, did little to reduce the dependency of blacks on white men and women for counsel and leadership. While Tappan was sharing his thoughts and experience with the white missionary teachers destined for the South, Richard H. Cain, the black minister, who would soon set out on that same pilgrimage, also drew on the past to urge that the traditional relationship between white and black reformers be reexamined. "We know how to serve others," the Reverend Cain observed in early 1865, "but, have not learned how to serve ourselves."

> We have always been *directed by others* in all the affairs of life: they have furnished the thoughts while we have been passive instruments, acting as we were acted upon, mere *automatons*. . . . The Anti-slavery Societies, the Abolition Societies, whose ostensible work has been to do battle for the Negro's elevation have never . . . thought it safe for them to advance colored men to places of trust.[85]

With emancipation, such questions assumed a new and critical importance. Few understood that more clearly than the Reverend Cain. If southern blacks needed instruction in how to act as free men and women, he suggested, both northern and southern blacks were desperately in need of experience "in the affairs of direction and government." The church and the schoolhouse seemed like ideal places in which to begin this necessary training. "We must take into our own hands the education of our race. . . . Honest, dignified whites may teach ever so well, it has not the effect to exalt the black man's opinion of his own race, because they have always been in the habit of seeing white men in honored positions, and respected." Anticipating by nearly half a century W. E. B. Du Bois's call for a "talented tenth" of educated, professional blacks whose leadership and example would help to uplift the mass of their people, the Reverend Cain, on the eve of his departure for Charleston, envisaged "an infusion of the intellectual development of the Northern colored men and women" into the South.

> Negro gentlemen and ladies must become teachers among them by example as well as by precept, teach them that though they be black, they are as good as any other class whose skin is whiter than theirs; teach them that complexions may differ but man is a man for all that. Finally, colored men in the North have got to come to this doctrine, that black men must think for themselves—act for themselves . . . [86]

## 9

BEFORE THE MISSIONARY SOCIETIES had dispatched their first schoolmarms to the South, and even as Union Army officers wrestled with the legal status of the contrabands, southern blacks had taken the first steps to teach themselves. Some of these pioneers belonged to the free Negro class, but among the early teachers were also newly freed or escaped slaves who had managed to acquire some rudimentary skills and now sought to share their knowledge with the less fortunate. In Hampton, Virginia, an elderly black who had been a slave of ex-President John Tyler opened a school in the basement of the abandoned Tyler mansion, while in that same neighborhood Mary Peake, a free Negro who had taught clandestinely before the war, seized the opportunity afforded by Union occupation to expand her teaching to include the newly created class of contrabands. "Some say we have not the same faculties and feelings with white folks," one of her pupils would observe. "What would the best soil produce without cultivation? We want to get wisdom. That is all we need. Let us get that, and we are made for time and eternity."[87]

The migration of black teachers from the North would gain headway later in the war, most of them the agents of black churches and the freedmen's aid societies. Charlotte Forten, who had previously taught school in New England and whose father had been active in the cause of black abolitionism and civil rights, accompanied the mostly white contingent of missionary teachers from Philadelphia to the Sea Islands of South Carolina, where she would spend nearly two years imparting not only basic reading and writing skills to her pupils but also an appreciation for the achievements of their race. "Talked to the children a little while to-day about the noble Toussaint [L'Ouverture]," she noted in her journal. "They listened very attentively. It is well that they sh'ld know what one of their color c'ld do for his race. I long to inspire them with courage and ambition (of a noble sort,) and high purpose." Perhaps more typical of the black missionary teachers was Virginia C. Green, who came to the Wood's plantation, on Davis Bend, Mississippi, where she set about organizing classes for 120 children. The freedmen sustained the school, four trustees chosen from among them controlled its operations, and in Miss Green they appear to have found a dedicated teacher. "I class myself with the freedmen," she wrote a Freedmen's Bureau officer. "Though I have never known servitude they are . . . my people. Born as far north as the lakes I have felt no freer because so many were less fortunate. . . . I look forward with impatience to the time when my people shall be strong, blest with education, purified and made prosperous by virtue and industry. The people on the plantation where I have labored I see tending slowly but steadily to this point."[88]

Not all the blacks who taught in the postwar South would have qualified for membership in Richard H. Cain's projected black intellectual elite. Fortunately for the Reverend Cain, who assumed a pastorate in Charleston, the individual who answered to the fullest his call for a talented elite to descend upon the South chose to settle in the same city. The credentials of Francis L. Cardozo were, indeed, impressive, exceeding those of most of the white teachers and superintendents. A freeborn mulatto, reputedly the son of a prominent Charleston economist and editor, Cardozo attended the University of Glasgow (from which he graduated with distinction), studied theology in Edinburgh and London, and returned to the United States to serve as pastor of the Temple Street Congregational Church in New Haven, Connecticut. Within weeks after the fall of Charleston, he resigned his pastorate to return to his native city as the principal of a Negro school operated under the auspices of the American Missionary Association. A complex and ambitious person, who found it difficult to brook any criticism, Cardozo shared with many of the white school officials a relatively low estimation of black teachers—at least in their present state of preparation. Presumably, the several blacks he employed on his own staff must have been distinguished, since Cardozo took considerable care in the selection and assignment of teachers and vowed to hire no blacks rather than one who might "disgrace" the entire cause. "I have placed the educated and experienced white Northern teachers in the highest and most responsible positions," he informed a northern AMA official, "and the colored ones in the lower and less responsible ones, where they may improve by the superiority of their *white* fellow-laborers, and whose positions afterwards they may be able to occupy." When subsequently confronted by two northern black teachers with his previously expressed preference for whites, Cardozo replied that he had always insisted upon competence in his staff members, regardless of color, and any reports to the contrary should be squelched since "it would hurt my influence very much."[89]

No visit to postwar Charleston was thought to be complete without calling on Cardozo and being guided through this showcase of the black educational effort in the South. To maintain that reputation, his critics would charge, he had begun to discriminate as carefully in the selection of pupils as in the assignment of teachers. By his own estimate, 200 of the 438 students in November 1867 were freeborn Negroes. Earlier that year, however, Sarah W. Stansbury, who had previously taught in Cardozo's school, expressed her immense relief over being transferred to a new post. "This is more like missionary work than any I have done since coming here. The children are all ex-slaves which is more than can be said of Mr. Cardozo's school—his own class and Mrs. Chippenfield's are composed, I should judge, entirely of freemen's children, so many of whom *owned slaves* before the war." What led to her break with Cardozo, she added, was his insistence that students who failed to pay their monthly tuition fees be sent home, thereby making the school even more exclusive. Still another former teacher charged that in the distribution of clothing gifts from the North, Cardozo had favored the children of "the *colored* people," who were best able to purchase such clothing, over "the *freed* people," who were by far the most needy. "I wish to do all I can for the *suffering* of any class," she wrote in protest; "but I am not willing to labor or beg for the 'free browns,' in a manner that will help to make the difference between them & the freed people, even greater than it was in slavery." Whether these various charges were valid or not may be less important than the characteristic way in which Cardozo dealt with them—he asked for the dismissal of both teachers.[90]

Like many of the missionary teachers and ministers, Cardozo assumed an active role in the community, aggressively defending the rights of blacks and warning against the "treacherous" class of whites seeking to regain political control of the state. Both his fame as an educator and his vigorous advocacy of civil rights propelled him into the political arena, and in 1867 he agreed to become a candidate for the constitutional convention. The way in which he chose to acknowledge the nomination was also characteristic. "I have no desire for the turbulent political scene," he wrote a friend in the North, "but being the *only educated colored* man here my friends thought it my duty to go if elected, and I consented to do so." That position ultimately launched a political career that culminated in his election as secretary of state of South Carolina.[91]

Although no doubt appreciating the talents of a Cardozo, the white officers and superintendents of the freedmen's aid societies might have also taken pains to note how truly exceptional he was compared to other black teachers. That was no less than what Cardozo himself would have conceded. Even if grudgingly, however, school officials came to recognize the strategic value of black teachers, both as examples for their people and because they were considered less likely than northern whites to incur "abuse and insult" in the interior counties. But in hiring black teachers, especially those who were native to the South, school administrators sometimes frankly confessed that they were sacrificing quality for color. The superintendent of the freedmen's schools in Montgomery, Alabama, defended the employment of three black instructors even though they were "inexperienced and defective in their mode of teaching." "We use them," he explained, "because they are of service to our cause. It is our policy to convert colored pupils into teachers as fast as possible. It is cheaper if not so beneficial and it has good effects in many ways." That explanation would not have impressed G. L. Eberhart, the state superintendent of freedmen's schools in Georgia. Like Cardozo, he advised "the most exacting care" in selecting black teachers. Unlike Cardozo, he expressed little confidence in their potential. "I am becoming daily more impressed with their total unfitness to assist in the moral and mental elevation of their own race. It appears as if Slavery had completely divested them of every moral attribute—every idea that leads to true moral rectitude."[92]

When the freedmen's aid societies and their educational representatives in the South scrutinized black candidates for teaching positions, their concern was not limited to questions of educational background and preparation. The experience with some black teachers made it incumbent upon the supervisors to avoid hiring anyone who might cause divisiveness within the harmonious "family" of teachers by agitating questions of social equality and fraternization. No matter how well qualified, a teacher who might be a source of controversy and embarrassment quickly outlived his or her welcome. In Wilmington, North Carolina, a freedmen's school official who would soon become the state superintendent of public instruction lavished considerable praise on one of the black women in his jurisdiction as "an excellent teacher and a faithful Christian." But he could neither tolerate nor understand her adamant refusal to be boarded with a black family rather than in the Mission House where the white teachers resided. "This is a delicate matter and must be handled in a delicate manner," he reported. Although anxious to hire qualified black teachers, he thought it unwise and inexpedient for them to come to the South in the company of white teachers or to board with white teachers.

> We are charged with endeavoring to bring about a condition of *social equality* between the blacks and the whites—we are charged with teaching the blacks that they have a right to demand from the whites social equality—now, if they can point to Mission families or teachers homes where there is complete social equality between colored and white, they have proved, to their own satisfaction at least, their assertion. They *can* say that if not in theory, we do in practice, teach social equality.

White teachers in any event could do more for the freedmen than black instructors, since "the colored people themselves, have more confidence in white teachers than in those of their own color."[93]

The question of where to quarter black teachers only pointed up the larger and persistent problem of how much social fraternization to permit and how far native white feelings and prejudices needed to be appeased. If black teachers assigned to the South had any way of knowing what to expect in this regard, that might have helped to ease tensions somewhat or at least given them the opportunity to reconsider their mission. Not until Blanche Harris and her sister had departed Oberlin for their new teaching posts in Natchez did the school official who accompanied them make it clear that public sentiment would not allow him to treat them in Mississippi as he had in Ohio. Although the two young black women in this instance preferred to board with a black family, "as we knew our influence would be greater if we were to board with our own people," they were asked instead to move into the Mission House, where they would room not with their white fellow teachers but with the domestic servants; moreover, Blanche Harris understood that her relations with the white teachers were to be kept at a minimum. "My room was to be my home," she observed in a letter protesting her treatment. Upon consulting with some of the local black residents, the Harris sisters resolved to rent a room in town rather than subject themselves to the double standard practiced in the Mission House. Before too many weeks had passed, however, they concluded that the school officials were determined to have them teach elsewhere in the county—or anyplace but Natchez.[94]

If some black teachers found it difficult to accept distinctions in living quarters between themselves and their white co-workers, still others came to resent the superintendents who treated them with exaggerated praise, but evaluated their classroom performance differently from that of their white peers. Outright hostility could be debilitating, but too much love from their co-workers might be equally demoralizing if it assumed the tone of condescension. To be confined to the least important positions or to be sent to the countryside while the choicer assignments in the cities were reserved for the better-educated whites also proved to be sources of friction, and some black teachers found the easy familiarity white superintendents presumed with them grating. How much longer, asked one discouraged black, would "our finely educated ladies" permit the same official to address them by their full names and title in Boston but only by their first name in the South? Such problems may have had their antecedents in the abolitionist movement, but few teachers took any comfort from that thought, if they were even aware of it. Too often, it appears, the sensitivities of black teachers were simply sacrificed to appease the sentiments of native whites and the ambivalent racial attitudes of some missionary educators. Whether subjected to the scowls of local citizens or to the paternal demeanor of co-workers, the black men and women who undertook the education of their southern brethren often had to rely on the inspiration of the classroom and the encouragement of the black community to sustain their efforts. "Sometimes we get discouraged and think we had better resign," Blanche Harris confessed at one point. "And then we know that we must suffer many things."[95]

The problems faced by the black teacher again pointed up the subservient role blacks were often forced to play in movements designed to assist their own people. Before the Civil War, differences over objectives, priorities, and roles, as well as growing concern over white patronization, had driven black abolitionists into independent agitation and organization, culminating in Martin R. Delany's emigrationist movement and Frederick Douglass' break with William Lloyd Garrison. The need for black activists to establish their own position and voice had also resulted in the National Convention of Colored Citizens in 1864. Although ideological and tactical differences between black and white activists may have been less marked when it came to educating the freedmen, the problem of how much responsibility should be assigned to blacks in that effort persisted, as did the need to define a relationship between the largely white freedmen's aid societies in the North and independent black activity in the South. "We do not object to any one coming South to teach, or superintend the education of our colored youth," a black editor wrote from Natchez in 1865, "but we would like to understand how it is that these missionary teachers desire so much to control all the school funds and property." When local blacks raised the money among themselves to purchase property for a school, as they did in several communities, why should they not exercise a larger voice—even the determining voice—in how that money was spent? Nor could this editor understand why the missionary societies presumed to send people to the South "who, while in the North make loud pretensions to Abolition, and when they get in the South partake so largely of that contemptible prejudice that they are ashamed to be seen in company with colored men."[96]

From the very outset, in fact, the movement to educate the freedmen had been biracial. The entrance of Union troops into a community often set in motion efforts among the black residents to collect sufficient funds to build a school and hire a teacher. When the blacks in Malden, West Virginia, the town to which Booker T. Washington and his family migrated after emancipation, discovered that a newly arrived eighteen-year-old black youth from Ohio knew how to read and write, they immediately hired him as a teacher and paid him whatever they could collect among themselves. In Natchez, the tuition fees collected from the pupils' parents sustained six schools for freedmen taught by black teachers; the black residents of Helena, Arkansas, voted to ask the Freedmen's Bureau to tax them for the support of schools for their children; in Nashville and Savannah, within weeks of Union occupation, blacks had organized their own school systems. In nearly every part of the South, reports of self-sustaining black schools suggested an impressive effort with a minimum of outside assistance. Nor should the commendable and extensive activity of the freedmen's aid societies obscure the effort mounted by the black churches, some of which preferred to establish their own schools side by side with those maintained by the white societies.[97]

What relationships these independent black efforts should enjoy with the northern benevolent societies posed a recurring problem, and the experience of Savannah in this regard suggested an all too familiar resolution of the problem. When the black citizens of that city convened in the aftermath of Union occupation, they heard the Reverend James Lynch and other dignitaries urge them to organize among themselves and develop their own programs and courses of action. Acting on this call, they formed the Savannah Educational Association to establish in turn a system of schools for the freedmen which would be managed and sustained by the community. But when the Reverend S. W. Magill, an agent of the American Missionary Association, came to Savannah and assessed the situation, he was appalled that neither the black board of education nor the black teachers possessed any experience in the management of schools or in teaching. "What a field opens before the benevolent!" he informed a northern officer of the Association. "It will not do of course to leave these people to themselves. . . . I fear they will be jealous & sullen if I attempt to place the management in the hands of our white teachers. But this must be done to make the schools effective." Ultimately, that was accomplished, but not until the director persuaded the black trustees to place confidence in their white friends. "It is a great point gained that they are convinced by their experience that they are not Sufficient of themselves."[98]

What transpired in Savannah suggested the forcefulness of a common assumption underscoring the missionary effort in the South—that black people emerging from the debilitating thralldom of bondage would require for some time the counsel and direction of their white allies. Even as they advised blacks to depend more on their own efforts and sought to inculcate black children with the virtues of self-help and self-reliance, these same "friends" might withhold their support or fail to encourage independent black efforts, question the wisdom and expediency of such efforts, or oppose them outright if they threatened to undermine their own authority. Observing this phenomenon as early as 1864, a black critic had to wonder why societies established for the relief and education of the freedmen, in which blacks initially played a prominent role, invariably fell into the hands of white managers, many of whom seemed to mistrust "the ability of colored men to do anything without the aid of the Saxon brain."[99]

Despite the occasional setbacks and discouragement, the energy expended by blacks to educate their children, like the simultaneous movement to worship by themselves, reflected a growing if not fully developed sense of community and racial pride, even as it sharpened the separation from and accentuated the differences with both their northern friends and native whites. It was not as though blacks consciously adopted a policy of self-imposed separation. But there did emerge a growing conviction that full admission to white society might have to be achieved through the development of independent and separate movements, organizations, and institutions. This would require not only self-recognition as a people and a community but the willingness to act on that consciousness. Neither illiteracy nor poverty, they also came to realize, would be extinguished in their own lifetimes, but even the poor and the illiterate in American society —white and black—possessed certain rights and could claim protection in the exercise of those rights. Ultimately, an elderly and illiterate freedman suggested, education would eliminate illiteracy among his people. But in exercising their freedom and attacking the critical problems that now beset them, they could ill afford to depend upon "book larnin' " alone.

> De Chaplain say we can learn to read in short time. Now dat may be so with dem who are mo' *heady*. God has not made all of us alike. Phaps some *will* get an education in a little while. I *knows* de *next generation*

*will.* But we'se a down trodden people. We hasn't had no chance at all. De most of us are slow and dull. We has bin kep down a *hundred years* and *I* think it will take a *hundred years to get us back agin.* Derefo' Mr Chaplain, I tink we better not wait for education.[100]

To define themselves as a people and to act upon their grievances, blacks in every one of the ex-Confederate states would begin to organize at some level. Freedmen and freeborn alike, the educated and the illiterate, preachers and field hands, teachers and artisans gathered together after church services, in the new schoolhouses, in town meetings, and in county and state conventions to discuss their condition and to frame a response. Previously barred by law, such meetings now took on additional significance as they set the stage for the entrance of freedmen into the political arena and for the fullest expression of their new status as black citizens.

# Chapter Ten

---

# BECOMING A PEOPLE

*We feel to bee a people.*

—A. H. HAINES,
BEAUFORT, SOUTH CAROLINA, OCTOBER 19, 1865[1]

*We want representative men, without regard to color, as long as they carry the brand of negro oppression. We need power and intellectual equality with the whites. It does not matter whether he be a pretty or ugly negro; a black negro or a mulatto. Whether he were a slave or a free negro; the question is, is he a negro at all? . . . We want power; it only comes through organization, and organization comes through unity. Our efforts must be one and inseparable, blended, tied, and bound together.*

—HENRY MCNEAL TURNER,
AUGUSTA, GEORGIA, JANUARY 4, 1866[2]

THE SCENE HAD NO REAL PRECEDENTS. Seeking to underscore that fact, a white reporter thought it nothing less than "the great sensation of the day" and a harbinger of "great and dreaded innovations." On September 29, 1865, more than 115 black men, most of them only recently slaves, filed into the African Methodist Episcopal Church in Raleigh, North Carolina, designated themselves a Convention of Freedmen, and elected a northern-born black minister who had never experienced slavery to preside over their deliberations. They had come together from all parts of the state, chosen in some fashion by their people and instructed by them to find ways to eradicate the legal inequities of the past that still circumscribed their new freedom. Meanwhile, several blocks from this site, the same number of white men, some of them former slaveholders, assembled in a legislative chamber to frame a civil government for North Carolina and to determine what they could preserve of a seemingly shattered past.

The dramatic contrasts in the meeting halls and purposes of these two conventions extended as well to the political and economic power whites and blacks wielded and to the occupations, class biases, attire, and formal education of the respective bodies. The distinctions in native intelligence and capacity for self-government were less discernible. Although the delegates to the Constitutional Convention were more literate, how they used their accumulated intelligence in the next six days of deliberations made that advantage less than obvious. If some of them retained charitable feelings for the former slave, in the belief that he bore no responsibility for his freedom, that did not mean they would entertain any foolish notions about his right to participate in the political life of the state.

Located in a back street of Raleigh, the church in which the Freedmen's Convention assembled was a modest wooden structure, scantily furnished, able to accommodate about 300 persons on the floor and another 100 in the gallery. During the four days of the convention, every seat would be filled with delegates and interested spectators, most of them also black. Affixed to the wall directly behind the pulpit, a lifelike bust of the martyred Abraham Lincoln remained shrouded in mourning more than five months after his assassination, and the inscription overhead repeated the classic words of his last inaugural address: "With malice toward none, with charity for all, with firmness in the right." That proved to be the spirit of this unique gathering. Several of the delegates, however, among them Abraham H. Galloway, a light-skinned man whose black mother had been a slave of the distinguished Galloway family, would have preferred less charity, more firmness, and at least a suggestion of malice if charity and firmness yielded no results. Whatever might have been Galloway's blood ties to the aristocratic clan whose name he bore, he harbored no affection for his former owners. Having escaped to Ohio in 1857, where he became an ardent abolitionist, Galloway returned to his native state after the war exuding what one observer called an "exceedingly radical and Jacobinical spirit." At this Raleigh gathering, he would agree to compromise his advocacy of immediate and universal manhood suffrage only if an educational test for voting was applied equally to both races. But he thought it unlikely that white North Carolinians would wish to disfranchise more than half of their eligible voters. And he refused to believe the threats of leading whites to exile themselves if blacks won political equality. "It wouldn't be six months," he thought, "before they would be putting their arms around our necks and begging us to vote [for] them for office."

Although Galloway called the Raleigh convention to order, the dominant mood was quickly established by the man the delegates chose as their permanent chairman—James W. Hood. Born in Pennsylvania, Hood had been a minister in Bridgeport, Connecticut, before coming South in 1864 as a missionary for the African Methodist Episcopal Zion Church. The election of a northern-born black to preside over a gathering of ex-slaves did not go unchallenged. "I myself am an adopted citizen of the State," Hood said in his defense, "having lived here for some two years, and if I am not a citizen here, I am not a citizen of any State." Upon hearing that some delegates were displeased with his election, he offered to resign, but the convention would not hear of it. In his opening address, Hood implored the delegates to refrain from "harsh language" and recrimination. "I say that we and the white people have to live here together. . . . We have been living together for a hundred years and more, and we have got to live together still; and the best way is to harmonize our feelings as much as possible, and to treat all men respectfully. Respectability will always gain respect . . ."

Voicing a similar moderation, James H. Harris, a native of North Carolina, emerged as the most influential figure of this and subsequent gatherings. Although born a slave, he had obtained his freedom in 1850 (his certificate of freedom described him as a nineteen-year-old "dark mulatoe" with a scar upon his head), migrated to Ohio, where he received some formal education, visited Liberia and Sierra Leone to observe the Afro-American settlements there, and returned to the United States in 1863 to help recruit blacks for military service. Two years later, as a delegate from Raleigh to the Freedmen's Convention, he shared with his new colleagues the results of his varied experiences. He had met enough northern whites, he told them, to know that the "intelligent white class in the South" remained the "best friends" of colored people. He had seen enough of the North to know the depth of racial animosities in that region, manifested in the exclusion of blacks from most non-menial employments and in wartime riots that ranked among the most "diabolical and murderous" exhibitions of racial hatred in history. He had come to recognize, too, that only the law of military necessity, not a benevolent crusade of the Union Army, had freed his people. Finally, his travels elsewhere in the world—"40,000 miles in search of a better country"—had convinced him that neither Africa nor the West Indies were places of asylum for American blacks. The freedmen's place was here on southern soil, and the only way to win the confidence of white men was to work faithfully and show "a patient and respectful demeanor." This was no time for recrimination, nor was this the proper moment for radical manifestos. If the present tensions and ill feeling were only permitted to subside, the freedmen would surely "receive what they had a right to claim." After all, he suggested, God was on their side, and he envisioned "a glorious future" for the black race in the South.

Like many of the postwar black conventions, the Raleigh conclave came to be dominated by those who thought it more expedient to request than to demand and who preferred to take their stand on the more abstract and less controversial principle of equality before the law rather than immediate admission to all political privileges. The effect of speeches such as those of Hood and Harris not only blunted the radicalism symbolized by Galloway but did much, said one relieved reporter, to disabuse the minds of fearful whites about the intent of these unprecedented and only recently prohibited meetings. Nevertheless, the delegates sometimes took a position at variance with this deliberately cultivated tone of moderation. The resolution revering the memory of John Brown would hardly have endeared them to the great mass of southern whites. Nor would native whites have appreciated the resolution praising the efforts of "that portion of the Republican party of which Messrs. Chase and Sumner and Stevens and Greeley are the heads" to secure blacks their rights through congressional action. And even as James Hood made his plea for conciliation, he rejected any return to the old days of subserviency, declared that blacks had waited long enough for their rights, and scoffed at the notion that they were unprepared to exercise those rights.

> People used to say it was not the time to abolish slavery, and used to tell us to wait until the proper time arrived; but it would only seem reasonable that the more slaves there were, the more difficult it would be to set them free. The best way is to give the colored man rights at once, and then they will practice them and the sooner know how to use them.

Nor did he hesitate to enumerate the rights which properly belonged to black people, as much as to their white fellow citizens.

> First, *the right to testify in courts of justice,* in order that we may defend our property and our rights. Secondly, *representation in the jury box.* It is the right of every man accused of any offence, to be tried by a jury of his peers. . . . Thirdly and finally, *the black man should have the right to carry his ballot to the ballot box.* These are the rights that we want—that we will contend for—and that, by the help of God, we will have, God being our defender.

That could hardly have been clearer. But the Appeals, Addresses, and Petitions adopted by the convention, and intended largely for white audiences, often failed to reflect the aggressive spirit with which individual blacks pressed their demands in speeches intended for their fellow delegates and the black spectators. With the Constitutional Convention meeting nearby, the Freedmen's Convention drew up an Address to that body which was the very model of circumspection—"moderate in tone," a white reporter wrote of it, and "unexceptionable in its phraseology and demands." Avoiding the issues of testimony in the courts, representation on juries, and suffrage, the Address acknowledged instead the powerlessness of the freedmen, their dependence upon "moral appeals to the hearts and consciences of the people," and their confidence in the "justice, wisdom, and patriotism" of the Constitutional Convention. Surely, that body would protect the interests of "all classes," including a people who were now "helpless" after 250 years of slavery, who had been raised in intimate association with the dominant race, and who in the Civil War had "remained throughout obedient and passive." Although they had no wish to return to slavery, they chose to emphasize the positive side of that sense of mutual obligations which had bound the masters and the slaves together. Rather than look to the North for protection and sympathy, they preferred to win their rights by "industry, sobriety and respectful demeanor." But whites needed to reciprocate this commitment by compensating them properly for their labor, by respecting the sanctity of their family relations, by providing for the education of their children, and by abolishing "oppressive laws" which made racial distinctions. "Is this asking too much?" the Address concluded.

The moderate tone of their appeals, the conspicuous omissions, the humble posture were all consistent with the conciliatory spirit that dominated the convention. The Raleigh newspapers, as did several northern reporters who were present, quickly lauded the Address as a product of good sense—"a wonderfully conservative document, undisfigured by the marks of levelling radicalism." Under the circumstances, the Constitutional Convention treated the Address with courtesy, while failing to act on the issues it raised. Like the "respect" and "confidence" which blacks accorded that body, the "courtesy" with which the whites responded seemed like so much playacting, with each side recognizing the inevitability of a prolonged struggle between them. Outside of the convention hall, the white delegates breathed precisely that spirit. "The niggers are having a convention, a'n't they?" one delegate asked a northern reporter. "What do they want? Equal rights, I suppose. How do they talk, anyhow? Going to vote, be they?" When informed that the blacks had been quite moderate in their speeches and that their principal demand had been the right to testify in the courts, the delegate quickly replied, "No, sir; they won't get that. It wouldn't do at all. No, sir. . . . The people won't have niggers giving evidence. They'll never get that. The people won't have it."

The tactics of accommodation failed to yield the expected concessions. If anything, the state's white leadership might have been encouraged to think they could return to the antebellum racial code with a minimum of resistance. Fortunately, the Freedmen's Convention had not left everything to the white man's sense of fair play. Before dispersing, the delegates agreed to organize a state Equal Rights League, instructed that organization to press for the repeal of all discriminatory laws, and proposed cooperation with any national group which might be formed with similar objectives. When the National Equal Rights League convened less than a month later in Cleveland, Ohio, James Harris was there to represent North Carolina. Alluding to his extensive travels, Harris declared on this occasion that he had found that "white men are white men" the world over.[3]

Less than a year after the Freedmen's Convention, blacks again gathered in the AME Church in Raleigh for a statewide meeting, but this time the rhetoric, the resolutions, and the appeals took on a more aggressive tone, as if to suggest that a year of "moderation" and "conciliation" had been sufficient time to test white intentions and intransigence. This time, too, the delegates recited their grievances with far more openness and with an obvious impatience: "In the counties of Jones, Duplin, Craven, Hyde, Halifax, and many others in this State, outrages are committed, such as killing, shooting and robbing the unprotected people for the most trifling offences, and, in frequent instances, for no offence at all." The perpetrators of this violence, the convention declared, were permitted to roam freely without any arrest for their crimes. Rather than appeal to the state legislature for a redress of grievances, the delegates expressed their "profound gratitude" for the recent actions of Congress, particularly the Freedmen's Bureau bill, the Civil Rights bill, and the proposed Fourteenth Amendment. They denounced taxation without representation as "in direct violation of the sacred rights of American citizens." And they urged blacks in every county, district, and village to organize branches of the Equal Rights League, so that the Federal government and the entire world would learn of the cruelties to which the freed slaves were being subjected.[4]

On January 14, 1868, delegates poured into Raleigh for still another Constitutional Convention to draft a new government and document for the state. But this body differed strikingly from its predecessor, both in spirit and in composition. This time blacks were not meeting separately several blocks away, drawing up "moral appeals" to the white conscience; instead, fifteen black delegates, duly elected by the eligible voters of the state, took their seats with the white delegates and prepared to participate fully in the deliberations. Presumably, the grievances and demands of the freed slaves would be reflected in the final results of the convention. Among others, James H. Harris, James W. Hood, and Abraham H. Galloway were on hand to make certain.

2

THE FREEDMEN'S CONVENTIONS marked the political debut of southern blacks. What made them so unprecedented was that men who had only recently been slaves, along with freeborn blacks, were expressing themselves in ways that had only recently been banned, gathering together for the first time, exchanging experiences, discussing the problems they faced in their particular counties, and sharing visions of a new South and a "redeemed" race. The scenes acted out in Raleigh were being duplicated in Mobile, Charleston, New Orleans, Vicksburg, Alexandria, Augusta, Nashville, Lexington, and Little Rock. Within a year after Appomattox, in nearly every ex-Confederate state, the local political activity which had begun with Federal occupation and the rallies celebrating emancipation culminated in the election of delegates to statewide conventions. And out of these gatherings would emerge a black leadership that would soon be called upon to help in the task of political reconstruction.

Perhaps as important as the conventions themselves was the local political activity that preceded them and the initial politicization of large numbers of blacks, both in the urban centers and in the countryside. Typical of such activity, the blacks of Edgecombe County, North Carolina, met in Tarboro to elect delegates to the state convention; they also took up a collection to defray the expenses of the trip to Raleigh and instructed the delegates on the most pressing concerns in their respective locales. The election of delegates might reveal as much about prevailing sentiments as the resolutions these local meetings passed. In Thomasville, Georgia, for example, blacks met in a grove near the edge of town and elected the Reverend Jared Wade, a literate clergyman and teacher, over Giles Price, an educated and fairly affluent blacksmith who had been free before the war and who had apparently offended some of his people by the generous and conspicuous support he had given the Confederacy.[5]

Where the election of delegates in mass meetings proved to be impossible or too dangerous, they were apt to be chosen after church services, by informal gatherings, or by clandestine neighborhood conferences. Even so, the cost and difficulty of travel to the state conventions kept some elected delegates away, while others might refuse to attend unless promised Federal protection when they returned to their homes. The absence of troops or of Federal officials had a way of reducing representation from the back-country or up-country counties, as in Louisiana and South Carolina. Ignoring the advice of local whites and threats to their lives and jobs, some delegates came to the state meetings at considerable personal and economic risk; others made a point of leaving during the night and returning with the least amount of notice, while some never returned after the local newspaper noted their presence at the convention. Isham Swett, a self-educated former slave and a barber in Fayetteville, North Carolina, attended the state conclave in Raleigh as a delegate. When the news became known, his white customers immediately withdrew their patronage. After attending the state convention in Macon, Georgia, several delegates remained in that city rather than return to their homes, fearing the strong stand they had taken on equal suffrage and civil rights would expose them instantly to roving white gangs. During the Convention of the Colored People of Virginia, Peter K. Jones, a delegate from Petersburg, asked, "Why are not more of you here?" and then suggested the answer: "Some of our people have been paid to stay away by our former masters. They told us that coming here would hurt us at home." At the same convention, a delegate from Williamsburg recited the difficulties in securing representation from his region, with former slaveholders doing everything in their power to prevent elected delegates from attending.[6]

Despite the absentees, most of the statewide conventions brought together a remarkable cross section of the black population. The sharp contrasts in attire, complexion, and demeanor, and the equally apparent differences in background and education, again impressed outside observers with the uniqueness of these assemblages. There were black soldiers in uniform, and nearly every convention recognized their symbolic importance by appointing at least one of them to some official position. Ministers appeared in substantial numbers, some of them dressed in black broadcloth and several of them only recently chaplains in the black regiments. If lawyers, farmers, and planters dominated the white constitutional conventions, clergymen, teachers, carpenters, mechanics, hotel waiters, barbers, household servants (including the former body servant of Jefferson Davis), and plantation hands made up the bulk of the black conventions. In Louisiana, where the freeborn mulattoes of New Orleans had met frequently since Federal occupation, the Convention of Colored Men that assembled in January 1865 was the first time delegates from the country parishes had participated, and that scene elicited a special comment from a black editor:

> There were seated side by side the rich and the poor, the literate and educated man, and the country laborer, hardly released from bondage, distinguished only by the natural gifts of the mind. There, the rich landowner, the opulent tradesman, seconded motions offered by humble mechanics and freedmen. Ministers of the gospel, officers and soldiers of the U.S. army, men who handle the sword or the pen, merchants and clerks, —all the classes of society were represented, and united in a common thought: the actual liberation from social and political bondage. It was a great spectacle, and one which will be remembered for generations to come.[7]

The leadership that emerged at the freedmen's conventions gained valuable experience for the roles many of them would subsequently play in Radical Reconstruction. Among the delegates to the state convention that assembled in Charleston in November 1865, for example, were a future lieutenant governor, state supreme court justice, and secretary of state of South Carolina, as well as several men destined to serve in the legislature and the United States Congress. The quality of black leadership, in South Carolina and elsewhere, immediately impressed outside observers, even skeptical native whites who had found the concept of blacks in such roles as either distasteful or incomprehensible. What remained open to question, however, was whether or not a "leader" commanded a significant following and constituency or was simply a self-appointed spokesman whose claims rested on his education, occupation, or northern origins. That was never an easy question to answer, though clergymen, who were in the most advantageous position to gather a following around them, tended to dominate postwar black political life.

In the early stages of organizational activity, especially in places like Charleston and New Orleans, the old free black communities contributed a disproportionate share of the leadership. But that dominance did not necessarily endure, particularly as some freed slaves quickly acquired an education and began to accumulate property. "It is remarkable," thought Richard H. Cain, who had come to Charleston in 1865, "that the former leading men in these parts, those whom we would have recognized as the great minds of the South among the colored people, have relapsed into secondary men; and the class who were hardly known, have come forward and assumed a bold front, and are asserting their manhood." In some states, moreover, as in Mississippi, blacks who had been free before the war were considered too dependent on whites to be entrusted with positions of leadership.[8]

Equally important in the early stages of political organization were northern blacks, most of them missionaries and teachers, who came to the South during and after the war, in some instances returning to a native land from which they had become exiles. Henry M. Turner, a freeborn South Carolinian who had already distinguished himself as an army chaplain and AME organizer, opened the Freedmen's Convention in Georgia in 1866 and shared political leadership in that state with Tunis G. Campbell, a Massachusetts-born black and Freedmen's Bureau agent who had established a virtually independent governnment in the Georgia Sea Islands. Richard H. Cain (a native of Virginia) and Francis L. Cardozo (a native of South Carolina), both of them ministers in Connecticut during the war, came to South Carolina in time to participate in the early convention movement, thereby joining an illustrious group that also included, as recent arrivals from the North, Martin R. Delany (a native of Virginia) and Jonathan J. Wright (a native of Pennsylvania), both of whom served for a time as Freedmen's Bureau agents.[9]

But the bulk of the delegates to the conventions were themselves freedmen who came out of the virtual anonymity of slavery to participate in the political life of their localities and states. Some of them were house servants and artisans who had acquired a rudimentary education and a degree of acculturation to white values; still others had spent their bondage in the fields and quarters, having little contact with whites except for the owner and overseer. For many of the freedmen, whatever their varied experiences in slavery, military service had exposed them for the first time to the outside world and helped to accelerate the transition from bondage to political activism and leadership. In South Carolina, Robert Smalls managed to construct a loyal constituency in the Sea Islands on the basis of his wartime exploits, as did Prince Rivers, a former coachman in Beaufort and a sergeant in the Union Army, who had impressed Colonel Higginson as a man "of apparently inexhaustible strength and activity" with extraordinary leadership powers. "He makes Toussaint perfectly intelligible; and if there should ever be a black monarchy in South Carolina, he will be its king."[10]

Not many of the freedmen in the black conventions initially assumed leadership roles. More often, the ministers, as the most educated and articulate members, effectively controlled the proceedings by displaying their oratorical talents and their political knowledge and, if necessary, by manipulating the finer points of parliamentary procedure with which most of the delegates were unfamiliar. But even if many of the ex-slaves "sat mute on the benches," as one observer described them, the delegates who most underscored the remarkable character of these conventions were those who came dressed in the cheapest homespun clothes, who could neither read nor write, whose faces and bodies still bore the marks of their recent bondage, and who spoke a language, said one reporter, "that no northern white man can understand." The only comparable assemblages in their experience had been for religious purposes, and if they spoke at all during the proceedings they might on occasion approximate in their gestures, shouts, and singsong oratory the rural prayer meetings they knew so intimately.[11]

When the ex-slave delegates pressed their grievances before the conventions, they lacked the style, the propensity for intellectual abstractions, and the ability to embellish their points with literary and biblical references that characterized, sometimes all too ostentatiously, their ministerial colleagues. But they spoke from their own individual experiences. "My dear brothers," one of them declared, "I don't place myself in this honorable convention as a Henry Clay or a Webster, fur I know I kin not do it, nor to speak afore you. I know I's a poor, destituted, onlarnt don't-know-A-from-B. I's been rocked in a hard cradle, from my youth up to the present age." Occasionally, they would rise to familiarize the delegates with conditions in their respective counties; some of them lost their patience altogether and scolded their more experienced colleagues for wasting precious time in parliamentary wrangling and trivialities and urged them to get on with the more pressing issues of freedom from economic oppression and the two-faced judicial system—issues that they confronted in their daily lives. Whatever their limitations in education and vocabulary, they often projected a wisdom that few of the wordy ministers and northern-educated delegates could surpass. "There is an eloquence in experience," one black reporter wrote after hearing an ex-slave relate the problems his people confronted, "which can never be had elsewhere; no, not even by the most polished culture of the schools." And if the white newspapers chose to dwell upon the ungrammatical utterances and plantation speech of some delegates, and mock their pretensions to oratory, several of the more literate blacks who were present saw no reason to be embarrassed. "I hope the reporters will take me down as saying 'dis,' 'dat,' 'de oder,' and the 'deformities of de constitution,'" James D. Lynch told the State Convention of the Colored People of Tennessee. "I know more of syntax than all of them put together." Nor would he tolerate the demeaning ways in which whites addressed black people, both the ex-slaves and the freeborn, outside the convention hall. "A white man said to me this morning, 'Well, Uncle, how are you getting along?' I was glad to know that I had a white nephew."[12]

That these were conventions of black people, called and managed and financed by black people, was a source of considerable pride. Although whites (usually Freedmen's Bureau officers) were invited to address them, and dignitaries (like Horace Greeley) sent messages replete with moral injunctions, the delegates wished to make clear that they were not the dupes of white men. A delegate to the Virginia freedmen's convention proudly asserted that the Appeal to the American People, which had just been read aloud, was "the production of our own people, and not the work of our northern friends." He knew the charge would be made and he wanted to forestall it. The point would have to be made more than once, that having been controlled and manipulated as slaves, they had no desire to perpetuate that relationship in freedom, even with whites who claimed to be their liberators. After all, some would argue, the underlying purpose of these meetings was to show the world that black people, most of them only recently slaves, were perfectly capable of coming together to discuss and act upon the critical issues of the day. In New Orleans, after a Federal official criticized the actions of a recent colored convention, the *Tribune* lashed out at his presumptuousness. "He seemed unwilling to understand that the Convention felt as colored men feel, while Mr. Conway could only feel as a white man feels. . . . We need no apprenticeship to take the place of slavery, no social minors, no political children."[13]

To proclaim their independence of white influence did not always make it so. Actually, the question of what relations they should sustain with their white friends remained an ongoing source of divisiveness within the ranks of black leadership. The matter came to a head at the Freedmen's Convention of Georgia in early 1866 when a majority committee report nominated a white Freedmen's Bureau official as president of the newly formed Georgia Equal Rights Association, while a minority report nominated a black clergyman. After some debate, the delegates elected the white man, who proceeded to commend them for the wisdom they had exercised "in choosing your President from among your white friends." But in Mobile, Alabama, when a black meeting considered a proposal to make a white man the editor of their newspaper, at least one participant strongly dissented. Such an appointment, he argued, would acknowledge that blacks still needed whites to act and think for them. "There is none but colored men that can truly sympathize with their race! None but those who have been subjected to the degrading influence of slavery that can truthfully lay our grievances before the world and claim its sympathy!"[14]

Since their white friends from the North were thought to be nearer to the sources of power, some blacks thought it in their best interests to cultivate close relationships, even at the risk of compromising their own independence. Still others deferred to them as men of experience and education who were in advantageous positions, whether as Freedmen's Bureau agents or the representatives of benevolent societies, to render them immediate relief and assistance. But in those places where a black leadership quickly emerged in the aftermath of the war, impatience with white dictation and advice manifested itself from the very outset. Not surprisingly, the *New Orleans Tribune* voiced the strongest opinions on this question. Without intending any disrespect for "our white friends," and while appreciating "the disinterestedness, the courage, the sound sense and the fraternal feeling they have displayed during their long crusade in behalf of liberty," the newspaper insisted that black people make their own policies, decide on priorities, and select leaders from among themselves. "Who can better know our interest than we do? Who is more competent to discern what is good for us than we are?" How blacks answered those questions went to the very heart of their freedom, and the *Tribune* thought their white friends could best demonstrate their friendship by immediately conceding that fact.

If we are men—as our friends contend we are—we are able to attend to our own business. There is no man in the world so perfectly identified with our own interest as to understand it better than we do ourselves. We listen respectfully to the addresses of our white friends; but we must deliberate and decide for ourselves. . . . We need friends, it is true; but we do not need tutors. The age of guardianship is past forever. We now think for ourselves, and we shall act for ourselves. [15]

Although blacks demonstrated a healthy skepticism about how much reliance they should place on their white friends, they were not always agreed on the amount of confidence they could place in themselves and in their own leaders and movements. With the critical problems they faced, and the need to project an image of harmony and responsibility to a skeptical white America, blacks could ill afford the factional struggles, acrimonious debates, and conflicts of personal ambition that pitted the dark-skinned against the light-skinned, the ex-slave against the freeborn, the native against the northern-born. No matter how often black leaders, newspapers, and meetings called for unity, the advent of freedom had a way of exacerbating old differences and introducing new divisions. During the Convention of the Freedmen of North Carolina, for example, one delegate could not restrain himself after a light-skinned Negro had criticized him for daring to oppose the northern-born black they had chosen for chairman. "I didn't come here," he shouted, "and no other man of this convention didn't come here, sir, to have the whip of slavery cracked over us by no slaveholder's son." With similar disdain, some blacks who had been free before the war resented being called "freedmen" and tried in every way to dissociate themselves from the former slaves.[16]

The sources of such divisiveness were familiar enough, reflecting as they did deeply rooted distinctions not only of color but of class, education, income, occupation, and acculturation to white society. Aside from being more literate and affluent than the ex-slaves, the mulattoes and free Negroes who made up the colored elites in cities like New Orleans, Charleston, and Washington, D.C., tended to lead a separate social life, married within their group, attended different churches, and preferred to send their children to private schools rather than to the newly established freedmen's schools. The Brown Fellowship Society of Charleston, which admitted only well-to-do mulattoes, and the Lotus Club of Washington, D.C., which excluded freedmen, exemplified the more extreme manifestations of this caste consciousness. Even the haughtiest house servants of Charleston and Washington, D.C., while thinking themselves superior to the "country niggers" who flocked to their cities after the war, might have been barred from "colored society" unless they possessed the necessary ancestral credentials.[17]

Having experienced the hostility of freeborn blacks, a newly freed slave found difficulty in making any sense out of it. "The free fellows felt themselves better than the slave, because of the fact, I suppose, that they were called free, while in reality they were no more free than the slave, until the war set both classes free." The problem he described became particularly acute in Washington, D.C., where upwards of 40,000 emancipated slaves from Virginia and Maryland confirmed the worst fears of inundation. Many of those who made up the old free Negro class, which had numbered less than 10,000 in 1860, reacted by withdrawing into their own social orbit, as if to draw a boundary between themselves and the "contrabands." John E. Bruce, an ex-slave who migrated to Washington with his mother during the war, would some years later pen a caustic commentary on the "fust families" that composed the colored elite of the nation's capital. The older citizens, he noted, manifested an exclusiveness that often bordered on the ludicrous. With an insatiable "love of display" and a frequently proclaimed pride in their ancestry ("forever and ever informing the uninitiated what a narrow escape they had from being born white"), they tried to assume the airs and manners of colored aristocrats "and wouldn't be caught dead with an ordinary Negro." If they lacked the means to live as aristocrats, they made up for it by their recollections of previous service to white dignitaries. "He has seen Daniel Webster, Henry Clay, Ben Wade and Joshua R. Giddings. He used to shave these great luminaries, which is the only consolation that the memories of departed days can now give him."[18]

Whether based on color or previous status, the distinctions separating blacks seldom assumed such importance outside of the few large urban centers. To make too much of the pretentiousness exhibited by members of these small elites would be to overlook the degree to which most mulattoes, free Negroes, and former slaves had always worked and lived together, sharing a common condition and plight and generally too preoccupied with survival and a hostile white society to cultivate any caste pretensions. When imposing restrictions and reinforcing racial segregation, moreover, whites would pay no attention to gradations of color or to the previous status of blacks. What a northern-born black leader observed of white attitudes in 1876 was no less true ten years earlier: "They call everybody a negro that is as black as the ace of spades or as white as snow, if they think he is a negro or know that he has negro blood in his veins."[19]

The sources of divisiveness persisted among blacks, and internal strife would occasionally surface and weaken their movements. But the common hostility they confronted usually forced the various groups that made up the black community to minimize and surmount their differences. Even in the large cities, the colored elites came to understand the futility of divorcing their cause from that of the mass of freedmen. "They must stand or fall together," the *New Orleans Tribune* proclaimed, and this mulatto organ consistently urged unity between the freemen and the freedmen.[20] Not simply the experience of a common oppression united them but the conviction that they could overcome it together. The black convention movement, as a vehicle for this unity, would play a major role in defining a common future.

WITH THE END OF THE WAR, black hopes and expectations seemed almost boundless. "Never was there a brighter prospect before any people," Richard H. Cain wrote from South Carolina, "than that presented to the colored people of the Southern states."[21] To take a conciliatory approach toward the former ruling class, now reeling under its wartime losses but still possessing considerable economic power, appeared to make sound political sense. If they could only share the future with whites, as equal participants in the body politic, black spokesmen vowed they would keep the peace, harbor no ill feelings or recriminations about the past, and no longer feel the need to look to the North for protection and sympathy. That hope (and implied threat if it were not realized) underlay much of the moderation that characterized the early postwar political activity of southern blacks.

Exulting in their freedom, but perceiving at the same time their powerlessness and vulnerability, the black conventions framed their addresses and manifestos for consideration by the state constitutional conventions and legislatures. Invariably, they appealed to the "wisdom, sense of justice, and magnanimous generosity" they expected from those bodies and which they professed to find in the hearts and minds of the white South. The pose they struck of a long-suffering but patient people seemed best calculated to win the approval of their white countrymen, many of whom had only recently come to know the true meaning of suffering, the separation of families, and defeat. The Convention of Colored People that gathered in Charleston in late 1865 grounded its appeal to "the White Inhabitants of South Carolina" in precisely that spirit:

> We have not come together in battle array to assume a boastful attitude and to talk loudly of high-sounding principles, or of unmeaning platitudes; nor do we pretend to any great boldness; for we remember your former wealth and greatness, and we know our poverty and weakness; and although we feel keenly our wrongs, still we come together, we trust, in a spirit of meekness and of patriotic good-will toward all the people of the State. [22]

To emphasize the mutuality of interest upon which a new South would rise, blacks attending the freedmen's conventions dwelled upon their own southern roots and how their lives, experiences, and destinies were interwoven with those of white Southerners. That kind of appeal would hopefully not only allay white apprehensions but lay to rest any new speculation about blacks expatriating themselves to some distant land. The South was their homeland, not Africa, not Central America, not even the northern United States, and they fully intended to make their homes in the regions they knew intimately and in which they had been born and reared along with their fellow whites.

> The dust of our fathers mingle with yours in the same grave yards; you have transmitted into our veins much of the rich blood which course through yours; we talk the same language, and worship the same God; our mothers have nursed you, and satisfied your hunger with our pap; our association with you have taught us to revere you. This is your country, but it is ours too; you were born here, so were we; your fathers fought for it, but our fathers fed them.[23]

To underscore their regional roots and loyalties, black spokesmen also thought this an appropriate time to remind white Southerners of how the slaves had remained peaceful and faithful "while your greatest trials were upon you" and when any rebellious behavior might have plunged the South into an even more costly bloodbath. Nearly every black convention repeated some variant of this theme, as if to suggest that their wartime conduct provided ample evidence not only of their essentially peaceful nature but of their ability to function responsibly under the most trying conditions.

> No race ever served a people more faithfully than we have served them who were our masters. When they were carrying on a war, the object of which was, to rivet our bonds still more firmly, and to make slavery perpetual, we at home conducted ourselves peaceably. We not only protected their wives and children, but tilled their fields and fed their armies. Did we, at any time rise against their helpless families, did we ever offer them insult of any kind?[24]

Actually, as both whites and blacks knew, the answers to those questions depended on individual experiences. The wartime record of slave behavior had been far more varied and complex, and the fidelity of blacks had often been fragile and fragmented. But for altogether different reasons, blacks and whites in the postwar years chose to ignore the wartime black Judases, the runaways, and the looters in favor of those who had stood by the side of their "white folks." Even as blacks recited their wartime loyalty, however, they claimed not to have been "indifferent spectators" to a war involving their very freedom and that their faithfulness suggested forbearance and Providential guidance rather than contentment with their condition. Seeking to explain their "docility and obedience," and their failure to avenge themselves on their oppressors during the Civil War, a statewide convention of Virginia blacks professed to see "the hand of an all-wise God, who has seen fit to hold the passions of His African children until He saw fit to stir the passions of the two sections of the country—that both North and South should suffer for the sin of slavery."[25]

Even the most effusive promises of continued loyalty and faithfulness were conditioned on whites responding in kind—that is, with good works that were commensurate with black expressions of good faith. While Alabama blacks acknowledged the affections they felt for those "among whom our lot is cast," they cautioned whites not to misinterpret those feelings as a willingness to forfeit or postpone "the rights of our common manhood." Similarly, the freedmen of Robeson County, North Carolina, were not necessarily averse to the conciliatory spirit that characterized the Freedmen's Convention of 1865, but they expected local whites to reciprocate by ceasing to beat them, drive them from their homes, and cheat them of their wages. Pending such developments, they promised to retain their skepticism about those native whites who were suddenly posing as their best friends. "We are ignorant, illiterate and all that, but we are not altogether so simple as to allow any person to impose himself on us as a friend when he has been our enemy and oppressor, until the arms of the United States struck the fetters from off our race." Recitals of wartime faithfulness, then, were apt to be accompanied by a clear statement of postwar expectations and aspirations, with black petitioners basing their case on the need for mutual respect and a common humanity. "It is contrary to nature," Georgia freedmen warned the state legislature, "to love that which is not lovely."[26]

While proudly proclaiming their love of the South, black spokesmen and nearly every black convention indicated a still higher loyalty. The allegiance they professed to the nation, the Federal government, and the Constitution took precedence over any regional identification. "We are part and parcel of the great American body politic," Kentucky blacks declared. "We love our country and her institutions. We are proud of her greatness, her glory and her might. We are intensely American." And being "intensely American," they had naturally sympathized with the Union cause in the Civil War. While blacks recited their wartime faithfulness, then, they might wish to make clear at the very same time the indispensable role many of them had played in crushing "the Slaveholder's Rebellion." How they chose to phrase their wartime services often depended on the audience they were addressing. In the Appeal they adopted for local consumption, Virginia blacks acknowledged their previous "docility and obedience." But in the Address they drew up for the United States Congress, the same convention delegates described the conduct of a people who had been neither "docile" nor "obedient."

> *We*, with scarce an exception, in our inmost souls espoused your cause, and watched, and prayed, and waited, and labored for *your* success. In spite of repeated discouragements we continued to flock to your lines, giving invaluable information, guiding your scouting parties and your minor expeditions, digging in your trenches, driving your teams, and in every way lightening the labors of your soldiers; concealing and aiding your soldiers who were escaping from the prison pens of a barbarous foe, and when reluctantly permitted, we rallied by myriads under your banner, and by the heroism illustrated at Fort Wagner, Port Hudson, Milliken's Bend and before Petersburg and Richmond, we demonstrated our

capacity to understand the *ideas* of the contest, and our worthiness to stand side by side with the bravest in fighting it out.

No less explicit, William H. Grey, the leading force of the Arkansas freedmen's convention, excoriated the "bastard republic" which had been established in the South, with slavery as its cornerstone, and revealed how his people had "thrown off the mask" and had provided the necessary force to break the back of the rebellion and save the Union. At first, he conceded, the mighty and educated northern Saxon had evinced little sympathy for the slave. But the American people suddenly awoke in 1862 to find him less of a fool than they had imagined. Beneath an exterior and "seeming respect" made up of endless chants of "yes, sir, massa" and "no, sir, massa," they discovered "a human soul, with a will and a purpose of its own." And Grey suggested that this discovery would have profound meaning for the nation. "We have now thrown off the mask, hereafter to do our own talking, and to use all legitimate means to get and to enjoy our political privileges. We don't want anybody to swear for us or to vote for us; we want to exercise those privileges for ourselves." The "peace and quiet" of Arkansas, he warned, depended on it.[27]

No matter how warmly they dwelled on the mutual affections and shared experiences of blacks and whites, no matter how genuine the professions of loyalty and the recitals of wartime faithfulness, none of the many postwar black meetings and conventions expressed the slightest tinge of nostalgia for the old days of slavery. That experience, as they viewed it, had been brutalizing and degrading. Although they might sympathize with the plight of former masters and mistresses and with the losses their "white folks" had sustained on the battlefield, such solicitude did not embrace the Confederate war effort or the "peculiar institution." In their overly conciliatory Address to the Constitutional Convention, North Carolina freedmen acknowledged an intimacy with whites "unknown to any other state of society" and "attachments for the white race which must be as enduring as life." But that same Address talked of having emerged from a bondage under which their race had "groaned" for 250 years and suffered indescribable "degradation." Even as the Kentucky Colored People's Convention acknowledged some former slaveholders as their "best friends," the view of bondage they incorporated in their Declaration of Sentiment was uncompromising: "that cursed system under which we so long groaned, which crushed every aspiration; debased us to the level with the beasts of the field; robbed us of every attribute of humanity, and prostituted our wives, our sisters, and daughters." Nor did the Virginia convention, although denying any ill will toward their former owners, hesitate to write into the Declaration of Rights and Wrongs an assessment of the "peculiar institution" as scathing as any prewar abolitionist might have conceived:

We have been compelled, under pain of death, to submit to injuries deeper and darker than the earth ever witnessed in the case of any other people. We have been forced to silence and inaction; to look on the infer-

nal spectacle of our sons groaning under the lash; our daughters ravished; our wives *violated*, and our firesides desolated, while we ourselves
have been led to the *shambles*, and sold like beasts of the field.

When that same convention debated the wording of its Appeal to the
American People, a delegate moved that the phrase "we feel no ill-will or
prejudice towards our former masters" be amended by striking out "our
former masters" and inserting "our former oppressors." The convention
agreed to the change.[28]

Having recalled the nightmare of slavery, black spokesmen could be
expected to voice a deep gratitude for their liberation and for the work of
northern benevolent associations and Federal officials in the South. But
praise for the North was often mixed with a bitter denunciation of northern emissaries who had allegedly betrayed their trust and mission. The
Alabama state convention found the actions of Union Army soldiers "a
source of great perplexity and discouragement to us"; far more scathing
condemnations of the occupation troops came from local meetings dealing
with local grievances, many of which spared few words to complain of daily
robberies and beatings by men wearing Union Army uniforms.[29] Nearly
every black convention endorsed the Freedmen's Bureau; nevertheless, the
praise was apt to be tempered with criticism of the actions and racial
attitudes of various local agents. In Georgia, two blacks were elected as
"Anti-Bureau" delegates to the state convention of 1866 but they may not
have reached their destination; after denouncing the Bureau at a local
meeting as "mischievous and creative of disturbances between the races,"
they were arrested and jailed by the same agent they had criticized. Several
months later, the convention in Georgia, although supportive of the Bureau, heard from a number of delegates about local agents who were indifferent to the fate of the freedmen, giving them no protection from hostile
whites and always siding with employers in labor disputes. Still another
convention that same year blamed the problems of the Bureau on the
appointment of native whites to official posts and urged that any new
openings be reserved exclusively for blacks or northern whites. Despite the
Bureau's shortcomings, blacks recognized that even the minimal protection it provided was better than none at all. In New Bern, North Carolina,
freedmen complained of the "atrocities" committed by several local Bureau
agents but thought them insufficient reason to dismantle the entire structure. "As a few leaky places in the roof of a man's house would not be
considered a sufficient ground for pulling it down and living out of doors
neither can we see sufficient reason in these abuses for removing the
Bureau but a greater reason why it should be perfected and maintained."[30]

Notwithstanding the often severe condemnations of slavery, the black
convention movement in its appeals and strategy reflected far greater
concern with the oppressions of the present than with the atrocities of the
past. But blacks willingly drew upon the past, and in particular the revolutionary heritage of the American people, to press their case for a future.
To be subjected to taxation without representation, said Missouri blacks,

was as "gross and outrageous" a violation of their rights as that which had moved colonists to wage a war for independence. Not only did blacks revive the issues of the American Revolution but they invoked its imagery as well. The Zion Church in Charleston, for example, where delegates to the state-wide black convention assembled in 1865, was compared to Faneuil Hall in Boston, where patriots had plotted the struggle against British tyranny, and Martin R. Delany, who spoke at the Charleston meeting, was introduced as "the Patrick Henry of his race in this, the second revolution for the rights of the colored man." The several conventions which drew up Declarations of Rights and Wrongs modeled their recitation of grievances on the most revered document of the nation—the Declaration of Independence—and black spokesmen borrowed heavily from it to underscore their claim to the "inalienable rights" guaranteed every American.[31]

Few moments in the freedmen's conventions were as dramatic and emotional as those set aside to hear the reports of individual delegates about conditions in their respective localities. Clerics, teachers, field hands, and urban artisans rose to their feet to describe the brutalities inflicted upon their people back home—the mutilated bodies fished out of local rivers, the restraints placed on black movement, the promised wages and crop shares that remained unpaid, the churches and schoolhouses set afire, the intimidation of their leaders, and a judicial system that operated largely to deprive them of justice rather than to redress their grievances. The same themes kept repeating themselves. They were taunted with their inferiority and ignorance by men who had conspired in the past to keep them illiterate and who now refused to accord them even minimal opportunities for an education. They were told of their incapacity for self-government and voting by men who had never taught them to be anything but slaves and who now refused to introduce them, even gradually, to any political responsibilities. They were denounced as cowards by men who had kept them disarmed and who now deprived them of any means to defend themselves.[32]

To strike a balance, as some conventions sought to do, between the need to articulate their grievances, to demand full citizenship, and to allay white suspicions of their actions proved to be a formidable undertaking. And it would ultimately fail, largely because blacks could neither resolve the contradiction between their advocacy of agitation and conciliation nor compromise any of the demands they thought absolutely indispensable to a free people. Few black activists, whatever their professions of conciliation, expected the deeply entrenched and pervasive racial ideology of the white South to wither away by itself. Their optimism about the future rested on their conviction that racial prejudices were susceptible to change through legislation, equal enforcement of the law, and relentless black agitation. To win their freedom, they had been entrusted with the rifle and the cartridge box. To maintain that freedom, they now insisted upon equal access to the ballot box, the jury box, and the schoolhouse. In drawing up their demands, delegates to the Convention of the Colored People of South

Carolina stated the minimal position assumed by nearly every black leader and meeting in the immediate post-emancipation years:

> We simply ask that we shall be recognized as *men*; that there be no obstructions placed in our way; that the same laws which govern *white men* shall govern *black men*; that we have the right of trial by a jury of our peers; that schools be established for the education of *colored children* as well as *white*, and that the advantages of both colors shall, in this respect, be *equal*; that no impediments be put in the way of our acquiring homesteads for ourselves and our people; that, in short, we be dealt with as others are—in equity and justice.[33]

The preponderance of concern in nearly every black convention lay with political and civil rights. Nothing, in fact, seems more perplexing about these meetings, with their often eloquent appeals, petitions, and declarations, than the virtual absence of any substantive economic content. To read the convention documents is to learn little about the most immediate and critical problem facing the great mass of former slaves—how they would fare as free laborers working for employers who had only recently been slaveholders. No convention debated the democratization of land proprietorship as an alternative to the perpetuation of the old dependency, nor did delegates express alarm over the eviction of ex-slaves from abandoned plantations which they claimed as their own. Only the Freedmen's Convention of Georgia went so far as to propose that slaves freed under the Emancipation Proclamation be paid for any labor performed after January 1, 1863.[34] But compensating black workers for years and decades of unpaid labor as slaves never even warranted the same consideration given in some white circles to compensating slaveholders for the losses they had sustained by emancipation.

While paying lip service to the land aspirations of the ex-slaves, the black convention movement rejected any interference with the rights of private property. Presuming to speak for the freedmen of Alabama, a state convention in Mobile declared that they neither desired nor expected to receive any man's property without giving him "a just equivalent." The Freedmen's Convention of Georgia suggested only that the Federal government dispose of Federal land in the South by offering it for sale to freedmen under reasonable terms. The black newspaper in Opelousas, Louisiana, envisioned families of freedmen in possession of independent homesteads, but it made clear at the same time that blacks harbored no confiscatory notions, such as those proposed "by some of the leaders of the Republican Party in the North."[35]

The restraint exercised by black leadership on this issue reflected more than its tacit acceptance of the prevailing middle-class ideology of white Americans. In their overriding concern for realizing the same rights to life, liberty, and property as whites enjoyed, black spokesmen did not wish to undermine their own position by appearing to advocate confiscation. Perhaps, too, they recognized the futility of that cause and the turmoil and resentment that would inevitably fall on their heads if any such policy were adopted. Whatever the reason, the black convention movement contented itself with demands for "even-handed justice" rather than "special privileges or favor," though such justice was apt to mean very little to propertyless laborers caught up in the web of indebtedness and dependency.

To listen to black leaders, the way for propertyless ex-slaves to achieve economic success differed in no significant respect from the advice traditionally proffered to propertyless whites. Rather than affirm the need for government action and planning to protect the interests of black agricultural laborers, the black convention movement, like most black newspapers, repeated the moral and economic injunctions and shibboleths that were standard fare in nineteenth-century American society: success came ultimately to the hard-working, the sober, the honest, and the educated, to those individuals who engaged in "faithful industry," practiced "judicious economy," cultivated habits of thrift and temperance, made their homes "models of neatness," and led moral, virtuous, Christian lives.[36] Jonathan C. Gibbs, destined to be a leading black force in Reconstruction politics in Florida, laid down a simple set of rules in the aftermath of the war: "If we can secure, for the next ten years, three clean shirts a week, a tooth brush, and spelling-book to every Freedman in South Carolina, I will go bail (a thing I seldom do) for the next hundred years, that we will have no more slavery, and both whites and blacks will be happier and better friends."[37] Nearly every black convention, cleric, editor, and self-professed leader repeated in one form or another these time-honored middle-class verities, discountenanced vagrancy and pauperism, and extolled the virtues of the Puritan work ethic. If blacks would only heed such advice, the doors that were now closed to them would swing open and they would achieve the respect and recognition of white Americans. That assumption would prove to be as naïve and mistaken as it was persistent.

When patronizing public places and riding in public transportation, the most successful blacks invariably found themselves sitting in separate compartments with the least successful blacks. Color, not class, made the essential difference, and the black convention movement addressed itself to this problem by insisting on equal access with whites to all public facilities. That was not the same thing as social equality, they assured whites, nor did they intend or desire to thrust themselves into the private lives and circles of whites. "We deem our own race, equal to all our wants of purely social enjoyment," the Freedmen's Convention of Georgia resolved. If anything, blacks sought protection from white miscegenationists and transgressors—that is, from a perverse form of "social equality" in which whites presumed to invade the sanctity of black families and approach their women with "insulting and degrading propositions."[38]

The equality blacks insisted upon was equality before the law, in which black testimony would be admitted into the courtroom and blacks seated on the juries. If this demand often loomed the largest, that was because many black spokesmen viewed it as essential for the protection of their lives and families and the necessary base on which suffrage and the acquisition of property would rest. Even if some whites still recoiled at the thought of black testimony and jurors, black leaders also perceived that these measures were deemed far less controversial than the right to vote and hold office. After all, blacks had enjoyed for some years the right of testimony in northern states which refused to permit them to vote, and many southern whites who were uncompromising on the suffrage issue seemed willing to yield on the lesser evil of equal rights in the courtroom, if only to restore the courts to civil authority. That would simply extend to blacks a right the Constitution already specified all free citizens should enjoy. Far less acceptable to whites were the proposals made by several black conventions that the proportion of blacks on juries reflect the racial composition of the region.[39]

After the Virginia black convention drew up a powerful Declaration of Rights and Wrongs, Henry Highland Garnet, a prewar abolitionist who participated in the meeting as an "honorary member," suggested a critical change in the wording. Since blacks were in no position to retaliate in the event whites refused to heed the Declaration, he thought it more respectful, "as humble petitioners," to use the word "ask" instead of "demand" when submitting their grievances to the American people. The delegates agreed with Garnet and approved his amendment. The question raised by Garnet's move was by no means trivial. With the many appeals, petitions, and declarations directed by these black conventions toward whites, what if no one bothered to listen and the constitutional conventions and state legislatures refused to act on even the most humbly worded requests? Few black spokesmen addressed themselves directly to this possibility, except to assure whites that they would never countenance insurrection or violence. No matter what happened to their memorial, Mississippi blacks told the forthcoming constitutional convention, "rest assured that we shall still remain your friends, and keep the Star Spangled Banner above us." Similarly, the Colored People's Convention in Alabama advised their people to be law-abiding, no matter what trials they might be forced to endure. "We must rather suffer wrong, if evil-minded men inflict wrong upon us than do wrong, while we seek to have those wrongs righted by law." That same meeting rejected insurrection as "inconsistent with our history as a people, and the farthest from our desires or possible intentions."[40]

While rejecting violent alternatives, black spokesmen and conventions tried to wield whatever leverage they thought they commanded to exact from native whites a recognition of their legal rights. The arguments they advanced, incorporating warnings of continued Federal intervention in the affairs of the South, revealed a certain political sagacity. In the event the constitutional conventions and legislatures rejected their demands, the white men who controlled those bodies should be prepared to pay a political price for their actions. If, for example, blacks who had loyally supported the Federal government had no right to representation, neither should whites who had lately taken up arms against the government complain of being denied representation in Congress. If blacks were deprived of the right of testimony or representation on the juries, southern whites should not expect to regain control over the judicial system. With similar shrewdness, blacks turned native white hostility to the Freedmen's Bureau to their own advantage by suggesting to Congress that the Bureau remained an "indispensable necessity" until such time as they were in a position to protect themselves through the vote, equal justice, and the right to bear arms.[41]

The ultimate leverage, as black spokesmen began to discern, lay in a reorganization of the ex-Confederate states that would provide the freed slaves with a political muscle commensurate with their electoral strength. That perception increasingly found its way into the black newspapers and conventions. While identifying themselves with their southern homeland and adopting a conciliatory stance toward the old ruling class, black spokesmen developed simultaneously a conception of postwar reconstruction that most native whites would have thought downright traitorous. And the longer whites persisted in denying them their demands and in writing white supremacy into the legal codes of the states, the more blacks would turn to the North and to Congress with their appeals. Even as blacks denied any insurrectionary intent, they gave their support and subsequently their votes to a reconstruction with revolutionary implications and possibilities.

4

———

"STRANGE, novel, and anomalous," the editor of the *New Orleans Tribune* wrote of the position of occupied Louisiana in the Union. He might have said the same of any of the ex-Confederate states. With few precedents to guide the victors, the proper legal status of the vanquished South defied any immediate or easy solution. That it became an issue at all stemmed from sharply conflicting notions about the content of southern reconstruction and whether the President or Congress should assume responsibility. For the ex-slave, the furious debate that raged in Washington, D.C., over this problem took on critical importance when its resolution spelled the difference between a congressional reconstruction in which blacks participated as political equals with whites and a presidential restoration in which they remained political mutes. "Be careful," the *Tribune* advised Congress, after assessing the results of President Lincoln's all too lenient proclamation of amnesty and reconstruction. "Magnanimity and amnesty are noble things; but do not deliver yourselves into the hands of your enemies—the enemies of progress, justice, and freedom."[42]

The skepticism with which southern whites greeted the conciliatory pronouncements of the black conventions resembled the suspicions they had often attached to the professions of loyalty emanating from their slaves. If anything, the evidence of possible duplicity seemed even more compelling when whites compared the many recitals of regional loyalty in the convention declarations with resolutions and petitions to Congress which suggested betrayal. The same North Carolina convention that had been so moderate in its demands and so loquacious in stating its identification with the South also praised the Radical faction of the Republican Party, including individuals like Thaddeus Stevens and Charles Sumner, who were an anathema to whites. Many of the same black meetings that advised their people to cultivate good relations with the white population also endorsed the Freedmen's Bureau, the Civil Rights bill, and the Fourteenth Amendment, any one of which aroused intense emotional responses from white Southerners. The same conventions and newpapers that cautioned their people against recriminations also urged Congress not to accept the elected representatives from the southern states until blacks had a voice in their selection. The Louisiana Equal Rights Convention even refused to memorialize the state legislature in 1865, lest such an action be misunderstood as recognizing the legitimacy of that body.[43]

The apparent contradictions in their pronouncements about conciliation and reconstruction were not viewed by blacks as contradictions at all. While wishing to live in racial harmony with their fellow whites, they asked only that the relationship henceforth be based on legal equality. While asking no indemnities for the past and expressing a willingness to forgive whites for the sins of slaveholding, they did insist upon security for the future. That consideration, more than any other, informed the attitude toward southern reconstruction developed in the immediate postwar years by a coterie of black leaders, many of whom would subsequently play a significant role in the political life of their respective states. Revealing at times a fine grasp of political strategy, they viewed the various proposals regarding amnesty for former Confederates as inseparable from their own claims to be admitted to all political privileges. That is, white men who had committed treason (as defined by the Constitution) by waging war against the United States could obviously not be trusted again with political power, unless they shared that power with blacks who had proven their loyalty to republican principles and to the sanctity of the Union. Nor could such power be safely reposed in the exclusive hands of southern Unionists, as President Lincoln envisioned, for their love of the Union reflected a desire to return to the past and their forced acceptance of the Emancipation Proclamation indicated no real concern for the condition or future of the ex-slave.[44]

Whatever might be done with the "political criminals" who had led the South out of the Union, the *New Orleans Tribune,* voicing the usually more radical position of the city's mulatto community, insisted that any magnanimity be within well-defined limits and acknowledge the need for a different organization of southern society.

> We are not enemies of amnesty, and we do not ask to visit the iniquity
> of the fathers upon the children unto the third and fourth generation of
> them that have Union and freedom. We are strong and generous enough
> to disdain retaliation, and let the assassins of Fort Pillow expiate their
> crime by a long and miserable existence. Although wronged to the last
> and deprived of our best blood by this unholy rebellion, we do not ask for
> the lives of the bloodthirsty foes. An amnesty sparing the lives of the
> culprits will be something magnanimous, and worthy of our great and
> generous Republic. But at the same time that we spare the lives of our
> vanquished foes, let their property be forfeited.

Considering the punishments usually meted out to a people defeated in
war, the editor's amnesty proposal seemed eminently fair. Rather than
execute or imprison the men who had betrayed the country, he suggested
only that the wealthy among them be reduced to poverty—that is, to a
condition already shared by millions of people who had stood by their
government and had fought and sacrificed their lives to preserve it. If many
whites who knew little of labor were thereby forced to work, that would
also be a most constructive form of rehabilitation.

> Let them go to work; let them handle the spade or the hoe, for their own
> benefit, as free laborers—we mean really free;—give them a chance for
> retrieving their fallen fortune. To work is holy, honorable and noble. Let
> them have a taste of it. . . . It is enough for the republic to spare the life
> of the rebels,—without restoring to them their plantations and palaces.
> The whole world will applaud the wisdom of the principle: amnesty for
> the persons, no amnesty for the property.[45]

Although large numbers of blacks—both the politically articulate and
the masses—might have sympathized with such "radical" notions of
amnesty and reconstruction, few black spokesmen publicly embraced a
position they deemed politically untenable. In subsequent years, in fact,
black leadership, although united in the determination to preserve the
gains of Reconstruction, sharply divided over the wisdom of removing
disfranchisement from ex-Confederate leaders. To permit them to return
to active political participation seemed like the best way to win their
approval of the work of black reconstructionists. But the democratic propensities of black leaders in this respect would also prove to be their undoing. The *New Orleans Tribune* clearly anticipated as much more than two
years before the advent of Radical Reconstruction. Neither the Civil War
nor emancipation, that newspaper argued, had really altered the mentality
of the old slaveholding class, nor should blacks expect any genuine conversion to racial egalitarianism and democratic principles.

> We must despair of this generation; for this generation has handled the
> whips and sold human flesh in the market; and they are corrupt. Let
> them die in peace. But, for God and the country's sake, do not make of

them Governors, Lieutenant Governors, Judges, Mayors, Sheriffs, Senators and Ministers to foreign countries. . . . We have had enough of shame and humiliation. The nation has washed out the black spot on her escutcheon. Shall we honor and obey, now, the very men who made the blot?[46]

Since the policies of Presidents Lincoln and Johnson seemed calculated to produce precisely that result, the warning had been well grounded.

Despite the disappointment over Lincoln's lenient amnesty program, his misplaced confidence in southern Unionists, and his "moderate" experiments in state reconstruction, the assassination of the President silenced his black critics and threw a stunned black community into deep mourning, as though it had lost its only white friend and protector. The President's initial doubts about the wisdom of emancipation and the enlistment of blacks were now forgotten, his equivocations on civil rights ignored, his schemes of colonization, expatriation, and reconstruction forgiven. Even the cold language and forced nature of his Emancipation Proclamation no longer seemed relevant, giving way to the legend of the Great Emancipator. "Hereafter, through all time," prophesied one black newspaper, "wherever the Black Race may be known in the world; whenever and wherever it shall lay the foundations of its power; build its cities and rear its temples, it will sacredly preserve if not deify the name of *'Abraham, the Martyr.'* " In heaping their praise on the fallen President, black clerics, editors, and common laborers tended to repeat the same themes and evoke the same images. He had completed the noble work begun by John Brown—"two martyrs, whose memories will live united in our bosoms." He was "the only President who ever had the courage to acknowledge the true manhood of the negro." He had been "the greatest earthly friend of the colored race," "a Martyr to his cause, and a Sacrifice to his country."[47] In a church on St. Helena Island, South Carolina, freedmen prayed for Lincoln as they would have prayed only for the Saviour himself. Christ had saved them from sin, Lincoln had rescued them from slavery, and more than one freedman thought them indistinguishable: "Lincoln died for we, Christ died for we, and me believe him de same mans." The manner of his death made him a logical black hero, victimized by the same spirit of malice and hatred that had brutalized black people for generations. For that very reason, the South could not escape responsibility by ascribing the act to "individual insanity," at least not in the view of numerous black spokesmen. To treat the assassin as a madman, they argued, would be to ignore the record of deliberate and rational oppression from which four million black men and women had only begun to emerge.[48]

Among substantial numbers of freedmen, the initial shock of Lincoln's death was compounded by apprehension over the future. If the President ("Massa Sam") and the government were one and the same, as some blacks assumed, the results of the war, including emancipation, appeared to be jeopardized. "We going to be slaves again?" more than one freedman thought to ask. To Jack Flowers, who had made a spectacular wartime escape to the Union lines in South Carolina, the assassination threatened to undo his exploit. "I 'spect it's no use to be here," he said dejectedly. "I might as well stayed where I was. It 'pears we can't be free, nohow. The rebs won't let us alone. If they can't kill us, they'll kill all our friens', sure." Former slaveholders had seized upon the President's death to taunt the freedmen about the suddenly dim prospects of freedom, a concerned missionary wrote from Florida, "and some of our people began to talk of going north to escape enslavement again, for as Massa Lincoln was gone they feared their hope was gone too." More typical may have been the many whites who expressed immediate concern over how the freed slaves would react to the assassination. Not unexpectedly, new rumors of insurrectionary conspiracies circulated and the white residents of a number of towns implored Federal authorities to double their precautions to keep the blacks quiet and orderly.[49]

To black spokesmen who had been openly critical of President Lincoln's reconstruction and amnesty programs, and to those who had repressed their misgivings, the significance of the assassination seemed abundantly clear. The President had been victimized by his own magnanimity. His confidence in southern redemption and repentance had been rewarded with an assassin's bullet. The *New Orleans Tribune,* which had been highly critical of the President, used the assassination to demonstrate that the nation's enemies had not yet been vanquished.

> Abraham Lincoln, the honest, the good, the religious man, who did not understand—be it said to his honor and glory—duplicity and trickery, believed in the protestations and solemn oaths of rebels. He was too confident, too lenient, and too mild. He was repaid with a pistol's bullet. He did not know—as we do—what chivalry is.

Upon hearing of the assassination, black clergymen attending a conference of the African Methodist Episcopal Church in Baltimore reacted in virtually the same manner, praising Lincoln's good works, forgiving his sins ("His errors were errors of the head, not of the heart"), and, most importantly, urging "a sterner course" and the application of "more rigid principles" toward the defeated South. If the American people heeded the obvious lesson of this event, black spokesmen declared, they would realize soon enough that most white Southerners remained "incorrigible rebels" who willingly and deceitfully took the oath of allegiance to recover their property and political power; the Rebels expected to win at the ballot box what they had lost on the battlefield, and President Lincoln had been naïve enough to believe their protestations of loyalty. Fortunately, his successor knew better. The future lay in good hands, most of these same black spokesmen agreed, for the new President understood "Southern pretenses and Southern excesses" from his own experience and he would now do his duty. "Agag is to be hewn into pieces," a confident black cleric proclaimed, "and

Samuel must come forward and wield the sword of destruction—that man is Andrew Johnson."[50]

Despite the grievous loss of Lincoln, then, black spokesmen were almost unanimous in their belief that Providence had chosen "a second Moses" to guide them to "the land of promise." None other than Andrew Johnson himself made that solemn pledge, in addressing the black people of Nashville: "Humble and unworthy as I am, if no other better shall be found, I will be your Moses, and lead you through the Red Sea of War and Bondage to a fairer future of Liberty and Peace." The *New Orleans Tribune*, with its own radical notions of reconstruction, thought well enough of the new President to predict that his previously expressed hostility to concentrations of political and economic power in the South presaged a vigorous policy of land confiscation and redistribution. Like Lincoln, Johnson was perceived as a man who exemplified the genius of democratic institutions, having risen from a humble station to the highest office in the land. He had proven his loyalty to the Union, and surely no man who had suffered "the malignity of the Rebels," as had Johnson, would seek to restore those "traitors" to power. Where Lincoln had equivocated, Johnson could be expected to be decisive. Where Lincoln had been overly magnanimous in his treatment of the ex-Confederates, Johnson, who knew these people far more intimately, would be firm and unyielding.[51]

The assessment of Johnson's personality traits proved accurate enough, but blacks had badly misjudged his politics and racial views. In upholding the principles of white supremacy, in expediting the pardon of ex-Confederate leaders, in seeking to restore political and economic power to the old ruling class, President Johnson would act all too decisively. And in opposing even minimal civil rights for blacks, he would be firm and unyielding. For some blacks, the disillusionment came earlier than for most. Even as black newspapers and leaders still voiced their confidence in the new President, field hands forced off the lands of pardoned Rebels suspected that the battle had already been lost. At least, that was the conclusion reached by a white teacher in the Sea Islands, as former masters returned to claim their lands.

> The people receive the rebels better than we expected, but the reason is that they believe Johnson is going to put them in their old masters' power again, and they feel that they must conciliate or be crushed. They no longer pray for the President—*our* President, as they used to call Lincoln —in the church. They keep an ominous silence and are very sad and troubled.[52]

For black spokesmen, the President's decision to pursue a "moderate" reconstruction plan, permitting the white South to reconstruct herself without black participation, prompted an initial disappointment that soon gave way to disbelief. What blacks had viewed (on Johnson's assurance) as an "experimental" policy, designed to test white loyalty and intentions, turned into a nightmare of repression, Black Codes, and unequal justice. But rather than give up the "experiment" as a failure, which black leaders had confidently expected, the President insisted that the new state governments be legitimized. And blacks were left to contemplate still again the betrayal of their expectations by a man they had only recently praised so unrestrainedly. "Johnson has sold us," Frederick Douglass wrote the publisher of the *New Orleans Tribune* in October 1865, but it remained for Congress "to pass upon the bargain." Two months later, as Congress prepared to convene, the *Tribune* voiced the now deepening black disillusionment with the President's policies. The editor urged Congress to assume control of reconstruction, to make "no compromises with a conservative and exclusively white-man loving administration," and to hold the President to his initial commitments. If treason were to be made "infamous," as Johnson had so often promised, the mode of punishment would have to be severer than the rapidly accumulating stack of executive pardons of former Confederate leaders suggested.[53]

The President's response to a delegation of black leaders in February 1866 did little to reassure the few blacks who still retained faith in him. At this none too harmonious exchange of views in the White House, Johnson introduced himself as "a friend of humanity, and especially the friend of the colored man." He offered once again, if they wished, to serve as their Moses to lead them from bondage to freedom. But he made it clear that he would not lead them to the ballot box, for that would only endanger their freedom and invite race war. Reaffirming his belief in government by consent of the governed, he interpreted that principle to mean that the white people in each state should determine the question of black suffrage. The President pointedly ignored the delegate who asked him if he would apply the principle of majority rule to states like South Carolina, where blacks comprised a majority of the population. Nor did he take kindly to Frederick Douglass' argument that blacks needed the vote to protect themselves from the already rampant violence which the President thought would be unleashed in the event of black suffrage. As the exchange became increasingly acrimonious, both sides thought it best to terminate the meeting, and Douglass told his fellow delegates: "The President sends us to the people, and we go to the people." After the "darkey delegation" left, President Johnson reportedly turned to a private secretary and exclaimed, "Those damned sons of bitches thought they had me in a trap! I know that damned Douglass; he's just like any nigger, and he would sooner cut a white man's throat than not." Whether the President actually made that remark, he proceeded to act in its spirit.[54]

Within months after the White House meeting, the break between the President and black leadership would be complete. James Lynch had acclaimed Andrew Johnson on July 4, 1865, as a firm champion of the African race, but by March 1866 he thought the President was "more to be pitied than feared." Henry M. Turner was less charitable, deeming the President dangerous as well as pitiful. "I charge Mr. Johnson with the murder of thousands of our people; for though he does not kill them personally, yet he abets, or gives aid to these murderers, so that it actually amounts to a direct encouragement." No longer the noble successor to the martyred Lincoln, Johnson now loomed for blacks as the new Jefferson Davis. Presuming to be a second Moses, he acted more like "a very excellent type of Pharaoh." Pretending to sympathize with the ex-slaves in their new freedom, he vetoed the legislation blacks deemed essential to preserve that freedom. And when he advised the states to reject the Fourteenth Amendment, blacks turned to Congress for an alternative to the callous disregard of human rights that distinguished the occupant of the White House. "The future looks dark," a black newspaper observed, "and we predict, that we are entering upon the greatest political contest that has ever agitated the people of the country—a contest, in which, we of the South must be for the most part spectators; not indifferent spectators, for it is about us that the political battle is fought. The issue is fairly joined."[55]

5

WITH THE ISSUE "fairly joined," the same urgency that prompted black leaders to look to Congress for relief also moved equal suffrage to the forefront of their demands. The initial hesitation to press that issue, as at the Freedmen's Convention in North Carolina in 1865, proved short-lived, particularly after the conciliatory appeals to the constitutional conventions and state legislatures had yielded only oppressive Black Codes and not even a hint of future political participation. For black leadership, the suffrage issue quickly assumed a significance that rivaled the emotional investment tens of thousands of black laborers had made in the idea of "forty acres and a mule." Both suffrage and land came to be regarded, albeit with sharply contrasting emphases by different classes of the black population, as indispensable to freedom. Only by winning the vote, black leaders told their people, would the other aspirations they cherished have a chance for fulfillment. "The only salvation for us besides the power of the Government," Virginia freedmen declared, "is in the *possession of the ballot*. Give us this, and we will protect ourselves."[56]

Political realism and the middle-class economic outlook of black leadership helped to determine the ordering of priorities. Predictably, then, the suffrage issue, not "forty acres and a mule," came to dominate the black conventions, newspapers, and oratory. While the demand for land raised the ugly specter of confiscation and the abrogation of the rights of property, the demand for the vote simply reaffirmed traditional American principles of equal opportunity, fair play, and government by the consent of the governed. To make this absolutely clear, black spokesmen invoked on every possible occasion the revolutionary traditions of the American nation and appealed to whites on the basis of their most cherished freedoms. If taxed to support national and state government, blacks demanded the right to participate in choosing the men who imposed and spent the taxes. If subjected to the laws of the land, blacks demanded a voice in selecting those who would make and administer the laws. "I tell you, sah," a North Carolina freedman explained to a northern visitor, "we ain't noways safe, 'long as dem people makes de laws we's got to be governed by. We's got to hab a voice in de 'pintin' of de law-makers. Den we knows our frens, and whose hans we's safe in." Few white Americans could quarrel with those sentiments without violating their own history and traditions. But if they did, blacks grounded their demand for suffrage on an even more direct appeal to the patriotic instincts of the American people.[57]

If blacks could be trusted with the musket, they could be trusted with the ballot, and the nation owed at least as much to those who had helped to defend it as to those who had tried to destroy it. Their claims to the suffrage, blacks maintained, had already been validated by the martyrdom of Crispus Attucks in the American Revolution, by the valor of black soldiers at the Battle of New Orleans in 1812 and most recently on the battlefields of the Civil War. This patriotic appeal was made frequently, if only because it seemed calculated to win sympathy in the North, where black leaders were now certain the final decision would be made. At the same time, blacks pressed their case on the basis of whites already permitted to vote. If men who had fought against the government could vote, why not loyal Americans who had remained steadfast in their support of the government? If "the very poorest and meanest of white men" and foreign immigrants barely acculturated to American values and principles (such as the "lowly" Irish) could be trusted to exercise the franchise, why not blacks whose roots were as deep as those of any American, including the President himself?[58]

By citing the admission of immigrants to political privileges, black leaders sought to make two important points. The case of the Irish suggested to them that wealth and literacy were not considered valid criteria for depriving any person of the suffrage. The fact that distinct ethnic groups like the Jews voted without restriction further suggested that political equality need not lead to social mixing, as some whites feared. "They enjoy all the privileges that any white American enjoys in this country," a black newspaper said of the Jews, but "there is not as much social commingling between the Jew and the white American as between the white American and the black man." In the view of the Colored American, a black newspaper in Augusta, Georgia, only three classes of the population could be properly deprived of the right to vote: foreigners, children, and women, whose "sphere is anywhere but in the arena of politics and government."[59] Although some black leaders were less dogmatic on the question of extending the vote to women, the issue was seldom raised lest it confuse and undermine the more urgent cause of black suffrage.

In petitioning the Constitutional Convention for suffrage rights, a black meeting in Charleston, South Carolina, frankly admitted the "deplorable ignorance" of the majority of their people. Nor did they expect "the ignorant" to be admitted to the exercise of privileges "which they might use to the injury of the State." While conceding this point, however, blacks in Charleston and elsewhere insisted that ignorance was not a deficiency peculiar to Afro-Americans but characterized large numbers of whites—North and South. If "the ignorant" were to be deprived of the vote, then, consistency demanded the disfranchisement of tens of thousands of whites. If, on the other hand, ignorant whites voted without undermining American institutions, ignorant blacks could be trusted as well. Although preferring universal manhood suffrage, black leaders were willing to accept educational and property tests, but only if they were applied honestly and equally to both races.[60] That would immediately enfranchise literate and propertied blacks, while encouraging others to emulate them. In the 1890s, black leaders would advance a similar proposal as a way of forestalling total disfranchisement. But whether in the 1860s or in the 1890s, black support for conditional suffrage rested on the false assumption that their white opponents objected only to ignorant and poor blacks voting and on the naïve belief that whites would disfranchise some of their own people. Actually, most black leaders knew better and suggested conditional suffrage only as a way of unveiling white hypocrisy and obtaining full suffrage. "Is a white voter required to know how to read and write?" a black newspaper asked. "To be a moral, a religious or a temperance man? Not in the least. . . . He enjoys his political rights simply because he is a man and a citizen." The black man asked for no less than that.[61]

To admit ignorant blacks to political privileges, white critics charged, would inevitably produce a massive pool of voters that could be easily manipulated by the employers who commanded their labor and by unscrupulous politicians who would play upon their expectations. Somehow, the black man as a voter could never be perceived as acting in his own best interests. Seeking to reject that stigma, black spokesmen, in addition to citing a wartime record of service to the Union, suggested that even under the most oppressive conditions of slavery, the black man had not necessarily been unmindful of what was best for himself and his family.

> Now, every candid minded man knows full well that the former slaves have always done just what their masters never wanted them to do. The master never wanted his slave to run away, or to eat his swine and cattle, no matter how injustly or inhumanly he was treated or how near starvation he might be. Yet it was done in both of these instances. In fact, to *"fool and worry old massa"* had become second nature to the slave.[62]

To the suggestion that the "superior knowledge and cunning" of the whites would overawe them at the polls, a black meeting in Virginia responded that unlike many enfranchised whites they could be depended upon not to vote for "traitors" or at the dictation of "the mitred priest" or the "rich rumseller." Nor would they ever abuse suffrage by voting to take their states out of the Union. "Mr. Judge, we always knows who's our friends and who isn't," a black preacher in Georgia assured a skeptical northern dignitary.

> We knows the difference between the Union ticket and the Rebel ticket. We may not know all about all the men that's on it; but we knows the difference between the Union and the Rebel parties. Yes, sir; we knows that much better than you do! Because, sir, some of our people stand behind these men at the table, and hear 'em talk; we see 'em in the house and by the wayside; and we *know* 'em from skin to core, better than you do or can do, till you live among 'em as long, and see as much of 'em as we have.[63]

With equal disdain, blacks dismissed the contention that they would necessarily vote for the old ruling class by virtue of the economic power it still wielded. "Have the employers of white voters always controlled their votes?" one black petition queried. "Let the history of elections answer." If former slaves voted the same way as their former masters, that would only suggest that their former masters had become enlightened enough to accept new ideas and political principles.[64]

The only legitimate test for suffrage, most blacks agreed, lay not in a person's literacy or economic well-being but in his loyalty to the government and democratic principles. The Civil War demonstrated to them the absence of any necessary correlation between property holding, literacy, and loyalty to the government; indeed, said one black newspaper, "the errors of ignorance have done less harm than have the graft and venality of the better informed." Having taken this position, blacks rejected the popular suggestion that they needed to be prepared for suffrage and should only be gradually introduced to political privileges. That, said the *New Orleans Tribune,* smacked too much of the calculated deceit whites had employed before the war to rationalize the perpetuation of slavery. "They talked of preparing and educating the blacks, so as to qualify them for liberty; but at the same time they were careful that the slaves should not educate or elevate themselves. If we admit the objection, it will hold good forever.... The actual enjoyment of new rights is the only way to get accustomed to and become fit for their exercise." Besides, to postpone suffrage until blacks acquired an education penalized them for previous restrictions over which they had no control and deprived the Union of their much-needed support at the polls.[65]

If whites required more than verbal assurances that blacks could exercise the vote responsibly, black leaders in some regions organized mock elections, scheduled them to coincide with the regular elections, and told their people to register and cast their ballots. As early as May 1865, blacks in Norfolk, Virginia, participated in the election of state legislators. Excluded from the regular political process, they held their own ward meetings, conducted a registration drive, improvised a polling place in the local

African Methodist Episcopal Church, and on election day voted their preference among the regular candidates. After tabulating the results, making
certain to add to them the votes of the black voters, they appealed to both
the state legislature and the United States Congress to recognize the legitimacy of their actions and the validity of their ballots. To no one's surprise,
they had voted almost unanimously for the "men of tried fidelity to the
Union, and of liberal sentiments."[66] Similar elections were reported in
places like Beaufort, South Carolina (November 8, 1864); Fernandina,
Florida (where black votes were counted in a mayoralty election); and New
Orleans.[67]

With the presence of an outspoken black press and an articulate,
well-organized leadership drawn from the free colored community, the
situation in New Orleans was unusual. Although slaves constituted more
than half the black population, the well-entrenched mulatto "aristocracy"
quickly assumed a dominant influence after Union occupation in April
1862. The tens of thousands of field hands who poured into the city from
the outlying rural districts during and immediately after the war might
have found this colored leadership both bewildering and alien. Enjoying
privileges not available to the slaves, such as the right to acquire property
(including slaves), they tended to be light-colored mulattoes, quadroons,
and octoroons, proud of their Creole heritage, literate and educated, and
occupying skilled and professional positions. Within this exclusive group,
moreover, classes existed, based upon gradations of wealth and color, ancestry, cultural pretensions, education, and church affiliation.[68]

No sooner had Union troops entered New Orleans than the demand for
full admission to political privileges surfaced in the colored community.
Obviously, the usual objections to extending the vote to poor and ignorant
blacks could hardly be sustained against such an educated, propertied, and
politically conscious colored population. When these blacks called for an
end to taxation without representation, as they immediately did, they were
not referring to future expectations of taxable property but to an already
prevailing condition. Hard-pressed as to how to respond to the demand for
voting privileges, whites ultimately came up with a solution that would
neatly resolve the difficulty while at the same time split the mulattoes from
the black freedmen and uphold the essential principles of white supremacy. The so-called Quadroon Bill introduced into the state legislature in
1864 defined as a "white person" anyone possessing no more than one
fourth of Negro blood and admitted such individuals to the same privileges
enjoyed by other whites, including the suffrage.

Not only was the proposition inviting but it promptly brought to a head
the charge that the mulatto community acted indifferently toward the
mass of black people in Louisiana, most of whom resided outside of New
Orleans and were only beginning to emerge from the degradation of slavery. But the response to the Quadroon Bill contradicted that assumption
soon enough. Neither the *New Orleans Tribune,* the principal voice of the
colored community, nor the colored leaders would lend any support to the

proposal; instead, they denounced it as divisive (creating distinctions of "white, white-washed and black") and preposterous ("If a quadroon has a right to vote, why not a mulatto? . . . If we take one-half or one-third of the colored population, to make citizens and voters, why not two-thirds or three-fourths?"). Not content with denouncing the bill, colored leaders thought this an ideal time to call for a coalition of blacks, regardless of color or previous condition, that would demand the immediate admission of all citizens on an equal basis to political and civil rights.

> The colored men of this country fully understand their position at the present time; they know that, in the Union there is strength; they are determined to be all emancipated from this absurd prejudice of caste; or perish as one man under its weight. Those that imagine that they are divided are much mistaken.

The Quadroon Bill went down to defeat, in part because many white legislators objected to any "black" people voting. But the debate had gone far to allay the freedmen's apprehensions about the motives and priorities of the free colored community.[69]

With their pleas for equal suffrage rejected, blacks in Louisiana coordinated their activities to participate in the November election of 1865. Whether their votes would be recognized or not, the *Tribune* urged every black man to register to vote and to preserve his certificate "as a testimony that he can in after-time bequeath to his children. It will show that in 1865 he was wide awake to the importance of obtaining his rights." Even as the Republican Party began to organize in Louisiana that same year, the *Tribune,* although designated the official party organ, implored the black population not to submerge themselves or their aspirations beneath the dictation of political expediency. "Let us be the allies of the Republicans, not their tools; let us retain our individuality, our banner, and our name."[70]

Elsewhere in the South, blacks also mounted campaigns to win the right of suffrage and to erase racial distinctions from the statute books. Whether that agitation took the form of Equal Rights Leagues, petitions, or mock elections, it attested to a growing political consciousness, particularly in the urban centers. But although blacks thereby gained valuable political experience, the impact of their meetings, petitions, and appeals on state and Federal legislative bodies and on white public opinion remained minimal. No matter how eloquently or forcefully they made known their grievances and demands, their political status rested ultimately on the fluctuating moods and machinations of white politicians in Washington and on the rapidly growing confrontation between President Andrew Johnson and the United States Congress. What helped to make possible the extension of the suffrage and civil rights to black Americans was not the activities of black activists (who lacked the necessary power to give force to their appeals), or the northern abolitionists (many of whom rested content with the achievement of emancipation), or even the Radical Republicans (most of whom would have stopped short of enfranchising blacks), but the insistence by the white governments in the South that the essentials of the old order be maintained without a modicum of concession and the equally unyielding determination of the President to validate the work and the spirit of those governments.

In adversity and defeat, blacks found the makings of their eventual triumph. Nor did the irony of the situation escape them.

> The unexpected policy of our *anomalous* President may be just as necessary to the great work of our enfranchisement in this country as were the defeats sustained by McClellan to the employment of colored soldiers and the recognition of our citizenship. . . . The brakes on the railroad car are often of more service than the locomotive. We often need the cloud more than the sunshine. . . . Paradoxical as it may seem, President Johnson's opposition to our political interests will finally result in securing them to us.[71]

Few political analysts could have been more discerning. Although some blacks claimed to regret the clash between the President and Congress, and even as most of them condemned the actions of the Johnson governments in the South, they were hardly averse to profiting from the blunders of their enemies. When ten of the eleven former Confederate states, at the urging of the President, rejected ratification of the Fourteenth Amendment, none expressed greater relief or joy than black leaders and newspapers. "Thank God, the Southern oligarchy are blind," the *New Orleans Tribune* observed. "This stubbornness of the conquered to refuse the mild and generous terms offered by the conqueror, can only bring the latter to exact stronger guaranties." Had the amendment been ratified, the *Tribune* noted, Congress would have been "morally obliged" to recognize the new southern governments and admit their "unpatriotic and illiberal" representatives. "But, thank God, the governing class of the South has not learned prudence yet. . . . Their folly will save us and save our liberties for the future. It is better for us that the work of reconstruction be protracted. Let the rebels do our work."[72]

To win the Civil War and preserve the Union, President Lincoln had been forced to issue the Emancipation Proclamation and to authorize the enlistment of black soldiers. To secure the peace and preserve the gains of the war, black leaders now believed, Congress would be forced to admit them to full participation in political life and to guarantee their civil rights. Confident of precisely that outcome, James Lynch told a state convention of Tennessee blacks in August 1865 to prepare themselves for political power.

> In the past struggle, when the nation stood trembling upon the verge of the precipice, the black man came to the rescue, his manhood was recognized in that hour of national trial, and why? From necessity . . . We were

needed to fill up the army, we were needed to supply the place of copper-head conscripts who had no stomach for the fight. . . . And the question of political power in this country will soon present another necessity which will give us the ballot box.

The return of the South to the Union with enhanced political representa-tion, made possible by abrogation of the three-fifths clause of the Constitu-tion, made this matter all the more urgent, and black spokesmen and newspapers never tired of reminding the North what it might expect if it refused to extend the vote to the former slaves. The "safety and protection" of the nation demanded no less. "Let us help you fight the rebels at the ballot-box," Tennessee blacks pleaded.[73]

With every blundering step made by President Johnson, black people came closer to a full recognition of their rights. But the victory, when it came, would be something less than a triumph of democratic principles. That is, Congress would yield to political necessity, not to the spirit of the Declaration of Independence or to black arguments about patriotic service to the country, taxation without representation, and the natural rights of man. Understandably, blacks would celebrate the triumph, while ignoring the mixed motives that made it possible. If they exuded a certain confi-dence, however, that may have reflected the experience of the past two years, in which they had prepared themselves for this eventuality. Few could contend, at least, that the privileges of voting and holding political office had suddenly been thrust upon a people who had previously given little or no consideration to political matters. By 1867, the issues had been clarified, leaders had emerged, and organizations were being formed to mobilize the mass of blacks who may not have been reached by the conven-tion movement and the black press.

# 6

NEARLY A HALF CENTURY after emancipation, W. E. B. Du Bois grappled with the problem of black identity. The Negro appeared to him as "a sort of seventh son, born with a veil, and gifted with second-sight in this Ameri-can world." Forced to view himself through the eyes of white men, to calculate his every move and word in terms of their expectations and demands, his vision permitted him no "true self-consciousness" but rather exposed him to a myriad of conflicting images.

It is a peculiar sensation, this double-consciousness, this sense of always looking at one's self through the eyes of others, of measuring one's soul by the tape of a world that looks on in amused contempt and pity. One ever feels his two-ness,—an American, a Negro; two souls, two thoughts, two unreconciled strivings; two warring ideals in one dark body, whose dogged strength alone keeps it from being torn asunder.

The history of the Afro-American, Du Bois contended, revolved around this perennial conflict—"this longing to attain self-conscious manhood, to merge his double self into a better and truer self." What seemed essential, however, was that blacks, while seeking admission to white society, not sacrifice their racial heritage and individuality.

> He would not bleach his Negro soul in a flood of white Americanism, for he knows that Negro blood has a message for the world. He simply wishes to make it possible for a man to be both a Negro and an American, without being cursed and spit upon by his fellows, without having the doors of Opportunity closed roughly in his face.[74]

Without the advantage of Du Bois's hindsight on Reconstruction and its tragic aftermath, blacks in the postwar years confronted the paradox of racial identity—how to define themselves as a people and as a race in relation to a society made up largely of whites who viewed themselves superior by virtue of the color of their skin, their Anglo-Saxon heritage, their mental endowments, and their future prospects. Since they aspired to the same rights exercised by white citizens, some blacks thought it imperative to underscore their Americanism, to demonstrate the ardor of their national loyalty, to disprove current theories of racial inferiority, and to show how much more acculturated they were to American ways and values than the recent arrivals from Europe. "We want to understand that we are no longer colored people, but Americans," John Mercer Langston told a black gathering in 1866.

> We have been called all manner of names. I have always called our people negroes. Perhaps you don't like it—I do. I want it to become synonymous with character. We are no longer negroes simply—no longer colored people simply, but a part of the great whole of the mighty American nation.[75]

To affirm their American identity, blacks noted the various cultures that made up the civilizations of the world and the emergence of a new "race" in the United States. Whether descended from Europeans or Africans, they suggested, Americans—white and black—were in the process of developing racial characteristics "as severely individual" as those of Europeans, Asians, and Africans. Surely, the voice of the AME Church would argue, no one could expect black people in the United States to be Africans after their lengthy residence in this land.

> To say that we could have preserved our African characteristics after dwelling for almost three centuries upon this continent, is most unphilosophical. Were it true we would be the most stolid race of the world —but whoever credited the negro for stolidity! The fact is, we are thoroughly Americans, and by reason of the fact that we have been here longer than the majority of the new American race, we have developed more fully than they, the characteristics by which it is to be known.

If the "negro character" differed in any respect from that of other citizens, the editorial concluded, the reason seemed abundantly apparent—"their character, is not American. Ours, is."[76]

So intent were some blacks on demonstrating their identification with American values that they contrasted the advantages they enjoyed by virtue of their long exposure to white Americans with their less fortunate brethren in Latin America and the Caribbean. The Negroes of the Spanish West Indies and Brazil were singled out, in particular, as "the lowest of our race on the American continent," largely because most of them were African-born and had not yet thrown off "its barbaric usages." Even the Haitians, although "a noble race" with a proud history, lacked "those elements of order, of cool deliberation, of submission to authority" necessary for good government. But blacks in the United States had learned their lessons from the best possible teachers.

> The American Negro, unlike his brethren, has been the pupil of the cool, aspiring, all conquering Saxon, and in no little measure he has partaken of all the greatness of his master. From him has he learned that form of government that is as surely destined to prevail the world over, as there is absolute worth in man . . .

Having resided by the side of their white brethren, blacks had imbibed the principles of republican government and Protestantism. "And being the most imitative of men, as saith his enemies, he bids fair to rival his great teacher."[77]

Even as blacks emphasized their American roots, they could not agree on whether they were Negro, colored, black, or African Americans. The ongoing debate over how they should be addressed revealed at the same time differences over how they conceptualized themselves as a race and a regard for how whites employed the various terms. The objections to "negro," for example, rested partly on its association with slavery and the tendency of whites to use it as a term of reproach. "We call each other colored people, black people, but not negro because we used that word in secesh times," a South Carolina freedman testified in 1863. Both "negro" and "black" also suggested unmixed ancestry and hence excluded large numbers of colored people. "Is your Chairman a negro?" James Lynch asked the delegates to a Convention of the Colored People of Tennessee. "Or your Secretary, or any of your officers, or your other members or those sergeants sitting over there? They are all mixed blood. We are not ashamed of the term 'negro,' but to call it a 'negro convention' is a lie. . . . It is very hard to tell whether there is any pure blood or not, because white men used to love colored women very much." Nor did "African" fare very well, particularly at a time when black leaders sought to educate their people to their Americanness. Henry M. Turner, a leader in the African Methodist Episcopal Church, agreed with several of his ministerial colleagues that the term "African" should be stricken from the title, if only because it suggested exclusion; on the other hand, "unlike the most of my race," he claimed pride in being called a Negro. "When I am walking the streets of a city, and hear some one say, there goes a negro preacher, or a negro chaplain, I feel a peculiar exaltedness." By the 1870s, the issue was far from settled, though "colored" seemed the most acceptable term, and a Louisiana newspaper indicated a willingness to accept "Negro" as long as it was capitalized, like any other nationality. "The French, German, Irish, Dutch, Japanese and other nationalities, are honored with a capital letter but the poor sons of Ham must bear the burden of a small n."[78]

Whatever terminology they used to describe themselves, some blacks preferred to look, act, and sound as little Negro, colored, or black as possible. By adopting the fashions, the life styles, the manners, and even the color of white society, they would be absorbed into the dominant society that much sooner. The advertisements appearing in black newspapers, for example, not only acknowledged the premium placed on whiteness but sought to place that aspiration within everyone's reach; if they could not turn white, they could purchase various devices calculated to bring them to the threshold of whiteness.

> *There cometh glad tidings of joy to all,*
> *To young and to old, to great and to small;*
> *The beauty which once was so precious and rare,*
> *Is free for all, and all may be fair.*
> BY THE USE OF CHASTELLAR'S WHITE LIQUID ENAMEL

Still other advertisements promised scientific treatments that would enable black women to excel "the famed beauty of the Caucasians."[79]

What they could not achieve with skin whiteners or hair treatments, some blacks hoped to attain by modeling their social functions and attire on white society. If they could not be absorbed into that society, they would establish their own society within a society—a replica of that from which they were excluded. Such pretentiousness, however, particularly when it manifested itself in lavish expenditures, provoked bitter responses in the black community. William J. Whipper, a northern-born black who settled in South Carolina after the war, berated the "worshippers of false gods" he found among his own people. *"Fashion* rules the hour," he wrote in 1866, "and, like menial slaves, we do its bidding. . . . The street, the church, and the ball-room are the theatres for its display of presumptive impudence." It simply made no sense. To obscure their lowly station in life, blacks were expending money on luxuries which they could ill afford, thereby compounding their poverty in a vain effort to hide it.

> Our real condition is obscured by falsehood. In our attempts to cheat others, we cheat ourselves. We wear fine clothing, silks, satins, broadcloth, and trinkets, for the purpose of representing our wealth, while

every person possessing a grain of common sense thinks quite to the contrary.

In their attempts to emulate whites, Whipper concluded, black people were totally ignoring the system of economy and industry that would ultimately enable them to achieve that objective. Making that point even more explicit, a black newspaper in Louisiana suggested that only the ownership of land would bring to blacks the respectability they now sought by indulging themselves in the white man's fashions and follies.

> Because we had to put up with a home-spun suit before emancipation we are determined to wear a silk one now no matter at what cost to our stomachs or our landlords. We are a poor people: everybody knows it: we are an ignorant people, the fact speaks for itself; we are an inexperienced people as every day's transactions will prove, and yet it is a painful fact that we will spend more time and money to appear what we are not, than it would cost to be what we pretend to be.

And yet this same newspaper that scorned lavish dress and entertainments featured articles describing fancy balls of colored people, the finery of their clothes, and the excellence of their repasts; indeed, in the very same issue and on the same page as the editorial on "Extravagance Among Colored People" appeared "The Fashion Department," with tips on "Summer Styles and Novelties." Similarly, the same newspapers that extolled the virtues of blackness and eloquently appealed to race pride often included advertisements on how black people could make themselves more white.[80]

The paradox did not lend itself to any easy or immediate resolution. But the frank discussion of such questions did force blacks to examine critically who they were and the nature of their relationship to white society. If some were naturally drawn toward the models and values of that society, still others thought the loss of racial distinctiveness too heavy a price to pay for admission. To ape the ways of a people who mocked, degraded, and ostracized them, moreover, in the expectation they could gain the respect of such people, would most likely be an exercise in futility and reinforce their feelings of inferiority. To shed their Negroness, whitewash their culture, and deny their ancestral homeland would result in still more self-hatred and self-deprecation. "They seemed to think that by repudiating the word 'colored' they would become white," a veteran black abolitionist observed; "that though they were as black a man as I, they, by rejecting that word colored would directly become as white as the natives of this country." James Lynch, before embarking on his political career in Mississippi, thought he understood the type all too well—those who placed no value on the ability of men of their own race, who adopted the opinions respecting them that most whites held, who preferred white men as religious instructors, teachers, physicians, and lawyers because they were white, who disparaged their own color and thereby paid homage to the alleged superiority of the Anglo-Saxon. And invariably, if such individuals should be flattered, feted, or rewarded by whites, "they will kiss the hands of the oppressor and ally themselves with the enemies or disparagers of their race."[81]

To counter the self-debasing images with which their people had been inculcated, black spokesmen needed to confront their cultural and national origins. While almost unanimously rejecting emigration and affirming their American heritage and identity, they might have been expected to harbor ambivalent feelings about their relationship to Africa. To identify with Africa raised the specter of a separate nationality, as well as awkward questions about backwardness and semi-barbarism, and might encourage those whites who still wished to return them there. For some blacks, in fact, the remoteness of Africa, both geographically and culturally, and the effects of race mixing in the United States only served to accentuate their Americanness. "We are not Africans," one black leader proclaimed, "but a mixed race, mingling Saxon, Indian, and African blood." Rather than deny the past, however, numerous black spokesmen preferred to embrace it as a source of racial pride. To reject emigration did not require blacks to reject Africa as their ancestral homeland, any more than English, Irish, and German Americans felt compelled to dissociate themselves from their national origins.

> Should a man despise his mother because she is black, or an African? All Africans are not black. If being born in Africa makes a man an African, then we are not Africans; but no matter where the place of our birth, we are still the descendants of Africans, and, of course, belong to that race.[82]

Nor did blacks necessarily subscribe to the prevailing image of Africa as a hopelessly backward, semi-barbaric Dark Continent with neither a past nor a future; on the contrary, the impressions conveyed in the black press tended to emphasize the rich and varied cultures and the ancient Negro empires from which they were descended. Africa had been the very cradle of civilization, with the black race acting as "the promoters and the originators of social progress." The first significant and "brilliant" culture in the world had been founded by the Egyptians, a mulatto people who had been instructed in the rudiments of art and industry by Ethiopians, a pure-black people. If portions of Africa now resembled a Dark Continent, for which the barbaric slave trade conducted by Europeans bore partial responsibility, that same darkness had once engulfed the Caucasian race and vestiges of it still existed among whites. "What should we think of the Caucasian race if we had to judge that race from the wild and naked brutes of Andaman, or even from the 'lazzaroni' of Naples?" Scoffing at the notion of African inferiority, a black leader in North Carolina noted that the Anglo-Saxon had once worn a "brass collar on his neck and the name of his Norman master marked on it." With equal cogency, the *New Orleans Tribune* asked, "Who are you that boast yourselves over the descendants of Africans? A few centuries ago, your forefathers were savages, in the wilds of Britain, Germany or Gaul; we Americans, of whatever nationality, are all alike descended from barbarians." The extent to which the black press and leadership reflected the conceptions of Africa that reposed in the great mass of Afro-Americans remains difficult to determine; many ex-slaves were no doubt too preoccupied with survival in the United States to concern themselves with such matters, while others may have been the subject of a caustic observation by the official voice of the African Methodist Episcopal Church: "It is possible, even now, for a negro to say, 'What have I to do with Africa?' and not be frowned down; nay, it is somewhat popular."[83]

What admittedly compounded the problem of identity and conceptions of Africa was the extent to which Americans, including many blacks, had been inculcated with the notion that whiteness was not only more acceptable but more beautiful and alluring. The slaves who thought they would turn white with emancipation were very few but those who resorted to artificial devices to approximate white features numbered in the thousands and laid the basis for several commercial fortunes in black cosmetology at the end of the century. Recognizing the importance of developing self-pride and racial consciousness in their people, some black spokesmen thought the aftermath of slavery a propitious time to question the premium placed on white, Western standards of beauty. Rather than view their blackness as a badge of degradation, they should be encouraged to embrace it as a symbol of strength and beauty, superior in many respects to the pale, pasty-complexioned Caucasians. Not only was blackness a color borne by their ancestors in Africa who had erected ancient and noble civilizations but it characterized a majority of the peoples of the world. Through their color, Afro-Americans could thus identify with the mass of mankind, "and who shall dare say that the time will not come, when the idea of wealth, power and intelligence will be associated with a dark skin, as it is now associated with a white one?"

> We are in the minority here, but we are the most numerous in the world as a whole. . . . Of the so-called white [race] there are three hundred and fifty million; of the brown there are five hundred and fifty million. So you see that we thus have a majority of two hundred million. If we were to raise the battle-cry of "Brown earth for brown men!" we could VOTE them out of this mundane sphere, and send them to the ghostly world, as not fit to live here.[84]

If the call for "Brown earth for brown men!" was as yet premature, the reality of black political power and even black majorities in the South was not. Although blacks remained a numerical minority in all but two of the ex-Confederate states, the acquisition of the ballot converted them instantly into a potent political force. Emboldened at the same time by a growing sense of racial and community identity, blacks prepared to become full partners in the remaking of southern society—in a reconstruction that promised to broaden the base of political participation and enable even an ex-slave to aspire to the "wealth, power and intelligence" long monopolized by a coterie of white-skinned natives.

## 7

THE LARGELY BLACK AUDIENCE that gathered in Savannah on April 2, 1867, listened as a prominent white Georgian advised them to be skeptical of any politician who tried to win their votes by telling them they were the equals of the white race. "Politicians have been the bane of all people," he warned, "and they will be your bane if you fail to act wisely and well in your new relations to the race which always has and always will be the predominant race in the world we live in. To fit you for the exercise of political rights you must be politically educated." If the audience received these remarks with a discernible lack of enthusiasm, they may have been both troubled by the content and anxious to hear the next speaker, James M. Simms, a preacher and former slave. No sooner had the former governor of Georgia introduced him than the Reverend Simms proceeded to set matters straight. White men, he declared, knew nothing of his people. Under slavery, most blacks had learned to dissimulate in the presence of their master, and he claimed to be no exception. But now, "for the first time," he no longer felt compelled to mask his views. No matter how illiterate or politically uneducated black people might be, he assured the crowd, they were not fools. As prospective voters, they knew enough to cast their ballots for a party which had always advocated principles of liberty and justice. Nor did they need to be "politically educated" to know not to elect "a rebel mayor" who tolerated the presence of "brutal policemen."

With considerable pride, the Reverend Simms alluded to the notable changes of the last decade. His audience no doubt suspected what lay behind the ardor with which the speaker now underscored his words. Nearly sixteen years earlier, Thomas Simms, his brother, had been returned in chains from Massachusetts as a fugitive slave and dragged through the streets of Savannah to the jail. Not far from that site, James Simms now stood, sharing a platform with white dignitaries and advising an assemblage made up largely of former slaves how to exercise their newly won rights as free men and citizens. The transition in the lives of the Simms brothers was no more extraordinary, however, than the political era which this and scores of similar meetings helped to launch. Neither white nor black spokesmen were oblivious to the implications. "Yes, we will be a power that will be felt in this country for all time to come," a black newspaper proclaimed, while a former Confederate official admitted as much as he surveyed the dim political scene: "The registration of voters shows that the political power will be in the hands of our late slaves. What shame! What humiliation for us. Would it not be better to take up arms and defend ourselves to the last against such infamy."[85]

With the passage of the Reconstruction Acts in March 1867, what came to be known as Radical or Congressional Reconstruction was under way. Until a popularly elected convention had framed a constitution acceptable to Congress, each of the unreconstructed southern states would remain under military rule. What made this proposed reconstruction "radical" was the stipulation that both races would vote for delegates to the conventions and no constitution would be acceptable unless it provided for black suffrage. Throughout the South, boards of registrars, usually composed of two whites and one black, began the process of enrolling qualified voters. With thousands of whites unable to qualify because of their roles in the Confederacy and still others refusing to register, the results were expected but no less startling. Of the 1,363,000 registered voters in the forthcoming elections, more than half of them—703,000—would be blacks, and they formed a majority of the electorate in Alabama, Florida, Louisiana, Mississippi, and South Carolina. When these figures were translated into local and county statistics, the results were sufficient to drive whites into even deeper despair. "Registration has closed here placing the negroes in a majority," a white resident of Savannah informed a business client, who was traveling in Europe. "I hope we shall be able to control them. If not, what a terrible prospect! You will probably find us in the throes of that revolution when you return."[86]

While canvassing Georgia and South Carolina for the Republican Party, Henry M. Turner expressed grave concern over how many of his people would exercise their new political power. The problem, as he discerned it, was not so much political apathy as the "foolish idea" that political involvement might compound their already precarious economic situation. Rather than take such risks, they would leave political matters to their "white friends and colored leaders."

> The result is that hundreds declare they will not register; others say, they do not care to either register or vote until things are more settled; others, again, say they cannot lose the time just now, crops are being laid by, and for every day they lose, from three to five dollars are deducted from their wages; while still others declare it is useless to register, for they have already been told that if they ever vote in harmony with Congress, or old Joe Brown, their throats will be cut from ear to ear . . .

To encourage full participation in the forthcoming elections, the Reverend Turner framed an urgent appeal to the "colored citizens" of Georgia and ordered that it be read in every AME church. More importantly, he proposed that the newly emerging black leadership in the state traverse the countryside in an effort to mobilize and register the thousands of freedmen not reached by urban rallies and newspapers. "What will it avail us for the larger cities to go right if we are to be dragged down to infamy and shame by the rural districts." And if the men remained indifferent to these appeals, Turner urged black women, though disfranchised, to organize themselves to help get out the vote.[87]

From the outset of registration, black leaders had recognized the need to educate their people to the uses of political power. With that objective in mind, black activists canvassed their respective counties and states, discussed with prospective voters the issues that should determine their selection of candidates, warned them that a failure to exercise their newly acquired rights might result in the forfeiture of those rights, and explained to them the mechanics of voter registration. Everywhere he traveled in the interior of South Carolina, Benjamin Franklin Randolph reported, he came across hundreds of his people who were at a loss to know how to register or vote, some of them the victims of "bad advice" and threats from their employers. "A short comprehensive lesson will any where satisfy them," he added, though local whites often made it difficult if not perilous for him to impart such instruction. (While canvassing these same districts the following year, Randolph was assassinated.) In urging blacks to register, a newspaper in Georgia framed its appeal in terms of black indebtedness to the North and the Republican Party. But the *New Orleans Tribune,* which no doubt would have seriously questioned any such obligations, chose to frame the issues so that few freedmen could afford to ignore them. "The vote is the means to reach the composition of juries, the dispensation of education, the organization of the militia and the police force, in such a manner that the interests of all races be represented and protected."[88]

Few prospective black voters needed any "political education" to recognize that their best interests lay with the party which had made possible their citizenship and franchise. But the candidates who might best advance Republican principles while acting on issues of daily concern to blacks were not so easily discerned. "They see clearly enough that the Republican party constitutes their political life boat," the *Tribune* observed. "But they claim the right to select the captains whom they can trust." In the many meetings called to mobilize support for the party, participants often utilized such occasions to define their concerns and to draw up a platform on which they expected candidates to run. Invariably, the demands included state-supported public schools (preferably without racial distinctions), unrestricted right of testimony, representation on juries, equal access to public facilities, and legislation that would ameliorate the plight of landless agricultural laborers.[89] Reflecting regional concerns, a former slave asked a political meeting in New Orleans to condemn the imminent introduction of Chinese coolie labor into the cotton and sugarcane fields, warning that such an immigration "will fill our jails, our lunatic asylums and our State prisons." In South Carolina, a black candidate coupled his opposition to confiscation with a promise to tax lands in such a way as to force the owners of large tracts to make some of that land available for purchase by freedmen. And when a black candidate in Georgia vowed to repeal taxes which discriminated against small farmers, he had only to share his personal experience with the audience. "Last year I rented a small farm of Dr. Simmons, of this county. After paying him the rent, I had 5 bales of cotton. On them I paid a tax of $15 a bale, making $75. It is needless for me to tell poor men how much I have needed that money this year. It would have breaded my family the whole year. I have felt its hardness."[90]

Not since the weeks preceding secession had the South witnessed as much intensive and enthusiastic political activity. But this time the participants were people who had been politically voiceless, most of them only a few years removed from slavery. When the Virginia Republican convention got under way in the African Church in Richmond, more than three thousand blacks waited outside to gain admittance, forcing party leaders to move the next day's session to Capitol Square. More important than any head counts, however, was the spirit in which black participants entered into these meetings, resembling in many instances the emotional fervor and call-and-response techniques they brought to their religious gatherings. More often than not, they heard what they had come to hear and cheered their avowed champions, while making certain the candidates understood their concerns. But if necessary, they revealed a political shrewdness capable of unmasking any candidate, white or black, old friends and professed converts alike. In Lebanon, Tennessee, a white Republican candidate and former slaveholder found his talk interrupted by a freedman who demanded to know if he had freed his slaves unconditionally. No less insistent was a freedman in Charlottesville, Virginia, who found unconvincing a candidate's recital of his Unionist record and opposition to secession. "While I believe a white man instantly who comes out flat-footed and says he was for the war, when there is no profit nor advantage in his saying so; when I hear another say that he was against the war ... I cannot help suspecting him instantly." And in Washington County, Georgia, a white candidate quickly discovered that he had stretched the credulity and patience of his audience too far when he sought to win them over by advocating social equality even if that resulted in intermarriage; the blacks shouted him down and refused to listen to the remainder of his speech. With slightly more toleration, an assemblage made up largely of freedmen listened to "a very intelligent, educated Negro" tell them that most of his people were not yet prepared to exercise the suffrage and he feared they would vote with their old masters as a way of gaining their good will. Before the speaker could proceed, an elderly freedman asked to be heard. "Every creature has got an instinct," he explained, punctuating each of his words. "The calf goes to the cow to suck, the bee to the hive. We's a poor, humble, degraded people, but we know our friends. We'd walk fifteen miles in war time to find out about the battle; we can walk fifteen miles and more to find how to vote."[91]

The overwhelmingly black participation in these meetings raised the inevitable cry that the Republican Party in the South had become a "black man's party" in fact as well as in spirit. When Laura Towne, the white schoolteacher, attended "a mass meeting of Republican citizens" in the Sea

Islands, she was surprised to find only one white man on the platform and few if any whites in the audience. Even white Republicans did not attend, she noted; "they are going to have a *white* party, they say." When one black speaker indicated he wanted no whites on the platform, the others took him to task for his intolerance. "What difference does skin make, my bredren, *I* would stand side by side a *white* man if he acted right. We mustn't be prejudiced against their color." After some further verbal exchanges of this kind, the assembled freedmen agreed that men should be judged by their acts, not by their color, and they invited whites to join them at their next meeting. When talk of a "black man's party" began to circulate in Louisiana, no doubt inspired by the aggressive stance of the New Orleans colored community, the black newspaper in St. Landry Parish recoiled at such a prospect and suggested it would be tantamount to political suicide. "Not only would we be crushed in the attempt, in most of the Southern States; but we may be sure the Northern States would not countenance our plan."[92]

With white men—both Northerners (Carpetbaggers) and natives (Scalawags)—assuming the prominent positions in the Republican Party, while remaining dependent on their overwhelmingly black constituencies, certain questions were bound to surface, and the talk of a "black man's party" only begins to suggest the dimensions of the problem. Forced in every state to coalesce with whites, what price would black leaders be willing to pay to maintain that coalition? Would the political influence they wielded, the posts they held in the party, and the number of elective and appointive offices they filled be commensurate with the electoral strength of their people? On the eve of Radical Reconstruction, black leaders in some instances acknowledged the need to defer to their more experienced and better-educated white allies. If nothing else, the fear persisted that if blacks pushed themselves too quickly into the center of the political arena, they would confirm the worst fears of native whites, fracture the party, and provoke a backlash in northern public opinion. When a leading clergyman in the AME Church advised blacks to restrict their political aspirations, he warned that "a colored ticket" would most likely turn thirty million white people against them. And when one overly enthusiastic abolitionist suggested that a Negro be nominated for Vice-President of the United States, many black leaders thought the proposal ill-timed and counterproductive. While he wished "to see black men (or colored, if you prefer the term) in every position socially and politically, attainable," Martin Delany wrote from South Carolina, such objectives need not be achieved at the cost of destroying the Republican Party and uniting "the conservative Negro hating elements North and South." Like Delany, black leaders found initially acceptable the maxim "Let us not attempt to reach the top of the tree without climbing by means of the lower branches," and thought it best to curb their political aspirations, leaving the more prestigious and conspicuous places to their white allies. "What fuel that would be to feed the flame of prejudice!" James H. Harris of North Carolina would declare in refusing a nomination to Congress in 1868. "I am not willing to sell out my race, for such a sale would my acceptance virtually be."[93]

Whatever considerations prompted some blacks initially to refuse nominations to public office, the projected political apprenticeship would be short-lived. Within two years of the elections to the constitutional conventions, Martin Delany himself told a political rally in Congo Square, New Orleans, that in every state in which blacks comprised a substantial portion of the electorate, "a *pro rata* of positions and places belong to them." That stand must have gratified those black spokesmen who from the very outset had advocated proportional representation and had warned their people not to concede anything to which their political strength entitled them; in Louisiana, in fact, where the population was nearly evenly divided between whites and blacks, the Republican Party in 1867 pledged itself to reserve half of all nominations and appointive offices for blacks. "That plank is our protection against absorption and intrigue," said the *New Orleans Tribune*. "It is the safeguard of the destinies of the African race in the State." Nor did the *Tribune* have much patience with those who argued for a delay of black political ambitions until they had acquired more education and experience. No people possessed more experience and education in the meaning of oppression than former slaves, the *Tribune* editor noted, and that fact alone would ensure democratic safeguards in any constitution they helped to frame.[94]

With the elections approaching, black canvassers and newspapers cautioned black voters about the critical importance of their political debut. If the "black vote" became the means by which "unscrupulous renegades" and "political vagrants" were elevated to office, the very legitimacy of this experiment in biracial democratic government might be jeopardized. Without wishing to reject the friendship and assistance of northern whites, the *New Orleans Tribune,* among other black spokesmen, found little reason to place any dependency on politicians who "cannot be so well informed as to our wants as we are ourselves." All too often, that same newspaper warned, their "good friends" from the North came to them "not through philanthropy, not for the affection they have for black men, but for the love of power and spoils which is devouring them." Such individuals invariably took credit for emancipating the slaves, offered blacks a "tutorage" that only perpetuated the dependency of slavery, and lavished praise on black people only when able to control them. If a Union officer came to them claiming their votes on the basis of his service in the war, the *Tribune* asked black voters to "unbutton his uniform coat and feel the heart throbs of the man within it." If, on the other hand, a former Confederate officer came to them professing to believe in Republican principles, the *Tribune* advised black voters to be skeptical of such sudden conversions. "After a five years' struggle we do not choose to join the Confederates today." And finally, the *Tribune* suggested that if any candidate replied to their demands with the familiar refrain of "too soon," it was to be interpreted as "a lack of courage" to carry out the reform at any time.

When will the right time come? Is it, per chance, after we will have separated for ten or twenty years the two races in different schools, and when we shall have realized the separation of this nation into two peoples? The difficulty, then, will be greater than it is today. A new order of things, based on separation, will have taken root. It will, then, be TOO LATE.[95]

Despite the emphasis placed on racial unity, black leaders were hardly immune to the usual political vices of sectarianism, dissimulation, and unbridled ambition. Nor did they necessarily agree on what relations they should sustain with the former slaveholding class or with their friends from the North. The extent to which they intended to act as "race men" if elected also tended to vary. Elick Mahaly, an ex-slave who ran for office in Crawford County, Georgia, demonstrated little of the moral fervor that could be found in the pages of the *New Orleans Tribune* or in the speeches of such Georgia blacks as Henry M. Turner and Tunis G. Campbell. He addressed himself almost exclusively to local agricultural problems and pledged himself to reconcile the interests of his own race with the need to ease the economic plight and political disabilities of the former slaveholding class. In offering himself to the voters in 1867, he played upon the theme of reconciliation.

I was born a slave on the plantation of Benjamin Lockett, Warren county, Miss. I remained with my old master until 1864, when I was brought to Georgia and sold to Mr. Isaac Dennis. My old master raised me as well as slaves are usually raised, giving me the rudiments of a common English education, and instilling into my youthful mind the principles of honesty and virtue. And I will say here, that I have never departed from them. . . . I am in favor of reconstruction under the military bills; though, if I am elected, I shall use my influence to have the disqualifications removed from all.[96]

But to have listened to the anguished cries of southern whites, the disaster they anticipated could best be summed up in an individual like the Reverend Nick Williams. This black preacher reportedly stormed through the interior of South Carolina in 1867, inculcating the minds of the freedmen with ideas subversive of the political and social order and bound to provoke a racial conflagration. Although skeptical of Reconstruction ("Will it put muskets in your hands or mine?"), he urged blacks to vote for none but their own color. The rights of the planter class to their lands, he declared, were no more legitimate than the previous rights they had claimed to their slaves. "Land we must have or we will die," and he expected no help in this regard from the North. Any agent of the Freedmen's Bureau could be easily bought—for as little as $2.50. The Negro in the North was treated no better than the slave in the South, perhaps even worse, and he advocated a massive exodus of northern blacks to the southern states, where they would combine with the freedmen to establish their own nation. That was the Reverend Williams' message, at least as white witnesses reported it. "No one can imagine, unless he was present among us," one such observer wrote, "the extent and character of the excitement among the negroes. All labour is suspended; our fodder withers in the fields; whilst crowds attend the reverend gentleman everywhere he goes." The district Freedmen's Bureau office was sufficiently alarmed to dispatch a detail of soldiers to arrest the Reverend Williams.[97]

If Elick Mahaly and Nick Williams pointed up the broad spectrum of black leadership and thought, the distinctions blurred in the minds of many southern whites. The quality and opinions of the individual were far less important than the nature of his aspirations. Whatever the range of views expressed, the spectacle of freedmen deliberating, nominating candidates, organizing politically, and preparing to cast ballots was enough to conjure up fearful images. "All society stands now like a cone on its Apex, with base up," a former governor of South Carolina observed on the eve of Radical rule. After Josiah Gorgas viewed his first freedmen's meeting, the first black policeman in Selma, and blacks being sworn in as voters, this prominent Alabaman and former Confederate officer could only brood about the extraordinary effort "to convert the Southern States into a Jamaica." No less alarmed and incredulous were those southern whites who saw in every political gathering of freedmen the specter of insurrection. "Threats of an incendiary & seditious character have been made by them," the mayor of a North Carolina town dutifully reported to the Freedmen's Bureau. "I am no alarmist, but I tell you in all sincerity that sooner or later, I fear a conflict will occur between the two races down here." Usually, as in this case, the Bureau agent reported that his investigation had failed to substantiate the charges.[98]

When Republicans gathered for a state convention in Richmond, the black workers in the tobacco factories informed their employers that they intended to stop work in order to attend the proceedings. About the same time, John H. Bills, the Tennessee planter, watched his laborers leave the fields to listen to Radical speakers in town; every one of them, he noted, had registered to vote, black registration in the district exceeded that of whites, and he wondered "to what depths of humiliation are we Comeing." Like Bills, many planters who had barely survived the transition to free labor now faced still further disruptions. After the freedmen had finally been persuaded not to expect any land redistribution or forty acres and a mule, the approach of the elections and constitutional conventions renewed precisely that kind of speculation. "You cannot be sure of any thing when Negro rule commences," a South Carolina planter wrote two months after passage of the Reconstruction Acts, "and I am making friends of the Mammon of unrighteousness as fast as possible. I still believe we can hold our own but the negroes will have to enjoy more of *the fruits* than before."[99] Once again, the Freedmen's Bureau dispatched its agents to the plantations to make clear to the laborers that the forthcoming constitutional conventions were powerless to effect any changes in the ownership of land. Still, despite even the denials of black leaders, many freedmen revived their hopes, and the idea persisted among them that the conventions they were helping to elect would take steps to ease their plight by making land available to them, whether through confiscation or taxation.[100] Some planters, in fact, may have been uncertain whether they had more to fear from the reactions of freedmen to still another betrayal of expectations or from the possible attempts by the new governments to gratify the demand for land.

Anticipating bad times, some whites appeared to invite the very worst times, as if their only chance for salvation lay in some plunge into the very depths of degradation. "Having reached bottom," Henry W. Ravenel confided to his diary in March 1867, "there is hope now that we may rise again to the surface in course of time." To expedite that ultimate triumph, some were content to allow their assumptions about black inferiority to work themselves out in public view. "Let the negroes alone," a prominent Charleston attorney advised, "give them the necessary amount of rope, let them have their representatives, *all black,* in the Convention, let their ignorance, incapacity, and excesses have full scope and accomplish its ends; dont attempt to modify it, with white sauce; let it be all black, and it will soon cure itself." The day the first black men entered the halls of Congress, William Heyward agreed, "then comes the revulsion," and the Yankees would no doubt be the first to deprive them of the ballot. "Such a Government as this cannot stand, and if when the next trial of the strength of parties comes on, they are nearly equal, neither will be disposed to yield to the other, then we may see another revolution."[101]

Before Radical Reconstruction had even begun, before a single black person had announced his candidacy for any office, the white South rushed to pronounce the entire experiment in biracial democratic government a total failure. It made no difference how blacks might choose to use their political power, even if they succeeded in establishing the most virtuous and competent governments in the history of the South. The sentence had already been handed down: this would be "the most galling tyranny and most stupendous system of organized robbery that is to be met with in history." Nothing that any Radical legislature or constitutional convention did in the next decade could have reversed this initial judgment. If the white South feared anything, in fact, it was not the likelihood of black failure but the possibility of black success. "There was one thing that the white South feared more than negro dishonesty, ignorance, and incompetency," W. E. B. Du Bois would write, "and that was negro honesty, knowledge, and efficiency." Neither at the outset nor at the end of Radical Reconstruction did whites deem corruption to be the essential issue. If they could barely distinguish between one black leader and another, they cared even less to distinguish between a corrupt government and an honest government. The issue was the right of black men to participate in any government on any level. And the most terrifying prospect of all remained the possibility that these people might actually learn the uses of political power. "If the negro is fit to make laws for the control of our conduct and property," a southern educator would warn some years later, "he is certainly fit to eat with us at our tables, to sleep in our beds, to be invited into our parlors, and to do all acts and things which a white man may do."[102]

The fears and despair which gripped portions of the white population drove them into the kinds of defensive preparations once associated with rumors of slave insurrections. "No man lives now at his ease," a resident of Rockingham, North Carolina, confessed. "When he lies down at night, although his doors and windows are locked and bolted, he puts his gun and pistol, in readiness, not knowing at what hour he may be called upon to use them." For those who lived in counties or states with a preponderance of blacks, the prospect of black majorities and black mayors, black legislators, black magistrates, and black jurors was almost impossible to grasp and precipitated frantic talk about migration. "What future can we look forward to for our children, different from what they would have, if they were in Jamaica?" a resident of Winnsboro, South Carolina, asked. "To live in a land where Free Negroes make the majority of the Inhabitants, as they do in this unfortunate State of ours, is to me revolting."[103]

But most whites neither migrated nor panicked. Since they had once guided the lives and thoughts of blacks as slaves, the assumption prevailed in some circles—albeit uneasily—that they could now exploit the "old ties" and the economic dependency of the freedmen to control them politically. If black suffrage was forced upon whites, a newspaper in Augusta, Georgia, warned, "we will take care to turn the African suffrages to other purposes than those designed by the Republican agitators. The negroes will be in our employ, under our care, and, if controlled by any, under *our* control. . . . We give fair warning that we stoop to conquer." With a certain degree of confidence, then, some white Democrats addressed themselves directly to the blacks in their vicinity, urging them not to abandon those who had always cared for them, those who knew them intimately, and those with whom their destiny lay. If they persisted in their political claims, however, they should at least know the futility of it all.

> It is impossible that your present power can endure, whether you use it for good or ill. . . . Let not your pride, nor yet your pretended friends, flatter you into the belief that you ever can or ever will, for any length of time, govern the white men of the South. The world has never seen such a spectacle, and its whole history, and especially the history of your race, gives no ground for the anticipation. . . . Your present power must surely and soon pass from you. Nothing that it builds will stand, and nothing will remain of it but the prejudices it may create.

Although some black spokesmen derived satisfaction from the sight of former slaveholders trying to win over the votes of former slaves, they did not minimize the seriousness of the effort. "They basely flatter us in order to better betray us," the *New Orleans Tribune* warned. "The deeper they bow, the more their detestation and desire for revenge are growing in their bosom."[104]

To consolidate any gains they might make among the freedmen, white Democrats even urged groups of "conservative colored men" to organize among themselves. Typical in this respect was a meeting in Montgomery, Alabama, in which black speakers pledged themselves to support in the forthcoming election "the policy of our own tried people, neighbors and friends, whose capital furnishes us employment and whose roofs shelter us, in preference to that inaugurated by strangers and their allies." The ways in which whites could assess the results of these efforts were easy enough. If the blacks voted with them on election day, that would be a triumph. But if they chose to remain at home, that would be sufficient. Less than a month after noting that most of his laborers had registered to vote, a planter in St. Martin Parish, Louisiana, exulted in what happened on election day: "Not one of the negroes left here to go and vote today. This has been a glorious day—All White!!!"[105]

If verbal appeals failed to achieve the desired results, as so often happened, southern whites fell back on the more effective weapons of economic coercion, intimidation, and violence. Within weeks after the passage of the Reconstruction Acts, for example, a Freedmen's Bureau agent in Sparta, Louisiana, requested a detachment of troops to protect the right of laborers to register to vote. Far less could be done, however, to counter the actions of employers who suddenly found they had no work for blacks who evinced any active interest in politics.

> This morning I discharged 3 of my hands. . . . I gave them from last Monday until Saturday night to decide as to whether or not they would vote. They being unwilling to give me a positive answer, I thereupon told them I would dispense with their services. . . . I retain two who promised me last week without any parley that they would stay at the mill & attend to their work.

With negotiations for new contracts coming in the wake of the first elections, employers like William Gamble of Henry County, Alabama, simply inserted a new clause which forbade the laborers to "*attend elections* or political meetings" without his consent. The beatings meted out to black voters, the assassination of black leaders, the intimidation of black candidates, and the breaking up of meetings suggested in 1867 some of the techniques of terrorism that would be embellished in the next few years to expedite the political emasculation of the freedmen.[106]

Despite the threats and economic coercion, blacks voted in overwhelming numbers in their first exercise of political power. On the eve of the election, laborers from the surrounding countryside began to pour into the towns, filling up the streets, attending last-minute rallies, marching in torchlight parades—partaking, in other words, of the traditional election eve festivities they had once watched from a distance. The next morning, lines formed outside the polling places as freedmen waited anxiously for the moment when they would cast their first vote. With rumors circulating that blacks expected to return from the polls with a mule and a deed to a forty-acre lot, a reporter in one town thought to ask a freedman waiting to vote whether he shared that expectation. "No Sah," he replied scornfully. "I spect to get nuffin but what I works hard for, and when I'se sick I'll get docked." If the lines were long and the process time-consuming, many freedmen seemed in no hurry, as though they wished to prolong the experience, some of them loitering around the polls long after they had voted. Seldom did the freedmen standing in line speak to each other, a reporter noted, apparently deeming silence more appropriate to the solemnity and "sacred importance" of the occasion. Noticing one of his laborers in line, an employer in Montgomery, Alabama, discharged him on the spot; the freedman smiled, looked down, said nothing, and voted.[107]

Except for a few sporadic skirmishes, election day in most of the South passed quietly—and with it, some mistakenly thought, the old political and social order.

# Notes

## Chapter One: "The Faithful Slave"

1. Ralph Ellison, *Shadow and Act* (New York, 1964), 92.

2. Orland Kay Armstrong, *Old Massa's People: The Old Slaves Tell Their Story* (Indianapolis, 1931), 200, 269.

3. Mary Boykin Chesnut, *A Diary from Dixie* (ed. Ben Ames Williams; Boston, 1949), 38. For white perceptions of slave reactions to the outbreak of the war, see also Duncan Clinch Heyward, *Seed from Madagascar* (Chapel Hill, N.C., 1937), 130, and William H. Russell, *My Diary North and South* (Boston, 1863), 84. For slave recollections of the bombardment of Fort Sumter, see Armstrong, *Old Massa's People,* 278.

4. Armstrong, *Old Massa's People,* 276–77; George P. Rawick (ed.), *The American Slave: A Composite Autobiography* (19 vols.; Westport, Conn., 1972), IV: Texas Narr. (Part 2), 174, 227; VI: Ala. Narr., 56; XIV: N.C. Narr. (Part 1), 62, 249; XVIII: Unwritten History of Slavery (Fisk Univ.), 3, 198.

5. Rawick (ed.), *American Slave,* XIV: N.C. Narr. (Part 1), 192. For a nearly identical recollection, see IV: Texas Narr. (Part 1), 122.

6. *Ibid.,* III: S.C. Narr. (Part 4), 171–72; IV: Texas Narr. (Part 2), 100; XII: Ga. Narr. (Part 2), 277–78; Whitelaw Reid, *After the War: A Southern Tour, May 1, 1865, to May 1, 1866* (London, 1866), 52; Weymouth T. Jordan, *Hugh Davis and His Alabama Plantation* (University, Ala., 1948), 155–56; Laura S. Haviland, *A Woman's Life-Work: Labors and Experiences* (Cincinnati, 1881), 264. Unable to provide properly for their own families, some planters bitterly protested the burdens of slave maintenance. See, e.g., Mary Ann Cobb to John B. Lamar, Nov. 11, 1861, in Kenneth Coleman (ed.), *Athens, 1861–1865* (Athens, Ga., 1969), 28; Rev. John Jones to Mrs. Mary Jones, Dec. 7, 1863, in Robert M. Myers (ed.), *The Children of Pride: A True Story of Georgia and the Civil War* (New Haven, 1972), 1121–22; and Chesnut, *Diary from Dixie,* 172, 243–44.

7. Letter from a slave to his mistress, in Robert S. Starobin (ed.), *Blacks in Bondage: Letters of American Slaves* (New York, 1974), 80–81; Francis B. Simkins and James W. Patton, *The Women of the Confederacy* (Richmond, 1936), 170–72; T. Conn Bryan, *Confederate Georgia* (Athens, Ga., 1953), 132.

8. Rawick (ed.), *American Slave,* IV: Texas Narr. (Part 2), 131; XVIII: Unwritten History, 206; XII: Ga. Narr. (Part 2), 277.

9. *Ibid.,* III: S.C. Narr. (Part 4), 48–50; VII: Okla. Narr., 46, 312. See also V: Texas Narr. (Part 3), 107, (Part 4), 97, 152; and Charles L. Perdue, Jr., Thomas E. Barden, and Robert K. Phillips (eds.), *Weevils in the Wheat: Interviews with Virginia Ex-Slaves* (Charlottesville, 1976), 335.

10. Rawick (ed.), *American Slave,* IX: Ark. Narr. (Part 3), 169, 174; IV: Texas Narr. (Part 2), 29; XIII: Ga. Narr. (Part 3), 300; II: S.C. Narr. (Part 1), 46. See also VI: Ala. Narr., 97, 226, 404; XII: Ga. Narr. (Part 2), 8; Armstrong, *Old Massa's People,* 316.

11. Rawick (ed.), *American Slave,* VI: Ala. Narr., 129–32; John W. Blassingame (ed.), *Slave Testimony: Two Centuries of Letters, Speeches, Interviews, and Autobiographies* (Baton Rouge, 1977), 660.

12. Rawick (ed.), *American Slave,* XVIII: Unwritten History, 14–15; XV: N.C. Narr. (Part 2), 25.

13. *Ibid.,* IV: Texas Narr. (Part 1), 187; Booker T. Washington, *Up from Slavery: An Autobiography* (New York, 1902), 12–13; Blassingame (ed.), *Slave Testimony,* 539.

14. Rawick (ed.), *American Slave,* III: S.C. Narr. (Part 3), 40; IV: Texas Narr. (Part 2), 100, V (Part 3), 260; XIV: N.C. Narr. (Part 1), 218–19.

15. David Macrae, *The Americans at Home* (Edinburgh, 1870; repr., New York, 1952), 209; J. T. Trowbridge, *The South: A*

*Tour of Its Battle-Fields and Ruined Cities, A Journey Through the Desolated States, and Talks with the People* (Hartford, 1867), 68.

16. Rawick (ed.), *American Slave,* IV: Texas Narr. (Part 1), 135; VII: Miss. Narr., 115; M. F. Armstrong and Helen W. Ludlow, *Hampton and Its Students* (New York, 1875), 110–11. See also Rupert S. Holland (ed.), *Letters and Diary of Laura M. Towne: Written from the Sea Islands of South Carolina, 1862–1884* (Cambridge, 1912), 29.

17. Bell I. Wiley (ed.), *Letters of Warren Akin: Confederate Congressman* (Athens, Ga., 1959), 5; Mrs. William Mason Smith to her family [Feb. 23, 1864], in Daniel E. Huger Smith et al. (eds.), *Mason Smith Family Letters, 1860–1868* (Columbia, S.C., 1950), 83.

18. Rawick (ed.), *American Slave,* V: Texas Narr. (Part 4), 192, 193–94.

19. *Ibid.,* VII: Okla. Narr., 88–90.

20. Simkins and Patton, *Women of the Confederacy,* 162; Bell I. Wiley, *Southern Negroes: 1861–1865* (New Haven, 1938), 51n.

21. Wiley, *Southern Negroes,* 52n.

22. E. C. Ball to W. J. Ball, July 23, 1863, Ball Family Papers, South Caroliniana Library, Univ. of South Carolina, Columbia; Simkins and Patton, *Women of the Confederacy,* 174.

23. Rawick (ed.), *American Slave,* IV: Texas Narr. (Part 1), 14–16. See also Blassingame (ed.), *Slave Testimony,* 537.

24. Rawick (ed.), *American Slave,* VII: Okla. Narr., 135; *New York Times,* quoting the Louisville correspondent of the *Cincinnati Commercial.* See also John K. Bettersworth, *Confederate Mississippi* (Baton Rouge, 1943), 163–64.

25. Rawick (ed.), *American Slave,* IV: Texas Narr. (Part 2), 77–78; VI: Ala. Narr., 224; Blassingame (ed.), *Slave Testimony,* 535. See also *Douglass' Monthly* (Rochester, N.Y.), IV (March 1862), 617; Perdue et al. (eds.), *Weevils in the Wheat,* 167; Starobin (ed.), *Blacks in Bondage,* 77–83; and Charles S. Sydnor, *A Gentleman of the Old Natchez Region: Benjamin L. C. Wailes* (Durham, N.C., 1938), 302–03.

26. Bryan, *Confederate Georgia,* 125; Wiley, *Southern Negroes,* 75–76.

27. Mrs. Mary Jones to Col. Charles C. Jones, Jr., June 5, 1863, in Myers (ed.), *Chil-*

*dren of Pride,* 1068; Simkins and Patton, *Women of the Confederacy,* 164; Russell, *My Diary North and South,* 208–09.

28. Chesnut, *Diary from Dixie,* 158–59; Kate Stone, *Brokenburn: The Journal of Kate Stone, 1861–1868* (ed. John Q. Anderson; Baton Rouge, 1972), 298.

29. Simkins and Patton, *Women of the Confederacy,* 164; Edmund Ruffin, *The Diary of Edmund Ruffin* (ed. William K. Scarborough; 2 vols.; Baton Rouge, 1972, 1976), I, 556–57. See also Russell, *My Diary North and South,* 131–32.

30. Robert F. Durden, *The Gray and the Black: The Confederate Debate on Emancipation* (Baton Rouge, 1972), 7–8; Russell, *My Diary North and South,* 188.

31. Durden, *The Gray and the Black,* 14, 168; John K. Bettersworth (ed.), *Mississippi in the Confederacy: As They Saw It* (Baton Rouge, 1961), 249. See also Benjamin Quarles, *The Negro in the Civil War* (Boston, 1953), 37, 49–50; John E. Johns, *Florida During the Civil War* (Gainesville, 1963), 174; E. Merton Coulter, "Slavery and Freedom in Athens, Georgia, 1860–66," in Elinor Miller and Eugene D. Genovese (eds.), *Plantation, Town, and County: Essays on the Local History of American Slave Society* (Urbana, Ill., 1974), 352; Coulter, *The Confederate States of America* (Baton Rouge, 1950), 256.

32. Memorial of Free Negroes, Jan. 10, 1861, quoted in George D. Terry, "From Free Men to Freedmen: Free Negroes in South Carolina, 1860–1866," seminar paper, Univ. of South Carolina, Columbia. For examples of free black support of the war, see also Emma E. Holmes, Ms. Diary, entry for Sept. 3, 1861, Univ. of South Carolina; Henry William Ravenel, *The Private Journal of Henry William Ravenel, 1859–1887* (ed. Arney R. Childs; Columbia, S.C., 1947), 50; Bettersworth (ed.), *Mississippi in the Confederacy,* 249; and Bryan, *Confederate Georgia,* 131. For the history of free blacks in the antebellum South, consult Ira Berlin, *Slaves Without Masters* (New York, 1974).

33. Blassingame (ed.), *Slave Testimony,* 174; James B. Sellers, *Slavery in Alabama* (University, Ala., 1950), 397–98.

34. Hope Summerell Chamberlain, *Old Days in Chapel Hill: Being the Life and Letters of Cornelia Phillips Spencer* (Chapel Hill, N.C., 1926), 131; Mrs. Nicholas Ware

Eppes [Susan Bradford Eppes], *The Negro of the Old South* (Chicago, 1925), 110; [Sallie A. Putnam], *In Richmond During the Confederacy* (New York, 1867; repr. 1961), 179–80; Emily Caroline Douglas, Ms. Autobiography, c. 1904, Emily Caroline Douglas Papers, Louisiana State University, Baton Rouge. See also Susan Dabney Smedes, *Memorials of a Southern Planter* (ed. Fletcher M. Green; New York, 1965), 184. For a description of an unusual statue erected in Fort Hill, South Carolina, dedicated to the faithfulness of the slaves during the Civil War, see Mason Crum, *Gullah: Negro Life in the Carolina Sea Islands* (Durham, N.C., 1940), 82.

35. Russell, *My Diary North and South*, 119, 131–32, 233, 257–58.

36. Mrs. Anna Andrews to Mrs. Courtney Jones, April 27, 1862, Andrews Papers, Duke University, Durham, N.C.

37. "Narrative of the Life and Adventures of Henry Bibb," reprinted in Gilbert Osofsky (ed.), *Puttin' On Ole Massa* (New York, 1969), 66; Rawick (ed.), *American Slave*, XVIII: Unwritten History, 134.

38. Ellison, *Shadow and Act*, 56; James Freeman Clarke, *Autobiography, Diary and Correspondence* (ed. Edward Everett Hale; Boston, 1891), 286.

39. *New York Times*, Dec. 30, 1861, Oct. 2, 1863; Henry Hitchcock, *Marching with Sherman: Passages from the Letters and Campaign Diaries of Henry Hitchcock* (ed. M. A. DeWolfe Howe; New Haven, 1927), 71.

40. *Cincinnati Daily Commercial*, reprinted in Frank Moore (ed.), *Rebellion Record* (11 vols.; New York, 1861–68), IV (Part IV), 10. For comparable slave responses, see *New York Times*, Nov. 20, 1861, Dec. 1, 1862.

41. George W. Nichols, *The Story of the Great March from the Diary of a Staff Officer* (New York, 1865), 60; Chesnut, *Diary from Dixie*, 158; Rawick (ed.), *American Slave*, IV: Texas Narr. (Part 1), 291. See also John Richard Dennett, *The South As It Is: 1865–1866* (ed. Henry M. Christman; New York, 1965), 174, and Blassingame (ed.), *Slave Testimony*, 383, 576.

42. Chesnut, *Diary from Dixie*, 159.

43. *Douglass' Monthly*, IV (Dec. 1861), 566. See also Bishop L. J. Coppin, *Unwritten History* (Philadelphia, 1919), 64; Blassingame (ed.), *Slave Testimony*, 616; Rawick (ed.), *American Slave*, III: S.C. Narr. (Part 4), 52–53; VIII: Ark. Narr. (Part 1), 281; XV: N.C. Narr. (Part 2), 199.

44. Rawick (ed.), *American Slave*, VII: Miss. Narr., 52; VIII: Ark. Narr. (Part 2), 122; XIV: N.C. Narr. (Part 1), 64, 334; XV: N.C. Narr. (Part 2), 229; XVIII: Unwritten History, 113. See also VII: Okla. Narr., 2; VII: Miss. Narr., 12; VIII: Ark. Narr. (Part 2), 105.

45. *Ibid.*, III: S.C. Narr. (Part 4), 52–53; Elizabeth H. Botume, *First Days Amongst the Contrabands* (Boston, 1893), 6–7; Chesnut, *Diary from Dixie*, 28. For a different account of the "spelling-out" story, see Work Projects Adm. (WPA), *The Negro in Virginia* (New York, 1940), 44.

46. Washington, *Up from Slavery*, 8–9; Rawick (ed.), *American Slave*, XIII: Ga. Narr. (Part 4), 348. See also III: S.C. Narr. (Part 4), 116; VI: Ala. Narr., 52; and Wiley, *Southern Negroes*, 18n.

47. Rawick (ed.), *American Slave*, V: Texas Narr. (Part 4), 42–43; XVII: Fla. Narr., 178.

48. *Ibid.*, VII: Okla. Narr., 117. See also Wiley, *Southern Negroes*, 17.

49. Susie King Taylor, *Reminiscences of My Life in Camp: With the 33d United States Colored Troops Late 1st S.C. Volunteers* (Boston, 1904), 8; Thomas Wentworth Higginson, *Army Life in a Black Regiment* (Boston, 1869), 34, 217. For a discussion of "The Sacred World of Black Slaves," see Lawrence W. Levine, *Black Culture and Black Consciousness: Afro-American Folk Thought from Slavery to Freedom* (New York, 1977), 3–80.

50. Rawick (ed.), *American Slave*, IV: Texas Narr. (Part 1), 11. See also XVIII: Unwritten History, 76.

51. Mrs. Octavia Victoria Rogers Albert, *The House of Bondage, or Charlotte Brooks and Other Slaves* (New York, 1891), 55–56; Rawick (ed.), *American Slave*, XII: Ga. Narr. (Part 1), 258.

52. Wiley, *Southern Negroes*, 106–07; Macrae, *Americans at Home*, 367.

53. Coppin, *Unwritten History*, 64–66; Russell, *My Diary North and South*, 147; Esther W. Douglass to Rev. Samuel Hunt, Feb. 1, 1866, American Missionary Assn. Ar-

chives, Amistad Research Center, Dillard University, New Orleans.

54. Blassingame (ed.), *Slave Testimony*, 377; Rawick (ed.), *American Slave*, XV: N.C. Narr. (Part 2), 426.

55. *New York Times*, May 16, 1861, also reprinted in *Douglass' Monthly*, IV (June 1861), 477; Rawick (ed.), *American Slave*, IV: Texas Narr. (Part 1), 11. For slave recollections of clandestine gatherings, see also Albert, *House of Bondage*, 12; H. C. Bruce, *The New Man: Twenty-nine Years a Slave, Twenty-nine Years a Free Man* (York, Pa., 1895; repr. New York, 1969), 99; Rawick (ed.), *American Slave*, IV and V: Texas Narr. (Part 1), 199, (Part 3), 240–41, (Part 4), 43, 154; VI: Ala. Narr., 68; VIII: Ark. Narr. (Part 1), 9; XIV: N.C. Narr. (Part 1), 419.

56. Ravenel, *Private Journal*, 269; *Douglass' Monthly*, IV (July, Dec. 1861), 487, 564; *New York Times*, May 16, June 2, 7, Dec. 8, 1861. After confirming the rumor of a slave conspiracy nearby, Edmund Ruffin confided to his diary on May 26, 1861, that many slaves, "as in this case, have learned that Lincoln's election was to produce general emancipation—& of course, many hoped for that, & since for northern military carrying out of that measure." *Diary*, II, 35.

57. *Douglass' Monthly*, IV (June 1861), 477; Wiley, *Southern Negroes*, 19. See also Bruce, *New Man*, 99–100; Washington, *Up from Slavery*, 8; and Blassingame (ed.), *Slave Testimony*, 616.

58. 39 Cong., 1 Sess., *Report of the Joint Committee on Reconstruction* (Washington, D.C., 1866), Part II, 177. For examples of how ex-slaves recalled the causes and issues of the war, see Armstrong, *Old Massa's People*, 265; Rawick (ed.), *American Slave*, VII: Miss. Narr., 40; XIII: Ga. Narr. (Part 3), 101; XIV: N.C. Narr. (Part 1), 317; XVII: Fla. Narr., 292–93; Perdue et al. (eds.), *Weevils in the Wheat*, 216; Blassingame (ed.), *Slave Testimony*, 640.

59. L. G. C. [Causey] to husband [R. J. Causey], Nov. 19, 1863, R. J. Causey Papers, Louisiana State Univ. For the strengthening of patrol laws, see Wiley, *Southern Negroes*, 33–34. For the operation of the patrol system during slavery, see Kenneth M. Stampp, *The Peculiar Institution: Slavery in the Ante-Bellum South* (New York, 1956), 214–15, and Eugene D. Genovese, *Roll, Jor-*

*dan, Roll: The World the Slaves Made* (New York, 1974), 617–19.

60. Brig. Gen. Richard Winter to Gov. John J. Pettus, June 6, 1862, in Bettersworth (ed.), *Mississippi in the Confederacy*, 77; Wiley, *Southern Negroes*, 36, 38; Ravenel, *Private Journal*, 130; George C. Rogers, Jr., *The History of Georgetown County, South Carolina* (Columbia, S.C., 1970), 406.

61. Johns, *Florida During the Civil War*, 152; Ruffin, *Diary*, II, 35–36. See also Putnam, *Richmond During the Confederacy*, 264–66; *Richmond Dispatch*, Nov. 13, 1862, quoted in *New York Times*, Nov. 23, 1862; Myers (ed.), *Children of Pride*, 1152–53; *Jackson Daily Mississippian*, April 15, 1863, in Bettersworth (ed.), *Mississippi in the Confederacy*, 238–39; Bryan, *Confederate Georgia*, 126. For efforts to restrict urban blacks, see, e.g., E. Merton Coulter, "Slavery and Freedom in Athens, Georgia, 1860–66," in Miller and Genovese (eds.), *Plantation, Town, and County*, 344–50.

62. Bernard H. Nelson, "Legislative Control of the Southern Free Negro, 1861–1865," *Catholic Historical Review*, XXXII (April 1946), 28–46; Vernon L. Wharton, *The Negro in Mississippi, 1865–1890* (Chapel Hill, N.C., 1947), 18; Bryan, *Confederate Georgia*, 131; Louis H. Manarin (ed.), *Richmond at War: The Minutes of the City Council, 1861–1865* (Chapel Hill, N.C., 1966), 346, 349; Berlin, *Slaves Without Masters*, 376.

63. Nancy and D. Willard to Micajah Wilkinson, May 15, 1862, Micajah Wilkinson Papers, Louisiana State Univ.; Bryan, *Confederate Georgia*, 126–27; Robert L. Kerby, *Kirby Smith's Confederacy: The Trans-Mississippi South, 1863–1865* (New York, 1972), 257. For the way in which College Hill, a Presbyterian community in Mississippi, dealt with a church member who had killed a "defiant" slave, see Maud M. Brown, "The War Comes to College Hill," *Journal of Mississippi History*, XVI (Jan. 1954), 28–30.

64. WPA, *Negro in Virginia*, 188.

65. Simkins and Patton, *Women of the Confederacy*, 162.

66. Rawick (ed.), *American Slave*, VII: Okla. Narr., 217–18, 220–22.

67. Albert V. House, Jr. (ed.), "Deterioration of a Georgia Rice Plantation During Four Years of Civil War," *Journal of South-*

ern History, IX (1943), 101–02; Louis Mani-
gault to "Mon Cher Pere" [Charles Mani-
gault], Nov. 24, Dec. 5, 1861, South Carolina
Dept. of Archives and History, Columbia;
Chesnut, *Diary from Dixie*, 216; D. E. Huger
Smith to Mrs. William Mason Smith, July
28, 1863, in Smith et al. (eds.), *Mason Smith
Family Letters*, 57.

68. Wiley, *Southern Negroes*, 6–7; Ra-
wick (ed.), *American Slave*, IV: Texas Narr.
(Part 1), 108; V (Part 3), 129; Simkins and
Patton, *Women of the Confederacy*, 174.

69. Albert, *House of Bondage*, 114–15;
Charles Nordhoff, *The Freedmen of South
Carolina: Some Account of Their Appear-
ance, Character, Condition, and Peculiar
Customs* [New York, 1863], 11–12; Mary
Williams Pugh to Richard L. Pugh, Nov. 9,
1862, in Katharine M. Jones (ed.), *Heroines
of Dixie: Confederate Women Tell Their
Story of the War* (Indianapolis, 1955), 184;
"Diary of John Berkley Grimball, 1858–
1865," *South Carolina Historical Magazine*,
LVI (1955), 166–67. See also *Douglass'
Monthly*, IV (March 1862), 617; Henry L.
Swint (ed.), *Dear Ones at Home: Letters from
Contraband Camps* (Nashville, 1966), 42;
Walter Clark, *The Papers of Walter Clark*
(eds. Aubrey Lee Brooks and Hugh Talmage
Lefler; 2 vols.; Chapel Hill, N.C., 1948), I, 94;
Hitchcock, *Marching with Sherman*, 70.

70. Rawick (ed.), *American Slave*, VII:
Okla. Narr., 221, 338; IV and V: Texas Narr.
(Part 3), 150, (Part 2), 154–55. The Texas
(IV–V) and Arkansas (VIII–XI) Narratives
contain numerous recollections of the war-
time migration. For a graphic description by
a young white woman, see Stone, *Broken-
burn*, 186–225. Still other accounts may be
found in Sir Arthur James Lyon Fremantle,
*Three Months in the Southern States: April–
June, 1863* (New York, 1864), 82, 86, 87;
Kerby, *Kirby Smith's Confederacy*, 255,
392–93; Jefferson D. Bragg, *Louisiana in the
Confederacy* (Baton Rouge, 1941), 216–17;
Wiley, *Southern Negroes*, 4–6.

71. Rawick (ed.), *American Slave*, IV
and V: Texas Narr. (Part 1), 108, (Part 3), 30,
79–80; VIII: Ark. Narr. (Part 2), 247.

72. Mary Williams Pugh to Richard L.
Pugh, Nov. 9, 1862, in Jones (ed.), *Heroines
of Dixie*, 184. See also Bragg, *Louisiana in
the Confederacy*, 217.

73. Chesnut, *Diary from Dixie*, 181–
82; Rawick (ed.), *American Slave*, IV and V:
Texas Narr. (Part 3), 129, (Part 2), 155.

74. Bayside Plantation Record, Louisi-
ana, Part II, 1862–66, Southern Historical
Collection, Univ. of North Carolina, Chapel
Hill; J. Carlyle Sitterson, *Sugar Country:
The Cane Sugar Industry in the South, 1753–
1950* (Lexington, Ky., 1953), 214–15.

75. "Diary of John Berkley Grimball,"
166–67, 213–14; House (ed.), "Deterioration
of a Georgia Rice Plantation," 107; Henry
Yates Thompson, *An Englishman in the
American Civil War: The Diaries of Henry
Yates Thompson, 1863* (ed. Christopher
Chancellor; New York, 1971), 113; Johns,
*Florida During the Civil War*, 152.

76. Wiley, *Southern Negroes*, 86–97.
For accounts of slave prices during the war,
see also Ruffin, *Diary*, II, 353, 466; Fremantle, *Three Months in the Southern States*, 62;
Bettersworth, *Confederate Mississippi*, 167–
69; and Bryan, *Confederate Georgia*, 130–31.

77. Rawick (ed.), *American Slave*, V:
Texas Narr. (Part 4), 195; XVI: Va. Narr., 6;
Perdue et al. (eds.), *Weevils in the Wheat*, 39;
Chesnut, *Diary from Dixie*, 497.

78. *Montgomery Advertiser*, quoted in
*Douglass' Monthly*, IV (Sept. 1861), 526;
*ibid.*, IV (July 1861), 481.

79. James H. Brewer, *The Confederate
Negro: Virginia's Craftsmen and Military
Laborers, 1861–1865* (Durham, N.C., 1969);
Wiley, *Southern Negroes*, 110–15; Coulter,
*Confederate States of America*, 258; Charles
B. Dew, *Ironmaker to the Confederacy: Jo-
seph R. Anderson and the Tredegar Iron
Works* (New Haven, 1966), 250; WPA, *Negro
in Virginia*, 193; Ruffin, *Diary*, II, 20; *New
York Times*, Feb. 11, 1864.

80. *Richmond Examiner*, quoted in
*New York Times*, Oct. 16, 1864. For the
efforts to mobilize black manpower for the
Confederate war effort, see Brewer, *Confederate Negro*, 6–11, 139–40; Wiley, *Southern
Negroes*, 114–22; Coulter, *Confederate States
of America*, 258–59; Bettersworth, *Confederate Mississippi*, 81–82; Bragg, *Louisiana in
the Confederacy*, 218; Bryan, *Confederate
Georgia*, 132–33; Johns, *Florida During the
Civil War*, 151; Kerby, *Kirby Smith's
Confederacy*, 56–57, 254–55; Ravenel, *Private Journal*, 46, 50, 96.

81. Wiley (ed.), *Letters of Warren Akin*, 33; Coulter, *Confederate States of America*, 259. For an owner who willingly sent her carriage driver for service on fortifications, see Mary Ann Cobb to F. W. C. Cook, July 12, 1864, in Coleman (ed.), *Athens, 1861–1865*, 94–95.

82. Brewer, *Confederate Negro*, 153–55; "Diary of Benjamin L. C. Wailes," quoted in Bettersworth (ed.), *Mississippi in the Confederacy*, 225–26. For conditions among the black military laborers, see also Wiley, *Southern Negroes*, 123–31; Bettersworth, *Confederate Mississippi*, 169–70; Bryan, *Confederate Georgia*, 133; Perdue et al. (eds.), *Weevils in the Wheat*, 325; *New York Times*, Sept. 6, 1863; *New York Tribune*, Jan. 26, 1865.

83. Bryan, *Confederate Georgia*, 132; Wiley, *Southern Negroes*, 124–25, 131–33; Quarles, *Negro in the Civil War*, 275; Perdue et al. (eds.), *Weevils in the Wheat*, 325.

84. Wiley, *Southern Negroes*, 132; Rawick (ed.), *American Slave*, IX: Ark. Narr. (Part 4), 182.

85. Jacob Stroyer, "My Life in the South," in William Loren Katz (ed.), *Five Slave Narratives* (New York, 1969), 35–36, 81–97.

86. Stephen Moore to Rachel Moore, July 8, 1862, Thomas J. Moore Papers, Univ. of South Carolina. For the life of the body servant, see also Armstrong, *Old Massa's People*, 282–91; WPA, *Negro in Virginia*, 193; Perdue et al. (eds.), *Weevils in the Wheat*, 167; Blassingame (ed.), *Slave Testimony*, 583; Rawick (ed.), *American Slave*, III: S.C. Narr. (Part 3), 154–55; IV: Texas Narr. (Part 2), 188–89; VI: Ala. Narr., 313–14; VII: Miss. Narr., 27–28; XII and XIII: Ga. Narr. (Part 2), 107–08, 325–26, (Part 3), 272; Wiley, *Southern Negroes*, 134–42.

87. Armstrong, *Old Massa's People*, 281; John F. Stegeman, *These Men She Gave: The Civil War Diary of Athens, Georgia* (Athens, Ga., 1964), 39–40; Rawick (ed.), *American Slave*, III: S. C. Narr. (Part 3), 154. See also Emma E. Holmes, Ms. Diary, entry for Oct. 14, 1862, Univ. of South Carolina.

88. WPA, *Negro in Virginia*, 193; Armstrong, *Old Massa's People*, 288–89, 295–99; Rawick (ed.), *American Slave*, III: S.

C. Narr. (Part 4), 3; IV: Texas Narr. (Part 2), 181; VII: Miss. Narr., 28; XII: Ga. Narr. (Part 2), 326; XIV: N.C. Narr. (Part 1), 115–16; Perdue et al. (eds.), *Weevils in the Wheat*, 196; Putnam, *Richmond During the Confederacy*, 178–79; Wiley, *Southern Negroes*, 143–45.

89. Rawick (ed.), *American Slave*, IV: Texas Narr. (Part 1), 278; Spencer B. King, Jr. (ed.), *Rebel Lawyer: Letters of Theodorick W. Montfort, 1861–1862* (Athens, Ga., 1965), 69, 77; Wiley, *Southern Negroes*, 141. See also *New York Times*, Sept. 30, 1862, Sept. 16, 1863, and Perdue et al. (eds.), *Weevils in the Wheat*, 168.

90. Wiley, *Southern Negroes*, 143n.; Rawick (ed.), *American Slave*, IV: Texas Narr. (Part 2), 188–89.

91. *Montgomery Weekly Mail*, Sept. 2, 1863, as quoted in Durden, *The Gray and the Black*, 32.

92. Joseph T. Wilson, *The Black Phalanx: A History of the Negro Soldiers of the United States in the Wars of 1775–1812, 1861–'65* (Hartford, 1888), 482; Wiley, *Southern Negroes*, 147–48n.; Gerald M. Capers, *Occupied City: New Orleans under the Federals, 1862–1865* (Lexington, Ky., 1965), 216–17; John W. Blassingame, *Black New Orleans, 1860–1880* (Chicago, 1973), 33–34; Quarles, *Negro in the Civil War*, 38; James M. McPherson, *The Negro's Civil War* (New York, 1965), 23–24.

93. McPherson, *Negro's Civil War*, 24; Quarles, *Negro in the Civil War*, 39; Dudley T. Cornish, *The Sable Arm: Negro Troops in the Union Army, 1861–1865* (New York, 1956), 67, 142.

94. Chesnut, *Diary from Dixie*, 203–04; *New Orleans Tribune*, Nov. 3, 1864. For the debate on slave enlistments, see Durden, *The Gray and the Black*, especially 29–100.

95. Durden, *The Gray and the Black*, 89, 95, 118–19; Wiley, *Southern Negroes*, 156–57; McPherson, *Negro's Civil War*, 244. See also Fremantle, *Three Months in the Southern States*, 282n.; Wiley (ed.), *Letters of Warren Akin*, 32–33; Ravenel, *Private Journal*, 201; *New York Times*, Sept. 12, 1863; Wiley, *Southern Negroes*, 152, 154–57; Coulter, *Confederate States of America*, 267–68; Bettersworth, *Confederate Mississippi*, 170–71; Bryan, *Confederate Georgia*, 133–34.

96. Durden, *The Gray and the Black,* 76; Wiley (ed.), *Letters of Warren Akin,* 117; Brooks and Lefler (eds.), *Papers of Walter Clark,* I, 140.

97. Durden, *The Gray and the Black,* 202–03; Wiley, *Southern Negroes,* 158–59; John S. Wise, *The End of an Era* (Boston, 1902), 394–95.

98. *New York Tribune,* April 4, 1865; Chesnut, *Diary from Dixie,* 456.

99. *Richmond Examiner,* Feb. 27, 1865, quoted in *New York Times,* March 5, 1865.

100. *New York Times,* Jan. 1, 1865; Hitchcock, *Marching with Sherman,* 128; Milo M. Quaife (ed.), *From the Cannon's Mouth: The Civil War Letters of General Alpheus S. Williams* (Detroit, 1959), 371.

101. Durden, *The Gray and the Black,* 44; Wiley, *Southern Negroes,* 160–61; Allan Nevins, *The War for the Union: The Organized War to Victory, 1864–1865* (New York, 1971), 278–79; Trowbridge, *The South: A Tour,* 208. For periodic reports of black "soldiers" in the Confederate Army, see *New York Times,* Aug. 17, 1861, Oct. 27, 1862, March 1, 14, May 14, 1863, March 23, 1865.

102. Rawick (ed.), *American Slave,* IV: Texas Narr. (Part 2), 134; XVI: Tenn. Narr., 12–13.

103. *Douglass' Monthly,* IV (June 1861), 477; *New York Times,* May 21, Dec. 15, 1861; House (ed.), "Deterioration of a Georgia Rice Plantation," 101; Sydnor, *A Gentleman of the Old Natchez Region,* 296; Bettersworth, *Confederate Mississippi,* 162.

104. *Douglass' Monthly,* IV (June 1861), 477; *New York Times,* May 11, 21, June 1, Dec. 15, 1861; Haviland, *A Woman's Life-Work,* 295–97; "Diary of Benjamin L. C. Wailes," in Bettersworth (ed.), *Mississippi in the Confederacy,* 234–35; Sydnor, *A Gentleman of the Old Natchez Region,* 296–97; Herbert Aptheker, *American Negro Slave Revolts* (New York, 1943), 363–65; Aptheker, "Notes on Slave Conspiracies in Confederate Mississippi," *Journal of Negro History,* XXIX (Jan. 1944), 75; Harvey Wish, "Slave Disloyalty under the Confederacy," *Journal of Negro History,* XXIII (Oct. 1938), 443; Bettersworth, *Confederate Mississippi,* 162; Bryan, *Confederate Georgia,* 127; Ruffin, *Diary,* II, 35.

105. *Cassville* (Ga.) *Standard,* quoted in *New York Times,* May 31, 1861; Ruffin, *Diary,* II, 35; Nancy and D. Willard to Micajah Wilkinson, May 28, 1861, Micajah Wilkinson Papers, Louisiana State Univ.; Wiley, *Southern Negroes,* 82.

106. Emma E. Holmes, Ms. Diary, entry for Sept. 29, 1862, Univ. of South Carolina; Aptheker, "Notes on Slave Conspiracies in Confederate Mississippi," 77.

107. Julia LeGrand, *The Journal of Julia LeGrand* (eds. Kate M. Rowland and Mrs. Morris E. Croxall; Richmond, 1911), 58–59. On Jan. 1, 1863, she wrote: "The long expected negro dinner did not come off." *Ibid.,* 61. For rumors of a general insurrection, see also Wish, "Slave Disloyalty under the Confederacy," 445–46; Wiley, *Southern Negroes,* 82–83.

108. *New York Times,* Jan. 25, 1863; L. G. C. [Causey] to her husband [R. J. Causey], Nov. 19, 1863, R. J. Causey Papers, Louisiana State Univ.

109. Wiley, *Southern Negroes,* 68; Aptheker, "Notes on Slave Conspiracies in Confederate Mississippi," 78–79; Elijah P. Marrs, *Life and History of the Rev. Elijah P. Marrs* (Louisville, 1885), quoted in McPherson, *Negro's Civil War,* 206–07. For a conspiracy by slaves near Laurinburg, North Carolina, to force themselves into the Union lines, see David P. Conyngham, *Sherman's March Through the South* (New York, 1865), 355.

110. "Memorial to the Senate and House of Representatives of Georgia," *Proceedings of the Freedmen's Convention of Georgia, Assembled at Augusta, January 10th, 1866* (Augusta, 1866), 18. For punishments meted out to suspected insurrectionists, see Bettersworth, *Confederate Mississippi,* 162–63; Sydnor, *A Gentleman of the Old Natchez Region,* 296–97; Wiley, *Southern Negroes,* 68, 82; Aptheker, *American Negro Slave Revolts,* 365–67; *New York Times,* Oct. 21, 1862, Oct. 29, 1863; John D. Winters, *The Civil War in Louisiana* (Baton Rouge, 1963), 307; Bryan, *Confederate Georgia,* 127.

111. Higginson, *Army Life in a Black Regiment,* 248.

112. *Ibid.,* 248; *Christian Recorder* (Philadelphia), June 28, 1862; *Anglo-African,* Sept. 21, 1861.

113. Susan R. Jervey and Charlotte St. J. Ravenel, *Two Diaries: From Middle St. John's, Berkeley, South Carolina, February–May, 1865* (St. John's Hunting Club, 1921; copy in South Caroliniana Library, Univ. of South Carolina), 7, 18; Durden, *The Gray and the Black,* 56. See also William G. Eliot, *The Story of Archer Alexander: From Slavery to Freedom, March 30, 1863* (Boston, 1885), 46; Blassingame (ed.), *Slave Testimony,* 359; Ruffin, *Diary,* II, 409–10; Charles E. Cauthen (ed.), *Family Letters of the Three Wade Hamptons, 1782–1901* (Columbia, S.C., 1953), 102; Nordhoff, *Freedmen of South Carolina,* 12; Oscar O. Winther (ed.), *With Sherman to the Sea: The Civil War Letters, Diaries & Reminiscences of Theodore F. Upson* (Bloomington, Ind., 1958), 73; John W. Hanson, *Historical Sketch of the Old Sixth Regiment of Massachusetts Volunteers* (Boston, 1866), 162; John Beatty, *The Citizen-Soldier; or Memoirs of a Volunteer* (Cincinnati, 1879), 132; *New York Times,* June 13, 1861, Nov. 3, 1862, May 9, 11, 1863, March 7, 1864, March 16, 1865; Wiley, *Southern Negroes,* 76–77; Wish, "Slave Disloyalty under the Confederacy," 446–47; Allan Nevins, *The War for the Union: The Organized War, 1863–1864* (New York, 1971), 415. For blacks as Union spies, see, e.g., WPA, *Negro in Virginia,* 199–200, and McPherson, *Negro's Civil War,* 147–49.

114. McPherson, *Negro's Civil War,* 150–53; John V. Hadley, *Seven Months a Prisoner; or Thirty-six Days in the Woods* (Indianapolis, 1868), 84; Wharton, *Negro in Mississippi,* 21.

115. James M. Guthrie, *Camp-Fires of the Afro-American* (Cincinnati [1899]), 306–16; Quarles, *Negro in the Civil War,* 71–74; Joel Williamson, *After Slavery: The Negro in South Carolina During Reconstruction, 1861–1877* (Chapel Hill, N.C., 1965), 6–7; Emma E. Holmes, Ms. Diary, entry for May 14, 1862, Univ. of South Carolina. For the subsequent testimony of Smalls before the American Freedmen's Inquiry Commission in 1863, see Blassingame (ed.), *Slave Testimony,* 373–79.

116. *New York Times,* June 2, 1861; Friends' Central Committee for the Relief of the Emancipated Negroes, *Letters from Joseph Simpson* (London, 1865), 23.

117. *Douglass' Monthly,* IV (July 1861), 487; *New York Times,* May 27, 1861; WPA, *Negro in Virginia,* 188–89; Willie Lee Rose, *Rehearsal for Reconstruction* (Indianapolis, 1964), 13–15; Louis S. Gerteis, *From Contraband to Freedman: Federal Policy Toward Southern Blacks, 1861–1865* (Westport, Conn., 1973), 11–17; Wiley, *Southern Negroes,* 175–76; Nevins, *War for the Union: The Organized War, 1863–1864,* 421–23; C. Peter Ripley, *Slaves and Freedmen in Civil War Louisiana* (Baton Rouge, 1976), 25–39.

118. Simkins and Patton, *Women of the Confederacy,* 163; Wiley, *Southern Negroes,* 9–10; *New York Times,* Nov. 20, 1861, May 7, 1864; Bettersworth, *Confederate Mississippi,* 164; Bragg, *Louisiana in the Confederacy,* 210; Blassingame, *Black New Orleans,* 26, 28; Johns, *Florida During the Civil War,* 63; *Douglass' Monthly,* IV (Dec. 1861), 565–66; Botume, *First Days Amongst the Contrabands,* 78.

119. *Douglass' Monthly,* IV (Sep. 1861), 526; Botume, *First Days Amongst the Contrabands,* 178–80; Armstrong and Ludlow, *Hampton and Its Students,* 111; Haviland, *A Woman's Life-Work,* 270; A. O. Howell, Jan. 19 and Feb. 6, 1864, American Missionary Assn. Archives; James E. Glazier to his parents, Feb. 28, 1862, Glazier Collection, Huntington Library, San Marino, Calif.; Ephraim M. Anderson, *Memoirs: Historical and Personal* (St. Louis, 1868), 364; Myers (ed.), *Children of Pride,* 957, 959; J. H. Easterby (ed.), *The South Carolina Rice Plantation: As Revealed in the Papers of Robert F. W. Allston* (Chicago, 1945), 289–90; Blassingame (ed.), *Slave Testimony,* 449–54, 456, 545–46; Rawick (ed.), *American Slave,* V: Texas Narr. (Part 3), 276; VIII: Ark. Narr. (Part 1), 169; Williamson, *After Slavery,* 6; *New York Times,* June 15, Oct. 27, Dec. 18, 1861, Jan. 14, 19, Feb. 9, Oct. 26, Dec. 16, 1862, March 9, June 26, July 12, Aug. 8, Nov. 10, 1863, May 7, 1864, March 2, 1865.

120. Quarles, *Negro in the Civil War,* 62; *New York Times,* Dec. 20, 1861, Nov. 15, 1862, May 7, 1864; Blassingame (ed.), *Slave Testimony,* 545; Winters, *Civil War in Louisiana,* 163, Higginson, *Army Life in a Black Regiment,* 11–12.

121. Chesnut, *Diary from Dixie*, 92–93; *Letters from Joseph Simpson*, 22; Higginson, *Army Life in a Black Regiment*, 71, 246; Haviland, *A Woman's Life-Work*, 270–71; Stone, *Brokenburn*, 202; Swint (ed.), *Dear Ones at Home*, 251; Bryan, *Confederate Georgia*, 128; *New York Times*, Dec. 26, 1861, Jan. 21, Feb. 9, Oct. 19, Nov. 29, 1862, June 14, 17, July 3, 12, 1863, July 17, 1864, April 2, 17, 1865; Blassingame (ed.), *Slave Testimony*, 450–51.

122. Myers (ed.), *Children of Pride*, 929–30, 934–35, 935, 939–40.

123. Rogers, *History of Georgetown County*, 406–07.

124. Easterby (ed.), *South Carolina Rice Plantation*, 199–200, 289–90, 291–92, 292–93. Having reached similar conclusions about defecting slaves, Edmund Ruffin could rationalize his son's decision to sell twenty-nine of those who had remained. "These were the fragments of sundry families, of which the other members had gone off in the several previous elopements—& who were therein active participators, as all the adults who remained were passive, knowing well the intentions of the others, & keeping their secret." Ruffin, *Diary*, II, 353.

125. Botume, *First Days Amongst the Contrabands*, 138–39, 140; *New York Times*, Dec. 12, 1862; Perdue et al. (eds.), *Weevils in the Wheat*, 64; Rose, *Rehearsal for Reconstruction*, 110. See also Ravenel, *Private Journal*, 115–16.

126. Higginson, *Army Life in a Black Regiment*, 247; Thompson, *An Englishman in the American Civil War*, 104; Ray Allen Billington (ed.), *The Journal of Charlotte L. Forten* (New York, 1953), 160.

127. Rawick (ed.), *American Slave*, V: Texas Narr. (Part 3), 83; Aptheker, *American Negro Slave Revolts*, 360–61.

128. John Eaton, *Grant, Lincoln and the Freedmen: Reminiscences of the Civil War* (New York, 1907; repr. 1969), 2; Emily Caroline Douglas, Ms. Autobiography, c.

1904, [167–68], Louisiana State Univ.; *New York Times*, Dec. 18, 1861. See also Blassingame (ed.), *Slave Testimony*, 173–74, 359.

129. Swint (ed.), *Dear Ones at Home*, 42; *New York Times*, June 16, 1861, Jan. 14, April 6, Dec. 16, 1862. See also Blassingame (ed.), *Slave Testimony*, 699–702, and Albert, *House of Bondage*, 114–15.

130. Towne, *Letters and Diary*, 24; *Letters from Joseph Simpson*, 26; P. J. Staudenraus (ed.), "A War Correspondent's View of St. Augustine and Fernandina: 1863," *Florida Historical Quarterly*, XLI (July 1962), 64; Julius Lester, *To Be a Slave* (New York, 1968), 29. See also Armstrong and Ludlow, *Hampton and Its Students*, 110–11; Haviland, *A Woman's Life-Work*, 268; Botume, *First Days Amongst the Contrabands*, 139; Rawick (ed.), *American Slave*, VIII: Ark. Narr. (Part 1), 169; XVIII: Unwritten History, 173.

131. *New York Times*, Dec. 18, 1861; Higginson, *Army Life in a Black Regiment*, 174; Albert, *House of Bondage*, 134–35.

132. Rawick (ed.), *American Slave*, XIV: N.C. Narr. (Part 1), 450; *Douglass' Monthly*, IV (Dec. 1861), 564.

133. Stone, *Brokenburn*, 28.

134. Chesnut, *Diary from Dixie*, 138, 139–40, 145–48, 151–52, 154, 176, 264–65.

135. Wise, *End of an Era*, 74; *Speech of James McDowell, Jr. (of Rockbridge) in the House of Delegates of Virginia, on the Slave Question* (Richmond, 1832), reprinted in Eric Foner (ed.), *Nat Turner* (Englewood Cliffs, N.J., 1971), 113. On January 4, 1862, Edmund Ruffin confided his recollections of the Nat Turner insurrection to his diary. *Diary*, II, 207–09.

136. Chesnut, *Diary from Dixie*, 38, 292–93.

137. Jones (ed.), *Heroines of Dixie*, 118.

138. Rawick (ed.), *American Slave*, IV: Texas Narr. (Part 2), 189.

## Chapter Two: Black Liberators

1. *Report of the Proceedings of a Meeting Held at Concert Hall, Philadelphia, on Tuesday Evening, November 3, 1863, to Take into Consideration the Condition of the Freed People of the South* (Philadelphia, 1863), 22.

2. George H. Hepworth, *The Whip, Hoe, and Sword; or, The Gulf-Department in '63* (Boston, 1864), 179.

3. W. E. B. Du Bois, *Black Reconstruction* (New York, 1935), 110.

4. *Christian Recorder,* April 23, May 28, 1864.

5. *Douglass' Monthly,* III (May 1861), 451.

6. Wiley, *Southern Negroes,* 301; *New York Times,* Oct. 18, 1862.

7. Roy P. Basler (ed.), *The Collected Works of Abraham Lincoln* (8 vols.; New Brunswick, N.J., 1953), V, 423; V. Jacque Voegeli, *Free but Not Equal: The Midwest and the Negro During the Civil War* (Chicago, 1967), 99; Bell I. Wiley, *The Life of Billy Yank: The Common Soldier of the Union* (Indianapolis, 1951), 120.

8. William C. Bryant II (ed.), "A Yankee Soldier Looks at the Negro," *Civil War History,* VII (1961), 144.

9. Cornish, *Sable Arm,* 9–10, 31; *Christian Recorder,* July 25, 1863.

10. *Christian Recorder,* Jan. 31, 1863.

11. Herbert Aptheker, "The Negro in the Union Navy," *Journal of Negro History,* XXXII (1947), 169–200 (for the experience of Robert Fitzgerald in the Union Navy, see Pauli Murray, *Proud Shoes: The Story of an American Family* (New York, 1956), 130–34); Cornish, *Sable Arm,* 33–58, 69–75; William F. Messner, "Black Violence and White Response: Louisiana, 1862," *Journal of Southern History,* XLI (1975), 28–30; *Douglass' Monthly,* V (Aug. 1862), 698–99; Wilson, *Black Phalanx,* 145–65; Rose, *Rehearsal for Reconstruction,* 144–48, 187–89; Towne, *Letters and Diary,* 41–54.

12. James M. McPherson, *The Struggle for Equality: Abolitionists and the Negro in the Civil War and Reconstruction* (Princeton, N.J., 1964), 197–202; Higginson, *Army Life in a Black Regiment,* 4.

13. Higginson, *Army Life in a Black Regiment,* 4–5, 10–11, 16–19, 25, 28–30.

14. E. Pershine Smith to Henry C. Carey, Jan. 5, 1863, Carey Papers, Edward Carey Gardiner Collection, Historical Society of Pennsylvania, Philadelphia; Winther (ed.), *With Sherman to the Sea,* 55.

15. Higginson, *Army Life in a Black Regiment,* 58–60; Higginson to Brig. Gen. Rufus Saxton, Feb. 1, 1863, in Guthrie, *Camp-Fires of the Afro-American,* 390–91.

16. Lary C. Rampp, "Negro Troop Activity in Indian Territory, 1863–1865," *Chronicles of Oklahoma,* XLVII (Spring 1969), 534–36; *New York Times,* Nov. 20, 1862; Henry T. Johns, *Life with the Forty-ninth Massachusetts Volunteers* (Washington, D.C., 1890), 248, 281–83; McPherson (ed.), *Negro's Civil War,* 185–87. See also *New York Times,* Feb. 23, April 1, Dec. 14, 1863; William Wells Brown, *The Negro in the American Rebellion* (Boston, 1880), 167–76; Albert, *House of Bondage,* 131–32.

17. Cornish, *Sable Arm,* 95, 114, 231, 251; Nevins, *War for the Union: The Organized War, 1863–1864,* 54n.; John W. Blassingame, "The Recruitment of Colored Troops in Kentucky, Maryland and Missouri, 1863–1865," *Historian,* XXIX (1967), 533–45; Basler (ed.), *Collected Works of Abraham Lincoln,* VII, 282; McPherson (ed.), *Negro's Civil War,* 192. See also *Christian Recorder,* Oct. 31, 1863.

18. Cornish, *Sable Arm,* 229–31; Wilson, *Black Phalanx,* 163–64. For examples of changing attitudes toward the use of black troops, see also Basler (ed.), *Collected Works of Abraham Lincoln,* V, 357, and VI, 149–50; John Mercer Langston, *From the Virginia Plantation to the National Capitol* (Hartford, 1894), 205–11; Voegeli, *Free but Not Equal,* 105.

19. *Record of Action of the Convention Held at Poughkeepsie, N.Y., July 15th and 16th, 1863, for the Purpose of Facilitating the Introduction of Colored Troops into the Service of the United States* (New York, 1863), 6, 7, 8; *Douglass' Monthly,* V (March 1863), 801, (April 1863), 819; *New York Times,* Jan. 11, 1864. See also *Christian Recorder,* July 18, 1863; *New York Times,* Feb. 20, March 26, 1864; H. Ford Douglass to Frederick Douglass, Jan. 8, 1863, in *Douglass' Monthly,* V (Feb. 1863), 786; Blassingame (ed.), *Slave Testimony,* 372.

20. *Christian Recorder,* June 20, 1863. See also *ibid.,* June 27, July 11, 18, 1863; *Douglass' Monthly,* V (April 1863), 818–19, (Aug. 1863), 852.

21. *Douglass' Monthly,* V (Aug. 1863), 851, (April 1863), 818.

22. Wiley, *Southern Negroes,* 306; *New York Times,* July 27, 31, Aug. 2, 1863.

23. Wiley, *Southern Negroes,* 306–07; Rose, *Rehearsal for Reconstruction,* 269–70; George H. Gordon, *A War Diary of Events in the War of the Great Rebellion, 1863–1865* (Boston, 1882), 275.

24. *New York Times,* April 4, 1864; Wilson, *Black Phalanx,* 130–32; John Hope Franklin (ed.), *The Diary of James T. Ayers: Civil War Recruiter* (Springfield, Ill., 1947), xvi, 5, 26–8; McPherson, *Negro's Civil War,* 206.

25. Wilson, *Black Phalanx,* 130–32; Blassingame, "Recruitment of Colored Troops in Kentucky, Maryland and Missouri, 1863–1865," 543–44; Henry G. Pearson, *The Life of John A. Andrew: Governor of Massachusetts, 1861–1865* (2 vols.; Boston, 1904), II, 144–45; Cornish, *Sable Arm,* 182; Franklin (ed.), *Diary of James T. Ayers,* 46.

26. John A. Hedrick to Benjamin S. Hedrick, March 13, 1864, Benjamin S. Hedrick Papers, Duke Univ.; McPherson, *Negro's Civil War,* 170; Blassingame, "Recruitment of Colored Troops in Kentucky, Maryland and Missouri, 1863–1865," 539.

27. Elizabeth Ware Pearson (ed.), *Letters from Port Royal* (Boston, 1906), 177, 185–90, 239, 282–84; Towne, *Letters and Diary,* 107; Rose, *Rehearsal for Reconstruction,* 266–68, 269, 328–29; *New York Times,* Jan. 25, 1863, March 1, 1865; Bruce, *The New Man,* 107; Wiley, *Southern Negroes,* 309–10; *Report of the Proceedings of a Meeting, Philadelphia, November 3, 1863,* 22.

28. Pearson (ed.), *Letters from Port Royal,* 185; Salmon P. Chase to David Hunter, Feb. 14, 1863, Main File, Huntington Library.

29. *New York Times,* March 1, 1863; *Christian Recorder,* July 18, 1863.

30. *Christian Recorder,* Feb. 28, July 11, 1863. See also *Record of Action of the Convention Held at Poughkeepsie, N.Y., July 15th and 16th, 1863,* 11–12.

31. Pearson, *Life of John Andrew,* II, 71–84; Luis F. Emilio, *History of the Fifty-fourth Regiment of Massachusetts Volunteer Infantry, 1863–1865* (Boston, 1891), 1–18; Cornish, *Sable Arm,* 105–10; McPherson, *Struggle for Equality,* 202–06; *Douglass' Monthly,* V (March 1863), 801.

32. Emilio, *History of the Fifty-fourth Regiment,* 19–34; Pearson, *Life of John Andrew,* II, 86–89; Cornish, *Sable Arm,* 147–48; McPherson, *Struggle for Equality,* 206; Quarles, *Negro in the Civil War,* 10–12; Frank A. Rollin, *Life and Public Services of Martin R. Delany* (Boston, 1883), 145; *New York Times,* May 29, 1863.

33. Emilio, *History of the Fifty-fourth Regiment,* 67–104; Brown, *Negro in the American Rebellion,* 198–211; McPherson, *Struggle for Equality,* 211–12; Lewis Douglass to Amelia Loguen, July 20, 1863, Carter G. Woodson Collection, Library of Congress.

34. *New York Times,* May 24, 1863.

35. McPherson, *Negro's Civil War,* 143–44, 173; William H. Parham to Jacob C. White, Aug. 7, 1863, Jacob C. White, Jr., Papers, American Negro Historical Society Papers, Historical Society of Pennsylvania.

36. *Christian Recorder,* July 26, 1862.

37. Cornish, *Sable Arm,* 184–85; *Christian Recorder,* June 11, 1864; *Douglass' Monthly,* V (March 1863), 801.

38. *Christian Recorder,* Aug. 13, April 2, 1864. See also *ibid.,* March 5, June 11, July 23, 1864.

39. *Ibid.,* Aug. 13, Feb. 13, March 5, 19, 1864; Rollin, *Life and Public Services of Martin R. Delany,* 146–54; *Douglass' Monthly,* V (Aug. 1863), 849; *Life and Times of Frederick Douglass* (Hartford, 1882), 421.

40. *Life and Times of Frederick Douglass,* 421–25.

41. *Christian Recorder,* March 5, April 23, July 30, Aug. 27, 1864. For life in the camp and the grievances of black soldiers, as expressed in letters from the soldiers, see *Christian Recorder* for 1863 and 1864.

42. *Ibid.,* Feb. 20, March 5, April 23, June 11, Aug. 13, 1864.

43. *Ibid.,* July 23, June 11, 1864. See also the identical argument of a Pennsylvania black soldier in *ibid.,* Aug. 13, 1864, and of a soldier from the 54th Mass. Rgt. in Brown, *Negro in the American Rebellion,* 250–51.

44. *Christian Recorder,* July 11, Aug. 27, 1864.

45. *Ibid.,* May 28, July 23, 1864; Higginson, *Army Life in a Black Regiment,* 252. For the refusal to accept pay, see also *Christian Recorder,* June 11, July 23, 30, Aug. 13, 27, 1864.

46. *Christian Recorder,* Sept. 12, 1863, June 25, July 2, 1864; McPherson, *Negro's Civil War,* 200–01; McPherson, *Struggle for Equality,* 217; Emilio, *History of the Fifty-fourth Regiment,* 190–91; Brown, *Negro in the American Rebellion,* 251–52; Higginson, *Army Life in a Black Regiment,* 280.

47. *Douglass' Monthly,* V (Aug. 1863), 852; *Christian Recorder,* July 18, 1863; John S. Rock to the soldiers of the 5th Rgt. of U.S. Heavy Artillery, Natchez, Miss., May 30, 1864, Ms. address in George L. Ruffin Papers, Howard Univ., Washington, D.C.; McPherson, *Negro's Civil War,* 175–76; Headquarters, Supervisory Committee on Colored Enlistments, "To Men of Color," broadside, Historical Society of Pennsylvania. Similar sentiments may be found in *Christian Recorder,* July 11, 1863.

48. *Christian Recorder,* Sept. 17, 1864.

49. *Ibid.,* Nov. 5, 1864.

50. McPherson, *Struggle for Equality,* 217–19; Higginson, *Army Life in a Black Regiment,* 287–89; *Christian Recorder,* Nov. 5, 1864; Emilio, *History of the Fifty-fourth Regiment,* 220–21, 227–28. On March 3, 1865, Congress enacted a law giving full retroactive pay to all black regiments that had been promised equal pay at the time of enlistment.

51. *New York Times,* June 14, 1864; William E. Farrison, *William Wells Brown* (Chicago, 1969), 382; Blassingame (ed.), *Slave Testimony,* 378, 384; Herbert Aptheker (ed.), *A Documentary History of the Negro People in the United States* (New York, 1951), 486–87. For similar sentiments, see *Christian Recorder,* April 23, June 11, July 23, 1864, and *New Orleans Tribune,* Aug. 25, 1864. On the appointment of black officers, see Cornish, *Sable Arm,* 214–17.

52. Rollin, *Life and Public Services of Martin R. Delany,* 141–43; *Christian Recorder,* Feb. 14, 1863.

53. Rollin, *Life and Public Services of Martin R. Delany,* 166–8, 200–02, 209–26.

54. *Richmond Dispatch,* Aug. 5, 1864, reprinted in *New York Times,* Aug. 12, 1864; Emma E. Holmes, Ms. Diary, entry for July 16, 1863, Univ. of South Carolina.

55. Colin Clarke to Maxwell Clarke, Feb. 10, 1864, Williams-Chesnut-Manning Papers, Univ. of South Carolina. For comparable sentiments, see House (ed.), "Deterio-

ration of a Georgia Rice Plantation During Four Years of Civil War," 107.

56. Cornish, *Sable Arm,* 160, 162–63, 167.

57. *Ibid.,* 159–62; Wilson, *Black Phalanx,* 316–18.

58. Cornish, *Sable Arm,* 163, 169, 172–73, 177–78; *New York Times,* Dec. 2, 1863, Jan. 28, March 26, 1864; Aptheker (ed.), *Documentary History,* 487–88; Williamson, *After Slavery,* 21; Kerby, *Kirby Smith's Confederacy,* 111.

59. Cornish, *Sable Arm,* 170–72. For reports of prisoner exchanges, see *Christian Recorder,* Feb. 25, 1865, and Williamson, *After Slavery,* 21.

60. Bell I. Wiley, *The Life of Johnny Reb: The Common Soldier of the Confederacy* (Indianapolis, 1943), 314–15; Cornish, *Sable Arm,* 164, 176–77.

61. *Christian Recorder,* July 26, 1862, Feb. 14, June 13, 1863, April 2, 1864; *New York Times,* May 20, 1863; *Douglass' Monthly,* V (Aug. 1863), 849–50.

62. Basler (ed.), *Collected Works of Abraham Lincoln,* VI, 357, VII, 302–03; *Life and Times of Frederick Douglass,* 423–24; *Christian Recorder,* April 23, 1864.

63. *Christian Recorder,* April 23, 1864; Cornish, *Sable Arm,* 173–75; Brown, *Negro in the American Rebellion,* 235–47; McPherson, *Negro's Civil War,* 217–21.

64. *Christian Recorder,* June 11, April 30, 1864. See also "The Capture of Fort Pillow," an editorial in *ibid.,* April 23, 1864.

65. Farrison, *William Wells Brown,* 391–92.

66. McPherson, *Negro's Civil War,* 225; Kerby, *Kirby Smith's Confederacy,* 312; Cornish, *Sable Arm,* 176–77; Wilson, *Black Phalanx,* 347–48.

67. *Christian Recorder,* Aug. 13, 1864; McPherson, *Negro's Civil War,* 222. See also *New York Times,* Aug. 26, 27, Oct. 1, 1864.

68. Higginson, *Army Life in a Black Regiment,* 173–74; Rose, *Rehearsal for Reconstruction,* 243–44; Sarah Bradford, *Harriet Tubman: The Moses of Her People* (2nd ed., 1886; repr. New York, 1961), 99–102.

69. *Christian Recorder,* April 9, June 18, 1864; March 18, April 1, 1865; Rawick (ed.), *American Slave,* XVII: Fla. Narr., 161. See also "Letter from South Carolina," in *Christian Recorder,* Feb. 25, 1865.

70. *New York Times,* Feb. 28, 1864; Rawick (ed.), *American Slave,* XVII: Fla. Narr., 82; *Christian Recorder,* April 15, 1865.

71. *Christian Recorder,* May 28, June 25, 1864, April 15, 1865.

72. *Ibid.,* May 28, 1864, March 25, April 15, 1865; Emma E. Holmes, Ms. Diary, entry for May 3, 1865, Univ. of South Carolina.

73. *New York Tribune,* March 2, 1865; *Christian Recorder,* April 15, 1865; Lt. Col. John S. Bogert, 103rd U.S. Colored Troops, to his parents, Feb. 24, 1865, Univ. of South Carolina; McPherson, *Negro's Civil War,* 236–37; Rollin, *Life and Public Services of Martin R. Delany,* 197–98.

74. Maxwell Clarke to Mrs. John Laurence Manning, Oct. 12, 1863, Williams-Chesnut-Manning Papers, Univ. of South Carolina; Jervey and Ravenel, *Two Diaries,* 7; *Christian Recorder,* June 25, 1864; Reid, *After the War,* 213; *Christian Recorder,* May 27, 1865.

75. *New York Times,* Dec. 5, 1863; Eliza Frances Andrews, *The War-Time Journal of a Georgia Girl, 1864–1865* (New York, 1908), 261–62; Johns, *Life with the Forty-ninth Massachusetts Volunteers,* 295–96; Simkins and Patton, *Women of the Confederacy,* 238. For similar views of native whites, see, e.g., Ravenel, *Private Journal,* 212–14; Jervey and Ravenel, *Two Diaries,* 7, 8–9, 11, 18, 31–33, 34; Stone, *Brokenburn,* 297–98.

76. *Christian Recorder,* May 6, 27, 1865.

77. Rawick (ed.), *American Slave,* XVIII: Unwritten History, 253.

78. Cornish, *Sable Arm,* 287–88; Wiley, *Southern Negroes,* 341–44; McPherson, *Negro's Civil War,* 143–47; Bryant (ed.), "A Yankee Soldier Looks at the Negro," 147.

79. Cornish, *Sable Arm,* 288; Wiley, *Life of Billy Yank,* 124–25, 134–37.

80. McPherson, *Negro's Civil War,* 183; Johns, *Life with the Forty-ninth Massachusetts Volunteers,* 154; Bryant (ed.), "A Yankee Soldier Looks at the Negro," 141; Wilson, *Black Phalanx,* 280–83; Johns, *Life with the Forty-ninth Massachusetts Volunteers,* 167, 168; McPherson, *Negro's Civil War,* 172; *New York Times,* June 14, 1864, May 17, 1863.

81. Wilson, *Black Phalanx,* 280, 282, 283; Gordon, *War Diary of Events,* 275; Higginson, *Army Life in a Black Regiment,* 29, 259.

82. Cornish, *Sable Arm,* 55, 261–64, 267, 288–89; *Christian Recorder,* Aug. 13, 1864.

83. McPherson, *Negro's Civil War,* 237; Rawick (ed.), *American Slave,* XVIII: Unwritten History, 150–51; IV: Texas Narr. (Part 1), 232; Hepworth, *Whip, Hoe, and Sword,* 187.

84. Johns, *Life with the Forty-ninth Massachusetts Volunteers,* 294–95; Lt. Col. John S. Bogert, 103rd U.S. Colored Troops, to his parents, Feb. 1, 17, 1865, Univ. of South Carolina.

85. *New York Times,* Aug. 21, 1863; George O. Jewett to Dexter Jewett, July 18, 1863, Main File, Henry E. Huntington Library; Wiley, *Life of Billy Yank,* 121. See also *New York Times,* April 16, 1863, Oct. 30, 1864, March 12, 1865; Joel Cook, *The Siege of Richmond* (Philadelphia, 1862), 75–76.

86. Cornish, *Sable Arm,* 147. See also *New York Times,* April 21, 1863; Bryant (ed.), "A Yankee Soldier Looks at the Negro," 146; Wilson, *Black Phalanx,* 298, 310–11.

87. Towne, *Letters and Diary,* 94; *New York Times,* Oct. 3, 1862; Johns, *Life with the Forty-ninth Massachusetts Volunteers,* 169.

88. Quoted in introduction to Higginson, *Army Life in a Black Regiment,* Collier Books reprint edition (New York, 1962), 19–20. On self-pride and the postwar expectations of black soldiers, see also *Christian Recorder,* Aug. 13, 1864 (Sgt. John C. Brock and Cpl. Abram C. Simms), March 18 (Sgt. John C. Brock and Pvt. Henry C. Hoyle), April 8 (George A. Watkins), 15 (William Waters), May 13 (J. N. Drake), 27 (Cpl. William Gibson and Pvt. W. A. Freeman); *New York Times,* Feb. 20, 1864, and Brown, *Negro in the American Rebellion,* 280–81 (Cpl. Spencer McDowell).

89. *New York Tribune,* June 8, 1863, quoted in Guthrie, *Camp-Fires of the Afro-American,* 366; Du Bois, *Black Reconstruction,* 104, 110. For similar sentiments, see *New York Times,* Aug. 21, 1863, and *New Era,* July 28, 1870.

90. *New York Times,* Aug. 17, 1865; Haviland, *A Woman's Life-Work,* 314–15. See also Ephraim McDowell Anderson, *Memoirs: Historical and Personal* (St. Louis, 1868), 400–01; Perdue et al. (eds.), *Weevils in the Wheat,* 179.

## Chapter Three: Kingdom Comin'

1. Higginson, *Army Life in a Black Regiment,* 217–18.

2. Louis Manigault to "Mon Cher Pere" [Charles Manigault], Nov. 24, Dec. 5, 1861, Louis Manigault Letters, South Carolina Department of Archives and History, Columbia; Louis Manigault to Charles W. Henry, April 10, 1863, with enclosure containing description and cropped photograph of a runaway slave, Manigault Family Letters, South Caroliniana Library, Univ. of South Carolina; Louis Manigault, Memos on Overseers, Gowrie Plantation (Savannah River), Feb. 1, 1857, Dec. 20, 1858, and "Visit to 'Gowrie' and 'East Hermitage' Plantations," March 1867, Manigault Plantation Records, Southern Historical Collection, Univ. of North Carolina; House (ed.), "Deterioration of a Georgia Rice Plantation During Four Years of Civil War," 98–117; Ulrich B. Phillips (ed.), *Plantation and Frontier: 1649–1863* (2 vols.; Cleveland, 1910), I, 138, 320–21, II, 32–33, in John R. Commons et al. (eds.), *A Documentary History of American Industrial Society* (10 vols.; Cleveland, 1910–11). See also James M. Clifton, "A Half-Century of a Georgia Rice Plantation," *North Carolina Historical Review,* XLVII (1970), 388–415.

3. Rawick (ed.), *American Slave,* XIV: N.C. Narr. (Part 1), 279; John Houston Bills, Ms. Diary, entry for Jan. 10, 1863, Univ. of North Carolina; *New York Times,* April 12, 1862 (the incident was related by "C.H.W.," a *Times* correspondent writing from Centreville, Virginia).

4. Jervey and Ravenel, *Two Diaries,* 5; Washington, *Up from Slavery,* 19–20.

5. Heyward, *Seed from Madagascar,* 135; S. H. Boineau to Charles Heyward, Jan. 6, 1865, Univ. of South Carolina; Jones (ed.), *Heroines of Dixie,* 196–97; Catherine Barbara Broun, Ms. Diary, entry for Jan. 1, 1864, Univ. of North Carolina. See also Ravenel, *Private Journal,* 205; Susan Bradford Eppes, *Through Some Eventful Years* (Macon, 1926; repr. Gainesville, 1968), 168.

6. Rawick (ed.), *American Slave,* VI: Ala. Narr., 270. For similar recollections, see III: S.C. Narr. (Part 4), 14, and XIV: N.C. Narr. (Part 1), 128. The song "Ol' Gen'ral Bragg's A-Mowin' Down de Yankees" also captured much of this feeling. Newman Ivey White (ed.), *North Carolina Folklore* (7 vols.; Durham, N.C., 1952–64), II, 543–44.

7. See e.g., Rawick (ed.), *American Slave,* XIV: N.C. Narr. (Part 1), 86.

8. Macrae, *Americans at Home,* 133; Rawick (ed.), *American Slave,* VI: Ala. Narr., 270–71.

9. Wiley, *Southern Negroes,* 19; *New York Tribune,* March 2, 1865; Rawick (ed.), *American Slave,* III: S.C. Narr. (Part 3), 202; V: Texas Narr. (Part 3), 158; XIV: N.C. Narr. (Part 1), 249–50.

10. John Houston Bills, Ms. Diary, entry for Jan. 14, 1863, Univ. of North Carolina; Perdue et al. (eds.), *Weevils in the Wheat,* 144. See also Stone, *Brokenburn,* 33, 35, and Rawick (ed.), *American Slave,* VII: Miss. Narr., 63–64.

11. Rawick (ed.), *American Slave,* XII: Ga. Narr. (Part 2), 278; V: Texas Narr. (Part 3), 230; II: S.C. Narr. (Part 1), 118–19; Smedes, *Memorials of a Southern Planter,* 188–89. See also Rawick (ed.), *American Slave,* II and III: S. C. Narr. (Part 1), 72, 248, (Part 2), 19, 54, 325, (Part 3), 26, (Part 4), 225; VI: Ala. Narr., 49–50, 89, 99, 144, 225, 331, 373, 420; VII: Okla. Narr., 106; XIV: N.C. Narr. (Part 1), 419; Jacob Stroyer, "My Life in the South," in Katz (ed.), *Five Slave Narratives,* 36; Washington, *Up from Slavery,* 19; Elizabeth W. Allston Pringle, *Chronicles of Chicora Wood* (New York, 1922), 221–24, 227–28; *The Diary of Dolly Lunt Burge* (ed. James I. Robertson; Athens, Ga., 1962), 91–92, 100; Matthew Page Andrews (ed.), *The Women of the South in War Times* (Baltimore, 1920), 237–38; Chesnut, *Diary from Dixie,* 475; and Katharine M. Jones (ed.), *When Sherman Came: Southern Women and the "Great March"* (Indianapolis, 1964), 116, 252.

12. *When the World Ended: The Diary of Emma LeConte* (ed. Earl S. Miers; New York, 1957), 31, 41; Wiley, *Southern Negroes*, 71; Jervey and Ravenel, *Two Diaries*, 10; Pringle, *Chronicles of Chicora Wood*, 234; Mrs. Mary Jones to Col. Charles C. Jones, Jr., May 19, 1863, in Myers (ed.), *Children of Pride*, 1062.

13. Chesnut, *Diary from Dixie*, 306; Jones (ed.), *Heroines of Dixie*, 232; Rawick (ed.), *American Slave*, IV: Texas Narr. (Part 2), 241.

14. Rawick (ed.), *American Slave*, II: S.C. Narr. (Part 1), 247, (Part 2), 20, 157; Stone, *Brokenburn*, 198, 203; Wise, *End of an Era*, 208, 210. See also Myers (ed.), *Children of Pride*, 885–86.

15. Rawick (ed.), *American Slave*, X: Ark. Narr. (Part 5), 136; *Black Republican* (New Orleans), May 20, 1865. For different versions and some recollections of the song, see White (ed.), *North Carolina Folklore*, II, 541–43, and Rawick (ed.), *American Slave*, II: S.C. Narr. (Part 2), 197; IV: Texas Narr. (Part 2), 28–29; XVIII: Unwritten History, 232.

16. *Douglass' Monthly*, IV (Jan. 1862), 580.

17. Stone, *Brokenburn*, 168–69; Nevins, *War for the Union: The Organized War, 1863–1864*, 417.

18. Towne, *Letters and Diary*, 27–29, 94–95; Rose, *Rehearsal for Reconstruction*, 17, 104–05, 108–09; Rawick (ed.), *American Slave*, III: S.C. Narr. (Part 3), 203. See also Forten, *Journal*, 144; *New York Times*, Dec. 1, 1861; Ruffin, *Diary*, II, 173; Isabella Middleton Leland (ed.), "Middleton Correspondence, 1861–1865," *South Carolina Historical Magazine*, LXIII (1962), 38.

19. P. L. Rainwater (ed.), "Letters of James Lusk Alcorn," *Journal of Southern History*, III (1937), 200–01; Ravenel, *Private Journal*, 210–11, 212.

20. Rawick (ed.), *American Slave*, XV: N.C. Narr. (Part 2), 200; VI: Ala. Narr., 420; XVII: Fla. Narr., 45; XIII: Ga. Narr. (Part 4), 145; *New York Times*, May 10, 1864; Haviland, *A Woman's Life-Work*, 274.

21. Rawick (ed.), *American Slave*, XVIII: Unwritten History, 253; IV: Texas Narr. (Part 1), 279–80; XIV: N.C. Narr. (Part 1), 157. For a Unionist planter who freed his slaves and offered to pay them for their labor, as the Yankee troops approached, see Haviland, *A Woman's Life-Work*, 315–16.

22. Rawick (ed.), *American Slave*, VII: Okla. Narr., 275–77, 281. For a similar story, see III: S.C. Narr. (Part 4), 26–27.

23. Haviland, *A Woman's Life-Work*, 274; Rawick (ed.), *American Slave*, II: S.C. Narr. (Part 2), 329.

24. Emma E. Holmes, Ms. Diary, entry for March 31, 1865, Univ. of South Carolina.

25. John Houston Bills, Ms. Diary, entry for July 11, 1864, Univ. of North Carolina; Sarah Morgan Dawson, *A Confederate Girl's Diary* (Boston, 1913), 277–78.

26. Andrews, *War-Time Journal of a Georgia Girl*, 127–28, 355.

27. Rawick (ed.), *American Slave*, XVII: Fla. Narr., 161–62. The song is also recalled in XVIII: Unwritten History, 32.

28. *Ibid.*, XIV: N.C. Narr. (Part 1), 24–25.

29. Botume, *First Days Amongst the Contrabands*, 13. For comparable experiences, see Higginson, *Army Life in a Black Regiment*, 173–74; *New York Times*, April 16, June 19, 1863; Rawick (ed.), *American Slave*, III: S.C. Narr. (Part 3), 28.

30. Rawick (ed.), *American Slave*, II: S.C. Narr. (Part 2), 236, 335; VII: Miss. Narr., 131; XV: N.C. Narr. (Part 2), 428; *New York Times*, June 19, 1863.

31. Rawick (ed.), *American Slave*, XIV: N.C. Narr. (Part 1), 178; XVIII: Unwritten History, 198; III: S.C. Narr. (Part 4), 23–24; Hitchcock, *Marching with Sherman*, 84; Fremantle, *Three Months in the Southern States*, 94; Botume, *First Days Amongst the Contrabands*, 55; Leland (ed.), "Middleton Correspondence, 1861–1865," 101; Jervey and Ravenel, *Two Diaries*, 17–18; Rawick (ed.), *American Slave*, XIV: N.C. Narr. (Part 1), 250.

32. Nichols, *The Great March*, 59; Rawick (ed.), *American Slave*, XI: Mo. Narr., 54; IX: Ark. Narr. (Part 3), 198.

33. Armstrong, *Old Massa's People*, 301–02; *New York Times*, June 14, 1863.

34. Nichols, *The Great March*, 59; Armstrong and Ludlow, *Hampton and Its Students*, 83; Dennett, *The South As It Is*, 320. For images of the Yankees, as imparted by masters and mistresses, and for the reactions of slaves, see also Towne, *Letters and Diary*, 27, 29; Wiley (ed.), *Letters of Warren*

*Akin,* 21; Taylor, *Reminiscences of My Life in Camp,* 7–8; Dennett, *The South As It Is,* 174, 319; Haviland, *A Woman's Life-Work,* 264; Swint (ed.), *Dear Ones at Home,* 42, 107, 252; Johns, *Life with the Forty-ninth Massachusetts Volunteers,* 179; James E. Glazier to his parents, Feb. 28, 1862, Glazier Collection, Huntington Library; *New York Times,* July 19, Aug. 8, Dec. 4, 1861, Jan. 20, April 12, Nov. 9, 1862; Blassingame (ed.), *Slave Testimony,* 383; Rawick (ed.), *American Slave,* VII: Miss. Narr., 162; XIII: Ga. Narr. (Part 3), 162; XIV: N.C. Narr. (Part 1), 136, 192, 214, 277; Wiley, *Southern Negroes,* 12–13; Hitchcock, *Marching with Sherman,* 64, 70, 84.

35. Wiley, *Southern Negroes,* 14; Rawick (ed.), *American Slave,* VIII and IX: Ark. Narr. (Part 2), 348, (Part 3), 173; VI: Ala. Narr., 15; Johns, *Life with the Forty-ninth Massachusetts Volunteers,* 141.

36. Hepworth, *Whip, Hoe, and Sword,* 141; M. Waterbury, *Seven Years Among the Freedmen* (3rd ed.; Chicago, 1893), 87; WPA, *Negro in Virginia,* 201–02; Perdue et al. (eds.), *Weevils in the Wheat,* 277. For the reactions of slaves to the arrival of the Yankees, see also Beatty, *Citizen-Soldier,* 119, 124–25; Chesnut, *Diary from Dixie,* 525; George T. Stevens, *Three Years in the Sixth Corps* (Albany, N.Y., 1866), 59; *New York Times,* April 14, Nov. 23, 1862, May 19, June 7, 1863, Dec. 23, 1864, March 6, 1865; *New York Tribune,* March 2, 4, 6, 1865; Rawick (ed.), *American Slave,* II and III: S.C. Narr. (Part 1), 142, (Part 4), 196; IX: Ark. Narr. (Part 4), 241; XII: Ga. Narr. (Part 1), 159; Armstrong and Ludlow, *Hampton and Its Students,* 83.

37. *New York Tribune,* March 2, 1865; Rawick (ed.), *American Slave,* II: S.C. Narr. (Part 1), 151; Wiley, *Southern Negroes,* 15; Nichols, *The Great March,* 161–62; Swint (ed.), *Dear Ones at Home,* 186–87.

38. Rawick (ed.), *American Slave,* II: S.C. Narr. (Part 2), 210–11; VI: Ala. Narr., 53. For similar recollections, see II and III: S.C. Narr. (Part 1), 40, 43, 53, 105–06, 128, 235–36, 259, 264, (Part 2), 32, 290, (Part 3), 26, 91, 102, 144, 192–93, 195, (Part 4), 209, 257–58; VI: Ala. Narr., 79, 99–100, 162–63, 270, 405; XIV and XV: N.C. Narr. (Part 1), 406, 425, (Part 2), 149; XVI: Va. Narr., 19; Perdue et al. (eds.), *Weevils in the Wheat,* 55, 108, 311.

39. Jervey and Ravenel, *Two Diaries,* 32; Easterby (ed.), *South Carolina Rice Plantation,* 208–09; Rawick (ed.), *American Slave,* XII: Ga. Narr. (Part 1), 248, (Part 2), 278, 282–83; VI: Ala. Narr., 190. For examples of these diverse reactions, see also Jervey and Ravenel, *Two Diaries,* 10–11; Ravenel, *Private Journal,* 213, 220; Smedes, *Memorials of a Southern Planter,* 193; Rawick (ed.), *American Slave,* II and III: S.C. Narr. (Part 2), 20, (Part 3), 91; V: Texas Narr. (Part 3), 228; VI: Ala. Narr., 190; VII: Miss. Narr., 14; VIII: Ark. Narr. (Part 2), 181; XIII: Ga. Narr. (Part 3), 256; XIV: N.C. Narr. (Part 1), 25; XVI: Va. Narr., 52; Perdue et al. (eds.), *Weevils in the Wheat,* 187.

40. Dawson, *A Confederate Girl's Diary,* 193; Rawick (ed.), *American Slave,* VI: Ala. Narr., 163, 373; II: S.C. Narr. (Part 1), 31; XII: Ga. Narr. (Part 1), 248. See also VI: Ala. Narr., 391–92, and IX: Ark. Narr. (Part 3), 198.

41. Rose, *Rehearsal for Reconstruction,* 64; Rawick (ed.), *American Slave,* II: S.C. Narr. (Part 1), 177; VIII: Ark. Narr. (Part 1), 312; VII: Miss. Narr., 39. See also III: S.C. Narr. (Part 3), 26, 252–53; V: Texas Narr. (Part 3), 270; VI: Ala. Narr., 50; VII: Okla. Narr., 167; X: Ark. Narr. (Part 5), 193; XIV: N.C. Narr. (Part 1), 293; Jones (ed.), *When Sherman Came,* 262.

42. Emma E. Holmes, Ms. Diary, entry for March 4, 1865, Univ. of South Carolina; Pringle, *Chronicles of Chicora Wood,* 233; Rawick (ed.), *American Slave,* II: S.C. Narr. (Part 1), 77; James W. Silver (ed.), *Mississippi in the Confederacy: As Seen in Retrospect* (Baton Rouge, 1961), 266. See also Burge, *Diary,* 102; Smedes, *Memorials of a Southern Planter,* 198; LeConte, *When the World Ended,* 51; Myers (ed.), *Children of Pride,* 1233, 1240; Jones (ed.), *When Sherman Came,* 7–8, 58, 232; Swint (ed.), *Dear Ones at Home,* 160; Chesnut, *Diary from Dixie,* 539; Macrae, *Americans at Home,* 259; *New York Times,* Dec. 27, 1864; Blassingame (ed.), *Slave Testimony,* 455; Perdue et al. (eds.), *Weevils in the Wheat,* 121; Rawick (ed.), *American Slave,* VII: Okla. Narr., 37; VII: Miss. Narr., 64; VIII: Ark. Narr. (Part 2), 10; XIV and XV: N.C. Narr. (Part 1), 256, (Part 2), 75.

43. Emma E. Holmes, Ms. Diary, entry for March 4, 1863, Univ. of South Carolina; Myers (ed.), *Children of Pride,* 1237.

44. Rawick (ed.), *American Slave*, IX and XI: Ark. Narr. (Part 3), 21, (Part 7), 240.

45. Wiley, *Life of Billy Yank*, 40–41.

46. Bryant (ed.), "A Yankee Soldier Looks at the Negro," 136; Wiley, *Life of Billy Yank*, 112–13.

47. *New York Times*, Nov. 14, 1861 (reprinted without comment in *Douglass' Monthly*, IV [Dec. 1861], 566); Rose, *Rehearsal for Reconstruction*, 64–65.

48. Nordhoff, *Freedmen of South Carolina*, 24–25; Johns, *Life with the Forty-ninth Massachusetts Volunteers*, 165, 138.

49. Johns, *Life with the Forty-ninth Massachusetts Volunteers*, 140, 164–65. See also Hepworth, *Whip, Hoe, and Sword*, 159–60, 163–64.

50. Wiley, *Life of Billy Yank*, 109; Fremantle, *Three Months in the Southern States*, 89. See also Bryant (ed.), "A Yankee Soldier Looks at the Negro," 134–35; Rev. Joel Grant to Prof. Henry Cowles, April 10, 1863, American Missionary Assn. Archives; Wiley, *Life of Billy Yank*, 42, 43, 112, 281.

51. Wiley, *Life of Billy Yank*, 109, 111–12; Henry A. Anderson to Miss Salina Saltsgiver, May 24, 1863, Henry Anderson Papers, Louisiana State Univ.

52. Wiley, *Life of Billy Yank*, 119; Rawick (ed.), *American Slave*, XIV: N.C. Narr. (Part 1), 96, 251; II: S.C. Narr. (Part 1), 105; Bryant (ed.), "A Yankee Soldier Looks at the Negro," 138–39. See also *Facts Concerning the Freedmen* (Boston: The Emancipation League, 1863), 9; John Oliver to Rev. S. S. Jocelyn, Aug. 5, 1862; C. P. Day to W. E. Whiting, Aug. 22, 1862; Rev. Joel Grant to Prof. Henry Cowles, April 10, 1863; Isaac S. Hubbs to Rev. S. S. Jocelyn and George Whipple, Jan. 8, 1864; A. O. Howell, Jan. 19, Feb. 6, 1864, American Missionary Assn. Archives; *Christian Recorder*, June 10, July 8, 1865; *New York Times*, Jan. 25, Feb. 5, July 20, 1863; Beatty, *Citizen-Soldier*, 132; John Beatty, *Memoirs of a Volunteer, 1861–1863* (ed. Harvey S. Ford; New York, 1946), 115; George F. Noyes, *The Bivouac and the Battlefield* (New York, 1863), 44; Winters, *Civil War in Louisiana*, 175–76. For native white views of Yankee mistreatment of slaves, see, e.g., Myers (ed.), *Children of Pride*, 1244, and Andrews, *War-Time Journal of a Georgia Girl*, 287, 331–32.

53. Wiley, *Life of Billy Yank*, 114–15, 118; Myrta Lockett Avary, *Dixie after the*

War (New York, 1906), 187; *New York Times*, Dec. 11, 1863.

54. Johns, *Life with the Forty-ninth Massachusetts Volunteers*, 139; *Christian Recorder*, Aug. 6, 1864; *New York Times*, Oct. 3, 1862; Wiley, *Life of Billy Yank*, 117; Emma E. Holmes, Ms. Diary, entry for Aug. 14, 1865, Univ. of South Carolina; *South Carolina Leader* (Charleston), Nov. 25, 1865.

55. Wiley, *Life of Billy Yank*, 114; George Whipple to Rev. S. S. Jocelyn, Aug. 1, 1862, American Missionary Assn. Archives; Myers (ed.), *Children of Pride*, 1230; Nevins, *War for the Union: The Organized War, 1863–1864*, 31; Perdue et al. (eds.), *Weevils in the Wheat*, 121; McPherson, *Negro's Civil War*, 113.

56. Swint (ed.), *Dear Ones at Home*, 169, 61. For similar examples of black disillusionment and protest, see *New Orleans Tribune*, July 8, 16, 1865; *Christian Recorder*, April 30, 1864, June 10, July 8, 1865; Rose, *Rehearsal for Reconstruction*, 240–41.

57. Wiley, *Life of Billy Yank*, 41, 115–16; James E. Glazier to his parents, Feb. 28, 1862, Glazier Collection, Huntington Library. See also Andrew J. Bennett, *The Story of the First Massachusetts Light Battery* (Boston, 1886), 100–01; Stevens, *Three Years in the Sixth Corps*, 273–74; Nevins, *War for the Union: The Organized War, 1863–1864*, 416.

58. Wiley, *Life of Billy Yank*, 41, 43.

59. Johns, *Life with the Forty-ninth Massachusetts Volunteers*, 170–71; Henrietta Stratton Jaquette (ed.), *South after Gettysburg: Letters of Cornelia Hancock, 1863–1868* (New York, 1956), 63–64. See also Bryant (ed.), "A Yankee Soldier Looks at the Negro," 136.

60. Thomas J. Myers to his wife, Feb. 26, 1865, Thomas J. Myers Papers, Univ. of North Carolina; Conyngham, *Sherman's March Through the South*, 275–78; Rose, *Rehearsal for Reconstruction*, 332; Emma E. Holmes, Ms. Diary, entry for May 3, 1865, Univ. of South Carolina; Pearson (ed.), *Letters from Port Royal*, 293–94; Towne, *Letters and Diary*, 148; Nichols, *The Great March*, 71; Winther (ed.), *With Sherman to the Sea*, 136, 138; Bryan, *Confederate Georgia*, 128; *New York Tribune*, Jan. 9, 1865. For slaves leaving with the Union forces, see also Beatty, *Citizen Soldier*, 141; Bennett, *Story*

of the First Massachusetts Light Battery, 153–54; Rev. Horace James, *Annual Report of the Superintendent of Negro Affairs in North Carolina, 1864* (Boston, n.d.), 36–37; Bryant (ed.), "A Yankee Soldier Looks at the Negro," 145–46; *New York Times,* Dec. 2, 1861, Dec. 18, 1862, April 6, 16, 18, May 9, June 5, 28, Aug. 8, 1863, Jan. 9, March 7, May 27, 1864, March 21, 1865; Rawick (ed.), *American Slave,* VIII: Ark. Narr. (Part 2), 110; XIV: N.C. Narr. (Part 1), 171–72; Wharton, *Negro in Mississippi,* 46–47; Williamson, *After Slavery,* 24–25; Bradford, *Harriet Tubman,* 99–101.

61. *Black Republican,* May 13, 1865; Eaton, *Grant, Lincoln and the Freedmen,* 2; Rose, *Rehearsal for Reconstruction,* 322, 332. See also Thompson, *An Englishman in the American Civil War,* 98; Elijah P. Burton, *Diary of E. P. Burton, Surgeon, 7th Regiment, Illinois* (Des Moines, 1939), 6, 8; Horace James, *Report of the Superintendent of Negro Affairs in North Carolina, 1864,* 57–58 (Appendix).

62. William F. Messner, "Black Violence and White Response: Louisiana, 1862," *Journal of Southern History,* XLI (1975), 21; Francis G. Peabody, *Education for Life: The Story of Hampton Institute* (New York, 1922), 34. For conditions in the contraband camps, see also Hannibal Hamlin to the Freedman's Relief Assn. of Philadelphia, June 6, 1862; Hamlin to Joseph M. Truman, Jr., June 13 and Sept. 9, 1862; George E. Baker to Truman, March 3, 1863; Lizzie MacLaurin to the Bethany Scholars, April 4, 1864, Papers of the Pennsylvania Society for Promoting the Abolition of Slavery, Historical Society of Pennsylvania; Rev. Joel Grant to Prof. Henry Cowles, April 10, 1863; A. O. Howell (Superintendent of Freedmen Camp, Natchez), Jan. 19 and Feb. 6, 1864; L. A. Eberhart to Rev. C. H. Fowler, Feb. 1, 1864, American Missionary Assn. Archives; Burton, *Diary,* 8; Jaquette (ed.), *South after Gettysburg,* 33–50; *New York Times,* March 20, Oct. 27, 28, Dec. 9, 1862, Jan. 18, Aug. 9, Nov. 12, 1863, Feb. 26, 1865. For Federal policy toward the contrabands, see Gerteis, *From Contraband to Freedman,* and Wiley, *Southern Negroes,* 175–294.

63. Myers (ed.), *Children of Pride,* 986, 1197–98; *New York Times,* Nov. 8, 1862, March 26, 1865; Stone, *Brokenburn,* 128; G.

P. Whittington, (ed.), "Concerning the Loyalty of Slaves in North Louisiana in 1863: Letters from John H. Ransdell to Governor Thomas O. Moore, dated 1863," *Louisiana Historical Quarterly,* XIV (1931), 492. "The contrabands are curious as to what shall be their fate. One or two told me that after working on our entrenchments it would go hard with them if their masters returned. One inquired suspiciously why his master's name was taken down." *New York Times,* July 20, 1861.

64. Nichols, *The Great March,* 62. See also *ibid.,* 83; Mary Ames, *From a New England Woman's Diary in Dixie in 1865* (Springfield, Mass., 1906), 64; *New York Times,* Dec. 18, 1861.

65. Cornelia Phillips Spencer, *The Last Ninety Days of the War in North Carolina* (New York, 1866), 186–87; *New York Times,* Dec. 1, 1862.

66. Wilmer Shields to William Newton Mercer, Dec. 11, 1863, Jan. 25, 1864, June 10 (incl. enclosure: "List of Negroes who have remained, been absent and returned, and are now on the plantations"), Sept. 20, 1865, Dec. 4, 1866, W. N. Mercer Papers, Louisiana State Univ.

67. Alexander F. Pugh, Ms. Plantation Diary, entries for Oct. 27, 28, 30, 31, Nov. 1, 2, 5, 6, 1862, Nov. 3, 1863, A. F. Pugh Papers, Louisiana State Univ.; Annette Koch to [Christian D. Koch], June 27, 1863, Christian D. Koch Papers, Louisiana State Univ.; Okar to Gustave Lauve, June 26, 1863, Gustave Lauve Papers, Louisiana State Univ.

68. John H. Ransdell to Gov. Thomas O. Moore, May 24, 26, 31, 1863, in Whittington (ed.), "Concerning the Loyalty of Slaves in North Louisiana," 491–93, 495, 497. For the rapid erosion of slavery in Louisiana and Mississippi, see also, e.g., Samuel A. Agnew (Miss.), Ms. Diary, entry for Oct. 29, 1862, Univ. of North Carolina; Bayside Plantation Record (Bayou Teche, La.), entries for April 10, May 1, 3, 4, 1863, Univ. of North Carolina; Louisa T. Lovell (Palmyra plantation, near Natchez) to Capt. Joseph Lovell, Feb. 7, 1864, Quitman Papers, Univ. of North Carolina; Emily Caroline Douglas (Adams Co., Miss.), Ms. Autobiography, 167–68, Louisiana State Univ.; *New York Times,* Dec. 1, 1862, Oct. 17, 1863; Sitterson, *Sugar Country,* 209–11; William K. Scarborough,

The *Overseer: Plantation Management in the Old South* (Baton Rouge, 1966), 153–55; F. W. Smith (ed.), "The Yankees in New Albany: Letters of Elizabeth Jane Beach, July 29, 1864," *Journal of Mississippi History,* II (Jan. 1940), 46; Ripley, *Slaves and Freedmen in Civil War Louisiana,* 14–23; James L. Roark, *Masters Without Slaves: Southern Planters in the Civil War and Reconstruction* (New York, 1977), 112–17.

69. Thompson, *An Englishman in the American Civil War,* 94; John Houston Bills, Ms. Diary, entries for Jan. 10, 14, May 18, 27, June 1, 3, 5, 8, 16, Aug. 21, 29, Oct. 8, 17, 1863 (incl. "Memoranda 1863: List of Servants Carried Off by Federal Army and Value"), Feb. 10, 11, July 11, 1864, Univ. of North Carolina.

70. Myers (ed.), *Children of Pride,* 1241, 1243, 1247.

71. Okar to Gustave Lauve, June 26, 1863, Gustave Lauve Papers, Louisiana State Univ.; Andrews, *War-Time Journal of a Georgia Girl,* 183. See also Wiley, *Southern Negroes,* 12; Bettersworth (ed.), *Mississippi in the Confederacy,* 240; Williamson, *After Slavery,* 24. For slaves who returned only to leave again, see, e.g., Wilmer Shields to William N. Mercer, June 10, 1865, Mercer Papers, Louisiana State Univ.; Sydnor, *A Gentleman of the Old Natchez Region,* 297; Sitterson, *Sugar Country,* 211.

72. Stone, *Brokenburn,* 185; John H. Bills, Ms. Diary, entries for Sept. 22, 24, 1863, Univ. of North Carolina; Myers (ed.), *Children of Pride,* 1263; WPA, *Negro in Virginia,* 202; Rawick (ed.), *American Slave,* II: S.C. Narr. (Part 2), 145; Ruffin, *Diary,* II, 409–10; Stone, *Brokenburn,* 179. See also Rainwater (ed.), "Letters of James Lusk Alcorn," 201; Easterby (ed.), *South Carolina Rice Plantation,* 207; Whittington (ed.), "Concerning the Loyalty of Slaves in North Carolina in 1863," 501. Edmund Ruffin, Jr., offered amnesty "for the past insubordination" to his returning slaves, "provided their future conduct should be good, as it had been generally previously." Ruffin, *Diary,* II, 367–68.

73. Ravenel, *Private Journal,* 251; Rose, *Rehearsal for Reconstruction,* 16–17, 106–08; *New York Times,* Nov. 20, 1861; Botume, *First Days Amongst the Contrabands,* 11, 33–34; *Christian Recorder,* Nov.

30, 1861. Few towns were sacked as thoroughly as Beaufort. Although an estimated 3,000 slaves helped to level Jackson, Mississippi, that was a joint operation with Union troops; in nearby Yazoo City, however, the blacks themselves burned down fourteen houses and the courthouse, and the proliferation of arson attempts elsewhere, some of them spectacularly successful, gave rise to new fears of a general insurrection. Silver (ed.), *Mississippi in the Confederacy,* 268–69; Harvey Wish, "Slave Disloyalty under the Confederacy," *Journal of Negro History,* XXIII (1938), 444; Williamson, *After Slavery,* 51.

74. Jervey and Ravenel, *Two Diaries,* 12; D. E. H. Smith (ed.), *Mason Smith Family Letters,* 193, 218; Easterby (ed.), *South Carolina Rice Plantation,* 208. See also Ruffin, *Diary,* II, 598; Ravenel, *Private Journal,* 216; Leland (ed.), "Middleton Correspondence, 1861–1865," 106; Ada Sterling, *A Belle of the Fifties: Memoirs of Mrs. Clay, of Alabama* (New York, 1905), 182; Stone, *Brokenburn,* 210; D. E. H. Smith (ed.), *Mason Smith Family Letters,* 188, 189; Elias Horry Deas to Anne Deas, Aug. 12, 1865, Deas Papers, Univ. of South Carolina.

75. Ravenel, *Private Journal,* 217; Leland (ed.), "Middleton Correspondence, 1861–1865," 107; Stone, *Brokenburn,* 193, 203; Williamson, *After Slavery,* 5–6. See also Jervey and Ravenel, *Two Diaries,* 11, 12, 33, 35, 37; Dawson, *Confederate Girl's Diary,* 178; D. E. H. Smith (ed.), *Mason Smith Family Letters,* 187; *New York Times,* Dec. 21, 1862; Whittington (ed.), "Concerning the Loyalty of Slaves in North Louisiana in 1863," 492; Jones (ed.), *When Sherman Came,* 268.

76. John H. Bills, Ms. Diary, entry for Feb. 11, 1864, Univ. of North Carolina; Easterby (ed.), *South Carolina Rice Plantation,* 208–10, 328; Pringle, *Chronicles of Chicora Wood,* 268–69. For comparable scenes, see, e.g., Elias Horry Deas to Anne Deas, May 5, 1865, Deas Papers, Univ. of South Carolina; Edward Lynch to Joseph Glover [June 1865], Glover-North Papers, Univ. of South Carolina; Avary, *Dixie after the War,* 341–42.

77. Towne, *Letters and Diary,* 34; *New York Times,* Nov. 20, 1861, Nov. 16, 20, Dec. 21, 1862; Pringle, *Chronicles of Chicora*

*Wood,* 269; Sitterson, *Sugar Country,* 212.

78. Easterby (ed.), *South Carolina Rice Plantation,* 213; Genovese, *Roll, Jordan, Roll,* 605; *New York Times,* Dec. 29, 1863; *Christian Recorder,* Nov. 26, 1862. See also Rawick (ed.), *American Slave,* IV: Texas Narr. (Part 2), 163; XII: Ga. Narr. (Part 2), 119; XVI: Tenn. Narr., 12.

79. Samuel A. Agnew, Ms. Diary, entries for Oct. 31, Nov. 1, 1862, Univ. of North Carolina; Louisa T. Lovell to Capt. Joseph Lovell, Feb. 7, 1864, Quitman Papers, Univ. of North Carolina. See also Sitterson, *Sugar Country,* 214.

80. Sitterson, *Sugar Country,* 212; Nevins, *War for the Union: The Organized War, 1863–1864,* 376–77; Jones (ed.), *Heroines of Dixie,* 118; Emily Caroline Douglas, Ms. Autobiography, 168, Louisiana State Univ.

81. *New York Times,* Dec. 1, 1862, Oct. 30, 1864; Rawick (ed.), *American Slave,* XVII: Fla. Narr., 246; Sitterson, *Sugar Country,* 220; Wiley, *Southern Negroes,* 74; Scarborough, *The Overseer,* 153–54. See also Clayton Jones, "Mississippi Agriculture," *Journal of Mississippi History,* XXIV (April 1962), 138; Sitterson, "The McCollams: A Planter Family of the Old and New South," in Miller and Genovese (eds.), *Plantation, Town, and County,* 296; Ruffin, *Diary,* II, 317, 320; Ravenel, *Private Journal,* 211–12; Jervey and Ravenel, *Two Diaries,* 36; Stone, *Brokenburn,* 175; Savannah Writers' Project, *Savannah River Plantations* (Savannah, 1947), 324; John H. Bills, Ms. Diary, entries from Jan. 10, 1863, to Dec. 14, 1864, Univ. of North Carolina.

82. For a discussion of the overseer under slavery, see Genovese, *Roll, Jordan, Roll,* 12–21, and Scarborough, *The Overseer.*

83. Nevins, *War for the Union: The Organized War, 1863–1864,* 377; *New York Times,* Oct. 26, 1862 (the dispatch was written by the New Orleans correspondent of the *Times* on Oct. 16).

84. Pringle, *Chronicles of Chicora Wood,* 264–65.

85. Easterby (ed.), *South Carolina Rice Plantation,* 213, 218, 328–29. See also Scarborough, *The Overseer,* 163–64.

86. Joseph LeConte, *'Ware Sherman: A Journal of Three Months' Personal Experience in the Last Days of the Confederacy* (Berkeley, Calif., 1938), 133–34; Emma E.

Holmes, Ms. Diary, entry for June 15, 1865, Univ. of South Carolina; Leland (ed.), "Middleton Correspondence, 1861–1865," 100–01; Jervey and Ravenel, *Two Diaries,* 53.

87. Wish, "Slave Disloyalty under the Confederacy," 444; Wiley, *Southern Negroes,* 81; *Christian Recorder,* May 28, 1864; Perdue et al. (eds.), *Weevils in the Wheat,* 162; Dawson, *Confederate Girl's Diary,* 185. For other examples, see Stone, *Brokenburn,* 205; Emma E. Holmes, Ms. Diary, entry for End of May 1865, Univ. of South Carolina; Gerteis, *From Contraband to Freedman,* 114.

88. Jervey and Ravenel, *Two Diaries,* 36; LeGrand, *Journal,* 130; Scarborough, *The Overseer,* 154–55; Sitterson, *Sugar Country,* 209–10.

89. Ruffin, *Diary,* II, 318; *New York Times,* Oct. 17, 1863; Myers (ed.), *Children of Pride,* 1248; Gerteis, *From Contraband to Freedman,* 114; Rogers, *History of Georgetown County,* 422; Bragg, *Louisiana in the Confederacy,* 216; Williamson, *After Slavery,* 46, 51–52.

90. Alexander F. Pugh, Ms. Plantation Diary, entry for Nov. 5, 1862, A. F. Pugh Papers, Louisiana State Univ.; Scarborough, *The Overseer,* 153; Williamson, *After Slavery,* 52; Messner, "Black Violence and White Response: Louisiana, 1862," 22.

91. Chesnut, *Diary from Dixie,* 532; Ravenel, *Private Journal,* 218, 223.

92. W. McKee Evans, *Ballots and Fence Rails: Reconstruction on the Lower Cape Fear* (Chapel Hill, N.C., 1966), 76; Stone, *Brokenburn,* 197.

93. Typical examples may be found in Emma E. Holmes, Ms. Diary, entries for March 4, 11, 1865, Univ. of South Carolina; Everard Green Baker, Ms. Diary, entry for Dec. 26, 1862, Univ. of North Carolina; Jervey and Ravenel, *Two Diaries,* 22; Stone, *Brokenburn,* 298; LeConte, *'Ware Sherman,* 32; Avary, *Dixie after the War,* 196; Myers (ed.), *Children of Pride,* 1218–19; Easterby (ed.), *South Carolina Rice Plantation,* 207–08; *New York Tribune,* March 23, 1865; Simkins and Patton, *Women of the Confederacy,* 164–65; Jones (ed.), *When Sherman Came,* 68, 134.

94. Chesnut, *Diary from Dixie,* 528.

95. Wiley, *Southern Negroes,* 70; Nevins, *War for the Union: The Organized War to Victory, 1864–1865,* 296–97; Smedes, *Me-*

morials of a Southern Planter, 194–95; Ra-
wick (ed.), *American Slave*, XIV: N.C. Narr.
(Part 1), 11–12. For other examples, see
Emma E. Holmes, Ms. Diary, entry for
March 4, 1865, Univ. of South Carolina;
Jones (ed.), *When Sherman Came*, 21; Ra-
wick (ed.), *American Slave*, XIV: N.C. Narr.
(Part 1), 250.

96. Washington, *Up from Slavery*, 19;
Rawick (ed.), *American Slave*, III: S.C. Narr.
(Part 3), 170; VII: Okla. Narr., 337–38; Trow-
bridge, *The South*, 391; Emma E. Holmes,
Ms. Diary, entry for March 31, 1865, Univ.
of South Carolina.

97. Emma E. Holmes, Ms. Diary, entry
for End of May, 1865, Univ. of South
Carolina; Dawson, *Confederate Girl's Diary*,
212; Chesnut, *Diary from Dixie*, 544. Two
months earlier, on May 2, 1865, Mary Chesnut had noted in her diary: "The fidelity of
the Negroes is the principal topic everywhere. There seems not a single case of a
Negro who betrayed his master ..." *Ibid.*,
527–28.

98. Ravenel, *Private Journal*, 221. See
also LeConte, *'Ware Sherman*, 105–06, 125.

99. Andrews (ed.), *Women of the South
in War Times*, 239; Rawick (ed.), *American
Slave*, III: S.C. Narr. (Part 3), 26. For similar
examples of slave "betrayal," see Ella Gertrude (Clanton) Thomas, Ms. Journal, entry
for Dec. 12, 1864, Duke Univ.; Robert Philip
Howell, Ms. Memoirs [17], Univ. of North
Carolina; Jervey and Ravenel, *Two Diaries*,
35; Smedes, *Memorials of a Southern
Planter*, 194; Andrews (ed.), *Women of the
South in War Times*, 263–64; Jones (ed.),
*When Sherman Came*, 21–22, 235, 243; Bettersworth (ed.), *Mississippi in the Confederacy*, 210; Johns, *Life with the Forty-ninth
Massachusetts Volunteers*, 191; Rawick
(ed.), *American Slave*, II: S. C. Narr. (Part 1),
69, (Part 2), 329–30; V: Texas Narr. (Part 3),
245; VI: Ala. Narr., 78–79; VII: Okla. Narr.,
211; XIV: N.C. Narr. (Part 1), 76; Hepworth,
*Whip, Hoe, and Sword*, 142–44.

100. *New York Times*, July 29, 1863,
Dec. 12, 1861; Catherine Barbara Broun, Ms.
Diary, entry for May 1, 1864, Univ. of North
Carolina.

101. Hepworth, *Whip, Hoe, and
Sword*, 144–45; Stone, *Brokenburn*, 209.

102. Smedes, *Memorials of a Southern
Planter*, 197; House (ed.), "Deterioration of a

Georgia Rice Plantation During Four Years
of Civil War," 107; Ella Gertrude (Clanton)
Thomas, Ms. Journal, entry for Dec. 12,
1864, Duke Univ.

103. Chesnut, *Diary from Dixie*, 503;
Pringle, *Chronicles of Chicora Wood*, 236;
Emma E. Holmes, Ms. Diary, entry for
End of May 1865, Univ. of South Carolina.
See also Jervey and Ravenel, *Two Diaries*,
35.

104. Bell I. Wiley, *The Plain People of
the Confederacy* (Baton Rouge, 1944), 83;
Robert Philip Howell, Ms. Memoirs [17–18],
Univ. of North Carolina; Bryant (ed.), "A
Yankee Soldier Looks at the Negro," 145;
John H. Bills, Ms. Diary, entry for May 18,
1865; House (ed.), "Deterioration of a
Georgia Rice Plantation During Four Years
of Civil War," 102; "Visit to 'Gowrie' and
'East Hermitage' Plantations," March 1867,
Manigault Plantation Records, Univ. of
North Carolina. See also Easterby (ed.),
*South Carolina Rice Plantation*, 190, and
Stone, *Brokenburn*, 193, 195, 198, 199, 203,
208–09, 363.

105. Mrs. Elizabeth Jane Beach to her
parents, July 29, 1864, in Smith (ed.), "The
Yankees in New Albany," 46; Andrews,
*War-Time Journal of a Georgia Girl*, 321–22.

106. Avary, *Dixie after the War*, 190;
Lillian A. Pereyra, *James Lusk Alcorn: Persistent Whig* (Baton Rouge, 1966), 79.

107. Rawick (ed.), *American Slave*,
XVIII: Unwritten History, 221; II: S.C. Narr.
(Part 1), 225. For a discussion of the house
servant in slavery, see Genovese, *Roll, Jordan, Roll*, 328–65.

108. Smedes, *Memorials of a Southern
Planter*, 198; Pringle, *Chronicles of Chicora
Wood*, 253; Wiley, *Southern Negroes*, 73. For
house servants who "behaved outra-
geously," see also Okar to Gustave Lauve,
June 26, 1863, Gustave Lauve Papers, Louisiana State Univ.; John H. Bills, Ms. Diary,
entry for Aug. 21, 29, 1865, Univ. of North
Carolina; Louisa T. Lovell to Capt. Joseph
Lovell, Feb. 7, 1864, Quitman Papers, Univ.
of North Carolina; Myers (ed.), *Children of
Pride*, 1248; D. E. H. Smith (ed.), *Mason
Smith Family Letters*, 192; Stone, *Brokenburn*, 173, 176; Easterby (ed.), *South
Carolina Rice Plantation*, 207; Chesnut, *Diary from Dixie*, 354; Jones (ed.), *When Sherman Came*, 130.

109. *Richmond Examiner,* quoted in Frank Moore (ed.), *The Rebellion Record* (11 vols.; New York, 1861–68), IV, Part IV, 101–02; Andrews, *War-Time Journal of a Georgia Girl,* 344. See also Ravenel, *Private Journal,* 218, 221, 251, 269–70, and Leland (ed.), "Middleton Correspondence," 100.

110. House (ed.), "Deterioration of a Georgia Rice Plantation During Four Years of Civil War," 102; LeGrand, *Journal,* 263; Dennett, *The South As It Is,* 261–63. On June 19, 1862, Edmund Ruffin made this entry in his diary: "Why this property & Marlbourne should be especially losers of slaves, cannot be understood, for nowhere were they better cared for, or better managed & treated, according to their condition of slavery." *Diary,* II, 346.

111. Myers (ed.), *Children of Pride,* 427; Du Bois, *Black Reconstruction,* 9.

112. Murray, *Proud Shoes,* 159–60.

113. "Narrative of William Wells Brown," in Osofsky (ed.), *Puttin' On Ole Massa,* 212; Philip S. Foner (ed.), *The Life and Writings of Frederick Douglass* (4 vols.; New York, 1950–55), I, 157; *Narrative of the Life of Frederick Douglass, an American Slave* (3rd English ed.; Wortley, 1846), 40, 99.

114. Scarborough, *The Overseer,* 16–19, 82–84, 93–94; Genovese, *Roll, Jordan, Roll,* 365–88; E. L. Pierce, *The Negroes at Port Royal* (Boston, 1862), 8–10; Rose, *Rehearsal for Reconstruction,* 132–33; S. H. Boineau to Charles Heyward, Nov. 24, 1864, Univ. of South Carolina.

115. Rawick (ed.), *American Slave,* VI: Ala. Narr., 66; Higginson, *Army Life in a*

*Black Regiment,* 219. For the fate of the driver in the postwar period, see below, Chapter 8.

116. Jesse Belflowers to Adele Petigru Allston, Oct. 19, 1864, in Easterby (ed.), *South Carolina Rice Plantation,* 310; Jervey and Ravenel, *Two Diaries,* 17–18; Hitchcock, *Marching with Sherman,* 69–70; D. E. H. Smith (ed.), *Mason Smith Family Letters,* 237; Genovese, *Roll, Jordan, Roll,* 387; Ruffin, *Diary,* II, 317.

117. John H. Ransdell to Gov. Thomas O. Moore, May 24, 1863, in Whittington (ed.), "Concerning the Loyalty of Slaves in North Louisiana in 1863," 493; Louis Manigault to Charles Manigault, Nov. 24, 1861, South Carolina Dept. of Archives and History, Columbia; Pierce, *Negroes at Port Royal,* 8–10; Rose, *Rehearsal for Reconstruction,* 20, 80–81.

118. Rawick (ed.), *American Slave,* VII: Okla. Narr., 251, 253–55.

119. Stone, *Brokenburn,* 171; Grace B. Elmore, Ms. Diary, entry for March 4, 1865, Univ. of North Carolina.

120. Wiley, *Southern Negroes,* 143n.; *New York Times,* April 2, 1865; Genovese, *Roll, Jordan, Roll,* 99; Hitchcock, *Marching with Sherman,* 121–23.

121. Genovese, *Roll, Jordan, Roll,* 112.

122. "Visit to 'Gowrie' and 'East Hermitage' Plantations," March 23, 1867, Manigault Plantation Records, Univ. of North Carolina.

123. Rawick (ed.), *American Slave,* VI: Ala. Narr., 81–82.

124. *Ibid.,* II: S.C. Narr. (Part 1), 151.

## Chapter Four: Slaves No More

1. Irwin Silber (ed.), *Soldier Songs and Home-Front Ballads of the Civil War* (New York, 1964), 41; WPA, *Negro in Virginia,* 212; Perdue et al. (eds.), *Weevils in the Wheat,* 117.

2. WPA, *Negro in Virginia,* 164–65, 201.

3. John B. Jones, *A Rebel War Clerk's Diary at the Confederate States Capital* (2 vols.; Philadelphia, 1866; repr. in one volume, ed. Earl Schenck Miers, 1958), 528–30; Nevins, *War for the Union: The Organized*

*War to Victory, 1864–1865,* 294; Swint (ed.), *Dear Ones at Home,* 90; Rembert W. Patrick, *The Fall of Richmond* (Baton Rouge, 1960), 41–58; Jones (ed.), *Heroines of Dixie,* 398; Putnam, *Richmond During the Confederacy,* 363–64.

4. *Christian Recorder,* April 8, 15, 22, 1865; Rawick (ed.), *American Slave,* XVI: Va. Narr., 35–37; Perdue et al. (eds.), *Weevils in the Wheat,* 103, 145–46. See also *New York Tribune,* April 6, 1865.

5. *Christian Recorder,* April 22, 1865.

See also *Black Republican,* May 20, 1865; WPA, *Negro in Virginia,* 212; Jones, *Rebel War Clerk's Diary,* 530.

6. Putnam, *Richmond During the Confederacy,* 367; Patrick, *Fall of Richmond,* 68–69; Phoebe Yates Pember, *A Southern Woman's Story: Life in Confederate Richmond* (Jackson, Tenn., 1959), 135.

7. *New York Times,* April 11, 1865; McPherson, *Negro's Civil War,* 67–68; Patrick, *Fall of Richmond,* 115. See also *Christian Recorder,* April 22, 1865.

8. Hope R. Daggett to Rev. George Whipple, April 1865; Mary E. Watson to Rev. George Whipple, May 1, 1865; Miss Frances Littlefield to Rev. George Whipple, May 1, 1865, American Missionary Assn. Archives.

9. Haviland, *A Woman's Life-Work,* 414–15.

10. WPA, *Negro in Virginia,* 205, 210; Rawick (ed.), *American Slave,* XVI: Va. Narr., 3, 5–6; Perdue et al. (eds.), *Weevils in the Wheat,* 36–39.

11. Patrick, *Fall of Richmond,* 117–18; *New York Times,* April 30, 1865.

12. WPA, *Negro in Virginia,* 266.

13. Rawick (ed.), *American Slave,* XVII: Fla. Narr., 103. See also XIV: N.C. Narr. (Part 1), 97–98. For a description of a plantation near Huntsville, Alabama, where both slaves and the master disclaimed any knowledge of emancipation, see Franklin (ed.), *Diary of James T. Ayers,* 26–29. The Emancipation Proclamation, formally declared on January 1, 1863, applied only to those states (or portions thereof) "this day in rebellion against the United States." The loyal border slave states (Kentucky, Missouri, Maryland, and Delaware) and Tennessee were thereby excluded from its provisions, along with thirteen Federal-occupied parishes in Louisiana (including New Orleans), forty-eight counties in West Virginia, and seven counties in Virginia which were "for the present, left precisely as if this proclamation were not issued." Wherever Union troops were in command, however, slaves generally assumed they were free.

14. Grace B. Elmore, Ms. Diary, entry for March 4, 1865, Univ. of North Carolina; *New York Times,* Dec. 30, 1861; *Christian Recorder,* May 6, 1865.

15. *New York Times,* June 2, 1863; Rawick (ed.), *American Slave,* II: S. C. Narr. (Part 2), 329–30; Jones (ed.), *When Sherman Came,* 235–36.

16. "Look to the Future," *Louisiana Democrat* (Alexandria), June 3, 1863, quoted in Whittington (ed.), "Concerning the Loyalty of Slaves in North Louisiana in 1863," 489–90.

17. Whittington (ed.), "Concerning the Loyalty of Slaves in North Louisiana in 1863," 494, 500, 501; Rainwater (ed.), "Letters of James Lusk Alcorn," 201, 202.

18. *New York Times,* April 14, 1864.

19. Jervey and Ravenel, *Two Diaries,* 41; Rawick (ed.), *American Slave,* XIV: N.C. Narr. (Part 1), 97; Blassingame (ed.), *Slave Testimony,* 541; Scarborough, *The Overseer,* 149. See also Rawick (ed.), *American Slave,* XV: N.C. Narr. (Part 2), 310–11.

20. Rawick (ed.), *American Slave,* VII: Okla. Narr., 95–96.

21. *Ibid.,* XII: Ga. Narr. (Part 1), 248. See also VI: Ala. Narr., 225.

22. *Ibid.,* XVII: Fla. Narr., 81; VII: Miss. Narr., 81; XIII: Ga. Narr. (Part 3), 64. See also III: S.C. Narr. (Part 3), 136; V: Texas Narr. (Part 3), 204; WPA, *Negro in Virginia,* 208.

23. Rawick (ed.), *American Slave,* XII: Ga. Narr. (Part 1), 262. See also VI: Ala. Narr., 239–40.

24. *New York Times,* March 30, April 4, 1865; *New York Tribune,* April 4, 1865; Williamson, *After Slavery,* 47–48. For other post-emancipation celebrations, see *New York Times,* Jan. 3, 1864 (Norfolk), Jan. 23 and Aug. 1 (Savannah), July 12 (Louisville), 14 (Raleigh), 1865; *New York Tribune,* Jan. 13 (Key West), July 8 (Mobile), 12 (Raleigh and Columbia), 1865.

25. Rollin, *Life and Public Services of Martin R. Delany,* 193–95; Williamson, *After Slavery,* 48–49.

26. Chesnut, *Diary from Dixie,* 520–21; Trowbridge, *The South,* 291; Andrews, *War-Time Journal of a Georgia Girl,* 308. For similar reactions, see D. E. H. Smith (ed.), *Mason Smith Family Letters,* 232; LeConte, *When the World Ended,* 85–86.

27. Myers (ed.), *Children of Pride,* 1273–74.

28. Smedes, *Memorials of a Southern Planter,* 216–17; Ella Gertrude (Clanton)

Thomas, Ms. Journal, entry for May 8, 1865, Duke Univ.; Williamson, *After Slavery*, 34.

29. Avary, *Dixie after the War*, 152; Haviland, *A Woman's Life-Work*, 256; Burge, *Diary*, 112–113.

30. Grace B. Elmore, Ms. Diary, entry for May 24, 30, 1865, Univ. of North Carolina; Emma E. Holmes, Ms. Diary, entry for End of May, June 15, Aug. 25, 1865, Univ. of South Carolina.

31. Ravenel, *Private Journal*, 231, 232, 238, 239–40.

32. Rawick (ed.), *American Slave*, V: Texas Narr. (Part 4), 133; Williamson, *After Slavery*, 33.

33. Rawick (ed.), *American Slave*, XII: Ga. Narr. (Part 2), 326; IV: Texas Narr. (Part 1), 264, (Part 2), 168.

34. *Ibid.*, IX: Ark. Narr. (Part 3), 115, 29; VII: Okla. Narr., 114; V: Texas Narr. (Part 4), 22; Macrae, *Americans at Home*, 211.

35. Mrs. Laura E. Buttolph to Mrs. Mary Jones, June 30, 1865, in Myers (ed.) *Children of Pride*, 1279. See also Burge, *Diary*, 113.

36. Rawick (ed.), *American Slave*, VIII: Ark. Narr. (Part 2), 128; XIII: Ga. Narr. (Part 4), 348–49. See also XII: Ga. Narr. (Part 2), 133; XIV: N.C. Narr. (Part 1), 60.

37. Col. J. L. Haynes to Capt. B. F. Henry, July 8, 1865, Records of the Assistant Commissioners, Mississippi (Letters Received), Bureau of Refugees, Freedmen, and Abandoned Lands (hereafter cited as Freedmen's Bureau), National Archives, Washington, D.C. See also Wharton, *Negro in Mississippi*, 48, and Joe M. Richardson, *The Negro in the Reconstruction of Florida, 1865–1877* (Tallahassee, 1965), 13–14.

38. 39 Cong., 1 Sess., House Exec. Doc. 70, *Freedmen's Bureau* (Washington, D.C., 1866), 9–10, 99, 154. For recollections of such meetings by ex-slaves, see Rawick (ed.), *American Slave*, III: S.C. Narr. (Part 3), 178; VIII: Ark. Narr. (Part 1), 37–38; XIII: Ga. Narr. (Part 4), 34.

39. Rawick (ed.), *American Slave*, IV and V: Texas Narr. (Part 2), 45–46, (Part 3), 70; Ravenel, *Private Journal*, 213–14.

40. Rawick (ed.), *American Slave*, II: S.C. Narr. (Part 1), 225; Macrae, *Americans at Home*, 209; *Black Republican*, April 29,

1865; *Christian Recorder*, Aug. 19, 1865. See also *Christian Recorder*, July 1, 1865; Dennett, *The South As It Is*, 26; Perdue et al. (eds.), *Weevils in the Wheat*, 94; Wharton, *Negro in Mississippi*, 47; Williamson, *After Slavery*, 33.

41. Rawick (ed.), *American Slave*, IV and V: Texas Narr. (Part 2), 179, (Part 3), 12, 78. For similar recollections, see IV: Texas Narr. (Part 1), 115, 164, (Part 2), 8, 248; VIII and IX: Ark. Narr. (Part 1), 334, (Part 3), 156. For the concern of Federal officials, see 39 Cong., 1 Sess., *Report of the Joint Committee on Reconstruction*, Part IV, 37; House Exec. Doc. 70, *Freedmen's Bureau*, 146; Senate Exec. Doc. 27, *Reports of the Assistant Commissioners of the Freedmen's Bureau made since December 1, 1865* (Washington, D.C., 1866), 83.

42. Rawick (ed.), *American Slave*, VII: Okla. Narr., 293–94; E. Merton Coulter, "Slavery and Freedom in Athens, Georgia, 1860–66," in Miller and Genovese (eds.), *Plantation, Town, and County*, 361; *Christian Recorder*, Aug. 19, 1865, Jan. 20, 1866; Dennett, *The South As It Is*, 121–22.

43. Rawick (ed.), *American Slave*, XIV: N.C. Narr. (Part 1), 60.

44. WPA, *Negro in Virginia*, 209.

45. Kathryn L. Morgan, "Caddy Buffers: Legends of a Middle Class Negro Family in Philadelphia," *Keystone Folklore Quarterly*, XI (Summer 1966), 75.

46. Washington, *Up from Slavery*, 20; Rawick (ed.), *American Slave*, IV and V: Texas Narr. (Part 2), 78, (Part 4), 82; XIII: Ga. Narr. (Part 3), 256, 85.

47. *Ibid.*, VII: Okla. Narr., 282; XVI: Tenn. Narr., 15.

48. *Ibid.*, III: S.C. Narr. (Part 4), 119; V: Texas Narr. (Part 4), 138; Blassingame (ed.), *Slave Testimony*, 586. Nearly all of the ex-slaves interviewed by the WPA had a vivid and often detailed recollection of the master's announcement of freedom. See, e.g., Rawick (ed.), *American Slave*, IV and V: Texas Narr. (Part 1), 82, 161–62, 208, (Part 2), 78, 199, (Part 3), 33, 36, 216, 234, (Part 4), 60, 124; VII: Okla. Narr., 150–51, 169; X: Ark. Narr. (Part 5), 18, (Part 6), 27; XII: Ga. Narr. (Part 1), 111; XV: N.C. Narr. (Part 2), 85–86; XVI: Tenn. Narr., 15.

49. *Ibid.*, IV and V: Texas Narr. (Part 1), 208, (Part 2), 78, (Part 3), 33; Francis W.

Dawson to [Joseph A. Reeks], June 13, 1865, F. W. Dawson Papers, Duke Univ.

50. Ravenel, *Private Journal*, 219; *New Orleans Picayune*, as reprinted in *Semi-Weekly Louisianian* (New Orleans), June 18, 1871; *Loyal Georgian* (Augusta), March 17, 1866. See also Burge, *Diary*, 98.

51. Rawick (ed.), *American Slave*, VII: Okla. Narr., 299; IV: Texas Narr. (Part 1), 255; XIII: Ga. Narr. (Part 3), 256; VI: Ala. Narr., 41. See also XIV: N.C. Narr. (Part 1), 280–81.

52. *Ibid.*, IV and V: Texas Narr. (Part 1), 122, (Part 3), 66; XV: N.C. Narr. (Part 2), 85–86.

53. *Ibid.*, VIII: Ark. Narr. (Part 2), 14; IV and V: Texas Narr. (Part 2), 139, (Part 3), 192. See also II: S.C. Narr. (Part 1), 314; IV: Texas Narr. (Part 1), 110, 167; XII: Ga. Narr. (Part 1), 102; XVI: Ky. Narr., 108.

54. Ravenel, *Private Journal*, 240; Rawick (ed.), *American Slave*, VIII: Ark. Narr. (Part 2), 186; V: Texas Narr. (Part 3), 228. See also IV: Texas Narr. (Part 1), 71, 162; VIII: Ark. Narr. (Part 1), 349; XII: Ga. Narr. (Part 2), 236; Evans, *Ballots and Fence Rails*, 74–75; 39 Cong., 1 Sess., *Report of the Joint Committee on Reconstruction*, Part II, 226; John William De Forest, *A Union Officer in the Reconstruction* (eds. James H. Croushore and David M. Potter; New Haven, 1948), 112–13; Perdue et al (eds.), *Weevils in the Wheat*, 3–4.

55. Avary, *Dixie after the War*, 183–85.

56. Rawick (ed.), *American Slave*, XVII: Fla. Narr., 130.

57. *Ibid.*, IV: Texas Narr. (Part 2), 6–8; XI: Mo. Narr., 313–16; III: S. C. Narr. (Part 3), 278; XII: Ga. Narr. (Part 2), 278. See also XVIII: Unwritten History, 62, and IV: Texas Narr. (Part 1), 142.

58. Perdue et al. (eds.), *Weevils in the Wheat*, 294; Rawick (ed.), *American Slave*, IV and V: Texas Narr. (Part 1), 52, (Part 3), 53, 261; X: Ark. Narr. (Part 6), 27A. See also XVI: Tenn. Narr., 15, and Botume, *First Days Amongst the Contrabands*, 59.

59. Rawick (ed.), *American Slave*, VII: Okla. Narr., 283; Heyward, *Seed from Madagascar*, 141.

60. Josiah Gorgas, Ms. Journal, entry for June 15, 1865, Univ. of North Carolina.

61. Genovese, *Roll, Jordan, Roll*, 79,

103; *Narrative of the Life of Frederick Douglass*, 48; Rawick (ed.), *American Slave*, IV: Texas Narr. (Part 1), 296.

62. Avary, *Dixie after the War*, 181; Chamberlain, *Old Days in Chapel Hill*, 130; A. A. Taylor, *The Negro in the Reconstruction of Virginia* (Washington, D.C., 1926), 73; Sidney Andrews, *The South since the War: As Shown by Fourteen Weeks of Travel and Observation in Georgia and the Carolinas* (Boston, 1866), 25; Emma E. Holmes, Ms. Diary, entry for June 15, 1865, Univ. of South Carolina; Myers (ed.), *Children of Pride*, 1278.

63. Chesnut, *Diary from Dixie*, 532, 529. For the attempts of former slaveholding families to perform the house labor themselves, see below, Chapter 7.

64. Trowbridge, *The South*, 187; Elias Horry Deas to Anne Deas, July 15, 1865, Deas Papers, Univ. of South Carolina.

65. Myers (ed.), *Children of Pride*, 1294, 1296; Charles S. Johnson, *Shadow of the Plantation* (Chicago, 1934), 131; Trowbridge, *The South*, 155–56.

66. Elias Horry Deas to Anne Deas, Aug. 12, 1865, Deas Papers, Univ. of South Carolina; Edward Lynch to Joseph Glover [c. June 1865], Glover-North Papers, Univ. of South Carolina.

67. Botume, *First Days Amongst the Contrabands*, 233. For white families who preferred to retain their former slaves, see, e.g., Myers (ed.), *Children of Pride*, 1323; *Colored Tennessean* (Nashville), Oct. 14, 1865; WPA, *Negro in Virginia*, 221.

68. *New York Tribune*, Dec. 8, 1865; Edward Lynch to Joseph Glover [c. June 1865], Univ. of South Carolina. For a discussion of the insurrection panic of 1865, see below, Chapter 8.

69. Higginson, *Army Life in a Black Regiment*, 249–50.

70. Towne, *Letters and Diary*, 34–35; Nordhoff, *Freedmen of South Carolina*, 7.

71. Eaton, *Grant, Lincoln, and the Freedmen*, 35; Ella Gertrude (Clanton) Thomas, Ms. Journal, entry for May 17, 1865, Duke Univ.; Colored People to the Governor of Mississippi, Dec. 3, 1865, Petition of the Freedmen of Claiborne County, Miss., filed in the Records of the Assistant Commissioners, Mississippi (Letters Received), Freedmen's Bureau; Elizabeth

Keckley, *Behind the Scenes: Or, Thirty Years a Slave, and Four Years in the White House* (New York, 1868), 73–74.

72. Rawick (ed.), *American Slave,* II: S.C. Narr. (Part 1), 69; Edward Lynch to Joseph Glover [c. June 1865], Univ. of South Carolina; Spencer, *Last Ninety Days of the War in North Carolina,* 187; Chamberlain, *Old Days in Chapel Hill,* 123.

73. Macrae, *Americans at Home,* 348. See also Botume, *First Days Amongst the Contrabands,* 142.

74. W. E. Towne to Bvt. Maj. Gen. Rufus Saxton, Aug. 17, 1865, Records of the Assistant Commissioners, South Carolina (Letters Received), Freedmen's Bureau; Rawick (ed.), *American Slave,* VI: Ala. Narr., 80.

75. De Forest, *Union Officer in the Reconstruction,* 65.

76. Rawick (ed.), *American Slave,* VII: Okla. Narr., 131, 133; W. E. Towne to Bvt. Maj. Gen. Rufus Saxton, Aug. 17, 1865, Records of the Assistant Commissioners, South Carolina (Letters Received), Freedmen's Bureau; Dennett, *The South As It Is,* 199–200.

77. Armstrong and Ludlow, *Hampton and Its Students,* 105; Rawick (ed.), *American Slave,* IV: Texas Narr. (Part 2), 189; Macrae, *Americans at Home,* 317. See also Forten, *Journal,* 134.

78. Armstrong and Ludlow, *Hampton and Its Students,* 109–14.

79. Reid, *After the War,* 478; Emma E. Holmes, Ms. Diary, entry for June 15, 1865, Univ. of South Carolina. For the similar experience of Pierce Butler and his daughter, Frances Leigh, as they returned to their extensive rice plantations in Georgia, see Frances B. Leigh, *Ten Years on a Georgia Plantation since the War* (London, 1883), 14–15, 21–22.

80. Chesnut, *Diary from Dixie,* 540. A similar experience may be found in Edward Lynch to Joseph Glover [c. June 1865], Univ. of South Carolina.

81. Edward Barnwell Heyward to "Tat" [Catherine Maria Clinch Heyward] [c. 1867], Heyward Family Papers, Univ. of South Carolina; Heyward, *Seed from Madagascar,* 154–55.

82. Avary, *Dixie after the War,* 341–45.

83. Easterby (ed.), *South Carolina Rice Plantation,* 209–11, 328–29; Pringle, *Chronicles of Chicora Wood,* 260–75.

84. Rawick (ed.), *American Slave,* III: S.C. Narr. (Part 4), 54; Eppes, *Through Some Eventful Years,* 272; Heyward, *Seed from Madagascar,* 138, 147; Jervey and Ravenel, *Two Diaries* (entry for Feb. 27, 1865), 6; Rawick (ed.), *American Slave,* VII: Okla. Narr., 273; V: Texas Narr. (Part 3), 216; VII: Miss Narr., 94; Lyle Saxon, Edward Dreyer, and Robert Tallant (eds.), *Gumbo Ya-Ya: A Collection of Louisiana Folk Tales* (Cambridge, 1945), 256.

85. Rawick (ed.), *American Slave,* X: Ark. Narr. (Part 6), 65–66. See also XIII: Ga. Narr. (Part 4), 170; XIV: N.C. Narr. (Part 1), 335; WPA, *Negro in Virginia,* 209.

86. Rawick (ed.), *American Slave,* VIII: Ark. Narr. (Part 2), 50; XIV: N.C. Narr. (Part 1), 145.

87. *Ibid.,* V: Texas Narr. (Part 4), 109; VI: Ala. Narr., 381; III: S.C. Narr. (Part 3), 141. See also II: S.C. Narr. (Part 2), 340, and V: Texas Narr. (Part 3), 16.

88. *Ibid.,* II: S.C. Narr. (Part 1), 142; Andrews (ed.), *Women of the South in War Times,* 192–93; Eppes, *Negro of the Old South,* 119. For other examples, see Rawick (ed.), *American Slave,* V: Texas Narr. (Part 4), 144–46: VI: Ala. Narr., 219; VIII: Ark. Narr. (Part 1), 65, 147, (Part 2), 75–76; XIII: Ga. Narr. (Part 4), 347.

89. Rawick (ed.), *American Slave,* IV: Texas Narr. (Part 2), 78; III: S.C. Narr. (Part 4), 119; Armstrong, *Old Massa's People,* 315; Blassingame (ed.), *Slave Testimony,* 492.

90. Avary, *Dixie after the War,* 183; Caroline R. Ravenel to D. E. Huger Smith, July 26 [1865], in D. E. H. Smith (ed.), *Mason Smith Family Letters,* 225. For similar sentiments, see Rawick (ed.), *American Slave,* VIII: Ark. Narr. (Part 2), 76, and Pringle, *Chronicles of Chicora Wood,* 283–84.

91. Rawick (ed.), *American Slave,* XVIII: Unwritten History, 202; IV: Texas Narr. (Part 1), 234; Genovese, *Roll, Jordan, Roll,* 29–30. For a classic example of such testimony, see Rawick (ed.), *American Slave,* VII: Okla. Narr., 71–72.

92. W. L. DeRosset to Louis Henry DeRosset, June 20, 1866, DeRosset Family Papers, Univ. of North Carolina.

93. Rawick (ed.), *American Slave,* IV: Texas Narr. (Part 1), 200, (Part 2), 133;

Washington, *Up from Slavery*, 21. For other examples, see Heyward, *Seed from Madagascar*, 129; WPA, *Negro in Virginia*, 211; Rawick (ed.), *American Slave*, III: S.C. Narr. (Part 3), 178; IV and V: Texas Narr. (Part 1), 241, (Part 2), 211, (Part 3), 257, (Part 4), 82, 172–73; VII: Okla. Narr., 133; VIII: Ark. Narr. (Part 1), 9, 38, (Part 2), 153; XII and XIII: Ga. Narr. (Part 1), 50, 181–82, 271, (Part 4), 112; Blassingame (ed.), *Slave Testimony*, 661.

94. Rawick (ed.), *American Slave*, IV: Texas Narr. (Part 2), 133; XVII: Fla. Narr., 160–61; WPA, *Negro in Virginia*, 211.

95. Rawick (ed.), *American Slave*, VII: Okla. Narr., 301; Wiley, *Southern Negroes*, 22; WPA, *Negro in Virginia*, 209–10.

96. *New York Tribune*, April 6, 1865; *New York Times*, Jan. 17, 1864.

97. Grace B. Elmore, Ms. Diary, entry for May 30, 1865, Univ. of North Carolina; Josiah Gorgas, Ms. Journal, entry for June 15, 1865, Univ. of North Carolina; Rawick (ed.), *American Slave*, VII: Okla. Narr., 133.

98. Grace B. Elmore, Ms. Diary, entry for May 30, 1865, Univ. of North Carolina; D. E. H. Smith (ed.), *Mason Smith Family Letters*, 192; Williamson, *After Slavery*, 37.

99. Rawick (ed.), *American Slave*, VII: Okla. Narr., 151. See also IV: Texas Narr. (Part 1), 277.

100. "Narrative of William Wells Brown," in Osofsky (ed.), *Puttin' On Ole Massa*, 220; "Extracts from Letters from Mississippi," in *American Freedman*, III (July 1869), 20.

101. Rawick (ed.), *American Slave*, VII: Okla. Narr., 29.

## Chapter Five: How Free Is Free?

1. William Francis Allen, Charles Pickard Ware, and Lucy McKim Garrison (eds.), *Slave Songs of the United States* (New York, 1867; repr. 1965), 94; Higginson, *Army Life in a Black Regiment*, 218.

2. Andrews, *The South since the War*, 188.

3. Eppes, *Negro of the Old South*, 121–22, 130, 138–39.

4. Trowbridge, *The South*, 68; Avary, *Dixie after the War*, 190. For the same imagery, see also Rawick (ed.), *American Slave*, VIII: Ark. Narr. (Part 1), 227.

5. Coulter, "Slavery and Freedom in Athens, Georgia, 1860–66," in Miller and Genovese (eds.), *Plantation, Town, and County*, 360; *Cincinnati Enquirer*, as quoted in *Cleveland Leader*, May 22, 1865.

6. Avary, *Dixie after the War*, 193. For an ex-slave who thought staying with her "white folks" after emancipation would help to turn her white, see Rawick (ed.), *American Slave*, V: Texas Narr. (Part 3), 6.

7. Rawick (ed.), *American Slave*, VII: Okla. Narr., 165–67.

8. Eppes, *Negro of the Old South*, 143, 133; Rawick (ed.), *American Slave*, II: S.C. Narr. (Part 2), 329; William W. Ball, *The State That Forgot: South Carolina's Surrender to Democracy* (Indianapolis, 1932), 129.

9. WPA, *Negro in Virginia*, 212; Pearson (ed.), *Letters from Port Royal*, 181; H. G. Spaulding, "Under the Palmetto," as reprinted in Bruce Jackson (ed.), *The Negro and His Folklore in Nineteenth-Century Periodicals* (Austin, 1967), 71; Higginson, *Army Life in a Black Regiment*; Waterbury, *Seven Years Among the Freedmen*, 76.

10. Nevins, *War for the Union: The Organized War, 1863–1864*, 414; *New York Times*, Nov. 12, 1865; Richardson, *Negro in the Reconstruction of Florida*, 10–11; Grace B. Elmore, Ms. Diary, entry for May 24, 1865, Univ. of North Carolina.

11. Reid, *After the War*, 370; Rawick (ed.), *American Slave*, VIII: Ark. Narr. (Part 1), 170; Williamson, *After Slavery*, 8; *New York Times*, Oct. 13, 1862. For similar expressions, see *National Freedman*, II (Jan. 15, 1866), 22; Miss Emma B. Eveleth to Rev. Samuel Hunt, May 2, 1866, American Missionary Assn. Archives; Perdue et al. (eds.), *Weevils in the Wheat*, 44.

12. H. R. Brinkerhoff to Maj. Gen. O. O. Howard, July 8, 1865, Records of the Assistant Commissioners, Mississippi (Letters Received), Freedmen's Bureau; Rawick (ed.), *American Slave*, XIV: N.C. Narr. (Part 1), 286–89.

13. Reid, *After the War*, 419–20; Tay-

lor, *Negro in the Reconstruction of Virginia,* 82. See also Rawick (ed.), *American Slave,* XVIII: Unwritten Historv. 267.

14. Forten, *Journal,* 139; Rawick (ed.), *American Slave,* VII: Okla. Narr., 209.

15. Rawick (ed.), *American Slave,* IX: Ark. Narr. (Part 3), 78; Chesnut, *Diary from Dixie,* 532.

16. Rawick (ed.), *American Slave,* V: Texas Narr. (Part 3), 153.

17. *Ibid.,* XIV and XV: N.C. Narr. (Part 1), 76, (Part 2), 351; VII: Okla. Narr., 51. See also *National Freedman,* II (Jan. 15, 1866), 23.

18. Haviland, *A Woman's Life-Work,* 468; Rawick (ed.), *American Slave,* XVIII: Unwritten History, 274; Swint (ed.), *Dear Ones at Home,* 99. See also Haviland, *A Woman's Life-Work,* 266–67.

19. 39 Cong., 1 Sess., Senate Exec. Doc. 27, *Reports of the Assistant Commissioners of the Freedmen's Bureau made since December 1, 1865,* 151; 38 Cong., 1 Sess., Senate Exec. Doc. 53, *Preliminary Report Touching the Condition and Management of Emancipated Refugees, Made to the Secretary of War by the American Freedmen's Inquiry Commission, June 30, 1863* (Washington, D.C., 1864), 3–4; De Forest, *Union Officer in the Reconstruction,* 36; Dennett, *The South As It Is,* 130. See also *National Freedman,* I (Sept. 15, 1865), 255–56, III (July 1869), 20; *New York Tribune,* Dec. 2, 1865.

20. Genovese, *Roll, Jordan, Roll,* 451; Herbert G. Gutman, *The Black Family in Slavery and Freedom, 1750–1925* (New York, 1976), 264–65.

21. Rawick (ed.), *American Slave,* IX: Ark. Narr. (Part 4), 183; Blassingame (ed.), *Slave Testimony,* 593; Perdue et al. (eds.), *Weevils in the Wheat,* 264–65; *National Anti-Slavery Standard,* Aug. 19, 1865, as quoted in Blassingame (ed.), *Slave Testimony,* 144n.

22. Botume, *First Days Amongst the Contrabands,* 163–64. See also Reid, *After the War,* 220–21.

23. Waterbury, *Seven Years Among the Freedmen,* 74–75, 76.

24. *Colored Tennessean,* Aug. 12, Oct. 14, 1865. For other examples, see *Christian Recorder,* April 13, 1863; *Black Republican,* April 15, 22, 29, May 13, 20, 1865; *Colored American* (Augusta, Ga.), Dec. 30, 1865, Jan.

13, 1866; *Colored Tennessean,* March 24, 31, 1866; *Tennessean,* July 18, 1866; *New Era* (Washington, D.C.), July 28, 1870.

25. Swint (ed.), *Dear Ones at Home,* 242–43. See also *ibid.,* 56–57, and Botume, *First Days Amongst the Contrabands,* 154–56.

26. *New York Times,* Sept. 8, 1865; Fanny Smart to Adam Smart, Feb. 13, 1866, filed with the Records of the Assistant Commissioners, Mississippi (Letters Received), Freedmen's Bureau.

27. Albert, *House of Bondage,* 102–17.

28. Rawick (ed.), *American Slave,* II: S.C. Narr. (Part 1), 231, 39. For post-emancipation "reunions" of married partners living on separate places, see, e.g., II and III: S.C. Narr. (Part 2), 82, (Part 4), 111; IV: Texas Narr. (Part 2), 158; XIII: Ga. Narr. (Part 3), 117, 212; XIV and XV: N.C. Narr. (Part 1), 286–89, (Part 2), 369; Blassingame (ed.), *Slave Testimony,* 661. The question of where a couple would settle sometimes proved difficult to resolve, with the husband or wife not always willing to leave a "secure" plantation for the uncertainty of the road or the place where the other spouse worked. See, e.g., Rawick (ed.), *American Slave,* V: Texas Narr. (Part 3), 131, and XIII: Ga. Narr. (Part 4), 165, 166.

29. Rawick (ed.), *American Slave,* IV: Texas Narr. (Part 1), 213; VII: Miss. Narr., 53–54; 39 Cong., 1 Sess., Senate Exec. Doc. 27, *Reports of the Assistant Commissioners of the Freedmen's Bureau* [1865–66], 151–52.

30. Rawick, (ed.), *American Slave,* XVI: Tenn. Narr., 19–21; VII: Miss. Narr., 13–15.

31. *Ibid.,* XIV: N.C. Narr. (Part 1), 248–52. See also XIII: Ga. Narr. (Part 3), 117, and Chesnut, *Diary from Dixie,* 533.

32. Rawick (ed.), *American Slave,* VII: Miss. Narr., 151–55; VI: Ala. Narr., 176–77; V: Texas Narr. (Part 4), 118–20. See also VI: Ala. Narr., 102.

33. For a discussion of the critical role of kinship and familial patterns in the culture of the slaves, see Gutman, *Black Family in Slavery and Freedom.*

34. Rawick (ed.), *American Slave,* IV: Texas Narr. (Part 1), 28–29. On the impact of the various apprenticeship or "binding out" arrangements, see, e.g., Affidavit of Caroline Johnson, April 10, 1866, Freed-

men's Bureau, Georgia, Registers of Letters Received; Wm. H. Beadle to Col. E. Whittlesey, March 10, 1866, and George S. Hawley to Lt. Fred H. Beecher, May 18, 1866, in Records of the Assistant Commissioners, North Carolina (Letters Received), Freedmen's Bureau; William Daniel to John A. Needles, May 6, 1865, Papers of the Pennsylvania Society for Promoting the Abolition of Slavery, XI: 1839–1868, Historical Society of Pennsylvania; De Forest, *Union Officer in the Reconstruction,* 112–13; Gutman, *Black Family in Slavery and Freedom,* 207–09.

35. Macrae, *Americans at Home,* 318. For a discussion of how slaveholders tended to regard marital and family ties, see Genovese, *Roll, Jordan, Roll,* 452–58, 475–76, and Stampp, *The Peculiar Institution,* 341–43.

36. Rawick (ed.), *American Slave,* XVIII: Unwritten History, 2.

37. *Ibid.,* XIV: N.C. Narr. (Part 1), 423; Swint (ed.), *Dear Ones at Home,* 217. For wartime disruptions of families, see Rawick (ed.), *American Slave,* II: S.C. Narr. (Part 2), 84; XVI: Va. Narr., 14; Gutman, *Black Family in Slavery and Freedom,* 22–23, 371–75, 583–84; C. Peter Ripley, "The Black Family in Transition: Louisiana, 1860–1865," *Journal of Southern History,* XLI (1975), 369–80.

38. WPA, *Negro in Virginia,* 80; Stampp, *The Peculiar Institution,* 344; Perdue et al. (eds.), *Weevils in the Wheat,* 118; Rawick (ed.), *American Slave,* II: S.C. Narr. (Part 2), 235–36.

39. *National Freedman,* II (May 1866), 143; WPA, *Negro in Virginia,* 82–83. See also Botume, *First Days Amongst the Contrabands,* 157–58; *New York Tribune,* April 4, 1865; Rawick (ed.), *American Slave,* XVIII: Unwritten History, 58; Reid, *After the War,* 126–27; Gutman, *Black Family in Slavery and Freedom,* 415.

40. 38 Cong., 1 Sess., Senate Exec. Doc. 53, *Preliminary Report Touching the Condition and Management of Emancipated Refugees ... by the American Freedmen's Inquiry Commission,* 3–4; Rev. Joseph Warren, *Extracts from Reports of Superintendents of Freedmen ..., First Series, May, 1864* (Vicksburg, 1864), 38, 40–41; Rawick (ed.), *American Slave,* XVIII: Unwritten History, 124; *New York Tribune,* Sept. 8,

1865; Botume, *First Days Amongst the Contrabands,* 158. For other examples of mass marriages, see Haviland, *A Woman's Life-Work,* 267; *New Orleans Tribune,* Oct. 5, 1864; Swint (ed.), *Dear Ones at Home,* 33n., 121.

41. Grace B. Elmore, Ms. Diary, entry for March 4, 1865, Univ. of North Carolina; *New York Times,* March 2, 1867.

42. Botume, *First Days Amongst the Contrabands,* 160–61; Williamson, *After Slavery,* 307–08; Wharton, *Negro in Mississippi,* 44; De Forest, *Union Officer in the Reconstruction,* 56n.; *New York Times,* June 3, 1865; Gutman, *Black Family in Slavery and Freedom,* 414, 417–18, 420.

43. Gutman, *Black Family in Slavery and Freedom,* 421; Botume, *First Days Amongst the Contrabands,* 154–56 (see also 162–63).

44. *New York Times,* Nov. 28, 1863. See also Nordhoff, *Freedmen of South Carolina,* 23; Swint (ed.), *Dear Ones at Home,* 33–34; Andrews, *War-Time Journal of a Georgia Girl,* 320.

45. Wharton, *Negro in Mississippi,* 228; Reid, *After the War,* 282n.; Gutman, *Black Family in Slavery and Freedom,* 389.

46. Leigh, *Ten Years on a Georgia Plantation,* 164; Clinton B. Fisk, *Plain Counsels for Freedmen: In Sixteen Brief Lectures* (Boston, 1866), 28–35 (serialized in *Free Man's Press,* Austin, Texas, Aug. 15, 22, Sept. 5, 12, 1868); Armstrong and Ludlow, *Hampton and Its Students,* 85.

47. George Parliss, Vicksburg, Miss., to Lt. Stuart Eldridge, April 9, 1866; Thomas H. Norton, Meridian, Miss., to Maj. A. W. Preston, Aug. 3, 1867; James DeGrey, Clinton, La., to William H. Webster, Sept. 10, 1867; and James DeGrey, Ms. Tri-Monthly Report, Dec. 31, 1867, Records of the Assistant Commissioners, Mississippi and Louisiana (Letters Received), Freedmen's Bureau; De Forest, *Union Officer in the Reconstruction,* 102; Swint (ed.), *Dear Ones at Home,* 121–22.

48. F. W. Loring and C. F. Atkinson, *Cotton Culture and the South Considered with Reference to Emigration* (Boston, 1869), 13, 136; Myers (ed.), *Children of Pride,* 1370. See also Loring and Atkinson, *Cotton Culture and the South,* 4, 15, 20, 137. See below,

Chapter 8, for female labor and contract negotiations.

49. Rawick (ed.), *American Slave,* XIX: God Struck Me Dead, 135; Towne, *Letters and Diary,* 183–84.

50. Samuel A. Agnew, Ms. Diary, entry for Jan. 8, 1867, Univ. of North Carolina; A. Marshall to "My Dear Niece," Jan. 20, 1867, Joseph Belknap Smith Papers, Duke Univ. See also Avary, *Dixie after the War,* 192; Richardson, *Negro in the Reconstruction of Florida,* 63; *New York Times,* April 29, 1867.

51. Fisk, *Plain Counsels for Freedmen,* 25–35. For women employed in the cotton barns, see, e.g., Botume, *First Days Amongst the Contrabands,* 235–36.

52. Avary, *Dixie after the War,* 362.

53. Swint (ed.), *Dear Ones at Home,* 123–24. See also *The Bulletin* (Louisville), Sept. 24, 1881.

54. Ellison, *Shadow and Act,* 147–48.

55. Rawick (ed.), *American Slave,* VIII: Ark. Narr. (Part 2), 52; "Narrative of William Wells Brown," in Osofsky (ed.), *Puttin' On Ole Massa,* 217–18.

56. Stroyer, "My Life in the South," in Katz (ed.), *Five Slave Narratives,* 14; Rawick (ed.), *American Slave,* IV: Texas Narr. (Part 2), 177; Botume, *First Days Amongst the Contrabands,* 45–46. See also Rawick (ed.), *American Slave,* IV: Texas Narr. (Part 2), 27, and XVIII: Unwritten History, 46.

57. Blassingame (ed.), *Slave Testimony,* 374; Heyward, *Seed from Madagascar,* 97–98; Smedes, *Memorials of a Southern Planter,* 71. For other examples, see Stroyer, "My Life in the South," in Katz (ed.), *Five Slave Narratives,* 14, and D. E. H. Smith (ed.), *Mason Smith Family Letters,* 226n.

58. Rawick (ed.), *American Slave,* VIII: Ark. Narr. (Part 1), 105; Swint (ed.), *Dear Ones at Home,* 37; Reid, *After the War,* 532; Lester, *To Be a Slave,* 147.

59. Rawick (ed.), *American Slave,* IX: Ark. Narr. (Part 3), 120. For other examples of ex-slaves who chose to take their former master's surname, see II: S.C. Narr. (Part 1), 327; IV and V: Texas Narr. (Part 2), 192, (Part 3), 5; XI: Ark. Narr. (Part 7), 245.

60. *Ibid.,* IV: Texas Narr. (Part 2), 192.

61. *Ibid.,* IX: Ark. Narr. (Part 3), 105; II: S.C. Narr. (Part 2), 117, 238, 266; IV:

Texas Narr. (Part 1), 54. For other examples, see II and III: S.C. Narr. (Part 1), 14, (Part 3), 59–60; IV: Texas Narr. (Part 1), 137, (Part 2), 237; VIII: Ark. Narr. (Part 1), 296.

62. Botume, *First Days Amongst the Contrabands,* 49; Quarles, *Negro in the Civil War,* 288; *National Freedman,* II (May 1866), 144. For a discussion of naming practices, both in slavery and in freedom, see also Genovese, *Roll, Jordan, Roll,* 443–50; Gutman, *Black Family in Slavery and Freedom,* 185–201, 230–56, and Williamson, *After Slavery,* 310–11.

63. D. E. H. Smith (ed.), *Mason Smith Family Letters,* 226; Andrews, *War-Time Journal of a Georgia Girl,* 346–47.

64. Rawick, (ed.), *American Slave,* XII: Ga. Narr. (Part 1), 351; Rainwater (ed.), "Letters of James Lusk Alcorn," 207.

65. Rawick (ed.), *American Slave,* V: Texas Narr. (Part 4), 149; *Christian Recorder,* March 17, 1866. See also Friends' Central Committee for the Relief of the Emancipated Negroes, *Letters from Joseph Simpson* (London, 1865), 23.

66. Bertram W. Doyle, *The Etiquette of Race Relations in the South: A Study in Social Control* (Chicago, 1937), 2, 3, 15, 53, 191; Blassingame (ed.), *Slave Testimony,* 488; Rawick (ed.), *American Slave,* XIV: N.C. Narr. (Part 1), 22, 26; X: Ark. Narr. (Part 5), 286; II: S.C. Narr. (Part 2), 95; XVIII: Unwritten History, 43, 44; Swint (ed.), *Dear Ones at Home,* 28; WPA, *Negro in Virginia,* 216.

67. Louis Manigault, "Visit to 'Gowrie' and 'East Hermitage' Plantations," March 1867, Manigault Plantation Records, Univ. of North Carolina; Smedes, *Memorials of a Southern Planter,* 217; Reid, *After the War,* 568–69.

68. *Christian Recorder,* Nov. 18, 1865; Swint (ed.), *Dear Ones at Home,* 73; Higginson, *Army Life in a Black Regiment,* 28–29; Macrae, *Americans at Home,* 311; Andrews, *The South since the War,* 229. See also Botume, *First Days Amongst the Contrabands,* 48.

69. *New York Times,* June 26, 1864; Chesnut, *Diary from Dixie,* 486; Dr. Ethelred Philips to Dr. James J. Philips, Oct. 24, 1865, Nov. 8, 1866, James J. Philips Collection, Univ. of North Carolina.

70. Swint (ed.), *Dear Ones at Home,* 189.

71. "Carleton" to *Boston Journal,* Feb. 13, 1865, reprinted in *National Freedman,* I (April 1, 1865), 83.

72. Dennett, *The South As It Is,* 168–69; 39 Cong., 1 Sess., *Report of the Joint Committee on Reconstruction,* Part II, 108.

73. Trowbridge, *The South,* 238–39.

74. Evans, *Ballots and Fence Rails,* 79; Dennett, *The South As It Is,* 42. See also Reid, *After the War,* 419–20.

75. Reid, *After the War,* 84, 152; Dennett, *The South As It Is,* 116.

76. *Narrative of the Life of Frederick Douglass,* 79.

77. Reid, *After the War,* 386–87, 387n.–88n.; Andrews, *War-Time Journal of a Georgia Girl,* 251, 282, 322–23, 351; Taylor, *Negro in the Reconstruction of Virginia,* 79–80; Grace B. Elmore, Ms. Diary, entry for July 13, 1865, Univ. of North Carolina; Emma E. Holmes, Ms. Diary, entry for March 31, 1865, Univ. of South Carolina; Andrews, *The South since the War,* 186–87; *New York Times,* Nov. 28, 1863; Rawick (ed.), *American Slave,* XII: Ga. Narr. (Part 1), 325; Elias Horry Deas to Anne Deas, July 15, 1865, Deas Papers, Univ. of South Carolina; Francis W. Dawson to [Joseph A. Reeks], June 13, 1865, F. W. Dawson Papers, Duke Univ.; Francis D. Richardson to Gen. St. John R. Liddell, July 31, 1866, John R. Liddell and Family Papers, Louisiana State Univ.

78. Dennett, *The South As It Is,* 137; Henry W. Ravenel to [Augustin Louis] Taveau, June 27, 1865, A. L. Taveau Papers, Duke Univ.

79. Andrews, *War-Time Journal of a Georgia Girl,* 351; Reid, *After the War,* 410n.–11n. See also Dennett, *The South As It Is,* 183.

80. John Hammond Moore (ed.), *The Juhl Letters to the Charleston Courier: A View of the South, 1865–1871* (Athens, Ga., 1974) (Aug. 24, 1865, and Jan. 26, 1866), 29–30, 72; Samuel A. Agnew, Ms. Diary, entry for July 20, 1865, Univ. of North Carolina; Dr. Ethelred Philips to Dr. James J. Philips, Nov. 8, 1866, James J. Philips Collection, Univ. of North Carolina.

81. J. H. Young to James W. White, Aug. 5, 1867, White Papers, Univ. of North Carolina.

82. Gilbert Thomas Stephenson, *Race Distinctions in American Law* (New York, 1911), 209; Wharton, *Negro in Mississippi,* 230; *Workingman's Advocate,* July 21, 1866.

83. Avary, *Dixie after the War,* 194.

84. *New Orleans Tribune,* Jan. 13, Feb. 28, June 25, Aug. 8, 1865; *Loyal Georgian,* July 6, 1867; *Freedman's Press,* July 18, 1868; *New York Times,* Aug. 17, 1865, March 22, June 2, 1866, April 29, May 18, June 19, 1867; *New York Tribune,* July 21, Aug. 22, 1865; Reid, *After the War,* 386n., 421; Andrews, *The South since the War,* 11; Dennett, *The South As It Is,* 293; Trowbridge, *The South,* 352; Alrutheus A. Taylor, *The Negro in Tennessee, 1865–1880* (Washington, D.C., 1941), 226–27; Taylor, *Negro in the Reconstruction of Virginia,* 52. For an example of integrated travel preceding black agitation on the subject, see the protest of a white Virginian after traveling by rail from Pittsburgh to Richmond, as quoted in *New York Times,* April 16, 1866.

85. Stephenson, *Race Distinctions in American Law,* 208–09; *American Freedman,* I (July 1866), 59; William H. Dixon, *New America* (2 vols.; London, 1867), II, 330–32; Reid, *After the War,* 386n., 421; Dennett, *The South As It Is,* 293; *Richmond Enquirer,* Sept. 7, 1867, as quoted in Taylor, *Negro in the Reconstruction of Virginia,* 52–53.

86. *New Orleans Tribune,* May 16, 1867; *New York Times,* Feb. 25, March 5, 1866; Taylor, *Negro in the Reconstruction of Virginia,* 53–54; *Colored American,* Dec. 30, 1865.

87. Wharton, *Negro in Mississippi,* 232–33; *The Confederate Records of the State of Georgia* (5 vols.; Atlanta, 1909), IV, 568; Trowbridge, *The South,* 161. For a denial of discrimination in "lunatic asylums" in New Orleans, see *New Orleans Tribune,* Oct. 19, 1866.

88. *Loyal Georgian,* July 6, 1867; *New Orleans Tribune,* Aug. 8, 1865; Williamson, *After Slavery,* 275–76.

89. *New Orleans Tribune,* May 5, 1867. For agitation in other cities, see, e.g., *Loyal Georgian,* July 6, 1867 (Savannah); *Christian Recorder,* June 2, 1866 (Baltimore); *New York Times,* July 9, 1867 (Mobile), May 27, 1867 (Nashville).

90. S. W. Ramsay, Office of the Charleston City Railway Company, Report of the Board of Directors, April 29, 1867, and John S. Riggs to R. K. Scott, May 3, 1867, Records of the Assistant Commissioners, South Carolina (Letters Received), Freedmen's Bureau; *New Orleans Tribune*, May 5, 28, 1867; *New York Times*, Jan. 7, March 27, 28, April 2, 5, May 27, 1867; Swint (ed.), *Dear Ones at Home*, 221, 225; Williamson, *After Slavery*, 281–83.

91. WPA, *Negro in Virginia*, 241–42; Taylor, *Negro in the Reconstruction of Virginia*, 52; *New York Times*, May 1, 4, 8, 1867; *New Orleans Tribune*, July 8, 1867. For litigation and rulings by Union officers, see *New Orleans Tribune*, May 8, July 7, 1867; *Freedman's Press*, July 18, 1868; *National Freedman*, I (Dec. 15, 1865), 362; *New York Times*, April 21, 22, May 18, June 19, July 10, Aug. 21, Sept. 8, 21, 1867.

92. *New Orleans Tribune*, Jan. 13, Feb. 28, May 21, June 25, Aug. 8, 20, 25, 29, 31, Sept. 1, 1865, April 30, May 1, 4, 7, 8, 9, 1867; *New York Times*, Nov. 5, 20, 1862, May 8, 16, 1867; J. C. Reid, Superintendent of the New Orleans and Carrollton Railroad Company, New Orleans, to Hon. E. Heath, Mayor of New Orleans, May 5, 1867, Pierre G. T. Beauregard Papers, Louisiana State Univ.

93. Macrae, *Americans at Home*, 297.

94. Trowbridge, *The South*, 352–53.

95. Chesnut, *Diary from Dixie*, 21–22.

96. *New York Times*, Sept. 17, 1865; *New Orleans Tribune*, Aug. 15, 1865; 39 Cong., 1 Sess., *Report of the Joint Committee on Reconstruction*, Part II, 56.

97. De Forest, *Union Officer in the Reconstruction*, 132; *Christian Recorder*, Feb. 24, 1866. Turner's remarks were also printed in *Colored American*, Jan. 13, 1866. For similar sentiments, see *Christian Recorder*, Aug. 27, 1864, Feb. 18, 1865.

98. *Colored American*, Jan. 6, 1866.

99. Avary, *Dixie after the War*, 377; *New York Times*, Feb. 4, 1866; Edmund Rhett to Maj. Gen. Scott, Aug. 12, 1866, Records of the Assistant Commissioners, South Carolina (Letters Received), Freedmen's Bureau.

100. Andrews, *War-Time Journal of a Georgia Girl*, 223; Ravenel, *Private Journal*, 246. For similar expressions of alarm over the stationing of black troops in their vicinity, see Dennett, *The South As It Is*, 32–33; *National Freedman*, I (Sept. 15, 1865), 264; Swint (ed.), *Dear Ones at Home*, 170; Andrews, *War-Time Journal of a Georgia Girl*, 231–32, 263–64, 338; D. E. H. Smith (ed.), *Mason Smith Family Letters*, 170; Emma E. Holmes, Ms. Diary, entry for April 7, 1865, Univ. of South Carolina; Grace B. Elmore, Ms. Diary, entry for July 13, 1865, Univ. of North Carolina; Dr. Ethelred Philips to Dr. James J. Philips, Aug. 2, 1865, James J. Philips Collection, Univ. of North Carolina.

101. Reid, *After the War*, 422n., 279. For other examples of conflict between returning Confederate soldiers and black troops, see Charles E. Cauthen (ed.), *Family Letters of the Three Wade Hamptons, 1782–1901* (Columbia, S.C., 1953), 129–30; Andrews, *The South since the War*, 28; *New York Times*, May 23, 26, 28, 1865.

102. D. E. H. Smith (ed.), *Mason Smith Family Letters*, 181; Ravenel, *Private Journal*, 245, 251; Emma E. Holmes, Ms. Diary, entry for March 31, 1865, Univ. of South Carolina; Petition of 18 Planters, Pineville, Charleston District, Sept. 1, 1865, Trenholm Papers, Univ. of North Carolina; 39 Cong., 1 Sess., *Report of the Joint Committee on Reconstruction*, Part II, 178; *New York Times*, Oct. 11, 1865; Evans, *Ballots and Fence Rails*, 79–80, 81; J. G. De Roulhac Hamilton, *Reconstruction in North Carolina* (New York, 1914), 158–61; Jack D. L. Holmes, "The Underlying Causes of the Memphis Race Riot of 1866," *Tennessee Historical Review*, XVII (1958), 217.

103. Evans, *Ballots and Fence Rails*, 79n.; Charles W. Ramsdell, *Reconstruction in Texas* (New York, 1910), 130–31; Andrews, *The South since the War*, 221.

104. Ravenel, *Private Journal*, 245–46, 247, 251; Andrews, *War-Time Journal of a Georgia Girl*, 362–63; Rev. John Hamilton Cornish, Ms. Diary, entry for June 18, 1865, Univ. of North Carolina.

105. John W. Burbidge to Joseph Glover, July 28, 1865, Glover-North Papers, Univ. of South Carolina; E. M. Jenkins and other citizens to Bvt. Maj. Gen. R. K. Scott, June 13, 1866, with endorsement by Maj. J. E. Cornelius; Frederick Reed to Bvt. Maj. Gen. R. K. Scott, June 13, 1866, Records of the Assistant Commissioners, South

Carolina (Letters Received), Freedmen's Bureau. See also Maj. George D. Reynolds to Lt. Stuart Eldridge, Oct. 5, 1865, Records of the Assistant Commissioners, Mississippi (Letters Received), Freedmen's Bureau; 39 Cong., 1 Sess., Senate Exec. Doc. 27, *Reports of the Assistant Commissioners of the Freedmen's Bureau* [1865–1866], 126.

106. *Christian Recorder,* Sept. 9, Oct. 21, 1865. For racial clashes among Union soldiers, see John C. Chavis to James Redpath [June 16, 1865], Univ. of South Carolina; *New York Times,* July 24, 1865, May 17, 1866; Williamson, *After Slavery,* 258; Evans, *Ballots and Fence Rails,* 63–64; Ravenel, *Private Journal,* 246; Dennett, *The South As It Is,* 193–94, 255.

107. *Christian Recorder,* Sept. 9, 1865; Evans, *Ballots and Fence Rails,* 65.

108. *Christian Recorder,* Sept. 9, 1865; Christian A. Fleetwood to Dr. James Hall, June 8, 1865, Carter G. Woodson Collection, Library of Congress.

109. Ravenel, *Private Journal,* 274, 288–89; Nevins, *War for the Union: The Organized War to Victory, 1864–1865,* 367; *New York Times,* Oct. 17, 1866.

110. Dennett, *The South As It Is,* 319; *Christian Recorder,* Dec. 2, 1865; D. E. H. Smith (ed.), *Mason Smith Family Letters,* 232–33; A. R. Salley to "My Dear Aunt," Nov. 13, 1865, Bruce, Jones, Murchison Papers, Univ. of South Carolina.

111. *Christian Recorder,* Sept. 9, Aug. 19, 1865; A. H. Haines to President Andrew Johnson, Records of the Assistant Commissioners, South Carolina (Letters Received), Freedmen's Bureau; Rawick (ed.), *American Slave,* XVIII: Unwritten History, 173. For assaults on discharged black soldiers, see *New Orleans Tribune,* July 26, 28, Aug. 31, 1865; *New York Times,* June 21, 1866; 39 Cong., 1 Sess., House Exec. Doc. 70, *Freedmen's Bureau,* 203, 236, 237, 238; Senate Exec. Doc. 27, *Reports of the Assistant Commissioners of the Freedmen's Bureau* [1865–1866], 6.

112. Rawick, (ed.), *American Slave,* XVIII: Unwritten History, 127; *South Carolina Leader* (Charleston), March 31, 1866. For black Union veterans who returned to the old plantations, see Rawick (ed.), *American Slave,* V: Texas Narr. (Part

3), 155; VII: Okla. Narr., 253; XVI: Kansas Narr., 9.

113. Reid, *After the War,* 558–62.

114. *New Orleans Tribune,* Aug. 31, 1865. "When de war ended, I goes back to my mastah and he treated me like his brother. Guess he wuz scared of me 'cause I had so much ammunition on me." Rawick (ed.), *American Slave,* XVI: Va. Narr., 43.

115. Andrews, *War-Time Journal of a Georgia Girl,* 341–43.

116. Reid, *After the War,* 352.

117. Trowbridge, *The South,* 314; Dennett, *The South As It Is,* 194.

118. Andrews, *The South since the War,* 100; Trowbridge, *The South,* 429–30.

119. 39 Cong., 1 Sess., *Report of the Joint Committee on Reconstruction,* Part III, 146; House Exec. Doc. 70, *Freedmen's Bureau,* 201–07. The reports of assaults and murders are voluminous, not all of them easily verifiable. See, e.g., 39 Cong., 1 Sess., *Report of the Joint Committee on Reconstruction,* Part III, 8–9, 146; House Exec. Doc. 70, *Freedmen's Bureau,* 201–07, 236–38, 248–49; George L. Childs, Office of the Provost Court, Charlottesville, Va., Sept. 20, 1865, Brock Collection, Henry E. Huntington Library; Bvt. Col. A. E. Niles, Kingstree, S.C., to Bvt. Maj. Gen. R. K. Scott, Dec. 10, 1866, Records of the Assistant Commissioners, South Carolina (Letters Received), Freedmen's Bureau; Letters from Anonymous (colored), Macon, Ga., April 13, 1866, Rebecca Lightfoot (freedwoman), Augusta, Ga., March 24, 1866, Freedmen's Bureau, Georgia (Registers of Letters Received); Trowbridge, *The South,* 463, 581; Dennett, *The South As It Is,* 125–26, 195–96, 221–22; *New Orleans Tribune,* July 14, Aug. 3, 1865; *New York Times,* Oct. 22, 1865, Jan. 8, Feb. 12, 27, Oct. 31, 1866, Jan. 12, Feb. 4, Aug. 5, 22, 30, Dec. 26, 1867. For reports of whites committing rape on black women, see *Loyal Georgian,* Jan. 27, Oct. 13, 1866; 39 Cong., 1 Sess., House Exec. Doc. 70, *Freedmen's Bureau,* 204, 207.

120. Dennett, *The South As It Is,* 110; *Loyal Georgian,* Oct. 13, 1866. For other expressions of concern by native whites, see R. W. Flournoy, New Albany, Miss., to Rep. Thaddeus Stevens, Nov. 20, 1865, Stevens Papers, Library of Congress; Trowbridge, *The South,* 499–500.

121. Trowbridge, *The South*, 314, 576; 39 Cong., 1 Sess., *Report of the Joint Committee on Reconstruction*, Part II, 127, Part III, 8; House Exec. Doc. 70, *Freedmen's Bureau*, 248–49; Williamson, *After Slavery*, 97.

122. *Christian Recorder*, June 23, 1866; Albert, *House of Bondage*, 139–40. For examples of organized violence, see Lt. Col. H. R. Brinkerhoff, Clinton, Miss., to Maj. Gen. O. O. Howard, July 8, 1865, Records of the Assistant Commissioners, Mississippi (Letters Received), Freedmen's Bureau; 39 Cong., 1 Sess., House Exec. Doc. 70, *Freedmen's Bureau*, 201–06, 237–38; *Report of the Joint Committee on Reconstruction*, Part III, 146; Andrews, *War-Time Journal of a Georgia Girl*, 343; Andrews, *The South since the War*, 118, 220; Williamson, *After Slavery*, 97; Richardson, *Negro in the Reconstruction of Florida*, 164; *New York Times*, May 10, July 6, Aug. 29, 1866, Jan. 4, May 16, 1867.

123. Cornelia P. Spencer to Eliza North, March 10, 1866, in Chamberlain, *Old Days in Chapel Hill*, 131; Trowbridge, *The South*, 572; Moore (ed.), *The Juhl Letters* (July 22, 1865), 23.

124. Dennett, *The South As It Is*, 261; *Loyal Georgian*, Oct. 13, 1865; Trowbridge, *The South*, 499–500.

125. Swint (ed.), *Dear Ones at Home*, 165–69; Ravenel, *Private Journal*, 287–89; Williamson, *After Slavery*, 258–59; Taylor, *Negro in the Reconstruction of Virginia*, 83; *New Orleans Tribune*, May 10, 12, 14, 1867; *New York Times*, July 24, 1865, April 3, 17, May 3, June 26, July 25, Aug. 20, 1866.

126. 39 Cong., 1 Sess., House Report 101, *Memphis Riots and Massacres* (Washington, D.C., 1866); William S. McFeely, *Yankee Stepfather: General O. O. Howard and the Freedmen* (New Haven, 1968), 274–82; Holmes, "The Underlying Causes of the Memphis Race Riot of 1866," 195–221; *American Freedman*, I (July 1866), 50–51; *New York Times*, May 3, 4, 7, 10, 11, 17, June 29, July 26, 1866; Taylor, *Negro in Tennessee*, 85–87.

127. 39 Cong., 2 Sess., House Report 16, *New Orleans Riots* (Washington, D.C., 1866); McFeely, *Yankee Stepfather*, 282–87; *New York Times*, July 29, 31, Aug. 1, 4, 5, 7, 8, 10, 11, 16, 17, 24, Oct. 14, 1866.

128. Dennett, *The South As It Is*, 150–51.

129. On March 22, 1865, the *New Orleans Tribune* concluded that during the last twenty years of slavery, colored residents had fared better before the courts than at the present time. For the legal system and slaves, see Stampp, *The Peculiar Institution*, 217–31.

130. *New York Times*, July 29, 1866; David Humphreys to Bvt. Maj. Gen. Swayne, Nov. 25, 1865, Records of the Assistant Commissioners, Alabama (Letters Received), Freedmen's Bureau; Coulter, "Slavery and Freedom in Athens, Georgia, 1860–66," in Miller and Genovese (eds.), *Plantation, Town, and County*, 361.

131. *New York Times*, Oct. 28, 1866; Julius J. Fleming to Gen. Scott, Sept. 15, 1866, Records of the Assistant Commissioners, South Carolina (Letters Received), Freedmen's Bureau.

132. De Forest, *Union Officer in the Reconstruction*, 1–14. For the varied record of the provost courts and the Freedmen's Bureau in meting out equal justice, see Capt. George R. Hurlbut to Capt. George L. Childs, Sept. 30, 1865, and Col. Orlando Brown to Capt. Frank P. Crandon, Aug. 31, 1865, Brock Collection, Henry E. Huntington Library; Henry Crocheron et al. to Gen Swayne, Nov. 24, 1865, Records of the Assistant Commissioners, Alabama; Julius J. Fleming to Gen. Scott, Sept. 15, 1866, Records of the Assistant Commissioners, South Carolina; Bvt. Maj. Thomas H. Norton to Maj. A. W. Preston, Aug. 3, 1867, Records of the Assistant Commissioners, Mississippi (Letters Received), Freedmen's Bureau; *New Orleans Tribune*, Aug. 14, 1865; Trowbridge, *The South*, 446; Dennett, *The South As It Is*, 223; William W. Rogers, *Thomas County, 1865–1900* (Tallahassee, 1973), 407; Williamson, *After Slavery*, 327; Richardson, *Negro in the Reconstruction of Florida*, 41–42, 51–52; Martin Abbott, *The Freedmen's Bureau in South Carolina, 1865–1872* (Chapel Hill, N.C., 1967), 100–02; McFeely, *Yankee Stepfather*, 267–73; George R. Bentley, *A History of the Freedmen's Bureau* (Philadelphia, 1955), 152–68.

133. William Daniel to John A. Needles, May 6, 1865, Pennsylvania Society for

Promoting the Abolition of Slavery, Historical Society of Pennsylvania; John Baker to Maj. Gen. Thomas J. Woods, May 20, 1866, and Bvt. Maj. Thomas H. Norton to Maj. A. W. Preston, Aug. 3, 1867, Records of the Assistant Commissioners, Mississippi; Julius J. Fleming to Gen. Scott, Sept. 15, 1866, Records of the Assistant Commissioners, South Carolina (Letters Received), Freedmen's Bureau; 39 Cong., 2 Sess., Senate Exec. Doc. 6, *Reports of the Assistant Commissioners of Freedmen* (Washington, D.C., 1867), 32, 60, 123; *Freedmen's Affairs in Kentucky and Tennessee, Report of Brevet Major General Carlin . . .* (Washington, D.C., 1868), 30; *Report of the Joint Committee on Reconstruction*, Part III, 8; *New Orleans Tribune*, Nov. 29, 1865; *Loyal Georgian*, Feb, 24, 1866; *New York Times*, Sept. 26, 1866, April 14, 1867; Richardson, *Negro in the Reconstruction of Florida*, 40, 44–46, 47–48; Taylor, *Negro in Tennessee*, 41.

134. Trowbridge, *The South*, 435–36; Macrae, *Americans at Home*, 139.

135. *New York Times*, July 29, 1866; Trowbridge, *The South*, 464, 446–47.

136. *New York Times*, Aug. 30, 1867; Dennett, *The South As It Is*, 221; Trowbridge, *The South*, 463; 39 Cong., 1 Sess., *Report of the Joint Committee on Reconstruction*, Part III, 8; House Exec. Doc. 70, *Freedmen's Bureau*, 201; Richardson, *Negro in the Reconstruction of Florida*, 164; Bvt. Col. A. E. Niles to Bvt. Maj. Gen. R. K. Scott, Dec. 10, 1866, Records of the Assistant Commissioners, South Carolina; Capt. W. G. Wedemeyer to Bvt. Maj. S. G. Greene, July 25, 1868, Records of the Assistant Commissioners, Mississippi (Letters Received), Freedmen's Bureau.

137. Richardson, *Negro in the Reconstruction of Florida*, 40–41, 44; Trowbridge, *The South*, 499; Stampp, *The Peculiar Institution*, 220.

138. *New Orleans Tribune*, July 14, Nov. 29, 1865; Dennett, *The South As It Is*, 128; Reid, *After the War*, 51n.–52n.; 39 Cong., 1 Sess., *Report of the Joint Committee on Reconstruction*, Part II, 213. See also Ira Pettibone to "Bro. Whitney," Feb. 22, 1865, American Missionary Assn. Archives.

139. Andrews, *The South since the War*, 189; Dennett, *The South As It Is*, 75.

See also Dennett, *The South As It Is*, 111, 157, 168, 181; *New York Times*, Sept. 10, Oct. 1, 1865; Wharton, *Negro in Mississippi*, 134–35.

140. Dennett, *The South As It Is*, 54, 132.

141. *Convention of the Freedmen of North Carolina* (Raleigh, 1865), 5; Thomas W. Knox, *Camp-fire and Cotton Field: Southern Adventure in Time of War* (New York, 1865), 337. For examples of black jurymen, see *Colored American*, Dec. 30, 1865; *New Orleans Tribune*, July 4, 1867; *New York Times*, Aug. 25, 30, Sept. 1, Oct. 20, 1867; Williamson, *After Slavery*, 329; Wharton, *Negro in Mississippi*, 137.

142. William V. Turner to Gen. Wager Swayne, Nov. 17, 1865, and Prince Murell et al. to Gen. Wager Swayne, Dec. 17, 1865, Records of the Assistant Commissioners, Alabama (Letters Received), Freedmen's Bureau; *New Orleans Tribune*, Nov. 11, Dec. 27, 1865, Sept. 2, 1866; *Christian Recorder*, Sept. 22, 1866. For protests of police abuses, see also C. P. Head et al., Vicksburg, to Brig. Gen. Samuel Thomas, April 17, 1866, Records of the Assistant Commissioners, Mississippi (Letters Received); *New Orleans Tribune*, May 10, 1865; 39 Cong., 1 Sess., *Report of the Joint Committee on Reconstruction*, Part II, 185. For examples of black police, see *New Orleans Tribune*, June 4, 6, 11, July 3, 1867; *New York Times*, Aug. 3, 10, Oct. 28, 1867. On the need for black police, see *New Orleans Tribune*, May 10, 1867.

143. *Loyal Georgian*, Feb. 24, 1866; *New Orleans Tribune*, July 14, 1865.

144. Swint (ed.), *Dear Ones at Home*, 169; *New Orleans Tribune*, March 22, June 7, July 18, 26, Aug. 31, 1865, Aug. 31, Sept. 1, 1866.

145. William Johnson to his parents, July 12, 1867, Main File, Henry E. Huntington Library; Letter from L. J. Leavy, July 4, 1866, Freedmen's Bureau, Georgia (Registers of Letters Received); *New York Times*, April 2, 1866; "Report of the Commissioner of the Bureau of Refugees, Freedmen and Abandoned Lands, November 1, 1866," in *Report of the Secretary of War* (Washington, D.C., 1867), Appendix, 733; Rev. Horace James, *Annual Report of the Superintendent*

of Negro Affairs in North Carolina, 1864 ... (Boston, n.d.), 21. See also *New York Times*, May 27, July 1, 1866.

146. James McMahon, City Clerk, Columbia, to Col. Mansfield, May 29, 1866; Col. Mansfield to Col. H. W. Smith, May 30, 1866; Letter from "a colored woman," May 16, 1866, Records of the Assistant Commissioners, South Carolina (Letters Received), Freedmen's Bureau.

## Chapter Six: The Feel of Freedom: Moving About

1. Eppes, *Negro of the Old South*, 134.

2. Perdue et al. (eds.), *Weevils in the Wheat*, 213.

3. Myers (ed.), *Children of Pride*, 1292–93.

4. Ella Gertrude (Clanton) Thomas, Ms. Journal, entries for Dec. 12, 1864, May 7 to Oct. 9, 1865, Sept. 17, 1866, Duke Univ.

5. A. R. Salley to "My Dear Aunt," Nov. 13, 1865, Bruce, Jones, Murchison Papers, Univ. of South Carolina.

6. Eppes, *Negro of the Old South*, 134.

7. Dr. Ethelred Philips to Dr. James J. Philips, Jan. 21, 1866, James J. Philips Collection, Univ. of North Carolina; Ball, *The State That Forgot*, 128; Emma E. Holmes, Ms. Diary, entry for June 15, 1865, Univ. of South Carolina. For freed slaves who equated departure with freedom, see also Duncan McLaurin to Gov. E. Hawley, May 23, 1866, McLaurin Papers, Duke Univ.; 39 Cong., 1 Sess., *Report of the Joint Committee on Reconstruction*, Part II, 99, 187, Part III, 118, 173; *National Freedman*, I (Nov. 15, 1865), 327; Rawick (ed.), *American Slave*, XVII: Fla. Narr., 103.

8. Mrs. Edward Smith Tennent to "My Dear Aunt" [Hattie Taylor], July 2, 1865, Dr. Edward Smith Tennent Papers, Univ. of South Carolina. For similar laments, see Hope L. Jones to "Aunt," Feb. 28, 1866, Bruce, Jones, Murchison Papers, and Emma E. Holmes, Ms. Diary, Aug. 22, 1865, Univ. of South Carolina; Chamberlain, *Old Days in Chapel Hill*, 88; Myers (ed.), *Children of Pride*, 1248, 1274; Ravenel, *Private Journal*, 244; D. E. H. Smith (ed.), *Mason Smith Family Letters*, 205; *New York Times*, March 9, 1865; Peter Kolchin, *First Freedom: The Responses of Alabama's Blacks to Emancipation and Reconstruction* (Westport, Conn., 1972), 6.

9. Rawick (ed.), *American Slave*, VIII: Ark. Narr. (Part 2), 14. See also II: S.C. Narr. (Part 1), 142; IV and V: Texas Narr. (Part 1), 162, 209, (Part 3), 192, (Part 4), 1.

10. *Ibid.*, IV: Texas Narr. (Part 2), 81–85; Armstrong, *Old Massa's People*, 319. See also Haviland, *A Woman's Life-Work*, 266; Rawick (ed.), *American Slave*, XIV: N.C. Narr. (Part 1), 215.

11. Rawick (ed.), *American Slave*, XIII: Ga. Narr. (Part 3), 293; Sarah M. Payne to Mary M. Clendenin, Sept. 30, 1865, Historical Society of Pennsylvania; Dennett, *The South As It Is*, 13–14.

12. Chesnut, *Diary from Dixie*, 538; Rawick (ed.), *American Slave*, XV: N.C. Narr. (Part 2), 290; XIII: Ga. Narr. (Part 3), 162. See also II: S.C. Narr. (Part 2), 84; VII: Miss. Narr., 28, 29–30.

13. Trowbridge, *The South*, 209; Rawick (ed.), *American Slave*, IX: Ark. Narr. (Part 4), 183–84.

14. Andrews, *The South since the War*, 25–26.

15. *New Orleans Tribune*, Nov. 12, 1865.

16. Eppes, *Through Some Eventful Years*, 284–85; Avary, *Dixie after the War*, 188.

17. Simkins and Patton, *Women of the Confederacy*, 251; LeConte, *When the World Ended*, 41, 112.

18. Grace B. Elmore, Ms. Diary, entry for May 30, 1865, Univ. of North Carolina; Mrs. Mary Jones to Mrs. Mary S. Mallard, Nov. 17, 1865, in Myers (ed.), *Children of Pride*, 1308.

19. Eppes, *Through Some Eventful Years*, 279–80, 285–86.

20. See, e.g., Dennett, *The South As It Is*, 127–28; *National Freedman*, I (July 15, 1865), 182; Rawick (ed.), *American Slave*, IV: Texas Narr. (Part 1), 60.

21. Dennett, *The South As It Is*, 223; 39 Cong., 1 Sess., House Exec. Doc. 70, *Freedmen's Bureau*, 388–89; *New York Times*, Aug. 2, 1865.

22. *New York Times*, Aug. 31, 1865, April 9, 1866. See also 39 Cong., 1 Sess., *Report of the Joint Committee on Reconstruc-*

tion, *Part III*, 142. On the role of the Union Army and the Freedmen's Bureau, see below, Chapters 7 and 8.

23. Ella Gertrude (Clanton) Thomas, Ms. Journal, entry for May 1865, Duke Univ.

24. H. R. Brinkerhoff to Maj. Gen. O. O. Howard, July 8, 1865, John L. Barnett to "Colonel," June 27, 1865, Records of the Assistant Commissioners, Mississippi and North Carolina (Letters Received), Freedmen's Bureau. See also Trowbridge, *The South*, 332, 461.

25. Dennett, *The South As It Is*, 364.

26. *Ibid.*, 226–27, 364–65. See also Andrews, *The South since the War*, 207, 221; Botume, *First Days Amongst the Contrabands*, 209–10.

27. 39 Cong., 1 Sess., Senate Exec. Doc. 27, *Reports of the Assistant Commissioners of the Freedmen's Bureau* [1865–1866], 85; Rawick (ed.), *American Slave*, IV: Texas Narr. (Part 1), 159; *New York Tribune*, July 25, 1865.

28. Rawick (ed.), *American Slave*, VI: Ala. Narr., 102; VII: Miss. Narr., 154–55; IV: Texas Narr. (Part 1), 14–16. See also Leigh, *Ten Years on a Georgia Plantation*, 14, 33–35.

29. Rawick (ed.), *American Slave*, XIV: N.C. Narr. (Part 1), 6–7; XIII: Ga. Narr. (Part 3), 207–08; De Forest, *Union Officer in the Reconstruction*, 36–37. See also Dennett, *The South As It Is*, 229, and Botume, *First Days Amongst the Contrabands*, 209–10.

30. *New York Times*, Nov. 28, 1863; Rawick (ed.), *American Slave*, X: Ark. Narr. (Part 5), 17, 18; C. W. Clarke to Col. Samuel Thomas, June 29, 1865, Records of the Assistant Commissioners, Mississippi (Letters Received), Freedmen's Bureau.

31. Higginson, *Army Life in a Black Regiment*, 266; *New York Tribune*, Nov. 10, 1865. See also *New York Times*, Aug. 5, 1864, Sept. 29, 1865.

32. Williamson, *After Slavery*, 110; 39 Cong., 1 Sess., *Report of the Joint Committee on Reconstruction*, Part II, 56. See also Blassingame (ed.), *Slave Testimony*, 384. On the postwar black conventions, see below, Chapter 10.

33. Rawick (ed.), *American Slave*, IV: Texas Narr. (Part 1), 300; Richardson, *Negro in the Reconstruction of Florida*, 75–78;

Trowbridge, *The South*, 460. On interstate migration patterns, see Wharton, *Negro in Mississippi*, 107; Williamson, *After Slavery*, 108–09; Richardson, *Negro in the Reconstruction of Florida*, 75–76; Kolchin, *First Freedom*, 20–21; De Forest, *Union Officer in the Reconstruction*, 130–31; Moore (ed.), *The Juhl Letters*, 143. In mid-1866, Oliver O. Howard, head of the Freedmen's Bureau, authorized transportation for delegates elected by the freedmen of Roanoke Island to visit plantations in Texas and explore employment opportunities there. If the investigation justified migration, freedmen in "the large and destitute settlements" would then be induced to move. O. O. Howard to Bvt. Maj. Gen. J. Robinson, Aug. 22, 1866, Records of the Assistant Commissioners, North Carolina (Letters Received), Freedmen's Bureau.

34. Reid, *After the War*, 562–63; Rawick (ed.), *American Slave*, XI: Mo. Narr., 117; XIII: Ga. Narr. (Part 4), 90–91.

35. Wharton, *Negro in Mississippi*, 109; Kolchin, *First Freedom*, 12–19, 22–23.

36. Andrews, *The South since the War*, 350–52.

37. Rawick (ed.), *American Slave*, IV: Texas Narr. (Part 2), 133. See also Macrae, *Americans at Home*, 324.

38. Rawick (ed.), *American Slave*, XIV: N.C. Narr. (Part 1), 124; V: Texas Narr. (Part 4), 39; Trowbridge, *The South*, 155–56; Weymouth T. Jordan, *Hugh Davis and His Alabama Plantation* (University, Ala., 1948), 160; Ephraim M. Anderson, *Memoirs: Historical and Personal* (St. Louis, 1868), 364; George Parliss to Stuart Eldridge, April 9, 1866, Records of the Assistant Commissioners, Mississippi (Letters Received), Freedmen's Bureau. See also *National Freedman*, I (Nov. 15, 1865), 327; Perdue et al. (eds.), *Weevils in the Wheat*, 262.

39. *Loyal Georgian*, March 3, 1866; Reid, *After the War*, 69; *New York Times*, Sept. 2, 1865.

40. *New York Times*, Dec. 10, 1865.

41. Loring and Atkinson, *Cotton Culture and the South*, 9, 13–14; Wharton, *Negro in Mississippi*, 126–27, 128; Williamson, *After Slavery*, 38, 159–62; Taylor, *Negro in Tennessee*, 141–42; *The Union* (New Orleans), July 14, 1863.

42. Dew, *Ironmaker to the Confeder-*

*acy,* 313–14. With the end of the war, the need to reconstruct shattered railroad tracks and build new lines produced immediate opportunities for freedmen to leave the fields for work that would be more remunerative. See, e.g., Loring and Atkinson, *Cotton Culture and the South,* 13–14, 17; *New York Times,* Feb. 24, 1867; Reid, *After the War,* 331; Capt. J. H. Weber to Col. Samuel Thomas, July 1, 1865, Records of the Assistant Commissioners, Mississippi (Letters Received), Freedmen's Bureau; Taylor, *Negro in the Reconstruction of Virginia,* 114; Taylor, *Negro in Tennessee,* 152–53; Wharton, *Negro in Mississippi,* 125.

43. Rawick (ed.), *American Slave,* XVI: Va. Narr., 7–8, 55–56.

44. Wharton, *Negro in Mississippi,* 106–07; Kolchin, *First Freedom,* 10; Taylor, *Negro in the Reconstruction of Virginia,* 32–34; Williamson, *After Slavery,* 108; Nevins, *War for the Union: The Organized War, 1863–1864,* 363–64; *New York Times,* Aug. 6, 1865.

45. Josiah Gorgas, Ms. Journal, entry for June 2, 1865, Univ. of North Carolina; Kolchin, *First Freedom,* 10.

46. Ravenel, *Private Journal,* 244; Margaret L. Montgomery (ed.), "Alabama Freedmen: Some Reconstruction Documents," *Phylon,* XIII (3rd Quarter 1952), 145; Kolchin, *First Freedom,* 7; Myers (ed.), *Children of Pride,* 1263, 1292; *New York Times,* July 17, 1865; Elias Horry Deas to Anne Deas, Aug. 12, 1865, Deas Papers, Univ. of South Carolina; Capt. William A. Poillon to Brig. Gen. Wager Swayne, Nov. 1865, Records of the Assistant Commissioners, Alabama (Letters Received), Freedmen's Bureau.

47. *Baton Rouge Advocate,* Feb. 21, 1866, quoted in Dennett, *The South As It Is,* 343–44; *Memphis Daily Avalanche,* March 15, 1866, quoted in Holmes, "The Underlying Causes of the Memphis Race Riot of 1866," 203n. See also *New York Times,* Sept. 1, 1865; Elias Horry Deas to Anne Deas, Aug. 12, 1865, Deas Papers, Univ. of South Carolina; Edward Lynch to Joseph Glover [c. June 1865], Glover-North Papers, Univ. of South Carolina; Wharton, *Negro in Mississippi,* 53; Richardson, *Negro in the Reconstruction of Florida,* 33–34.

48. Elias Horry Deas to Anne Deas,

Aug. 12, 1865, Deas Papers, Univ. of South Carolina; *New York Times,* Sept. 2, 1865; Emma E. Holmes, Ms. Diary, entry for June 15, 1865, Univ. of South Carolina.

49. Emma E. Holmes, Ms. Diary, entry for End of May 1865, Univ. of South Carolina; Rawick (ed.), *American Slave,* XIII: Ga. Narr. (Part 4), 235.

50. Elias Horry Deas to Anne Deas, July, Aug. 12, 1865, Deas Papers, Univ. of South Carolina.

51. 39 Cong., 1 Sess., House Exec. Doc. 70, *Freedmen's Bureau,* 231.

52. *Loyal Georgian,* April 10, 1867; *Christian Recorder,* Dec. 16, 1865; *Black Republican,* April 29, 1865. For similar advice, see *Colored Tennessean,* Oct. 14, 1865.

53. *New York Tribune,* June 12, 17, 27, July 16, Aug. 8, 1865; *New York Times,* June 15, 1865; *New Orleans Tribune,* Aug. 26, 1865.

54. *Christian Recorder,* July 21, 1866. See also, e.g., *ibid.,* June 10, July 8, 1865; *New Orleans Tribune,* July 8, 1865; *New York Times,* June 11, 1865, July 29, 1866; *The Union,* April 9, 1864.

55. *New York Times,* July 7, 1865; Henry Crocheron et al. to Gen. Swayne, Nov. 24, 1865, Records of the Assistant Commissioners, Alabama (Letters Received), Freedmen's Bureau; *Christian Recorder,* June 10, 1865. For a black protest meeting in Selma, Ala., see *New York Times,* Nov. 12, 1865.

56. Kolchin, *First Freedom,* 7; *New Orleans Tribune,* July 22, 26, 29, 1865; 39 Cong., 2 Sess., Senate Exec. Doc. 6, *Reports of the Assistant Commissioners of Freedmen,* 129; *New York Times,* Oct. 28, 1865.

57. *The Union,* April 9, 1864; *New Orleans Tribune,* Aug. 18, 1864, July 16, 26, 1865; *New York Times,* Feb. 2, 1863, Sept. 28, Nov. 13, 1865; *New York Tribune,* June 12, 1865; 39 Cong., 1 Sess., Senate Exec. Doc. 27, *Reports of the Assistant Commissioners of the Freedmen's Bureau* [1865–1866], 51; 39 Cong., 2 Sess., Senate Exec. Doc. 6, *Reports of the Assistant Commissioners of Freedmen,* 129.

58. *Christian Recorder,* July 1, 1865; *National Freedman,* I (Aug. 15, 1865), 200; *New York Times,* June 25, July 16, 1865; 39 Cong., 1 Sess., Senate Exec. Doc. 27, *Reports of the Assistant Commissioners of the Freed-*

*men's Bureau* [1865–1866], 8; *New Orleans Tribune,* Oct. 12, 1865.

59. Wharton, *Negro in Mississippi,* 53; Kolchin, *First Freedom,* 7.

60. Seleg G. Wright to Rev. George Whipple, April 1, 7, 1864; "An Officer of the U.S.A." [apparently S. G. Wright], April 4, 1864, Ms. article intended for release to newspaper, American Missionary Assn. Archives; *Christian Recorder,* July 1, 1865. See also "Abstract of a Report of a Visit to Natchez," in Warren, *Extracts from Reports of Superintendents of Freedmen.*

61. *New Orleans Tribune,* Aug. 8, 1865.

62. Prince Murell et al., Tuscaloosa, Ala., Dec. 17, 1865; C. P. Head et al., Vicksburg, to Brig. Gen. Samuel Thomas, April 17, 1866; Jim Leigh et al., Tuscumbia, Ala., Nov. 27, 1865, Records of the Assistant Commissioners, Alabama and Mississippi (Letters Received), Freedmen's Bureau.

63. Trowbridge, *The South,* 453–54; *New York Times,* Aug. 6, 1865 (quoting the *Petersburg Daily Index*). See also *New York Times,* June 16, Aug. 6, 1865, Dec. 4, 1866; Ravenel, *Private Journal,* 238–39; Wharton, *Negro in Mississippi,* 127; Williamson, *After Slavery,* 162; Charles H. Wesley, *Negro Labor in the United States, 1850–1925* (New York, 1927), 218.

64. Rawick (ed.), *American Slave,* XIV: N.C. Narr. (Part 1), 277.

65. See, e.g., *ibid.,* IV and V: Texas Narr. (Part 1), 280, (Part 2), 142, (Part 4), 77; VI: Ala. Narr., 280–81, 420; VIII: Ark. Narr. (Part 2), 63–64; XIII: Ga. Narr. (Part 3), 177, (Part 4), 172; 39 Cong., 1 Sess., *Report of the Joint Committee on Reconstruction,* Part II, 99.

66. 39 Cong., 1 Sess., Senate Exec. Doc. 27, *Reports of the Assistant Commissioners of the Freedmen's Bureau* [1865–1866], 65.

67. Lt. Col. H. R. Brinkerhoff to Maj. Gen. O. O. Howard, July 8, 1865, Records of the Assistant Commissioners, Mississippi (Letters Received), Freedmen's Bureau; 39 Cong., 1 Sess., House Exec. Doc. 70, *Freedmen's Bureau,* 288; Rawick (ed.), *American Slave,* XV: N.C. Narr. (Part 2), 41.

68. Walter L. Fleming, *Civil War and Reconstruction in Alabama* (New York, 1905), 272; Rawick (ed.), *American Slave,* XIV: N.C. Narr. (Part 1), 407; III: S.C. Narr.

(Part 3), 265–66. For movement back to the plantations, see also Trowbridge, *The South,* 251–52; 39 Cong., 1 Sess., Senate Exec. Doc. 27, *Reports of the Assistant Commissioners of the Freedmen's Bureau* [1865–1866], 13; Capt. J. H. Weber to Col. Samuel Thomas, July 1, 1865, Records of the Assistant Commissioners, Mississippi (Letters Received), Freedmen's Bureau; Myers (ed.), *Children of Pride,* 1296; Williamson, *After Slavery,* 40–41.

69. Rawick (ed.), *American Slave,* XIV: N.C. Narr. (Part 1), 407; Trowbridge, *The South,* 537–38.

70. Leigh, *Ten Years on a Georgia Plantation,* 22; Chesnut, *Diary from Dixie,* 531; 39 Cong., 1 Sess., *Report of the Joint Committee on Reconstruction,* Part II, 80. See also Avary, *Dixie after the War,* 185–86; Easterby (ed.), *South Carolina Rice Plantation,* 216; Trowbridge, *The South,* 491–92.

71. Rawick (ed.), *American Slave,* XIV: N.C. Narr. (Part 1), 26.

72. Andrews, *The South since the War,* 25; Perdue et al. (eds.), *Weevils in the Wheat,* 213.

73. Rawick (ed.), *American Slave,* IV: Texas Narr. (Part 2), 105; XIV: N.C. Narr. (Part 1), 178. See also V: Texas Narr. (Part 4), 32.

74. *Ibid.,* VII: Miss. Narr., 173; IV: Texas Narr. (Part 2), 88; Perdue et al. (eds.), *Weevils in the Wheat,* 228–29.

75. Rawick (ed.), *American Slave,* XIV: N.C. Narr. (Part 1), 300; XIII: Ga. Narr. (Part 3), 64. For similar recollections, see, e.g., II and III: S.C. Narr. (Part 1), 334–35, (Part 2), 263, (Part 3), 236–37, (Part 4), 80; IV and V: Texas Narr. (Part 1), 3, (Part 2), 128, 161–62, (Part 3), 130, (Part 4), 72; VII: Okla. Narr., 340; Miss. Narr., 154; XII and XIII: Ga. Narr. (Part 2), 263, (Part 3), 39; XIV: N.C. Narr. (Part 1), 172, 239; XVII: Fla. Narr., 376.

76. *Ibid.,* VIII: Ark. Narr. (Part 1), 14, 189; IV: Texas Narr. (Part 1), 65.

77. *Ibid.,* II: S.C. Narr. (Part 2), 216. For variations of this theme, see also IV and V: Texas Narr. (Part 1), 64–65, (Part 2), 128, (Part 3), 161, 164, (Part 4), 25; XII and XIII: Ga. Narr. (Part 2), 70–71, (Part 3), 301; XIV and XV: N.C. Narr. (Part 1), 136–37, 294, (Part 2), 103.

78. *Ibid.*, II: S.C. Narr. (Part 1), 5–6.

79. *Ibid.*, III: S.C. Narr. (Part 3), 51. For recollections of "hard times," especially in the first winter of freedom, see also VI: Ala. Narr., 226; VII: Okla. Narr., 294; VIII and X: Ark. Narr. (Part 2), 6, 161, (Part 5), 124; XIV and XV: N.C. Narr. (Part 1), 186, (Part 2), 268.

80. *Ibid.*, XVI: Tenn. Narr., 6; VII: Okla. Narr., 202.

81. *Ibid.*, VII: Miss. Narr., 39–41.

82. *Ibid.*, XII and XIII: Ga. Narr. (Part 3), 29, (Part 2), 8; VII: Miss. Narr., 41.

83. *Ibid.*, VI: Ala. Narr., 405–06; IV: Texas Narr. (Part 1), 82–83; VII: Okla. Narr., 51.

84. Williamson, *After Slavery*, 36–37; Emma E. Holmes, Ms. Diary, entry for End of May 1865, Univ. of South Carolina; Rawick (ed.), *American Slave*, VI: Ala. Narr., 167.

85. Rawick (ed.), *American Slave*, XIV: N.C. Narr. (Part 1), 335–38.

86. Mrs. William Mason Smith to Mrs. Edward L. Cottenet, July 12, 1865, in D. E. H. Smith (ed.), *Mason Smith Family Letters*, 221.

87. Isabella A. Soustan to "Master Man" [probably George C. Taylor], July 10, 1865, George C. Taylor Collection, Univ. of North Carolina.

88. Alice Dabney to "My Dear Old Master" [Thomas Dabney], Feb. 10, 1867, in Smedes, *Memorials of a Southern Planter*, 234–35. Susan Dabney Smedes, the daughter of Thomas Dabney, added that the letter had been written "with Alice's own hand."

89. Jake to "Mas William" [William D. Simpson], Feb. 5, 1867, Simpson Papers, Univ. of North Carolina.

90. *Cincinnati Commercial*, reprinted in *New York Tribune*, Aug. 22, 1865, as a "letter dictated by a servant." For other reprints of the letter, see "Letter from a Freedman to His Old Master: Written just as he dictated it," in Lydia Maria Child (ed.), *The Freedmen's Book* (Boston, 1865), 265–67, and Carter G. Woodson (ed.), *The Mind of the Negro as Reflected in Letters Written During the Crisis 1800–1860* (Washington, D.C., 1926), 537–39.

## Chapter Seven: Back to Work: The Old Compulsions

1. *South Carolina Leader*, Dec. 16, 1865.

2. W. L. DeRosset to Louis Henry DeRosset, June 20, 1866, DeRosset Family Papers, Univ. of North Carolina.

3. Dr. Ethelred Philips to Dr. James J. Philips, Aug. 2, 1865, James J. Philips Collection, Univ. of North Carolina; Trowbridge, *The South*, 390–91.

4. Ravenel, *Private Journal*, 269; William Henry Stiles to Elizabeth Anne Mackay, Sept. 22, 1865, Mackay-Stiles Collection, Univ. of North Carolina; Kolchin, *First Freedom*, 23.

5. Donald MacRae to Julia MacRae, Sept. 4, 1865, MacRae Papers, Duke Univ.; Dennett, *The South As It Is*, 83–84

6. *Ibid.*, 26.

7. Rawick (ed.), *American Slave*, V: Texas Narr. (Part 4), 50; IX: Ark. Narr. (Part 3), 156; Abraham to "My Dear Master" [Joseph Glover], May 15, 1865, and John W. Burbidge to Joseph Glover, June 26, 1865, Glover-North Papers, Univ. of South Carolina; Knox, *Camp-fire and Cotton Field*, 374.

8. Rev. John Hamilton Cornish, Ms. Diary, entry for June 19, 1865, Univ. of North Carolina. See also Rawick (ed.), *American Slave*, XI: Mo. Narr., 272–73.

9. Knox, *Camp-fire and Cotton Field*, 337; *New York Times*, Feb. 12, 1865; Bell I. Wiley, "Vicissitudes of Early Reconstruction Farming in the Lower Mississippi Valley," *Journal of Southern History*, III (1937), 451–52.

10. Loring and Atkinson, *Cotton Culture and the South*, 5, 6, 9, 11, 22, 106, 109–10; Trowbridge, *The South*, 391, 392; Myers (ed.), *Children of Pride*, 1309; *New York Times*, April 12, 1867; Kolchin, *First Freedom*, 9; Easterby (ed.), *South Carolina Rice Plantation*, 330. Most of the volume by Loring and Atkinson consists of responses by cotton planters to a circular asking for "detailed facts and opinions relative to the la-

bor, the methods of cotton culture, and the general condition and capacities of the South."

11. Loring and Atkinson, *Cotton Culture and the South*, 10.

12. *Ibid.*, 8; Edward Barnwell Heyward to "Tat" [Catherine Maria Clinch Heyward], May 5, 1867, Heyward Family Papers, Univ. of South Carolina; William E. Bayley to Commanding Officer, July 3, 1865, Records of the Assistant Commissioners, Mississippi (Letters Received), Freedmen's Bureau.

13. Loring and Atkinson, *Cotton Culture and the South*, 4, 110. See also William Henry Stiles to Elizabeth Anne Mackay, Sept. 22, 1865, Mackay-Stiles Collection, and Samuel A. Agnew, Ms. Diary, entry for July 24, 1865, Univ. of North Carolina; George Parliss to Lt. Stuart Eldridge, April 9, 1866, Records of the Assistant Commissioners, Mississippi (Letters Received), Freedmen's Bureau; Wilmer Shields to William Newton Mercer, July 10, 1866, Mercer Papers, Louisiana State Univ.

14. Leigh, *Ten Years on a Georgia Plantation*, 24–26, 57.

15. Wiley, "Vicissitudes of Early Reconstruction Farming in the Lower Mississippi Valley," 449–50; Avary, *Dixie after the War*, 189–90. See also Wilmer Shields to William Newton Mercer, Sept. 20, 1865, Mercer Papers, Louisiana State Univ.

16. Reid, *After the War*, 460–64.

17. Jordan, *Hugh Davis and His Alabama Plantation*, 151–62. Similar frustrations are described in Elias Horry Deas to Anne Deas, Oct. 20, 1866, Deas Papers, Univ. of South Carolina.

18. Andrews, *The South since the War*, 22; Mary C. Simms Oliphant, Alfred Taylor Odell, and T. C. Duncan Eaves (eds.), *The Letters of William Gilmore Simms* (5 vols.; Columbia, S.C., 1952–56), IV, 557, 567, 602; W. W. Bateman to John L. Manning, Aug. 2, 1865, Williams-Chesnut-Manning Papers, Univ. of South Carolina; Grace B. Elmore, Ms. Diary, entry for March 4, 1865, Univ. of North Carolina; John Moore to Mrs. Joseph R. Snyder, Oct. 11, 1866, Kean-Prescott Papers, Univ. of North Carolina; Trowbridge, *The South*, 118–19; Dennett, *The South As It Is*, 42, 78, 191; Reid, *After the War*, 164–

65, 186, 298, 318; 39 Cong., 1 Sess., Senate Exec. Doc. 2, "Report of Carl Schurz on the States of South Carolina, Georgia, Alabama, Mississippi, and Louisiana," in *Message of the President of the United States*, 16–17, 27; *National Freedman*, I (Aug. 15, 1865), 224; De Forest, *Union Officer in the Reconstruction*, 100–01.

19. Loring and Atkinson, *Cotton Culture and the South*, 4, 6, 13.

20. *New York Times*, Dec 31, 1861; *Christian Recorder*, June 17, 1865; Macrae, *Americans at Home*, 324.

21. Dennett, *The South As It Is*, 191; Leigh, *Ten Years on a Georgia Plantation*, 55.

22. Waterbury, *Seven Years Among the Freedmen*, 71.

23. Charles Stearns, *The Black Man of the South, and the Rebels* (New York, 1872), 43–46.

24. Williamson, *After Slavery*, 51; Eppes, *Negro of the Old South*, 115–17; Eppes, *Through Some Eventful Years*, 282–83.

25. William Henry Stiles to Elizabeth Anne Mackay, Sept. 22, 1865, Mackay-Stiles Collection, Univ. of North Carolina; Leigh, *Ten Years on a Georgia Plantation*, 52; Emma E. Holmes, Ms. Diary, entry for July 17, 1865, Univ. of South Carolina.

26. Easterby (ed.), *South Carolina Rice Plantation*, 212, 215; D. E. H. Smith (ed.), *Mason Smith Family Letters*, 248; Myers (ed.), *Children of Pride*, 1280, 1287, 1308–09.

27. Myers (ed.), *Children of Pride*, 1280; Williamson, *After Slavery*, 40; Leigh, *Ten Years on a Georgia Plantation*, 38; Jones (ed.), *Heroines of Dixie*, 268–69.

28. S. D. G. Niles to Maj. Gen. T. J. Wood, June 13, 1866, Records of the Assistant Commissioners, Mississippi (Letters Received), Freedmen's Bureau; Rawick (ed.), *American Slave*, VI: Ala. Narr., 176–77; VII: Miss. Narr., 54.

29. Ella Gertrude (Clanton) Thomas, Ms. Journal, entries for May 27, 29, 1865, Duke Univ.

30. Dr. Ethelred Philips to Dr. James J. Philips, Oct. 24, 1865, James J. Philips Collection, Univ. of North Carolina; LeGrand, *Journal*, 263–64; D. E. H. Smith (ed.), *Mason Smith Family Letters*, 223; Emma E.

Holmes, Ms. Diary, entries for Aug. 22, Oct. 1, 1865, Univ. of South Carolina; James C. Bonner, "Plantation Experiences of a New York Woman," *North Carolina Historical Review,* XXIII (1956), 546.

31. Grace B. Elmore, Ms. Diary, entries for March 4, May 24, 30, 1865, Univ. of North Carolina.

32. Donald MacRae to Julia MacRae, Sept. 4, 1865, MacRae Papers, Duke Univ.

33. Dr. Ethelred Philips to Dr. James J. Philips, June 17, 1867, James J. Philips Collection, Univ. of North Carolina. See also Eppes, *Through Some Eventful Years,* 311.

34. William Heyward to James Gregorie, June 4, 1868, Gregorie-Elliott Collection, Univ. of North Carolina; Loring and Atkinson, *Cotton Culture and the South,* 5 (see also 11, 85, 87, 93).

35. Richardson, *Negro in the Reconstruction of Florida,* 54; *New York Times,* Oct. 8, 1865; 39 Cong., 2 Sess., Senate Exec. Doc. 6, *Reports of the Assistant Commissioners of Freedmen* [Jan. 3, 1867], 159; Loring and Atkinson, *Cotton Culture and the South,* 84, 87, 94; Claude H. Nolen, *The Negro's Image in the South: The Anatomy of White Supremacy* (Lexington, Ky., 1967), 173–77; Reid, *After the War,* 397.

36. C. W. Clarke to Col. Samuel Thomas, June 29, 1865, Records of the Assistant Commissioners, Mississippi (Letters Received), Freedmen's Bureau; Theodore B. Wilson, *The Black Codes of the South* (University, Ala., 1965), 45; 39 Cong., 2 Sess., Senate Exec. Doc. 6, *Reports of the Assistant Commissioners of Freedmen* [Jan. 3, 1867], 159; Taylor, *Negro in the Reconstruction of Virginia,* 109; Williamson, *After Slavery,* 117.

37. Moore (ed.), *The Juhl Letters* (Aug. 7, 1866), 108; Reid, *After the War,* 276; Taylor, *Negro in the Reconstruction of Virginia,* 122; Edward Barnwell Heyward to Allen C. Izard, July 16, 1866, Heyward Family Papers, Univ. of South Carolina.

38. Loring and Atkinson, *Cotton Culture and the South,* 71; Taylor, *Negro in the Reconstruction of Virginia,* 74–75; 39 Cong., 1 Sess., *Report of the Joint Committee on Reconstruction,* Part II, 109.

39. Richardson, *Negro in the Reconstruction of Florida,* 53.

40. Mrs. McKenzie Parker to Mrs.

William Mason Smith, Nov. 6, 1865, in D. E. H. Smith (ed.), *Mason Smith Family Letters,* 246; Grace B. Elmore, Ms. Diary, entry for July 13, 1865, Univ. of North Carolina. See also Eppes, *Through Some Eventful Years,* 309–10.

41. Bryant (ed.), "A Yankee Soldier Looks at the Negro," 145; Sarah M. Payne to Mary M. Clendenin, Sept. 30, 1865, Historical Society of Pennsylvania; Ella Gertrude (Clanton) Thomas, Ms. Journal, entries for May [26], 29, 1865, Duke Univ.

42. Emma E. Holmes, Ms. Diary, entry for May 3, 1865, Univ. of South Carolina; Avary, *Dixie after the War,* 188–89; Myers (ed.), *Children of Pride,* 1280.

43. Jervey and Ravenel, *Two Diaries,* 36; Simkins and Patton, *Women of the Confederacy,* 255; William Heyward to James Gregorie, June 4, 1868, Gregorie-Elliott Collection, Univ. of North Carolina. See also LeConte, *When the World Ended,* 54.

44. Andrews, *War-Time Journal of a Georgia Girl,* 373–74, 375.

45. *Ibid.,* 374–75.

46. LeGrand, *Journal,* 99–100; Andrews, *War-Time Journal of a Georgia Girl,* 375–76, 378–80.

47. Emma E. Holmes, Ms. Diary, entries for End of May, June 15, Aug. 14, 25, 1865, Univ. of South Carolina.

48. Andrews, *War-Time Journal of a Georgia Girl,* 374; Chesnut, *Diary from Dixie,* 488; Stone, *Brokenburn,* 7–9. For the daily tasks of a housemaid under slavery, as recalled by an ex-slave who had assisted her mother, see Rawick (ed.), *American Slave,* VI: Ala. Narr., 416–17.

49. Eppes, *Through Some Eventful Years,* 310; Eppes, *Negro of the Old South,* 137, 139–40.

50. Trowbridge, *The South,* 328–29.

51. Rawick (ed.), *American Slave,* II: S.C. Narr. (Part 1), 22; Waterbury, *Seven Years Among the Freedmen,* 40.

52. D. E. H. Smith (ed.), *Mason Smith Family Letters,* 222; Hope L. Jones to "My Dear Aunt," Feb. 28, 1866, Bruce-Jones-Murchison Papers, Univ. of South Carolina.

53. Trowbridge, *The South,* 291.

54. Dennett, *The South As It Is,* 15; Williamson, *After Slavery,* 73. See also Moore (ed.), *The Juhl Letters* (Aug. 31, 1865), 34.

55. Charles L. Wagandt, *The Mighty Revolution: Negro Emancipation in Maryland, 1862–1864* (Baltimore, 1964), 42; 39 Cong., 1 Sess., *Report of the Joint Committee on Reconstruction*, Part IV, 16.

56. Andrews, *The South since the War*, 364; Fleming, *Civil War and Reconstruction in Alabama*, 386; Myers (ed.), *Children of Pride*, 1338. See also Moore (ed.), *The Juhl Letters* (Dec. 31, 1865), 59.

57. Andrews, *War-Time Journal of a Georgia Girl*, 340; Trowbridge, *The South*, 491.

58. Wharton, *Negro in Mississippi*, 54; Dennett, *The South As It Is*, 6, 15, 102–03; Reid, *After the War*, 337; Trowbridge, *The South*, 78–79; Macrae, *Americans at Home*, 132, 294–95; Haviland, *A Woman's Life Work*, 306; Loring and Atkinson, *Cotton Culture and the South*, 6–7, 11; Myers (ed.), *Children of Pride*, 1244; Moore (ed.), *The Juhl Letters* (Jan. 26, 1866), 71; *Selma Mirror*, as quoted in *New Orleans Tribune*, Dec. 19, 1865; 39 Cong., 1 Sess., *Report of the Joint Committee on Reconstruction*, Part II, 109.

59. Dennett, *The South As It Is*, 290; Grace B. Elmore, Ms. Diary, entry for March 4, 1865, Univ. of North Carolina. For similar predictions, see, e.g., Loring and Atkinson, *Cotton Culture and the South*, 6–7, 20; Trowbridge, *The South*, 78; Macrae, *Americans at Home*, 295; Duncan McLaurin to Gov. E. Hawley, May 23, 1866, McLaurin Papers, Duke Univ.; Roark, *Masters Without Slaves*, 138.

60. Loring and Atkinson, *Cotton Culture and the South*, 9; Hepworth, *Whip, Hoe, and Sword*, 49–50; 39 Cong., 1 Sess., *Report of the Joint Committee on Reconstruction*, Part II, 130; Dennett, *The South As It Is*, 15; Reid, *After the War*, 164–65. Planters would use this argument repeatedly to explain violations of labor contracts by blacks and the folly of monthly wage payments in cash.

61. Andrews, *The South since the War*, 364.

62. Macrae, *Americans at Home*, 321; 39 Cong., 1 Sess., *Report of the Joint Committee on Reconstruction*, Part III, 136; Moore (ed.), *The Juhl Letters* (July 22, 1865), 20; Dennett, *The South As It Is*, 15. On Dec. 2, 1866, the *New Orleans Tribune* reprinted this lament from the *Brandon* (Miss.) *Republican:* "Alas! he [the freedman] cannot sing and dance with the same zest now. He has no old master to furnish him food and raiment; no kind mistress to take care of him when he gets sick; no comfortable cabin to live in; no thick clothing to shield him from the storms; no banjo to pick, and his heart is so heavy he can't sing and dance. Candidly, we have not seen or heard of a real old fashioned negro frolic since the poor darkey was set free."

63. Trowbridge, *The South*, 136, 332.

64. Reid, *After the War*, 218.

65. Dennett, *The South As It Is*, 65.

66. Col. Samuel Thomas, Asst. Commissioner, Bureau of Refugees, Freedmen, and Abandoned Lands for Mississippi and N.E. Louisiana, to Gen. Carl Schurz, Sept. 28, 1865, in 39 Cong., 1 Sess., Senate Exec. Doc. 2, "Report of Carl Schurz on the States of South Carolina, Georgia, Alabama, Mississippi, and Louisiana," in *Message of the President of the United States*, 81.

67. Andrews, *The South since the War*, 398.

68. Reid, *After the War*, 25, 44, 291, 337; Andrews, *The South since the War*, 398; 39 Cong., 1 Sess., Senate Exec. Doc. 2, "Report of Carl Schurz," 16–17; Wharton, *Negro in Mississippi*, 83; *New York Times*, Sept. 17, 1865.

69. *Macon Telegraph*, May 16, 1865, quoted in *New York Times*, June 16, 1865; Trowbridge, *The South*, 573; Reid, *After the War*, 343–44.

70. Ravenel, *Private Journal*, 256; Walter L. Fleming (ed.), *Documentary History of Reconstruction* (2 vols.; Cleveland, 1906–07), I, 282–83; Wharton, *Negro in Mississippi*, 84–85, 91–92; Wilson, *Black Codes of the South*, 74.

71. Andrews, *The South since the War*, 157–58; Dennett, *The South As It Is*, 161–62; Reid, *After the War*, 361.

72. *New York Times*, June 17, 1865; Dennett, *The South As It Is*, 133; Wharton, *Negro in Mississippi*, 84; Otto H. Olsen, *Carpetbagger's Crusade: The Life of Albion Winegar Tourgee* (Baltimore, 1965), 34.

73. *New Orleans Daily South*, Nov. 19, 1865, quoted in Reid, *After the War*, 411; *Edgefield* (S.C.) *Advertiser*, Oct. 25, 1865, quoted in Wilson, *Black Codes of the South*,

145; Fleming (ed.), *Documentary History of Reconstruction*, I, 298–99.

74. The discussion of the Black Codes is based on the enactments compiled in "Laws in Relation to Freedmen," 39 Cong., 2 Sess., Senate Exec. Doc. 6, *Freedmen's Affairs*, 170–230; Edward McPherson, *The Political History of the United States of America During the Period of Reconstruction* (Washington, D.C., 1880), 29–44; and Fleming (ed.), *Documentary History of Reconstruction*, I, 273–312. See also Wharton, *Negro in Mississippi*, 83–89; Williamson, *After Slavery*, 72–76; Stampp, *Era of Reconstruction*, 79–80; and Wilson, *Black Codes of the South*, 65–80, 96–116. In examining the state legislation regarding the freedmen, care must be taken not to confuse laws proposed with those actually enacted; the northern press was not always clear on this point.

75. *New Orleans Tribune*, July 15, 19, 30, Aug. 20, 1865. For the Louisiana parish laws, see also 39 Cong., 1 Sess., Senate Exec. Doc. 2, "Report of Carl Schurz," 92–96.

76. Trowbridge, *The South*, 373; Wilson, *Black Codes of the South*, 143; Wharton, *Negro in Mississippi*, 83.

77. Colored People to the Governor of Mississippi, Petition of the Freedmen of Claiborne County, Miss., Dec. 3, 1865, in Records of the Assistant Commissioners, Mississippi (Letters Received), Freedmen's Bureau.

78. *South Carolina Leader*, Dec. 16, 1865; *Loyal Georgian*, Feb 17, 1866. For black protest, see also *Colored American*, Jan. 6, 13, 1866; *Loyal Georgian*, Feb. 3, 1866; *South Carolina Leader*, Dec. 23, 1865.

79. McPherson, *Political History of the United States of America During the Period of Reconstruction*, 36–38, 41–42; Williamson, *After Slavery*, 77–79; Fleming, *Civil War and Reconstruction in Alabama*, 378–79, 382–83; Wharton, *Negro in Mississippi*, 90–93; Taylor, *Negro in the Reconstruction of Virginia*, 18; Richardson, *Negro in the Reconstruction of Florida*, 43; Wilson, *Black Codes of the South*, 96–115.

80. Wharton, *Negro in Mississippi*, 91, 92; *New Orleans Tribune*, Aug. 20, 1865.

81. Sitterson, *Sugar Country*, 235; Stampp, *The Peculiar Institution*, 146; Andrews, *The South since the War*, 25. For sim-

ilar sentiments, see also Jordan, *Hugh Davis and His Alabama Plantation*, 161; Trowbridge, *The South*, 390–91, 393; 39 Cong., 1 Sess., *Report of the Joint Committee on Reconstruction*, Part III, 5, 24–25.

82. Dennett, *The South As It Is*, 53. See also *ibid.*, 77–82; Trowbridge, *The South*, 389; C. W. Clarke to Col. Samuel Thomas, June 29, 1865, Records of the Assistant Commissioners, Mississippi (Letters Received), Freedmen's Bureau.

83. Dennett, *The South As It Is*, 129, 261, 252.

84. Andrews, *The South since the War*, 205, 362.

85. Rawick (ed.), *American Slave*, IV and V: Texas Narr. (Part 1), 280, (Part 3), 83–84. See also XIV: N.C. Narr. (Part 1), 72.

86. *Ibid.*, VIII: Ark. Narr. (Part 2), 284; Trowbridge, *The South*, 291–92.

87. Andrews, *The South since the War*, 26; 39 Cong., 1 Sess., *Report of the Joint Committee on Reconstruction*, Part III, 3; Stone, *Brokenburn*, 368–69.

88. Trowbridge, *The South*, 427–28; Rawick (ed.), *American Slave*, XVIII: Unwritten History, 138. See also V: Texas Narr. (Part 3), 261.

89. Williamson, *After Slavery*, 88; John W. Burbidge to Joseph Glover, July 28, 1865, Glover-North Papers, Univ. of South Carolina; Rev. John Jones to Mrs. Jones, July 26, 1865, in Myers (ed.), *Children of Pride*, 1282–83. See also Dr. Ethelred Philips to Dr. James J. Philips, Aug. 2, 1865, James J. Philips Collection, Univ. of North Carolina; H. A. Johnson to "Dear Friend Samuel," July 14, 1865, Univ. of North Carolina; Emma E. Holmes, Ms. Diary, entry for June 15, 1865, Univ. of South Carolina; Easterby (ed.), *South Carolina Rice Plantation*, 210–211; Oliphant et al. (eds.), *Letters of William Gilmore Simms*, IV, 505; LeConte, *When the World Ended*, 105, 115–16.

90. For the Union Army and the expulsion of freed slaves from the cities and towns, see above, Chapter 6. For the military role in imposing order on the plantations, se•, e.g., Petition of 18 Planters, Pineville, Charleston District, Sept. 1, 1865, Trenholm Papers, Univ. of North Carolina; Ravenel, *Private Journal*, 223; Richardson, *Negro in*

the Reconstruction of Florida, 56; *New York Times*, June 16, 1865.

91. Col. William E. Bayley to Commanding Officer, Vicksburg, Miss., July 3, 1865, Records of the Assistant Commissioners, Mississippi (Letters Received), Freedmen's Bureau; *New Orleans Tribune*, April 11, 1865.

92. Eppes, *Negro of the Old South*, 125; Ball, *The State That Forgot*, 128; Reid, *After the War*, 419. See also Myers (ed.), *Children of Pride*, 1292–93.

93. Towne, *Letters and Diary*, 20; Knox, *Camp-fire and Cotton Field*, 316–17.

94. On wartime Federal labor policies in the South, see Gerteis, *From Contraband to Freedman;* Eaton, *Grant, Lincoln, and the Freedmen;* and Wiley, *Southern Negroes*, esp. 230–59. On white and black lessees, see *Christian Recorder*, July 16, 1864; *New Orleans Tribune*, July 11, 1865; *Report of the General Superintendent of Freedmen, Department of the Tennessee and State of Arkansas for 1864* (Memphis, 1865), 14–15, 50; Knox, *Camp-fire and Cotton Field*, 320–21; *National Freedman*, I (Feb. 1, May 1, July 15, 1865), 16–17, 121, 187; *New York Times*, Nov. 13, 28, 1863, Aug. 2, Sept. 26, 1865; and the experience of Isaac Shoemaker in Roark, *Masters Without Slaves*, 118–19. On the Davis Bend project, see Col. Samuel Thomas, "Report of a Trip to Davis Bend, Waterproof and Natchez," in Warren, *Extracts from Reports of Superintendents of Freedmen;* Reid, *After the War*, 279–87; Trowbridge, *The South*, 383–84; Knox, *Camp-fire and Cotton Field*, 353; *National Freedman*, I (Feb. 1, 1865), 25; *New Orleans Tribune*, July 9, 29, 1865; *New York Times*, Oct. 2, 1864, Aug. 22, 1865; Joseph E. Davis and Benjamin F. Montgomery, Article of Agreement, Oct. 31, 1865, Records of the Assistant Commissioners, Mississippi (Letters Received), Freedmen's Bureau; *Semi-Weekly Louisianian*, May 14, 1871; *New National Era*, April 20, 1871; and Wharton, *Negro in Mississippi*, 38–42. After the war, Davis leased two plantations to Benjamin T. Montgomery, his former slave and plantation manager, who subsequently purchased the plantations and became a successful planter.

95. Emma E. Holmes, Ms. Diary, entry for June 15, 1865, Univ. of South Carolina.

96. Knox, *Camp-fire and Cotton Field*,

364–69; *Black Republican*, April 15, 1865; *New York Times*, Dec. 22, 1862, Jan. 16, March 5, April 17, 1863, Sept. 25, 1864; Sitterson, *Sugar Country*, 220–23; Gerteis, *From Contraband to Freedman*, 65–82; Wiley, *Southern Negroes*, 210–21; Messner, "Black Violence and White Response: Louisiana, 1862," 31–37.

97. *New Orleans Tribune*, Aug. 13, Dec. 8, 1864, Jan. 28, Feb. 7, 18, March 14, 19, April 1, 9, July 29, 1865. See also *ibid.*, Oct. 16, 1864, March 16, April 13, 1865. For a meeting to protest the labor system and the reaction of Federal authorities, see *ibid.*, March 18, 19, 28, 29, 30, 1865.

98. *New Orleans Tribune*, Oct. 12, 1864; Gerteis, *From Contraband to Freedman*, 90, 113–14.

99. Messner, "Black Violence and White Response: Louisiana, 1862," 36–37.

100. Ruffin, *Diary*, II, 601–03, 670–72.

101. Thomas Smith to Capt. J. H. Weber, Nov. 3, 1865, Records of the Assistant Commissioners, Mississippi (Letters Received), Freedmen's Bureau.

102. *Free Man's Press*, Sept. 12, 1868; 39 Cong., 1 Sess., House Exec. Doc. 70, *Freedmen's Bureau*, 263–64.

103. Lt. George Parliss to Lt. Stuart Eldridge, April 9, 1866; Capt. A. Preston to Eldridge, June 7, 1866; R. H. Willoughby to Bvt. Maj. A. M. Crawford, July 27, 1867; Capt. William A. Poillon to Brig. Gen. Wager Swayne, Nov. 1865; Capt. J. H. Weber to Col. Samuel Thomas, July 1, 1865, Records of the Assistant Commissioners, Mississippi (Parliss, Preston, Weber), South Carolina (Willoughby), Alabama (Poillon) (Letters Received), Freedmen's Bureau; 39 Cong., 1 Sess., House Exec. Doc. 70, *Freedmen's Bureau*, 2–3. For advice to freedmen, see also *ibid.*, 2–3, 34–35, 92–93, 124–25, 231–32, 263–64, 309, 395, and 39 Cong., 1 Sess., *Report of the Joint Committee on Reconstruction*, Part II, 230–31; *Colored Tennessean*, Oct. 14, 1865; and Dennett, *The South As It Is*, 250.

104. S. D. G. Niles to Maj. Gen. T. J. Wood, June 13, 1866, Records of the Assistant Commissioners, Mississippi (Letters Received), Freedmen's Bureau; Dennett, *The South As It Is*, 251–52. For native white praise of the Bureau, see also David Humphreys to Bvt. Maj. Gen. Swayne, Nov. 25,

1865, Records of the Assistant Commissioners, Alabama (Letters Received), Freedmen's Bureau; Moore (ed.), *The Juhl Letters* (Sept. 4, 1865), 37–38; 39 Cong., 1 Sess., Senate Exec. Doc. 27, *Reports of the Assistant Commissioners of the Freedmen's Bureau* [1865–1866], 81; Dennett, *The South As It Is,* 291–92; *New York Times,* Sept. 13, 1865; Taylor, *Negro in Tennessee,* 14–15; and Wharton, *Negro in Mississippi,* 78. For hostile white views, see Leigh, *Ten Years on a Georgia Plantation,* 33–34; Reid, *After the War,* 577–78; 39 Cong., 1 Sess., *Report of the Joint Committee on Reconstruction,* Part II, 113, 123; Wharton, *Negro in Mississippi,* 78.

105. 39 Cong., 1 Sess., *Report of the Joint Committee on Reconstruction,* Part II, 230; House Exec. Doc. 70, *Freedmen's Bureau,* 231; Fisk, *Plain Counsels for Freedmen,* 12. See also O. O. Howard in *National Freedman,* I (Aug. 15, 1865), 234–35, and Col. J. L. Haynes to Capt. B. F. Henry, July 8, 1865, Records of the Assistant Commissioners, Mississippi (Letters Received), Freedmen's Bureau.

106. 39 Cong., 1 Sess., House Exec. Doc. 70, *Freedmen's Bureau,* 219–20. See also Capt. William A. Poillon to Brig. Gen. Wager Swayne, Nov. 1865, and Lt. George Parliss to Lt. Stuart Eldridge, April 9, 1866, Records of the Assistant Commissioners, Alabama and Mississippi (Letters Received), Freedmen's Bureau.

107. Williamson, *After Slavery,* 87, 91; Richardson, *Negro in the Reconstruction of Florida,* 57–58, 62; Wharton, *Negro in Mississippi,* 74–77; Horace James to the Secretaries of the American Missionary Association, Oct. 20, 1865, American Missionary Assn. Archives. For the work of the Bureau, see also *Autobiography of Oliver Otis Howard* (2 vols.; New York, 1907); "Of the Dawn of Freedom," in W. E. B. Du Bois, *The Souls of Black Folk* (Chicago, 1903), 13–40; Bentley, *A History of the Freedmen's Bureau;* McFeely, *Yankee Stepfather;* Abbott, *The Freedmen's Bureau in South Carolina;* Howard A. White, *The Freedmen's Bureau in Louisiana* (Baton Rouge, 1970).

108. Andrews, *The South since the War,* 23–24; *Christian Recorder,* Dec. 1, 1866. For critical observations of Bureau personnel and their treatment of the freed-

men, see letters and affidavits from Bacchus Brinson (colored), Augusta, Ga., March 21, 1866, Berry Chalman (freedman), Augusta, Ga., May 24, 1866, William Davis and others (freedmen), March 31, 1866, Margaret J. McMurry (white), Marietta, Ga., Oct. 25, 1866, and M. V. Jordan, Miller Co., Ga., Oct. 27, 1866, in Freedmen's Bureau (Registers of Letters Received), Georgia. See also black testimony on the Bureau in *Christian Recorder,* Aug. 12, 1865, May 26, June 9, 1866, and Trowbridge, *The South,* 465.

109. On black Bureau agents, see, e.g., the letters and reports of Martin R. Delany and B. F. Randolph, Records of the Assistant Commissioners, South Carolina (Letters Received), and of J. J. Wright, Records of the Subdivision of Beaufort, South Carolina, Freedmen's Bureau.

110. *New Orleans Tribune,* Dec. 14, 23, 1865.

111. De Forest, *Union Officer in the Reconstruction,* 39, 41–42. See also Dennett, *The South As It Is,* 109–10, 221.

112. *New Orleans Tribune,* Oct. 31, 1867; De Forest, *Union Officer in the Reconstruction,* 29–30. For typical cases handled by a Bureau agent, see, e.g., Reports of J. J. Wright, Records of the Subdivision of Beaufort, South Carolina, and the Tri-Monthly Reports of James DeGrey, as submitted to William H. Webster, Records of the Assistant Commissioners, Louisiana (Letters Received), Freedmen's Bureau; Dennett, *The South As It Is,* 125–26; and De Forest, *Union Officer in the Reconstruction,* 28–36.

113. Dennett, *The South As It Is,* 73–74. See also the testimony of Lorenzo Ivy in Armstrong and Ludlow, *Hampton and Its Students,* 80.

114. *Christian Recorder,* June 23, 1866; Affidavit of Bacchus Brinson, Augusta, Ga., March 21, 1866, Freedmen's Bureau (Registers of Letters Received), Georgia; Amos McCollough to Gen. O. O. Howard, May 6, 1866, Records of the Assistant Commissioners, North Carolina (Letters Received), Freedmen's Bureau.

115. 39 Cong., 2 Sess., Senate Exec. Doc. 6, *Reports of the Assistant Commissioners of Freedmen* [Jan. 3, 1867], 113, 116; Capt. Randolph Stoops to Capt. George L. Childs, July 15, 1865, and Statement of

Frederick Nicholas and Miner Poindexter of Columbia, Fluvanna Co., Virginia, June 28, 1865, Brock Collection, Henry E. Huntington Library.

116. Lt. George Parliss to Lt. Stuart Eldridge, April 9, 1866, Capt. J. H. Weber to Col. Samuel Thomas, July 1, 1865, Maj. George D. Reynolds to Lt. Stuart Eldridge, Oct. 5, 1865, Records of the Assistant Commissioners, Mississippi (Letters Received), Freedmen's Bureau.

117. *New Orleans Tribune*, Oct. 31, 1867; Lt. C. W. Clarke to Col. Samuel Thomas, June 29, 1865, Records of the Assistant Commissioners, Mississippi (Letters Received), Freedmen's Bureau.

118. *New Orleans Tribune*, Aug. 31, Oct. 22, 1865.

## Chapter Eight: Back to Work: The New Dependency

1. Henry Lee Swint, *The Northern Teacher in the South, 1862–1870* (Nashville, 1941), 89.

2. *Christian Recorder*, Sept. 30, 1865.

3. Nordhoff, *Freedmen of South Carolina*, 7–8.

4. Botume, *First Days Amongst the Contrabands*, 237; Towne, *Letters and Diary*, 31; *New Orleans Tribune*, Oct. 11, Nov. 21, 1865.

5. Lt. Edward M. Stoeber to Bvt. Maj. Taylor, July 24, 1865; "Memorandum of Extracts from Speech by Major Delany, African, at the Brick Church, St. Helena Island, South Carolina, Sunday, July 23, 1865," submitted by Lt. Alexander Whyte, Jr., to Col. Charles H. Howard, Records of the Assistant Commissioners, South Carolina (Letters Received), Freedmen's Bureau. For the speech's repercussions, see also W. E. Towne to Bvt. Maj. Gen. Saxton, Aug. 17, 1865, in the same records.

6. *Loyal Georgian*, Jan. 20, 1866.

7. *New York Times*, April 30, 1865; 39 Cong., 1 Sess., Senate Exec. Doc. 53, *Preliminary Report . . . by the American Freedmen's Inquiry Commission, June 30, 1863*, 6–7. For favorable views of black labor, see also, e.g., W. E. Towne to Bvt. Maj. Gen. Saxton, Aug. 17, 1865, Records of the Assistant Commissioners, South Carolina (Letters Received), Freedmen's Bureau; A. C. Voris to Maj. George A. Hicks, Oct. 21, 1865, Brock Collection, Henry E. Huntington Library; 39 Cong., 1 Sess., *Report of the Joint Committee on Reconstruction*, Part I, 117–18, Part II, 5, 13, 42, 43, 182, 247; Loring and Atkinson, *Cotton Culture and the South*, 8–9, 10; Reid, *After the War*, 569–70; Trowbridge, *The South*, 138, 162, 581; *Colored Tennessean*, March 24, 1866; *Christian Recorder*, Aug.

19, Sept. 30, 1865; *New York Times*, April 8, Oct. 1, Nov. 12, 1865.

8. Trowbridge, *The South*, 150. See also *ibid.*, 288; Reid, *After the War*, 385; and *New York Times*, Oct. 6, 1866.

9. Reid, *After the War*, 385; Trowbridge, *The South*, 230n.–31n.; Swint (ed.), *Dear Ones at Home*, 233.

10. *New Orleans Tribune*, July 16, 1865.

11. Williamson, *After Slavery*, 102.

12. Scarborough, *The Overseer*, 153; *New York Times*, June 21, 1863. See also Rawick (ed.), *American Slave*, VIII: Ark. Narr. (Part 1), 71.

13. *New York Times*, March 19, 1864. For wartime articulation of demands by black laborers, see also Towne, *Letters and Diary*, 24; *New York Times*, Oct. 14, 1862, June 21, 1863; Annette Koch to Christian D. Koch, June 27, 1863, Koch Papers, Louisiana State Univ.; Sitterson, *Sugar Country*, 209; Scarborough, *The Overseer*, 155; LeConte, *'Ware Sherman*, 56; Ravenel, *Private Journal*, 215, 216; Knox, *Camp-fire and Cotton Field*, 374.

14. Hepworth, *Whip, Hoe, and Sword*, 29–30. For a similar incident, resulting in the dismissal of the overseer, see *New York Times*, Oct. 17, 1863.

15. Towne, *Letters and Diary*, 24; Pearson (ed.), *Letters from Port Royal*, 250, 300–01, 303–04.

16. Patrick, *Fall of Richmond*, 118–19; Rawick (ed.), *American Slave*, XI: Mo. Narr., 115; VII: Okla. Narr., 184–85.

17. Jones, *Heroines of Dixie*, 119–20; Jervey and Ravenel, *Two Diaries*, 13.

18. Ravenel, *Private Journal*, 212, 214–18; Myers (ed.), *Children of Pride*, 1284.

19. Trowbridge, *The South*, 428.

20. 39 Cong., 1 Sess., *Report of the Joint Committee on Reconstruction,* Part II, 109; Jonathan Worth to Col. Whittlesey, Nov. 23, 1865, in J. G. De Roulhac Hamilton (ed.), *The Correspondence of Jonathan Worth* (2 vols.; Raleigh, 1909), I, 451; *Letters from Joseph Simpson* (May 16, 1865), 12. See also Margaret L. Montgomery, "Alabama Freedmen: Some Reconstruction Documents," *Phylon,* XIII (1952), 245; Trowbridge, *The South,* 495; *National Freedman,* I (Aug. 15, 1865), 226.

21. Dr. Ethelred Philips to Dr. James J. Philips, Aug. 2, 1865, James J. Philips Collection, Univ. of North Carolina; Myers (ed.), *Children of Pride,* 1241, 1371, 1405, 1412.

22. For examples of these concerns, see 39 Cong., 1 Sess., *Report of the Joint Committee on Reconstruction,* Part II, 54, 56; *Loyal Georgian,* Jan. 27, 1866; Wiley, *Southern Negroes,* 231–33; Rose, *Rehearsal for Reconstruction,* 79, 82; Dennett, *The South As It Is,* 254–55.

23. *New Orleans Tribune,* Nov. 30, 1864, Jan. 28, 29, Feb. 2, March 1, 8, July 16, 1865. See also Richard H. Cain in *Christian Recorder,* June 17, 1865.

24. *Christian Recorder,* March 25, 1865; Evans, *Ballots and Fence Rails,* 68–69.

25. Patrick, *Fall of Richmond,* 125.

26. McPherson, *Negro's Civil War,* 294; Maj. George D. Reynolds to Lt. Stuart Eldridge, Oct. 5, 1865, Records of the Assistant Commissioners, Mississippi (Letters Received), Freedmen's Bureau. For additional evidence of freedmen's land expectations, see Capt. William A. Poillon to Brig. Gen. Wager Swayne, Nov. 1865, Records of the Assistant Commissioners, Alabama (Letters Received), Freedmen's Bureau; Bvt. Brig. Gen. Alvin C. Voris to Maj. George A. Hicks, Oct. 7, 1865, Brock Collection, Henry E. Huntington Library; 39 Cong., 2 Sess., Senate Exec. Doc. 6, *Reports of the Assistant Commissioners of Freedmen* [Jan. 3, 1867], 4; 39 Cong., 1 Sess., House Exec. Doc. 70, *Freedmen's Bureau,* 394; J. S. Fullerton, *Report of the Administration of Freedmen's Affairs in Louisiana* (Washington, D.C., 1865), 2; Dennett, *The South As It Is,* 188–89.

27. Andrews, *The South since the War,* 97–98; Thomas Smith to Capt. J. H. Weber, Nov. 3, 1865, Records of the Assistant Commissioners, Mississippi (Letters Received), Freedmen's Bureau; *Letters from Joseph Simpson* (May 29, 1865), 13; Manuel Gottlieb, "The Land Question in Georgia During Reconstruction," *Science and Society,* III (1939), 360.

28. D. E. H. Smith (ed.), *Mason Smith Family Letters,* 234; Elias Horry Deas to Anne Deas, Aug. 12, 1865, Deas Papers, Univ. of South Carolina; Josiah Gorgas, Ms. Journal, entry for Aug. 30, 1865, Univ. of North Carolina; Samuel A. Agnew, Ms. Diary, entry for Nov. 3, 1865, Univ. of North Carolina; Petition of 18 Planters, Pineville, Charleston District, Sept. 1, 1865, Trenholm Papers, Univ. of North Carolina; Donald MacRae to Julia MacRae, Sept. 4, 1865, MacRae Papers, Duke Univ.; Ravenel, *Private Journal,* 258; Oliphant et al. (eds.), *Letters of William Gilmore Simms,* IV, 528, 560; Leigh, *Ten Years on a Georgia Plantation,* 27–28; Gottlieb, "The Land Question in Georgia During Reconstruction," 359; Savannah Writers' Project, *Savannah River Plantations* (Savannah, 1947), 324; Heyward, *Seed from Madagascar,* 150–51; Easterby (ed.), *South Carolina Rice Plantation,* 207; Andrews, *The South since the War,* 232–33.

29. The text of the meeting with the black ministers may be found in *National Freedman,* I (April 1, 1865), 98–101, and in *New York Tribune,* Feb. 13, 1865. On Sherman's Order No. 15 and the land policy of the Freedmen's Bureau, see Williamson, *After Slavery,* 59–63; McFeely, *Yankee Stepfather,* 104–05; and the testimony of Gen. Rufus Saxton in 39 Cong., 1 Sess., *Report of the Joint Committee on Reconstruction,* Part II, 221.

30. Trowbridge, *The South,* 151; Edward Barnwell Heyward to Catherine Maria Clinch Heyward, May 5, 1867, Heyward Family Papers, Univ. of South Carolina; Reid, *After the War,* 564, 59. For similar sentiments, see Dennett, *The South As It Is,* 341–42, and 39 Cong., 1 Sess., *Report of the Joint Committee on Reconstruction,* Part III, 77.

31. 39 Cong., 1 Sess., *Report of the Joint Committee on Reconstruction,* Part II, 191, Part III, 31; Rawick (ed.), *American Slave,* IV and V: Texas Narr. (Part 2), 179, (Part 3), 78; XIV: N.C. Narr. (Part 1), 219;

Perdue et al. (eds.), *Weevils in the Wheat*, 291.

32. Bradford, *Harriet Tubman*, 102; Eppes, *Negro of the Old South*, 133.

33. Rawick (ed.), *American Slave*, VI: Ala. Narr., 314–15; Maj. George D. Reynolds to Lt. Stuart Eldridge, Oct. 5, 1865, and Capt. William A. Poillon to Brig. Gen. Wager Swayne, Nov. 1865, Records of the Assistant Commissioners, Mississippi and Alabama (Letters Received), Freedmen's Bureau; 39 Cong., 1 Sess., House Exec. Doc. 70, *Freedmen's Bureau*, 4–5; WPA, *Negro in Virginia*, 218. For instructions to Bureau agents regarding the land expectations of blacks, see also *Freedmen's Bureau*, 34, 95, 135, 147, 162–63, 309, 367–68.

34. *Black Republican*, April 15, 1865; *Christian Recorder*, Aug. 26, 1865. See also *Colored Tennessean*, Oct. 14, 1865.

35. W. E. Towne to Bvt. Maj. Gen. Saxton, Aug. 17, 1865, Records of the Assistant Commissioners, South Carolina (Letters Received), Freedmen's Bureau; Armstrong, *Old Massa's People*, 334–35; Rawick (ed.), *American Slave*, III: S.C. Narr. (Part 3), 45; Williamson, *After Slavery*, 166; Rose, *Rehearsal for Reconstruction*, 200–01, 214–15; Richardson, *Negro in the Reconstruction of Florida*, 73, 75–76, 79–81.

36. *New York Times*, May 12, 1867; WPA, *Negro in Virginia*, 219–20; Fleming, *Civil War and Reconstruction in Alabama*, 447–48; Richardson, *Negro in the Reconstruction of Florida*, 74–75.

37. 39 Cong., 2 Sess., Senate Exec. Doc. 6, *Reports of the Assistant Commissioners of Freedmen* [Jan. 3, 1867], 120; Rawick (ed.), *American Slave*, VII: Miss. Narr., 97–98, 147; Wharton, *Negro in Mississippi*, 60; Richardson, *Negro in the Reconstruction of Florida*, 76; Dennett, *The South As It Is*, 73.

38. E. Merton Coulter, *The South During Reconstruction, 1865–1877* (Baton Rouge, 1947), 109; Gottlieb, "The Land Question in Georgia During Reconstruction," 364; *New Orleans Tribune*, April 19, May 6, 1865; McFeely, *Yankee Stepfather*, 95, 203; "Petition from Colored Citizens of Roanoke Island," enclosed in Bvt. Maj. Daniel Hart to Commanding Officer, Post of Goldsboro, N.C., Dec. 28, 1867, Records of the Assistant

Commissioners, North Carolina (Letters Received), Freedmen's Bureau.

39. Dennett, *The South As It Is*, 248–51; Gottlieb, "The Land Question in Georgia During Reconstruction," 364.

40. Botume, *First Days Amongst the Contrabands*, 195–99; Armstrong and Ludlow, *Hampton and Its Students*, 181; *Autobiography of Oliver Otis Howard*, II, 238–39; Andrews, *The South since the War*, 212; Ames, *From a New England Woman's Diary in Dixie*, 95–103.

41. Ames, *From a New England Woman's Diary in Dixie*, 98, 99–103; McFeely, *Yankee Stepfather*, 156–57.

42. *New York Times*, Oct. 10, 12, 13, 19, 1867; *New Era*, July 7, 1870; WPA, *Negro in Virginia*, 218. For a similar confrontation in Hampton, Virginia, see *National Freedman*, I (Sept. 15, 1865), 267–68, and *New York Tribune*, Aug. 25, 1865.

43. Avary, *Dixie after the War*, 345; Lt. Erastus W. Everson to Bvt. Maj. Henry W. Smith, Jan. 30, 1866, Records of the Assistant Commissioners, South Carolina (Letters Received), Freedmen's Bureau; Ravenel, *Private Journal*, 271–72; *New York Times*, Feb. 5, 1866; Trowbridge, *The South*, 539–40. See also Williamson, *After Slavery*, 82–85.

44. Dennett, *The South As It Is*, 291; William Heyward to James Gregorie, June 4, 1868, Gregorie-Elliott Collection, Univ. of North Carolina; Myers (ed.), *Children of Pride*, 1308–09; Trowbridge, *The South*, 393. For agreements among planters not to sell or rent lands to blacks, see Douglas G. Manning to Mrs. John L. Manning, Dec. 25, 1865, Williams-Chesnut-Manning Papers, Univ. of South Carolina; *South Carolina Leader*, Dec. 16, 1865; 39 Cong., 1 Sess., House Exec. Doc. 70, *Freedmen's Bureau*, 371; Andrews, *The South since the War*, 206; *New York Times*, Jan. 27, 29, 1866; Taylor, *Negro in the Reconstruction of Virginia*, 106–07. See also Dennett, *The South As It Is*, 344–45, and Reid, *After the War*, 564–65.

45. Allen S. Izard to Mrs. William Mason Smith, Sept. 15, 1865, in D. E. H. Smith (ed.), *Mason Smith Family Letters*, 231.

46. 39 Cong., 1 Sess., Senate Exec. Doc. 27, *Reports of the Assistant Commissioners of the Freedmen's Bureau* [1865–1866], 36–37.

47. Heyward, *Seed from Madagascar,* 140. See also the contracts cited in note 49.

48. Williamson, *After Slavery,* 97; H. A. Moore, Jr., to Maj. Gen Scott, April 19, 1866, Records of the Assistant Commissioners, South Carolina (Letters Received), Freedmen's Bureau.

49. Contracts between Joseph Glover and freedmen, Aug. 13, 1865, to Jan. 1, 1866, and Jan. 1, 1866, to Jan. 1, 1867, Glover-North Papers, Univ. of South Carolina; Contracts between Elias Horry Deas and freedmen, Sept. 7, 1865, and March 3, 1866, Deas Papers, Univ. of South Carolina; Felix Shank to Capt. M. Whalen (Freedmen's Bureau agent), July 14, 1868, including contract with freedman, Feb. 5, 1868, and Contracts between A. J. and J. W. Shank and Enos (freedman) and Augustus (freedman), Jan. 5, 1867, Joseph Belknap Smith Papers, Duke Univ.; "Form of Contracts between planters and freedmen, as substantially adopted by the Darlington meeting, revised and adopted by the mass meeting of Sumter, Kershaw and Clarendon planters, Dec. 21, 1865, and approved by Maj. Gen. Saxton, of the Freedmen's Bureau," in 39 Cong., 1 Sess., *Report of the Joint Committee on Reconstruction,* Part II, 241–42; "A Freedmen's Contract, 1865," in Easterby (ed.), *South Carolina Rice Plantation,* 354–55; "Terms of Agreement between Charles and E. B. Heyward, Esqrs., and certain labourers," June 5, 1865, in Heyward, *Seed from Madagascar,* 139–40; Dennett, *The South As It Is,* 281–83; Lt. C. W. Clarke to Col. Samuel Thomas, June 29, 1865, Records of the Assistant Commissioners, Mississippi (Letters Received), Freedmen's Bureau; Rogers, *Thomas County, 1865–1900,* 30–31; Bryan, *Confederate Georgia,* 136; Loring and Atkinson, *Cotton Culture and the South,* 28.

50. H. A. Moore, Jr., to Maj. Gen Scott, April 19, 1866, Records of the Assistant Commissioners, South Carolina (Letters Received), Freedmen's Bureau; Rollin, *Martin R. Delany,* 261–62.

51. Trowbridge, *The South,* 386. On hours of labor, see contracts cited in note 49.

52. Trowbridge, *The South,* 367–68; Lt. George Parliss to Lt. Stuart Eldridge, April 9, 1866, Records of the Assistant Commissioners, Mississippi (Letters Received), Freedmen's Bureau.

53. Leigh, *Ten Years on a Georgia Plantation,* 33, 56; Trowbridge, *The South,* 430; Dennett, *The South As It Is,* 291; Pierce, *The Negroes at Port Royal,* 9; Heyward, *Seed from Madagascar,* 157; "Visit to 'Gowrie' and 'East Hermitage' Plantations," March 1867, Manigault Plantation Records, Univ. of North Carolina. For contract provisions regarding the driver or black foreman, see also Elias H. Deas contract with freedmen, March 3, 1866, Deas Papers, Univ. of South Carolina, and 39 Cong., 1 Sess., *Report of the Joint Committee on Reconstruction,* Part II, 241–42.

54. Trowbridge, *The South,* 391; Reid, *After the War,* 490. The estimates of compensation rates are based on the archival records and published reports of the Freedmen's Bureau, the accounts of postwar travelers in the South (especially Sidney Andrews, John R. Dennett, J. T. Trowbridge, and Whitelaw Reid), and the black press.

55. Dennett, *The South As It Is,* 321–22; Reid, *After the War,* 526; *Report of the General Superintendent of Freedmen, Department of the Tennessee and State of Arkansas for 1864,* 31. On compensation by shares, see, e.g., the Glover and Deas contracts with freedmen cited in note 49; John H. Bills, Ms. Diary, entry for Dec. 31, 1866, Univ. of North Carolina; Dr. Ethelred Philips to Dr. James J. Philips, Jan. 21, 1866, James J. Philips Collection, Univ. of North Carolina; Myers (ed.), *Children of Pride,* 1363; Easterby (ed.), *South Carolina Rice Plantation,* 210, 216; D. E. H. Smith (ed.), *Mason Smith Family Letters,* 264; Heyward, *Seed from Madagascar,* 139; and the archival records and published reports of the Freedmen's Bureau. Although domestic servants were often paid on a daily or weekly basis, some contracts compensated them with a share of the proceeds from sale of the crop. See, e.g., Williamson, *After Slavery,* 159, and Wharton, *Negro in Mississippi,* 126–27.

56. Trowbridge, *The South,* 392; Reid, *After the War,* 343; Dennett, *The South As It Is,* 82; Leigh, *Ten Years on a Georgia Plantation,* 26; *New York Times,* Oct. 2, 1866; Moore (ed.), *The Juhl Letters* (Aug. 11, 1866), 113. For the experience of a planter in South Carolina who tried both systems, see William M. Hazzard to Gen. R. K. Scott,

March 11, 1868, Records of the Assistant Commissioners, South Carolina (Letters Received), Freedmen's Bureau.

57. J. W. Alvord, *Report on Schools and Finances of Freedmen, for January, 1866,* 24; *New National Era,* April 13, 1871; De Forest, *Union Officer in the Reconstruction,* 28; Trowbridge, *The South,* 424; 39 Cong., 1 Sess., Senate Exec. Doc. 27, *Reports of the Assistant Commissioners of the Freedmen's Bureau* [1865–1866], 36–37. For the pervasiveness of these fears and the grounds on which they were based, see *ibid.,* 21, 25; John P. Bardwell to Rev. M. E. Strieby, Nov. 20, 1865, American Missionary Assn. Archives; *New York Times,* Aug. 20, Oct. 14, 1865; Dennett, *The South As It Is,* 73; Leigh, *Ten Years on a Georgia Plantation,* 84.

58. Trowbridge, *The South,* 565.

59. Richardson, *Negro in the Reconstruction of Florida,* 63; *New Orleans Tribune,* Dec. 8, 1864.

60. Reid, *After the War,* 291n.

61. Rawick (ed.), *American Slave,* XIII: Ga. Narr. (Part 4), 170–71.

62. Bvt. Brig. Gen. Alvin C. Voris to Maj. George A. Hicks, Oct. 7, 1865, Brock Collection, Henry E. Huntington Library; Thomas Smith to Capt. J. H. Weber, Nov. 3, 1865, Records of the Assistant Commissioners, Mississippi (Letters Received), Freedmen's Bureau; 39 Cong., 1 Sess., House Exec. Doc. 70, *Freedmen's Bureau,* 252; *Report of the Joint Committee on Reconstruction,* Part II, 238. See also *ibid.,* 247; H. A. Johnson to "Dear Friend Samuel," July 14, 1865, Univ. of North Carolina; and Williamson, *After Slavery,* 38.

63. Williamson, *After Slavery,* 66; H. W. Ravenel to Augustin L. Taveau, June 27, 1865, Taveau Papers, Duke Univ. On the Freedmen's Bureau and rations, see also Botume, *First Years Amongst the Contrabands,* 260; Rev. Horace James, *Annual Report of the Superintendent of Negro Affairs in North Carolina* [1864–1865], Appendix, 57; "Report of the Commissioner of the Bureau of Refugees, Freedmen and Abandoned Lands, November 1, 1866," in *Report of the Secretary of War* (Washington, D.C., 1867), Appendix, 712; Avary, *Dixie after the War,* 211–12.

64. *New York Times,* June 27, 1865; Douglas G. Manning to Mrs. John L. Manning, Dec. 25, 1865, Williams-Chesnut-

Manning Papers, Univ. of South Carolina. See also *South Carolina Leader,* Dec. 16, 1865; *New Orleans Tribune,* July 4, 1865; 39 Cong., 1 Sess., House Exec. Doc. 70, *Freedmen's Bureau,* 371; Trowbridge, *The South,* 229; Andrews, *The South since the War,* 206; Taylor, *Negro in the Reconstruction of Virginia,* 106.

65. Trowbridge, *The South,* 427.

66. Lorenzo James to Brig. Gen. Wager Swayne, Nov. 20, 1865, Records of the Assistant Commissioners, Alabama (Letters Received), Freedmen's Bureau; Ravenel, *Private Journal,* 222; 39 Cong., 1 Sess., *Report of the Joint Committee on Reconstruction,* Part II, 55, 228; Williamson, *After Slavery,* 97.

67. William E. Bayley to Commanding Officer, Vicksburg, July 3, 1865, Records of the Assistant Commissioners, Mississippi (Letters Received), Freedmen's Bureau; Heyward, *Seed from Madagascar,* 142; 39 Cong., 1 Sess., *Report of the Joint Committee on Reconstruction,* Part III, 167; *New York Times,* Aug. 22, 1865; Myers (ed.), *Children of Pride,* 1323; B. F. Blow vs. Jerry Marvast and Abram Marvast (freedmen), Lowndes County, before J. A. Pruitt, Justice of the Peace (acting as agent of the Freedmen's Bureau), Sept. 12, 1865, Records of the Assistant Commissioners, Alabama (Letters Received), Freedmen's Bureau; Stearns, *Black Man of the South, and The Rebels,* 170–71.

68. 39 Cong., 1 Sess., *Report of the Joint Committee on Reconstruction,* Part II, 229; Rogers, *History of Georgetown County,* 433.

69. Felix Shank to Capt. M. Whalen, July 14, 1868, including contract with freedman, Feb. 5, 1868, Joseph Belknap Smith Papers, Duke Univ.; Andrews, *The South since the War,* 206; *New York Times,* Aug. 20, 1865. On Saturday and Sunday work, see also S. D. G. Niles to Maj. Gen. T. J. Wood, June 13, 1866, James DeGrey to William H. Webster, Sept. 10, 1867, Records of the Assistant Commissioners, Mississippi and Louisiana (Letters Received), Freedmen's Bureau; Loring and Atkinson, *Cotton Culture and the South,* 12; Stearns, *Black Man of the South, and The Rebels,* 46; Dennett, *The South As It Is,* 222.

70. William H. Stiles to his wife [Elizabeth A. Mackay], Sept. 22, 1865, Mackay-

Stiles Collection, Univ. of North Carolina; Reid, *After the War,* 530.

71. Andrews, *The South since the War,* 203; R. H. Willoughby to Bvt. Maj. A. M. Crawford, July 27, 1867, Records of the Assistant Commissioners, South Carolina (Letters Received), Freedmen's Bureau; Reid, *After the War,* 572–73.

72. Andrews, *The South since the War,* 204; Lt. George Parliss to Lt. Stuart Eldridge, April 9, 1866, Maj. M. R. Delany to Bvt. Lt. Col. H. W. Smith, Aug. 1, 1866, Records of the Assistant Commissioners, Mississippi and South Carolina (Letters Received), Freedmen's Bureau; 39 Cong., 2 Sess., Senate Exec. Doc. 6, *Reports of the Assistant Commissioners of Freedmen* [Jan. 3, 1867], 51–52; *New York Times,* Sept. 12, 1866; De Forest, *Union Officer in the Reconstruction,* 29.

73. McFeely, *Yankee Stepfather,* 157; Col. J. L. Haynes to Capt. B. F. Henry, July 8, 1865, Records of the Assistant Commissioners, Mississippi (Letters Received), Freedmen's Bureau; Richardson, *Negro in the Reconstruction of Florida,* 64; Bvt. Maj. Thomas H. Norton to Maj. A. W. Preston, Aug. 3, 1867, B. F. Blow vs. Jerry Marvast and Abram Marvast (freedmen), Lowndes County, before J. A. Pruitt, Justice of the Peace (acting as agent of the Freedmen's Bureau), Sept. 12, 1865, Records of the Assistant Commissioners, Mississippi and Alabama (Letters Received), Freedmen's Bureau.

74. McFeely, *Yankee Stepfather,* 121; S. D. G. Niles to Maj. Gen. T. J. Wood, June 16, 1866, Lorenzo James to Brig. Gen. Wager Swayne, Aug. 16, 1865, Records of the Assistant Commissioners, Mississippi and Alabama (Letters Received), Freedmen's Bureau.

75. Dennett, *The South As It Is,* 56.

76. Armstrong and Ludlow, *Hampton and Its Students,* 79–80.

77. 39 Cong., 1 Sess., *Report of the Joint Committee on Reconstruction,* Part II, 191; Trowbridge, *The South,* 363–64. For additional examples of freedmen defrauded of their pay or shares, see Rawick (ed.), *American Slave,* III: S.C. Narr. (Part 3), 15; V: Texas Narr. (Part 4), 117; XIV: N.C. Narr. (Part 1), 49, 420; Bvt. Brig. Gen. Alvin C. Voris to Maj. George A. Hicks, Oct. 2, 1865,

Brock Collection, Henry E. Huntington Library; Maj. M. R. Delany to Bvt. Lt. Col. H. W. Smith, Aug. 1, 1866, H. S. Van Eaton to Bvt. Maj. Gen. A. C. Gillem, Nov. 24, 1867, Records of the Assistant Commissioners, South Carolina and Mississippi (Letters Received), Freedmen's Bureau; Andrews, *The South since the War,* 322–23, 368; Trowbridge, *The South,* 362–64; *Loyal Georgian,* Jan. 27, 1866; 39 Cong., 1 Sess., *Report of the Joint Committee on Reconstruction,* Part II, 52, 222, 225, 259.

78. *Christian Recorder,* March 31, 1866. See also Dennett, *The South As It Is,* 331–32, 338–39.

79. Wiley, "Vicissitudes of Early Reconstruction Farming in the Lower Mississippi Valley," 448; Wilmer Shields to William Newton Mercer, Dec. 19, 1865, Mercer Papers, Louisiana State Univ.; Rogers, *History of Georgetown County,* 432.

80. Eppes, *Negro of the Old South,* 128–29; Reid, *After the War,* 527; Andrews, *The South since the War,* 322; Leigh, *Ten Years on a Georgia Plantation,* 76.

81. Reid, *After the War,* 527–28.

82. Trowbridge, *The South,* 366; Richardson, *Negro in the Reconstruction of Florida,* 60; 40 Cong., 2 Sess., House Exec. Doc. 1, *Report of the Commissioner of the Bureau of Refugees, Freedmen, and Abandoned Lands, November 1, 1867,* 681; *Colored Tennessean,* Oct. 4, 1865.

83. Leigh, *Ten Years on a Georgia Plantation,* 76–77; Bvt. Maj. Thomas H. Norton to Maj. A. W. Preston, Aug. 3, 1867, Records of the Assistant Commissioners, Mississippi (Letters Received), Freedmen's Bureau. See also Dennett, *The South As It Is,* 332, 338.

84. De Forest, *Union Officer in the Reconstruction,* 73–75. See also Capt. A. Preston to Lt. Stuart Eldridge, June 7, 1866, Records of the Assistant Commissioners, Mississippi (Letters Received), Freedmen's Bureau.

85. Trowbridge, *The South,* 363; Macrae, *Americans at Home,* 323–24; Rawick (ed.), *American Slave,* VII: Okla. Narr., 283; Maj. and Bvt. Lt. Col. J. E. Cornelius to Bvt. Maj. Edward L. Deane, Dec. 22, 1866, Records of the Assistant Commissioners, South Carolina (Letters Received), Freedmen's Bureau. See also Ames, *From a New*

England Woman's Diary in Dixie, 120, and
WPA, Negro in Virginia, 221.

86. Donald MacRae to Julia MacRae,
Sept. 4, 1865, MacRae Papers, Duke Univ.;
Dr. Ethelred Philips to Dr. James J. Philips,
Aug. 2, 1865, James J. Philips Collection,
Univ. of North Carolina. For fears and ex-
pectations of an "emancipation insurrec-
tion," see also Edward Lynch to Joseph
Glover [c. June 1865], John W. Burbidge to
Joseph Glover, July 28, 1865, Glover-North
Papers, Univ. of South Carolina; A. R. Sal-
ley to "My Dear Aunt," Nov. 13, 1865,
Bruce-Jones-Murchison Papers, Univ. of
South Carolina; Samuel A. Agnew, Ms. Di-
ary, entries for Nov. 3, 21, 22, 1865, Univ. of
North Carolina; Jabez Curry to Gov. Lewis
Parsons, Sept. 29, 1865, John Swanson to
Gov. Parsons, Oct. 3, 1865, Thomas Smith to
Capt. J. H. Weber, Nov. 3, 1865, Records of
the Assistant Commissioners, Alabama
(Curry and Swanson) and Mississippi
(Smith) (Letters Received), Freedmen's Bu-
reau; South Carolina Leader, Dec. 23, 1865;
New Orleans Tribune, Oct. 21, 1865; New
York Times, Nov. 12, 1865; Dennett, The
South As It Is, 190, 275; Andrews, The South
since the War, 27; Reid, After the War, 386–
87; Williamson, After Slavery, 249–52;
Wharton, Negro in Mississippi, 59, 218–19.

87. Sebastian Kraft to President An-
drew Johnson, Aug. [April?] 28, 1865,
Records of the Assistant Commissioners,
South Carolina (Letters Received), Freed-
men's Bureau; Reid, After the War, 386;
Dennett, The South As It Is, 190.

88. Williamson, After Slavery, 249–50,
250–51; Reid, After the War, 387n.–89n.

89. 39 Cong., 1 Sess., Report of the
Joint Committee on Reconstruction, Part III,
30; John P. Bardwell to Rev. M. E. Strieby,
Nov. 4, 1865, American Missionary Assn.
Archives; Moore (ed.), The Juhl Letters (Oct.
28, 1865), 51; South Carolina Leader, Dec. 9,
1865; Dennett, The South As It Is, 240–41;
Col. James C. Beecher to Maj. Kinsman, Oct.
7, 1865, W. E. Towne to Bvt. Maj. Gen. Saxton, Aug. 17, 1865, Records of the Assistant
Commissioners, South Carolina (Letters Received), Freedmen's Bureau.

90. Andrews, War-Time Journal of a
Georgia Girl, 315–16; Leigh, Ten Years on a
Georgia Plantation, 35–37; D. E. H. Smith
(ed.), Mason Smith Family Letters, 232–33,

237; Ella Gertrude (Clanton) Thomas, Ms.
Journal, entry for July 23, 1865, Duke
Univ.; Williamson, After Slavery, 250–51,
and the sources cited in note 86.

91. Samuel A. Agnew, Ms. Diary, entries for Nov. 3, 24, 1865, Univ. of North
Carolina; W. E. Towne to Bvt. Maj. Gen. Saxton, Aug. 17, 1865, Records of the Assistant
Commissioners, South Carolina (Letters Received), Freedmen's Bureau. See also
Wilmer Shields to William N. Mercer, Dec.
19, 1865, Mercer Papers, Louisiana State
Univ.; Dennett, The South As It Is, 240; Andrews, The South since the War, 27; New
Orleans Tribune, Oct. 21, 1865; D. E. H.
Smith (ed.), Mason Smith Family Letters,
232; Chesnut, Diary from Dixie, 532;
Thomas Smith to Capt. J. H. Weber, Nov. 3,
1865, Records of the Assistant Commissioners, Mississippi (Letters Received), Freedmen's Bureau.

92. 39 Cong., 1 Sess., Report of the
Joint Committee on Reconstruction, Part III,
142; South Carolina Leader, Dec. 16, 1865;
Dennett, The South As It Is, 193; New York
Times, Sept. 7, Dec. 1, 1865; Williamson, Af-
ter Slavery, 251–52; Wharton, Negro in Re-
construction, 59, 218; Evans, Ballots and
Fence Rails, 130.

93. New Orleans Tribune, Oct. 21, Dec.
27, 1865, Dec. 19, 1867; South Carolina
Leader, Dec. 23, 1865; Christian Recorder,
Dec. 30, 1865, Feb. 24, 1866; New York
Times, Dec. 31, 1865.

94. New Orleans Tribune, Oct. 21,
1865; Andrews, The South since the War,
207.

95. Burge, Diary, 114; Dennett, The
South As It Is, 275; 39 Cong., 1 Sess., Report
of the Joint Committee on Reconstruction,
Part II, 192, Part III, 30, 31; New York
Times, Dec. 27, 28, 29, 1865; Moore (ed.), The
Juhl Letters (Dec. 25, 1865), 57; Evans, Bal-
lots and Fence Rails, 131; Samuel A. Agnew,
Ms. Diary, entry for Nov. 26, 1865, Univ. of
North Carolina.

96. Easterby (ed.), South Carolina Rice
Plantation, 224–25; Leigh, Ten Years on a
Georgia Plantation, 131–32. See also New
Orleans Tribune, Dec. 19, 1867.

97. Botume, First Days Amongst the
Contrabands, 204–06. See also Christian
Recorder, Feb. 24, 1866. The Emancipation
Day celebration in Richmond is described

in Haviland, *A Woman's Life-Work,* 401–02.

98. Samuel A. Agnew, Ms. Diary, entries for Dec. 5, 25, 1865, Univ. of North Carolina; Wilmer Shields to William N. Mercer, Dec. 19, 1865, Mercer Papers, Louisiana State Univ.; Easterby (ed.), *South Carolina Rice Plantation,* 215–16; Capt. D. Corbin to H. W. Smith, Feb. 1, 1866, Records of the Assistant Commissioners, South Carolina (Letters Received), Freedmen's Bureau. See also Dennett, *The South As It Is,* 188.

99. E. W. Everson to Bvt. Maj. Edward Deane, Jan. 17, 1867, Records of the Assistant Commissioners, South Carolina (Letters Received), Freedmen's Bureau; Moore (ed.), *The Juhl Letters* (Jan. 29, 1866), 73–74; Montgomery, "Alabama Freedmen: Some Reconstruction Documents," 250; *New York Times,* Jan. 8, 1866; Kolchin, *First Freedom,* 9–10; Williamson, *After Slavery,* 39, 105–06.

100. Ravenel, *Private Journal,* 272; Eppes, *Negro of the Old South,* 128, 130–31.

101. *New York Times,* Feb. 28, 1868; 39 Cong., 1 Sess., *Report of the Joint Committee on Reconstruction,* Part III, 167; Reid, *After the War,* 446–47. See also 39 Cong., 1 Sess., House Exec. Doc. 70, *Freedmen's Bureau,* 273; Sarah M. Payne to Mary Clendenin, Dec. 14, 1867, Historical Society of Pennsylvania; and Reid, *After the War,* 455.

102. Leigh, *Ten Years on a Georgia Plantation,* 87–91.

103. Bragg, *Louisiana in the Confederacy,* 213–14; Wiley, *Southern Negroes,* 236–37; Allen S. Izard to Mrs. William Mason Smith, Sept. 26, 1865, in D. E. H. Smith (ed.), *Mason Smith Family Letters,* 236.

104. *South Carolina Leader,* Dec. 9, 1865; Dennett, *The South As It Is,* 203. For black views on the respective merits of the share and wage systems, see also Maj. M. R. Delany to Bvt. Lt. Col. H. W. Smith, Aug. 1, 1866, and B. F. Randolph to Bvt. Maj. Gen. R. K. Scott, Aug. 6, 1867, Records of the Assistant Commissioners, South Carolina (Letters Received), Freedmen's Bureau.

105. Leigh, *Ten Years on a Georgia Plantation,* 90–91; Reid, *After the War,* 507; Williamson, *After Slavery,* 93–94; Contract between Elias H. Deas and freedmen, March 3, 1866, Deas Papers, Univ. of South Carolina; Contract between Felix Shank and

freedman, Feb. 5, 1868, and between A. J. and J. W. Shank and Enos, Jan. 5, 1867, Joseph Belknap Smith Papers, Duke Univ.; Reid, *After the War,* 464; Lt. George Parliss to Lt. Stuart Eldridge, April 9, 1866, James DeGrey to Lt. J. M. Lee, Nov. 10, 1867, Records of the Assistant Commissioners, Mississippi and Louisiana (Letters Received), Freedmen's Bureau. The demand for a five-day workweek (which no working class, white or black, enjoyed in 1865) may also be found in John H. Bills, Ms. Diary, entry for Sept. 9, 1865, Univ. of North Carolina; Wilmer Shields to William N. Mercer, Dec. 12, 1866, Mercer Papars, Louisiana State Univ.; S. D. G. Niles to Maj. Gen. T. J. Wood, June 13, 1866, Records of the Assistant Commissioners, Mississippi (Letters Received), Freedmen's Bureau; Loring and Atkinson, *Cotton Culture and the South,* 12; Williamson, *After Slavery,* 91–92.

106. Emma E. Holmes, Ms. Diary, entry for Jan. 15, 1866, Univ. of South Carolina; Rogers, *History of Georgetown County,* 431–32; Williamson, *After Slavery,* 104–05.

107. Wilmer Shields to William N. Mercer, Sept. 21, Nov. 18, 21, Dec. 1, 12, 26, 1866, Jan. 1, 6, 9, 16, Feb. 6, 13, May 22, 1867, Mercer Papers, Louisiana State Univ.

108. John H. Bills, Ms. Diary, entry for July 29, 1865, Univ. of North Carolina; Easterby (ed.), *South Carolina Rice Plantation,* 223; Williamson, *After Slavery,* 100; Samuel A. Agnew, Ms. Diary, entries for Jan. 1, 3, 1867, Univ. of North Carolina; Reid, *After the War,* 446–47.

109. Joe M. Richardson (ed.), "A Northerner Reports on Florida: 1866," *Florida Historical Quarterly,* XL (1962), 383; Esther W. Douglass to Rev. Samuel Hunt, Feb. 1, 1866, American Missionary Assn. Archives.

110. Lt. George Parliss to Lt. Stuart Eldridge, April 9, 1866, Bvt. Lt. Col. B. F. Smith to Bvt. Maj. H. W. Smith, Jan. 21, 1866, Records of the Assistant Commissioners, Mississippi and South Carolina (Letters Received), Freedmen's Bureau. See also *New York Times,* Nov. 30, 1866, and Stearns, *Black Man of the South, and The Rebels,* 47–48.

111. Bvt. Maj. Thomas H. Norton to Maj. A. W. Preston, Aug. 3, 1867, Lt. George

Parliss to Lt. Stuart Eldridge, April 9, 1866, Records of the Assistant Commissioners, Mississippi (Letters Received), Freedmen's Bureau. See also, in the South Carolina records, Bvt. Maj. Erastus Everson to Bvt. Lt. Col. H. W. Smith, June 15, 1866, and M. J. Kirk to Maj. M. R. Delany, May 24, 1866.

112. Edmund Rhett to Maj. Gen. Scott, Aug. 12, 1866, James DeGrey to William H. Webster, Sept. 10, 1867, Bvt. Lt. Col. B. F. Smith to Bvt. Maj. H. W. Smith, Feb. 21, 1866, Records of the Assistant Commissioners, South Carolina (Rhett and Smith) and Louisiana (DeGrey) (Letters Received), Freedmen's Bureau; *New York Times,* Sept. 5, 1867; Stearns, *Black Man of the South, and The Rebels,* 47–48.

113. Moore (ed.), *The Juhl Letters* (Nov. 17, 1866), 134–37; *New York Times,* June 22, Aug. 16, 1866. See also *New Orleans Tribune,* Sept. 27, 1865; *New York Times,* Aug. 17, Dec. 5, 1866; and, for a joint white-black protest in Raleigh on rents, Fisk P. Brewer to George Whipple, May 27, 1867, American Missionary Assn. Archives.

114. Lt. James M. Johnston to Bvt. Maj. A. M. Crawford, Dec. 17, 1866, Records of the Assistant Commissioners, South Carolina (Letters Received), Freedmen's Bureau. See also *New York Times,* Dec. 30, 1866; J. R. Grady (sheriff, Lillington, Harnett Co.) to Post Commander, Aug. 27, 1867, E. W. Everson to Bvt. Maj. Edward Deane, Jan. 17, 18, 1867, Everson to Lt. Crawford, June 19, 1867, Records of the Assistant Commissioners, North Carolina and South Carolina (Letters Received), Freedmen's Bureau.

115. [name deleted] to Gov. Jonathan Worth, Nov. 29, 1866, in Gov. Worth to Col. Bomford, Dec. 3, 1866, Records of the Assistant Commissioners, North Carolina (Letters Received), Freedmen's Bureau.

116. J. J. Pringle Smith to Mrs. Robert Smith, Jan. 13, 1867, in D. E. H. Smith (ed.), *Mason Smith Family Letters,* 273; Rogers, *History of Georgetown County,* 433; James DeGrey to Lt. J. M. Lee, Nov. 15, 1867, Records of the Assistant Commissioners, Louisiana (Letters Received), Freedmen's Bureau.

117. Reid, *After the War,* 546–50.

118. Lt. Erastus Everson to Bvt. Maj. Henry W. Smith, Jan. 30, 1866, R. H. Wil-

loughby to Bvt. Maj. A. M. Crawford, July 27, 1867, Records of the Assistant Commissioners, South Carolina (Letters Received), and J. J. Wright to Bvt. Gen. Gile, June 3, 1867, Records of the Subdivision of Beaufort, S.C., Freedmen's Bureau.

119. McFeely, *Yankee Stepfather,* 202–03; Lt. and Bvt. Brig. Gen. H. Neide to Bvt. Maj. Edward L. Deane, Feb. 9, 1867, Bvt. Maj. Gen. R. K. Scott to Maj. Gen. O. O. Howard, Feb. 14, 1867, Records of the Assistant Commissioners, South Carolina (Letters Received), Freedmen's Bureau.

120. *Workingman's Advocate,* April 28, June 2, 1866; *New York Times,* April 18, May 24, Dec. 6, 1866, Feb. 10, May 15, June 15, 1867; Taylor, *Negro in the Reconstruction of Virginia,* 120.

121. *New Orleans Tribune,* May 17, 1867; Trowbridge, *The South,* 405.

122. *Christian Recorder,* Dec. 2, 1865; *New Orleans Tribune,* Dec. 20, 22, 23, 24, 25, 1865.

123. Williamson, *After Slavery,* 92–93. For the action of a Bureau officer in the South Carolina low country when faced with a "combination" among the blacks on several plantations, see Capt. D. Corbin to H. W. Smith, Feb. 1, 1866, Records of the Assistant Commissioners, South Carolina (Letters Received), Freedmen's Bureau.

124. *South Carolina Leader,* Dec. 16, 1865; Reid, *After the War,* 464. See also Dennett, *The South As It Is,* 247.

125. Dennett, *The South As It Is,* 15, 114–15, 276–77; *Colored American,* Jan. 6, 1866; Moore (ed.), *The Juhl Letters* (July 4, 1866), 103; Bvt. Lt. Col. B. F. Smith to Bvt. Maj. H. W. Smith, Jan. 21, 1866, Records of the Assistant Commissioners, South Carolina (Letters Received), Freedmen's Bureau.

126. Everard Green Baker, Ms. Diary, entries for Dec. 26, 1862, May 31, 1865, Jan. 13, July 17, 1866, May 29, 1867, Univ. of North Carolina; Genovese, *Roll, Jordan, Roll,* 90.

127. Easterby (ed.), *South Carolina Rice Plantation,* 18–19; Dr. Ethelred Philips to Dr. James J. Philips, Aug. 2, Oct. 24, 1865, Nov. 8, 1866, June 17, Dec. 1, 1867, James J. Philips Collection, Univ. of North Carolina.

128. Myers (ed.), *Children of Pride,* 1340–41, 1366, 1369, 1374, 1376, 1403, 1429.

129. Moore, (ed.), *The Juhl Letters* (Oct. 7, 1866), 125; Trowbridge, *The South*, 545.

130. Lt. Erastus Everson to Bvt. Maj. Henry W. Smith, Jan. 30, 1866, Bvt. Lt. Col. B. F. Smith to Bvt. Maj. Henry W. Smith, Jan. 21, 1866, Records of the Assistant Commissioners, South Carolina (Letters Received), Freedmen's Bureau; *Autobiography of Oliver Otis Howard*, II, 239; Andrews, *The South since the War*, 212.

131. Loring and Atkinson, *Cotton Culture and the South*, 4; Reid, *After the War*, 463; Leigh, *Ten Years on a Georgia Plantation*, 57–58, 78–79. For other examples of the yearning for landownership and the movement toward tenantry, see Loring and Atkinson, *Cotton Culture and the South*, 5, 14, 121, 145; Ravenel, *Private Journal*, 272; Reid, *After the War*, 533; Trowbridge,

*The South*, 362; Macrae, *Americans at Home*, 210; *Christian Recorder*, Dec. 30, 1865; *National Freedman*, I (Nov. 15, 1865), 337.

132. For examples of "tenantry" contracts, see Dennett, *The South As It Is*, 282–83. See also *ibid.*, 108–09.

133. Loring and Atkinson, *Cotton Culture and the South*, 13.

134. Rawick (ed.), *American Slave*, VIII: Ark. Narr. (Part 2), 63–64.

135. Andrews, *The South since the War*, 370 (also reprinted in *New York Times*, Jan. 7, 1866). For a similar assessment, see Botume, *First Days Amongst the Contrabands*, 197.

136. Rawick (ed.), *American Slave*, IV: Texas Narr. (Part 2), 134.

137. *Ibid.*, XIV: N.C. Narr. (Part 1), 361–62.

## Chapter Nine: The Gospel and the Primer

1. *Christian Recorder*, May 26, 1866.

2. Reid, *After the War*, 510.

3. *Christian Recorder*, Jan. 31, 1863, Feb. 25, Aug. 5, Dec. 30, 1865, Jan. 20, 1866.

4. B. F. Randolph to Bvt. Maj. Gen. Rufus Saxton, Aug. 31, 1865, Records of the Assistant Commissioners, South Carolina (Letters Received), Freedmen's Bureau.

5. *Christian Recorder*, April 15, 1865 (editorial); Rose, *Rehearsal for Reconstruction*, 217; James M. McPherson, "The New Puritanism: Values and Goals of Freedmen's Education in America," in Lawrence Stone (ed.), *The University in Society* (2 vols.; Princeton, 1974), II, 615; Daniel A. Payne, *Recollections of Seventy Years* (Nashville, 1888; repr. New York, 1969), 163n.

6. Swint (ed.), *Dear Ones at Home*, 24; *American Freedman*, III (April 1868), 400. On the problems missionaries encountered with black speech, see also Swint (ed.), *Dear Ones at Home*, 62; Pearson (ed.), *Letters from Port Royal*, 34–35, 90; Botume, *First Days Amongst the Contrabands*, 277.

7. *Christian Recorder*, Sept. 29, 1866.

8. Rawick (ed.), *American Slave*, V: Texas Narr. (Part 4), 184.

9. Thomas W. Cardozo to Samuel Hunt, June 23, 1865, Thomas D. S. Tucker to

"Dear Friends of the Association," Nov. 27, 1862, Tucker to George Whipple, Dec. 24, 1862, American Missionary Assn. Archives.

10. Ralph Ellison, *Invisible Man* (New York, 1952), 3.

11. *Christian Recorder*, Sept. 7, 1861, June 27, 1863.

12. Genovese, *Roll, Jordan, Roll*, 234; *Christian Recorder*, July 25, 1863.

13. *Christian Recorder*, May 27, 1865.

14. J. W. C. Pennington to "My Esteemed Friend," May 25, 1870, American Missionary Assn. Archives; *Christian Recorder*, June 29, 1867. See also Amos Gerry Beman to Rev. George Whipple, Feb. 25, 1867, in "Documents," *Journal of Negro History*, XXII (1937), 222–26.

15. *Christian Recorder*, June 16, 1866 (H. M. Turner and A. Waddell letters).

16. Marcia Colton to Rev. George Whipple, May 19, June 14, July 9, Oct. 7, Nov. 1, 1864, American Missionary Assn. Archives.

17. *Christian Recorder*, July 1, March 18, 1865; Thomas W. Cardozo to Samuel Hunt, June 23, 1865, American Missionary Assn. Archives; Elizabeth Kilham, "Sketches in Color: IV," in Jackson (ed.), *The Negro and His Folklore*, 133. For the

reactions of white missionaries to black religious worship in the South, see the sources cited in notes 19 and 20.

18. *Christian Recorder,* July 14, 1866 (editorial); Timothy Lyman to Rev. M. E. Strieby, Feb, 27, 1865, American Missionary Assn. Archives.

19. Rev. Joel Grant to Prof. Henry Cowles, April 10, 1863, H. S. Beals to Rev. S. S. Jocelyn, April 28, 1863, Martha L. Kellogg to Rev. S. S. Jocelyn, Sept. 3, 1863, American Missionary Assn. Archives; *National Freedman,* I (Sept. 15, 1865), 264 (Rev. Henry J. Fox); *New York Times,* Nov. 28, 1863. See also Waterbury, *Seven Years Among the Freedmen,* 18–19, and Macrae, *Americans at Home,* 353–75.

20. H. S. Beals to Rev. S. S. Jocelyn, April 28, Aug. 18, 1863, William G. Kephart to Lewis Tappan, May 9, 1864, Augustus C. Stickle to Jacob R. Shipherd, July 9, 1867, Timothy Lyman to Rev. M. E. Strieby, Feb. 27, 1865, Rev. W. T. Richardson to Rev. George Whipple, July 3, 1863, Mary E. Burdick to Rev. George Whipple, March 8, 1864, American Missionary Assn. Archives; *National Freedman,* I (Oct. 15, 1865), 285 (M. J. Ringler); Towne, *Letters and Diary,* 20; Swint (ed.), *Dear Ones at Home,* 21–22, 58. See also Pearson (ed.), *Letters from Port Royal,* 26–28; Ames, *From a New England Woman's Diary in Dixie,* 81–82; Higginson, *Army Life in a Black Regiment,* 17–18.

21. Rawick (ed.), *American Slave,* III: S.C. Narr. (Part 3), 5; Higginson, *Army Life in a Black Regiment,* 253.

22. Swint, *The Northern Teacher in the South,* 42; Timothy Lyman to Rev. M. E. Strieby, Feb. 27, 1865, H. S. Beals to Rev. S. S. Jocelyn, April 28, 1863, William G. Kephart to Lewis Tappan, May 9, 1864, Louise A. Woodbury to Rev. S. S. Jocelyn, Sept. 7, 1863, American Missionary Assn. Archives.

23. Kilham, "Sketches in Color: IV," in Jackson (ed.), *The Negro and His Folklore,* 125–31.

24. *Christian Recorder,* Aug. 5, 1865. On the "peculiar fitness" of blacks for missionary and teaching positions in the South, see also, e.g., *ibid.,* Nov. 28, 1863 (editorial), Feb. 6, 1864 (R. H. Cain and T. H. C. Hinton), Feb. 11 (J. Lynch), March 18 ("Junius"), April 15 (editorial), Sept. 9 (J. Lynch), Sept.

23 (A. Crummell), 1865, Feb. 24, 1866, and June 29, 1867 (R. H. Cain).

25. Sella Martin to M. E. Strieby, March 20, 1866, American Missionary Assn. Archives; *Christian Recorder,* Feb. 11, 1865 (James H. Payne).

26. Towne, *Letters and Diary,* 55; *Christian Recorder,* June 16, 1866 (A. Waddell), Dec. 30 and Aug. 5, 1865 (H. M. Turner). For commendation of the work of the white benevolent societies, especially the American Missionary Assn. and the National Freedmen's Relief Assn., see, e.g., *Christian Recorder,* June 3, 1865 (Meeting of the South Carolina Conference), and Feb. 27, 1864 (J. Lynch).

27. Edward P. Smith to M. E. Strieby, July 21, 1865, American Missionary Assn. Archives; Blassingame (ed.), *Slave Testimony,* 495, 420; Rawick (ed.), *American Slave,* IV: Texas Narr. (Part 1), 198, (Part 2), 167; Perdue et al. (eds.), *Weevils in the Wheat,* 322. On ex-slave recollections of white preachers, see also, e.g., Blassingame (ed.), *Slave Testimony,* 420, 538, 642; Rawick (ed.), *American Slave,* V: Texas Narr. (Part 3), 213, (Part 4), 7; VIII and X: Ark. Narr. (Part 1), 35, (Part 2), 294, (Part 5), 36–37; XVIII: Unwritten History, 45, 76, 98, 310.

28. Blassingame (ed.), *Slave Testimony,* 643; Rawick (ed.), *American Slave,* II: S.C. Narr. (Part 1), 241; IV: Texas Narr. (Part 1), 199; Haviland, *A Woman's Life-Work,* 321.

29. Rev. L. S. Burkhead, "History of the Difficulties of the Pastorate of the Front Street Methodist Church, Wilmington, N.C., for the Year 1865," in *An Annual Publication of Historical Papers Published by the Historical Society of Trinity College, Durham, N.C.,* Series VIII (1908–09), 35–118. For a black view of the "difficulties," see *Christian Recorder,* April 15, 1865 ("Arnold").

30. *Christian Recorder,* Feb. 24, 1866 (R. H. Cain), Jan. 21 and Feb. 4, 1865 (J. Lynch), March 24, 1866 (H. M. Turner). See also *ibid.,* Jan. 29, 1870 ("Our Record").

31. *Ibid.,* Oct. 14, 1865, Sept. 8, 1866; Rawick (ed.), *American Slave,* II: S.C. Narr. (Part 1), 35–36.

32. H. Shelton Smith, *In His Image, But . . . : Racism in Southern Religion, 1780–*

*1910* (Durham, N.C., 1972), 229–31; Ralph E. Morrow, *Northern Methodism and Reconstruction* (East Lansing, Mich., 1956), 129; Wharton, *Negro in Mississippi,* 260–61; Williamson, *After Slavery,* 196–97; Kolchin, *First Freedom,* 111–13.

33. Morrow, *Northern Methodism and Reconstruction,* 136; *Christian Recorder,* March 5, 1870 ("Separate Churches"), March 26, 1864 (J. D. S. Hall), June 17, 1865 (R. H. Cain). For the struggle between the AME and the Methodist Episcopal Church, including the conflicts over church property, see also *Christian Recorder,* March 12 (J. D. S. Hall), June 25 (J. Lynch), 1864, April 15 ("Arnold"), May 13 (H. M. Turner), June 3 (S.C. Conference), Aug. 5 and Oct. 7 (H. R. Revels), Oct. 21 (J. Lynch), 1865, Sept. 21, 1867 ("True Position of AME Church"); Coppin, *Unwritten History,* 117–18; Morrow, *Northern Methodism and Reconstruction,* 139–40; and Williamson, *After Slavery,* 181–91.

34. Reid, *After the War,* 519–20; Rev. A. G. Smith to "Dear Sir," Sept. 25, 1867, Records of the Assistant Commissioners, North Carolina (Letters Received), Freedmen's Bureau.

35. Avary, *Dixie after the War,* 203–04.

36. *Mobile News,* reprinted in *New Orleans Tribune,* Sept. 9, 1865. See also Kolchin, *First Freedom,* 118–19.

37. *New York Times,* July 1, 1867; *Christian Recorder,* June 16, 1866. The war had exacerbated the sectional split in the national churches, prompting some southern whites to prefer that black congregations affiliate with the independent black churches rather than with the MEC (North). *Christian Recorder,* Oct. 21, 1865 (J. Lynch), Sept. 21, 1867 ("True Position of the AME Church").

38. *New York Times,* Nov. 28, 1863.

39. *Missionary Record,* reprinted in *Semi-Weekly Louisianian,* April 21, 1872; *Christian Recorder,* May 26, 1866 (Address of the Bishops). For criticism of ministers in politics, see *Christian Recorder,* Feb. 1, 1868, and *Louisianian,* Feb. 16, 1871.

40. *Christian Recorder,* Jan. 29, 1870 ("Our Record"). On the activities of H. M. Turner, see *ibid.,* June 9, 1866, Aug. 17, 1867, Feb. 1, 1868, March 6, 1869; on R. H.

Cain, *ibid.,* Sept. 8, 1866, and Williamson, *After Slavery,* 206–07; on J. C. Gibbs, *Christian Recorder,* Sept. 16, 1865, Sept. 8, 1866, and Richardson, *Negro in the Reconstruction of Florida,* 94; on J. Lynch, *Christian Recorder,* June 8, 22, 1867, *Weekly Louisianian,* Jan. 4, 1873, and Wharton, *Negro in Mississippi,* 154–55.

41. Macrae, *Americans at Home,* 368.

42. Blassingame (ed.), *Slave Testimony,* 598; *Missionary Record* (Charleston), July 5, 1873; J. W. Alvord, *Eighth Semi-Annual Report on Schools for Freedmen, July 1, 1869* (Washington, D.C., 1869), 46.

43. Genovese, *Roll, Jordan, Roll,* 562; Reid, *After the War,* 145.

44. Louis R. Harlan, *Booker T. Washington: The Making of a Black Leader, 1856–1901* (New York, 1972), 14; Washington, *Up from Slavery,* 6–7, 26–32, 37.

45. Botume, *First Days Amongst the Contrabands,* 259; Blassingame (ed.), *Slave Testimony,* 174.

46. Dennett, *The South As It Is,* 322; Rose, *Rehearsal for Reconstruction,* 46. On the theme of "knowledge is power," see also, e.g., "State Convention of the Colored People of South Carolina," in *South Carolina Leader,* Nov. 25, 1865; *Loyal Georgian,* Jan. 20, 1866; and 39 Cong., 1 Sess., House Exec. Doc. 70, *Freedmen's Bureau,* 334.

47. *National Freedman,* I (Aug. 15, 1865), 217 (W. T. Briggs); (Dec. 15, 1865), 350 (S. K. Whiting); Quarles, *Negro in the Civil War,* 292; Waterbury, *Seven Years Among the Freedmen,* 81. For the intensity of the freedmen's commitment to education, see also, e.g., Esther W. Douglass to Rev. Samuel Hunt, Dec. 27, 1865, American Missionary Assn. Archives; *South Carolina Leader,* Dec. 9, 1865; *National Freedman,* I (Dec. 15, 1865), 351–52 (H. C. Fisher); *American Freedman,* I (June 1866), 46 (G. H. Allan); Botume, *First Days Amongst the Contrabands,* 57; Trowbridge, *The South,* 251; 39 Cong., 2 Sess., Senate Exec. Doc. 6, *Reports of the Assistant Commissioners of Freedmen* [Jan. 3, 1867], 105; Alvord, *Eighth Semi-Annual Report on Schools for Freedmen, July 1, 1869,* 45.

48. Murray, *Proud Shoes,* 182; Mrs. William L. Coan to M. E. Strieby, Sept. 23, 1864, American Missionary Assn. Archives; Waterbury, *Seven Years Among the Freed-*

*men,* 19; Asa B. Whitfield to Julia A. Shearman, April 17, 1867, American Missionary Assn. Archives. For the appeals of two black teachers for assistance, see Jonathan J. Wright to Rev. Samuel Hunt, Dec. 4, 1865, Feb. 5, 1866, and T. G. Steward to John A. Rockwell, Nov. 6, 1867, American Missionary Assn. Archives.

49. Trowbridge, *The South,* 466; *National Freedman,* I (April 1, 1865), 93 (M. E. Jones and N. J. McCullough); Harriet B. Greeley to Rev. George Whipple, April 29, 1865, American Missionary Assn. Archives. On the difficulty of adjusting work schedules to schooling, see also Rawick (ed.), *American Slave,* XIII: Ga. Narr. (Part 3), 117; XIV: N.C. Narr. (Part 1), 277; XVI: Tenn. Narr., 29; *American Freedman,* III (June 1868), 431 (L. M. Towne); and Helen M. Jones to S. G. Wright, Jan. 13, 1866, American Missionary Assn. Archives.

50. J. W. Alvord, *Report on Schools and Finances of Freedmen for July, 1866* (Washington, D.C., 1866), 16 (Helena, Ark.); Ames, *From a New England Woman's Diary in Dixie,* 108–09 (Seabrook); *New York Times,* Jan. 13, 19, 1862 (Lawrence); Williamson, *After Slavery,* 211 (Charleston); Reid, *After the War,* 246 (New Orleans); W. T. Richardson to M. E. Strieby, Jan. 2, 1865 (Savannah), and Rev. W. F. Eaton to Rev. George Whipple, May 26, 1865 (King plantation, St. Simon's Island), American Missionary Assn. Archives; *Colored Tennessean,* March 24, 1866 (Douglass school); *National Freedman,* I (Feb. 1, 1865), 11–12 (Savannah); Trowbridge, *The South,* 490 (Augusta), 509–10 (Savannah). See also Swint, *Northern Teacher in the South,* 79–80 (Richmond); Wiley, *Southern Negroes,* 271 (La.); Trowbridge, *The South,* 337 (Tenn.); Haviland, *A Woman's Life-Work,* 321–22 (New Orleans ); *New York Tribune,* July 7, 1865 (Richmond).

51. *Colored Tennessean,* Oct. 14, 1865; J. W. Alvord, *Fourth Semi-Annual Report on Schools for Freedmen, July 1, 1867* (Washington, D.C., 1867), 83, and *Ninth Semi-Annual Report on Schools for Freedmen, January 1, 1870* (Washington, D.C., 1870), 46; Rawick (ed.), *American Slave,* IV: Texas Narr. (Part 2), 48. On the plantation schools, see also J. W. Alvord, *Third Semi-Annual Report on Schools for Freedmen, January 1,*

*1867* (Washington, D.C., 1867), 25–26; *Colored Tennessean,* March 24, 1866; B. F. Randolph to Bvt. Maj. Gen. R. K. Scott, March 15, 1867, Records of the Assistant Commissioners, South Carolina (Letters Received), Freedmen's Bureau; S. S. Ashley to Rev. Samuel Hunt, March 7, 1866, American Missionary Assn. Archives; *National Freedman,* II (April 1866), 118 (F. A. Fiske); Waterbury, *Seven Years Among the Freedmen,* 18; Stearns, *Black Man of the South, and The Rebels,* 196–99; Trowbridge, *The South,* 289; Reid, *After the War,* 511; *New York Times,* Oct. 17, 1865, May 27, 1867.

52. Chesnut, *Diary from Dixie,* 199–200; Mary E. Burdick to George Whipple, March 8, 1864, American Missionary Assn. Archives.

53. McPherson, "The New Puritanism: Values and Goals of Freedmen's Education in America," 624–25. On the educational work of the Freedmen's Bureau, see, in addition to the archival records and official reports, Abbott, *Freedmen's Bureau in South Carolina,* 82–98; White, *Freedmen's Bureau in Louisiana,* 166–200; and Bentley, *History of the Freedmen's Bureau,* 169–84.

54. Marcia Colton to Rev. George Whipple, June 14, 1864, American Missionary Assn. Archives; Lydia Maria Child to Sarah S. Shaw, April 8, 1866, Shaw Family Papers, New York Public Library; *American Freedman,* I (April 1866), 3 (editorial). See also *National Freedman,* I (March 1, 1865), 44 (annual report).

55. Botume, *First Days Amongst the Contrabands,* 31–32; Josiah Beardsley, Feb. 15, 1865, Marcia Colton to Rev. George Whipple, June 14, 1864, American Missionary Assn. Archives; Ames, *From a New England Woman's Diary in Dixie,* 25–26; Rose, *Rehearsal for Reconstruction,* 58. On missionary comparisons of the blacks and the Irish, see also Towne, *Letters and Diary,* 6; Pearson (ed.), *Letters from Port Royal,* 11, 15, 18, 75.

56. George N. Greene to George Whipple, May 15, 1865, H. S. Beals to Rev. Samuel Hunt, Dec. 30, 1865, Frank H. Green to George Whipple, July 7, 1864, American Missionary Assn. Archives; Swint, *Northern Teacher in the South,* 41; *National Freed-*

*man,* I (Feb. 1, 1865), 14 (Juliet B. Smith); *American Freedman,* III (April 1869), 7 (Lucy Eastman).

57. *National Freedman,* I (April 1, 1865), 92 (Fannie Graves and Annie P. Merriam); S. S. Ashley to Col. N. A. McLean, Feb. 7, 1866, American Missionary Assn. Archives.

58. Towne, *Letters and Diary,* 26; *New National Era,* April 13, 1871. On the respective merits of practical and classical education, see also *New Era,* May 5, 1870 ("Genius and Its Exactions").

59. *Christian Recorder,* Aug. 5, 1865; Quarles, *Negro in the Civil War,* 291; Wiley, *Southern Negroes,* 287. On the content of instruction, see also, e.g., Swint, *Northern Teacher in the South,* 80–90; Towne, *Letters and Diary,* 163; *Extracts from Letters of Teachers and Superintendents of the New England Educational Commission for Freedmen* (4th Series, Jan. 1, 1864; Boston, 1864), 8–10; Stearns, *Black Man in the South, and The Rebels,* 59–64; *Christian Recorder,* Sept. 29, 1866 ("Impressions of Charleston"); *New York Tribune,* June 2, 1865; *New Era,* Feb. 24, 1870 (J. W. Alvord).

60. A. L. Etheridge to William T. Briggs, June 7, 1864, Edwin S. Williams to S. S. Jocelyn, April 26, 1863, American Missionary Assn. Archives; Forten, *Journal,* 131.

61. Sarah J. Foster to E. P. Smith, Jan. 3, 1868, W. L. Coan to George Whipple, Oct. 6, 1864, American Missionary Assn. Archives; Reid, *After the War,* 249–50; Botume, *First Days Amongst the Contrabands,* 257; *New York Tribune,* Dec. 2, 1865.

62. *National Freedman,* II (April 1866), 115 (Chloe Merrick); *American Freedman,* III (May 1868), 412.

63. Mary E. Burdick to George Whipple, March 8, 1864, American Missionary Assn. Archives. On comparisons of white and black students and the aptness of blacks for various fields of study, see Josiah Beardsley, Feb. 15, 1865 (Ms. apparently intended for publication in *The American Missionary*), G. H. Hyde to W. E. Whiting, Feb. 26, 1862, William G. Kephart to Lewis Tappan, May 9, 1864, John Silsby to Rev. George Whipple, Sept. 14, 1866, Elliot Whipple to Rev. E. P. Smith, June 17, 1867, American

Missionary Assn. Archives; *National Freedman,* I (April 1, 1865), 92, (July 15, 1865), 191–92, (Aug. 15, 1865), 217; *Extracts from Letters of Teachers and Superintendents of the New England Educational Commission for Freedmen* (4th series, Jan. 1, 1864), 3, 7, 9; 39 Cong., 1 Sess., *Report of the Joint Committee on Reconstruction,* Part II, 91, 256; Dennett, *The South As It Is,* 207; Trowbridge, *The South,* 337; Reid, *After the War,* 255; Macrae, *Americans at Home,* 342–45; *New York Times,* Aug. 6, 17, 1865; *New York Tribune,* July 7, 1865. On comparisons of black and mulatto students, see *Loyal Georgian,* March 17, 1866; *National Freedman,* I (Aug. 15, 1865), 218; Nordhoff, *Freedmen of South Carolina,* 9.

64. Botume, *First Days Amongst the Contrabands,* 107–09; *National Freedman,* I (Sept. 15, 1865), 251; *Christian Recorder,* July 1, 1865; Reid, *After the War,* 15–17, 246–53; Dennett, *The South As It Is,* 206–08, 211, 304.

65. *Freedom's Journal,* June 1, 1827; Frank H. Green to Rev. George Whipple, Aug. 12, 1864, American Missionary Assn. Archives; *Christian Recorder,* May 6, 1865 (J. C. Gibbs).

66. Rev. W. T. Richardson to Mrs. E. A. Lane, April 29, 1865, American Missionary Assn. Archives; *Christian Recorder,* July 8, 1865 (G.N.Y.).

67. Asa B. Whitfield to Julia A. Shearman, April 17, 1867, American Missionary Assn. Archives.

68. 39 Cong., 1 Sess., *Report of the Joint Committee on Reconstruction,* Part II, 247; Moore (ed.), *The Juhl Letters* (Sept. 18, 1866), 120.

69. Richardson, *Negro in the Reconstruction of Florida,* 100; N. A. McLean to Rev. S. S. Ashley, Feb. 20, 1866, American Missionary Assn. Archives; J. W. Alvord, *Eighth Semi-Annual Report on Schools for Freedmen, July 1, 1869,* 54. See also John Silsby to Rev. George Whipple, Sept. 14, 1866, American Missionary Assn. Archives; *National Freedman,* I (Nov. 15, 1865), 316 (B. W. Pond).

70. Botume, *First Days Amongst the Contrabands,* 4; [Prof. Bennett Puryear], *The Public School in Its Relation to the Negro* (Richmond, 1877), 11. See also 39 Cong.,

1 Sess., Senate Exec. Doc. 2, "Report of Carl Schurz," 25; Evans, *Ballots and Fence Rails*, 226–27.

71. Nolen, *Negro's Image in the South*, 127–28.

72. 39 Cong., 1 Sess., *Report of the Joint Committee on Reconstruction*, Part II, 55, 86, 143, 183, 252; B. F. Whittemore to Bvt. Maj. H. W. Smith, Dec. 30, 1865, Records of the Assistant Commissioners, South Carolina (Letters Received), Freedmen's Bureau; D. C. Jencks to Rev. Samuel Hunt, Dec. 21, 1865, American Missionary Assn. Archives.

73. D. T. Allen to Rev. C. H. Fowler, Jan. 1, 1864, American Missionary Assn. Archives; Amos McCollough et al. to Gen. O. O. Howard, May 6, 1866, Charles F. Mayerhoff to Col. Samuel Thomas, April 2, 1866, R. F. Campbell to Col. Samuel Thomas, April 5, 1866, Records of the Assistant Commissioners, North Carolina and Mississippi (Letters Received), Freedmen's Bureau. On native white reaction to black schools and the reception accorded teachers of freedmen, see also John P. Bardwell to George Whipple, April 28, May 4, 1866, William L. Clark to Rev. E. P. Smith, Nov. 19, 1867, Rev. George W. Honey to Rev. M. E. Strieby, Feb. 21, 1866, Addie Warren to John P. Bardwell, May 6, 1866, American Missionary Assn. Archives; *National Freedman*, I (Nov. 15, 1865), 324 (M. Anderson), (Dec. 15, 1865), 347 (A. B. Corliss), 360 (W. J. Albert), II (May 1866), 149; *American Freedman*, III (June 1868), 427; Waterbury, *Seven Years Among the Freedmen*, 19; Office of the Board of Education for Freedmen, Dept. of the Gulf, *Report* (Feb. 28, 1865), 8–9; Trowbridge, *The South*, 188, 228, 490; *Loyal Georgian*, May 9, 1867; Swint, *Northern Teacher in the South*, 94–142.

74. *Christian Recorder*, June 16, 1866; *New Orleans Tribune*, Dec. 29, 1865, Sept. 5, 1866; John P. Bardwell to George Whipple, April 28, 1866, American Missionary Assn. Archives; *National Freedman*, I (Nov. 15, 1865), 328 (C. Kennedy).

75. 39 Cong., 1 Sess., *Report of the Joint Committee on Reconstruction*, Part II, 253; Towne, *Letters and Diary*, 178. See also J. W. Alvord, *Eighth Semi-Annual Report on Schools for Freedmen, July 1, 1869*, 23;

*Loyal Georgian*, July 6, 1867 (G. L. Eberhart); *New York Tribune*, Dec. 2, 1865.

76. Sallie Coit to Emily, April 15, 1868, William N. Tillinghast Papers, Duke Univ.; A. W. Moore to E. H. Dabbs, April 30, 1870, A. L. Burt Papers, Duke Univ.

77. Reid, *After the War*, 152; Botume, *First Days Amongst the Contrabands*, 257–58. For examples of racial mixing in the freedmen's schools, see Rev. Fisk P. Brewer to Rev. George Whipple, Nov. 8, 1866 ("I would not have it made too public till we can show more decided results"), American Missionary Assn. Archives; *American Freedman*, I (June 1866), 43 (F. P. Brewer), 44 (E. B. Adams), (July 1866), 80; Swint (ed.), *Dear Ones at Home*, 204; Richardson, *Negro in the Reconstruction of Florida*, 108–09. On the fate of the "experiment" in Raleigh, see Fisk P. Brewer to George Whipple, Feb. 6, 1867, American Missionary Assn. Archives.

78. *American Freedman*, I (April 1866), 5–6, (May 1866), 23–24; H. S. Beals to Rev. E. P. Smith, Feb. 15, 1867, Rev. S. J. Whiton to Rev. E. P. Smith, Feb. 16, 1867, Rev. S. J. Whiton to Rev. George Whipple, Feb. 28, 1867, Rev. S. J. Whiton to Rev. E. P. Smith, March 4, 1867, John Scott to Rev. E. P. Smith, March 6, 1867, Hyman Thompson to Rev. George Whipple, March 1867, American Missionary Assn. Archives.

79. *New York Times*, Dec. 15, 1867.

80. *New Orleans Tribune*, April 26, 1867, Jan. 22, 1869. See also *ibid.*, Feb. 17, 23, 1865, July 24, Oct. 24, 29, 1867; William T. Nicholls to "Cousin Tom," Col. W. W. Pugh Papers, Louisiana State Univ.; J. W. Alvord, *Tenth Semi-Annual Report on Schools for Freedmen, July 1, 1870*, 48.

81. Avary, *Dixie after the War*, 312; Mary to Missouria Stokes, June 1868, Missouria Stokes Papers, Duke Univ.; Miss. S. W. Stansbury to Rev. E. P. Smith, May 21, 1867, American Missionary Assn. Archives.

82. G. L. Eberhart to Rev. Samuel Hunt, May 23, June 4, 1866, American Missionary Assn. Archives. See also J. E. Bryant to Rev. George Whipple, June 12, 1866, Davis Tillson to Rev. Whipple, July 4, 1866.

83. *American Freedman*, I (Nov. 1866), 114 (editorial); Martha L. Kellogg to Rev. George Whipple, Dec. 17, 1866, American Missionary Assn. Archives.

84. On the question of racial mixing in the abolitionist movement, see, e.g., Leon F. Litwack, *North of Slavery: The Negro in the Free States, 1790–1860* (Chicago, 1961), 216–23.

85. Lewis Tappan, *Caste: A Letter to a Teacher Among the Freedmen* (New York [1867]), 9; *Christian Recorder,* Jan. 7, 1865.

86. *Christian Recorder,* April 23, 1864, June 29, 1867, Jan. 7, 1865. See also the sources cited in note 24.

87. *New York Times,* Dec. 8, 1861; WPA, *Negro in Virginia,* 263.

88. Forten, *Journal,* 133; Virginia C. Green to A. W. Preston, Oct. 24, 1866, Records of the Assistant Commissioners, Mississippi (Letters Received), Freedmen's Bureau. See also Jonathan J. Wright to Rev. Samuel Hunt, Feb. 5, 1866, T. G. Steward to John A. Rockwell, Nov. 6, 1867, American Missionary Assn. Archives.

89. Francis L. Cardozo to Rev. George Whipple, July 5, 1865, Cardozo to Rev. M. E. Strieby, Aug. 13, 1866, Cardozo to Rev. Samuel Hunt, Dec. 2, 1865, Jan. 13 [1866]. On the progress of his school, see Cardozo to Hunt, Oct. 10, Nov. 7, 22, Dec. 2, 15, 1865, Cardozo to Whipple, Oct. 21, 1865, Jan. 27, 1866, American Missionary Assn. Archives.

90. Francis L. Cardozo, School Report for November 1867, Sarah W. Stansbury to E. P. Smith, Jan. 30, 1867, Cardozo to E. P. Smith, Dec. 24, 1866, Jane A. Van Allen to E. P. Smith, Feb. 16, 1867, Cardozo to E. P. Smith, April 9, 1867, American Missionary Assn. Archives. For visits to Cardozo's school, see Dennett, *The South As It Is,* 217–18; Macrae, *Americans at Home,* 266–69; Cardozo to Rev. Samuel Hunt, March 10, 1866, Jonathan J. Wright to Hunt, Dec. 4, 1865, American Missionary Assn. Archives.

91. Francis L. Cardozo to Rev. George Whipple, Oct. 21, 1865, Cardozo to E. P. Smith, Nov. 4, 1867, American Missionary Assn. Archives. On his preparations for the constitutional convention and the prospect of his candidacy for secretary of state of South Carolina, see Cardozo to E. P. Smith, Dec. 7, 1867, Jan. 2, March 9, 1868, American Missionary Assn. Archives.

92. C. W. Buckley to Rev. George Whipple, March 13, 1866, G. L. Eberhart to Ira Pettibone, Oct. 19, 1866, American Missionary Assn. Archives. On the preference for black teachers in the "interior," see J. W. Alvord, *Seventh Semi-Annual Report on Schools for Freedmen, January 1, 1869,* 24.

93. S. S. Ashley to Rev. Samuel Hunt, Jan. 22, 1866, American Missionary Assn. Archives. On the preference for white teachers, see also *American Freedman,* I (Oct. 1866), 106 (W. D. Newsome); Reid, *After the War,* 511. On the objections of free-born "colored people" to "a teacher born in bondage, unless of a very light complexion," see J. W. Alvord, *Ninth Semi-Annual Report on Schools for Freedmen, January 1, 1870,* 15–16.

94. Blanche Harris to Rev. George Whipple, Jan. 23, March 10, 1866, John P. Bardwell to Whipple, March 20, April 2, 1866, Rev. Palmer Litts to Whipple, April 27, 1866, Addie Warren to John P. Bardwell, May 6, 1866, John P. Bardwell to Rev. Samuel Hunt, June 22, 1866, Mary Still to Hunt, Feb. 19, 1866, American Missionary Assn. Archives.

95. *Christian Recorder,* Sept. 8, 1866 (T.W.C.); Blanche Harris to Rev. George Whipple, March 10, 1866, American Missionary Assn. Archives.

96. *Christian Recorder,* Dec. 2, 1865 ("Editorial Correspondence").

97. Washington, *Up from Slavery,* 28; John P. Bardwell to Rev. M. E. Strieby, Nov. 20, 1865, American Missionary Assn. Archives; *New York Times,* June 22, 1866, Aug. 21, 1863. On black support of schools and teachers and independent educational efforts, see also, e.g., B. F. Randolph to Bvt. Maj. Gen. R. K. Scott, March 15, 1867, Records of the Assistant Commissioners, South Carolina (Letters Received), Freedmen's Bureau; De Forest, *Union Officer in the Reconstruction,* 118–21; Trowbridge, *The South,* 228, 251; 39 Cong., 1 Sess., *Report of the Joint Committee on Reconstruction,* Part II, 251, 254, 256, 257; Blassingame (ed.), *Slave Testimony,* 386; *Loyal Georgian,* July 6, 1867; *New York Times,* Sept. 2, 10, 1865.

98. *Christian Recorder,* Jan. 21, 1865 (J. Lynch); W. T. Richardson to Rev. M. E. Strieby, Jan. 2, 1865, Richardson to Rev. George Whipple, Jan. 10, 1865, Rev. S. W. Magill to Whipple, Feb. 3, 6, 26, 1865, American Missionary Assn. Archives.

99. *Christian Recorder,* Aug. 27, 1864 ("Junius").

100. T. K. Noble to Rev. George Whipple, Sept. 29, 1865, American Missionary Assn. Archives.

## Chapter Ten: Becoming a People

1. A. H. Haines to President Andrew Johnson, Oct. 19, 1865, Records of the Assistant Commissioners, South Carolina (Letters Received), Freedmen's Bureau.

2. *Christian Recorder,* Jan. 20, 1866.

3. Discussion of the Freedmen's Convention of North Carolina and the political activity among blacks which preceded and immediately followed it is based on *Convention of the Freedmen of North Carolina: Official Proceedings* [Raleigh, 1865]; *Christian Recorder,* Oct. 28, 1865 (same as official proceedings, except for additional speech by James Harris; also includes a report of a mass meeting in Edgecombe Co.); *National Freedman,* I (Oct. 15, 1865), 289, 301–02; *New York Times,* May 19 and Sept. 17 (New Bern), Oct. 7 and 9 (state conv ), 1865; *New York Tribune,* Oct. 7 (state conv.), 24 (Edgecombe Co.), 1865; *New Orleans Tribune,* Sept. 24 (Robeson Co., N.C.), Oct. 19 (Wilmington), 1865; Dennett, *The South As It Is,* 148–54, 156, 175–77; Andrews, *The South since the War,* 119–31, 162, 188; Evans, *Ballots and Fence Rails,* 87–93, 110–12; Perrin Busbee to Benjamin S. Hedrick, Jan. 8, 1866, B. S. Hedrick Papers, Duke Univ.; James H. Harris Papers, 1850 to 1873, State Dept. of Archives and History, Raleigh, N.C.; *Proceedings of the First Annual Meeting of the National Equal Rights League, Held in Cleveland, Ohio, October 19, 20, and 21, 1865* (Philadelphia, 1865), 4.

4. *New York Times,* Oct. 11, 1866; *New Orleans Tribune,* Oct. 27, 1866.

5. *Christian Recorder,* Oct. 28, 1865; Rogers, *Thomas County, 1865–1900,* 8, 13.

6. Andrews, *The South since the War,* 131, 188; Dennett, *The South As It Is,* 149, 175; *New York Times,* Oct. 24, 1865, Nov. 19, 1866; *Proceedings of the Convention of the Colored People of Virginia, Held in the City of Alexandria, Aug. 2, 3, 4, 5, 1865* (Alexandria, 1865), 4, 11.

7. *New Orleans Tribune,* Jan. 15, 1865.

8. *Christian Recorder,* April 21, 1866.

9. See, e.g., *Loyal Georgian,* July 6, 1867 (H. M. Turner); *Christian Recorder,* Sept. 30 (R. H. Cain), Nov. 25 (T. G. Campbell), 1865, April 21, 1866 (R. H. Cain), May 4 (J. J. Wright), 11 (H. M. Turner), Aug. 17 (H. M. Turner), Oct. 12 (M. R. Delany), 1867, Feb. 1, 1868 (H. M. Turner), June 26, 1869 (M. R. Delany); Cardozo to Rev. George Whipple, Oct. 21, 1865, Cardozo to Rev. E. P. Smith, Nov. 4, 1867, March 9, 1868, Wright to Rev. Samuel Hunt, Dec. 4, 1865, American Missionary Assn. Archives; T. G. Campbell, *Sufferings of the Rev. T. G. Campbell and His Family, in Georgia* (Washington, D.C., 1877); H. M. Turner, "Speech on the Eligibility of Colored Members to Seats in the Georgia Legislature . . . September 3d, 1868," in George A. Singleton, *The Romance of African Methodism: A Study of the African Methodist Episcopal Church* (New York, 1952), Appendix B, 1–16.

10. Williamson, *After Slavery,* 26–30; Higginson, *Army Life in a Black Regiment,* 57–58.

11. Dennett, *The South As It Is,* 150; Andrews, *The South since the War,* 123, 131.

12. Dennett, *The South As It Is,* 150–51; *New Orleans Tribune,* May 7, 1867 (Letter from Mobile); "Proceedings of the State Convention of the Colored People of Tennessee," in *Colored Tennessean,* Aug. 12, 1865.

13. *Convention of the Colored People of Virginia* (Aug. 1865), 10; *New Orleans Tribune,* March 15, 1865. For Horace Greeley's message, see *Convention of the Freedmen of North Carolina* (Sept.–Oct. 1865), 9–11.

14. *Proceedings of the Freedmen's Convention of Georgia, Assembled at Augusta, January 10th, 1866* (Augusta, 1866), 21, 23; *New Orleans Tribune,* July 18, 1865 (Letter from Mobile).

15. *New Orleans Tribune,* Jan. 20, Feb. 1, 1865. Similar editorial advice may be found in the issues of March 7, April 25, 1865, May 1, 19, June 12, 1867.

16. Dennett, *The South As It Is,* 152–53; J. W. Alvord, *Seventh Semi-Annual Report on Schools for Freedmen, January 1, 1869,* 50.

17. On free-born "colored society," see Berlin, *Slaves Without Masters;* Marina Wikramanayake, *A World in Shadow: The Free Black in Antebellum South Carolina* (Columbia, S.C., 1973); Constance McLaughlin Green, *The Secret City: A History of Race Relations in the Nation's Capital* (Princeton, 1967); and Blassingame, *Black New Orleans.*

18. Bruce, *The New Man,* 79; W. L. Tilden, Washington, D.C., Feb. 12, 1866 (Ms. report), American Missionary Assn. Archives; John E. Bruce, *Washington's Colored Society* (n.p., 1877; typewritten copy in Schomburg Collection, New York Public Library).

19. Williamson, *After Slavery,* 314. For an examination of "colored society," as "moulded by outside forces," see Rev. T. G. Steward, "Colored Society," *Christian Recorder,* Nov. 9, 16, 23, Dec. 14, 28, 1876, Jan. 11, 18, 1877.

20. *New Orleans Tribune,* Feb. 19, 1869. For similar sentiments, see the issues of Dec. 6, 29, 1864, March 28, June 30, 1865. But for the persistence of divisiveness, see, e.g., *Semi-Weekly Louisianian,* May 25, 1871.

21. *Christian Recorder,* April 21, 1866.

22. *New York Tribune,* Nov. 29, 1865 (Convention of Colored People, South Carolina).

23. *Freedmen's Convention of Georgia* (Jan. 1866), 19. See also *Convention of the Freedmen of North Carolina* (Sept.–Oct. 1865), 14.

24. *Colored American,* Jan. 6, 1866. See also *New York Tribune,* Nov. 29, 1865 (Convention of Colored People, South Carolina); *Freedmen's Convention of Georgia* (Jan. 1866), 18.

25. *Convention of the Freedmen of North Carolina* (Sept.–Oct. 1865), 13; *Convention of the Colored People of Virginia* (Aug. 1865), 9.

26. *National Freedman,* I (Dec. 15, 1865), 364 (Convention of Colored People, Alabama); *New Orleans Tribune,* Sept. 24, 1865 (Address of Freedmen of Robeson Co., N.C.); *Freedmen's Convention of Georgia*

(Jan. 1866), 19. More than a hundred years later, at the peak of the civil rights struggle in the South, Malcolm X would make a similar pronouncement on the limits of black forbearance: "It's simply not possible to love a man whose chief purpose in life is to humiliate you, and still be what is considered a normal human being."

27. *Colored Tennessean,* March 31, 1866 (Kentucky Colored People's Convention); *New York Tribune,* Nov. 29, 1865 (Convention of Colored People, South Carolina); *Convention of the Colored People of Virginia* (Aug. 1865), 9, 21; *Proceedings of the Convention of Colored Citizens of the State of Arkansas Held in Little Rock . . . Nov. 30, Dec. 1 and 2* (Helena, 1866), 3–4.

28. *Convention of the Freedmen of North Carolina* (Sept.–Oct. 1865), 13; *Colored Tennessean,* March 31, 1866 (Kentucky Colored People's Convention); *Convention of the Colored People of Virginia* (Aug. 1865), 9, 10, 12.

29. Montgomery, "Alabama Freedmen: Some Reconstruction Documents," 248; *New York Times,* Nov. 12, 1865 (Selma, Ala.).

30. *New York Times,* June 20, 1866; *American Freedman,* I (Sept. 1866), 87 (Georgia Equal Rights Assn. meeting); *Proceedings of the Convention of the Equal Rights and Educational Association of Georgia, Assembled at Macon, October 29th, 1866* (Augusta, 1866), 17; S. W. Laidler to Thaddeus Stevens, May 7, 1866, Stevens Papers, Library of Congress (New Bern freedmen's meeting). Praise for the work of the Freedmen's Bureau was voiced by conventions in Alabama (1865), Georgia (1866), Kentucky (1867), North Carolina (1865), South Carolina (1865), Tennessee (1865), and Virginia (1865).

31. [State Exec. Comm. for Equal Political Rights in Missouri], *An Address by the Colored People of Missouri to the Friends of Equal Rights* (St. Louis, 1865), 3; *South Carolina Leader,* Nov. 25, 1865 (Convention of Colored People); "Our Wrongs and Rights," *Convention of the Colored People of Virginia* (Aug. 1865), 12–13.

32. *American Freedman,* I (Sept. 1866), 87–88 (Georgia Equal Rights Assn. meeting); *Freedmen's Convention of Georgia* (Jan. 1866), 16–17; *Proceedings of the State*

*Convention of Colored Men, Held at Lexington, Kentucky, in the A.M.E. Church, November 26th, 27th, and 28th, 1867* (Frankfort, 1867), 5–6; *Convention of the Colored People of Virginia* (Aug. 1865), 12.

33. *Colored Tennessean*, Aug. 12, 1865 (Convention of the Colored People); *New York Tribune*, Nov. 29, 1865 (Convention of Colored People, South Carolina).

34. *Freedmen's Convention of Georgia* (Jan. 1866), 30. The address drawn up by the freedmen of North Carolina to the Constitutional Convention did complain of "unscrupulous and avaricious employers" who expelled blacks from the plantations and refused adequate compensation (*Convention of the Freedmen of North Carolina*, Sept.–Oct. 1865), and Tennessee and Georgia blacks demanded "just compensation" for labor performed (*Colored Tennessean*, Aug. 12, 1865; *Freedmen's Convention of Georgia*, Jan. 1866, 29).

35. *National Freedman*, I (Dec. 15, 1865), 364 (Convention of Colored People, Alabama); *Freedmen's Convention of Georgia* (Jan. 1866), 30; *St. Landry Progress* (Opelousas, La.), Sept. 7, 1867. For opposition to confiscation, see also *New Orleans Tribune*, June 12, 1867 (Radical Republican convention, Louisiana, June 1867), and *New York Times*, May 26, 1867 (James Harris of N.C.). The Alabama convention of 1867 called for the confiscation of property of employers who discharged blacks for exercising their civil rights (*New Orleans Tribune*, May 4, 1867), and Beverly Nash, a South Carolina black leader, thought the confiscation question should be settled by Congress and "we should make no expression of opinion about it" (*New York Times*, Aug. 9, 1867). For pro-confiscation sentiment, see *New Orleans Tribune*, Sept. 10, 24, 1864, April 19, May 6, 1865, and *New National Era*, Jan. 26, 1871.

36. See, e.g., Montgomery, "Alabama Freedmen: Some Reconstruction Documents," 247, 249 (Colored People's Convention, 1865); *New York Tribune*, Dec. 30, 1865 (Colored Convention of Maryland); *Colored Tennessean*, March 31, 1866 (Kentucky Colored People's Convention); *Freedmen's Convention of Georgia* (Jan. 1866), 30.

37. *Christian Recorder*, Feb. 3, 1866. For similar sentiments, see, e.g., *Christian Recorder*, April 8 ("What Shall We Do to Be Respected?"), Aug. 26 (Charleston Corr.), Sept. 30 (H. H. Garnet), Dec. 9, 16, 23 (Advice to Freedmen), 1865; March 10 ("Trying Moment"), 17 ("The Jew and the Black Gentile"), 24 (Emigration), April 21 (S.C. Corr.), May 19 ("Get Land"), Aug. 18 ("Colored Conventions"), 25 (J. M. Langston), Sept. 22 ("Our Great Need"), 1866; Sept. 14 (J. M. Langston), Nov. 30 ("Self-Reliance the Key to Success"), 1867; *Colored American*, Jan. 6, 1866; *Black Republican*, April 15, 1865; *Free Man's Press*, Aug. 1 ("Learn a Trade"), Sept. 5, 1868.

38. *Address by the Colored People of Missouri*, 3; *Colored Tennessean*, March 31, 1866 (Kentucky Colored People's Convention); *Freedmen's Convention of Georgia* (Jan. 1866), 29–30; *Christian Recorder*, Feb. 24, 1866 (H. M. Turner); *Convention of Colored Men, Kentucky* (Nov. 1867), 7. On equal access to public facilities, see, e.g., the Georgia (Jan. and Oct. 1866) and Kentucky (1867) conventions.

39. *Convention of Colored Men, Kentucky* (Nov. 1867), 8–9; *Convention of the Freedmen of North Carolina* (Sept.–Oct. 1865), 5; *Freedmen's Convention of Georgia* (Jan. 1866), 19–20, 29.

40. *Convention of the Colored People of Virginia* (Aug. 1865), 11; *New Orleans Tribune*, May 30, 1865 (Memorial of the Colored Men of Mississippi); Montgomery, "Alabama Freedmen: Some Reconstruction Documents," 248, 249 (Colored People's Convention, 1865).

41. *Freedmen's Convention of Georgia* (Jan. 1866), 29; *New Orleans Tribune*, May 30, 1865 (Memorial of the Colored Men of Mississippi); *Colored Tennessean*, Aug. 12, 1865 (Convention of the Colored People); *Convention of the Colored People of Virginia* (Aug. 1865), 20; S. W. Laidler to Thaddeus Stevens, May 7, 1866, Stevens Papers, Library of Congress (New Bern freedmen's meeting); *Convention of Colored Men, Kentucky* (Nov. 1867), 7; *New York Tribune*, Nov. 29, 1865 (Convention of Colored People, South Carolina).

42. *New Orleans Tribune*, Aug. 9, 1864, April 6, 1865. See also the issues of Jan. 3, April 28, and July 23, 1865.

43. *Ibid.*, Jan. 14, 15, Feb. 5, 9, 14, 18, 19, 1865.

44. *Convention of the Colored People of*

*Virginia* (Aug. 1865), 21; *New Orleans Tribune*, March 25, May 28, 1865.

45. *New Orleans Tribune*, April 19, 1865. See also the issue of Nov. 25, 1866, which urged the election of "colored" judges and legislators. "But we want to fight that political contest squarely and fairly, under the banner of suffrage to all, and not by attempting the impracticable and impossible work of suppressing the minority."

46. *Ibid.*, June 4, 1865.

47. *Black Republican*, April 22, 1865; *New Orleans Tribune*, April 20, 1865; *Proceedings of the Forty-eighth Annual Session of the Baltimore Conference of the African Methodist Episcopal Church, April 13th, 1865* (Baltimore, 1865), 8; *Christian Recorder*, April 22, 1865. See also *Christian Recorder*, June 3, 1865 (S.C. Conference), May 5, 1865 (J. C. Brock).

48. Towne, *Letters and Diary*, 159–60, 162; *Black Republican*, April 22, 1865.

49. *New York Times*, May 13, 1865; Pearson (ed.), *Letters from Port Royal*, 310–11; Botume, *First Days Amongst the Contrabands*, 173–75, 178; Harriet B. Greeley to Rev. George Whipple, April 29, 1865, American Missionary Assn. Archives; *Black Republican*, April 29, 1865.

50. *New Orleans Tribune*, April 22, 28, 21, 1865; *Proceedings of the Forty-eighth Session of the Baltimore Conf. of the AME Church, April 13, 1865,* 9–10.

51. Martin Abbott, "Freedom's Cry: Negroes and Their Meetings in South Carolina, 1865–1869," *Phylon*, XX (Fall 1959), 264 (Charleston Mutual Aid Society); *New Orleans Tribune*, May 2, 6, April 22, July 27, 1865; *Black Republican*, April 22, 1865.

52. Towne, *Letters and Diary*, 167.

53. *New Orleans Tribune*, July 27, 30, Aug. 3, Sept. 9, Oct. 27, Dec. 9, 30, 1865. For a more hopeful view of Johnson, see *South Carolina Leader*, Oct. 21, Dec. 9, 1865.

54. McPherson, *The Political History of the United States of America During the Period of Reconstruction*, 52–55; LaWanda and John H. Cox, *Politics, Principle, & Prejudice, 1865–66* (Glencoe, Ill., 1963), 163. For black response to the interview, see *New York Times*, Feb. 9, 1866; *Christian Recorder*, Feb. 17, 1866.

55. *Christian Recorder*, March 3,

April 14, Sept. 8, 1866; *Loyal Georgian*, March 3, 1866. For black disillusionment with Johnson, see also *New Orleans Tribune*, Sept. 11, 15, 1866; *Christian Recorder*, Jan. 19, March 9, 1867; *Loyal Georgian*, March 17, Oct. 13, 1866.

56. *Convention of the Colored People of Virginia* (Aug. 1865), 21.

57. Reid, *After the War*, 52. For the "taxation without representation is tyranny" argument, see *Convention of Colored Citizens of Arkansas* (1866), 6; *Freedmen's Convention of Georgia* (Jan. 1866), 18; *Convention of Colored Men, Kentucky* (Nov. 1867), 7; *Christian Recorder*, Oct. 28, 1865 (Edgecombe, Co., N.C.); *New York Times*, Oct. 11, 1866 (Convention of Freedmen, North Carolina); *New York Tribune*, Nov. 29, 1865 (Convention of Colored People, South Carolina); *Loyal Georgian*, Oct. 13, 1866; *New Orleans Tribune*, Nov. 16, 1865; *Black Republican*, April 29, 1865.

58. *Address by the Colored People of Missouri* (1865); *New York Times*, Sept. 17, 1865 (A. H. Galloway at the Convention of Freedmen, N.C.); *The Union* (New Orleans), Dec. 1, 1863 (P. B. S. Pinchback); *Freedmen's Convention of Georgia* (Jan. 1866), 29; *Equal Suffrage. Address from the Colored Citizens of Norfolk, Virginia, to the People of the United States* (New Bedford, Mass., 1865); *Christian Recorder*, Oct. 28, 1865 (Edgecombe Co., N.C.), May 19, 1866.

59. *Christian Recorder*, July 14, 1866; *Colored American*, Jan. 13, 1866.

60. Herbert Aptheker, "South Carolina Negro Conventions, 1865," *Journal of Negro History*, XXXI (1946), 94; *Loyal Georgian*, Feb. 17, 1866; *Colored Tennessean*, Oct. 7, 1865; *New Orleans Tribune*, Nov. 18, 1864, Dec. 15, 1866; *Freedmen's Convention of Georgia* (Jan. 1866), 19; *Proceedings of the Council of the Georgia Equal Rights Association, Assembled at Augusta, Ga., April 4th, 1866* (Augusta, 1866), 13; *New York Times*, Sept. 17, 1865 (A. H. Galloway at the Convention of Freedmen, N.C.); Dennett, *The South As It Is*, 27.

61. *New Orleans Tribune*, Nov. 18, 1864.

62. *Ibid.*, Aug. 1, 1865.

63. *Convention of the Colored People of Virginia* (Aug. 1865), 21–22; Reid, *After the War*, 144.

64. *Convention of the Colored People of Virginia* (Aug. 1865), 22.

65. *New Orleans Tribune*, Dec. 9, Nov. 18, 1864. See also the issue of May 4, 1865 ("Fallacy of 'Preparation' ").

66. *National Freedman*, I (Aug. 15, 1865), 220; *New York Times*, June 4, 1865; *Equal Suffrage. Address from the Colored Citizens of Norfolk, Va.* (1865), 9–15.

67. On the "election" in Beaufort, see *The Mission of the United States Republic: An Oration Delivered by Rev. James Lynch ... July 4, 1865* (Augusta, 1865), 10; on a mayoralty election in Fernandina, see Reid, *After the War*, 160; on the registration and voting in New Orleans, see *New Orleans Tribune*, June 17, 23, 24, 30, July 12, 21, 28, Aug. 4, 18, 22, Sept. 2, 10, 17, 19, Nov. 7, 8, 10, 15, 1865.

68. Blassingame, *Black New Orleans*, 1–22.

69. *New Orleans Tribune*, Nov. 15, 16, 1864.

70. *Ibid.*, Sept. 2, 26, 1865.

71. *Christian Recorder*, May 19, 1866.

72. *New Orleans Tribune*, Nov. 11, Oct. 23, 1866.

73. *Colored Tennessean*, Aug. 12, 1865 (Convention of the Colored People); *New York Times*, April 25, 1865 (Petition from "the colored men of East Tennessee"). See also *New Orleans Tribune*, April 4, July 25, 1865, Sept. 13, 1866.

74. Du Bois, *The Souls of Black Folk*, 3–4.

75. *Christian Recorder*, Aug. 25, 1866. See also "The Negro an Inferior Race," in *ibid.*, Nov. 20, 1869 (D. A. Straker)

76. *Ibid.*, Oct. 4, 1877 ("Race Characteristics").

77. *Ibid.*, Nov. 21, 1868 ("The American Negro").

78. Blassingame (ed.), *Slave Testimony*, 381; *Colored Tennessean*, Aug. 12, 1865 (Convention of the Colored People); *Christian Recorder*, Jan. 23, 1864 (H. M. Turner); *Weekly Louisianian*, Dec. 7, 1878 ("Spell It with a Capital"). On objections to "negro," see also *New Era*, Aug. 18, 1870; nevertheless, the editor of *Weekly Louisianian* (Dec. 12, 1874) thought few if any "intelligent colored citizens" objected to the term, "though they very properly resent the contemptuous one when spelt with two

gs." On gradations of color, see *New Orleans Tribune*, May 23, 1865. For the debate over whether to strike "African" from the name of the African Methodist Episcopal Church, see *Christian Recorder*, Nov. 21, Dec. 19, 1863, April 9, 1864, March 25, April 1, 8, May 6, 1865; *New Orleans Tribune*, June 9, 1865.

79. *Loyal Georgian*, April 10, 1867; *New Era*, Feb. 3, 1870.

80. *Christian Recorder*, June 16, 1866; *Semi-Weekly Louisianian*, June 15, 1871.

81. *Semi-Weekly Louisianian*, March 10, 1872 (H. H. Garnet); *Christian Recorder*, May 13, 1865.

82. *Christian Recorder*, March 25 (J. Lynch), April 8 (G. Rue), 1865.

83. *New Orleans Tribune*, Aug. 13, 1865, Feb. 18, 1869; Evans, *Ballots and Fence Rails*, 90; *Christian Recorder*, Nov. 27, 1869.

84. *Christian Recorder*, June 30, 1866, Oct. 21, 1865.

85. *New Orleans Tribune*, April 13, 1867 (Savannah meeting); *Christian Recorder*, Jan. 5, 1867; Josiah Gorgas, Ms. Journal, entry for July 9, 1867, Univ. of North Carolina.

86. William S. Basinger to George W. J. DeRenne, Aug. 12, 1867, DeRenne Papers, Duke Univ.

87. *Loyal Georgian*, July 6, 1867.

88. B. F. Randolph to Bvt. Maj. Gen. R. K. Scott, Aug. 6, 1867, Records of the Assistant Commissioners, South Carolina (Letters Received), Freedmen's Bureau (Randolph's assassination was announced in *Christian Recorder*, Oct. 31, 1868); *New Orleans Tribune*, May 12, 1867. See also *Loyal Georgian*, July 6, 1867 ("A Word on Registration").

89. *New Orleans Tribune*, May 24, 1867. On the demands voiced by black political rallies, see, e.g., *Christian Recorder*, May 4, 1867 (Beaufort, S.C.); *New Orleans Tribune*, May 4 (Mobile), 10 (St. Louis), 1867; *New York Times*, Jan. 27 (Georgetown, D.C.), March 19 (Savannah), 27 (Charleston), April 2 (Savannah), 19 (Mobile), 24 (Petersburg, Va.), May 4 (Mobile), 8 (Talladega, Ala.), 9 (Jefferson Co., Fla.), 1867.

90. *New York Times*, Oct. 28, Aug. 9, 31, 1867.

91. *Loyal Georgian*, Aug. 10, 1867;

*New York Times,* June 30, May 20, Sept. 25, 1867; *Loyal Georgian,* April 10, 1867. But Thomas W. Stringer, a black political leader in Mississippi, thought his people "more or less mistrustful" of all the candidates. "They know that there are but few southerners that will do altogether right by them in making the laws, and that northerners with a few exceptions, that are eligible, are no better." *Christian Recorder,* May 11, 1867.

92. Towne, *Letters and Diary,* 182–83; *St. Landry Progress,* Nov. 16, 1867.

93. *New York Times,* May 28, 1867; *Christian Recorder,* Oct. 11, 1867 (M. R. Delany); *Free Press* (Charleston), April 5, 1868. On black political aspirations, see also *Christian Recorder,* Aug. 10 ("A Colored Man for Vice-President of the United States" and "Who Are Our Friends?"), Nov. 30 (J. C. Sampson), 1867; *New York Times,* Aug. 6, 9, Oct. 22, 1867.

94. *Christian Recorder,* June 26, 1869 (M. R. Delany); *New Orleans Tribune,* June 12, 13, 14, 18, June 25, 29, July 11, 12, 31, 1867.

95. *New Orleans Tribune,* May 17, June 12, May 19, Dec. 24, June 9, April 21, May 1, July 31, 1867.

96. *Macon Telegraph,* reprinted in *St. Landry Progress,* Oct. 5, 1867.

97. Edward Deane, Asst. Commissioner, Freedmen's Bureau, Charleston, S.C., to Headquarters, Sub-Asst. Commissioner, Darlington, S.C., Aug. 24, 1867, with a newspaper clipping on the Rev. Nick Williams from *Charleston Mercury,* Aug. 24, 1867, instructions to investigate "the truth of the statements contained therein," and an endorsement by the commanding officer in Darlington that he had already dispatched troops to arrest Williams. Records of the Assistant Commissioners, South Carolina (Letters Received), Freedmen's Bureau. The arrest is also reported in *New York Times,* Sept. 9, 1867.

98. F. W. Pickens to Adele Petigru Allston, Nov. 22, 1867, in Easterby (ed.), *South Carolina Rice Plantation,* 237; Josiah Gorgas, Ms. Journal, entries for March 9, July 14, Aug. 25, 1867, Univ. of North Carolina; Abner S. Williams, Mayor of Williamston, North Carolina, to Hon. Jonathan Worth, Sept. 8, 1866, Lt. C. W. Dodge to Lt. Col.

Stephen Moore, Sept. 28, 1866, Records of the Assistant Commissioners, North Carolina (Letters Received), Freedmen's Bureau. See H. S. Van Eaton to Bvt. Maj. Gen. A. Gillem, Nov. 24, 1867, Records of the Assistant Commissioners, Mississippi (Letters Received), Freedmen's Bureau.

99. *Loyal Georgian,* Aug. 10, 1867; John H. Bills, Ms. Diary, entries for July 16, 17, 29, 1867, Univ. of North Carolina; Edward Barnwell Heyward to "Tat" [Catherine Maria Clinch Heyward], May 5, 1867, Heyward Family Papers, Univ. of South Carolina.

100. Lt. H. R. Williams to Lt. Merritt Barber, Feb. 10, 1868, Records of the Assistant Commissioners, Mississippi (Letters Received), Freedmen's Bureau; *New York Times,* Jan. 30, 1868 (Bureau circular, Albany, Ga.). For reports that the impending elections had revived hopes among freedmen of land redistribution, see Fisk P. Brewer to Rev. George Whipple, May 27, 1867, American Missionary Assn. Archives; Sarah M. Payne to Mary Clendenin, Dec. 14, 1867, Historical Society of Pennsylvania; Robert Philip Howell, Ms. Memoirs, 24, Univ. of North Carolina; Mrs. Mary Jones to Mrs. Mary S. Mallard, May 15, 1867, in Myers (ed.), *Children of Pride,* 1382; *New York Times,* May 18, June 14, July 23, Aug. 13, Oct. 11, 1867, Feb. 28, 1868.

101. Ravenel, *Private Journal,* 306; Theodore G. Barker to Benjamin Allston, Oct. 10, 1867, in Easterby (ed.), *South Carolina Rice Plantation,* 235; William Heyward to James Gregorie, June 4, 1868, Gregorie-Elliott Collection, Univ. of North Carolina. The same suggestion was made in a Macon newspaper, as quoted in *New York Times,* Aug. 13, 1867.

102. Henry Middleton to Mr. and Mrs. J. Francis Fisher, May 29, 1867, Cadwalader Collection (J. F. Fisher section), Historical Society of Pennsylvania; W. E. B. Du Bois, "Reconstruction and Its Benefits," *American Historical Review,* XV (1910), 795; Puryear, *The Public School in Its Relation to the Negro,* 14.

103. Walter K. Steele to W. W. Lenoir, Jan. 5, 1868, Lenoir Papers, Univ. of North Carolina; G. I. Crafts to William Porcher Miles, April 13, 1867, William P. Miles Collection, Univ. of North Carolina. Similar

sentiments are expressed in John C. MacRae to Donald MacRae, March 17, 1867, MacRae Papers, Duke Univ., and in Dr. Ethelred Philips to Dr. James J. Philips, Dec. 1, 1867, James J. Philips Collection, Univ. of North Carolina.

104. *Augusta* (Ga.) *Chronicle,* as quoted in *New Orleans Tribune,* Nov. 22, 1865; *Free Press,* April 11, 1868; *New Orleans Tribune,* April 9, 17, 1867. For white appeals to black voters, see also Jacob R. Davis, "To the Colored Voters of the 18th District of Georgia" [1868?], Joseph Belknap Smith Papers, Duke Univ.; *New York Times,* March 21, April 8, June 19, Aug. 25, 1867. For black response to these appeals, see *New Orleans Tribune,* April 9 ("The Enemy's Plan"), Nov. 27, Dec. 14, 21, 1867; *New York Times,* May 25, 1867.

105. *New Orleans Tribune,* Dec. 13, 1867; Paul L. De Clouet, Ms. Diary, entry for Nov. 3, 1868, Alexandre E. De Clouet Papers, Louisiana State Univ. For reports of the activities of "conservative" blacks, see *New Orleans Tribune,* April 9, Dec. 14, 1867; *New York Times,* April 2, 15, 21, Sept. 1, Nov. 21, 22, 26, 1867. For black response, including alleged threats of violence, see "Conservative Negroes," in Charles N. Hunter scrapbook, Nov. 30, 1867, Duke Univ.; J. N. Huske to "Dear Joe," Aug. 17, 1868, William N. Tillinghast Papers, Duke Univ.; *New Orleans Tribune,* April 13, 1867; *New York Times,* Oct. 23, 1867.

106. E. W. Demus to Capt. William C. Sterling, April 24, 1867, Records of the Assistant Commissioners, Louisiana (Letters Received), Freedmen's Bureau; George R. Ghiselin to Dr. Thomas J. McKie, Nov. 2, 1868, T. J. McKie Papers, Duke Univ.; Jacob Black, Chairman of Board of Registration, Eufala, Ala., to Hon. Albert Griffin, Feb. 22, 1868, Thaddeus Stevens Papers, Library of Congress. For reports of violence, intimidation, and economic coercion, see also Thad K. Pruess, Oxford, Miss., to Maj. A. W. Preston, July 31, 1867, William E. Dove, Georgetown, S.C., to Bvt. Maj. H. C. Egbert, June 6, 1868, Lt. W. G. Sprague, Aberdeen, Miss., to Maj. John Tyler, July 2, 1868, Emanuel Handy [freedman candidate for the legislature], Hazlehurst, Miss., to Gen. A. C. Gillem, July 5, 1868, Records of the Assistant Commissioners, Mississippi and South Carolina (Letters Received), Freedmen's Bureau; A. Y. Sharpe to Mrs. Lucy M. Young, Aug. 31, 1868, William D. Simpson Papers, Univ. of North Carolina; Moore (ed.), *The Juhl Letters* (May 7, 1867), 155–56; *New York Times,* April 7, Oct. 3, Dec. 14, 20, 1867.

107. *New York Times,* Feb. 15, 1868 (Montgomery, Ala.). See also *Christian Recorder,* Nov. 16, 1867 (Norfolk); *New York Times,* June 4 (Washington, D.C.), Aug. 2 (Knoxville and Memphis), Oct. 29 (Augusta and Richmond), 30 (Macon and Savannah), 1867.

# Selected Bibliography

*This bibliography is confined to books, articles, and government documents that have been cited more than once in the Notes.*

Abbott, Martin. *The Freedmen's Bureau in South Carolina, 1865–1872.* Chapel Hill, 1967.

*An Address by the Colored People of Missouri to the Friends of Equal Rights.* [State Executive Committee for Equal Political Rights in Missouri] St. Louis, 1865.

[African Methodist Episcopal Church]. *Proceedings of the Forty-eighth Annual Session of the Baltimore Conference of the African Methodist Episcopal Church, April 13th, 1865.* Baltimore, 1865.

Albert, Mrs. Octavia V. Rogers. *The House of Bondage, or Charlotte Brooks and Other Slaves.* New York, 1891.

Alvord, John W. *Semi-Annual Report on Schools for Freedmen.* Washington, D.C., 1867–1870.

Ames, Mary. *From a New England Woman's Diary in Dixie in 1865.* Springfield, Mass., 1906.

Anderson, Ephraim M. *Memoirs: Historical and Personal; including the Campaigns of the First Missouri Confederate Brigade.* St. Louis, 1868.

Andrews, Eliza Frances. *The War-Time Journal of a Georgia Girl, 1864–1865.* New York, 1908.

Andrews, Matthew Page (ed.). *The Women of the South in War Times.* Baltimore, 1920.

Andrews, Sidney. *The South Since the War: As Shown by Fourteen Weeks of Travel and Observation in Georgia and the Carolinas.* Boston, 1866.

Aptheker, Herbert. *American Negro Slave Revolts.* New York, 1943.

——. *A Documentary History of the Negro People in the United States.* New York, 1951.

——. "Notes on Slave Conspiracies in Confederate Mississippi." *Journal of Negro History* XXIX (1944), 75–79.

Armstrong, Mrs. M. F., and Helen W. Ludlow. *Hampton and Its Students. By Two of Its Teachers.* New York, 1875.

Armstrong, Orland Kay. *Old Massa's People: The Old Slaves Tell Their Story.* Indianapolis, 1931.

Avary, Myrta Lockett. *Dixie After the War.* New York, 1906.

Ball, William W. *The State That Forgot: South Carolina's Surrender to Democracy.* Indianapolis, 1932.

Basler, Roy P. (ed.). *The Collected Works of Abraham Lincoln.* 8 vols. New Brunswick, N.J., 1953.

Beatty, John. *The Citizen Soldier; or Memoirs of a Volunteer.* Cincinnati, 1879.

Bennett, Andrew J. *The Story of the First Massachusetts Light Battery.* Boston, 1886.

Bentley, George R. *A History of the Freedmen's Bureau.* Philadelphia, 1955.

Berlin, Ira. *Slaves Without Masters: The Free Negro in the Antebellum South.* New York, 1974.

Bettersworth, John K. *Confederate Mississippi.* Baton Rouge, 1943.

—— (ed.). *Mississippi in the Confederacy: As They Saw It.* Baton Rouge, 1961.

Blassingame, John W. *Black New Orleans, 1860–1880.* Chicago, 1973.

——. "The Recruitment of Colored Troops in Kentucky, Maryland and Missouri, 1863–1865." *The Historian* XXIX (1967), 533–45.

—— (ed.). *Slave Testimony: Two Centuries of Letters, Speeches, Interviews, and Autobiographies.* Baton Rouge, 1977.

Botume, Elizabeth Hyde. *First Days Amongst the Contrabands.* Boston, 1893.

Bradford, Sarah. *Harriet Tubman: The Moses of Her People.* 2nd ed. 1886; repr. New York, 1961.

Bragg, Jefferson D. *Louisiana in the Confederacy.* Baton Rouge, 1941.

Brewer, James H. *The Confederate Negro: Virginia's Craftsmen and Military Laborers, 1861–1865.* Durham, 1969.

Brooks, Aubrey Lee, and Hugh Talmage Lefler (eds.). *The Papers of Walter Clark.* 2 vols. Chapel Hill, 1948.

Brown, William Wells. "Narrative of William Wells Brown." In Gilbert Osofsky (ed.), *Puttin' On Ole Massa.* New York, 1969.

———. *The Negro in the American Rebellion: His Heroism and His Fidelity.* Boston, 1880.

Bruce, H. C. *The New Man. Twenty-nine Years a Slave. Twenty-nine Years a Free Man.* York, Pa., 1895; repr. New York, 1969.

Bruce, John E. *Washington's Colored Society.* n.p., 1877 (typewritten copy in Schomburg Center for Research in Black Culture, New York Public Library).

Bryan, Thomas C. *Confederate Georgia.* Athens, 1953.

Bryant, William C. II (ed.). "A Yankee Soldier Looks at the Negro." *Civil War History* VII (1961), 133–48.

Burge, Dolly L. *The Diary of Dolly Lunt Burge,* edited by James I. Robertson. Athens, 1962.

Burton, Elijah P. *Diary of E. P. Burton, Surgeon 7th Reg. Ill. 3rd Brig. 2nd Div. 16 A.C.* Des Moines, 1939.

[Campbell, Tunis G.]. *Sufferings of the Rev. T. G. Campbell and His Family, in Georgia.* Washington, D.C., 1877.

Cauthen, Charles E. (ed.). *Family Letters of the Three Wade Hamptons, 1782–1901.* Columbia, S.C., 1953.

Chamberlain, Hope Summerell. *Old Days in Chapel Hill: Being the Life and Letters of Cornelia Phillips Spencer.* Chapel Hill, 1926.

Chesnut, Mary Boykin. *A Diary from Dixie,* edited by Ben Ames Williams. Boston, 1949.

Coleman, Kenneth (ed.). *Athens, 1861–1865.* Athens, 1969.

[Convention of Colored Citizens of Arkansas]. *Proceedings of the Convention of Colored Citizens of the State of Arkansas, Held in Little Rock. Thursday, Friday and Saturday, Nov. 30, Dec. 1 and 2.* Helena, Ark., 1866.

[Convention of Colored Men, Kentucky]. *Proceedings of the State Convention of Colored Men, Held at Lexington, Kentucky, in the A.M.E. Church, November 26th, 27th, and 28th, 1867.* Frankfort, Ky., 1867.

[Convention of the Colored People of Virginia]. *Proceedings of the Colored People of Va., Held in the City of Alexandria, Aug. 2, 3, 4, 5, 1865.* Alexandria, 1865.

[Convention of the Equal Rights and Educational Assn. of Georgia]. *Proceedings of the Convention of the Equal Rights and Educational Association of Georgia, Assembled at Macon, October 29th, 1866.* Augusta, 1866.

*Convention of the Freedmen of North Carolina: Official Proceedings.* [Raleigh, 1865].

Conyngham, David P. *Sherman's March Through the South.* New York, 1865.

Coppin, Bishop L. J. *Unwritten History.* Philadelphia, 1919.

Cornish, Dudley Taylor. *The Sable Arm: Negro Troops in the Union Army, 1861–1865.* New York, 1956.

Coulter, E. Merton. *The Confederate States of America, 1861–1865.* Baton Rouge, 1950.

———. "Slavery and Freedom in Athens, Georgia, 1860–1866." In Elinor Miller and Eugene D. Genovese (eds.), *Plantation, Town, and County: Essays on the Local History of American Slave Society,* 337–64. Urbana, 1974.

[Council of the Georgia Equal Rights Assn.]. *Proceedings of the Council of the Georgia Equal Rights Association. Assembled at Augusta, Ga. April 4th, 1866.* Augusta, 1866.

Dawson, Sarah Morgan. *A Confederate Girl's Diary.* Boston, 1913.

De Forest, John William. *A Union Officer in the Reconstruction,* edited by James H. Croushore and David M. Potter. New Haven, 1948.

Dennett, John Richard. *The South As It Is, 1865–1866,* edited by Henry M. Christman. New York, 1965.

Dew, Charles B. *Ironmaker to the Confederacy: Joseph R. Anderson and the Tredegar Iron Works.* New Haven, 1966.

Douglass, Frederick. *Life and Times of Frederick Douglass.* Written by Himself. Hartford, Conn., 1882.

———. *Narrative of the Life of Frederick Douglass, an American Slave.* Written by Himself. 3rd English ed. Wortley, near Leeds, 1846.

Du Bois, W. E. Burghardt. *Black Reconstruction, 1860–1880.* New York, 1935.

————. *The Souls of Black Folk.* Chicago, 1903.

Durden, Robert F. *The Gray and the Black: The Confederate Debate on Emancipation.* Baton Rouge, 1972.

Easterby, J. H. (ed.). *The South Carolina Rice Plantation: As Revealed in the Papers of Robert F. W. Allston.* Chicago, 1945.

Eaton, John. *Grant, Lincoln and the Freedmen: Reminiscences of the Civil War With Special Reference to the Work for the Contrabands and Freedmen of the Mississippi Valley.* New York, 1907; repr. New York, 1969.

Ellison, Ralph. *Shadow and Act.* New York, 1964.

Emilio, Luis F. *History of the Fifty-Fourth Regiment of Massachusetts Volunteer Infantry, 1863–1865.* Boston, 1891.

Eppes, Mrs. Nicholas Ware [Susan Bradford Eppes]. *The Negro of the Old South: A Bit of Period History.* Chicago, 1925.

————. *Through Some Eventful Years.* Macon, 1926; repr. Gainesville, 1968.

*Equal Suffrage. Address from the Colored Citizens of Norfolk, Virginia, to the People of the United States. Also An Account of the Agitation Among the Colored People of Virginia for Equal Rights.* New Bedford, Mass., 1865.

Evans, W. McKee. *Ballots and Fence Rails: Reconstruction on the Lower Cape Fear.* Chapel Hill, 1967.

Farrison, William E. *William Wells Brown: Author and Reformer.* Chicago, 1969.

Fisk, Clinton B. *Plain Counsels for Freedmen: In Sixteen Brief Lectures.* Boston, 1866.

Fisk University. *Unwritten History of Slavery.* In George P. Rawick, *The American Slave: A Composite Autobiography,* Vol. 18. Westport, Conn., 1972.

Fleming, Walter L. *Civil War and Reconstruction in Alabama.* New York, 1905.

———— (ed.). *Documentary History of Reconstruction.* 2 vols. Cleveland, 1906–07.

Forten, Charlotte L. *The Journal of Charlotte L. Forten,* edited by Ray Allen Billington. New York, 1953.

Franklin, John Hope (ed.). *The Diary of James T. Ayers: Civil War Recruiter.* Springfield, Ill., 1947.

[Freedmen's Convention of Georgia]. *Proceedings of the Freedmen's Convention of Georgia, Assembled at Augusta, January 10th, 1866.* Augusta, 1866.

Fremantle, Arthur James Lyon. *Three Months in the Southern States: April–June, 1863.* New York, 1864.

Genovese, Eugene D. *Roll, Jordan, Roll: The World the Slaves Made.* New York, 1974.

Gerteis, Louis S. *From Contraband to Freedman: Federal Policy Toward Southern Blacks, 1861–1865.* Westport, Conn., 1973.

Gordon, George H. *A War Diary of Events in the War of the Great Rebellion, 1863–1865.* Boston, 1882.

Gottlieb, Manuel. "The Land Question During Reconstruction." *Science and Society* III (1939), 356–88.

Grimball, John Berkley. "Diary of John Berkley Grimball, 1858–1865." *South Carolina Historical Magazine* LVI (1955), 8–30, 92–114, 157–80, 205–25; LVII (1956), 28–50, 88–102.

Guthrie, James M. *Camp-Fires of the Afro-American; or, The Colored Man as a Patriot.* Cincinnati, [1899].

Gutman, Herbert G. *The Black Family in Slavery and Freedom, 1750–1925.* New York, 1976.

Haviland, Laura S. *A Woman's Life-Work: Labors and Experiences.* Cincinnati, 1881.

Hepworth, George H. *The Whip, Hoe, and Sword; or, The Gulf-Department in '63.* Boston, 1864.

Heyward, Duncan Clinch. *Seed From Madagascar.* Chapel Hill, 1937.

Higginson, Thomas Wentworth. *Army Life in a Black Regiment.* Boston, 1870.

Hitchcock, Henry. *Marching With Sherman: Passages from the Letters and Campaign Diaries of Henry Hitchcock,* edited by M. A. DeWolfe Howe. New Haven, 1927.

Holmes, Jack D. L. "The Underlying Causes of the Memphis Race Riot of 1866." *Tennessee Historical Quarterly* XVII (1958), 195–221.

House, Albert V., Jr. (ed.). "Deterioration of a Georgia Rice Plantation During Four Years of Civil War." *Journal of Southern History* IX (1943), 98–113.

Howard, Oliver Otis. *Autobiography of Oliver Otis Howard.* 2 vols. New York, 1907.

Jackson, Bruce (ed.). *The Negro and His Folklore in Nineteenth-Century Periodicals.* Austin, 1967.

James, Rev. Horace. *Annual Report of the Superintendent of Negro Affairs in North Carolina*, 1864. Boston, n.d.

Jaquette, Henrietta S. (ed.). *South After Gettysburg: Letters of Cornelia Hancock, 1863–1868.* New York, 1956.

Jervey, Susan R., and Charlotte St. J. Ravenel. *Two Diaries: From Middle St. John's, Berkeley, South Carolina, February–May, 1865. Journals Kept by Miss Susan R. Jervey and Miss Charlotte St. J. Ravenel, at Northampton and Pooshee Plantations, and Reminiscences of Mrs. (Waring) Henagan. With Two Contemporary Reports from Federal Officials.* St. John's Hunting Club, 1921.

Johns, Henry T. *Life With the Forty-Ninth Massachusetts Volunteers.* Washington, D.C., 1890.

Johns, John E. *Florida During the Civil War.* Gainesville, 1963.

Jones, John B. *A Rebel War Clerk's Diary at the Confederate States Capital,* edited by Earl S. Miers. New York, 1961.

Jones, Katharine M. (ed.). *Heroines of Dixie: Confederate Women Tell Their Story of the War.* Indianapolis, 1955.

—— (ed.). *When Sherman Came: Southern Women and the "Great March."* Indianapolis, 1964.

Jordan, Weymouth T. *Hugh Davis and His Alabama Plantation.* University, Ala., 1948.

Katz, William Loren (ed.). *Five Slave Narratives.* New York, 1969.

Kerby, Robert L. *Kirby Smith's Confederacy: The Trans-Mississippi South, 1863–1865.* New York, 1972.

Knox, Thomas W. *Camp-Fire and Cotton-Field: Southern Adventure in Time of War. Life With the Union Armies, and Residence on a Louisiana Plantation.* Cincinnati, 1865.

Kolchin, Peter. *First Freedom: The Responses of Alabama's Blacks to Emancipation and Reconstruction.* Westport, Conn., 1972.

LeConte, Emma. *When the World Ended: The Diary of Emma LeConte,* edited by Earl S. Miers. New York, 1957.

LeConte, Joseph. *'Ware Sherman: A Journal of Three Months' Personal Experience in the Last Days of the Confederacy.* Berkeley, Calif., 1938.

LeGrand, Julia. *The Journal of Julia LeGrand,* edited by Kate M. Rowland and Mrs. Morris E. Croxall. Richmond, 1911.

Leigh, Frances B. *Ten Years on a Georgia Plantation Since the War.* London, 1883.

Leland, Isabella Middleton (ed.). "Middleton Correspondence, 1861–1865." *South Carolina Historical Magazine* LXIII (1962), 33–41, 61–70, 164–74, 204–10; LXIV (1963), 28–38, 95–104, 158–68, 212–19; LXV (1964), 33–44, 98–109.

Lester, Julius. *To Be a Slave.* New York, 1968.

Loring, F. W., and C. F. Atkinson. *Cotton Culture and the South Considered With Reference to Emigration.* Boston, 1869.

Lynch, Rev. James. *The Mission of the United States Republic: An Oration. Delivered by Rev. James Lynch, at the Parade Ground, Augusta, Ga., July 4, 1865.* Augusta, 1865.

McFeely, William S. *Yankee Stepfather: General O. O. Howard and the Freedmen.* New Haven, 1968.

McPherson, Edward. *The Political History of the United States of America During the Period of Reconstruction, From April 15, 1865, to July 15, 1870.* Washington, D.C., 1880.

McPherson, James M. *The Negro's Civil War: How American Negroes Felt and Acted During the War for the Union.* New York, 1965.

——. "The New Puritanism: Values and Goals of Freedmen's Education in America." In Lawrence Stone (ed.), *The University in Society,* 2 vols. Princeton, 1974.

——. *The Struggle for Equality: Abolitionists and the Negro in the Civil War and Reconstruction.* Princeton, 1964.

Macrae, David. *The Americans At Home.* Edinburgh, 1870; repr. New York, 1952.

Messner, William F. "Black Violence and White Response: Louisiana, 1862." *Journal of Southern History* XLI (1975), 19–38.

Miller, Elinor, and Eugene D. Genovese (eds.). *Plantation, Town, and County: Essays on the Local History of American Slave Society.* Urbana, Ill., 1974.

Montgomery, Margaret L. (ed.). "Alabama Freedmen: Some Reconstruction Documents." *Phylon,* Third Quarter (1952), 245–51.

Moore, Frank (ed.). *Rebellion Record.* 11 vols. New York, 1861–68.

Moore, John Hammond (ed.). *The Juhl Letters to the Charleston Courier: A View of the South, 1865–1871.* Athens, 1974.

Morrow, Ralph E. *Northern Methodism and Reconstruction.* East Lansing, 1956.

Murray, Pauli. *Proud Shoes: The Story of an American Family.* New York, 1956.

Myers, Robert Manson (ed.). *The Children of Pride: A True Story of Georgia and the Civil War.* New Haven, 1972.

Nevins, Allan. *The War for the Union: The Organized War to Victory, 1863–1864.* New York, 1971.

——. *The War for the Union: The Organized War to Victory, 1864–1865.* New York, 1971.

[New England Educational Commission for Freedmen]. *Extracts from Letters of Teachers and Superintendents of the New-England Educational Commission for Freedmen.* Fourth Series, January 1, 1864. Boston, 1864.

Nichols, George W. *The Story of the Great March from the Diary of a Staff Officer.* New York, 1865.

Nolen, Claude H. *The Negro's Image in the South: The Anatomy of White Supremacy.* Lexington, 1967.

Nordhoff, Charles. *The Freedmen of South-Carolina: Some Account of Their Appearance, Character, Condition, and Peculiar Customs.* [New York, 1863].

Oliphant, Mary C., Alfred Taylor Odell, and T. C. Duncan Eaves (eds.). *The Letters of William Gilmore Simms.* 5 vols. Columbia, S.C., 1952–56.

Osofsky, Gilbert (ed.). *Puttin' On Ole Massa: The Slave Narratives of Henry Bibb, William Wells Brown, and Solomon Northup.* New York, 1969.

Patrick, Rembert W. *The Fall of Richmond.* Baton Rouge, 1960.

Pearson, Elizabeth Ware (ed.). *Letters from Port Royal: Written at the Time of the Civil War.* Boston, 1906.

Pearson, Henry Greenleaf. *The Life of John A. Andrew: Governor of Massachusetts, 1861–1865.* 2 vols. Boston, 1904.

Perdue, Charles L., Jr., Thomas E. Barden, and Robert K. Phillips (eds.). *Weevils in the Wheat: Interviews with Virginia Ex-Slaves.* Charlottesville, 1976.

Pierce, E. L. *The Negroes at Port Royal: Report of E. L. Pierce, Government Agent, to the Hon. Salmon P. Chase, Secretary of the Treasury.* Boston, 1862.

Pringle, Elizabeth W. Allston. *Chronicles of Chicora Wood.* New York, 1922.

[Puryear, Prof. Bennett]. *The Public School in Its Relation to the Negro.* By Civis. Richmond, 1877.

Putnam, Sallie A. *In Richmond During the Confederacy.* New York, 1867; repr. 1961.

Quarles, Benjamin. *The Negro in the Civil War.* Boston, 1953.

Rainwater, P. L. (ed.). "Letters of James Lusk Alcorn." *Journal of Southern History* III (1937), 196–209.

Ravenel, Henry William. *The Private Journal of Henry William Ravenel, 1859–1887,* edited by Arney Robinson Childs. Columbia, S.C., 1947.

Rawick, George P. (ed.). *The American Slave: A Composite Autobiography.* 19 vols. Westport, Conn., 1972.

*Record of Action of the Convention Held at Poughkeepsie, N.Y., July 15th and 16th, 1863, For the Purpose of Facilitating the Introduction of Colored Troops into the Service of the United States.* New York, 1863.

Reid, Whitelaw. *After the War: A Southern Tour, May 1, 1865, to May 1, 1866.* Cincinnati, 1866.

"Report of the Commissioner of the Bureau of Refugees, Freedmen and Abandoned Lands, November 1, 1866." In *Report of the Secretary of War,* Appendix. Washington, D.C., 1867.

*Report of the General Superintendent of Freedmen, Department of the Tennessee and State of Arkansas for 1864.* Memphis, 1865.

*Report of the Proceedings of a Meeting Held at Concert Hall, Philadelphia, On Tuesday Evening, November 3, 1863, To Take Into Consideration the Condition of the Freed People of the South.* Philadelphia, 1863.

Richardson, Joe M. *The Negro in the Reconstruction of Florida, 1865–1877.* Tallahassee, 1965.

Ripley, C. Peter. *Slaves and Freedmen in Civil War Louisiana.* Baton Rouge, 1976.

Roark, James L. *Masters Without Slaves: Southern Planters in the Civil War and Reconstruction.* New York, 1977.

Rogers, George C. *The History of Georgetown County, South Carolina.* Columbia, 1970.

Rogers, William Warren. *Thomas County, 1865–1900.* Tallahassee, 1973.

Rollin, Frank A. *Life and Public Services of Martin R. Delany.* Boston, 1883.

Rose, Willie Lee. *Rehearsal for Reconstruction: The Port Royal Experiment.* Indianapolis, 1964.

Ruffin, Edmund. *The Diary of Edmund Ruffin,* edited by William K. Scarborough. 2 vols. Baton Rouge, 1972, 1976

Russell, William Howard. *My Diary North and South.* Boston, 1863.

Savannah Writers' Project. *Savannah River Plantations.* Savannah, 1947.

Scarborough, William K. *The Overseer: Plantation Management in the Old South.* Baton Rouge, 1966.

Silver, James W. (ed.). *Mississippi in the Confederacy: As Seen in Retrospect.* Baton Rouge, 1961.

Simkins, Francis B., and James W. Patton. *The Women of the Confederacy.* Richmond, 1936.

[Simpson, Joseph]. Friends' Central Committee for the Relief of the Emancipated Negroes, London, 9th Month 1st, 1865. *Letters from Joseph Simpson, Manchester.* [London, 1865].

Sitterson, J. Carlyle. *Sugar Country: The Cane Sugar Industry in the South, 1753–1950.* Lexington, Ky., 1953.

Smedes, Susan Dabney. *Memorials of a Southern Planter,* edited by Fletcher M. Green. New York, 1965.

Smith, Daniel E. Huger, Alice R. Huger Smith, and Arney R. Childs (eds.). *Mason Smith Family Letters, 1860–1868.* Columbia, S.C., 1950.

Smith, F. W. (ed.). "The Yankees in New Albany: Letter of Elizabeth Jane Beach, July 29th, 1864." *Journal of Mississippi History* II (1940), 42–48.

Spencer, Cornelia Phillips. *The Last Ninety Days of the War in North Carolina.* New York, 1866.

Stampp, Kenneth M. *The Peculiar Institution: Slavery in the Ante-Bellum South.* New York, 1956.

Starobin, Robert S. (ed.). *Blacks in Bondage: Letters of American Slaves.* New York, 1974.

Stearns, Charles. *The Black Man of the South, and the Rebels; or, The Characteristics of the Former, and the Recent Outrages of the Latter.* New York, 1872.

Stephenson, Gilbert T. *Race Distinctions in American Law.* New York, 1911.

Stevens, George T. *Three Years in the Sixth Corps.* Albany, 1866.

Stone, Kate. *Brokenburn: The Journal of Kate Stone, 1861–1868,* edited by John Q. Anderson. Baton Rouge, 1972.

Stroyer, Jacob. "My Life in the South." In William Loren Katz (ed.), *Five Slave Narratives.* New York, 1969.

Swint, Henry L. (ed.). *Dear Ones at Home: Letters from Contraband Camps.* Nashville, 1966.

———. *The Northern Teacher in the South, 1862–1870.* Nashville, 1941.

Sydnor, Charles S. *A Gentleman of the Old Natchez Region: Benjamin L. C. Wailes.* Durham, 1938.

Taylor, Alrutheus A. *The Negro in Tennessee, 1865–1880.* Washington, D.C., 1941.

———. *The Negro in the Reconstruction of Virginia.* Washington, D.C., 1926.

Taylor, Susie King. *Reminiscences of My Life in Camp: With the 33d United States Colored Troops Late 1st S.C. Volunteers.* Boston, 1904.

Thompson, Henry Yates. *An Englishman in the American Civil War: The Diaries of Henry Yates Thompson,* edited by Christopher Chancellor. New York, 1971.

Towne, Laura M. *Letters and Diary of Laura M. Towne: Written from the Sea Islands of South Carolina, 1862–1884,* edited by Rupert Sargent Holland. Cambridge, 1912.

Trowbridge, J. T. *The South: A Tour of Its Battle-Fields and Ruined Cities, A Journey Through the Desolated States, and Talks with the People.* Hartford, 1866.

U.S. 38th Cong., 1st Sess., Senate Executive Document 53. *Preliminary Report Touching the Condition and Management of Emancipated Refugees, Made to the Secretary of War by the American Freedmen's Inquiry Commission, June 30, 1863.* Washington, D.C., 1864.

U.S. 39th Cong., 1st Sess., House Executive Document 70. *Freedmen's Bureau. Letter from the Secretary of War . . . transmitting a report, by the Commissioner of the Freedmen's Bureau, of all orders issued by him or any assistant commissioner.* Washington, D.C., 1866.

U.S. 39th Cong., 1st Sess., House Report 101. *Memphis Riots and Massacres.* Washington, D.C., 1866.

U.S. 39th Cong., 1st Sess. *Report of the Joint Committee on Reconstruction.* Washington, D.C., 1866.

U.S. 39th Cong., 1st Sess., Senate Executive Document 2. "Report of Carl Schurz on the States of South Carolina, Georgia, Alabama, Mississippi, and Louisiana." In *Message of the President of the United States.* Washington, D.C., 1865.

U.S. 39th Cong., 1st Sess., Senate Executive Document 27. *Reports of the Assistant Commissioners of the Freedmen's Bureau made since December 1, 1865 and up until March 1, 1866.* Washington, D.C., 1866.

U.S. 39th Cong., 2nd Sess., House Report 16. *New Orleans Riots.* Washington, D.C., 1866.

U.S. 39th Cong., 2nd Sess., Senate Executive Document 6. "Laws in Relation to Freedmen." In *Freedmen's Affairs,* 170–230. Washington, D.C., 1867.

U.S. 39th Cong., 2nd Sess., Senate Executive Document 6. *Reports of the Assistant Commissioners of Freedmen.* Washington, D. C., 1867.

U.S. 40th Cong., 2nd Sess., House Executive Document 1. *Report of the Commissioner of the Bureau of Refugees, Freedmen, and Abandoned Lands, November 1, 1867.* Washington, D.C., 1867.

Voegeli, V. Jacque. *Free but Not Equal: The Midwest and the Negro During the Civil War.* Chicago, 1967.

Warren, Rev. Joseph. *Extracts from Reports of Superintendents of Freedmen . . . , First Series, May, 1864.* Vicksburg, 1864.

Washington, Booker T. *Up from Slavery: An Autobiography.* New York, 1902.

Waterbury, M. *Seven Years Among the Freedmen.* 3rd ed. Chicago, 1893.

Wharton, Vernon Lane. *The Negro in Mississippi, 1865–1890.* Chapel Hill, 1947.

White, Howard A. *The Freedmen's Bureau in Louisiana.* Baton Rouge, 1970.

White, Newman Ivey (ed.). *North Carolina Folklore.* 7 vols. Durham, 1952–64.

Whittington, G. P. (ed.). "Concerning the Loyalty of Slaves in North Louisiana in 1863: Letters from John H. Ransdell to Governor Thomas O. Moore, dated 1863." *Louisiana Historical Quarterly* XIV (1931), 487–502.

Wiley, Bell Irvin (ed.). *Letters of Warren Akin: Confederate Congressman.* Athens, 1959.

———. *The Life of Billy Yank: The Common Soldier of the Union.* Indianapolis, 1952.

———. *The Life of Johnny Reb: The Common Soldier of the Confederacy.* Indianapolis, 1943.

———. *Southern Negroes, 1861–1865.* New Haven, 1938.

———. "Vicissitudes of Early Reconstruction Farming in the Lower Mississippi Valley." *Journal of Southern History* III (1937), 441–52.

Williamson, Joel. *After Slavery: The Negro in South Carolina During Reconstruction, 1861–1877.* Chapel Hill, 1965.

Wilson, Joseph T. *The Black Phalanx: A History of the Negro Soldiers of the United States in the Wars of 1775–1812, 1861–'65.* Hartford, 1888.

Wilson, Theodore B. *The Black Codes of the South.* University, Ala., 1965.

Winters, John D. *The Civil War in Louisiana.* Baton Rouge, 1963.

Winther, Oscar Osburn (ed.) *With Sherman to the Sea: The Civil War Letters, Diaries & Reminiscences of Theodore F. Upson.* Bloomington, 1958.

Wise, John S. *The End of an Era.* Boston, 1902.

Wish, Harvey. "Slave Disloyalty Under the Confederacy." *Journal of Negro History* XXIII (1938), 435–50.

Work Projects Administration, Virginia. *The Negro in Virginia.* New York, 1940.

## MANUSCRIPT SOURCES

*Amistad Research Center, Dillard University, New Orleans*
    American Missionary Association Papers (This collection was consulted when still housed in the Fisk University Library, Nashville, Tennessee.)

*Duke University Library, Durham, North Carolina*

Andrews Papers

Armisted L. Burt Papers

Henry S. Clark Papers

Francis W. Dawson Papers

DeRenne Papers

Benjamin S. Hedrick Papers

Charles N. Hunter Scrapbook

MacRae Papers

T. J. McKie Papers

McLaurin Papers

Joseph Belknap Smith Papers

Missouria Stokes Papers

Augustin L. Taveau Papers

William N. Tillinghast Papers

Ella Gertrude (Clanton) Thomas Journal

*Historical Society of Pennsylvania, Philadelphia*

American Negro Historical Society Papers, Jacob C. White, Jr., Papers

Cadwalader Collection, J. F. Fisher Section, Henry Middleton and Wife

Edward Carey Gardiner Collection, Carey Papers

Sarah P. Miller Payne, Letters to Mary Clendenin and Nancy Hartshorne Clendenin Freeman, 1865–1872

Pennsylvania Society for Promoting the Abolition of Slavery Papers

*Howard University Library, Washington, D.C.*

George L. Ruffin Papers

*Henry E. Huntington Library, San Marino, California*

Brock Collection

Glazier Collection

Main File

*Library of Congress, Washington, D.C.*

Thaddeus Stevens Papers

Carter G. Woodson Collection

*Louisiana State Department of Archives and History, Louisiana State University, Baton Rouge*

Henry Anderson Papers

Gustave Lauve Papers

Pierre G. T. Beauregard Papers

St. John R. Liddell and Family Papers

R. J. Causey Papers

William N. Mercer Papers

Alexander E. De Clouet Papers

Alexander F. Pugh and Family Papers

Emily Caroline Douglas Papers

W. W. Pugh Papers

Christian D. Koch Papers

Micajah Wilkinson Papers

*National Archives, Washington, D.C.*

Bureau of Refugees, Freedmen, and Abandoned Lands (Freedmen's Bureau)

Records of the Assistant Commissioners (Letters Received)

Records of the Subordinate Field Offices

Registers of Letters Received

*New York Public Library, New York*

Shaw Family Papers

*North Carolina State Department of Archives and History, Raleigh*

James H. Harris Papers

*Schomburg Center for Research in Black Culture, New York Public Library*

John E. Bruce Papers

*South Carolina Department of Archives and History, Columbia*

Manigault Papers

*South Caroliniana Library, University of South Carolina, Columbia*

Ball Family Papers

Heyward Family Papers

John S. Bogert Papers

Emma E. Holmes Diary

Bruce-Jones-Murchison Papers

Miscellaneous Correspondence

Bonds Conway Papers

Thomas J. Moore Papers

Deas Papers

Dr. Edward Smith Tennent Papers

Glover-North Family Papers

Williams-Chesnut-Manning Papers

*Southern Historical Collection, University of North Carolina, Chapel Hill*

Samuel A. Agnew Diary

Josiah Gorgas Journal

Avery Family Papers

Gregorie-Elliott Family Papers

Everard Green Baker Diaries

Robert Philip Howell Memoirs

Bayside Plantation Records

Kean-Prescott Family Papers

Jesse and Overton Bernard Diaries

Lenoir Family Papers

John Houston Bills Diary

William Gaston Lewis Papers

Catherine Barbara Broun Diary

Mackay-Stiles Papers

John Hamilton Cornish Diary

Manigault Plantation Records

De Rosset Family Papers

William Porcher Miles Papers

Belle Edmondson Diary

Miscellaneous Correspondence

Grace B. Elmore Diaries

Thomas J. Myers Papers

James J. Philips Collection
Quitman Papers
William D. Simpson Papers

George C. Taylor Collection
Trenholm Papers
James W. White Papers

## NEWSPAPERS

*Anglo-African* (New York)
*Black Republican* (New Orleans)
*Bulletin* (Louisville)
*Christian Recorder* (Philadelphia)
*Colored American* (Augusta, Ga.)
*Colored Tennessean* (Nashville)
*Douglass' Monthly* (Rochester)
*Freedman's Press* (Austin, Texas)
*Free Man's Press* (Austin, Texas)
*Free Press* (Charleston, S.C.)
*Louisianian* (New Orleans)
*Loyal Georgian* (Augusta)
*Missionary Record* (Charleston, S.C.)

*New Era* (Washington, D.C.)
*New National Era* (Washington, D.C.)
*New Orleans Tribune* (New Orleans)
*New York Times* (New York)
*New York Tribune* (New York)
*St. Landry Progress* (Opelousas, La.)
*Semi-Weekly Louisianian* (New Orleans)
*South Carolina Leader* (Charleston)
*Tennessean* (Nashville)
*The Union* (New Orleans)
*Weekly Louisianian* (New Orleans)
*Workingman's Advocate* (Chicago)

# Index

## A Note About the Author

Leon F. Litwack was born in Santa Barbara, California, in 1929. He received his B.A., M.A., and Ph.D. from the University of California at Berkeley, where he is currently Professor of History. Mr. Litwack has also taught at the universities of Wisconsin and South Carolina and at Colorado College. He has been the recipient of a Guggenheim Fellowship, a Distinguished Teaching Award, and a National Endowment for the Humanities Film Grant, with which he produced *To Look for America* in 1971.